THE DECLINE AND FALL
OF THE ROMAN EMPIRE

The Decline and Fall

OF THE

ROMAN EMPIRE

by EDWARD GIBBON

VOLUME II

395 A.D.—1185 A.D.

THE MODERN LIBRARY

NEW YORK

The material included in this volume is taken from Every-
man's Library. This edition was prepared by Oliphant
Smeaton, who reprinted all of Gibbon's own notes and
added to them the material set off in brackets and signed
with the initials *O.S.*

THE MODERN LIBRARY
is published by RANDOM HOUSE, INC.
New York, New York
Manufactured in the United States of America

CONTENTS

CONTENTS

THE

HISTORY OF THE DECLINE AND FALL

OF THE

ROMAN EMPIRE

CHAPTER XXVII (340–397 A.D.)

Death of Gratian—Ruin of Arianism—St. Ambrose—First Civil War, against Maximus—Character, Administration, and Penance, of Theodosius—Death of Valentinian II.—Second Civil War, against Eugenius—Death of Theodosius

THE fame of Gratian, before he had accomplished the twentieth year of his age, was equal to that of the most celebrated princes. His gentle and amiable disposition endeared him to his private friends, the graceful affability of his manners engaged the affection of the people; the men of letters, who enjoyed the liberality, acknowledged the taste and eloquence of their sovereign; his valour and dexterity in arms were equally applauded by the soldiers; and the clergy considered the humble piety of Gratian as the first and most useful of his virtues. The victory of Colmar had delivered the West from a formidable invasion, and the grateful provinces of the East ascribed the merits of Theodosius to the author of *his* greatness and of the public safety. Gratian survived those memorable events only four or five years, but he survived his reputation, and, before he fell a victim to rebellion, he had lost, in a great measure, the respect and confidence of the Roman world.

The remarkable alteration of his character or conduct may not be imputed to the arts of flattery, which had besieged the son of Valentinian from his infancy, nor to the headstrong passion which that gentle youth appears to have escaped. A more attentive view of the life of Gratian may perhaps suggest the true cause of the disappointment of the public hopes. His apparent virtues, instead of being the hardy productions of experience and adversity, were the premature and artificial fruits of a royal education. The anxious tenderness of his father was continually employed to bestow on him those advantages which he might perhaps esteem the more highly as he himself had been deprived of them, and the most skilful masters of every science and of every art had laboured to form the mind and body of the young prince.[1] The knowledge which they painfully communicated was dis-

---

[1] Valentinian was less attentive to the religion of his son; since he intrusted the education of Gratian to Ausonius, a professed Pagan. (Mém. de l'Académie des Inscriptions, tom. xv. p. 125-138). The poetical fame of Ausonius condemns the taste of his age.

played with ostentation and celebrated with lavish praise. His soft and tractable disposition received the fair impression of their judicious precepts, and the absence of passion might easily be mistaken for the strength of reason.   His preceptors gradually rose to the rank and consequence of ministers of state,[2] and, as they wisely dissembled their secret authority, he seemed to act with firmness, with propriety, and with judgment on the most important occasions of his life and reign. But the influence of this elaborate instruction did not penetrate beyond the surface, and the skilful preceptors, who so accurately guided the steps of their royal pupil, could not infuse into his feeble and indolent character the vigorous and independent principle of action which renders the laborious pursuit of glory essentially necessary to the happiness and almost to the existence of the hero.   As soon as time and accident had removed those faithful counsellors from the throne, the emperor of the West insensibly descended to the level of his natural genius, abandoned the reins of government to the ambitious hands which were stretched forwards to grasp them, and amused his leisure with the most frivolous gratifications.   A public sale of favour and injustice was instituted, both in the court and in the provinces, by the worthless delegates of his power, whose merit it was made *sacrilege* to question.[3]   The conscience of the credulous prince was directed by saints and bishops,[4] who procured an Imperial edict to punish, as a capital offence, the violation, the neglect, or even the ignorance of the divine law.[5]   Among the various arts which had exercised the youth of Gratian, he had applied himself, with singular inclination and success, to manage the horse, to draw the bow, and to dart the javelin; and these qualifications, which might be useful to a soldier, were prostituted to the viler purposes of hunting.   Large parks were enclosed for the Imperial pleasures, and plentifully stocked with every species of wild beasts, and Gratian neglected the duties and even the dignity of his rank to consume whole days in the vain display of his dexterity and boldness in the chase.   The pride and wish of the Roman emperor to excel in an art in which he might be surpassed by the meanest of his slaves reminded the numerous spectators of the examples of

[2] Ausonius was successively promoted to the Prætorian præfecture of Italy (A.D. 377) and of Gaul (A.D. 378) ; and was at length invested with the consulship (A.D. 379).   He expressed his gratitude in a servile and insipid piece of flattery (Actio Gratiarum, p. 699-736 [ed. Toll. Amst. 1671]), which has survived more worthy productions.

[3] Disputare de principali judicio non oportet.   Sacrilegii enim instar est dubitare, an is dignus sit, quem elegerit imperator.   Codex Justinian. l. ix. tit. xxix. leg. 2.   This convenient law was revived and promulgated, after the death of Gratian, by the feeble court of Milan.

[4] Ambrose composed, for his instruction, a theological treatise on the faith of the Trinity: and Tillemont (Hist. des Empereurs, tom. v. p. 158, 169) ascribes to the archbishop the merit of Gratian's intolerant laws.

[5] Qui divinæ legis sanctitatem [aut] nesciendo omittunt, aut negligendo violant, et offendunt, sacrilegium committunt.   Codex Justinian. l. ix. tit. xxix. leg. 1.   Theodosius indeed may claim his share in the merit of this comprehensive law.

Nero and Commodus; but the chaste and temperate Gratian was a stranger to their monstrous vices, and his hands were stained only with the blood of animals.[6]

The behaviour of Gratian, which degraded his character in the eyes of mankind, could not have disturbed the security of his reign if the army had not been provoked to resent their peculiar injuries. As long as the young emperor was guided by the instructions of his masters, he professed himself the friend and pupil of the soldiers; many of his hours were spent in the familiar conversation of the camp, and the health, the comforts, the rewards, the honours of his faithful troops, appeared to be the object of his attentive concern. But, after Gratian more freely indulged his prevailing taste for hunting and shooting, he naturally connected himself with the most dexterous ministers of his favourite amusement. A body of the Alani was received into the military and domestic service of the palace, and the admirable skill which they were accustomed to display in the unbounded plains of Scythia was exercised on a more narrow theatre in the parks and enclosures of Gaul. Gratian admired the talents and customs of these favourite guards, to whom alone he intrusted the defence of his person; and, as if he meant to insult the public opinion, he frequently showed himself to the soldiers and people with the dress and arms, the long bow, the sounding quiver, and the fur garments of a Scythian warrior. The unworthy spectacle of a Roman prince who had renounced the dress and manners of his country filled the minds of the legions with grief and indignation.[7] Even the Germans, so strong and formidable in the armies of the empire, affected to disdain the strange and horrid appearance of the savages of the North, who, in the space of a few years, had wandered from the banks of the Volga to those of the Seine. A loud and licentious murmur was echoed through the camps and garrisons of the West; and as the mild indolence of Gratian neglected to extinguish the first symptoms of discontent, the want of love and respect was not supplied by the influence of fear. But the subversion of an established government is always a work of some real, and of much apparent difficulty; and the throne of Gratian was protected by the sanctions of custom, law, religion, and the nice balance of the civil and military powers which had been established by the policy of Constantine. It is not very important to inquire from what causes the revolt of Britain was produced. Accident is commonly the parent of disorder: the seeds of rebellion happened to fall on a soil which was supposed to be more fruitful than any other in tyrants and

---

[6] Ammianus (xxxi. 10) and the younger Victor [Epit. c. 47] acknowledge the virtues of Gratian; and accuse, or rather lament, his degenerate taste. The odious parallel of Commodus is saved by "licet incruentus;" and perhaps Philostorgius (l. x. c. 10 [5], and Godefroy, p. 412) has guarded, with some similar reserve, the comparison of Nero.

[7] Zosimus (l. iv. [c. 35] p. 247) and the younger Victor ascribe the revolution to the favour of the Alani and the discontent of the Roman troops. Dum exercitum negligeret, et paucos ex Alanis, quos ingenti auro ad se transtulerat, anteferret veteri ac Romano militi [Epit. c. 47].

usurpers;[8] the legions of that sequestered island had been long famous for a spirit of presumption and arrogance;[9] and the name of Maximus was proclaimed by the tumultuary but unanimous voice both of the soldiers and of the provincials. The emperor, or the rebel, for his title was not yet ascertained by fortune, was a native of Spain, the countryman, the fellow-soldier, and the rival of Theodosius, whose elevation he had not seen without some emotions of envy and resentment; the events of his life had long since fixed him in Britain, and I should not be unwilling to find some evidence for the marriage which he is said to have contracted with the daughter of a wealthy lord of Caernarvonshire.[10] But this provincial rank might justly be considered as a state of exile and obscurity, and, if Maximus had obtained any civil or military office, he was not invested with the authority either of governor or general.[11] His abilities and even his integrity are acknowledged by the partial writers of the age, and the merit must indeed have been conspicuous that could extort such a confession in favour of the vanquished enemy of Theodosius. The discontent of Maximus might incline him to censure the conduct of his sovereign, and to encourage, perhaps without any views of ambition, the murmurs of the troops. But in the midst of the tumult he artfully or modestly refused to ascend the throne, and some credit appears to have been given to his own positive declaration that he was compelled to accept the dangerous present of the Imperial purple.[12]

But there was danger likewise in refusing the empire, and, from the moment that Maximus had violated his allegiance to his lawful sovereign, he could not hope to reign, or even to live, if he confined his moderate ambition within the narrow limits of Britain. He boldly and wisely resolved to prevent the designs of Gratian; the youth of the island crowded to his standard, and he invaded Gaul with a fleet and

---

[8] Britannia fertilis provincia tyrannorum, is a memorable expression used by Jerom in the Pelagian controversy, and variously tortured in the disputes of our national antiquaries. The revolutions of the last age appeared to justify the image of the sublime Bossuet, "cette ile, plus orageuse que les mers qui l'environment."

[9] Zosimus says of the British soldiers, τῶν ἄλλων ἁπάντων πλέον αὐθαδείᾳ καὶ θυμῷ νικωμένους [l. c.].

[10] Helena the daughter of Eudda. Her chapel may still be seen at Caersegont, now Caer-narvon. (Carte's Hist. of England, vol. i. p. 168, from Rowland's Mona Antiqua.) The prudent reader may not perhaps be satisfied with such Welch evidence.

[11] Camden (vol. i. introduct. p. ci) appoints him governor of Britain; and the father of our antiquities is followed, as usual, by his blind progeny. Pacatus and Zosimus had taken some pains to prevent this error or fable; and I shall protect myself by their decisive testimonies. Regali habitû exulem suum, illi exules orbis induerunt (in Panegyr. Vet. xii. 23), and the Greek historian still less equivocally, αὐτὸς (Maximus) δὲ οὐδὲ εἰς ἀρχὴν ἔντιμον ἔτυχε προελθών (l. iv. [c. 35] p. 248).

[12] Sulpicius Severus, Dialog. ii. 7. Orosius, l. vii. c. 34, p. 556. They both acknowledge (Sulpicius had been his subject) his innocence and merit. It is singular enough that Maximus should be less favourably treated by Zosimus, the partial adversary of his rival.

THE ROMAN EMPIRE 5

army which were long afterwards remembered as the emigration of a considerable part of the British nation.[13] The emperor, in his peaceful residence of Paris, was alarmed by their hostile approach, and the darts which he idly wasted on lions and bears might have been employed more honourably against the rebels. But his feeble efforts announced his degenerate spirit and desperate situation, and deprived him of the resources which he still might have found in the support of his subjects and allies. The armies of Gaul, instead of opposing the march of Maximus, received him with joyful and loyal acclamations, and the shame of the desertion was transferred from the people to the prince. The troops whose station more immediately attached them to the service of the palace abandoned the standard of Gratian the first time that it was displayed in the neighbourhood of Paris. The emperor of the West fled towards Lyons with a train of only three hundred horse, and in the cities along the road, where he hoped to find a refuge, or at least a passage, he was taught by cruel experience that every gate is shut against the unfortunate. Yet he might still have reached in safety the dominions of his brother, and soon have returned with the forces of Italy and the East, if he had not suffered himself to be fatally deceived by the perfidious governor of the Lyonnese province. Gratian was amused by protestations of doubtful fidelity, and the hopes of a support which could not be effectual, till the arrival of Andragathius, the general of the cavalry of Maximus, put an end to his suspense. That resolute officer executed, without remorse, the orders or the intentions of the usurper. Gratian, as he rose from supper, was delivered into the hands of the assassin, and his body was denied to the pious and pressing entreaties of his brother Valentinian.[14] The death of the emperor was followed by that of his powerful general Mellobaudes, the king of the Franks, who maintained to the last moment of his life the ambiguous reputation which is the just recompense of obscure and subtle policy.[15] These executions might be necessary to the public safety, but the successful usurper, whose power was acknowledged by all the provinces of the West, had the merit and the

[13] Archbishop Usher (Antiquitat. Britan. Eccles. p. 107, 108) has diligently collected the legends of the island and the continent. The whole emigration consisted of 30,000 soldiers and 100,000 plebeians, who settled in Bretagne. Their destined brides, St. Ursula with 11,000 noble and 60,000 plebeian virgins, mistook their way, landed at Cologne, and were all most cruelly murdered by the Huns. But the plebeian sisters have been defrauded of their equal honours; and, what is still harder, John Trithemius presumes to mention the *children* of these British *virgins*.

[14] Zosimus (l. iv. [c. 35] p. 248, 249) has transported the death of Gratian from Lugdunum in Gaul (Lyons) to Singidunum in Mæsia. Some hints may be extracted from the Chronicles; some lies may be detected in Sozomen (l. vii. c. 13) and Socrates (l. v. c. 11). Ambrose is our most authentic evidence (tom. i. Enarrat. in Psalm lxi. p. 961, tom. ii. Epist. xxiv. p. 888, etc., and de Obitû Valentinian. Consolat. No. 28, p. 1182).

[15] Pacatus (xii. 28) celebrates his fidelity; while his treachery is marked in Prosper's Chronicle as the cause of the ruin of Gratian. Ambrose, who has occasion to exculpate himself, only condemns the death of Vallio, a faithful servant of Gratian (tom. ii. Epist. xxiv. p. 891, edit. Benedict.).

satisfaction of boasting that, except those who had perished by the chance of war, his triumph was not stained by the blood of the Romans.[16]

The events of this revolution had passed in such rapid succession that it would have been impossible for Theodosius to march to the relief of his benefactor before he received the intelligence of his defeat and death. During the season of sincere grief or ostentatious mourning the Eastern emperor was interrupted by the arrival of the principal chamberlain of Maximus; and the choice of a venerable old man for an office which was usually exercised by eunuchs announced to the court of Constantinople the gravity and temperance of the British usurper. The ambassador condescended to justify or excuse the conduct of his master, and to protest, in specious language, that the murder of Gratian had been perpetrated, without his knowledge or consent, by the precipitate zeal of the soldiers. But he proceeded, in a firm and equal tone, to offer Theodosius the alternative of peace or war. The speech of the ambassador concluded with a spirited declaration that, although Maximus, as a Roman and as the father of his people, would choose rather to employ his forces in the common defence of the republic, he was armed and prepared, if his friendship should be rejected, to dispute in a field of battle the empire of the world. An immediate and peremptory answer was required, but it was extremely difficult for Theodosius to satisfy, on this important occasion, either the feelings of his own mind or the expectations of the public. The imperious voice of honour and gratitude called aloud for revenge. From the liberality of Gratian he had received the Imperial diadem; his patience would encourage the odious suspicion that he was more deeply sensible of former injuries than of recent obligations; and if he accepted the friendship, he must seem to share the guilt, of the assassin. Even the principles of justice and the interest of society would receive a fatal blow from the impunity of Maximus, and the example of successful usurpation would tend to dissolve the artificial fabric of government, and once more to replunge the empire in the crimes and calamities of the preceding age. But, as the sentiments of gratitude and honour should invariably regulate the conduct of an individual, they may be overbalanced in the mind of a sovereign by the sense of superior duties, and the maxims both of justice and humanity must permit the escape of an atrocious criminal if an innocent people would be involved in the consequences of his punishment. The assassin of Gratian had usurped, but he actually possessed, the most warlike provinces of the empire; the East was exhausted by the misfortunes, and even by the success, of the Gothic war; and it was seriously to be apprehended that, after the vital strength of the republic had been wasted in a doubtful and destructive contest, the feeble conqueror

---

[16] He protested, nullum ex adversariis nisi inacie occubuisse. Sulp. Severus in Vit. B. Martin. c. 23. The orator of Theodosius bestows reluctant, and therefore weighty, praise on his clemency. Si cui ille, pro ceteris, sceleribus, suit, *minus crudelis* fuisse videtur (Panegyr. Vet. xii. 28).

would remain an easy prey to the barbarians of the north. These weighty considerations engaged Theodosius to dissemble his resentment and to accept the alliance of the tyrant. But he stipulated that Maximus should content himself with the possession of the countries beyond the Alps. The brother of Gratian was confirmed and secured in the sovereignty of Italy, Africa, and the Western Illyricum, and some honourable conditions were inserted in the treaty to protect the memory and the laws of the deceased emperor.[17] According to the custom of the age, the images of the three Imperial colleagues were exhibited to the veneration of the people; nor should it be lightly supposed that, in the moment of a solemn reconciliation, Theodosius secretly cherished the intention of perfidy and revenge.[18]

The contempt of Gratian for the Roman soldiers had exposed him to the fatal effects of their resentment. His profound veneration for the Christian clergy was rewarded by the applause and gratitude of a powerful order, which has claimed in every age the privilege of dispensing honours, both on earth and in heaven.[19] The orthodox bishops bewailed his death, and their own irreparable loss; but they were soon comforted by the discovery that Gratian had committed the sceptre of the East to the hands of a prince whose humble faith and fervent zeal were supported by the spirit and abilities of a more vigorous character. Among the benefactors of the church, the fame of Constantine has been rivalled by the glory of Theodosius. If Constantine had the advantage of erecting the standard of the cross, the emulation of his successor assumed the merit of subduing the Arian heresy, and of abolishing the worship of idols in the Roman world. Theodosius was the first of the emperors baptised in the true faith of the Trinity. Although he was born of a Christian family, the maxims, or at least the practice, of the age encouraged him to delay the ceremony of his initiation till he was admonished of the danger of delay by the serious illness which threatened his life towards the end of the first year of his reign. Before he again took the field against the Goths, he received the sacrament of baptism[20] from Acholius, the orthodox bishop of Thessalonica:[21] and as the emperor ascended from the holy font, still glowing with the warm feelings of regeneration, he dictated a solemn edict, which proclaimed his own faith, and prescribed the religion of his subjects. "It

[17] Ambrose mentions the laws of Gratian, quas non abrogavit hostis (tom. ii. Epist. xvii. p. 827).
[18] Zosimus, l. iv. [c. 37] p. 251, 252. We may disclaim his odious suspicions, but we cannot reject the treaty of peace which the friends of Theodosius have absolutely forgotten, or slightly mentioned.
[19] Their oracle, the archbishop of Milan, assigns to his pupil Gratian a high and respectable place in heaven (tom. ii. de Obit. Val. Consol. p. 1193).
[20] For the baptism of Theodosius, see Sozomen (l. vii. c. 4), Socrates (l. v. c. 6), and Tillemont (Hist. des Empereurs, tom. v. p. 728).
[21] Ascolius, or Acholius, was honoured by the friendship and the praises of Ambrose, who styles him, murus fidei atque sanctitatis (tom. ii. Epist. xv. p. 820); and afterwards celebrates his speed and diligence in running to Constantinople, Italy, etc. (Epist. xvi. p. 822)—a virtue which does not appertain either to a *wall* or a *bishop*.

is our pleasure (such is the Imperial style) that all the nations which are governed by our clemency and moderation should steadfastly adhere to the religion which was taught by St. Peter to the Romans, which faithful tradition has preserved, and which is now professed by the pontiff Damascus, and by Peter, bishop of Alexandria, a man of apostolic holiness. According to the discipline of the apostles, and the doctrine of the Gospel, let us believe the sole deity of the Father, the Son, and the Holy Ghost, under an equal majesty and a pious Trinity. We authorise the followers of this doctrine to assume the title of Catholic Christians; and as we judge that all others are extravagant madmen, we brand them with the infamous name of Heretics, and declare that their conventicles shall no longer usurp the respectable appellation of churches. Besides the condemnation of Divine justice, they must expect to suffer the severe penalties, which our authority, guided by heavenly wisdom, shall think proper to inflict upon them."[22] The faith of a soldier is commonly the fruit of instruction, rather than of inquiry; but as the emperor always fixed his eyes on the visible landmarks of orthodoxy which he had so prudently constituted, his religious opinions were never affected by the specious texts, the subtle arguments, and the ambiguous creeds of the Arian doctors. Once indeed he expressed a faint inclination to converse with the eloquent and learned Eunomius, who lived in retirement at a small distance from Constantinople. But the dangerous interview was prevented by the prayers of the Empress Flacilla, who trembled for the salvation of her husband; and the mind of Theodosius was confirmed by a theological argument adapted to the rudest capacity. He had lately bestowed on his eldest son Arcadius the name and honours of Augustus, and the two princes were seated on a stately throne to receive the homage of their subjects. A bishop, Amphilochius of Iconium, approached the throne, and, after saluting with due reverence the person of his sovereign, he accosted the royal youth with the same familiar tenderness which he might have used towards a plebeian child. Provoked by this insolent behaviour, the monarch gave orders that the rustic priest should be instantly driven from his presence. But while the guards were forcing him to the door, the dexterous polemic had time to execute his design, by exclaiming, with a loud voice, "Such is the treatment, O emperor! which the King of heaven has prepared for those impious men who affect to worship the Father, but refuse to acknowledge the equal majesty of his divine Son." Theodosius immediately embraced the bishop of Iconium, and never forgot the important lesson which he received from this dramatic parable.[23]

Constantinople was the principal seat and fortress of Arianism; and,

[22] Codex Theodos. l. xvi. tit. i. leg. 2, with Godefroy's Commentary, tom. vi. p. 5-9. Such an edict deserved the warmest praises of Baronius, auream sanctionem, edictum pium et salutare.—sic itur ad astra.

[23] Sozomen, l. vii. c. 6. Theodoret, l. v. c. 16. Tillemont is displeased (Mém. Ecclés. tom. vi. p. 627, 628) with the terms of "rustic bishop," "obscure city." Yet I must take leave to think that both Amphilochius and Iconium were objects of inconsiderable magnitude in the Roman empire.

in a long interval of forty years,[24] the faith of the princes and prelates who reigned in the capital of the East was rejected in the purer schools of Rome and Alexandria. The archiepiscopal throne of Macedonius, which had been polluted with so much Christian blood, was successively filled by Eudoxus and Damophilus. Their diocese enjoyed a free importation of vice and error from every province of the empire; the eager pursuit of religious controversy afforded a new occupation to the busy idleness of the metropolis: and we may credit the assertion of an intelligent observer, who describes, with some pleasantry, the effects of their loquacious zeal. "This city," says he, "is full of mechanics and slaves, who are all of them profound theologians, and preach in the shops and in the streets. If you desire a man to change a piece of silver, he informs you wherein the Son differs from the Father; if you ask the price of a loaf, you are told, by way of reply, that the Son is inferior to the Father; and if you inquire whether the bath is ready, the answer is, that the Son was made out of nothing."[25] The heretics, of various denominations, subsisted in peace under the protection of the Arians of Constantinople, who endeavoured to secure the attachment of those obscure sectaries, while they abused, with unrelenting severity, the victory which they had obtained over the followers of the council of Nice. During the partial reigns of Constantius and Valens, the feeble remnant of the Homoousians was deprived of the public and private exercise of their religion; and it has been observed, in pathetic language, that the scattered flock was left without a shepherd to wander on the mountains, or to be devoured by rapacious wolves.[26] But as their zeal, instead of being subdued, derived strength and vigour from oppression, they seized the first moments of imperfect freedom, which they acquired by the death of Valens, to form themselves into a regular congregation, under the conduct of an episcopal pastor. Two natives of Cappadocia, Basil and Gregory Nazianzen,[27] were distinguished above all their contemporaries[28] by the rare union of profane eloquence

[24] Sozomen, l. vii. c. 5. Socrates, l. v. c. 7. Marcellin. in Chron. The account of forty years must be dated from the election or intrusion of Eusebius, who wisely exchanged the bishopric of Nicomedia for the throne of Constantinople.

[25] See Jortin's Remarks on Ecclesiastical History, vol. iv. p. 71. The thirty-third Oration of Gregory Nazianzen affords indeed some similar ideas, even some still more ridiculous; but I have not yet found the *words* of this remarkable passage, which I allege on the faith of a correct and liberal scholar.

[26] See the thirty-second Oration of Gregory Nazianzen, and the account of his own life, which he has composed in 1800 iambics. Yet every physician is prone to exaggerate the inveterate nature of the disease which he has cured.

[27] I confess myself deeply indebted to the *two* Lives of Gregory Nazianzen, composed with very different views, by Tillemont (Mém. Ecclés. tom. ix. p. 305–560, 692–731), and Le Clerc (Bibliothèque Universelle, tom. xviii. p. 1–128).

[28] Unless Gregory Nazianzen mistook thirty years in his own age, he was born, as well as his friend Basil, about the year 329. The preposterous chronology of Suidas has been graciously received, because it removes the

and of orthodox piety. These orators, who might sometimes be compared, by themselves and by the public, to the most celebrated of the ancient Greeks, were united by the ties of the strictest friendship. They had cultivated, with equal ardour, the same liberal studies in the schools of Athens; they had retired, with equal devotion, to the same solitude in the deserts of Pontus; and every spark of emulation or envy appeared to be totally extinguished in the holy and ingenious breasts of Gregory and Basil. But the exaltation of Basil, from a private life to the archiepiscopal throne of Cæsarea, discovered to the world, and perhaps to himself, the pride of his character; and the first favour which he condescended to bestow on his friend was received, and perhaps was intended, as a cruel insult.[29] Instead of employing the superior talents of Gregory in some useful and conspicuous station, the haughty prelate selected, among the fifty bishoprics of his extensive province, the wretched village of Sasima,[30] without water, without verdure, without society, situate at the junction of three highways, and frequented only by the incessant passage of rude and clamorous waggoners. Gregory submitted with reluctance to this humiliating exile: he was ordained bishop of Sasima; but he solemnly protests that he never consummated his spiritual marriage with this disgusting bride. He afterwards consented to undertake the government of his native church of Nazianzus,[31] of which his father had been bishop above five-and-forty years. But as he was still conscious that he deserved another audience and another theatre, he accepted, with no unworthy ambition, the honourable invitation which was addressed to him from the orthodox party of Constantinople. On his arrival in the capital, Gregory was entertained in the house of a pious and charitable kinsman; the most

scandal of Gregory's father, a saint likewise, begetting children after he became a bishop (Tillemont, Mém. Ecclés. tom. ix. p. 693-697).

[29] Gregory's Poem on his own Life contains some beautiful lines (tom. ii. p. 8 [ed. Paris, 1609]), which burst from the heart, and speak the pangs of injured and lost friendship:—

$$\ldots\ldots \pi \acute{o} \nu o \iota \ \kappa o \iota \nu o \grave{\iota} \ \lambda \acute{o} \gamma \omega \nu,$$
$$O \mu \acute{o} \sigma \tau \epsilon \gamma \acute{o} s \ \tau \epsilon \ \kappa a \grave{\iota} \ \sigma \upsilon \nu \acute{\epsilon} \sigma \tau \iota o s \ \beta \acute{\iota} o s,$$
$$N o \hat{\upsilon} s \ \epsilon \hat{\iota} s \ \acute{\epsilon} \nu \ \acute{a} \mu \phi o \hat{\iota} \nu \ldots$$
$$\Delta \iota \epsilon \sigma \kappa \acute{\epsilon} \delta a \sigma \tau a \iota \ \pi \acute{a} \nu \tau a, \ \kappa \acute{a} \rho \rho \iota \pi \tau a \iota \ \chi a \mu a \acute{\iota}.$$
$$A \mathring{\upsilon} \rho a \iota \ \phi \acute{\epsilon} \rho o \upsilon \sigma \iota \ \tau \grave{a} s \ \pi a \lambda a \iota \grave{a} s \ \acute{\epsilon} \lambda \pi \acute{\iota} \delta a s.$$

In A Midsummer Night's Dream, Helena addresses the same pathetic complaint to her friend Hermia:—

        Is all the counsel that we two have shared,
        The sisters' vows, etc.

Shakespeare had never read the poems of Gregory Nazianzen; he was ignorant of the Greek language; but his mother-tongue, the language of Nature, is the same in Cappadocia and in Britain.

[30] This unfavourable portrait of Sasima is drawn by Gregory Nazianzen (tom. ii. de Vita suâ, p. 7, 8). Its precise situation, forty-nine miles from Archelais, and thirty-two from Tyana, is fixed in the Itinerary of Antoninus (p. 144, edit. Wesseling).

[31] The name of Nazianzus has been immortalised by Gregory; but his native town, under the Greek or Roman title of Diocæsarea (Tillemont, Mém. Ecclés. tom. ix. p. 692), is mentioned by Pliny (vi. 3), Ptolemy, and Hierocles (Itinerar. Wesseling, p. 709). It appears to have been situate on the edge of Isauria.

spacious room was consecrated to the uses of religious worship; and the name of *Anastasia* was chosen to express the resurrection of the Nicene faith. This private conventicle was afterwards converted into a magnificent church; and the credulity of the succeeding age was prepared to believe the miracles and visions which attested the presence, or at least the protection, of the Mother of God.[32] The pulpit of the Anastasia was the scene of the labours and triumphs of Gregory Nazianzen; and in the space of two years he experienced all the spiritual adventures which constitute the prosperous or adverse fortunes of a missionary.[33] The Arians, who were provoked by the boldness of his enterprise, represented his doctrine as if he had preached three distinct and equal Deities; and the devout populace was excited to suppress, by violence and tumult, the irregular assemblies of the Athanasian heretics. From the cathedral of St. Sophia there issued a motley crowd "of common beggars, who had forfeited their claim to pity; of monks, who had the appearance of goats or satyrs; and of women, more terrible than so many Jezebels." The doors of the Anastasia were broken open; much mischief was perpetrated, or attempted, with sticks, stones, and firebrands; and as a man lost his life in the affray, Gregory, who was summoned the next morning before the magistrate, had the satisfaction of supposing that he publicly confessed the name of Christ. After he was delivered from the fear and danger of a foreign enemy, his infant church was disgraced and distracted by intestine faction. A stranger, who assumed the name of Maximus [34] and the cloak of a Cynic philosopher, insinuated himself into the confidence of Gregory, deceived and abused his favourable opinion, and, forming a secret connection with some bishops of Egypt, attempted, by a clandestine ordination, to supplant his patron in the episcopal seat of Constantinople. These mortifications might sometimes tempt the Cappadocian missionary to regret his obscure solitude. But his fatigues were rewarded by the daily increase of his fame and his congregation; and he enjoyed the pleasure of observing that the greater part of his numerous audience retired from his sermons satisfied with the eloquence of the preacher,[35] or dissatisfied with the manifold imperfections of their faith and practice.[36]

[32] See Ducange, Constant. Christiana, l. iv. p. 141, 142. The θεία δύναμις of Sozomen (l. vii. c. 5) is interpreted to mean the Virgin Mary.

[33] Tillemont (Mém. Ecclés. tom. ix. p. 432, etc.) diligently collects, enlarges, and explains, the oratorical and poetical hints of Gregory himself.

[34] He pronounced an oration (tom. i. Orat. xxiii. p. 409) in his praise; but after their quarrel the name of Maximus was changed into that of Heron (see Jerom, tom. i. in Catalog. Script. Eccles. p. 301 [tom. ii. p. 930, ed. Vallars.]). I touch slightly on these obscure and personal squabbles.

[35] Under the modest emblem of a dream, Gregory (tom. ii. Carmen ix. p. 78) describes his own success with some human complacency. Yet it should seem, from his familiar conversation with his auditor St. Jerom (tom. i. Epist. ad Nepotian, p. 14 [tom. i. p. 261, ed. Vallars.]), that the preacher understood the true value of popular applause.

[36] Lacrimæ auditorum laudes tuæ sint, is the lively and judicious advice of St. Jerom [loc. cit.].

The catholics of Constantinople were animated with joyful confidence by the baptism and edict of Theodosius; and they impatiently waited the effects of his gracious promise. Their hopes were speedily accomplished; and the emperor, as soon as he had finished the operations of the campaign, made his public entry into the capital at the head of a victorious army. The next day after his arrival he summoned Damophilus to his presence, and offered that Arian prelate the hard alternative of subscribing to the Nicene creed, or of instantly resigning, to the orthodox believers, the use and possession of the episcopal palace, the cathedral of St. Sophia, and all the churches of Constantinople. The zeal of Damophilus, which in a catholic saint would have been justly applauded, embraced, without hesitation, a life of poverty and exile,[37] and his removal was immediately followed by the purification of the Imperial city. The Arians might complain, with some appearance of justice. that an inconsiderable congregation of sectaries should usurp the hundred churches which they were insufficient to fill, whilst the far greater part of the people was cruelly excluded from every place of religious worship. Theodosius was still inexorable; but as the angels who protected the catholic cause were only visible to the eyes of faith, he prudently reinforced those heavenly legions with the more effectual aid of temporal and carnal weapons, and the church of St. Sophia was occupied by a large body of the Imperial guards. If the mind of Gregory was susceptible of pride, he must have felt a very lively satisfaction when the emperor conducted him through the streets in solemn triumph, and, with his own hand, respectfully placed him on the archiepiscopal throne of Constantinople. But the saint (who had not subdued the imperfections of human virtue) was deeply affected by the mortifying consideration that his entrance into the fold was that of a wolf rather than of a shepherd; that the glittering arms which surrounded his person were necessary for his safety; and that he alone was the object of the imprecations of a great party, whom, as men and citizens, it was impossible for him to despise. He beheld the innumerable multitude, of either sex, and of every age, who crowded the streets, the windows, and the roofs of the houses; he heard the tumultuous voice of rage, grief, astonishment, and despair; and Gregory fairly confesses that on the memorable day of his installation the capital of the East wore the appearance of a city taken by storm, and in the hands of a barbarian conqueror.[38] About six weeks afterwards, Theodosius declared his resolution of expelling from all the churches of his dominions the bishops and their clergy who should obstinately refuse to believe, or at least to profess, the doctrine of the council of Nice. His lieutenant Sapor was

[37] Socrates (l. v. c. 7) and Sozomen (l. vii. c. 5) relate the evangelical words and actions of Damophilus without a word of approbation. He considered, says Socrates, that it is difficult to *resist* the powerful; but it was easy, and would have been profitable, to *submit.*

[38] See Gregory Nazianzen, tom. ii. de Vitâ suâ, p. 21, 22. For the sake of posterity, the bishop of Constantinople records a stupendous prodigy. In the month of November, it was a cloudy morning, but the sun broke forth when the procession entered the church.

armed with the ample powers of a general law, a special commission, and a military force;[39] and this ecclesiastical revolution was conducted with so much discretion and vigour, that the religion of the emperor was established, without tumult or bloodshed, in all the provinces of the East. The writings of the Arians, if they had been permitted to exist,[40] would perhaps contain the lamentable story of the persecution which afflicted the church under the reign of the impious Theodosius; and the sufferings of *their* holy confessors might claim the pity of the disinterested reader. Yet there is reason to imagine that the violence of zeal and revenge was in some measure eluded by the want of resistance; and that, in their adversity, the Arians displayed much less firmness than had been exerted by the orthodox party under the reigns of Constantius and Valens. The moral character and conduct of the hostile sects appear to have been governed by the same common principles of nature and religion: but a very material circumstance may be discovered, which tended to distinguish the degrees of their theological faith. Both parties in the schools, as well as in the temples, acknowledged and worshipped the divine majesty of Christ; and, as we are always prone to impute our own sentiments and passions to the Diety, it would be deemed more prudent and respectful to exaggerate than to circumscribe the adorable perfections of the Son of God. The disciple of Athanasius exulted in the proud confidence that he had entitled himself to the divine favour, while the follower of Arius must have been tormented by the secret apprehension that he was guilty perhaps of an unpardonable offence by the scanty praise and parsimonious honours which he bestowed on the Judge of the World. The opinions of Arianism might satisfy a cold and speculative mind; but the doctrine of the Nicene Creed, most powerfully recommended by the merits of faith and devotion, was much better adapted to become popular and successful in a believing age.

The hope that truth and wisdom would be found in the assemblies of the orthodox clergy induced the emperor to convene, at Constantinople, a synod of one hundred and fifty bishops, who proceeded, without much difficulty or delay, to complete the theological system which had been established in the council of Nice. The vehement disputes of the fourth century had been chiefly employed on the nature of the Son of God; and the various opinions which were embraced concerning the *Second*, were extended and transferred, by a natural analogy, to the *Third* person of the Trinity.[41] Yet it was found, or it

[39] Of the three ecclesiastical historians, Theodoret alone (l. v. c. 2) has mentioned this important commission of Sapor, which Tillemont (Hist. des Empereurs, tom. v. p. 728), judiciously removes from the reign of Gratian to that of Theodosius.

[40] I do not reckon Philostorgius, though he mentions (l. ix. c. 19) the expulsion of Damophilus. The Eunomian historian has been carefully strained through an orthodox sieve.

[41] Le Clerc has given a curious extract (Bibliothèque Universelle, tom. xviii. p. 91-105) of the theological sermons which Gregory Nazianzen pronounced at Constantinople against the Arians, Eunomians, Macedonians, etc. He tells the Macedonians, who deified the Father and the Son, without the

was thought, necessary, by the victorious adversaries of Arianism, to explain the ambiguous language of some respectable doctors; to confirm the faith of the catholics; and to condemn an unpopular and inconsistent sect of Macedonians, who freely admitted that the Son was consubstantial to the Father, while they were fearful of seeming to acknowledge the existence of *Three* Gods. A final and unanimous sentence was pronounced to ratify the equal Deity of the Holy Ghost: the mysterious doctrine has been received by all the nations, and all the churches, of the Christian world; and their grateful reverence has assigned to the bishops of Theodosius the second rank among the general councils.[42]   Their knowledge of religious truth may have been preserved by tradition, or it may have been communicated by inspiration; but the sober evidence of history will not allow much weight to the personal authority of the Fathers of Constantinople.   In an age when the ecclesiastics had scandalously degenerated from the model of apostolical purity, the most worthless and corrupt were always the most eager to frequent and disturb the episcopal assemblies.   The conflict and fermentation of so many opposite interests and tempers inflamed the passions of the bishops: and their ruling passions were the love of gold and the love of dispute.   Many of the same prelates who now applauded the orthodox piety of Theodosius had repeatedly changed, with prudent flexibility, their creeds and opinions; and in the various revolutions of the church and state, the religion of their sovereign was the rule of their obsequious faith.   When the emperor suspended his prevailing influence, the turbulent synod was blindly impelled by the absurd or selfish motives of pride, hatred, and resentment.   The death of Meletius, which happened at the council of Constantinople, presented the most favourable opportunity of terminating the schism of Antioch, by suffering his aged rival, Paulinus, peaceably to end his days in the episcopal chair.   The faith and virtues of Paulinus were unblemished.   But his cause was supported by the Western churches; and the bishops of the synod resolved to perpetuate the mischiefs of discord, by the hasty ordination of a perjured candidate,[43] rather than to betray the imagined dignity of the East, which had been illustrated by the birth and death of the Son of God.   Such unjust and disorderly proceedings forced the gravest members of the assembly to dissent and to secede; and the clamorous majority, which remained masters of the

Holy Ghost, that they might as well be styled *Tritheists as Ditheists.* Gregory himself was almost a Tritheist, and his monarchy of heaven resembles a well-regulated aristocracy.

[42] The first general council of Constantinople now triumphs in the Vatican; but the popes had long hesitated, and their hesitation perplexes and almost staggers the humble Tillemont (Mém. Ecclés. tom. ix. p. 499, 500).

[43] Before the death of Meletius, six or eight of his most popular ecclesiastics, among whom was Flavian, had *abjured,* for the sake of peace, the bishopric of Antioch (Sozomen, l. vii. c. 3, 11; Socrates, l. v. c. 5). Tillemont thinks it his duty to disbelieve the story; but he owns that there are many circumstances in the life of Flavian which *seem* inconsistent with the praises of Chrysostom and the character of a saint (Mém. Ecclés. tom. x. p. 541).

field of battle, could be compared only to wasps or magpies, to a flight of cranes, or to a flock of geese.[44]

A suspicion may possibly arise that so unfavourable a picture of ecclesiastical synods has been drawn by the partial hand of some obstinate heretic or some malicious infidel. But the name of the sincere historian who has conveyed this instructive lesson to the knowledge of posterity must silence the impotent murmurs of superstition and bigotry. He was one of the most pious and eloquent bishops of the age; a saint, and a doctor of the church; the scourge of Arianism, and the pillar of the orthodox faith; a distinguished member of the council of Constantinople, in which, after the death of Meletius, he exercised the functions of president: in a word—Gregory Nazianzen himself. The harsh and ungenerous treatment which he experienced,[45] instead of derogating from the truth of his evidence, affords an additional proof of the spirit which actuated the deliberations of the synod. Their unanimous suffrage had confirmed the pretensions which the bishop of Constantinople derived from the choice of the people and the approbation of the emperor. But Gregory soon became the victim of malice and envy. The bishops of the East, his strenuous adherents, provoked by his moderation in the affairs of Antioch, abandoned him, without support, to the adverse faction of the Egyptians, who disputed the validity of his election and rigorously asserted the obsolete canon that prohibited the licentious practice of episcopal translations. The pride, or the humility, of Gregory, prompted him to decline a contest which might have been imputed to ambition and avarice; and he publicly offered, not without some mixture of indignation, to renounce the government of a church which had been restored, and almost created by his labours. His resignation was accepted by the synod, and by the emperor, with more readiness than he seems to have expected. At the time when he might have hoped to enjoy the fruits of his victory, his episcopal throne was filled by the senator Nectarius; and the new archbishop, accidentally recommended by his easy temper and venerable aspect, was obliged to delay the ceremony of his consecration till he had previously despatched the rites of his baptism.[46] After this remarkable experience of the ingratitude of princes and prelates, Gregory retired once more to his

[44] Consult Gregory Nazianzen, de Vitâ suâ, tom. ii. p. 25-28. His general and particular opinion of the clergy and their assemblies may be seen in verse and prose (tom. i. Orat. i. p. 33; Epist. lv. p. 814, tom. ii.; Carmen x. p. 81). Such passages are faintly marked by Tillemont, and fairly produced by Le Clerc.

[45] See Gregory, tom. ii. de Vitâ suâ, p. 28-31. The fourteenth, twenty-seventh, and thirty-second Orations were pronounced in the several stages of this business. The peroration of the last (tom. i. p. 528), in which he takes a solemn leave of men and angels, the city and the emperor, the East and the West, etc., is pathetic, and almost sublime.

[46] The whimsical ordination of Nectarius is attested by Sozomen (l. vii. c. 8); but Tillemont observes (Mém. Ecclés. tom. ix. p. 719), Après tout, ce narré de Sozomène est si honteux pour tous ceux qu'il y mêle, et surtout pour Théodose, qu'il vaut mieux travailler à le détruire qu'à le soutenir: an admirable canon of criticism!

obscure solitude of Cappadocia, where he employed the remainder of his life, about eight years, in the exercises of poetry and devotion. The title of Saint has been added to his name: but the tenderness of his heart,[47] and the elegance of his genius, reflect a more pleasing lustre on the memory of Gregory Nazianzen.

It was not enough that Theodosius had suppressed the insolent reign of Arianism, or that he had abundantly revenged the injuries which the catholics sustained from the zeal of Constantius and Valens. The orthodox emperor considered every heretic as a rebel against the supreme powers of heaven and of earth; and each of those powers might exercise their peculiar jurisdiction over the soul and body of the guilty. The decrees of the council of Constantinople had ascertained the true standard of the faith; and the ecclesiastics who governed the conscience of Theodosius suggested the most effectual methods of persecution. In the space of fifteen years he promulgated at least fifteen severe edicts against the heretics,[48] more especially against those who rejected the doctrine of the Trinity; and to deprive them of every hope of escape, he sternly enacted that, if any laws or rescripts should be alleged in their favour, the judges should consider them as the illegal productions, either of fraud or forgery. The penal statutes were directed against the ministers, the assemblies, and the persons of the heretics; and the passions of the legislator were expressed in the language of declamation and invective. I. The heretical teachers, who usurped the sacred titles of Bishops or Presbyters, were not only excluded from the privileges and emoluments so liberally granted to the orthodox clergy, but they were exposed to the heavy penalties of exile and confiscation, if they presumed to preach the doctrine, or to practise the rites, of their *accursed* sects. A fine of ten pounds of gold (above four hundred pounds sterling) was imposed on every person who should dare to confer, or receive, or promote, an heretical ordination: and it was reasonably expected that, if the race of pastors could be extinguished, their helpless flocks would be compelled, by ignorance and hunger, to return within the pale of the catholic church. II. The rigorous prohibition of conventicles was carefully extended to every possible circumstance in which the heretics could assemble with the intention of worshipping God and Christ according to the dictates of their conscience. Their religious meetings, whether public or secret, by day or by night, in cities or in the country, were equally proscribed by the edicts of Theodosius; and the building, or ground, which had been used for that illegal purpose, was forfeited to the Imperial domain. III. It was supposed that the error of the heretics could proceed only from the obstinate temper of their minds; and that such a temper was a fit object of censure and punishment. The anathemas of the church were fortified by a sort of

---

[47] I can only be understood to mean that such was his natural temper when it was not hardened or inflamed by religious zeal. From his retirement he exhorts Nectarius to prosecute the heretics of Constantinople.

[48] See the Theodosian Code, l. xvi. tit. v. leg. 6-23, with Godefroy's commentary on each law, and his general summary, or *Paratitlon*, tom. vi. p. 104-110.

civil excommunication, which separated them from their fellow-citizens by a peculiar brand of infamy; and this declaration of the supreme magistrate tended to justify, or at least to excuse, the insults of a fanatic populace. The sectaries were gradually disqualified for the possession of honourable or lucrative employments; and Theodosius was satisfied with his own justice, when he decreed that, as the Eunomians distinguished the nature of the Son from that of the Father, they should be incapable of making their wills, or of receiving any advantage from testamentary donations. The guilt of the Manichæan heresy was esteemed of such magnitude that it could be expiated only by the death of the offender; and the same capital punishment was inflicted on the Audians, or *Quartodecimans*,[49] who should dare to perpetrate the atrocious crime of celebrating on an improper day the festival of Easter. Every Roman might exercise the right of public accusation; but the office of *Inquisitors* of the Faith, a name so deservedly abhorred, was first instituted under the reign of Theodosius. Yet we are assured that the execution of his penal edicts was seldom enforced; and that the pious emperor appeared less desirous to punish than to reclaim or terrify his refractory subjects.[50]

The theory of persecution was established by Theodosius, whose justice and piety have been applauded by the saints; but the practice of it, in the fullest extent, was reserved for his rival and colleague, Maximus, the first among the Christian princes who shed the blood of his Christian subjects on account of their religious opinions. The cause of the Priscillianists,[51] a recent sect of heretics who disturbed the provinces of Spain, was transferred, by appeal, from the synod of Bordeaux to the Imperial consistory of Trèves; and by the sentence of the Prætorian præfect, seven persons were tortured, condemned, and executed. The first of these was Priscillian [52] himself, bishop of Avila,[53] in Spain, who adorned the advantages of birth and fortune by the accomplishments of eloquence and learning. Two presbyters and two deacons accompanied their beloved master in his death, which they esteemed as a glorious martyrdom; and the number of religious victims was com-

---

[49] They always kept their Easter, like the Jewish Passover, on the fourteenth day of the first moon after the vernal equinox; and thus pertinaciously opposed the Roman church and Nicene synod, which had *fixed* Easter to a Sunday. Bingham's Antiquities, I. xx. c. 5, vol. ii. p. 309, fol. edit.

[50] Sozomen, l. vii. c. 12.

[51] See the Sacred History of Sulpicius Severus (l. ii. p. 437-452, edit. Lugd. Bat. 1647), a correct and original writer. Dr. Lardner (Credibility, etc., part ii. vol. ix. p. 256-350) has laboured this article with pure learning, good sense, and moderation. Tillemont (Mém. Ecclés. tom. viii. p. 491–527) has raked together all the dirt of the fathers—a useful scavenger!

[52] Sulpicius Severus mentions the arch-heretic with esteem and pity. Felix profecto, si non pravo studio corrupisset optimum ingenium; prorsus multa in eo animi et corporis bona cerneres. (Hist. Sacra, l. ii. p. 439.) Even Jerom (tom. i. in Script. Eccles. p. 302 [tom. ii. p. 934, ed. Vallars.]) speaks with temper of Priscillian and Latronian.

[53] The bishopric (in Old Castile) is now worth 20,000 ducats a year (Busching's Geography, vol. ii. p. 308), and is therefore much less likely to produce the author of a new heresy.

pleted by the execution of Latronian, a poet, who rivalled the fame of the ancients; and of Euchrocia, a noble matron of Bordeaux, the widow of the orator Delphidius.[54] Two bishops, who had embraced the sentiments of Priscillian, were condemned to a distant and dreary exile;[55] and some indulgence was shown to the meaner criminals who assumed the merit of an early repentance. If any credit could be allowed to confessions extorted by fear or pain, and to vague reports, the offspring of malice and credulity, the heresy of the Priscillianists would be found to include the various abominations of magic, of impiety, and of lewdness.[56] Priscillian, who wandered about the world in the company of his spiritual sisters, was accused of praying stark-naked in the midst of the congregation; and it was confidently asserted, that the effects of his criminal intercourse with the daughter of Euchrocia had been suppressed by means still more odious and criminal. But an accurate, or rather a candid inquiry, will discover that, if the Priscillianists violated the laws of nature, it was not by the licentiousness, but by the austerity of their lives. They absolutely condemned the use of the marriage-bed; and the peace of families was often disturbed by indiscreet separations. They enjoined, or recommended, a total abstinence from all animal food; and their continual prayers, fasts, and vigils, inculcated a rule of strict and perfect devotion. The speculative tenets of the sect, concerning the person of Christ and the nature of the human soul, were derived from the Gnostic and Manichæan system; and this vain philosophy, which had been transported from Egypt to Spain, was ill adapted to the grosser spirits of the West. The obscure disciples of Priscillian suffered, languished, and gradually disappeared: his tenets were rejected by the clergy and people, but his death was the subject of a long and vehement controversy; while some arraigned, and others applauded, the justice of his sentence. It is with pleasure that we can observe the humane inconsistency of the most illustrious saints and bishops, Ambrose of Milan [57] and Martin of Tours,[58] who, on this occasion, asserted the cause of toleration. They pitied the unhappy men who had been executed at Trèves; they refused to hold communion with their episcopal murderers; and if Martin deviated from that generous resolution, his motives were laudable, and his repentance was exemplary. The bishops of Tours and Milan pronounced, without hesitation, the

[54] Exprobrabatur mulieri viduæ nimia religio, et diligentius culta divinitas (Pacat. in Panegyr. Vet. xii. 29). Such was the idea of a humane though ignorant polytheist.
[55] One of them was sent in Syllinam insulam quæ ultra Britanniam est. What must have been the ancient condition of the rocks of Scilly (Camden's Britannia, vol. ii. p. 1519)?
[56] The scandalous calumnies of Augustin, pope Leo, etc., which Tillemont swallows like a child, and Lardner refutes like a man, may suggest some candid suspicions in favour of the older Gnostics.
[57] Ambrose, tom. ii. Epist. xxiv. p. 891.
[58] In the Sacred History, and the Life of St. Martin, Sulpicius Severus uses some caution; but he declares himself more freely in the Dialogues (iii. 15). Martin was reproved, however, by his own conscience and by an angel; nor could he afterwards perform miracles with so much ease.

eternal damnation of heretics; but they were surprised and shocked by the bloody image of their temporal death, and the honest feelings of nature resisted the artificial prejudices of theology. The humanity of Ambrose and Martin was confirmed by the scandalous irregularity of the proceedings against Priscillian and his adherents. The civil and ecclesiastical ministers had transgressed the limits of their respective provinces. The secular judge had presumed to receive an appeal, and to pronounce a definitive sentence, in a matter of faith and episcopal jurisdiction. The bishops had disgraced themselves by exercising the functions of accusers in a criminal prosecution. The cruelty of Ithacius,[59] who beheld the tortures, and solicited the death of the heretics, provoked the just indignation of mankind; and the vices of that profligate bishop were admitted as a proof that his zeal was instigated by the sordid motives of interest. Since the death of Priscillian, the rude attempts of persecution have been refined and methodised in the holy office, which assigns their distinct parts to the ecclesiastical and secular powers. The devoted victim is regularly delivered by the priest to the magistrate, and by the magistrate to the executioner: and the inexorable sentence of the church, which declares the spiritual guilt of the offender, is expressed in the mild language of pity and intercession.

Among the ecclesiastics who illustrated the reign of Theodosius, Gregory Nazianzen was distinguished by the talents of an eloquent preacher; the reputation of miraculous gifts added weight and dignity to the monastic virtues of Martin of Tours;[60] but the palm of episcopal vigour and ability was justly claimed by the intrepid Ambrose.[61] He was descended from a noble family of Romans; his father had exercised the important office of Prætorian præfect of Gaul; and the son, after passing through the studies of a liberal education, attained, in the regular gradation of civil honours, the station of consular of Liguria, a province which included the Imperial residence of Milan. At the age of thirty-four, and before he had received the sacrament of baptism, Ambrose, to his own surprise and to that of the world, was suddenly transformed from a governor to an archbishop. Without the least mixture, as it is said, of art or intrigue, the whole body of the people unanimously saluted him with the episcopal title; the concord and perseverance of their acclamations were ascribed to a preternatural impulse; and the reluctant magistrate was compelled to undertake a spiritual office for which he was not prepared by the habits and occupa-

---

[59] The catholic presbyter (Sulp. Sever. l. ii. p. 448), and the Pagan orator (Pacat. in Panegyr. Vet. xxi. 29), reprobate with equal indignation the character and conduct of Ithacius.

[60] The Life of St. Martin, and the Dialogues concerning his miracles, contain facts adapted to the grossest barbarism, in a style not unworthy of the Augustin age. So natural is the alliance between good taste and good sense, that I am always astonished by this contrast.

[61] The short and superficial Life of St. Ambrose, by his deacon Paulinus (Appendix ad edit. Benedict. p. i.-xv.), has the merit of original evidence. Tillemont (Mém. Ecclés. tom. x. p. 78-306) and the Benedictine editors (p. xxxi.-lxiii.) have laboured with their usual diligence.

tions of his former life.   But the active force of his genius soon qualified him to exercise, with zeal and prudence, the duties of his ecclesiastical jurisdiction; and while he cheerfully renounced the vain and
splendid trappings of temporal greatness, he condescended, for the
good of the church, to direct the conscience of the emperors, and to
control the administration of the empire.   Gratian loved and revered
him as a father; and the elaborate treatise on the faith of the Trinity
was designed for the instruction of the young prince.   After his tragic
death, at a time when the Empress Justina trembled for her own safety,
and for that of her son Valentinian, the archbishop of Milan was despatched on two different embassies to the court of Trèves.   He exercised, with equal firmness and dexterity, the powers of his spiritual and
political characters; and perhaps contributed, by his authority and eloquence, to check the ambition of Maximus, and to protect the peace of
Italy.[62]   Ambrose had devoted his life and his abilities to the service of
the church.   Wealth was the object of his contempt; he had renounced
his private patrimony; and he sold, without hesitation, the consecrated
plate for the redemption of captives.   The clergy and people of Milan
were attached to their archbishop; and he deserved the esteem, without
soliciting the favour, or apprehending the displeasure, of his feeble
sovereigns.

The government of Italy, and of the young emperor, naturally devolved to his mother Justina, a woman of beauty and spirit, but who,
in the midst of an orthodox people, had the misfortune of professing
the Arian heresy, which she endeavoured to instil into the mind of
her son.   Justina was persuaded that a Roman emperor might claim, in
his own dominions, the public exercise of his religion; and she proposed to the archbishop, as a moderate and reasonable concession,
that he should resign the use of a single church, either in the city or suburbs of Milan.   But the conduct of Ambrose was governed by very
different principles.[63]   The palaces of the earth might indeed belong to
Cæsar, but the churches were houses of God; and, within the limits of
his diocese, he himself, as the lawful successor of the apostles, was the
only minister of God.   The privileges of Christianity, temporal as well
as spiritual, were confined to the true believers; and the mind of Ambrose was satisfied that his own theological opinions were the standard
of truth and orthodoxy.   The archbishop, who refused to hold any conference or negotiation with the instruments of Satan, declared, with
modest firmness, his resolution to die a martyr rather than to yield to
the impious sacrilege; and Justina, who resented the refusal as an act
of insolence and rebellion, hastily determined to exert the Imperial prerogative of her son.   As she desired to perform her public devotions on

[62] Ambrose himself (tom. ii. Epist. xxiv. p. 888-891) gives the emperor a
very spirited account of his own embassy.
[63] His own representation of his principles and conduct (tom. ii. Epist.
xx. xxi. xxii. p. 852-880) is one of the curious monuments of ecclesiastical
antiquity.   It contains two letters to his sister Marcellina, with a petition
to Valentinian, and the sermon *de Basilicis non tradendis*.

the approaching festival of Easter, Ambrose was ordered to appear before the council. He obeyed the summons with the respect of a faithful subject, but he was followed, without his consent, by an innumerable people: they pressed, with impetuous zeal, against the gates of the palace; and the affrighted ministers of Valentinian, instead of pronouncing a sentence of exile on the archbishop of Milan, humbly requested that he would interpose his authority to protect the person of the emperor, and to restore the tranquillity of the capital. But the promises which Ambrose received and communicated were soon violated by a perfidious court; and, during six of the most solemn days which Christian piety has set apart for the exercise of religion, the city was agitated by the irregular convulsions of tumult and fanaticism. The officers of the household were directed to prepare, first the Portian, and afterwards the new, *Basilica,* for the immediate reception of the emperor and his mother. The splendid canopy and hangings of the royal seat were arranged in the customary manner; but it was found necessary to defend them, by a strong guard, from the insults of the populace. The Arian ecclesiastics who ventured to show themselves in the streets were exposed to the most imminent danger of their lives; and Ambrose enjoyed the merit and reputation of rescuing his personal enemies from the hands of the enraged multitude.

But while he laboured to restrain the effects of their zeal, the pathetic vehemence of his sermons continually inflamed the angry and seditious temper of the people of Milan. The characters of Eve, of the wife of Job, of Jezebel, of Herodias, were indecently applied to the mother of the emperor; and her desire to obtain a church for the Arians was compared to the most cruel persecutions which Christianity had endured under the reign of Paganism. The measures of the court served only to expose the magnitude of the evil. A fine of two hundred pounds of gold was imposed on the corporate body of merchants and manufacturers: an order was signified, in the name of the emperor, to all the officers and inferior servants of the courts of justice, that, during the continuance of the public disorders, they should strictly confine themselves to their houses: and the ministers of Valentinian imprudently confessed that the most respectable part of the citizens of Milan was attached to the cause of their archbishop. He was again solicited to restore peace to his country, by a timely compliance with the will of his sovereign. The reply of Ambrose was couched in the most humble and respectful terms, which might, however, be interpreted as a serious declaration of civil war. " His life and fortune were in the hands of the emperor; but he would never betray the church of Christ, or degrade the dignity of the episcopal character. In such a cause he was prepared to suffer whatever the malice of the dæmon could inflict; and he only wished to die in the presence of his faithful flock, and at the foot of the altar; *he* had not contributed to excite, but it was in the power of God alone to appease, the rage of the people: he deprecated the scenes of blood and confusion which were likely to ensue; and it was his fervent prayer that he might not survive to behold the ruin of a flourishing city, and perhaps the desolation of all Italy." [64]   The obstinate bigotry of Justina would have endangered the empire of her son, if, in this contest with the church and people of Milan, she could have depended on the active obedience of the troops of the palace.   A large body of Goths had marched to occupy the *Basilica,* which was the object of the dispute: and it might be expected from the Arian principles and barbarous manners of these foreign mercenaries, that they would not entertain any scruples in the execution of the most sanguinary orders. They were encountered on the sacred threshold by the archbishop, who, thundering against them a sentence of excommunication, asked them, in the tone of a father and a master, Whether it was to invade the house of God that they had implored the hospitable protection of the republic?   The suspense of the barbarians allowed some hours for a more effectual negotiation; and the empress was persuaded by the advice of her wisest counsellors to leave the catholics in possession of all the churches of Milan; and to dissemble, till a more convenient season, her intentions of revenge.   The mother of Valentinian could never forgive the triumph of Ambrose: and the royal youth uttered a passionate exclamation, that his own servants were ready to betray him into the hands of an insolent priest.

The laws of the empire, some of which were inscribed with the name of Valentinian, still condemned the Arian heresy, and seemed to excuse the resistance of the catholics.   By the influence of Justina, an edict of toleration was promulgated in all the provinces which were subject to the court of Milan; the free exercise of their religion was granted to those who professed the faith of Rimini; and the emperor declared that all persons who should infringe this sacred and salutary constitution should be capitally punished, as the enemies of the public peace.[65]   The character and language of the archbishop of Milan may justify the suspicion that his conduct soon afforded a reasonable ground, or at least a specious pretence, to the Arian ministers, who watched the opportunity of surprising him in some act of disobedience to a law which he strangely represents as a law of blood and tyranny.   A sentence of easy and honourable banishment was pronounced, which enjoined Ambrose to depart from Milan without delay, whilst it permitted him to choose the place of his exile and the number of his companions.   But the authority of the saints, who have preached and

---

[64] Retz had a similar message from the queen to request that he would appease the tumult of Paris.   It was no longer in his power, etc.   A quoi j'ajoutai tout ce que vous pouvez vous imaginer de respect, de douleur, de regret, et de soumission, etc. (Mémoires, tom. i. p. 140).   Certainly I do not compare either the causes or the men; yet the coadjutor himself had some idea (p. 84) of imitating St. Ambrose.

[65] Sozomen alone (l. vii. c. 13) throws this luminous fact into a dark and perplexed narrative.

practised the maxims of passive loyalty, appeared to Ambrose of less moment than the extreme and pressing danger of the church. He boldly refused to obey; and his refusal was supported by the unanimous consent of his faithful people.[66] They guarded by turns the person of their archbishop; the gates of the cathedral and the episcopal palace were strongly secured; and the Imperial troops, who had formed the blockade, were unwilling to risk the attack of that impregnable fortress. The numerous poor, who had been relieved by the liberality of Ambrose, embraced the fair occasion of signalising their zeal and gratitude; and as the patience of the multitude might have been exhausted by the length and uniformity of nocturnal vigils, he prudently introduced into the church of Milan the useful institution of a loud and regular psalmody. While he maintained this arduous contest, he was instructed, by a dream, to open the earth in a place where the remains of two martyrs, Gervasius and Protasius,[67] had been deposited above three hundred years. Immediately under the pavement of the church two perfect skeletons were found,[68] with the heads separated from their bodies, and a plentiful effusion of blood. The holy relics were presented, in solemn pomp, to the veneration of the people; and every circumstance of this fortunate discovery was admirably adapted to promote the designs of Ambrose. The bones of the martyrs, their blood, their garments, were supposed to contain a healing power; and the preternatural influence was communicated to the most distant objects, without losing any part of its original virtue. The extraordinary cure of a blind man,[69] and the reluctant confessions of several dæmoniacs, appeared to justify the faith and sanctity of Ambrose; and the truth of those miracles is attested by Ambrose himself, by his secretary Paulinus, and by his proselyte, the celebrated Augustin, who, at that time, professed the art of rhetoric in Milan. The reason of the present age may possibly approve the incredulity of Justina and her Arian court, who derided the theatrical representations which were exhibited by the

[66] Excubabat pia plebs in ecclesiâ mori parata cum episcopo suo . . . Nos adhuc frigidi excitabamur tamen civitate attonitâ atque turbatâ. Augustin. Confession. l. ix. c. 7.

[67] Tillemont, Mém. Ecclés. tom. ii. p. 78, 498. Many churches in Italy, Gaul, etc., were dedicated to these unknown martyrs, of whom St. Gervase seems to have been more fortunate than his companion.

[68] Invenimus miræ magnitudinis viros duos, ut prisca ætas ferebat, tom. ii. Epist. xxii. p. 875. The size of these skeletons was fortunately, or skilfully, suited to the popular prejudice of the gradual decrease of the human stature, which has prevailed in every age since the time of Homer.

Grandiaque effossis mirabitur ossa sepulchris.

[69] Ambros. tom. ii. Epist. xxii. p. 875. Augustin. Confes. l. ix. c. 7, de Civitat. Dei, l. xxii. c. 8. Paulin. in Vitâ St. Ambros. c. 14, in Append. Benedict. p. 4. The blind man's name was Severus; he touched the holy garment, recovered his sight, and devoted the rest of his life (at least twenty-five years) to the service of the church. I should recommend this miracle to our divines, if it did not prove the worship of relics as well as the Nicene creed.

contrivance, and at the expense, of the archbishop.[70]   Their effect,
however, on the minds of the people, was rapid and irresistible; and the
feeble sovereign of Italy found himself unable to contend with the favourite of Heaven.   The powers likewise of the earth interposed in the
defence of Ambrose: the disinterested advice of Theodosius was the genuine result of piety and friendship; and the mask of religious zeal
concealed the hostile and ambitious designs of the tyrant of Gaul.[71]

The reign of Maximus might have ended in peace and prosperity,
could he have contented himself with the possession of three ample
countries, which now constitute the three most flourishing kingdoms of
modern Europe.   But the aspiring usurper, whose sordid ambition was
not dignified by the love of glory and of arms, considered his actual
forces as the instruments only of his future greatness, and his success was the immediate cause of his destruction.   The wealth which he
extorted [72] from the oppressed provinces of Gaul, Spain, and Britain,
was employed in levying and maintaining a formidable army of barbarians, collected, for the most part, from the fiercest nations of Germany.   The conquest of Italy was the object of his hopes and preparations; and he secretly meditated the ruin of an innocent youth, whose
government was abhorred and despised by his catholic subjects.   But as
Maximus wished to occupy, without resistance, the passes of the Alps, he
received, with perfidious smiles, Domninus of Syria, the ambassador of
Valentinian, and pressed him to accept the aid of a considerable body
of troops for the service of a Pannonian war.   The penetration of Ambrose had discovered the snares of an enemy under the professions of
friendship;[73] but the Syrian Domninus was corrupted or deceived by the
liberal favour of the court of Trèves; and the council of Milan obstinately rejected the suspicion of danger with a blind confidence, which
was the effect not of courage, but of fear.   The march of the auxiliaries
was guided by the ambassador; and they were admitted, without distrust, into the fortresses of the Alps.   But the crafty tyrant followed,
with hasty and silent footsteps, in the rear; and as he diligently intercepted all intelligence of his motions, the gleam of armour and the dust
excited by the troops of cavalry first announced the hostile approach of
a stranger to the gates of Milan.   In this extremity, Justina and her son
might accuse their own imprudence and the perfidious arts of Maximus;
but they wanted time, and force, and resolution to stand against the
Gauls and Germans, either in the field or within the walls of a large and

[70] Paulin. in Vit. St. Ambros. c. 5 [15], in Append. Benedict. p. 5.
[71] Tillemont, Mém. Ecclés. tom. x. p. 190, 750.   He partially allows the
mediation of Theodosius, and capriciously rejects that of Maximus, though
it is attested by Prosper, Sozomen, and Theodoret.
[72] The modest censure of Sulpicius (Dialog. iii. 15 [p. 576] inflicts a much
deeper wound than the feeble declamation of Pacatus (xii. 25, 26).
[73] Esto tutior adversus hominem, pacis involucro [bellum] tegentem, was
the wise caution of Ambrose (tom. ii. p, 891) after his return from his second
embassy.

disaffected city. Flight was their only hope; Aquileia their only refuge: and, as Maximus now displayed his genuine character, the brother oɪ Gratian might expect the same fate from the hands of the same assassin. Maximus entered Milan in triumph; and if the wise archbishop refused a dangerous and criminal connection with the usurper, he might indirectly contribute to the success of his arms by inculcating from the pulpit the duty of resignation rather than that of resistance.[74] The unfortunate Justina reached Aquileia in safety; but she distrusted the strength of the fortifications; she dreaded the event of a siege; and she resolved to implore the protection of the great Theodosius, whose power and virtue were celebrated in all the countries of the West. A vessel was secretly provided to transport the Imperial family; they embarked with precipitation in one of the obscure harbours of Venetia, or Istria; traversed the whole extent of the Hadriatic and Ionian seas; turned the extreme promontory of Peloponnesus; and, after a long but successful navigation, reposed themselves in the port of Thessalonica. All the subjects of Valentinian deserted the cause of a prince who, by his abdication, had absolved them from the duty of allegiance; and if the little city of Æmona, on the verge of Italy, had not presumed to stop the career of his inglorious victory, Maximus would have obtained without a struggle the sole possession of the Western empire.

Instead of inviting his royal guests to the palace of Constantinople, Theodosius had some unknown reasons to fix their residence at Thessalonica; but these reasons did not proceed from contempt or indifference, as he speedily made a visit to that city, accompanied by the greatest part of his court and senate. After the first tender expressions of friendship and sympathy, the pious emperor of the East gently admonished Justina that the guilt of heresy was sometimes punished in this world as well as in the next; and that the public profession of the Nicene faith would be the most efficacious step to promote the restoration of her son, by the satisfaction which it must occasion both on earth and in heaven. The momentous question of peace or war was referred by Theodosius to the deliberation of his council; and the arguments which might be alleged on the side of honour and justice had acquired, since the death of Gratian, a considerable degree of additional weight. The persecution of the Imperial family, to which Theodosius himself had been indebted for his fortune, was now aggravated by recent and repeated injuries. Neither oaths nor treaties could restrain the boundless ambition of Maximus; and the delay of vigorous and decisive measures, instead of prolonging the blessings of peace, would expose the Eastern empire to the danger of an hostile invasion. The barbarians who had passed the Danube had lately assumed the character of soldiers and subjects, but their native fierceness was yet untamed; and the operations of a war, which would exercise their valour and diminish

[74] Baronius (A.D. 387, No. 63) applies to this season of public distress some of the penitential sermons of the archbishop.

their numbers, might tend to relieve the provinces from an intolerable oppression. Notwithstanding these specious and solid reasons, which were approved by a majority of the council, Theodosius still hesitated whether he should draw the sword in a contest which could no longer admit any terms of reconciliation; and his magnanimous character was not disgraced by the apprehensions which he felt for the safety of his infant sons, and the welfare of his exhausted people. In this moment of anxious doubt, while the fate of the Roman world depended on the resolution of a single man, the charms of the princess Galla most powerfully pleaded the cause of her brother Valentinian.[75] The heart of Theodosius was softened by the tears of beauty; his affections were insensibly engaged by the graces of youth and innocence; the art of Justina managed and directed the impulse of passion; and the celebration of the royal nuptials was the assurance and signal of the civil war. The unfeeling critics, who consider every amorous weakness as an indelible stain on the memory of a great and orthodox emperor, are inclined on this occasion to dispute the suspicious evidence of the historian Zosimus. For my own part, I shall frankly confess that I am willing to find, or even to seek, in the revolutions of the world some traces of the mild and tender sentiments of domestic life; and amidst the crowd of fierce and ambitious conquerors, I can distinguish, with peculiar complacency, a gentle hero who may be supposed to receive his armour from the hands of love. The alliance of the Persian king was secured by the faith of treaties; the martial barbarians were persuaded to follow the standard or to respect the frontiers of an active and liberal monarch; and the dominions of Theodosius, from the Euphrates to the Hadriatic, resounded with the preparations of war both by land and sea. The skilful disposition of the forces of the East seemed to multiply their numbers, and distracted the attention of Maximus. He had reason to fear that a chosen body of troops, under the command of the intrepid Arbogastes, would direct their march along the banks of the Danube, and boldly penetrate through the Rhætian provinces into the centre of Gaul. A powerful fleet was equipped in the harbours of Greece and Epirus, with an apparent design that, as soon as the passage had been opened by a naval victory, Valentinian and his mother should land in Italy, proceed without delay to Rome, and occupy the majestic seat of religion and empire. In the meanwhile Theodosius himself advanced, at the head of a brave and disciplined army, to encounter his unworthy rival, who, after the siege of Æmona, had fixed his camp in the neighbourhood of Siscia, a city of Pannonia, strongly fortified by the broad and rapid stream of the Save.

[75] The flight of Valentinian and the love of Theodosius for his sister are related by Zosimus (l. iv. [c. 43] p. 263, 264). Tillemont produces some weak and ambiguous evidence to antedate the second marriage of Theodosius (Hist. des Empereurs, tom. v. p. 740), and consequently to refute ces contes de Zosime qui seroient trop contraires à la piété de Théodose.

The veterans, who still remembered the long resistance, and successive resources, of the tyrant Magnentius, might prepare themselves for the labours of three bloody campaigns. But the contest with his successor, who, like him, had usurped the throne of the West, was easily decided in the term of two months,[76] and within the space of two hundred miles. The superior genius of the emperor of the East might prevail over the feeble Maximus, who in this important crisis showed himself destitute of military skill or personal courage; but the abilities of Theodosius were seconded by the advantage which he possessed of a numerous and active cavalry. The Huns, the Alani, and, after their example, the Goths themselves, were formed into squadrons of archers, who fought on horseback, and confounded the steady valour of the Gauls and Germans by the rapid motions of a Tartar war. After the fatigue of a long march in the heat of summer they spurred their foaming horses into the waters of the Save, swam the river in the presence of the enemy, and instantly charged and routed the troops who guarded the high ground on the opposite side. Marcellinus, the tyrant's brother, advanced to support them with the select cohorts, which were considered as the hope and strength of the army. The action, which had been interrupted by the approach of night, was renewed in the morning; and, after a sharp conflict, the surviving remnant of the bravest soldiers of Maximus threw down their arms at the feet of the conqueror. Without suspending his march, to receive the loyal acclamations of the citizens of Æmona, Theodosius pressed forwards to terminate the war by the death or captivity of his rival, who fled before him with the diligence of fear. From the summit of the Julian Alps he descended with such incredible speed into the plain of Italy that he reached Aquileia on the evening of the first day; and Maximus, who found himself encompassed on all sides, had scarcely time to shut the gates of the city. But the gates could not long resist the effort of a victorious enemy; and the despair, the disaffection, the indifference of the soldiers and people hastened the downfall of the wretched Maximus. He was dragged from his throne, rudely stripped of the Imperial ornaments, the robe, the diadem, and the purple slippers; and conducted, like a malefactor, to the camp and presence of Theodosius, at a place about three miles from Aquileia. The behaviour of the emperor was not intended to insult, and he showed some disposition to pity and forgive the tyrant of the West, who had never been his personal enemy, and was now become the object of his contempt. Our sympathy is the most forcibly excited by the misfortunes to which we are exposed; and the spectacle of a proud competitor now prostrate at his feet could not fail of producing very serious and solemn thoughts in the mind of the victorious emperor. But the feeble emotion of involuntary pity was checked by his regard for public justice and the memory of Gratian;

[76] See Godefroy's Chronology of the Laws, Cod. Theodos. tom. i. p. cxix.

and he abandoned the victim to the pious zeal of the soldiers, who drew him out of the Imperial presence and instantly separated his head from his body. The intelligence of his defeat and death was received with sincere or well-dissembled joy: his son Victor, on whom he had conferred the title of Augustus, died by the order, perhaps by the hand, of the bold Arbogastes; and all the military plans of Theodosius were successfully executed. When he had thus terminated the civil war, with less difficulty and bloodshed than he might naturally expect, he employed the winter months of his residence at Milan to restore the state of the afflicted provinces; and early in the spring he made, after the example of Constantine and Constantius, his triumphal entry into the ancient capital of the Roman empire.[77]

The orator, who may be silent without danger, may praise without difficulty and without reluctance;[78] and posterity will confess that the character of Theodosius[79] might furnish the subject of a sincere and ample panegyric. The wisdom of his laws and the success of his arms rendered his administration respectable in the eyes both of his subjects and of his enemies. He loved and practised the virtues of domestic life, which seldom hold their residence in the palaces of kings. Theodosius was chaste and temperate; he enjoyed, without excess, the sensual and social pleasures of the table, and the warmth of his amorous passions was never diverted from their lawful objects. The proud titles of Imperial greatness were adorned by the tender names of a faithful husband, an indulgent father; his uncle was raised, by his affectionate esteem, to the rank of a second parent; Theodosius embraced, as his own, the children of his brother and sister, and the expressions of his regard were extended to the most distant and obscure branches of his numerous kindred. His familiar friends were judiciously selected from among those persons who, in the equal intercourse of private life, had appeared before his eyes without a mask; the consciousness of personal and superior merit enabled him to despise the accidental distinction of the purple, and he proved by his conduct that he had forgotten all the injuries, while he most gratefully remembered all the favours and ser-

[77] Besides the hints which may be gathered from chronicles and ecclesiastical history, Zosimus (l. iv. [c. 40, seq.] p. 259-267), Orosius (l. vii. c. 35), and Pacatus (in Panegyr. Vet. xii. 30-47), supply the loose and scanty materials of this civil war. Ambrose (tom. ii. Epist. xl. p. 952, 953) darkly alludes to the well-known events of a magazine surprised, an action at Petovio, a Sicilian, perhaps a naval, victory, etc. Ausonius (p. 236, edit. Toll.) applauds the peculiar merit and good fortune of Aquileia.

[78] Quam promptum laudare principem, tam tutum siluisse de principe (Pacat. in Panegyr. Vet. xii. 2). Latinus Pacatus Drepanius, a native of Gaul, pronounced this oration at Rome (A.D. 388). He was afterwards proconsul of Africa; and his friend Ausonius praises him as a poet second only to Virgil. See Tillemont, Hist. des Empereurs, tom. v p 303.

[79] See the fair portrait of Theodosius by the younger Victor; the strokes are distinct and the colours are mixed. The praise of Pacatus is too vague: and Claudian always seems afraid of exalting the father above the son.

vices which he had received before he ascended the throne of the Roman empire. The serious or lively tone of his conversation was adapted to the age, the rank, or the character of his subjects whom he admitted into his society; and the affability of his manners displayed the image of his mind. Theodosius respected the simplicity of the good and virtuous: every art, every talent, of an useful or even of an innocent nature, was rewarded by his judicious liberality; and, except the heretics, whom he persecuted with implacable hatred, the diffusive circle of his benevolence was circumscribed only by the limits of the human race. The government of a mighty empire may assuredly suffice to occupy the time and the abilities of a mortal; yet the diligent prince, without aspiring to the unsuitable reputation of profound learning, always reserved some moments of his leisure for the instructive amusement of reading. History, which enlarged his experience, was his favourite study. The annals of Rome, in the long period of eleven hundred years, presented him with a various and splendid picture of human life; and it has been particularly observed that, whenever he perused the cruel acts of Cinna, of Marius, or of Sylla, he warmly expressed his generous detestation of those enemies of humanity and freedom. His disinterested opinion of past events was usefully applied as the rule of his own actions, and Theodosius has deserved the singular commendation that his virtues always seemed to expand with his fortune; the season of his prosperity was that of his moderation, and his clemency appeared the most conspicuous after the danger and success of the civil war. The Moorish guards of the tyrant had been massacred in the first heat of the victory, and a small number of the most obnoxious criminals suffered the punishment of the law. But the emperor showed himself much more attentive to relieve the innocent than to chastise the guilty. The oppressed subjects of the West, who would have deemed themselves happy in the restoration of their lands, were astonished to receive a sum of money equivalent to their losses; and the liberality of the conqueror supported the aged mother and educated the orphan daughters of Maximus.[80] A character thus accomplished might almost excuse the extravagant supposition of the orator Pacatus that, if the elder Brutus could be permitted to revisit the earth, the stern republican would abjure, at the feet of Theodosius, his hatred of kings; and ingenuously confess that such a monarch was the most faithful guardian of the happiness and dignity of the Roman people.[81]

Yet the piercing eye of the founder of the republic must have discerned two essential imperfections, which might, perhaps, have abated his recent love of despotism. The virtuous mind of Theodosius was

[80] Ambros. tom. ii. Epist. xl. p. 955. Pacatus, from the want of skill or of courage, omits this glorious circumstance.

[81] Pacat. in Panegyr. Vet. xii. 20.

often relaxed by indolence,[82] and it was sometimes inflamed by passion.[83] In the pursuit of an important object his active courage was capable of the most vigorous exertions; but as soon as the design was accomplished, or the danger was surmounted, the hero sunk into inglorious repose, and, forgetful that the time of a prince is the property of his people, resigned himself to the enjoyment of the innocent but trifling pleasures of a luxurious court. The natural disposition of Theodosius was hasty and choleric; and, in a station where none could resist and few would dissuade the fatal consequence of his resentment, the humane monarch was justly alarmed by the consciousness of his infirmity and of his power. It was the constant study of his life to suppress or regulate the intemperate sallies of passion; and the success of his efforts enhanced the merit of his clemency. But the painful virtue which claims the merit of victory is exposed to the danger of defeat; and the reign of a wise and merciful prince was polluted by an act of cruelty which would stain the annals of Nero or Domitian. Within the space of three years the inconsistent historian of Theodosius must relate the generous pardon of the citizens of Antioch, and the inhuman massacre of the people of Thessalonica.

The lively impatience of the inhabitants of Antioch was never satisfied with their own situation, or with the character and conduct of their successive sovereigns. The Arian subjects of Theodosius deplored the loss of their churches; and, as three rival bishops disputed the throne of Antioch, the sentence which decided their pretensions excited the murmurs of the two unsuccessful congregations. The exigencies of the Gothic war, and the inevitable expense that accompanied the conclusion of the peace, had constrained the emperor to aggravate the weight of the public impositions; and the provinces of Asia, as they had not been involved in the distress, were the less inclined to contribute to the relief of Europe. The auspicious period now approached of the tenth year of his reign; a festival more grateful to the soldiers, who received a liberal donative, than to the subjects, whose voluntary offerings had been long since converted into an extraordinary and oppressive burden. The edicts of taxation interrupted the repose and pleasures of Antioch; and the tribunal of the magistrate was besieged by a suppliant crowd, who, in pathetic, but at first in respectful language, solicited the redress of their grievances. They were gradually incensed by the pride of their haughty rulers, who treated their complaints as a criminal resist-

---

[82] Zosimus, 1. iv. [c. 50] p. 271, 272. His partial evidence is marked by an air of candour and truth. He observes these vicissitudes of sloth and activity, not as a vice but as a singularity in the character of Theodosius.
[86] This choleric temper is acknowledged and excused by Victor [Epit. c. 48]. Sed habes (says Ambrose in decent and manly language to his sovereign) naturæ impetum, quem si quis lenire velit, cito vertes ad misericordiam: si quis stimulet, in magis exsuscitas, ut eum revocare vix possis (tom. ii. Epist. li. p. 998). Theodosius (Claud. in iv. Cons. Hon. 266, etc.) exhorts his son to moderate his anger.

ance; their satirical wit degenerated into sharp and angry invectives; and, from the subordinate powers of government, the invectives of the people insensibly rose to attack the sacred character of the emperor himself. Their fury, provoked by a feeble opposition, discharged itself on the images of the Imperial family which were erected, as objects of public veneration, in the most conspicuous places of the city. The statues of Theodosius, of his father, of his wife Flaccilla, of his two sons Arcadius and Honorius, were insolently thrown down from their pedestals, broken in pieces, or dragged with contempt through the streets; and the indignities which were offered to the representations of Imperial majesty sufficiently declared the impious and treasonable wishes of the populace. The tumult was almost immediately suppressed by the arrival of a body of archers; and Antioch had leisure to reflect on the nature and consequences of her crime.[84] According to the duty of his office, the governor of the province despatched a faithful narrative of the whole transaction, while the trembling citizens intrusted the confession of their crime and the assurances of their repentance to the zeal of Flavian their bishop, and to the eloquence of the senator Hilarius, the friend, and most probably the disciple, of Libanius,[85] whose genius on this melancholy occasion was not useless to his country. But the two capitals, Antioch and Constantinople, were separated by the distance of eight hundred miles; and, notwithstanding the diligence of the Imperial posts, the guilty city was severely punished by a long and dreadful interval of suspense. Every rumour agitated the hopes and fears of the Antiochians, and they heard with terror that their sovereign, exasperated by the insult which had been offered to his own statues, and more especially to those of his beloved wife, had resolved to level with the ground the offending city, and to massacre, without distinction of age or sex, the criminal inhabitants,[86] many of whom were actually driven, by their apprehensions, to seek a refuge in the mountains of Syria and the adjacent desert. At length, twenty-four days after the sedition, the general Hellebicus, and Cæsarius, master of the offices, declared the will of the emperor and the sentence of Antioch. That proud capital was degraded from the rank of a city; and the metropolis of the East, stripped of its lands, its privileges, and its revenues, was subjected, under the humiliating denomination of a village, to the juris-

[84] The Christians and Pagans agreed in believing that the sedition of Antioch was excited by the dæmons. A gigantic woman (says Sozomen, l. vii. c. 23) paraded the streets with a scourge in her hand. An old man, says Libanius (Orat. xii. p. 396), transformed himself into a youth, then a boy, etc.

[85] Zosimus, in his short and disingenuous account (l. iv. [c. 41] p. 258, 259), is certainly mistaken in sending Libanius himself to Constantinople. His own orations fix him at Antioch.

[86] Libanius (Orat. i. p. 6, edit. Venet.) declares, that under such a reign the fear of a massacre was groundless and absurd, especially in the emperor's absence; for his presence, according to the eloquent slave, might have given a sanction to the most bloody acts.

diction of Laodicea.[87] The baths, the circus, and the theatres were shut; and, that every source of plenty and pleasure might at the same time be intercepted, the distribution of corn was abolished by the severe instructions of Theodosius. His commissioners then proceeded to inquire into the guilt of individuals—of those who had perpetrated, and of those who had not prevented, the destruction of the sacred statues. The tribunal of Hellebicus and Cæsarius, encompassed with armed soldiers, was erected in the midst of the Forum. The noblest and most wealthy of the citizens of Antioch appeared before them in chains; the examination was assisted by the use of torture, and their sentence was pronounced or suspended, according to the judgment of these extraordinary magistrates. The houses of the criminals were exposed to sale, their wives and children were suddenly reduced from affluence and luxury to the most abject distress, and a bloody execution was expected to conclude the horrors of a day [88] which the preacher of Antioch, the eloquent Chrysostom, has represented as a lively image of the last and universal judgment of the world. But the ministers of Theodosius performed with reluctance the cruel task which had been assigned them; they dropped a gentle tear over the calamities of the people, and they listened with reverence to the pressing solicitations of the monks and hermits, who descended in swarms from the mountains.[89] Hellebicus and Cæsarius were persuaded to suspend the execution of their sentence; and it was agreed that the former should remain at Antioch, while the latter returned, with all possible speed, to Constantinople, and presumed once more to consult the will of his sovereign. The resentment of Theodosius had already subsided; the deputies of the people, both the bishop and the orator, had obtained a favourable audience; and the reproaches of the emperor were the complaints of injured friendship rather than the stern menaces of pride and power. A free and general pardon was granted to the city and citizens of Antioch; the prison-doors were thrown open; the senators, who despaired of their lives, recovered the possession of their houses and estates; and the capital of the East was restored to the enjoyment of her ancient dignity and splendour. Theodosius condescended to praise the senate of Constantinople, who had generously interceded for their distressed brethren; he rewarded the eloquence of Hilarius with the government of Palestine, and dismissed the bishop of Antioch with the warmest expressions of respect and gratitude. A thousand new statues arose to the

[87] Laodicea, on the sea-coast, sixty-five miles from Antioch (see Noris, Epoch. Syro-Maced. Dissert. iii. p. 230). The Antiochians were offended that the dependent city of Seleucia should presume to intercede for them.

[88] As the days of the tumult depend on the *movable* festival of Easter, they can only be determined by the previous determination of the year. The year 387 has been preferred, after a laborious inquiry, by Tillemont (Hist. des Emp. tom. v. p. 741-744) and Montfaucon (Chrysostom, tom. xiii. p. 105-110).

[89] Chrysostom opposes *their* courage, which was not attended with much risk, to the cowardly flight of the Cynics.

clemency of Theodosius; the applause of his subjects was ratified by the approbation of his own heart; and the emperor confessed that, if the exercise of justice is the most important duty, the indulgence of mercy is the most exquisite pleasure of a sovereign.[90]

The sedition of Thessalonica is ascribed to a more shameful cause, and was productive of much more dreadful consequences. That great city, the metropolis of all the Illyrian provinces, had been protected from the dangers of the Gothic war by strong fortifications and a numerous garrison. Botheric, the general of those troops, and, as it should seem from his name, a barbarian, had among his slaves a beautiful boy, who excited the impure desires of one of the charioteers of the circus. The insolent and brutal lover was thrown into prison by the order of Botheric; and he sternly rejected the importunate clamours of the multitude, who, on the day of the public games, lamented the absence of their favourite, and considered the skill of a charioteer as an object of more importance than his virtue. The resentment of the people was embittered by some previous disputes; and, as the strength of the garrison had been drawn away for the service of the Italian war, the feeble remnant, whose numbers were reduced by desertion, could not save the unhappy general from their licentious fury. Botheric and several of his principal officers were inhumanly murdered; their mangled bodies were dragged about the streets; and the emperor, who then resided at Milan, was surprised by the intelligence of the audacious and wanton cruelty of the people of Thessalonica. The sentence of a dispassionate judge would have inflicted a severe punishment on the authors of the crime; and the merit of Botheric might contribute to exasperate the grief and indignation of his master. The fiery and choleric temper of Theodosius was impatient of the dilatory forms of a judicial inquiry; and he hastily resolved that the blood of his lieutenant should be expiated by the blood of the guilty people. Yet his mind still fluctuated between the counsels of clemency and of revenge; the zeal of the bishops had almost extorted from the reluctant emperor the promise of a general pardon; his passion was again inflamed by the flattering suggestions of his minister Rufinus; and, after Theodosius had despatched the messengers of death, he attempted, when it was too late, to prevent the execution of his orders. The punishment of a Roman city was blindly committed to the undistinguishing sword of the barbarians; and the hostile preparations were concerted with the dark and perfidious artifice of an illegal conspiracy. The people of Thessalonica were

[90] The sedition of Antioch is represented in a lively and almost dramatic manner by two orators who had their respective shares of interest and merit. See Libanius (Orat. xiv. xv. [xii. xiii.] p. 389-420, edit. Morel.; Orat. i. p. 1-14, Venet. 1754) and the twenty orations of St. John Chrysostom, de Statuis (tom. ii. p. 1-225, edit. Montfaucon). I do not pretend to *much* personal acquaintance with Chrysostom; but Tillemont (Hist. des Empereurs, tom. v. p. 263-283) and Hermant (Vie de St. Chrysostome, tom. i. p. 137-224) had read him with pious curiosity and diligence.

treacherously invited, in the name of their sovereign, to the games of the circus; and such was their insatiate avidity for those amusements that every consideration of fear or suspicion was disregarded by the numerous spectators. As soon as the assembly was complete, the soldiers, who had secretly been posted round the circus, received the signal, not of the races, but of a general massacre. The promiscuous carnage continued three hours, without discrimination of strangers or natives, of age or sex, of innocence or guilt; the most moderate accounts state the number of the slain at seven thousand; and it is affirmed by some writers that more than fifteen thousand victims were sacrificed to the manes of Botheric. A foreign merchant, who had probably no concern in his murder, offered his own life and all his wealth to supply the place of *one* of his two sons; but while the father hesitated with equal tenderness, while he was doubtful to choose, and unwilling to condemn, the soldiers determined his suspense by plunging their daggers at the same moment into the breasts of the defenceless youths. The apology of the assassins, that they were obliged to produce the prescribed number of heads, serves only to increase, by an appearance of order and design, the horrors of the massacre, which was executed by the commands of Theodosius. The guilt of the emperor is aggravated by his long and frequent residence at Thessalonica. The situation of the unfortunate city, the aspect of the streets and buildings, the dress and faces of the inhabitants, were familiar, and even present, to his imagination; and Theodosius possessed a quick and lively sense of the existence of the people whom he destroyed.[91]

The respectful attachment of the emperor for the orthodox clergy had disposed him to love and admire the character of Ambrose, who united all the episcopal virtues in the most eminent degree. The friends and ministers of Theodosius imitated the example of their sovereign; and he observed, with more surprise than displeasure, that all his secret counsels were immediately communicated to the archbishop, who acted from the laudable persuasion that every measure of civil government may have some connection with the glory of God and the interest of the true religion. The monks and populace of Callinicum, an obscure town on the frontier of Persia, excited by their own fanaticism, and by that of their bishop, had tumultuously burnt a conventicle of the Valentinians and a synagogue of the Jews. The seditious prelate was condemned by the magistrate of the provinces either to rebuild the synagogue or to repay the damage; and this mod-

---

[91] The original evidence of Ambrose (tom. ii. Epist. li. p. 998), Augustin (de Civitat. Dei, v. 26), and Paulinus (in Vit. Ambros. c. 24), is delivered in vague expressions of horror and pity. It is illustrated by the subsequent and unequal testimonies of Sozomen (l. vii. c. 25), Theodoret (l. v. c. 17), Theophanes (Chronograph. p. 62 [tom. i. p. 113, ed. Bonn.]), Cedrenus (p. 317 [tom. i. p. 556, ed. Bonn.]), and Zonaras (tom. ii. l. xiii. [c. 18] p. 34). Zosimus *alone,* the partial enemy of Theodosius, most unaccountably passes over in silence the worst of his actions.

erate sentence was confirmed by the emperor. But it was not confirmed by the archbishop of Milan.[92] He dictated an epistle of censure and reproach, more suitable perhaps if the emperor had received the mark of circumcision and renounced the faith of his baptism. Ambrose considers the toleration of the Jewish as the persecution of the Christian religion; boldly declares that he himself and every true believer would eagerly dispute with the bishop of Callinicum the merit of the deed and the crown of martyrdom; and laments, in the most pathetic terms, that the execution of the sentence would be fatal to the fame and salvation of Theodosius. As this private admonition did not produce an immediate effect, the archbishop from his pulpit [93] publicly addressed the emperor on his throne;[94] nor would he consent to offer the oblation of the altar till he had obtained from Theodosius a solemn and positive declaration which secured the impunity of the bishop and monks of Callinicum. The recantation of Theodosius was sincere;[95] and, during the term of his residence at Milan, his affection for Ambrose was continually increased by the habits of pious and familiar conversation.

When Ambrose was informed of the massacre of Thessalonica, his mind was filled with horror and anguish. He retired into the country to indulge his grief and to avoid the presence of Theodosius. But as the archbishop was satisfied that a timid silence would render him the accomplice of his guilt, he represented in a private letter the enormity of the crime, which could only be effaced by the tears of penitence. The episcopal vigour of Ambrose was tempered by prudence; and he contented himself with signifying [96] an indirect sort of excommunication, by the assurance that he had been warned in a vision not to offer the oblation in the name or in the presence of Theodosius, and by the advice that he would confine himself to the use of prayer, without presuming to approach the altar of Christ, or to receive the holy eucharist with those hands that were still polluted with the blood of

[92] See the whole transaction in Ambrose (tom. ii. Epist. xl. xli. p. 946-956), and his biographer Paulinus (c. 23). Bayle and Barbeyrac (Morales des Pères, c. xvii. p. 325, etc.) have justly condemned the archbishop.

[93] His sermon is a strange allegory of Jeremiah's rod, of an almond-tree, of the woman who washed and anointed the feet of Christ. But the peroration is direct and personal.

[94] Hodie, Episcope, de me proposuisti. Ambrose modestly confessed it; but he sternly reprimanded Timesius, general of the horse and foot, who had presumed to say that the monks of Callinicum deserved punishment.

[95] Yet, five years afterwards, when Theodosius was absent from his spiritual guide, he tolerated the Jews, and condemned the destruction of their synagogues. Cod. Theodos. l. xvi. tit. viii. leg. 9, with Godefroy's Commentary, tom. vi. p. 225.

[96] Ambros. tom. ii. Epist. li. p. 997-1001. His epistle is a miserable rhapsody on a noble subject. Ambrose could act better than he could write. His compositions are destitute of taste or genius; without the spirit of Tertullian, the copious elegance of Lactantius, the lively wit of Jerom, or the grave energy of Augustin.

an innocent people. The emperor was deeply affected by his own reproaches and by those of his spiritual father; and after he had bewailed the mischievous and irreparable consequences of his rash fury, he proceeded in the accustomed manner to perform his devotions in the great church of Milan. He was stopped in the porch by the archbishop, who, in the tone and language of an ambassador of Heaven, declared to his sovereign that private contrition was not sufficient to atone for a public fault or to appease the justice of the offended Deity. Theodosius humbly represented that, if he had contracted the guilt of homicide, David, the man after God's own heart, had been guilty not only of murder but of adultery. " You have imitated David in his crime, imitate then his repentance," was the reply of the undaunted Ambrose. The rigorous conditions of peace and pardon were accepted; and the public penance of the emperor Theodosius has been recorded as one of the most honourable events in the annals of the church. According to the mildest rules of ecclesiastical discipline which were established in the fourth century, the crime of homicide was expiated by the penitence of twenty years:[97] and as it was impossible in the period of human life to purge the accumulated guilt of the massacre of Thessalonica, the murderer should have been excluded from the holy communion till the hour of his death. But the archbishop, consulting the maxims of religious policy, granted some indulgence to the rank of his illustrious penitent, who humbled in the dust the pride of the diadem; and the public edification might be admitted as a weighty reason to abridge the duration of his punishment. It was sufficient that the emperor of the Romans, stripped of the ensigns of royalty, should appear in a mournful and suppliant posture; and that, in the midst of the church of Milan, he should humbly solicit, with sighs and tears, the pardon of his sins.[98] In this spiritual cure Ambrose employed the various methods of mildness and severity. After a delay of about eight months Theodosius was restored to the communion of the faithful; and the edict, which interposes a salutary interval of thirty days between the sentence and the execution, may be accepted as the worthy fruits of his repentance.[99] Posterity has applauded the

[97] According to the discipline of St. Basil (Canon lvi.), the voluntary homicide was *four* years a mourner; *five* an hearer; *seven* in a prostrate state; and *four* in a standing posture. I have the original (Beveridge, Pandect. tom. ii. p. 47-151) and a translation (Chardon, Hist. des Sacremens, tom. iv. p. 219-277) of the Canonical Epistles of St. Basil.

[98] The penance of Theodosius is authenticated by Ambrose (tom. ii. de Obit. Theodos. c. 34, p. 1207), Augustin (de Civitat. Dei, v. 26), and Paulinus (in Vit. Ambros. c. 24). Socrates is ignorant; Sozomen (l. vii. c. 25) concise; and the copious narrative of Theodoret (l. v. c. 18) must be used with precaution.

[99] Codex Theodos. l. ix. tit. xl. leg. 13. The date and circumstances of this law are perplexed with difficulties; but I feel myself inclined to favour the honest efforts of Tillemont (Hist. des Emp. tom. v. p. 721) and Pagi (Critica, tom. i. p. 578).

virtuous firmness of the archbishop: and the example of Theodosius may prove the beneficial influence of those principles which could force a monarch, exalted above the apprehension of human punishment, to respect the laws and ministers of an invisible Judge. " The prince," says Montesquieu, " who is actuated by the hopes and fears of religion, may be compared to a lion, docile only to the voice, and tractable to the hand, of his keeper." [100] The motions of the royal animal will therefore depend on the inclination and interest of the man who has acquired such dangerous authority over him; and the priest who holds in his hand the conscience of a king may inflame or moderate his sanguinary passions. The cause of humanity and that of persecution have been asserted by the same Ambrose with equal energy and with equal success.

After the defeat and death of the tyrant of Gaul, the Roman world was in the possession of Theodosius. He derived from the choice of Gratian his honourable title to the provinces of the East; he had acquired the West by the right of conquest; and the three years which he spent in Italy were usefully employed to restore the authority of the laws and to correct the abuses which had prevailed with impunity under the usurpation of Maximus and the minority of Valentinian. The name of Valentinian was regularly inserted in the public acts, but the tender age and doubtful faith of the son of Justina appeared to require the prudent care of an orthodox guardian, and his specious ambition might have excluded the unfortunate youth, without a struggle and almost without a murmur, from the administration and even from the inheritance of the empire. If Theodosius had consulted the rigid maxims of interest and policy, his conduct would have been justified by his friends, but the generosity of his behaviour on this memorable occasion has extorted the applause of his most inveterate enemies. He seated Valentinian on the throne of Milan, and, without stipulating any present or future advantages, restored him to the absolute dominion of all the provinces from which he had been driven by the arms of Maximus. To the restitution of his ample patrimony Theodosius added the free and generous gift of the countries beyond the Alps which his successful valour had recovered from the assassin of Gratian.[101] Satisfied with the glory which he had acquired by revenging the death of his benefactor and delivering the West from the yoke of tyranny, the emperor returned from Milan to Constantinople, and, in the peaceful possession of the East, insensibly relapsed into his former habits of luxury and indolence. Theodosius discharged his obligation to the brother, he indulged his conjugal tenderness to the sister, of

---

[100] Un prince qui aime la religion, et qui la craint, est un lion qui cède à la main qui le flatte, ou à la voix qui l'appaise. Esprit des Loix, l. xxiv. c. 2.

[101] Τοῦτο περὶ τοὺς εὐεργέτας καθῆκον ἔδοξεν εἶναι, is the niggard praise of Zosimus himself (l. iv. [c. 48] p. 267). Augustin says, with some happiness of expression, Valentinianum . . misericordissimâ veneratione restituit.

Valentinian; and posterity, which admires the pure and singular glory of his elevation, must applaud his unrivalled generosity in the use of victory.

The empress Justina did not long survive her return to Italy, and, though she beheld the triumph of Theodosius, she was not allowed to influence the government of her son.[102] The pernicious attachment to the Arian sect which Valentinian had imbibed from her example and instructions was soon erased by the lessons of a more orthodox education. His growing zeal for the faith of Nice, and his filial reverence for the character and authority of Ambrose, disposed the catholics to entertain the most favourable opinion of the virtues of the young emperor of the West.[103] They applauded his chastity and temperance, his contempt of pleasure, his application to business, and his tender affection for his two sisters, which would not, however, seduce his impartial equity to pronounce an unjust sentence against the meanest of his subjects. But this amiable youth, before he had accomplished the twentieth year of his age, was oppressed by domestic treason, and the empire was again involved in the horrors of a civil war. Arbogastes,[104] a gallant soldier of the nation of the Franks, held the second rank in the service of Gratian. On the death of his master he joined the standard of Theodosius, contributed, by his valour and military conduct, to the destruction of the tyrant, and was appointed, after the victory, master-general of the armies of Gaul. His real merit and apparent fidelity had gained the confidence both of the prince and people; his boundless liberality corrupted the allegiance of the troops; and, whilst he was universally esteemed as the pillar of the state, the bold and crafty barbarian was secretly determined either to rule or to ruin the empire of the West. The important commands of the army were distributed among the Franks; the creatures of Arbogastes were promoted to all the honours and offices of the civil government; the progress of the conspiracy removed every faithful servant from the presence of Valentinian; and the emperor, without power and without intelligence, insensibly sunk into the precarious and dependent condition of a captive.[105] The indignation which he expressed, though it might arise only from the rash and impatient temper of youth, may be candidly ascribed to the generous spirit of a prince who felt that he

---

[102] Sozomen, l. vii. c. 14. His chronology is very irregular.

[103] See Ambrose (tom. ii. de Obit. Valentinian. c. 15, etc., p. 1178, c. 36, etc.. p. 1184). When the young emperor gave an entertainment, he fasted himself; he refused to see an handsome actress, etc. Since he ordered his wild beasts to be killed, it is ungenerous in Philostorgius (l. xi. c. 1) to reproach him with the love of that amusement.

[104] Zosimus (l. iv. [c. 53] p. 275) praises the enemy of Theodosius. But he is detested by Socrates (l. v. c. 25) and Orosius (l. vii. c. 35).

[105] Gregory of Tours (l. ii. c. 9, p. 165, in the second volume of the Historians of France) has preserved a curious fragment of Sulpicius Alexander. an historian far more valuable than himself.

was not unworthy to reign. He secretly invited the archbishop of Milan to undertake the office of a mediator, as the pledge of his sincerity and the guardian of his safety. He contrived to apprise the emperor of the East of his helpless situation, and he declared that, unless Theodosius could speedily march to his assistance, he must attempt to escape from the palace, or rather prison, of Vienne, in Gaul, where he had imprudently fixed his residence in the midst of the hostile faction. But the hopes of relief were distant and doubtful; and, as every day furnished some new provocation, the emperor, without strength or counsel, too hastily resolved to risk an immediate contest with his powerful general. He received Arbogastes on the throne, and, as the count approached with some appearance of respect, delivered to him a paper which dismissed him from all his employments. "My authority," replied Arbogastes, with insulting coolness, "does not depend on the smile or the frown of a monarch;" and he contemptuously threw the paper on the ground. The indignant monarch snatched at the sword of one of the guards, which he struggled to draw from its scabbard, and it was not without some degree of violence that he was prevented from using the deadly weapon against his enemy or against himself. A few days after this extraordinary quarrel, in which he had exposed his resentment and his weakness, the unfortunate Valentinian was found strangled in his apartment, and some pains were employed to disguise the manifest guilt of Arbogastes, and to persuade the world that the death of the young emperor had been the voluntary effect of his own despair.[106] His body was conducted with decent pomp to the sepulchre of Milan, and the archbishop pronounced a funeral oration to commemorate his virtue and his misfortunes.[107] On this occasion the humanity of Ambrose tempted him to make a singular breach in his theological system, and to comfort the weeping sisters of Valentinian by the firm assurance that their pious brother, though he had not received the sacrament of baptism, was introduced, without difficulty, into the mansions of eternal bliss.[108]

The prudence of Arbogastes had prepared the success of his ambitious designs, and the provincials, in whose breasts every sentiment of patriotism or loyalty was extinguished, expected, with tame resignation, the unknown master whom the choice of a Frank might place on the Imperial throne. But some remains of pride and prejudice still opposed the elevation of Arbogastes himself, and the judicious barba-

[106] Godefroy (Dissertat. ad Philostorg. p. 429-434) has diligently collected all the circumstances of the death of Valentinian II. The variations and the ignorance of contemporary writers prove that it was secret.

[107] De Obitû Valentinian. tom. ii. p. 1173-1196. He is forced to speak a discreet and obscure language: yet he is much bolder than any layman, or perhaps any other ecclesiastic, would have dared to be.

[108] See c. 51, p. 1188; c. 75, p. 1193. Dom Chardon (Hist. des Sacremens, tom. i. p. 86), who owns that St. Ambrose most strenuously maintains the indispensable necessity of baptism, labours to reconcile the contradiction.

rians thought it more advisable to reign under the name of some dependent Roman. He bestowed the purple on the rhetorician Eugenius,[109] whom he had already raised from the place of his domestic
secretary to the rank of master of the offices. In the course both of
his private and public service the count had always approved the attachment and abilities of Eugenius; his learning and eloquence, supported by the gravity of his manners, recommended him to the esteem
of the people, and the reluctance with which he seemed to ascend the
throne may inspire a favourable prejudice of his virtue and moderation. The ambassadors of the new emperor were immediately despatched to the court of Theodosius, to communicate, with affected
grief, the unfortunate accident of the death of Valentinian, and, without
mentioning the name of Arbogastes, to request that the monarch of the
East would embrace as his lawful colleague the respectable citizen who
had obtained the unanimous suffrage of the armies and provinces of
the West.[110] Theodosius was justly provoked that the perfidy of a
barbarian should have destroyed in a moment the labours and the
fruit of his former victory; and he was excited by the tears of his
beloved wife [111] to revenge the fate of her unhappy brother, and once
more to assert by arms the violated majesty of the throne. But as
the second conquest of the West was a task of difficulty and danger,
he dismissed, with splendid presents and an ambiguous answer, the
ambassadors of Eugenius, and almost two years were consumed in the
preparations of the civil war. Before he formed any decisive resolution, the pious emperor was anxious to discover the will of Heaven;
and as the progress of Christianity had silenced the oracles of Delphi
and Dodona, he consulted an Egyptian monk, who possessed, in the
opinion of the age, the gift of miracles and the knowledge of futurity.
Eutropius, one of the favourite eunuchs of the palace of Constantinople, embarked for Alexandria, from whence he sailed up the Nile
as far as the city of Lycopolis, or of Wolves, in the remote province
of Thebais.[112] In the neighbourhood of that city, and on the summit

[109] Quem sibi Germanus famulum delegerat exul,
is the contemptuous expression of Claudian (iv. Cons. Hon. 74). Eugenius
professed Christianity; but his secret attachment to Paganism (Sozomen, l.
vii. c. 22; Philostorg. l. xi. c. 2) is probable in a grammarian, and would
secure the friendship of Zosimus (l. iv. [c. 54] p. 276, 277).
[110] Zosimus (l. iv. [c. 55] p. 278) mentions this embassy; but he is diverted
by another story from relating the event.
[111] Συνετάραξεν ἡ τούτου γαμετὴ Γάλλα τὰ βασίλεια, τὸν ἀδελφὸν ὀλοφυρομένη.
Zosim. l. iv. [c. 55] p. 277. He afterwards says ([c. 57] p. 280) that Galla
died in childbed [A.D. 394.—S.]; and intimates that the affliction of her husband was extreme but short.
[112] Lycopolis is the modern Siut, or Osiot, a town of Said, about the size of
St. Denys, which drives a profitable trade with the kingdom of Sennaar, and
has a very convenient fountain, "cujus potû signa virginitatis eripiuntur."
See D'Anville, Description de l'Egypte, p. 181. Abulfeda, Descript. Egypt. p.
14; and the curious Annotations, p. 25, 92, of his editor Michaelis.

of a lofty mountain, the holy John [113] had constructed with his own hands an humble cell, in which he had dwelt above fifty years, without opening his door, without seeing the face of a woman, and without tasting any food that had been prepared by fire or any human art. Five days of the week he spent in prayer and meditation, but on Saturdays and Sundays he regularly opened a small window, and gave audience to the crowd of suppliants who successively flowed from every part of the Christian world. The eunuch of Theodosius approached the window with respectful steps, proposed his questions concerning the event of the civil war, and soon returned with a favourable oracle, which animated the courage of the emperor by the assurance of a bloody but infallible victory.[114] The accomplishment of the prediction was forwarded by all the means that human prudence could supply. The industry of the two master-generals, Stilicho and Timasius, was directed to recruit the numbers and to revive the discipline of the Roman legions. The formidable troops of barbarians marched under the ensigns of their national chieftains. The Iberian, the Arab, and the Goth, who gazed on each other with mutual astonishment, were enlisted in the service of the same prince; and the renowned Alaric acquired, in the school of Theodosius, the knowledge of the art of war which he afterwards so fatally exerted for the destruction of Rome.[115]

The emperor of the West, or, to speak more properly, his general Arbogastes, was instructed by the misconduct and misfortune of Maximus how dangerous it might prove to extend the line of defence against a skilful antagonist, who was free to press or to suspend, to contract or to multiply, his various methods of attack.[116] Arbogastes fixed his station on the confines of Italy; the troops of Theodosius were permitted to occupy, without resistance, the provinces of Pannonia, as

[113] The Life of John of Lycopolis is described by his two friends, Rufinus (1. ii. c. i. p. 449) and Palladius (Hist. Lausiac. c. 43, p. 738), in Rosweyde's great Collection of the Vitæ Patrum. Tillemont (Mém. Ecclés. tom. x. p. 718, 720) has settled the chronology.
[114] Sozomen, 1. vii. c. 22. Claudian (in Eutrop. 1. i. 312) mentions the eunuch's journey: but he most contemptuously derives the Egyptian dreams and the oracles of the Nile.
[115] Zosimus, 1. iv. [c. 57] p. 280; Socrates, 1. vii. 10. Alaric himself (de Bell. Getico, 524) dwells with more complacency on his early exploits against the Romans.
   . . . Tot Augustos Hebro qui teste fugavi.
Yet his vanity could scarcely have proved this *plurality* of flying emperors.
[116] Claudian (in iv. Cons. Honor. 77, etc.) contrasts the military plans of the two usurpers:—
      . . . Novitas audere priori
    Suadebat; cautumque dabant exempla sequentem.
    His nova moliri præceps: his quærere tuta
    Providus. Hic fusis, collectis viribus ille;
    Hic vagus excurrens; hic intra claustra reductus;
    Dissimiles, sed morte pares . . .

far as the foot of the Julian Alps; and even the passes of the mountains were negligently, or perhaps artfully, abandoned to the bold invader. He descended from the hills, and beheld, with some astonishment, the formidable camp of the Gauls and Germans that covered with arms and tents the open country which extends to the walls of Aquileia and the banks of the Frigidus,[117] or Cold River.[118] This narrow theatre of the war circumscribed by the Alps and the Hadriatic, did not allow much room for the operations of military skill; the spirit of Arbogastes would have disdained a pardon; his guilt extinguished the hope of a negotiation; and Theodosius was impatient to satisfy his glory and revenge by the chastisement of the assassins of Valentinian. Without weighing the natural and artificial obstacles that opposed his efforts, the emperor of the East immediately attacked the fortifications of his rivals, assigned the post of honourable danger to the Goths, and cherished a secret wish that the bloody conflict might diminish the pride and numbers of the conquerors. Ten thousand of those auxiliaries, and Bacurius, general of the Iberians, died bravely on the field of battle. But the victory was not purchased by their blood; the Gauls maintained their advantage, and the approach of night protected the disorderly flight, or retreat, of the troops of Theodosius. The emperor retired to the adjacent hills, where he passed a disconsolate night, without sleep, without provisions, and without hopes,[119] except that strong assurance which, under the most desperate circumstances, the independent mind may derive from the contempt of fortune and of life. The triumph of Eugenius was celebrated by the insolent and dissolute joy of his camp, whilst the active and vigilant Arbogastes secretly detached a considerable body of troops to occupy the passes of the mountains and to encompass the rear of the Eastern army. The dawn of day discovered to the eyes of Theodosius the extent and the extremity of his danger, but his apprehensions were soon dispelled by a friendly message from the leaders of those troops, who expressed their inclination to desert the standard of the tyrant. The honourable and lucrative rewards which they stipulated as the price of their perfidy were granted without hesitation, and, as ink and paper could not easily be procured, the emperor subscribed on his own tablets the ratification of the treaty. The spirit of his soldiers was revived by this seasonable reinforcement, and they

[117] The Frigidus, a small though memorable stream in the country of Goretz, now called the Vipao, falls into the Sontius, or Lisonzo, above Aquileia, some miles from the Hadriatic. See D'Anville's ancient and modern maps, and the Italia Antiqua of Cluverius (tom. i. p. 188).
[118] Claudian's wit is intolerable: the snow was dyed red; the cold river smoked; and the channel must have been choked with carcasses if the current had not been swelled with blood.
[119] Theodoret affirms that St. John and St. Philip appeared to the waking or sleeping emperor, on horseback, etc. This is the first instance of apostolic chivalry, which afterwards became so popular in Spain and in the Crusades.

again marched with confidence to surprise the camp of a tyrant whose principal officers appeared to distrust either the justice or the success of his arms. In the heat of the battle a violent tempest,[120] such as is often felt among the Alps, suddenly arose from the East. The army of Theodosius was sheltered by their position from the impetuosity of the wind, which blew a cloud of dust in the faces of the enemy, disordered their ranks, wrested their weapons from their hands, and diverted or repelled their ineffectual javelins. This accidental advantage was skilfully improved: the violence of the storm was magnified by the superstitious terrors of the Gauls, and they yielded without shame to the invisible powers of heaven, who seemed to militate on the side of the pious emperor. His victory was decisive, and the deaths of his two rivals were distinguished only by the difference of their characters. The rhetorician Eugenius, who had almost acquired the dominion of the world, was reduced to implore the mercy of the conqueror, and the unrelenting soldiers separated his head from his body as he lay prostrate at the feet of Theodosius. Arbogastes, after the loss of a battle in which he had discharged the duties of a soldier and a general, wandered several days among the mountains. But when he was convinced that his cause was desperate, and his escape impracticable, the intrepid barbarian imitated the example of the ancient Romans, and turned his sword against his own breast. The fate of the empire was determined in a narrow corner of Italy; and the legitimate successor of the house of Valentinian embraced the archbishop of Milan, and graciously received the submission of the provinces of the West. Those provinces were involved in the guilt of rebellion; while the inflexible courage of Ambrose alone had resisted the claims of successful usurpation. With a manly freedom, which might have been fatal to any other subject, the archbishop rejected the gifts of Eugenius, declined his correspondence, and withdrew himself from Milan to avoid the odious presence of a tyrant whose downfall he predicted in discreet and ambiguous language. The merit of Ambrose was applauded by the conqueror, who secured the attachment of the people by his alliance with the church: and the clemency of Theodosius is ascribed to the humane intercession of the archbishop of Milan.[121]

[120] Te propter, gelidis Aquilo de monte procellis
Obruit adversas acies; revolutaque tela
Vertit in auctores, et turbine reppulit hastas.
O nimium dilecte Deo, cui fundit ab antris
Æolus armatas hiemes; cui militat Æther,
Et conjurati veniunt ad classica venti.

These famous lines of Claudian (in iii. Cons. Honor. 93, etc., A.D. 396) are alleged by his contemporaries, Augustin and Orosius, who suppress the Pagan deity of Æolus, and add some circumstances from the information of eye-witnesses. Within four months after the victory, it was compared by Ambrose to the miraculous victories of Moses and Joshua.

[121] The events of this civil war are gathered from Ambrose (tom. ii. Epist. xlii. p. 1022), Paulinus (in Vit. Ambros. c. 26-34), Augustin (de Civitat. Dei,

After the defeat of Eugenius, the merit, as well as the authority, of
Theodosius was cheerfully acknowledged by all the inhabitants of the
Roman world. The experience of his past conduct encouraged the
most pleasing expectations of his future reign; and the age of the emperor, which did not exceed fifty years, seemed to extend the prospect
of the public felicity. His death, only four months after his victory,
was considered by the people as an unforeseen and fatal event, which
destroyed in a moment the hopes of the rising generation. But the
indulgence of ease and luxury had secretly nourished the principles of
disease.[122]   The strength of Theodosius was unable to support the
sudden and violent transition from the palace to the camp; and the
increasing symptoms of a dropsy announced the speedy dissolution of
the emperor. The opinion, and perhaps the interest, of the public had
confirmed the division of the Eastern and Western empires; and the
two royal youths, Arcadius and Honorius, who had already obtained,
from the tenderness of their father, the title of Augustus, were destined
to fill the thrones of Constantinople and of Rome. Those princes were
not permitted to share the danger and glory of the civil war;[123] but
as soon as Theodosius had triumphed over his unworthy rivals, he
called his younger son, Honorius, to enjoy the fruits of the victory, and
to receive the sceptre of the West from the hands of his dying father.
The arrival of Honorius at Milan was welcomed by a splendid exhibition of the games of the circus; and the emperor, though he was oppressed by the weight of his disorder, contributed by his presence
to the public joy. But the remains of his strength were exhausted by
the painful effort which he made to assist at the spectacles of the
morning. Honorius supplied, during the rest of the day, the place of
his father; and the great Theodosius expired in the ensuing night.
Notwithstanding the recent animosities of a civil war, his death was
universally lamented. The barbarians, whom he had vanquished, and
the churchmen, by whom he had been subdued, celebrated with loud
and sincere applause the qualities of the deceased emperor which appeared the most valuable in their eyes. The Romans were terrified by
the impending dangers of a feeble and divided administration; and
every disgraceful moment of the unfortunate reigns of Arcadius and
Honorius revived the memory of their irreparable loss.

v. 26), Orosius (l. vii. c. 35), Sozomen (l. vii. c. 24), Theodoret (l. v. c. 24),
Zosimus (1 iv. [c. 58], p. 281, 282), Claudian (in iii. Cons. Hon. 63-105; in
iv. Cons. Hon. 70-117), and the Chronicles published by Scaliger.
    [122] This disease, ascribed by Socrates (l. v. c. 26) to the fatigues of war, is
represented by Philostorgius (l. xi. c. 2) as the effect of sloth and intemperance;
for which Photius calls him an impudent liar (Godefroy, Dissert. p. 438).
    [123] Zosimus supposes that the boy Honorius accompanied his father (l. iv.
[c. 58] p. 280). Yet the quanto flagrabant pectora voto is all that flattery would
allow to a contemporary poet, who clearly describes the emperor's refusal,
and the journey of Honorius, *after* the victory (Claudian in iii. Cons. 78-125).

In the faithful picture of the virtues of Theodosius, his imperfections have not been dissembled; the act of cruelty, and the habits of indolence, which tarnished the glory of one of the greatest of the Roman princes. An historian perpetually adverse to the fame of Theodosius has exaggerated his vices and their pernicious effects; he boldly asserts that every rank of subjects imitated the effeminate manners of their sovereign; that every species of corruption polluted the course of public and private life; and that the feeble restraints of order and decency were insufficient to resist the progress of that degenerate spirit which sacrifices, without a blush, the consideration of duty and interest to the base indulgence of sloth and appetite.[124]   The complaints of contemporary writers, who deplore the increase of luxury and depravation of manners, are commonly expressive of their peculiar temper and situation.   There are few observers who possess a clear and comprehensive view of the revolutions of society, and who are capable of discovering the nice and secret springs of action which impel, in the same uniform direction, the blind and capricious passions of a multitude of individuals.   If it can be affirmed, with any degree of truth, that the luxury of the Romans was more shameless and dissolute in the reign of Theodosius than in the age of Constantine, perhaps, or of Augustus, the alteration cannot be ascribed to any beneficial improvements which had gradually increased the stock of national riches.   A long period of calamity or decay must have checked the industry and diminished the wealth of the people; and their profuse luxury must have been the result of that indolent despair which enjoys the present hour and declines the thoughts of futurity.   The uncertain condition of their property discouraged the subjects of Theodosius from engaging in those useful and laborious undertakings which require an immediate expense, and promise a slow and distant advantage.   The frequent examples of ruin and desolation tempted them not to spare the remains of a patrimony which might, every hour, become the prey of the rapacious Goth.   And the mad prodigality which prevails in the confusion of a shipwreck or a siege may serve to explain the progress of luxury amidst the misfortunes and terrors of a sinking nation.

The effeminate luxury, which infected the manners of courts and cities, had instilled a secret and destructive poison into the camps of the legions; and their degeneracy has been marked by the pen of a military writer, who had accurately studied the genuine and ancient principles of Roman discipline.   It is the just and important observation of Vegetius, that the infantry was invariably covered with defensive armour from the foundation of the city to the reign of the emperor Gratian.   The relaxation of discipline and the disuse of exercise rendered the soldiers less able and less willing to support the fatigues of the service; they complained of the weight of the armour, which

[124] Zosimus. l. iv. [c. 33] p. 244.

they seldom wore; and they successively obtained the permission of laying aside both their cuirasses and their helmets. The heavy weapons of their ancestors, the short sword and the formidable *pilum,* which had subdued the world, insensibly dropped from their feeble hands. As the use of the shield is incompatible with that of the bow, they reluctantly marched into the field, condemned to suffer either the pain of wounds or the ignominy of flight, and always disposed to prefer the more shameful alternative. The cavalry of the Goths, the Huns, and the Alani, had felt the benefits and adopted the use of defensive armour; and, as they excelled in the management of missile weapons, they easily overwhelmed the naked and trembling legions, whose heads and breasts were exposed, without defence, to the arrows of the barbarians. The loss of armies, the destruction of cities, and the dishonour of the Roman name, ineffectually solicited the successors of Gratian to restore the helmets and cuirasses of the infantry. The enervated soldiers abandoned their own and the public defence; and their pusillanimous indolence may be considered as the immediate cause of the downfall of the empire.[125]

CHAPTER XXVIII (378-420 A.D.)

Final Destruction of Paganism—Introduction of the Worship of Saints and Relics among the Christians

THE ruin of Paganism, in the age of Theodosius, is perhaps the only example of the total extirpation of any ancient and popular superstition, and may therefore deserve to be considered as a singular event in the history of the human mind. The Christians, more especially the clergy, had impatiently supported the prudent delays of Constantine and the equal toleration of the elder Valentinian; nor could they deem their conquest perfect or secure as long as their adversaries were permitted to exist. The influence which Ambrose and his brethren had acquired over the youth of Gratian and the piety of Theodosius was employed to infuse the maxims of persecution into the breasts of their Imperial proselytes. Two specious principles of religious jurisprudence were established, from whence they deduced a direct and rigorous conclusion against the subjects of the empire who still adhered to the ceremonies of their ancestors: *that* the magistrate is, in some measure, guilty of the crimes which he neglects to prohibit or to punish; and *that* the idolatrous worship of fabulous deities and real dæmons is the most abominable crime against the supreme majesty of the Creator.

---

[125] Vegetius, de Re Militari, l. i. c. 20. The series of calamities, which he marks, compel us to believe that the *Hero* to whom he dedicates his book is the last and most inglorious of the Valentinians.

The laws of Moses and the examples of Jewish history [1] were hastily, perhaps erroneously, applied by the clergy to the mild and universal reign of Christianity.[2] The zeal of the emperors was excited to vindicate their own honour and that of the Deity; and the temples of the Roman world were subverted about sixty years after the conversion of Constantine.

From the age of Numa to the reign of Gratian, the Romans preserved the regular succession of the several colleges of the sacerdotal order.[3] Fifteen PONTIFFS exercised their supreme jurisdiction over all things and persons that were consecrated to the service of the gods; and the various questions which perpetually arose in a loose and traditionary system were submitted to the judgment of their holy tribunal. Fifteen grave and learned AUGURS observed the face of the heavens, and prescribed the actions of heroes according to the flight of birds. Fifteen keepers of the Sibylline books (their name of QUINDECEMVIRS was derived from their number) occasionally consulted the history of future, and, as it should seem, of contingent events. Six VESTALS devoted their virginity to the guard of the sacred fire and of the unknown pledges of the duration of Rome, which no mortal had been suffered to behold with impunity.[4] Seven EPULOS prepared the table of the gods, conducted the solemn procession, and regulated the ceremonies of the annual festival. The three FLAMENS of Jupiter, of Mars, and of Quirinus, were considered as the peculiar ministers of the three most powerful deities, who watched over the fate of Rome and of the universe. The KING of the SACRIFICES represented the person of Numa and of his successors in the religious functions, which could be performed only by royal hands. The confraternities of the SALIANS, the LUPERCALS, etc., practised such rites as might extort a smile of

[1] St. Ambrose (tom. ii. de Obit. Theodos. p. 1208 [ed. Bened.]) expressly praises and recommends the zeal of Josiah in the destruction of idolatry. The language of Julius Firmicus Maternus on the same subject (de Errore Profan. Relig. p. 467, edit. Gronov. [Rotterod. 1743]) is piously inhuman. Nec filio jubet (the Mosaic Law) parci, nec fratri, et per amatam conjugem gladium vindicem ducit, etc.

[2] Bayle (tom. ii. p. 406, in his Commentaire Philosophique) justifies and limits these intolerant laws by the temporal reign of Jehovah over the Jews. The attempt is laudable.

[3] See the outlines of the Roman hierarchy in Cicero (de Legibus, ii. 7, 8), Livy (i. 20), Dionysius Halicarnassensis (l. ii. [c. 63, sqq.] p. 119-129, edit. Hudson), Beaufort (République Romaine, tom. i. p. 1-90), and Moyle (vol. i. p. 10-55). The last is the work of an English whig, as well as of a Roman antiquary.

[4] These mystic, and perhaps imaginary, symbols have biven birth to various fables and conjectures. It seems probable that the Palladium was a small statue (three cubits and a half high) of Minerva, with a lance and distaff; that it was usually inclosed in a *seria*, or barrel; and that a similar barrel was placed by its side to disconcert curiosity or sacrilege. See Mezeriac (Comment. sur les Epitres d'Ovide, tom. i. p. 60-66) and Lipsius (tom. iii. p. 610 de Vestâ, etc., c. 10).

contempt from every reasonable man, with a lively confidence of recommending themselves to the favour of the immortal gods. The authority which the Roman priests had formerly obtained in the counsels of the republic was gradually abolished by the establishment of monarchy and the removal of the seat of empire. But the dignity of their sacred character was still protected by the laws and manners of their country; and they still continued, more especially the college of pontiffs, to exercise in the capital, and sometimes in the provinces, the rights of their ecclesiastical and civil jurisdiction. Their robes of purple, chariots of state, and sumptuous entertainments attracted the admiration of the people; and they received, from the consecrated lands and the public revenue, an ample stipend, which liberally supported the splendour of the priesthood and all the expenses of the religious worship of the state. As the service of the altar was not incompatible with the command of armies, the Romans, after their consulships and triumphs, aspired to the place of pontiff or of augur; the seats of Cicero [5] and Pompey were filled, in the fourth century, by the most illustrious members of the senate; and the dignity of their birth reflected additional splendour on their sacerdotal character. The fifteen priests who composed the college of pontiffs enjoyed a more distinguished rank as the companions of their sovereign; and the Christian emperors condescended to accept the robe and ensigns which were appropriated to the office of supreme pontiff. But when Gratian ascended the throne, more scrupulous or more enlightened, he sternly rejected those profane symbols; [6] applied to the service of the state or of the church the revenues of the priests and vestals; abolished their honours and immunities; and dissolved the ancient fabric of Roman superstition, which was supported by the opinions and habits of eleven hundred years. Paganism was still the constitutional religion of the senate. The hall or temple in which they assembled was adorned by the statue and altar of Victory; [7] a majestic female standing on a globe, with flowing garments, expanded wings, and a crown of laurel in her outstretched hand. [8] The senators were sworn on the altar of the goddess to observe

[5] Cicero frankly (ad Atticum, 1. ii. Epist. 5) or indirectly (ad Familiar. 1. xv. Epist. 4) confesses that the *Augurate* is the supreme object of his wishes. Pliny is proud to tread in the footsteps of Cicero (1. iv. Epist. 8), and the chain of tradition might be continued from history and marbles.

[6] Zosimus, 1. iv. [c. 36] p. 249, 250 I have suppressed the foolish pun about *Pontifex* and *Maximus*.

[With regard to Gibbon's statement that Gratian, when he ascended the throne, sternly rejected the use of the Pagan symbols, and applied them to the service of the Christian Church, this is a mistake. It was at a later period of his life that this occurred.—O. S.]

[7] This statue was transported from Tarentum to Rome, placed in the *Curia Julia* by Cæsar, and decorated by Augustus with the spoils of Egypt.

[8] Prudentius (1. ii. [in Symm.] in initio) has drawn a very awkward portrait of Victory; but the curious reader will obtain more satisfaction from Montfaucon's Antiquities (tom. i. p. 341).

the laws of the emperor and of the empire; and a solemn offering of
wine and incense was the ordinary prelude of their public deliberations.[9] The removal of this ancient monument was the only injury
which Constantius had offered to the superstition of the Romans. The
altar of Victory was again restored by Julian, tolerated by Valentinian,
and once more banished from the senate by the zeal of Gratian.[10]
But the emperor yet spared the statues of the gods which were exposed
to the public veneration: four hundred and twenty-four temples, or
chapels, still remained to satisfy the devotion of the people, and in
every quarter of Rome the delicacy of the Christians was offended
by the fumes of idolatrous sacrifice.[11]

But the Christians formed the least numerous party in the senate of
Rome;[12] and it was only by their absence that they could express their
dissent from the legal, though profane, acts of a Pagan majority. In
that assembly the dying embers of freedom were, for a moment, revived
and inflamed by the breath of fanaticism. Four respectable deputa-
tions were successively voted to the Imperial court,[13] to represent the
grievances of the priesthood and the senate, and to solicit the restoration of the altar of Victory. The conduct of this important business
was intrusted to the eloquent Symmachus,[14] a wealthy and noble senator, who united the sacred characters of pontiff and augur with the
civil dignities of proconsul of Africa and præfect of the city. The
breast of Symmachus was animated by the warmest zeal for the cause
of expiring Paganism; and his religious antagonists lamented the abuse
of his genius and the inefficacy of his moral virtues.[15] The orator,
whose petition is extant to the emperor Valentinian, was conscious of
the difficulty and danger of the office which he had assumed. He cautiously avoids every topic which might appear to reflect on the religion
of his sovereign; humbly declares that prayers and entreaties are his

[9] See Suetonius (in August. c. 35) and the Exordium of Pliny's Panegyric.
[10] These facts are mutually allowed by the two advocates Symmachus and
Ambrose.
[11] The *Notitia Urbis,* more recent than Constantine, does not find one
Christian church worthy to be named among the edifices of the city. Ambrose
(tom. ii. Epist. xvii. p. 825) deplores the public scandals of Rome, which
continually offended the eyes, the ears, and the nostrils of the faithful.
[12] Ambrose repeatedly affirms, in contradiction to common sense (Moyle's
Works, vol. ii. p. 147), that the Christians had a majority in the senate.
[13] The *first* (A.D. 382) to Gratian, who refused them audience. The *second*
(A.D. 384) to Valentinian, when the field was disputed by Symmachus and
Ambrose. The *third* (A.D. 388) to Theodosius; and the *fourth* (A.D. 392) to
Valentinian. Lardner (Heathen Testimonies, vol. iv. p. 372-399) fairly represents the whole transaction.
[14] Symmachus, who was invested with all the civil and sacerdotal honours,
represented the emperor under the two characters of *Pontifex Maximus* and
Princeps Senatus. See the proud inscription at the head of his works.
[15] As if any one, says Prudentius (in Symmach. i. 639), should dig in the
mud with an instrument of gold and ivory. Even saints, and polemic saints,
treat this adversary with respect and civility.

only arms; and artfully draws his arguments from the schools of rhetoric rather than from those of philosophy. Symmachus endeavours to seduce the imagination of a young prince, by displaying the attributes of the goddess of Victory; he insinuates that the confiscation of the revenues which were consecrated to the service of the gods was a measure unworthy of his liberal and disinterested character; and maintains that the Roman sacrifices would be deprived of their force and energy, if they were no longer celebrated at the expense as well as in the name of the republic. Even scepticism is made to supply an apology for superstition. The great and incomprehensible *secret* of the universe eludes the inquiry of man. Where reason cannot instruct, custom may be permitted to guide; and every nation seems to consult the dictates of prudence, by a faithful attachment to those rites and opinions which have received the sanction of ages. If those ages have been crowned with glory and prosperity—if the devout people has frequently obtained the blessings which they have solicited at the altars of the gods—it must appear still more advisable to persist in the same salutary practice, and not to risk the unknown perils that may attend any rash innovations. The test of antiquity and success was applied with singular advantage to the religion of Numa; and ROME herself, the celestial genius that presided over the fates of the city, is introduced by the orator to plead her own cause before the tribunal of the emperors. " Most excellent princes," says the venerable matron, " fathers of your country! pity and respect my age, which has hitherto flowed in an uninterrupted course of piety. Since I do not repent, permit me to continue in the practice of my ancient rites. Since I am born free, allow me to enjoy my domestic institutions. This religion has reduced the world under my laws. These rites have repelled Hannibal from the city, and the Gauls from the Capitol. Were my grey hairs reserved for such intolerable disgrace? I am ignorant of the new system that I am required to adopt; but I am well assured that the correction of old age is always an ungrateful and ignominious office." [16] The fears of the people supplied what the discretion of the orator had suppressed; and the calamities which afflicted or threatened the declining empire were unanimously imputed by the Pagans to the new religion of Christ and of Constantine.

But the hopes of Symmachus were repeatedly baffled by the firm and dexterous opposition of the archbishop of Milan, who fortified the emperors against the fallacious eloquence of the advocate of Rome. In this controversy Ambrose condescends to speak the language of a

[16] See the fifty-fourth Epistle of the tenth book of Symmachus [p. 289, ed. Paris, 1604]. In the form and disposition of his ten books of Epistles, he imitated the younger Pliny, whose rich and florid style he was supposed by his friends to equal or excel (Macrob. Saturnal, l. v. c. i.). But the luxuriancy of Symmachus consists of barren leaves, without fruits, and even without flowers. Few facts and few sentiments can be extracted from his verbose correspondence.

philosopher, and to ask, with some contempt, why it should be thought necessary to introduce an imaginary and invisible power as the cause of those victories, which were sufficiently explained by the valour and discipline of the legions. He justly derides the absurd reverence for antiquity, which could only tend to discourage the improvements of art and to replunge the human race into their original barbarism. From thence gradually rising to a more lofty and theological tone, he pronounces that Christianity alone is the doctrine of truth and salvation, and that every mode of Polytheism conducts its deluded votaries through the paths of error to the abyss of eternal perdition.[17] Arguments like these, when they were suggested by a favourite bishop, had power to prevent the restoration of the altar of Victory; but the same arguments fell with much more energy and effect from the mouth of a conqueror, and the gods of antiquity were dragged in triumph at the chariot-wheels of Theodosius.[18] In a full meeting of the senate the emperor proposed, according to the forms of the republic, the important question, whether the worship of Jupiter or that of Christ should be the religion of the Romans? The liberty of suffrages, which he affected to allow, was destroyed by the hopes and fears that his presence inspired; and the arbitrary exile of Symmachus was a recent admonition that it might be dangerous to oppose the wishes of the monarch. On a regular division of the senate, Jupiter was condemned

[17] See Ambrose (tom. ii. Epist. xvii. xviii. p. 825-833). The former of these epistles is a short caution; the latter is a formal reply to the petition or *libel* of Symmachus. The same ideas are more copiously expressed in the poetry, if it may deserve that name, of Prudentius, who composed his two books against Symmachus (A.D. 404) while that senator was still alive. It is whimsical enough that Montesquieu (Considérations, etc., c. xix. tom. iii. p. 487) should overlook the two professed antagonists of Symmachus, and amuse himself with descanting on the more remote and indirect confutations of Orosius, St. Augustin, and Salvian.

[18] See Prudentius (in Symmach. l. i. 545, etc.). The Christian agrees with the Pagan Zosimus (l. iv. [c. 59] p. 283) in placing this visit of Theodosius after the *second* civil war, gemini bis victor cæde Tyranni (l. i 410). But the time and circumstances are better suited to his first triumph

[The truth of the statement has been questioned that "at a full meeting of the senate the emperor proposed, according to the forms of the republic, whether the worship of Jupiter or of Christ should be the religion of the Romans." It is remarkable that Zosimus and Prudentius concur in asserting the fact of the question being solemnly deliberated by the senate, though with directly opposite results. Zosimus declares that the majority of the assembly adhered to the ancient religion of Rome. Gibbon has taken the authority of Prudentius, who, as a Latin writer, though a poet, deserves more credit than the Greek historian. Both writers concur in placing this scene after the second triumph of Theodosius. But it has been almost demonstrated by Pagi and Tillemont that Theodosius did not visit Rome after the defeat of Eugenius. It is extremely improbable that the Christian emperor would submit such a question to the senate, whose authority was nearly obsolete, except on one occasion, which was almost hailed as an epoch in the restoration of her ancient privileges. The silence of Ambrose on an event so striking and redounding so much to the honour of Christianity is of great weight.—O. S.]

and degraded by the sense of a very large majority; and it is rather surprising that any members should be found bold enough to declare, by their speeches and votes, that they were still attached to the interest of an abdicated deity.[19]   The hasty conversion of the senate must be attributed either to supernatural or to sordid motives; and many of these reluctant proselytes betrayed, on every favourable occasion, their secret disposition to throw aside the mask of odious dissimulation.   But they were gradually fixed in the new religion, as the cause of the ancient became more hopeless; they yielded to the authority of the emperor, to the fashion of the times, and to the entreaties of their wives and children,[20] who were instigated and governed by the clergy of Rome and the monks of the East.   The edifying example of the Anician family was soon imitated by the rest of the nobility: the Bassi, the Paullini, the Gracchi, embraced the Christian religion; and " the luminaries of the world, the venerable assembly of Catos (such are the high-flown expressions of Prudentius), were impatient to strip themselves of their pontifical garment—to cast the skin of the old serpent—to assume the snowy robes of baptismal innocence—and to humble the pride of the consular fasces before the tombs of the martyrs." [21]   The citizens, who subsisted by their own industry, and the populace, who were supported by the public liberality, filled the churches of the Lateran and Vatican with an incessant throng of devout proselytes.   The decrees of the senate, which proscribed the worship of idols, were ratified by the general consent of the Romans;[22] the splendour of the Capitol was defaced, and the solitary temples were abandoned to ruin and contempt.[23]   Rome submitted to the yoke of the

[19] Prudentius, after proving that the sense of the senate is declared by a legal majority, proceeds to say (609, etc.),

> Adspice quam pleno subsellia nostra Senatû
> Decernant infame Jovis pulvinar, et omne
> Idolum longe purgatâ ex urbe fugandum.
> Qua vocat egregii sententia Principis, illuc
> Libera, tum pedibus, tum corde, frequentia transit.

Zosimus ascribes to the conscript fathers an heathenish courage which few of them are found to possess.

[20] Jerom specifies the pontiff Albinus, who was surrounded with such a believing family of children and grandchildren as would have been sufficient to convert even Jupiter himself—an extraordinary proselyte! (tom. i. ad Lætam, p. 54 [Ep. cvii. tom. i. p. 671, ed. Vallars.]).

[21] Exsultare Patres videas, pulcherrima mundi
> Lumina; Conciliumque senûm gestire Catonum
> Candidiore togâ niveum pietatis amictum
> Sumere; et exuvias deponere pontificales.

The fancy of Prudentius is warmed and elevated by victory.

[21] Prudentius, after he has described the conversion of the senate and people, asks, with some truth and confidence,

> Et dubitamus adhuc Romam, tibi, Christe, dicatam
> In leges transisse tuas?

[22] Jerom exults in the desolation of the Capitol and the other temples of Rome (tom. i. p. 54, tom. ii. p. 95).

[Theodosius seized the funds bestowed by the public for the expense of

Gospel; and the vanquished provinces had not yet lost their reverence for the name and authority of Rome.

The filial piety of the emperors themselves engaged them to proceed with some caution and tenderness in the reformation of the eternal city. Those absolute monarchs acted with less regard to the prejudices of the provincials. The pious labour, which had been suspended near twenty years since the death of Constantius,[24] was vigorously resumed, and finally accomplished, by the zeal of Theodosius. Whilst that warlike prince yet struggled with the Goths, not for the glory, but for the safety of the republic, he ventured to offend a considerable party of his subjects, by some acts which might perhaps secure the protection of Heaven, but which must seem rash and unseasonable in the eye of human prudence. The success of his first experiments against the Pagans encouraged the pious emperor to reiterate and enforce his edicts of proscription: the same laws which had been originally published in the provinces of the East, were applied, after the defeat of Maximus, to the whole extent of the Western empire; and every victory of the orthodox Theodosius contributed to the triumph of the Christian and catholic faith.[25] He attacked superstition in her most vital part, by prohibiting the use of sacrifices, which he declared to be criminal as well as infamous; and if the terms of his edicts more strictly condemned the impious curiosity which examined the entrails of the victims,[26] every subsequent explanation tended to involve in the same guilt the general practice of *immolation,* which essentially constituted the religion of the Pagans. As the temples had been erected for the purpose of sacrifice, it was the duty of a benevolent prince to remove from his subjects the dangerous temptation of offending against the laws which he had enacted.

sacrifices, says Zosimus. This is not so. The public sacrifices ceased not only because they were positively prohibited, but because the public treasury would no longer bear the expense. The public and the private sacrifices in the provinces, which were not under the same regulations with those of the capital, continued to take place. In Rome, however, many Pagan ceremonies, which were without sacrifice, remained in full force. The gods were invoked, the temples were frequented, the pontificates inscribed, according to ancient usage among the family titles of honour, so that it cannot be said that Paganism was completely suppressed by Theodosius.—O. S.]

[24] Libanius (Orat. pro Templis, p. 10, Genev. 1634, published by James Godefroy, and now extremely scarce) accuses Valentinian and Valens of prohibiting sacrifices. Some partial order may have been issued by the Eastern emperor; but the idea of any general law is contradicted by the silence of the Code and the evidence of ecclesiastical history.

[25] See his laws in the Theodosian Code, l. xvi. tit. x. leg. 7-11.

[26] Homer's sacrifices are not accompanied with any inquisition of entrails (see Feithius, Antiquitat. Homer. l. i. c. 10, 16. The Tuscans, who produced the first *Haruspices,* subdued both the Greeks and the Romans (Cicero de Divinatione, ii. 23).

[In opposition to the statement that the Tuscans introduced Pagan worship by divination into Greece and Rome, it may be stated that the Greeks observed the entrails of victims as early as the Persian war. Cf. the famous passage in Æschylus, Prometheus Bound, 493 *sqq.,* where Prometheus is said to have taught mortals the art.—O. S.]

A special commission was granted to Cynegius, the Prætorian præfect of the East, and afterwards to the counts Jovius and Gaudentius, two officers of distinguished rank in the West, by which they were directed to shut the temples, to seize or destroy the instruments of idolatry, to abolish the privileges of the priests, and to confiscate the consecrated property for the benefit of the emperor, of the church, or of the army.[27] Here the desolation might have stopped: and the naked edifices, which were no longer employed in the service of idolatry, might have been protected from the destructive rage of fanaticism.   Many of those temples were the most splendid and beautiful monuments of Grecian architecture: and the emperor himself was interested not to deface the splendour of his own cities, or to diminish the value of his own possessions. Those stately edifices might be suffered to remain, as so many lasting trophies of the victory of Christ.   In the decline of the arts, they might be usefully converted into magazines, manufactures, or places of public assembly: and perhaps, when the walls of the temple had been sufficiently purified by holy rites, the worship of the true Deity might be allowed to expiate the ancient guilt of idolatry.   But as long as they subsisted, the Pagans fondly cherished the secret hope that an auspicious revolution, a second Julian, might again restore the altars of the gods: and the earnestness with which they addressed their unavailing prayers to the throne [28] increased the zeal of the Christian reformers to extirpate, without mercy, the root of superstition.   The laws of the emperors exhibit some symptoms of a milder disposition:[29] but their cold and languid efforts were insufficient to stem the torrent of enthusiasm and rapine, which was conducted, or rather impelled, by the spiritual rulers of the church.   In Gaul, the holy Martin, bishop of Tours,[30] marched at the head of his faithful monks to destroy the idols, the temples, and the consecrated trees of his extensive diocese; and, in the execution of this

[27] Zosimus, l. iv. [c. 37] p. 245, 249. Theodoret, l. v. c. 21. Idatius in Chron. Prosper. Aquitan. l. iii. c. 38 apud Baronium, Annal. Eccles. A.D. 389, No. 52. Libanius (pro Templis, p. 10) labours to prove that the commands of Theodosius were not direct and positive.

[28] Cod. Theodos. l. xvi. tit. x. leg. 8, 18.   There is room to believe that this temple of Edessa, which Theodosius wished to save for civil uses, was soon afterwards a heap of ruins (Libanius pro Templis. p. 26, 27, and Godefroy's notes, p. 59).

[Libanius appears to be the best authority for the East where, under Theodosius, the work of devastation was carried on with very different degrees of violence, according to the temper of the local authorities and of the clergy, and more especially the neighbourhood of the more fanatical monks. Neander says that the prohibition of sacrifice would be easily misconstrued into an order for the destruction of the buildings in which sacrifices were performed. (*Geschichte der Christlichen Religion*, vol. ii. p. 156.   An abuse of this kind led to this remarkable oration by Libanius.—O. S.]

[29] See this curious oration of Libanius pro Templis, pronounced, or rather composed, about the year 390.   I have consulted with advantage Dr. Lardner's version and remarks (Heathen Testimonies, vol. iv. p. 135-163).

[30] See the Life of Martin by Sulpicius Severus, c. 9-14.   The saint once mistook (as Don Quixote might have done) an harmless funeral for an idolatrous procession, and imprudently committed a miracle.

arduous task, the prudent reader will judge whether Martin was supported by the aid of miraculous powers or of carnal weapons. In Syria, the divine and excellent Marcellus,[31] as he is styled by Theodoret, a bishop animated with apostolic fervour, resolved to level with the ground the stately temples within the diocese of Apamea. His attack was resisted by the skill and solidity with which the temple of Jupiter had been constructed. The building was seated on an eminence: on each of the four sides the lofty roof was supported by fifteen massy columns, sixteen feet in circumference; and the large stones of which they were composed were firmly cemented with lead and iron. The force of the strongest and sharpest tools had been tried without effect. It was found necessary to undermine the foundations of the columns, which fell down as soon as the temporary wooden props had been consumed with fire; and the difficulties of the enterprise are described under the allegory of a black dæmon, who retarded, though he could not defeat, the operations of the Christian engineers. Elated with victory, Marcellus took the field in person against the powers of darkness; a numerous troop of soldiers and gladiators marched under the episcopal banner, and he successively attacked the villages and country temples of the diocese of Apamea. Whenever any resistance or danger was apprehended, the champion of the faith, whose lameness would not allow him either to fight or fly, placed himself at a convenient distance, beyond the reach of darts. But this prudence was the occasion of his death; he was surprised and slain by a body of exasperated rustics; and the synod of the province pronounced, without hesitation, that the holy Marcellus had sacrificed his life in the cause of God. In the support of this cause, the monks, who rushed with tumultuous fury from the desert, distinguished themselves by their zeal and diligence. They deserved the enmity of the Pagans; and some of them might deserve the reproaches of avarice and intemperance, which they indulged at the expense of the people, who foolishly admired their tattered garments, loud psalmody, and artificial paleness.[32] A small number of temples was protected by the fears, the venality, the taste, or the prudence of the civil and ecclesiastical governors. The temple of the Celestial Venus at Carthage, whose sacred precincts formed a circumference of two miles, was judiciously converted into a Christian church;[33] and a similar consecration has preserved inviolate the majestic dome of the Pantheon at Rome.[34] But in almost every

[31] Compare Sozomen (1. vii. c. 15) with Theodoret (1. v. c. 21). Between them they relate the crusade and death of Marcellus.

[32] Libanius pro Templis, p. 10-13. He rails at these black-garbed men, the Christian monks, who eat more than elephants. Poor elephants! *they* are temperate animals.

[33] Prosper. Aquitan. 1. iii. c. 38, apud Baronium; Annal. Eccles. A.D. 389, No. 58, etc. The temple had been shut some time, and the access to it was overgrown with brambles.

[34] Donatus, Roma Antiqua et Nova, 1. iv. c. 4, p. 468. This consecration was performed by Pope Boniface IV. I am ignorant of the favourable circumstances which had preserved the Pantheon above two hundred years after the reign of Theodosius.

province of the Roman world, an army of fanatics, without authority and without discipline, invaded the peaceful inhabitants; and the ruin of the fairest structures of antiquity still displays the ravages of *those* barbarians who alone had time and inclination to execute such laborious destruction.

In this wide and various prospect of devastation, the spectator may distinguish the ruins of the temple of Serapis, at Alexandria.[35] Serapis does not appear to have been one of the native gods, or monsters, who sprung from the fruitful soil of superstitious Egypt.[36] The first of the Ptolemies had been commanded, by a dream, to import the mysterious stranger from the coast of Pontus, where he had been long adored by the inhabitants of Sinope; but his attributes and his reign were so imperfectly understood, that it became a subject of dispute whether he represented the bright orb of day, or the gloomy monarch of the subterraneous regions.[37] The Egyptians, who were obstinately devoted to the religion of their fathers, refused to admit this foreign deity within the walls of their cities.[38] But the obsequious priests, who were seduced by the liberality of the Ptolemies, submitted, without resistance, to the power of the god of Pontus: an honourable and domestic genealogy was provided; and this fortunate usurper was introduced into the throne and bed of Osiris,[39] the husband of Isis, and the celestial monarch of Egypt. Alexandria, which claimed his peculiar protection, gloried in the name of the city of Serapis. His temple,[40] which rivalled the pride and magnificence of the Capitol, was erected on the spacious summit of an

[35] Sophronius composed a recent and separate history (Jerom. in Script. Eccles. tom. i. p. 303), which has furnished materials to Socrates (1. v. c. 16), Theodoret (1. v. c. 22), and Rufinus (1. ii. c. 22). Yet the last, who had been at Alexandria before and after the event, may deserve the credit of an original witness.

[36] Gerard Vossius (Opera, tom. v. p. 80, and de Idololatriâ, 1. i. c. 29) strives to support the strange notion of the Fathers, that the patriarch Joseph was adored in Egypt as the bull Apis and the god Serapis. [Modern writers are agreed that the worship of Serapis was not so strange to the ancient Egyptians as the narrative of Tacitus would imply. Serapis appears to have been worshipped by the ancient Egyptians as the god of the lower world, and hence to have been identified by the Ptolemies with the Jupiter, Dis, or Pluto of Sinope. He was the Osiris of the lower world, and among the Greeks and Romans took the place of this deity. See Guigniaut, Sérapis et son Origine.—O.S.]

[37] Origo dei nondum nostris celebrata, Ægyptiorum antistites *sic* memorant, etc. Tacit. Hist. iv. 83. The Greeks who had travelled into Egypt were alike ignorant of this new deity.

[38] Macrobius, Saturnal. 1. i. c. 7. Such a living fact decisively proves his foreign extraction.

[39] At Rome, Isis and Serapis were united in the same temple. The precedency which the queen assumed may seem to betray her unequal alliance with the stranger of Pontus. But the superiority of the female sex was established in Egypt as a civil and religious institution (Diodor. Sicul. tom. i. i. [c. 27] p. 31, edit. Wesseling), and the same order is observed in Plutarch's Treatise of Isis and *Osiris;* whom he identifies with Serapis.

[40] Ammianus (xxii. 16). The Exposito totius Mundi (p. 8, in Hudson's Geograph. Minor. tom. iii.), and Rufinus (1. ii. c. 22), celebrate the *Serapeum* as one of the wonders of the world.

artificial mount, raised one hundred steps above the level of the adjacent parts of the city; and the interior cavity was strongly supported by arches, and distributed into vaults and subterraneous apartments. The consecrated buildings were surrounded by a quadrangular portico; the stately halls and exquisite statues displayed the triumph of the arts; and the treasures of ancient learning were preserved in the famous Alexandrian library, which had arisen with new splendour from its ashes.[41] After the edicts of Theodosius had severely prohibited the sacrifices of the Pagans, they were still tolerated in the city and temple of Serapis; and this singular indulgence was imprudently ascribed to the superstitious terrors of the Christians themselves: as if they had feared to abolish those ancient rites which could alone secure the inundations of the Nile, the harvests of Egypt, and the subsistence of Constantinople.[42]

At that time [43] the archiepiscopal throne of Alexandria was filled by Theophilus,[44] the perpetual enemy of peace and virtue; a bold, bad

[41] See Mémoires de l'Acad. des Inscriptions, tom. ix. p. 397-416. The *old* library of the Ptolemies was *totally* consumed in Cæsar's Alexandrian war. Marc Antony gave the whole collection of Pergamus (200,000 volumes) to Cleopatra, as the foundation of the *new* library of Alexandria.
[Some statements of Gibbon regarding the libraries of Alexandria require some modification. In the Alexandria of the Ptolemies there were two libraries, the larger one in the quarter named the *Bruchium,* and the smaller one was the *Serapeum*—called the daughter of the other, and situated in the quarter called Rhacotis. The former was totally destroyed in the conflagration of the Bruchium, during Cæsar's Alexandrian war; but the latter, which was of great value, remained uninjured. It is probable that the collection of Pergamus was placed in the Bruchium after the fire, as that quarter was without a library, and the queen was anxious to repair the ravages occasioned by the Civil War. If this supposition is correct, two Alexandrian libraries continued to exist after the time of Cæsar, and this is rendered still more probable by the fact that, during the first three centuries of the Christian era, the Bruchium was still the literary quarter of Alexandria. But a great change took place in the time of Aurelian. This emperor, in suppressing the revolt of Firmus in Egypt A.D. 273, is said to have destroyed the Bruchium, and though this statement is hardly to be taken literally, the Bruchium ceased from this time to be included within the walls of Alexandria, and was regarded only as a suburb of the city. Whether the great library in the Bruchium with the museum and its other literary establishments perished at this time, we do not know; but the Serapeum for the next century takes its place as the literary quarter of Alexandria, and becomes the chief library of the city. Hence many writers erroneously speak of the Serapeum as if it had been from the beginning the great Alexandrian library.—O. S.]
[42] Libanius (pro Templis, p. 21) indiscreetly provokes his Christian masters by this insulting remark.
[43] We may choose between the date of Marcellinus (A.D. 389) or that of Prosper (A.D. 391). Tillemont (Hist. des. Emp. tom. v. p. 310, 756) prefers the former, and Pagi the latter.
[With regard to "the chapel of Bacchus" which Theophilus overthrew, Sozomen calls it "a temple of Bacchus," but as Dr. Smith says, we may conclude it was a temple of Osiris, as the Greeks gave to this deity the name of Bacchus. Socrates calls the temple a Mithreum.—O. S.]
[44] Tillemont, Mém. Ecclés. tom. xi. p. 441-500. The ambiguous situation of Theophilus—a *saint,* as the friend of Jerom; a *devil,* as the enemy of Chrysostom—produces a sort of impartiality; yet, upon the whole, the balance is justly inclined against him.

man, whose hands were alternately polluted with gold and with blood. His pious indignation was excited by the honours of Serapis; and the insults which he offered to an ancient chapel of Bacchus convinced the Pagans that he meditated a more important and dangerous enterprise. In the tumultuous capital of Egypt, the slightest provocation was sufficient to inflame a civil war. The votaries of Serapis, whose strength and numbers were much inferior to those of their antagonists, rose in arms at the instigation of the philosopher Olympius,[45] who exhorted them to die in the defence of the altars of the gods. These Pagan fanatics fortified themselves in the temple, or rather fortress, of Serapis; repelled the besiegers by daring sallies and a resolute defence; and, by the inhuman cruelties which they exercised on their Christian prisoners, obtained the last consolation of despair. The efforts of the prudent magistrate were usefully exerted for the establishment of a truce till the answer of Theodosius should determine the fate of Serapis. The two parties assembled without arms, in the principal square; and the Imperial rescript was publicly read. But when a sentence of destruction against the idols of Alexandria was pronounced, the Christians sent up a shout of joy and exultation, whilst the unfortunate Pagans, whose fury had given way to consternation, retired with hasty and silent steps, and eluded, by their flight or obscurity, the resentment of their enemies. Theophilus proceeded to demolish the temple of Serapis, without any other difficulties than those which he found in the weight and solidity of the materials; but these obstacles proved so insuperable that he was obliged to leave the foundations, and to content himself with reducing the edifice itself to a heap of rubbish, a part of which was soon afterwards cleared away, to make room for a church erected in honour of the Christian martyrs. The valuable library of Alexandria was pillaged or destroyed; and near twenty years afterwards, the appearance of the empty shelves excited the regret and indignation of every spectator whose mind was not totally darkened by religious prejudice.[46] The compositions of ancient genius, so many of which have irretrievably perished, might surely have been excepted from the wreck of idolatry, for the amusement and instruction of succeeding ages; and either the zeal or the avarice of the archbishop [47]

[45] Lardner (Heathen Testimonies, vol. iv. p. 411) has alleged a beautiful passage from Suidas, or rather from Damascius, which shows the devout and virtuous Olympius, not in the light of a warrior, but of a prophet.
[46] Nos vidimus armaria librorum, quibus direptis, exinanita ea a nostris hominibus, nostris temporibus memorent. Orosius, l. vi. c. 15, p. 421, edit. Havercamp. Though a bigot and a controversial writer, Orosius seems to blush.
[Gibbon seems to think that the whole of the Serapeum was destroyed, but this was not the case. It was only the sanctuary of the god that was levelled with the ground, and the library, the halls and the other buildings in the consecrated ground remained standing long afterwards. Moreover, if we credit the story of the destruction of the Alexandrian library by the Arabs under Amrou, which there seems no good reason to doubt, we must conclude that the library in the Serapeum existed down to A.D. 638.—O. S.]
[47] Eunapius, in the Lives of Antoninus and Ædesius, execrates the sacrilegious rapine of Theophilus. Tillemont (Mém. Ecclés. tom. xiii. p. 453)

might have been satiated with the rich spoils which were the reward of his victory. While the images and vases of gold and silver were carefully melted, and those of a less valuable metal were contemptuously broken and cast into the streets, Theophilus laboured to expose the frauds and vices of the ministers of the idols: their dexterity in the management of the loadstone; their secret methods of introducing an human actor into a hollow statue; and their scandalous abuse of the confidence of devout husbands and unsuspecting females.[48] Charges like these may seem to deserve some degree of credit, as they are not repugnant to the crafty and interested spirit of superstition. But the same spirit is equally prone to the base practice of insulting and calumniating a fallen enemy; and our belief is naturally checked by the reflection that it is much less difficult to invent a fictitious story than to support a practical fraud. The colossal statue of Serapis [49] was involved in the ruin of his temple and religion. A great number of plates of different metals, artificially joined together, composed the majestic figure of the deity, who touched on either side the walls of the sanctuary. The aspect of Serapis, his sitting posture, and the sceptre which he bore in his left hand, were extremely similar to the ordinary representations of Jupiter. He was distinguished from Jupiter by the basket, or bushel, which was placed on his head; and by the emblematic monster which he held in his right hand; the head and body of a serpent branching into three tails, which were again terminated by the triple heads of a dog, a lion, and a wolf. It was confidently affirmed that, if any impious hand should dare to violate the majesty of the god, the heavens and the earth would instantly return to their original chaos. An intrepid soldier, animated by zeal, and armed with a weighty battle-axe, ascended the ladder; and even the Christian multitude expected with some anxiety the event of the combat.[50] He aimed a vigorous stroke against the cheek of Serapis; the cheek fell to the ground; the thunder was still silent, and both the heavens and the earth continued

quotes an epistle of Isidore of Pelusium, which reproaches the primate with the *idolatrous* worship of gold, the auri *sacra* fames.

[48] Rufinius names the priest of Saturn who, in the character of the god, familiarly conversed with many pious ladies of quality; till he betrayed himself, in a moment of transport, when he could not disguise the tone of his voice. The authentic and impartial narrative of Æschines (see Bayle, Dictionnaire Critique, SCAMANDRE), and the adventure of Mundus (Joseph. Antiquitat. Judaic. l. xviii. c. 3 [§ 4], p. 877, edit. Havercamp), may prove that such amorous frauds have been practised with success.

[49] See the images of Serapis, in Montfaucon (tom. ii. p. 297): but the description of Macrobius (Saturnal. l. i. c. 20) is much more picturesque and satisfactory.

[50] Sed fortes tremuere manus, motique verendâ
Majestate loci, si robora sacra ferirent
In sua credebant reditturas membra secures.

(Lucan. iii. 429.) "Is it true" (said Augustus to a veteran of Italy, at whose house he supped) "that the man who gave the first blow to the golden statue of Anaitis was instantly deprived of his eyes and of his life?"—"*I was* that man" (replied the clear-sighted veteran), "and you now sup on one of the legs of the goddess." (Plin. Hist. Natur. xxxiii. 24.)

to preserve their accustomed order and tranquillity. The victorious soldier repeated his blows: the huge idol was overthrown and broken in pieces; and the limbs of Serapis were ignominiously dragged through the streets of Alexandria. His mangled carcase was burnt in the amphitheatre, amidst the shouts of the populace; and many persons attributed their conversion to this discovery of the impotence of their tutelar deity. The popular modes of religion, that propose any visible and material objects of worship, have the advantage of adapting and familiarising themselves to the senses of mankind; but this advantage is counterbalanced by the various and inevitable accidents to which the faith of the idolater is exposed. It is scarcely possible that, in every disposition of mind, he should preserve his implicit reverence for the idols, or the relics, which the naked eye and the profane hand are unable to distinguish from the most common productions of art or nature; and, if, in the hour of danger, their secret and miraculous virtue does not operate for their own preservation, he scorns the vain apologies of his priests, and justly derides the object and the folly of his superstitious attachment.[51]   After the fall of Serapis, some hopes were still entertained by the Pagans that the Nile would refuse his annual supply to the impious masters of Egypt; and the extraordinary delay of the inundation seemed to announce the displeasure of the river-god.   But this delay was soon compensated by the rapid swell of the waters.   They suddenly rose to such an unusual height as to comfort the discontented party with the pleasing expectation of a deluge; till the peaceful river again subsided to the well-known and fertilising level of sixteen cubits, or about thirty English feet.[52]

The temples of the Roman empire were deserted or destroyed; but the ingenious superstition of the Pagans still attempted to elude the laws of Theodosius, by which all sacrifices had been severely prohibited. The inhabitants of the country, whose conduct was less exposed to the eye of malicious curiosity, disguised their *religious* under the appearance of *convivial* meetings.   On the days of solemn festivals they assembled in great numbers under the spreading shade of some consecrated trees; sheep and oxen were slaughtered and roasted; and this rural entertainment was sanctified by the use of incense and by the hymns which were sung in honour of the gods.   But it was alleged that, as no part of the animal was made a burnt-offering, as no altar was provided to receive the blood, and as the previous oblation of salt cakes and the concluding ceremony of libations were carefully omitted, these festal meetings did not involve the guests in the guilt or penalty of an illegal sacrifice.[53]

[51] The History of the Reformation affords frequent examples of the sudden change from superstition to contempt.

[52] Sozomen, l. vii. c. 20.   I have supplied the measure.   The same standard of the inundation, and consequently of the cubit, has uniformly subsisted since the time of Herodotus.   See Fréret, in the Mém. de l'Académie des Inscriptions, tom. xvi. p. 344-353.   Greaves's Miscellaneous Works, vol. i. p. 233.   The Egyptian cubit is about twenty-two inches of the English measure.

[53] Libanius (pro Templis, p. 15, 16, 17) pleads their cause with gentle and insinuating rhetoric.   From the earliest age such feasts had enlivened the

Whatever might be the truth of the facts or the merit of the distinction,[54] these vain pretences were swept away by the last edict of Theodosius, which inflicted a deadly wound on the superstition of the Pagans.[55] This prohibitory law is expressed in the most absolute and comprehensive terms. "It is our will and pleasure," says the emperor, "that none of our subjects, whether magistrates or private citizens, however exalted or however humble may be their rank and condition, shall presume in any city or in any place to worship an inanimate idol by the sacrifice of a guiltless victim." The act of sacrificing and the practice of divination by the entrails of the victim are declared (without any regard to the object of the inquiry) a crime of high treason against the state, which can be expiated only by the death of the guilty. The rites of Pagan superstition which might seem less bloody and atrocious are abolished as highly injurious to the truth and honour of religion; luminaries, garlands, frankincense, and libations of wine are specially enumerated and condemned; and the harmless claims of the domestic genius, of the household gods, are included in this rigorous proscription. The use of any of these profane and illegal ceremonies subjects the offender to the forfeiture of the house or estate where they have been performed; and if he has artfully chosen the property of another for the scene of his impiety, he is compelled to discharge, without delay, a heavy fine of twenty-five pounds of gold, or more than one thousand pounds sterling. A fine not less considerable is imposed on the connivance of the secret enemies of religion who shall neglect the duty of their respective stations, either to reveal or to punish the guilt of idolatry. Such was the persecuting spirit of the laws of Theodosius, which were repeatedly enforced by his sons and grandsons, with the loud and unanimous applause of the Christian world.[56]

In the cruel reigns of Decius and Diocletian Christianity had been proscribed, as a revolt from the ancient and hereditary religion of the empire; and the unjust suspicions which were entertained of a dark and dangerous faction were in some measure countenanced by the inseparable

country: and those of Bacchus (Georgic. ii. 380) had produced the theatre of Athens. See Godefroy, ad loc., Liban., and Codex Theodos. tom. vi. p. 284 [ed. Lugd. 1665].

[54] Honorius tolerated these rustic festivals (A.D. 399). "Absque ullo sacrificio, atque ullâ superstitione damnabili." But nine years afterwards he found it necessary to reiterate and enforce the same proviso (Codex Theodos. l. xvi. tit. x. leg. 17, 19).

[55] Cod. Theodos. l. xvi. tit. x. leg. 12. Jortin (Remarks on Eccles. History, vol. iv. p. 134) censures, with becoming asperity, the style and sentiment of this intolerant law.

[56] Such a charge should not be lightly made; but it may surely be justified by the authority of St. Augustin, who thus addresses the Donatists: "Quis nostrûm, quis vestrûm non laudat leges ab Imperatoribus datas adversus sacrificia Paganorum? Et certe longe ibi pœna severior constituta est; illius quippe impietatis capitale supplicium est." Epist. xciii. No. 10 [tom. ii. p. 308, ed. Bened. 1797], quoted by Le Clerc (Bibliothèque Choisie, tom. viii. p. 277), who adds some judicious reflections on the intolerance of the victorious Christians.

union and rapid conquests of the catholic church. But the same excuses of fear and ignorance cannot be applied to the Christian emperors, who violated the precepts of humanity and of the Gospel. The experience of ages had betrayed the weakness as well as folly of Paganism; the light of reason and of faith had already exposed to the greatest part of mankind the vanity of idols; and the declining sect, which still adhered to their worship, might have been permitted to enjoy in peace and obscurity the religious customs of their ancestors. Had the Pagans been animated by the undaunted zeal which possessed the minds of the primitive believers, the triumph of the church must have been stained with blood; and the martyrs of Jupiter and Apollo might have embraced the glorious opportunity of devoting their lives and fortunes at the foot of their altars. But such obstinate zeal was not congenial to the loose and careless temper of Polytheism. The violent and repeated strokes of the orthodox princes were broken by the soft and yielding substance against which they were directed; and the ready obedience of the Pagans protected them from the pains and penalties of the Theodosian Code.[57] Instead of asserting that the authority of the gods was superior to that of the emperor, they desisted, with a plaintive murmur, from the use of those sacred rites which their sovereign had condemned. If they were sometimes tempted by a sally of passion, or by the hopes of concealment, to indulge their favourite superstition, their humble repentance disarmed the severity of the Christian magistrate, and they seldom refused to atone for their rashness by submitting, with some secret reluctance, to the yoke of the Gospel. The churches were filled with the increasing multitude of these unworthy proselytes, who had conformed, from temporal motives, to the reigning religion; and whilst they devoutly imitated the postures and recited the prayers of the faithful, they satisfied their conscience by the silent and sincere invocation of the gods of antiquity.[58] If the Pagans wanted patience to suffer, they wanted spirit to resist; and the scattered myriads, who deplored the ruin of the temples, yielded, without a contest, to the fortune of their adversaries. The disorderly opposition [59] of the peasants of Syria and the populace of Alexandria to the rage of private fanaticism was silenced by the name and authority of the emperor. The Pagans of the West, without contributing to the elevation of Eugenius, disgraced by their partial attachment the cause and character of the usurper. The clergy vehemently exclaimed that he aggravated the crime of rebellion by the guilt of apostasy; that, by his permission,

---

[57] Orosius, l. vii. c. 28, p. 537. Augustin (Enarrat. in Psalm cxl. apud Lardner, Heathen Testimonies, vol. iv. p. 458) insults their cowardice. " Quis eorum comprehensus est in sacrificio (cum his legibus ista prohiberentur) et non negavit ? "

[58] Libanius (pro Templis, p. 17, 18) mentions, without censure, the occasional conformity, and as it were theatrical play, of these hypocrites.

[59] Libanius concludes his apology (p. 32) by declaring to the emperor that, unless he expressly warrants the destruction of the temples, ἴσθι τοὺς τῶν ἀγρῶν δεσπότας, καὶ αὐτοῖς, καὶ τῷ νόμῳ βοηθήσοντας, the proprietors will defend themselves and the laws.

the altar of Victory was again restored; and that the idolatrous symbols of Jupiter and Hercules were displayed in the field against the invincible standard of the cross. But the vain hopes of the Pagans were soon annihilated by the defeat of Eugenius; and they were left exposed to the resentment of the conqueror, who laboured to deserve the favour of Heaven by the extirpation of idolatry.[60]

A nation of slaves is always prepared to applaud the clemency of their master who, in the abuse of absolute power, does not proceed to the last extremes of injustice and oppression. Theodosius might undoubtedly have proposed to his Pagan subjects the alternative of baptism or of death; and the eloquent Libanius has praised the moderation of a prince who never enacted, by any positive law, that all his subjects should immediately embrace and practise the religion of their sovereign.[61] The profession of Christianity was not made an essential qualification for the enjoyment of the civil rights of society, nor were any peculiar hardships imposed on the sectaries who credulously received the fables of Ovid and obstinately rejected the miracles of the Gospel. The palace, the schools, the army, and the senate were filled with declared and devout Pagans; they obtained, without distinction, the civil and military honours of the empire. Theodosius distinguished his liberal regard for virtue and genius by the consular dignity which he bestowed on Symmachus,[62] and by the personal friendship which he expressed to Libanius;[63] and the two eloquent apologists of Paganism were never required either to change or to dissemble their religious opinions. The Pagans were indulged in the most licentious freedom of speech and writing; the historical and philosophic remains of Eunapius, Zosimus,[64] and the fanatic teachers of the school of Plato, betray the most furious animosity, and contain the sharpest invectives, against the sentiments and conduct of their victorious adversaries. If these audacious libels were publicly known,

[60] Paulinus, in Vit. Ambros. c. 26. Augustin de Civitat. Dei, 1. v. c. 26. Theodoret, 1. v. c. 24.

[61] Libanius suggests the form of a persecuting edict which Theodosius might enact (pro Templis, p. 31) : a rash joke and a dangerous experiment. Some princes would have taken his advice.

[62] Denique pro meritis terrestribus æqua rependens
Munera, sacricolis summos impertit honores,
Dux bonus, et certare sinit cum laude suorum:
Nec pago implicitos per debita culmina mundi
Ire viros prohibet.
Ipse magistratum tibi consulis, ipse tribunal
Contulit.
                              Prudent. in Symmach. i. 617, etc.

[63] Libanius (pro Templis, p. 32) is proud that Theodosius should thus distinguish a man who even in his *presence* would swear by Jupiter. Yet this presence seems to be no more than a figure of rhetoric.

[64] Zosimus, who styles himself Count and Ex-advocate of the Treasury, reviles, with partial and indecent bigotry, the Christian princes, and even the father of his sovereign. His work must have been privately circulated, since it escaped the invectives of the ecclesiastical historians prior to Evagrius (l. iii. c. 40-41), who lived towards the end of the sixth century.

we must applaud the good sense of the Christian princes, who viewed with a smile of contempt the last struggles of superstition and despair.[65] But the Imperial laws which prohibited the sacrifices and ceremonies of Paganism were rigidly executed; and every hour contributed to destroy the influence of a religion which was supported by custom rather than by argument. The devotion of the poet or the philosopher may be secretly nourished by prayer, meditation, and study; but the exercise of public worship appears to be the only solid foundation of the religious sentiments of the people, which derive their force from imitation and habit. The interruption of that public exercise may consummate, in the period of a few years, the important work of a national revolution. The memory of theological opinions cannot long be preserved without the artificial helps of priests, of temples, and of books.[66] The ignorant vulgar, whose minds are still agitated by the blind hopes and terrors of superstition, will be soon persuaded by their superiors to direct their vows to the reigning deities of the age; and will insensibly imbibe an ardent zeal for the support and propagation of the new doctrine, which spiritual hunger at first compelled them to accept. The generation that arose in the world after the promulgation of the Imperial laws was attracted within the pale of the catholic church: and so rapid, yet so gentle, was the fall of Paganism, that only twenty-eight years after the death of Theodosius the faint and minute vestiges were no longer visible to the eye of the legislator.[67]

The ruin of the Pagan religion is described by the sophists as a dreadful and amazing prodigy, which covered the earth with darkness and restored the ancient dominion of chaos and of night. They relate in solemn and pathetic strains that the temples were converted into sepulchres, and that the holy places, which had been adorned by the statues of the gods, were basely polluted by the relics of Christian martyrs. " The monks " (a race of filthy animals, to whom Eunapius is tempted to refuse the name of men) " are the authors of the new worship, which, in the place of those deities who are conceived by the understanding, has substituted the meanest and most contemptible slaves. The heads, salted and pickled, of those infamous malefactors, who for the multitude of their crimes have suffered a just and ignominious death; their bodies, still marked by the impression of the lash and the scars of those tortures which were inflicted by the sentence of the magistrate; such " (continues Eunapius) " are the gods which the

[65] Yet the Pagans of Africa complained that the times would not allow them to answer with freedom the City of God; nor does St. Augustin (v. 26) deny the charge.

[66] The Moors of Spain, who secretly preserved the Mahometan religion above a century, under the tyranny of the Inquisition, possessed the Koran, with the peculiar use of the Arabic tongue. See the curious and honest story of their expulsion in Geddes (Miscellanies, vol. i. p. 1-198).

[67] Paganos qui supersunt, quanquam jam nullos esse credamus, etc. Cod Theodos. l. xvi. tit. x. leg. 22, A.D. 423. The younger Theodosius was afterwards satisfied that his judgment had been somewhat premature.

earth produces in our days; such are the martyrs, the supreme arbitrators of our prayers and petitions to the Deity, whose tombs are now consecrated as the objects of the veneration of the people." [68] Without approving the malice, it is natural enough to share the surprise of the sophist, the spectator of a revolution which raised those obscure victims of the laws of Rome to the rank of celestial and invisible protectors of the Roman empire. The grateful respect of the Christians for the martyrs of the faith was exalted, by time and victory, into religious adoration; and the most illustrious of the saints and prophets were deservedly associated to the honours of the martyrs. One hundred and fifty years after the glorious deaths of St. Peter and St. Paul, the Vatican and the Ostian road were distinguished by the tombs, or rather by the trophies, of those spiritual heroes. [69] In the age which followed the conversion of Constantine, the emperors, the consuls, and the generals of armies devoutly visited the sepulchres of a tentmaker and a fisherman; [70] and their venerable bones were deposited under the altars of Christ, on which the bishops of the royal city continually offered the unbloody sacrifice. [71] The new capital of the Eastern world, unable to produce any ancient and domestic trophies, was enriched by the spoils of dependent provinces. The bodies of St. Andrew, St. Luke, and St. Timothy had reposed near three hundred years in the obscure graves from whence they were transported, in solemn pomp, to the church of the apostles, which the magnificence of Constantine had founded on the banks of the Thracian Bosphorus. [72] About fifty years afterwards the same banks were honoured by the presence of Samuel, the judge and prophet of the people of Israel. His ashes, deposited in a golden vase, and covered with a silken veil, were delivered by the bishops into each other's hands. The relics of Samuel were received by the people with the same joy and reverence which they would have shown to the living prophet; the highways, from Palestine

[68] See Eunapius, in the Life of the sophist Ædesius; in that of Eustathius he foretells the ruin of Paganism, καὶ τι μυθῶδες, καὶ ἀειδὲς, σκότος τυραννήσει τὰ ἐπὶ γης κάλλιστα.

[69] Caius (apud Euseb. Hist. Eccles. l. ii. c. 25), a Roman presbyter, who lived in the time of Zephyrinus (A.D. 202-219), is an early witness of this superstitious practice.

[70] Chrysostom. Quod Christus sit Deus. Tom. i. nov. edit. No. 9. I am indebted for this quotation to Benedict the XIVth's pastoral letter on the Jubilee of the year 1750. See the curious and entertaining letters of M. Chais, tom. iii.

[71] Male facit ergo Romanus episcopus? qui, super mortuorum hominum, Petri and Pauli, secundum nos, ossa veneranda . . . offert Domino sacrificia, et tumulos eorum, Christi arbitratur altaria. Jerom. tom. ii. advers. Vigilant. p. 153. [Tom. ii. p. 395, ed. Vallars.]

[72] Jerom (tom. ii. p. 122 [contra Vigilant. c. 5, tom. ii. p. 391, ed. Vallars.]) bears witness to these translations, which are neglected by the ecclesiastical historians. The passion of St. Andrew at Patræ is described in an epistle from the clergy of Achaia, which Baronius (Annal. Eccles. A.D. 60, No. 34) wishes to believe, and Tillemont is forced to reject. St. Andrew was adopted as the spiritual founder of Constantinople (Mém. Ecclés. tom. i. p. 317-323, 588-594).

to the gates of Constantinople, were filled with an uninterrupted procession; and the emperor Arcadius himself, at the head of the most illustrious members of the clergy and senate, advanced to meet his extraordinary guest, who had always deserved and claimed the homage of kings.[73] The example of Rome and Constantinople confirmed the faith and discipline of the catholic world. The honours of the saints and martyrs, after a feeble and ineffectual murmur of profane reason,[74] were universally established; and in the age of Ambrose and Jerom something was still deemed wanting to the sanctity of a Christian church, till it had been consecrated by some portion of holy relics, which fixed and inflamed the devotion of the faithful. In the long period of twelve hundred years, which elapsed between the reign of Constantine and the reformation of Luther, the worship of saints and relics corrupted the pure and perfect simplicity of the Christian model; and some symptoms of degeneracy may be observed even in the first generations which adopted and cherished this pernicious innovation.

I. The satisfactory experience that the relics of saints were more valuable than gold or precious stones [75] stimulated the clergy to multiply the treasures of the church. Without much regard for truth or probability, they invented names for skeletons, and actions for names. The fame of the apostles, and of the holy men who had imitated their virtues, was darkened by religious fiction. To the invincible band of genuine and primitive martyrs they added myriads of imaginary heroes, who had never existed, except in the fancy of crafty or credulous legendaries; and there is reason to suspect that Tours might not be the only diocese in which the bones of a malefactor were adored instead of those of a saint.[76] A superstitious practice, which tended to increase the temptations of fraud and credulity, insensibly extinguished the light of history and of reason in the Christian world.

II. But the progress of superstition would have been much less rapid and victorious if the faith of the people had not been assisted by the seasonable aid of visions and miracles to ascertain the authenticity and virtue of the most suspicious relics. In the reign of the younger Theo-

[73] Jerom (tom. ii. p. 122 [l. c. ed. Vallars.]) pompously describes the translation of Samuel, which is noticed in all the chronicles of the times.
[74] The Presbyter Vigilantius, the protestant of his age, firmly, though ineffectually, withstood the superstition of monks, relics, saints, fasts, etc., for which Jerom compares him to the Hydra, Cerberus, the Centaurs, etc., and considers him only as the organ of the Dæmon (tom. ii. p. 120-126 [tom. ii. p. 387-402, ed. Vallars.]). Whoever will peruse the controversy of St. Jerom and Vigilantius, and St. Augustin's account of the miracles of St. Stephen, may speedily gain some idea of the spirit of the Fathers.
[75] M. de Beausobre (Hist. du Manichéisme, tom. ii. p. 648) has applied a worldly sense to the pious observation of the clergy of Smyrna, who carefully preserved the relics of St. Polycarp the martyr.
[76] Martin of Tours (see his Life, c. 8, by Sulpicius Severus) extorted this confession from the mouth of the dead man. The error is allowed to be natural; the discovery is supposed to be miraculous. Which of the two was likely to happen most frequently?

dosius, Lucian,[77] a presbyter of Jerusalem, and the ecclesiastical minister
of the village of Caphargamala, about twenty miles from the city, related
a very singular dream, which, to remove his doubts, had been repeated
on three successive Saturdays. A venerable figure stood before him, in
the silence of the night, with a long beard, a white robe, and a gold rod;
announced himself by the name of Gamaliel; and revealed to the astonished presbyter, that his own corpse, with the bodies of his son Abibas,
his friend Nicodemus, and the illustrious Stephen, the first martyr of the
Christian faith, were secretly buried in the adjacent field. He added,
with some impatience, that it was time to release himself and his companions from their obscure prison; that their appearance would be salutary to a distressed world; and that they had made choice of Lucian to
inform the bishop of Jerusalem of their situation and their wishes. The
doubts and difficulties which still retarded this important discovery were
successively removed by new visions; and the ground was opened by the
bishop, in the presence of an innumerable multitude. The coffins of
Gamaliel, of his son, and of his friend, were found in regular order; but
when the fourth coffin, which contained the remains of Stephen, was
shown to the light, the earth trembled, and an odour such as that of Paradise was smelt, which instantly cured the various diseases of seventy-three
of the assistants. The companions of Stephen were left in their peaceful
residence of Caphargamala; but the relics of the first martyr were transported, in solemn procession, to a church constructed in their honour on
Mount Sion; and the minute particles of those relics, a drop of blood,[78]
or the scrapings of a bone, were acknowledged, in almost every province
of the Roman world, to possess a divine and miraculous virtue. The
grave and learned Augustin,[79] whose understanding scarcely admits the
excuse of credulity, has attested the innumerable prodigies which were
performed in Africa by the relics of St. Stephen; and this marvellous
narrative is inserted in the elaborate work of the City of God, which the
bishop of Hippo designed as a solid and immortal proof of the truth of
Christianity. Augustin solemnly declares that he has selected those
miracles only which were publicly certified by the persons who were
either the objects, or the spectators, of the power of the martyr. Many
prodigies were omitted or forgotten; and Hippo had been less favourably

[77] Lucian composed in Greek his original narrative, which has been translated by Avitus, and published by Baronius (Annal. Eccles. A.D. 415, No. 7-16).
The Benedictine editors of St. Augustin have given (at the end of the work
De Civitate Dei) two several copies, with many various readings. It is the
character of falsehood to be loose and inconsistent. The most incredible parts
of the legend are smoothed and softened by Tillemont (Mém. Ecclés. tom.
ii. p. 9, etc.).
[78] A phial of St. Stephen's blood was annually liquefied at Naples till he
was superseded by St. Januarius (Ruinart. Hist. Persecut. Vandal. p. 529).
[79] Augustin composed the two-and-twenty books de Civitate Dei in the space
of thirteen years, A.D. 413-426. (Tillemont, Mém. Ecclés. tom. xiv. p. 608,
etc.) His learning is too often borrowed, and his arguments are too often
his own; but the whole work claims the merit of a magnificent design, vigorously, and not unskilfully, executed.

treated than the other cities of the province. And yet the bishop enumerates above seventy miracles, of which three were resurrections from the dead, in the space of two years, and within the limits of his own diocese.[80]   If we enlarge our view to all the diocese, and all the saints, of the Christian world, it will not be easy to calculate the fables, and the errors, which issued from this inexhaustible source. But we may surely be allowed to observe that a miracle, in that age of superstition and credulity, lost its name and its merit, since it could scarcely be considered as a deviation from the ordinary and established laws of nature.

III. The innumerable miracles, of which the tombs of the martyrs were the perpetual theatre, revealed to the pious believer the actual state and constitution of the invisible world; and his religious speculations appeared to be founded on the firm basis of fact and experience. Whatever might be the condition of vulgar souls in the long interval between the dissolution and the resurrection of their bodies, it was evident that the superior spirits of the saints and martyrs did not consume that portion of their existence in silent and inglorious sleep.[81]   It was evident (without presuming to determine the place of their habitation, or the nature of their felicity) that they enjoyed the lively and active consciousness of their happiness, their virtue, and their powers; and that they had already secured the possession of their eternal reward. The enlargement of their intellectual faculties surpassed the measure of the human imagination; since it was proved by *experience* that they were capable of hearing and understanding the various petitions of their numerous votaries, who, in the same moment of time, but in the most distant parts of the world, invoked the name and assistance of Stephen or of Martin.[82]   The confidence of their petitioners was founded on the persuasion that the saints, who reigned with Christ, cast an eye of pity upon earth; that they were warmly interested in the prosperity of the catholic church; and that the individuals who imitated the example of their faith and piety were the peculiar and favourite objects of their

[80] See Augustin de Civitat. Dei, l. xxii. c. 22, and the Appendix, which contains two books of St. Stephen's miracles, by Evodius, bishop of Uzalis. Freculphus (apud Basnage, Hist. des Juifs, tom. viii. p. 249) has preserved a Gallic or Spanish proverb, "Whoever pretends to have read all the miracles of St. Stephen, he lies."

[81] Burnet (de Statû Mortuorum, p. 56-84) collects the opinions of the Fathers, as far as they assert the sleep or repose of human souls till the day of judgment. He afterwards exposes (p. 91, etc.) the inconveniences which must arise if they possessed a more active and sensible existence.

[82] Vigilantius placed the souls of the prophets and martyrs, either in the bosom of Abraham (in loco refrigerii), or else under the altar of God. Nec posse [de] suis tumulis et ubi voluerint adesse præsentes. But Jerom (tom. ii. p. 122 [tom. ii. p. 392, ed. Vallars.]) sternly refutes this *blasphemy.* Tu Deo leges pones? Tu apostolis vincula injicies, ut usque ad diem judicii teneantur custodiâ, nec sint cum Domino suo; de quibus scriptum est, Sequuntur Agnum quocunque vadit. Si Agnus ubique, ergo, et hi, qui cum Agno sunt, ubique esse credendi sunt. Et cum diabolus et dæmones toto vagentur in orbe, etc.

most tender regard. Sometimes, indeed, their friendship might be influenced by considerations of a less exalted kind: they viewed with partial affection the places which had been consecrated by their birth, their residence, their death, their burial, or the possession of their relics. The meaner passions of pride, avarice, and revenge, may be deemed unworthy of a celestial breast; yet the saints themselves condescended to testify their grateful approbation of the liberality of their votaries; and the sharpest bolts of punishment were hurled against those impious wretches who violated their magnificent shrines, or disbelieved their supernatural power.[83] Atrocious, indeed, must have been the guilt, and strange would have been the scepticism, of those men, if they had obstinately resisted the proofs of a divine agency, which the elements, the whole range of the animal creation, and even the subtle and invisible operations of the human mind, were compelled to obey.[84] The immediate, and almost instantaneous, effects, that were supposed to follow the prayer, or the offence, satisfied the Christians of the ample measure of favour and authority which the saints enjoyed in the presence of the Supreme God; and it seemed almost superfluous to inquire whether they were continually obliged to intercede before the throne of grace, or whether they might not be permitted to exercise, according to the dictates of their benevolence and justice, the delegated powers of their subordinate ministry. The imagination, which had been raised by a painful effort to the contemplation and worship of the Universal Cause, eagerly embraced such inferior objects of adoration as were more proportioned to its gross conceptions and imperfect faculties. The sublime and simple theology of the primitive Christians was gradually corrupted: and the MONARCHY of heaven, already clouded by metaphysical subtleties, was degraded by the introduction of a popular mythology which tended to restore the reign of polytheism.[85]

IV. As the objects of religion were gradually reduced to the standard of the imagination, the rites and ceremonies were introduced that seemed most powerfully to affect the senses of the vulgar. If, in the beginning of the fifth century,[86] Tertullian, or Lactantius,[87] had been suddenly

[83] Fleury, Discours sur l'Hist. Ecclésiastique, iii. p. 80.

[84] At Minorca, the relics of St. Stephen converted in eight days 540 Jews; with the help, indeed, of some wholesome severities, such as burning the synagogue, driving the obstinate infidels to starve among the rocks, etc. See the original letter of Severus bishop of Minorca (ad calcem St. Augustin. de Civ. Dei), and the judicious remarks of Basnage (tom. viii. p. 245-251).

[85] Mr. Hume (Essays, vol. ii. p. 434) observes, like a philosopher, the natural flux and reflux of polytheism and theism.

[86] D'Aubigné (see his own Mémoires, p. 156-160) frankly offered, with the consent of the Huguenot ministers, to allow the first 400 years as the rule of faith. The Cardinal du Perron haggled for forty years more, which were indiscreetly given. Yet neither party would have found their account in this foolish bargain.

[87] The worship practised and inculcated by Tertullian, Lactantius, Arnobius, etc., is so *extremely* pure and spiritual, that their declamations against the Pagan sometimes glance against the Jewish ceremonies.

raised from the dead, to assist at the festival of some popular saint or martyr,[88] they would have gazed with astonishment and indignation on the profane spectacle which had succeeded to the pure and spiritual worship of a Christian congregation. As soon as the doors of the church were thrown open, they must have been offended by the smoke of incense, the perfume of flowers, and the glare of lamps and tapers, which diffused, at noon-day, a gaudy, superfluous, and, in their opinion, a sacrilegious light. If they approached the balustrade of the altar, they made their way through the prostrate crowd, consisting, for the most part, of strangers and pilgrims, who resorted to the city on the vigil of the feast; and who already felt the strong intoxication of fanaticism, and, perhaps, of wine. Their devout kisses were imprinted on the walls and pavement of the sacred edifice; and their fervent prayers were directed, whatever might be the language of their church, to the bones, the blood, or the ashes of the saint, which were usually concealed, by a linen or silken veil, from the eyes of the vulgar. The Christians frequented the tombs of the martyrs, in the hope of obtaining, from their powerful intercession, every sort of spiritual, but more especially of temporal, blessings. They implored the preservation of their health, or the cure of their infirmities; the fruitfulness of their barren wives, or the safety and happiness of their children. Whenever they undertook any distant or dangerous journey, they requested that the holy martyrs would be their guides and protectors on the road; and if they returned without having experienced any misfortune, they again hastened to the tombs of the martyrs, to celebrate, with grateful thanksgivings, their obligations to the memory and relics of those heavenly patrons. The walls were hung round with symbols of the favours which they had received; eyes, and hands, and feet, of gold and silver: and edifying pictures, which could not long escape the abuse of indiscreet or idolatrous devotion, represented the image, the attributes, and the miracles of the tutelar saint. The same uniform original spirit of superstition might suggest, in the most distant ages and countries, the same methods of deceiving the credulity, and of affecting the senses of mankind:[89] but it must ingenuously be confessed that the ministers of the catholic church imitated the profane model which they were impatient to destroy. The most respectable bishops had persuaded themselves that the ignorant rustics would more cheerfully renounce the superstitions of Paganism, if they found some resemblance, some compensation, in the bosom of Christianity. The religion of Con-

---

[88] Faustus the Manichæan accuses the Catholics of idolatry. Vertitis idola in martyres . . . quos votis similibus colitis. M. de Beausobre (Hist. Critique du Manichéisme, tom. ii. p. 629-700), a protestant, but a philosopher, has represented, with candour and learning, the introduction of *Christian idolatry* in the fourth and fifth centuries.

[89] The resemblance of superstition, which could not be imitated, might be traced from Japan to Mexico. Warburton has seized this idea, which he distorts by rendering it too general and absolute (Divine Legation, vol. iv. p. 126, etc.).

stantine achieved, in less than a century, the final conquest of the Roman empire: but the victors themselves were insensibly subdued by the arts of their vanquished rivals.[90]

CHAPTER XXIX (386-398 A.D.)

Final Division of the Roman Empire between the Sons of Theodosius—Reign of Arcadius and Honorius—Administration of Rufinus and Stilicho—Revolt and Defeat of Gildo in Africa

THE genius of Rome expired with Theodosius, the last of the successors of Augustus and Constantine who appeared in the field at the head of their armies, and whose authority was universally acknowledged throughout the whole extent of the empire. The memory of his virtues still continued, however, to protect the feeble and inexperienced youth of his two sons. After the death of their father, Arcadius and Honorius were saluted, by the unanimous consent of mankind, as the lawful emperors of the East and of the West; and the oath of fidelity was eagerly taken by every order of the state; the senates of old and new Rome, the clergy, the magistrates, the soldiers, and the people. Arcadius, who then was about eighteen years of age, was born in Spain in the humble habitation of a private family. But he received a princely education in the palace of Constantinople; and his inglorious life was spent in that peaceful and splendid seat of royalty, from whence he appeared to reign over the provinces of Thrace, Asia Minor, Syria, and Egypt, from the Lower Danube to the confines of Persia and Æthiopia. His younger brother, Honorius, assumed, in the eleventh year of his age, the nominal government of Italy, Africa, Gaul, Spain, and Britain; and the troops which guarded the frontiers of his kingdom were opposed, on one side, to the Caledonians, and on the other to the Moors. The great and martial præfecture of Illyricum was divided between the two princes: the defence and possession of the provinces of Noricum, Pannonia and Dalmatia, still belonged to the Western empire; but the two large dioceses of Dacia and Macedonia, which Gratian had intrusted to the valour of Theodosius, were for ever united to the empire of the East. The boundary in Europe was not very different from the line which now separates the Germans and the Turks; and the respective advantages of territory, riches, populousness, and military strength, were fairly balanced and compensated in this final and permanent division of the Roman empire. The hereditary sceptre of the sons of Theodosius appeared to be the gift of nature and of their father; the generals and ministers had been accustomed to adore the majesty of the royal infants; and the army

[90] The imitation of Paganism is the subject of Dr. Middleton's agreeable letter from Rome. Warburton's animadversions obliged him to connect (vol. iii. p. 120-132) the history of the two religions, and to prove the antiquity of the Christian copy.

and people were not admonished of their rights, and of their power, by the dangerous example of a recent election. The gradual discovery of the weakness of Arcadius and Honorius, and the repeated calamities of their reign, were not sufficient to obliterate the deep and early impressions of loyalty. The subjects of Rome, who still reverenced the persons, or rather the names, of their sovereigns, beheld with equal abhorrence the rebels who opposed, and the ministers who abused, the authority of the throne.

Theodosius had tarnished the glory of his reign by the elevation of Rufinus, an odious favourite, who in an age of civil and religious faction has deserved, from every party, the imputation of every crime. The strong impulse of ambition and avarice [1] had urged Rufinus to abandon his native country, an obscure corner of Gaul,[2] to advance his fortune in the capital of the East: the talent of bold and ready elocution [3] qualified him to succeed in the lucrative profession of the law; and his success in that profession was a regular step to the most honourable and important employments of the state. He was raised, by just degrees, to the station of master of the offices. In the exercise of his various functions, so essentially connected with the whole system of civil government, he acquired the confidence of a monarch who soon discovered his diligence and capacity in business, and who long remained ignorant of the pride, the malice, and the covetousness of his disposition. These vices were concealed beneath the mask of profound dissimulation;[4] his passions were subservient only to the passions of his master; yet, in the horrid massacre of Thessalonica, the cruel Rufinus inflamed the fury, without imitating the repentance, of Theodosius. The minister, who viewed with proud indifference the rest of mankind, never forgave the appearance of an injury; and his personal enemies had forfeited, in his opinion, the merit of all public services. Promotus, the master-general of the infantry, had saved the empire from the invasion of the Ostrogoths; but he indignantly supported the pre-eminence of a rival whose character and profession he despised; and, in the midst of a public council, the impatient soldier was provoked to chastise with a blow the indecent pride of the favourite. This act of violence was represented to the emperor as an insult which it was incumbent on *his* dignity to resent. The disgrace and exile of Promotus were signified by a peremptory order to repair without delay to a military station on the banks of the Danube; and the death of that general (though he was slain in a skirmish with the

[1] Alecto, envious of the public felicity, convenes an infernal synod; Megæra recommends her pupil Rufinus, and excites him to deeds of mischief, etc. But there is as much difference between Claudian's fury and that of Virgil, as between the characters of Turnus and Rufinus.

[2] It is evident (Tillemont, Hist. des Emp. tom. v. p. 770), though De Marca is ashamed of his countryman, that Rufinus was born at Elusa, the metropolis of Novempopulania, now a small village of Gascony (D'Anville, Notice de l'Ancienne Gaule, p. 289).

[3] Philosotorgius, l. xi. c. 3, with Godefroy's Dissert. p. 440.

[4] A passage of Suidas is expressive of his profound dissimulation; βαθυγνώμων ἄνθρωπος καὶ κρυψίνους.

barbarians) was imputed to the perfidious arts of Rufinus.[5] The sacrifice of an hero gratified his revenge; the honours of the consulship elated his vanity; but his power was still imperfect and precarious as long as the important posts of præfect of the East, and of præfect of Constantinople, were filled by Tatian [6] and his son Proculus, whose united authority balanced for some time the ambition and favour of the master of the offices. The two præfects were accused of rapine and corruption in the administration of the laws and finances. For the trial of these illustrious offenders the emperor constituted a special commission: several judges were named to share the guilt and reproach of injustice; but the right of pronouncing sentence was reserved to the president alone, and that president was Rufinus himself. The father, stripped of the præfecture of the East, was thrown into a dungeon; but the son, conscious that few ministers can be found innocent where an enemy is their judge, had secretly escaped; and Rufinus must have been satisfied with the least obnoxious victim, if despotism had not condescended to employ the basest and most ungenerous artifice. The prosecution was conducted with an appearance of equity and moderation which flattered Tatian with the hope of a favourable event: his confidence was fortified by the solemn assurances and perfidious oaths of the president, who presumed to interpose the sacred name of Theodosius himself; and the unhappy father was at last persuaded to recall, by a private letter, the fugitive Proculus. He was instantly seized, examined, condemned, and beheaded in one of the suburbs of Constantinople, with a precipitation which disappointed the clemency of the emperor. Without respecting the misfortunes of a consular senator, the cruel judges of Tatian compelled him to behold the execution of his son: the fatal cord was fastened round his own neck; but in the moment when he expected, and perhaps desired, the relief of a speedy death, he was permitted to consume the miserable remnant of his old age in poverty and exile.[7] The punishment of the two præfects might perhaps be excused by the exceptionable parts of their own conduct; the enmity of Rufinus might be palliated by the jealous and unsociable nature of ambition. But he indulged a spirit of revenge, equally repugnant to prudence and to justice, when he degraded their native country of Lycia from the rank of Roman provinces, stigmatised a guiltless people with a mark of ignominy, and declared that the countrymen of

---

[5] Zosimus, l. iv. [c. 51] p. 272, 273.

[6] Zosimus, who describes the fall of Tatian and his son (l. iv. [c. 52] p. 273, 274), asserts their innocence; and even *his* testimony may outweigh the charges of their enemies (Cod. Theod. tom iv. p. 489), who accuse them of oppressing the *Curiæ*. The connection of Tatian with the Arians, while he was præfect of Egypt (A.D. 373), inclines Tillemont to believe that he was guilty of every crime (Hist. des Emp. tom. v. p. 360; Mém. Ecclés. tom. vi. p. 589).

[7] ————Juvenum rorantia colla
Ante patrum vultus strictâ cecidere securi.
Ibat grandævus nato moriente superstes
Post trabeas exsul.   In Rufin. i. 248.

The *facts* of Zosimus explain the *allusions* of Claudian; but his classic interpreters were ignorant of the fourth century. The *fatal cord* I found, with the help of Tillemont, in a sermon of St. Asterius of Amasea.

Tatian and Proculus should for ever remain incapable of holding any employment of honour or advantage under the Imperial government.[8] The new præfect of the East (for Rufinus instantly succeeded to the vacant honours of his adversary) was not diverted, however, by the most criminal pursuits from the performance of the religious duties which in that age were considered as the most essential to salvation. In the suburb of Chalcedon, surnamed the *Oak*, he had built a magnificent villa, to which he devoutly added a stately church consecrated to the apostles St. Peter and St. Paul, and continually sanctified by the prayers and penance of a regular society of monks. A numerous and almost general synod of the bishops of the Eastern empire was summoned to celebrate at the same time the dedication of the church and the baptism of the founder. This double ceremony was performed with extraordinary pomp; and when Rufinus was purified in the holy font from all the sins that he had hitherto committed, a venerable hermit of Egypt rashly proposed himself as the sponsor of a proud and ambitious statesman.[9]

The character of Theodosius imposed on his minister the task of hypocrisy, which disguised, and sometimes restrained, the abuse of power; and Rufinus was apprehensive of disturbing the indolent slumber of a prince still capable of exerting the abilities and the virtue which had raised him to the throne.[10] But the absence, and soon afterwards the death, of the emperor confirmed the absolute authority of Rufinus over the person and dominions of Arcadius, a feeble youth, whom the imperious præfect considered as his pupil, rather than his sovereign. Regardless of the public opinion, he indulged his passions without remorse and without resistance; and his malignant and rapacious spirit rejected every passion that might have contributed to his own glory or the happiness of the people. His avarice,[11] which seems to have prevailed in his

---

[8] This odious law is recited and repealed by Arcadius (A.D. 396), in the Theodosian Code, l. ix. tit. xxxviii. leg. 9. The sense, as it is explained by Claudian (in Rufin. i. 232) and Godefroy (tom. iii. p. 279), is perfectly clear.
————Exscindere cives
Funditus, et nomen gentis delere laborat.
The scruples of Pagi and Tillemont can arise only from their zeal for the glory of Theodosius.

[9] Ammonius   . Rufinum propriis manibus suscepit sacro fonte mundatum. See Rosweyde's Vitæ Patrum, p. 947. [Heraclidis Paradisus in Append. ad Vit. Patr. p. 941 *b*.] Sozomen (l. viii. c. 17) mentions the church and monastery: and Tillemont (Mém. Ecclés. tom. ix. p. 593) records this synod, in which St. Gregory of Nyssa performed a conspicuous part.

[10] Montesquieu (Esprit des Loix, l. xii. c. 12) praises one of the laws of Theodosius, addressed to the præfect Rufinus (l. ix. tit. iv. leg. unic.), to discourage the prosecution of treasonable or sacrilegious words. A tyrannical statute always proves the existence of tyranny; but a laudable edict may only contain the specious professions or ineffectual wishes of the prince or his ministers. This, I am afraid, is a just though mortifying canon of criticism.
[11] ————fluctibus auri
Expleri calor ille nequit————
        .   .   .   .   .
Congestæ cumulantur opes; orbisque rapinas
Accipit una domus.

corrupt mind over every other sentiment, attracted the wealth of the East by the various arts of partial and general extortion—oppressive taxes, scandalous bribery, immoderate fines, unjust confiscations, forced or fictitious testaments, by which the tyrant despoiled of their lawful inheritance the children of strangers or enemies; and the public sale of justice, as well as of favour, which he instituted in the palace of Constantinople. The ambitious candidate eagerly solicited, at the expense of the fairest part of his patrimony, the honours and emoluments of some provincial government; the lives and fortunes of the unhappy people were abandoned to the most liberal purchaser; and the public discontent was sometimes appeased by the sacrifice of an unpopular criminal, whose punishment was profitable only to the præfect of the East, his accomplice and his judge. If avarice were not the blindest of the human passions, the motives of Rufinus might excite our curiosity, and we might be tempted to inquire with what view he violated every principle of humanity and justice to accumulate those immense treasures which he could not spend without folly nor possess without danger. Perhaps he vainly imagined that he laboured for the interest of an only daughter, on whom he intended to bestow his royal pupil and the august rank of empress of the East. Perhaps he deceived himself by the opinion that his avarice was the instrument of his ambition. He aspired to place his fortune on a secure and independent basis, which should no longer depend on the caprice of the young emperor; yet he neglected to conciliate the hearts of the soldiers and people by the liberal distribution of those riches which he had acquired with so much toil and with so much guilt. The extreme parsimony of Rufinus left him only the reproach and envy of ill-gotten wealth; his dependents served him without attachment; the universal hatred of mankind was repressed only by the influence of servile fear. The fate of Lucian proclaimed to the East that the præfect, whose industry was much abated in the despatch of ordinary business, was active and indefatigable in the pursuit of revenge. Lucian, the son of the præfect Florentius, the oppressor of Gaul and the enemy of Julian, had employed a considerable part of his inheritance, the fruit of rapine and corruption, to purchase the friendship of Rufinus and the high office of count of the East. But the new magistrate imprudently departed from the maxims of the court and of the times, disgraced his benefactor by the contrast of a virtuous and temperate administration, and presumed to refuse an act of injustice which might have tended to the profit of the emperor's uncle. Arcadius was easily persuaded to resent the supposed insult; and the præfect of the East resolved to execute in person the cruel vengeance which he meditated against this ungrateful delegate of his power. He performed with incessant speed the journey of seven or eight hundred miles from Constantinople to Antioch, entered

---

This character (Claudian, in Rufin. i. 184-220) is confirmed by Jerom, a disinterested witness (dedecus insatiabilis avaritiæ, tom. i. ad Heliodor. p. 26 [Epist. lx. tom. i. p. 342, ed. Vallars.]), by Zosimus (l. v. [c. 1] p. 286), and by Suidas, who copied the history of Eunapius.

the capital of Syria at the dead of night, and spread universal consternation among a people ignorant of his design, but not ignorant of his character. The count of the fifteen provinces of the East was dragged, like
the vilest malefactor, before the arbitrary tribunal of Rufinus. Notwithstanding the clearest evidence of his integrity, which was not impeached
even by the voice of an accuser, Lucian was condemned, almost without
a trial, to suffer a cruel and ignominious punishment. The ministers of
the tyrant, by the order and in the presence of their master, beat him on
the neck with leather throngs armed at the extremities with lead; and
when he fainted under the violence of the pain, he was removed in a close
litter to conceal his dying agonies from the eyes of the indignant city.
No sooner had Rufinus perpetrated this inhuman act, the sole object of
his expedition, than he returned, amidst the deep and silent curses of a
trembling people, from Antioch to Constantinople; and his diligence was
accelerated by the hope of accomplishing, without delay, the nuptials
of his daughter with the emperor of the East.[12]

But Rufinus soon experienced that a prudent minister should constantly secure his royal captive by the strong, though invisible, chain of
habit; and that the merit, and much more easily the favour of the absent,
are obliterated in a short time from the mind of a weak and capricious
sovereign. While the præfect satiated his revenge at Antioch, a secret
conspiracy of the favourite eunuchs, directed by the great chamberlain
Eutropius, undermined his power in the palace of Constantinople. They
discovered that Arcadius was not inclined to love the daughter of
Rufinus, who had been chosen without his consent for his bride, and
they contrived to substitute in her place the fair Eudoxia, the daughter
of Bauto,[13] a general of the Franks in the service of Rome, and who was
educated, since the death of her father, in the family of the sons of
Promotus. The young emperor, whose chastity had been strictly guarded
by the pious care of his tutor Arsenius,[14] eagerly listened to the artful
and flattering descriptions of the charms of Eudoxia; he gazed with impatient ardour on her picture, and he understood the necessity of concealing his amorous designs from the knowledge of a minister who was so
deeply interested to oppose the consummation of his happiness. Soon
after the return of Rufinus, the approaching ceremony of the royal nuptials was announced to the people of Constantinople, who prepared to
celebrate with false and hollow acclamations the fortune of his daughter.

[12] ——Cætera segnis;
     Ad facinus velox; penitus regione remotas
     Impiger ire vias.
This allusion of Claudian (in Rufin. i. 241) is again explained by the circumstantial narrative of Zosimus (l. v. [c. 2] p. 288, 289).
   [13] Zosimus (l. iv. [c. 33] p. 243) praises the valour, prudence, and integrity
of Bauto the Frank. See Tillemont, Hist. des Empereurs, tom. v. p. 771.
   [14] Arsenius escaped from the palace of Constantinople, and passed fifty-five
years in rigid penance in the monasteries of Egypt. See Tillemont, Mém.
Ecclés. tom. xiv. p. 676-702; and Fleury, Hist. Eccles. tom. v. p. 1, etc.; but
the latter, for want of authentic materials, has given too much credit to the
legend of Metaphrastes.

A splendid train of eunuchs and officers issued, in hymeneal pomp, from the gates of the palace, bearing aloft the diadem, the robes, and the inestimable ornaments of the future empress. The solemn procession passed through the streets of the city, which were adorned with garlands and filled with spectators; but when it reached the house of the sons of Promotus, the principal eunuch respectfully entered the mansion, invested the fair Eudoxia with the Imperial robes, and conducted her in triumph to the palace and bed of Arcadius.[15] The secrecy and success with which this conspiracy against Rufinus had been conducted imprinted a mark of indelible ridicule on the character of a minister who had suffered himself to be deceived, in a post where the arts of deceit and dissimulation constitute the most distinguished merit. He considered, with a mixture of indignation and fear, the victory of an aspiring eunuch who had secretly captivated the favour of his sovereign; and the disgrace of his daughter, whose interest was inseparably connected with his own, wounded the tenderness, or at least the pride, of Rufinus. At the moment when he flattered himself that he should become the father of a line of kings, a foreign maid, who had been educated in the house of his implacable enemies, was introduced into the Imperial bed; and Eudoxia soon displayed a superiority of sense and spirit to improve the ascendant which her beauty must acquire over the mind of a fond and youthful husband. The emperor would soon be instructed to hate, to fear, and to destroy the powerful subject whom he had injured; and the consciousness of guilt deprived Rufinus of every hope, either of safety or comfort, in the retirement of a private life. But he still possessed the most effectual means of defending his dignity, and perhaps of oppressing his enemies. The præfect still exercised an uncontrolled authority over the civil and military government of the East: and his treasures, if he could resolve to use them, might be employed to procure proper instruments for the execution of the blackest designs that pride, ambition, and revenge could suggest to a desperate statesman. The character of Rufinus seemed to justify the accusations that he conspired against the person of his sovereign to seat himself on the vacant throne; and that he had secretly invited the Huns and the Goths to invade the provinces of the empire and to increase the public confusion. The subtle præfect, whose life had been spent in the intrigues of the palace, opposed with equal arms the artful measures of the eunuch Eutropius; but the timid soul of Rufinus was astonished by the hostile approach of a more formidable rival, of the great Stilicho, the general, or rather the master, of the empire of the West.[16]

[15] This story (Zosimus, l. v. [c. 3] p. 290) proves that the hymeneal rites of antiquity were still practised, without idolatry, by the Christians of the East; and the bride was *forcibly* conducted from the house of her parents to that of her husband. Our form of marriage requires, with less delicacy, the express and public consent of a virgin.

[16] Zosimus (l. v. [c. 4] p. 290), Orosius (l. vii. c. 37), and the Chronicle of Marcellinus. Claudian (in Rufin. ii. 7-100) paints, in lively colours, the distress and guilt of the præfect.

The celestial gift, which Achilles obtained, and Alexander envied, of a poet worthy to celebrate the actions of heroes, has been enjoyed by Stilicho, in a much higher degree than might have been expected from the declining state of genius and of art. The muse of Claudian,[17] devoted to his service, was always prepared to stigmatise his adversaries, Rufinus or Eutropius, with eternal infamy; or to paint, in the most splendid colours, the victories and virtues of a powerful benefactor. In the review of a period indifferently supplied with authentic materials, we cannot refuse to illustrate the annals of Honorius from the invectives, or the panegyrics, of a contemporary writer; but as Claudian appears to have indulged the most ample privilege of a poet and a courtier, some criticism will be requisite to translate the language of fiction or exaggeration into the truth and simplicity of historic prose. His silence concerning the family of Stilicho may be admitted as a proof that his patron was neither able nor desirous to boast of a long series of illustrious progenitors, and the slight mention of his father, an officer of barbarian cavalry in the service of Valens, seems to countenance the assertion that the general who so long commanded the armies of Rome was descended from the savage and perfidious race of the Vandals.[18] If Stilicho had not possessed the external advantages of strength and stature, the most flattering bard, in the presence of so many thousand spectators, would have hesitated to affirm that he surpassed the measure of the demi-gods of antiquity; and that, whenever he moved, with lofty steps, through the streets of the capital, the astonished crowd made room for the stranger, who displayed, in a private condition, the awful majesty of a hero. From his earliest youth he embraced the profession of arms; his prudence and valour were soon distinguished in the field; the horsemen and archers of the East admired his superior dexterity; and in each degree of his military promotions, the public judgment always prevented and approved the choice of the sovereign. He was named by Theodosius to ratify a solemn treaty with the monarch of Persia: he supported, during that important embassy, the dignity of the Roman name; and after his return to Constantinople his merit was rewarded by an intimate and honourable alliance with the Imperial family. Theodosius had been prompted, by a pious motive of fraternal affection, to adopt, for his own, the daughter of his brother Honorius; the beauty and accomplishments of Serena [19] were universally admired by the obsequious court; and Stilicho obtained the preference over a crowd of rivals who ambitiously disputed the hand of

[17] Stilicho, directly or indirectly, is the perpetual theme of Claudian. The youth and private life of the hero are vaguely expressed in the poem on his first consulship, 35-140.
[18] Vandalorum imbellis, avaræ, perfidæ, et dolosæ gentis genere editus. Orosius, l. vii. c. 38. Jerom (tom. i. ad Gerontiam, p. 93) calls him a semi-barbarian.
[19] Claudian, in an imperfect poem, has drawn a fair, perhaps a flattering, portrait of Serena. That favourite niece of Theodosius was born, as well as her sister Thermantia, in Spain; from whence, in their earliest youth, they were honourably conducted to the palace of Constantinople.

the princess, and the favour of her adoptive father.[20] The assurance that the husband of Serena would be faithful to the throne which he was permitted to approach engaged the emperor to exalt the fortunes, and to employ the abilities, of the sagacious and intrepid Stilicho. He rose through the successive steps of master of the horse, and count of the domestics, to the supreme rank of master-general of all the cavalry and infantry of the Roman, or at least of the Western, empire;[21] and his enemies confessed that he invariably disdained to barter for gold the rewards of merit, or to defraud the soldiers of the pay and gratifications which they deserved or claimed from the liberality of the state.[22] The valour and conduct which he afterwards displayed in the defence of Italy against the arms of Alaric and Radagaisus may justify the fame of his early achievements; and in an age less attentive to the laws of honour or of pride, the Roman generals might yield the pre-eminence of rank to the ascendant of superior genius.[23] He lamented and revenged the murder of Promotus, his rival and his friend; and the massacre of many thousands of the flying Bastarnæ is represented by the poet as a bloody sacrifice which the Roman Achilles offered to the names of another Patroclus. The virtues and victories of Stilicho deserved the hatred of Rufinus: and the arts of calumny might have been successful, if the tender and vigilant Serena had not protected her husband against his domestic foes, whilst he vanquished in the field the enemies of the empire.[24] Theodosius continued to support an unworthy minister, to whose diligence he delegated the government of the palace and of the East; but when he marched against the tyrant Eugenius, he associated his faithful general to the labours and glories of the civil war; and in the last moments of his life the dying monarch recommended to Stilicho the care of his sons and of the republic.[25] The ambition and the abilities of

[20] Some doubt may be entertained whether this adoption was legal, or only metaphorical (see Ducange, Fam. Byzant. p. 75). An old inscription gives Stilicho the singular title of *Pro-gener Divi Theodosii.*

[21] Claudian (Laus Serenæ, 190, 193) expresses, in poetic language, the "dilectus equorum," and the "gemino mox idem culmine duxit agmina." The inscription adds, "count of the domestics," an important command, which Stilicho, in the height of his grandeur, might prudently retain.

[22] The beautiful lines of Claudian (in i. Cons. Stilich. ii. 113) display *his* genius : but the integrity of Stilicho (in the military administration) is much more firmly established by the unwilling evidence of Zosimus (l. v. [c. 34] p. 345).

[23] ——Si bellica nubes
Ingrueret, quamvis annis et jure minori,
Cedere grandævos equitum peditumque magistros
Adspiceres.   Claudian, Laus Seren. v. 196, etc.
A modern general would deem their submission either heroic patriotism or abject servility.

[24] Compare the poem on the first consulship (i. 95-115) with the *Laus Serenæ* (227-237, where it unfortunately breaks off). We may perceive the deep, inveterate malice of Rufinus.

[25] ——Quem *fratribus* ipse
Discedens, clipeum defensoremque dedisti.
(iv. Cons. Hon. 432.)

Stilicho were not unequal to the important trust; and he claimed the
guardianship of the two empires during the minority of Arcadius and
Honorius.[26] The first measure of his administration, or rather of his
reign, displayed to the nations the vigour and activity of a spirit worthy
to command. He passed the Alps in the depth of winter; descended the
stream of the Rhine, from the fortress of Basel to the marshes of Batavia;
reviewed the state of the garrisons; repressed the enterprises of the Germans; and, after establishing along the banks a firm and honourable
peace, returned with incredible speed to the palace of Milan.[27] The
person and court of Honorius were subject to the master-general of the
West; and the armies and provinces of Europe obeyed, without hesitation, a regular authority, which was exercised in the name of their young
sovereign. Two rivals only remained to dispute the claims, and to
provoke the vengeance, of Stilicho. Within the limits of Africa, Gildo,
the Moor, maintained a proud and dangerous independence; and the
minister of Constantinople asserted his equal reign over the emperor
and the empire of the East.

The impartiality which Stilicho affected, as the common guardian of
the royal brothers, engaged him to regulate the equal division of the
arms, the jewels, and the magnificent wardrobe and furniture of the
deceased emperor.[28] But the most important object of the inheritance
consisted of the numerous legions, cohorts, and squadrons, of Romans
or barbarians, whom the event of the civil war had united under the
standard of Theodosius. The various multitudes of Europe and Asia,
exasperated by recent animosities, were overawed by the authority
of a single man; and the rigid discipline of Stilicho protected the lands
of the citizen from the rapine of the licentious soldier.[29] Anxious, however, and impatient to relieve Italy from the presence of this formidable
host, which could be useful only on the frontiers of the empire, he
listened to the just requisition of the minister of Arcadius, declared his

Yet the nomination was private (iii. Cons. Hon. 142—cunctos discedere . . .
jubet—and may therefore be suspected. Zosimus and Suidas apply to Stilicho
and Rufinus the same equal title of 'Επίτροποι, guardians or procurators.
[26] The Roman law distinguishes two sorts of *minority,* which expired at
the age of fourteen and of twenty-five. The one was subject to the *tutor,*
or guardian, of the person; the other, to the *curator,* or trustee, of the estate
(Heineccius, Antiquitat. Rom. ad Jurisprudent. pertinent. l. i. tit. xxii. xxiii.
p. 218-232). But these legal ideas were never accurately transferred into the
constitution of an elective monarchy.
[27] See Claudian (i. Cons. Stilich. i. 188-242) ; but he must allow more than
fifteen days for the journey and return between Milan and Leyden.
[28] I. Cons. Stilich. ii. 88-94. Not only the robes and diadems of the deceased
emperor, but even the helmets, sword-hilts, belts, cuirasses, etc., were enriched
with pearls, emeralds, and diamonds.
[29] ——Tantoque remoto
Principe, mutatas orbis non sensit habenas.
This high commendation (i. Cons. Stil. i. 149) may be justified by the fears
of the dying emperor (de Bell. Gildon. 292-301), and the peace and good
order which were enjoyed after his death (i. Cons. Stil. i. 150-168).

intention of reconducting in person the troops of the East, and dexterously employed the rumour of a Gothic tumult to conceal his private designs of ambition and revenge.[30] The guilty soul of Rufinus was alarmed by the approach of a warrior and a rival wnose enmity he deserved; he computed, with increasing terror, the narrow space of his life and greatness; and, as the last hope of safety, he interposed the authority of the emperor Arcadius. Stilicho, who appears to have directed his march along the sea-coast of the Hadriatic, was not far distant from the city of Thessalonica when he received a peremptory message to recall the troops of the East, and to declare that *his* nearer approach would be considered, by the Byzantine court, as an act of hostility. The prompt and unexpected obedience of the general of the West convinced the vulgar of his loyalty and moderation; and, as he had already engaged the affection of the Eastern troops, he recommended to their zeal the execution of his bloody design, which might be accomplished in his absence, with less danger perhaps, and with less reproach. Stilicho left the command of the troops of the East to Gainas, the Goth, on whose fidelity he firmly relied, with an assurance at least that the hardy barbarian would never be diverted from his purpose by any consideration of fear or remorse. The soldiers were easily persuaded to punish the enemy of Stilicho and of Rome; and such was the general hatred which Rufinus had excited, that the fatal secret, communicated to thousands, was faithfully preserved during the long march from Thessalonica to the gates of Constantinople. As soon as they had resolved his death, they condescended to flatter his pride; the ambitious præfect was seduced to believe that those powerful auxiliaries might be tempted to place the diadem on his head: and the treasures which he distributed with a tardy and reluctant hand were accepted by the indignant multitude as an insult rather than as a gift. At the distance of a mile from the capital, in the field of Mars, before the palace of Hebdomon, the troops halted; and the emperor, as well as his minister, advanced, according to ancient custom, respectfully to salute the power which supported their throne. As Rufinus passed along the ranks, and disguised, with studied courtesy, his innate haughtiness, the wings insensibly wheeled from the right and left, and enclosed the devoted victim within the circle of their arms. Before he could reflect on the danger of his situation, Gainas gave the signal of death; a daring and forward soldier plunged his sword into the breast of the guilty præfect, and Rufinus fell, groaned, and expired, at the feet of the affrighted emperor. If the agonies of a moment could expiate the crimes of a whole life, or if the outrages inflicted on a breathless corpse could be the object of pity, our humanity might perhaps be

[30] Stilicho's march and the death of Rufinus are described by Claudian (in Rufin. l. ii. 101-453), Zosimus (l. v. [c. 7] p. 296, 297), Sozomen (l. viii. c. 1), Socrates (l. vi. c. 1), Philostorgius (l. xi. c. 3, with Godefroy, p. 441), and the Chronicle of Marcellinus.

affected by the horrid circumstances which accompanied the murder of Rufinus. His mangled body was abandoned to the brutal fury of the populace of either sex, who hastened in crowds, from every quarter of the city, to trample on the remains of the haughty minister, at whose frown they had so lately trembled. His right hand was cut off, and carried through the streets of Constantinople, in cruel mockery, to extort contributions for the avaricious tyrant, whose head was publicly exposed, borne aloft on the point of a long lance.[31] According to the savage maxims of the Greek republics, his innocent family would have shared the punishment of his crimes. The wife and daughter of Rufinus were indebted for their safety to the influence of religion. *Her* sanctuary protected them from the raging madness of the people; and they were permitted to spend the remainder of their lives in the exercises of Christian devotion in the peaceful retirement of Jerusalem.[32]

The servile poet of Stilicho applauds with ferocious joy this horrid deed, which, in the execution, perhaps of justice, violated every law of nature and society, profaned the majesty of the prince, and renewed the dangerous examples of military licence. The contemplation of the universal order and harmony had satisfied Claudian of the existence of the Deity; but the prosperous impunity of vice appeared to contradict his moral attributes; and the fate of Rufinus was the only event which could dispel the religious doubts of the poet.[33] Such an act might vindicate the honour of Providence; but it did not much contribute to the happiness of the people. In less than three months they were informed of the maxims of the new administration, by a singular edict, which established the exclusive right of the treasury over the spoils of Rufinus; and silenced, under heavy penalties, the presumptuous claims of the subjects of the Eastern empire who had been injured by his rapacious tyranny.[34] Even Stilicho did not derive from the murder of his rival the fruit which he had proposed; and though he gratified his revenge, his ambition was disappointed. Under the name of a favourite, the weakness of Arcadius required a master,

[31] The *dissection* of Rufinus, which Claudian performs with the savage coolness of an anatomist (in Rufin. ii. 405-415), is likewise specified by Zosimus [v. c. 7] and Jerom (tom. i. p. 26 [Epist. lx. tom. i. p. 342, ed. Vallars.]).

[32] The Pagan Zosimus mentions their sanctuary and pilgrimage. The sister of Rufinus, Sylvania, who passed her life at Jerusalem, is famous in monastic history. 1. The studious virgin had diligently, and even repeatedly, perused the commentators on the Bible, Origen, Gregory, Basil, etc., to the amount of five millions of lines. 2. At the age of threescore she could boast that she had never washed her hands, face, or any part of her whole body, except the tips of her fingers, to receive the communion. See the Vitæ Patrum, p. 779, 977.

[33] See the beautiful exordium of his invective against Rufinus, which is curiously discussed by the sceptic Bayle, Dictionnaire Critique, RUFIN. Not. E.

[34] See the Theodosian Code, l. ix. tit. xlii. leg. 14, 15. The new ministers attempted, with inconsistent avarice, to seize the spoils of their predecessor and to provide for their own future security.

but he naturally preferred the obsequious arts of the eunuch Eutropius, who had obtained his domestic confidence; and the emperor contemplated with terror and aversion the stern genius of a foreign warrior. Till they were divided by the jealousy of power, the sword of Gainas, and the charms of Eudoxia, supported the favour of the great chamberlain of the palace: the perfidious Goth, who was appointed mastergeneral of the East, betrayed, without scruple, the interest of his benefactor; and the same troops who had so lately massacred the enemy of Stilicho were engaged to support, against him, the independence of the throne of Constantinople. The favourites of Arcadius fomented a secret and irreconcilable war against a formidable hero, who aspired to govern and to defend the two empires of Rome and the two sons of Theodosius. They incessantly laboured, by dark and treacherous machinations, to deprive him of the esteem of the prince, the respect of the people, and the friendship of the barbarians. The life of Stilicho was repeatedly attempted by the dagger of hired assassins; and a decree was obtained from the senate of Constantinople, to declare him an enemy of the republic, and to confiscate his ample possessions in the provinces of the East. At a time when the only hope of delaying the ruin of the Roman name depended on the firm union and reciprocal aid of all the nations to whom it had been gradually communicated, the subjects of Arcadius and Honorius were instructed, by their respective masters, to view each other in a foreign and even hostile light; to rejoice in their mutual calamities; and to embrace, as their faithful allies, the barbarians whom they excited to invade the territories of their countrymen.[35] The natives of Italy affected to despise the servile and effeminate Greeks of Byzantium, who presumed to imitate the dress, and to usurp the dignity, of Roman senators;[36] and the Greeks had not yet forgot the sentiments of hatred and contempt which their polished ancestors had so long entertained for the rude inhabitants of the West. The distinction of two governments, which soon produced the separation of two nations, will justify my design of suspending the series of the Byzantine history, to prosecute, without interruption, the disgraceful but memorable reign of Honorius.

The prudent Stilicho, instead of persisting to force the inclinations of a prince and people who rejected his government, wisely abandoned Arcadius to his unworthy favourites; and his reluctance to involve the two empires in a civil war displayed the moderation of a minister who

[35] See Claudian (i. Cons. Stilich. l. i. 275, 292, 296, l. ii. 83), and Zosimus, l. v. [c. 11] p. 302.
[36] Claudian turns the consulship of the eunuch Eutropius into a national reflection (l. ii. 135):

　　　　　　—— Plaudentem cerne senatum,
　　Et Byzantinos proceres, Graiosque Quirites:
　　O patribus plebes, O digni consule patres.

It is curious to observe the first symptoms of jealousy and schism between old and new Rome, between the Greeks and Latins.

had so often signalised his military spirit and abilities. But if Stilicho had any longer endured the revolt of Africa, he would have betrayed the security of the capital, and the majesty of the Western emperor, to the capricious insolence of a Moorish rebel. Gildo,[37] the brother of the tyrant Firmus, had preserved and obtained, as the reward of his apparent fidelity, the immense patrimony which was forfeited by treason; long and meritorious service in the armies of Rome raised him to the dignity of a military count; the narrow policy of the court of Theodosius had adopted the mischievous expedient of supporting a legal government by the interest of a powerful family; and the brother of Firmus was invested with the command of Africa. His ambition soon usurped the administration of justice and of the finances, without account and without control; and he maintained, during a reign of twelve years, the possession of an office from which it was impossible to remove him without the danger of a civil war. During those twelve years the provinces of Africa groaned under the dominion of a tyrant who seemed to unite the unfeeling temper of a stranger with the partial resentments of domestic faction. The forms of law were often superseded by the use of poison; and if the trembling guests who were invited to the table of Gildo presumed to express their fears, the insolent suspicion served only to excite his fury, and he loudly summoned the ministers of death. Gildo alternately indulged the passions of avarice and lust;[38] and if his *days* were terrible to the rich, his *nights* were not less dreadful to husbands and parents. The fairest of their wives and daughters were prostituted to the embraces of the tyrant; and afterwards abandoned to a ferocious troop of barbarians and assassins, the black or swarthy natives of the desert, whom Gildo considered as the only guardians of his throne. In the civil war between Theodosius and Eugenius, the count, or rather the sovereign of Africa, maintained a haughty and suspicious neutrality; refused to assist either of the contending parties with troops or vessels, expected the declaration of fortune, and reserved for the conqueror the vain professions of his allegiance. Such professions would not have satisfied the master of the Roman world: but the death of Theodosius, and the weakness

---

[37] Claudian may have exaggerated the vices of Gildo; but his Moorish extraction, his notorious actions, and the complaints of St. Augustin, may justify the poet's invectives. Baronius (Annal. Eccles. A.D. 398, No. 35-56) has treated the African rebellion with skill and learning.

[38] Instat terribilis vivis, morientibus hæres,
Virginibus raptor, thalamis obscenus adulter.
Nulla quies: oritur prædâ cessante libido,
Divitibusque dies, et nox metuenda maritis.
────── Mauris clarissima quæque
Fastidita datur.

De Bello Gildonico, 165, 189.

Baronius condemns, still more severely, the licentiousness of Gildo; as his wife, his daughter, and his sister, were examples of perfect chastity. The adulteries of the African soldiers are checked by one of the Imperial laws.

and discord of his sons, confirmed the power of the Moor, who condescended, as a proof of his moderation, to abstain from the use of the diadem, and to supply Rome with the customary tribute, or rather subsidy, of corn.   In every division of the empire, the five provinces of Africa were invariably assigned to the West; and Gildo had consented to govern that extensive country in the name of Honorius; but his knowledge of the character and designs of Stilicho soon engaged him to address his homage to a more distant and feeble sovereign. The ministers of Arcadius embraced the cause of a perfidious rebel; and the delusive hope of adding the numerous cities of Africa to the empire of the East tempted them to assert a claim which they were incapable of supporting either by reason or by arms.[39]

When Stilicho had given a firm and decisive answer to the pretensions of the Byzantine court, he solemnly accused the tyrant of Africa before the tribunal which had formerly judged the kings and nations of the earth; and the image of the republic was revived, after a long interval, under the reign of Honorius.   The emperor transmitted an accurate and ample detail of the complaints of the provincials, and the crimes of Gildo, to the Roman senate; and the members of that venerable assembly were required to pronounce the condemnation of the rebel.   Their unanimous suffrage declared him the enemy of the republic; and the decree of the senate added a sacred and legitimate sanction to the Roman arms.[40]   A people who still remembered that their ancestors had been the masters of the world would have applauded, with conscious pride, the representation of ancient freedom, if they had not long since been accustomed to prefer the solid assurance of bread to the unsubstantial visions of liberty and greatness.   The subsistence of Rome depended on the harvests of Africa; and it was evident that a declaration of war would be the signal of famine.   The præfect Symmachus, who presided in the deliberations of the senate, admonished the minister of his just apprehension that, as soon as the revengeful Moor should prohibit the exportation of corn, the tranquillity, and perhaps the safety, of the capital would be threatened by the hungry rage of a turbulent multitude.[41]   The prudence of Stilicho conceived, and executed without delay, the most effectual measure for the relief of the Roman people.   A large and seasonable supply of corn, collected in the inland provinces of Gaul, was embarked on the rapid stream of the Rhone, and transported by an easy navigation from the Rhone to the Tiber.   During the whole term of the African war, the granaries

[39] Inque tuam sortem numerosas transtulit urbes.
Claudian (de Bell. Gildonico, 230-324) has touched, with political delicacy, the intrigues of the Byzantine court, which are likewise mentioned by Zosimus (i. v. [c. 11] p. 302).
[40] Symmachus (l. iv. epist. 4) expresses the judicial forms of the senate; and Claudian (i. Cons. Stilich. l. i. 325, etc.) seems to feel the spirit of a Roman.
[41] Claudian finely displays these complaints of Symmachus, in a speech of the goddess of Rome before the throne of Jupiter (de Bell. Gildon. 28-128).

of Rome were continually filled, her dignity was vindicated from the humiliating dependence, and the minds of an immense people were quieted by the calm confidence of peace and plenty.[42]

The cause of Rome, and the conduct of the African war, were intrusted by Stilicho to a general active and ardent to avenge his private injuries on the head of the tyrant. The spirit of discord which prevailed in the house of Nabal had excited a deadly quarrel between two of his sons, Gildo and Mascezel.[43] The usurper pursued, with implacable rage, the life of his younger brother, whose courage and abilities he feared; and Mascezel, oppressed by superior power, took refuge in the court of Milan; where he soon received the cruel intelligence that his two innocent and helpless children had been murdered by their inhuman uncle. The affliction of the father was suspended only by the desire of revenge. The vigilant Stilicho already prepared to collect the naval and military forces of the Western empire; and he had resolved, if the tyrant should be able to wage an equal and doubtful war, to march against him in person. But as Italy required his presence, and as it might be dangerous to weaken the defence of the frontier, he judged it more advisable that Mascezel should attempt this arduous adventure at the head of a chosen body of Gallic veterans, who had lately served under the standard of Eugenius. These troops, who were exhorted to convince the world that they could subvert, as well as defend, the throne of an usurper, consisted of the *Jovian,* the *Herculian,* and the *Augustan* legions; of the *Nervian* auxiliaries; of the soldiers who displayed in their banners the symbol of a *lion;* and of the troops which were distinguished by the auspicious names of *Fortunate* and *Invincible.* Yet such was the smallness of their establishments, or the difficulty of recruiting, that these *seven* bands,[44] of high dignity and reputation in the service of Rome, amounted to no more than five thousand effective men.[45] The fleet of galleys and transports sailed in tempestuous weather from the port of Pisa, in Tuscany, and steered their course to the little island of Capraria, which had borrowed that name from the wild goats, its original inhabi-

---

[42] See Claudian (in Eutrop. l. i. 401, etc.; i. Cons. Stil. l. i. 306, etc.; ii. Cons. Stilich. 91, etc.).

[43] He was of a mature age, since he had formerly (A.D. 373) served against his brother Firmus (Ammian. xxix. 5). Claudian, who understood the court of Milan, dwells on the injuries, rather than the merits, of Mascezel (de Bell. Gild. 389-414). The Moorish war was not worthy of Honorius or Stilicho, etc.

[44] Claudian, Bell. Gild. 415-423. The change of discipline allowed him to use indifferently the names of *Legio, Cohors, Manipulus.* See the *Notitia Imperii,* S. 38, 40.

[45] Orosius (l. vii. c. 36, p. 565) qualifies this account with an expression of doubt (ut aiunt); and it scarcely coincides with the δυνάμεις ἀδρὰς of Zosimus (l. v. [c. 11] p. 303). Yet Claudian, after some declamation about Cadmus's soldiers, frankly owns that Stilicho sent a small army, lest the rebel should fly, ne timeare times (i. Cons. Stilich. l. i. 314, etc.).

tants, whose place was now occupied by a new colony of a strange and savage appearance. " The whole island (says an ingenious traveller of those times) is filled, or rather defiled, by men who fly from the light. They call themselves *Monks* or solitaries, because they choose to live alone, without any witnesses of their actions. They fear the gifts of fortune, from the apprehension of losing them; and, lest they should be miserable, they embrace a life of voluntary wretchedness. How absurd is their choice! how perverse their understanding! to dread the evils, without being able to support the blessings, of the human condition. Either this melancholy madness is the effect of disease, or else the consciousness of guilt urges these unhappy men to exercise on their own bodies the tortures which are inflicted on fugitive slaves by the hand of justice." [46] Such was the contempt of a profane magistrate for the monks of Capraria, who were revered by the pious Mascezel as the chosen servants of God.[47] Some of them were persuaded, by his entreaties, to embark on board the fleet; and it is observed, to the praise of the Roman general, that his days and nights were employed in prayer, fasting, and the occupation of singing psalms. The devout leader, who with such a reinforcement appeared confident of victory, avoided the dangerous rocks of Corsica, coasted along the eastern side of Sardinia, and secured his ships against the violence of the south wind, by casting anchor in the safe and capacious harbour of Cagliari, at the distance of one hundred and forty miles from the African shores.[48]

Gildo was prepared to resist the invasion with all the forces of Africa. By the liberality of his gifts and promises, he endeavoured to secure the doubtful allegiance of the Roman soldiers, whilst he attracted to his standard the distant tribes of Gætulia and Æthiopia. He proudly reviewed an army of seventy thousand men, and boasted, with the rash presumption which is the forerunner of disgrace, that his numerous cavalry would trample under their horses' feet the troops of Mascezel, and involve, in a cloud of burning sand, the natives of the cold regions of Gaul and Germany.[49] But the Moor who commanded the legions of Honorius was too well acquainted with the manners of the countrymen to entertain any serious apprehension of a

[46] Claud. Rutil. Numatian. Itinerar. lib. i. 439-448. He afterwards (*ib.* 515-526) mentions a religious madman on the isle of Gorgona. For such profane remarks, Rutilius and his accomplices are styled, by his commentator Barthius, rabiosi canes diaboli. Tillemont (Mém. Ecclés. tom. xii. p. 471) more calmly observes that the unbelieving poet praises where he means to censure.

[47] Orosius, l. vii. c. 36, p. 564. Augustin commends two of these savage saints of the Isle of Goats (Epist. lxxxi. apud Tillemont, Mém. Ecclés. tom. xiii. p. 317, and Baronius, Annal. Eccles. A.D. 398, No. 51).

[48] Here the first book of the Gildonic war is terminated. The rest of Claudian's poem has been lost; and we are ignorant *how* or *where* the army made good their landing in Africa.

[49] Orosius must be responsible for the account. The presumption of Gildo and his various train of barbarians is celebrated by Claudian (i. Cons. Stil. l. i. 345-355).

naked and disorderly host of barbarians, whose left arm, instead of a shield, was protected only by a mantle; who were totally disarmed as soon as they had darted their javelin from their right hand; and whose horses had never been taught to bear the control, or to obey the guidance, of the bridle. He fixed his camp of five thousand veterans in the face of a superior enemy, and, after the delay of three days, gave the signal of a general engagement.[50] As Mascezel advanced before the front with fair offers of peace and pardon, he encountered one of the foremost standard-bearers of the Africans, and, on his refusal to yield, struck him on the arm with his sword. The arm and the standard sunk under the weight of the blow, and the imaginary act of submission was hastily repeated by all the standards of the line. At this signal the disaffected cohorts proclaimed the name of their lawful sovereign; the barbarians, astonished by the defection of their Roman allies, dispersed, according to their custom, in tumultuary flight; and Mascezel obtained the honours of an easy and almost bloodless victory.[51] The tyrant escaped from the field of battle to the sea-shore, and threw himself into a small vessel, with the hope of reaching in safety some friendly port of the empire of the East; but the obstinacy of the wind drove him back into the harbour of Tabraca,[52] which had acknowledged, with the rest of the province, the dominion of Honorius, and the authority of his lieutenant. The inhabitants, as a proof of their repentance and loyalty, seized and confined the person of Gildo in a dungeon; and his own despair saved him from the intolerable torture of supporting the presence of an injured and victorious brother.[53] The captives and the spoils of Africa were laid at the feet of the emperor; but Stilicho, whose moderation appeared more conspicuous and more sincere in the midst of prosperity, still affected to consult the laws of the republic, and referred to the senate and people of Rome the judgment of the most illustrious criminals.[54] Their trial was public

[50] St. Ambrose, who had been dead about a year, revealed in a vision the time and place of the victory. Mascezel afterwards related his dream to Paulinus, the original biographer of the saint, from whom it might easily pass to Orosius.

[51] Zosimus (l. v. [c. 11] p. 303) supposes an obstinate combat; but the narrative of Orosius appears to conceal a real fact under the disguise of a miracle.

[52] Tabraca lay between the two Hippos (Cellarius, tom. ii. p. 112; D'Anville, tom. iii. p. 84). Orosius has distinctly named the field of battle, but our ignorance cannot define the precise situation.

[53] The death of Gildo is expressed by Claudian (i. Cons. Stil. l. 357) and his best interpreters, Zosimus and Orosius.

[54] Claudian (iii. Cons. Stilich. 99-119) describes their trial (tremuit quos Africa nuper, cernunt rostra reos), and applauds the restoration of the ancient constitution. It is here that he introduces the famous sentence so familiar to the friends of despotism:

——Nunquam libertas gratior exstat
Quam sub rege pio.

But the freedom which depends on royal piety scarcely deserves that appellation.

and solemn; but the judges, in the exercise of this obsolete and precarious jurisdiction, were impatient to punish the African magistrates who had intercepted the subsistence of the Roman people. The rich and guilty province was oppressed by the Imperial ministers, who had a visible interest to multiply the number of the accomplices of Gildo; and if an edict of Honorius seems to check the malicious industry of informers, a subsequent edict, at the distance of ten years, continues and renews the prosecution of the offences which had been committed in the time of the general rebellion.[55] The adherents of the tyrant who escaped the first fury of the soldiers and the judges might derive some consolation from the tragic fate of his brother, who could never obtain his pardon for the extraordinary services which he had performed. After he had finished an important war in the space of a single winter, Mascezel was received at the court of Milan with loud applause, affected gratitude, and secret jealousy;[56] and his death, which perhaps was the effect of accident, has been considered as the crime of Stilicho. In the passage of a bridge, the Moorish prince, who accompanied the master-general of the West, was suddenly thrown from his horse into the river; the officious haste of the attendants was restrained by a cruel and perfidious smile which they observed on the countenance of Stilicho; and while they delayed the necessary assistance, the unfortunate Mascezel was irrecoverably drowned.[57]

The joy of the African triumph was happily connected with the nuptials of the emperor Honorius, and of his cousin Maria, the daughter of Stilicho; and this equal and honourable alliance seemed to invest the powerful minister with the authority of a parent over his submissive pupil. The muse of Claudian was not silent on this propitious day;[58] he sung, in various and lively strains, the happiness of the royal pair, and the glory of the hero who confirmed their union and supported their throne. The ancient fables of Greece, which had almost ceased to be the object of religious faith, were saved from oblivion by the genius of poetry. The picture of the Cyprian grove, the seat of harmony and love; the triumphant progress of Venus over her native seas, and the mild influence which her presence diffused in the palace of Milan, express to every age the natural sentiments of the heart in the just and pleasing language of allegorical fiction. But

[55] See the Theodosian Code, l. ix. tit. xxxix. leg. 3, tit. xl. leg. 19.

[56] Stilicho, who claimed an equal share in all the victories of Theodosius and his son, particularly asserts that Africa was recovered by the wisdom of *his* counsels (see an inscription produced by Baronius).

[57] I have softened the narrative of Zosimus, which, in its crude simplicity, is almost incredible (l. v. [c. 11] p. 303). Orosius damns the victorious general (p. 538 [lib. vii. c. 36]) for violating the right of sanctuary.

[58] Claudian, as the poet laureat, composed a serious and elaborate epithalamium of 340 lines; besides some gay Fescennines, which were sung in a more licentious tone on the wedding night.

the amorous impatience which Claudian attributes to the young prince [59] must excite the smiles of the court; and his beauteous spouse (if she deserved the praise of beauty) had not much to fear or to hope from the passions of her lover. Honorius was only in the fourteenth year of his age; Serena, the mother of his bride, deferred, by art or persuasion, the consummation of the royal nuptials; Maria died a virgin, after she had been ten years a wife; and the chastity of the emperor was secured by the coldness, or perhaps the debility, of his constitution.[60] His subjects, who attentively studied the character of their young sovereign, discovered that Honorius was without passions, and consequently without talents; and that his feeble and languid disposition was alike incapable of discharging the duties of his rank, or of enjoying the pleasures of his age. In his early youth he made some progress in the exercises of riding and drawing the bow; but he soon relinquished these fatiguing occupations, and the amusement of feeding poultry became the serious and daily care of the monarch of the West,[61] who resigned the reins of empire to the firm and skilful hand of his guardian Stilicho. The experience of history will countenance the suspicion that a prince who was born in the purple received a worse education than the meanest peasant of his dominions, and that the ambitious minister suffered him to attain the age of manhood without attempting to excite his courage or to enlighten his understanding.[62] The predecessors of Honorius were accustomed to animate by their example, or at least by their presence, the valour of the legions; and the dates of their laws attest the perpetual activity of their motions through the provinces of the Roman world. But the son of Theodosius passed the slumber of his life a captive in his palace, a stranger in his country, and the patient, almost the indifferent, spectator of the ruin of the Western empire, which was repeatedly attacked, and finally subverted, by the arms of the barbarians. In the eventful history of a reign of twenty-eight years, it will seldom be necessary to mention the name of the emperor Honorius.

[59] ——— Calet obvius ire
Jam princeps, tardumque cupit discedere solem.
Nobilis haud aliter *sonipes*—

(de Nuptiis Honor. et Mariæ, 287) and more freely in the Fescennines 112-126 [iv. 14].

Dices, *O quoties,* hoc mihi dulcius
Quam flavos *decies* vincere Sarmatas.

.   .   .   .

Tum victor mandido prosilias toro
Nocturni referens vulnera prœlii.

[60] See Zosimus, l. v. [c. 28] p. 333.

[61] Procopius de Bell. Vandal. l. i. c. 2 [tom. i. p. 316, ed. Bonn.]. I have borrowed the general practice of Honorius, without adopting the singular, and, indeed, improbable tale, which is related by the Greek historian.

[62] The lessons of Theodosius, or rather Claudian (iv. Cons. Honor. 214-418) might compose a fine institution for the future prince of a great and free nation. It was far above Honorius and his degenerate subjects.

CHAPTER XXX (395-408 A.D.)

Revolt of the Goths—They plunder Greece—Two great Invasions of Italy by Alaric and Radagaisus—They are repulsed by Stilicho—The Germans overrun Gaul—Usurpation of Constantine in the West—Disgrace and Death of Stilicho

IF the subjects of Rome could be ignorant of their obligations to the great Theodosius, they were too soon convinced how painfully the spirit and abilities of their deceased emperor had supported the frail and mouldering edifice of the republic. He died in the month of January; and before the end of the winter of the same year, the Gothic nation was in arms.[1] The barbarian auxiliaries erected their independent standard, and boldly avowed the hostile designs which they had long cherished in their ferocious minds. Their countrymen, who had been condemned by the conditions of the last treaty to a life of tranquillity and labour, deserted their farms at the first sound of the trumpet, and eagerly resumed the weapons which they had reluctantly laid down. The barriers of the Danube were thrown open; the savage warriors of Scythia issued from their forests; and the uncommon severity of the winter allowed the poet to remark "that they rolled their ponderous waggons over the broad and icy back of the indignant river."[2] The unhappy natives of the provinces to the south of the Danube submitted to the calamities which, in the course of twenty years, were almost grown familiar to their imagination; and the various troops of barbarians who gloried in the Gothic name were irregularly spread from the woody shores of Dalmatia to the walls of Constantinople.[3] The interruption, or at least the diminution, of the subsidy which the Goths had received from the prudent liberality of Theodosius, was the specious pretence of their revolt: the affront was embittered by their contempt for the unwarlike sons of Theodosius; and their resentment was inflamed by the weakness or treachery of the minister of Arcadius. The frequent visits of Rufinus to the camp of the barbarians, whose

[1] The revolt of the Goths and the blockade of Constantinople are distinctly mentioned by Claudian (in Rufin. 1. ii. 7-100), Zosimus (l. v. [c. 5] p. 292), and Jornandes (de Rebus Geticis, c. 29).

[2]
—— Alii per terga ferocis
Danubi solidata ruunt; expertaque remos
Frangunt stagna rotis.   [Claud. ib. v. 24.]

Claudian and Ovid often amuse their fancy by interchanging the metaphors and properties of *liquid* water and *solid* ice. Much false wit has been expended in this easy exercise.

[3] Jerom. tom. i. p. 26 [Epist. lx. tom. i. p. 342, ed. Vallars.]. He endeavours to comfort his friend Heliodorus, bishop of Altinum, for the loss of his nephew Nepotian, by a curious recapitulation of all the public and private misfortunes of the times. See Tillemont, Mém. Ecclés. tom. xii. p. 200, etc.

arms and apparel he affected to imitate, were considered as a sufficient evidence of his guilty correspondence; and the public enemy, from a motive either of gratitude or of policy, was attentive, amidst the general devastation, to spare the private estates of the unpopular præfect. The Goths, instead of being impelled by the blind and headstrong passions of their chiefs, were now directed by the bold and artful genius of Alaric. That renowned leader was descended from the noble race of the Balti,[4] which yielded only to the royal dignity of the Amali: he had solicited the command of the Roman armies; and the Imperial court provoked him to demonstrate the folly of their refusal, and the importance of their loss. Whatever hopes might be entertained of the conquest of Constantinople, the judicious general soon abandoned an impracticable enterprise. In the midst of a divided court and a discontented people, the emperor Arcadius was terrified by the aspect of the Gothic arms: but the want of wisdom and valour was supplied by the strength of the city; and the fortifications, both of the sea and land, might securely brave the impotent and random darts of the barbarians. Alaric disdained to trample any longer on the prostrate and ruined countries of Thrace and Dacia, and he resolved to seek a plentiful harvest of fame and riches in a province which had hitherto escaped the ravages of war.[5]

The character of the civil and military officers on whom Rufinus had devolved the government of Greece confirmed the public suspicion that he had betrayed the ancient seat of freedom and learning to the Gothic invader. The proconsul Antiochus was the unworthy son of a respectable father; and Gerontius, who commanded the provincial troops, was much better qualified to execute the oppressive orders of a tyrant than to defend, with courage and ability, a country most remarkably fortified by the hand of nature. Alaric had traversed, without resistance, the plains of Macedonia and Thessaly, as far as the foot of Mount Oeta, a steep and woody range of hills, almost impervious to his cavalry. They stretched from east to west, to the edge of the sea-shore; and left, between the precipice and the Malian Gulf, an interval of three hundred feet, which in some places was contracted

---

[4] *Baltha,* or *bold:* origo mirifica, says Jornandes (c. 29). This illustrious race long continued to flourish in France, in the Gothic province of Septimania, or Languedoc, under the corrupted appellation of *Baux:* and a branch of that family afterwards settled in the kingdom of Naples (Grotius in Prolegom. ad Hist. Gothic. p. 53). The lords of Baux, near Arles, and of seventy-nine subordinate places, were independent of the counts of Provence (Longuerue, Description de la France, tom. i. p. 357).

[5] Zosimus (l. v. [c. 5] p. 293-295) is our best guide for the conquest of Greece: but the hints and allusion of Claudian are so many rays of historic light.

[6] Compare Herodotus (l. vii. c. 176) and Livy (xxxvi. 15). The narrow entrance of Greece was probably enlarged by each successive ravisher

to a road capable of admitting only a single carriage.[6] In this narrow
pass of Thermopylæ, where Leonidas and the three hundred Spartans
had gloriously devoted their lives, the Goths might have been stopped,
or destroyed, by a skilful general; and perhaps the view of that sacred
spot might have kindled some sparks of military ardour in the breasts
of the degenerate Greeks. The troops which had been posted to defend
the straits of Thermopylæ retired, as they were directed, without attempting to disturb the secure and rapid passage of Alaric;[7] and the
fertile fields of Phocis and Bœotia were instantly covered by a deluge
of barbarians, who massacred the males of an age to bear arms, and
drove away the beautiful females, with the spoil and cattle of the
flaming villages. The travellers who visited Greece several years afterwards could easily discover the deep and bloody traces of the march
of the Goths; and Thebes was less indebted for her preservation to the
strength of her seven gates than to the eager haste of Alaric, who
advanced to occupy the city of Athens and the important harbour of
the Piræus. The same impatience urged him to prevent the delay and
danger of a siege, by the offer of a capitulation; and as soon as the
Athenians heard the voice of the Gothic herald, they were easily persuaded to deliver the greatest part of their wealth, as the ransom of
the city of Minerva and its inhabitants. The treaty was ratified by
solemn oaths, and observed with mutual fidelity. The Gothic prince,
with a small and select train, was admitted within the walls; he indulged himself in the refreshment of the bath, accepted a splendid banquet which was provided by the magistrate, and affected to show that
he was not ignorant of the manners of civilised nations.[8] But the
whole territory of Attica, from the promontory of Sunium to the town
of Megara, was blasted by his baleful presence; and, if we may use the
comparison of a contemporary philosopher, Athens itself resembled
the bleeding and empty skin of a slaughtered victim. The distance
between Megara and Corinth could not much exceed thirty miles;
but the *bad road*, an expressive name, which it still bears among the
Greeks, was, or mighty easily have been made, impassable for the
march of an enemy. The thick and gloomy woods of Mount Cithæron
covered the inland country; the Scironian rocks approached the water's
edge, and hung over the narrow and winding path, which was confined

[7] He passed, says Eunapius (in Vit. Philosoph. p. 93, edit. Commelin, 1596),
through the straits, διὰ τῶν τυλῶν (of Thermopylæ) παρῆλθεν, σώπερ διὰ σταδίου
καὶ ἱπποκρότου πεδίου τρέχων.
[8] In obedience to Jerom and Claudian (in Rufin. l. ii. 191), I have mixed
some darker colours in the mild representation of Zosimus, who wished to
soften the calamities of Athens.
    Nec fera Cecropias traxissent vincula matres.
Synesius (Epist. cxxxv. p. 272, edit. Petav.) observes that Athens, whose
sufferings he imputes to the proconsul's avarice, was at that time less famous
for her schools of philosophy than for her trade of honey.

above six miles along the sea-shore.[9] The passage of those rocks, so infamous in every age, was terminated by the isthmus of Corinth; and a small body of firm and intrepid soldiers might have successfully defended a temporary entrenchment of five or six miles from the Ionian to the Ægean Sea. The confidence of the cities of Peloponnesus in their natural rampart had tempted them to neglect the care of their antique walls; and the avarice of the Roman governors had exhausted and betrayed the unhappy province.[10] Corinth, Argos, Sparta, yielded without resistance to the arms of the Goths; and the most fortunate of the inhabitants were saved by death from beholding the slavery of their families and the conflagration of their cities.[11] The vases and statues were distributed among the barbarians, with more regard to the value of the materials than to the elegance of the workmanship; the female captives submitted to the laws of war; the enjoyment of beauty was the reward of valour; and the Greeks could not reasonably complain of an abuse which was justified by the example of the heroic times.[12] The descendants of that extraordinary people, who had considered valour and discipline as the walls of Sparta, no longer remembered the generous reply of their ancestors to an invader more formidable than Alaric. " If thou art a god, thou wilt not hurt those who have never injured thee; if thou art a man, advance—and thou

[9] ———Vallata mari Scironia rupes,
Et duo continuo connectens æquora muro
Isthmos.

Claudian de Bell. Getico, 188.
The Scironian rocks are described by Pausanias (l. i. c. 44, p. 107, edit. Kuhn) and our modern travellers Wheeler (p. 436) and Chandler (p. 298). Hadrian made the road passable for two carriages [Pausan. i. c. 44, § 6, ed. Bekker].

[10] Claudian (in Rufin. l. ii. 186, and de Bello Getico, 611, etc.) vaguely, though forcibly, delineates the scene of rapine and destruction.

[With regard to Alaric's invasion of Greece, Prof. Bury points out that although there is no record that Alaric burnt down the Temple of Eleusis, it is certain that the invasion of the Goths was coincident with the end of the Eleusinian mysteries. At the same time we must remember that the edicts of Theodosius had exercised a repressive influence upon the worship. Then, as to Athens, there can be no doubt that it surrendered and was spared by Alaric, also that its glorious art treasures were not pillaged. In fact, as Gregorovius remarks, Athens suffered less from Alaric than from the invasion in the time of Dexippus.—O. S.]

[11] Τρὶς μάκαρες Δαναοὶ καὶ τετράκις, etc. These generous lines of Homer (Odyss. l. v. 306) were transcribed by one of the captive youths of Corinth: and the tears of Mummius may prove that the rude conqueror, though he was ignorant of the value of an original picture, possessed the purest source of good taste, a benevolent heart (Plutarch, Symposiac. l. ix. tom. ii. p. 737, edit. Wechel. [tom. viii. p. 939, ed. Reiske]).

[12] Homer perpetually describes the exemplary patience of these female captives, who gave their charms, and even their hearts, to the murderers of their fathers, brothers, etc. Such a passion (of Eriphile for Achilles) is touched with admirable delicacy by Racine.

wilt find men equal to thyself." [13]   From Thermopylæ to Sparta the
leader of the Goths pursued his victorious march without encountering
any mortal antagonists; but one of the advocates of expiring Paganism
has confidently asserted that the walls of Athens were guarded by the
goddess Minerva, with her formidable Ægis, and by the angry phantom of Achilles,[14] and that the conqueror was dismayed by the presence
of the hostile deities of Greece. In an age of miracles it would perhaps
be unjust to dispute the claim of the historian Zosimus to the common
benefit, yet it cannot be dissembled that the mind of Alaric was ill prepared to receive, either in sleeping or waking visions, the impressions of
Greek superstition. The songs of Homer and the fame of Achilles had
probably never reached the ear of the illiterate *barbarian;* and the
Christian faith, which he had devoutly embraced, taught him to despise
the imaginary deities of Rome and Athens. The invasion of the Goths,
instead of vindicating the honours, contributed, at least accidently, to
extirpate the last remains of Paganism; and the mysteries of Ceres,
which had subsisted eighteen hundred years, did not survive the destruction of Eleusis and the calamities of Greece.[15]

The last hope of a people who could no longer depend on their arms,
their gods, or their sovereign, was placed in the powerful assistance of
the general of the West; and Stilicho, who had not been permitted to
repulse, advanced to chastise the invaders of Greece.[16] A numerous fleet
was equipped in the ports of Italy; and the troops, after a short and
prosperous navigation over the Ionian Sea, were safely disembarked
on the isthmus, near the ruins of Corinth. The woody and mountainous
country of Arcadia, the fabulous residence of Pan and the Dryads,
became the scene of a long and doubtful conflict between two generals
not unworthy of each other. The skill and perseverance of the Roman
at length prevailed; and the Goths, after sustaining a considerable loss
from disease and desertion, gradually retreated to the lofty mountain
of Pholoe, near the sources of the Peneus, and on the frontiers of Elis—
a sacred country, which had formerly been exempted from the calamities
of war.[17] The camp of the barbarians was immediately besieged; the

[13] Plutarch (in Pyrrho [c. 26], tom. ii. p. 471, edit. Brian) gives the genuine
answer in the Laconic dialect. Pyrrhus attacked Sparta with 25,000 foot,
2000 horse, and 24 elephants: and the defence of that open town is a fine comment on the laws of Lycurgus, even in the last stage of decay.
[14] Such, perhaps, as Homer (Iliad, xx. 164) has so nobly painted him.
[15] Eunapius (in Vit. Philosoph. p. 90-93) intimates that a troop of monks
betrayed Greece and followed the Gothic camp.
[16] For Stilicho's Greek war compare the honest narrative of Zosimus (1. v.
[c. 7] p. 295, 296) with the curious circumstantial flattery of Claudian (i.
Cons. Stilich. 1. i. 172-186; iv. Cons. Hon. 459-487). As the event was not
glorious, it is artfully thrown into the shade.
[17] The troops who marched through Elis delivered up their arms. This
security enriched the Eleans, who were lovers of a rural life. Riches begat
pride: they disdained their privilege, and they suffered. Polybius advises
them to retire once more within their magic circle. See a learned and judicious

waters of the river [18] were diverted into another channel; and while they laboured under the intolerable pressure of thirst and hunger, a strong line of circumvallation was formed to prevent their escape. After these precautions Stilicho, too confident of victory, retired to enjoy his triumph in the theatrical games and lascivious dances of the Greeks; his soldiers, deserting their standards, spread themselves over the country of their allies, which they stripped of all that had been saved from the rapacious hands of the enemy. Alaric appears to have seized the favourable moment to execute one of those hardy enterprises in which the abilities of a general are displayed with more genuine lustre than in the tumult of a day of battle. To extricate himself from the prison of Peloponnesus it was necessary that he should pierce the entrenchments which surrounded his camp; that he should perform a difficult and dangerous march of thirty miles, as far as the Gulf of Corinth; and that he should transport his troops, his captives, and his spoil, over an arm of the sea, which, in the narrow interval between Rhium and the opposite shore, is at least half a mile in breadth.[19] The operations of Alaric must have been secret, prudent, and rapid, since the Roman general was confounded by the intelligence that the Goths, who had eluded his efforts, were in full possession of the important province of Epirus. This unfortunate delay allowed Alaric sufficient time to conclude the treaty which he secretly negotiated with the ministers of Constantinople. The apprehension of a civil war compelled Stilicho to retire, at the haughty mandate of his rivals, from the dominions of Arcadius; and he respected, in the enemy of Rome, the honourable character of the ally and servant of the emperor of the East.

A Grecian philosopher,[20] who visited Constantinople soon after the death of Theodosius, published his liberal opinions concerning the duties of kings and the state of the Roman republic. Synesius observes

discourse on the Olympic games, which Mr. West has prefixed to his translation of Pindar.

[18] Claudian (in iv. Cons. Hon. 480) alludes to the fact without naming the river; perhaps the Alpheus (i. Cons. Stil. l. i. 185).

—— Et Alpheus Geticis angustus acervis
Tardior ad Siculos etiamnum pergit amores.

Yet I should prefer the Peneus, a shallow stream in a wide and deep bed which runs through Elis and falls into the sea below Cyllene. It had been joined with the Alpheus to cleanse the Augean stable. (Cellarius, tom. i. p. 760. Chandler's Travels, p. 286.)

[19] Strabo, l. viii. p. 517 [p. 335, ed. Casaub.]. Plin. Hist. Natur. iv. 3. Wheeler, p. 308. Chandler, p. 275. They measured from different points the distance between the two lands.

[20] Synesius passed three years (A.D. 397-400) at Constantinople as deputy from Cyrene to the emperor Arcadius. He presented him with a crown of gold, and pronounced before him the instructive oration de Regno (p. 1-32, edit. Petav. Paris, 1612). The philosopher was made bishop of Ptolemais, A.D. 410, and died about 430. See Tillemont, Mém. Ecclés. tom. xii. p. 499, 554, 683-685.

and deplores the fatal abuse which the imprudent bounty of the late emperor had introduced into the military service. The citizens and subjects had purchased an exemption from the indispensable duty of defending their country, which was supported by the arms of barbarian mercenaries. The fugitives of Scythia were permitted to disgrace the illustrious dignities of the empire; their ferocious youth, who disdained the salutary restraint of laws, were more anxious to acquire the riches than to imitate the arts of a people the object of their contempt and hatred; and the power of the Goths was the stone of Tantalus, perpetually suspended over the peace and safety of the devoted state. The measures which Synesius recommends are the dictates of a bold and generous patriot. He exhorts the emperor to revive the courage of his subjects by the example of manly virtue; to banish luxury from the court and from the camp; to substitute, in the place of the barbarian mercenaries, an army of men interested in the defence of their laws and of their property; to force, in such a moment of public danger, the mechanic from his shop and the philosopher from his school; to rouse the indolent citizen from his dream of pleasure; and to arm, for the protection of agriculture, the hands of the laborious husbandman. At the head of such troops, who might deserve the name and would display the spirit of Romans, he animates the son of Theodosius to encounter a race of barbarians who were destitute of any real courage; and never to lay down his arms till he had chased them far away into the solitudes of Scythia, or had reduced them to the state of ignominious servitude which the Lacedæmonians formerly imposed on the captive Helots.[21] The court of Arcadius indulged the zeal, applauded the eloquence, and neglected the advice of Synesius. Perhaps the philosopher, who addresses the emperor of the East in the language of reason and virtue which he might have used to a Spartan king, had not condescended to form a practicable scheme, consistent with the temper and circumstances of a degenerate age. Perhaps the pride of the ministers, whose business was seldom interrupted by reflection, might reject, as wild and visionary, every proposal which exceeded the measure of their capacity, and deviated from the forms and precedents of office. While the oration of Synesius and the downfall of the barbarians were the topics of popular conversation, an edict was published at Constantinople which declared the promotion of Alaric to the rank of master-general of the Eastern Illyricum. The Roman provincials, and the allies who had respected the faith of treaties, were justly indignant that the ruin of Greece and Epirus should be so liberally rewarded. The Gothic conqueror was received as a lawful magistrate in the cities which he had so lately besieged. The fathers whose sons he had massacred, the husbands whose wives he had violated, were subject to his authority; and the success of his rebellion encouraged the ambition of every leader of the foreign

[21] Synesius de Regno, p. 21-26.

mercenaries. The use to which Alaric applied his new command distinguishes the firm and judicious character of his policy. He issued his orders to the four magazines and manufactures of offensive and defensive arms, Margus, Ratiaria, Naissus, and Thessalonica, to provide his troops with an extraordinary supply of shields, helmets, swords, and spears; the unhappy provincials were compelled to forge the instruments of their own destruction; and the barbarians removed the only defect which had sometimes disappointed the efforts of their courage.[22] The birth of Alaric, the glory of his past exploits, and the confidence in his future designs, insensibly united the body of the nation under his victorious standards; and, with the unanimous consent of the barbarian chieftains, the master-general of Illyricum was elevated, according to ancient custom, on a shield, and solemnly proclaimed king of the Visigoths.[23] Armed with this double power, seated on the verge of the two empires, he alternately sold his deceitful promises to the courts of Arcadius and Honorius,[24] till he declared and executed his resolution of invading the dominions of the West. The provinces of Europe which belonged to the Eastern emperor were already exhausted, those of Asia were inaccessible, and the strength of Constantinople had resisted his attack. But he was tempted by the fame, the beauty, the wealth of Italy, which he had twice visited; and he secretly aspired to plant the Gothic standard on the walls of Rome, and to enrich his army with the accumulated spoils of three hundred triumphs.[25]

[22] ——————— qui fœdera rumpit
Ditatur: qui servat, eget: vastator Achivæ
Gentis, et Epirum nuper populatus inultam
Præsidet Illyrico: jam, quos obsedit, amicos
Ingreditur muros; illis responsa daturus
Quorum conjugibus potitur, natosque peremit.
Claudian in Eutrop. l. ii. 212. Alaric applauds his own policy (de Bell. Getic. 533-543) in the use which he had made of this Illyrian jurisdiction.

[23] Jornandes, c. 29, p. 651 [ed. Grot. 1655; p. 81, ed. Lugd. B. 1597]. The Gothic historian adds, with unusual spirit, Cum suis deliberans suasit suo labore quærere regna, quam alienis per otium subjacere.
[Some annotators think that it was more likely that Alaric was proclaimed king in 395 A.D. after the death of Theodosius.—O. S.]

[24] —— Discors odiisque anceps civilibus orbis
Non sua vis tutata diu, dum fœdera fallax
Ludit, et alternæ perjuria venditat aulæ.
Claudian de Bell. Get. 565.

[25] Alpibus Italiæ ruptis penetrabis ad *Urbem*.
This authentic prediction was announced by Alaric, or at least by Claudian (de Bell. Getico, 547), seven years before the event. But as it was not accomplished within the term which has been rashly fixed, the interpreters escaped through an ambiguous meaning.
[Claudian states that a voice had foretold to Alaric that he would plant his standard on the walls of Rome. Cf. Claudian, *De Bello Getico*, 546-7.
Rumpe omnes, Alarice mores: hoc impiger anno
Alpibus Italiæ ruptis penetrabis ad urbem.
In Koch's edition of Claudian the fact is indicated that the first and last letters of the two lines spell ROMA.—O. S.]

The scarcity of facts,[26] and the uncertainty of dates,[27] oppose our attempts to describe the circumstances of the first invasion of Italy by the arms of Alaric. His march, perhaps from Thessalonica, through the warlike and hostile country of Pannonia, as far as the foot of the Julian Alps; his passage of those mountains, which were strongly guarded by troops and entrenchments; the siege of Aquileia, and the conquest of the provinces of Istria and Venetia, appear to have employed a considerable time. Unless his operations were extremely cautious and slow, the length of the interval would suggest a probable suspicion that the Gothic king retreated towards the banks of the Danube, and reinforced his army with fresh swarms of barbarians, before he again attempted to penetrate into the heart of Italy. Since the public and important events escape the diligence of the historian, he may amuse himself with contemplating for a moment the influence of the arms of Alaric on the fortunes of two obscure individuals, a presbyter of Aquileia, and an husbandman of Verona. The learned Rufinus, who was summoned by his enemies to appear before a Roman synod,[28] wisely preferred the dangers of a besieged city; and the barbarians, who furiously shook the walls of Aquileia, might save him from the cruel sentence of another heretic, who, at the request of the same bishops, was severely whipped and condemned to perpetual exile on a desert island.[29] The *old man* [30] who had passed

[26] Our best materials are 970 verses of Claudian, in the poem on the Getic war, and the beginning of that which celebrates the sixth consulship of Honorius. Zosimus is totally silent; and we are reduced to such scraps, or rather crumbs, as we can pick from Orosius and the Chronicles.

[27] Notwithstanding the gross errors of Jornandes, who confounds the Italian wars of Alaric (c. 29), his date of the consulship of Stilicho and Aurelian (A.D. 400) is firm and respectable. It is certain from Claudian (Tillemont, Hist. des Emp. tom. v. p. 804), that the battle of Pollentia was fought A.D. 403; but we cannot easily fill the interval.

[As regards Alaric in Italy, the events which Gibbon supposes to have taken place in 400-402 are uncertain. We know that Alaric crossed the Alps early in the winter of 401 A.D., probably October (Claudian vi. *Cons. Honor.* 440, *Bell Get.* 471), entered Italy in November of that same year, and fought the battle of Pollentia on Easter Day 402. Alaric was in Istria late in 402 or early in 403, and the battle of Verona was fought in the summer (probably June) of that year, 403. Bury thinks that after Pollentia there must have been another engagement at Asta. The 17th Appendix to Prof. Bury's third volume is worthy of the most careful study by all interested in this question. There is, however, no authority for Gibbon's statement that Honorius on his way to Arles took refuge in Asta. It is (says Dr. W. Smith) simply an hypothesis to account for the presence of Alaric in Liguria, and rests only on Claudian's mention of Asta in conjunction with Pollentia.—O. S.]

[28] Tantum Romanæ urbis judicium fugis, ut magis obsidionem barbaricam, quam *pacatæ* urbis judicium velis sustinere. Jerom, tom. ii. p. 239. Rufinus understood his own danger; the *peaceful* city was inflamed by the beldam Marcella and the rest of Jerom's faction.

[29] Jovinian, the enemy of fasts and of celibacy, who was persecuted and insulted by the furious Jerom (Jortin's Remarks, vol. iv. p. 104, etc.). See the original edict of banishment in the Theodosian Code, l. xvi. tit. v. leg. 53.

[30] This epigram (de Sene Veronensi qui surburbium nusquam egressus est)

his simple and innocent life in the neighbourhood of Verona, was a
stranger to the quarrels both of kings and of bishops; *his* pleasures, his
desires, his knowledge, were confined within the little circle of his
paternal farm; and a staff supported his aged steps on the same ground
where he had sported in his infancy. Yet even this humble and rustic
felicity (which Claudian describes with so much truth and feeling) was
still exposed to the undistinguishing rage of war. His trees, his old
contemporary trees,[31] must blaze in the conflagration of the whole
country; a detachment of Gothic cavalry might sweep away his cottage
and his family; and the power of Alaric could destroy this happiness,
which he was not able either to taste or to bestow. " Fame," says the
poet, " encircling with terror her gloomy wings, proclaimed the march
of the barbarian army, and filled Italy with consternation:" the apprehensions of each individual were increased in just proportion to the
measure of his fortune: and the most timid, who had already embarked
their valuable effects, meditated their escape to the island of Sicily or
the African coast. The public distress was aggravated by the fears and
reproaches of superstition.[32] Every hour produced some horrid tale of
strange and portentous accidents: the Pagans deplored the neglect of
omens and the interruption of sacrifices; but the Christians still derived
some comfort from the powerful intercession of the saints and martyrs.[33]

The emperor Honorius was distinguished, above his subjects, by the
pre-eminence of fear as well as of rank. The pride and luxury in which
he was educated had not allowed him to suspect that there existed on the
earth any power presumptuous enough to invade the repose of the successor of Augustus. The arts of flattery concealed the impending danger
till Alaric approached the palace of Milan. But when the sound of war
had awakened the young emperor, instead of flying to arms with the
spirit, or even the rashness, of his age, he eagerly listened to those timid
counsellors who proposed to convey his sacred person and his faithful
attendants to some secure and distant station in the provinces of Gaul.

is one of the earliest and most pleasing compositions of Claudian. Cowley's
imitation (Hurd's edition, vol. ii. p. 241) has some natural and happy strokes:
but it is much inferior to the original portrait, which is evidently drawn from
the life.

[31] Ingentem meminit parvo qui germine quercum
     Æquævumque videt consenuisse nemus.

A neighbouring wood born with himself he sees,
And loves his old contemporary trees.

In this passage Cowley is perhaps superior to his original; and the English
poet, who was a good botanist, has concealed the *oaks* under a more general
expression.

[32] Claudian de Bell. Get. 199-266. He may seem prolix: but fear and superstition occupied as large a space in the minds of the Italians.

[33] From the passages of Paulinus which Baronius has produced (Annal.
Eccles. A.D. 403, No. 51) it is manifest that the general alarm had pervaded
all Italy, as far as Nola in Campania, where that famous penitent had fixed
his abode.

Stilicho alone [34] had courage and authority to resist this disgraceful measure, which would have abandoned Rome and Italy to the barbarians; but as the troops of the palace had been lately detached to the Rhætian frontier, and as the resource of new levies was slow and precarious, the general of the West could only promise that, if the court of Milan would maintain their ground during his absence, he would soon return with an army equal to the encounter of the Gothic king. Without losing a moment (while each moment was so important to the public safety), Stilicho hastily embarked on the Larian lake, ascended the mountains of ice and snow amidst the severity of an Alpine winter, and suddenly repressed, by his unexpected presence, the enemy, who had disturbed the tranquillity of Rhætia.[35] The barbarians, perhaps some tribes of the Alemanni, respected the firmness of a chief who still assumed the language of command; and the choice which he condescended to make of a select number of their bravest youth was considered as a mark of his esteem and favour. The cohorts, who were delivered from the neighbouring foe, diligently repaired to the Imperial standard; and Stilicho issued his orders to the most remote troops of the West, to advance, by rapid marches, to the defence of Honorius and of Italy. The fortresses of the Rhine were abandoned; and the safety of Gaul was protected only by the faith of the Germans, and the ancient terror of the Roman name. Even the legion which had been stationed to guard the wall of Britain against the Caledonians of the North was hastily recalled;[36] and a numerous body of the cavalry of the Alani was persuaded to engage in the service of the emperor, who anxiously expected the return of his general. The prudence and vigour of Stilicho were conspicuous on this occasion, which revealed, at the same time, the weakness of the falling empire. The legions of Rome, which had long since languished in the gradual decay of discipline and courage, were exterminated by the Gothic and civil wars; and it was found impossible without exhausting and exposing the provinces, to assemble an army for the defence of Italy.

When Stilicho seemed to abandon his sovereign in the unguarded palace of Milan, he had probably calculated the term of his absence, the distance of the enemy, and the obstacles that might retard their march. He principally depended on the rivers of Italy, the Adige, the Mincius,

[34] Solus erat Stilicho, etc., is the exclusive commendation which Claudian bestows (de Bell. Get. 267), without condescending to except the emperor. How insignificant must Honorius have appeared in his own court!
[35] The face of the country and the hardiness of Stilicho are finely described (de Bell. Get. 340-363).
[36] Venit et extremis legio prætenta Britannis
Quæ Scoto dat frena truci.
De Bell. Get. 416.
Yet the most rapid march from Edinburgh, or Newcastle, to Milan, must have required a longer space of time than Claudian seems willing to allow for the duration of the Gothic war.

the Oglio, and the Addua, which, in the winter or spring, by the fall of
rains, or by the melting of the snows, are commonly swelled into broad
and impetuous torrents.[37]   But the season happened to be remarkably
dry; and the Goths could traverse, without impediment, the wide and
stony beds, whose centre was faintly marked by the course of a shallow
stream.   The bridge and passage of the Addua was secured by a strong
detachment of the Gothic army; and as Alaric approached the walls,
or rather the suburbs, of Milan, he enjoyed the proud satisfaction of
seeing the emperor of the Romans fly before him.   Honorius, accompanied by a feeble train of statesmen and eunuchs, hastily retreated
towards the Alps, with a design of securing his person in the city of
Arles, which had often been the royal residence of his predecessors.
But Honorius [38] had scarcely passed the Po before he was overtaken
by the speed of the Gothic cavalry;[39] since the urgency of the danger
compelled him to seek a temporary shelter within the fortification of
Asta, a town of Liguria or Piemont, situate on the banks of the Tana-
rus.[40]   The siege of an obscure place, which contained so rich a prize,
and seemed incapable of a long resistance, was instantly formed,
and indefatigably pressed, by the king of the Goths; and the bold
declaration, which the emperor might afterwards make, that his breast
had never been susceptible of fear, did not probably obtain much credit
even in his own court.[41]   In the last and almost hopeless extremity, after
the barbarians had already proposed the indignity of a capitulation, the
Imperial captive was suddenly relieved by the fame, the approach, and
at length the presence, of the hero whom he had so long expected.   At
the head of a chosen and intrepid vanguard, Stilicho swam the stream
of the Addua, to gain the time which he must have lost in the attack
of the bridge; the passage of the Po was an enterprise of much less
hazard and difficulty; and the successful action, in which he cut his
way through the Gothic camp under the walls of Asta, revived the hopes

[37] Every traveller must recollect the face of Lombardy (see Fontenelle, tom.
v. p. 279), which is often tormented by the capricious and irregular abundance
of waters.   The Austrians before Genoa were encamped in the dry bed of
the Polcevera. "Ne sarebbe" (says Muratori) "mai passato per mente a
que' buoni Alemanni, che quel picciolo torrente potesse, per cosi dire, in un
instante cangiarsi in un terribil gigante." (Annal. d'Italia, tom. xvi. p. 443,
Milan, 1753, 8vo. edit.)

[38] Claudian does not clearly answer our question, Where was Honorius himself?   Yet the flight is marked by the pursuit; and my idea of the Gothic
war is justified by the Italian critics, Sigonius (tom. i. p. ii. p. 369, de Imp.
Occident. l. x.) and Muratori (Annali d'Italia, tom. iv. p. 45).

[39] One of the roads may be traced in the Itineraries (p. 98, 288, 294, with
Wesseling's Notes).   Asta lay some miles on the right hand.

[40] Asta, or Asti, a Roman colony, is now the capital of a pleasant county,
which, in the sixteenth century, devolved to the dukes of Savoy (Leandro
Alberti, Descrizzione d'Italia, p. 382).

[41] Nec me timor impulit ullus. He might hold this proud language the next
year at Rome, five hundred miles from the scene of danger (vi. Cons.
Hon. 449).

and vindicated the honour of Rome. Instead of grasping the fruit of his victory, the barbarian was gradually invested, on every side, by the troops of the West, who successively issued through all the passes of the Alps; his quarters were straitened; his convoys were intercepted; and the vigilance of the Romans prepared to form a chain of fortifications, and to besiege the lines of the besiegers. A military council was assembled of the long-haired chiefs of the Gothic nation; of aged warriors, whose bodies were wrapped in furs, and whose stern countenances were marked with honourable wounds. They weighed the glory of persisting in their attempt against the advantage of securing their plunder; and they recommended the prudent measure of a seasonable retreat. In this important debate, Alaric displayed the spirit of the conqueror of Rome; and after he had reminded his countrymen of their achievements and of their designs, he concluded his animating speech by the solemn and positive assurance that he was resolved to find in Italy either a kingdom or a grave.[42]

The loose discipline of the barbarians always exposed them to the danger of a surprise; but, instead of choosing the dissolute hours of riot and intemperance, Stilicho resolved to attack the *Christian* Goths whilst they were devoutly employed in celebrating the festival of Easter.[43] The execution of the stratagem, or, as it was termed by the clergy, of the sacrilege, was intrusted to Saul, a barbarian and a Pagan, who had served, however, with distinguished reputation among the veteran generals of Theodosius. The camp of the Goths, which Alaric had pitched in the neighbourhood of Pollentia,[44] was thrown into confusion by the sudden and impetuous charge of the Imperial cavalry; but, in a few moments, the undaunted genius of their leader gave them an order and a field of battle; and, soon as they had recovered from their astonishment, the pious confidence that the God of the Christians would assert their cause added new strength to their native valour. In this engagement, which was long maintained with equal courage and success, the chief of the Alani, whose diminutive and savage form concealed a magnanimous soul, approved his suspected loyalty, by the zeal

---

[42] Hanc ego vel victor regno, vel morte tenebo
    Victus, humum.
The speeches (de Bell. Get. 479-549) of the Gothic Nestor and Achilles are strong, characteristic, adapted to the circumstances, and possibly not less genuine than those of Livy.

[43] Orosius (l. vii. c. 37) is shocked at the impiety of the Romans, who attacked on Easter Sunday such pious Christians. Yet, at the same time, public prayers were offered at the shrine of St. Thomas of Edessa for the destruction of the Arian robber. See Tillemont (Hist. des. Emp. tom. v. p. 529), who quotes a homily which has been erroneously ascribed to St. Chrysostom.

[44] The vestiges of Pollentia are twenty-five miles to the south-east of Turin. *Urbs,* in the same neighbourhood, was a royal chase of the kings of Lombardy, and a small river, which excused the prediction, "penetrabis ad urbem." (Cluver. Ital. Antiq. tom. i. p. 83-85.)

with which he fought and fell in the service of the republic; and the fame of this gallant barbarian has been imperfectly preserved in the verses of Claudian, since the poet, who celebrates his virtue, has omitted the mention of his name. His death was followed by the flight and dismay of the squadrons which he commanded; and the defeat of the wing of cavalry might have decided the victory of Alaric, if Stilicho had not immediately led the Roman and barbarian infantry to the attack. The skill of the general, and the bravery of the soldiers, surmounted every obstacle. In the evening of the bloody day, the Goths retreated from the field of battle; the entrenchments of their camp were forced, and the scene of rapine and slaughter made some atonement for the calamities which they had inflicted on the subjects of the empire.[45] The magnificent spoils of Corinth and Argos enriched the veterans of the West; the captive wife of Alaric, who had impatiently claimed his promise of Roman jewels and Patrician handmaids,[46] was reduced to implore the mercy of the insulting foe; and many thousand prisoners, released from the Gothic chains, dispersed through the provinces of Italy the praises of their heroic deliverer. The triumph of Stilicho [47] was compared by the poet, and perhaps by the public, to that of Marius; who, in the same part of Italy, had encountered and destroyed another army of Northern barbarians. The huge bones and the empty helmets of the Cimbri and of the Goths would easily be confounded by succeeding generations; and posterity might erect a common trophy to the memory of the two most illustrious generals, who had vanquished, on the same memorable ground, the two most formidable enemies of Rome.[48]

The eloquence of Claudian [49] has celebrated, with lavish applause, the victory of Pollentia, one of the most glorious days in the life of

[45] Orosius wishes, in doubtful words, to insinuate the defeat of the Romans. "Pugnantes vicimus, victores victi sumus." Prosper (in Chron.) makes it an equal and bloody battle; but the Gothic writers, Cassiodorus (in Chron.) and Jornandes (de Reb. Get. c. 30), claim a decisive victory.

[46] Demens Ausonidum gemmata monilia matrum,
Romanasque altâ famulas cervice petebat.
                                        De Bell. Get. 627.
[From these lines of Claudian by no possible stretch of ingenuity can be wrung any authority whereon to base the statement that Alaric's wife fell a captive into the victor's hands.—O. S.]

[47] Claudian (de Bell. Get. 580-647) and Prudentius (in Symmach. l. ii. 694-719) celebrate, without ambiguity, the Roman victory of Pollentia. They are poetical and party writers; yet some credit is due to the most suspicious witnesses who are checked by the recent notoriety of facts.

[48] Claudian's peroration is strong and elegant; but the identity of the Cimbric and Gothic fields must be understood (like Virgil's Philippi, Georgic i. 490) according to the loose geography of a poet. Vercellæ and Pollentia are sixty miles from each other; and the latitude is still greater if the Cimbri were defeated in the wide and barren plain of Verona (Maffei, Verona Illustrata, p. i. p. 54-62).

[49] Claudian and Prudentius must be strictly examined, to reduce the figures and extort the historic sense of those poets.

his patron; but his reluctant and partial muse bestows more genuine praise on the character of the Gothic king. His name is, indeed, branded with the reproachful epithets of pirate and robber, to which the conquerors of every age are so justly entitled; but the poet of Stilicho is compelled to acknowledge that Alaric possessed the invincible temper of mind which rises superior to every misfortune, and derives new resources from adversity. After the total defeat of his infantry, he escaped, or rather withdrew, from the field of battle, with the greatest part of his cavalry entire and unbroken. Without wasting a moment to lament the irreparable loss of so many brave companions, he left his victorious enemy to bind in chains the captive images of a Gothic king;[50] and boldly resolved to break through the unguarded passes of the Apennine, to spread desolation over the fruitful face of Tuscany, and to conquer or die before the gates of Rome. The capital was saved by the active and incessant diligence of Stilicho; but he respected the despair of his enemy; and, instead of committing the fate of the republic to the chance of another battle, he proposed to purchase the absence of the barbarians. The spirit of Alaric would have rejected such terms, the permission of a retreat, and the offer of a pension, with contempt and indignation; but he exercised a limited and precarious authority over the independent chieftains who had raised him, for *their* service, above the rank of his equals; they were still less disposed to follow an unsuccessful general, and many of them were tempted to consult their interest by a private negotiation with the minister of Honorius. The king submitted to the voice of his people, ratified the treaty with the empire of the West, and repassed the Po with the remains of the flourishing army which he had led into Italy. A considerable part of the Roman forces still continued to attend his motions: and Stilicho, who maintained a secret correspondence with some of the barbarian chiefs, was punctually appraised of the designs that were formed in the camp and council of Alaric. The king of the Goths, ambitious to signalise his retreat by some splendid achievement, had resolved to occupy the important city of Verona, which commands the principal passage of the Rhætian Alps; and, directing his march through the territories of those German tribes whose alliance would restore his exhausted strength, to invade, on the side of the Rhine, the wealthy and unsuspecting provinces of Gaul. Ignorant of the treason which had already betrayed his bold and judicious enterprise, he advanced towards the passes of the mountains, already possessed by the Imperial troops; where he was exposed, almost at the same instant, to a general attack in the front, on his

[50] Et gravant en airain ses frêles avantages
    De mes états conquis enchainer les images.
The practice of exposing in triumph the images of kings and provinces was familiar to the Romans. The bust of Mithridates himself was twelve feet high, of massy gold (Freinshem. Supplement. Livian. ciii. 47).

flanks, and in the rear. In this bloody action, at a small distance from the walls of Verona, the loss of the Goths was not less heavy than that which they had sustained in the defeat of Pollentia; and their valiant king, who escaped by the swiftness of his horse, must either have been slain or made prisoner, if the hasty rashness of the Alani had not disappointed the measures of the Roman general. Alaric secured the remains of his army on the adjacent rocks; and prepared himself, with undaunted resolution, to maintain a siege against the superior numbers of the enemy, who invested him on all sides. But he could not oppose the destructive progress of hunger and disease; nor was it possible for him to check the continual desertion of his impatient and capricious barbarians. In this extremity he still found resources in his own courage, or in the moderation of his adversary; and the retreat of the Gothic king was considered as the deliverance of Italy.[51] Yet the people, and even the clergy, incapable of forming any rational judgment of the business of peace and war, presumed to arraign the policy of Stilicho, who so often vanquished, so often surrounded, and so often dismissed the implacable enemy of the republic. The first moment of the public safety is devoted to gratitude and joy; but the second is diligently occupied by envy and calumny.[52]

The citizens of Rome had been astonished by the approach of Alaric; and the diligence with which they laboured to restore the walls of the capital confessed their own fears, and the decline of the empire. After the retreat of the barbarians, Honorius was directed to accept the dutiful invitation of the senate, and to celebrate, in the Imperial city, the auspicious era of the Gothic victory, and of his sixth consulship.[53] The suburbs and the streets, from the Milvian bridge to the Palatine mount, were filled by the Roman people, who, in the space of an hundred years, had only thrice been honoured with the presence of their sovereigns. While their eyes were fixed on the chariot where Stilicho was deservedly seated by the side of his royal pupil, they applauded the pomp of a triumph which was not stained, like that of Constantine or of Theodosius, with civil blood. The procession passed under a lofty arch, which had been purposely erected: but in less than seven years, the Gothic conquerors of Rome might read, if they were able to read, the superb inscription of that monument, which attested the total defeat and destruction of their nation.[54] The emperor resided

[51] The Getic war and the sixth consulship of Honorius obscurely connect the events of Alaric's retreat and losses.

[52] Taceo de Alarico . . . sæpe victo, sæpe concluso, semperque dimisso. Orosius, l. vii. c. 37, p. 567. Claudian (vi. Cons. Hon. 320) drops the curtain with a fine image.

[53] The remainder of Claudian's poem on the sixth consulship of Honorius describes the journey, the triumph, and the games (330-660).

[54] See the inscription in Mascou's History of the Ancient Germans, viii. 12. The words are positive and indiscreet: Getarum nationem in omne, ævum domitam, etc.

several months in the capital, and every part of his behaviour was regulated with care to conciliate the affection of the clergy, the senate, and the people of Rome. The clergy was edified by his frequent visits, and liberal gifts, to the shrines of the apostles. The senate, who, in the triumphal procession, had been excused from the humiliating ceremony of preceding on foot the Imperial chariot, was treated with the decent reverence which Stilicho always affected for that assembly. The people was repeatedly gratified by the attention and courtesy of Honorius in the public games, which were celebrated on that occasion with a magnificence not unworthy of the spectator. As soon as the appointed number of chariot-races was concluded, the decoration of the circus was suddenly changed; the hunting of wild beasts afforded a various and splendid entertainment; and the chase was succeeded by a military dance, which seems, in the lively description of Claudian, to present the image of a modern tournament.

In these games of Honorius, the inhuman combats of gladiators [55] polluted for the last time the amphitheatre of Rome. The first Christian emperor may claim the honour of the first edict which condemned the art and amusement of shedding human blood; [56] but this benevolent law expressed the wishes of the prince, without reforming an inveterate abuse which degraded a civilised nation below the condition of savage cannibals. Several hundred, perhaps several thousand, victims were annually slaughtered in the great cities of the empire; and the month of December, more peculiarly devoted to the combats of gladiators, still exhibited to the eyes of the Roman people a grateful spectacle of blood and cruelty. Amidst the general joy of the victory of Pollentia, a Christian poet exhorted the emperor to extirpate, by his authority, the horrid custom which had so long resisted the voice of humanity and religion.[57] The pathetic representations of Prudentius were less effectual than the generous boldness of Telemachus, an Asiatic monk, whose death was more useful to mankind than his life.[58] The Romans were provoked by the interruption of their pleasures; and the rash monk, who had descended into the arena, to separate the gladiators, was overwhelmed under a shower of stones. But the madness of the people soon subsided: they respected the

[55] On the curious though horrid subject of the gladiators, consult the two books of the Saturnalia of Lipsius, who, as an *antiquarian,* is inclined to excuse the practice of *antiquity* (tom. iii. p. 483-545).

[56] Cod. Theodos. l. xv. tit. xii. leg. i. The Commentary of Godefroy affords large materials (tom. v. p. 396) for the history of gladiators.

[57] See the peroration of Prudentius (in Symmach l. ii. 1121-1131), who had doubtless read the eloquent invective of Lactantius (Divin. Institut. l. vi. c. 20). The Christian apologists have not spared these bloody games, which were introduced in the religious festivals of Paganism.

[58] Theodoret, l. v. c. 26. I wish to believe the story of St. Telemachus. Yet no church has been dedicated, no altar has been erected, to the only monk who died a martyr in the cause of humanity.

memory of Telemachus, who had deserved the honours of martyrdom; and they submitted, without a murmur, to the laws of Honorius, which abolished for ever the human sacrifices of the amphitheatre. The citizens, who adhered to the manners of their ancestors, might perhaps insinuate that the last remains of a martial spirit were preserved in this school of fortitude, which accustomed the Romans to the sight of blood, and to the contempt of death: a vain and cruel prejudice, so nobly confuted by the valour of ancient Greece and of modern Europe! [59]

The recent danger to which the person of the emperor had been exposed in the defenceless palace of Milan urged him to seek a retreat in some inaccessible fortress of Italy, where he might securely remain, while the open country was covered by a deluge of barbarians. On the coast of the Hadriatic, about ten or twelve miles from the most southern of the seven mouths of the Po, the Thessalians had founded the ancient colony of RAVENNA,[60] which they afterwards resigned to the natives of Umbria. Augustus, who had observed the opportunity of the place, prepared, at the distance of three miles from the old town, a capacious harbour for the reception of two hundred and fifty ships of war. This naval establishment, which included the arsenals and magazines, the barracks of the troops, and the houses of the artificers, derived its origin and name from the permanent station of the Roman fleet; the intermediate space was soon filled with buildings and inhabitants, and the three extensive and populous quarters of Ravenna gradually contributed to form one of the most important cities of Italy. The principal canal of Augustus poured a copious stream of the waters of the Po through the midst of the city, to the entrance of the harbour; the same waters were introduced into the profound ditches that encompassed the walls; they were distributed by a thousand subordinate canals into every part of the city, which they divided into a variety of small islands; the communication was maintained only by the use of boats and bridges; and the houses of Ravenna, whose appearance may be compared to that of Venice, were raised on the foundation of wooden piles. The adjacent country, to the distance of many miles, was a deep and impassable morass; and the artificial causeway

---

[59] Crudele gladiatorum spectaculum et inhumanum *nonnullis* videri solet; et *haud scio* an ita sit, ut nunc fit. Cicero Tusculan. ii. 17. He faintly censures the *abuse,* and warmly defends the *use,* of these sports; oculis nulla poterat esse fortior contra dolorem et mortem disciplina. Seneca (Epist. v. i.) shows the feelings of a man.

[60] This account of Ravenna is drawn from Strabo (l. v. p. 327 [p. 213, ed. Casaub.]), Pliny (iii. 20), Stephen of Byzantium (sub voce ῾Ράβεννα, p. 651, edit. Berkel.), Claudian (in vi. Cons. Honor. 494, etc)., Sidonius Apollinaris (l. i. Epist. 5, 8), Jornandes (de Reb. Get. c. 29), Procopius (de Bell. Gothic. l. i. c. i. p. 309, edit. Louvre [tom. ii. p. 8, ed. Bonn]), and Cluverius (Ital. Antiq. tom. i. p. 301-307). Yet I still want a local antiquarian, and a good topographical map.

which connected Ravenna with the continent might be easily guarded or destroyed on the approach of an hostile army. These morasses were interspersed, however, with vineyards; and though the soil was exhausted by four or five crops, the town enjoyed a more plentiful supply of wine than of fresh water.[61] The air, instead of receiving the sickly and almost pestilential exhalations of low and marshy grounds, was distinguished, like the neighbourhood of Alexandria, as uncommonly pure and salubrious; and this singular advantage was ascribed to the regular tides of the Hadriatic, which swept the canals, interrupted the unwholesome stagnation of the waters, and floated, every day, the vessels of the adjacent country into the heart of Ravenna. The gradual retreat of the sea has left the modern city at the distance of four miles from the Hadriatic, and as early as the fifth or sixth century of the Christian era the port of Augustus was converted into pleasant orchards, and a lonely grove of pines covered the ground where the Roman fleet once rode at anchor.[62] Even this alteration contributed to increase the natural strength of the place, and the shallowness of the water was a sufficient barrier against the large ships of the enemy. This advantageous situation was fortified by art and labour; and in the twentieth year of his age the emperor of the West, anxious only for his personal safety, retired to the perpetual confinement of the walls and morasses of Ravenna. The example of Honorius was imitated by his feeble successors, the Gothic kings, and afterwards the Exarchs, who occupied the throne and palace of the emperors; and till the middle of the eighth century Ravenna was considered as the seat of government and the capital of Italy.[63]

The fears of Honorius were not without foundation, nor were his precautions without effect. While Italy rejoiced in her deliverance from the Goths, a furious tempest was excited among the nations of Germany, who yielded to the irresistible impulse that appears to have been gradually communicated from the eastern extremity of the continent of Asia. The Chinese annals, as they have been interpreted by the learned industry of the present age, may be usefully applied to reveal the secret and remote causes of the fall of the Roman empire.

[61] Martial (Epigram iii. 56, 57) plays on the trick of the knave who had sold him wine instead of water; but he seriously declares that a cistern at Ravenna is more valuable than a vineyard. Sidonius complains that the town is destitute of fountains and aqueducts, and ranks the want of fresh water among the local evils, such as the croaking of frogs, the stinging of gnats, etc.

[62] The fable of Theodore and Honoria, which Dryden has so admirably transplanted from Boccaccio (Giornata iii. novell. viii.) was acted in the wood of *Chiassi,* a corrupt word from *Classis,* the naval station, which, with the intermediate road or suburb, the *Via Cæsaris,* constituted the *triple* city of Ravenna.

[63] From the year 404 the dates of the Theodosian Code became sedentary at Constantinople and Ravenna. See Godefroy's Chronology of the Laws, tom. i. p. cxlviii., etc.

The extensive territory to the north of the great wall was possessed after the flight of the Huns by the victorious Sienpi; who were sometimes broken into independent tribes, and sometimes re-united under a supreme chief; till at length, styling themselves *Topa,* or masters of the earth, they acquired a more solid consistence and a more formidable power. The Topa soon compelled the pastoral nations of the eastern desert to acknowledge the superiority of their arms; they invaded China in a period of weakness and intestine discord; and these fortunate Tartars, adopting the laws and manners of the vanquished people, founded an Imperial dynasty, which reigned near one hundred and sixty years over the northern provinces of the monarchy. Some generations before they ascended the throne of China, one of the Topa princes had enlisted in his cavalry a slave of the name of Moko, renowned for his valour, but who was tempted, by the fear of punishment, to desert his standard, and to range the desert at the head of an hundred followers. This gang of robbers and outlaws swelled into a camp, a tribe, a numerous people, distinguished by the appellation of *Geougen;* and their hereditary chieftains, the posterity of Moko the slave, assumed their rank among the Scythian monarchs. The youth of Toulun, the greatest of his descendants, was exercised by those misfortunes which are the school of heroes. He bravely struggled with adversity, broke the imperious yoke of the Topa, and became the legislator of his nation and the conqueror of Tartary. His troops were distributed into regular bands of an hundred and of a thousand men; cowards were stoned to death; the most splendid honours were proposed as the reward of valour; and Toulun, who had knowledge enough to despise the learning of China, adopted only such arts and institutions as were favourable to the military spirit of his government. His tents, which he removed in the winter season to a more southern latitude, were pitched during the summer on the fruitful banks of the Selinga. His conquests stretched from Corea far beyond the river Irtish. He vanquished, in the country to the north of the Caspian sea, the nation of the *Huns;* and the new title of *Khan,* or *Cagan,* expressed the fame and power which he derived from this memorable victory.[64]

The chain of events is interrupted, or rather is concealed, as it passes from the Volga to the Vistula, through the dark interval which separates the extreme limits of the Chinese and of the Roman geography. Yet the temper of the barbarians, and the experience of successive emigrations, sufficiently declare that the Huns, who were oppressed by the arms of the Geougen, soon withdrew from the presence of an insulting victor. The countries towards the Euxine were already occupied by their kindred tribes; and their hasty flight, which they soon

[64] See M. de Guignes, Hist. des Huns, tom. i. p. 179-189, tom. ii. p. 295, 334-338.

converted into a bold attack, would more naturally be directed towards the rich and level plains through which the Vistula gently flows into the Baltic sea. The North must again have been alarmed and agitated by the invasion of the Huns; and the nations who retreated before them must have pressed with incumbent weight on the confines of Germany.[65] The inhabitants of those regions which the ancients have assigned to the Suevi, the Vandals, and the Burgundians, might embrace the resolution of abandoning to the fugitives of Sarmatia their woods and morasses, or at least of discharging their superfluous numbers on the provinces of the Roman empire.[66] About four years after the victorious Toulun had assumed the title of Khan of the Geougen, another barbarian, the haughty Rhodogast, or Radagaisus,[67] marched from the northern extremities of Germany almost to the gates of Rome, and left the remains of his army to achieve the destruction of the West. The Vandals, the Suevi, and the Burgundians, formed the strength of this mighty host; but the Alani, who had found an hospitable reception in their new seats, added their active cavalry to the heavy infantry of the Germans; and the Gothic adventurers crowded so eagerly to the standard of Radagaisus, that, by some historians, he has been styled the King of the Goths. Twelve thousand warriors, distinguished above the vulgar by their noble birth or their valiant deeds, glittered in the van;[68] and the whole multitude, which was not less than two hundred thousand fighting men, might be increased, by the accession of women, of children, and of slaves, to the amount of four hundred thousand persons. This formidable emigration issued from the same coast of the Baltic which had poured forth the myriads of the Cimbri and Teutones to assault Rome and Italy in the vigour of the republic. After the departure of those barbarians, their native country, which was marked by the vestiges of their greatness, long ramparts and gigantic moles,[69] remained, during some ages, a vast and dreary solitude; till the human species was renewed by the powers of generation, and the vacancy was filled by the influx of new inhabi-

[65] Procopius (de Bell. Vandal. l. i. c. iii. p. 182 [ed. Paris; tom. i. p. 319, ed. Bonn]) has observed an emigration from the Palus Mæotis to the north of Germany, which he ascribes to famine. But his views of ancient history are strangely darkened by ignorance and error.

[66] Zosimus (l. v. [c. 26] p. 331) uses the general description of the nations beyond the Danube and the Rhine. Their situation, and consequently their names, are manifestly shown, even in the various epithets which each ancient writer may have casually added.

[67] The name of Rhadagast was that of a local deity of the Obotrites (in Mecklenburg). A hero might naturally assume the appellation of his tutelar god; but it is not probable that the barbarians should worship an unsuccessful hero. See Mascou, Hist. of the Germans, viii. 14.

[68] Olympiodorus (apud Photium, p. 180 [p. 57, ed. Bekker]) uses the Latin word Ὀπτιμάτοι, which does not convey any precise idea. I suspect that they were the princes and nobles with their faithful companions—the knights with their squires, as they would have been styled some centuries afterwards.

[69] Tacit. de Moribus Germanorum, c. 37.

tants. The nations who now usurp an extent of land which they are unable to cultivate would soon be assisted by the industrious poverty of their neighbours, if the government of Europe did not protect the claims of dominion and property.

The correspondence of nations was in that age so imperfect and precarious, that the revolutions of the North might escape the knowledge of the court of Ravenna, till the dark cloud, which was collected along the coast of the Baltic, burst in thunder upon the banks of the Upper Danube. The emperor of the West, if his ministers disturbed his amusements by the news of the impending danger, was satisfied with being the occasion and the spectator of the war.[70] The safety of Rome was intrusted to the counsels and the sword of Stilicho; but such was the feeble and exhausted state of the empire, that it was impossible to restore the fortifications of the Danube, or to prevent by a vigorous effort the invasion of the Germans.[71] The hopes of the vigilant minister of Honorius were confined to the defence of Italy. He once more abandoned the provinces, recalled the troops, pressed the new levies, which were rigorously exacted and pusillanimously eluded; employed the most efficacious means to arrest or allure the deserters; and offered the gift of freedom and of two pieces of gold to all the slaves who would enlist.[72] By these efforts he painfully collected from the subjects of a great empire an army of thirty or forty thousand men, which, in the days of Scipio or Camillus, would have been instantly furnished by the free citizens of the territory of Rome.[73] The thirty legions of Stilicho were reinforced by a large body of barbarian auxiliaries; the faithful Alani were personally attached to his service; and the troops of Huns and of Goths, who marched under the banners of their native princes Huldin and Sarus, were animated by interest and resentment to oppose the ambition of Radagaisus. The king of the confederate Germans passed without resistance the Alps,

[70] ——— Cujus agendi
Spectator vel causa fui,
Claudian, vi. Cons. Hon. 439,
is the modest language of Honorius, in speaking of the Gothic war, which he had seen somewhat nearer.

[71] Zosimus (l. v. [c. 26] p. 331) transports the war and the victory of Stilicho beyond the Danube. A strange error, which is awkwardly and imperfectly cured by reading "Ἄρνον for "Ἴστρον (Tillemont, Hist. des Emp. tom. v. p. 807). In good policy, we must use the service of Zosimus, without esteeming or trusting him.

[72] Codex Theodos. l. vii. tit. xiii. leg. 16. The date of this law (A.D. 406, May 18) satisfies me, as it had done Godefroy (tom. ii. p. 387), of the true year of the invasion of Radagaisus. Tillemont, Pagi, and Muratori, prefer the preceding year; but they are bound, by certain obligations of civility and respect, to St. Paulinus of Nola.

[73] Soon after Rome had been taken by the Gauls, the senate, on a sudden emergency, armed ten legions, 3000 horse and 42,000 foot—a force which the city could not have sent forth under Augustus (Livy, vii. 25). This declaration may puzzle an antiquary, but it is clearly explained by Montesquieu.

the Po, and the Apennine; leaving on one hand the inaccessible palace
of Honorius securely buried among the marshes of Ravenna, and, on
the other, the camp of Stilicho, who had fixed his head-quarters at
Ticinum, or Pavia, but who seems to have avoided a decisive battle
till he had assembled his distant forces. Many cities of Italy were
pillaged or destroyed; and the siege of Florence [74] by Radagaisus is
one of the earliest events in the history of that celebrated republic,
whose firmness checked and delayed the unskilful fury of the barbarians. The senate and people trembled at their approach within an
hundred and eighty miles of Rome, and anxiously compared the danger which they had escaped with the new perils to which they were
exposed. Alaric was a Christian and a soldier, the leader of a disciplined army; who understood the laws of war, who respected the
sanctity of treaties, and who had familiarly conversed with the subjects of the empire in the same camps and the same churches. The
savage Radagaisus was a stranger to the manners, the religion, and
even the language of the civilised nations of the South. The fierceness
of his temper was exasperated by cruel superstition; and it was universally believed that he had bound himself by a solemn vow to reduce
the city into a heap of stones and ashes, and to sacrifice the most
illustrious of the Roman senators on the altars of those gods who were
appeased by human blood. The public danger, which should have reconciled all domestic animosities, displayed the incurable madness of
religious faction. The oppressed votaries of Jupiter and Mercury respected, in the implacable enemy of Rome, the character of a devout
Pagan; loudly declared that they were more apprehensive of the sacrifices than of the arms of Radagaisus; and secretly rejoiced in the
calamities of their country, which condemned the faith of their Christian adversaries.[75]

Florence was reduced to the last extremity; and the fainting courage
of the citizens was supported only by the authority of St. Ambrose,
who had communicated in a dream the promise of a speedy deliverance.[76] On a sudden they beheld from their walls the banners of
Stilicho, who advanced with his united force to the relief of the faith-

[74] Machiavel has explained, at least as a philosopher, the origin of Florence,
which insensibly descended, for the benefit of trade, from the rock of Fæsulæ
to the banks of the Arno (Istoria Florentina, tom. i. l. ii. p. 36; Londra, 1747).
The triumvirs sent a colony to Florence, which, under Tiberius (Tacit. Annal.
i. 79), deserved the reputation and name of a *flourishing* city. See Culver.
Ital. Antiq. tom. i. p. 507, etc.
[75] Yet the Jupiter of Radagaisus, who worshipped Thor and Woden, was
very different from the Olympic or Capitoline Jove. The accommodating
temper of polytheism might unite those various and remote deities; but the
genuine Romans abhorred the human sacrifices of Gaul and Germany.
[76] Paulinus (in Vit. Ambros. c. 50) relates this story, which he received from
the mouth of Pansophia herself, a religious matron of Florence. Yet the
archbishop soon ceased to take an active part in the business of the world,
and never became a popular saint.

ful city, and who soon marked that fatal spot for the grave of the bar-barian host. The apparent contradictions of those writers who variously relate the defeat of Radagaisus, may be reconciled without offering much violence to their respective testimonies. Orosius and Augus-tin, who were intimately connected by friendship and religion, ascribe this miraculous victory to the providence of God rather than to the valour of man.[77] They strictly exclude every idea of chance, or even of bloodshed, and positively affirm that the Romans, whose camp was the scene of plenty and idleness, enjoyed the distress of the barbarians slowly expiring on the sharp and barren ridge of the hills of Fæsulæ, which rise above the city of Florence. Their extravagant assertion that not a single soldier of the Christian army was killed, or even wounded, may be dismissed with silent contempt; but the rest of the narrative of Augustin and Orosius is consistent with the state of the war and the character of Stilicho. Conscious that he commanded the *last* army of the republic, his prudence would not expose it in the open field to the headstrong fury of the Germans. The method of surrounding the enemy with strong lines of circumvallation, which he had twice em-ployed against the Gothic king, was repeated on a larger scale and with more considerable effect. The examples of Cæsar must have been familiar to the most illiterate of the Roman warriors; and the fortifica-tions of Dyrrachium, which connected twenty-four castles by a per-petual ditch and rampart of fifteen miles, afforded the model of an en-trenchment which might confine and starve the most numerous host of barbarians.[78] The Roman troops had less degenerated from the indus-try than from the valour of their ancestors; and if the servile and laborious work offended the pride of the soldiers, Tuscany could supply many thousand peasants who would labour, though perhaps they would not fight, for the salvation of their native country. The imprisoned multitude of horses and men [79] was gradually destroyed by famine rather than by the sword; but the Romans were exposed during the progress of such an extensive work to the frequent attacks of an im-

---

[77] Augustin de Civitat. Dei. v. 23. Orosius, l. vii. c. 37, p. 567-571. The two friends wrote in Africa ten or twelve years after the victory, and their authority is implicitly followed by Isidore of Seville (in Chron. p. 713, edit. Grot.). How many interesting facts might Orosius have inserted in the vacant space which is devoted to pious nonsense !

[78] Franguntur montes, planumque per ardua Cæsar
　　 Ducit opus: pandit fossas, turritaque summis
　　 Disponit castella jugis, magnoque recessû
　　 Amplexus fines, saltus, nemorosaque tesqua
　　 Et silvas, vastâque feras indagine claudit.

Yet the simplicity of truth (Cæsar, de Bell. Civ. iii. 44) is far greater than the amplifications of Lucan (Pharsal. l. vi. 29-63).

[79] The rhetorical expressions of Orosius, " in arido et aspero montis jugo, " " in unum ac parvum verticem, " are not very suitable to the encampment of a great army. But Fæsulæ, only three miles from Florence, might afford space for the head-quarters of Radagaisus, and would be comprehended within the circuit of the Roman lines.

patient enemy. The despair of the hungry barbarians would precipitate them against the fortifications of Stilicho; the general might sometimes indulge the ardour of his brave auxiliaries, who eagerly pressed
to assault the camp of the Germans; and these various incidents might
produce the sharp and bloody conflicts which dignify the narrative of
Zosimus and the Chronicles of Prosper and Marcellinus.[80] A seasonable supply of men and provisions had been introduced into the walls
of Florence, and the famished host of Radagaisus was in its turn besieged. The proud monarch of so many warlike nations, after the
loss of his bravest warriors, was reduced to confide either in the faith
of a capitulation, or in the clemency of Stilicho.[81] But the death of
the royal captive, who was ignominiously beheaded, disgraced the triumph of Rome and of Christianity; and the short delay of his execution was sufficient to brand the conqueror with the guilt of cool and
deliberate cruelty.[82] The famished Germans who escaped the fury of
the auxiliaries were sold as slaves, at the contemptible price of as
many single pieces of gold; but the difference of food and climate
swept away great numbers of those unhappy strangers; and it was observed that the inhuman purchasers, instead of reaping the fruits of
their labour, were soon obliged to provide the expense of their inter-
ment. Stilicho informed the emperor and the senate of his success,
and deserved a second time the glorious title of Deliverer of Italy.[83]

The fame of the victory, and more especially of the miracle, has
encouraged a vain persuasion that the whole army, or rather nation,
of Germans who migrated from the shores of the Baltic miserably
perished under the walls of Florence. Such indeed was the fate of
Radagaisus himself, of his brave and faithful companions, and of more
than one-third of the various multitude of Sueves and Vandals, of
Alani and Burgundians, who adhered to the standard of their general.[84] The union of such an army might excite our surprise, but the
causes of separation are obvious and forcible: and pride of birth, the
insolence of valour, the jealousy of command, the impatience of subor-

[80] See Zosimus, 1. v. [c. 26] p. 331, and the Chronicles of Prosper and
Marcellinus.
[81] Olympiodorus (apud Photium, p. 180 [p. 57, ed. Bekk.]), uses an expression (προσηταιρίσατο) which would denote a strict and friendly alliance,
and render Stilicho still more criminal. The paulisper retentus, deinde interfectus, of Orosius [p. 570], is sufficiently odious.
[82] Orosius, piously inhuman, sacrifices the king and people—Agag and
the Amalekites—without a symptom of compassion. The bloody actor is less
detestable than the cool, unfeeling historian.
[83] And Claudian's muse, was she asleep? had she been ill-paid? Methinks
the seventh consulship of Honorius (A.D. 407) would have furnished the subject of a noble poem. Before it was discovered that the state could no longer
be saved, Stilicho (after Romulus, Camillus, and Marius) might have been
worthily surnamed the fourth founder of Rome.
[84] A luminous passage of Prosper's Chronicle, "*In tres partes, per diversos
principes, divisus exercitus,*" reduces the miracle of Florence, and connects
the history of Italy, Gaul, and Germany.

dination, and the obstinate conflict of opinions, of interests, and of passions, among so many kings and warriors, who were untaught to yield or to obey. After the defeat of Radagaisus, two parts of the German host, which must have exceeded the number of one hundred thousand men, still remained in arms between the Apennine and the Alps, or between the Alps and the Danube. It is uncertain whether they attempted to revenge the death of their general; but their irregular fury was soon diverted by the prudence and firmness of Stilicho, who opposed their march and facilitated their retreat, who considered the safety of Rome and Italy as the great object of his care, and who sacrificed with too much indifference the wealth and tranquillity of the distant provinces.[85]   The barbarians acquired, from the junction of some Pannonian deserters, the knowledge of the country and of the roads, and the invasion of Gaul, which Alaric had designed, was executed by the remains of the great army of Radagaisus.[86]

Yet if they expected to derive any assistance from the tribes of Germany who inhabited the banks of the Rhine, their hopes were disappointed. The Alemanni preserved a state of inactive neutrality, and the Franks distinguished their zeal and courage in the defence of the empire. In the rapid progress down the Rhine which was the first act of the administration of Stilicho, he had applied himself with peculiar attention to secure the alliance of the warlike Franks, and to remove the irreconcilable enemies of peace and of the republic. Marcomir, one of their kings, was publicly convicted before the tribunal of the Roman magistrate of violating the faith of treaties. He was sentenced to a mild but distant exile in the province of Tuscany; and this degradation of the regal dignity was so far from exciting the resentment of his subjects, that they punished with death the turbulent Sunno, who attempted to revenge his brother, and maintained a dutiful allegiance to the princes who were established on the throne by the choice of Stilicho.[87]   When the limits of Gaul and Germany were

[85] Orosius and Jerom positively charge him with instigating the invasion. "Excitatæ a Stilichone gentes," etc. They must mean *indirectly*. He saved Italy at the expense of Gaul.

[86] The Count de Buat is satisfied that the Germans who invaded Gaul were the *two-thirds* that yet remained of the army of Radagaisus. See the Histoire Ancienne des Peuples de l'Europe (tom. vii. p. 87, 121, Paris, 1772), an elaborate work, which I had not the advantage of perusing till the year 1777. As early as 1771, I find the same idea expressed in a rough draught of the present History. I have since observed a similar intimation in Mascou (viii. 15). Such agreement, without mutual communication, may add some weight to our common sentiment.

[87] —— Provincia missos
Expellet citius fasces, quam Francia reges
Quos dederis.

Claudian (i. Cons. Stil. l. i. 235, etc.) is clear and satisfactory. These kings of France are unknown to Gregory of Tours; but the author of the Gesta Francorum mentions both Sunno and Marcomir, and names the latter as the father of Pharamond (in tom. ii. p. 543). He seems to write from good materials, which he did not understand.

shaken by the northern emigration, the Franks bravely encountered the single force of the Vandals, who, regardless of the lessons of adversity, had again separated their troops from the standard of their barbarian allies. They paid the penalty of their rashness; and twenty thousand Vandals, with their king Godigisclus, were slain in the field of battle. The whole people must have been extirpated if the squadrons of the Alani, advancing to their relief, had not trampled down the infantry of the Franks, who, after an honourable resistance, were compelled to relinquish the unequal contest. The victorious confederates pursued their march, and on the last day of the year, in a season when the waters of the Rhine were most probably frozen, they entered without opposition the defenceless provinces of Gaul. This memorable passage of the Suevi, the Vandals, the Alani, and the Burgundians, who never afterwards retreated, may be considered as the fall of the Roman empire in the countries beyond the Alps; and the barriers, which had so long separated the savage and the civilised nations of the earth, were from that fatal moment levelled with the ground.[88]

While the peace of Germany was secured by the attachment of the Franks and the neutrality of the Alemanni, the subjects of Rome, unconscious of their approaching calamities, enjoyed the state of quiet and prosperity which had seldom blessed the frontiers of Gaul. Their flocks and herds were permitted to graze in the pastures of the barbarians; their huntsmen penetrated, without fear or danger, into the darkest recesses of the Hercynian wood.[89] The banks of the Rhine were crowned, like those of the Tiber, with elegant houses and well-cultivated farms; and if a poet descended the river, he might express his doubt on which side was situated the territory of the Romans.[90] This scene of peace and plenty was suddenly changed into a desert; and the prospect of the smoking ruins could alone distinguish the solitude of nature from the desolation of man. The flourishing city of Mentz was surprised and destroyed, and many thousand Christians were inhumanly massacred in the church. Worms perished after a long and obstinate siege; Strasburg, Spires, Rheims, Tournay, Arras, Amiens, experienced the cruel oppression of the German yoke; and the

[88] See Zosimus (l. vi. [c. 3] p. 373), Orosius (l. vii. c. 40, p. 576), and the Chronicles. Gregory of Tours (l. ii. c. 9, p. 165, in the second volume of the Historians of France) has preserved a valuable fragment of Renatus Profuturus Frigeridus, whose three names denote a Christian, a Roman subject, and a semi-barbarian.

[89] Claudian (i. Cons. Stil. l. i. 221, etc.; l. ii. 186) describes the peace and prosperity of the Gallic frontier. The Abbé Dubos (Hist. Critique, etc., tom. i. p. 174) would read *Alba* (a nameless rivulet of the Ardennes) instead of *Albis;* and expatiates on the danger of the Gallic cattle grazing beyond the *Elbe.* Foolish enough! In poetical geography, the Elbe and the Hercynian signify any river or any wood in Germany. Claudian is not prepared for the strict examination of our antiquaries.

[90] ———Geminasque viator
Cum videat ripas, quæ sit Romana requirat.

consuming flames of war spread from the banks of the Rhine over the greatest part of the seventeen provinces of Gaul. That rich and extensive country, as far as the ocean, the Alps, and the Pyrenees, was delivered to the barbarians, who drove before them in a promiscuous crowd the bishop, the senator, and the virgin, laden with the spoils of their houses and altars.[91] The ecclesiastics, to whom we are indebted for this vague description of the public calamities, embraced the opportunity of exhorting the Christians to repent of the sins which had provoked the Divine Justice, and to renounce the perishable goods of a wretched and deceitful world. But as the Pelagian controversy,[92] which attempts to sound the abyss of grace and predestination, soon became the serious employment of the Latin clergy, the Providence which had decreed, or foreseen, or permitted, such a train of moral and natural evils, was rashly weighed in the imperfect and fallacious balance of reason. The crimes and the misfortunes of the suffering people were presumptuously compared with those of their ancestors, and they arraigned the Divine Justice, which did not exempt from the common destruction, the feeble, the guiltless, the infant portion of the human species. These idle disputants overlooked the invariable laws of nature, which have connected peace with innocence, plenty with industry, and safety with valour. The timid and selfish policy of the court of Ravenna might recall the Palatine legions for the protection of Italy; the remains of the stationary troops might be unequal to the arduous task; and the barbarian auxiliaries might prefer the unbounded licence of spoil to the benefits of a moderate and regular stipend. But the provinces of Gaul were filled with a numerous race of hardy and robust youth, who, in the defence of their houses, their families, and their altars, if they had dared to die, would have deserved to vanquish. The knowledge of their native country would have enabled them to oppose continual and insuperable obstacles to the progress of an invader; and the deficiency of the barbarians in arms as well as in discipline removed the only pretence which excuses the submission of a populous country to the inferior numbers of a veteran army. When France was invaded by Charles the Fifth, he inquired of a prisoner how many *days* Paris might be distant from the frontier; " Perhaps *twelve*, but they will be days of battle:" [93] such was the gallant answer which checked

[91] Jerom, tom. i. p. 93 [Epist. cxxiii. c. 16, tom. i. p. 908, ed. Vallars.]. See, in the first volume of the Historians of France, p. 777, 782, the proper extracts from the Carmen de Providentiâ Divinâ, and Salvian. The anonymous poet was himself a captive, with his bishop and fellow-citizens.

[92] The Pelagian doctrine, which was first agitated A.D. 405, was condemned, in the space of ten years, at Rome and Carthage. St. Augustin fought and conquered; but the Greek church was favourable to his adversaries; and (what is singular enough) the people did not take any part in a dispute which they could not understand.

[93] See the Mémoires de Guillaume du Bellay, l. vi. In French, the original reproof is less obvious and more pointed, from the double sense of the word *journée,* which alike signifies a day's travel or a battle.

THE ROMAN EMPIRE

the arrogance of that ambitious prince. The subjects of Honorius and those of Francis I. were animated by a very different spirit; and in less than two years the divided troops of the savages of the Baltic, whose numbers, were they fairly stated, would appear contemptible, advanced without a combat to the foot of the Pyrenæan mountains.

In the early part of the reign of Honorius, the vigilance of Stilicho had successfully guarded the remote island of Britain from her incessant enemies of the ocean, the mountains, and the Irish coast.[94] But those restless barbarians could not neglect the fair opportunity of the Gothic war, when the walls and stations of the province were stripped of the Roman troops. If any of the legionaries were permitted to return from the Italian expedition, their faithful report of the court and character of Honorius must have tended to dissolve the bounds of allegiance, and to exasperate the seditious temper of the British army. The spirit of revolt, which had formerly disturbed the age of Gallienus, was revived by the capricious violence of the soldiers; and the unfortunate, perhaps the ambitious, candidates, who were the objects of their choice, were the instruments, and at length the victims, of their passion.[95] Marcus was the first whom they placed on the throne, as the lawful emperor of Britain and of the West. They violated, by the hasty murder of Marcus, the oath of fidelity which they had imposed on themselves; and *their* disapprobation of his manners may seem to inscribe an honourable epitaph on his tomb. Gratian was the next whom they adorned with the diadem and the purple; and, at the end of four months, Gratian experienced the fate of his predecessor. The memory of the great Constantine, whom the British legions had given to the church and to the empire, suggested the singular motive of their third choice. They discovered in the ranks a private soldier of the name of Constantine, and their impetuous levity had already seated him on the throne, before they perceived his incapacity to sustain the weight of that glorious appellation.[96] Yet the authority of Constantine was less precarious, and his government was more successful, than the

[94] Claudian (i. Cons. Stil. l. ii. 250). It is supposed that the Scots of Ireland invaded by sea the whole western coast of Britain; and some slight credit may be given even to Nennius and the Irish traditions (Carte's Hist. of England, vol. i, p. 169). Whitaker's Genuine History of the Britons, p. 199. The sixty-six Lives of St. Patrick, which were extant in the ninth century, must have contained as many thousand lies; yet we may believe that, in one of these Irish inroads, the future apostle was led away captive (Usher, Antiquit. Eccles. Britann. p. 431; and Tillemont, Mém. Ecclés. tom. xvi. p. 456, 782, etc.).

[95] The British usurpers are taken from Zosimus (l. vi. [c. 2] p. 371-375), Orosius (l. vii. v. 40, p. 576, 577), Olympiodorus (apud Photium, p. 180, 181 [p. 57, ed. Bekker]), the ecclesiastical historians, and the Chronicles. The Latins are ignorant of Marcus.

[96] Cum in Constantino *inconstantiam* . . . execrarentur (Sidonius Apollinaris, l. v. Epist. 9, p. 139, edit. secund. Sirmond.). Yet Sidonius might be tempted, by so fair a pun, to stigmatise a prince who had disgraced his grandfather.

transient reigns of Marcus and of Gratian. The danger of leaving his inactive troops in those camps which had been twice polluted with blood and sedition urged him to attempt the reduction of the Western provinces. He landed at Boulogne with an inconsiderable force; and after he had reposed himself some days, he summoned the cities of Gaul, which had escaped the yoke of the barbarians, to acknowledge their lawful sovereign. They obeyed the summons without reluctance. The neglect of the court of Ravenna had absolved a deserted people from the duty of allegiance; their actual distress encouraged them to accept any circumstances of change, without apprehension, and, perhaps, with some degree of hope; and they might flatter themselves that the troops, the authority, and even the name of a Roman emperor, who fixed his residence in Gaul, would protect the unhappy country from the rage of the barbarians. The first successes of Constantine against the detached parties of the Germans were magnified by the voice of adulation into splendid and decisive victories, which the re-union and insolence of the enemy soon reduced to their just value. His negotiations procured a short and precarious truce; and if some tribes of the barbarians were engaged, by the liberality of his gifts and promises, to undertake the defence of the Rhine, these expensive and uncertain treaties, instead of restoring the pristine vigour of the Gallic frontier, served only to disgrace the majesty of the prince, and to exhaust what yet remained of the treasures of the republic. Elated however with this imaginary triumph, the vain deliverer of Gaul advanced into the provinces of the South, to encounter a more pressing and personal danger. Sarus the Goth was ordered to lay the head of the rebel at the feet of the emperor Honorius; and the forces of Britain and Italy were unworthily consumed in this domestic quarrel. After the loss of his two bravest generals, Justinian and Nevigastes, the former of whom was slain in the field of battle, the latter in a peaceful but treacherous interview, Constantine fortified himself within the walls of Vienna. The place was ineffectually attacked seven days; and the Imperial army supported, in a precipitate retreat, the ignominy of purchasing a secure passage from the freebooters and outlaws of the Alps.[97] Those mountains now separated the dominions of two rival monarchs: and the fortifications of the double frontier were guarded by the troops of the empire, whose arms would have been more usefully employed to maintain the Roman limits against the barbarians of Germany and Scythia.

On the side of the Pyrenees, the ambition of Constantine might be justified by the proximity of danger; but his throne was soon established by the conquest, or rather submission, of Spain, which yielded to the influence of regular and habitual subordination, and received

[97] *Bagaudæ* is the name which Zosimus applies to them; perhaps they deserved a less odious character (see Dubos, Hist. Critique, tom. i. p. 203). We shall hear of them again.

the laws and magistrates of the Gallic præfecture. The only opposition which was made to the authority of Constantine proceeded not so much from the powers of government, or the spirit of the people, as from the private zeal and interest of the family of Theodosius. Four brothers [98] had obtained, by the favour of their kinsman, the deceased emperor, an honourable rank, and ample possessions, in their native country; and the grateful youths resolved to risk those advantages in the service of his son. After an unsuccessful effort to maintain their ground at the head of the stationary troops of Lusitania, they retired to their estates; where they armed and levied, at their own expense, a considerable body of slaves and dependents, and boldly marched to occupy the strong posts of the Pyrenæan mountains. This domestic insurrection alarmed and perplexed the sovereign of Gaul and Britain; and he was compelled to negotiate with some troops of barbarian auxiliaries, for the service of the Spanish war. They were distinguished by the title of *Honorians;* [99] a name which might have reminded them of their fidelity to their lawful sovereign; and if it should candidly be allowed that the *Scots* were influenced by any partial affection for a British prince, the *Moors* and the *Marcomanni* could be tempted only by the profuse liberality of the usurper, who distributed among the barbarians the military, and even the civil, honours of Spain. The nine bands of *Honorians,* which may be easily traced on the establishment of the Western empire, could not exceed the number of five thousand men; yet this inconsiderable force was sufficient to terminate a war which had threatened the power and safety of Constantine. The rustic army of the Theodosian family was surrounded and destroyed in the Pyrenees: two of the brothers had the good fortune to escape by sea to Italy or the East; the other two, after an interval of suspense, were executed at Arles; and if Honorius could remain insensible of the public disgrace, he might perhaps be affected by the personal misfortunes of his generous kinsmen. Such were the feeble arms which decided the possession of the Western provinces of Europe, from the wall of Antoninus to the Columns of Hercules. The events of peace and war have undoubtedly been diminished by the narrow and imperfect view of the historians of the times, who were equally ignorant of the causes and of the effects of the most important revolutions. But the total decay of the national strength had annihilated even the last resource of a despotic government; and the revenue of exhausted pro-

[98] Verinianus, Didymus, Theodosius, and Lagodius, who in modern courts would be styled princes of the blood, were not distinguished by any rank or privileges above the rest of their fellow-subjects.

[99] These *Honoriani* or *Honoriaci* consisted of two bands of Scots or Attacotti, two of Moors, two of Marcomanni, the Victores, the Ascarii, and the Gallicani (Notitia Imperii, sect. xxxviii. edit. Lab.). They were part of the sixty-five *Auxilia Palatina,* and are properly styled ἐν τῇ αὐλῇ τάξεις by Zosimus (l. vi. [c. 4] p. 374).

vinces could no longer purchase the military service of a discontented and pusillanimous people.

The poet, whose flattery has ascribed to the Roman eagle the victories of Pollentia and Verona, pursues the hasty retreat of Alaric from the confines of Italy, with a horrid train of imaginary spectres, such as might hover over an army of barbarians which was almost exterminated by war, famine, and disease.[100]   In the course of this unfortunate expedition, the king of the Goths must indeed have sustained a considerable loss; and his harassed forces required an interval of repose to recruit their numbers and revive their confidence.   Adversity had exercised and displayed the genius of Alaric; and the fame of his valour invited to the Gothic standard the bravest of the barbarian warriors, who, from the Euxine to the Rhine, were agitated by the desire of rapine and conquest.   He had deserved the esteem, and he soon accepted the friendship, of Stilicho himself.   Renouncing the service of the emperor of the East, Alaric concluded, with the court of Ravenna, a treaty of peace and alliance, by which he was declared master-general of the Roman armies throughout the præfecture of Illyricum; as it was claimed, according to the true and ancient limits, by the minister of Honorius.[101]   The execution of the ambitious design, which was either stipulated or implied in the articles of the treaty, appears to have been suspended by the formidable irruption of Radagaisus; and the neutrality of the Gothic king may perhaps be compared to the indifference of Cæsar, who, in the conspiracy of Catiline, refused either to assist or to oppose the enemy of the republic.   After the defeat of the Vandals, Stilicho resumed his pretensions to the provinces of the East; appointed civil magistrates for the administration of justice and of the finances; and declared his impatience to lead to the gates of Constantinople the united armies of the Romans and of the Goths.   The prudence, however, of Stilicho, his aversion to civil war, and his perfect knowledge of the weakness of the state, may countenance the suspicion that domestic peace, rather than foreign conquest, was the object of his policy; and that his principal care was to employ the forces of Alaric at a distance from Italy.   This design could not long escape the penetration of the Gothic king, who continued to hold a doubtful, and perhaps a treacherous, correspondence with the rival courts; who protracted, like a dissatisfied mercenary, his languid operations of Thessaly and Epirus; and who soon returned to claim the extravagant reward of his ineffectual services.   From his camp near

[100] ——— Comitantur euntem
Pallor, et atra Fames; et saucia lividus ora
Luctus; et inferno stridentes agmine Morbi.
                    Claudian in vi. Cons. Hon. 321, etc.
[101] These dark transactions are investigated by the Count de Buat (Hist. des Peuples de l'Europe, tom. vii. c. iii.-viii. p. 69-206), whose laborious accuracy may sometimes fatigue a superficial reader.

Æmona,[102] on the confines of Italy, he transmitted to the emperor of
the West a long account of promises, of expenses, and of demands;
called for immediate satisfaction, and clearly intimated the consequences of a refusal. Yet, if his conduct was hostile, his language was
decent and dutiful. He humbly protessed himself the friend of Stilicho, and the soldier of Honorius; offered his person and his troops to
march, without delay, against the usurper of Gaul; and solicited, as
a permanent retreat for the Gothic nation, the possession of some
vacant province of the Western empire.

The political and secret transactions of two statesmen who laboured
to deceive each other and the world must for ever have been concealed
in the impenetrable darkness of the cabinet, if the debates of a popular
assembly had not thrown some rays of light on the correspondence of
Alaric and Stilicho. The necessity of finding some artificial support
for a government which, from a principle, not of moderation, but of
weakness, was reduced to negotiate with its own subjects, had insensibly revived the authority of the Roman senate: and the minister of
Honorius respectfully consulted the legislative council of the republic.
Stilicho assembled the senate in the palace of the Cæsars; represented,
in a studied oration, the actual state of affairs; proposed the demands
of the Gothic king; and submitted to their consideration the choice of
peace or war. The senators, as if they had been suddenly awakened
from a dream of four hundred years, appeared on this important occasion to be inspired by the courage, rather than by the wisdom, of their
predecessors. They loudly declared, in regular speeches or in tumultuary acclamations, that it was unworthy of the majesty of Rome to
purchase a precarious and disgraceful truce from a barbarian king;
and that, in the judgment of a magnanimous people, the chance of ruin
was always preferable to the certainty of dishonour. The minister,
whose pacific intentions were seconded only by the voices of a few
servile and venal followers, attempted to allay the general ferment, by
an apology for his own conduct, and even for the demands of the
Gothic prince. " The payment of a subsidy, which had excited the
indignation of the Romans, ought not (such was the language of Stilicho) to be considered in the odious light either of a tribute or of a
ransom, extorted by the menaces of a barbarian enemy. Alaric had
faithfully asserted the just pretensions of the republic to the provinces
which were usurped by the Greeks of Constantinople: he modestly required the fair and stipulated recompense of his services; and if he
had desisted from the prosecution of his enterprise, he had obeyed, in
his retreat, the peremptory, though private, letters of the emperor him-

[102] See Zosimus, l. v. [c. 29] p. 334, 335. He interrupts his scanty narrative
to relate the fable of Æmona, and of the ship Argo, which was drawn overland from that place to the Hadriatic. Sozomen (l. viii. c. 25; l. ix. c. 4) and
Socrates (l. vii. c. 10) cast a pale and doubtful light, and Orosius (l. vii. c.
38, p. 571) is abominably partial.

self. These contradictory orders (he would not dissemble the errors of his own family) had been procured by the intercession of Serena. The tender piety of his wife had been too deeply affected by the discord of the royal brothers, the sons of her adopted father; and the sentiments of nature had too easily prevailed over the stern dictates of the public welfare." These ostensible reasons, which faintly disguise the obscure intrigues of the palace of Ravenna, were supported by the authority of Stilicho; and obtained, after a warm debate, the reluctant approbation of the senate. The tumult of virtue and freedom subsided; and the sum of four thousand pounds of gold was granted, under the name of a subsidy, to secure the peace of Italy, and to conciliate the friendship of the king of the Goths. Lampadius alone, one of the most illustrious members of the assembly, still persisted in his dissent; exclaimed with a loud voice, " This is not a treaty of peace, but of servitude;" [103] and escaped the danger of such bold opposition by immediately retiring to the sanctuary of a Christian church.

But the reign of Stilicho drew towards its end; and the proud minister might perceive the symptoms of his approaching disgrace. The generous boldness of Lampadius had been applauded; and the senate, so patiently resigned to a long servitude, rejected with disdain the offer of invidious and imaginary freedom. The troops, who still assumed the name and prerogatives of the Roman legions, were exasperated by the partial affection of Stilicho for the barbarians: and the people imputed to the mischievous policy of the minister the public misfortunes, which were the natural consequence of their own degeneracy. Yet Stilicho might have continued to brave the clamours of the people, and even of the soldiers, if he could have maintained his dominion over the feeble mind of his pupil. But the respectful attachment of Honorius was converted into fear, suspicion, and hatred. The crafty Olympius,[104] who concealed his vices under the mask of Christian piety, had secretly undermined the benefactor by whose favour he was promoted to the honourable offices of the Imperial palace. Olympius revealed to the unsuspecting emperor, who had attained the twenty-fifth year of his age, that he was without weight or authority in his own government; and artfully alarmed his timid and indolent disposition by a lively picture of the designs of Stilicho, who already

[103] Zosimus, l. v. [c. 29] p. 338, 339. He repeats the words of Lampadius as they were spoken in Latin, " Non est ista pax, sed pactio servitutis," and then translates them into Greek for the benefit of his readers.

[104] He came from the coast of the Euxine, and exercised a splendid office, λαμπρᾶς δὲ στρατείας ἐν τοῖς βασιλείοις ἠξιωμένος. His actions justify his character, which Zosimus (l. v. [c. 32] p. 340) exposes with visible satisfaction. Augustin revered the piety of Olympius, whom he styles a true son of the church (Baronius, Annal. Eccles. A.D. 408, No. 19, etc.; Tillemont, Mém. Eccles. tom. xiii. p. 467, 468). But these praises, which the African saint so unworthily bestows, might proceed as well from ignorance as from adulation.

meditated the death of his sovereign, with the ambitious hope of placing the diadem on the head of his son Eucherius. The emperor was
instigated by his new favourite to assume the tone of independent dignity; and the minister was astonished to find that secret resolutions
were formed in the court and council, which were repugnant to his
interest, or to his intentions. Instead of residing in the palace of
Rome, Honorius declared that it was his pleasure to return to the
secure fortress of Ravenna. On the first intelligence of the death of
his brother Arcadius, he prepared to visit Constantinople, and to regulate, with the authority of a guardian, the provinces of the infant
Theodosius.[105] The representation of the difficulty and expense of
such a distant expedition checked this strange and sudden sally of
active diligence; but the dangerous project of showing the emperor
to the camp of Pavia, which was composed of the Roman troops, the
enemies of Stilicho and his barbarian auxiliaries, remained fixed and
unalterable. The minister was pressed, by the advice of his confidant,
Justinian, a Roman advocate, of a lively and penetrating genius, to
oppose a journey so prejudicial to his reputation and safety. His
strenuous, but ineffectual, efforts confirmed the triumph of Olympius;
and the prudent lawyer withdrew himself from the impending ruin of
his patron.

In the passage of the emperor through Bologna a mutiny of the
guards was excited and appeased by the secret policy of Stilicho, who
announced his instructions to decimate the guilty, and ascribed to his
own intercession the merit of their pardon. After this tumult, Honorius
embraced, for the last time, the minister whom he now considered as a
tyrant, and proceeded on his way to the camp of Pavia, where he was
received by the loyal acclamations of the troops who were assembled
for the service of the Gallic war. On the morning of the fourth day he
pronounced, as he had been taught, a military oration in the presence
of the soldiers, whom the charitable visits and artful discourses of
Olympius had prepared to execute a dark and bloody conspiracy. At
the first signal they massacred the friends of Stilicho, the most illustrious officers of the empire; two Prætorian præfects, of Gaul and of
Italy; two masters-general of the cavalry and infantry; the master of
the offices, the quæstor, the treasurer, and the count of the domestics.
Many lives were lost, many houses were plundered; the furious sedition
continued to rage till the close of the evening; and the trembling emperor, who was seen in the streets of Pavia without his robes or diadem,
yielded to the persuasions of his favourite, condemned the memory of
the slain, and solemnly approved the innocence and fidelity of their
assassins. The intelligence of the massacre of Pavia filled the mind of

[105] Zosimus, 1. v. [c. 31] p. 338, 339. Sozomen, 1. ix. c. 4. Stilicho offered
to undertake the journey to Constantinople, that he might divert Honorius
from the vain attempt. The Eastern empire would not have obeyed, and
could not have been conquered.

Stilicho with just and gloomy apprehensions, and he instantly summoned, in the camp of Bologna, a council of the confederate leaders who were attached to his service, and would be involved in his ruin. The impetuous voice of the assembly called aloud for arms and for revenge; to march, without a moment's delay, under the banners of a hero whom they had so often followed to victory; to surprise, to oppress, to extirpate the guilty Olympius and his degenerate Romans, and perhaps to fix the diadem on the head of their injured general. Instead of executing a resolution which might have been justified by success, Stilicho hesitated till he was irrecoverably lost. He was still ignorant of the fate of the emperor; he distrusted the fidelity of his own party; and he viewed with horror the fatal consequences of arming a crowd of licentious barbarians against the soldiers and people of Italy. The confederates, impatient of his timorous and doubtful delay, hastily retired with fear and indignation. At the hour of midnight Sarus, a Gothic warrior, renowned among the barbarians themselves for his strength and valour, suddenly invaded the camp of his benefactor, plundered the baggage, cut in pieces the faithful Huns who guarded his person, and penetrated to the tent, where the minister, pensive and sleepless, meditated on the dangers of his situation. Stilicho escaped with difficulty from the sword of the Goths, and after issuing a last and generous admonition to the cities of Italy to shut their gates against the barbarians, his confidence or his despair urged him to throw himself into Ravenna, which was already in the absolute possession of his enemies. Olympius, who had assumed the dominion of Honorius, was speedily informed that his rival had embraced, as a suppliant, the altar of the Christian church. The base and cruel disposition of the hypocrite was incapable of pity or remorse; but he piously affected to elude, rather than to violate, the privilege of the sanctuary. Count Heraclian, with a troop of soldiers, appeared at the dawn of day before the gates of the church of Ravenna. The bishop was satisfied by a solemn oath that the Imperial mandate only directed them to secure the person of Stilicho: but as soon as the unfortunate minister had been tempted beyond the holy threshold, he produced the warrant for his instant execution. Stilicho supported with calm resignation the injurious names of traitor and parricide; repressed the unseasonable zeal of his followers, who were ready to attempt an ineffectual rescue; and, with a firmness not unworthy of the last of the Roman generals, submitted his neck to the sword of Heraclian.[106]

The servile crowd of the palace, who had so long adored the fortune of Stilicho, affected to insult his fall; and the most distant connection

[106] Zosimus (l. v. [c. 30, sqq.] p. 336-345) has copiously, though not clearly, related the disgrace and death of Stilicho. Olympiodorus (apud Phot. p. 177 [p. 56, ed. Bekker]), Orosius (l. vii. c. 38, p. 571, 572), Sozomen (l. ix. c. 4), and Philostorgius (l. xi. c. 3, l. xii. c. 2), afford supplemental hints.

with the master-general of the West, which had so lately been a title to wealth and honours, was studiously denied, and rigorously punished. His family, united by a triple alliance with the family of Theodosius, might envy the condition of the meanest peasant. The flight of his son Eucherius was intercepted; and the death of that innocent youth soon followed the divorce of Thermantia, who filled the place of her sister Maria, and who, like Maria, had remained a virgin in the Imperial bed.[107] The friends of Stilicho who had escaped the massacre of Pavia were persecuted by the implacable revenge of Olympius, and the most exquisite cruelty was employed to extort the confession of a treasonable and sacrilegious conspiracy. They died in silence; their firmness justified the choice,[108] and perhaps absolved the innocence, of their patron; and the despotic power which could take his life without a trial, and stigmatise his memory without a proof, has no jurisdiction over the impartial suffrage of posterity.[109] The services of Stilicho are great and manifest; his crimes, as they are vaguely stated in the language of flattery and hatred, are obscure, at least, and improbable. About four months after his death an edict was published, in the name of Honorius, to restore the free communication of the two empires, which had been so long interrupted by the *public enemy*.[110] The minister, whose fame and fortune depended on the prosperity of the state, was accused of betraying Italy to the barbarians, whom he repeatedly vanquished at Pollentia, at Verona, and before the walls of Florence. His pretended design of placing the diadem on the head of his son Eucherius could not have been conducted without preparations or accomplices; and the ambitious father would not surely have left the future emperor, till the twentieth year of his age, in the humble station of tribune of the notaries. Even the religion of Stilicho was arraigned by the malice of his rival. The seasonable, and almost miraculous, deliverance was devoutly celebrated by the applause of the clergy, who asserted that the restoration of idols and the persecution of the church would have been the first measure of the reign of Eucherius. The son of Stilicho, however, was educated in the bosom of Christianity, which his father

[107] Zosimus, 1. v. [c. 28] p. 333. The marriage of a Christian with two sisters scandalises Tillemont (Hist. des Empereurs, tom. v. p. 557), who expects, in vain, that Pope Innocent I. should have done something in the way either of censure or of dispensation.

[108] Two of his friends are honourably mentioned (Zosimus, 1. v. [c. 35] p. 346)—Peter, chief of the school of notaries, and the great chamberlain Deuterius. Stilicho had secured the bedchamber; and it is surprising that, under a feeble prince, the bedchamber was not able to secure him.

[109] Orosius (1. vii. c. 38, p. 571, 572) seems to copy the false and furious manifestos which were dispersed through the provinces by the new administration.

[110] See the Theodosian Code, 1. vii. tit. xvi. leg. 1; 1. ix. tit. xlii. leg. 22. Stilicho is branded with the name of *prædo publicus*, who employed his wealth *ad omnem ditandam, inquietandamque Barbariem.*

had uniformly professed and zealously supported.[111]   Serena had borrowed her magnificent necklace from the statue of Vesta;[112] and the Pagans execrated the memory of the sacrilegious minister, by whose order the Sibylline books, the oracles of Rome, had been committed to the flames.[113]   The pride and power of Stilicho constituted his real guilt.   An honourable reluctance to shed the blood of his countrymen appears to have contributed to the success of his unworthy rival; and it is the last humiliation of the character of Honorius, that posterity has not condescended to reproach him with his base ingratitude to the guardian of his youth and the support of his empire.

Among the train of dependents whose wealth and dignity attracted the notice of their own times, *our* curiosity is excited by the celebrated name of the poet Claudian, who enjoyed the favour of Stilicho, and was overwhelmed in the ruin of his patron.   The titular offices of tribune and notary fixed his rank in the Imperial court: he was indebted to the powerful intercession of Serena for his marriage with a rich heiress of the province of Africa;[114] and the statue of Claudian, erected in the forum of Trajan, was a monument of the taste and liberality of the Roman senate.[115]   After the praises of Stilicho became offensive and criminal, Claudian was exposed to the enmity of a powerful and unforgiving courtier whom he had provoked by the insolence of wit.   He had compared, in a lively epigram, the opposite characters of two Prætorian præfects of Italy; he contrasts the innocent repose of a philosopher, who sometimes resigned the hours of business to slumber, perhaps to study, with the interested diligence of a rapacious minister, indefatigable in the pursuit of unjust or sacrilegious gain.   " How happy," continues Claudian, " how happy might it be for the people of Italy if Mallius

[111] Augustin himself is satisfied with the effectual laws which Stilicho had enacted against heretics and idolaters, and which are still extant in the Code. He only applies to Olympius for their confirmation (Baronius, Annal. Eccles. A.D. 408, No. 19).

[112] Zosimus, l. v. [c. 38] p. 351.   We may observe the bad taste of the age, in dressing their statues with such awkward finery.

[113] See Rutilius Numatianus (Itinerar. l. ii. 41-60), to whom religious enthusiasm has dictated some elegant and forcible lines.   Stilicho likewise stripped the gold plates from the doors of the Capitol, and read a prophetic sentence which was engraven under them (Zosimus, l. v. [c. 38] p. 352). These are foolish stories; yet the charge of *impiety* adds weight and credit to the praise, which Zosimus reluctantly bestows, of his virtues.

[114] At the nuptials of Orpheus (a modest comparison!) all the parts of animated nature contributed their various gifts, and the gods themselves enriched their favourite.   Claudian had neither flocks, nor herds, nor vines, nor olives.   His wealthy bride was heiress to them all.   But he carried to Africa a recommendatory letter from Serena, his Juno, and was made happy (Epist. ii. ad Serenam).

[115] Claudian feels the honour like a man who deserved it (in præfat. Bell. Get.).   The original inscription, on marble, was found at Rome, in the fifteenth century, in the house of Pomponius Lætus.   The statue of a poet, far superior to Claudian, should have been erected, during his lifetime, by the men of letters, his countrymen and contemporaries.   It was a noble design.

could be constantly awake, and if Hadrian would always sleep! " [116]
The repose of Mallius was not disturbed by this friendly and gentle
admonition; but the cruel vigilance of Hadrian watched the opportunity
of revenge, and easily obtained from the enemies of Stilicho the trifling
sacrifice of an obnoxious poet. The poet concealed himself, however,
during the tumult of the revolution, and, consulting the dictates of
prudence rather than of honour, he addressed, in the form of an epistle,
a suppliant and humble recantation to the offended præfect. He deplores, in mournful strains, the fatal indiscretion into which he had been
hurried by passion and folly; submits to the imitation of his adversary
the generous examples of the clemency of gods, of heroes, and of lions;
and expresses his hope that the magnanimity of Hadrian will not trample
on a defenseless and contemptible foe, already humbled by disgrace and
poverty, and deeply wounded by the exile, the tortures, and the death
of his dearest friends. [117] Whatever might be the success of his prayer or
the accidents of his future life, the period of a few years levelled in the
grave the minister and the poet: but the name of Hadrian is almost sunk
in oblivion, while Claudian is read with pleasure in every country which
has retained or acquired the knowledge of the Latin language. If we
fairly balance his merits and his defects, we shall acknowledge that
Claudian does not either satisfy or silence our reason. It would not be
easy to produce a passage that deserves the epithet of sublime or
pathetic; to select a verse that melts the heart or enlarges the imagination. We should vainly seek in the poems of Claudian the happy invention and artificial conduct of an interesting fable, or the just and
lively representation of the characters and situations of real life. For
the service of his patron he published occasional panegyrics and invectives, and the design of these slavish compositions encouraged his propensity to exceed the limits of truth and nature. These imperfections,
however, are compensated in some degree by the poetical virtues of
Claudian. He was endowed with the rare and precious talent of raising
the meanest, of adoring the most barren, and of diversifying the most
similar topics; his colouring, more especially in descriptive poetry, is
soft and splendid; and he seldom fails to display, and even to abuse, the
advantages of a cultivated understanding, a copious fancy, an easy and
sometimes forcible expression, and a perpetual flow of harmonious

[116] See Epigram xxx. :—
> Mallius indulget somno noctesque diesque:
> Insomnis *Pharius* sacra, profana, rapit.
> Omnibus, hoc, Italæ gentes, exposcite votis,
> Mallius ut vigilet, dormiat ut Pharius.

Hadrian was a Pharian (of Alexandria). See his public life in Godefroy,
Cod. Theodos. tom. vi. p. 364. Maliius did not always sleep. He composed
some elegant dialogues on the Greek systems of natural philosophy (Claud.
in Mall. Theodor. Cons. 61-112).

[117] See Claudian's first Epistle. Yet in some places an air of irony and in'
dignation betrays his secret reluctance.

versification. To these commendations, independent of any accidents of time and place, we must add the peculiar merit which Claudian derived from the unfavourable circumstances of his birth. In the decline of arts and of empire, a native of Egypt,[118] who had received the education of a Greek, assumed in a mature age the familiar use and absolute command of the Latin language;[119] soared above the heads of his feeble contemporaries; and placed himself, after an interval of three hundred years, among the poets of ancient Rome.[120]

CHAPTER XXXI (408-449 A.D.)

Invasion of Italy by Alaric—Manners of the Roman Senate and People—Rome is thrice besieged, and at length pillaged, by the Goths—Death of Alaric —The Goths evacuate Italy—Fall of Constantine—Gaul and Spain are occupied by the Barbarians—Independence of Britain

THE incapacity of a weak and distracted government may often assume the appearance and produce the effects of a treasonable correspondence with the public enemy. If Alaric himself had been introduced into the council of Ravenna, he would probably have advised the same measures which were actually pursued by the ministers of Honorius.[1] The king of the Goths would have conspired, perhaps with some reluctance, to destroy the formidable adversary by whose arms, in Italy as well as in Greece, he had been twice overthrown. *Their* active and interested hatred laboriously accomplished the disgrace and ruin of the great Stilicho. The valour of Sarus, his fame in arms, and his personal or hereditary influence over the confederate barbarians, could recommend him only to the friends of their country who despised or detested the worthless characters of Turpilio, Varanes, and Vigilantius. By the pressing instances of the new favourites, these generals, unworthy as

[118] National vanity has made him a Florentine, or a Spaniard. But the first Epistle of Claudian proves him a native of Alexandria (Fabricius, Biblioth. Latin. tom. iii. p. 191-202, edit. Ernest.).

[119] His first Latin verses were composed during the consulship of Probinus, A.D. 395:—

Romanos bibimus primum, te consule, fontes,
    Et Latiæ cessit Graia Thalia togæ.

Besides some Greek epigrams, which are still extant, the Latin poet had composed, in Greek, the Antiquities of Tarsus, Anazarbus, Berytus, Nice, etc. It is more easy to supply the loss of good poetry than of authentic history.

[120] Strada (Prolusion v. vi.) allows him to contend with the five heroic poets, Lucretius, Virgil, Ovid, Lucan, and Statius. His patron is the accomplished courtier Balthazar Castiglione. His admirers are numerous and passionate. Yet the rigid critics reproach the exotic weeds or flowers which spring too luxuriantly in his Latian soil.

[1] The series of events, from the death of Stilicho to the arrival of Alaric before Rome, can only be found in Zosimus, l. v. [c. 35-37] p. 347-350.

they had shown themselves of the name of soldiers,[2] were promoted to the command of the cavalry, of the infantry, and of the domestic troops. The Gothic prince would have subscribed with pleasure the edict which the fanaticism of Olympius dictated to the simple and devout emperor. Honorius excluded all persons who were adverse to the catholic church from holding any office in the state; obstinately rejected the service of all those who dissented from his religion; and rashly disqualified many of his bravest and most skilful officers who adhered to the Pagan worship or who had imbibed the opinions of Arianism.[3] These measures, so advantageous to an enemy, Alaric would have approved, and might perhaps have suggested; but it may seem doubtful whether the barbarian would have promoted his interest at the expense of the inhuman and absurd cruelty which was perpetrated by the direction, or at least with the connivance, of the Imperial ministers. The foreign auxiliaries who had been attached to the person of Stilicho lamented his death; but the desire of revenge was checked by a natural apprehension for the safety of their wives and children, who were detained as hostages in the strong cities of Italy, where they had likewise deposited their most valuable effects. At the same hour, and as if by a common signal, the cities of Italy were polluted by the same horrid scenes of universal massacre and pillage, which involved in promiscuous destruction the families and fortunes of the barbarians. Exasperated by such an injury, which might have awakened the tamest and most servile spirit, they cast a look of indignation and hope towards the camp of Alaric, and unanimously swore to pursue with just and implacable war the perfidious nation that had so basely violated the laws of hospitality. By the imprudent conduct of the ministers of Honorius the republic lost the assistance, and deserved the enmity, of thirty thousand of her bravest soldiers; and the weight of that formidable army, which alone might have determined the event of the war, was transferred from the scale of the Romans into that of the Goths.

In the arts of negotiation, as well as in those of war, the Gothic king maintained his superior ascendant over an enemy whose seeming changes proceeded from the total want of counsel and design. From his camp, on the confines of Italy, Alaric attentively observed the revolutions of the palace, watched the progress of faction and discontent, disguised the hostile aspect of a barbarian invader, and assumed the more popular appearance of the friend and ally of the great Stilicho; to whose virtues, when they were no longer formidable, he could pay a just tribute of

---

[2] The expression of Zosimus is strong and lively, καταφρόνησιν ἐμποιῆσαι τοῖς πολεμίοις ἀρκοῦντας, sufficient to excite the contempt of the enemy.

[3] Eos qui catholicæ sectæ sunt inimici, intra palatium militare prohibemus. Nullus nobis sit aliquâ ratione conjunctus, qui a nobis fide et religione discordat. Cod. Theodos, 1. xvi. tit. v. leg. 42, and Godefroy's Commentary, tom. vi. p. 164. This law was applied in the utmost latitude and rigorously executed. Zosimus, l. v. [c. 46] p. 364.

sincere praise and regret. The pressing invitation of the malcontents, who urged the king of the Goths to invade Italy, was enforced by a lively sense of his personal injuries; and he might speciously complain that the Imperial ministers still delayed and eluded the payment of the four thousand pounds of gold which had been granted by the Roman senate either to reward his services or to appease his fury. His decent firmness was supported by an artful moderation, which contributed to the success of his designs. He required a fair and reasonable satisfaction; but he gave the strongest assurances that, as soon as he had obtained it, he would immediately retire. He refused to trust the faith of the Romans, unless Aëtius and Jason, the sons of two great officers of state, were sent as hostages to his camp: but he offered to deliver in exchange several of the noblest youths of the Gothic nation. The modesty of Alaric was interpreted by the ministers of Ravenna as a sure evidence of his weakness and fear. They disdained either to negotiate a treaty or to assemble an army; and with a rash confidence, derived only from their ignorance of the extreme danger, irretrievably wasted the decisive moments of peace and war. While they expected, in sullen silence, that the bar- barians should evacuate the confines of Italy, Alaric, with bold and rapid marches, passed the Alps and the Po; hastily pillaged the cities of Aquileia, Altinum, Concordia, and Cremona, which yielded to his arms; increased his forces by the accession of thirty thousand auxiliaries; and, without meeting a single enemy in the field, advanced as far as the edge of the morass which protected the impregnable residence of the emperor of the West. Instead of attempting the hopeless siege of Ravenna, the prudent leader of the Goths proceeded to Rimini, stretched his ravages along the sea-coast of the Hadriatic, and meditated the conquest of the ancient mistress of the world. An Italian hermit, whose zeal and sanctity were respected by the barbarians themselves, encountered the victorious monarch, and boldly denounced the indignation of Heaven against the oppressors of the earth: but the saint himself was confounded by the solemn asseveration of Alaric that he felt a secret and præter- natural impulse, which directed, and even compelled, his march to the gates of Rome. He felt that his genius and his fortune were equal to the most arduous enterprises; and the enthusiasm which he communi- cated to the Goths insensibly removed the popular and almost supersti- tious reverence of the nations for the majesty of the Roman name. His troops, animated by the hopes of spoil, followed the course of the Flaminian way, occupied the unguarded passes of the Apennine,[4] de- scended into the rich plains of Umbria; and, as they lay encamped on the banks of the Clitumnus, might wantonly slaughter and devour the

---

Addison (see his Works, vol. ii. p. 54, edit. Baskerville) has given a very picturesque description of the road through the Apennine. The Goths were not at leisure to observe the beauties of the prospect; but they were pleased to find that the Saxa Intercisa, a narrow passage which Vespasian had cut through the rock (Cluver. Italia Antiq. tom. i. p. 618), was totally neglected.

milk-white oxen which had been so long reserved for the use of Roman triumphs.[5] A lofty situation and a seasonable tempest of thunder and lightning preserved the little city of Narni: but the king of the Goths, despising the ignoble prey, still advanced with unabated vigour; and after he had passed through the stately arches, adorned with the spoils of barbaric victories, he pitched his camp under the walls of Rome.[6]

During a period of six hundred and nineteen years the seat of empire had never been violated by the presence of a foreign enemy. The unsuccessful expedition of Hannibal [7] served only to display the character of the senate and people; of a senate degraded, rather than ennobled, by the comparison of an assembly of kings; and of a people to whom the ambassador of Pyrrhus ascribed the inexhaustible resources of the Hydra.[8] Each of the senators in the time of the Punic war had accomplished his term of military service, either in a subordinate or a superior station; and the decree which invested with temporary command all those who had been consuls, or censors, or dictators, gave the republic the immediate assistance of many brave and experienced generals. In the beginning of the war the Roman people consisted of two hundred and fifty thousand citizens of an age to bear arms.[9] Fifty thousand had already died in the defence of their country; and the twenty-three legions which were employed in the different camps of Italy, Greece, Sardinia, Sicily, and Spain, required about one hundred thousand men. But there

[5] Hinc albi, Clitumne, Greges, et maxima taurus
Victima sæpe, tuo perfusi flumine sacro,
Romanos ad templa Deum duxere triumphos.
Georg. ii. 147.
Besides Virgil, most of the Latin poets, Propertius, Lucan, Silius Italicus, Claudian, etc., whose passages may be found in Cluverius and Addison, have celebrated the triumphal victims of Clitumnus.

[6] Some ideas of the march of Alaric are borrowed from the journey of Honorius over the same ground (see Claudian in vi. Cons. Hon. 494-522). The measured distance between Ravenna and Rome was 254 Roman miles. Itinerar. Wesseling, p. 126.

[7] The march and retreat of Hannibal are described by Livy, l. xxvi. c. 7, 8, 9, 10, 11; and the reader is made a spectator of the interesting scene.

[8] These comparisons were used by Cineas, the counsellor of Pyrrhus, after his return from his embassy, in which he had diligently studied the discipline and manners of Rome. See Plutarch in Pyrrho [c. 19], tom. ii. p. 459.

[9] In the three census which were made of the Roman people about the time of the second Punic war, the numbers stand as follows (see Livy, Epitom. l. xx. Hist. l. xxvii. 36, xxix. 37), 270, 213, 137, 108, 214,000. The fall of the second and the rise of the third appears so enormous, that several critics, notwithstanding the unanimity of the MSS., have suspected some corruption of the text of Livy. (See Drakenborch ad xxvii. 36, and Beaufort, République Romaine, tom. i. p. 325.) They did not consider that the second census was taken only at Rome, and that the numbers were diminished, not only by the death, but likewise by the absence, of many soldiers. In the third census, Livy expressly affirms that the legions were mustered by the care of particular commissaries. From the numbers on the list we must always deduct one-twelfth above threescore and incapable of bearing arms. See Population de la France, p. 72.

still remained an equal number in Rome and the adjacent territory who were animated by the same intrepid courage; and every citizen was trained from his earliest youth in the discipline and exercises of a soldier. Hannibal was astonished by the constancy of the senate, who, without raising the siege of Capua or recalling their scattered forces, expected his approach. He encamped on the banks of the Anio, at the distance of three miles from the city: and he was soon informed that the ground on which he had pitched his tent was sold for an adequate price at a public auction; and that a body of troops was dismissed by an opposite road to reinforce the legions of Spain.[10] He led his Africans to the gates of Rome, where he found three armies in order of battle prepared to receive him; but Hannibal dreaded the event of a combat from which he could not hope to escape unless he destoyed the last of his enemies; and his speedy retreat confessed the invincible courage of the Romans.

From the time of the Punic war the uninterrupted succession of senators had preserved the name and image of the republic; and the degenerate subjects of Honorius ambitiously derived their descent from the heroes who had repulsed the arms of Hannibal and subdued the nations of the earth. The temporal honours which the devout Paula [11] inherited and despised are carefully recapitulated by Jerom, the guide of her conscience and the historian of her life. The genealogy of her father, Rogatus, which ascended as high as Agamemnon, might seem to betray a Grecian origin; but her mother, Blæsilla, numbered the Scipios, Æmilius Paulus, and the Gracchi in the list of her ancestors; and Toxotius, the husband of Paula, deduced his royal lineage from Æneas, the father of the Julian line. The vanity of the rich, who desired to be noble, was gratified by these lofty pretensions. Encouraged by the applause of their parasites, they easily imposed on the credulity of the vulgar; and were countenanced in some measure by the custom of adopting the name of their patron, which had always prevailed among the freedmen and clients of illustrious families. Most of those families, however, attacked by so many causes of external violence or internal decay, were gradually extirpated: and it would be more reasonable to seek for a lineal descent of twenty generations

[10] Livy considers these two incidents as the effects only of chance and courage. I suspect that they were both managed by the admirable policy of the senate. [As a parallel instance to what is related of Hannibal, compare the remarkable transaction in Jerom, xxxii. 6, 44, where the prophet purchases his uncle's estate at the approach of the Babylonian captivity, in his undoubting confidence in the future restoration of the people. In the latter case it was the triumph of religious faith, in the other of national pride.—O. S.]

[11] See Jerom, tom. i. p. 169, 170, ad Eustochium [Epist. cviii. tom. i. p. 684, ed. Vallars.]; he bestows on Paula the splendid titles of Gracchorum stirps, soboles Scipionum, Pauli hæres, cujus vocabulum trahit, Martiæ Papyriæ Matris Africani vera et germana propago. This particular description supposes a more solid title than the surname of Julius, which Toxotius shared with a thousand families of the western provinces. See the Index of Tacitus, of Gruter's Inscriptions, etc.

among the mountains of the Alps or in the peaceful solitude of Apulia, than on the theatre of Rome, the seat of fortune, of danger, and of perpetual revolutions. Under each successive reign and from every province of the empire a crowd of hardy adventurers, rising to eminence by their talents or their vices, usurped the wealth, the honours, and the palaces of Rome; and oppressed or protected the poor and humble remains of consular families, who were ignorant, perhaps, of the glory of their ancestors.[12]

In the time of Jerom and Claudian the senators unanimously yielded the pre-eminence to the Anician line; and a slight view of *their* history will serve to appreciate the rank and antiquity of the noble families which contended only for the second place.[13]

During the five first ages of the city the name of the Anicians was unknown; they appear to have derived their origin from Præneste; and the ambition of those new citizens was long satisfied with the plebeian honours of tribunes of the people.[14] One hundred and sixty-eight years before the Christian era the family was ennobled by the prætorship of Anicius, who gloriously terminated the Illyrian war by the conquest of the nation and the captivity of their king.[15] From the triumph of that general three consulships in distant periods mark the succession of the Anician name.[16] From the reign of Diocletian to the final extinction of the Western empire that name shone with a lustre which was not eclipsed in the public estimation by the majesty

[12] Tacitus (Annal. iii. 55) affirms that, between the battle of Actium and the reign of Vespasian, the senate was gradually filled with *new* families from the Municipia and colonies of Italy.

[13] Nec quisquam Procerum tentet (licet ære vetusto
  Floreat, et claro cingatur Roma senatû)
  Se jactare parem; sed primâ sede relictâ
  Aucheniis, de jure licet certare secundo.
      Claud. in Prob. et Olybrii Coss. 18.
Such a compliment paid to the obscure name of the Auchenii has amazed the critics; but they all agree that, whatever may be the true reading, the sense of Claudian can be applied only to the Anician family.

[14] The earliest date on the annals of Pighius is that of M. Anicius Gallus, Trib. Pl. A.U.C. 506. Another Tribune, Q. Anicius, A.U.C. 508, is distinguished by the epithet of Prænestinus. Livy (xlv. 43) places the Anicii below the great families of Rome.

[15] Livy, xliv. 30, 31, xlv. 3, 26, 43. He fairly appreciates the merit of Anicius, and justly observes that his fame was clouded by the superior lustre of the Macedonian, which preceded the Illyrian, triumph.

[16] The dates of the three consulships are A.U.C. 593, 818, 967: the two last under the reigns of Nero and Caracalla. The second of these consuls distinguished himself only by his infamous flattery (Tacit. Annal. xv. 74); but even the evidence of crimes, if they bear the stamp of greatness and antiquity, is admitted, without reluctance, to prove the genealogy of a noble house.

[There is still an earlier instance of a member of the family attaining one of the higher offices of the state. Quintus Anicius Prænestinus was curule ædile with Q. Flavius, the celebrated scribe of Appius Claudius Cæcus, B.C. 304. Cf. Pliny. *Hist. Nat.* lib. xxxiii. c. 1, s. 6.—O. S.]

of the Imperial purple.[17]   The several branches to whom it was communicated united, by marriage or inheritance, the wealth and titles of
the Annian, the Petronian, and the Olybrian houses; and in each generation the number of consulships was multiplied by an hereditary
claim.[18]   The Anician family excelled in faith and in riches: they were
the first of the Roman senate who embraced Christianity; and it is
probable that Anicius Julian, who was afterwards consul and præfect
of the city, atoned for his attachment to the party of Maxentius by
the readiness with which he accepted the religion of Constantine.[19]
Their ample patrimony was increased by the industry of Probus, the
chief of the Anician family, who shared with Gratian the honours of
the consulship, and exercised four times the high office of Prætorian
præfect.[20]   His immense estates were scattered over the wide extent
of the Roman world; and though the public might suspect or disap-
prove the methods by which they had been acquired, the generosity and
magnificence of that fortunate statesman deserved the gratitude of his
clients and the admiration of strangers.[21]   Such was the respect entertained for his memory, that the two sons of Probus, in their earliest
youth and at the request of the senate, were associated in the consular
dignity: a memorable distinction, without example in the annals of
Rome.[22]

" The marbles of the Anician palace," were used as a proverbial expression of opulence and splendour;[23] but the nobles and senators of

[17] In the sixth century the nobility of the Anician name is mentioned (Cassiodor. Variar. l. x. Ep. 11, 12) with singular respect by the minister of a
Gothic king of Italy.

[18] —— Fixus in omnes
Cognatos procedit honos; quemcumque requiras
Hâc de stirpe virum, certum est de Consule nasci.
Per fasces numerantur avi, semperque renatâ
Nobilitate virent, et prolem fata sequuntur.
(Claudian in Prob. et Olyb. Consulat. 12, etc.)   The Annii, whose name
seems to have merged in the Anician, mark the Fasti with many consulships
from the time of Vespasian to the fourth century.

[19] The title of first Christian senator may be justified by the authority of
Prudentius (in Symmach. i. 553) and the dislike of the Pagans to the Anician
family. See Tillemont, Hist. des Empereurs, tom. iv. p. 183, v. p. 44. Baron.
Annal. A.D. 312, No. 78; A.D. 322, No. 2.

[20] Probus . . . claritudine generis et potentiâ et opûm amplitudine cognitus
Orbi Romano, per quem universum pœne patrimonia sparsa possedit, juste an
secus non judicioli est nostri. Ammian. Marcellin. xxvii. 11. His children
and widow erected for him a magnificent tomb in the Vatican, which was
demolished in the time of pope Nicholas V. to make room for the new church
of St. Peter. Baronius, who laments the ruin of this Christian monument,
has diligently preserved the inscriptions and basso-relievos. See Annal. Eccles.
A.D. 395, No. 5-17.

[21] Two Persian satraps travelled to Milan and Rome to hear St. Ambrose
and to see Probus. (Paulin. in Vit. Ambros.) Claudian (in Cons. Probin.
et. Olybr. 30-60) seems at a loss how to express the glory of Probus.

[22] See the poem which Claudian addressed to the two noble youths.

[23] Secundinus, the Manichæan, ap. Baron. Annal. Eccles. A.D. 390, No. 34.

Rome aspired in due gradation to imitate that illustrious family. The accurate description of the city, which was composed in the Theodosian age, enumerates one thousand seven hundred and eighty *houses,* the residence of wealthy and honourable citizens.[24] Many of these stately mansions might almost excuse the exaggeration of the poet—that Rome contained a multitude of palaces, and that each palace was equal to a city, since it included within its own precincts everything which could be subservient either to use or luxury: markets, hippodromes, temples, fountains, baths, porticos, shady groves, and artificial aviaries.[25] The historian Olympiodorus, who represents the state of Rome when it was besieged by the Goths,[26] continues to observe that several of the richest senators received from their estates an annual income of four thousand pounds of gold, above one hundred and sixty thousand pounds sterling; without computing the stated provision of corn and wine, which, had they been sold, might have equalled in value one-third of the money. Compared to this immoderate wealth, an ordinary revenue of a thousand or fifteen hundred pounds of gold might be considered as no more than adequate to the dignity of the senatorian rank, which required many expenses of a public and ostentatious kind. Several examples are recorded in the age of Honorius of vain and popular nobles who celebrated the year of their prætorship by a festival which lasted seven days and cost above one hundred thousand pounds sterling.[27] The estates of the Roman senators, which so far exceed the

[24] See Nardini, Roma Antica, p. 89, 498, 500.
[25] Quid loquar inclusas inter laquearia silvas?
  Vernula quâ vario carmine ludit avis?
    Claud. Rutil. Numatian. Itinerar. ver. 111.
The poet lived at the time of the Gothic invasion. A moderate palace would have covered Cincinnatus's farm of four acres (Val. Max. iv. 4, 7). In laxitatem ruris excurrunt, says Seneca, Epist. 114. See a judicious note of Mr. Hume, Essays, vol. i. p. 562, last 8vo edition.
[26] This curious account of Rome in the reign of Honorius is found in a fragment of the historian Olympiodorus, ap. Photium, p. 197 [p. 63, ed. Bekker].
[27] The sons of Alypius [Olympius in Bekker's ed.], of Symmachus, and of Maximus, spent, during their respective prætorships, twelve, or twenty, or forty, *centenaries* (or hundredweight of gold). See Olympiodor. ap. Phot. p. 197 [p. 63, ed. Bekker]. This popular estimation allows some latitude; but it is difficult to explain a law in the Theodosian Code (l. vi. tit. iv. leg. 5) which fixes the expense of the first prætor at 25,000, of the second at 20,000, and of the third at 15,000 *folles.* The name of *follis* (see Mém. de l'Académie des Inscriptions, tom. xxviii. p. 727) was equally applied to a purse of 125 pieces of silver, and to a small copper coin of the value of $\frac{1}{2625}$ part of that purse. In the former sense, the 25,000 *folles* would be equal to £150,000; in the latter to five or six pounds sterling. The one appears extravagant, the other is ridiculous. There must have existed some third and middle value, which is here understood; but ambiguity is an inexcusable fault in the language of laws.
[The centenarium was a hundred pounds weight of gold, and from the time of Constantine, the pound contained 72 solidi. Supposing the solidus to be worth only 10s. English, the prætorship of Symmachus cost £72,000, and that of Maximus £144,000. In the passage from the Theodosian Code,

proportion of modern wealth, were not confined to the limits of Italy. Their possessions extended far beyond the Ionian and Ægean seas to the most distant provinces: the city of Nicopolis, which Augustus had founded as an eternal monument of the Actian victory, was the property of the devout Paula;[28] and it is observed by Seneca, that the rivers which had divided hostile nations now flowed through the lands of private citizens.[29] According to their temper and circumstances, the estates of the Romans were either cultivated by the labour of their slaves, or granted, for a certain and stipulated rent, to the industrious farmer. The economical writers of antiquity strenuously recommend the former method wherever it may be practicable; but if the object should be removed by its distance or magnitude from the immediate eye of the master, they prefer the active care of an old hereditary tenant, attached to the soil and interested in the produce, to the mercenary administration of a negligent, perhaps an unfaithful, steward.[30]

The opulent nobles of an immense capital, who were never excited by the pursuit of military glory, and seldom engaged in the occupations of civil government, naturally resigned their leisure to the business and amusements of private life. At Rome commerce was always held in contempt; but the senators, from the first age of the republic, increased their patrimony and multiplied their clients by the lucrative practice of usury, and the obsolete laws were eluded or violated by the mutual inclinations and interest of both parties.[31] A considerable mass of treasure must always have existed at Rome, either

quoted by Gibbon, the *follis* means a purse of 125 pieces of silver, and as this *follis* was equal to £5 11s. nearly (according to Mommsen) 25,000 *folles* = £143,750. This sum is prodigious, but it is nearly the same as what was expended by Maximus in his prætorship. Savigny makes the solidus equal to 10s., but Mommsen prefers 12s. as being its approximate value.—O. S.]

[28] Nicopolis . . . in Actiaco littore sita possessionis vestræ nunc pars vel maxima est. Jerom. in præfat. Comment. ad Epistol. ad Titum, tom. ix. p. 243. M. de Tillemont supposes, strangely enough, that it was part of Agamemnon's inheritance. Mém. Ecclés. tom. xii. p. 85.

[29] Seneca, Epist. lxxxix. His language is of the declamatory kind: but declamation could scarcely exaggerate the avarice and luxury of the Romans. The philosopher himself deserved some share of the reproach, if it be true that his rigorous exaction of *Quadringenties,* above three hundred thousand pounds, which he had lent at high interest, provoked a rebellion in Britain. (Dion Cassius, l. lxii. [c. 2] p. 1003.) According to the conjecture of Gale (Antoninus's Itinerary in Britain, p. 92), the same Faustinus possessed an estate near Bury, in Suffolk, and another in the kingdom of Naples.

[30] Volusius, a wealthy senator (Tacit. Annal. iii. 30), always preferred tenants born on the estate. Columella, who received this maxim from him, argues very judiciously on the subject. De Re Rusticâ, l. i. c. 7, p. 408, edit. Gesner. Leipzig, 1735.

[31] Valesius (ad Ammian. xiv. 6) has proved, from Chrysostom and Augustin, that the senators were not allowed to lend money at usury. Yet it appears from the Theodosian Code (see Godefroy ad l. ii. tit. xxxiii. tom. i. p. 230-239) that they were permitted to take six per cent, or one-half of the legal interest; and, what is more singular, this permission was granted to the *young* senators.

in the current coin of the empire, or in the form of gold and silver plate; and there were many sideboards in the time of Pliny which contained more solid silver than had been transported by Scipio from vanquished Carthage.[32] The greater part of the nobles, who dissipated their fortunes in profuse luxury, found themselves poor in the midst of wealth, and idle in a constant round of dissipation. Their desires were continually gratified by the labour of a thousand hands; of the numerous train of their domestic slaves, who were actuated by the fear of punishment; and of the various professions of artificers and merchants, who were more powerfully impelled by the hopes of gain. The ancients were destitute of many of the conveniences of life which have been invented or improved by the progress of industry; and the plenty of glass and linen has diffused more real comforts among the modern nations of Europe than the senators of Rome could derive from all the refinements of pompous or sensual luxury.[33] Their luxury and their manners have been the subject of minute and laborious disquisition; but as such inquiries would divert me too long from the design of the present work, I shall produce an authentic state of Rome and its inhabitants which is more peculiarly applicable to the period of the Gothic invasion. Ammianus Marcellinus, who prudently chose the capital of the empire as the residence the best adapted to the historian of his own times, has mixed with the narrative of public events a lively representation of the scenes with which he was familiarly conversant. The judicious reader will not always approve the asperity of censure, the choice of circumstances, or the style of expression; he will perhaps detect the latent prejudices and personal resentments which soured the temper of Ammianus himself; but he will surely observe, with philosophic curiosity, the interesting and original picture of the manners of Rome.[34]

[32] Plin. Hist. Natur. xxxiii. 50. He states the silver at only 4380 pounds, which is increased by Livy (xxx. 45) to 100,023; the former seems too little for an opulent city, the latter too much for any private sideboard.
[33] The learned Arbuthnot (Tables of Ancient Coins, etc., p. 153) has observed with humour, and I believe with truth, that Augustus had neither glass to his windows nor a shirt to his back. Under the lower empire the use of linen and glass became somewhat more common.
[This is altogether wrong. The discovery of glass in common use in Pompeii has rather spoilt the point of Arbuthnot's jest. Glass was in general use in the reign of Augustus, and linen became common in that of Tiberius.— O. S.]
[34] It is incumbent on me to explain the liberties which I have taken with the text of Ammianus. 1. I have melted down into one piece the sixth chapter of the fourteenth and the fourth of the twenty-eighth book. 2. I have given order and connection to the confused mass of materials. 3. I have softened *some* extravagant hyperboles and pared away some superfluities of the original. 4. I have developed some observations which were insinuated rather than expressed. With these allowances my version will be found, not literal indeed, but faithful and exact.

" The greatness of Rome (such is the language of the historian) was founded on the rare and almost incredible alliance of virtue and of fortune. The long period of her infancy was employed in a laborious struggle against the tribes of Italy, the neighbours and enemies of the rising city. In the strength and ardour of youth she sustained the storms of war, carried her victorious arms beyond the seas and the mountains, and brought home triumphal laurels from every country of the globe. At length, verging towards old age, and sometimes conquering by the terror only of her name, she sought the blessings of ease and tranquillity. The VENERABLE CITY, which had trampled on the necks of the fiercest nations, and established a system of laws, the perpetual guardians of justice and freedom, was content, like a wise and wealthy parent, to devolve on the Cæsars, her favourite sons, the care of governing her ample patrimony.[35] A secure and profound peace, such as had been once enjoyed in the reign of Numa, succeeded to the tumults of a republic; while Rome was still adored as the queen of the earth, and the subject nations still reverenced the name of the people and the majesty of the senate. But this native splendour (continues Ammianus) is degraded and sullied by the conduct of some nobles, who, unmindful of their own dignity and of that of their country, assume an unbounded licence of vice and folly. They contend with each other in the empty vanity of titles and surnames, and curiously select or invent the most lofty and sonorous appellations—Reburrus or Fabunius, Pagonius or Tarrasius [36]—which may impress the ears of the vulgar with astonishment and respect. From a vain ambition of perpetuating their memory, they affect to multiply their likeness in statues of bronze and marble; nor are they satisfied unless those statues are covered with plates of gold; an honourable distinction, first granted to Acilius the consul, after he had subdued by his arms and counsels the power of king Antiochus. The ostentation of displaying, of magnifying perhaps, the rent-roll of the estates which they possess in all the provinces, from the rising to the setting sun, provokes the just resentment of every man who recollects that their poor and invincible ancestors were not distinguished from the meanest of the soldiers by the

---

[35] Claudian, who seems to have read the history of Ammianus, speaks of this great revolution in a much less courtly style:

> Postquam jura ferox in se communia Cæsar
> Transtulit; et lapsi mores; desuetaque priscis
> Artibus, in gremium pacis servile recessi.

De Bell. Gildonico, v. 49.

[36] The minute diligence of antiquarians has not been able to verify these extraordinary names. I am of opinion that they were invented by the historian himself, who was afraid of any personal satire or application. It is certain, however, that the simple denominations of the Romans were gradually lengthened to the number of four, five, or even seven, pompous surnames; as, for instance, Marcus Mæcius Mæmmius Furius Balburius Cæcilianus Placidus. See Norris, Cenotaph. Pisan. Dissert. iv. p. 438.

delicacy of their food or the splendour of their apparel. But the modern nobles measure their rank and consequence according to the loftiness of their chariots,[37] and the weighty magnificence of their dress. Their long robes of silk and purple float in the wind; and as they are agitated, by art or accident, they occasionally discover the under garments, the rich tunics, embroidered with the figures of various animals.[38] Followed by a train of fifty servants, and tearing up the pavement, they move along the streets with the same impetuous speed as if they travelled with post-horses; and the example of the senators is boldly imitated by the matrons and ladies, whose covered carriages are continually driving round the immense space of the city and suburbs. Whenever these persons of high distinction condescend to visit the public baths, they assume, on their entrance, a tone of loud and insolent command, and appropriate to their own use the conveniences which were designed for the Roman people. If, in these places of mixed and general resort, they meet any of the infamous ministers of their pleasures, they express their affection by a tender embrace, while they proudly decline the salutations of their fellow-citizens, who are not permitted to aspire above the honour of kissing their hands or their knees. As soon as they have indulged themselves in the refreshment of the bath, they resume their rings and the other ensigns of their dignity, select from their private wardrobe of the finest linen, such as might suffice for a dozen persons, the garments the most agreeable to their fancy, and maintain till their departure the same haughty demeanour, which perhaps might have been excused in the great Marcellus after the conquest of Syracuse. Sometimes indeed these heroes undertake more arduous achievements: they visit their estates in Italy, and procure themselves, by the toil of servile hands, the amusements of the chase.[39] If at any time, but more especially on a hot day, they have courage to sail in their painted galleys from the Lucrine

[37] The *carrucæ*, or coaches of the Romans, were often of solid silver curiously carved and engraved; and the trappings of the mules or horses were embossed with gold. This magnificence continued from the reign of Nero to that of Honorius; and the Appian way was covered with the splendid equipages of the nobles, who came out to meet St. Melania when she returned to Rome six years before the Gothic siege (Seneca, Epist. lxxxvii.; Plin. Hist. Natur. xxxiii. 49; Paulin. Nolan. apud Baron. Annal. Eccles. A.D. 397, No. 5). Yet pomp is well exchanged for convenience; and a plain modern coach that is hung upon springs is much preferable to the silver or gold *carts* of antiquity, which rolled on the axletree, and were exposed, for the most part, to the inclemency of the weather.

[38] In a homily of Asterius, bishop of Amasia, M. de Valois has discovered (ad Ammian. xiv. 6) that this was a new fashion; that bears, wolves, lions, and tigers, woods, hunting-matches, etc., were represented in embroidery; and that the more pious coxcombs substituted the figure or legend of some favourite saint.

[39] See Pliny's Epistles, i. 6. Three large wild boars were allured and taken in the toils without interrupting the studies of the philosophic sportsman.

lake [40] to their elegant villas on the sea-coast of Puteoli and Caieta,[41] they compare their own expeditions to the marches of Cæsar and Alexander.   Yet should a fly presume to settle on the silken folds of their gilded umbrellas, should a sunbeam penetrate through some unguarded and imperceptible chink, they deplore their intolerable hardships, and lament in affected language that they were not born in the land of the Cimmerians,[42] the regions of eternal darkness.   In these journeys into the country [43] the whole body of the household marches with their master.   In the same manner as the cavalry and infantry, the heavy and the light armed troops, the advanced guard and the rear, are marshalled by the skill of their military leaders, so the domestic officers, who bear a rod as an ensign of authority, distribute and arrange the numerous train of slaves and attendants.   The baggage and wardrobe move in the front, and are immediately followed by a multitude of cooks and inferior ministers employed in the service of the kitchens and of the table.   The main body is composed of a promiscuous crowd of slaves, increased by the accidental concourse of idle or dependent plebeians.   The rear is closed by the favourite band of eunuchs, distributed from age to youth, according to the order of seniority.   Their numbers and their deformity excite the horror of the indignant spectators, who are ready to execrate the memory of Semiramis for the cruel art which she invented of frustrating the purposes of nature, and of blasting in the bud the hopes of future generations.   In the exercise of domestic jurisdiction the nobles of Rome express an exquisite sensibility for any personal injury, and a contemptuous indifference for the rest of the human species.   When they have called for warm water, if a slave has been tardy in his obedience, he is instantly chas-

[40] The change from the inauspicious word *Avernus,* which stands in the text, is immaterial.   The two lakes, Avernus and Lucrinus, communicated with each other, and were fashioned by the stupendous moles of Agrippa into the Julian port, which opened through a narrow entrance into the gulf of Puteoli.   Virgil, who resided on the spot, has described (Georgic ii. 161) this work at the moment of its execution: and his commentators, especially Catrou, have derived much light from Strabo, Suetonius, and Dion.   Earthquakes and volcanoes have changed the face of the country, and turned the Lucrine lake, since the year 1538, into the Monte Nuovo.   See Camillo Pellegrino Discorsi della Campania Felice, p. 239, 244, etc. Antonii Sanfelicii Campania, p. 13, 88.
[41] The regna Cumana et Puteolana; loca cætero quivalde expetenda, interpellantium autem multitudine pæne fugienda.   Cicero ad Attic. xiv. 16.
[42] The proverbial expression of *Cimmerian darkness* was originally borrowed from the description of Homer (in the eleventh book of the Odyssey) which he applies to a remote and fabulous country on the shores of the ocean.   See Erasmi Adagia, in his Works, tom. ii. p. 593, the Leyden edition.
[43] We may learn from Seneca Epist. cxxiii., three curious circumstances relative to the journeys of the Romans.   1. They were preceded by a troop of Numidian light-horse, who announced by a cloud of dust the approach of a great man.   2. Their baggage-mules transported not only the precious vases but even the fragile vessels of crystal and *murra,* which last is almost proved, by the learned French translator of Seneca (tom. iii. p. 402-422), to mean the

tised with three hundred lashes; but should the same slave commit a wilful murder, the master will mildly observe that he is a worthless fellow, but that if he repeats the offence he shall not escape punishment. Hospitality was formerly the virtue of the Romans; and every stranger who could plead either merit or misfortune was relieved or rewarded by their generosity. At present, if a foreigner, perhaps of no contemptible rank, is introduced to one of the proud and wealthy senators, he is welcomed indeed in the first audience with such warm professions and such kind inquiries, that he retires enchanted with the affability of his illustrious friend, and full of regret that he had so long delayed his journey to Rome, the native seat of manners as well as of empire. Secure of a favourable reception, he repeats his visit the ensuing day, and is mortified by the discovery that his person, his name, and his country are already forgotten. If he still has resolution to persevere, he is gradually numbered in the train of dependents, and obtains the permission to pay his assiduous and unprofitable court to a haughty patron, incapable of gratitude or friendship, who scarcely deigns to remark his presence, his departure, or his return. Whenever the rich prepare a solemn and popular entertainment,[44] whenever they celebrate with profuse and pernicious luxury their private banquets, the choice of the guests is the subject of anxious deliberation. The modest, the sober, and the learned are seldom preferred; and the nomenclators, who are commonly swayed by interested motives, have the address to insert in the list of invitations the obscure names of the most worthless of mankind. But the frequent and familiar companions of the great are those parasites who practise the most useful of all arts, the art of flattery; who eagerly applaud each word and every action of their immortal patron; gaze with rapture on his marble columns and variegated pavements, and strenuously praise the pomp and elegance which he is taught to consider as a part of his personal merit. At the Roman tables the birds, the *squirrels*,[45] or the fish, which appear of an

porcelain of China and Japan. 3. The beautiful faces of the young slaves were covered with a medicated crust, or ointment, which secured them against the effects of the sun and frost.

[44] Distributio solemnium sportularum. The *sportulæ*, or *sportellæ*, were small baskets supposed to contain a quantity of hot provisions of the value of 100 quadrantes, or twelvepence halfpenny, which were ranged in order in the hall, and ostentatiously distributed to the hungry or servile crowd who waited at the door. This indelicate custom is very frequently mentioned in the epigrams of Martial and the satires of Juvenal. See likewise Suetonius, in Claud. c. 21; in Neron. c. 16; in Domitian. c. 4, 7. These baskets of provisions were afterwards converted into large pieces of gold and silver coin, or plate, which were mutually given and accepted even by the persons of the highest rank (see Symmach. Epist. iv. 55, ix. 124, and Miscell. p. 256 [ed. Paris, 1604]), on solemn occasions, of consulships, marriages, etc.

[45] The want of an English name obliges me to refer to the common genus of squirrels, the Latin *glis,* the French *loir;* a little animal who inhabits the woods and remains torpid in cold weather (see Plin. Hist. Natur. viii. 82; Buffon, Hist. Naturelle, tom. viii. 158; Pennant's Synopsis of Quadrupeds, p. 289).

uncommon size, are contemplated with curious attention; a pair of scales is accurately applied to ascertain their real weight; and, while the more rational guests are disgusted by the vain and tedious repetition, notaries are summoned to attest by an authentic record the truth of such a marvellous event. Another method of introduction into the houses and society of the great is derived from the profession of gaming, or, as it is more politely styled, of play. The confederates are united by a strict and indissoluble bond of friendship, or rather of conspiracy; a superior degree of skill in the *Tesserarian* art (which may be interpreted the game of dice and tables [46]) is a sure road to wealth and reputation. A master of that sublime science, who in a supper or assembly is placed below a magistrate, displays in his countenance the surprise and indignation which Cato might be supposed to feel when he was refused the prætorship by the votes of a capricious people. The acquisition of knowledge seldom engages the curiosity of the nobles, who abhor the fatigue and disdain the advantages of study; and the only books which they peruse are the Satires of Juvenal, and the verbose and fabulous histories of Marius Maximus.[47] The libraries which they have inherited from their fathers are secluded, like dreary sepulchres, from the light of day.[48] But the costly instruments of the theatre, flutes, and enormous lyres, and hydraulic organs, are constructed for their use; and the harmony of vocal and instrumental music is incessantly repeated in the palaces of Rome. In those palaces sound is preferred to sense, and the care of the body to that of the mind. It is allowed as a salutary maxim, that the light and frivolous

The art of rearing and fattening great numbers of *ghers* was practised in Roman villas as a profitable article of rural economy (Varro, de Re Rusticâ, iii. 15). The excessive demand of them for luxurious tables was increased by the foolish prohibitions of the censors; and it is reported that they are still esteemed in modern Rome, and are frequently sent as presents by the Colonna princes (see Brotier, the last editor of Pliny, tom. ii. p. 458, apud Barbou, 1779).

[46] This game, which might be translated by the more familiar names of *trictrac*, or *backgammon*, was a favourite amusement of the gravest Romans; and old Mucius Scævola, the lawyer, had the reputation of a very skilful player. It was called *ludus duodecim scriptorum*, from the twelve *scripta* or lines which equally divided the *alveolus* or table. On these the two armies, the white and the black, each consisting of fifteen men, or *calculi*, were regularly placed and alternately moved according to the laws of the game and the chances of the *tesseræ* or dice. Dr. Hyde, who diligently traces the history and varieties of the *nerdiludium* (a name of Persic etymology) from Ireland to Japan, pours forth on this trifling subject a copious torrent of classic and Oriental learning. See Syntagma Dissertat. tom. ii. p. 217-405.

[47] Marius Maximus, homo omnium verbosissimus, qui et mythistoricis se voluminibus implicavit. Vopiscus in Hist. August. p. 242 [Vopisc. Firm. c. 1.] He wrote the Lives of the Emperors from Trajan to Alexander Severus. See Gerard Vossius de Historicis Latin. l. ii. c. 3, in his Works, vol. iv. p. 57.

[48] This satire is probably exaggerated. The Saturnalia of Macrobius, and the Epistles of Jerom, afford satisfactory proofs that Christian theology and classic literature were studiously cultivated by several Romans of both sexes and of the highest rank.

suspicion of a contagious malady is of sufficient weight to excuse the visits of the most intimate friends; and even the servants who are despatched to make the decent inquiries are not suffered to return home till they have undergone the ceremony of a previous ablution. Yet this selfish and unmanly delicacy occasionally yields to the more imperious passion of avarice. The prospect of gain will urge a rich and gouty senator as far as Spoleto; every sentiment of arrogance and dignity is subdued by the hopes of an inheritance, or even of a legacy; and a wealthy childless citizen is the most powerful of the Romans. The art of obtaining the signature of a favourable testament, and sometimes of hastening the moment of its execution, is perfectly understood; and it has happened that in the same house, though in different apartments, a husband and a wife, with the laudable design of overreaching each other, have summoned their respective lawyers, to declare at the same time their mutual but contradictory intentions. The distress which follows and chastises extravagant luxury often reduces the great to the use of the most humiliating expedients. When they desire to borrow, they employ the base and supplicating style of the slave in the comedy; but when they are called upon to pay, they assume the royal and tragic declamation of the grandsons of Hercules. If the demand is repeated, they readily procure some trusty sycophant. instructed to maintain a charge of poison, or magic, against the insolent creditor, who is seldom released from prison till he has signed a discharge of the whole debt. These vices, which degrade the moral character of the Romans, are mixed with a puerile superstition that disgraces their understanding. They listen with confidence to the predictions of haruspices, who pretend to read in the entrails of victims the signs of future greatness and prosperity; and there are many who do not presume either to bathe or to die, or to appear in public, till they have diligently consulted, according to the rules of astrology, the situation of Mercury and the aspect of the moon.[49] It is singular enough that this vain credulity may often be discovered among the profane sceptics who impiously doubt or deny the existence of a celestial power."

In populous cities, which are the seat of commerce and manufactures, the middle ranks of inhabitants, who derive their subsistence from the dexterity or labour of their hands, are commonly the most prolific, the most useful, and, in that sense, the most respectable part of the community. But the plebeians of Rome, who disdained such sedentary and servile arts, had been oppressed from the earliest times by the weight of debt and usury, and the husbandman, during the term of his military service, was obliged to abandon the cultivation of his

[49] Macrobius, the friend of these Roman nobles, considered the stars as the cause, or at least the signs, of future events (de Somn. Scipion. l. i. c. 19, p. 68).

farm.[50]   The lands of Italy, which had been originally divided among
the families of free and indigent proprietors, were insensibly purchased
or usurped by the avarice of the nobles; and in the age which preceded
the fall of the republic, it was computed that only two thousand citizens
were possessed of any independent substance.[51]   Yet as long as the
people bestowed by their suffrages the honours of the state, the command of the legions, and the administration of wealthy provinces, their
conscious pride alleviated in some measure the hardships of poverty;
and their wants were seasonably supplied by the ambitious liberality of
the candidates, who aspired to secure a venal majority in the thirty-
five tribes, or the hundred and ninety-three centuries, of Rome.   But
when the prodigal commons had imprudently alienated not only the
use, but the *inheritance,* of power, they sunk, under the reign of the
Cæsars, into a vile and wretched populace, which must, in a few generations, have been totally extinguished, if it had not been continually
recruited by the manumission of slaves and the influx of strangers.   As
early as the time of Hadrian it was the just complaint of the ingenuous
natives that the capital had attracted the vices of the universe and the
manners of the most opposite nations.   The intemperance of the Gauls,
the cunning and levity of the Greeks, the savage obstinacy of the
Egyptians and Jews, the servile temper of the Asiatics, and the dissolute, effeminate prostitution of the Syrians, were mingled in the various
multitude, which, under the proud and false denomination of Romans,
presumed to despise their fellow-subjects, and even their sovereigns,
who dwelt beyond the precincts of the ETERNAL CITY.[52]

Yet the name of that city was still pronounced with respect: the
frequent and capricious tumults of its inhabitants were indulged with
impunity; and the successors of Constantine, instead of crushing the
last remains of the democracy by the strong arm of military power,
embraced the mild policy of Augustus, and studied to relieve the poverty and to amuse the idleness of an innumerable people.[53]   I. For

[50] The histories of Livy (see particularly vi. 36) are full of the extortions
of the rich and the sufferings of the poor debtors.   The melancholy story
of a brave old soldier (Dionys. Hal. 1. vi. c. 26, p. 347, edit. Hudson, and
Livy, ii. 23) must have been frequently repeated in those primitive times,
which have been so undeservedly praised.

[51] Non esse in civitate duo millia hominum qui rem haberent.   Cicero, Offic.
ii. 21, and Comment. Paul. Manut, in edit. Græv.   This vague computation
was made A.U.C. 649, in a speech of the tribune Philippus, and it was his object,
as well as that of the Gracchi (see Plutarch), to deplore, and perhaps to exaggerate, the misery of the common people.

[52] See the third Satire (60-125) of Juvenal, who indignantly complains,
——— Quamvis quota portio fæcia Achæi !
Jampridem Syrus in Tiberim defluxit Orontes ;
Et linguam et mores, etc.
Seneca, when he proposes to comfort his mother (Consolat. ad Helv. c. 6)
by the reflection that a great part of mankind were in a state of exile, re-
minds her how few of the inhabitants of Rome were born in the city.

[53] Almost all that is said of the bread, bacon, oil, wine, etc., may be found

the convenience of the lazy plebeians, the monthly distributions of corn were converted into a daily allowance of bread; a great number of ovens were constructed and maintained at the public expense; and at the appointed hour, each citizen, who was furnished with a ticket, ascended the flight of steps which had been assigned to his peculiar quarter or division, and received, either as a gift or at a very low price, a loaf of bread of the weight of three pounds for the use of his family. II. The forests of Lucania, whose acorns fattened large droves of wild hogs,[54] afforded, as a species of tribute, a plentiful supply of cheap and wholesome meat. During five months of the year a regular allowance of bacon was distributed to the poorer citizens; and the annual consumption of the capital, at a time when it was much declined from its former lustre, was ascertained, by an edict of Valentinian the Third, at three millions six hundred and twenty-eight thousand pounds.[55] III. In the manners of antiquity the use of oil was indispensable for the lamp as well as for the bath, and the annual tax which was imposed on Africa for the benefit of Rome amounted to the weight of three millions of pounds, to the measure, perhaps, of three hundred thousand English gallons. IV. The anxiety of Augustus to provide the metropolis with sufficient plenty of corn was not extended beyond that necessary article of human subsistence; and when the popular clamour accused the dearness and scarcity of wine, a proclamation was issued by the grave reformer to remind his subjects that no man could reasonably complain of thirst, since the aqueducts of Agrippa had introduced into the city so many copious streams of pure and salubrious water.[56] This rigid sobriety was insensibly relaxed; and, although the generous design of Aurelian [57] does not appear to have been executed in its full extent, the use of wine was allowed on

in the fourteenth book of the Theodosian Code, which expressly treats of the *police* of the great cities. See particularly the titles iii. iv. xv. xvi. xvii. xxiv. The collateral testimonies are produced in Godefroy's Commentary, and it is needless to transcribe them. According to a law of Theodosius, which appreciates in money the military allowance, a piece of gold (eleven shillings) was equivalent to eighty pounds of bacon, or to eighty pounds of oil, or to twelve modii (or pecks) of salt (Cod. Theod. l. viii. tit. iv. leg. 17). This equation, compared with another seventy pounds of bacon for an *amphora* (Cod. Theod. l. xiv. tit. iv. leg. 4), fixes the price of wine at about sixteen-pence the gallon.

[54] The anonymous author of the Description of the World (p. 14, in tom. iii. Geograph. Minor. Hudson) observes of Lucania, in his barbarous Latin, Regio obtima, et ipsa omnibus habundans, et lardum multum foras emittit: propter quod est in montibus, cujus æscam animalium variam.
[55] See Novell. ad calcem Cod. Theod. D. Valent. l. i. tit. xv. [tom. vi. App. p. 28, ed. Gothofr.]. This law was published at Rome, June 29th, A.D. 452
[56] Sueton. in August. c. 42. The utmost debauch of the emperor himself, in his favourite wine of Rhætia, never exceeded a *sextarius* (an English pint). Id. c. 77. Torrentius ad loc. and Arbuthnot's Tables, p. 86.
[57] His design was to plant vineyards along the sea-coast of Etruria (Vopiscus, in Hist. August. p. 225 [in Aurel. c. 48]), the dreary, unwholesome, uncultivated *Maremme* of modern Tuscany.

very easy and liberal terms. The administration of the public cellars was delegated to a magistrate of honourable rank; and a considerable part of the vintage of Campania was reserved for the fortunate inhabitants of Rome.

The stupendous aqueducts, so justly celebrated by the praises of Augustus himself, replenished the *Thermæ*, or baths, which had been constructed in every part of the city with Imperial magnificence. The baths of Antoninus Caracalla, which were open, at stated hours, for the indiscriminate service of the senators and the people, contained above sixteen hundred seats of marble; and more than three thousand were reckoned in the baths of Diocletian.[58] The walls of the lofty apartments were covered with curious mosaics, that imitated the art of the pencil in the elegance of design and the variety of colours. The Egyptian granite was beautifully encrusted with the precious green marble of Numidia; the perpetual stream of hot water was poured into the capacious basins through so many wide mouths of bright and massy silver; and the meanest Roman could purchase, with a small copper coin, the daily enjoyment of a scene of pomp and luxury which might excite the envy of the kings of Asia.[59] From these stately palaces issued a swarm of dirty and ragged plebeians, without shoes and without a mantle; who loitered away whole days in the street or Forum to hear news and to hold disputes; who dissipated in extravagant gaming the miserable pittance of their wives and children; and spent the hours of the night in obscure taverns and brothels in the indulgence of gross and vulgar sensuality.[60]

But the most lively and splendid amusement of the idle multitude depended on the frequent exhibition of public games and spectacles. The piety of Christian princes had suppressed the inhuman combats of gladiators; but the Roman people still considered the Circus as their home, their temple, and the seat of the republic. The impatient crowd rushed at the dawn of day to secure their places, and there were many who passed a sleepless and anxious night in the adjacent porticos. From the morning to the evening, careless of the sun or of the rain, the spectators, who sometimes amounted to the number of four hundred thousand, remained in eager attention; their eyes fixed on the horses and charioteers, their minds agitated with hope and fear for the success of the *colours* which they espoused; and the happiness of

[58] Olympiodor, apud Phot. p. 197 [p. 63, ed. Bekker].
[59] Seneca (Epistol. lxxxvi.) compares the baths of Scipio Africanus, at his villa of Liternum, with the magnificence (which was continually increasing) of the public baths of Rome, long before the stately Thermæ of Antoninus and Diocletian were erected. The *quadrans* paid for admission was the quarter of the *as*, about one-eighth of an English penny.
[60] Ammianus (l. xiv. c. 6, and l. xxviii. c. 4), after describing the luxury and pride of the nobles of Rome, exposes, with equal indignation, the vices and follies of the common people.

Rome appeared to hang on the event of a race.[61] The same immoderate ardour inspired their clamours and their applause as often as
they were entertained with the hunting of wild beasts and the various
modes of theatrical representation. These representations in modern
capitals may deserve to be considered as a pure and elegant school of
taste, and perhaps of virtue. But the Tragic and Comic Muse of the
Romans, who seldom aspired beyond the imitation of Attic genius,[62]
had been almost totally silent since the fall of the republic;[63] and their
place was unworthily occupied by licentious farce, effeminate music,
and splendid pageantry. The pantomimes,[64] who maintained their
reputation from the age of Augustus to the sixth century, expressed,
without the use of words, the various fables of the gods and heroes of
antiquity; and the perfection of their art, which sometimes disarmed
the gravity of the philosopher, always excited the applause and wonder
of the people. The vast and magnificent theatres of Rome were filled
by three thousand female dancers, and by three thousand singers, with
the masters of the respective choruses. Such was the popular favour
which they enjoyed, that, in a time of scarcity, when all strangers
were banished from the city, the merit of contributing to the public
pleasures exempted *them* from a law which was strictly executed against
the professors of the liberal arts.[65]

It is said that the foolish curiosity of Elagabalus attempted to discover, from the quantity of spiders' webs, the number of the inhabi-

---

[61] Juvenal, Satir. xi. 191, etc. The expressions of the historian Ammianus
are not less strong and animated than those of the satirist; and both the one
and the other painted from the life. The numbers which the great Circus was
capable of receiving are taken from the *original Notitiæ* of the city. The differences between them prove that they did not transcribe each other; but the
sum may appear incredible, though the country on these occasions flocked to
the city.

[62] Sometimes, indeed, they composed original pieces.
———— Vestigia Græca
Ausi deserere et celebrare domestica facta.
Horat. Epistol. ad Pisones, 285, and the learned though perplexed note of
Dacier, who might have allowed the name of tragedies to the *Brutus* and the
Decius of Pacuvius, or to the *Cato* of Maternus. The *Octavia,* ascribed to one
of the Senecas, still remains a very unfavourable specimen of Roman tragedy.

[63] In the time of Quintillian and Pliny a tragic poet was reduced to the imperfect method of hiring a great room, and reading his play to the company,
whom he invited for that purpose. (See Dialog. de Oratoribus, c. 9, 10, and
Plin. Epistol. vii. 17.)

[64] See the dialogue of Lucian, entitled de Saltatione, tom. ii. p. 265-317, edit.
Reitz. The pantomimes obtained the honourable name of χειροσόφοι; and it
was required that they should be conversant with almost every art and science.
Burette (in the Mémoires de l'Académie des Inscriptions, tom. i. p. 127, etc.)
has given a short history of the art of pantomimes.

[65] Ammianus, l. xiv. c. 6. He complains, with decent indignation, that the
streets of Rome were filled with crowds of females, who might have given
children to the state, but whose only occupation was to curl and dress their
hair, and jactari volubilibus gyris, dum exprimunt innumera simulacra, quæ
finxere fabulæ theatrales.

tants of Rome. A more rational method of inquiry might not have been undeserving of the attention of the wisest princes, who could easily have resolved a question so important for the Roman government and so interesting to succeeding ages. The births and deaths of the citizens were duly registered; and if any writer of antiquity had condescended to mention the annual amount, or the common average, we might now produce some satisfactory calculation which would destroy the extravagant assertions of critics, and perhaps confirm the modest and probable conjectures of philosophers.[66] The most diligent researches have collected only the following circumstances, which, slight and imperfect as they are, may tend in some degree to illustrate the question of the populousness of ancient Rome. I. When the capital of the empire was besieged by the Goths, the circuit of the walls was accurately measured by Ammonius, the mathematician, who found it equal to twenty-one miles.[67] It should not be forgotten that the form of the city was almost that of a circle, the geometrical figure which is known to contain the largest space within any given circumference. II. The architect Vitruvius, who flourished in the Augustan age, and whose evidence, on this occasion, has peculiar weight and authority, observes that the innumerable habitations of the Roman people would have spread themselves far beyond the narrow limits of the city; and that the want of ground, which was probably contracted on every side by gardens and villas, suggested the common, though inconvenient, practice of raising the houses to a considerable height in the air.[68] But the loftiness of these buildings, which often consisted of hasty work and insufficient materials, was the cause of frequent and fatal accidents; and it was repeatedly enacted by Augustus, as well as by Nero, that the height of private edifices within the walls of Rome should not exceed the measure of seventy feet from the ground.[69]

[66] Lipsius (tom. iii. p. 423, de Magnitud. Romana, l. iii. c. 3) and Isaac Vossius (Observat. Var. p. 26-34) have indulged strange dreams, of four, or eight, or fourteen millions in Rome. Mr. Hume (Essays, vol. i. p. 450-457), with admirable good sense and scepticism, betrays some secret disposition to extenuate the populousness of ancient times.

[67] Olympiodor. ap. Phot. p. 197 [p. 63, ed. Bekker]. See Fabricius, Biblioth. Græc. tom. ix. p. 400.

[The name of the mathematician was Ammon, not Ammonius, and notwithstanding this statement in Olympiodorus, the actual circumference of the walls of Rome could not have exceeded twelve miles.—O. S.]

[68] In eâ autem majestate urbis, et vicium infinitâ frequentiâ innumerabiles habitationes opus fuit explicare. Ergo cum recipere non posset area plana tantam multitudinem [ad habitandum] in urbe, ad auxilium altitudinis ædificiorum res ipsa coëgit devenire. Vitruv. ii. 8. This passage, which I owe to Vossius, is clear, strong, and comprehensive.

[69] The successive testimonies of Pliny, Aristides, Claudian, Rutilius, etc., prove the insufficiency of these restrictive edicts. See Lipsius, de Magnitud. Romana, l. iii. c. 4.

——— Tabulata tibi jam tertia fumant;
Tu nescis; nam si gradibus trepidatur ab imis
Ultimus ardebit, quem tegula sola tuetur
A pluviâ.   Juvenal, Satir. iii. 191.

III. Juvenal [70] laments, as it should seem from his own experience, the hardships of the poorer citizens, to whom he addresses the salutary advice of emigrating, without delay, from the smoke of Rome, since they might purchase in the little towns of Italy a cheerful, commodious dwelling at the same price which they annually paid for a dark and miserable lodging. House-rent was therefore immoderately dear: the rich acquired, at an enormous expense, the ground, which they covered with palaces and gardens; but the body of the Roman people was crowded into a narrow space; and the different floors and apartments of the same house were divided, as it is still the custom of Paris and other cities, among several families of plebeians. **IV.** The total number of houses in the fourteen regions of the city is accurately stated in the description of Rome composed under the reign of Theodosius, and they amount to forty-eight thousand three hundred and eighty-two.[71] The two classes of *domus* and of *insulæ*, into which they are divided, include all the habitations of the capital, of every rank and condition, from the marble palace of the Anicii, with a numerous establishment of freedmen and slaves, to the lofty and narrow lodging-house where the poet Codrus and his wife were permitted to hire a wretched garret immediately under the tiles. If we adopt the same average which, under similar circumstances, has been found applicable to Paris,[72] and indifferently allow about twenty-five persons for each house, of every degree, we may fairly estimate the inhabitants of Rome at twelve hundred thousand: a number which cannot be thought excessive for the capital of a mighty empire, though it exceeds the populousness of the greatest cities of modern Europe.[73]

[70] Read the whole third Satire, but particularly 166, 223, etc. The description of a crowded *insula,* or lodging-house, in Petronius (c. 95, 97), perfectly tallies with the complaints of Juvenal; and we learn from legal authority that, in the time of Augustus (Heineccius, Hist. Juris Roman. c. iv. p. 181), the ordinary rent of the several *cœnacula,* or apartments of an *insula,* annually produced forty thousand sesterces, between three and four hundred pounds sterling (Pandect. l. xix. tit. ii. No. 30), a sum which proves at once the large extent and high value of those common buildings.

[71] This sum total is composed of 1780 *domus,* or great houses, of 46,602 *insulæ,* or plebeian habitations (see Nardini, Roma Antica, l. iii. p. 88) ; and these numbers are ascertained by the agreement of the texts of the different *Notitiæ.* Nardini, l. viii. p. 498, 500.

[72] See that accurate writer M. de Messance, Recherches sur la Population, p. 175-187. From probable or certain grounds he assigns to Paris 23,565 houses, 71,114 families, and 576,630 inhabitants.

[73] This computation is not very different from that which M. Brotier, the last editor of Tacitus (tom. ii. p. 380), has assumed from similar principles; though he seems to aim at a degree of precision which it is neither possible nor important to obtain.

[Since the time of Gibbon, the populousness of ancient Rome has been investigated by several writers, whose names are below. De la Malle has reduced the population to 562,000 souls, and Höck to 2,265,000. The estimate of the former is much too low. The most important datum for estimating the population is the statement in the Monumentum Ancyranum, that the plebs

Such was the state of Rome under the reign of Honorius, at the time when the Gothic army formed the siege, or rather the blockade, of the city.[74] By a skilful disposition of his numerous forces, who impatiently watched the moment of an assault, Alaric encompassed the walls, commanded the twelve principal gates, intercepted all communication with the adjacent country, and vigilantly guarded the navigation of the Tiber, from which the Romans derived the surest and most plentiful supply of provisions. The first emotions of the nobles and of the people were those of surprise and indignation, that a vile barbarian should dare to insult the capital of the world; but their arrogance was soon humbled by misfortune; and their unmanly rage, instead of being directed against an enemy in arms, was meanly exercised on a defenceless and innocent victim. Perhaps in the person of Serena the Romans might have respected the niece of Theodosius, the aunt, nay even the adoptive mother, of the reigning emperor; they abhorred the widow of Stilicho; and they listened with credulous passion to the tale of calumny which accused her of maintaining a secret and criminal correspondence with the Gothic invader. Actuated, or overawed, by the same popular frenzy, the senate, without requiring any evidence of her guilt, pronounced the sentence of her death. Serena was ignominiously strangled; and the infatuated multitude were astonished to find that this cruel act of injustice did not immediately produce the retreat of the barbarians and the deliverance of the city. That unfortunate city gradually experienced the distress of scarcity, and at length the horrid calamities of famine. The daily allowance of three pounds of bread was reduced to one-half, to one-third, to nothing; and the price of corn still continued to rise in a rapid and extravagant proportion.

urbana in the year 5 B.C. consisted of 320,000 males. This number contains neither children under 11 years of age (Suetonius, Aug. 41), nor senators, nor equites, nor slaves. The females and children under eleven must have been at least double, which would make the plebs urbana 640,000. Höck supposes that as the 320,000 were the persons who received the *congiaria* from the state, they were only the poorer members of the plebs urbana, and that the whole number of the latter amounted to 1,250,000. Mommsen, however, has satisfactorily proved that all Roman citizens received the *congiaria,* with the exception of the senators and the equites. The latter may have been about 10,000. The number of slaves was immense, and was at least equal to or double the male population. In addition to these we must reckon the military and the great mass of foreigners always resident in Rome, so that the population could not have been far short of 2,000,000. If this should be considered too large a number to be distributed among the 1780 domus and the 46,602 insulæ, it must be remembered that the domus were large palaces, and the insulæ contained numerous separate dwellings, being divided from other edifices by a space of at least five feet, whence their name. Besides this, the slaves were very densely crowded, and lived in cellars and subterranean dwellings under the public edifices.—O. S.]

[74] For the events of the first siege of Rome, which are often confounded with those of the second and third, see Zosimus, l. v. [c. 38-42] p. 350-354; Sozomen, l. ix. c. 6; Olympiodorus, ap. Phot. p. 180 [p. 57, ed. Bekk.]; Philostorgius, l. xii. c. 3; and Godefroy, Dissertat. p. 467-475.

The poorer citizens, who were unable to purchase the necessaries of life, solicited the precarious charity of the rich; and for a while the public misery was alleviated by the humanity of Læta, the widow of the emperor Gratian, who had fixed her residence at Rome, and consecrated, to the use of the indigent, the princely revenue which she annually received from the grateful successors of her husband.[75] But these private and temporary donatives were insufficient to appease the hunger of a numerous people; and the progress of famine invaded the marble palaces of the senators themselves. The persons of both sexes, who had been educated in the enjoyment of ease and luxury, discovered how little is requisite to supply the demands of nature; and lavished their unavailing treasures of gold and silver to obtain the coarse and scanty sustenance which they would formerly have rejected with disdain. The food the most repugnant to sense or imagination, the aliments the most unwholesome and pernicious to the constitution, were eagerly devoured, and fiercely disputed, by the rage of hunger. A dark suspicion was entertained that some desperate wretches fed on the bodies of their fellow-creatures whom they had secretly murdered; and even mothers (such was the horrid conflict of the two most powerful instincts implanted by nature in the human breast), even mothers are said to have tasted the flesh of their slaughtered infants! [76] Many thousands of the inhabitants of Rome expired in their houses, or in the streets, for want of sustenance; and as the public sepulchres without the walls were in the power of the enemy, the stench which arose from so many putrid and unburied carcasses infected the air; and the miseries of famine were succeeded and aggravated by the contagion of a pestilential disease. The assurances of speedy and effectual relief, which were repeatedly transmitted from the court of Ravenna, supported, for some time, the fainting resolution of the Romans, till at length the despair of any human aid tempted them to accept the offers of a preternatural deliverance. Pompeianus, præfect of the city, had been persuaded, by the art or fanaticism of some Tuscan diviners, that, by the mysterious force of spells and sacrifices, they could extract the lightning from the clouds, and point those celestial fires against the camp of the barbarians.[77] The important secret was com-

[75] The mother of Læta was named Pissumena. Her father, family, and country are unknown. Ducange, Fam. Byzantin. p. 59.

[76] Ad nefandos cibos erupit esurientium rabies, et sua invicem membra aniarunt, dum mater non parcit lactenti infantiæ; et recipit utero, quem paullò ante effuderat. Jerom. ad. Principiam, tom. i. p. 121 [Ep. cxxvii. tom. i. p. 953, ed. Vallars.]. The same horrid circumstance is likewise told of the sieges of Jerusalem and Paris. For the latter, compare the tenth book of the Henriade, and the Journal de Henri IV. tom. i. p. 47-83; and observe that a plain narrative of facts is much more pathetic than the most laboured descriptions of epic poetry.

[77] Zosimus (l. v. [c. 41] p. 355, 356) speaks of these ceremonies like a Greek unacquainted with the national superstition of Rome and Tuscany. I suspect that they consisted of two parts, the secret and the public; the former

municated to Innocent, the bishop of Rome; and the successor of St.
Peter is accused, perhaps without foundation, of preferring the safety
of the republic to the rigid severity of the Christian worship. But
when the question was agitated in the senate; when it was proposed,
as an essential condition, that those sacrifices should be performed in
the Capitol, by the authority and in the presence of the magistrates;
the majority of that respectable assembly, apprehensive either of the
Divine or of the Imperial displeasure, refused to join in an act which
appeared almost equivalent to the public restoration of Paganism.[78]

The last resource of the Romans was in the clemency, or at least in
the moderation, of the king of the Goths. The senate, who in this
emergency assumed the supreme powers of government, appointed two
ambassadors to negotiate with the enemy. This important trust was
delegated to Basilius, a senator of Spanish extraction, and already conspicuous in the administration of provinces; and to John, the first
tribune of the notaries, who was peculiarly qualified, by his dexterity in
business, as well as by his former intimacy with the Gothic prince.
When they were introduced into his presence, they declared, perhaps
in a more lofty style than became their abject condition, that the
Romans were resolved to maintain their dignity, either in peace or
war; and that, if Alaric refused them a fair and honourable capitulation, he might sound his trumpets, and prepare to give battle to an
innumerable people, exercised in arms and animated by despair. "The
thicker the hay, the easier it is mowed," was the concise reply of the
barbarian; and this rustic metaphor was accompanied by a loud and
insulting laugh, expressive of his contempt for the menaces of an unwarlike populace, enervated by luxury before they were emaciated by
famine. He then condescended to fix the ransom which he would accept as the price of his retreat from the walls of Rome: *all* the gold
and silver in the city, whether it were the property of the state, or of
individuals; *all* the rich and precious movables; and *all* the slaves who
could prove their title to the name of *barbarians*. The ministers of
the senate presumed to ask, in a modest and suppliant tone, " If such,

were probably an imitation of the arts and spells by which Numa had drawn
down Jupiter and his thunder on Mount Aventine.
———— Quid agant laqueis, quæ carmina dicant,
Quâque trahant superis sedibus arte Jovem,
Scire nefas homini.
The *ancilia* or shields of Mars, the *pignora Imperii*, which were carried in
solemn procession on the calends of March, derived their origin from this
mysterious event (Ovid. Fast. iii. 259-398). It was probably designed to
revive this ancient festival, which had been suppressed by Theodosius. In
that case we recover a chronological date (March the 1st, A.D. 409) which
has not hitherto been observed.
[78] Sozomen (l. ix. c. 6) insinuates that the experiment was actually though
unsuccessfully made, but he does not mention the name of Innocent; and
Tillemont (Mém. Ecclés. tom. x. p. 645) is determined not to believe that a
pope could be guilty of such impious condescension.

O king! are your demands, what do you intend to leave us? " " YOUR LIVES," replied the haughty conqueror: they trembled and retired. Yet before they retired, a short suspension of arms was granted, which allowed some time for a more temperate negotiation. The stern features of Alaric were insensibly relaxed; he abated much of the rigour of his terms; and at length consented to raise the siege, on the immediate payment of five thousand pounds of gold, of thirty thousand pounds of silver, of four thousand robes of silk, of three thousand pieces of fine scarlet cloth, and of three thousand pounds weight of pepper.[79] But the public treasury was exhausted; the annual rents of the great estates in Italy and the provinces were intercepted by the calamities of war; the gold and gems had been exchanged, during the famine, for the vilest sustenance; the hoards of secret wealth were still concealed by the obstinacy of avarice; and some remains of consecrated spoils afforded the only resource that could avert the impending ruin of the city. As soon as the Romans had satisfied the rapacious demands of Alaric, they were restored, in some measure, to the enjoyment of peace and plenty. Several of the gates were cautiously opened; the importation of provisions from the river and the adjacent country was no longer obstructed by the Goths; the citizens resorted in crowds to the free market which was held during three days in the suburbs; and while the merchants who undertook this gainful trade made a considerable profit, the future subsistence of the city was secured by the ample magazines which were deposited in the public and private granaries. A more regular discipline than could have been expected was maintained in the camp of Alaric; and the wise barbarian justified his regard for the faith of treaties, by the just severity with which he chastised a party of licentious Goths who had insulted some Roman citizens on the road to Ostia. His army, enriched by the contributions of the capital, slowly advanced into the fair and fruitful province of Tuscany, where he proposed to establish his winter-quarters; and the Gothic standard became the refuge of forty thousand barbarian slaves, who had broke their chains, and aspired, under the command of their great deliverer, to revenge the injuries and the disgrace of their cruel servitude. About the same time he received a more honourable reinforcement of Goths and Huns, whom Adolphus,[80] the brother of his wife, had conducted, at his pressing invitation, from the banks of the

[79] Pepper was a favourite ingredient of the most expensive Roman cookery, and the best sort commonly sold for fifteen denarii, or ten shillings, the pound. See Pliny, Hist. Natur. xii. 14. It was brought from India; and the same country, the coast of Malabar, still affords the greatest plenty; but the improvement of trade and navigation has multiplied the quantity and reduced the price. See Histoire Politique et Philosophique, etc., tom. i. p. 457.

[80] This Gothic chieftain is called, by Jornandes and Isidore, *Athaulphus;* by Zosimus and Orosius, *Ataulphus;* and by Olympiodorus, *Adaoulphus.* I have used the celebrated name of *Adolphus,* which seems to be authorised by the practice of the Swedes, the sons or brothers of the ancient Goths.

Danube to those of the Tiber, and who had cut their way, with some difficulty and loss, through the superior numbers of the Imperial troops. A victorious leader, who united the daring spirit of a barbarian with the art and discipline of a Roman general, was at the head of an hundred thousand fighting men; and Italy pronounced with terror and respect the formidable name of Alaric.[81]

At the distance of fourteen centuries we may be satisfied with relating the military exploits of the conquerors of Rome, without presuming to investigate the motives of their political conduct. In the midst of his apparent prosperity, Alaric was conscious, perhaps, of some secret weakness, some internal defect; or perhaps the moderation which he displayed was intended only to deceive and disarm the easy credulity of the ministers of Honorius. The king of the Goths repeatedly declared that it was his desire to be considered as the friend of peace and of the Romans. Three senators, at his earnest request, were sent ambassadors to the court of Ravenna, to solicit the exchange of hostages and the conclusion of the treaty; and the proposals which he more clearly expressed during the course of the negotiations could only inspire a doubt of his sincerity, as they might seem inadequate to the state of his fortune. The barbarian still aspired to the rank of master-general of the armies of the West; he stipulated an annual subsidy of corn and money; and he chose the provinces of Dalmatia, Noricum, and Venetia for the seat of his new kingdom, which would have commanded the important communication between Italy and the Danube. If these modest terms should be rejected, Alaric showed a disposition to relinquish his pecuniary demands, and even to content himself with the possession of Noricum; an exhausted and impoverished country, perpetually exposed to the inroads of the barbarians of Germany.[82] But the hopes of peace were disappointed by the weak obstinacy, or interested views, of the minister Olympius. Without listening to the salutary remonstrances of the senate, he dismissed their ambassadors under the conduct of a military escort, too numerous for a retinue of honour, and too feeble for an army of defence. Six thousand Dalmatians, the flower of the Imperial legions, were ordered to march from Ravenna to Rome, through an open country which was occupied by the formidable myriads of the barbarians. These brave legionaries, encompassed and betrayed, fell a sacrifice to ministerial folly; their general, Valens, with an hundred soldiers, escaped from the field of battle; and one of the ambassadors, who could no longer claim the protection of the law of nations, was obliged to purchase his freedom with a ransom of thirty thousand pieces of gold. Yet Alaric, instead of resenting this act of impotent hostility, immediately renewed

[81] The treaty between Alaric and the Romans, etc., is taken from Zosimus, l. v. [c. 41, sqq.] p. 354, 355, 358, 359, 362, 363. The additional circumstances are too few and trifling to require any other quotation.
[82] Zosimus, l. v. [c. 48] p. 367, 368, 369.

his proposals of peace, and the second embassy of the Roman senate, which derived weight and dignity from the presence of Innocent, bishop of the city, was guarded from the dangers of the road by a detachment of Gothic soldiers.[83]

Olympius [84] might have continued to insult the just resentment of a people who loudly accused him as the author of the public calamities, but his power was undermined by the secret intrigues of the palace. The favourite eunuchs transferred the government of Honorius and the empire to Jovius, the Prætorian præfect—an unworthy servant, who did not atone by the merit of personal attachment for the errors and misfortunes of his administration. The exile, or escape, of the guilty Olympius reserved him for more vicissitudes of fortune: he experienced the adventures of an obscure and wandering life; he again rose to power; he fell a second time into disgrace; his ears were cut off—he expired under the lash—and his ignominious death afforded a grateful spectacle to the friends of Stilicho. After the removal of Olympius, whose character was deeply tainted with religious fanaticism, the Pagans and heretics were delivered from the impolitic proscription which excluded them from the dignities of the state. The brave Gennerid,[85] a soldier of barbarian origin, who still adhered to the worship of his ancestors, had been obliged to lay aside the military belt; and though he was repeatedly assured by the emperor himself that laws were not made for persons of his rank or merit, he refused to accept any partial dispensation, and persevered in honourable disgrace till he had extorted a general act of justice from the distress of the Roman government. The conduct of Gennerid in the important station to which he was promoted or restored, of master-general of Dalmatia, Pannonia, Noricum, and Rhætia, seemed to revive the discipline and spirit of the republic. From a life of idleness and want his troops were soon habituated to severe exercise and plentiful subsistence, and his private generosity often supplied the rewards which were denied by the avarice or poverty of the court of Ravenna. The valour of Gennerid, formidable to the adjacent barbarians, was the firmest bulwark of the Illyrian frontier; and his vigilant care assisted the empire with a reinforcement of ten thousand Huns, who arrived on the confines of

[83] Zosimus, l. v. [c. 45] p. 360, 361, 362. The bishop, by remaining at Ravenna, escaped the impending calamities of the city. Orosius, l. vii. c. 39, p. 573.

[84] For the adventures of Olympius and his successors in the ministry, see Zosimus, l. v. [c. 46] p. 363, 365, 366; and Olympiodor. ap. Phot. p. 180, 181 [p. 57, ed. Bekk.].

[85] Zosimus (l. v. [c. 46] p. 364) relates this circumstance with visible complacency, and celebrates the character of Gennerid as the last glory of expiring Paganism. Very different were the sentiments of the council of Carthage, who deputed four bishops to the court of Ravenna, to complain of the law which had been just enacted, that all conversions to Christianity should be free and voluntary. See Baronius, Annal. Eccles. A.D. 409, No. 12; A.D. 410, No. 47, 48.

Italy, attended by such a convoy of provisions, and such a numerous train of sheep and oxen, as might have been sufficient not only for the march of an army but for the settlement of a colony. But the court and councils of Honorius still remained a scene of weakness and distraction, of corruption and anarchy. Instigated by the præfect Jovius, the guards rose in furious mutiny and demanded the heads of two generals and of the two principal eunuchs. The generals, under a perfidious promise of safety, were sent on ship-board and privately executed; while the favour of the eunuchs procured them a mild and secure exile at Milan and Constantinople. Eusebius the eunuch and the barbarian Allobich succeeded to the command of the bed-chamber and of the guards; and the mutual jealousy of the subordinate ministers was the cause of their mutual destruction. By the insolent order of the count of the domestics, the great chamberlain was shamefully beaten to death with sticks before the eyes of the astonished emperor; and the subsequent assassination of Allobich, in the midst of a public procession, is the only circumstance of his life in which Honorius discovered the faintest symptom of courage or resentment. Yet before they fell, Eusebius and Allobich had contributed their part to the ruin of the empire by opposing the conclusion of a treaty which Jovius, from a selfish, and perhaps a criminal motive, had negotiated with Alaric, in a personal interview under the walls of Rimini. During the absence of Jovius the emperor was persuaded to assume a lofty tone of inflexible dignity, such as neither his situation nor his character could enable him to support; and a letter, signed with the name of Honorius, was immediately despatched to the Prætorian præfect, granting him a free permission to dispose of the public money, but sternly refusing to prostitute the military honours of Rome to the proud demands of a barbarian. This letter was imprudently communicated to Alaric himself; and the Goth, who in the whole transaction had behaved with temper and decency, expressed in the most outrageous language his lively sense of the insult so wantonly offered to his person and to his nation. The conference of Rimini was hastily interrupted; and the præfect Jovius, on his return to Ravenna, was compelled to adopt, and even to encourage, the fashionable opinions of the court. By his advice and example the principal officers of the state and army were obliged to swear that, without listening in *any* circumstances to *any* conditions of peace, they would still persevere in perpetual and implacable war against the enemy of the republic. This rash engagement opposed an insuperable bar to all future negotiation. The ministers of Honorius were heard to declare that, if they had only invoked the name of the Deity, they would consult the public safety, and trust their souls to the mercy of Heaven: but they had sworn by the sacred head of the emperor himself; they had touched in solemn ceremony that august seat of majesty and wisdom; and the violation of their oath would expose them to the temporal penalties of sacrilege and rebellion.[86]

While the emperor and his court enjoyed with sullen pride the security of the marshes and fortifications of Ravenna, they abandoned Rome, almost without defence, to the resentment of Alaric. Yet such was the moderation which he still preserved, or affected, that as he moved with his army along the Flaminian way he successively despatched the bishops of the towns of Italy to reiterate his offers of peace, and to conjure the emperor that he would save the city and its inhabitants from hostile fire and the sword of the barbarians.[87] These impending calamities were however averted, not indeed by the wisdom of Honorius, but by the prudence or humanity of the Gothic king, who employed a milder, though not less effectual, method of conquest. Instead of assaulting the capital he successfully directed his efforts against the *Port* of Ostia, one of the boldest and most stupendous works of Roman magnificence.[88] The accidents to which the precarious subsistence of the city was continually exposed in a winter navigation and an open road had suggested to the genius of the first Cæsar the useful design which was executed under the reign of Claudius. The artificial moles which formed the narrow entrance advanced far into the sea, and firmly repelled the fury of the waves, while the largest vessels securely rode at anchor within three deep and capacious basins which received the northern branch of the Tiber about two miles from the ancient colony of Ostia.[89] The Roman *Port* insensibly swelled to

[86] Zosimus, l. v. [c. 47-49] p. 367, 368, 369. This custom of swearing by the head, or life, or safety, or genius, of the sovereign, was of the highest antiquity, both in Egypt (Genesis xlii. 15) and Scythia. It was soon transferred, by flattery, to the Cæsars; and Tertullian complains that it was the only oath which the Romans of his time affected to reverence. See an elegant Dissertation of the Abbé Massieu on the Oaths of the Ancients, in the Mém. de l'Académie des Inscriptions, tom. i. p. 208, 209.

[87] Zosimus, l. v. [c. 50] p. 368, 369. I have softened the expressions of Alaric, who expatiates in too florid a manner on the history of Rome.

[88] See Sueton. in Claud. c. 20; Dion Cassius, l. lx. [c. 11] p. 949, edit. Reimar; and the lively description of Juvenal, Satir. xii. 75, etc. In the sixteenth century, when the remains of this Augustan port were still visible, the antiquarians sketched the plan (see D'Anville, Mém. de l'Académie des Inscriptions, tom. xxx. p. 198), and declared with enthusiasm that all the monarchs of Europe would be unable to execute so great a work (Bergier, Hist. des Grands Chemins des Romains, tom. ii. p. 356).

[89] The *Ostia Tiberina* (see Cluver. Italia Antiq. l. iii. p. 870-879), in the plural number, the two mouths of the Tiber, were separated by the Holy Island, an equilateral triangle, whose sides were each of them computed at about two miles. The colony of Ostia was founded immediately beyond the left, or southern, and the *Port* immediately beyond the right, or northern, branch of the river; and the distance between their remains measures something more than two miles on Cingolani's map. In the time of Strabo the sand and mud deposited by the Tiber had choked the harbour of Ostia; the progress of the same cause has added much to the size of the Holy Island, and gradually left both Ostia and the Port at a considerable distance from the shore. The dry channels (fiumi morti) and the large estuaries (stagno

the size of an episcopal city,[90] where the corn of Africa was deposited in spacious granaries for the use of the capital. As soon as Alaric was in possession of that important place he summoned the city to surrender at discretion; and his demands were enforced by the positive declaration that a refusal, or even a delay, should be instantly followed by the destruction of the magazines on which the life of the Roman people depended. The clamours of that people and the terror of famine subdued the pride of the senate; they listened without reluctance to the proposal of placing a new emperor on the throne of the unworthy Honorius; and the suffrage of the Gothic conqueror bestowed the purple on Attalus, præfect of the city. The grateful monarch immediately acknowledged his protector as master-general of the armies of the West; Adolphus, with the rank of count of the domestics, obtained the custody of the person of Attalus; and the two hostile nations seemed to be united in the closest bands of friendship and alliance.[91]

The gates of the city were thrown open, and the new emperor of the Romans, encompassed on every side by the Gothic arms, was conducted in tumultuous procession to the palace of Augustus and Trajan. After he had distributed the civil and military dignities among his favourites and followers, Attalus convened an assembly of the senate, before whom, in a formal and florid speech, he asserted his resolution of restoring the majesty of the republic, and of uniting to the empire the provinces of Egypt and the East which had once acknowledged the sovereignty of Rome. Such extravagant promises inspired every reasonable citizen with a just contempt for the character of an unwarlike usurper, whose elevation was the deepest and most ignominious wound which the republic had yet sustained from the insolence of the barbarians. But the populace, with their usual levity, applauded the change of masters. The public discontent was favourable to the rival of Honorius; and the sectaries, oppressed by his persecuting edicts, expected some degree of countenance, or at least of toleration, from a

di Ponente, di Levante) mark the changes of the river and the efforts of the sea. Consult, for the present state of this dreary and desolate tract, the excellent map of the ecclesiastical state by the mathematicians of Benedict XIV.; an actual survey of the *Agro Romano,* in six sheets, by Cingolani, which contains 113,819 *rubbia* (about 570,000 acres) ; and the large topographical map of Ameti, in eight sheets.

[90] As early as the third (Lardner's Credibility of the Gospel, part ii. vol. iii. p. 89-92), or at least the fourth century (Carol. a Sancto Paulo, Notit. Eccles. p. 47), the Port of Rome was an episcopal city, which was demolished, as it should seem, in the ninth century, by pope Gregory IV., during the incursions of the Arabs. It is now reduced to an inn, a church, and the house or palace of the bishop, who ranks as one of six cardinal bishops of the Roman church. See Eschinard, Descrizione di Roma et dell' Agro Romano, p. 328.

[91] For the elevation of Attalus, consult Zosimus, l. vi. [c. 6, 7] p. 377-380; Sozomen, l. ix. c. 8, 9; Olympiodor. ap. Phot. p. 180, 181 [p. 57, ed. Bekk.]; Philostorg. l. xii. c. 3, and Godefroy, Dissertat. p. 470.

prince who, in his native country of Ionia, had been educated in the
Pagan superstition, and who had since received the sacrament of baptism from the hands of an Arian bishop.[92] The first days of the reign
of Attalus were fair and prosperous. An officer of confidence was sent
with an inconsiderable body of troops to secure the obedience of Africa;
the greatest part of Italy submitted to the terror of the Gothic powers;
and though the city of Bologna made a vigorous and effectual resistance, the people of Milan, dissatisfied perhaps with the absence of
Honorius, accepted with loud acclamations the choice of the Roman
senate. At the head of a formidable army, Alaric conducted his royal
captive almost to the gates of Ravenna; and a solemn embassy of the
principal ministers—of Jovius the Prætorian præfect, of Valens, master
of the cavalry and infantry, of the quæstor Potamius, and of Julian,
the first of the notaries—was introduced with martial pomp into the
Gothic camp. In the name of their sovereign they consented to acknowledge the lawful election of his competitor, and to divide the
provinces of Italy and the West between the two emperors. Their
proposals were rejected with disdain; and the refusal was aggravated
by the insulting clemency of Attalus, who condescended to promise that
if Honorius would instantly resign the purple he should be permitted
to pass the remainder of his life in the peaceful exile of some remote
island.[93] So desperate indeed did the situation of the son of Theodosius appear to those who were the best acquainted with his strength
and resources, that Jovius and Valens, his minister and his general,
betrayed their trust, infamously deserted the sinking cause of their
benefactor, and devoted their treacherous allegiance to the service of
his more fortunate rival. Astonished by such examples of domestic
treason, Honorius trembled at the approach of every servant, at the
arrival of every messenger. He dreaded the secret enemies who might
lurk in his capital, his palace, his bed-chamber; and some ships lay
ready in the harbour of Ravenna to transport the abdicated monarch
to the dominions of his infant nephew, the emperor of the East.

But there *is* a Providence (such at least was the opinion of the historian Procopius [94]) that watches over innocence and folly, and the
pretensions of Honorius to its peculiar care cannot reasonably be disputed. At the moment when his despair, incapable of any wise or
manly resolution, meditated a shameful flight, a seasonable reinforce-

[92] We may admit the evidence of Sozomen for the Arian baptism, and
that of Philostorgius for the Pagan education, of Attalus. The visible joy
of Zosimus, and the discontent which he imputes to the Anician family, are
very unfavourable to the Christianity of the new emperor.

[93] He carried his insolence so far as to declare that he should mutilate
Honorius before he sent him into exile. But this assertion of Zosimus [l. vi.
c. 8] is destroyed by the more impartial testimony of Olympiodorus, who
attributes the ungenerous proposal (which was absolutely rejected by Attalus)
to the baseness and perhaps the treachery of Jovius.

[94] Procop. de Bell. Vandal. l. i. c. 2 [tom. i. p. 318, ed. Bonn].

ment of four thousand veterans unexpectedly landed in the port of Ravenna. To these valiant strangers, whose fidelity had not been corrupted by the factions of the court, he committed the walls and gates of the city, and the slumbers of the emperor were no longer disturbed by the apprehension of imminent and internal danger. The favourable intelligence which was received from Africa suddenly changed the opinions of men and the state of public affairs. The troops and officers whom Attalus had sent into that province were defeated and slain, and the active zeal of Heraclian maintained his own allegiance and that of his people. The faithful count of Africa transmitted a large sum of money, which fixed the attachment of the Imperial guards; and his vigilance in preventing the exportation of corn and oil introduced famine, tumult and discontent into the walls of Rome. The failure of the African expedition was the source of mutual complaint and recrimination in the party of Attalus, and the mind of his protector was insensibly alienated from the interest of a prince who wanted spirit to command or docility to obey. The most imprudent measures were adopted, without the knowledge or against the advice of Alaric, and the obstinate refusal of the senate to allow in the embarkation the mixture even of five hundred Goths, betrayed a suspicious and distrustful temper which in their situation was neither generous nor prudent. The resentment of the Gothic king was exasperated by the malicious arts of Jovius, who had been raised to the rank of patrician, and who afterwards excused his double perfidy by declaring without a blush that he had only *seemed* to abandon the service of Honorius more effectually to ruin the cause of the usurper. In a large plain near Rimini, and in the presence of an innumerable multitude of Romans and barbarians, the wretched Attalus was publicly despoiled of the diadem and purple; and those ensigns of royalty were sent by Alaric as the pledge of peace and friendship to the son of Theodosius.[95] The officers who returned to their duty were reinstated in their employments, and even the merit of a tardy repentance was graciously allowed; but the degraded emperor of the Romans, desirous of life and insensible of disgrace, implored the permission of following the Gothic camp in the train of a haughty and capricious barbarian.[96]

The degradation of Attalus removed the only real obstacle to the conclusion of the peace, and Alaric advanced within three miles of Ravenna to press the irresolution of the Imperial ministers, whose insolence soon returned with the return of fortune. His indignation was kindled by the report that a rival chieftain, that Sarus, the personal

[95] See the cause and circumstances of the fall of Attalus in Zosimus, l. vi. [c. 9-12], p. 380-383. Sozomen, l. ix. c. 8. Philostorg. l. xii. c. 3. The two acts of indemnity in the Theodosian Code, l. ix. tit. xxxviii. leg. 11, 12, which were published the 12th of February and the 8th of August, A.D. 410, evidently relate to this usurper.

[96] In hoc, Alaricus, imperatore, facto, infecto, refecto, ac defecto . . . mimum risit, et ludum spectavit imperii. Orosius, l. vii. c. 42, p. 582.

enemy of Adolphus, and the hereditary foe of the house of Balti, had been received into the palace. At the head of three hundred followers that fearless barbarian immediately sallied from the gates of Ravenna, surprised and cut in pieces a considerable body of Goths, re-entered the city in triumph, and was permitted to insult his adversary by the voice of a herald, who publicly declared that the guilt of Alaric had for ever excluded him from the friendship and alliance of the emperor.[97] The crime and folly of the court of Ravenna was expiated a third time by the calamities of Rome. The king of the Goths, who no longer dissembled his appetite for plunder and revenge, appeared in arms under the walls of the capital; and the trembling senate, without any hopes of relief, prepared by a desperate resistance to delay the ruin of their country. But they were unable to guard against the secret conspiracy of their slaves and domestics, who either from birth or interest were attached to the cause of the enemy. At the hour of midnight the Salarian gate was silently opened, and the inhabitants were awakened by the tremendous sound of the Gothic trumpet. Eleven hundred and sixty-three years after the foundation of Rome, the Imperial city, which had subdued and civilised so considerable a part of mankind, was delivered to the licentious fury of the tribes of Germany and Scythia.[98]

The proclamation of Alaric, when he forced his entrance into a vanquished city, discovered, however, some regard for the laws of humanity and religion. He encouraged his troops boldly to seize the rewards of valour, and to enrich themselves with the spoils of a wealthy and effeminate people; but he exhorted them at the same time to spare the lives of the unresisting citizens, and to respect the churches of the apostles St. Peter and St. Paul as holy and inviolable sanctuaries. Amidst the horrors of a nocturnal tumult several of the Christian Goths displayed the fervour of a recent conversion; and some instances of their uncommon piety and moderation are related, and perhaps adorned, by the zeal of ecclesiastical writers.[99] While the barbarians roamed

---

[97] Zosimus, l. vi. [c. 13] p. 384. Sozomen, l. ix. c. 9. Philostorgius. l. xii. c. 3. In this place the text of Zosimus is mutilated, and we have lost the remainder of his sixth and last book, which ended with the sack of Rome. Credulous and partial as he is, we must take our leave of that historian with some regret.

[98] Adest Alaricus, trepidam Romam obsidet, turbat, irrumpit. Orosius, l. vii. c. 39, p. 573. He despatches this great event in seven words; but he employs whole pages in celebrating the devotion of the Goths. I have extracted from an improbable story of Procopius the circumstances which had an air of probability. Procop. de Bell. Vandal. l. i. c. 2 [tom. i. p. 315, ed. Bonn]. He supposes that the city was surprised while the senators slept in the afternoon; but Jerom, with more authority and more reason, affirms that it was in the night, nocte Moab capta est; nocte cecidit murus ejus, tom. i. p. 121. ad Principiam [Epist. cxxvii. c. 12, tom. i. p. 953, ed. Vallars.].

[99] Orosius (l. vii. c. 39, p. 573-576) applauds the piety of the Christian Goths without seeming to perceive that the greatest part of them were Arian heretics. Jornandes (c. 30, p. 653 [p. 86, ed. Lugd. B. 1597]) and Isidore

through the city in quest of prey, the humble dwelling of an aged virgin, who had devoted her life to the service of the altar, was forced open by one of the powerful Goths. He immediately demanded, though in civil language, all the gold and silver in her possession, and was astonished at the readiness with which she conducted him to a splendid hoard of massy plate of the richest materials and the most curious workmanship. The barbarian viewed with wonder and delight this valuable acquisition, till he was interrupted by a serious admonition, addressed to him in the following words: " These," said she, " are the consecrated vessels belonging to St. Peter: if you presume to touch them, the sacrilegious deed will remain on your conscience. For my part, I dare not keep what I am unable to defend." The Gothic captain, struck with reverential awe, despatched a messenger to inform the king of the treasure which he had discovered, and received a per-emptory order from Alaric, that all the consecrated plate and ornaments should be transported, without damage or delay, to the church of the apostle. From the extremity, perhaps, of the Quirinal hill to the distant quarter of the Vatican, a numerous detachment of Goths, marching in order of battle through the principal streets, protected with glittering arms the long train of their devout companions who bore aloft on their heads the sacred vessels of gold and silver, and the martial shouts of the barbarians were mingled with the sound of religious psalmody. From all the adjacent houses a crowd of Christians hastened to join this edifying procession, and a multitude of fugitives, without distinction of age or rank, or even of sect, had the good fortune to escape to the secure and hospitable sanctuary of the Vatican. The learned work concerning the *City of God* was professedly composed by St. Augustin, to justify the ways of Providence in the destruction of the Roman greatness. He celebrates with peculiar satisfaction this memorable triumph of Christ, and insults his adversaries by challenging them to produce some similar example of a town taken by storm, in which the fabulous gods of antiquity had been able to protect either themselves or their deluded votaries.[100]

In the sack of Rome some rare and extraordinary examples of barbarian virtue have been deservedly applauded. But the holy precincts of the Vatican and the apostolic churches could receive a very small proportion of the Roman people: many thousand warriors, more especially of the Huns who served under the standard of Alaric, were strangers to the name, or at least to the faith, of Christ, and we may

of Seville (Chron. p. 714, edit. Grot.), who were both attached to the Gothic cause, have repeated and embellished these edifying tales. According to Isidore, Alaric himself was heard to say that he waged war with the Romans, and not with the Apostles. Such was the style of the seventh century; two hundred years before, the fame and merit had been ascribed, not to the Apostles, but to Christ.

[100] See Augustin, de Civitat. Dei, l. i. c. 1-6. He particularly appeals to the examples of Troy, Syracuse, and Tarentum.

suspect, without any breach of charity or candour, that in the hour
of savage licence, when every passion was inflamed and every restraint
was removed, the precepts of the Gospel seldom influenced the behaviour of the Gothic Christians.   The writers the best disposed to
exaggerate their clemency have freely confessed that a cruel slaughter
was made of the Romans,[101] and that the streets of the city were filled
with dead bodies, which remained without burial during the general
consternation.   The despair of the citizens was sometimes converted
into fury; and whenever the barbarians were provoked by opposition,
they extended the promiscuous massacre to the feeble, the innocent, and
the helpless.   The private revenge of forty thousand slaves was exercised
without pity or remorse; and the ignominious lashes which they had
formerly received were washed away in the blood of the guilty or
obnoxious families.   The matrons and virgins of Rome were exposed
to injuries more dreadful, in the apprehension of chastity, than death
itself; and the ecclesiastical historian has selected an example of female
virtue for the admiration of future ages.[102]   A Roman lady, of singular
beauty and orthodox faith, had excited the impatient desires of a
young Goth, who, according to the sagacious remark of Sozomen, was
attached to the Arian heresy.   Exasperated by her obstinate resistance,
he drew his sword, and, with the anger of a lover, slightly wounded her
neck.   The bleeding heroine still continued to brave his resentment and
to repel his love, till the ravisher desisted from his unavailing efforts,
respectfully conducted her to the sanctuary of the Vatican, and gave six
pieces of gold to the guards of the church on condition that they should
restore her inviolate to the arms of her husband.   Such instances of
courage and generosity were not extremely common.   The brutal
soldiers satisfied their sensual appetites without consulting either the
inclination or the duties of their female captives; and a nice question
of casuistry was seriously agitated, Whether those tender victims, who

---

[101] Jerom (tom. i. p. 121, ad Principiam [Ep. cxxvii. tom. i. p. 953, ed.
Vallars.]) has applied to the sack of Rome all the strong expressions of
Virgil:—

> Quis cladem illius noctis, quis funera fando,
> Explicet, etc.

Procopius (1. i. c. 2 [tom. i. p. 316, ed. Bonn]) positively affirms that great
numbers were slain by the Goths. Augustin (de Civ. Dei, l. i. c. 12, 13)
offers Christian comfort for the death of those whose bodies (*multa corpora*)
had remained (*in tantâ strage*) unburied. Baronius, from the different writings of the Fathers, has thrown some light on the sack of Rome. Annal.
Eccles. A.D. 410, No. 16-44.

[102] Sozomen, l. ix. c. 10. Augustin (de Civitat. Dei, l. i. c. 17) intimates
that some virgins or matrons actually killed themselves to escape violation;
and though he admires their spirit, he is obliged, by his theology, to condemn
their rash presumption. Perhaps the good bishop of Hippo was too easy in the
belief, as well as too rigid in the censure, of this act of female heroism. The
twenty maidens (if they ever existed) who threw themselves into the Elbe
when Magdeburg was taken by storm, have been multiplied to the number
of twelve hundred. See Harte's History of Gustavus Adolphus, vol. i. p. 308.

had inflexibly refused their consent to the violation which they sustained, had lost, by their misfortune, the glorious crown of virginity.[103] There were other losses indeed of a more substantial kind and more general concern. It cannot be presumed that all the barbarians were at all times capable of perpetrating such amorous outrages; and the want of youth, or beauty, or chastity, protected the greatest part of the Roman women from the danger of a rape. But avarice is an insatiate and universal passion; since the enjoyment of almost every object that can afford pleasure to the different tastes and tempers of mankind may be procured by the possession of wealth. In the pillage of Rome a just preference was given to gold and jewels, which contain the greatest value in the smallest compass and weight; but, after these portable riches had been removed by the more diligent robbers, the palaces of Rome were rudely stripped of their splendid and costly furniture. The sideboards of massy plate, and the variegated wardrobes of silk and purple, were irregularly piled in the waggons that always followed the march of a Gothic army. The most exquisite works of art were roughly handled or wantonly destroyed: many a statue was melted for the sake of the precious materials; and many a vase, in the division of the spoil, was shivered into fragments by the stroke of a battle-axe. The acquisition of riches served only to stimulate the avarice of the rapacious barbarians, who proceeded by threats, by blows, and by tortures, to force from their prisoners the confession of hidden treasure.[104] Visible splendour and expense were alleged as the proof of a plentiful fortune; the appearance of poverty was imputed to a parsimonious disposition; and the obstinacy of some misers, who endured the most cruel torments before they would discover the secret object of their affection, was fatal to many unhappy wretches, who expired under the lash for refusing to reveal their imaginary treasures. The edifices of Rome, though the damage has been much exaggerated, received some injury from the violence of the Goths. At their entrance through the Salarian gate they fired the adjacent houses to guide their march and to distract the attention of the citizens; the flames, which encountered no obstacle in the disorder of the night, consumed many

[103] See Augustin, de Civitat. Dei. l. i. c. 16-18. He treats the subject with remarkable accuracy: and after admitting that there cannot be any crime where there is no consent, he adds, Sed quia non solum quod ad dolorem, verum etiam quod ad libidinem, pertinet, in corpore alieno perpetrari potest; quicquid tale factum fuerit, etsi retentam constantissimo animo pudicitiam non excutit, pudorem tamen incutit, ne credatur factum cum mentis etiam voluntate, quod fieri fortasse sine carnis aliquâ voluptate non potuit. In c. 18 he makes some curious distinctions between moral and physical virginity.
[104] Marcella, a Roman lady, equally respectable for her rank, her age, and her piety, was thrown on the ground and cruelly beaten and whipped, cæsam fustibus flagellisque, etc. Jerom, tom. i. p. 121, ad Principiam [Ep. cxxvii. c. 13, tom. i. p. 953, ed. Vallars.]. See Augustin, de Civ. Dei, l. i. c. 10. The modern Sacco di Roma, p. 208, gives an idea of the various methods of torturing prisoners for gold.

private and public buildings, and the ruins of the palace of Sallust [105] remained in the age of Justinian a stately monument of the Gothic conflagration.[106] Yet a contemporary historian has observed that fire could scarcely consume the enormous beams of solid brass, and that the strength of man was insufficient to subvert the foundations of ancient structures. Some truth may possibly be concealed in his devout assertion, that the wrath of Heaven supplied the imperfections of hostile rage, and that the proud Forum of Rome, decorated with the statues of so many gods and heroes, was levelled in the dust by the stroke of lightning.[107] Whatever might be the numbers of equestrian or plebeian rank who perished in the massacre of Rome, it is confidently affirmed that only one senator lost his life by the sword of the enemy.[108] But it was not easy to compute the multitudes who, from an honourable station and a prosperous fortune, were suddenly reduced to the miserable condition of captives and exiles. As the barbarians had more occasion for money than for slaves, they fixed at a moderate price the redemption of their indigent prisoners; and the ransom was often paid by the benevolence of their friends, or the charity of strangers.[109] The captives, who were regularly sold, either in open market or by private contract, would have legally regained their native freedom, which it was impossible for a citizen to lose

[105] The historian Sallust, who usefully practised the vices which he has so eloquently censured, employed the plunder of Numidia to adorn his palace and gardens on the Quirinal hill. The spot where the house stood is now marked by the church of St. Susanna, separated only by a street from the baths of Diocletian, and not far distant from the Salarian gate. See Nardini, Roma Antica, p. 192, 193, and the great Plan of Modern Rome, by Nolli.
[106] The expressions of Procopius are distinct and moderate (de Bell. Vandal. l. i. c. 2 [tom. i. p. 316, ed. Bonn]). The chronicle of Marcellinus speaks too strongly, partem urbis Romæ cremavit; and the words of Philostorgius ἐν ἐρειπίοις δὲ της πόλεως κειμένης, l. xii. c. 3) convey a false and exaggerated idea. Bargæus has composed a particular dissertation (see tom. iv. Antiquit. Rom. Græv.) to prove that the edifices of Rome were not subverted by the Goths and Vandals.
[107] Orosius, l. ii. c. 19, p. 143. He speaks as if he disapproved all statues; vel Deum vel hominem mentiuntur. They consisted of the kings of Alba and Rome from Æneas, the Romans illustrious either in arms or arts, and the deified Cæsars. The expression which he uses of Forum is somewhat ambiguous, since there existed five principal Fora; but as they were all contiguous and adjacent, in the plain which is surrounded by the Capitoline, the Quirinal, the Esquiline, and the Palatine hills, they might fairly be considered as one. See the Roma Antiqua of Donatus, p. 162-201, and the Roma Antica of Nardini, p. 212-273. The former is more useful for the ancient descriptions, the latter for the actual topography.
[108] Orosius (l. ii. c. 19, p. 142) compares the cruelty of the Gauls and the clemency of the Goths. Ibi vix quemquam inventum senatorem, qui vel absens evaserit; hic vix quemquam requiri, qui forte ut latens perierit. But there is an air of rhetoric, and perhaps of falsehood, in this antithesis; and Socrates (l. vii. c. 10) affirms, perhaps by an opposite exaggeration, that many senators were put to death with various and exquisite tortures.
[109] Multi . . . Christiani captivi ducti sunt. Augustin. de Civ. Dei, l. i. c. 14; and the Christians experienced no peculiar hardships.

or to alienate.[110] But as it was soon discovered that the vindication of
their liberty would endanger their lives, and that the Goths, unless they
were tempted to sell, might be provoked to murder their useless prisoners,
the civil jurisprudence had been already qualified by a wise regulation,
that they should be obliged to serve the moderate term of five years, till
they had discharged by their labour the price of their redemption.[111]
The nations who invaded the Roman empire had driven before them,
into Italy, whole troops of hungry and affrighted provincials, less apprehensive of servitude than of famine. The calamities of Rome and Italy
dispersed the inhabitants to the most lonely, the most secure, the most
distant places of refuge. While the Gothic cavalry spread terror and
desolation along the sea-coast of Campania and Tuscany, the little island
of Igilium, separated by a narrow channel from the Argentarian promontory, repulsed, or eluded, their hostile attempts; and at so small a distance from Rome, great numbers of citizens were securely concealed in
the thick woods of that sequestered spot.[112] The ample patrimonies
which many senatorian families possessed in Africa invited them, if they
had time and prudence to escape from the ruin of their country, to embrace the shelter of that hospitable province. The most illustrious of
these fugitives was the noble and pious Proba,[113] the widow of the præfect Petronius. After the death of her husband, the most powerful subject of Rome, she had remained at the head of the Anician family, and
successively supplied, from her private fortune, the expense of the consulships of her three sons. When the city was besieged and taken by

[110] See Heineccius, Antiquitat. Juris Roman. tom. i. p. 96.
[111] Appendix Cod. Theodos. xvi. in Sirmond. Opera, tom. i. p. 735. This
edict was published on the 11th of December, A.D. 408, and is more reasonable
than properly belonged to the ministers of Honorius.
[112]   Eminus Igilii sylvosa cacumina miror;
               Quem fraudare nefas laudis honore suæ.
            Hæc proprios nuper tutata est insula saltus;
               Sive loci ingenio, seu domini genio.
            Gurgite cum modico victricibus obstitit armis,
               Tanquam longinquo dissociata mari.
            Hæc multos lacerâ suscepit ab urbe fugatos,
               Hic fessis posito certa timore salus.
            Plurima terreno populaverat æquora bello,
               Contra naturam classe timendus eques:
            Unum, mira fides, vario discrimine portum!
               Tam prope Romanis, tam procul esse Getis.
                                    Rutilius, in Itinerar. l. i. 325.
The island is now called Giglio. See Cluver. Ital. Antiq. l. ii. p. 502.
[113] As the adventures of Proba and her family are connected with the life
of St. Augustin, they are diligently illustrated by Tillemont, Mém. Ecclés.
tom. xiii. p. 620-635. Some time after their arrival in Africa, Demetrias
took the veil and made a vow of virginity; an event which was considered
as of the highest importance to Rome and to the world. All the *Saints* wrote
congratulatory letters to her; that of Jerom is still extant (tom. i. p. 62-73,
ad Demetriad. de servandâ Virginitat. [Epist. cxxx. tom. i. p. 969, ed. Vallars.]), and contains a mixture of absurd reasoning, spirited declamation, and
curious facts, some of which relate to the siege and sack of Rome.

the Goths, Proba supported with Christian resignation the loss of immense riches; embarked in a small vessel, from whence she beheld, at sea, the flames of her burning palace; and fled with her daughter Læta, and her grand-daughter, the celebrated virgin Demetrias, to the coast of Africa. The benevolent profusion with which the matron distributed the fruits or the price of her estates contributed to alleviate the misfortunes of exile and captivity. But even the family of Proba herself was not exempt from the rapacious oppression of Count Heraclian, who basely sold, in matrimonial prostitution, the noblest maidens of Rome to the lust or avarice of the Syrian merchants. The Italian fugitives were dispersed through the provinces, along the coast of Egypt and Asia, as far as Constantinople and Jerusalem; and the village of Bethlehem, the solitary residence of St. Jerom and his female converts, was crowned with illustrious beggars, of either sex and every age, who excited the public compassion by the remembrance of their past fortune.[114] This awful catastrophe of Rome filled the astonished empire with grief and terror. So interesting a contrast of greatness and ruin disposed the fond credulity of the people to deplore, and even to exaggerate, the afflictions of the queen of cities. The clergy, who applied to recent events the lofty metaphors of Oriental prophecy, were sometimes tempted to confound the destruction of the capital and the dissolution of the globe.

There exists in human nature a strong propensity to depreciate the advantages, and to magnify the evils, of the present times. Yet, when the first emotions had subsided, and a fair estimate was made of the real damage, the more learned and judicious contemporaries were forced to confess that infant Rome had formerly received more essential injury from the Gauls than she had now sustained from the Goths in her declining age.[115] The experience of eleven centuries has enabled posterity to produce a much more singular parallel; and to affirm with confidence, that the ravages of the barbarians whom Alaric had led from the banks of the Danube were less destructive than the hostilities exercised by the troops of Charles the Fifth, a catholic prince, who styled himself Emperor of the Romans.[116] The Goths evacuated the city at the end of

[114] See the pathetic complaint of Jerom (tom. v. p. 400) in his preface to the second book of his Commentaries on the Prophet Ezekiel.

[115] Orosius, though with some theological partiality, states this comparison, l. ii. c. 19, p. 142, l. vii. c. 39, p. 575. But, in the history of the taking of Rome by the Gauls, everything is uncertain, and perhaps fabulous. See Beaufort sur l'Incertitude, etc., de l'Histoire Romaine, p. 356; and Melot, in the Mém. de l'Académie des Inscript. tom. xv. p. 1-21.

[116] The reader who wishes to inform himself of the circumstances of this famous event may peruse an admirable narrative in Dr. Robertson's History of Charles V. vol. ii. p. 283; or consult the Annali d'Italia of the learned Muratori, tom. xiv. p. 230-244, octavo edition. If he is desirous of examining the originals, he may have recourse to the eighteenth book of the great, but unfinished, history of Guicciardini. But the account which most truly deserves the name of authentic and original is a little book, entitled *Il Sacco di Roma,* composed, within less than a month after the assault of the city, by the *brother* of the historian Guicciardini, who appears to have been an able magistrate and a dispassionate writer.

six days, but Rome remained above nine months in the possession of the Imperialists; and every hour was stained by some atrocious act of cruelty, lust, and rapine. The authority of Alaric preserved some order and moderation among the ferocious multitude which acknowledged him for their leader and king; but the constable of Bourbon had gloriously fallen in the attack of the walls; and the death of the general removed every restraint of discipline from an army which consisted of three independent nations, the Italians, the Spaniards, and the Germans. In the beginning of the sixteenth century the manners of Italy exhibited a remarkable scene of the depravity of mankind. They united the sanguinary crimes that prevail in an unsettled state of society, with the polished vices which spring from the abuse of art and luxury; and the loose adventurers, who had violated every prejudice of patriotism and superstition to assault the palace of the Roman pontiff, must deserve to be considered as the most profligate of the *Italians*. At the same era the *Spaniards* were the terror both of the Old and New World; but their high-spirited valour was disgraced by gloomy pride, rapacious avarice, and unrelenting cruelty. Indefatigable in the pursuit of fame and riches, they had improved, by repeated practice, the most exquisite and effectual methods of torturing their prisoners: many of the Castilians who pillaged Rome were familiars of the holy inquisition; and some volunteers, perhaps, were lately returned from the conquest of Mexico. The *Germans* were less corrupt than the Italians, less cruel than the Spaniards; and the rustic, or even savage aspect of those Tramontane warriors often disguised a simple and merciful disposition. But they had imbibed, in the first fervour of the Reformation, the spirit, as well as the principles, of Luther. It was their favourite amusement to insult, or destroy, the consecrated objects of catholic superstition; they indulged, without pity or remorse, a devout hatred against the clergy of every denomination and degree who form so considerable a part of the inhabitants of modern Rome; and their fanatic zeal might aspire to subvert the throne of Antichrist, to purify, with blood and fire, the abominations of the spiritual Babylon.[117]

The retreat of the victorious Goths, who evacuated Rome on the sixth day,[118] might be the result of prudence, but it was not surely the effect of fear.[119] At the head of an army encumbered with rich and weighty spoils, their intrepid leader advanced along the Appian Way into the southern provinces of Italy, destroying whatever dared to oppose his

[117] The furious spirit of Luther, the effect of temper and enthusiasm, has been forcibly attacked (Bossuet, Hist. des Variations des Eglises Protestantes, livre i. p. 20-36) and feebly defended (Seckendorf, Comment. de Lutheranismo, especially l. i. No. 78, p. 120, and l. iii. No. 122, p. 556).

[118] Marcellinus, in Chron. Orosius (l. vii. c. 39, p. 575), asserts that he left Rome on the *third* day; but this difference is easily reconciled by the successive motions of great bodies of troops.

[119] Socrates (l. vii. c. 10) pretends, without any colour of truth or reason, that Alaric fled on the report that the armies of the Eastern empire were in full march to attack him.

passage, and contenting himself with the plunder of the unresisting country. The fate of Capua, the proud and luxurious metropolis of Campania, and which was respected, even in its decay, as the eighth city of the empire,[120] is buried in oblivion; whilst the adjacent town of Nola [121] has been illustrated, on this occasion, by the sanctity of Paulinus,[122] who was successively a consul, a monk, and a bishop. At the age of forty he renounced the enjoyment of wealth and honour, of society and literature, to embrace a life of solitude and penance; and the loud applause of the clergy encouraged him to despise the reproaches of his worldly friends, who ascribed this desperate act to some disorder of the mind or body.[123] An early and passionate attachment determined him to fix his humble dwelling in one of the suburbs of Nola, near the miraculous tomb of St. Felix, which the public devotion had already surrounded with five large and populous churches. The remains of his fortune, and of his understanding, were dedicated to the service of the glorious martyr; whose praise, on the day of his festival, Paulinus never failed to celebrate by a solemn hymn; and in whose name he erected a sixth church, of superior elegance and beauty, which was decorated with many curious pictures from the history of the Old and New Testament. Such assiduous zeal secured the favour of the saint,[124] or at least of the people; and, after fifteen years' retirement, the Roman consul was compelled to accept the bishopric of Nola, a few months before the city was invested by the Goths. During the siege, some religious persons were satisfied that they had seen, either in dreams or visions, the divine form of their tutelar patron; yet it soon appeared by the event, that Felix wanted power, or inclination, to preserve the flock of which he had formerly been the shepherd. Nola was not saved from the general devastation;[125] and the captive bishop was protected only by the general opinion of his innocence and poverty. Above four years elapsed from

[120] Ausonius de Claris Urbibus, p. 233, edit. Toll. The luxury of Capua had formerly surpassed that of Sybaris itself. See Athenæus Deipnosophist. l. xii. [c. 36] p. 528, edit. Casaubon.

[121] Forty-eight years before the foundation of Rome (about 800 before the Christian era) the Tuscans built Capua and Nola, at the distance of twenty-three miles from each other: but the latter of the two cities never emerged from a state of mediocrity.

[122] Tillemont (Mém. Ecclés. tom. xiv. p. 1-146) has compiled, with his usual diligence, all that relates to the life and writings of Paulinus, whose retreat is celebrated by his own pen and by the praises of St. Ambrose, St. Jerom, St. Augustin, Sulpicius Severus, etc., his Christian friends and contemporaries.

[123] See the affectionate letters of Ausonius (Epist. xix.-xxv. p. 650-698, edit. Toll.) to his colleague, his friend, and his disciple, Paulinus. The religion of Ausonius is still a problem (see Mém. de l'Académie des Inscriptions, tom. xv. p. 123-138). I believe that it was such in his own time, and consequently that in his heart he was a Pagan.

[124] The humble Paulinus once presumed to say that he believed St. Felix *did* love him; at least, as a master loves his little dog.

[125] See Jornandes, de Reb. Get. c. 30, p. 653. Philostorgius, l. xii. c. 3. Augustin, de Civ. Dei, l. i. c. 10. Baronius, Annal. Eccles. A.D. 410, No. 45, 46.

the successful invasion of Italy by the arms of Alaric, to the voluntary retreat of the Goths under the conduct of his successor Adolphus; and, during the whole time, they reigned without control over a country which, in the opinion of the ancients, had united all the various excellences of nature and art. The prosperity, indeed, which Italy had attained in the auspicious age of the Antonines, had gradually declined with the decline of the empire. The fruits of a long peace perished under the rude grasp of the barbarians; and they themselves were in-capable of tasting the more elegant refinements of luxury which had been prepared for the use of the soft and polished Italians. Each soldier, however, claimed an ample portion of the substantial plenty, the corn and cattle, oil and wine, that was daily collected and con-sumed, in the Gothic camp; and the principal warriors insulted the villas and gardens, once inhabited by Lucullus and Cicero, along the beauteous coast of Campania. Their trembling captives, the sons and daughters of Roman senators, presented, in goblets of gold and gems, large draughts of Falernian wine to the haughty victors, who stretched their huge limbs under the shade of plane-trees,[126] arti-ficially disposed to exclude the scorching rays, and to admit the genial warmth, of the sun. These delights were enhanced by the memory of past hardships: the comparison of their native soil, the bleak and barren hills of Scythia, and the frozen banks of the Elbe and Danube, added new charms to the felicity of the Italian climate.[127]

Whether fame, or conquest, or riches were the object of Alaric, he pursued that object with an indefatigable ardour which could neither be quelled by adversity nor satiated by success. No sooner had he reached the extreme land of Italy than he was attracted by the neighbouring prospect of a fertile and peaceful island. Yet even the possession of Sicily he considered only an an intermediate step to the important expedition which he already meditated against the continent of Africa. The straits of Rhegium and Messina [128] are twelve miles in length, and in the

---

[126] The *platanus,* or plane-tree, was a favourite of the ancients, by whom it was propagated, for the sake of shade, from the East to Gaul. Pliny, Hist. Natur. xii. 3, 4, 5. He mentions several of an enormous size; one in the Imperial villa at Velitræ, which Caligula called his nest, as the branches were capable of holding a large table, the proper attendants, and the emperor himself, whom Pliny quaintly styles *pars umbræ;* an expression which might, with equal reason, be applied to Alaric.

[127] The prostrate South to the destroyer yields
Her boasted titles and her golden fields;
With grim delight the brood of winter view
A brighter day, and skies of azure hue;
Scent the new fragrance of the opening rose,
And quaff the pendent vintage as it grows.

See Gray's Poems, published by Mr. Mason, p. 197. Instead of compiling tables of chronology and natural history, why did not Mr. Gray apply the powers of his genius to finish the philosophic poem of which he has left such an exquisite specimen?

[128] For the perfect description of the Straits of Messina, Scylla, Charybdis,

narrowest passage about one mile and a half broad; and the fabulous monsters of the deep, the rocks of Scylla and the whirlpool of Charybdis, could terrify none but the most timid and unskilled mariners. Yet as soon as the first division of the Goths had embarked, a sudden tempest arose, which sunk or scattered many of the transports; their courage was daunted by the terrors of a new element; and the whole design was defeated by the premature death of Alaric, which fixed, after a short illness, the fatal term of his conquests. The ferocious character of the barbarians was displayed in the funeral of a hero whose valour and fortune they celebrated with mournful applause. By the labour of a captive multitude they forcibly diverted the course of the Busentinus, a small river that washes the walls of Consentia. The royal sepulchre, adorned with the splendid spoils and trophies of Rome, was constructed in the vacant bed; the waters were then restored to their natural channel; and the secret spot where the remains of Alaric had been deposited was for ever concealed by the inhuman massacre of the prisoners who had been employed to execute the work.[129]

The personal animosities and hereditary feuds of the barbarians were suspended by the strong necessity of their affairs; and the brave Adolphus, the brother-in-law of the deceased monarch, was unanimously elected to succeed to his throne. The character and political system of the new king of the Goths may be best understood from his own conversation with an illustrious citizen of Narbonne, who afterwards, in a pilgrimage to the Holy Land, related it to St. Jerom, in the presence of the historian Orosius. " In the full confidence of valour and victory, I once aspired (said Adolphus) to change the face of the universe; to obliterate the name of Rome; to erect on its ruins the dominion of the Goths; and to acquire, like Augustus, the immortal fame of the founder of a new empire. By repeated experiments I was gradually convinced that laws are essentially necessary to maintain and regulate a well-constituted state; and that the fierce untractable humour of the Goths was incapable of bearing the salutary yoke of laws and civil government. From that moment I proposed to myself a different object of glory and ambition; and it is now my sincere wish that the gratitude of future ages should acknowledge the merit of a stranger, who employed the sword of the Goths, not to subvert, but to restore and maintain, the prosperity of the Roman empire." [130] With these pacific views the successor of Alaric suspended the operations of war, and seriously negotiated with the Imperial court a treaty of friendship and alliance. It was the interest of the ministers of Honorius, who were now released

---

etc., see Cluverius (Ital. Antiq. l. iv. p. 1293, and Silicia Antiq. l. i. p. 60-76), who had diligently studied the ancients and surveyed with a curious eye the actual face of the country.

[129] Jornandes, de Reb. Get. c. 30, p. 654 [p. 87, ed. Lugd. B. 1597].

[130] Orosius, l. vii. c. 43, p. 584, 585. He was sent by St. Augustin, in the year 415, from Africa to Palestine, to visit St. Jerom and to consult with him on the subject of Pelagian controversy.

from the obligation of their extravagant oath, to deliver Italy from
the intolerable weight of the Gothic powers; and they readily accepted
their service against the tyrants and barbarians who infested the provinces beyond the Alps.[131]   Adolphus, assuming the character of a
Roman General, directed his march from the extremity of Campania
to the southern provinces of Gaul.   His troops, either by force or agreement, immediately occupied the cities of Narbonne, Toulouse, and
Bordeaux; and though they were repulsed by Count Boniface from
the walls of Marseilles, they soon extended their quarters from the
Mediterranean to the ocean.   The oppressed provincials might exclaim that the miserable remnant which the enemy had spared was
cruelly ravished by their pretended allies; yet some specious colours
were not wanting to palliate or justify the violence of the Goths.
The cities of Gaul which they attacked might perhaps be considered as
in a state of rebellion against the government of Honorius: the articles
of the treaty or the secret instructions of the court might sometimes be
alleged in favour of the seeming usurpations of Adolphus; and the
guilt of any irregular unsuccessful act of hostility might always be imputed, with an appearance of truth, to the ungovernable spirit of a barbarian host impatient of peace or discipline.   The luxury of Italy had
been less effectual to soften the temper than to relax the courage of the
Goths; and they had imbibed the vices, without imitating the arts and
institutions, of civilised society.[132]

The professions of Adolphus were probably sincere, and his attachment to the cause of the republic was secured by the ascendant which a
Roman princess had acquired over the heart and understanding of the
barbarian king. Placidia,[133] the daughter of the great Theodosius, and of
Galla, his second wife, had received a royal education in the palace of
Constantinople; but the eventful story of her life is connected with the
revolutions which agitated the Western empire under the reign of her
brother Honorius.   When Rome was first invested by the arms of Alaric,
Placidia, who was then about twenty years of age, resided in the city;
and her ready consent of the death of her cousin Serena has a cruel and
ungrateful appearance, which, according to the circumstances of the action, may be aggravated or excused by the consideration of her tender
age.[134]   The victorious barbarians detained, either as a hostage or a cap-

---

[131] Jornandes supposes, without much probability, that Adolphus visited and
plundered Rome a second time (more locustarum erasit).   Yet he agrees with
Orosius in supposing that a treaty of peace was concluded between the Gothic
prince and Honorius.   See Oros. l. vii. c. 43, p. 584, 585.   Jornandes, de Reb.
Geticis, c. 31, p. 654, 655 [p. 88, ed. Lugd. B.].

[132] The retreat of the Goths from Italy and their first transactions in Gaul
are dark and doubtful.   I have derived much assistance from Mascou (Hist.
of the Ancient Germans, l. viii. c. 29, 35, 36, 37), who has illustrated and
connected the broken chronicles and fragments of the times.

[133] See an account of Placidia in Ducange, Fam. Byzant. p. 72; and Tillemont, Hist. des Empereurs, tom. v. p. 260, 386, etc., tom. vi. p. 240.

[134] Zosim. l. v. [c. 38] p. 350.

tive,[135] the sister of Honorius; but while she was exposed to the disgrace of following round Italy the motions of a Gothic camp, she experienced, however, a decent and respectful treatment. The authority of Jornandes, who praises the beauty of Placidia, may perhaps be counterbalanced by the silence, the expressive silence, of her flatterers: yet the splendour of her birth, the bloom of youth, the elegance of manners, and the dexterous insinuations which she condescended to employ, made a deep impression on the mind of Adolphus; and the Gothic king aspired to call himself the brother of the emperor. The ministers of Honorius rejected with disdain the proposal of an alliance so injurious to every sentiment of Roman pride; and repeatedly urged the restitution of Placidia as an indispensable condition of the treaty of peace. But the daughter of Theodosius submitted without reluctance to the desires of the conqueror, a young and valiant prince, who yielded to Alaric in loftiness of stature, but who excelled in the more attractive qualities of grace and beauty. The marriage of Adolphus and Placidia [136] was consummated before the Goths retired from Italy; and the solemn, perhaps the anniversary, day of their nuptials was afterwards celebrated in the house of Ingenuus, one of the most illustrious citizens of Narbonne in Gaul. The bride, attired and adorned like a Roman empress, was placed on a throne of state; and the king of the Goths, who assumed on this occasion the Roman habit, contented himself with a less honourable seat by her side. The nuptial gift, which, according to the custom of his nation,[137] was offered to Placidia, consisted of the rare and magnificent spoils of her country. Fifty beautiful youths, in silken robes, carried a basin in each hand; and one of these basins was filled with pieces of gold, the other with precious stones of an inestimable value. Attalus, so long the sport of fortune and of the Goths, was appointed to lead the

[135] Zosim. l. vi. [c. 12] p. 383. Orosius (l. vii. c. 40, p. 576) and the Chronicles of Marcellinus and Idatius seem to suppose that the Goths did not carry away Placidia till after the last siege of Rome.

[136] See the pictures of Adolphus and Placidia, and the account of their marriage, in Jornandes, de Reb. Geticis, c. 31, p. 654, 655 [p. 88, ed. Lugd. B.] With regard to the place where the nuptials were stipulated, or consummated, or celebrated, the MSS. of Jornandes vary between two neighbouring cities, Forli and Imola (Forum Livii and Forum Cornelii). It is fair and easy to reconcile the Gothic historian with Olympiodorus (see Mascou, l. viii. c. 36) : but Tillemont grows peevish, and swears that it is not worth while to try to conciliate Jornandes with any good authors.

[137] The Visigoths (the subjects of Adolphus) restrained, by subsequent laws, the prodigality of conjugal love. It was illegal for a husband to make any gift or settlement for the benefit of his wife during the first year of their marriage; and his liberality could not at any time exceed the tenth part of his property. The Lombards were somewhat more indulgent: they allowed the *morgingcap* immediately after the wedding night; and this famous gift, the reward of virginity, might equal the fourth part of the husband's substance. Some cautious maidens, indeed, were wise enough to stipulate beforehand a present which they were too sure of not deserving. See Montesquieu, Esprit des Loix, l. xix. c. 25. Muratori, delle Antichità Italiane, tom. i. Dissertazione xx. p. 243.

chorus of the Hymeneal song; and the degraded emperor might aspire
to the praise of a skilful musician. The barbarians enjoyed the insolence of their triumph; and the provincials rejoiced in this alliance,
which tempered, by the mild influence of love and reason, the fierce
spirit of their Gothic lord.[138]

The hundred basins of gold and gems presented to Placidia at her nuptial feast formed an inconsiderable portion of the Gothic treasures; of
which some extraordinary specimens may be selected from the history
of the successors of Adolphus. Many curious and costly ornaments of
pure gold, enriched with jewels, were found in their palace of Narbonne
when it was pillaged in the sixth century by the Franks: sixty cups or
chalices: fifteen *patens,* or plates, for the use of the communion; twenty
boxes, or cases, to hold the books of the gospels: this consecrated
wealth [139] was distributed by the son of Clovis among the churches of
his dominions, and his pious liberality seems to upbraid some former
sacrilege of the Goths. They possessed, with more security of conscience,
the famous *missorium,* or great dish for the service of the table, of massy
gold, of the weight of five hundred pounds, and of far superior value,
from the precious stones, the exquisite workmanship, and the tradition
that it had been presented by Aëtius, the patrician, to Torismond, king
of the Goths. One of the successors of Torismond purchased the aid of
the French monarch by the promise of this magnificent gift. When he
was seated on the throne of Spain, he delivered it with reluctance to the
ambassadors of Dagobert; despoiled them on the road; stipulated, after a long negotiation, the inadequate ransom of two hundred thousand
pieces of gold; and preserved the *missorium* as the pride of the Gothic
treasury.[140] When that treasury, after the conquest of Spain, was
plundered by the Arabs, they admired and they have celebrated another
object still more remarkable; a table of considerable size, of one single
piece of solid emerald,[141] encircled with three rows of fine pearls, supported by three hundred and sixty-five feet of gems and massy gold, and

[138] We owe the curious detail of this nuptial feast to the historian Olympiodorus, ap. Photium, p. 185, 188 [p. 59, ed. Bekk.].
[139] See in the great collection of the Historians of France by Dom Bouquet,
tom. ii. Greg. Turonens. l. iii. c. 10, p. 191. Gesta Regum Francorum, c. 23,
p. 557. The anonymous writer, with an ignorance worthy of his times, supposes that these instruments of Christian worship had belonged to the temple
of Solomon. If he has any meaning, it must be that they were found in the
sack of Rome.
[140] Consult the following original testimonies in the Historians of France,
tom. ii. Fredegarii Scholastici Chron. c. 73, p. 441. Fredegar. Fragment. iii.
p. 463. Gesta Regis Dagobert. c. 29, p. 587. The accession of Sisenand to
the throne of Spain happened A.D. 631. The 200,000 pieces of gold were appropriated by Dagobert to the foundation of the church of St. Denys.
[141] The president Goguet (Origine des Loix, etc., tom. ii. p. 239) is of opinion
that the stupendous pieces of emerald, the statues and columns which antiquity has placed in Egypt, at Gades, at Constantinople, were in reality
artificial compositions of coloured glass. The famous emerald dish which
is shown at Genoa is supposed to countenance the suspicion.

estimated at the price of five hundred thousand pieces of gold.[142] Some portion of the Gothic treasures might be the gift of friendship or the tribute of obedience; but the far greater part had been the fruits of war and rapine, the spoils of the empire, and perhaps of Rome.

After the deliverance of Italy from the oppression of the Goths, some secret counsellor was permitted, amidst the factions of the palace, to heal the wounds of that afflicted country.[143] By a wise and humane regulation the eight provinces which had been the most deeply injured— Campania, Tuscany, Picenum, Samnium, Apulia, Calabria, Bruttium, and Lucania—obtained an indulgence of five years; the ordinary tribute was reduced to one-fifth, and even that fifth was destined to restore and support the useful institution of the public posts. By another law the lands which had been left without inhabitants or cultivation were granted, with some diminution of taxes, to the neighbours who should occupy or the strangers who should solicit them; and the new possessors were secured against the future claims of the fugitive proprietors. About the same time a general amnesty was published in the name of Honorius, to abolish the guilt and memory of all the *involuntary* offences which had been committed by his unhappy subjects during the term of the public disorder and calamity. A decent and respectful attention was paid to the restoration of the capital; the citizens were encouraged to rebuild the edifices which had been destroyed or damaged by hostile fire; and extraordinary supplies of corn were imported from the coast of Africa. The crowds that so lately fled before the sword of the barbarians were soon recalled by the hopes of plenty and pleasure; and Albinus, præfect of Rome, informed the court, with some anxiety and surprise, that in a single day he had taken an account of the arrival of fourteen thousand strangers.[144] In less than seven years the vestiges of the Gothic invasion were almost obliterated, and the city appeared to resume its former splendour and tranquillity. The venerable matron replaced her crown of laurel, which had been ruffled by the storms of war, and was still amused in the last moment of her decay with the prophecies of revenge, of victory, and of eternal dominion.[145]

[142] Elmacin. Hist. Saracenica, l. i. p. 85; Roderic. Tolet. Hist. Arab. c. 9. Cardonne, Hist. de l'Afrique et de l'Espagne sous les Arabes, tom. i. p. 83. It was called the Table of Solomon, according to the custom of the Orientals, who ascribe to that prince every ancient work of knowledge or magnificence.

[143] His three laws are inserted in the Theodosian Code, l. xi. tit. xxviii. leg. 7; l. xiii. tit. xi. leg. 12; l. xv. tit. xiv. leg. 14. The expressions of the last are very remarkable, since they contain not only a pardon, but an apology.

[144] Olympiodorus ap. Phot. p. 188 [p. 59, ed. Bekk.]. Philostorgius (l. xii. c. 5) observes, that when Honorius made his triumphal entry he encouraged the Romans, with his hand and voice (χειρὶ καὶ γλώττη), to rebuild their city; and the Chronicle of Prosper commends Heraclian, qui in Romanæ urbis reparationem strenuum exhibuerat ministerium.

[145] The date of the voyage of Claudius Rutilius Numatianus is clogged with some difficulties; but Scaliger has deduced from astronomical characters that he left Rome the 24th of September, and embarked at Porto the 9th of October, A.D. 416. See Tillemont, Hist. des Empereurs, tom. v. p. 820. In

This apparent tranquillity was soon disturbed by the approach of an hostile armament from the country which afforded the daily subsistence of the Roman people. Heraclian, count of Africa, who under the most difficult and distressful circumstances had supported with active loyalty the cause of Honorius, was tempted in the year of his consulship to as-sume the character of a rebel and the title of emperor. The ports of Af-rica were immediately filled with the naval forces, at the head of which he prepared to invade Italy; and his fleet, when it cast anchor at the mouth of the Tiber, indeed surpassed the fleets of Xerxes and Alexander, if *all* the vessels, including the royal galley and the smallest boat, did ac-tually amount to the incredible number of three thousand two hun-dred.[146] Yet with such an armament, which might have subverted or re-stored the greatest empires of the earth, the African usurper made a very faint and feeble impression on the provinces of his rival. As he marched from the port along the road which leads to the gates of Rome, he was en-countered, terrified, and routed by one of the Imperial captains; and the lord of this mighty host, deserting his fortune and his friends, ignomini-ously fled with a single ship.[147] When Heraclian landed in the harbour of Carthage, he found that the whole province, disdaining such an un-worthy ruler, had returned to their allegiance. The rebel was beheaded in the ancient temple of Memory, his consulship was abolished,[148] and the remains of his private fortune, not exceeding the moderate sum of four thousand pounds of gold, were granted to the brave Constantius, who had already defended the throne which he afterwards shared with his feeble sovereign. Honorius viewed with supine indifference the calami-ties of Rome and Italy,[149] but the rebellious attempts of Attalus and Heraclian against his personal safety awakened for a moment the torpid instinct of his nature. He was probably ignorant of the causes and events which preserved him from these impending dangers; and as Italy was no longer invaded by any foreign or domestic enemies, he peaceably

this poetical Itinerary, Rutilius (l. i. 115, etc.) addresses Rome in a high strain of congratulation:

> Erige crinales lauros, seniumque sacrati
> Verticis in virides, Roma, recinge comas, etc.

[146] Orosius composed his history in Africa only two years after the event; yet his authority seems to be overbalanced by the improbability of the fact. The Chronicle of Marcellinus gives Heraclian 700 ships and 3000 men: the latter of these numbers is ridiculously corrupt; but the former would please me very much.

[147] The Chronicle of Idatius affirms, without the least appearance of truth, that he advanced as far as Otriculum, in Umbria, where he was overthrown in a great battle, with the loss of fifty thousand men.

[148] See Cod. Theod. l. xv. tit. xiv. leg. 13. The legal acts performed in his name, even the manumission of slaves, were declared invalid till they had been formally repealed.

[149] I have disdained to mention a very foolish, and probably a false, report (Procop. de Bell. Vandal. l. i. c. 2 [tom. i. p. 316, ed. Bonn]), that Honorius was alarmed by the *loss* of Rome till he understood that it was not a favour-ite chicken of that name, but *only* the capital of the world, which had been lost. Yet even this story is some evidence of the public opinion.

existed in the palace of Ravenna, while the tyrants beyond the Alps were repeatedly vanquished in the name and by the lieutenants of the son of Theodosius.[150]   In the course of a busy and interesting narrative I might possibly forget to mention the death of such a prince, and I shall therefore take the precaution of observing in this place that he survived the last siege of Rome about thirteen years.

The usurpation of Constantine, who received the purple from the legions of Britain, had been successful, and seemed to be secure.   His title was acknowledged from the wall of Antoninus to the Columns of Hercules, and, in the midst of the public disorder, he shared the dominion and the plunder of Gaul and Spain with the tribes of barbarians whose destructive progress was no longer checked by the Rhine or Pyrenees.   Stained with the blood of the kinsmen of Honorius, he extorted from the court of Ravenna, with which he secretly corresponded, the ratification of his rebellious claims.   Constantine engaged himself by a solemn promise to deliver Italy from the Goths, advanced as far as the banks of the Po, and, after alarming rather than assisting his pusillanimous ally, hastily returned to the palace of Arles, to celebrate with intemperate luxury his vain and ostentatious triumph.   But this transient prosperity was soon interrupted and destroyed by the revolt of Count Gerontius, the bravest of his generals, who, during the absence of his son Constans, a prince already invested with the Imperial purple, had been left to command in the provinces of Spain.   For some reason of which we are ignorant, Gerontius, instead of assuming the diadem, placed it on the head of his friend Maximus, who fixed his residence at Tarragona, while the active count pressed forwards through the Pyrenees to surprise the two emperors Constantine and Constans before they could prepare for their defence.   The son was made prisoner at Vienne, and immediately put to death; and the unfortunate youth had scarcely leisure to deplore the elevation of his family, which had tempted or compelled him sacrilegiously to desert the peaceful obscurity of the monastic life. The father maintained a siege within the walls of Arles; but those walls must have yielded to the assailants had not the city been unexpectedly relieved by the approach of an Italian army.   The name of Honorius, the proclamation of a lawful emperor, astonished the contending parties of the rebels.   Gerontius, abandoned by his own troops, escaped to the confines of Spain, and rescued his name from oblivion by the Roman courage which appeared to animate the last moments of his life. In the middle of the night a great body of his perfidious soldiers surrounded and attacked his house, which he had strongly barricaded. His wife, a

---

[150] The materials for the lives of all these tyrants are taken from six contemporary historians, two Latins and four Greeks: Orosius, l. vii. c. 42, p. 581, 582, 583; Renatus Profuturus Frigeridus, apud Gregor. Turon. l. ii. c. 9, in the Historians of France, tom. ii. p. 165, 166; Zosimus, l. vi. [c. 2] p. 370, 371; Olympiodorus, apud Phot. p. 180, 181, 184, 185 [p. 57 sqq., ed. Bekk.]; Sozomen, l. ix. c. 12, 13, 14, 15; and Philostorgius, l. xii. c. 5, 6, with Godefroy's Dissertations, p. 477-481; besides the four Chronicles of Prosper Tyro, Prosper of Aquitain, Idatius, and Marcellinus.

valiant friend of the nation of the Alani, and some faithful slaves, were still attached to his person; and he used with so much skill and resolution a large magazine of darts and arrows, that above three hundred of the assailants lost their lives in the attempt. His slaves, when all the missile weapons were spent, fled at the dawn of day; and Gerontius, if he had not been restrained by conjugal tenderness, might have imitated their example; till the soldiers, provoked by such obstinate resistance, applied fire on all sides to the house. In this fatal extremity he complied with the request of his barbarian friend and cut off his head. The wife of Gerontius, who conjured him not to abandon her to a life of misery and disgrace, eagerly presented her neck to his sword: and the tragic scene was terminated by the death of the count himself, who after three ineffectual strokes, drew a short dagger and sheathed it in his heart.[151] The unprotected Maximus, whom he had invested with the purple, was indebted for his life to the contempt that was entertained of his power and abilities. The caprice of the barbarians, who ravaged Spain, once more seated this Imperial phantom on the throne: but they soon resigned him to the justice of Honorius; and the tyrant Maximus, after he had been shown to the people of Ravenna and Rome, was publicly executed.

The general, Constantius was his name, who raised by his approach the siege of Arles and dissipated the troops of Gerontius, was born a Roman; and this remarkable distinction is strongly expressive of the decay of military spirit among the subjects of the empire. The strength and majesty which were conspicuous in the person of that general [152] marked him in the popular opinion as a candidate worthy of the throne which he afterwards ascended. In the familiar intercourse of private life his manners were cheerful and engaging: nor would he sometimes disdain, in the license of convivial mirth, to vie with the pantomimes themselves in the exercises of their ridiculous profession. But when the trumpet summoned him to arms; when he mounted his horse, and, bending down (for such was his singular practice) almost upon the neck, fiercely rolled his large animated eyes round the field, Constantius then struck terror into his foes and inspired his soldiers with the assurance of victory. He had received from the court of Ravenna the important commission of extirpating rebellion in the provinces of the West; and the pretended emperor Constantine, after enjoying a short and anxious respite, was again besieged in his capital by the arms of a more formidable enemy. Yet this interval allowed time for a successful negotiation with

---

[151] The praises which Sozomen has bestowed on this act of despair appear strange and scandalous in the mouth of an ecclesiastical historian. He observes (p. 379 [ed. Cantab. 1720]) that the wife of Gerontius was a *Christian;* and that her death was worthy of her religion, and of immortal fame.

[152] Εἶδος ἄξιον τυραννίδος, is the expression of Olympiodorus, which he seems to have borrowed from *Æolus,* a tragedy of Euripides, of which some fragments only are now extant (Euripid. Barnes, tom. ii. p. 443, ver. 38). This allusion may prove that the ancient tragic poets were still familiar to the Greeks of the fifth century.

the Franks and Alemanni; and his ambassador, Edobic, soon returned at the head of an army to disturb the operations of the siege of Arles. The Roman general, instead of expecting the attack in his lines, boldly, and perhaps wisely, resolved to pass the Rhone and to meet the barbarians. His measures were conducted with so much skill and secrecy, that, while they engaged the infantry of Constantius in the front, they were suddenly attacked, surrounded, and destroyed by the cavalry of his lieutenant Ulphilas, who had silently gained an advantageous post in their rear. The remains of the army of Edobic were preserved by flight or submission, and their leader escaped from the field of battle to the house of a faithless friend, who too clearly understood that the head of his obnoxious guest would be an acceptable and lucrative present for the Imperial general. On this occasion Constantius behaved with the magnanimity of a genuine Roman. Subduing or suppressing every sentiment of jealousy, he publicly acknowledged the merit and services of Ulphilas; but he turned with horror from the assassin of Edobic, and sternly intimated his commands that the camp should no longer be polluted by the presence of an ungrateful wretch who had violated the laws of friendship and hospitality. The usurper, who beheld from the walls of Arles the ruin of his last hopes, was tempted to place some confidence in so generous a conqueror. He required a solemn promise for his security; and after receiving, by the imposition of hands, the sacred character of a Christian presbyter, he ventured to open the gates of the city. But he soon experienced that the principles of honour and integrity, which might regulate the ordinary conduct of Constantius, were superseded by the loose doctrines of political morality. The Roman general indeed refused to sully his laurels with the blood of Constantine; but the abdicated emperor and his son Julian were sent, under a strong guard, into Italy; and before they reached the palace of Ravenna they met the ministers of death.

At a time when it was universally confessed that almost every man in the empire was superior in personal merit to the princes whom the accident of their birth had seated on the throne, a rapid succession of usurpers, regardless of the fate of their predecessors, still continued to arise. This mischief was peculiarly felt in the provinces of Spain and Gaul, where the principles of order and obedience had been extinguished by war and rebellion. Before Constantine resigned the purple, and in the fourth month of the siege of Arles, intelligence was received in the Imperial camp that Jovinus had assumed the diadem at Mentz, in the Upper Germany, at the instigation of Goar, king of the Alani, and of Guntiarius, king of the Burgundians; and that the candidate on whom they had bestowed the empire advanced with a formidable host of barbarians from the banks of the Rhine to those of the Rhone. Every circumstance is dark and extraordinary in the short history of the reign of Jovinus. It was natural to expect that a brave and skilful general, at the head of a victorious army, would have asserted, in a field of battle, the justice of the cause of Honorius. The hasty retreat of Constantius might be justified by weighty reasons; but he resigned without a struggle the possession of Gaul; and Dardanus, the Prætorian præfect, is recorded as the only magistrate who refused to yield obedience to the usurper.[153] When the Goths, two years after the siege of Rome, established their quarters in Gaul, it was natural to suppose that their inclinations could be divided only between the emperor Honorius, with whom they had formed a recent alliance, and the degraded Attalus, whom they reserved in their camp for the occasional purpose of acting the part of a musician or a monarch. Yet in a moment of disgust (for which it is not easy to assign a cause or a date) Adolphus connected himself with the usurper of Gaul; and imposed on Attalus the ignominious task of negotiating the treaty which ratified his own disgrace. We are again surprised to read, that, instead of considering the Gothic alliance as the firmest support of his throne, Jovinus upbraided, in dark and ambiguous language, the officious importunity of Attalus; that, scorning the advice of his great ally, he invested with the purple his brother Sebastian; and that he most imprudently accepted the service of Sarus, when that gallant chief, the soldier of Honorius, was provoked to desert the court of a prince who knew not how to reward or punish. Adolphus, educated among a race of warriors, who esteemed the duty of revenge as the most precious and sacred portion of their inheritance, advanced with a body of ten thousand Goths to encounter the hereditary enemy of the house of Balti. He attacked Sarus at an unguarded moment, when he was accompanied only by eighteen or twenty of his valiant followers. United by friendship, animated by despair, but at length oppressed by multitudes, this band of heroes deserved the esteem, without exciting the compassion, of their enemies; and the lion was no sooner taken in the toils [154] than he was instantly despatched. The death of Sarus dissolved the loose alliance which Adolphus still maintained with the usurpers of Gaul. He again listened to the dictates of love and prudence; and soon satisfied the brother of Placidia, by the assurance that he would immediately transmit to the palace of Ravenna the heads of the two tyrants, Jovinus and Sebastian. The king of the Goths executed his promise without difficulty or delay: the helpless brothers, unsupported by any personal merit, were abandoned by their barbarian auxiliaries; and the short opposition of Valentia was expiated by the ruin of one of the oldest cities of Gaul. The

[153] Sidonius Apollinaris (l. v. Epist. 9, p. 139, and Not. Sirmond. p. 58), after stigmatising the *inconstancy* of Constantine, the *facility* of Jovinus, the *perfidy* of Gerontius, continues to observe that *all* the vices of these tyrants were united in the person of Dardanus. Yet the præfect supported a respectable character in the world, and even in the church; held a devout correspondence with St. Augustin and St. Jerom; and was complimented by the latter (tom. iii. p. 66) with the epithets of Christianorum Nobilissime and Nobilium Christianissime.

[154] The expression may be understood almost literally: Olympiodorus says, μόλις σάκκοις ἐζώγρησαν. Σάκκος (or σάκος) may signify a sack or a loose garment; and this method of entangling and catching an enemy, laciniis contortis, was much practised by the Huns (Ammian. xxxi. 2). Il fut pris vif avec des filets, is the translation of Tillemont, Hist. des Empereurs, tom. v. p. 608.

emperor chosen by the Roman senate, who had been promoted, degraded, insulted, restored, again degraded, and again insulted, was finally abandoned to his fate; but when the Gothic king withdrew his protection, he was restrained, by pity or contempt, from offering any violence to the person of Attalus. The unfortunate Attalus, who was left without subjects or allies, embarked in one of the ports of Spain, in search of some secure and solitary retreat; but he was intercepted at sea, conducted to the presence of Honorius, led in triumph through the streets of Rome or Ravenna, and publicly exposed to the gazing multitude, on the second step of the throne of his *invincible* conqueror. The same measure of punishment with which, in the days of his prosperity, he was accused of menacing his rival, was inflicted on Attalus himself: he was condemned, after the amputation of two fingers, to a perpetual exile in the isle of Lipari, where he was supplied with the decent necessaries of life. The remainder of the reign Honorius was undisturbed by rebellion; and it may be observed that in the space of five years seven usurpers had yielded to the fortune of a prince who was himself incapable either of counsel or of action.

The situation of Spain, separated on all sides from the enemies of Rome, by the sea, by the mountains, and by intermediate provinces, had secured the long tranquillity of that remote and sequestered country; and we may observe, as a sure symptom of domestic happiness, that, in a period of four hundred years, Spain furnished very few materials to the history of the Roman empire. The footsteps of the barbarians, who, in the reign of Gallienus, had penetrated beyond the Pyrenees, were soon obliterated by the return of peace; and in the fourth century of the Christian era, the cities of Emerita or Merida, of Corduba, Seville, Bracara, and Tarragona, were numbered with the most illustrious of the Roman world. The various plenty of the animal, the vegetable, and the mineral kingdoms, was improved and manufactured by the skill of an industrious people; and the peculiar advantages of naval stores contributed to support an extensive and profitable trade.[155] The arts and sciences flourished under the protection of the emperors; and if the character of the Spaniards was enfeebled by peace and servitude, the hostile approach of the Germans, who had spread terror and desolation from the Rhine to the Pyrenees, seemed to rekindle some sparks of military ardour. As long as the defence of the mountains was intrusted to the hardy and faithful militia of the country, they successfully repelled the frequent attempts of the barbarians. But no sooner had the national troops been compelled to resign their post to the Honorian bands in the service of Constantine,

[155] Without recurring to the more ancient writers, I shall quote three respectable testimonies which belong to the fourth and seventh centuries: the Expositio totius Mundi (p. 16, in the third volume of Hudson's Minor Geographers), Ausonius (de Claris Urbibus, p. 242, edit. Toll.), and Isidore of Seville (Præfat. ad Chron. ap Grotium, Hist. Goth. p. 707). Many particulars relative to the fertility and trade of Spain may be found in Nonnius, Hispania, Illustrata; and in Huet, Hist. du Commerce des Anciens, c. 40, p. 228-234.

than the gates of Spain were treacherously betrayed to the public enemy, about ten months before the sack of Rome by the Goths.[156]   The consciousness of guilt, and the thirst of rapine, prompted the mercenary guards of the Pyrenees to desert their station; to invite the arms of the Suevi, the Vandals, and the Alani; and to swell the torrent which was poured with irresistible violence from the frontiers of Gaul to the sea of Africa.   The misfortunes of Spain may be described in the language of its most eloquent historian, who has concisely expressed the passionate, and perhaps exaggerated, declamations of contemporary writers.[157]   " The irruption of these nations was followed by the most dreadful calamities: as the barbarians exercised their indiscriminate cruelty on the fortunes of the Romans and the Spaniards, and ravaged with equal fury the cities and the open country.   The progress of famine reduced the miserable inhabitants to feed on the flesh of their fellow-creatures; and even the wild beasts, who multiplied, without control, in the desert, were exasperated by the taste of blood and the impatience of hunger boldly to attack and devour their human prey.   Pestilence soon appeared, the inseparable companion of famine; a large proportion of the people was swept away; and the groans of the dying excited only the envy of their surviving friends.   At length the barbarians, satiated with carnage and rapine, and afflicted by the contagious evils which they themselves had introduced, fixed their permanent seats in the depopulated country.   The ancient Gallicia, whose limits included the kingdom of Old Castille, was divided between the Suevi and the Vandals; the Alani were scattered over the provinces of Carthagena and Lusitania, from the Mediterranean to the Atlantic Ocean; and the fruitful territory of Bætica was allotted to the Silingi, another branch of the Vandalic nation.   After regulating this partition, the conquerors contracted with their new subjects some reciprocal engagements of protection and obedience: the lands were again cultivated; and the towns and villages were again occupied by a captive people.   The greatest part of the Spaniards was even disposed to prefer this new condition of poverty and barbarism to the severe oppressions of the Roman government; yet there were many who still asserted their native freedom, and who refused, more especially in the mountains of Gallicia, to submit to the barbarian yoke.[158]

The important present of the heads of Jovinus and Sebastian had approved the friendship of Adolphus, and restored Gaul to the obedience

---

[156] The date is accurately fixed in the Fasti and the Chronicle of Idatius. Orosius (l. vii. c. 40, p. 578) imputes the loss of Spain to the treachery of the Honorians; while Sozomen (l. ix. c. 12) accuses only their negligence.

[157] Idatius wishes to apply the prophecies of Daniel to these national calamities, and is therefore obliged to accommodate the circumstances of the event to the terms of the prediction.

[158] Mariana de Rebus Hispanicis, l. v. c. 1, tom. i. p. 148. Hag. Comit. 1733. He had read in Orosius (l. vii c. 41, p. 579) that the barbarians had turned their swords into ploughshares; and that many of the provincials preferred inter Barbaros pauperem libertatem, quam inter Romanos tributariam solicitudinem, sustinere.

of his brother Honorius. Peace was incompatible with the situation and temper of the king of the Goths. He readily accepted the proposal of turning his victorious arms against the barbarians of Spain; the troops of Constantius intercepted his communication with the seaports of Gaul, and gently pressed his march towards the Pyrenees:[159] he passed the mountains, and surprised, in the name of the emperor, the city of Barcelona. The fondness of Adolphus for his Roman bride was not abated by time or possession; and the birth of a son, surnamed, from his illustrious grandsire, Theodosius, appeared to fix him for ever in the interest of the public. The loss of that infant, whose remains were deposited in a silver coffin in one of the churches near Barcelona, afflicted his parents; but the grief of the Gothic king was suspended by the labours of the field; and the course of his victories was soon interrupted by domestic treason He had imprudently received into his service one of the followers of Sarus, a barbarian of a daring spirit, but of a diminutive stature, whose secret desire of revenging the death of his beloved patron was continually irritated by the sarcasms of his insolent master. Adolphus was assassinated in the palace of Barcelona; the laws of the succession were violated by a tumultuous faction;[160] and a stranger to the royal race, Singeric, the brother of Sarus himself, was seated on the Gothic throne. The first act of his reign was the inhuman murder of the six children of Adolphus, the issue of a former marriage, whom he tore, without pity, from the feeble arms of a venerable bishop.[161] The unfortunate Placidia, instead of the respectful compassion which she might have excited in the most savage breasts, was treated with cruel and wanton insult. The daughter of the emperor Theodosius, confounded among a crowd of vulgar captives, was compelled to march on foot above twelve miles, before the horse of a barbarian, the assassin of an husband whom Placidia loved and lamented.[162]

But Placidia soon obtained the pleasure of revenge; and the view of her ignominious sufferings might rouse an indignant people against the tyrant, who was assassinated on the seventh day of his usurpation. After the death of Singeric, the free choice of the nation bestowed the Gothic sceptre on Wallia, whose warlike and ambitious temper appeared, in the beginning of his reign, extremely hostile to the republic. He marched in arms from Barcelona to the shores of the Atlantic Ocean, which the

[159] This mixture of force and persuasion may be fairly inferred from comparing Orosius and Jornandes, the Roman and the Gothic historian.

[160] According to the system of Jornandes (c. 33, p. 659 [ed. Grot.]), the true hereditary right to the Gothic sceptre was vested in the *Amali;* but those princes, who were the vassals of the Huns, commanded the tribes of the Ostrogoths in some distant parts of Germany or Scythia.

[161] The murder is related by Olympiodorus; but the number of the children is taken from an epitaph of suspected authority.

[162] The death of Adolphus was celebrated at Constantinople with illuminations and Circensian games. (See Chron. Alexandrin.) It may seem doubtful whether the Greeks were actuated on this occasion by their hatred of the barbarians or of the Latins.

ancients revered and dreaded as the boundary of the world. But when he reached the southern promontory of Spain,[163] and, from the rock now covered by the fortress of Gibralter, contemplated the neighbouring and fertile coast of Africa, Wallia resumed the designs of conquest which had been interrupted by the death of Alaric. The winds and waves again disappointed the enterprise of the Goths; and the minds of a superstitious people were deeply affected by the repeated disasters of storms and shipwrecks. In this disposition, the successor of Adolphus no longer refused to listen to a Roman ambassador, whose proposals were enforced by the real, or supposed, approach of a numerous army, under the conduct of the brave Constantius. A solemn treaty was stipulated and observed: Placidia was honourably restored to her brother; six hundred thousand measures of wheat were delivered to the hungry Goths;[164] and Wallia engaged to draw his sword in the service of the empire. A bloody war was instantly excited among the barbarians of Spain; and the contending princes are said to have addressed their letters, their ambassadors, and their hostages, to the throne of the Western emperor, exhorting him to remain a tranquil spectator of their contest, the events of which must be favourable to the Romans by the mutual slaughter of their common enemies.[165] The Spanish war was obstinately supported, during three campaigns, with desperate valour and various success; and the martial achievements of Wallia diffused through the empire the superior renown of the Gothic hero. He exterminated the Silingi, who had irretrievably ruined the elegant plenty of the province of Bætica. He slew, in battle, the king of the Alani; and the remains of those Scythian wanderers who escaped from the field, instead of choosing a new leader, humbly sought a refuge under the standard of the Vandals, with whom they were ever afterwards confounded. The Vandals themselves, and the Suevi, yielded to the efforts of the invincible Goths. The promiscuous multitude of barbarians, whose retreat had been intercepted, were driven into the mountains of Gallicia; where they still continued, in a narrow compass and on a barren soil, to exercise their domestic and implacable hostilities. In the pride of victory, Wallia was faithful to his engagements: he restored his Spanish conquests to the obedience of Honorius; and the tyranny of the Imperial officers soon reduced an op-

[163] Quòd *Tartessiacis* avus hujus Vallia *terris*
Vandalicas turmas, et juncti Martis Alanos
Stravit, et occiduam texêre cadavera *Calpen.*
Sidon. Appollinar. in Panegyr. Anthem. 363,
p. 300, edit. Sirmond.

[164] This supply was very acceptable: the Goths were insulted by the Vandals of Spain with the epithet of *Truli,* because in their extreme distress they had given a piece of gold for a *trula,* or about half a pound of flour. Olympiod. apud Phot. p. 189 [p. 60, ed. Bekk.].

[165] Orosius inserts a copy of these pretended letters. Tu cum omnibus pacem habe, omniumque obsides accipe; nos nobis configimus, nobis perimus, tibi vincimus; immortalis vero quæstus erit Reipublicæ tuæ, si utrique pereamus [p. 586]. The idea is just; but I cannot persuade myself that it was entertained or expressed by the barbarians.

pressed people to regret the time of their barbarian servitude. While the event of the war was still doubtful, the first advantages obtained by the arms of Wallia had encouraged the court of Ravenna to decree the honours of a triumph to their feeble sovereign He entered Rome like the ancient conquerors of nations; and if the monuments of servile corruption had not long since met with the fate which they deserved, we should probably find that a crowd of poets and orators, of magistrates and bishops, applauded the fortune, the wisdom, and the invincible courage of the emperor Honorius.[166]

Such a triumph might have been justly claimed by the ally of Rome, if Wallia, before he repassed the Pyrenees, had extirpated the seeds of the Spanish war. His victorious Goths, forty-three years after they had passed the Danube, were established, according to the faith of treaties, in the possession of the second Aquitain, a maritime province between the Garonne and the Loire, under the civil and ecclesiastical jurisdiction of Bourdeaux. That metropolis, advantageously situated for the trade of the ocean, was built in a regular and elegant form; and its numerous inhabitants were distinguished among the Gauls by their wealth, their learning, and the politeness of their manners. The adjacent province, which has been fondly compared to the garden of Eden, is blessed with a fruitful soil and a temperate climate; the face of the country displayed the arts and the rewards of industry; and the Goths, after their martial toils, luxuriously exhausted the rich vineyards of Aquitain.[167] The Gothic limits were enlarged by the additional gift of some neighbouring dioceses; and the successors of Alaric fixed their royal residence at Toulouse, which included five populous quarters, or cities, within the spacious circuit of its walls. About the same time, in the last years of the reign of Honorius, the GOTHS, the BURGUNDIANS, and the FRANKS, obtained a permanent seat and dominion in the provinces of Gaul. The liberal grant of the usurper Jovinus to his Burgundian allies was confirmed by the lawful emperor; the lands of the First, or Upper, Germany were ceded to those formidable barbarians; and they gradually occupied, either by conquest or treaty, the two provinces which still retain, with the titles of *Duchy* and of *County*, the national appellation of Burgundy.[168] The Franks, the valiant and faithful allies of the Roman re-

---

[166] Romam triumphans ingreditur is the formal expression of Prosper's Chronicle. The facts which relate to the death of Adolphus and the exploits of Wallia are related from Olympiodorus (ap Phot. p. 188 [p. 59, 60, ed. Bekk.]), Orosius (l. vii. c. 43, p. 584-587), Jornandes (de Rebus Geticis, c. 31, 32), and the Chronicles of Idatius and Isidore.

[167] Ausonius (de Claris Urbibus, p. 257-262 [No. 14]) celebrates Bourdeaux with the partial affection of a native. See in Salvian (de Gubern. Dei, p. 228, Paris, 1608) a florid description of the provinces of Aquitain and Novempopulania.

[168] Orosius (l. vii. c. 32, p. 550) commends the mildness and modesty of these Burgundians, who treated their subjects of Gaul as their Christian brethren. Mascou has illustrated the origin of their kingdom in the four first annotations at the end of his laborious History of the Ancient Germans, vol. ii. p. 555-572 of the English translation.

public, were soon tempted to imitate the invaders whom they had so bravely resisted. Trèves, the capital of Gaul, was pillaged by their lawless bands; and the humble colony which they so long maintained in the district of Toxandria, in Brabant, insensibly multiplied along the banks of the Meuse and Scheld, till their independent power filled the whole extent of the Second, or Lower, Germany. These facts may be sufficiently justified by historic evidence; but the foundation of the French monarchy by Pharamond, the conquests, the laws, and even the existence of that hero, have been justly arraigned by the impartial severity of modern criticism.[169]

The ruin of the opulent provinces of Gaul may be dated from the establishment of these barbarians, whose alliance was dangerous and oppressive, and who were capriciously impelled, by interest or passion, to violate the public peace. A heavy and partial ransom was imposed on the surviving provincials who had escaped the calamities of war; the fairest and most fertile lands were assigned to the rapacious strangers, for the use of their families, their slaves, and their cattle; and the trembling natives relinquished with a sigh the inheritance of their fathers. Yet these domestic misfortunes, which are seldom the lot of a vanquished people, had been felt and inflicted by the Romans themselves, not only in the insolence of foreign conquest, but in the madness of civil discord. The Triumvirs proscribed eighteen of the most flourishing colonies of Italy, and distributed their lands and houses to the veterans who revenged the death of Cæsar, and oppressed the liberty of their country. Two poets, of unequal fame, have deplored, in similar circumstances, the loss of their patrimony; but the legionaries of Augustus appear to have surpassed, in violence and injustice, the barbarians who invaded Gaul under the reign of Honorius. It was not without the utmost difficulty that Virgil escaped from the sword of the centurion who had usurped his farm in the neighbourhood of Mantua;[170] but Paulinus of Bourdeaux received a sum of money from his Gothic purchaser, which he accepted with pleasure and surprise; and, though it was much inferior to the real value of his estate, this act of rapine was disguised by some colours of

---

[169] See Mascou, l. viii. c. 43, 44, 45. Except in a short and suspicious line of the Chronicle of Prosper (in tom. i. p. 638), the name of Pharamond is never mentioned before the seventh century. The author of the Gesta Francorum (in tom. ii. p. 543) suggests, probably enough, that the choice of Pharamond, or at least of a king, was recommended to the Franks by his father Marcomir, who was an exile in Tuscany.

[170]   O Lycida, vivi pervenimus: advena nostri
          (Quod nunquam veriti sumus) ut possessor agelli
          Diceret: Hæc mea sunt; veteres migrate coloni.
          Nunc victi tristes, etc.

See the whole of the ninth eclogue, with the useful Commentary of Servius. Fifteen miles of the Mantuan territory were assigned to the veterans, with a reservation in favour of the inhabitants of three miles round the city. Even in this favour they were cheated by Alfenus Varus, a famous lawyer and one of the commissioners, who measured eight hundred paces of water and morass.

moderation and equity.[171]   The odious name of conquerors was softened
into the mild and friendly appellation of the *guests* of the Romans; and
the barbarians of Gaul, more especially the Goths, repeatedly declared
that they were bound to the people by the ties of hospitality, and to the
emperor by the duty of allegiance and military service.   The title of
Honorius and his successors, their laws and their civil magistrates, were
still respected in the provinces of Gaul, of which they had resigned the
possession to the barbarian allies; and the kings, who exercised a supreme and independent authority over their native subjects, ambitiously
solicited the more honourable rank of master-generals of the Imperial
armies.[172]   Such was the involuntary reverence which the Roman name
still impressed on the minds of those warriors who had borne away in
triumph the spoils of the Capitol.

   Whilst Italy was ravaged by the Goths, and a succession of feeble tyrants oppressed the provinces beyond the Alps, the British island separated itself from the body of the Roman empire.   The regular forces
which guarded that remote province had been gradually withdrawn; and
Britain was abandoned, without defence, to the Saxon pirates and the
savages of Ireland and Caledonia.   The Britons, reduced to this extremity, no longer relied on the tardy and doubtful aid of a declining monarchy.   They assembled in arms, repelled the invaders, and rejoiced in the
important discovery of their own strength.[173]   Afflicted by similar calamities, and actuated by the same spirit, the Armorican provinces (a name
which comprehended the maritime countries of Gaul between the Seine
and the Loire)[174] resolved to imitate the example of the neighbouring
island.   They expelled the Roman magistrate, who acted under the authority of the usurper Constantine; and a free government was established among a people who had so long been subject to the arbitrary
will of a master.   The independence of Britain and Armorica was soon
confirmed by Honorius himself, the lawful emperor of the West; and the
letters by which he committed to the new states the care of their own
safety might be interpreted as an absolute and perpetual abdication of the
exercise and rights of sovereignty.   This interpretation was, in some
measure, justified by the event.   After the usurpers of Gaul had successively fallen, the maritime provinces were restored to the empire.   Yet
their obedience was imperfect, and precarious: the vain, the inconstant,

[171] See the remarkable passage of the Eucharisticon of Paulinus, 575, apud
Mascou, l. viii. c. 42.
[172] This important truth is established by the accuracy of Tillemont (Hist.
des Emp. tom. v. p. 641) and by the ingenuity of the Abbé Dubos (Hist. de
l'Etablissement de la Monarchie Françoise dans les Gaules, tom. i. p. 259).
[173] Zosimus (l. vi. [c. 5] 376 [c. 10], 383) relates in a few words the revolt of
Britain and Armorica.   Our antiquarians, even the great Camden himself,
have been betrayed into many gross errors by their imperfect knowledge of
the history of the continent.
[174] The limits of Armorica are defined by two national geographers, Messieurs
de Valois and d'Anville, in their *Notitias* of Ancient Gaul.   The word had
been used in a more extensive, and was afterwards contracted to a much nar-
rower, signification.

rebellious disposition of the people, was incompatible either with freedom or servitude;[175] and Armorica, though it could not long maintain
the form of a republic,[176] was agitated by frequent and destructive
revolts. Britain was irrecoverably lost.[177] But as the emperors wisely
acquiesced in the independence of a remote province, the separation
was not embittered by the reproach of tyranny or rebellion; and the
claims of allegiance and protection were succeeded by the mutual and
voluntary offices of national friendship.[178]

This revolution dissolved the artificial fabric of civil and military government; and the independent country, during a period of forty years,
till the descent of the Saxons, was ruled by the authority of the clergy,
the nobles, and the municipal towns.[179] I. Zosimus, who alone has preserved the memory of this singular transaction, very accurately observes
that the letters of Honorius were addressed to the *cities* of Britain.[180]
Under the protection of the Romans, ninety-two considerable towns had
arisen in the several parts of that great province; and, among these,
thirty-three cities were distinguished above the rest by their superior
privileges and importance.[181] Each of these cities, as in all the other

[175] Gens inter geminos notissima clauditur amnes,
    Armoricana prius veteri cognomine dicta.
    Torva, ferox, ventosa, procax, incauta, rebellis;
    Inconstans, disparque sibi novitatis amore;
    Prodiga verborum, sed non et prodiga facti.
Erricus, Monach. in Vit. St. Germani, l. v. apud Vales. Notit. Galliarum,
p. 43. Valesius alleges several testimonies to confirm this character; to which
I shall add the evidence of the presbyter Constantine (A.D. 488), who, in the
Life of St. Germain, calls the Armorican rebels mobilem et indisciplinatum
populum. See the Historians of France, tom. i. p. 643.

[176] I thought it necessary to enter my protest against this part of the system
of the Abbé Dubos, which Montesquieu has so vigorously opposed. See Esprit
des Loix, l. xxx. c. 24.

[177] Βρετανννίαν μέντοι 'Ρωμαῖοι ἀνασώσασθαι οὐκέτι ἔσχον, are the words of
Procopius (de Bell. Vandal. l. i. c. 2, p. 181, Louvre edition [tom. i. p. 318,
ed. Bonn]), in a very important passage which has been too much neglected.
Even Bede (Hist. Gent. Anglican. l. i. c. 12, p. 50, edit. Smith) acknowledges
that the Romans finally left Britain in the reign of Honorius. Yet our modern
historians and antiquarians extend the term of their dominion; and there
are some who allow only the interval of a few months between their departure and the arrival of the Saxons.

[178] Bede has not forgot the occasional aid of the legions against the Scots
and Picts; and more authentic proof will hereafter be produced that the independent Britons raised 12,000 men for the service of the emperor Anthemius
in Gaul.

[179] I owe it to myself and to historic truth to declare that some *circumstances*
in this paragraph are founded only on conjecture and analogy. The stub-
bornness of our language has sometimes forced me to deviate from the *con-
ditional* into the *indicative* mood.

[180] Πρὸς τὰς ἐν Βρεταννίᾳ πόλεις. Zosimus, l. vi. [c. 10] p. 383.

[181] Two cities of Britain were *municipia*, nine *colonies*, ten *Latii jure donatæ*,
twelve *stipendiariæ* of eminent note. This detail is taken from Richard of
Cirencester, de Sitû Britanniæ, p. 36; and though it may not seem probable
that he wrote from the MSS. of a Roman general, he shows a genuine knowledge of antiquity, very extraordinary for a monk of the fourteenth century.

provinces of the empire, formed a legal corporation, for the purpose of regulating their domestic policy; and the powers of municipal government were distributed among annual magistrates, a select senate, and the assembly of the people, according to the original model of the Roman constitution.[182] The management of a common revenue, the exercise of civil and criminal jurisdiction, and the habits of public counsel and command, were inherent to these petty republics; and when they asserted their independence, the youth of the city, and of the adjacent districts, would naturally range themselves under the standard of the magistrate. But the desire of obtaining the advantages, and of escaping the burthens, of political society, is a perpetual and inexhaustible source of discord; nor can it reasonably be presumed that the restoration of British freedom was exempt from tumult and faction. The pre-eminence of birth and fortune must have been frequently violated by bold and popular citizens; and the haughty nobles, who complained that they were become the subjects of their own servants,[183] would sometimes regret the reign of an arbitrary monarch. II. The jurisdiction of each city over the adjacent country was supported by the patrimonial influence of the principal senators; and the smaller towns, the villages, and the proprietors of land, consulted their own safety by adhering to the shelter of these rising republics. The sphere of their attraction was proportioned to the respective degrees of their wealth and populousness; but the hereditary lords of ample possessions, who were not oppressed by the neighbourhood of any powerful city, aspired to the rank of independent princes, and boldly exercised the rights of peace and war. The gardens and villas, which exhibited some faint imitation of Italian elegance, would soon be converted into strong castles, the refuge, in time of danger, of the adjacent country: [184] the produce of the land was applied to purchase arms and horses; to maintain a military force of slaves, of peasants, and of licentious followers: and the chieftain might assume, within his own domain, the powers of a civil magistrate. Several of these British chiefs might be the genuine posterity of ancient kings; and many more would be tempted to adopt this honourable genealogy, and to vindicate their hereditary claims, which had been suspended by the usurpation of the Cæsars.[185] Their situation and their hopes would

---

[182] See Maffei, Verona Illustrata, part. i. 1. v. p. 83-106.

[183] Leges restituit, libertatemque reducit,
Et servos famulis non sinit esse suis.
Itinerar. Rutil. 1. i. 215.

[184] An inscription (apud Sirmond, Not. ad Sidon. Appollinar. p. 59) describes a castle, cum muris et portis, tuitioni omnium, erected by Dardanus on his own estate near Sisteron in the second Narbonnese, and named by him Theopolis.

[185] The establishment of their power would have been easy indeed if we could adopt the impracticable scheme of a lively and learned antiquarian, who supposes that the British monarchs of the several tribes continued to reign, though with subordinate jurisdiction, from the time of Claudius to that of Honorius. See Whitaker's History of Manchester, vol. i. p. 247-257.

dispose them to affect the dress, the language, and the customs of their ancestors. If the *princes* of Britain relapsed into barbarism, while the *cities* studiously preserved the laws and manners of Rome, the whole island must have been gradually divided by the distinction of two national parties; again broken into a thousand subdivisions of war and faction by the various provocations of interest and resentment. The public strength, instead of being united against a foreign enemy, was consumed in obscure and intestine quarrels; and the personal merit which had placed a successful leader at the head of his equals might enable him to subdue the freedom of some neighbouring cities, and to claim a rank among the *tyrants* [186] who infested Britain after the dissolution of the Roman government. III. The British church might be composed of thirty or forty bishops,[187] with an adequate proportion of the inferior clergy; and the want of riches (for they seem to have been poor) [188] would compel them to deserve the public esteem by a decent and exemplary behaviour. The interest, as well as the temper, of the clergy, was favourable to the peace and union of their distracted country: those salutary lessons might be frequently inculcated in their popular discourses; and the episcopal synods were the only councils that could pretend to the weight and authority of a national assembly. In such councils, where the princes and magistrates sat promiscuously with the bishops, the important affairs of the state, as well as of the church, might be freely debated, differences reconciled, alliances formed, contributions imposed, wise resolutions often concerted, and sometimes executed; and there is reason to believe, that, in moments of extreme danger, a *Pendragon*, or Dictator, was elected by the general consent of the Britons. These pastoral cares, so worthy of the episcopal character, were interrupted, however, by zeal and superstition; and the British clergy incessantly laboured to eradicate the Pelagian heresy, which they abhorred as the peculiar disgrace of their native country.[189]

It is somewhat remarkable, or rather it is extremely natural, that the revolt of Britain and Armorica should have introduced an appearance of liberty into the obedient provinces of Gaul. In a solemn edict,[190]

---

[186] Ἀλλ᾽ οὖσα ὑπὸ τυράννοις ἀπ᾽ αὐτοῦ ἔμενε. Procopius, de Bell. Vandal. l. i. c. 2, p. 181 [ed. Paris; tom. i. p. 318, ed. Bonn]. Britannia fertilis provincia tyrannorum, was the expression of Jerom in the year 415 (tom. ii. p. 255, ad Ctesiphont. [Epist. cxxxiii. c. 9, tom. i. p. 1032, ed. Vallars.]). By the pilgrims who resorted every year to the Holy Land, the monk of Bethlem received the earliest and most accurate intelligence.

[187] See Bingham's Eccles. Antiquities, vol. i. l. ix. c. 6, p. 394.

[188] It is reported of *three* British bishops who assisted at the council of Rimini, A.D. 359, tam pauperes fuisse ut nihil [proprium] haberent. Sulpicius Severus, Hist. Sacra, l. ii. p. 420. Some of their brethren, however, were in better circumstances.

[189] Consult Usher, de Antiq. Eccles. Britannicar. c. 8-12.

[190] See the correct text of this edict, as published by Sirmond (Not. ad Sidon. Apollin. p. 147). Hincmar of Rheims, who assigns a place to the *bishops*, had probably seen (in the ninth century) a more perfect copy. Dubos, Hist. Critique de la Monarchie Françoise, tom. i. p. 241-255.

filled with the strongest assurances of that paternal affection which princes so often express, and so seldom feel, the emperor Honorius promulgated his intention of convening an annual assembly of the *seven provinces:* a name peculiarly appropriated to Aquitain and the ancient Narbonnese, which had long since exchanged their Celtic rudeness for the useful and elegant arts of Italy.[191]   Arles, the seat of government and commerce, was appointed for the place of the assembly, which regularly continued twenty-eight days, from the fifteenth of August to the thirteenth of September of every year.   It consisted of the Prætorian præfect of the Gauls; of seven provincial governors, one consular, and six presidents; of the magistrates, and perhaps the bishops, of about sixty cities; and of a competent, though indefinite, number of the most honourable and opulent *possessors* of land, who might justly be considered as the representatives of their country.   They were empowered to interpret and communicate the laws of their sovereign; to expose the grievances and wishes of their constituents; to moderate the excessive or unequal weight of taxes; and to deliberate on every subject of local or national importance that could tend to the restoration of the peace and prosperity of the seven provinces.   If such an institution, which gave the people an interest in their own government, had been universally establishd by Trajan or the Antonines, the seeds of public wisdom and virtue might have been cherished and propagated in the empire of Rome.   The privileges of the subject would have secured the throne of the monarch; the abuses of an arbitrary administration might have been prevented, in some degree, or corrected, by the interposition of these representative assemblies; and the country would have been defended against a foreign enemy by the arms of natives and freemen.   Under the mild and generous influence of liberty, the Roman empire might have remained invincible and immortal; or if its excessive magnitude, and the instability of human affairs, had opposed such perpetual continuance, its vital and constituent members might have separately preserved their vigour and independence.   But in the decline of the empire, when every principle of health and life had been exhausted, the tardy application of this partial remedy was incapable of producing any important or salutary effects.   The emperor Honorius expresses his surprise that he must compel the reluctant provinces to accept a privilege which they should ardently have solicited.   A fine of three, or even five, pounds of gold was imposed on the absent representatives, who seem to have declined this imaginary gift of a free constitution, as the last and most cruel insult of their oppressors.

[191] It is evident from the *Notitia* that the seven provinces were the Viennensis, the maritime Alps, the first and second Narbonnese, Novempopulania, and the first and second Aquitain.   In the room of the first Aquitain, the Abbé Dubos, on the authority of Hincmar, desires to introduce the first Lugdunensis or Lyonnese.

CHAPTER XXXII (395-1453 A.D.)

Arcadius Emperor of the East—Administration and Disgrace of Eutropius—Revolt of Gainas—Persecution of St. John Chrysostom—Theodosius II. Emperor of the East—His Sister Pulcheria—His Wife Eudocia—The Persian War, and Division of Armenia

THE division of the Roman world between the sons of Theodosius marks the final establishment of the empire of the East, which, from the reign of Arcadius to the taking of Constantinople by the Turks, subsisted one thousand and fifty-eight years in a state of premature and perpetual decay. The sovereign of that empire assumed and obstinately retained the vain, and at length fictitious, title of Emperor of the ROMANS; and the hereditary appellations of CÆSAR and AUGUSTUS continued to declare that he was the legitimate successor of the first of men, who had reigned over the first of nations. The palace of Constantinople rivalled, and perhaps excelled, the magnificence of Persia; and the eloquent sermons of St. Chrysostom[1] celebrate, while they condemn, the pompous luxury of the reign of Arcadius. "The emperor," says he, "wears on his head either a diadem or a crown of gold, decorated with precious stones of inestimable value. These ornaments and his purple garments are reserved for his sacred person alone; and his robes of silk are embroidered with the figures of golden dragons. His throne is of massy gold. Whenever he appears in public he is surrounded by his courtiers, his guards, and his attendants. Their spears, their shields, their cuirasses, the bridles and trappings of their horses, have either the substance or the appearance of gold; and the large splendid boss in the midst of their shield is encircled with smaller bosses, which represent the shape of the human eye. The two mules that draw the chariot of the monarch are perfectly white, and shining all over with gold. The chariot itself, of pure and solid gold, attracts the admiration of the spectators, who contemplate the purple curtains, the snowy carpet, the size of the precious stones, and the resplendent plates of gold, that glitter as they are agitated by the motion of the carriage. The Imperial pictures are white, on a blue ground; the emperor appears seated on his throne, with his arms, his horses, and his guards beside him; and his vanquished enemies in chains at his feet." The successors of Constantine established their perpetual residence in the royal city which he had erected on the verge of Europe and Asia. Inaccessible to the menaces of their enemies,

---

[1] Father Montfaucon, who, by the command of his Benedictine superiors, was compelled (see Longueruana, tom. i. p. 205) to execute the laborious edition of St. Chrysostom, in thirteen volumes in folio (Paris, 1738), amused himself with extracting from that immense collection of morals some curious *antiquities,* which illustrate the manners of the Theodosian age (see Chrysostom, Opera, tom. xiii. p. 192-196), and his French Dissertation, in the Mémoires de l'Acad. des Inscriptions, tom. xiii. p. 474-490.

and perhaps to the complaints of their people, they received with each wind the tributary productions of every climate; while the impregnable strength of their capital continued for ages to defy the hostile attempts of the barbarians. Their dominions were bounded by the Hadriatic and the Tigris; and the whole interval of twenty-five days' navigation, which separated the extreme cold of Scythia from the torrid zone of Æthiopia,[2] was comprehended within the limits of the empire of the East. The populous countries of that empire were the seat of art and learning, of luxury and wealth; and the inhabitants, who had assumed the language and manners of Greeks, styled themselves, with some appearance of truth, the most enlightened and civilised portion of the human species. The form of government was a pure and simple monarchy; the name of the ROMAN REPUBLIC, which so long preserved a faint tradition of freedom, was confined to the Latin provinces; and the princes of Constantinople measured their greatness by the servile obedience of their people. They were ignorant how much this passive disposition enervates and degrades every faculty of the mind. The subjects who had resigned their will to the absolute commands of a master were equally incapable of guarding their lives and fortunes against the assaults of the barbarians or of defending their reason from the terrors of superstition.

The first events of the reign of Arcadius and Honorius are so intimately connected, that the rebellion of the Goths and the fall of Rufinus have already claimed a place in the history of the West. It has already been observed that Eutropius,[3] one of the principal eunuchs of the palace of Constantinople, succeeded the haughty minister whose ruin he had accomplished and whose vices he soon imitated. Every order of the state bowed to the new favourite; and their tame and obsequious submission encouraged him to insult the laws, and, what is still more difficult and dangerous, the manners of his country. Under the weakest of the predecessors of Arcadius the reign of the eunuchs had been secret and almost invisible. They insinuated themselves into the confidence of the prince; but their ostensible functions were confined

[2] According to the loose reckoning, that a ship could sail with a fair wind 1000 stadia, or 125 miles, in the revolution of a day and night, Diodorus Siculus computes ten days from the Palus Mæotis to Rhodes, and four days from Rhodes to Alexandria. The navigation of the Nile, from Alexandria to Syene, under the tropic of Cancer, required, as it was against the stream, ten days more. Diodor. Sicul. tom. i. l. iii. [c. 33] p. 200, edit. Wesseling. He might, without much impropriety, measure the extreme heat from the verge of the torrid zone; but he speaks of the Mæotis, in the 47th degree of northern latitude, as if it lay within the polar circle.
[3] Barthius, who adored his author with the blind superstition of a commentator, gives the preference to the two books which Claudian composed against Eutropius, above all his other productions (Baillet, Jugemens des Savans, tom. iv. p. 227). They are indeed a very elegant and spirited satire, and would be more valuable in an historical light, if the invective were less vague and more temperate.

to the menial service of the wardrobe and Imperial bedchamber. They might direct in a whisper the public counsels, and blast by their malicious suggestions the fame and fortunes of the most illustrious citizens; but they never presumed to stand forward in the front of empire,[4] or to profane the public honours of the state. Eutropius was the first of his artificial sex who dared to assume the character of a Roman magistrate and general.[5] Sometimes, in the presence of the blushing senate, he ascended the tribunal to pronounce judgment or to repeat elaborate harangues; and sometimes appeared on horseback, at the head of his troops, in the dress and armour of a hero. The disregard of custom and decency always betrays a weak and ill-regulated mind; nor does Eutropius seem to have compensated for the folly of the design by any superior merit or ability in the execution. His former habits of life had not introduced him to the study of the laws or the exercises of the field; his awkward and unsuccessful attempts provoked the secret contempt of the spectators; the Goths expressed their wish that *such* a general might always command the armies of Rome; and the name of the minister was branded with ridicule, more pernicious, perhaps, than hatred to a public character. The subjects of Arcadius were exasperated by the recollection that this deformed and decrepit eunuch,[6] who so perversely mimicked the actions of a man, was born in the most abject conditions of servitude; that before he entered the Imperial palace he had been successively sold and purchased by an hundred masters, who had exhausted his youthful strength in every mean and infamous office, and at length dismissed him in his old age to freedom and poverty.[7] While these dis-

[4] After lamenting the progress of the eunuchs in the Roman palace, and defining their proper functions, Claudian adds,

——— A fronte recedant
Imperii.

In Eutrop. i. 422.
Yet it does not appear that the eunuch had assumed any of the efficient offices of the empire, and he is styled only Præpositus sacri cubiculi in the edict of his banishment. See Cod. Theod. l. ix. tit. xl. leg. 17.

[5] Jamque oblita sui, nec sobria divitiis mens
In miseras leges hominumque negotia ludit:
Judicat eunuchus . . .
Arma etiam violare parat. . . .

Claudian (in Eutrop. i. 229-270), with that mixture of indignation and humour which always pleases in a satiric poet, describes the insolent folly of the eunuch, the disgrace of the empire, and the joy of the Goths.

——— Gaudet, cum viderit, hostis,
Et sentit jam deesse viros.

[6] The poet's lively description of his deformity (i. 110-125) is confirmed by the authentic testimony of Chrysostom (tom. iii. [in Eutrop. i. c. 3] p. 384, edit. Montfaucon), who observes that, when the paint was washed away, the face of Eutropius appeared more ugly and wrinkled than that of an old woman. Claudian remarks (i. 469), and the remark must have been founded on experience, that there was scarcely any interval between the youth and the decrepit age of a eunuch.

[7] Eutropius appears to have been a native of Armenia or Assyria. His

graceful stories were circulated, and perhaps exaggerated, in private conversations, the vanity of the favourite was flattered with the most extraordinary honours. In the senate, in the capital, in the provinces, the statues of Eutropius were erected, in brass or marble, decorated with the symbols of his civil and military virtues, and inscribed with the pompous title of the third founder of Constantinople. He was promoted to the rank of *patrician,* which began to signify, in a popular and even legal acceptation, the father of the emperor: and the last year of the fourth century was polluted by the *consulship* of an eunuch and a slave. This strange and inexpiable prodigy [8] awakened, however, the prejudices of the Romans. The effeminate consul was rejected by the West as an indelible stain to the annals of the republic; and without invoking the shades of Brutus and Camillus, the colleague of Eutropius, a learned and respectable magistrate,[9] sufficiently represented the different maxims of the two administrations.

The bold and vigorous mind of Rufinus seems to have been actuated by a more sanguinary and revengeful spirit; but the avarice of the eunuch was not less insatiate than that of the præfect.[10] As long as he despoiled the oppressors who had enriched themselves with the plunder of the people, Eutropius might gratify his covetous disposition without much envy or injustice: but the progress of his rapine soon invaded the wealth which had been acquired by lawful inheritance or laudable industry. The usual methods of extortion were practised and improved; and Claudian has sketched a lively and original picture of the public auction of the state. " The impotence of the eunuch " (says that agreeable satirist) " has served only to stimulate his avarice: the same hand which, in his servile condition, was exercised in petty thefts to unlock the coffers of his master, now grasps the riches of the world; and this infamous broker of the empire appreciates and divides the Roman prov-

three services, which Claudian more particularly describes, were these:—1. He spent many years as the catamite of Ptolemy, a groom or soldier of the Imperial stables 2. Ptolemy gave him to the old general Arintheus, for whom he very skilfully exercised the profession of a pimp. 3. He was given, on her marriage, to the daughter of Arintheus; and the future consul was employed to comb her hair, to present the silver ewer, to wash and to fan his mistress in hot weather. See l. i. 31-137.

[8] Claudian (l. i. in Eutrop. 1-22), after enumerating the various prodigies of monstrous births, speaking animals, showers of blood or stones, double suns, etc., adds, with some exaggeration,
        Omnia cesserunt eunucho consule monstra.
The first book concludes with a noble speech of the goddess of Rome to her favourite Honorius, deprecating the *new* ignominy to which she was exposed.

[9] Fl. Mallius Theodorus, whose civil honours and philosophical works have been celebrated by Claudian in a very elegant panegyric.

[10] Μεθύων δέ ἤδη τῷ πλούτῳ, drunk with riches, is the forcible expression of Zosimus (l. v. [c. 10] p. 301); and the avarice of Eutropius is equally execrated in the Lexicon of Suidas and the Chronicle of Marcellinus. Chrysostom had often admonished the favourite of the vanity and danger of immoderate wealth, tom. iii. p. 381 [in Eutrop. i. c. 1].

inces from Mount Hæmus to the Tigris. One man, at the expense of his villa, is made proconsul of Asia; a second purchases Syria with his wife's jewels; and a third laments that he has exchanged his paternal estate for the government of Bithynia. In the antechamber of Eutropius a large tablet is exposed to public view, which marks the respective prices of the provinces. The different value of Pontus, of Galatia, of Lydia is accurately distinguished. Lycia may be obtained for so many thousand pieces of gold; but the opulence of Phrygia will require a more considerable sum. The eunuch wishes to obliterate by the general disgrace his personal ignominy; and as he has been sold himself, he is desirous of selling the rest of mankind. In the eager contention, the balance, which contains the fate and fortunes of the province, often trembles on the beam; and till one of the scales is inclined by a superior weight, the mind of the impartial judge remains in anxious suspense.[11] Such " (continues the indignant poet) " are the fruits of Roman valour, of the defeat of Antiochus, and of the triumph of Pompey." This venal prostitution of public honours secured the impunity of *future* crimes; but the riches which Eutropius derived from confiscation were *already* stained with injustice; since it was decent to accuse and to condemn the proprietors of the wealth which he was impatient to confiscate. Some noble blood was shed by the hand of the executioner; and the most inhospitable extremities of the empire were filled with innocent and illustrious exiles. Among the generals and consuls of the East, Abundantius [12] had reason to dread the first effects of the resentment of Eutropius. He had been guilty of the unpardonable crime of introducing that abject slave to the palace of Constantinople; and some degree of praise must be allowed to a powerful and ungrateful favourite who was satisfied with the disgrace of his benefactor. Abundantius was stripped of his ample fortunes by an Imperial rescript, and banished to Pityus, on the Euxine, the last frontier of the Roman world; where he subsisted by the precarious mercy of the barbarians till he could obtain, after the fall of Eutropius, a milder exile at Sidon in Phœnicia. The destruction of Timasius [13] required a more serious and regular mode of attack. That

---

[11] —— certantum sæpe duorum
      Diversum suspendit onus: cum pondere judex
      Vergit, et in geminas nutat provincia lances.
Claudian (i. 192-209) so curiously distinguishes the circumstances of the sale that they all seem to allude to particular anecdotes.

[12] Claudian (in Eutrop. i. 154-170) mentions the *guilt* and exile of Abundantius; nor could he fail to quote the example of the artist who made the first trial of the brazen bull which he presented to Phalaris. See Zosimus, l. v. [c. 10] p. 302; Jerom, tom. i. p. 26 [Ep. lx. c. 16, tom. i. p. 342, ed. Vallars.]. The difference of place is easily reconciled; but the decisive authority of Asterius of Amasia (Orat. iv. p. 76, apud Tillemont, Hist. des Empereurs, tom. v. p. 435) must turn the scale in favour of Pityus.

[13] Suidas (most probably from the history of Eunapius) has given a very unfavourable picture of Timasius. The account of his accuser, the judges, trial, etc., is perfectly agreeable to the practice of ancient and modern courts.

great officer, the master-general of the armies of Theodosius, had signalised his valour by a decisive victory which he obtained over the
Goths of Thessaly; but he was too prone, after the example of his sovereign, to enjoy the luxury of peace and to abandon his confidence to
wicked and designing flatterers. Timasius had despised the public
clamour by promoting an infamous dependent to the command of a
cohort; and he deserved to feel the ingratitude of Bargus, who was
secretly instigated by the favourite to accuse his patron of a treasonable
conspiracy. The general was arraigned before the tribunal of Arcadius
himself; and the principal eunuch stood by the side of the throne to
suggest the questions and answers of his sovereign. But as this form of
trial might be deemed partial and arbitrary, the further inquiry into
the crimes of Timasius was delegated to Saturnius and Procopius; the
former of consular rank, the latter still respected as the father-in-law
of the emperor Valens. The appearances of a fair and legal proceeding
were maintained by the blunt honesty of Procopius; and he yielded with
reluctance to the obsequious dexterity of his colleague, who pronounced
a sentence of condemnation against the unfortunate Timasius. His immense riches were confiscated in the name of the emperor and for the
benefit of the favourite; and he was doomed to perpetual exile at Oasis,
a solitary spot in the midst of the sandy deserts of Libya.[14] Secluded
from all human converse, the master-general of the Roman armies was
lost for ever to the world; but the circumstances of his fate have been
related in a various and contradictory manner. It is insinuated that
Eutropius despatched a private order for his secret execution.[15] It was
reported that in attempting to escape from Oasis he perished in the
desert of thirst and hunger, and that his dead body was found on the
sands of Libya.[16] It has been asserted with more confidence that his
son Syagrius, after successfully eluding the pursuit of the agents and
emissaries of the court, collected a band of African robbers; that he
rescued Timasius from the place of his exile; and that both the father
and the son disappeared from the knowledge of mankind.[17] But the

(See Zosimus, 1. v. [c. 9] p. 298, 299, 300.) I am almost tempted to quote
the romance of a great master (Fielding's Works, vol. iv. p. 49, etc., 8vo.
edit.), which may be considered as the history of human nature.
[14] The great Oasis was one of the spots in the sands of Libya, watered
with springs, and capable of producing wheat, barley, and palm-trees. It
was about three days' journey from north to south, about half a day in
breadth, and at the distance of about five days' march to the west of Abydus,
on the Nile. See D'Anville, Description de l'Egypte, p. 186, 187, 188. The
barren desert which encompasses Oasis (Zosimus 1. v. [c. 9] p. 300) has
suggested the idea of comparative fertility, and even the epithet of the *happy
island* (Herodot. iii. 26).
[15] The line of Claudian, in Eutrop. 1. i. 180,
       Marmaricus claris violatur cædibus Hammon,
evidently alludes to *his* persuasion of the death of Timasius.
[16] Sozomen, 1. viii. c. 7. He speaks from report, ὥς τινος ἐπυθόμην.
[17] Zosimus, 1. v. [c. 9] p. 300. Yet he seems to suspect that this rumour was
spread by the friends of Eutropius.

ungrateful Bargus, instead of being suffered to possess the reward of guilt, was soon afterwards circumvented and destroyed by the more powerful villainy of the minister himself, who retained sense and spirit enough to abhor the instrument of his own crimes.

The public hatred and the despair of individuals continually threatened, or seemed to threaten, the personal safety of Eutropius, as well as of the numerous adherents who were attached to his fortune and had been promoted by his venal favour. For their mutual defence he contrived the safeguard of a law which violated every principle of humanity and justice.[18] I. It is enacted, in the name and by the authority of Arcadius, that all those who shall conspire, either with subjects or with strangers, against the lives of any of the persons whom the emperor considers as the members of his own body, shall be punished with death and confiscation. This species of fictitious and metaphorical treason is extended to protect not only the *illustrious* officers of the state and army who are admitted into the sacred consistory, but likewise the principal domestics of the palace, the senators of Constantinople, the military commanders, and the civil magistrates of the provinces: a vague and indefinite list, which, under the successors of Constantine, included an obscure and numerous train of subordinate ministers. II. This extreme severity might perhaps be justified, had it been only directed to secure the representatives of the sovereign from any actual violence in the execution of their office. But the whole body of Imperial dependents claimed a privilege, or rather impunity, which screened them in the loosest moments of their lives from the hasty, perhaps the justifiable, resentment of their fellow-citizens: and, by a strange perversion of the laws, the same degree of guilt and punishment was applied to a private quarrel and to a deliberate conspiracy against the emperor and the empire. The edict of Arcadius most positively and most absurdly declares that in such cases of treason, *thoughts* and *actions* ought to be punished with equal severity; that the knowledge of a mischievous intention, unless it be instantly revealed, becomes equally criminal with the intention itself;[19] and that those rash men who shall presume to solicit the pardon of traitors shall themselves be branded with public

[18] See the Theodosian Code, 1. ix. tit. 14, ad legem Corneliam de Sicariis, leg. 3, and the Code of Justinian, 1. ix. tit. viii. ad legem Juliam de Majestate, leg. 5. The alteration of the *title,* from murder to treason, was an improvement of the subtle Tribonian. Godefroy, in a formal dissertation, which he has inserted in his Commentary, illustrates this law of Arcadius, and explains all the difficult passages which had been perverted by the jurisconsults of the darker ages. See tom. iii. p. 88-111.

[19] Bartolus understands a simple and naked consciousness, without any sign of approbation or concurrence. For this opinion, says Baldus, he is now roasting in hell. For my own part, continues the discreet Heineccius (Element. Jur. Civil. 1. iv. p. 411), I must approve the theory of Bartolus; but in practise I should incline to the sentiment of Baldus. Yet Bartolus was gravely quoted by the lawyers of Cardinal Richelieu; and Eutropius was indirectly guilty of the murder of the virtuous De Thou.

and perpetual infamy. III. " With regard to the sons of the traitors "
(continues the emperor), " although they ought to share the punishment,
since they will probably imitate the guilt of their parents, yet, by the
special effect of our Imperial lenity, we grant them their lives; but, at
the same time, we declare them incapable of inheriting, either on the
father's or on the mother's side, or of receiving any gift or legacy from
the testament either of kinsmen or of strangers.   Stigmatised with
hereditary infamy, excluded from the hopes of honours or fortune, le
them endure the pangs of poverty and contempt till they shall consider
life as a calamity and death as a comfort and relief." In such words, so
well adapted to insult the feelings of mankind, did the emperor, or
rather his favourite eunuch, applaud the moderation of a law which
transferred the same unjust and inhuman penalties to the children of
all those who had seconded or who had not disclosed these fictitious
conspiracies.   Some of the noblest regulations of Roman jurisprudence
have been suffered to expire; but this edict, a convenient and forcible
engine of ministerial tyranny, was carefully inserted in the codes of
Theodosius and Justinian; and the same maxims have been revived in
modern ages to protect the electors of Germany and the cardinals of the
church of Rome.[20]

Yet these sanguinary laws, which spread terror among a disarmed
and dispirited people, were of too weak a texture to restrain the bold
enterprise of Tribigild [21] the Ostrogoth.   The colony of that warlike nation, which had been planted by Theodosius in one of the most fertile
districts of Phrygia,[22] impatiently compared the slow returns of laborious husbandry with the successful rapine and liberal rewards of Alaric;
and their leader resented, as a personal affront, his own ungracious reception in the palace of Constantinople.   A soft and wealthy province in
the heart of the empire was astonished by the sound of war, and the
faithful vassal who had been disregarded or oppressed was again respected as soon as he resumed the hostile character of a barbarian.   The
vineyards and fruitful fields between the rapid Marsyas and the winding
Mæander [23] were consumed with fire; the decayed walls of the cities

[20] Godefroy, tom. iii. p. 89.   It is, however, suspected that this law, so
repugnant to the maxims of Germanic freedom, has been surreptitiously added
to the golden bull.

[21] A copious and circumstantial narrative (which he might have reserved
for more important events) is bestowed by Zosimus (l. v. [c. 10, *sqq.*] p. 304-
312) on the revolt of Tribigild and Gainas.   See likewise Socrates, l. vi.
c. 6, and Sozomen, l. viii. c. 4.   The second book of Claudian against Eutropius
is a fine though imperfect piece of history.

[22] Claudian (in Eutrop. l. ii. 237-250) very accurately observes that the
ancient name and nation of the Phrygians extended very far on every side,
till their limits were contracted by the colonies of the Bithynians of Thrace,
of the Greeks, and at last of the Gauls.   His description (ii. 257-272) of the
fertility of Phrygia, and of the four rivers that produced gold, is just and
picturesque.

[23] Xenophon, Anabasis, l. i. [c. 2, § 8] p. 11, 12, edit. Hutchinson; Strabo,

crumbled into dust at the first stroke of an enemy; the trembling inhabitants escaped from a bloody massacre to the shores of the Hellespont; and a considerable part of Asia Minor was desolated by the rebellion of Tribigild. His rapid progress was checked by the resistance of the peasants of Pamphylia; and the Ostrogoths, attacked in a narrow pass between the city of Selgæ,[24] a deep morass, and the craggy cliffs of Mount Taurus, were defeated with the loss of their bravest troops. But the spirit of their chief was not daunted by misfortune, and his army was continually recruited by swarms of barbarians and outlaws who were desirous of exercising the profession of robbery under the more honourable names of war and conquest. The rumours of the success of Tribigild might for some time be suppressed by fear, or disguised by flattery; yet they gradually alarmed both the court and the capital. Every misfortune was exaggerated in dark and doubtful hints, and the future designs of the rebels became the subject of anxious conjecture. Whenever Tribigild advanced into the inland country, the Romans were inclined to suppose that he meditated the passage of Mount Taurus and the invasion of Syria. If he descended towards the sea, they imputed, and perhaps suggested, to the Gothic chief the more dangerous project of arming a fleet in the harbours of Ionia, and of extending his depredations along the maritime coast, from the mouth of the Nile to the port of Constantinople. The approach of danger and the obstinacy of Tribigild, who refused all terms of accommodation, compelled Eutropius to summon a council of war.[25] After claiming for himself the privilege of a veteran soldier, the eunuch intrusted the guard of Thrace and the Hellespont to Gainas the Goth, and the command of the Asiatic army to his favourite Leo; two generals who differently but effectually promoted the cause of the rebels. Leo,[26] who from the bulk of his body and the dulness of his mind was surnamed the Ajax of the East, had deserted his original trade of a woolcomber, to exercise with much less skill and success the military profession; and his uncertain operations were capriciously framed and executed with an ignorance of real difficulties and a timorous neglect of every favourable oppor-

l. xii. p. 865, edit. Amstel. [p. 577, ed. Casaub.] ; Q. Curt. l. iii. c. 1. Claudian compares the junction of the Marsyas and Mæander to that of the Saone and the Rhône, with this difference, however, that the smaller of the Phrygian rivers is not accelerated but retarded by the larger.

[24] Selgæ, a colony of the Lacedæmonians, had formerly numbered twenty thousand citizens; but in the age of Zosimus it was reduced to a πολίχνη, or small town. See Cellarius, Geograph. Antiq. tom. ii. p. 117.

[25] The council of Eutropius, in Claudian, may be compared to that of Domitian in the fourth Satire of Juvenal. The principal members of the former were, juvenes protervi lascivique senes; one of them had been a cook, a second a woolcomber. The language of their original profession exposes their assumed dignity; and their trifling conversation about tragedies, dancers, etc., is made still more ridiculous by the importance of the debate.

[26] Claudian (l. ii. 376-461) has branded him with infamy; and Zosimus, in more temperate language, confirms his reproaches. L. v. [c. 14] p. 305.

tunity. The rashness of the Ostrogoths had drawn them into a dis-advantageous position between the rivers Melas and Eurymedon, where they were almost besieged by the peasants of Pamphylia; but the arrival of an Imperial army, instead of completing their destruction, afforded the means of safety and victory. Tribigild surprised the unguarded camp of the Romans in the darkness of the night, seduced the faith of the greater part of the barbarian auxiliaries, and dissipated without much effort the troops which had been corrupted by the relaxation of discipline and the luxury of the capital. The discontent of Gainas, who had so boldly contrived and executed the death of Rufinus, was irritated by the fortune of his unworthy successor; he accused his own dishonourable patience under the servile reign of an eunuch; and the ambitious Goth was convicted, at least in the public opinion, of secretly fomenting the revolt of Tribigild, with whom he was connected by a domestic as well as by a national alliance.[27] When Gainas passed the Hellespont, to unite under his standard the remains of the Asiatic troops, he skilfully adapted his motions to the wishes of the Ostrogoths, abandoning by his retreat the country which they desired to invade, or facilitating by his approach the desertion of the barbarian auxiliaries. To the Imperial court he repeatedly magnified the valour, the genius, the inexhaustible resources of Tribigild, confessed his own inability to prosecute the war, and extorted the permission of negotiating with his invincible adversary. The conditions of peace were dictated by the haughty rebel; and the peremptory demand of the head of Eutropius revealed the author and the design of this hostile conspiracy.

The bold satirist, who has indulged his discontent by the partial and passionate censure of the Christian emperors, violates the dignity rather than the truth of history by comparing the son of Theodosius to one of those harmless and simple animals who scarcely feel that they are the property of their shepherd. Two passions, however—fear and conjugal affection—awakened the languid soul of Arcadius: he was terrified by the threats of a victorious barbarian, and he yielded to the tender eloquence of his wife Eudoxia, who, with a flood of artificial tears, presenting her infant children to their father, implored his justice for some real or imaginary insult which she imputed to the audacious eunuch.[28] The emperor's hand was directed to sign the condemnation of Eutropius; the magic spell, which during four years had bound the prince and the people, was instantly dissolved; and the acclamations that so lately hailed the merit and fortune of the favourite were converted into the clamours of the soldiers and people, who reproached his crimes and

[27] The *conspiracy* of Gainas and Tribigild, which is attested by the Greek historian, had not reached the ears of Claudian, who attributes the revolt of the Ostrogoth to his own *martial spirit* and the advice of his wife.

[28] This anecdote, which Philostorgius alone has preserved (l. xi. c. 6, and Gothofred, Dissertat. p. 451-456), is curious and important, since it connects the revolt of the Goths with the secret intrigues of the palace.

pressed his immediate execution. In this hour of distress and despair his only refuge was in the sanctuary of the church, whose privileges he had wisely, or profanely, attempted to circumscribe; and the most eloquent of the saints, John Chrysostom, enjoyed the triumph of protecting a prostrate minister, whose choice had raised him to the ecclesiastical throne of Constantinople. The archbishop, ascending the pulpit of the cathedral that he might be distinctly seen and heard by an innumerable crowd of either sex and of every age, pronounced a seasonable and pathetic discourse on the forgiveness of injuries and the instability of human greatness. The agonies of the pale and affrighted wretch, who lay grovelling under the table of the altar, exhibited a solemn and instructive spectacle; and the orator, who was afterwards accused of insulting the misfortunes of Eutropius, laboured to excite the contempt, that he might assuage the fury, of the people.[29] The powers of humanity, of superstition, and of eloquence prevailed. The empress Eudoxia was restrained, by her own prejudices or by those of her subjects, from violating the sanctuary of the church; and Eutropius was tempted to capitulate, by the milder arts of persuasion, and by an oath that his life should be spared.[30] Careless of the dignity of their sovereign, the new ministers of the palace immediately published an edict, to declare that his late favourite had disgraced the names of consul and patrician, to abolish his statues, to confiscate his wealth, and to inflict a perpetual exile in the island of Cyprus.[31] A despicable and decrepit eunuch could no longer alarm the fears of his enemies; nor was he capable of enjoying what yet remained—the comforts of peace, of solitude, and of a happy climate. But their implacable revenge still envied him the last moments of a miserable life, and Eutropius had no sooner touched the shores of Cyprus than he was hastily recalled. The vain hope of eluding, by a

---

[29] See the Homily [i. in Eutrop.] of Chrysostom, tom. iii. p. 381-386, of which the exordium is particularly beautiful; Socrates, l. vi. c. 5; Sozomen, l. viii. c. 7. Montfaucon (in his Life of Chrysostom, tom. xiii. p. 135) too hastily supposes that Tribigild was *actually* in Constantinople, and that he commanded the soldiers who were ordered to seize Eutropius. Even Claudian, a Pagan poet (Præfat. ad. l. ii. in Eutrop. 27), has mentioned the flight of the eunuch to the sanctuary.

Suppliciterque pias humilis prostratus ad aras
Mitigat iratas voce tremente nurus.

[30] Chrysostom, in another homily [in Eutr. ii. c. 1] (tom. iii. p. 386), affects to declare that Eutropius would not have been taken, had he not deserted the church. Zosimus (l. v. [c. 18] p. 313), on the contrary, pretends that his enemies forced him (ἐξαρπάσαντες αὐτὸν) from the sanctuary. Yet the promise is an evidence of some treaty; and the strong assurance of Claudian (Præfat. ad. l. ii. 46),

Sed tamen exemplo non feriere tuo,

may be considered as an evidence of some promise.

[31] Cod. Theod. l. ix. tit. xl. leg. 14 [leg. 17]. The date of that law (Jan. 17, A.D. 399) is erroneous and corrupt, since the fall of Eutropius could not happen till the autumn of the same year. See Tillemont, Hist. des Empereurs, tom. v. p. 780.

change of place, the obligation of an oath, engaged the empress to transfer the scene of his trial and execution from Constantinople to the adjacent suburb of Chalcedon. The consul Aurelian pronounced the sentence; and the motives of that sentence expose the jurisprudence of a despotic government. The crimes which Eutropius had committed against the people might have justified his death; but he was found guilty of harnessing to his chariot the *sacred* animals, who, from their breed or colour, were reserved for the use of the emperor alone.[32]

While this domestic revolution was transacted, Gainas[33] openly revolted from his allegiance, united his forces at Thyatira in Lydia with those of Tribigild, and still maintained his superior ascendant over the rebellious leader of the Ostrogoths. The confederate armies advanced without resistance to the straits of the Hellespont and the Bosphorus, and Arcadius was instructed to prevent the loss of his Asiatic dominions by resigning his authority and his person to the faith of the barbarians. The church of the holy martyr Euphemia, situate on a lofty eminence near Chalcedon,[34] was chosen for the place of the interview. Gainas bowed with reverence at the feet of the emperor, whilst he required the sacrifice of Aurelian and Saturninus, two ministers of consular rank; and their naked necks were exposed by the haughty rebel to the edge of the sword, till he condescended to grant them a precarious and disgraceful respite. The Goths, according to the terms of the agreement, were immediately transported from Asia into Europe; and their victorious chief, who accepted the title of master-general of the Roman armies, soon filled Constantinople with his troops, and distributed among his dependents the honours and rewards of the empire. In his early youth Gainas had passed the Danube as a suppliant and a fugitive: his elevation had been the work of valour and fortune, and his indiscreet or perfidious conduct was the cause of his rapid downfall. Notwithstanding the vigorous opposition of the archbishop, he importunately claimed for his Arian sectaries the possession of a peculiar church, and the pride of the catholics was offended by the public toleration of heresy.[35] Every quarter of Constantinople was filled with tumult and disorder; and the barbarians gazed with such ardour on the rich shops of the jewellers

[32] Zosimus, l. v. [c. 18] p. 313. Philostorgius, l. xi. c. 6.
[33] Zosimus (l. v. [c. 18-22] p. 313-323), Socrates (l. vi. c. 4 [6]), Sozomen (l. viii. c. 4), and Theodoret (l. v. c. 32, 33), represent, though with some various circumstances, the conspiracy, defeat, and death of Gainas.
[34] Ὁσίας Εὐφημίας μαρτύριον is the expression of Zosimus himself (l. v. [c. 18] p. 314), who inadvertently uses the fashionable language of the Christians. Evagrius describes (l. ii. c. 3) the situation, architecture, relics, and miracles of that celebrated church, in which the general council of Chalcedon was afterwards held.
[35] The pious remonstrances of Chrysostom, which do not appear in his own writings, are strongly urged by Theodoret; but his insinuation that they were successful is disproved by facts. Tillemont (Hist. des. Empereurs, tom. v. p. 383) has discovered that the emperor, to satisfy the rapacious demands of Gainas, was obliged to melt the plate of the church of the Apostles.

and the tables of the bankers which were covered with gold and silver, that it was judged prudent to remove those dangerous temptations from their sight. They resented the injurious precaution; and some alarming attempts were made during the night to attack and destroy with fire the Imperial palace.[36]   In this state of mutual and suspicious hostility, the guards and the people of Constantinople shut the gates, and rose in arms to prevent or to punish the conspiracy of the Goths.   During the absence of Gainas his troops were surprised and oppressed; seven thousand barbarians perished in this bloody massacre.   In the fury of the pursuit the catholics uncovered the roof, and continued to throw down flaming logs of wood till they overwhelmed their adversaries, who had retreated to the church or conventicle of the Arians.   Gainas was either innocent of the design or too confident of his success; he was astonished by the intelligence that the flower of his army had been ingloriously destroyed; that he himself was declared a public enemy; and that his countryman Fravitta, a brave and loyal confederate, had assumed the management of the war by sea and land.   The enterprises of the rebel against the cities of Thrace were encountered by a firm and well-ordered defence: his hungry soldiers were soon reduced to the grass that grew on the margin of the fortifications; and Gainas, who vainly regretted the wealth and luxury of Asia, embraced a desperate resolution of forcing the passage of the Hellespont.   He was destitute of vessels, but the woods of the Chersonesus afforded materials for rafts, and his intrepid barbarians did not refuse to trust themselves to the waves.   But Fravitta attentively watched the progress of their undertaking.   As soon as they had gained the middle of the stream, the Roman galleys,[37] impelled by the full force of oars, of the current, and of a favourable wind, rushed forwards in compact order and with irresistible weight, and the Hellespont was covered with the fragments of the Gothic shipwreck.   After the destruction of his hopes and the loss of many thousands of his bravest soldiers, Gainas, who could no longer aspire to govern or to subdue the Romans, determined to resume the independence of a savage life.   A light and active body of barbarian horse, disengaged from their infantry and baggage, might perform in eight or ten days a march of three hundred miles from the Hellespont to the Danube;[38] the garrisons of

[36] The ecclesiastical historians, who sometimes guide and sometimes follow the public opinion, most confidently assert that the palace of Constantinople was guarded by legions of angels.

[37] Zosimus (l. v. [c. 20] p. 319) mentions these galleys by the name of *Liburnians*, and observes that they were as swift (without explaining the difference between them) as the vessels with fifty oars; but that they were far inferior in speed to the *triremes*, which had been long disused.   Yet he reasonably concludes, from the testimony of Polybius, that galleys of a still larger size had been constructed in the Punic wars.   Since the establishment of the Roman empire over the Mediterranean, the useless art of building large ships of war had probably been neglected, and at length forgotten.

[38] Chishull (Travels, p. 61-63, 72-76) proceeded from Gallipoli, through Hadrianople, to the Danube, in about fifteen days.   He was in the train of an

that important frontier had been gradually annihilated; the river in the month of December would be deeply frozen; and the unbounded prospect of Scythia was open to the ambition of Gainas. This design was secretly communicated to the national troops, who devoted themselves to the fortunes of their leader; and before the signal of departure was given, a great number of provincial auxiliaries, whom he suspected of an attachment to their native country, were perfidiously massacred. The Goths advanced by rapid marches through the plains of Thrace, and they were soon delivered from the fear of pursuit by the vanity of Fravitta, who, instead of extinguishing the war, hastened to enjoy the popular applause, and to assume the peaceful honours of the consulship. But a formidable ally appeared in arms to vindicate the majesty of the empire, and to guard the peace and liberty of Scythia.[39] The superior forces of Uldin, king of the Huns, opposed the progress of Gainas; an hostile and ruined country prohibited his retreat; he disdained to capitulate; and after repeatedly attempting to cut his way through the ranks of the enemy, he was slain, with his desperate followers, in the field of battle. Eleven days after the naval victory of the Hellespont, the head of Gainas, the inestimable gift of the conqueror, was received at Constantinople with the most liberal expressions of gratitude; and the public deliverance was celebrated by festivals and illuminations. The triumphs of Arcadius became the subject of epic poems;[40] and the monarch, no longer oppressed by any hostile terrors, resigned himself to the mild and absolute dominion of his wife, the fair and artful Eudoxia, who has sullied her fame by the persecution of St. John Chrysostom.

After the death of the indolent Nectarius, the successor of Gregory Nazianzen, the church of Constantinople was distracted by the ambition of rival candidates, who were not ashamed to solicit, with gold or flattery, the suffrage of the people or of the favourite. On this occasion Eutropius seems to have deviated from his ordinary maxims; and his uncorrupted judgment was determined only by the superior merit of a stranger. In a late journey into the East he had admired the sermons of John, a native and presbyter of Antioch, whose name has been

English ambassador, whose baggage consisted of seventy-one waggons. That learned traveller has the merit of tracing a curious and unfrequented route.

[39] The narrative of Zosimus, who actually leads Gainas beyond the Danube, must be corrected by the testimony of Socrates [l. vi. c. 6] and Sozomen [l. viii. c. 4], that he was killed in *Thrace,* and by the precise and authentic dates of the Alexandrian or Paschal Chronicle, p. 307 [ed. Paris; tom. i. p. 567, ed. Bonn]. The naval victory of the Hellespont is fixed to the month Apellæus, the tenth of the calends of January (December 23); the head of Gainas was brought to Constantinople the third of the nones of January (January 3), in the month Audynæus.

[40] Eusebius Scholasticus acquired much fame by his poem on the Gothic war, in which he had served. Near forty years afterwards, Ammonius recited another poem on the same subject, in the presence of the emperor Theodosius. See Socrates, l. vi. c. 6.

distinguished by the epithet of Chrysostom, or the Golden Mouth.[41] A private order was despatched to the governor of Syria; and as the people might be unwilling to resign their favourite preacher, he was transported, with speed and secrecy, in a post-chariot, from Antioch to Constantinople. The unanimous and unsolicited consent of the court, the clergy, and the people ratified the choice of the minister; and, both as a saint and as an orator, the new archbishop surpassed the sanguine expectations of the public. Born of a noble and opulent family in the capital of Syria, Chrysostom had been educated, by the care of a tender mother, under the tuition of the most skilful masters. He studied the art of rhetoric in the school of Libanius; and that celebrated sophist, who soon discovered the talents of his disciple, ingenuously confessed that John would have deserved to succeed him had he not been stolen away by the Christians. His piety soon disposed him to receive the sacrament of baptism; to renounce the lucrative and honourable profession of the law; and to bury himself in the adjacent desert, where he subdued the lusts of the flesh by an austere penance of six years. His infirmities compelled him to return to the society of mankind; and the authority of Meletius devoted his talents to the service of the church: but in the midst of his family, and afterwards on the archiepiscopal throne, Chrysostom still persevered in the practice of the monastic virtues. The ample revenues, which his predecessors had consumed in pomp and luxury, he diligently applied to the establishment of hospitals; and the multitudes who were supported by his charity preferred the eloquent and edifying discourses of their archbishop to the amusements of the theatre or the circus. The monuments of that eloquence, which was admired near twenty years at Antioch and Constantinople, have been carefully preserved; and the possession of near one thousand sermons or homilies has authorised the critics [42] of suc-

---

[41] The sixth book of Socrates, the eighth of Sozomen, and the fifth of Theodoret, afford curious and authentic materials for the Life of John Chrysostom. Besides those general historians, I have taken for my guides the four principal biographers of the saint:—1. The author of a partial and passionate Vindication of the Archbishop of Constantinople, composed in the form of a dialogue, and under the name of his zealous partisan, Palladius, bishop of Helenopolis (Tillemont, Mém. Ecclés. tom. xi. p. 500-533). It is inserted among the works of Chrysostom, tom. xiii. p. 1-90, edit. Montfaucon. 2. The moderate Erasmus (tom. iii. Epist. MCL. p. 1331-1347, edit. Lugd. Bat.). His vivacity and good sense were his own; his errors, in the uncultivated state of ecclesiastical antiquity, were almost inevitable. 3. The learned Tillemont (Mém. Ecclésiastiques, tom. xi. p. 1-405, 547-626, etc. etc.), who compiles the Lives of the saints with incredible patience and religious accuracy. He has minutely searched the voluminous works of Chrysostom himself. 4. Father Montfaucon, who has perused those works with the curious diligence of an editor, discovered several new homilies, and again reviewed and composed the Life of Chrysostom (Opera Chrysostom. tom. xiii. p. 91-177).

[42] As I am *almost* a stranger to the voluminous sermons of Chrysostom, I have given my confidence to the two most judicious and moderate of the ecclesiastical critics, Erasmus (tom. iii. p. 1344) and Dupin (Bibliothèque Ec-

ceeding times to appreciate the genuine merit of Chrysostom. They unanimously attribute to the Christian orator the free command of an elegant and copious language; the judgment to conceal the advantages which he derived from the knowledge of rhetoric and philosophy; an inexhaustible fund of metaphors and similitudes, of ideas and images, to vary and illustrate the most familiar topics; the happy art of engaging the passions in the service of virtue, and of exposing the folly as well as the turpitude of vice almost with the truth and spirit of a dramatic representation.

The pastoral labours of the archbishop of Constantinople provoked and gradually united against him two sorts of enemies; the aspiring clergy, who envied his success, and the obstinate sinners, who were offended by his reproofs. When Chrysostom thundered from the pulpit of St. Sophia against the degeneracy of the Christians, his shafts were spent among the crowd, without wounding or even marking the character of any individual. When he declaimed against the peculiar vices of the rich, poverty might obtain a transient consolation from his invectives: but the guilty were still sheltered by their numbers; and the reproach itself was dignified by some ideas of superiority and enjoyment. But as the pyramid rose towards the summit, it insensibly diminished to a point; and the magistrates, the ministers, the favourite eunuchs, the ladies of the court,[43] the empress Eudoxia herself, had a much larger share of guilt to divide among a smaller proportion of criminals. The personal applications of the audience were anticipated or confirmed by the testimony of their own conscience; and the intrepid preacher assumed the dangerous right of exposing both the offence and the offender to the public abhorrence. The secret resentment of the court encouraged the discontent of the clergy and monks of Constantinople, who were too hastily reformed by the fervent zeal of their archbishop. He had condemned from the pulpit the domestic females of the clergy of Constantinople, who, under the name of servants or sisters, afforded a perpetual occasion either of sin or of scandal. The silent and solitary ascetics, who had secluded themselves from the world, were entitled to the warmest approbation of Chrysostom; but he despised and stigmatised, as the disgrace of their holy profession, the crowd of degenerate monks, who, from some unworthy motives of pleasure or

clésiastique, tom. iii. p. 38) ; yet the good taste of the former is sometimes vitiated by an excessive love of antiquity, and the good sense of the latter is always restrained by prudential considerations

[43] The females of Constantinople distinguished themselves by their enmity or their attachment to Chrysostom. Three noble and opulent widows—Marsa, Castricia, and Eugraphia—were the leaders of the persecution (Pallad. Dialog. tom. xiii. p. 14 [c. 4, p. 35, ed. Paris, 1680]). It was impossible that they should forgive a preacher who reproached their affectation to conceal, by the ornaments of dress, their age and ugliness (Pallad. p. 27). Olympias, by equal zeal, displayed in a more pious cause, has obtained the title of saint. See Tillemont, Mém. Ecclés. tom. xi. p. 416-440.

profit, so frequently infested the streets of the capital. To the voice of persuasion the archbishop was obliged to add the terrors of authority; and his ardour in the exercise of ecclesiastical jurisdiction was not always exempt from passion; nor was it always guided by prudence. Chrysostom was naturally of a choleric disposition.[44] Although he struggled, according to the precepts of the Gospel, to love his private enemies, he indulged himself in the privilege of hating the enemies of God and of the church; and his sentiments were sometimes delivered with too much energy of countenance and expression. He still maintained, from some considerations of health or abstinence, his former habits of taking his repasts alone; and this inhospitable custom,[45] which his enemies imputed to pride, contributed at least to nourish the infirmity of a morose and unsocial humour. Separated from that familiar intercourse which facilitates the knowledge and the despatch of business, he reposed an unsuspecting confidence in his deacon Serapion; and seldom applied his speculative knowledge of human nature to the particular characters either of his dependents or of his equals. Conscious of the purity of his intentions, and perhaps of the superiority of his genius, the archbishop of Constantinople extended the jurisdiction of the Imperial city, that he might enlarge the sphere of his pastoral labours; and the conduct which the profane imputed to an ambitious motive, appeared to Chrysostom himself in the light of a sacred and indispensable duty. In his visitation through the Asiatic provinces he deposed thirteen bishops of Lydia and Phrygia; and indiscreetly declared that a deep corruption of simony and licentiousness had infected the whole episcopal order.[46] If those bishops were innocent, such a rash and unjust condemnation must excite a well-grounded discontent. If they were guilty, the numerous associates of their guilt would soon discover that their own safety depended on the ruin of the archbishop, whom they studied to represent as the tyrant of the Eastern church. This ecclesiastical conspiracy was managed by Theophilus,[47] archbishop of Alexandria, an active and ambitious prelate, who displayed

[44] Sozomen, and more especially Socrates, have defined the real character of Chrysostom with a temperate and impartial freedom very offensive to his blind admirers. Those historians lived in the next generation, when party violence was abated, and had conversed with many persons intimately acquainted with the virtues and imperfections of the saint.

[45] Palladius (tom. xiii. p. 40, etc. [c. xii. p. 102, ed. Paris, 1680]) very seriously defends the archbishop. 1. He never tasted wine. 2. The weakness of his stomach required a peculiar diet. 3. Business, or study, or devotion, often kept him fasting till sunset. 4. He detested the noise and levity of great dinners. 5. He saved the expense for the use of the poor. 6. He was apprehensive, in a capital like Constantinople, of the envy and reproach of partial invitations.

[46] Chrysostom declares his free opinion (tom. ix. hom. iii. in Act. Apostol. p. 29) that the number of bishops who might be saved bore a very small proportion to those who would be damned.

[47] See Tillemont, Mém. Ecclés. tom. xi. p. 441-500.

the fruits of rapine in monuments of ostentation. His national dislike
to the rising greatness of a city which degraded him from the second
to the third rank in the Christian world was exasperated by some personal disputes with Chrysostom himself.[48]   By the private invitation
of the empress, Theophilus landed at Constantinople, with a stout
body of Egyptian mariners, to encounter the populace; and a train of
dependent bishops, to secure by their voices the majority of a synod.
The synod [49] was convened in the suburb of Chalcedon, surnamed
the *Oak*, where Rufinus had erected a stately church and monastery;
and their proceedings were continued during fourteen days or sessions.
A bishop and a deacon accused the archbishop of Constantinople; but
the frivolous or improbable nature of the forty-seven articles which
they presented against him may justly be considered as a fair and unexceptionable panegyric.   Four successive summons were signified to
Chrysostom; but he still refused to trust either his person or his reputation in the hands of his implacable enemies, who, prudently declining
the examination of any particular charges, condemned his contumacious
disobedience, and hastily pronounced a sentence of deposition.   The
synod of the *Oak* immediately addressed the emperor to ratify and
execute their judgment, and charitably insinuated that the penalties of
treason might be inflicted on the audacious preacher, who had reviled,
under the name of Jezebel, the empress Eudoxia herself. The archbishop
was rudely arrested, and conducted through the city, by one of the
Imperial messengers, who landed him, after a short navigation, near the
entrance of the Euxine; from whence, before the expiration of two
days, he was gloriously recalled.

The first astonishment of his faithful people had been mute and
passive: they suddenly rose with unanimous and irresistible fury. Theophilus escaped, but the promiscuous crowd of monks and Egyptian
mariners was slaughtered without pity in the streets of Constantinople.[50]
A seasonable earthquake justified the interposition of Heaven; the

[48] I have purposely omitted the controversy which arose among the monks
of Egypt concerning Origenism and Anthropomorphism, the dissimulation and
violence of Theophilus, his artful management of the simplicity of Epiphanius,
the persecution and flight of the *long* or tall brothers, the ambiguous support
which they received at Constantinople from Chrysostom, etc. etc.

[49] Photius (p. 53-60 [p. 17, *sqq.* ed. Bekk.]) has preserved the original acts of
the synod of the Oak, which destroy the false assertion that Chrysostom was
condemned by no more than thirty-six bishops, of whom twenty-nine were
Egyptians.   Forty-five bishops subscribed his sentence. See Tillemont, Mém.
Ecclés. tom. xi. p. 595.

[50] Palladius owns (p. 30 [c. 8, p. 75]) that if the people of Constantinople
had found Theophilus, they would certainly have thrown him into the sea.
Socrates mentions (l. vi. c. 17) a battle between the mob and the sailors of
Alexandria, in which many wounds were given, and some lives were lost.   The
massacre of the monks is observed only by the Pagan Zosimus (l. v. [c. 23]
p. 324), who acknowledges that Chrysostom had a singular talent to lead the
illiterate multitude, ἦν γὰρ ὁ ἄνθρωπος ἄλογον ὄχλον ὑπαγαγέσθαι δεινός.

torrent of sedition rolled forwards to the gates of the palace; and the empress, agitated by fear or remorse, threw herself at the feet of Arcadius, and confessed that the public safety could be purchased only by the restoration of Chrysostom. The Bosphorus was covered with innumerable vessels; the shores of Europe and Asia were profusely illuminated; and the acclamations of a victorious people accompanied, from the port to the cathedral, the triumph of the archbishop, who too easily consented to resume the exercise of his functions, before his sentence had been legally reversed by the authority of an ecclesiastical synod. Ignorant, or careless, of the impending danger, Chrysostom indulged his zeal, or perhaps his resentment; declaimed with peculiar asperity against *female* vices; and condemned the profane honours which were addressed, almost in the precincts of St. Sophia, to the statue of the empress. His imprudence tempted his enemies to inflame the haughty spirit of Eudoxia, by reporting, or perhaps inventing, the famous exordium of a sermon, " Herodias is again furious; Herodias again dances; she once more requires the head of John:" an insolent allusion, which, as a woman and a sovereign, it was impossible for her to forgive.[51] The short interval of a perfidious truce was employed to concert more effectual measures for the disgrace and ruin of the archbishop. A numerous council of the Eastern prelates, who were guided from a distance by the advice of Theophilus, confirmed the validity, without examining the justice, of the former sentence; and a detachment of barbarian troops was introduced into the city, to suppress the emotions of the people. On the vigil of Easter the solemn administration of baptism was rudely interrupted by the soldiers, who alarmed the modesty of the naked catechumens, and violated, by their presence, the awful mysteries of the Christian worship. Arsacius occupied the church of St. Sophia and the archiepiscopal throne. The catholics retreated to the baths of Constantine, and afterwards to the fields, where they were still pursued and insulted by the guards, the bishops, and the magistrates. The fatal day of the second and final exile of Chrysostom was marked by the conflagration of the cathedral, of the senate-house, and of the adjacent buildings; and this calamity was imputed, without proof, but not without probability, to the despair of a persecuted faction.[52]

Cicero might claim some merit if his voluntary banishment preserved the peace of the republic;[53] but the submission of a Chrysostom was

---

[51] See Socrates, l. vi. c. 18. Sozomen, l. viii. c. 20. Zosimus (l. v. [c. 24] p. 324, 327) mentions, in general terms, his invectives against Eudoxia. The homily which begins with those famous words is rejected as spurious. Montfaucon, tom. xiii. p. 151. Tillemont, Mém. Ecclés. tom. xi. p. 603.

[52] We might naturally expect such a charge from Zosimus (l. v. [c. 24] p. 327; but it is remarkable enough that it should be confirmed by Socrates, l. vi. c. 18, and the Paschal Chronicle, p. 307 [ed. Paris; tom. i. p. 568, ed. Bonn].

[53] He displays those specious motives (Post Reditum, c. 13, 14) in the language of an orator and a politician.

the indispensable duty of a Christian and a subject. Instead of listening to his humble prayer that he might be permitted to reside at Cyzicus or Nicomedia, the inflexible empress assigned for his exile the remote and desolate town of Cucusus, among the ridges of Mount Taurus, in the Lesser Armenia. A secret hope was entertained that the archbishop might perish in a difficult and dangerous march of seventy days in the heat of summer, through the provinces of Asia Minor, where he was continually threatened by the hostile attacks of the Isaurians, and the more implacable fury of the monks. Yet Chrysostom arrived in safety at the place of his confinement; and the three years which he spent at Cucusus, and the neighbouring town of Arabissus, were the last and most glorious of his life. His character was consecrated by absence and persecution; the faults of his administration were no longer remembered; but every tongue repeated the praises of his genius and virtue: and the respectful attention of the Christian world was fixed on a desert spot among the mountains of Taurus. From that solitude the archbishop, whose active mind was invigorated by misfortunes, maintained a strict and frequent correspondence [54] with the most distant provinces; exhorted the separate congregation of his faithful adherents to persevere in their allegiance; urged the destruction of the temples of Phœnicia, and the extirpation of heresy in the isle of Cyprus; extended his pastoral care to the missions of Persia and Scythia; negotiated, by his ambassadors, with the Roman pontiff and the emperor Honorius; and boldly appealed, from a partial synod, to the supreme tribunal of a free and general council. The mind of the illustrious exile was still independent; but his captive body was exposed to the revenge of the oppressors, who continued to abuse the name and authority of Arcadius.[55] An order was despatched for the instant removal of Chrysostom to the extreme desert of Pityus: and his guards so faithfully obeyed their cruel instructions, that, before he reached the sea-coast of the Euxine, he expired at Comana, in Pontus, in the sixtieth year of his age. The succeeding generation acknowledged his innocence and merit. The archbishops of the East, who might blush that their predecessors had been the enemies of Chrysostom, were grad-

[54] Two hundred and forty-two of the epistles of Chrysostom are still extant (Opera, tom. iii. p. 528-736 [ed. Bened.]). They are addressed to a great variety of persons, and show a firmness of mind much superior to that of Cicero in his exile. The fourteenth epistle contains a curious narrative of the dangers of his journey.

[55] After the exile of Chrysostom, Theophilus published an *enormous* and *horrible* volume against him, in which he perpetually repeats the polite expressions of hostem humanitatis, sacrilegorum principem, immundum dæmonem; he affirms that John Chrysostom had delivered his soul to be adulterated by the devil; and wishes that some farther punishment, adequate (if possible) to the magnitude of his crimes, may be inflicted on him. St. Jerom, at the request of his friend Theophilus, translated this edifying performance from Greek into Latin. See Facundus Hermian. Defens. pro iii. Capitul. 1 vi. c. 5 [p. 260, ed. Paris, 1629], published by Sirmond, Opera, tom. ii. p. 595, 596, 597.

ually disposed, by the firmness of the Roman pontiff, to restore the honours of that venerable name.[56] At the pious solicitation of the clergy and people of Constantinople, his relics, thirty years after his death, were transported from their obscure sepulchre to the royal city.[57] The emperor Theodosius advanced to receive them as far as Chalcedon; and, falling prostrate on the coffin, implored, in the name of his guilty parents, Arcadius and Eudoxia, the forgiveness of the injured saint.[58]

Yet a reasonable doubt may be entertained whether any stain of hereditary guilt could be derived from Arcadius to his successor. Eudoxia was a young and beautiful woman, who indulged her passions and despised her husband: Count John enjoyed, at least, the familiar confidence of the empress; and the public named him as the real father of Theodosius the younger.[59] The birth of a son was accepted, however, by the pious husband as an event the most fortunate and honourable to himself, to his family, and to the Eastern world: and the royal infant, by an unprecedented favour, was invested with the titles of Cæsar and Augustus. In less than four years afterwards, Eudoxia, in the bloom of youth, was destroyed by the consequences of a miscarriage; and this untimely death confounded the prophecy of a holy bishop,[60] who, amidst the universal joy, had ventured to foretell that she should behold the long and auspicious reign of her glorious son. The catholics applauded the justice of Heaven, which avenged the persecution of St. Chrysostom; and perhaps the emperor was the only person who sincerely bewailed the loss of the haughty and rapacious Eudoxia. Such a domestic misfortune afflicted *him* more deeply than the public calamities of the East [61]—the licentious excursions, from Pontus to Palestine,

[56] His name was inserted by his successor Atticus in the dyptics of the church of Constantinople, A.D. 418. Ten years afterwards he was revered as a saint. Cyril, who inherited the place and the passions of his uncle Theophilus, yielded with much reluctance. See Facund. Hermian. l. iv. c. 1 [p. 142, ed Par. 1629]; Tillemont, Mém. Ecclés. tom. xiv. p. 277-283.

[57] Socrates, l. vii. c. 45; Theodoret, l. v. c. 36. This event reconciled the Joanites, who had hitherto refused to acknowledge his successors. During his lifetime the Joanites were respected by the catholics as the true and orthodox communion of Constantinople. Their obstinacy gradually drove them to the brink of schism.

[58] According to some accounts (Baronius, Annal. Eccles. A.D. 438, No. 9, 10), the emperor was forced to send a letter of invitation and excuses before the body of the ceremonious saint could be moved from Comana.

[59] Zosimus, l. v. [c. 18] p. 315. The chastity of an empress should not be impeached without producing a witness; but it is astonishing that the witness should write and live under a prince whose legitimacy he dared to attack. We must suppose that this history was a party libel, privately read and circulated by the Pagans. Tillemont (Hist. des Empereurs, tom. v. p. 782) is not averse to brand the reputation of Eudoxia.

[60] Porphyry of Gaza. His zeal was transported by the order which he had obtained for the destruction of eight Pagan temples of that city. See the curious details of his life (Baronius, A.D. 401, No. 17-51), originally written in Greek, or perhaps in Syriac, by a monk, one of his favourite deacons.

[61] Philostorg. l. xi. c. 8, and Godefroy, Dissertat. p. 457.

of the Isaurian robbers, whose impunity accused the weakness of the government; and the earthquakes, the conflagrations, the famine, and the flights of locusts,[62] which the popular discontent was equally disposed to attribute to the incapacity of the monarch. At length, in the thirty-first year of his age, after a reign (if we may abuse that word) of thirteen years, three months, and fifteen days, Arcadius expired in the palace of Constantinople. It is impossible to delineate his character; since, in a period very copiously furnished with historical materials, it has not been possible to remark one action that properly belongs to the son of the great Theodosius.

The historian Procopius [63] has indeed illuminated the mind of the dying emperor with a ray of human prudence, or celestial wisdom. Arcadius considered, with anxious foresight, the helpless condition of his son Theodosius, who was no more than seven years of age, the dangerous factions of a minority, and the aspiring spirit of Jezdegerd, the Persian monarch. Instead of tempting the allegiance of an ambitious subject by the participation of supreme power, he boldly appealed to the magnanimity of a king, and placed, by a solemn testament, the sceptre of the East in the hands of Jezdegerd himself. The royal guardian accepted and discharged this honourable trust with unexampled fidelity; and the infancy of Theodosius was protected by the arms and councils of Persia. Such is the singular narrative of Procopius; and his veracity is not disputed by Agathias,[64] while he presumes to dissent from his judgment, and to arraign the wisdom of a Christian emperor, who so rashly, though so fortunately, committed his son and his dominions to the unknown faith of a stranger, a rival, and a heathen. At the distance of one hundred and fifty years, this political question might be debated in the court of Justinian; but a prudent historian will refuse to examine the *propriety,* till he has ascertained the *truth,* of the testament of Arcadius. As it stands without a parallel in the history of the world, we may justly require that it should be attested by the positive and unanimous evidence of contemporaries. The strange novelty of the event, which excites our distrust, must have attracted their notice; and their universal silence annihilates the vain tradition of the succeeding age.

[62] Jerom (tom. vi. p. 73, 76) describes in lively colours the regular and destructive march of the locusts, which spread a dark cloud between heaven and earth over the land of Palestine. Seasonable winds scattered them, partly into the Dead Sea and partly into the Mediterranean.

[63] Procopius, de Bell. Persic. l. i. c. 2, p. 8, edit. Louvre [tom. i. p. 14, ed. Bonn].

[64] Agathias, l. iv. [c. 26] p. 136, 137 [p. 264, ed. Bonn]. Although he confesses the prevalence of the tradition, he asserts that Procopius was the first who had committed it to writing. Tillemont (Hist. des Empereurs, tom. vi. p. 597) argues very sensibly on the merits of this fable. His criticism was not warped by any ecclesiastical authority: both Procopius and Agathias are half Pagans.

The maxims of Roman jurisprudence, if they could fairly be trans-ferred from private property to public dominion, would have adjudged to the emperor Honorius the guardianship of his nephew, till he had attained, at least, the fourteenth year of his age. But the weakness of Honorius, and the calamities of his reign, disqualified him from prose-cuting this natural claim; and such was the absolute separation of the two monarchies, both in interest and affection, that Constantinople would have obeyed with less reluctance the orders of the Persian, than those of the Italian court. Under a prince whose weakness is disguised by the external signs of manhood and discretion, the most worthless favourites may secretly dispute the empire of the palace, and dictate to submissive provinces the commands of a master whom they direct and despise. But the ministers of a child, who is incapable of arming them with the sanction of the royal name, must acquire and exercise an independent authority. The great officers of the state and army, who had been appointed before the death of Arcadius, formed an aristoc-racy which might have inspired them with the idea of a free republic; and the government of the Eastern empire was fortunately assumed by the præfect Anthemius,[65] who obtained, by his superior abilities, a lasting ascendant over the minds of his equals. The safety of the young emperor proved the merit and integrity of Anthemius; and his prudent firmness sustained the force and reputation of an infant reign. Uldin, with a formidable host of barbarians, was encamped in the heart of Thrace; he proudly rejected all terms of accommodation; and, pointing to the rising sun, declared to the Roman ambassadors that the course of that planet should alone terminate the conquests of the Huns. But the desertion of his confederates, who were privately con-vinced of the justice and liberality of the Imperial ministers, obliged Uldin to repass the Danube: the tribe of the Scyrri, which composed his rear-guard, was almost extirpated; and many thousand captives were dispersed, to cultivate, with servile labour, the fields of Asia.[66] In the midst of the public triumph, Constantinople was protected by a strong enclosure of new and more extensive walls; the same vigilant care was applied to restore the fortifications of the Illyrian cities; and a plan was judiciously conceived, which, in the space of seven years, would have secured the command of the Danube, by establishing on that river a perpetual fleet of two hundred and fifty armed vessels.[67]

---

[65] Socrates, l. vii. c. 1. Anthemius was the grandson of Philip, one of the ministers of Constantius, and the grandfather of the emperor Anthemius. After his return from the Persian embassy, he was appointed consul and Prætorian præfect of the East, in the year 405; and held the præfecture about ten years. See his honours and praises in Godefroy, Cod. Theod. tom. vi. p. 350; Tillemont, Hist. des Emp. tom. vi. p. 1, etc.

[66] Sozomen, l. ix. c. 5. He saw some Scyrri at work near Mount Olympus, in Bithynia, and cherished the vain hope that those captives were the last of the nation.

[67] Cod. Theod. l. vii. tit. xvii.; l. xv. tit. i. leg. 49.

But the Romans had so long been accustomed to the authority of a monarch, that the first, even among the females of the Imperial family, who displayed any courage or capacity, was permitted to ascend the vacant throne of Theodosius. His sister Pulcheria,[68] who was only two years older than himself, received at the age of sixteen the title of *Augusta;* and though her favour might be sometimes clouded by caprice or intrigue, she continued to govern the Eastern empire near forty years; during the long minority of her brother, and after his death in her own name, and in the name of Marcian, her nominal husband. From a motive either of prudence or religion, she embraced a life of celibacy; and notwithstanding some aspersions on the chastity of Pulcheria,[69] this resolution, which she communicated to her sisters Arcadia and Marina, was celebrated by the Christian world as the sublime effort of heroic piety. In the presence of the clergy and people the three daughters of Arcadius [70] dedicated their virginity to God; and the obligation of their solemn vow was inscribed on a tablet of gold and gems, which they publicly offered in the great church of Constantinople. Their palace was converted into a monastery, and all males—except the guides of their conscience, the saints who had forgotten the distinction of sexes—were scrupulously excluded from the holy threshold. Pulcheria, her two sisters, and a chosen train of favourite damsels, formed a religious community: they renounced the vanity of dress, interrupted by frequent fasts their simple and frugal diet, allotted a portion of their time to works of embroidery, and devoted several hours of the day and night to the exercises of prayer and psalmody. The piety of a Christian virgin was adorned by the zeal and liberality of an empress. Ecclesiastical history describes the splendid churches which were built at the expense of Pulcheria in all the provinces of the East, her charitable foundations for the benefit of strangers and the poor, the ample donations which she assigned for the perpetual maintenance of monastic societies, and the active severity with which she laboured to suppress the opposite heresies of Nestorius and Eutyches. Such virtues were supposed to deserve the peculiar favour of the Deity: and the relics of martyrs, as well as the knowledge of future events, were communicated in visions and revelations to the

[68] Sozomen has filled three chapters with a magnificent panegyric of Pulcheria (l. ix. c. 1, 2, 3); and Tillemont (Mémoires Ecclés. tom. xv. p. 171-184) has dedicated a separate article to the honour of St. Pulcheria, virgin and empress.

[69] Suidas (Excerpta, p. 68, in Script. Byzant.) pretends, on the credit of the Nestorians, that Pulcheria was exasperated against their founder, because he censured her connection with the beautiful Paulinus, and her incest with her brother Theodosius.

[70] See Ducange, Famil. Byzantin. p. 70. Flaccilla, the eldest daughter, either died before Arcadius, or, if *she* lived till the year 431 (Marcellin. Chron.), some defect of mind or body must have excluded her from the honours of her rank.

Imperial saint.[71]   Yet the devotion of Pulcheria never diverted her indefatigable attention from temporal affairs; and she alone, among all the descendants of the great Theodosius, appears to have inherited any share of his manly spirit and abilities.   The elegant and familiar use which she had acquired both of the Greek and Latin languages was readily applied to the various occasions of speaking or writing on public business: her deliberations were maturely weighed; her actions were prompt and decisive; and while she moved without noise or ostentation the wheel of government, she discreetly attributed to the genius of the emperor the long tranquillity of his reign.   In the last years of his peaceful life Europe was indeed afflicted by the arms of Attila; but the more extensive provinces of Asia still continued to enjoy a profound and permanent repose.   Theodosius the younger was never reduced to the disgraceful necessity of encountering and punishing a rebellious subject: and since we cannot applaud the vigour, some praise may be due to the mildness and prosperity, of the administration of Pulcheria.

The Roman world was deeply interested in the education of its master.   A regular course of study and exercise was judiciously instituted; of the military exercises of riding, and shooting with the bow; of the liberal studies of grammar, rhetoric, and philosophy: the most skilful masters of the East ambitiously solicited the attention of their royal pupil, and several noble youths were introduced into the palace to animate his diligence by the emulation of friendship.   Pulcheria alone discharged the important task of instructing her brother in the arts of government; but her precepts may countenance some suspicion of the extent of her capacity or of the purity of her intentions.   She taught him to maintain a grave and majestic deportment; to walk, to hold his robes, to seat himself on his throne in a manner worthy of a great prince; to abstain from laughter, to listen with condescension, to return suitable answers; to assume by turns a serious or a placid countenance; in a word, to represent with grace and dignity the external figure of a Roman emperor.   But Theodosius [72] was never excited to support the

---

[71] She was admonished, by repeated dreams, of the place where the relics of the forty martyrs had been buried.   The ground had successively belonged to the house and garden of a woman of Constantinople, to a monastery of Macedonian monks, and to a church of St. Thrysus, erected by Cæsarius, who was consul A.D. 397; and the memory of the relics was almost obliterated. Notwithstanding the charitable wishes of Dr. Jortin (Remarks, tom. iv. p. 234), it is not easy to acquit Pulcheria of some share in the pious fraud, which must have been transacted when she was more than five-and-thirty years of age.

[72] There is a remarkable difference between the two ecclesiastical historians who in general bear so close a resemblance.   Sozomen (l. ix. c. 1) ascribes to Pulcheria the government of the empire and the education of her brother, whom he scarcely condescends to praise.   Socrates, though he affectedly disclaims all hopes of favour or fame, composes an elaborate panegyric on the emperor, and cautiously suppresses the merits of his sister (l. vii. c. 22, 42).

weight and glory of an illustrious name; and, instead of aspiring to imitate his ancestors, he degenerated (if we may presume to measure the degrees of incapacity) below the weakness of his father and his uncle. Arcadius and Honorius had been assisted by the guardian care of a parent, whose lessons were enforced by his authority and example. But the unfortunate prince who is born in the purple must remain a stranger to the voice of truth; and the son of Arcadius was condemned to pass his perpetual infancy encompassed only by a servile train of women and eunuchs. The ample leisure which he acquired by neglecting the essential duties of his high office was filled by idle amusements and unprofitable studies. Hunting was the only active pursuit that could tempt him beyond the limits of the palace; but he most assiduously laboured, sometimes by the light of a midnight lamp, in the mechanic occupations of painting and carving; and the elegance with which he transcribed religious books entitled the Roman emperor to the singular epithet of *Calligraphes,* or a fair writer. Separated from the world by an impenetrable veil, Theodosius trusted the persons whom he loved; he loved those who were accustomed to amuse and flatter his indolence; and as he never perused the papers that were presented for the royal signature, the acts of injustice the most repugnant to his character were frequently perpetrated in his name. The emperor himself was chaste, temperate, liberal, and merciful; but these qualities—which can only deserve the name of virtues when they are supported by courage and regulated by discretion—were seldom beneficial, and they sometimes proved mischievous, to mankind. His mind, enervated by a royal education, was oppressed and degraded by abject superstition: he fasted, he sung psalms, he blindly accepted the miracles and doctrines with which his faith was continually nourished. Theodosius devoutly worshipped the dead and living saints of the catholic church; and he once refused to eat till an insolent monk, who had cast an excommunication on his sovereign, condescended to heal the spiritual wound which he had inflicted.[73]

The story of a fair and virtuous maiden, exalted from a private condition to the Imperial throne, might be deemed an incredible romance, if such a romance had not been verified in the marriage of Theodosius. The celebrated Athenais [74] was educated by her father

Philostorgius (l. xii. c. 7) expresses the influence of Pulcheria in gentle and courtly language, τὰς βασιλικὰς σημειώσεις ὑπηρετουμένη καὶ διευθύνουσα. Suidas (Excerpt. p. 53) gives a true character of Theodosius; and I have followed the example of Tillemont (tom. vi. p. 25) in borrowing some strokes from the modern Greeks.

[73] Theodoret, l. v. c. 37. The bishop of Cyrrhus, one of the first men of his age for his learning and piety, applauds the obedience of Theodosius to the divine laws.

[74] Socrates (l. vii. c. 21) mentions her name (Athenais, the daughter of Leontius, an Athenian sophist), her baptism, marriage, and poetical genius. The most ancient account of her history is in John Malala (part ii. p. 20, 21,

Leontius in the religion and sciences of the Greeks; and so advantageous was the opinion which the Athenian philosopher entertained of his contemporaries, that he divided his patrimony between his two sons, bequeathing to his daughter a small legacy of one hundred pieces of gold, in the lively confidence that her beauty and merit would be a sufficient portion. The jealousy and avarice of her brothers soon compelled Athenais to seek a refuge at Constantinople, and with some hopes, either of justice or favour, to throw herself at the feet of Pulcheria. That sagacious princess listened to her eloquent complaint, and secretly destined the daughter of the philosopher Leontius for the future wife of the emperor of the East, who had now attained the twentieth year of his age. She easily excited the curiosity of her brother by an interesting picture of the charms of Athenais: large eyes, a well-proportioned nose, a fair complexion, golden locks, a slender person, a graceful demeanour, an understanding improved by study, and a virtue tried by distress. Theodosius, concealed behind a curtain in the apartment of his sister, was permitted to behold the Athenian virgin: the modest youth immediately declared his pure and honourable love, and the royal nuptials were celebrated amidst the acclamations of the capital and the provinces. Athenais, who was easily persuaded to renounce the errors of Paganism, received at her baptism the Christian name of Eudocia: but the cautious Pulcheria withheld the title of Augusta till the wife of Theodosius had approved her fruitfulness by the birth of a daughter, who espoused fifteen years afterwards the emperor of the West. The brothers of Eudocia obeyed, with some anxiety, her Imperial summons; but as she could easily forgive their fortunate unkindness, she indulged the tenderness, or perhaps the vanity, of a sister, by promoting them to the rank of consuls and præfects. In the luxury of the palace she still cultivated those ingenuous arts which had contributed to her greatness, and wisely dedicated her talents to the honour of religion and of her husband. Eudocia composed a poetical paraphrase of the first eight books of the Old Testament and of the prophecies of Daniel and Zechariah; a cento of the verses of Homer, applied to the life and miracles of Christ, the legend of St. Cyprian, and a panegyric on the Persian victories of Theodosius; and her writings, which were applauded by a servile and superstitious age, have not been disdained by the candour of impartial criticism.[75] The fondness of the

edit. Venet. 1733 [p. 354, 355, ed. Bonn]) and in the Paschal Chronicle (p. 311, 312 [ed. Paris; tom. i. p. 576, 577, ed. Bonn]). Those authors had probably seen original pictures of the empress Eudocia. The modern Greeks, Zonaras, Cedrenus, etc., have displayed the love, rather than the talent, of fiction. From Nicephorus, indeed, I have ventured to assume her age. The writer of a romance would not have *imagined* that Athenais was near twenty-eight years old when she inflamed the heart of a young emperor.

[75] Socrates, l. vii. c. 21. Photius, p. 413-420 [p. 128, 129, ed. Bekk.]. The Homeric cento is still extant, and has been repeatedly printed; but the claim of Eudocia to that insipid performance is disputed by the critics. See Fa-

emperor was not abated by time and possession; and Eudocia, after the marriage of her daughter, was permitted to discharge her grateful vows by a solemn pilgrimage to Jerusalem. Her ostentatious progress through the East may seem inconsistent with the spirit of Christian humility: she pronounced from a throne of gold and gems an eloquent oration to the senate of Antioch, declared her royal intention of enlarging the walls of the city, bestowed a donative of two hundred pounds of gold to restore the public baths, and accepted the statues which were decreed by the gratitude of Antioch. In the Holy Land her alms and pious foundations exceeded the munificence of the great Helena; and though the public treasure might be impoverished by this excessive liberality, she enjoyed the conscious satisfaction of returning to Constantinople with the chains of St. Peter, the right arm of St. Stephen, and the undoubted picture of the Virgin, painted by St. Luke.[76] But this pilgrimage was the fatal term of the glories of Eudocia. Satiated with empty pomp, and unmindful perhaps of her obligations to Pulcheria, she ambitiously aspired to the government of the Eastern empire: the palace was distracted by female discord; but the victory was at last decided by the superior ascendant of the sister of Theodosius. The execution of Paulinus, master of the offices, and the disgrace of Cyrus, Prætorian præfect of the East, convinced the public that the favour of Eudocia was insufficient to protect her most faithful friends, and the uncommon beauty of Paulinus encouraged the secret rumour that his guilt was that of a successful lover.[77] As soon as the empress perceived that the affection of Theodosius was irretrievably lost, she requested the permission of retiring to the distant solitude of Jerusalem. She obtained her request, but the jealousy of Theodosius, or the vindictive spirit of Pulcheria, pursued her in her last retreat; and Saturninus, count of the domestics, was directed to punish with death two ecclesiastics, her most favoured servants. Eudocia instantly revenged them by the assassination of the count: the furious passions which she indulged on this suspicious occasion seemed to justify the severity of Theodosius; and the empress, ignominiously stripped of the honours of her rank,[78] was disgraced, perhaps unjustly, in the eyes of the world. The remainder of the life of Eudocia, about sixteen years, was spent in exile and devotion; and the

bricius, Biblioth. Græc. tom. i. p. 357. The *Ionia*, a miscellaneous dictionary of history and fable, was compiled by another empress of the name of Eudocia who lived in the eleventh century; and the work is still extant in manuscript.

[76] Baronius (Annal. Eccles. A.D. 438, 439) is copious and florid; but he is accused of placing the lies of different ages on the same level of authenticity

[77] In this short view of the disgrace of Eudocia I have imitated the caution of Evagrius (l. i. c. 21) and Count Marcellinus (in Chron. A.D. 440 and 444 [p. 26]). The two authentic dates assigned by the latter overturn a great part of the Greek fictions; and the celebrated story of the *apple*, etc., is fit only for the Arabian Nights, where something not very unlike it may be found.

[78] Priscus (in Excerpt. Legat. p. 69 [ed. Paris; p. 208, ed. Bonn]), a contemporary and a courtier, drily mentions her Pagan and Christian names without adding any title of honour or respect.

approach of age, the death of Theodosius, the misfortunes of her only daughter, who was led a captive from Rome to Carthage, and the society of the Holy Monks of Palestine, insensibly confirmed the religious temper of her mind. After a full experience of the vicissitudes of human life, the daughter of the philosopher Leontius expired at Jerusalem, in the sixty-seventh year of her age; protesting with her dying breath that she had never transgressed the bounds of innocence and friendship.[79]

The gentle mind of Theodosius was never inflamed by the ambition of conquest or military renown; and the slight alarm of a Persian war scarcely interrupted the tranquillity of the East. The motives of this war were just and honourable. In the last year of the reign of Jezdegerd, the supposed guardian of Theodosius, a bishop, who aspired to the crown of martyrdom, destroyed one of the fire-temples of Susa.[80] His zeal and obstinacy were revenged on his brethren: the Magi excited a cruel persecution; and the intolerant zeal of Jezdegerd was imitated by his son Varanes, or Bahram, who soon afterwards ascended the throne. Some Christian fugitives, who escaped to the Roman frontier, were sternly demanded, and generously refused; and the refusal, aggravated by commercial disputes, soon kindled a war between the rival monarchies. The mountains of Armenia, and the plains of Mesopotamia, were filled with hostile armies; but the operations of two successive campaigns were not productive of any decisive or memorable events. Some engagements were fought, some towns were besieged, with various and doubtful success: and if the Romans failed in their attempt to recover the long-lost possession of Nisibis, the Persians were repulsed from the walls of a Mesopotamian city by the valour of a martial bishop, who pointed his thundering engine in the name of St. Thomas the Apostle. Yet the splendid victories which the incredible speed of the messenger Palladius repeatedly announced to the palace of Constantinople were celebrated with festivals and panegyrics. From these panegyrics the historians [81] of the age might borrow their extraordinary, and perhaps fabulous, tales; of the proud challenge of a Persian hero, who was entangled by the net, and despatched by the

---

[79] For the *two* pilgrimages of Eudocia, and her long residence at Jerusalem, her devotion, alms, etc., see Socrates (l. vii. c. 47) and Evagrius (l. i. c. 20, 21, 22). The Paschal Chronicle may sometimes deserve regard; and, in the domestic history of Antioch, John Malala becomes a writer of good authority. The Abbé Guenée, in a memoir on the fertility of Palestine, of which I have only seen an extract, calculates the gifts of Eudocia at 20,488 pounds of gold, above 800,000 pounds sterling.

[80] Theodoret, l. v. c. 39. Tillemont, Mém. Ecclés. tom. xii. p. 356-364. Assemanni, Bibliot. Oriental. tom. iii. p. 396, tom. iv. p. 61. Theodoret blames the rashness of Abdas, but extols the constancy of his martyrdom. Yet I do not clearly understand the casuistry which prohibits our repairing the damage which we have unlawfully committed.

[81] Socrates (l. vii. c. 18, 19, 20, 21) is the best author for the Persian war. We may likewise consult the three Chronicles, the Paschal, and those of Marcellinus and Malala.

sword, of Areobindus the Goth; of the ten thousand *Immortals,* who
were slain in the attack of the Roman camp; and of the hundred
thousand Arabs, or Saracens, who were impelled by a panic terror to
throw themselves headlong into the Euphrates. Such events may be
disbelieved or disregarded; but the charity of a bishop, Acacius of
Amida, whose name might have dignified the saintly calendar, shall not
be lost in oblivion. Boldly declaring that vases of gold and silver are
useless to a God who neither eats nor drinks, the generous prelate sold
the plate of the church of Amida; employed the price in the redemption
of seven thousand Persian captives; supplied their wants with affectionate liberality; and dismissed them to their native country, to inform
their king of the true spirit of the religon which he persecuted. The
practice of benevolence in the midst of war must always tend to assuage
the animosity of contending nations; and I wish to persuade myself
that Acacius contributed to the restoration of peace. In the conference
which was held on the limits of the two empires, the Roman ambassadors degraded the personal character of their sovereign, by a vain
attempt to magnify the extent of his power, when they seriously advised
the Persians to prevent, by a timely accommodation, the wrath of a
monarch who was yet ignorant of this distant war. A truce of one
hundred years was solemnly ratified; and although the revolutions of
Armenia might threaten the public tranquillity, the essential conditions
of this treaty were respected near fourscore years by the successors of
Constantine and Artaxerxes.

Since the Roman and Parthian standards first encountered on the
banks of the Euphrates, the kingdom of Armenia [82] was alternately
oppressed by its formidable protectors; and in the course of this
History, several events, which inclined the balance of peace and war,
have been already related. A disgraceful treaty had resigned Armenia
to the ambition of Sapor; and the scale of Persia appeared to preponderate. But the royal race of Arsaces impatiently submitted to the
house of Sassan; the turbulent nobles asserted, or betrayed, their
hereditary independence; and the nation was still attached to the
Christian princes of Constantinople. In the beginning of the fifth
century Armenia was divided by the progress of war and faction; [83] and

[82] This account of the ruin and division of the kingdom of Armenia is
taken from the third book of the Armenian history of Moses of Chorene.
Deficient as he is in every qualification of a good historian, his local information, his passions, and his prejudices are strongly expressive of a native and
contemporary. Procopius (de Ædificiis, l. iii. c. 1-5) relates the same facts
in a very different manner; but I have extracted the circumstances, the most
probable in themselves and the least inconsistent with Moses of Chorene.

[83] The western Armenians used the Greek language and characters in their
religious offices; but the use of that hostile tongue was prohibited by the
Persians in the eastern provinces, which were obliged to use the Syriac, till
the invention of the Armenian letters by Mesrobes in the beginning of the
fifth century, and the subsequent version of the Bible into the Armenian language; an event which relaxed the connection of the church and nation with
Constantinople.

the unnatural division precipitated the downfall of that ancient monarchy. Chosroes, the Persian vassal, reigned over the eastern and most extensive portion of the country; while the western province acknowledged the jurisdiction of Arsaces, and the supremacy of the emperor Arcadius. After the death of Arsaces, the Romans suppressed the regal government, and imposed on their allies the condition of subjects. The military command was delegated to the count of the Armenian frontier; the city of Theodosiopolis [84] was built and fortified in a strong situation, on a fertile and lofty ground, near the sources of the Euphrates; and the dependent territories were ruled by five satraps, whose dignity was marked by a peculiar habit of gold and purple. The less fortunate nobles, who lamented the loss of their king, and envied the honours of their equals, were provoked to negotiate their peace and pardon at the Persian court; and, returning with their followers to the palace of Artaxata, acknowledged Chosroes for their lawful sovereign. About thirty years afterwards, Artasires, the nephew and successor of Chosroes, fell under the displeasure of the haughty and capricious nobles of Armenia; and they unanimously desired a Persian governor in the room of an unworthy king. The answer of the archbishop Isaac, whose sanction they earnestly solicited, is expressive of the character of a superstitious people. He deplored the manifest and inexecusable vices of Artasires; and declared that he should not hesitate to accuse him before the tribunal of a Christian emperor, who would punish, without destroying, the sinner. " Our king," continued Isaac, " is too much addicted to licentious pleasures, but he has been purified in the holy water of baptism. He is a lover of women, but he does not adore the fire or the elements. He may deserve the reproach of lewdness, but he is an undoubted catholic; and his faith is pure, though his manners are flagitious. I will never consent to abandon my sheep to the rage of devouring wolves; and you would soon repent your rash exchange of the infirmities of a believer, for the specious virtues of an heathen." [85] Exasperated by the firmness of Isaac, the factious nobles accused both the king and the archbishop as the secret adherents of the emperor; and absurdly rejoiced in the sentence of condemnation, which, after a partial hearing, was solemnly pronounced by Bahram himself. The descendants of Arsaces were degraded from the royal dignity,[86] which

[84] Moses Choren. 1. iii. c. 59, p. 309 and p. 358 [ed. Whiston, Lond. 1736]. Procopius, de Ædificiis, 1. iii. c. 5. Theodosiopolis stands, or rather stood, about thirty-five miles to the east of Arzeroum, the modern capital of Turkish Armenia. See D'Anville, Géographie Ancienne, tom. ii. p. 99, 100.

[85] Moses Choren. 1. iii. c. 63, p. 316. According to the institution of St. Gregory, the Apostle of Armenia, the archbishop was always of the royal family; a circumstance which, in some degree, corrected the influence of the sacerdotal character, and united the mitre with the crown.

[86] A branch of the royal house of Arsaces still subsisted with the rank and possessions (as it should seem) of Armenian satraps. See Moses Choren. 1 iii. c. 65, p. 321.

they had possessed above five hundred and sixty years;[87] and the dominions of the unfortunate Artasires, under the new and significant appellation of Persarmenia, were reduced into the form of a province. This usurpation excited the jealousy of the Roman government; but the rising disputes were soon terminated by an amicable, though unequal, partition of the ancient kingdom of Armenia; and a territorial acquisition, which Augustus might have despised, reflected some lustre on the declining empire of the younger Theodosius.

CHAPTER XXXIII (423-455 A.D.)

Death of Honorius—Valentinian III. Emperor of the West—Administration of his Mother Placidia—Aëtius and Boniface—Conquest of Africa by the Vandals

DURING a long and disgraceful reign of twenty-eight years, Honorius, emperor of the West, was separated from the friendship of his brother, and afterwards of his nephew, who reigned over the East; and Constantinople beheld, with apparent indifference and secret joy, the calamities of Rome. The strange adventures of Placidia gradually renewed and cemented the alliance of the two empires. The daughter of the great Theodosius had been the captive and the queen of the Goths; she lost an affectionate husband; she was dragged in chains by his insulting assassin; she tasted the pleasure of revenge, and was exchanged, in the treaty of peace, for six hundred thousand measures of wheat. After her return from Spain to Italy, Placidia experienced a new persecution in the bosom of her family. She was averse to a marriage which had been stipulated without her consent; and the brave Constantius, as a noble reward for the tyrants whom he had vanquished, received, from the hand of Honorius himself, the struggling and reluctant hand of the widow of Adolphus. But her resistance ended with the ceremony of the nuptials; nor did Placidia refuse to become the mother of Honoria and Valentinian the Third, or to assume and exercise an absolute dominion over the mind of her grateful husband. The generous soldier, whose time had hitherto been divided between social pleasure and military service, was taught new lessons of avarice and ambition: he extorted the title of Augustus; and the servant of Honorius was associated to the empire of the West. The death of Constantius, in the seventh month of his reign, instead of diminishing, seemed to increase,

---

[87] Valarsaces was appointed king of Armenia by his brother the Parthian monarch, immediately after the defeat of Antiochus Sidetes (Moses Choren. l. ii. c. 2, p. 85), one hundred and thirty years before Christ. Without depending on the various and contradictory periods of the reigns of the last kings, we may be assured that the ruin of the Armenian kingdom happened after the council of Chalcedon, A.D. 431 (l. iii. c. 61, p. 312) ; and under Varanes, or Bahram, king of Persia (l. iii. c. 64, p. 317), who reigned from A.D. 420 to 440. See Assemanni, Bibliot. Oriental. tom. iii. p. 396.

the power of Placidia; and the indecent familiarity [1] of her brother, which might be no more than the symptoms of a childish affection, were universally attributed to incestuous love. On a sudden, by some base intrigues of a steward and a nurse, this excessive fondness was converted into an irreconcilable quarrel: the debates of the emperor and his sister were not long confined within the walls of the palace; and as the Gothic soldiers adhered to their queen, the city of Ravenna was agitated with bloody and dangerous tumults, which could only be appeased by the forced or voluntary retreat of Placidia and her children. The royal exiles landed at Constantinople, soon after the marriage of Theodosius, during the festival of the Persian victories. They were treated with kindness and magnificence; but as the statues of the emperor Constantius had been rejected by the Eastern court, the title of Augusta could not decently be allowed to his widow. Within a few months after the arrival of Placidia a swift messenger announced the death of Honorius, the consequence of a dropsy; but the important secret was not divulged till the necessary orders had been despatched for the march of a large body of troops to the sea-coast of Dalmatia. The shops and the gates of Constantinople remained shut during seven days; and the loss of a foreign prince, who could neither be esteemed nor regretted, was celebrated with loud and affected demonstrations of the public grief.

While the ministers of Constantinople deliberated, the vacant throne of Honorius was usurped by the ambition of a stranger. The name of the rebel was John; he filled the confidential office of *Primicerius*, or principal secretary; and history has attributed to his character more virtues than can easily be reconciled with the violation of the most sacred duty. Elated by the submission of Italy, and the hope of an alliance with the Huns, John presumed to insult by an embassy, the majesty of the Eastern emperor; but when he understood that his agents had been banished, imprisoned, and at length chased away with deserved ignominy, John prepared to assert by arms the injustice of his claims. In such a cause the grandson of the great Theodosius should have marched in person; but the young emperor was easily diverted by his physicians from so rash and hazardous a design; and the conduct of the Italian expedition was prudently intrusted to Ardaburius and his son Aspar, who had already signalised their valour against the Persians. It was resolved that Ardaburius should embark with the infantry; whilst Aspar, at the head of the cavalry, conducted Placidia, and her son Valentinian, along the sea-coast of the Hadriatic. The

---

[1] Τὰ συνεχῆ κατὰ στόμα φιλήματα, is the expression of Olympiodorus (apud Photium, p. 196 [p. 62 b, ed. Bekk.]) ; who means, perhaps, to describe the same caresses which Mahomet bestowed on his *daughter* Phatemah. Quando (says the prophet himself), quando subit mihi desiderium Paradisi, osculor eam, et ingero linguam meam in os ejus. But this sensual indulgence was justified by miracle and mystery; and the anecdote has been communicated to the public by the Reverend Father Maracci, in his Version and Confutation of the Koran, tom. i. p. 32.

march of the cavalry was performed with such active diligence, that they surprised, without resistance, the important city of Aquileia; when the hopes of Aspar were unexpectedly confounded by the intelligence that a storm had dispersed the Imperial fleet, and that his father, with only two galleys, was taken and carried a prisoner into the port of Ravenna. Yet this incident, unfortunate as it might seem, facilitated the conquest of Italy. Ardaburius employed, or abused, the courteous freedom which he was permitted to enjoy, to revive among the troops a sense of loyalty and gratitude; and, as soon as the conspiracy was ripe for execution, he invited, by private messages, and pressed the approach of Aspar. A shepherd, whom the popular credulity transformed into an angel, guided the Eastern cavalry, by a secret, and, it was thought, an impassable road, through the morasses of the Po: the gates of Ravenna, after a short struggle, were thrown open; and the defenceless tyrant was delivered to the mercy, or rather to the cruelty, of the conquerors. His right hand was first cut off, and after he had been exposed, mounted on an ass, to the public derision, John was beheaded in the circus of Aquileia. The emperor Theodosius, when he received the news of the victory, interrupted the horse-races; and singing, as he marched through the streets, a suitable psalm, conducted his people from the Hippodrome to the church, where he spent the remainder of the day in grateful devotion.[2]

In a monarchy which, according to various precedents, might be considered as elective, or hereditary, or patrimonial, it was impossible that the intricate claims of female and collateral succession should be clearly defined;[3] and Theodosius, by the right of consanguinity or conquest, might have reigned the sole legitimate emperor of the Romans. For a moment, perhaps, his eyes were dazzled by the prospect of unbounded sway; but his indolent temper gradually acquiesced in the dictates of sound policy. He contented himself with the possession of the East; and wisely relinquished the laborious task of waging a distant and doubtful war against the barbarians beyond the Alps, or of securing the obedience of the Italians and Africans, whose minds were alienated by the irreconcilable difference of language and interest. Instead of listening to the voice of ambition, Theodosius resolved to imitate the moderation of his grandfather, and to seat his cousin Valentinian on the throne of the West. The royal infant was distinguished at Constantinople by the title of *Nobilissimus*: he was promoted, before

[2] For these revolutions of the Western empire consult Olympiodor. apud Phot. p. 192, 193, 196, 197, 200 [p. 61-63, ed. Bekk.]; Sozomen, l. ix. c. 16; Socrates, l. vii. 23, 24; Philostorgius, l. xii. c. 10, 11 [12-14], and Godefroy, Dissertat. p. 486; Procopius, de Bell. Vandal. l. i. c. 3, p. 182, 183 [ed. Paris; tom. i. p. 319 *seqq.* ed. Bonn]; Theophanes, in Chronograph, p. 72, 73 [ed. Par.; tom. i. p. 129-131, ed. Bonn]; and the Chronicles.

[3] See Grotius de Jure Belli et Pacis, l. ii. c. 7. He has laboriously, but vainly, attempted to form a reasonable system of jurisprudence from the various and discordant modes of royal succession, which have been introduced by fraud or force, by time or accident.

his departure from Thessalonica, to the rank and dignity of *Cæsar*: and, after the conquest of Italy, the patrician Helion, by the authority of Theodosius, and in the presence of the senate, saluted Valentinian the Third by the name of Augustus, and solemnly invested him with the diadem and the Imperial purple.[4] By the agreement of the three females who governed the Roman world, the son of Placidia was betrothed to Eudoxia, the daughter of Theodosius and Athenais; and, as soon as the lover and his bride had attained the age of puberty, this honourable alliance was faithfully accomplished. At the same time, as a compensation, perhaps, for the expenses of the war, the Western Illyricum was detached from the Italian dominions, and yielded to the throne of Constantinople.[5] The emperor of the East acquired the useful dominion of the rich and maritime province of Dalmatia, and the dangerous sovereignty of Pannonia and Noricum, which had been filled and ravaged above twenty years by a promiscuous crowd of Huns, Ostrogoths, Vandals, and *Bavarians*. Theodosius and Valentinian continued to respect the obligations of their public and domestic alliance; but the unity of the Roman government was finally dissolved. By a positive declaration, the validity of all future laws was limited to the dominions of their peculiar author; unless he should think proper to communicate them, subscribed with his own hand, for the approbation of his independent colleague.[6]

Valentinian, when he received the title of Augustus, was no more than six years of age; and his long minority was intrusted to the guardian care of a mother who might assert a female claim to the succession of the Western empire. Placidia envied, but she could not equal, the reputation and virtues of the wife and sister of Theodosius; the elegant genius of Eudocia, the wise and successful policy of Pulcheria. The mother of Valentinian was jealous of the power which she was incapable of exercising:[7] she reigned twenty-five years, in the name of her son; and the character of that unworthy emperor grad-

---

[4] The original writers are not agreed (see Muratori, Annali d'Italia, tom. iv. p. 139) whether Valentinian received the Imperial diadem at Rome or Ravenna. In this uncertainty, I am willing to believe that some respect was shown to the senate.

[5] The Count de Buat (Hist. des Peuples de l'Europe, tom. vii. p. 292-300) has established the reality, explained the motives, and traced the consequences, of this remarkable cession.

[6] See the first *Novel* of Theodosius, by which he ratifies and communicates (A.D. 438) the Theodosian Code. About 40 years before that time the unity of legislation had been proved by an exception. The Jews, who were numerous in the cities of Apulia and Calabria, produced a law of the East to justify their exemption from municipal offices (Cod. Theod. l. xvi. tit. viii. leg. 13) ; and the Western emperor was obliged to invalidate, by a special edict, the law, quam constat meis partibus esse damnosam. Cod. Theod. l. xi. [xii.] tit. i. leg. 158.

[7] Cassiodorus (Variar. l. xi. Epist. i. p. 238 [p. 161, ed. Venet.]) has compared the regencies of Placidia and Amalasuntha. He arraigns the weakness of the mother of Valentinian, and praises the virtues of his royal mistress. On this occasion flattery seems to have spoken the language of truth.

ually countenanced the suspicion that Placidia had enervated his youth by a dissolute education, and studiously diverted his attention from every manly and honourable pursuit. Amidst the decay of military spirit, her armies were commanded by two generals, Aëtius [8] and Boniface,[9] who may be deservedly named as the last of the Romans. Their union might have supported a sinking empire; their discord was the fatal and immediate cause of the loss of Africa. The invasion and defeat of Attila has immortalised the fame of Aëtius; and though time has thrown a shade over the exploits of his rival, the defence of Marseilles, and the deliverance of Africa, attest the military talents of Count Boniface. In the field of battle, in partial encounters, in single combats, he was still the terror of the barbarians: the clergy, and particularly his friend Augustin, were edified by the Christian piety which had once tempted him to retire from the world; the people applauded his spotless integrity; the army dreaded his equal and inexorable justice, which may be displayed in a very singular example. A peasant, who complained of the criminal intimacy between his wife and a Gothic soldier, was directed to attend his tribunal the following day: in the evening the count, who had diligently informed himself of the time and place of the assignation, mounted his horse, rode ten miles into the country, surprised the guilty couple, punished the soldier with instant death, and silenced the complaints of the husband, by presenting him, the next morning, with the head of the adulterer. The abilities of Aëtius and Boniface might have been usefully employed against the public enemies in separate and important commands; but the experience of their past conduct should have decided the real favour and confidence of the empress Placidia. In the melancholy season of her exile and distress, Boniface alone had maintained her cause with unshaken fidelity; and the troops and treasures of Africa had essentially contributed to extinguish the rebellion. The same rebellion had been supported by the zeal and activity of Aëtius, who brought an army of sixty thousand Huns from the Danube to the confines of Italy, for the service of the usurper. The untimely death of John compelled him to accept an advantageous treaty; but he still continued, the subject and the soldier of Valentinian, to entertain a secret, perhaps a treasonable, correspondence with his barbarian allies, whose retreat had been pur-

---

[8] Philostorgius, l. xii. c. 12 [14], and Godefroy's Dissertat. p. 493, etc.; and Renatus Frigeridus, apud Gregor. Turon. l. ii. c. 8, in tom. ii. p. 163. The father of Aëtius was Gaudentius, an illustrious citizen of the province of Scythia and master-general of the cavalry: his mother was a rich and noble Italian. From his earliest youth, Aëtius, as a soldier and a hostage, had conversed with the barbarians.

[9] For the character of Boniface see Olympiodorus, apud Phot. p 196 [p. 62 b, ed. Bekk.]; and St. Augustin, apud Tillemont, Mémoires Ecclés. tom. xiii. p. 712-715, 886. The bishop of Hippo at length deplored the fall of his friend, who, after a solemn vow of chastity, had married a second wife of the Arian sect, and who was suspected of keeping several concubines in his house.

chased by liberal gifts and more liberal promises. But Aëtius possessed an advantage of singular moment in a female reign: he was present: he beseiged with artful and assiduous flattery the palace of Ravenna; disguised his dark designs with the mask of loyalty and friendship; and at length deceived both his mistress and his absent rival, by a subtle conspiracy which a weak woman and a brave man could not easily suspect. He secretly persuaded [10] Placidia to recall Boniface from the government of Africa; he secretly advised Boniface to disobey the Imperial summons: to the one, he represented the order as a sentence of death; to the other, he stated the refusal as a signal of revolt; and when the credulous and unsuspectful count had armed the province in his defence, Aëtius applauded his sagacity in foreseeing the rebellion which his own perfidy had excited. A temperate inquiry into the real motives of Boniface would have restored a faithful servant to his duty and to the republic; but the arts of Aëtius still continued to betray and to inflame, and the count was urged by persecution to embrace the most desperate counsels. The success with which he eluded or repelled the first attacks could not inspire a vain confidence that, at the head of some loose disorderly Africans, he should be able to withstand the regular forces of the West, commanded by a rival whose military character it was impossible for him to despise. After some hesitation, the last struggles of prudence and loyalty, Boniface despatched a trusty friend to the court, or rather to the camp, of Gonderic, king of the Vandals, with the proposal of a strict alliance, and the offer of an advantageous and perpetual settlement.

After the retreat of the Goths the authority of Honorius had obtained a precarious establishment in Spain, except only in the province of Gallicia, where the Suevi and the Vandals had fortified their camps in mutual discord and hostile independence. The Vandals prevailed, and their adversaries were besieged in the Nervasian hills, between Leon and Oviedo, till the approach of Count Asterius compelled, or rather provoked, the victorious barbarians to remove the scene of the war to the plains of Bætica. The rapid progress of the Vandals soon required a more effectual opposition, and the master-general Castinus marched against them with a numerous army of Romans and Goths. Vanquished in battle by an inferior enemy, Castinus fled with dishonour to Tarragona; and this memorable defeat, which has been represented as the punishment, was most probably the effect, of his rash presumption.[11] Seville and Carthagena became the reward, or rather

[10] Procopius (de Bell. Vandal. l. i. c. 3, 4, p. 182-186 [tom. i. p. 319-328, ed. Bonn]) relates the fraud of Aëtius, the revolt of Boniface, and the loss of Africa. This anecdote, which is supported by some collateral testimony (see Ruinart, Hist. Persecut. Vandal. p. 420, 421) seems agreeable to the practice of ancient and modern courts, and would be naturally revealed by the repentance of Boniface.
[11] See the Chronicles of Prosper and Idatius [Sirmond, Op. tom. ii. p. 298]. Salvian (de Gubernat. Dei, l. vii. p. 246, Paris, 1608) ascribes the victory of the Vandals to their superior piety. They fasted, they prayed, they carried

the prey, of the ferocious conquerors; and the vessels which they found in the harbour of Carthagena might easily transport them to the isles of Majorca and Minorca, where the Spanish fugitives, as in a secure recess, had vainly concealed their families and their fortunes. The experience of navigation, and perhaps the prospect of Africa, encouraged the Vandals to accept the invitation which they received from Count Boniface, and the death of Gonderic served only to forward and animate the bold enterprise. In the room of a prince not conspicuous for any superior powers of the mind or body, they acquired his bastard brother, the terrible Genseric;[12] a name which in the destruction of the Roman empire has reserved an equal rank with the names of Alaric and Attila. The king of the Vandals is described to have been of a middle stature, with a lameness in one leg, which he had contracted by an accidental fall from his horse. His slow and cautious speech seldom declared the deep purposes of his soul: he disdained to imitate the luxury of the vanquished, but he indulged the sterner passions of anger and revenge. The ambition of Genseric was without bounds and without scruples, and the warrior could dexterously employ the dark engines of policy to solicit the allies who might be useful to his success, or to scatter among his enemies the seeds of hatred and contention. Almost in the moment of his departure he was informed that Hermanric, king of the Suevi, had presumed to ravage the Spanish territories which he was resolved to abandon. Impatient of the insult, Genseric pursued the hasty retreat of the Suevi as far as Merida, precipitated the king and his army into the river Anas, and calmly returned to the sea-shore to embark his victorious troops. The vessels which transported the Vandals over the modern Straits of Gibralter, a channel only twelve miles in breadth, were furnished by the Spaniards, who anxiously wished their departure, and by the African general, who had implored their formidable assistance.[13]

Our fancy, so long accustomed to exaggerate and multiply the martial swarms of barbarians that seemed to issue from the North, will perhaps be surprised by the account of the army which Genseric mustered on the coast of Mauritania. The Vandals, who in twenty years

a Bible in the front of the Host, with the design, perhaps, of reproaching the perfidy and sacrilege of their enemies.

[12] Gizericus (his name is variously expressed) staturâ mediocris et equi casû claudicans, animo profundus, sermone rarus, luxuriæ contemptor, irâ turbidus, habendi cupidus, ad solicitandas gentes providentissimus, semina contentionum jacere, odia miscere paratus. Jornandes, de Rebus Geticis, c. 33, p. 657. This portrait, which is drawn with some skill and a strong likeness, must have been copied from the Gothic history of Cassiodorus.

[13] See the Chronicle of Idatius. That bishop, a Spaniard and a contemporary, places the passage of the Vandals in the month of May, of the year of Abraham (which commences in October) 2444. This date, which coincides with A.D. 429, is confirmed by Isidore, another Spanish bishop, and is justly preferred to the opinion of those writers who have marked for that event one of the two preceding years. See Pagi Critica, tom. ii. p. 205, etc.

had penetrated from the Elbe to Mount Atlas, were united under the command of their warlike king; and he reigned with equal authority over the Alani, who had passed within the term of human life from the cold of Scythia to the excessive heat of an African climate. The hopes of the bold enterprise had excited many brave adventurers of the Gothic nation, and many desperate provincials were tempted to repair their fortunes by the same means which had occasioned their ruin. Yet this various multitude amounted only to fifty thousand effective men; and though Genseric artfully magnified his apparent strength by appointing eighty *chiliarchs,* or commanders of thousands, the fallacious increase of old men, of children, and of slaves, would scarcely have swelled his army to the number of fourscore thousand persons.[14] But his own dexterity and the discontents of Africa soon fortified the Vandal powers by the accession of numerous and active allies. The parts of Mauritania which border on the great desert and the Atlantic ocean were filled with a fierce and untractable race of men, whose savage temper had been exasperated rather than reclaimed by their dread of the Roman arms. The wandering Moors,[15] as they gradually ventured to approach the sea-shore and the camp of the Vandals, must have viewed with terror and astonishment the dress, the armour, the martial pride and discipline of the unknown strangers who had landed on their coast; and the fair complexions of the blue-eyed warriors of Germany formed a very singular contrast with the swarthy or olive hue which is derived from the neighbourhood of the torrid zone. After the first difficulties had in some measure been removed which arose from the mutual ignorance of their respective language, the Moors, regardless of any future consequence, embraced the alliance of the enemies of Rome, and a crowd of naked savages rushed from the woods and valleys of Mount Atlas, to satiate their revenge on the polished tyrants who had injuriously expelled them from the native sovereignty of the land.

The persecution of the Donatists [16] was an event not less favourable to the designs of Genseric. Seventeen years before he landed in Africa,

[14] Compare Procopius (de Bell. Vandal. l. i. c. 5, p. 190 [tom. i. p. 334, ed. Bonn]) and Victor Vitensis (de Persecutione Vandal. l. i. c. 1, p. 3, edit. Ruinart). We are assured by Idatius that Genseric evacuated Spain, cum Vandalis *omnibus* eorumque familiis [Sirm. Op. tom. ii. p. 299]; and Possidius (in Vit. Augustin. c. 28, apud Ruinart, p. 427) describes his army as manus ingens immanium gentium Vandalorum et Alanorum, commixtam secum habens Gothorum gentem, aliarumque diversarum personas.

[15] For the manners of the Moors see Procopius (de Bell. Vandal. l. ii. c. 6, p. 249 [tom. i. p. 434, ed. Bonn]); for their figure and complexion, M. de Buffon (Histoire Naturelle, tom. iii. p. 430). Procopius says in general that the Moors had joined the Vandals before the death of Valentinian (de Bell. Vandal. l. i. c. 5, p. 190 [tom. i. p. 334, ed. Bonn]); and it is probable that the independent tribes did not embrace any uniform system of policy.

[16] See Tillemont, Mémoires Ecclés. tom. xiii. p. 516-558; and the whole series of the persecution, in the original monuments, published by Dupin at the end of Optatus, p. 323-515.

a public conference was held at Carthage by the order of the magistrate. The catholics were satisfied that, after the invincible reasons which they had alleged, the obstinacy of the schismatics must be inexcusable and voluntary, and the emperor Honorius was persuaded to inflict the most rigorous penalties on a faction which had so long abused his patience and clemency. Three hundred bishops,[17] with many thousands of the inferior clergy, were torn from their churches, stripped of their ecclesiastical possessions, banished to the islands, and proscribed by the laws, if they presumed to conceal themselves in the provinces of Africa. Their numerous congregations, both in cities and in the country, were deprived of the rights of citizens and of the exercise of religious worship. A regular scale of fines, from ten to two hundred pounds of silver, was curiously ascertained, according to the distinctions of rank and fortune, to punish the crime of assisting at schismatic conventicle; and if the fine had been levied five times without subduing the obstinacy of the offended, his future punishment was referred to the discretion of the Imperial court.[18]   By these severities, which obtained the warmest approbation of St. Augustin,[19] great numbers of Donatists were reconciled to the catholic church; but the fanatics who still persevered in their opposition were provoked to madness and despair; the distracted country was filled with tumult and bloodshed; the armed troops of Circumcellions alternately pointed their rage against themselves or against their adversaries; and the calendar of martyrs received on both sides a considerable augmentation.[20]   Under these circumstances Genseric, a Christian, but an enemy of the orthodox communion, showed himself to the Donatists as a powerful deliverer, from whom they might reasonably expect the repeal of the odious and oppressive edicts of the Roman emperors.[21]   The conquest of Africa

[17] The Donatist bishops, at the conference of Carthage, amounted to 279; and they asserted that their whole number was not less than 400. The Catholics had 286 present, 120 absent, besides sixty-four vacant bishoprics.

[18] The fifth title of the sixteenth book of the Theodosian Code exhibits a series of the Imperial laws against the Donatists, from the year 400 to the year 428. Of these the 54th law, promulgated by Honorius, A.D. 414, is the most severe and effectual.

[19] St. Augustin altered his opinion with regard to the proper treatment of heretics. His pathetic declaration of pity and indulgence for the Manichæans has been inserted by Mr. Locke (vol. iii. p. 469) among the choice specimens of his commonplace book. Another philosopher, the celebrated Bayle (tom. ii. p. 445-496), has refuted, with superfluous diligence and ingenuity, the arguments by which the bishop of Hippo justified, in his old age, the persecution of the Donatists.

[20] See Tillemont, Mém. Ecclés. tom. xiii. p. 586-592, 806. The Donatists boasted of *thousands* of these voluntary martyrs. Augustin asserts, and probably with truth, that these numbers were much exaggerated; but he sternly maintains that it was better that *some* should burn themselves in this world than that *all* should burn in hell flames.

[21] According to St. Augustin and Theodoret, the Donatists were inclined to the principles, or at least to the party, of the Arians, which Genseric supported. Tillemont, Mém. Ecclés. tom. vi. p. 68.

was facilitated by the active zeal or the secret favour of a domestic faction; the wanton outrages against the churches and the clergy, of which the Vandals are accused, may be fairly imputed to the fanaticism of their allies; and the intolerant spirit which disgraced the triumph of Christianity contributed to the loss of the most important province of the West.[22]

The court and the people were astonished by the strange intelligence that a virtuous hero, after so many favours and so many services, had renounced his allegiance and invited the barbarians to destroy the province entrusted to his command. The friends of Boniface, who still believed that his criminal behaviour might be excused by some honourable motive, solicited, during the absence of Aëtius, a free conference with the Count of Africa; and Darius, an officer of high distinction, was named for the important embassy.[23]   In their first interview at Carthage the imaginary provocations were mutually explained, the opposite letters of Aëtius were produced and compared, and the fraud was easily detected. Placidia and Boniface lamented their fatal error, and the count had sufficient magnanimity to confide in the forgiveness of his sovereign, or to expose his head to her future resentment. His repentance was fervent and sincere; but he soon discovered that it was no longer in his power to restore the edifice which he had shaken to its foundations. Carthage and the Roman garrisons returned with their general to the allegiance of Valentinian, but the rest of Africa was still distracted with war and faction; and the inexorable king of the Vandals, disdaining all terms of accommodation, sternly refused to relinquish the possession of his prey. The band of veterans who marched under the standard of Boniface, and his hasty levies of provincial troops, were defeated with considerable loss; the victorious barbarians insulted the open country; and Carthage, Cirta, and Hippo Regius, were the only cities that appeared to rise above the general inundation.

The long and narrow tract of the African coast was filled with frequent monuments of Roman art and magnificence; and the respective degrees of improvement might be accurately measured by the distance from Carthage and the Mediterranean. A simple reflection will impress every thinking mind with the clearest idea of fertility and cultivation:

[22] See Baronius, Annal. Eccles. A.D. 428, No. 7, A.D. 439, No. 35. The cardinal, though more inclined to seek the cause of great events in heaven than on the earth, has observed the apparent connection of the Vandals and the Donatists. Under the reign of the barbarians, the schismatics of Africa enjoyed an obscure peace of one hundred years; at the end of which we may again trace them by the light of the Imperial persecutions. See Tillemont, Mém. Ecclés. tom. vi. p. 192, etc.

[23] In a confidential letter to Count Boniface, St. Augustin, without examining the grounds of the quarrel, piously exhorts him to discharge the duties of a Christian and a subject; to extricate himself without delay from his dangerous and guilty situation; and even, if he could obtain the consent of his wife, to embrace a life of celibacy and penance (Tillemont, Mém. Ecclés. tom. xiii. p. 890). The bishop was intimately connected with Darius, the minister of peace (id. tom. xiii. p. 928).

the country was extremely populous; the inhabitants reserved a liberal subsistence for their own use; and the annual exportation, particularly of wheat, was so regular and plentiful, that Africa deserved the name of the common granary of Rome and of mankind. On a sudden the seven fruitful provinces, from Tangier to Tripoli, were overwhelmed by the invasion of the Vandals, whose destructive rage has perhaps been exaggerated by popular animosity, religious zeal, and extravagant declamation. War in its fairest form implies a perpetual violation of humanity and justice; and the hostilities of barbarians are inflamed by the fierce and lawless spirit which incessantly disturbs their peaceful and domestic society. The Vandals, where they found resistance, seldom gave quarter; and the deaths of the valiant countrymen were expiated by the ruin of the cities under whose walls they had fallen. Careless of the distinction of age, or sex, or rank, they employed every species of indignity and torture to force from the captives a discovery of their hidden wealth. The stern policy of Genseric justified his frequent examples of military execution: he was not always the master of his own passions or of those of his followers; and the calamities of war were aggravated by the licentiousness of the Moors and the fanaticism of the Donatists. Yet I shall not easily be persuaded that it was the common practice of the Vandals to extirpate the olives and other fruit trees of a country where they intended to settle: nor can I believe that it was a usual stratagem to slaughter great numbers of their prisoners before the walls of a besieged city, for the sole purpose of infecting the air and producing a pestilence, of which they themselves must have been the first victims.[24]

The generous mind of Count Boniface was tortured by the exquisite distress of beholding the ruin which he had occasioned, and whose rapid progress he was unable to check. After the loss of a battle he retired to Hippo Regius, where he was immediately besieged by an enemy who considered him as the real bulwark of Africa. The maritime colony of *Hippo*,[25] about two hundred miles westward of Carthage, had formerly acquired the distinguishing epithet of *Regius* from the residence of Numidian kings; and some remains of trade and

---

[24] The original complaints of the desolation of Africa are contained—.1. In a letter from Capreolus, bishop of Carthage, to excuse his absence from the council of Ephesus (ap. Ruinart, p. 428). 2. In the Life of St. Augustin by his friend and colleague Possidius (ap. Ruinart, p. 427). 3. In the History of the Vandalic Persecution, by Victor Vitensis (l. i. c. 1, 2, 3, edit. Ruinart). The last picture, which was drawn sixty years after the event, is more expressive of the author's passions than of the truth of facts.

[25] See Cellarius, Geograph. Antiq. tom. ii. part ii. p. 112. Leo African. in Ramusio, tom. i. fol. 70. L'Afrique de Marmol, tom. ii. p. 434, 437. Shaw's Travels, p. 46, 47. The old Hippo Regius was finally destroyed by the Arabs in the seventh century; but a new town, at the distance of two miles, was built with the materials; and it contained in the sixteenth century about three hundred families of industrious, but turbulent, manufacturers. The adjacent territory is renowned for a pure air. a fertile soil, and plenty of exquisite fruit.

populousness still adhere to the modern city, which is known in Europe by the corrupted name of Bona. The military labours and anxious reflections of Count Boniface were alleviated by the edifying conversation of his friend St. Augustin;[26] till that bishop, the light and pillar of the catholic church, was gently released, in the third month of the siege and in the seventy-sixth year of his age, from the actual and the impending calamities of his country. The youth of Augustin had been stained by the vices and errors which he so ingenuously confesses; but from the moment of his conversion to that of his death the manners of the bishop of Hippo were pure and austere, and the most conspicuous of his virtues was an ardent zeal against heretics of every denomination —the Manichæans, the Donatists, and the Pelagians, against whom he waged a perpetual controversy. When the city, some months after his death, was burnt by the Vandals, the library was fortunately saved which contained his voluminous writings—two hundred and thirty-two separate books or treatises on theological subjects, besides a complete exposition of the psalter and the gospel, and a copious magazine of epistles and homilies.[27] According to the judgment of the most impartial critics, the superficial learning of Augustin was confined to the Latin language;[28] and his style, though sometimes animated by the eloquence of passion, is usually clouded by false and affected rhetoric. But he possessed a strong, capacious, argumentative mind; he boldly sounded the dark abyss of grace, predestination, free-will, and original sin; and the rigid system of Christianity which he framed or restored [29] has been entertained with public applause and secret reluctance by the Latin church.[30]

[26] The Life of St. Augustin, by Tillemont, fills a quarto volume (Mém. Ecclés. tom. xiii.) of more than one thousand pages; and the diligence of that learned Jansenist was excited, on this occasion, by factious and devout zeal for the founder of his sect.

[27] Such at least is the account of Victor Vitensis (de Persecut. Vandal. l. i. c. 3); though Gennadius seems to doubt whether any person had read, or even collected, all the works of St. Augustin (see Hieronym. Opera, tom. i. p. 319, in Catalog. Scriptor. Eccles.). They have been repeatedly printed; and Dupin (Bibliothèque Ecclés. tom. iii. p. 158-257) has given a large and satisfactory abstract of them as they stand in the last edition of the Benedictines. My personal acquaintance with the bishop of Hippo does not extend beyond the Confessions and the City of God.

[28] In his early youth (Confess. i. 14) St. Augustin disliked and neglected the study of Greek; and he frankly owns that he read the Platonists in a Latin version (Confess. vii. 9). Some modern critics have thought that his ignorance of Greek disqualified him from expounding the Scriptures; and Cicero or Quintilian would have required the knowledge of that language in a professor of rhetoric.

[29] These questions were seldom agitated from the time of St. Paul to that of St. Augustin. I am informed that the Greek fathers maintain the natural sentiments of the Semi-Pelagians; and that the orthodoxy of St. Augustin was derived from the Manichæan school.

[30] The church of Rome has canonised Augustin and reprobated Calvin. Yet, as the real difference between them is invisible even to a theological microscope, the Molinists are oppressed by the authority of the saint, and

By the skill of Boniface, and perhaps by the ignorance of the Vandals, the siege of Hippo was protracted above fourteen months: the sea
was continually open; and when the adjacent country had been exhausted by irregular rapine, the besiegers themselves were compelled
by famine to relinquish their enterprise. The importance and danger
of Africa were deeply felt by the regent of the West. Placidia implored
the assistance of her Eastern ally; and the Italian fleet and army were
reinforced by Aspar, who sailed from Constantinople with a powerful
armament. As soon as the force of the two empires was united under
the command of Boniface, he boldly marched against the Vandals;
and the loss of a second battle irretrievably decided the fate of Africa.
He embarked with the precipitation of despair, and the people of Hippo
were permitted, with their families and effects, to occupy the vacant
place of the soldiers, the greatest part of whom were either slain or
made prisoners by the Vandals. The count, whose fatal credulity had
wounded the vitals of the republic, might enter the palace of Ravenna
with some anxiety, which was soon removed by the smiles of Placidia.
Boniface accepted with gratitude the rank of patrician and the dignity
of master-general of the Roman armies; but he must have blushed at
the sight of those medals in which he was represented with the name
and attributes of victory.[31] The discovery of his fraud, the displeasure
of the empress, and the distinguished favour of his rival, exasperated
the haughty and perfidious soul of Aëtius. He hastily returned from
Gaul to Italy, with a retinue, or rather with an army, of barbarian followers; and such was the weakness of the government, that the two
generals decided their private quarrel in a bloody battle. Boniface was
successful; but he received in the conflict a mortal wound from the
spear of his adversary, of which he expired within a few days, in such
Christian and charitable sentiments that he exhorted his wife, a rich
heiress of Spain, to accept Aëtius for her second husband. But
Aëtius could not derive any immediate advantage from the generosity
of his dying enemy: he was proclaimed a rebel by the justice of Placidia; and though he attempted to defend some strong fortresses,
erected on his patrimonial estate, the Imperial power soon compelled
him to retire into Pannonia, to the tents of his faithful Huns. The

the Jansenists are disgraced by their resemblance to the heretic. In the
meanwhile the Protestant Arminians stand aloof and deride the mutual perplexity of the disputants (see a curious Review of the Controversy by Le
Clerc, Bibliothèque Universelle, tom. xiv. p. 144-398). Perhaps a reasoner
still more independent may smile in *his* turn when he peruses an Arminian
Commentary on the Epistle to the Romans.
[31] Ducange, Fam. Byzant. p. 67. On one side, the head of Valentinian; on
the reverse, Boniface with a scourge in one hand and a palm in the other,
standing in a triumphal car, which is drawn by four horses, or, in another
medal, by four stags; an unlucky emblem! I should doubt whether another
example can be found of the head of a subject on the reverse of an Imperial
medal. See Science des Médailles, by the Père Jobert, tom. i. p. 132-150, edit.
of 1739, by the Baron de la Bastie.

republic was deprived by their mutual discord of the service of her two most illustrious champions.[32]

It might naturally be expected, after the retreat of Boniface, that the Vandals would achieve without resistance or delay the conquest of Africa. Eight years however elapsed from the evacuation of Hippo to the reduction of Carthage. In the midst of that interval the ambitious Genseric, in the full tide of apparent prosperity, negotiated a treaty of peace, by which he gave his son Hunneric for an hostage, and consented to leave the Western emperor in the undisturbed possession of the three Mauritanias.[33] This moderation, which cannot be imputed to the justice, must be ascribed to the policy, of the conqueror. His throne was encompassed with domestic enemies, who accused the baseness of his birth, and asserted the legitimate claims of his nephews, the sons of Gonderic. Those nephews, indeed, he sacrificed to his safety; and their mother, the widow of the deceased king, was precipitated by his order into the river Ampsaga. But the public discontent burst forth in dangerous and frequent conspiracies; and the warlike tyrant is supposed to have shed more Vandal blood by the hand of the executioner than in the field of battle.[34] The convulsions of Africa, which had favoured his attack, opposed the firm establishment of his power; and the various seditions of the Moors and Germans, the Donatists and catholics, continually disturbed or threatened the unsettled reign of the conqueror. As he advanced towards Carthage he was forced to withdraw his troops from the Western provinces; the sea-coast was exposed to the naval enterprises of the Romans of Spain and Italy; and, in the heart of Numidia, the strong inland city of Cirta still persisted in obstinate independence.[35] These difficulties were gradually subdued by the spirit, the perserverance, and the cruelty of Genseric, who alternately applied the arts of peace and war to the establishment of his African kingdom. He subscribed a solemn treaty, with the hope of deriving some advantage from the term of its continuance and the moment of its violation. The vigilance of his enemies was relaxed by the protestations of friendship which concealed his hostile approach; and Carthage was at length surprised by the Vandals, five hun-

[32] Procopius (de Bell. Vandal. l. i. c. 3, p. 185 [tom. i. p. 325, ed. Bonn]) continues the history of Boniface no farther than his return to Italy. His death is mentioned by Prosper [Ann. 432] and Marcellinus; the expression of the latter, that Aëtius the day before had provided himself with a *longer* spear, implies something like a regular duel.

[33] See Procopius, de Bell. Vandal. l. i. c. 4, p. 186 [tom. i. p. 327, ed. Bonn]. Valentinian published several humane laws to relieve the distress of his Numidian and Mauritanian subjects; he discharged them in a great measure from the payment of their debts, reduced their tribute to one-eighth, and gave them a right of appeal from their provincial magistrates to the præfect of Rome. Cod. Theod. tom. vi. Novell. p. 11, 12.

[34] Victor Vitensis, de Persecut. Vandal. l. ii. c. 5, p. 26. The cruelties of Genseric towards his subjects are strongly expressed in Prosper's Chronicle, A.D. 442.

[35] Possidius, in Vit. Augustin. c. 28, apud Ruinart, p. 428.

dred and eighty-five years after the destruction of the city and republic by the younger Scipio.[36]

A new city had arisen from its ruins, with the title of a colony; and though Carthage might yield to the royal prerogatives of Constantinople, and perhaps to the trade of Alexandria, or the splendour of Antioch, she still maintained the second rank in the West; as the *Rome* (if we may use the style of contemporaries) of the African world. That wealthy and opulent metropolis [37] displayed, in a dependent condition, the image of a flourishing republic. Carthage contained the manufactures, the arms, and the treasures of the six provinces. A regular subordination of civil honours gradually ascended from the procurators of the streets and quarters of the city to the tribunal of the supreme magistrate, who, with the title of proconsul, represented the state and dignity of a consul of ancient Rome. Schools and *gymnasia* were instituted for the education of the African youth; and the liberal arts and manners, grammar, rhetoric, and philosophy, were publicly taught in the Greek and Latin languages. The buildings of Carthage were uniform and magnificent: a shady grove was planted in the midst of the capital; the *new* port, a secure and capacious harbour, was subservient to the commercial industry of citizens and strangers; and the splendid games of the circus and theatre were exhibited almost in the presence of the barbarians. The reputation of the Carthaginians was not equal to that of their country, and the reproach of Punic faith still adhered to their subtle and faithless character.[38] The habits of trade and the abuse of luxury had corrupted their manners; but their impious contempt of monks and the shameless practice of unnatural lusts are the two abominations which excite the pious vehemence of Salvian, the preacher of the age.[39] The king of the Vandals severely reformed the vices of a voluptuous people; and the ancient, noble, ingenuous freedom of Carthage (these expressions of Victor are not with-

[36] See the Chronicles of Idatius, Isidore, Prosper, and Marcellinus. They mark the same year, but different days, for the surprisal of Carthage.
[37] The picture of Carthage, as it flourished in the fourth and fifth centuries, is taken from the Expositio totius Mundi, p. 17, 18, in the third volume of Hudson's Minor Geographers; from Ausonius de Claris Urbibus, p. 228, 229; and principally from Salvian, de Gubernatione Dei, l. vii. p. 257, 258. I am surprised that the *Notitia* should not place either a mint or an arsenal at Carthage, but only a gynecæum, or female manufacture.
[38] The anonymous author of the Expositio totius Mundi compares, in his barbarous Latin, the country and the inhabitants; and, after stigmatising their want of faith, he coolly concludes, Difficile autem inter eos inventitur bonus, tamen in multis pauci boni esse possunt. P. 18.
[39] He declares that the peculiar vices of each country were collected in the sink of Carthage (l. vii. p. 257). In the indulgence of vice the Africans applauded their manly virtue. Et illi se magis virilis fortitudinis esse crederent, qui maxime viros feminei usûs probrositate fregissent (p. 268). The streets of Carthage were polluted by effeminate wretches, who publicly assumed the countenance, the dress, and the character, of women (p. 264). If a monk appeared in the city, the holy man was pursued with impious scorn and ridicule; detestantibus ridentium cachinnis (p. 289).

out energy) was reduced by Genseric into a state of ignominious servitude. After he had permitted his licentious troops to satiate their rage
and avarice, he instituted a more regular system of rapine and oppression. An edict was promulgated, which enjoined all persons, without fraud or delay, to deliver their gold, silver, jewels, and valuable
furniture or apparel to the royal officers; and the attempt to secrete any
part of their patrimony was inexorably punished with death and torture as an act of treason against the state. The lands of the procon-
sular province, which formed the immediate district of Carthage, were
accurately measured and divided among the barbarians; and the conqueror reserved for his peculiar domain the fertile territory of Byzacium
and the adjacent parts of Numidia and Gætulia.[40]

It was natural enough that Genseric should hate those whom he had
injured: the nobility and senators of Carthage were exposed to his
jealousy and resentment; and all those who refused the ignominious
terms which their honour and religion forbade them to accept were
compelled by the Arian tyrant to embrace the condition of perpetual
banishment. Rome, Italy, and the provinces of the East, were filled
with a crowd of exiles, of fugitives and of ingenuous captives, who
solicited the public compassion: and the benevolent epistles of Theodoret still preserve the names and misfortunes of Cælestian and
Maria.[41] The Syrian bishop deplores the misfortunes of Cælestian,
who, from the state of a noble and opulent senator of Carthage, was
reduced, with his wife, and family, and servants, to beg his bread in
a foreign country; but he applauds the resignation of the Christian
exile, and the philosophic temper which, under the pressure of such
calamities, could enjoy more real happiness than was the ordinary
lot of wealth and prosperity. The story of Maria, the daughter of the
magnificent Eudæmon, is singular and interesting. In the sack of Carthage she was purchased from the Vandals by some merchants of Syria,
who afterwards sold her as a slave in their native country. A female attendant, transported in the same ship, and sold in the same family,
still continued to respect a mistress whom fortune had reduced to the
common level of servitude; and the daughter of Eudæmon received
from her grateful affection the domestic services which she had once
required from her obedience. This remarkable behaviour divulged
the real condition of Maria, who, in the absence of the bishop of Cyrrhus, was redeemed from slavery by the generosity of some soldiers of
the garrison. The liberality of Theodoret provided for her decent
maintenance; and she passed ten months among the deaconesses of the
church, till she was unexpectedly informed that her father, who had
escaped from the ruin of Carthage, exercised an honourable office in
one of the Western provinces. Her filial impatience was seconded

---

[40] Compare Procopius, de Bell. Vandal. l. i. c. 5, p. 189, 190 [tom. i. p. 332
sqq., ed. Bonn]; and Victor Vitensis, de Persecut. Vandal. l. i. c. 4.
[41] Ruinart (p. 444-457) has collected from Theodoret and other authors the
misfortunes real and fabulous, of the inhabitants of Carthage.

by the pious bishop: Theodoret, in a letter still extant, recommends
Maria to the bishop of Ægæ, a maritime city of Cilicia, which was
frequented, during the annual fair, by the vessels of the West; most
earnestly requesting that his colleague would use the maiden with a
tenderness suitable to her birth; and that he would intrust her to the
care of such faithful merchants as would esteem it a sufficient gain if
they restored a daughter, lost beyond all human hope, to the arms of
her afflicted parent.

Among the insipid legends of ecclesiastical history, I am tempted
to distinguish the memorable fable of the SEVEN SLEEPERS;[42] whose
imaginary date corresponds with the reign of the younger Theodosius,
and the conquest of Africa by the Vandals.[43] When the emperor Decius
persecuted the Christians, seven noble youths of Ephesus concealed
themselves in a spacious cavern in the side of an adjacent mountain
where they were doomed to perish by the tyrant, who gave orders that
the entrance should be firmly secured with a pile of huge stones. They
immediately fell into a deep slumber, which was miraculously prolonged, without injuring the powers of life, during a period of one hundred and eighty-seven years. At the end of that time, the slaves of
Adolius, to whom the inheritance of the mountain had descended, removed the stones, to supply materials for some rustic edifice: the light
of the sun darted into the cavern, and the Seven Sleepers were permitted to awake. After a slumber, as they thought of a few hours,
they were pressed by the calls of hunger; and resolved that Jamblichus,
one of their number, should secretly return to the city to purchase bread
for the use of his companions. The youth (if we may still employ
that appellation) could no longer recognise the once familiar aspect of
his native country; and his surprise was increased by the appearance of
a large cross, triumphantly erected over the principal gate of Ephesus.
His singular dress and obsolete language confounded the baker, to
whom he offered an ancient medal of Decius as the current coin of the
empire; and Jamblichus, on the suspicion of a secret treasure, was
dragged before the judge. Their mutual inquiries produced the amazing discovery that two centuries were almost elapsed since Jamblichus
and his friends had escaped from the rage of a Pagan tyrant. The

[42] The choice of fabulous circumstances is of small importance; yet I have
confined myself to the narrative which was translated from the Syriac by
the care of Gregory of Tours (de Gloriâ Martyrûm, l. i. c. 95, in Max. Bibliothecâ Patrum, tom. xi. p. 856), to the Greek acts of their martyrdom (apud
Photium, p. 1400, 1401 [p. 467, ed. Bekk.]), and to the Annals of the Patriarch
Eutychius (tom. i. p. 391, 531, 532, 535, vers. Pocock [Oxon. 1658]).

[43] Two Syriac writers, as they are quoted by Assemanni (Bibliot. Oriental.
tom. i. p. 336, 338), place the resurrection of the Seven Sleepers in the year
736 (A.D. 425) or 748 (A.D. 437) of the era of the Seleucides. Their Greek
acts, which Photius had read, assign the date of the thirty-eighth year of
the reign of Theodosius, which may coincide either with A.D. 439 or 446.
The period which had elapsed since the persecution of Decius is easily ascertained; and nothing less than the ignorance of Mahomet or the legendaries
could suppose an interval of three or four hundred years.

bishop of Ephesus, the clergy, the magistrates, the people, and, as it is said, the emperor Theodosius himself, hastened to visit the cavern of the Seven Sleepers; who bestowed their benediction, related their story, and at the same instant peaceably expired. The origin of this marvellous fable cannot be ascribed to the pious fraud and credulity of the *modern* Greeks, since the authentic tradition may be traced within half a century of the supposed miracle. James of Sarug, a Syrian bishop, who was born only two years after the death of the younger Theodosius, has devoted one of his two hundred and thirty homilies to the praise of the young men of Ephesus.[44] Their legend, before the end of the sixth century, was translated from the Syriac into the Latin language, by the care of Gregory of Tours. The hostile communions of the East preserve their memory with equal reverence; and their names are honourably inscribed in the Roman, the Abyssinian, and the Russian calendar.[45] Nor has their reputation been confined to the Christian world. This popular tale, which Mahomet might learn when he drove his camels to the fairs of Syria, is introduced, as a divine revelation, into the Koran.[46] The story of the Seven Sleepers has been adopted and adorned by the nations, from Bengal to Africa, who profess the Mahometan religion;[47] and some vestiges of a similar tradition have been discovered in the remote extremities of Scandinavia.[48] This easy and universal belief, so expressive of the sense of mankind, may be ascribed to the genuine merit of the fable itself. We imperceptibly advance from youth to age without observing the gradual, but incessant, change of human affairs; and even in our larger experience of

[44] James, one of the orthodox fathers of the Syrian church, was born A.D. 452; he began to compose his sermons A.D. 474; he was made bishop of Batnæ, in the district of Sarug and province of Mesopotamia, A.D. 519, and died A.D. 521. (Assemanni, tom. i. p. 288, 289.) For the homily *de Pueris Ephesinis*, see p. 335-339: though I could wish that Assemanni had translated the text of James of Sarug instead of answering the objections of Baronius.
[45] See the *Acta Sanctorum* of the Bollandists (Mensis Julii, tom. vi. p. 375-397). This immense calendar of Saints, in one hundred and twenty-six years (1644-1770), and in fifty volumes in folio, has advanced no farther than the 7th day of October. The suppression of the Jesuits has most probably checked an undertaking which, through the medium of fable and superstition, communicates much historical and philosophical instruction.
[46] See Maracci Alcoran. Sura xviii. tom. ii. p. 420-427, and tom. i. part iv. p. 103. With such an ample privilege Mahomet has not shown much taste or ingenuity. He has invented the dog (Al Rakim) of the Seven Sleepers; the respect of the sun, who altered his course twice a day that he might not shine into the cavern; and the care of God himself, who preserved their bodies from putrefaction by turning them to the right and left.
[47] See D'Herbelot, Bibliothèque Orientale, p. 139; and Renaudot, Hist. Patriarch. Alexandrin, p. 39, 40.
[48] Paul, the deacon of Aquileia (de Gestis Langobardorum, l. i. c. 4, p. 745, 746, edit. Grot.), who lived towards the end of the eighth century, has placed in a cavern under a rock on the shore of the ocean the Seven Sleepers of the North, whose long repose was respected by the barbarians. Their dress declared them to be Romans; and the deacon conjectures that they were reserved by Providence as the future apostles of those unbelieving countries.

history, the imagination is accustomed, by a perpetual series of causes and effects, to unite the most distant revolutions. But if the interval between two memorable eras could be instantly annihilated; if it were possible, after a momentary slumber of two hundred years, to display the *new* world to the eyes of a spectator who still retained a lively and recent impression of the *old,* his surprise and his reflections would furnish the pleasing subject of a philosophical romance. The scene could not be more advantageously placed than in the two centuries which elapsed between the reigns of Decius and of Theodosius the Younger. During this period the seat of government had been transported from Rome to a new city on the banks of the Thracian Bosphorus and the abuse of military spirit had been suppressed by an artificial system of tame and ceremonious servitude. The throne of the persecuting Decius was filled by a succession of Christian and orthodox princes, who had extirpated the fabulous gods of antiquity: and the public devotion of the age was impatient to exalt the saints and martyrs of the catholic church on the altars of Diana and Hercules. The union of the Roman empire was dissolved; its genius was humbled in the dust; and armies of unknown barbarians, issuing from the frozen regions of the North, had established their victorious reign over the fairest provinces of Europe and Africa.

CHAPTER XXXIV (376-453 A.D.)

The Character, Conquests, and Court of Attila, King of the Huns—Death of Theodosius the Younger—Elevation of Marcian to the Empire of the East

THE Western world was oppressed by the Goths and Vandals, who fled before the Huns; but the achievements of the Huns themselves were not adequate to their power and prosperity. Their victorious hordes had spread from the Volga to the Danube; but the public force was exhausted by the discord of independent chieftains; their valour was idly consumed in obscure and predatory excursions; and they often degraded their national dignity, by condescending, for the hopes of spoil, to enlist under the banners of their fugitive enemies. In the reign of ATTILA[1] the Huns again became the terrors of the world;

[1] The authentic materials for the history of Attila may be found in Jornandes (de Rebus Geticis, c. 34-50, p. 660-688, edit. Grot.) and Priscus (Excerpta de Legationibus, p. 33-76, Paris, 1648 [p. 140-220, ed. Bonn]). I have not seen the Lives of Attila, composed by Juvencus Cælius Calanus Dalmatinus, in the twelfth century, or by Nicolas Olahus, archbishop of Gran, in the sixteenth. See Mascou's History of the Germans, ix. 23, and Maffei Osservazioni Litterarie, tom. i. p. 88, 89. Whatever the modern Hungarians have added must be fabulous; and they do not seem to have excelled in the art of fiction. They suppose that when Attila invaded Gaul and Italy, married

and I shall now describe the character and actions of that formidable barbarian, who alternately insulted and invaded the East and the West and urged the rapid downfall ot the Roman Empire.

In the tide of emigration which impetuously rolled from the confines of China to those of Germany, the most powerful and populous tribes may commonly be found on the verge of the Roman provinces. The accumulated weight was sustained for a while by artificial barriers; and the easy condescension of the emperors invited, without satisfying, the insolent demands of the barbarians, who had acquired an eager appetite for the luxuries of civilised life. The Hungarians, who ambitiously insert the name of Attila among their native kings, may affirm with truth that the hordes which were subject to his uncle Roas, or Rugilas, had formed their encampments within the limits of modern Hungary,[2] in a fertile country which liberally supplied the wants of a nation of hunters and shepherds. In this advantageous situation, Rugilas, and his valiant brothers, who continually added to their power and reputation, commanded the alternative of peace or war with the two empires. His alliance with the Romans of the West was cemented by his personal friendship for the great Aëtius, who was always secure of finding in the barbarian camp an hospitable reception and a powerful support. At his solicitation, and in the name of John the usurper, sixty thousand Huns advanced to the confines of Italy; their march and their retreat were alike expensive to the state; and the grateful policy of Aëtius

innumerable wives, etc., he was one hundred and twenty years of age. Thevrocz Chron. p. i. c. 22, in Script. Hungar. tom. i. p. 76.

[Attila is the outstanding figure in this chapter, and under his German name, Etzel, is the hero of many well-known Scandinavian and German poems, of which the most perfect is the celebrated *Nibelungen Lied*. This poem and others reveal the impression which Attila made on his contemporaries and succeeding ages, and therefore deserve mention in connection with the history of the king of the Huns. In these poems Etzel or Attila appears in conflict with the Burgundians and Franks, and the destruction of Gundicarius, king of the Burgundians, by the Huns in 436 is supposed to be represented by the catastrophe of the *Nibelungen Lied*. Theodoric, the Ostrogoth, under the name of Dietrich of Bern, that is, Theodoric of Verona, is represented as the contemporary of Attila, though he was not born till two years after the death of Attila; and Siegfried, whose adventures form so prominent a part of the poem, is identified with much probability with Sigebert, king of Austrasia, who was assassinated in 575. See the Fall of the Nibelungers, London, 1850; Grimm, Die Deutsche Heldensage, p. 63.—O. S.]

[2] Hungary has been successively occupied by three Scythian colonies:—1. The Huns of Attila; 2. The Abares, in the sixth century; and, 3. The Turks or Magyars, A.D. 889, the immediate and genuine ancestors of the modern Hungarians, whose connection with the two former is extremely faint and remote. The *Prodromus* and *Notitia* of Matthew Belius appear to contain a rich fund of information concerning ancient and modern Hungary. I have seen the extracts in Bibliothèque Ancienne et Moderne, tom. xxii. p. 1-51, and Bibliothèque Raisonée, tom. xvi. p. 127-175.

[The modern Hungarians cannot claim to be the descendants of Attila and his Huns. The Magyars are a Finnish race, while the Huns were certainly Turks.—O. S.]

abandoned the possession of Pannonia to his faithful confederates. The Romans of the East were not less apprehensive of the arms of Rugilas, which threatened the provinces, or even the capital. Some ecclesiastical historians have destroyed the barbarians with lightning and pestilence;[3] but Theodosius was reduced to the more humble expedient of stipulating an annual payment of three hundred and fifty pounds of gold, and of disguising this dishonourable tribute by the title of general, which the king of the Huns condescended to accept. The public tranquillity was frequently interrupted by the fierce impatience of the barbarians and the perfidious intrigues of the Byzantine court. Four dependent nations, among whom we may distinguish the Bavarians, disclaimed the sovereignty of the Huns; and their revolt was encouraged and protected by a Roman alliance; till the just claims and formidable power of Rugilas were effectually urged by the voice of Eslaw, his ambassador. Peace was the unanimous wish of the senate: their decree was ratified by the emperor; and two ambassadors were named—Plinthas, a general of Scythian extraction, but of consular rank; and the quæstor Epigenes, a wise and experienced statesman, who was recommended to that office by his ambitious colleague.

The death of Rugilas suspended the progress of the treaty. His two nephews, Attila and Bleda, who succeeded to the throne of their uncle, consented to a personal interview with the ambassadors of Constantinople; but as they proudly refused to dismount, the business was transacted on horseback, in a spacious plain near the city of Margus, in the Upper Mæsia. The kings of the Huns assumed the solid benefits, as well as the vain honours, of the negotiation. They dictated the conditions of peace, and each condition was an insult on the majesty of the empire. Besides the freedom of a safe and plentiful market on the banks of the Danube, they required that the annual contribution should be augmented from three hundred and fifty to seven hundred pounds of gold; that a fine or ransom, of eight pieces of gold, should be paid for every Roman captive who had escaped from his barbarian master; that the emperor should renounce all treaties and engagements with the enemies of the Huns; and that all the fugitives who had taken refuge in the court or provinces of Theodosius should be delivered to the justice of their offended severeign. This justice was rigorously inflicted on some unfortunate youths of a royal race. They were crucified on the territories of the empire, by the command of Attila: and, as soon as the king of the Huns had impressed the Romans with the terror of his name, he indulged them in a short and arbitrary respite, whilst he subdued the rebellious or independent nations of Scythia and Germany.[4]

[3] Socrates, 1. vii. c. 43; Theodoret, 1. v. c. 37. Tillemont, who always depends on the faith of his ecclesiastical authors, strenuously contends (Hist. des. Emp. tom. vi. p. 136, 607) that the wars and personages were not the same.

[4] See Priscus, p. 47, 48 [ed. Par.; pp. 166-170, ed. Bonn], and Hist. des Peuples de l'Europe. tom. vii. c. xii. xiii. xiv. xv.

Attila, the son of Mundzuk, deduced his noble, perhaps his regal, descent [5] from the ancient Huns, who had formerly contended with the monarchs of China. His features, according to the observation of a Gothic historian, bore the stamp of his national origin; and the portrait of Attila exhibits the genuine deformity of a modern Calmuck;[6] a large head, a swarthy complexion, small deep-seated eyes, a flat nose, a few hairs in the place of a beard, broad shoulders, and a short square body, of nervous strength, though of a disproportioned form. The haughty step and demeanor of the king of the Huns expressed the consciousness of his superiority above the rest of mankind; and he had a custom of fiercely rolling his eyes, as if he wished to enjoy the terror which he inspired. Yet this savage hero was not inaccessible to pity; his suppliant enemies might confide in the assurance of peace or pardon; and Attila was considered by his subjects as a just and indulgent master. He delighted in war; but, after he had ascended the throne in a mature age, his head, rather than his hand, achieved the conquest of the North; and the fame of an adventurous soldier was usefully exchanged for that of a prudent and successful general. The effects of personal valour are so inconsiderable, except in poetry or romance, that victory, even among barbarians, must depend on the degree of skill with which the passions of the multitude are combined and guided for the service of a single man. The Scythian conquerors, Attila and Zingis, surpassed their rude countrymen in art, rather than in courage; and it may be observed that the monarchies, both of the Huns and of the Moguls, were erected by their founders on the basis of popular superstition. The miraculous conception, which fraud and credulity ascribed to the virgin mother of Zingis, raised him above the level of human nature; and the naked prophet, who, in the name of the Deity, invested him with the empire of the earth, pointed the valour of the Moguls with irresistible enthusiasm.[7] The religious arts of Attila were not less skilfully adapted to the character of his age and country. It was natural enough that the Scythians should adore, with peculiar devotion, the god of war; but as they were incapable of forming either an abstract idea or a corporeal representation, they worshipped their tutelar deity under the symbol of

[5] Priscus, p. 39 [p. 150, ed. Bonn]. The modern Hungarians have deduced his genealogy, which ascends, in the thirty-fifth degree, to Ham the son of Noah; yet they are ignorant of his father's real name. (De Guignes, Hist. des Huns, tom. ii. p. 297.)

[6] Compare Jornandes (c. 35, p. 661) with Buffon, Hist. Naturelle, tom. iii. p. 380. The former had a right to observe, originis suæ signa restituens. The character and portrait of Attila are probably transcribed from Cassiodorus.

[7] Abulpharag. Dynast. vers. Pocock, p. 281 [ed. Oxon. 1663]; Genealogical History of the Tartars, by Abulghazi Bahader Khan, part iii. c. 15, part iv. c. 3; Vie de Gengiscan, par Petit de la Croix, l. i. c. 1, 6. The relations of the missionaries who visited Tartary in the thirteenth century (see the seventh volume of the Histoire des Voyages) express the popular language and opinions; Zingis is styled the son of God, etc., etc.

an iron cimeter.[8] One of the shepherds of the Huns perceived that a heifer, who was grazing, had wounded herself in the foot, and curiously followed the track of the blood, till he discovered, among the long grass, the point of an ancient sword, which he dug out of the ground, and presented to Attila. That magnanimous, or rather that artful, prince accepted, with pious gratitude, this celestial favour; and, as the rightful possessor of the *sword of Mars*, asserted his divine and indefeasible claim to the dominion of the earth.[9] If the rites of Scythia were practised on this solemn occasion, a lofty altar, or rather pile of faggots, three hundred yards in length and in breadth, was raised in a spacious plain; and the sword of Mars was placed erect on the summit of this rustic altar, which was annually consecrated by the blood of sheep, horses, and of the hundredth captive.[10] Whether human sacrifices formed any part of the worship of Attila, or whether he propitiated the god of war with the victims which he continually offered in the field of battle, the favourite of Mars soon acquired a sacred character, which rendered his conquests more easy and more permanent; and the barbarian princes confessed, in the language of devotion or flattery, that they could not presume to gaze, with a steady eye, on the divine majesty of the king of the Huns.[11] His brother Bleda, who reigned over a considerable part of the nation, was compelled to resign his sceptre and his life. Yet even this cruel act was attributed to a supernatural impulse; and the vigour with which Attila wielded the sword of Mars convinced the world that it had been reserved alone for his invincible arm.[12] But the extent of his empire affords the only remaining evidence of the number and importance of his victories; and the Scythian monarch, however ignorant of the value of science and philosophy, might perhaps lament that his illiterate subjects were destitute of the art which could perpetuate the memory of his exploits.

[8] Nec templum apud eos visitur, aut delubrum, ne tugurium quidem culmo tectum cerni usquam potest; sed *gladius* barbarico ritû humi figitur nudus, eumque ut Martem regionum quas circumcircant præsulem verecundius colunt. Ammian. Marcellin. xxxi. 2, and the learned Notes of Lindenbrogius and Valesius.

[9] Priscus relates this remarkable story, both in his own text (p. 65 [p. 201, ed. Bonn]) and in the quotation made by Jornandes (c. 35, p. 662). He might have explained the tradition or fable, which characterised this famous sword, and the name as well as attributes of the Scythian deity whom he has translated into the Mars of the Greeks and Romans.

[10] Herodot. l. iv. c. 62. For the sake of economy, I have calculated by the smallest stadium. In the human sacrifices, they cut off the shoulder and arm of the victim, which they threw up into the air, and drew omens and presages from the manner of their falling on the pile.

[11] Priscus, p. 55 [p. 182, ed. Bonn]. A more civilised hero, Augustus himself, was pleased if the person on whom he fixed his eyes seemed unable to support their divine lustre. Sueton. in August. c. 79.

[12] The Count de Buat (Hist. des Peuples de l'Europe, tom. vii. p. 428, 429) attempts to clear Attila from the murder of his brother, and is almost inclined to reject the concurrent testimony of Jornandes and the contemporary Chronicles.

If a line of separation were drawn between the civilised and the savage climates of the globe; between the inhabitants of cities, who cultivated the earth, and the hunters and shepherds, who dwelt in tents, Attila might aspire to the title of supreme and sole monarch of the barbarians.[13] He alone, among the conquerors of ancient and modern times, united the two mighty kingdoms of Germany and Scythia; and those vague appellations, when they are applied to his reign, may be understood with an ample latitude. Thuringia, which stretched beyond its actual limits as far as the Danube, was in the number of his provinces; he interposed, with the weight of a powerful neighbour, in the domestic affairs of the Franks; and one of his lieutenants chastised, and almost exterminated, the Burgundians of the Rhine. He subdued the islands of the ocean, the kingdoms of Scandinavia, encompassed and divided by the waters of the Baltic; and the Huns might derive a tribute of furs from that northern region, which has been protected from all other conquerors by the severity of the climate and the courage of the natives. Towards the East, it is difficult to circumscribe the dominion of Attila over the Scythian deserts; yet we may be assured that he reigned on the banks of the Volga; that the king of the Huns was dreaded, not only as a warrior, but as a magician;[14] that he insulted and vanquished the khan of the formidable Geougen; and that he sent ambassadors to negotiate an equal alliance with the empire of China. In the proud review of the nations who acknowledged the sovereignty of Attila, and who never entertained, during his lifetime, the thought of a revolt, the Gepidæ and the Ostrogoths were distinguished by their numbers, their bravery, and the personal merit of their chiefs. The renowned Ardaric, king of the Gepidæ, was the faithful and sagacious counsellor of the monarch, who esteemed his intrepid genius, whilst he loved the mild and discreet virtues of the noble Walamir, king of the Ostrogoths. The crowd of vulgar kings, the leaders of so many martial tribes, who served under the standard of Attila, were ranged in the submissive order of guards and domestics round the person of their master. They watched his nod; they trembled at his frown; and at the first signal of his will, they executed, without murmur or hesitation, his stern and absolute commands. In time of peace, the dependent princes, with their national troops, attended the royal camp in regular succession; but when Attila collected his military force he was able to bring into the field an army

---

[13] Fortissimarum gentium dominus, qui inauditâ ante se potentiâ, solus Scythica et Germanica regna possedit. Jornandes, c. 49, p. 684; Priscus, p. 64, 65 [p. 199-201, ed. Bonn]. M. de Guignes, by his knowledge of the Chinese, has acquired (tom. ii. p. 295-301) an adequate idea of the empire of Attila.

[14] See Hist. des Huns, tom. ii. p. 296. The Geougen believed that the Huns could excite at pleasure storms of wind and rain. This phenomenon was produced by the stone *Gezi*, to whose magic power the loss of a battle was ascribed by the Mahometan Tartars of the fourteenth century. See Chere-feddin Ali, Hist. de Timur Bec, tom. i. p. 82, 83.

of five, or, according to another account, of seven hundred thousand barbarians.[15]

The ambassadors of the Huns might awaken the attention of Theodosius, by reminding him that they were his neighbours both in Europe and Asia; since they touched the Danube on one hand, and reached with the other as far as the Tanais. In the reign of his father Arcadius, a band of adventurous Huns had ravaged the provinces of the East, from whence they brought away rich spoils and innumerable captives. They advanced, by a secret path, along the shores of the Caspian Sea; traversed the snowy mountains of Armenia; passed the Tigris, the Euphrates, and the Halys; recruited their weary cavalry with the generous breed of Cappadocian horses; occupied the hilly country of Cilicia; and disturbed the festal songs and dances of the citizens of Antioch.[16] Egypt trembled at their approach; and the monks and

[15] Jornandes, c. 35, p. 661; c. 37, p. 667. See Tillemont, Hist. des Empereurs, tom. vi. p. 129, 138. Corneille has represented the pride of Attila to his subject kings, and his tragedy opens with these two ridiculous lines:—

> Ils ne sont pas venus, nos deux rois! qu'on leur die
> Qu'ils se font trop attendre, et qu'Attila s'ennuie.

The two kings of the Gepidæ and the Ostrogoths are profound politicians and sentimental lovers; and the whole piece exhibits the defects, without the genius, of the poet.

[16] ——— alii per Caspia claustra
> Armeniasque nives, inopino tramite ducti
> Invadunt Orientis opes : jam pascua fumant
> Cappadocum, volucrumque parens Argæus equorum.
> Jam rubet altus Halys, nec se defendit iniquo
> Monte Cilix ; Syriæ tractus vastantur amœni ;
> Assuetumque choris, et lætâ plebe canorum,
> Proterit imbellem sonipes hostilis Orontem.
>
> Claudian, in Rufin. l. ii. 28-35.

See likewise, in Eutrop. l. i. 243-251, and the strong description of Jerom, who wrote from his feelings, tom. i. p. 26, ad Heliodor. p. 200, ad Ocean. [p. 342 and 460 ed. Vallars.]. Philostorgius (l. ix. c. 8 [17]) mentions this irruption.

[Niebuhr, in his "Lectures on the History of Rome," says that "Gibbon's description of Attila's power is one of the weak parts of his work," and there are strong reasons for believing that the extent of Attila's power and dominions has been overstated. It must be remembered that the halo of fiction and romance around Attila is exclusively German, and as Attila was the conqueror of the Germans, there was a natural tendency on the part of that people to exaggerate the might of the monarch by whom they had been subdued. Our chief authority for the extent of Attila is Jornandes, who was himself a Goth. It is possible that many of the people mentioned in the list of Attila's hosts may have been simple confederates, or a portion of them may have been incorporated in his army as he passed through their country. Some notion may be formed of the real magnitude of Attila's kingdom by the extent of the kingdoms which were formed out of his dominions after his death. Suffice it to say that the area out of which they grew was limited to Pannonia, Western Dacia, Eastern Rhætia, and North Mœsia. It is probable that the sovereign sway of Attila was bounded by the eastern frontier of Bohemia on the west, and by the Mæotes, or thereabouts on the east. The northern boundary was uncertain, but it certainly did not extend as far north as Jornandes would lead us to suppose.—O. S.]

pilgrims of the Holy Land prepared to escape their fury by a speedy embarkation. The memory of this invasion was still recent in the minds of the Orientals. The subjects of Attila might execute, with superior forces, the design which these adventurers had so boldly attempted; and it soon became the subject of anxious conjecture whether the tempest would fall on the dominions of Rome or of Persia. Some of the great vassals of the king of the Huns, who were themselves in the rank of powerful princes, had been sent to ratify an alliance and society of arms with the emperor, or rather with the general, of the West. They related, during their residence at Rome, the circumstances of an expedition which they had lately made into the East. After passing a desert and a morass supposed by the Romans to be the lake Mæotis, they penetrated through the mountains, and arrived, at the end of fifteen days' march, on the confines of Media, where they advanced as far as the unknown cities of Basic and Cursic.[17] They encountered the Persian army in the plains of Media; and the air, according to their own expression, was darkened by a cloud of arrows. But the Huns were obliged to retire before the numbers of the enemy. Their laborious retreat was affected by a different road; they lost the greatest part of their booty; and at length returned to the royal camp, with some knowledge of the country, and an impatient desire of revenge. In the free conversation of the Imperial ambassadors, who discussed, at the court of Attila, the character and designs of their formidable enemy, the ministers of Constantinople expressed their hope that his strength might be diverted and employed in a long and doubtful contest with the princes of the house of Sassan. The more sagacious Italians admonished their Eastern brethren of the folly and danger of such a hope; and convinced them, *that* the Medes and Persians were incapable of resisting the arms of the Huns; and *that* the easy and important acquisition would exalt the pride, as well as power, of the conqueror. Instead of contenting himself with a moderate contribution and a military title, which equalled him only to the generals of Theodosius, Attila would proceed to impose a disgraceful and intolerable yoke on the necks of the prostrate and captive Romans, who would then be encompassed on all sides by the empire of the Huns.[18]

While the powers of Europe and Asia were solicitous to avert the impending danger, the alliance of Attila maintained the Vandals in the possession of Africa. An enterprise had been concerted between the courts of Ravenna and Constantinople for the recovery of that valuable province; and the ports of Sicily were already filled with the military and naval forces of Theodosius. But the subtle Genseric, who spread his

[17] [" The unknown cities of Basic and Cursic." Gibbon has fallen into a curious error here. Basic and Cursic are not the names of cities, but the names of the two commanders who were over the respective bands of Huns who invaded Persia.—O. S.]

[18] See the original conversation in Priscus, p. 64, 65 [ed. Par.; p. 198-201, ed. Bonn].

negotiations round the world, prevented their designs, by exciting the king of the Huns to invade the Eastern empire; and a trifling incident soon became the motive, or pretence, of a destructive war.[19] Under the faith of the treaty of Margus, a free market was held on the northern side of the Danube, which was protected by a Roman fortress surnamed Constantia. A troop of barbarians violated the commercial security; killed, or dispersed, the unsuspecting traders; and levelled the fortress with the ground. The Huns justified this outrage as an act of reprisal; alleged that the bishop of Margus had entered their territories, to discover and steal a secret treasure of their kings; and sternly demanded the guilty prelate, the sacrilegious spoil, and the fugitive subjects, who had escaped from the justice of Attila. The refusal of the Byzantine court was the signal of war; and the Mæsians at first applauded the generous firmness of their sovereign. But they were soon intimidated by the destruction of Viminiacum and the adjacent towns; and the people was persuaded to adopt the convenient maxim, that a private citizen, however innocent or respectable, may be justly sacrificed to the safety of his country. The bishop of Margus, who did not possess the spirit of a martyr, resolved to prevent the designs which he suspected. He boldly treated with the princes of the Huns; secured, by solemn oaths, his pardon and reward; posted a numerous detachment of barbarians, in silent ambush, on the banks of the Danube; and, at the appointed hour, opened, with his own hand, the gates of his episcopal city. This advantage, which had been obtained by treachery, served as a prelude to more honourable and decisive victories. The Illyrian frontier was covered by a line of castles and fortresses; and though the greatest part of them consisted only of a single tower, with a small garrison, they were commonly sufficient to repel, or to intercept, the inroads of an enemy who was ignorant of the art, and impatient of the delay, of a regular siege. But these slight obstacles were instantly swept away by the inundation of the Huns.[20] They destroyed, with fire and sword, the populous cities of Sirmium and Singidunum, of Ratiaria and Marcianopolis, of Naissus and Sardica; where every circumstance in the discipline of the people and the construction of the buildings had been gradually adapted to the sole purpose of defence. The whole breadth

[19] Priscus, p. 331. His history contained a copious and elegant account of the war (Evagrius, l. i. c. 17); but the extracts which relate to the embassies are the only parts that have reached our times. The original work was accessible, however, to the writers from whom we borrow our imperfect knowledge, Jornandes, Theophanes, Count Marcellinus, Prosper-Tyro, and the author of the Alexandrian, or Paschal, Chronicle. M. de Buat (Hist. des Peuples de l'Europe, tom. vii. c. xv.) has examined the cause, the circumstances, and the duration of this war; and will not allow it to extend beyond the year four hundred and forty-four.

[20] Procopius, de Ædificiis, l. iv. c. 5 [tom. iii. p. 286, ed. Bonn]. These fortresses were afterwards restored, strengthened, and enlarged by the emperor Justinian; but they were soon destroyed by the Abares, who succeeded to the power and possessions of the Huns.

of Europe, as it extends above five hundred miles from the Euxine to the Hadriatic, was at once invaded, and occupied, and desolated, by the myriads of barbarians whom Attila led into the field. The public danger and distress could not, however, provoke Theodosius to interrupt his amusements and devotion, or to appear in person at the head of the Roman legions. But the troops which had been sent against Genseric were hastily recalled from Sicily; the garrisons, on the side of Persia, were exhausted; and a military force was collected in Europe, formidable by their arms and numbers, if the generals had understood the science of command, and their soldiers the duty of obedience. The armies of the Eastern empire were vanquished in three successive engagements; and the progress of Attila may be traced by the fields of battle. The two former, on the banks of the Utus, and under the walls of Marcianopolis, were fought in the extensive plains between the Danube and Mount Hæmus. As the Romans were pressed by a victorious enemy, they gradually, and unskilfully, retired towards the Chersonesus of Thrace; and that narrow peninsula, the last extremity of the land, was marked by their third and irreparable defeat. By the destruction of this army, Attila acquired the indisputable possession of the field. From the Hellespont to Thermopylæ and the suburbs of Constantinople he ravaged, without resistance and without mercy, the provinces of Thrace and Macedonia. Heraclea and Hadrianople might, perhaps, escape this dreadful irruption of the Huns; but the words the most expressive of total extirpation and erasure are applied to the calamities which they inflicted on seventy cities of the Eastern empire.[21] Theodosius, his court, and the unwarlike people, were protected by the walls of Constantinople; but those walls had been shaken by a recent earthquake, and the fall of fifty-eight towers had opened a large and tremendous breach. The damage indeed was speedily repaired; but this accident was aggravated by a superstitious fear that Heaven itself had delivered the Imperial city to the shepherds of Scythia, who were strangers to the laws, the language, and the religion of the Romans.[22]

In all their invasions of the civilised empires of the South, the Scythian shepherds have been uniformly actuated by a savage and destructive spirit. The laws of war, that restrain the exercise of national rapine and murder, are founded on two principles of substantial interest: the knowledge of the permanent benefits which may be obtained by a moderate use of conquest, and a just apprehension lest the desolation which we inflict on the enemy's country may be retaliated on our own.

[21] Septuaginta civitates (says Prosper-Tyro) deprædatione vastatæ. The language of Count Marcellinus is still more forcible. Pene totam Europam, invasis *excisisque* civitatibus atque castellis, conrisit.

[22] Tillemont (Hist. des Empereurs, tom. vi. p. 106, 107) has paid great attention to this memorable earthquake, which was felt as far from Constantinople as Antioch and Alexandria, and is celebrated by all the ecclesiastical writers. In the hands of a popular preacher, an earthquake is an engine of admirable effect.

But these considerations of hope and fear are almost unknown in the pastoral state of nations. The Huns of Attila may without injustice be compared to the Moguls and Tartars before their primitive manners were changed by religion and luxury; and the evidence of Oriental history may reflect some light on the short and imperfect annals of Rome. After the Moguls had subdued the northern provinces of China, it was seriously proposed, not in the hour of victory and passion, but in calm deliberate council, to exterminate all the inhabitants of that populous country, that the vacant land might be converted to the pasture of cattle. The firmness of a Chinese mandarin,[23] who insinuated some principles of rational policy into the mind of Zingis, diverted him from the execution of this horrid design. But in the cities of Asia which yielded to the Moguls, the inhuman abuse of the rights of war was exercised with a regular form of discipline, which may, with equal reason though not with equal authority, be imputed to the victorious Huns. The inhabitants who had submitted to their discretion were ordered to evacuate their houses and to assemble in some plain adjacent to the city, where a division was made of the vanquished into three parts. The first class consisted of the soldiers of the garrison and the young men capable of bearing arms; and their fate was instantly decided: they were either enlisted among the Moguls, or they were massacred on the spot by the troops, who, with pointed spears and bended bows, had formed a circle round the captive multitude. The second class, composed of the young and beautiful women, of the artificers of every rank and profession, and of the more wealthy or honourable citizens, from whom a private ransom might be expected, was distributed in equal or proportionable lots. The remainder, whose life or death was alike useless to the conquerors, were permitted to return to the city, which in the meanwhile had been stripped of its valuable furniture; and a tax was imposed on those wretched inhabitants for the indulgence of breathing their native air. Such was the behaviour of the Moguls when they were not conscious of any extraordinary rigour.[24] But the most casual provocation, the slightest motive of caprice or convenience, often provoked them to involve a whole people in an indiscriminate massacre; and the ruin of some flourishing cities was executed with such unrelenting perseverance, that, according to their own expression, horses might run without stumbling over the ground where they had once stood. The three great capitals of Khorasan, Maru,

[23] He represented to the emperor of the Moguls that the four provinces (Petcheli, Chantong, Chansi, and Leaotong) which he already possessed might annually produce, under a mild administration, 500,000 ounces of silver, 400,000 measures of rice, and 800,000 pieces of silk. Gaubil, Hist. de la Dynastie des Mongous, p. 58, 59. Yelutchousay (such was the name of the mandarin) was a wise and virtuous minister who saved his country and civilised the conquerors. See p. 102, 103.

[24] Particular instances would be endless; but the curious reader may consult the Life of Gengiscan, by Petit de la Croix, the Histoire des Mongous, and the fifteenth book of the History of the Huns.

Neisabour, and Herat, were destroyed by the armies of Zingis; and the exact account which was taken of the slain amounted to four millions three hundred and forty-seven thousand persons.[25] Timur, or Tamerlane, was educated in a less barbarous age and in the profession of the Mahometan religion; yet, if Attila equalled the hostile ravages of Tamerlane,[26] either the Tartar or the Hun might deserve the epithet of the SCOURGE OF GOD.[27]

It may be affirmed with bolder assurance that the Huns depopulated the provinces of the empire by the number of Roman subjects whom they led away into captivity. In the hands of a wise legislator such an industrious colony might have contributed to diffuse through the deserts of Scythia the rudiments of the useful and ornamental arts; but these captives, who had been taken in war, were accidentally dispersed among the hordes that obeyed the empire of Attila. The estimate of their respective value was formed by the simple judgment of unenlightened and unprejudiced barbarians. Perhaps they might not understand the merit of a theologian profoundly skilled in the controversies of the Trinity and the Incarnation; yet they respected the ministers of every religion; and the active zeal of the Christian missionaries, without approaching the person or the palace of the monarch, successfully laboured in the propagation of the gospel.[28] The pastoral tribes, who were ignorant of the distinction of landed property, must have disregarded the use as well as the abuse of civil jurisprudence; and the skill of an eloquent lawyer could excite only their contempt or their abhorrence.[29]

---

[25] At Maru, 1,300,000; at Herat, 1,600,000; at Neisabour, 1,747,000. D'Herbelot, Bibliothèque Orientale, p. 380, 381. I use the orthography of D'Anville's maps. It must, however, be allowed, that the Persians were disposed to exaggerate their losses, and the Moguls to magnify their exploits.

[26] Cherefeddin Ali, his servile panegyrist, would afford us many horrid examples. In his camp before Delhi, Timur massacred 100,000 Indian prisoners, who had *smiled* when the army of their countrymen appeared in sight (Hist. de Timur Bec, tom. iii. p. 90). The people of Ispahan supplied 70,000 human skulls for the structure of several lofty towers (id. tom. i. p. 434). A similar tax was levied on the revolt of Bagdad (tom. iii. p. 370) ; and the exact account, which Cherefeddin was not able to procure from the proper officers, is stated by another historian (Ahmed Arabsiada, tom. ii. p. 175, vers. Manger) at 90,000 heads.

[27] The ancients, Jornandes, Priscus, etc., are ignorant of this epithet. The modern Hungarians have imagined that it was applied, by a hermit of Gaul, to Attila, who was pleased to insert it among the titles of his royal dignity. Mascou, ix. 23, and Tillemont, Hist. des Empereurs, tom. vi. p. 143.

[28] The missionaries of St. Chrysostom had converted great numbers of the Scythians, who dwelt beyond the Danube in tents and waggons. Theodoret, l. v. c. 31; Photius, p. 1517 [p. 508 b, ed. Bekk.]. The Mahometans, the Nestorians, and the Latin Christians, thought themselves secure of gaining the sons and grandsons of Zingis, who treated the rival missionaries with impartial favour.

[29] The Germans, who exterminated Varus and his legions, had been particularly offended with the Roman laws and lawyers. One of the barbarians, after the effectual precautions of cutting out the tongue of an advocate, and

The perpetual intercourse of the Huns and the Goths had communicated the familiar knowledge of the two national dialects; and the barbarians were ambitious of conversing in Latin, the military idiom even of the Eastern empire.[30] But they disdained the language and the sciences of the Greeks; and the vain sophist or grave philosopher who had enjoyed the flattering applause of the schools, was mortified to find that his robust servant was a captive of more value and importance than himself. The mechanic arts were encouraged and esteemed, as they tended to satisfy the wants of the Huns. An architect in the service of Onegesius, one of the favourites of Attila, was employed to construct a bath: but this work was a rare example of private luxury; and the trades of the smith, the carpenter, the armourer, were much more adapted to supply a wandering people with the useful instruments of peace and war. But the merit of the physician was received with universal favour and respect: the barbarians, who despised death, might be apprehensive of disease; and the haughty conqueror trembled in the presence of a captive to whom he ascribed perhaps an imaginary power of prolonging or preserving his life.[31] The Huns might be provoked to insult the misery of their slaves, over whom they exercised a despotic command;[32] but their manners were not susceptible of a refined system of oppression, and the efforts of courage and diligence were often recompensed by the gift of freedom. The historian Priscus, whose embassy is a source of curious instruction, was accosted in the camp of Attila by a stranger, who saluted him in the Greek language, but whose dress and figure displayed the appearance of a wealthy Scythian. In the siege of Viminiacum he had lost, according to his own account, his fortune and liberty: he became the slave of Onegesius; but his faithful services against the Romans and the Acatzires had gradually raised him to the rank of the native Huns, to whom he was attached by the domestic pledges of a new wife and several children. The spoils of war had restored and improved his private property; he was admitted to the table of his former lord; and the apostate Greek blessed the hour of his captivity, since it had been the introduction to a happy and independent state, which he

sewing up his mouth, observed with much satisfaction that the viper could no longer hiss. Florus, iv. 12.
[30] Priscus, p. 59 [p. 190, ed. Bonn]. It should seem that the Huns preferred the Gothic and Latin languages to their own, which was probably a harsh and barren idiom.
[31] Philip de Comines, in his admirable picture of the last moments of Lewis XI. (Mémoires, 1. vi. c. 12), represents the insolence of his physician, who, in five months, extorted 54,000 crowns and a rich bishopric from the stern avaricious tyrant.
[32] Priscus (p. 61 [p. 194, ed. Bonn]) extols the equity of the Roman laws, which protected the life of a slave. Occidere solent (says Tacitus of the Germans) non disciplinâ et servitate, sed impetu et irâ, ut inimicum, nisi quòd impune. De Moribus Germ. c. 25. The Heruli, who were the subjects of Attila, claimed and exercised the power of life and death over their slaves. See a remarkable instance in the second book of Agathias.

held by the honourable tenure of military service. This reflection naturally produced a dispute on the advantages and defects of the Roman government, which was severely arraigned by the apostate, and defended by Priscus in a prolix and feeble declamation. The freedman of Onegesius exposed, in true and lively colours, the vices of a declining empire of which he had so long been the victim; the cruel absurdity of the Roman princes, unable to protect their subjects against the public enemy, unwilling to trust them with arms for their own defence; the intolerable weight of taxes, rendered still more oppressive by the intricate or arbitrary modes of collection; the obscurity of numerous and contradictory laws; the tedious and expensive forms of judicial proceedings; the partial administration of justice; and the universal corruption which increased the influence of the rich and aggravated the misfortunes of the poor. A sentiment of patriotic sympathy was at length revived in the breast of the fortunate exile, and he lamented with a flood of tears the guilt or weakness of those magistrates who had perverted the wisest and most salutary institutions.[33]

The timid or selfish policy of the Western Romans had abandoned the Eastern empire to the Huns.[34] The loss of armies and the want of discipline or virtue were not supplied by the personal character of the monarch. Theodosius might still affect the style as well as the title of *Invincible Augustus,* but he was reduced to solicit the clemency of Attila who imperiously dictated these harsh and humiliating conditions of peace. I. The emperor of the East resigned, by an express or tacit convention, an extensive and important territory which stretched along the southern banks of the Danube, from Singidunum, or Belgrade, as far as Novæ, in the diocese of Thrace. The breadth was defined by the vague computation of fifteen days' journey; but, from the proposal of Attila to remove the situation of the national market, it soon appeared that he comprehended the ruined city of Naissus within the limits of his dominions. II. The king of the Huns required and obtained that his tribute or subsidy should be augmented from seven hundred pounds of gold to the annual sum of two thousand one hundred; and he stipulated the immediate payment of six thousand pounds of gold to defray the expenses, or to expiate the guilt, of the war. One might imagine that such a demand, which scarcely equalled the measure of private wealth, would have been readily discharged by the opulent empire of the East; and the public distress affords a remarkable proof of the impoverished, or at least of the disorderly, state of the finances. A large proportion of the taxes extorted from the people was detained and intercepted in their passage through the foulest channels to the treasury of Constantinople. The revenue was dissipated by Theodosius and his favourites in waste-

---

[33] See the whole conversation in Priscus, p. 59-62 [p. 189-197, ed. Bonn].
[34] Nova iterum Orienti assurgit ruina . . . quum nulla ab Occidentalibus ferrentur auxilia. Prosper-Tyro composed his Chronicle in the West; and his observation implies a censure.

ful and profuse luxury, which was disguised by the names of Imperial magnificence or Christian charity. The immediate supplies had been exhausted by the unforeseen necessity of military preparations. A personal contribution, rigorously but capriciously imposed on the members of the senatorian order, was the only expedient that could disarm without loss of time the impatient avarice of Attila: and the poverty of the nobles compelled them to adopt the scandalous resource of exposing to public auction the jewels of their wives and the hereditary ornaments of their palaces.[35] III. The king of the Huns appears to have established as a principle of national jurisprudence, that he could never lose the property which he had once acquired in the persons who had yielded either a voluntary or reluctant submission to his authority. From this principle he concluded, and the conclusions of Attila were irrevocable laws, that the Huns who had been taken prisoners in war should be released without delay and without ransom; that every Roman captive who had presumed to escape should purchase his right to freedom at the price of twelve pieces of gold; and that all the barbarians who had deserted the standard of Attila should be restored without any promise or stipulation of pardon. In the execution of this cruel and ignominious treaty the Imperial officers were forced to massacre several loyal and noble deserters who refused to devote themselves to certain death; and the Romans forfeited all reasonable claims to the friendship of any Scythian people by this public confession that they were destitute either of faith or power to protect the suppliant who had embraced the throne of Theodosius.[36]

The firmness of a single town, so obscure that except on this occasion it has never been mentioned by any historian or geographer, exposed the disgrace of the emperor and empire. Azimus, or Azimuntium, a small city of Thrace on the Illyrian borders,[37] had been distinguished by the martial spirit of its youth, the skill and reputation of the leaders whom they had chosen, and their daring exploits against the innumerable host of the barbarians. Instead of tamely expecting their approach, the

[35] According to the description, or rather invective, of Chrysostom, an auction of Byzantine luxury must have been very productive. Every wealthy house possessed a semicircular table of massy silver, such as two men could scarcely lift; a vase of solid gold of the weight of forty pounds; cups, dishes, of the same metal, etc.

[36] The articles of the treaty, expressed without much order or precision. may be found in Priscus (p. 34, 35, 36, 37, 53, etc. [ed. Par.; p. 142-148, 178, etc., ed. Bonn]). Count Marcellinus dispenses some comfort by observing— 1. *That* Attila himself solicited the peace and presents which he had formerly refused; and, 2. *That,* about the same time, the ambassadors of India presented a fine large tame tiger to the emperor Theodosius.

[37] Priscus, p. 35, 36 [p. 143, 144, ed. Bonn]. Among the hundred and eighty-two forts or castles of Thrace enumerated by Procopius (de Ædificiis, l. iv. c. xi. tom. ii. p. 92, edit. Paris [tom. iii. p. 306, ed. Bonn]), there is one of the name of *Esimontou,* whose position is doubtfully marked, in the neighbourhood of Anchialus and the Euxine Sea. The name and walls of Azimuntium might subsist till the reign of Justinian; but the race of its brave defenders had been carefully extirpated by the jealousy of the Roman princes.

Azimuntines attacked, in frequent and successful sallies, the troops of
the Huns, who gradually declined the dangerous neighbourhood, rescued
from their hands the spoil and the captives, and recruited their domestic
force by the voluntary association of fugitives and deserters. After the
conclusion of the treaty Attila still menaced the empire with implacable
war, unless the Azimuntines were persuaded or compelled to comply
with the conditions which their sovereign had accepted. The ministers
of Theodosius confessed, with shame and with truth, that they no longer
possessed any authority over a society of men who so bravely asserted
their natural independence; and the king of the Huns condescended to
negotiate an equal exchange with the citizens of Azimus. They
demanded the restitution of some shepherds, who with their cattle had
been accidentally surprised. A strict though fruitless inquiry was allowed; but the Huns were obliged to swear that they did not detain any
prisoners belonging to the city before they could recover two surviving
countrymen whom the Azimuntines had reserved as pledges for the safety
of their lost companions. Attila, on his side, was satisfied and deceived
by their solemn asseveration that the rest of the captives had been put
to the sword; and that it was their constant practice immediately to
dismiss the Romans and the deserters who had obtained the security of
the public faith. This prudent and officious dissimulation may be condemned or excused by the casuists as they incline to the rigid decree of
St. Augustin, or the milder sentiment of St. Jerom and St. Chrysostom: but every soldier, every statesman, must acknowledge that, if the
race of the Azimuntines had been encouraged and multiplied, the barbarians would have ceased to trample on the majesty of the empire.[38]

If would have been strange, indeed, if Theodosius had purchased, by
the loss of honour, a secure and solid tranquillity, or if his tameness
had not invited the repetition of injuries. The Byzantine court was
insulted by five or six successive embassies;[39] and the ministers of Attila
were uniformly instructed to press the tardy or imperfect execution of
the last treaty; to produce the names of fugitives and deserters who
were still protected by the empire; and to declare, with seeming moderation, that, unless their sovereign obtained complete and immediate satisfaction, it would be impossible for him, were it even his wish, to check
the resentment of his warlike tribes. Besides the motive of pride and
interest which might prompt the king of the Huns to continue this train

[38] The peevish dispute of St. Jerom and St. Augustin, who laboured by
different expedients to reconcile the *seeming* quarrel of the two apostles, St.
Peter and St. Paul, depends on the solution of an important question (Middleton's Works, vol. ii. p. 5-10), which has been frequently agitated by catholic
and protestant divines, and even by lawyers and philosophers of every age.
[39] Montesquieu (Considérations sur la Grandeur, etc., c. xix.) has delineated,
with a bold and easy pencil, some of the most striking circumstances of the
pride of Attila and the disgrace of the Romans. He deserves the praise
of having read the Fragments of Priscus, which have been too much disregarded.

of negotiation, he was influenced by the less honourable view of enriching his favourites at the expense of his enemies. The Imperial treasury was exhausted to procure the friendly offices of the ambassadors and their principal attendants, whose favourable report might conduce to the maintenance of peace. The barbarian monarch was flattered by the liberal reception of his ministers; he computed with pleasure the value and splendour of their gifts, rigorously exacted the performance of every promise which would contribute to their private emolument, and treated as an important business of state the marriage of his secretary Constantius.[40] That Gallic adventurer, who was recommended by Aëtius to the king of the Huns, had engaged his service to the ministers of Constantinople for the stipulated reward of a wealthy and noble wife; and the daughter of Count Saturninus was chosen to discharge the obligations of her country. The reluctance of the victim, some domestic troubles, and the unjust confiscation of her fortune, cooled the ardour of her interested lover; but he still demanded, in the name of Attila, an equivalent alliance; and, after many ambiguous delays and excuses, the Byzantine court was compelled to sacrifice to this insolent stranger the widow of Armatius, whose birth, opulence, and beauty placed her in the most illustrious rank of the Roman matrons. For these importunate and oppressive embassies Attila claimed a suitable return; he weighed, with suspicious pride, the character and station of the Imperial envoys; but he condescended to promise that he would advance as far as Sardica to receive any minister who had been invested with the consular dignity. The council of Theodosius eluded this proposal by representing the desolate and ruined condition of Sardica; and even ventured to insinuate that every officer of the army or household was qualified to treat with the most powerful princes of Scythia. Maximin,[41] a respectable courtier, whose abilities had been long exercised in civil and military employments, accepted with reluctance the troublesome, and perhaps dangerous, commission of reconciling the angry spirit of the king of the Huns. His friend, the historian Priscus,[42] embraced the opportunity of observing the barbarian

[40] See Priscus, p. 69, 71, 72, etc. [p. 208, 213, ed. Bonn]. I would fain believe that this adventurer was afterwards crucified by the order of Attila, on a suspicion of treasonable practices; but Priscus (p. 57 [p. 185, 186, ed. Bonn]) has too plainly distinguished *two* persons of the name of Constantius, who, from the similar events of their lives, might have been easily confounded.

[41] In the Persian treaty, concluded in the year 422, the wise and eloquent Maximin had been the assessor of Ardaburius (Socrates, l. vii. c. 20). When Marcian ascended the throne, the office of Great Chamberlain was bestowed on Maximin, who is ranked in a public edict among the four principal ministers of state (Novell. ad Calc. Cod. Theod. p. 31 [tit. ii.]). He executed a civil and military commission in the eastern provinces; and his death was lamented by the savages of Æthiopia, whose incursions he had repressed. See Priscus, p. 40, 41 [p. 153, 154, ed. Bonn].

[42] Priscus was a native of Panium in Thrace, and deserved by his eloquence an honourable place among the sophists of the age. His Byzantine history, which related to his own times, was comprised in seven books. See Fabricius

hero in the peaceful and domestic scenes of life: but the secret of the embassy, a fatal and guilty secret, was intrusted only to the interpreter Vigilius. The two last ambassadors of the Huns, Orestes, a noble subject of the Pannonian province, and Edecon, a valiant chieftain of the tribe of the Scyrri, returned at the same time from Constantinople to the royal camp. Their obscure names were afterwards illustrated by the extraordinary fortune and the contrast of their sons: the two servants of Attila became the fathers of the last Roman emperor of the West, and of the first barbarian king of Italy.

The ambassadors, who were followed by a numerous train of men and horses, made their first halt at Sardica, at the distance of three hundred and fifty miles, or thirteen days' journey, from Constantinople. As the remains of Sardica were still included within the limits of the empire, it was incumbent on the Romans to exercise the duties of hospitality. They provided, with the assistance of the provincials, a sufficient number of sheep and oxen, and invited the Huns to a splendid, or, at least, a plentiful supper. But the harmony of the entertainment was soon disturbed by mutual prejudice and indiscretion. The greatness of the emperor and the empire was warmly maintained by their ministers; the Huns, with equal ardour, asserted the superiority of their victorious monarch: the dispute was inflamed by the rash and unseasonable flattery of Vigilius, who passionately rejected the comparison of a mere mortal with the divine Theodosius; and it was with extreme difficulty that Maximin and Priscus were able to divert the conversation or to soothe the angry minds of the barbarians. When they rose from table the Imperial ambassador presented Edecon and Orestes with rich gifts of silk robes and Indian pearls, which they thankfully accepted. Yet Orestes could not forbear insinuating that *he* had not always been treated with such respect and liberality: and the offensive distinction which was implied between his civil office and the hereditary rank of his colleague seems to have made Edecon a doubtful friend and Orestes an irreconcilable enemy. After this entertainment they travelled about one hundred miles from Sardica to Naissus. That flourishing city, which had given birth to the great Constantine, was levelled with the ground; the inhabitants were destroyed or dispersed; and the appearance of some sick persons, who were still permitted to exist among the ruins of the churches, served only to increase the horror of the prospect. The surface of the country was covered with the bones of the slain; and the ambassadors, who directed their course to the north-west, were obliged to pass the hills of modern Servia before they descended into the flat and marshy grounds which are terminated by the Danube. The Huns were masters of the great river: their navigation was performed in large canoes, hollowed out of the trunk of a single tree; the ministers

Biblioth. Græc. tom. vi. p. 235, 236. Notwithstanding the charitable judgment of the critics, I suspect that Priscus was a Pagan.

of Theodosius were safely landed on the opposite bank; and their barbarian associates immediately hastened to the camp of Attila, which was
equally prepared for the amusements of hunting or of war. No sooner
had Maximin advanced about two miles from the Danube than he began
to experience the fastidious insolence of the conqueror. He was sternly
forbid to pitch his tents in a pleasant valley, lest he should infringe the
distant awe that was due to the royal mansion. The ministers of Attila
pressed him to communicate the business and the instructions which he
reserved for the ear of their sovereign. When Maximin temperately
urged the contrary practice of nations, he was still more confounded to
find that the resolutions of the Sacred Consistory, those secrets (says
Priscus) which should not be revealed to the gods themselves, had been
treacherously disclosed to the public enemy. On his refusal to comply
with such ignominious terms, the Imperial envoy was commanded instantly to depart; the order was recalled; it was again repeated; and
the Huns renewed their ineffectual attempts to subdue the patient firmness of Maximin. At length, by the intercession of Scotta, the brother
of Onegesius, whose friendship had been purchased by a liberal gift, he
was admitted to the royal presence; but, instead of obtaining a decisive
answer, he was compelled to undertake a remote journey towards the
North, that Attila might enjoy the proud satisfaction of receiving in the
same camp the ambassadors of the Eastern and Western empires. His
journey was regulated by the guides, who obliged him to halt, to hasten
his march, or to deviate from the common road, as it best suited the
convenience of the king. The Romans who traversed the plains of
Hungary suppose that they passed *several* navigable rivers, either in
canoes or portable boats; but there is reason to suspect that the winding
stream of the Theiss, or Tibiscus, might present itself in different places
under different names. From the contiguous villages they received a
plentiful and regular supply of provisions; mead instead of wine, millet
in the place of bread, and a certain liquor named *camus*, which, according to the report of Priscus, was distilled from barley.[43] Such fare might
appear coarse and indelicate to men who had tasted the luxury of Constantinople; but, in their accidental distress, they were relieved by the
gentleness and hospitality of the same barbarians, so terrible and so
merciless in war. The ambassadors had encamped on the edge of a
large morass. A violent tempest of wind and rain, of thunder and lightning, overturned their tents, immersed their baggage and furniture in
the water, and scattered their retinue, who wandered in the darkness

---

[43] The Huns themselves still continued to despise the labours of agriculture;
they abused the privilege of a victorious nation; and the Goths, their industrious subjects, who cultivated the earth, dreaded their neighbourhood, like
that of so many ravenous wolves (Priscus, p. 45 [p. 163, ed. Bonn]). In
the same manner the Sarts and Tadgics provide for their own subsistence, and
for that of the Usbec Tartars, their lazy and rapacious sovereigns. See
Genealogical History of the Tartars, p. 423, 455, etc.

of the night, uncertain of their road and apprehensive of some unknown danger, till they awakened by their cries the inhabitants of a neighbouring village, the property of the widow of Bleda. A bright illumination, and, in a few moments, a comfortable fire of reeds, was kindled by their officious benevolence: the wants, and even the desires, of the Romans were liberally satisfied; and they seem to have been embarrassed by the singular politeness of Bleda's widow, who added to her other favours the gift, or at least the loan, of a sufficient number of beautiful and obsequious damsels. The sunshine of the succeeding day was dedicated to repose, to collect and dry the baggage, and to the refreshment of the men and horses; but, in the evening, before they pursued their journey, the ambassadors expressed their gratitude to the bounteous lady of the village by a very acceptable present of silver cups, red fleeces, dried fruits, and Indian pepper. Soon after this adventure they rejoined the march of Attila, from whom they had been separated about six days; and slowly proceeded to the capital of an empire which did not contain, in the space of several thousand miles, a single city.

As far as we may ascertain the vague and obscure geography of Priscus, this capital appears to have been seated between the Danube, the Theiss, and the Carpathian hills, in the plains of Upper Hungary, and most probably in the neighbourhood of Jazberin, Agria, or Tokay.[44] In its origin it could be no more than an accidental camp, which, by the long and frequent residence of Attila, had insensibly swelled into a huge village, for the reception of his court, of the troops who followed his person, and of the various multitude of idle or industrious slaves and retainers.[45] The baths, constructed by Onegesius, were the only edifice of stone; the materials had been transported from Pannonia; and since the adjacent country was destitute even of large

[44] It is evident that Priscus passed the Danube and the Theiss, and that he did not reach the foot of the Carpathian hills. Agria, Tokay, and Jazberin are situate in the plains circumscribed by this definition. M. de Buat (Histoire des Peuples, etc., tom. vii. p. 461) has chosen Tokay; Otrokosci (p. 180, apud Mascou, ix. 23), a learned Hungarian, has preferred Jazberin, a place about thirty-six miles westward of Buda and the Danube.
[M. St. Martin considers the narrative of Priscus, the only authority of Count de Buat and of Gibbon, too vague to fix the position of Attila's camp. "It is worthy of remark that in the Hungarian traditions collected by Thevrocz, l. 2, c. 17, precisely on the left branch of the Danube, where Attila's residence was situated, in the same parallel stands the present city of Buda, in Hungarian Buduvur. It is for this reason that this city has retained for a long time among the Germans of Hungary the name of Etzelnburg or Etzelaburg, viz., the city of Attila. St. Martin sees no reason for not accepting the narration of the Hungarian historians.—O. S.]
[45] The royal village of Attila may be compared to the city of Karacorum, the residence of the successors of Zingis, which, though it appears to have been a more stable habitation, did not equal the size or splendour of the town and abbey of St. Denys in the 13th century (see Rubruquis, in the Histoire Générale des Voyages, tom. vii. p. 286). The camp of Aurengzebe, as it is so agreeably described by Bernier (tom. ii. p. 217-235), blended the manners of Scythia with the magnificence and luxury of Hindostan.

timber, it may be presumed that the meaner habitations of the royal village consisted of straw, of mud, or of canvas. The wooden houses of the more illustrious Huns were built and adorned with rude magnificence, according to the rank, the fortune, or the taste of the proprietors. They seem to have been distributed with some degree of order and symmetry; and each spot became more honourable as it approached the person of the sovereign. The palace of Attila, which surpassed all other houses in his dominions, was built entirely of wood, and covered an ample space of ground. The outward enclosure was a lofty wall, or palisade, of smooth square timber, intersected with high towers, but intended rather for ornament than defence. This wall, which seems to have encircled the declivity of a hill, comprehended a great variety of wooden edifices, adapted to the uses of royalty. A separate house was assigned to each of the numerous wives of Attila; and, instead of the rigid and illiberal confinement imposed by Asiatic jealousy, they politely admitted the Roman ambassadors to their presence, their table, and even to the freedom of an innocent embrace. When Maximin offered his presents to Cerca the principal queen, he admired the singular architecture of her mansion, the height of the round columns, the size and beauty of the wood, which was curiously shaped or turned, or polished or carved; and his attentive eye was able to discover some taste in the ornaments, and some regularity in the proportions. After passing through the guards who watched before the gate, the ambassadors were introduced into the private apartment of Cerca. The wife of Attila received their visit sitting, or rather lying, on a soft couch; the floor was covered with a carpet; the domestics formed a circle round the queen; and her damsels, seated on the ground, were employed in working the variegated embroidery which adorned the dress of the barbaric warriors. The Huns were ambitious of displaying those riches which were the fruit and evidence of their victories; the trappings of their horses, their swords, and even their shoes, were studded with gold and precious stones; and their tables were profusely spread with plates, and goblets, and vases of gold and silver, which had been fashioned by the labour of Grecian artists. The monarch alone assumed the superior pride of still adhering to the simplicity of his Scythian ancestors.[46] The dress of Attila, his arms, and the furniture of his horse, were plain, without ornament, and of a single colour. The royal table was served in wooden cups and platters; flesh was his only food; and the conqueror of the North never tasted the luxury of bread.

When Attila first gave audience to the Roman ambassadors on the banks of the Danube, his tent was encompassed with a formidable guard. The monarch himself was seated in a wooden chair. His stern

---

[46] When the Moguls displayed the spoils of Asia in the diet of Toncat, the throne of Zingis was still covered with the original black felt carpet on which he had been seated when he was raised to the command of his warlike countrymen. See Vie de Gengiscan, l. iv. c. 9.

countenance, angry gestures, and impatient tone astonished the firmness of Maximin; but Vigilius had more reason to tremble, since he distinctly understood the menace, that if Attila did not respect the law of nations, he would nail the deceitful interpreter to a cross, and leave his body to the vultures. The barbarians condescended, by producing an accurate list, to expose the bold falsehood of Vigilius, who had affirmed that no more than seventeen deserters could be found. But he arrogantly declared that he apprehended only the disgrace of contending with his fugitive slaves; since he despised their impotent efforts to defend the provinces which Theodosius had intrusted to their arms: " For what fortress " (added Attila), " what city, in the wide extent of the Roman empire, can hope to exist, secure and impregnable, if it is our pleasure that it should be erased from the earth? " He dismissed, however, the interpreter, who returned to Constantinople with his peremptory demand of more complete restitution, and a more splendid embassy. His anger gradually subsided, and his domestic satisfaction in a marriage which he celebrated on the road with the daughter of Eslam might perhaps contribute to mollify the native fierceness of his temper. The entrance of Attila into the royal village was marked by a very singular ceremony. A numerous troop of women came out to meet their hero and their king. They marched before him, distributed into long and regular files: the intervals between the files were filled by white veils of thin linen, which the women on either side bore aloft in their hands, and which formed a canopy for a chorus of young virgins, who chanted hymns and songs in the Scythian language. The wife of his favourite Onegesius, with a train of female attendants, saluted Attila at the door of her own house, on his way to the palace; and offered, according to the custom of the country, her respectful homage, by entreating him to taste the wine and meat which she had prepared for his reception. As soon as the monarch had graciously accepted her hospitable gift, his domestics lifted a small silver table to a convenient height, as he sat on horseback; and Attila, when he had touched the goblet with his lips, again saluted the wife of Onegesius, and continued his march. During his residence at the seat of empire his hours were not wasted in the recluse idleness of a seraglio; and the king of the Huns could maintain his superior dignity without concealing his person from the public view. He frequently assembled his council, and gave audience to the ambassadors of the nations; and his people might appeal to the supreme tribunal, which he held at stated times, and, according to the Eastern custom, before the principal gate of his wooden palace. The Romans, both of the East and of the West, were twice invited to the banquet where Attila feasted with the princes and nobles of Scythia. Maximin and his colleagues were stopped on the threshold, till they had made a devout libation to the health and prosperity of the king of the Huns; and were conducted, after this ceremony, to their respective seats in a spacious hall. The royal table and couch, covered with carpets and fine linen, was raised by several steps in the midst of the hall; and a son, an uncle, or perhaps a favourite king, were admitted to share the simple and homely repast of Attila. Two lines of small tables, each of which contained three or four guests, were ranged in order on either hand; the right was esteemed the most honourable, but the Romans ingenuously confess that they were placed on the left; and that Beric, an unknown chieftain, most probably of the Gothic race, preceded the representatives of Theodosius and Valentinian. The barbarian monarch received from his cupbearer a goblet filled with wine, and courteously drank to the health of the most distinguished guest, who rose from his seat and expressed, in the same manner, his loyal and respectful vows. This ceremony was successively performed for all, or at least for the illustrious persons of the assembly; and a considerable time must have been consumed, since it was thrice repeated as each course or service was placed on the table. But the wine still remained after the meat had been removed; and the Huns continued to indulge their intemperance long after the sober and decent ambassadors of the two empires had withdrawn themselves from the nocturnal banquet. Yet before they retired they enjoyed a singular opportunity of observing the manners of the nation in their convivial amusements. Two Scythians stood before the couch of Attila, and recited the verses which they had composed to celebrate his valour and his victories. A profound silence prevailed in the hall; and the attention of the guests was captivated by the vocal harmony, which revived and perpetuated the memory of their own exploits: a martial ardour flashed from the eyes of the warriors, who were impatient for battle; and the tears of the old men expressed their generous despair that they could no longer partake the danger and glory of the field.[47] This entertainment, which might be considered as a school of military virtue, was succeeded by a farce that debased the dignity of human nature. A Moorish and a Scythian buffoon successively excited the mirth of the rude spectators, by their deformed figure, ridiculous dress, antic gestures, absurd speeches, and the strange unintelligible confusion of the Latin, the Gothic, and the Hunnic languages; and the hall resounded with loud and licentious peals of laughter. In the midst of this intemperate riot, Attila alone, without a change of countenance, maintained his steadfast and inflexible gravity, which was never relaxed, except on the entrance of Irnac, the youngest of his sons: he embraced the boy with a smile of paternal tenderness, gently pinched him by the cheek, and betrayed a partial affection, which was justified by the assurance of his prophets that Irnac would be the future support of his family and empire. Two days afterwards the ambassadors received a second invitation; and they had reason to praise the politeness, as well as the hospitality, of Attila. The king

---

[47] If we may believe Plutarch (in Demetrio, tom. v. [c. 19] p. 24), it was the custom of the Scythians, when they indulged in the pleasures of the table, to awaken their languid courage by the martial harmony of twanging their bow-strings.

of the Huns held a long and familiar conversation with Maximin; but his civility was interrupted by rude expressions and haughty reproaches; and he was provoked, by a motive of interest, to support, with unbecoming zeal, the private claims of his secretary Constantius. " The emperor " (said Attila) " has long promised him a rich wife: Constantius must not be disappointed; nor should a Roman emperor deserve the name of liar." On the third day the ambassadors were dismissed; the freedom of several captives was granted, for a moderate ransom, to their pressing entreaties; and, besides the royal presents, they were permitted to accept from each of the Scythian nobles the honourable and useful gift of a horse. Maximin returned, by the same road, to Constantinople; and though he was involved in an accidental dispute with Beric, the new ambassador of Attila, he flattered himself that he had contributed, by the laborious journey, to confirm the peace and alliance of the two nations.[48]

But the Roman ambassador was ignorant of the treacherous design which had been concealed under the mask of the public faith. The surprise and satisfaction of Edecon, when he contemplated the splendour of Constantinople, had encouraged the interpreter Vigilius to procure for him a secret interview with the eunuch Chrysaphius,[49] who governed the emperor and the empire. After some previous conversation, and a mutual oath of secrecy, the eunuch, who had not, from his own feelings or experience, imbibed any exalted notions of ministerial virtue, ventured to propose the death of Attila, as an important service, by which Edecon might deserve a liberal share of the wealth and luxury which he admired. The ambassador of the Huns listened to the tempting offer; and professed, with apparent zeal, his ability, as well as readiness, to execute the bloody deed: the design was communicated to the master of the offices, and the devout Theodosius consented to the assassination of his invincible enemy. But this perfidious conspiracy was defeated by the dissimulation, or the repentance, of Edecon; and though he might exaggerate his inward abhorrence for the treason which he seemed to approve, he dexterously assumed the merit of an early and voluntary confession. If we *now* review the embassy of Maximin and the behaviour of Attila, we must applaud the barbarian, who respected the laws of hospitality, and generously entertained and dismissed the minis-

---

[48] The curious narrative of this embassy, which required few observations, and was not susceptible of any collateral evidence, may be found in Priscus, p. 49-70 [ed. Par.; p. 170-209, ed. Bonn]. But I have not confined myself to the same order; and I had previously extracted the historical circumstances, which were less intimately connected with the journey and business of the Roman ambassadors.

[49] M. de Tillemont has very properly given the succession of chamberlains who reigned in the name of Theodosius. Chrysaphius was the last, and, according to the unanimous evidence of history, the worst of these favourites (see Hist. des Empereurs, tom. vi. p. 117-119; Mém. Ecclés. tom. xv. p. 438). His partiality for his godfather, the heresiarch Eutyches, engaged him to persecute the orthodox party.

ter of a prince who had conspired against his life. But the rashness of
Vigilius will appear still more extraordinary, since he returned, conscious
of his guilt and danger, to the royal camp accompanied by his son, and
carrying with him a weighty purse of gold, which the favourite eunuch
had furnished, to satisfy the demands of Edecon and to corrupt the
fidelity of the guards. The interpreter was instantly seized and dragged
before the tribunal of Attila, where he asserted his innocence with
specious firmness, till the threat of inflicting instant death on his son
extorted from him a sincere discovery of the criminal transaction. Under
the name of ransom, or confiscation, the rapacious king of the Huns
accepted two hundred pounds of gold for the life of a traitor whom he
disdained to punish. He pointed his just indignation against a nobler
object. His ambassadors, Eslaw and Orestes, were immediately despatched to Constantinople with a peremptory instruction, which it was
much safer for them to execute than to disobey. They boldly entered
the Imperial presence with the fatal purse hanging down from the neck
of Orestes, who interrogated the eunuch Chrysaphius, as he stood beside
the throne, whether he recognised the evidence of his guilt. But the
office of reproof was reserved for the superior dignity of his colleague
Eslaw, who gravely addressed the emperor of the East in the following
words: " Theodosius is the son of an illustrious and respectable parent:
Attila likewise is descended from a noble race; and *he* has supported,
by his actions, the dignity which he inherited from his father Mundzuk.
But Theodosius has forfeited his paternal honours, and, by consenting
to pay tribute, has degraded himself to the condition of a slave. It is
therefore just that he should reverence the man whom fortune and merit
have placed above him, instead of attempting, like a wicked slave,
clandestinely to conspire against his master." The son of Arcadius,
who was accustomed only to the voice of flattery, heard with astonishment the severe language of truth: he blushed and trembled; nor did
he presume directly to refuse the head of Chrysaphius, which Eslaw
and Orestes were instructed to demand. A solemn embassy, armed
with full powers and magnificent gifts, was hastily sent to deprecate
the wrath of Attila; and his pride was gratified by the choice of Nomius
and Anatolius, two ministers of consular or patrician rank, of whom the
one was great treasurer, and the other was master-general of the armies
of the East. He condescended to meet these ambassadors on the banks
of the river Drenco; and though he at first affected a stern and haughty
demeanour, his anger was insensibly mollified by their eloquence and
liberality. He condescended to pardon the emperor, the eunuch, and
the interpreter; bound himself by an oath to observe the conditions of
peace; released a great number of captives; abandoned the fugitives
and deserters to their fate; and resigned a large territory, to the south
of the Danube, which he had already exhausted of its wealth and inhabitants. But this treaty was purchased at an expense which might
have supported a vigorous and successful war; and the subjects of The-

odosius were compelled to redeem the safety of a worthless favourite by oppressive taxes which they would more cheerfully have paid for his destruction.[50]

The emperor Theodosius did not long survive the most humiliating circumstance of an inglorious life. As he was riding or hunting in the neighbourhood of Constantinople, he was thrown from his horse into the river Lycus: the spine of his back was injured by the fall; and he expired some days afterwards, in the fiftieth year of his age, and the forty-third of his reign.[51] His sister Pulcheria, whose authority had been controlled both in civil and ecclesiastical affairs by the pernicious influence of the eunuchs, was unanimously proclaimed empress of the East; and the Romans, for the first time, submitted to a female reign. No sooner had Pulcheria ascended the throne than she indulged her own and the public resentment by an act of popular justice. Without any legal trial, the eunuch Chrysaphius was executed before the gates of the city; and the immense riches which had been accumulated by the rapacious favourite served only to hasten and to justify his punishment.[52] Amidst the general acclamations of the clergy and people, the empress did not forget the prejudice and disadvantage to which her sex was exposed; and she wisely resolved to prevent their murmurs by the choice of a colleague who would always respect the superior rank and virgin chastity of his wife. She gave her hand to Marcian, a senator, about sixty years of age, and the nominal husband of Pulcheria was solemnly invested with the Imperial purple. The zeal which he displayed for the orthodox creed, as it was established by the council of Chalcedon, would alone have inspired the grateful eloquence of the catholics. But the behaviour of Marcian in a private life, and afterwards on the throne, may support a more rational belief that he was qualified to restore and invigorate an empire which had been almost dissolved by the successive weakness of two hereditary monarchs. He was born in Thrace, and educated to the profession of arms; but Marcian's youth had been severely exercised by poverty and misfortune, since his only resource, when he first arrived at Constantinople, consisted in two hundred pieces of gold which he had borrowed of a friend. He passed nineteen years in the domestic and

---

[50] This secret conspiracy, and its important consequences, may be traced in the fragments of Priscus, p. 37, 38, 39, 54, 70, 71, 72 [p. 146-150, 180, 210-214, ed. Bonn]. The chronology of that historian is not fixed by any precise date; but the series of negotiations between Attila and the Eastern empire must be included within the three or four years which are terminated, A.D. 450, by the death of Theodosius.

[51] Theodorus the Reader (see Vales. Hist. Eccles. tom. iii. p. 563) and the Paschal Chronicle mention the fall without specifying the injury; but the consequence was so likely to happen, and so unlikely to be invented, that we may safely give credit to Nicephorus Callistus, a Greek of the fourteenth century.

[52] Pulcheriæ nutû (says Count Marcellinus) suâ cum avaritiâ interemptus est. She abandoned the eunuch to the pious revenge of a son whose father had suffered at his instigation.

military service of Aspar and his son Ardaburius; followed those powerful generals to the Persian and African wars; and obtained, by their influence, the honourable rank of tribune and senator.   His mild disposition and useful talents, without alarming the jealousy, recommended Marcian to the esteem and favour of his patrons; he had seen, perhaps he had felt, the abuses of a venal and oppressive administration; and his own example gave weight and energy to the laws which he promul gated for the reformation of manners.[53]

CHAPTER XXXV (419-455 A.D.)

Invasion of Gaul by Attila—He is repulsed by Aëtius and the Visigoths— Attila invades and evacuates Italy—The Deaths of Attila, Aëtius, and Valentinian the Third

IT was the opinion of Marcian, that war should be avoided as long as it is possible to preserve a secure and honourable peace; but it was likewise his opinion that peace cannot be honourable or secure, if the sovereign betrays a pusillanimous aversion to war.   This temperate courage dictated his reply to the demands of Attila, who insolently pressed the payment of the annual tribute.   The emperor signified to the barbarians that they must no longer insult the majesty of Rome by the mention of a tribute; that he was disposed to reward, with becoming liberality, the faithful friendship of his allies; but that, if they presumed to violate the public peace, they should feel that he possessed troops, and arms, and resolution, to repel their attacks.   The same language, even in the camp of the Huns, was used by his ambassador Apollonius, whose bold refusal to deliver the presents, till he had been admitted to a personal interview, displayed a sense of dignity, and a contempt of danger, which Attila was not prepared to expect from the degenerate Romans.[1]   He threatened to chastise the rash successor of Theodosius; but he hesitated, whether he should first direct his invincible arms against the Eastern or the Western empire.   While mankind awaited his decision with awful suspense, he sent an equal defiance to the courts of Ravenna and Constantinople; and his ministers saluted the two emperors with the same haughty declaration.   "Attila, *my* lord, and *thy* lord, commands thee to provide a palace for his immediate reception." [2]   But as the barbarian

[53] Procopius, de Bell. Vandal. l. i. c. 4 [tom. i. p. 325, *sqq.* ed. Bonn] ; Evagrius, l. ii. c. 1 ; Theophanes, p. 90, 91 [ed. Par.; tom. i. p. 161-164, ed. Bonn] ; Novell. ad Calcem Cod. Theod. tom. vi. p. 30.   The praises which St. Leo and the catholics have bestowed on Marcian are diligently transcribed by Baronius, as an encouragement for future princes.
[1] See Priscus, p. 39, 72 [p. 213, 214, ed. Bonn].
[2] The Alexandrian or Paschal Chronicle, which introduces this haughty message during the lifetime of Theodosius, may have anticipated the date;

despised, or affected to despise, the Romans of the East, whom he had so often vanquished, he soon declared his resolution of suspending the easy conquest till he had achieved a more glorious and important enterprise. In the memorable invasions of Gaul and Italy, the Huns were naturally attracted by the wealth and fertility of those provinces; but the particular motives and provocations of Attila can only be explained by the state of the Western empire under the reign of Valentinian, or, to speak more correctly, under the administration of Aëtius.[3]

After the death of his rival Boniface, Aëtius had prudently retired to the tents of the Huns; and he was indebted to their alliance for his safety and his restoration. Instead of the suppliant language of a guilty exile, he solicited his pardon at the head of sixty thousand barbarians; and the empress Placidia confessed, by a feeble resistance, that the condescension which might have been ascribed to clemency was the effect of weakness or fear. She delivered herself, her son Valentinian, and the Western empire, into the hands of an insolent subject; nor could Placidia protect the son-in-law of Boniface, the virtuous and faithful Sebastian,[4] from the implacable persecution which urged him from one kingdom to another, till he miserably perished in the service of the Vandals. The fortunate Aëtius, who was immediately promoted to the rank of patrician, and thrice invested with the honours of the consulship, assumed, with the title of master of the cavalry and infantry, the whole military power of the state; and he is sometimes styled, by contemporary writers, the duke, or general, of the Romans of the West. His prudence, rather than his virtue, engaged him to leave the grandson of Theodosius in the possession of the purple; and Valentinian was permitted to enjoy the peace and luxury of Italy, while the patrician appeared in the glorious light of a hero and a patriot, who supported near twenty years the ruins of the Western empire. The Gothic historian ingenuously confesses that Aëtius was born for the salvation of the Roman republic;[5] and the following portrait, though it is drawn in the fairest colours, must be

but the dull annalist was incapable of inventing the original and genuine style of Attila.

[3] The second book of the Histoire Critique de l'Etablissement de la Monarchie Françoise, tom. i. p. 189-424, throws great light on the state of Gaul when it was invaded by Attila; but the ingenious author, the Abbé Dubos, too often bewilders himself in system and conjecture.

[4] Victor Vitensis (de Persecut. Vandal. l. i. c. 6, p. 8, edit. Ruinart) calls him, acer consilio et strenuus in bello: but his courage, when he became unfortunate, was censured as desperate rashness; and Sebastian deserved, or obtained, the epithet of *præceps* (Sidon. Apollinar. Carmen ix. 281). His adventures at Constantinople, in Sicily, Gaul, Spain, and Africa, are faintly marked in the Chronicles of Marcellinus and Idatius. In his distress he was always followed by a numerous train; since he could ravage the Hellespont and Propontis and seize the city of Barcelona.

[5] Reipublicæ Romanæ singulariter natus, qui superbiam Suevorum, Francorumque barbariem immensis cœdibus servire Imperio Romano coëgisset. Jornandes de Rebus Geticis, c. 34, p. 660.

allowed to contain a much larger proportion of truth than of flattery.[6] " His mother was a wealthy and noble Italian, and his father Gauden- tius, who held a distinguished rank in the province of Scythia, gradually rose from the station of a military *domestic* to the dignity of master of the cavalry. Their son, who was enrolled almost in his infancy in the guards, was given as a hostage, first to Alaric, and afterwards to the Huns; and he successively obtained the civil and military honours of the palace, for which he was equally qualified by superior merit. The graceful figure of Aëtius was not above the middle stature; but his manly limbs were admirably formed for strength, beauty, and agility; and he excelled in the martial exercises of managing a horse, drawing a bow, and darting the javelin. He could patiently endure the want of food or of sleep; and his mind and body were alike capable of the most laborious efforts. He possessed the genuine courage that can despise not only dangers, but injuries: and it was impossible either to corrupt, or deceive, or intimidate the firm integrity of his soul." [7] The bar- barians, who had seated themselves in the Western provinces, were in- sensibly taught to respect the faith and valour of the patrician Aëtius. He soothed their passions, consulted their prejudices, balanced their interest, and checked their ambition. A seasonable treaty which he concluded with Genseric protected Italy from the depredations of the Vandals; the independent Britons implored and acknowledged his salu- tary aid; the Imperial authority was restored and maintained in Gaul and Spain; and he compelled the Franks and the Suevi, whom he had vanquished in the field, to become the useful confederates of the republic.

From a principle of interest, as well as gratitude, Aëtius assiduously cultivated the alliance of the Huns. While he resided in their tents as an hostage or an exile, he had familiarly conversed with Attila himself, the nephew of his benefactor; and the two famous antagonists appear to have been connected by a personal and military friendship, which they afterwards confirmed by mutual gifts, frequent embassies, and the education of Carpilio, the son of Aëtius, in the camp of Attila. By the specious professions of gratitude and voluntary attachment, the patrician might disguise his apprehensions of the Scythian conqueror, who pressed

[6] [Some valuable fragments of a poetical panegyric on Aëtius by Mero- baudes, a Spaniard, were recovered from a palimpsest MS. by the industry and sagacity of Niebuhr, and were reprinted in the edition of the Byzantine historians. The poet speaks in glowing terms of the long peace enjoyed under the administration of Aëtius. The poet was rewarded by a statue publicly dedicated to his honour in Rome.—O. S.]
[7] This portrait is drawn by Renatus Profuturus Frigeridus, a contem- porary historian, known only by some extracts which are preserved by Gregory of Tours (l. ii. c. 8, in tom. ii. p. 163). It was probably the duty, or at least the interest, of Renatus, to magnify the virtues of Aëtius; but he would have shown more dexterity if he had not insisted on his patient *forgiving* disposition.

the two empires with his innumerable armies. His demands were obeyed or eluded. When he claimed the spoils of a vanquished city, some vases of gold, which had been fraudulently embezzled, the civil and military governors of Noricum were immediately despatched to satisfy his complaints: [8] and it is evident, from their conversation with Maximin and Priscus in the royal village, that the valour and prudence of Aëtius had not saved the Western Romans from the common ignominy of tribute. Yet his dexterous policy prolonged the advantages of a salutary peace; and a numerous army of Huns and Alani, whom he had attached to his person, was employed in the defence of Gaul. Two colonies of these barbarians were judiciously fixed in the territories of Valence and Orleans; [9] and their active cavalry secured the important passages of the Rhône and of the Loire. These savage allies were not indeed less formidable to the subjects than to the enemies of Rome. Their original settlement was enforced with the licentious violence of conquest; and the province through which they marched was exposed to all the calamities of an hostile invasion.[10] Strangers to the emperor or the republic, the Alani of Gaul were devoted to the ambition of Aëtius; and though he might suspect that, in a contest with Attila himself, they would revolt to the standard of their national king, the patrician laboured to restrain, rather than to excite, their zeal and resentment against the Goths, the Burgundians, and the Franks.

The kingdom established by the Visigoths in the southern provinces of Gaul had gradually acquired strength and maturity; and the conduct of those ambitious barbarians, either in peace or war, engaged the perpetual vigilance of Aëtius. After the death of Wallia, the Gothic sceptre

[8] The embassy consisted of Count Romulus; of Promotus, president of Noricum; and of Romanus, the military duke. They were accompanied by Tatullus, an illustrious citizen of Petovio, in the same province, and father of Orestes, who had married the daughter of Count Romulus. See Priscus, p. 57, 65 [p. 185, 198, ed. Bonn]. Cassiodorus (Variar. i. 4) mentions another embassy which was executed by his father and Carpilio, son of Aëtius; and, as Attila was no more, he could safely boast of their manly, intrepid behaviour in his presence.

[9] Deserta Valentinæ urbis rura Alanis partienda traduntur. Prosper. Tyronis Chron. in Historiens de France, tom. i. p. 639. A few lines afterwards, Prosper observes that lands in the *ulterior* Gaul were assigned to the Alani. Without admitting the correction of Dubos (tom. i. p. 300), the reasonable supposition of *two* colonies or garrisons of Alani will confirm his arguments and remove his objections.

[10] See Prosper, Tyro, p. 639. Sidonius (Panegyr. Avit. 246) complains, in the name of Auvergne, his native country—

Litorius Scythicos equites tunc forte, subacto
Celsus Aremorico, Geticum rapiebat in agmen
Per terras, Arverne, tuas: qui proxima quæque
Discursu, flammis, ferro, feritate, rapinis,
Delebant; pacis fallentes nomen inane.

Another poet, Paulinus of Perigord, confirms the complaint:

Nam socium vix ferre queas, qui durior hoste.
See Dubos, tom. i. p. 330.

devolved to Theodoric, the son of the great Alaric; [11] and his prosperous reign of more than thirty years over a turbulent people may be allowed to prove that his prudence was supported by uncommon vigour, both of mind and body. Impatient of his narrow limits, Theodoric aspired to the possession of Arles, the wealthy seat of government and commerce; but the city was saved by the timely approach of Aëtius; and the Gothic king, who had raised the siege with some loss and disgrace, was persuaded, for an adequate subsidy, to divert the martial valour of his subjects in a Spanish war. Yet Theodoric still watched, and eagerly seized, the favourable moment of renewing his hostile attempts. The Goths besieged Narbonne, while the Belgic provinces were invaded by the Burgundians; and the public safety was threatened on every side by the apparent union of the enemies of Rome. On every side, the activity of Aëtius and his Scythian cavalry opposed a firm and successful resistance. Twenty thousand Burgundians were slain in battle; and the remains of the nation humbly accepted a dependent seat in the mountains of Savoy.[12] The walls of Narbonne had been shaken by the battering engines, and the inhabitants had endured the last extremities of famine, when Count Litorius, approaching in silence, and directing each horseman to carry behind him two sacks of flour, cut his way through the entrenchments of the besiegers. The siege was immediately raised; and the more decisive victory, which is ascribed to the personal conduct of Aëtius himself, was marked with the blood of eight thousand Goths. But in the absence of the patrician, who was hastily summoned to Italy by some public or private interest, Count Litorius succeeded to the command; and his presumption soon discovered that far different talents are required to lead a wing of cavalry, or to direct the operations of an important war. At the head of an army of Huns, he rashly advanced to the gates of Toulouse, full of careless contempt for an enemy whom his misfortunes had rendered prudent, and his situation made desperate. The predictions of the augurs had inspired Litorius with the profane confidence that he should enter the Gothic capital in triumph; and the trust which he reposed in his Pagan allies encouraged him to reject the fair conditions of peace which were repeatedly proposed by the bishops

[11] Theodoric II., the son of Theodoric I., declares to Avitus his resolution of repairing, or expiating, the fault which his *grandfather* had committed.

Quæ *noster,* peccavit *avus,* quem fuscat id unum,
Quod te, Roma, capit.

Sidon. Panegyric. Avit. 505.

This character, applicable only to the great Alaric, establishes the genealogy of the Gothic kings, which has hitherto been unnoticed.

[12] The name of *Sapaudia,* the origin of *Savoy,* is first mentioned by Ammianus Marcellinus [l. xv. c. 11]; and two military posts are ascertained by the Notitia within the limits of that province; a cohort was stationed at Grenoble in Dauphiné; and Ebredunum, or Iverdun, sheltered a fleet of small vessels which commanded the lake of Neufchâtel. See Valesius, Notit. Galliarum, p. 503. D'Anville, Notice de l'Ancienne Gaule, p. 284, 579.

in the name of Theodoric. The king of the Goths exhibited in his distress the edifying contrast of Christian piety and moderation; nor did he lay aside his sackcloth and ashes till he was prepared to arm for the combat. His soldiers, animated with martial and religious enthusiasm, assaulted the camp of Litorius. The conflict was obstinate; the slaughter was mutual. The Roman general, after a total defeat, which could be imputed only to his unskilful rashness, was actually led through the streets of Toulouse, not in his own, but in an hostile triumph; and the misery which he experienced, in a long and ignominious captivity, excited the compassion of the barbarians themselves.[13] Such a loss, in a country whose spirit and finances were long since exhausted, could not easily be repaired; and the Goths, assuming, in their turn, the sentiments of ambition and revenge, would have planted their victorious standards on the banks of the Rhône, if the presence of Aëtius had not restored strength and discipline to the Romans.[14] The two armies expected the signal of a decisive action; but the generals, who were conscious of each other's force, and doubtful of their own superiority, prudently sheathed their swords in the field of battle; and their reconciliation was permanent and sincere. Theodoric, king of the Visigoths, appears to have deserved the love of his subjects, the confidence of his allies, and the esteem of mankind. His throne was surrounded by six valiant sons, who were educated with equal care in the exercises of the barbarian camp, and in those of the Gallic schools: from the study of the Roman jurisprudence they acquired the theory, at least, of law and justice; and the harmonious sense of Virgil contributed to soften the asperity of their native manners.[15] The two daughters of the Gothic king were given in marriage to the eldest sons of the kings of the Suevi and of the Vandals, who reigned in Spain and Africa; but these illustrious alliances were pregnant with guilt and discord. The queen of the

---

[13] Salvian has attempted to explain the moral government of the Deity; a task which may be readily performed by supposing that the calamities of the wicked are *judgments,* and those of the righteous, *trials.*

[14] ———— Capto terrarum damna patebant
Litorio: in Rhodanum proprios producere fines,
Theudoridæ fixum; nec erat pugnare necesse,
Sed migrare Getis. Rabidam trux asperat iram
Victor; quôd sensit Scythicum sub mœnibus hostem
Imputat, et nihil est gravius, si forsitan unquam
Vincere contingat, trepido.
                                                    Panegyr. Avit. 300, etc.
Sidonius then proceeds, according to the duty of a panegyrist, to transfer the whole merit from Aëtius to his minister Avitus.

[15] Theodoric II. revered, in the person of Avitus, the character of his preceptor.
                    ———— Mihi Romula dudum
Per te jura placent; parvumque ediscere jussit
Ad tua verba pater, docili quo prisca *Maronis*
Carmine molliret Scythicos mihi pagina mores.
                                                    Sidon. Panegyric. Avit. 495, etc.

Suevi bewailed the death of an husband, inhumanly massacred by her brother. The princess of the Vandals was the victim of a jealous tyrant, whom she called her father. The cruel Genseric suspected that his son's wife had conspired to poison him; the supposed crime was punished by the amputation of her nose and ears; and the unhappy daughter of Theodoric was ignominiously returned to the court of Toulouse in that deformed and mutilated condition. This horrid act, which must seem incredible to a civilised age, drew tears from every spectator; but Theodoric was urged, by the feelings of a parent and a king, to revenge such irreparable injuries. The Imperial ministers, who always cherished the discord of the barbarians, would have supplied the Goths with arms, and ships, and treasures, for the African war; and the cruelty of Genseric might have been fatal to himself, if the artful Vandal had not armed, in his cause, the formidable power of the Huns. His rich gifts and pressing solicitations inflamed the ambition of Attila; and the designs of Aëtius and Theodoric were prevented by the invasion of Gaul.[16]

The Franks, whose monarchy was still confined to the neighbourhood of the Lower Rhine, had wisely established the right of hereditary succession in the noble family of the Merovingians.[17] These princes were elevated on a buckler, the symbol of military command; [18] and the royal fashion of long hair was the ensign of their birth and dignity. Their flaxen locks, which they combed and dressed with singular care, hung down in flowing ringlets on their back and shoulders; while the rest of the nation were obliged, either by law or custom, to shave the hinder part of their head, to comb their hair over the forehead, and to content themselves with the ornament of two small whiskers.[19] The lofty stature

[16] Our authorities for the reign of Theodoric I. are, Jornandes de Rebus Geticis, c. 34, 36, and the Chronicles of Idatius and the two Prospers, inserted in the Historians of France, tom. i. p. 612-640. To these we may add Salvian de Gubernatione Dei, l. vii. p. 243, 244, 245, and the Panegyric of Avitus by Sidonius.

[17] Reges Crinitos [super] se creavisse de primâ, et ut ita dicam, nobiliori suorum familiâ (Greg. Turon. l. ii. c. 9, p. 166, of the second volume of the Historians of France). Gregory himself does not mention the Merovingian name, which may be traced, however, to the beginning of the seventh century, as the distinctive appellation of the royal family, and even of the French monarchy. An ingenious critic has deduced the Merovingians from the great Maroboduus; and he has clearly proved that the prince who gave his name to the first race was more ancient than the father of Childeric. See Mémoires de l'Académie des Inscriptions, tom. xx. p. 52-90, tom. xxx. p. 557-587.

[18] This German custom, which may be traced from Tacitus to Gregory of Tours, was at length adopted by the emperors of Constantinople. From a MS. of the tenth century, Montfaucon has delineated the representation of a similar ceremony, which the ignorance of the age had applied to king David. See Monumens de la Monarchie Françoise, tom. i. Discours Préliminaire.

[19] Cæsaries prolixa . . . crinium flagellis per terga dismissis, etc. See the Preface to the third volume of the Historians of France and the Abbé Le Bœuf (Dissertat. tom. iii. p. 47-79). This peculiar fashion of the Mero-

of the Franks and their blue eyes denoted a Germanic origin; their close apparel accurately expressed the figure of their limbs; a weighty sword was suspended from a broad belt; their bodies were protected by a large shield: and these warlike barbarians were trained from their earliest youth to run, to leap, to swim; to dart the javelin or battle-axe with unerring aim; to advance without hesitation against a superior enemy; and to maintain, either in life or death, the invincible reputation of their ancestors.[20]   Clodion, the first of their long-haired kings whose name and actions are mentioned in authentic history, held his residence at Dispargum,[21] a village or fortress, whose place may be assigned between Louvain and Brussels.   From the report of his spies the king of the Franks was informed that the defenceless state of the second Belgic must yield, on the slightest attack, to the valour of his subjects.   He boldly penetrated through the thickets and morasses of the Carbonarian forest; [22] occupied Tournay and Cambray, the only cities which existed in the fifth century; and extended his conquests as far as the river Somme, over a desolate country whose cultivation and populousness are the effects of more recent industry.[23]   While Clodion lay encamped in the plains of Artois,[24] and celebrated with vain and ostentatious security the marriage perhaps of his son, the nuptial feast was interrupted by the unexpected and unwelcome presence of Aëtius, who had passed the Somme at the head of his light cavalry.   The tables, which had been spread under the shelter of a hill along the banks of a pleasant stream, were rudely overturned; the Franks were oppressed before they could recover their arms or their ranks, and their unavailing valour was fatal

vingians has been remarked by natives and strangers; by Priscus (tom. i. p. 608 [p. 152, ed. Bonn]), by Agathias (tom. ii. p. 49 [l. i. c. 3, p. 19, ed. Bonn]), and by Gregory of Tours (l. iii. 18, vi. 24, viii. 10, tom. ii. p. 196, 278, 316).

[20] See an original picture of the figure, dress, arms, and temper of the ancient Franks, in Sidonius Apollinaris (Panegyr., Majorian. 238-254) ; and such pictures, though coarsely drawn, have a real and intrinsic value.   Father Daniel (Hist. de la Milice Françoise, tom. i. p. 2-7) has illustrated the description.

[21] Dubos, Hist. Critique, etc., tom. i. p. 271, 272.   Some geographers have placed Dispargum on the German side of the Rhine.   See a note of the Benedictine Editors to the Historians of France, tom. ii. p. 166.

[22] The Carbonarian wood was that part of the great forest of the Ardennes which lay between the Escaut, or Scheldt, and the Meuse.   Vales. Notit. Gall. p. 126.

[23] Gregor. Turon, l. ii. c. 9, in tom. ii. p. 166, 167; Fredegar. Epitom. c. 9, p. 395; Gesta Reg. Francor. c. 5, in tom. ii. p. 544; Vit. St. Remig. ab Hincmar, in tom. iii. p. 373.

[24] —— Francus quâ Cloio patentes
Atrebatum terras pervaserat.

                                             Panegyr. Majorian. 212.
The precise spot was a town or village called Vicus *Helena;* and both the name and the place are discovered by modern geographers at Lens.   See Vales. Notit. Gall. p. 246.   Longuerue, Description de la France, tom. ii. p. 88.

only to themselves. The loaded waggons which had followed their march afforded a rich booty; and the virgin-bride with her female attendants submitted to the new lovers who were imposed on them by the chance of war. This advantage, which had been obtained by the skill and activity of Aëtius, might reflect some disgrace on the military prudence of Clodion; but the king of the Franks soon regained his strength and reputation, and still maintained the possession of his Gallic kingdom from the Rhine to the Somme.[25] Under his reign. and most probably from the enterprising spirit of his subjects, the three capitals, Mentz, Trèves, and Cologne, experienced the effects of hostile cruelty and avarice. The distress of Cologne was prolonged by the perpetual dominion of the same barbarians who evacuated the ruins of Trèves, and Trèves, which in the space of forty years had been four times besieged and pillaged, was disposed to lose the memory of her afflictions in the vain amusements of the circus.[26] The death of Clodion, after a reign of twenty years, exposed his kingdom to the discord and ambition of his two sons. Meroveus, the younger,[27] was persuaded to implore the protection of Rome; he was received at the Imperial court as the ally of Valentinian and the adopted son of the patrician Aëtius, and dismissed to his native country with splendid gifts and the strongest assurances of friendship and support. During his absence his elder brother had solicited with equal ardour the formidable aid of Attila; and the king of the Huns embraced an alliance which facilitated the passage of the Rhine, and justified by a specious and honourable pretence the invasion of Gaul.[28]

When Attila declared his resolution of supporting the cause of his

[25] See a vague account of the action in Sidonius, Panegyr. Majorian. 212-230. The French critics, impatient to establish their monarchy in Gaul, have drawn a strong argument from the silence of Sidonius, who dares not insinuate that the vanquished Franks were compelled to repass the Rhine. Dubos, tom. i. p. 322.

[26] Salvian (de Gubernat. Dei. l. vi.) has expressed, in vague and declamatory language, the misfortunes of these three cities, which are distinctly ascertained by the learned Mascou, Hist. of the Ancient Germans, ix. 21.

[27] Priscus in relating the contest does not name the two brothers; the second of whom he had seen at Rome, a beardless youth, with long flowing hair (Historians of France, tom. i. p. 607, 608 [p. 152, ed. Bonn]). The Benedictine Editors are inclined to believe that they were the sons of some unknown king of the Franks who reigned on the banks of the Neckar; but the arguments of M. de Foncemagne (Mém. de l'Académie, tom. viii. p. 464) seem to prove that the succession of Clodion was disputed by his two sons, and that the younger was Meroveus, the father of Childeric.
[What the relation was of Meroveus to Clodion is extremely doubtful. By some writers he is spoken of as a son, by others as an illegitimate son, by a third set as merely belonging to his race. Cf. Sismondi *Histoire des Français*, i. 117.—O. S.]

[28] Under the Merovingian race the throne was hereditary; but all the sons of the deceased monarch were equally entitled to their share of his treasures and territories. See the Dissertations of M. de Foncemagne, in the sixth and eighth volumes of the Mémoires de l'Académie.

allies the Vandals and the Franks, at the same time, and almost in the spirit of romantic chivalry, the savage monarch professed himself the lover and the champion of the princess Honoria. The sister of Valentinian was educated in the palace of Ravenna; and as her marriage might be productive of some danger to the state, she was raised, by the title of *Augusta*,[29] above the hopes of the most presumptuous subject. But the fair Honoria had no sooner attained the sixteenth year of her age than she detested the importunate greatness which must for ever exclude her from the comforts of honourable love: in the midst of vain and unsatisfactory pomp Honoria sighed, yielded to the impulse of nature, and threw herself into the arms of her chamberlain Eugenius. Her guilt and shame (such is the absurd language of imperious man) were soon betrayed by the appearances of pregnancy: but the disgrace of the royal family was published to the world by the imprudence of the empress Placidia, who dismissed her daughter, after a strict and shameful confinement, to a remote exile at Constantinople. The unhappy princess passed twelve or fourteen years in the irksome society of the sisters of Theodosius and their chosen virgins, to whose *crown* Honoria could no longer aspire, and whose monastic assiduity of prayer, fasting, and vigils she reluctantly imitated. Her impatience of long and hopeless celibacy urged her to embrace a strange and desperate resolution. The name of Attila was familiar and formidable at Constantinople, and his frequent embassies entertained a perpetual intercourse between his camp and the Imperial palace. In the pursuit of love, or rather of revenge, the daughter of Placidia sacrificed every duty and every prejudice, and offered to deliver her person into the arms of a barbarian of whose language she was ignorant, whose figure was scarcely human, and whose religion and manners she abhorred. By the ministry of a faithful eunuch she transmitted to Attila a ring, the pledge of her affection, and earnestly conjured him to claim her as a lawful spouse to whom he had been secretly betrothed. These indecent advances were received, however, with coldness and disdain; and the king of the Huns continued to multiply the number of his wives till his love was awakened by the more forcible passions of ambition and avarice. The invasion of Gaul was preceded and justified by a formal demand of the princess Honoria, with a just and equal share of the Imperial patrimony. His predecessors, the ancient Tanjous, had often addressed in the same hostile and peremptory manner the daughters of China; and the pretensions of Attila were not less offensive to the majesty of Rome. A firm but temperate refusal was communicated to his ambassadors. The right of female succession, though it might derive a specious argu-

---

[29] A medal is still extant which exhibits the pleasing countenance of Honoria, with the title of Augusta; and on the reverse, the improper legend of *Salus Reipublicæ* round the monogram of Christ. See Ducange, Famil. Byzantin. p. 67, 73.

ment from the recent examples of Placidia and Pulcheria, was strenuously denied, and the indissoluble engagements of Honoria were opposed to the claims of her Scythian lover.[30]   On the discovery of her
connection with the king of the Huns, the guilty princess had been sent
away, as an object of horror, from Constantinople to Italy: her life was
spared, but the ceremony of her marriage was performed with some obscure and nominal husband before she was immured in a perpetual
prison, to bewail those crimes and misfortunes which Honoria might have
escaped had she not been born the daughter of an emperor.[31]

A native of Gaul and a contemporary, the learned and eloquent Sidonius, who was afterwards bishop of Clermont, had made a promise to
one of his friends that he would compose a regular history of the war
of Attila. If the modesty of Sidonius had not discouraged him from the
prosecution of this interesting work,[32] the historian would have related
with the simplicity of truth those memorable events to which the poet,
in vague and doubtful metaphors, has concisely alluded.[33]   The kings
and nations of Germany and Scythia, from the Volga perhaps to the
Danube, obeyed the warlike summons of Attila.   From the royal village
in the plains of Hungary his standard moved towards the West, and
after a march of seven or eight hundred miles he reached the conflux
of the Rhine and the Neckar, where he was joined by the Franks who
adhered to his ally, the elder of the sons of Clodion.   A troop of light
barbarians who roamed in quest of plunder might choose the winter for
the convenience of passing the river on the ice, but the innumerable
cavalry of the Huns required such plenty of forage and provisions as
could be procured only in a milder season; the Hercynian forest supplied
materials for a bridge of boats, and the hostile myriads were poured with

[30] See Priscus, p. 39, 40 [p. 151, 152, ed. Bonn]. It might be fairly alleged
that, if females could succeed to the throne, Valentinian himself, who had
married the daughter and heiress of the younger Theodosius, would have
asserted her right to the Eastern empire.
[31] The adventures of Honoria are imperfectly related by Jornandes, de
Successione Regn. c. 97, and de Reb. Get. c. 42, p. 674; and in the Chronicles
of Prosper and Marcellinus; but they cannot be made consistent or probable, unless we separate, by an interval of time and place, her intrigue with
Eugenius and her invitation of Attila.
[32] Exegeras mihi, ut promitterem tibi Attilæ bellum stylo me posteris in-
timaturum . . . cœperam   scribere,   sed   operis   arrepti   fasce   perspecto,
tæduit inchoasse.   Sidon. Apoll. l. viii. Epist. 15, p. 246.
[33] ――――― Subito cum rupta tumultu
Barbaries totas in te transfuderat Arctos,
Gallia.   Pugnacem Rugum comitante Gelono,
Gepida trux sequitur; Scyrum Burgundio cogit:
Chunus, Bellonotus, Neurus, Basterna, *Toringus,*
Bructerus, ulvosâ vel quem Nicer abluit undâ
Prorumpit Francus.   Cecidit cito secta bipenni
Hercynia in lintres, et Rhenum texuit alno.
Et jam terrificis diffuderat Attila turmis
In campos, se, Belga, tuos.
                                                                    Panegyr. Avit. 319, etc.

resistless violence into the Belgic provinces.[34]   The consternation of Gaul was universal, and the various fortunes of its cities have been adorned by tradition with martyrdoms and miracles.[35]   Troyes was saved by the merits of St. Lupus; St. Servatius was removed from the world that he might not behold the ruin of Tongres; and the prayers of St. Genevieve diverted the march of Attila from the neighbourhood of Paris. But as the greatest part of the Gallic cities were alike destitute of saints and soldiers, they were besieged and stormed by the Huns, who practised, in the example of Metz,[36] their customary maxims of war. They involved in a promiscuous massacre the priests who served at the altar and the infants who, in the hour of danger, had been providently baptised by the bishop; the flourishing city was delivered to the flames, and a solitary chapel of St. Stephen marked the place where it formerly stood.   From the Rhine and the Moselle, Attila advanced into the heart of Gaul, crossed the Seine at Auxerre, and after a long and laborious march fixed his camp under the walls of Orleans.   He was desirous of securing his conquests by the possession of an advantageous post which commanded the passage of the Loire; and he depended on the secret invitation of Sangiban, king of the Alani, who had promised to betray the city and to revolt from the service of the empire.   But this treacherous conspiracy was detected and disappointed: Orleans had been strengthened with recent fortifications, and the assaults of the Huns were vigorously repelled by the faithful valour of the soldiers or citizens who defended the place.   The pastoral diligence of Anianus, a bishop of primitive sanctity and consummate prudence, exhausted every art of religious policy to support their courage till the arrival of

[34] The most authentic and circumstantial account of this war is contained in Jornandes (de Reb. Geticis, c. 36-41, p. 662-672), who has sometimes abridged, and sometimes transcribed, the larger history of Cassiodorus. Jornandes, a quotation which it would be superfluous to repeat, may be corrected and illustrated by Gregory of Tours, l. ii. c. 5, 6, 7, and the Chronicles of Idatius, Isidore, and the two Prospers.   All the ancient testimonies are collected and inserted in the Historians of France; but the reader should be cautioned against a supposed extract from the Chronicle of Idatius (among the fragments of Fredegarius, tom. ii. p. 462), which often contradicts the genuine text of the Gallician bishop.

[35] The *ancient* legendaries deserve some regard, as they are obliged to connect their fables with the real history of their own times. See the Lives of St. Lupus, St. Anianus, the bishops of Metz, Ste. Genevieve, etc., in the Historians of France, tom. i. p. 644, 645, 649, tom. iii. p. 369.

[36] The scepticism of the Count de Buat (Hist. des Peuples, tom. vii. p. 539, 540) cannot be reconciled with any principles of reason or criticism.   Is not Gregory of Tours precise and positive in his account of the destruction of Metz?   At the distance of no more than an hundred years could he be ignorant, could the people be ignorant of the fate of a city, the actual residence of his sovereigns, the kings of Austrasia?   The learned Count, who seems to have undertaken the apology of Attila and the barbarians, appeals to the false Idatius, *parcens* civitatibus Germaniæ et Galliæ, and forgets that the true Idatius had explicitly affirmed, plurimæ civitates *effractæ,* among which he enumerates Metz.

the expected succours. After an obstinate siege the walls were shaken by the battering rams; the Huns had already occupied the suburbs, and the people who were incapable of bearing arms lay prostrate in prayer. Anianus, who anxiously counted the days and hours, despatched a trusty messenger to observe from the rampart the face of the distant country. He returned twice without any intelligence that could inspire hope or comfort; but in his third report he mentioned a small cloud which he had faintly descried at the extremity of the horizon. " It is the aid of God! " exclaimed the bishop in a tone of pious confidence; and the whole multitude repeated after him " It is the aid of God." The remote object, on which every eye was fixed, became each moment larger and more distinct; the Roman and Gothic banners were gradually perceived; and a favourable wind, blowing aside the dust, discovered, in deep array, the impatient squadrons of Aëtius and Theodoric, who pressed forwards to the relief of Orleans.

The facility with which Attila had penetrated into the heart of Gaul may be ascribed to his insidious policy as well as to the terror of his arms. His public declarations were skilfully mitigated by his private assurances; he alternately soothed and threatened the Romans and the Goths; and the courts of Ravenna and Toulouse, mutually suspicious of each other's intentions, beheld with supine indifference the approach of their common enemy. Aëtius was the sole guardian of the public safety; but his wisest measures were embarrassed by a faction which, since the death of Placidia, infested the Imperial palace: the youth of Italy trembled at the sound of the trumpet; and the barbarians, who from fear or affection were inclined to the cause of Attila, awaited with doubtful and venal faith the event of the war. The patrician passed the Alps at the head of some troops whose strength and numbers scarcely deserved the name of an army.[37] But on his arrival at Arles or Lyons he was confounded by the intelligence that the Visigoths, refusing to embrace the defence of Gaul, had determined to expect within their own territories the formidable invader whom they professed to despise. The senator Avitus, who after the honourable exercise of the Prætorian præfecture had retired to his estate in Auvergne, was persuaded to accept the important embassy, which he executed with ability and success. He represented to Theodoric that an ambitious conqueror who aspired to the dominion of the earth could be resisted only by the firm and unanimous alliance of the powers whom he laboured to oppress. The lively eloquence of Avitus inflamed the Gothic warriors by the description of the injuries which their ancestors had suffered from the Huns, whose implacable fury still pursued them from the Danube to the foot of the

[37] ——— Vix liquerat Alpes
Aëtius, tenue, et rarum sine milite ducens
Robur, in auxiliis Geticum male credulus agmen
Incassum propriis præsumens adfore castris.
Panegyr. Avit. 328, etc.

Pyrenees. He strenuously urged that it was the duty of every Christian to save from sacrilegious violation the churches of God and the relics of the saints; that it was the interest of every barbarian who had acquired a settlement in Gaul to defend the fields and vineyards, which were cultivated for his use, against the desolation of the Scythian shepherds. Theodoric yielded to the evidence of truth, adopted the measure at once the most prudent and the most honourable, and declared that as the faithful ally of Aëtius and the Romans he was ready to expose his life and kingdom for the common safety of Gaul.[38] The Visigoths, who at that time were in the mature vigour of their fame and power, obeyed with alacrity the signal of war, prepared their arms and horses, and assembled under the standard of their aged king, who was resolved, with his two eldest sons, Torismond and Theodoric, to command in person his numerous and valiant people. The example of the Goths determined several tribes or nations that seemed to fluctuate between the Huns and the Romans. The indefatigable diligence of the patrician gradually collected the troops of Gaul and Germany, who had formerly acknowledged themselves the subjects or soldiers of the republic, but who now claimed the rewards of voluntary service and the rank of independent allies; the Læti, the Armoricans, the Breones, the Saxons, the Burgundians, the Sarmatians or Alani, the Ripuarians, and the Franks who followed Meroveus as their lawful prince. Such was the various army which, under the conduct of Aëtius and Theodoric, advanced by rapid marches to relieve Orleans, and to give battle to the innumerable host of Attila.[39]

On their approach the king of the Huns immediately raised the siege, and sounded a retreat to recall the foremost of his troops from the pillage of a city which they had already entered.[40] The valour of Attila was always guided by his prudence; and as he foresaw the fatal consequences of a defeat in the heart of Gaul, he repassed the Seine, and expected

[38] The policy of Attila, of Aëtius, and of the Visigoths, is imperfectly described in the Panegyric of Avitus and the thirty-sixth chapter of Jornandes. The poet and the historian were both biased by personal or national prejudices. The former exalts the merit and importance of Avitus; orbis, Avite, salus, etc.! The latter is anxious to show the Goths in the most favourable light. Yet their agreement, when they are fairly interpreted, is a proof of their veracity.

[39] The review of the army of Aëtius is made by Jornandes, c. 36, p. 664, edit. Grot. tom. ii. p. 23, of the Historians of France, with the notes of the Benedictine editor. The *Læti* were a promiscuous race of barbarians, born or naturalised in Gaul; and the Riparii, or *Ripuarii,* derived their name from their posts on the three rivers, the Rhine, the Meuse, and the Moselle; the *Armoricans* possessed the independent cities between the Seine and the Loire. A colony of *Saxons* had been planted in the diocese of Bayeux; the *Burgundians* were settled in Savoy; and the *Breones* were a warlike tribe of Rhætians, to the east of the lake of Constance.

[40] Aurelianensis urbis obsidio, oppugnatio, irruptio, nec direptio. Sidon. Apollin. l. viii. Epist. 15, p. 246. The preservation of Orleans might easily be turned into a miracle, obtained and foretold by the holy bishop.

the enemy in the plains of Châlons, whose smooth and level surface was adapted to the operations of his Scythian cavalry. But in this tumul-tuary retreat the vanguard of the Romans and their allies continually pressed, and sometimes engaged, the troops whom Attila had posted in the rear; the hostile columns, in the darkness of the night and the per-plexity of the roads, might encounter each other without design; and the bloody conflict of the Franks and Gepidæ, in which fifteen thou-sand [41] barbarians were slain, was a prelude to a more general and de-cisive action. The Catalaunian fields [42] spread themselves round Châ-lons, and extend, according to the vague measurement of Jornandes, to the length of one hundred and fifty, and the breadth of one hundred miles, over the whole province, which is entitled to the appellation of a *champaign* country.[43] This spacious plain was distinguished, however, by some inequalities of ground; and the importance of an height which commanded the camp of Attila was understood and disputed by the two generals. The young and valiant Torismond first occupied the sum-mit; the Goths rushed with irresistible weight on the Huns, who laboured to ascend from the opposite side: and the possession of this advantageous post inspired both the troops and their leaders with a fair assurance of victory. The anxiety of Attila prompted him to consult his priests and haruspices. It was reported that, after scrutinising the entrails of vic-tims and scraping their bones, they revealed, in mysterious language, his own defeat, with the death of his principal adversary; and that the barbarian, by accepting the equivalent, expressed his involuntary esteem for the superior merit of Aëtius. But the unusual despondency which seemed to prevail among the Huns engaged Attila to use the expedient, so familiar to the generals of antiquity, of animating his troops by a military oration; and his language was that of a king who had often fought and conquered at their head.[44] He pressed them to consider their past glory, their actual danger, and their future hopes. The same fortune which opened the deserts and morasses of Scythia to their unarmed valour, which had laid so many warlike nations pros-trate at their feet, had reserved the *joys* of this memorable field for

---

[41] The common editions read xcm; but there is some authority of manu-scripts (and almost any authority is sufficient) for the more reasonable number of xvm.

[42] Châlons, or Duro-Catalaunum, afterwards *Catalauni,* had formerly made a part of the territory of Rheims, from whence it is distant only twenty-seven miles. See Vales. Notit. Gall. p. 136; D'Anville, Notice de l'Ancienne Gaule, p. 212, 279.

[43] The name of Campania, or Champagne, is frequently mentioned by Gregory of Tours; and that great province, of which Rheims was the capital, obeyed the command of a duke. Vales. Notit. p. 120-123.

[44] I am sensible that these military orations are usually composed by the historian; yet the old Ostrogoths, who had served under Attila, might repeat his discourse to Cassiodorus; the ideas, and even the expressions, have an original Scythian cast; and I doubt whether an Italian of the sixth century would have thought of the hujus certaminis *gaudia.*

the consummation of their victories. The cautious steps of their enemies, their strict alliance, and their advantageous posts, he artfully
represented as the effects, not of prudence, but of fear. The Visigoths
alone were the strength and nerves of the opposite army, and the Huns
might securely trample on the degenerate Romans, whose close and
compact order betrayed their apprehensions, and who were equally
incapable of supporting the dangers or the fatigues of a day of battle.
The doctrine of predestination, so favourable to martial virtue, was
carefully inculcated by the king of the Huns; who assured his subjects
that the warriors, protected by Heaven, were safe and invulnerable
amidst the darts of the enemy; but that the unerring Fates would
strike their victims in the bosom of inglorious peace. " I myself,"
continued Attila, "will throw the first javelin, and the wretch who
refuses to imitate the example of his sovereign is devoted to inevitable
death." The spirit of the barbarians was rekindled by the presence,
the voice, and the example of their intrepid leader; and Attila, yielding
to their impatience, immediately formed his order of battle. At the
head of his brave and faithful Huns, he occupied in person the centre
of the line. The nations subject to his empire, the Rugians, the
Heruli, the Thuringians, the Franks, the Burgundians, were extended,
on either hand, over the ample space of the Catalaunian fields; the right
wing was commanded by Ardaric, king of the Gepidæ; and the three
valiant brothers who reigned over the Ostrogoths were posted on the
left to oppose the kindred tribes of the Visigoths. The disposition of
the allies was regulated by a different principle. Sangiban, the faithless
king of the Alani, was placed in the centre: where his motions might
be strictly watched, and his treachery might be instantly punished.
Aëtius assumed the command of the left, and Theodoric of the right
wing; while Torismond still continued to occupy the heights which
appear to have stretched on the flank, and perhaps the rear, of the
Scythian army. The nations from the Volga to the Atlantic were
assembled on the plain of Châlons; but many of these nations had
been divided by faction, or conquest, or emigration; and the appearance of similar arms and ensigns, which threatened each other, presented the image of a civil war.

The discipline and tactics of the Greeks and Romans form an
interesting part of their national manners. The attentive study of the
military operations of Xenophon, or Cæsar, or Frederic, when they
are described by the same genius which conceived and executed them,
may tend to improve (if such improvement can be wished) the art
of destroying the human species. But the battle of Châlons can
only excite our curiosity by the magnitude of the object; since it
was decided by the blind impetuosity of barbarians, and has been
related by partial writers, whose civil or ecclesiastical profession secluded them from the knowledge of military affairs. Cassiodorus, however, had familiarly conversed with many Gothic warriors who served

in that memorable engagement; " a conflict," as they informed him,
" fierce, various, obstinate, and bloody; such as could not be paralleled either in the present or in past ages." The number of the
slain amounted to one hundred and sixty-two thousand, or, according
to another account, three hundred thousand persons;[45] and these incredible exaggerations suppose a real and effective loss, sufficient to
justify the historian's remark that whole generations may be swept
away by the madness of kings in the space of a single hour. After
the mutual and repeated discharge of missile weapons, in which the
archers of Scythia might signalise their superior dexterity, the cavalry
and infantry of the two armies were furiously mingled in closer combat.
The Huns, who fought under the eyes of their king, pierced through
the feeble and doubtful centre of the allies, separated their wings from
each other, and wheeling, with a rapid effort, to the left, directed
their whole force against the Visigoths. As Theodoric rode along the
ranks to animate his troops, he received a mortal stroke from the
javelin of Andages, a noble Ostrogoth, and immediately fell from his
horse. The wounded king was oppressed in the general disorder and
trampled under the feet of his own cavalry; and this important death
served to explain the ambiguous prophecy of the haruspices. Attila
already exulted in the confidence of victory, when the valiant Torismond descended from the hills, and verified the remainder of the
prediction. The Visigoths, who had been thrown into confusion by
the flight, or defection, of the Alani, gradually restored their order
of battle; and the Huns were undoubtedly vanquished, since Attila
was compelled to retreat. He had exposed his person with the rashness of a private soldier; but the intrepid troops of the centre had
pushed forwards beyond the rest of the line; their attack was faintly
supported; their flanks were unguarded; and the conquerors of Scythia
and Germany were saved by the approach of the night from a total
defeat. They retired within the circle of waggons that fortified their
camp; and the dismounted squadrons prepared themselves for a defence to which neither their arms nor their temper were adapted. The
event was doubtful: but Attila had secured a last and honourable
resource. The saddles and rich furniture of the cavalry were collected
by his order into a funeral pile; and the magnanimous barbarian had
resolved, if his entrenchments should be forced, to rush headlong into
the flames, and to deprive his enemies of the glory which they might
have acquired by the death or captivity of Attila.[46]

[45] The expressions of Jornandes, or rather of Cassiodorus, are extremely
strong. Bellum atrox, multiplex, immane, pertinax, cui simile nulle usquam
narrat antiquitas: ubi talia gesta referuntur, ut nihil esset quod in vitâ suâ
conspicere potuisset egregius, qui hujus miraculi privaretur aspectû [c. 40,
p. 668]. Dubos (Hist. Critique, tom. i. p. 392, 393) attempts to reconcile the
162,000 of Jornandes with the 300,000 of Idatius and Isidore, by supposing
that the larger number included the total destruction of the war, the effects
of disease, the slaughter of the unarmed people, etc.

[46] The Count de Buat (Hist. des Peuples, etc., tom. vii. p. 554-573), still

But his enemies had passed the night in equal disorder and anxiety. The inconsiderate courage of Torismond was tempted to urge the pursuit, till he unexpectedly found himself, with a few followers, in the midst of the Scythian waggons. In the confusion of a nocturnal combat he was thrown from his horse; and the Gothic prince must have perished like his father, if his youthful strength and the intrepid zeal of his companions had not rescued him from this dangerous situation. In the same manner, but on the left of the line, Aëtius himself, separated from his allies, ignorant of their victory, and anxious for their fate, encountered and escaped the hostile troops that were scattered over the plains of Châlons; and at length reached the camp of the Goths, which he could only fortify with a slight rampart of shields till the dawn of day. The Imperial general was soon satisfied of the defeat of Attila, who still remained inactive within his entrenchments; and when he contemplated the bloody scene, he observed, with secret satisfaction, that the loss had principally fallen on the barbarians. The body of Theodoric, pierced with honourable wounds, was discovered under a heap of the slain: his subjects bewailed the death of their king and father; but their tears were mingled with songs and acclamations, and his funeral rites were performed in the face of a vanquished enemy. The Goths, clashing their arms, elevated on a buckler his eldest son Torismond, to whom they justly ascribed the glory of their success; and the new king accepted the obligation of revenge as a sacred portion of his paternal inheritance. Yet the Goths themselves were astonished by the fierce and undaunted aspect of their formidable antagonist; and their historian has compared Attila to a lion encompassed in his den and threatening his hunters with redoubled fury. The kings and nations who might have deserted his standard in the hour of distress were made sensible that the displeasure of their monarch was the most imminent and inevitable danger. All his instruments of martial music incessantly sounded a loud and animating strain of defiance; and the foremost troops, who advanced to the assault, were checked or destroyed by showers of arrows from every side of the entrenchments. It was determined in a general council of war to besiege the king of the Huns in his camp, to intercept his provisions, and to reduce him to the alternative of a disgraceful treaty or an unequal combat. But the impatience of the barbarians soon disdained these cautious and dilatory measures: and the mature policy of Aëtius was apprehensive that, after the extirpation of the Huns, the republic would be oppressed by the pride and power of the Gothic nation. The patrician exerted the superior ascendant of authority and reason to calm the passions which the son of Theodoric considered as a duty; represented, with seeming affection and real truth, the dangers of absence and delay; and persuaded Torismond to disappoint, by his speedy return, the ambitious designs of his brothers, who

depending on the *false,* and again rejecting the *true,* Idatius, has divided the defeat of Attila into two great battles; the former near Orleans, the latter in Champagne: in the one, Theodoric was slain; in the other, he was revenged.

might occupy the throne and treasures of Toulouse.[47] After the departure of the Goths, and the separation of the allied army, Attila was surprised at the vast silence that reigned over the plains of Châlons: the
suspicion of some hostile stratagem detained him several days within
the circle of his waggons, and his retreat beyond the Rhine confessed
the last victory which was achieved in the name of the Western empire.
Meroveus and his Franks, observing a prudent distance, and magnifying the opinion of their strength by the numerous fires which they
kindled every night, continued to follow the rear of the Huns till they
reached the confines of Thuringia. The Thuringians served in the army
of Attila: they traversed, both in their march and in their return, the
territories of the Franks; and it was perhaps in this war that they
exercised the cruelties which, about fourscore years afterwards, were
revenged by the son of Clovis. They massacred their hostages, as well
as their captives: two hundred young maidens were tortured with
exquisite and unrelenting rage; their bodies were torn asunder by wild
horses, or their bones were crushed under the weight of rolling waggons;
and their unburied limbs were abandoned on the public roads as a prey
to dogs and vultures. Such were those savage ancestors whose imaginary virtues have sometimes excited the praise and envy of civilised
ages![48]

Neither the spirit, nor the forces, nor the reputation of Attila were
impaired by the failure of the Gallic expedition. In the ensuing spring
he repeated his demand of the princess Honoria and her patrimonial
treasures. The demand was again rejeced or eluded; and the indignant
lover immediately took the field, passed the Alps, invaded Italy, and
besieged Aquileia with an innumerable host of barbarians. Those barbarians were unskilled in the methods of conducting a regular siege,
which, even among the ancients, required some knowledge, or at least
some practice, of the mechanic arts. But the labour of many thousand
provincials and captives, whose lives were sacrificed without pity, might
execute the most painful and dangerous work. The skill of the Roman
artists might be corrupted to the destruction of their country. The walls
of Aquileia were assaulted by a formidable train of battering rams,

[47] Jornandes de Rebus Geticis, c. 41, p. 671. The policy of Aëtius and the
behaviour of Torismond are extremely natural; and the patrician, according
to Gregory of Tours (l. ii. c. 7, p. 163), dismissed the prince of the Franks by
suggesting to him a similar apprehension. The false Idatius ridiculously
pretends that Aëtius paid a clandestine nocturnal visit to the kings of the
Huns and of the Visigoths; from each of whom he obtained a bribe of ten
thousand pieces of gold as the price of an undisturbed retreat.

[48] These cruelties, which are passionately deplored by Theodoric, the son
of Clovis (Gregory of Tours, l. iii. c. 10, p. 190), suit the time and circumstances of the invasion of Attila. His residence in Thuringia was long attested by popular tradition; and he is supposed to have assembled a *couroultai*,
or diet, in the territory of Eisenach. See Mascou, ix. 30, who settles with
nice accuracy the extent of ancient Thuringia, and derives its name from
the Gothic tribe of the Thervingi.

movable turrets, and engines that threw stones, darts, and fire;[49] and the monarch of the Huns employed the forcible impulse of hope, fear, emulation, and interest, to subvert the only barrier which delayed the conquest of Italy. Aquileia was at that period one of the richest, the most populous, and the strongest of the maritime cities of the Hadriatic coast. The Gothic auxiliaries, who appear to have served under their native princes, Alaric and Antala, communicated their intrepid spirit; and the citizens still remembered the glorious and successful resistance which their ancestors had opposed to a fierce, inexorable barbarian, who disgraced the majesty of the Roman purple. Three months were consumed without effect in the siege of Aquileia; till the want of provisions and the clamours of his army compelled Attila to relinquish the enterprise, and reluctantly to issue his orders that the troops should strike their tents the next morning, and begin their retreat. But as he rode round the walls, pensive, angry, and disappointed, he observed a stork preparing to leave her nest in one of the towers, and to fly with her infant family towards the country. He seized, with the ready penetration of a statesman, this trifling incident which chance had offered to superstition; and exclaimed, in a loud and cheerful tone, that such a domestic bird, so constantly attached to human society, would never have abandoned her ancient seats unless those towers had been devoted to impending ruin and solitude.[50] The favourable omen inspired an assurance of victory; the siege was renewed, and prosecuted with fresh vigour; a large breach was made in the part of the wall from whence the stork had taken her flight; the Huns mounted to the assault with irresistible fury; and the succeeding generation could scarcely discover the ruins of Aquileia.[51] After this dreadful chastisement, Attila pursued his march; and as he passed, the cities of Altinum, Concordia, and Padua were reduced into heaps of stones and ashes. The inland towns, Vicenza, Verona, and Bergamo, were exposed to the rapacious cruelty of the Huns. Milan and Pavia submitted, without resistance, to the loss of their wealth; and applauded

[49] Machinis constructis, omnibusque tormentorum generibus adhibitis. Jornandes, c. 42, p. 673. In the thirteenth century the Moguls battered the cities of China with large engines constructed by the Mahometans or Christians in their service. which threw stones from 150 to 300 pounds weight. In the defence of their country the Chinese used gunpowder, and even bombs, above an hundred years before they were known in Europe; yet even those celestial, or infernal, arms were insufficient to protect a pusillanimous nation. See Gaubil, Hist. des Mongous, p. 70, 71, 155, 157, etc.

[50] The same story is told by Jornandes and by Procopius (de Bell. Vandal. l. i. c. 4, p. 187, 188 [tom. i. p. 330, ed. Bonn]) : nor is it easy to decide which is the original. But the Greek historian is guilty of an inexcusable mistake in placing the siege of Aquileia *after* the death of Aëtius.

[51] Jornandes, about an hundred years afterwards, affirms that Aquileia was so completely ruined, ita ut vix ejus vestigia, ut appareant, reliquerint. See Jornandes de Reb. Geticis, c. 42, p. 673. Paul. Diacon. l. ii. c. 14, p. 785 [Grot. Hist. Goth.]. Liutprand, Hist. l. iii. c. 2. The name of Aquileia was sometimes applied to Forum Julii (Cividad del Friuli), the more recent capita! of the Venetian province.

the unusual clemency which preserved from the flames the public as well as private buildings, and spared the lives of the captive multitude. The popular traditions of Comum, Turin, or Modena may justly be suspected; yet they concur with more authentic evidence to prove that Attila spread his ravages over the rich plains of modern Lombardy, which are divided by the Po, and bounded by the Alps and Apennine.[52] When he took possession of the royal palace of Milan, he was surprised and offended at the sight of a picture which represented the Cæsars seated on their throne, and the princes of Scythia prostrate at their feet. The revenge which Attila inflicted on this monument of Roman vanity was harmless and ingenious. He commanded a painter to reverse the figures and the attitudes; and the emperors were delineated on the same canvas approaching in a suppliant posture to empty their bags of tributary gold before the throne of the Scythian monarch.[53] The spectators must have confessed the truth and propriety of the alteration; and were perhaps tempted to apply, on this singular occasion, the well-known fable of the dispute between the lion and the man.[54]

It is a saying worthy of the ferocious pride of Attila, that the grass never grew on the spot were his horse had trod. Yet the savage destroyer undesignedly laid the foundations of a republic which revived, in the feudal state of Europe, the art and spirit of a commercial industry. The celebrated name of Venice, or Venetia,[55] was formerly diffused over a large and fertile province of Italy, from the confines of Pannonia to the river Addua, and from the Po to the Rhætian and Julian Alps. Before the irruption of the barbarians, fifty Venetian cities flourished in peace and prosperity: Aquileia was placed in the most conspicuous station: but the ancient dignity of Padua was supported by agriculture and manufactures; and the property of five hundred citizens, who were entitled to

[52] In describing this war of Attila, a war so famous but so imperfectly known, I have taken for my guides two learned Italians who considered the subject with some peculiar advantages: Sigonius, de Imperio Occidentali, l. xiii. in his Works, tom. i. p. 495-502; and Muratori, Annali d'Italia, tom. iv. p. 229-236, 8vo edition.

[53] This anecdote may be found under two different articles (μεδιόλανον and κόρυκος) of the miscellaneous compilation of Suidas.

[54] Leo respondit, humanâ hoc pictum manû:
Videres hominem dejectum, si pingere
Leones scirent.
                      Appendix ad Phædrum, Fab. xxv.
The lion in Phædrus very foolishly appeals from pictures to the amphitheatre; and I am glad to observe that the native taste of La Fontaine (l. iii. fable x.) has omitted this most lame and impotent conclusion.

[55] Paul the Deacon (de Gestis Langobard, l. ii. c. 14 [seqq.], p. 784) describes the provinces of Italy about the end of the eighth century. *Venetia non solum in paucis insulis quas nunc Venetias dicimus, constat; sed ejus terminus a Pannoniæ finibus usque Adduam fluvium protelatur.* The history of that province till the age of Charlemagne forms the first and most interesting part of the Verona Illustrata (p. 1-388), in which the Marquis Scipio Maffei has shown himself equally capable of enlarged views and minute disquisitions.

the equestrian rank, must have amounted, at the strictest computation, to one million seven hundred thousand pounds. Many families of Aquileia, Padua, and the adjacent towns, who fled from the sword of the Huns, found a safe, though obscure, refuge in the neighbouring islands.[56] At the extremity of the Gulf, where the Hadriatic feebly imitates the tides of the ocean, near an hundred small islands are separated by shallow water from the continent, and protected from the waves by several long slips of land, which admit the entrance of vessels through some secret and narrow channels.[57] Till the middle of the fifth century these remote and sequestered spots remained without cultivation, with few inhabitants, and almost without a name. But the manners of the Venetian fugitives, their arts and their government, were gradually formed by their new situation; and one of the epistles of Cassiodorus,[58] which describes their condition about seventy years afterwards, may be considered as the primitive monument of the republic.[59] The minister of Theodoric compares them, in his quaint declamatory style, to waterfowl, who had fixed their nests on the bosom of the waves; and though he allows that the Venetian provinces had formerly contained many noble families, he

[56] This emigration is not attested by any contemporary evidence; but the fact is proved by the event, and the circumstances might be preserved by tradition. The citizens of Aquileia retired to the Isle of Gradus, those of Padua to Rivus Altus, or Rialto, where the city of Venice was afterwards built, etc.

[57] The topography and antiquities of the Venetian islands, from Gradus to Clodia, or Chioggia, are accurately stated in the Dissertatio Chorographica de Italiâ Medii Ævi, p. 151-155.

[58] Cassiodor. Variar. 1. xii. Epist. 24. Maffei (Verona Illustrata, part i. p. 240-254) has translated and explained this curious letter, in the spirit of a learned antiquarian and a faithful subject, who considered Venice as the only legitimate offspring of the Roman republic. He fixes the date of the epistle, and consequently the præfecture, of Cassiodorus, A.D. 523; and the Marquis's authority has the more weight as he had prepared an edition of his works and actually published a dissertation on the true orthography of his name. See Osservazioni Letterarie, tom. ii. p. 290-339.

[59] [Count Figliasi was the first to prove, in his *Memoirs of the Veneti*, that, from the most remote period, this nation, which occupied the country which has since been called the Venetian States, likewise inhabited the islands scattered upon the coast, and that from thence arose the names *Venetia prima* and *secunda*, of which the first applied to the mainland and the second to the islands and lagoons. From the time of the Pelasgi and of the Etrurians, the first Veneti inhabiting a fertile and pleasant country devoted themselves to agriculture; the second, placed in the midst of canals at the mouth of several rivers, conveniently situated with regard to the islands of Greece, as well as the fertile plains of Italy, applied themselves to navigation and commerce. Both submitted to the Romans a short time before the second Punic war; yet it was not till after the victory of Marius over the Cimbri that their country was reduced to a Roman province. Under the emperors, Venetia Prima obtained more than once by its calamities, a place in history. But the maritime province was occupied with fisheries, salt works, and commerce. The Romans have considered the inhabitants of this part as beneath the dignity of history, and have left them in obscurity. They dwelt there until their islands afforded a retreat to their ruined and fugitive compatriots. Cf. Sismondi, *Hist. des Repub. Italiennes*, vol. i. p. 313.—O. S.]

insinuates that they were now reduced by misfortune to the same level of humble poverty. Fish was the common, and almost the universal, food of every rank: their only treasure consisted in the plenty of salt which they extracted from the sea: and the exchange of that commodity, so essential to human life, was substituted in the neighbouring markets to the currency of gold and silver. A people whose habitations might be doubtfully assigned to the earth or water soon became alike familiar with the two elements; and the demands of avarice succeeded to those of necessity. The islanders, who, from Grado to Chiozza, were intimately connected with each other, penetrated into the heart of Italy, by the secure, though laborious, navigation of the rivers and inland canals. Their vessels, which were continually increasing in size and number, visited all the harbours of the Gulf; and the marriage which Venice annually celebrates with the Hadriatic was contracted in her early infancy. The epistle of Cassiodorus, the Prætorian præfect, is addressed to the maritime tribunes; and he exhorts them, in a mild tone of authority, to animate the zeal of their countrymen for the public service, which required their assistance to transport the magazines of wine and oil from the province of Istria to the royal city of Ravenna. The ambiguous office of these magistrates is explained by the tradition, that, in the twelve principal islands, twelve tribunes, or judges, were created by an annual and popular election. The existence of the Venetian republic under the Gothic kingdom of Italy is attested by the same authentic record which annihilates their lofty claim of original and perpetual independence.[60]

The Italians, who had long since renounced the exercise of arms, were surprised, after forty years' peace, by the approach of a formidable barbarian, whom they abhorred as the enemy of their religion as well as of their republic. Amidst the general consternation, Aëtius alone was incapable of fear; but it was impossible that he should achieve alone and unassisted any military exploits worthy of his former renown. The barbarians who had defended Gaul refused to march to the relief of Italy; and the succours promised by the Eastern emperor were distant and doubtful. Since Aëtius, at the head of his domestic troops, still maintained the field, and harassed or retarded the march of Attila, he never showed himself more truly great than at the time when his conduct was blamed by an ignorant and ungrateful people.[61] If the mind of Valen-

[60] See, in the second volume of Amelot de la Houssaie, Histoire du Gouvernement de Venise, a translation of the famous *Squittenio*. This book, which has been exalted far above its merits, is stained in every line with the disingenuous malevolence of party: but the principal evidence, genuine and apocryphal, is brought together, and the reader will easily choose the fair medium.

[61] Sirmond (Not. ad Sidon, Apollin. p. 19) has published a curious passage from the Chronicle of Prosper. Attila, redintegratis viribus, quas in Gallia amiserat, Italiam ingredi per Pannonias intendit; nihil duce nostro Aëtio secundum prioris belli opera prospiciente, etc. He reproaches Aëtius with neglecting to guard the Alps and with a design to abandon Italy; but this rash censure may at least be counterbalanced by the favourable testimonies of Idatius and Isidore.

tinian had been susceptible of any generous sentiments, he would have chosen such a general for his example and his guide. But the timid grandson of Theodosius, instead of sharing the dangers, escaped from the sound, of war; and his hasty retreat from Ravenna to Rome, from an impregnable fortress to an open capital, betrayed his secret intention of abandoning Italy as soon as the danger should approach his Imperial person. This shameful abdication was suspended, however, by the spirit of doubt and delay which commonly adheres to pusillanimous counsels, and sometimes corrects their pernicious tendency. The Western emperor, with the senate and people of Rome, embraced the more salutary resolution of deprecating, by a solemn and suppliant embassy, the wrath of Attila. This important commission was accepted by Avienus, who, from his birth and riches, his consular dignity, the numerous train of his clients, and his personal abilities, held the first rank in the Roman senate. The specious and artful character of Avienus [62] was admirably qualified to conduct a negotiation either of public or private interest: his colleague Trigetius had exercised the Prætorian præfecture of Italy; and Leo, bishop of Rome, consented to expose his life for the safety of his flock. The genius of Leo [63] was exercised and displayed in the public misfortunes; and he has deserved the appellation of *Great* by the successful zeal with which he laboured to establish his opinions and his authority, under the venerable names of orthodox faith and ecclesiastical discipline. The Roman ambassadors were introduced to the tent of Attila, as he lay encamped at the place where the slow-winding Mincius is lost in the foaming waves of the lake Benacus,[64] and trampled, with his Scythian cavalry, the farms of Catullus and Virgil.[65] The barbarian monarch listened with favourable, and even respectful, attention; and the deliverance of Italy was purchased by the immense ransom or dowry of the princess Honoria. The state of his army might facilitate the treaty and

[62] See the original portraits of Avienus and his rival Basilius delineated and contrasted in the epistles (i. 9, p. 22) of Sidonius. He had studied the characters of the two chiefs of the senate; but he attached himself to Basilius as the more solid and disinterested friend.

[63] The character and principles of Leo may be traced in one hundred and forty-one original epistles, which illustrate the ecclesiastical history of his long and busy pontificate, from A.D. 440 to 461. See Dupin, Bibliothèque Ecclésiastique, tom. iii. part ii. p. 120-165.

[64] —— tardis ingens ubi flexibus errat
Mincius, et tenerâ prætexit arundine ripas

.   .   .   .   .

Anne lacus tantos, te Lari maxime, teque
Fluctibus, et fremitu assurgens *Benace* marino.

[65] The Marquis Maffei (Verona Illustrata, part i. p. 95, 129, 221, part ii. p. 2, 6) has illustrated with taste and learning this interesting topography. He places the interview of Attila and St. Leo near Ariolica, or Ardelica, now Peschiera, at the conflux of the lake and river; ascertains the villa of Catullus, in the delightful peninsula of Sirmio, and discovers the Andes of Virgil in the village of Bandes, precisely situate, quâ se subducere colles incipiunt, where the Veronese hills imperceptibly slope down into the plain of Mantua.

hasten his retreat. Their martial spirit was relaxed by the wealth and indolence of a warm climate. The shepherds of the North, whose ordinary food consisted of milk and raw flesh, indulged themselves too freely in the use of bread, of wine, and of meat prepared and seasoned by the arts of cookery; and the progress of disease revenged in some measure the injuries of the Italians.[66] When Attila declared his resolution of carrying his victorious arms to the gates of Rome, he was admonished by his friends, as well as by his enemies, that Alaric had not long survived the conquest of the eternal city. His mind, superior to real danger, was assaulted by imaginary terrors; nor could he escape the influence of superstition, which had so often been subservient to his designs.[67] The pressing eloquence of Leo, his majestic aspect and sacerdotal robes, excited the veneration of Attila for the spiritual father of the Christians. The apparition of the two apostles of St. Peter and St. Paul, who menaced the barbarian with instant death if he rejected the prayer of their successor, is one of the noblest legends of ecclesiastical tradition. The safety of Rome might deserve the interposition of celestial beings; and some indulgence is due to a fable which has been represented by the pencil of Raphael and the chisel of Algardi.[68]

Before the king of the Huns evacuated Italy, he threatened to return more dreadful, and more implacable, if his bride, the princess Honoria, were not delivered to his ambassadors within the term stipulated by the treaty. Yet, in the meanwhile, Attila relieved his tender anxiety, by adding a beautiful maid, whose name was Ildico, to the list of his innumerable wives.[69] Their marriage was celebrated with barbaric pomp and festivity, at his wooden palace beyond the Danube; and the monarch, oppressed with wine and sleep, retired at a late hour from the banquet

[66] Si statim infesto agmine urbem petiissent, prande discrimen esset: sed in Venetiâ quo fere tractu Italia mollissima est, ipsâ soli cœlique clementiâ robur elanguit. Ad hoc panis usû carnisque coctæ, et dulcedine vini mitigatos, etc. This passage of Florus (iii. 3) is still more applicable to the Huns than to the Cimbri, and it may serve as a commentary on the *celestial* plague with which Idatius and Isidore have afflicted the troops of Attila.

[67] The historian Priscus had positively mentioned the effect which this example produced on the mind of Attila. Jornandes, c. 42, p. 673.

[68] The picture of Raphael is in the Vatican; the basso (or perhaps the alto) relievo of Algardi on one of the altars of St. Peter's (see Dubos, Réflexions sur la Poésie et sur la Peinture, tom. i. p. 519, 520). Baronius (Annal. Eccles. A.D. 452, No. 57, 58) bravely sustains the truth of the apparition; which is rejected, however, by the most learned and pious Catholics.

[69] Attila, ut Priscus historicus refert, extinctionis suæ tempore, puellam Ildico nomine, decoram valde, sibi [in] matrimonium post innumerabiles uxores . . . socians. Jornandes, c. 49, p. 683, 684. He afterwards adds (c. 50, p. 686) Filii Attilæ, quorum per licentiam libidinis pœne populus fuit. Polygamy has been established among the Tartars of every age. The rank of plebeian wives is regulated only by their personal charms: and the faded matron prepares, without a murmur, the bed which is destined for her blooming rival But in royal families the daughters of Khans communicate to their sons a prior right of inheritance. See Genealogical History, p. 406, 407, 408.

to the nuptial bed. His attendants continued to respect his pleasures or his repose the greatest part of the ensuing day, till the unusual silence alarmed their fears and suspicions; and, after attempting to awaken Attila by loud and repeated cries, they at length broke into the royal apartment. They found the trembling bride sitting by the bedside, hiding her face with her veil, and lamenting her own danger, as well as the death of the king, who had expired during the night.[70] An artery had suddenly burst: and as Attila lay in a supine posture, he was suffocated by a torrent of blood, which, instead of finding a passage through the nostrils, regurgitated into the lungs and stomach. His body was solemnly exposed in the midst of the plain, under a silken pavilion; and the chosen squadrons of the Huns, wheeling round in measured evolutions, chanted a funeral song to the memory of a hero, glorious in his life, invincible in his death, the father of his people, the scourge of his enemies, and the terror of the world. According to their national custom, the barbarians cut off a part of their hair, gashed their faces with unseemly wounds, and bewailed their valiant leader as he deserved, not with the tears of women, but with the blood of warriors. The remains of Attila were enclosed within three coffins of gold, of silver, and of iron, and privately buried in the night: the spoils of nations were thrown into his grave; the captives who had opened the ground were inhumanly massacred; and the same Huns, who had indulged such excessive grief, feasted, with dissolute and intemperate mirth, about the recent sepulchre of their king. It was reported at Constantinople that, on the fortunate night in which he expired, Marcian beheld in a dream the bow of Attila broken asunder: and the report may be allowed to prove how seldom the image of that formidable barbarian was absent from the mind of a Roman emperor.[71]

The revolution which subverted the empire of the Huns established the fame of Attila, whose genius alone had sustained the huge and disjointed fabric. After his death the boldest chieftains aspired to the rank of kings; the most powerful kings refused to acknowledge a superior; and the numerous sons whom so many various mothers bore to the deceased monarch divided and disputed like a private inheritance the sovereign command of the nations of Germany and Scythia. The bold Ardaric felt and represented the disgrace of this servile partition; and his subjects, the warlike Gepidæ, with the Ostrogoths, under the conduct of three valiant brothers, encouraged their allies to vindicate the

[70] The report of her *guilt* reached Constantinople, where it obtained a very different name; and Marcellinus observes, that the tyrant of Europe was slain in the night by the hand and the knife of a woman. Corneille, who has adapted the genuine account to his tragedy, describes the irruption of blood in forty bombast lines, and Attila exclaims, with ridiculous fury,

———— S'il ne veut s'arrêter (*his blood*),
(Dit-il) on me payera ce qui m'en va coûter.

[71] The curious circumstances of the death and funeral of Attila are related by Jornandes (c. 49, p. 683, 684, 685), and were probably transcribed from Priscus.

rights of freedom and royalty. In a bloody and decisive conflict on the banks of the river Netad in Pannonia, the lance of the Gepidæ, the sword of the Goths, the arrows of the Huns, the Suevic infantry, the light arms of the Heruli, and the heavy weapons of the Alani, encountered or supported each other; and the victory of Ardaric was accompanied with the slaughter of thirty thousand of his enemies. Ellac, the eldest son of Attila, lost his life and crown in the memorable battle of Netad; his early valour had raised him to the throne of the Acatzires, a Scythian people, whom he subdued; and his father, who loved the superior merit, would have envied the death, of Ellac.[72] His brother Dengisich, with an army of Huns still formidable in their flight and ruin, maintained his ground above fifteen years on the banks of the Danube. The palace of Attila, with the old country of Dacia, from the Carpathian hills to the Euxine, became the seat of a new power which was erected by Ardaric, king of the Gepidæ. The Pannonian conquests, from Vienna to Sirmium, were occupied by the Ostrogoths; and the settlements of the tribes who had so bravely asserted their native freedom were irregularly distributed according to the measure of their respective strength. Surrounded and oppressed by the multitude of his father's slaves, the kingdom of Dengisich was confined to the circle of his waggons; his desperate courage urged him to invade the Eastern empire: he fell in battle, and his head, ignominiously exposed in the Hippodrome, exhibited a grateful spectacle to the people of Constantinople. Attila had fondly or superstitiously believed that Irnac, the youngest of his sons, was destined to perpetuate the glories of his race. The character of that prince, who attempted to moderate the rashness of his brother Dengisich, was more suitable to the declining condition of the Huns; and Irnac, with his subject hordes, retired into the heart of the Lesser Scythia. They were soon overwhelmed by a torrent of new barbarians, who followed the same road which their own ancestors had formerly discovered. The *Geougen*, or Avares, whose residence is assigned by the Greek writers to the shores of the ocean, impelled the adjacent tribes; till at length the Igours of the North, issuing from the cold Siberian regions which produce the most valuable furs, spread themselves over the desert as far as the Borysthenes and the Caspian gates, and finally extinguished the empire of the Huns.[73]

Such an event might contribute to the safety of the Eastern empire

[72] See Jornandes, de Rebus Geticis, c. 50, p. 685, 686, 687, 688. His distinction of the national arms is curious and important. Nam ibi admirandum reor fuisse spectaculum, ubi cernere erat cunctis, pugnantem Gothum ense furentem, Gepidam in vulnere suorum cuncta tela frangentem, Suevum pede, Hunnum sagittâ præsumere, Alanum gravi, Herulum, levi, armaturâ, aciem instruere. I am not precisely informed of the situation of the river Netad.

[73] Two modern historians have thrown much new light on the ruin and division of the empire of Attila—M. de Buat, by his laborious and minute diligence (tom. viii. p. 3-31, 68-94) ; and M. de Guignes, by his extraordinary knowledge of the Chinese language and writers. See Hist. des Huns, tom. ii. p. 315-319.

under the reign of a prince who conciliated the friendship, without for-feiting the esteem, of the barbarians. But the emperor of the West, the feeble and dissolute Valentinian, who had reached his thirty-fifth year without attaining the age of reason or courage, abused this apparent security to undermine the foundations of his own throne by the murder of the patrician Aëtius. From the instinct of a base and jealous mind, he hated the man who was universally celebrated as the terror of the bar-barians and the support of the republic; and his new favourite, the eunuch Heraclius, awakened the emperor from the supine lethargy which might be disguised during the life of Placidia [74] by the excuse of filia* piety. The fame of Aëtius, his wealth and dignity, the numerous and martial train of barbarian followers, his powerful dependents who filled the civil offices of the state, and the hopes of his son Gaudentius, who was already contracted to Eudoxia, the emperor's daughter, had raised him above the rank of a subject. The ambitious designs, of which he was secretly accused, excited the fears as well as the resentment of Valentinian. Aëtius himself, supported by the consciousness of his merit, his services, and perhaps his innocence, seems to have maintained a haughty and indiscreet behaviour. The patrician offended his sovereign by an hostile declaration; he aggravated the offence by compelling him to ratify with a solemn oath a treaty of reconciliation and alliance; he pro-claimed his suspicions, he neglected his safety; and from a vain confidence that the enemy whom he despised was incapable even of a manly crime, he rashly ventured his person in the palace of Rome. Whilst he urged, perhaps with intemperate vehemence, the marriage of his son, Valentinian, drawing his sword—the first sword he had ever drawn—plunged it in the breast of a general who had saved his empire: his courtiers and eunuchs ambitiously struggled to imitate their master; and Aëtius, pierced with an hundred wounds, fell dead in the royal presence. Boethius, the Prætorian præfect, was killed at the same moment; and before the event could be divulged, the principal friends of the patrician were summoned to the palace and separately murdered. The horrid deed, palliated by the specious names of justice and necessity, was immediately communi-cated by the emperor to his soldiers, his subjects, and his allies. The nations who were strangers or enemies to Aëtius generously deplored the unworthy fate of a hero; the barbarians who had been attached to his service dissembled their grief and resentment; and the public contempt which had been so long entertained for Valentinian was at once converted into deep and universal abhorrence. Such sentiments seldom pervade the walls of a palace; yet the emperor was confounded by the honest reply of a Roman whose approbation he had not disdained to solicit. " I

[74] Placidia died at Rome, November 27, A.D. 450. She was buried at Ra-venna, where her sepulchre, and even her corpse, seated in a chair of cypress-wood, were preserved for ages. The empress received many compliments from the orthodox clergy; and St. Peter Chrysologus assured her that her zeal for the Trinity had been recompensed by an august trinity of children. See Tillemont, Hist. des Emp. tom. vi. p. 240.

am ignorant, sir, of your motives or provocations; I only know that you have acted like a man who cuts off his right hand with his left." [75]

The luxury of Rome seems to have attracted the long and frequent visits of Valentinian, who was consequently more despised at Rome than in any other part of his dominions. A republican spirit was insensibly revived in the senate, as their authority, and even their supplies, became necessary for the support of his feeble government. The stately demeanour of an hereditary monarch offended their pride, and the pleasures of Valentinian were injurious to the peace and honour of noble families. The birth of the empress Eudoxia was equal to his own, and her charms and tender affection deserved those testimonies of love which her inconstant husband dissipated in vague and unlawful amours. Petronius Maximus, a wealthy senator of the Anician family, who had been twice consul, was possessed of a chaste and beautiful wife: her obstinate resistance served only to irritate the desires of Valentinian, and he resolved to accomplish them either by stratagem or force. Deep gaming was one of the vices of the court; the emperor, who, by chance or contrivance, had gained from Maximus a considerable sum, uncourteously exacted his ring as a security for the debt, and sent it by a trusty messenger to his wife, with an order in her husband's name that she should immediately attend the empress Eudoxia. The unsuspecting wife of Maximus was conveyed in her litter to the Imperial palace; the emissaries of her impatient lover conducted her to a remote and silent bed-chamber; and Valentinian violated, without remorse, the laws of hospitality. Her tears when she returned home, her deep affliction, and the bitter reproaches against a husband whom she considered as the accomplice of his own shame, excited Maximus to a just revenge; the desire of revenge was stimulated by ambition; and he might reasonably aspire, by the free suffrage of the Roman senate, to the throne of a detested and despicable rival. Valentinian, who supposed that every human breast was devoid like his own of friendship and gratitude, had imprudently admitted among his guards several domestics and followers of Aëtius. Two of these, of barbarian race, were persuaded to execute a sacred and honourable duty by punishing with death the assassin of their patron; and their intrepid courage did not long expect a favourable moment. Whilst Valentinian amused himself in the field of Mars with the spectacle of some military sports, they suddenly rushed upon him with drawn weapons, despatched the guilty Heraclius, and stabbed the emperor to the heart, without the least opposition from his numerous train, who seemed to rejoice in the tyrant's death. Such was the fate of Valentinian the Third,[76] the last Roman

---

[75] Aëtium Placidus mactavit semivir amens, is the expression of Sidonius (Panegyr. Avit. 359). The poet knew the world, and was not inclined to flatter a minister who had injured or disgraced Avitus and Majorian, the successive heroes of his song.

[76] With regard to the cause and circumstances of the deaths of Aëtius and Valentinian, our information is dark and imperfect. Procopius (de Bell. Vandal. l. i. c. 4, p. 186, 187, 188 [tom. i. p. 327-331, ed. Bonn]) is a fabulous

emperor of the family of Theodosius. He faithfully imitated the hered·
itary weakness of his cousin and his two uncles, without inheriting the
gentleness, the purity, the innocence, which alleviate in their characters
the want of spirit and ability. Valentinian was less excusable, since he
had passions without virtues: even his religion was questionable; and
though he never deviated into the paths of heresy, he scandalised the
pious Christians by his attachment to the profane arts of magic and
divination.

As early as the time of Cicero and Varro it was the opinion of the
Roman augurs that the *twelve vultures* which Romulus had seen, represented the *twelve centuries* assigned for the fatal period of his c'ty.[77]
This prophecy, disregarded perhaps in the season of health and prosperity,
inspired the people with gloomy apprehensions when the twelfth century,
clouded with disgrace and misfortune, was almost elapsed;[78] and even
posterity must acknowledge with some surprise that the arbitrary interpretation of an accidental or fabulous circumstance has been seriously
verified in the downfall of the Western empire. But its fall was announced by a clearer omen than the flight of vultures: the Roman government appeared every day less formidable to its enemies, more odious
and oppressive to its subjects.[79] The taxes were multiplied with the public
distress; economy was neglected in proportion as it became necessary;
and the injustice of the rich shifted the unequal burden from themselves
to the people, whom they defrauded of the *indulgences* that might sometimes have alleviated their misery. The severe inquisition, wh'ch confiscated their goods and tortured their persons, compelled the subjects of
Valentinian to prefer the more simple tyranny of the barbarians, to fly
to the woods and mountains, or to embrace the vile and abject condition

writer for the events which precede his own memory. His narrative must
therefore be supplied and corrected by five or six Chronicles, none of which
were composed in Rome or Italy, and which can only express, in broken
sentences, the popular rumours as they were conveyed to Gaul, Spain, Africa,
Constantinople, or Alexandria.

[77] This interpretation of Vettius, a celebrated augur, was quoted by Varro
in the xviiith book of his Antiquities. Censorinus, de Die Natali, c. 17, p. 90,
91, edit. Havercamp.

[78] According to Varro, the twelfth century would expire A.D. 447; but the
uncertainty of the true era of Rome might allow some latitude of anticipation or delay. The poets of the age, Claudian (de Bell. Getico, 265) and
Sidonius (in Panegyr. Avit. 357), may be admitted as fair witnesses of the
popular opinion.

> Tunc reputant annos, interceptoque volatû
> Vulturis, incidunt properatis sæcula metis.
>
> .   .   .   .   .
>
> Jam prope fata tui bissenas Vulturis alas
> Implebant; scis namque tuos, scis, Roma, labores.

See Dubos, Hist. Critique, tom. i. p. 340-346.

[79] The fifth book of Salvian is filled with pathetic lamentations and vehement
invectives. His immoderate freedom serves to prove the weakness, as well
as the corruption, of the Roman government. His book was published after
the loss of Africa (A.D. 439), and before Attila's war (A.D. 451).

of mercenary servants.   They abjured and abhorred the name of Roman
citizens, which had formerly excited the ambition of mankind.   The
Armorican provinces of Gaul and the greatest part of Spain were thrown
into a state of disorderly independence by the confederations of the
Bagaudæ, and the Imperial ministers pursued with proscriptive laws and
ineffectual arms the rebels whom they had made.[80]   If all the barbarian
conquerors had been annihilated in the same hour, their total destruction
would not have restored the empire of the West: and if Rome still survived, she survived the loss of freedom, of virtue, and of honour.

CHAPTER XXXVI (439-490 A.D.)

*Sack of Rome by Genseric, King of the Vandals—His Naval Depredations
—Succession of the last Emperors of the West, Maximus, Avitus,
Majorian, Severus, Anthemius, Olybrius, Glycerius, Nepos, Augustulus—
Total Extinction of the Western Empire—Reign of Odoacer, the first
Barbarian King of Italy*

THE loss or desolation of the provinces from the Ocean to the Alps impaired the glory and greatness of Rome: her internal prosperity was
irretrievably destroyed by the separation of Africa.   The rapacious Vandals confiscated the patrimonial estates of the senators, and intercepted
the regular subsidies which relieved the poverty and encouraged the
idleness of the plebeians.   The distress of the Romans was soon aggravated by an unexpected attack; and the province, so long cultivated for
their use by industrious and obedient subjects, was armed against them
by an ambitious barbarian.   The Vandals and Alani, who followed the
successful standard of Genseric, had acquired a rich and fertile territory, which stretched along the coast above ninety days' journey from
Tangier to Tripoli; but their narrow limits were pressed and confined,
on either side, by the sandy desert and the Mediterranean.   The discovery and conquest of the Black nations, that might dwell beneath
the torrid zone, could not tempt the rational ambition of Genseric; but
he cast his eyes towards the sea; he resolved to create a naval power,
and his bold resolution was executed with steady and active perseverance.   The woods of Mount Atlas afforded an inexhaustible nursery

[80] The Bagaudæ of Spain, who fought pitched battles with the Roman troops,
are repeatedly mentioned in the Chronicle of Idatius.   Salvian has described
their distress and rebellion in very forcible language.   Itaque nomen civium
Romanorum . . . nunc ultro repudiatur ac fugitur, nec vile tamen [tantum]
sed etiam abominabile pœne habetur . . . Et hinc est ut etiam hi qui ad barbaros non confugiunt, barbari tamen esse coguntur, scilicet ut est pars magna
Hispanorum, et non minima Gallorum . . . De Bagaudis nunc mihi sermo est,
qui per malos judices et cruentos spoliati, afflicti, necati postquam jus Romanæ
libertatis amiserant, etiam honorem Romani nominis perdiderunt . . . Vocamus
rebelles, vocamus perditos quos esse compulimus criminosos.   De Gubernat.
Dei, l. v. p. 158, 159.

of timber; his new subjects were skilled in the arts of navigation and shipbuilding; he animated his daring Vandals to embrace a mode of warfare which would render every maritime country accessible to their arms; the Moors and Africans were allured by the hopes of plunder; and, after an interval of six centuries, the fleets that issued from the port of Carthage again claimed the empire of the Mediterranean. The success of the Vandals, the conquest of Sicily, the sack of Palermo, and the frequent descents on the coast of Lucania, awakened and alarmed the mother of Valentinian and the sister of Theodosius. Alliances were formed; and armaments, expensive and ineffectual, were prepared for the destruction of the common enemy, who reserved his courage to encounter those dangers which his policy could not prevent or elude. The designs of the Roman government were repeatedly baffled by his artful delays, ambiguous promises, and apparent concessions; and the interposition of his formidable confederate, the king of the Huns, recalled the emperors from the conquest of Africa to the care of their domestic safety. The revolutions of the palace, which left the Western empire without a defender and without a lawful prince, dispelled the apprehensions and stimulated the avarice of Genseric. He immediately equipped a numerous fleet of Vandals and Moors, and cast anchor at the mouth of the Tiber, about three months after the death of Valentinian and the elevation of Maximus to the Imperial throne.

The private life of the senator Petronius Maximus[1] was often alleged as a rare example of human felicity. His birth was noble and illustrious, since he descended from the Anician family; his dignity was supported by an adequate patrimony in land and money; and these advantages of fortune were accompanied with liberal arts and decent manners, which adorn or imitate the inestimable gifts of genius and virtue. The luxury of his palace and table was hospitable and elegant. Whenever Maximus appeared in public, he was surrounded by a train of grateful and obsequious clients;[2] and it is possible that among these clients he might deserve and possess some real friend. His merit was rewarded by the favour of the prince and senate: he thrice exercised the office of Prætorian præfect of Italy; he was twice invested with the consulship, and he obtained the rank of patrician. These civil honours were not incompatible with the enjoyment of leisure and tranquillity; his hours, according to the demands of pleasure or reason, were accurately distributed by a water-clock; and this avarice of time may be allowed to prove the sense which Maximus entertained of his

[1] Sidonius Apollinaris composed the thirteenth epistle of the second book to refute the paradox of his friend Serranus, who entertained a singular though generous enthusiasm for the deceased emperor. This epistle, with some indulgence, may claim the praise of an elegant composition; and it throws much light on the character of Maximus.

[2] Clientum prævia, pedisequa, circumfusa, populositas, is the train which Sidonius himself (l. i. Epist. 9) assigns to another senator of consular rank.

own happiness. The injury which he received from the emperor Valen₁ tinian appears to excuse the most bloody revenge. Yet a philosophei might have reflected, that, if the resistance of his wife had been sincere, her chastity was still inviolate, and that it could never be restored if she had consented to the will of the adulterer. A patriot would have hesitated before he plunged himself and his country into those inevitable calamities which must follow the extinction of the royal house of Theodosius.

The imprudent Maximus disregarded these salutary considerations: he gratified his resentment and ambition; he saw the bleeding corpse of Valentinian at his feet; and he heard himself saluted Emperor by the unanimous voice of the senate and people. But the day of his inauguration was the last day of his happiness. He was imprisoned (such is the lively expression of Sidonius) in the palace; and after passing a sleepless night, he sighed that he had attained the summit of his wishes, and aspired only to descend from the dangerous elevation. Oppressed by the weight of the diadem, he communicated his anxious thoughts to his friend and quæstor Fulgentius; and when he looked back with unavailing regret on the secure pleasures of his former life, the emperor exclaimed, " O fortunate Damocles, thy reign began and ended with the same dinner:" a well-known allusion, which Fulgentius afterwards repeated as an instructive lesson for princes and subjects.[3]

The reign of Maximus continued about three months. His hours, of which he had lost the command, were disturbed by remorse, or guilt, or terror; and his throne was shaken by the seditions of the soldiers, the people, and the confederate barbarians. The marriage of his son Palladius with the eldest daughter of the late emperor might tend to establish the hereditary succession of his family; but the violence which he offered to the empress Eudoxia could proceed only from the blind impulse of lust or revenge. His own wife, the cause of these tragic events, had been seasonably removed by death; and the widow of Valentinian was compelled to violate her decent mourning, perhaps her real grief, and to submit to the embraces of a presumptuous usurper, whom she suspected as the assassin of her deceased husband. These suspicions were soon justified by the indiscreet confession of Maximus himself; and he wantonly provoked the hatred of his reluctant bride, who was still conscious that she descended from a line of emperors. From the East, however, Eudoxia could not hope to obtain any effectual assistance: her father and her aunt Pulcheria were dead; her mother

[3] Districtus ensis cui super impiâ
Cervice pendet, non *Siculæ dapes*
Dulcem elaborabunt saporem :
Non avium citharæque cantus
Somnum reducent.

                                    Horat. Carm. iii. 1.
Sidonius concludes his letter with the story of Damocles, which Cicero (Tusculan. v. 20, 21) had so inimitably told.

languished at Jerusalem in disgrace and exile; and the sceptre of Constantinople was in the hands of a stranger.   She directed her eyes towards Carthage; secretly implored the aid of the king of the Vandals; and persuaded Genseric to improve the fair opportunity of disguising his rapacious designs by the specious names of honour, justice, and compassion.[4]   Whatever abilities Maximus might have shown in a subordinate station, he was found incapable of administering an empire: and though he might easily have been informed of the naval preparations which were made on the opposite shores of Africa, he expected with supine indifference the approach of the enemy, without adopting any measures of defence, of negotiation, or of a timely retreat. When the Vandals disembarked at the mouth of the Tiber, the emperor was suddenly roused from his lethargy by the clamours of a trembling and exasperated multitude.   The only hope which presented itself to his astonished mind was that of a precipitate flight, and he exhorted the senators to imitate the example of their prince.   But no sooner did Maximus appear in the streets than he was assaulted by a shower of stones: a Roman or a Burgundian soldier claimed the honour of the first wound; his mangled body was ignominiously cast into the Tiber; the Roman people rejoiced in the punishment which they had inflicted on the author of the public calamities; and the domestics of Eudoxia signalised their zeal in the service of their mistress.[5]

On the third day after the tumult, Genseric boldly advanced from the port of Ostia to the gates of the defenceless city.   Instead of a sally of the Roman youth, there issued from the gates an unarmed and venerable procession of the bishop at the head of his clergy.[6]   The fearless spirit of Leo, his authority and eloquence, *again* mitigated the fierceness of a barbarian conqueror: the king of the Vandals promised to spare the unresisting multitude, to protect the buildings from fire, and to exempt the captives from torture; and although such orders were neither seriously given, nor strictly obeyed, the mediation of Leo was glorious to himself, and in some degree beneficial to his country.   But Rome and its inhabitants were delivered to the licentiousness of the Vandals and

---

[4] Notwithstanding the evidence of Procopius, Evagrius, Idatius, Marcellinus, etc., the learned Muratori (Annali d'Italia, tom. iv. p. 249) doubts the reality of this invitation, and observes, with great truth, " Non si può dii quanto sia facile il popolo a sognare e spacciar voci false."   But his argument, from the interval of time and place, is extremely feeble.   The figs which grew near Carthage were produced to the senate of Rome on the third day.

[5] . . . Infidoque tibi Burgundio ductu
Extorquet trepidas mactandi principis iras.
Sidon. in Panegyr. Avit. 442.
A remarkable line, which insinuates that Rome and Maximus were betrayed by their Burgundian mercenaries.

[6] The apparent success of pope Leo may be justified by Prosper, and the *Historia Miscellan.;* but the improbable notion of Baronius (A.D. 455, No. 13) that Genseric spared the three apostolical churches is not countenanced even by the doubtful testimony of the *Liber Pontificalis.*

Moors, whose blind passions revenged the injuries of Carthage. The pillage lasted fourteen days and nights; and all that yet remained of public or private wealth, of sacred or profane treasure, was diligently transported to the vessels of Genseric. Among the spoils, the splendid relics of two temples, or rather of two religions, exhibited a memorable example of the vicissitudes of human and divine things. Since the abolition of Paganism, the Capitol had been violated and abandoned; yet the statues of the gods and heroes were still respected, and the curious roof of gilt bronze was reserved for the rapacious hands of Genseric.[7] The holy instruments of the Jewish worship,[8] the gold table, and the gold candlestick with seven branches, originally framed according to the particular instructions of God himself, and which were placed in the sanctuary of his temple, had been ostentatiously displayed to the Roman people in the triumph of Titus. They were afterwards deposited in the temple of Peace; and at the end of four hundred years, the spoils of Jerusalem were transferred from Rome to Carthage, by a barbarian who derived his origin from the shores of the Baltic. These ancient monuments might attract the notice of curiosity as well as of avarice. But the Christian churches, enriched and adorned by the prevailing superstition of the times, afforded more plentiful materials for sacrilege; and the pious liberality of pope Leo, who melted six silver vases, the gift of Constantine, each of an hundred pounds weight, is an evidence of the damage which he attempted to repair. In the forty-five years that had elapsed since the Gothic invasion, the pomp and luxury of Rome were in some measure restored; and it was difficult either to escape, or to satisfy, the avarice of a conqueror who possessed leisure to collect, and ships to transport, the wealth of the capital. The Imperial ornaments of the palace, the magnificent furniture and wardrobe, the sideboards of massy plate, were accumulated with disorderly rapine: the gold and silver amounted to several thousand talents; yet even the brass and copper were laboriously removed. Eudoxia herself, who advanced to meet her friend and deliverer, soon bewailed the imprudence of her own conduct. She was rudely stripped of her jewels; and the unfortunate empress, with her two daughters, the only surviving remains of the great Theodosius, was compelled, as a captive, to follow the

---

[7] The profusion of Catulus, the first who gilt the roof of the Capitol, was not universally approved (Plin. Hist. Natur. xxxiii. 18); but it was far exceeded by the emperor's, and the external gilding of the temple cost Domitian 12,000 talents (£2,400,000). The expressions of Claudian and Rutilius (*luce metalli æmula . . . fastigia astris*, and *confunduntque vagos delubra micantia visus*) manifestly prove that this splendid covering was not removed either by the Christians or the Goths (see Donatus, Roma Antiqua, l. ii. c. 6, p. 125). It should seem that the roof of the Capitol was decorated with gilt statues, and chariots drawn by four horses.

[8] The curious reader may consult the learned and accurate treatise of Hadrian Reland, de Spoliis Templi Hierosolymitani in Arcû Titiano Romæ conspicuis, in 12mo. Trajecti ad Rhenum, 1716.

haughty Vandal, who immediately hoisted sail, and returned with a prosperous navigation to the port of Carthage.[9] Many thousand Romans of both sexes, chosen for some useful or agreeable qualifications, reluctantly embarked on board the fleet of Genseric; and their distress was aggravated by the unfeeling barbarians, who, in the division of the booty, separated the wives from their husbands, and the children from their parents. The charity of Deogratias, bishop of Carthage,[10] was their only consolation and support. He generously sold the gold and silver plate of the church to purchase the freedom of some, to alleviate the slavery of others, and to assist the wants and infirmities of a captive multitude, whose health was impaired by the hardships which they had suffered in the passage from Italy to Africa. By his order, two spacious churches were converted into hospitals: the sick were distributed in convenient beds, and liberally supplied with food and medicines; and the aged prelate repeated his visits both in the day and night, with an assiduity that surpassed his strength, and a tender sympathy which enhanced the value of his services. Compare this scene with the field of Cannæ; and judge between Hannibal and the successor of St. Cyprian.[11]

The deaths of Aëtius and Valentinian had relaxed the ties which held the barbarians of Gaul in peace and subordination. The sea-coast was infested by the Saxons; the Alemanni and the Franks advanced from the Rhine to the Seine; and the ambition of the Goths seemed to meditate more extensive and permanent conquests. The emperor Maximus relieved himself, by a judicious choice, from the weight of these distant cares; he silenced the solicitations of his friends, listened to the voice of fame, and promoted a stranger to the general command of the forces in Gaul. Avitus,[12] the stranger whose merit was so nobly rewarded, descended from a wealthy and honourable family in the diocese of Auvergne. The convulsions of the times urged him to embrace, with the same ardour, the civil and military professions; and the indefati-

[9] The vessel which transported the relics of the Capitol was the only one of the whole fleet that suffered shipwreck. If a bigoted sophist, a Pagan bigot, had mentioned the accident, he might have rejoiced that this cargo of sacrilege was lost in the sea.

[10] See Victor Vitensis, de Persecut. Vandal. l. i. c. 8, p. 11, 12, edit. Ruinart. Deogratias governed the church of Carthage only three years. If he had not been privately buried, his corpse would have been torn piecemeal by the mad devotion of the people.

[11] The general evidence for the death of Maximus, and the sack of Rome by the Vandals, is comprised in Sidonius (Panegyr. Avit. 441-450), Procopius (de Bell. Vandal. l. i. c. 4, 5, p. 188, 189 [tom. i. p. 332, ed. Bonn.], and l. ii. c. 9, p. 255 [tom. i. p. 445, *sq.,* ed. Bonn]), Evagrius (l. ii. c. 7), Jornandes (de Reb. Geticis, c. 45, p. 677), and the Chronicles of Idatius, Prosper, Marcellinus, and Theophanes, under the proper year.

[12] The private life and elevation of Avitus must be deduced, with becoming suspicion, from the panegyric pronounced by Sidonius Apollinaris, his subject, and his son-in-law.

gable youth blended the studies of literature and jurisprudence with the exercise of arms and hunting. Thirty years of his life were laudably spent in the public service; he alternately displayed his talents in war and negotiation; and the soldier of Aëtius, after executing the most important embassies, was raised to the station of Prætorian præfect of Gaul. Either the merit of Avitus excited envy, or his moderation was desirous of repose, since he calmly retired to an estate which he possessed in the neighbourhood of Clermont. A copious stream, issuing from the mountain, and falling headlong in many a loud and foaming cascade, discharged its waters into a lake about two miles in length, and the villa was pleasantly seated on the margin of the lake. The baths, the porticoes, the summer and winter apartments, were adapted to the purposes of luxury and use; and the adjacent country afforded the various prospects of woods, pastures, and meadows.[13] In this retreat, where Avitus amused his leisure with books, rural sports, the practice of husbandry, and the society of his friends,[14] he received the Imperial diploma, which constituted him master-general of the cavalry and infantry of Gaul. He assumed the military command; the barbarians suspended their fury; and whatever means he might employ, whatever concessions he might be forced to make, the people enjoyed the benefits of actual tranquillity. But the fate of Gaul depended on the Visigoths; and the Roman general, less attentive to his dignity than to the public interest, did not disdain to visit Toulouse in the character of an ambassador. He was received with courteous hospitality by Theodoric, the king of the Goths; but while Avitus laid the foundations of a solid alliance with that powerful nation, he was astonished by the intelligence that the emperor Maximus was slain, and that Rome had been pillaged by the Vandals. A vacant throne, which he might ascend without guilt or danger, tempted his ambition:[15] and the Visigoths were easily persuaded to support his claim by their irresistible suffrage. They loved the person of Avitus; they respected his virtues; and they were not insensible of the advantage, as well as honour, of giving an emperor

[13] After the example of the younger Pliny, Sidonius (1. ii. Epist. 2) has laboured the florid, prolix, and obscure description of his villa, which bore the name (*Avitacum*), and had been the property, of Avitus. The precise situation is not ascertained. Consult, however, the notes of Savaron and Sirmond.

[14] Sidonius (1. ii. Epist. 9) has described the country life of the Gallic nobles, in a visit which he made to his friends, whose estates were in the neighbourhood of Nismes. The morning hours were spent in the *sphæristerium* or tennis-court, or in the library, which was furnished with *Latin* authors, profane and religious—the former for the men, the latter for the ladies. The table was twice served, at dinner and supper, with hot meat (boiled and roast) and wine. During the intermediate time, the company slept, took the air on horseback, and used the warm bath.

[15] Seventy lines of panegyric (505-575) which describe the importunity of Theodoric and of Gaul, struggling to overcome the modest reluctance of Avitus, are blown away by three words of an honest historian. Romanum *ambisset* Imperium (Greg. Turon. 1. ii. c. 11, in tom. ii. p. 168).

to the West. The season was now approaching in which the annual assembly of the seven provinces was held at Arles; their deliberations might perhaps be influenced by the presence of Theodoric and his martial brothers; but their choice would naturally incline to the most illustrious of their countrymen. Avitus, after a decent resistance, accepted the Imperial diadem from the representatives of Gaul; and his election was ratified by the acclamations of the barbarians and provincials. The formal consent of Marcian, emperor of the East, was solicited and obtained; but the senate, Rome, and Italy, though humbled by their recent calamities, submitted with a secret murmur to the presumption of the Gallic usurper.

Theodoric, to whom Avitus was indebted for the purple, had acquired the Gothic sceptre by the murder of his elder brother Torismond; and he justified this atrocious deed by the design which his predecessor had formed of violating his alliance with the empire.[16] Such a crime might not be incompatible with the virtues of a barbarian; but the manners of Theodoric were gentle and humane; and posterity may contemplate without terror the original picture of a Gothic king, whom Sidonius had intimately observed in the hours of peace and of social intercourse. In an epistle, dated from the court of Toulouse, the orator satisfies the curiosity of one of his friends, in the following description:[17] " By the majesty of his appearance, Theodoric would command the respect of those who are ignorant of his merit; and although he is born a prince, his merit would dignify a private station. He is of a middle stature, his body appears rather plump than fat, and in his well-proportioned limbs agility is united with muscular strength.[18] If you examine his countenance, you will distinguish a high forehead, large shaggy eyebrows, an aquiline nose, thin lips, a regular set of white teeth, and a fair complexion, that blushes more frequently from modesty than from anger. The ordinary distribution of his time, as far as it is exposed to the public view, may be concisely represented. Before daybreak he repairs, with a small train, to his domestic chapel, where the service is performed by the Arian clergy; but those who presume to interpret his secret sentiments consider this assiduous devotion as the effect of habit and policy. The rest of the morning is employed in the administration of his king-

---

[16] Isidore, archbishop of Seville, who was himself of the blood-royal of the Goths, acknowledges and almost justifies (Hist. Goth. p. 718) the crime which their slave Jornandes had basely dissembled (c. 43, p. 675).

[17] This elaborate description (l. i. Ep. ii. p. 2-7) was dictated by some political motive. It was designed for the public eye, and had been shown by the friends of Sidonius before it was inserted in the collection of his epistles. The first book was published separately. See Tillemont, Mémoires Ecclés. tom. xvi. p. 264.

[18] I have suppressed, in this portrait of Theodoric, several minute circumstances and technical phrases, which could be tolerable, or indeed intelligible, to those only who, like the contemporaries of Sidonius, had frequented the markets where naked slaves were exposed to sale (Dubos, Hist. Critique, tom. i. p. 404).

dom. His chair is surrounded by some military officers of decent aspect and behaviour: the noisy crowd of his barbarian guards occupies the hall of audience, but they are not permitted to stand within the veils or curtains that conceal the council-chamber from vulgar eyes. The ambassadors of the nations are successively introduced: Theodoric listens with attention, answers them with discreet brevity, and either announces or delays, according to the nature of their business, his final resolution. About eight (the second hour) he rises from his throne, and visits either his treasury or his stables. If he chooses to hunt, or at least to exercise himself on horseback, his bow is carried by a favourite youth; but when the game is marked, he bends it with his own hand, and seldom misses the object of his aim: as a king, he disdains to bear arms in such ignoble warfare; but as a soldier, he would blush to accept any military service which he could perform himself. On common days his dinner is not different from the repast of a private citizen; but every Saturday many honourable guests are invited to the royal table, which, on these occasions, is served with the elegance of Greece, the plenty of Gaul, and the order and diligence of Italy.[19] The gold or silver plate is less remarkable for its weight than for the brightness and curious workmanship: the taste is gratified without the help of foreign and costly luxury; the size and number of the cups of wine are regulated with a strict regard to the laws of temperance; and the respectful silence that prevails is interrupted only by grave and instructive conversation. After dinner Theodoric sometimes indulges himself in a short slumber; and as soon as he wakes he calls for the dice and tables, encourages his friends to forget the royal majesty, and is delighted when they freely express the passions which are excited by the incidents of play. At this game, which he loves as the image of war, he alternately displays his eagerness, his skill, his patience, and his cheerful temper. If he loses, he laughs: he is modest and silent if he wins. Yet, notwithstanding this seeming indifference, his courtiers choose to solicit any favour in the moments of victory; and I myself, in my applications to the king, have derived some benefit from my losses.[20] About the ninth hour (three o'clock) the tide of business again returns, and flows incessantly till after sunset, when the signal of the royal supper dismisses the weary crowd of suppliants and pleaders. At the supper, a more familiar repast, buffoons and pantomimes are sometimes introduced, to divert, not to offend, the company by their ridiculous wit: but female singers, and the soft effeminate modes of music, are severely banished, and such martial tunes as animate the soul to deeds of valour are alone grateful

[19] Videas ibi elegantiam Græcam, abundantiam Gallicanam; celeritatem Italam; publicam pompam, privatam diligentiam, regiam disciplinam.

[20] Tunc etiam ego aliquid obsecraturus feliciter vincor, et mihi tabula perit ut causa salvetur [p. 6]. Sidonius of Auvergne was not a subject of Theodoric; but he might be compelled to solicit either justice or favour at the court of Toulouse.

to the ear of Theodoric. He retires from table; and the nocturnal guards are immediately posted at the entrance of the treasury, the palace, and the private apartments."

When the king of the Visigoths encouraged Avitus to assume the purple, he offered his person and his forces as a faithful soldier of the republic.[21] The exploits of Theodoric soon convinced the world that he had not degenerated from the warlike virtues of his ancestors. After the establishment of the Goths in Aquitain, and the passage of the Van-dals into Africa, the Suevi, who had fixed their kingdom in Gallicia, aspired to the conquest of Spain, and threatened to extinguish the feeble remains of the Roman dominion. The provincials of Carthagena and Tarragona, afflicted by an hostile invasion, represented their injuries and their apprehensions. Count Fronto was despatched, in the name of the emperor Avitus, with advantageous offers of peace and alliance; and Theodoric interposed his weighty mediation to declare that, unless his brother-in-law, the king of the Suevi, immediately retired, he should be obliged to arm in the cause of justice and of Rome. " Tell him," replied the haughty Rechiarius, " that I despise his friendship and his arms; but that I shall soon try whether he will dare to expect my arrival under the walls of Toulouse." Such a challenge urged Theodoric to prevent the bold designs of his enemy: he passed the Pyrenees at the head of the Visigoths; the Franks and Burgundians served under his standard; and though he professed himself the dutiful servant of Avitus, he privately stipulated, for himself and his successors, the absolute pos-session of his Spanish conquests. The two armies, or rather the two nations, encountered each other on the banks of the river Urbicus, about twelve miles from Astorga; and the decisive victory of the Goths appeared for a while to have extirpated the name and kingdom of the Suevi. From the field of battle Theodoric advanced to Braga, their metropolis, which still retained the splendid vestiges of its ancient com-merce and dignity.[22] His entrance was not polluted with blood; and the Goths respected the chastity of their female captives, more espe-cially of the consecrated virgins: but the greatest part of the clergy and people were made slaves, and even the churches and altars were confounded in the universal pillage. The unfortunate king of the Suevi had escaped to one of the ports of the ocean; but the obstinacy of the

---

[21] Theodoric himself had given a solemn and voluntary promise of fidelity, which was understood both in Gaul and Spain:—

―――― Romæ sum, te duce, Amicus,
Principe te, MILES.

Sidon. Panegyr. Avit. 511.

[22] Quæque sinû pelagi jactat se Bracara dives.

Auson. de Claris Urbibus, p. 245 [Emerita, ix.].

From the design of the king of the Suevi, it is evident that the navigation from the ports of Gallicia to the Mediterranean was known and practised. The ships of Bracara, or Braga, cautiously steered along the coast, without daring to lose themselves in the Atlantic.

winds opposed his flight: he was delivered to his implacable rival; and Rechiarius, who neither desired nor expected mercy, received, with manly constancy, the death which he would probably have inflicted. After this bloody sacrifice to policy or resentment, Theodoric carried his victorious arms as far as Merida, the principal town of Lusitania, without meeting any resistance, except from the miraculous powers of St. Eulalia; but he was stopped in the full career of success, and recalled from Spain before he could provide for the security of his conquests. In his retreat towards the Pyrenees he revenged his disappointment on the country through which he passed; and, in the sack of Polentia and Astorga, he showed himself a faithless ally, as well as a cruel enemy. Whilst the king of the Visigoths fought and vanquished in the name of Avitus, the reign of Avitus had expired; and both the honour and the interest of Theodoric were deeply wounded by the disgrace of a friend whom he had seated on the throne of the Western empire.[23]

The pressing solicitations of the senate and people persuaded the emperor Avitus to fix his residence at Rome, and to accept the consulship for the ensuing year. On the first day of January, his son-in-law, Sidonius Apollinaris, celebrated his praises in a panegyric of six hundred verses; but this composition, though it was rewarded with a brass statue,[24] seems to contain a very moderate proportion either of genius or of truth. The poet, if we may degrade that sacred name, exaggerates the merit of a sovereign and a father; and his prophecy of a long and glorious reign was soon contradicted by the event. Avitus, at a time when the Imperial dignity was reduced to a pre-eminence of toil and danger, indulged himself in the pleasures of Italian luxury: age had not extinguished his amorous inclinations; and he is accused of insulting, with indiscreet and ungenerous raillery, the husbands whose wives he had seduced or violated.[25] But the Romans were not inclined either to excuse his faults or to acknowledge his virtues. The several parts of the empire became every day more alienated from each other; and the stranger of Gaul was the object of popular hatred and contempt. The senate asserted their legitimate claim in the election of an emperor; and their authority, which had been originally derived from the old constitution, was again fortified by the actual weakness of a declining monarchy. Yet even such a monarchy might have resisted the votes

[23] This Suevic war is the most authentic part of the Chronicle of Idatius, who, as bishop of Iria Flavia, was himself a spectator and a sufferer. Jornandes (c. 44, p. 675, 676, 677) has expatiated with pleasure on the Gothic victory.

[24] In one of the porticoes or galleries belonging to Trajan's library, among the statues of famous writers and orators. Sidon. Apoll. l. ix. Epist. 16, p. 284; Carm. viii. p. 350.

[25] Luxuriose agere volens a senatoribus projectus est, is the concise expression of Gregory of Tours (l. ii. c. xi. in tom. ii. p. 168). An old Chronicle (in tom. ii. p. 649) mentions an indecent jest of Avitus, which seems more applicable to Rome than to Trèves.

of an unarmed senate, if their discontent had not been supported, or
perhaps inflamed, by Count Ricimer, one of the principal commanders
of the barbarian troops who formed the military defence of Italy. The
daughter of Wallia, king of the Visigoths, was the mother of Ricimer;
but he was descended, on the father's side, from the nation of the
Suevi:[26] his pride or patriotism might be exasperated by the misfortunes of his countrymen; and he obeyed with reluctance an emperor
in whose elevation he had not been consulted. His faithful and important services against the common enemy rendered him still more formidable;[27] and, after destroying on the coast of Corsica a fleet of Vandals, which consisted of sixty galleys, Ricimer returned in triumph
with the appellation of the Deliverer of Italy. He chose that moment
to signify to Avitus that his reign was at an end; and the feeble emperor, at a distance from his Gothic allies, was compelled, after a short
and unavailing struggle, to abdicate the purple. By the clemency, however, or the contempt of Ricimer,[28] he was permitted to descend from
the throne to the more desirable station of bishop of Placentia: but
the resentment of the senate was still unsatisfied; and their inflexible
severity pronouncd the sentence of his death. He fled towards the Alps,
with the humble hope, not of arming the Visigoths in his cause, but of
securing his person and treasures in the sanctuary of Julian, one of the
tutelar saints of Auvergne.[29] Disease, or the hand of the executioner,
arrested him on the road; yet his remains were decently transported to
Brivas, or Brioude, in his native province, and he reposed at the feet
of his holy patron.[30] Avitus left only one daughter, the wife of Sidonius Apollinaris, who inherited the patrimony of his father-in-law;
lamenting, at the same time, the disappointment of his public and
private expectations. His resentment prompted him to join, or at least
to countenance, the measures of a rebellious faction in Gaul; and the

[26] Sidonius (Panegyr. Anthem. 302 [360], etc.) praises the royal birth of
Ricimer, the lawful heir, as he chooses to insinuate, both of the Gothic and
Suevic kingdoms.
[27] See the Chronicle of Idatius. Jornandes (c. xliv. p. 676 [c. 45, p. 678])
styles him, with some truth, virum egregium, et pene tunc in Italiâ ad exercitum singularem.
[28] Parcens innocentiæ Aviti, is the compassionate but contemptuous language
of Victor Tunnunensis (in Chron. apud Scaliger Euseb.). In another place
he calls him vir totius simplicitatis. This commendation is more humble, but
it is more solid and sincere, than the praises of Sidonius.
[29] He suffered, as it is supposed, in the persecution of Diocletian (Tillemont,
Mém. Ecclés. tom. v. p. 279, 696). Gregory of Tours, his peculiar votary, has
dedicated to the glory of Julian the Martyr an entire book (de Gloriâ Marty-
rum, l. ii. in Max. Bibliot. Patrum, tom. xi. p. 861-871), in which he relates
about fifty foolish miracles performed by his relics.
[30] Gregory of Tours (l. ii. c. xi. p. 168) is concise, but correct, in the reign
of his countryman. The words of Idatius, "caret imperio, caret et vitâ" [Hist.
de France, i. p. 621], seem to imply that the death of Avitus was violent; but
it must have been secret, since Evagrius (l. ii. c. 7) could suppose that he died
of the plague.

poet had contracted some guilt, which it was incumbent on him to expiate by a new tribute of flattery to the succeeding emperor.[31]

The successor of Avitus presents the welcome discovery of a great and heroic character, such as sometimes arise, in a degenerate age, to vindicate the honour of the human species. The emperor Majorian has deserved the praises of his contemporaries and of posterity; and these praises may be strongly expressed in the words of a judicious and disinterested historian: " That he was gentle to his subjects; that he was terrible to his enemies; and that he excelled in *every* virtue *all* his predecessors who had reigned over the Romans." [32] Such a testimony may justify at least the panegyric of Sidonius; and we may acquiesce in the assurance that, although the obsequious orator would have flattered with equal zeal the most worthless of princes, the extraordinary merit of his object confined him, on this occasion, within the bounds of truth.[33] Majorian derived his name from his maternal grandfather, who, in the reign of the great Theodosius, had commanded the troops of the Illyrian frontier. He gave his daughter in marriage to the father of Majorian, a respectable officer, who administered the revenues of Gaul with skill and integrity; and generously preferred the friendship of Aëtius to the tempting offers of an insidious court. His son, the future emperor, who was educated in the profession of arms, displayed, from his early youth, intrepid courage, premature wisdom, and unbounded liberality in a scanty fortune. He followed the standard of Aëtius, contributed to his success, shared, and sometimes eclipsed, his glory, and at last excited the jealousy of the patrician, or rather of his wife, who forced him to retire from the service.[34] Majorian, after the death of Aëtius, was recalled and promoted: and his intimate connec-

---

[31] After a modest appeal to the examples of his brethren, Virgil and Horace, Sidonius honestly confesses the debt, and promises payment:—

Sic mihi diverso nuper sub Marte cadenti
Jussisti placido victor ut essem animo.
Serviat ergo tibi servati lingua poetæ,
Atque meæ vitæ laus tua sit pretium.
Sidon. Apoll. Carm. iv. p. 308.

See Dubos, Hist. Critique, tom. i. p. 448, etc.

[32] The words of Procopius deserve to be transcribed: αὖτος γὰρ ὁ Μαιορῖνος ξύμπαντας τοὺς πώποτε 'Ρωμαίων βεβασιλευκότας ὑπεραίρων ἀρετῇ πάσῃ; and afterwards, ἀνὴρ τὰ μὲν εἰς τοὺς ὑπηκόους μέτριος γεγονώς, φοβερὸς δὲ τὰ ἐς τοὺς παλεμίους (de Bell. Vandal. l. i. c. 7, p. 194 [tom. i. p. 340 and 342, ed. Bonn])—a concise but comprehensive definition of royal virtue.

[33] The Panegyric was pronounced at Lyons before the end of the year 458, while the emperor was still consul. It has more art than genius, and more labour than art. The ornaments are false or trivial; the expression is feeble and prolix; and Sidonius wants the skill to exhibit the principal figure in a strong and distinct light. The private life of Majorian occupies about two hundred lines, 107-305.

[34] She pressed his immediate death, and was scarcely satisfied with his disgrace. It should seem that Aëtius, like Belisarius and Marlborough, was governed by his wife, whose fervent piety, though it might work miracles (Gregor. Turon. l. ii. c. 7, p. 162), was not incompatible with base and sanguinary counsels.

tion with Count Ricimer was the immediate step by which he ascended the throne of the Western empire. During the vacancy that succeeded the abdication of Avitus, the ambitious barbarian, whose birth excluded him from the Imperial dignity, governed Italy, with the title of Patrician; resigned to his friend the conspicuous station of master-general of the cavalry and infantry, and, after an interval of some months, consented to the unanimous wish of the Romans, whose favour Majorian had solicited by a recent victory over the Alemanni.[35] He was invested with the purple at Ravenna: and the epistle which he addressed to the senate will best describe his situation and his sentiments. " Your election, Conscript Fathers! and the ordinance of the most valiant army, have made me your emperor.[36] May the propitious Deity direct and prosper the counsels and events of my administration to your advantage and to the public welfare! For my own part, I did not aspire, I have submitted, to reign; nor should I have discharged the obligations of a citizen if I had refused, with base and selfish ingratitude, to support the weight of those labours which were imposed by the republic. Assist, therefore, the prince whom you have made; partake the duties which you have enjoined; and may our common endeavours promote the happiness of an empire which I have accepted from your hands. Be assured that, in our times, justice shall resume her ancient vigour, and that virtue shall become not only innocent but meritorious. Let none, except the authors themselves, be apprehensive of *delations*,[37] which, as a subject, I have always condemned, and, as a prince, will severely punish. Our own vigilance, and that of our father, the patrician Ricimer, shall regulate all military affairs and provide for the safety of the Roman world, which we have saved from foreign and domestic enemies.[38] You now understand the maxims of my government: you may

[35] The Alemanni had passed the Rhætian Alps, and were defeated in the *Campi Canini*, or Valley of Bellinzone, through which the Ticino flows, in its descent from Mount Adula, to the Lago Maggiore (Cluver. Italia Antiq. tom. i. p. 100. 101). This boasted victory over *nine hundred* barbarians (Panegyr. Majorian. 373, etc.) betrays the extreme weakness of Italy.

[36] Imperatorem me factum, P. C. electionis vestræ arbitrio, et fortissimi exercitûs ordinatione agnoscite (Novell. Majorian. tit. iii. p. 34, ad Calcem Cod. Theodos.). Sidonius proclaims the unanimous voice of the empire:—

      —— Postquam ordine vobis
   Ordo omnis regnum dederat; *plebs, curia, miles,*
   Et *collega simul.*   [Carm. v.] 386.

This language is ancient and constitutional; and we may observe that the *clergy* were not yet considered as a distinct order of the state.

[37] Either *dilationes*, or *delationes*, would afford a tolerable reading; but there is much more sense and spirit in the latter, to which I have therefore given the preference.

[38] Ab externo hoste et a domesticâ clade liberavimus: by the latter, Majorian must understand the tyranny of Avitus, whose death he consequently avowed as a meritorious act. On this occasion Sidonius is fearful and obscure; he describes the twelve Cæsars, the nations of Africa, etc., that he may escape the dangerous name of Avitus (305-369).

confide in the faithful love and sincere assurances of a prince who has formerly been the companion of your life and dangers, who still glories in the name of senator, and who is anxious that you should never repent of the judgment which you have pronounced in his favour." The emperor, who, amidst the ruins of the Roman world, revived the ancient language of law and liberty, which Trajan would not have disclaimed, must have derived those generous sentiments from his own heart, since they were not suggested to his imitation by the customs of his age or the example of his predecessors.[39]

The private and public actions of Majorian are very imperfectly known: but his laws, remarkable for an original cast of thought and expression, faithfully represent the character of a sovereign who loved his people, who sympathised in their distress, who had studied the causes of the decline of the empire, and who was capable of applying (as far as such reformation was practicable) judicious and effectual remedies to the public disorders.[40] His regulations concerning the finances manifestly tended to remove, or at least to mitigate, the most intolerable grievances. I. From the first hour of his reign he was solicitous (I translate his own words) to relieve the *weary* fortunes of the provincials, oppressed by the accumulated weight of indictions and superindictions.[41] With this view, he granted an universal amnesty, a final and absolute discharge of all arrears of tribute, of all debts which, under any pretence, the fiscal officers might demand from the people. This wise dereliction of obsolete, vexatious, and unprofitable claims, improved and purified the sources of the public revenue; and the subject, who could now look back without despair, might labour with hope and gratitude for himself and for his country. II. In the assessment and collection of taxes Majorian restored the ordinary jurisdiction of the provincial magistrates, and suppressed the extraordinary commissions which had been introduced in the name of the emperor himself or of the Prætorian præfects. The favourite servants who obtained such irregular powers were insolent in their behaviour and arbitrary in their demands: they affected to despise the subordinate tribunals, and they were discontented if their fees and profits did not twice exceed the sum which they condescended to pay into the treasury. One instance of their extortion would appear incredible were it not authenticated by the legislator himself. They exacted the whole payment in gold: but they refused the current coin of the empire, and

---

[39] See the whole edict or epistle of Majorian to the senate (Novell. tit. iv. p. 34.) Yet the expression *regnum nostrum* bears some taint of the age, and does not mix kindly with the word *respublica,* which he frequently repeats.

[40] See the laws of Majorian (they are only nine in number, but very long and various), at the end of the Theodosian Code, Novell. l. iv. p. 32-37. Godefroy has not given any commentary on these additional pieces.

[41] Fessas provincialium variâ atque multiplici tributorum exactione fortunas, et extraordinariis fiscalium solutionum oneribus attritas, etc. Novell. Majorian. tit. iv. p. 34.

would accept only such ancient pieces as were stamped with the names of Faustina or the Antonines. The subject who was unprovided with these curious medals had recourse to the expedient of compounding with their rapacious demands; or, if he succeeded in the research, his imposition was doubled according to the weight and value of the money of former times.[42]   III. " The municipal corporations (says the emperor), the lesser senates (so antiquity has justly styled them), deserve to be considered as the heart of the cities and the sinews of the republic.   And yet so low are they now reduced, by the injustice of magistrates and the venality of collectors, that many of their members, renouncing their dignity and their country, have taken refuge in distant and obscure exile."   He urges, and even compels, their return to their respective cities; but he removes the grievance which had forced them to desert the exercise of their municipal functions.   They are directed, under the authority of the provincial magistrates, to resume their office of levying the tribute; but, instead of being made responsible for the whole sum assessed on their district, they are only required to produce a regular account of the payments which they have actually received, and of the defaulters who are still indebted to the public.   IV. But Majorian was not ignorant that these corporate bodies were too much inclined to retaliate the injustice and oppression which they had suffered, and he therefore revives the useful office of the *defenders of cities.* He exhorts the people to elect, in a full and free assembly, some man of discretion and integrity who would dare to assert their privileges, to represent their grievances, to protect the poor from the tyranny of the rich, and to inform the emperor of the abuses that were committed under the sanction of his name and authority.

The spectator who casts a mournful view over the ruins of ancient Rome is tempted to accuse the memory of the Goths and Vandals for the mischief which they had neither leisure, nor power, nor perhaps inclination, to perpetrate.   The tempest of war might strike some lofty turrets to the ground; but the destruction which undermined the foundations of those massy fabrics was prosecuted, slowly and silently, dur-

---

[42] The learned Greaves (vol. i. p. 329, 330, 331) has found, by a diligent inquiry, that *aurei* of the Antonines weighed one hundred and eighteen, and those of the fifth century only sixty-eight English grains.   Majorian gives currency to all gold coin, excepting only the *Gallic solidus,* from its deficiency, not in the weight, but in the standard.

[Until about the time of Constantine, " Defensor " was the title of persons who were employed in municipal matters of merely a temporary kind.   But about the first half or the middle of the fourth century the Defensores appear as regularly established functionaries.   Their title is Defensor Civitatis, Plebis, Loci.   They were elected by the whole town, and not merely by the decurions, and, unlike the magistrates, who were chosen from the decurions, they could not be taken from the latter body.   The office was, at its origin, held for five years, but after the time of Justinian only for two.   The principal business of the decurion was to protect the town against the oppression of the governor. Cf. Savigny, *Geschichte des Romischen Rechts,* vol. i. p. 88.—O. S.]

ing a period of ten centuries; and the motives of interest, that afterwards operated without shame or control, were severely checked by the taste and spirit of the emperor Majorian. The decay of the city had gradually impaired the value of the public works. The circus and theatres might still excite, but they seldom gratified, the desires of the people: the temples which had escaped the zeal of the Christians were no longer inhabited either by gods or men; the diminished crowds of the Romans were lost in the immense space of their baths and porticoes; and the stately libraries and halls of justice became useless to an indolent generation whose repose was seldom disturbed either by study or business. The monuments of consular or Imperial greatness were no longer revered as the immortal glory of the capital: they were only esteemed as an inexhaustible mine of materials, cheaper, and more convenient, than the distant quarry. Specious petitions were continually addressed to the easy magistrates of Rome which stated the want of stones or bricks for some necessary service: the fairest forms of architecture were rudely defaced for the sake of some paltry or pretended repairs; and the degenerate Romans, who converted the spoil to their own emolument, demolished, with sacrilegious hands, the labours of their ancestors. Majorian, who had often sighed over the desolation of the city, applied a severe remedy to the growing evil.[43] He reserved to the prince and senate the sole cognisance of the extreme cases which might justify the destruction of an ancient edifice; imposed a fine of fifty pounds of gold (two thousand pounds sterling) on every magistrate who should presume to grant such illegal and scandalous licence; and threatened to chastise the criminal obedience of their subordinate officers by a severe whipping and the amputation of both their hands. In the last instance the legislator might seem to forget the proportion of guilt and punishment; but his zeal arose from a generous principle, and Majorian was anxious to protect the monuments of those ages in which he would have desired and deserved to live. The emperor conceived that it was his interest to increase the number of his subjects; that it was his duty to guard the purity of the marriage-bed: but the means which he employed to accomplish these salutary purposes are of an ambiguous, and perhaps exceptionable, kind. The pious maids who consecrated their virginity to Christ were restrained from taking the veil till they had reached their fortieth year. Widows under that age were compelled to form a second alliance within the term of five years,

[43] The whole edict (Novell. Majorian. tit. vi. p. 35) is curious. "Antiquarum ædium dissipatur speciosa constructio; et ut [earum] aliquid reparetur, magna diruuntur. Hinc jam occasio nascitur, ut etiam unusquisque privatum ædificium construens, per gratiam judicum ... præsumere de publicis locis necessaria, et transferre non dubitet," etc. With equal zeal, but with less power, Petrarch, in the fourteenth century, repeated the same complaints (Vie de Petrarque, tom. i. p. 326, 327). If I prosecute this History, I shall not be unmindful of the decline and fall of the *city* of Rome—an interesting object, to which my plan was originally confined.

by the forfeiture of half their wealth to their nearest relations or to the state. Unequal marriages were condemned or annulled. The punishment of confiscation and exile was deemed so inadequate to the guilt of adultery, that, if the criminal returned to Italy, he might, by the express declaration of Majorian, be slain with impunity.[44]

While the emperor Majorian assiduously laboured to restore the happiness and virtue of the Romans, he encountered the arms of Genseric, from his character and situation their most formidable enemy. A fleet of Vandals and Moors landed at the mouth of the Liris or Garigliano; but the Imperial troops surprised and attacked the disorderly barbarians, who were encumbered with the spoils of Campania; they were chased with slaughter to their ships, and their leader, the king's brother-in-law, was found in the number of the slain.[45] Such vigilance might announce the character of the new reign, but the strictest vigilance and the most numerous forces were insufficient to protect the long-extended coast of Italy from the depredations of a naval war. The public opinion had imposed a nobler and more arduous task on the genius of Majorian. Rome expected from him alone the restitution of Africa, and the design which he formed of attacking the Vandals in their new settlements was the result of bold and judicious policy. If the intrepid emperor could have infused his own spirit into the youth of Italy; if he could have revived in the field of Mars the manly exercises in which he had always surpassed his equals; he might have marched against Genseric at the head of a *Roman* army. Such a reformation of national manners might be embraced by the rising generation; but it is the misfortune of those princes who laboriously sustain a declining monarchy, that, to obtain some immediate advantage, or to avert some impending danger, they are forced to countenance, and even to multiply, the most pernicious abuses. Majorian, like the weakest of his predecessors, was reduced to the disgraceful expedient of substituting barbarian auxiliaries in the place of his unwarlike subjects: and his superior abilities could only be displayed in the vigour and dexterity with which he wielded a dangerous instrument, so apt to recoil on the hand that used it. Besides the confederates who were already engaged in the service of the empire, the fame of his liberality and valour attracted the nations of the Danube, the Borysthenes, and perhaps of the Tanais. Many thousands of the bravest subjects of Attila, the Gepidæ, the Ostrogoths, the Rugians, the Burgundians, the Suevi, the Alani, assembled in the plains of Liguria, and their formidable strength was bal-

[44] The emperor chides the lenity of Rogatian, consular of Tuscany, in a style of acrimonius reproof, which sounds almost like personal resentment (Novell. tit. ix. p. 37). The law of Majorian which punished obstinate widows was soon afterwards repealed by his successor Severus (Novell. Sever. tit. i. p. 37).

[45] Sidon. Panegyr. Majorian. 385-440.

anced by their mutual animosities.[46] They passed the Alps in a severe winter. The emperor led the way on foot and in complete armour, sounding with his long staff the depth of the ice or snow, and encouraging the Scythians, who complained of the extreme cold, by the cheerful assurance that they should be satisfied with the heat of Africa. The citizens of Lyons had presumed to shut their gates: they soon implored, and experienced, the clemency of Majorian. He vanquished Theodoric in the field, and admitted to his friendship and alliance a king whom he had found not unworthy of his arms. The beneficial though precarious reunion of the greatest part of Gaul and Spain was the effect of persuasion as well as of force;[47] and the independent Bagaudæ, who had escaped or resisted the oppression of former reigns, were disposed to confide in the virtues of Majorian. His camp was filled with barbarian allies; his throne was supported by the zeal of an affectionate people; but the emperor had foreseen that it was impossible without a maritime power to achieve the conquest of Africa. In the first Punic war the republic had exerted such incredible diligence that, within sixty days after the first stroke of the axe had been given in the forest, a fleet of one hundred and sixty galleys proudly rode at anchor in the sea.[48] Under circumstances much less favourable, Majorian equalled the spirit and perseverance of the ancient Romans. The woods of the Apennine were felled; the arsenals and manufactures of Ravenna and Misenum were restored; Italy and Gaul vied with each other in liberal contributions to the public service; and the Imperial navy of three hundred large galleys, with an adequate proportion of transports and smaller vessels, was collected in the secure and capacious harbour of Carthagena in Spain.[49] The intrepid countenance of Majorian animated his troops with a confidence of victory; and if we might credit the historian Procopius, his courage sometimes hurried him beyond the bounds of prudence. Anxious to explore with his own eyes the state of

[46] The review of the army, and passage of the Alps, contain the most tolerable passages of the Panegyric (470-552). M. de Buat (Hist. des Peuples, etc., tom. viii. p. 49-55) is a more satisfactory commentator than either Savaron or Sirmond.

[47] Τὰ μὲν ὅπλοις, τα δὲ λόγοις, is the just and forcible distinction of Priscus (Excerpt. Legat. p. 42 [p. 156, ed. Bonn]), in a short fragment which throws much light on the history of Majorian. Jornandes has suppressed the defeat and alliance of the Visigoths, which were solemnly proclaimed in Gallicia, and are marked in the Chronicle of Idatius.

[48] Florus, l. ii. c. 2. He amuses himself with the poetical fancy that the trees had been transformed into ships; and, indeed, the whole transaction, as it is related in the first book of Polybius, deviates too much from the probable course of human events.

[49] Interea duplici texis dum littore classem
Inferno superoque mari, cadit omnis in æquor
Silva tibi, etc.
                    Sidon. Panegyr. Majorian. 441-461.
The number of ships, which Priscus fixes at 300, is magnified, by an indefinite comparison with the fleets of Agamemnon, Xerxes, and Augustus.

the Vandals, he ventured, after disguising the colour of his hair, to visit Carthage in the character of his own ambassador: and Genseric was afterwards mortified by the discovery that he had entertained and dismissed the emperor of the Romans. Such an anecdote may be rejected as an improbable fiction, but it is a fiction which would not have been imagined unless in the life of a hero.[50]

Without the help of a personal interview, Genseric was sufficiently acquainted with the genius and designs of his adversary. He practised his customary arts of fraud and delay, but he practised them without success. His applications for peace became each hour more submissive, and perhaps more sincere; but the inflexible Majorian had adopted the ancient maxim that Rome could not be safe as long as Carthage existed in a hostile state. The king of the Vandals distrusted the valour of his native subjects, who were enervated by the luxury of the South;[51] he suspected the fidelity of the vanquished people, who abhorred him as an Arian tyrant; and the desperate measure which he executed of reducing Mauritania into a desert[52] could not defeat the operations of the Roman emperor, who was at liberty to land his troops on any part of the African coast. But Genseric was saved from impending and inevitable ruin by the treachery of some powerful subjects, envious or apprehensive of their master's success. Guided by their secret intelligence, he surprised the unguarded fleet in the bay of Carthagena: many of the ships were sunk, or taken, or burnt; and the preparations of three years were destroyed in a single day.[53] After this event the behaviour of the two antagonists showed them superior to their fortune. The Vandal, instead of being elated by this accidental victory, immediately renewed his solicitations for peace. The emperor of the West, who was capable of forming great designs and of supporting heavy disappointments, consented to a treaty, or rather to a suspension of arms, in the full assurance that before he could restore his navy he should be supplied with provocations to justify a second war. Majorian returned to Italy to

[50] Procopius de Bell. Vandal. l. i. c. 7, p. 194 [tom. i. p. 341, ed. Bonn]. When Genseric conducted his unknown guest into the arsenal of Carthage, the arms clashed of their own accord. Majorian had tinged his yellow locks with a black colour.

[51]   Spoliisque potitus
Immensis, robur luxû jam perdidit omne,
Quo valuit dum pauper erat.
                              Panegyr. Majorian. 330.
He afterwards applies to Genseric, unjustly as it should seem, the vices of his subjects.

[52] He burnt the villages and poisoned the springs (Priscus, p. 42 [p. 156, ed. Bonn]). Dubos (Hist. Critique, tom. i. p. 475) observes that the magazines which the Moors buried in the earth might escape his destructive search. Two or three hundred pits are sometimes dug in the same place, and each pit contains at least four hundred bushels of corn. Shaw's Travels, p. 139.

[53] Idatius, who was safe in Gallicia from the power of Ricimer, boldly and honestly declares, Vandali per proditores admoniti, etc.: he dissembles, however, the name of the traitor.

prosecute his labours for the public happiness; and as he was conscious of his own integrity, he might long remain ignorant of the dark conspiracy which threatened his throne and his life. The recent misfortune of Carthagena sullied the glory which had dazzled the eyes of the multitude: almost every description of civil and military officers were exasperated against the Reformer, since they all derived some advantage from the abuses which he endeavoured to suppress; and the patrician Ricimer impelled the inconstant passions of the barbarians against a prince whom he esteemed and hated. The virtues of Majorian could not protect him from the impetuous sedition which broke out in the camp near Tortona at the foot of the Alps. He was compelled to abdicate the Imperial purple; five days after his abdication it was reported that he died of a dysentery,[54] and the humble tomb which covered his remains was consecrated by the respect and gratitude of succeeding generations.[55] The private character of Majorian inspired love and respect. Malicious calumny and satire excited his indignation, or, if he himself were the object, his contempt; but he protected the freedom of wit, and in the hours which the emperor gave to the familiar society of his friends he could indulge his taste for pleasantry without degrading the majesty of his rank.[56]

It was not perhaps without some regret that Ricimer sacrificed his friend to the interest of his ambition: but he resolved in a second choice to avoid the imprudent preference of superior virtue and merit. At his command the obsequious senate of Rome bestowed the Imperial title on Libius Severus, who ascended the throne of the West without emerging from the obscurity of a private condition. History has scarcely deigned to notice his birth, his elevation, his character, or his death. Severus expired as soon as his life became inconvenient to his patron;[57] and it would be useless to discriminate his nominal reign in

[54] Procop. de Bell. Vandal. l. i. c. 7, p. 194 [tom. i. p. 342, ed. Bonn]. The testimony of Idatius is fair and impartial: "Majorianum de Galliis Romam redeuntem, et Romano imperio vel nomini res necessarias ordinantem, Richimer livore percitus, et *invidorum* consilio fultus, fraude interficit circumventum" [Sirmondi Op. tom. ii. p. 311]. Some read *Suevorum,* and I am unwilling to efface either of the words, as they express the different accomplices who united in the conspiracy against Majorian.

[55] See the Epigrams of Ennodius, No. cxxxv. inter Sirmond. Opera, tom. i. p. 1903. It is flat and obscure; but Ennodius was made bishop of Pavia fifty years after the death of Majorian, and his praise deserves credit and regard.

[56] Sidonius gives a tedious account (l. i. Epist. xi. p. 25-31) of a supper at Arles, to which he was invited by Majorian a short time before his death. He had no intention of praising a deceased emperor; but a casual disinterested remark, " Subrisit Augustus; ut erat, auctoritate servatâ, cum se communioni dedisset, joci plenus," outweighs the six hundred lines of his venal panegyric.

[57] Sidonius (Panegyr. Anthem. 317) dismisses him to heaven:—
Auxerat Augustus naturæ lege Severus
Divorum numerum.
And an old list of the emperors, composed about the time of Justinian, praises his piety, and fixes his residence at Rome (Sirmond. Not. ad Sidon, p. 111, 112).

the vacant interval of six years between the death of Majorian and the elevation of Anthemius. During that period the government was in the hands of Ricimer alone; and although the modest barbarian disclaimed the name of king, he accumulated treasures, formed a separate army, negotiated private alliances, and ruled Italy with the same independent and despotic authority which was afterwards exercised by Odoacer and Theodoric. But his dominions were bounded by the Alps; and two Roman generals, Marcellinus and Ægidius, maintained their allegiance to the republic, by rejecting with disdain the phantom which he styled an emperor. Marcellinus still adhered to the old religion; and the devout Pagans, who secretly disobeyed the laws of the church and state, applauded his profound skill in the science of divination. But he possessed the more valuable qualifications of learning, virtue, and courage;[58] the study of the Latin literature had improved his taste, and his military talents had recommended him to the esteem and confidence of the great Aëtius, in whose ruin he was involved. By a timely flight Marcellinus escaped the rage of Valentinian, and boldly asserted his liberty amidst the convulsions of the Western empire. His voluntary or reluctant submission to the authority of Majorian was rewarded by the government of Sicily and the command of an army stationed in that island to oppose or to attack the Vandals; but his barbarian mercenaries, after the emperor's death, were tempted to revolt by the artful liberality of Ricimer. At the head of a band of faithful followers the intrepid Marcellinus occupied the province of Dalmatia, assumed the title of patrician of the West, secured the love of his subjects by a mild and equitable reign, built a fleet which claimed the dominion of the Hadriatic, and alternately alarmed the coasts of Italy and of Africa.[59] Ægidius, the master-general of Gaul, who equalled, or at least who imitated, the heroes of ancient Rome,[60] proclaimed his immortal resentment against the assassins of his beloved master. A brave and numerous army was attached to his standard: and though he was prevented by the arts of Ricimer and the arms of the Visigoths from marching to the gates of Rome, he maintained his independent sovereignty beyond the Alps and rendered the name of Ægidius respectable both in peace and war. The Franks, who had punished with exile the youthful follies of Childeric, elected the Roman general for their king; his vanity rather than his ambition was gratified by that singular honour; and

---

[58] Tillemont, who is always scandalised by the virtues of infidels, attributes this advantageous portrait of Marcellinus (which Suidas has preserved) to the partial zeal of some Pagan historian (Hist. des Empereurs. tom. vi. p. 330).

[59] Procopius de Bell. Vandal. l. i. c. 6, p. 191 [tom. i. p. 336, ed. Bonn]. In various circumstances of the life of Marcellinus, it is not easy to reconcile the Greek historian with the Latin Chronicles of the times.

[60] I must apply to Ægidius the praises which Sidonius (Panegyr. Majorian. 553) bestows on a nameless master-general, who commanded the rear-guard of Majorian. Idatius, from public report, commends his Christian piety; and Priscus mentions (p. 42 [p. 156, 157, ed. Bonn]) his military virtues.

when the nation at the end of four years repented of the injury which they had offered to the Merovingian family, he patiently acquiesced in the restoration of the lawful prince. The authority of Ægidius ended only with his life, and the suspicions of poison and secret violence, which derived some countenance from the character of Ricimer, were eagerly entertained by the passionate credulity of the Gauls.[61]

The kingdom of Italy, a name to which the Western empire was gradually reduced, was afflicted, under the reign of Ricimer, by the incessant depredations of the Vandal pirates.[62] In the spring of each year they equipped a formidable navy in the port of Carthage, and Genseric himself, though in a very advanced age, still commanded in person the most important expeditions. His designs were concealed with impenetrable secrecy till the moment that he hoisted sail. When he was asked by his pilot what course he should steer, "Leave the determination to the winds (replied the barbarian, with pious arrogance): *they* will transport us to the guilty coast whose inhabitants have provoked the divine justice;" but if Genseric himself deigned to issue more precise orders, he judged the most wealthy to be the most criminal. The Vandals repeatedly visited the coasts of Spain, Liguria, Tuscany, Campania, Lucania, Bruttium, Apulia, Calabria, Venetia, Dalmatia, Epirus, Greece, and Sicily: they were tempted to subdue the island of Sardinia, so advantageously placed in the centre of the Mediterranean; and their arms spread desolation or terror from the Columns of Hercules to the mouth of the Nile. As they were more ambitious of spoil than of glory, they seldom attacked any fortified cities, or engaged any regular troops in the open field. But the celerity of their motions enabled them almost at the same time to threaten and to

[61] Greg. Turon. l. ii. c. 12, in tom. ii. p. 168. The Père Daniel, whose ideas were superficial and modern, has started some objections against the story of Childeric (Hist. de France, tom. i. Préface Historique, p. lxxviii. etc.) ; but they have been fairly satisfied by Dubos (Hist. Critique, tom. i. p. 460-510), and by two authors who disputed the prize of the Academy of Soissons (p. 131-177, 310-339). With regard to the term of Childeric's exile, it is necessary either to prolong the life of Ægidius beyond the date assigned by the Chronicle of Idatius, or to correct the text of Gregory, by reading *quarto* anno, instead of *octavo*.

[62] The naval war of Genseric is described by Priscus (Excerpta Legation. p. 42 [p. 157, ed. Bonn]), Procopius (de Bell. Vandal. l. i. c. 5, p. 189, 190, and c. 22, p. 228 [tom. i. p. 332, *sqq.,* and p. 399, ed. Bonn]), Victor Vitensis (de Persecut. Vandal. l. i. c. 17, and Ruinart, p. 467-481), and in the three panegyrics of Sidonius, whose chronological order is absurdly transposed in the editions both of Savaron and Sirmond. (Avit. Carm. vii. 441-451. Majorian. Carm. v. 327-350, 385-440. Anthem. Carm. ii. 348-386.) In one passage the poet seems inspired by his subject, and expresses a strong idea by a lively image:—

—— Hinc Vandalus hostis
Urget; et in nostrum numerosâ classe quotannis
Militat excidium; conversoque ordine fati
Torrida Caucaseos infert mihi Byrsa furores.

[Carm. ii. 347.]

attack the most distant objects which attracted their desires; and as they always embarked a sufficient number of horses, they had no sooner landed than they swept the dismayed country with a body of light cavalry. Yet, notwithstanding the example of their king, the native Vandals and Alani insensibly declined this toilsome and perilous warfare; the hardy generation of the first conquerors was almost extinguished, and their sons, who were born in Africa, enjoyed the delicious baths and gardens which had been acquired by the valour of their fathers. Their place was readily supplied by a various multitude of Moors and Romans, of captives and outlaws; and those desperate wretches, who had already violated the laws of their country, were the most eager to promote the atrocious acts which disgraced the victories of Genseric. In the treatment of his unhappy prisoners he sometimes consulted his avarice, and sometimes indulged his cruelty; and the massacre of five hundred noble citizens of Zante or Zacynthus, whose mangled bodies he cast into the Ionian Sea, was imputed by the public indignation to his latest posterity.

Such crimes could not be excused by any provocations, but the war which the king of the Vandals prosecuted against the Roman empire was justified by a specious and reasonable motive. The widow of Valentinian, Eudoxia, whom he had led captive from Rome to Carthage, was the sole heiress of the Theodosian house; her elder daughter, Eudocia, became the reluctant wife of Hunneric, his eldest son; and the stern father, asserting a legal claim which could not easily be refuted or satisfied, demanded a just proportion of the Imperial patrimony. An adequate, or at least a valuable, compensation was offered by the Eastern emperor to purchase a necessary peace. Eudoxia and her younger daughter Placidia, were honourably restored, and the fury of the Vandals was confined to the limits of the Western empire. The Italians, destitute of a naval force, which alone was capable of protecting their coasts, implored the aid of the more fortunate nations of the East, who had formerly acknowledged in peace and war the supremacy of Rome. But the perpetual division of the two empires had alienated their interest and their inclinations; the faith of a recent treaty was alleged; and the Western Romans, instead of arms and ships, could only obtain the assistance of a cold and ineffectual mediation. The haughty Ricimer, who had long struggled with the difficulties of his situation, was at length reduced to address the throne of Constantinople in the humble language of a subject; and Italy submitted, as the price and security of the alliance, to accept a master from the choice of the emperor of the East.[63] It is not the purpose of the present chapter, or even of the

---

[63] The poet himself is compelled to acknowledge the distress of Ricimer:—

Præterea invictus Ricimer, quem publica fata
Respiciunt, *proprio* solus vix *Marte* repellit
Piratam per rura vabum.

[Carm. ii. 352.]

Italy addresses her complaint to the Tiber; and Rome, at the solicitation of

present volume, to continue the distinct series of the Byzantine history; but a concise view of the reign and character of the emperor Leo may explain the last efforts that were attempted to save the falling empire of the West.[64]

Since the death of the younger Theodosius, the domestic repose of Constantinople had never been interrupted by war or faction. Pulcheria had bestowed her hand, and the sceptre of the East, on the modest virtue of Marcian: he gratefully reverenced her august rank and virgin chastity; and, after her death, he gave his people the example of the religious worship that was due to the memory of the Imperial saint.[65] Attentive to the prosperity of his own dominions, Marcian seemed to behold with indifference the misfortunes of Rome; and the obstinate refusal of a brave and active prince to draw his sword against the Vandals was ascribed to a secret promise which had formerly been exacted from him when he was a captive in the power of Genseric.[66] The death of Marcian, after a reign of seven years, would have exposed the East to the danger of a popular election, if the superior weight of a single family had not been able to incline the balance in favour of the candidate whose interest they supported. The patrician Aspar might have placed the diadem on on his own head, if he would have subscribed the Nicene creed.[67] During three generations the armies of the East were successively commanded by his father, by himself, and by his son Ardaburius; his barbarian guards formed a military force that overawed the palace and the capital; and the liberal distribution of his immense treasures rendered Aspar as popular as he was powerful. He recommended the obscure name of Leo of Thrace, a military tribune, and the principal steward of his household. His nomination was unanimously ratified by the senate; and the servant of Aspar received the Imperial crown from the hands of the patriarch or bishop, who was permitted to express, by this unusual ceremony, the suffrage of the Deity.[68] This

the river-god, transports herself to Constantinople, renounces her ancient claims, and implores the friendship of Aurora, the goddess of the East. This fabulous machinery, which the genius of Claudian had used and abused, is the constant and miserable resource of the muse of Sidonius.

[64] The original authors of the reigns of Marcian, Leo, and Zeno, are reduced to some imperfect fragments, whose deficiencies must be supplied from the more recent compilations of Theophanes, Zonaras, and Cedrenus.

[65] St. Pulcheria died A.D. 453, four years before her nominal husband; and her festival is celebrated on the 10th of September by the modern Greeks: she bequeathed an immense patrimony to pious, or at least to ecclesiastical uses. See Tillemont. Mémoires Ecclés. tom. xv. p. 181-184.

[66] See Procopius de Bell. Vandal. l. i. c. 4, p. 185 [tom. i. p. 325, ed. Bonn].

[67] From this disability of Aspar to ascend the throne, it may be inferred that the stain of *Heresy* was perpetual and indelible, while that of *Barbarism* disappeared in the second generation.

[68] Theophanes, p. 95 [ed. Par.; tom. i. p. 170, ed. Bonn]. This appears to be the first origin of a ceremony which all the Christian princes of the world have since adopted; and from which the clergy have deduced the most formidable consequences.

emperor, the first of the name of Leo, has been distinguished by the title of the *Great*, from a succession of princes who gradually fixed in the opinion of the Greeks a very humble standard of heroic, or at least of royal, perfection. Yet the temperate firmness with which Leo resisted the oppression of his benefactor showed that he was conscious of his duty and of his prerogative. Aspar was astonished to find that his influence could no longer appoint a præfect of Constantinople: he presumed to reproach his sovereign with a breach of promise, and, insolently shaking his purple, " It is not proper (said he) that the man who is invested with this garment should be guilty of lying." " Nor is it proper (replied Leo) that a prince should be compelled to resign his own judgment, and the public interest, to the will of a subject." [69] After this extraordinary scene, it was impossible that the reconciliation of the emperor and the patrician could be sincere; or, at least, that it could be solid and permanent. An army of Isaurians [70] was secretly levied and introduced into Constantinople; and while Leo undermined the authority, and prepared the disgrace, of the family of Aspar, his mild and cautious behaviour restrained them from any rash and desperate attempts, which might have been fatal to themselves or their enemies. The measures of peace and war were affected by this internal revolution. As long as Aspar degraded the majesty of the throne, the secret correspondence of religion and interest engaged him to favour the cause of Genseric. When Leo had delivered himself from the ignominious servitude, he listened to the complaints of the Italians; resolved to extirpate the tyranny of the Vandals; and declared his alliance with his colleague Anthemius, whom he solemnly invested with the diadem and purple of the West.

The virtues of Anthemius have perhaps been magnified, since the Imperial descent, which he could only deduce from the usurper Procopius, has been swelled into a line of emperors.[71] But the merit of his immediate parents, their honours, and their riches, rendered Anthemius one of the most illustrious subjects of the East. His father, Procopius, obtained, after his Persian embassy, the rank of general and patrician; and the name of Anthemius was derived from his maternal grandfather, the celebrated præfect, who protected, with so much ability and success,

---

[69] Cedrenus (p. 346 [ed. Par.; tom. i. p. 607, ed. Bonn]), who was conversant with the writers of better days, has preserved the remarkable words of Aspar, Βασιλεῦ, τὸν ταύτην τὴν ἀλουργίδα περιβεβλημένον οὐ Χρῆ διαψεύδεσθαι.

[70] The power of the Isaurians agitated the Eastern empire in the two succeeding reigns of Zeno and Anastasius; but it ended in the destruction of those barbarians, who maintained their fierce independence about two hundred and thirty years.

[71] ——— Tali tu civis ab urbe
Procopio genitore micas; cui prisca propago
Augustis venit a *proavis*.

The poet (Sidon. Panegyr. Anthem. 67-306) then proceeds to relate the private life and fortunes of the future emperor, with which he must have been very imperfectly acquainted.

the infant reign of Theodosius. The grandson of the præfect was raised above the condition of a private subject by his marriage with Euphemia, the daughter of the emperor Marcian. This splendid alliance, which might supersede the necessity of merit, hastened the promotion of Anthemius to the successive dignities of count, of master-general, of consul, and of patrician; and his merit or fortune claimed the honours of a victory which was obtained on the banks of the Danube over the Huns. Without indulging an extravagant ambition, the son-in-law of Marcian might hope to be his successor; but Anthemius supported the disappointment with courage and patience; and his subsequent elevation was universally approved by the public, who esteemed him worthy to reign till he ascended the throne.[72] The emperor of the West marched from Constantinople, attended by several counts of high distinction, and a body of guards almost equal to the strength and numbers of a regular army: he entered Rome in triumph, and the choice of Leo was confirmed by the senate, the people, and the barbarian confederates of Italy.[73] The solemn inauguration of Anthemius was followed by the nuptials of his daughter and the patrician Ricimer; a fortunate event, which was considered as the firmest security of the union and happiness of the state. The wealth of two empires was ostentatiously displayed; and many senators completed their ruin, by an expensive effort to disguise their poverty. All serious business was suspended during this festival; the courts of justice were shut; the streets of Rome, the theatres, the places of public and private resort, resounded with hymenæal song and dances: and the royal bride, clothed in silken robes, with a crown on her head, was conducted to the palace of Ricimer, who had changed his military dress for the habit of a consul and a senator. On this memorable occasion, Sidonius, whose early ambition had been so fatally blasted, appeared as the orator of Auvergne, among the provincial deputies who addressed the throne with congratulations or complaints.[74] The calends of January were now approaching, and the venal poet, who had loved Avitus and esteemed Majorian, was persuaded by his friends to celebrate, in heroic verse, the merit, the felicity, the second consulship, and the future triumphs of the emperor Anthemius. Sidonius pronounced, with assurance and success, a panegyric which is still extant; and whatever might be the imperfections, either of the subject or of the composition, the welcome flatterer was immediately rewarded with the præfecture of Rome; a dignity

[72] Sidonius discovers, with tolerable ingenuity, that this disappointment added new lustre to the virtues of Anthemius (210, etc.), who declined one sceptre, and reluctantly accepted another (22, etc.).

[73] The poet again celebrates the unanimity of all orders of the state (15-22); and the Chronicle of Idatius mentions the forces which attended his march.

[74] Interveni etenim nuptiis Patricii Ricimeris, cui filia perennis Augusti in spem publicæ securitatis copulabatur. The journey of Sidonius from Lyons, and the festival of Rome, are described with some spirit. L. i. Epist. 5, p. 9-13; Epist. 9, p. 21.

which placed him among the illustrious personages of the empire, till he wisely preferred the more respectable character of a bishop, and a saint.[75]

The Greeks ambitiously commend the piety and catholic faith of the emperor whom they gave to the West; nor do they forget to observe that, when he left Constantinople, he converted his palace into the pious foundation of a public bath, a church, and an hospital for old men.[76] Yet some suspicious appearances are found to sully the theological fame of Anthemius. From the conversation of Philotheus, a Macedonian sectary, he had imbibed the spirit of religious toleration; and the heretics of Rome would have assembled with impunity, if the bold and vehement censure which pope Hilary pronounced in the church of St. Peter had not obliged him to abjure the unpopular indulgence.[77] Even the Pagans, a feeble and obscure remnant, conceived some vain hopes, from the indifference, or partiality, of Anthemius; and his singular friendship for the philosopher Severus, whom he promoted to the consulship, was ascribed to a secret project of reviving the ancient worship of the gods.[78] These idols were crumbled into dust: and the mythology which had once been the creed of nations was so universally disbelieved, that it might be employed without scandal, or at least without suspicion, by Christian poets.[79] Yet the vestiges of superstition were not absolutely obliterated, and the festival of the Lupercalia, whose origin had preceded the foundation of Rome, was still celebrated under the reign of Anthemius. The savage and simple rites were expressive of an early state of society before the invention of arts and agriculture. The rustic deities who presided over the toils and pleasures of the pastoral life, Pan, Faunus, and their train of satyrs, were such

[75] Sidonius (l. i. Epist. 9, p. 23, 24) very fairly states his motive, his labour, and his reward. "Hic ipse Panegyricus, si non judicium, certe eventum, boni operis, accepit." He was made bishop of Clermont A.D. 471. Tillemont, Mém. Ecclés. tom. xvi. p. 750.

[76] The palace of Anthemius stood on the banks of the Propontis. In the ninth century, Alexius, the son-in-law of the emperor Theophilus, obtained permission to purchase the ground, and ended his days in a monastery which he founded on that delightful spot. Ducange, Constantinopolis Christiana, p. 117, 152.

[77] Papa Hilarius . . . apud beatum Petrum Apostolum, palam ne id fieret, clarâ voce constrinxit, in tantum ut non ea facienda cum interpositione juramenti idem promitteret Imperator. Gelasius Epistol. ad Andronicum, apud Baron. A.D. 467, No. 3. The cardinal observes, with some complacency, that it was much easier to plant heresies at Constantinople than at Rome.

[78] Damascius, in the Life of the philosopher Isidore, apud Photium, p. 1040 [p. 340a, ed. Bekk.]. Damascius, who lived under Justinian, composed another work, consisting of 570 præternatural stories of souls, dæmons, apparitions, the dotage of Platonic Paganism.

[79] In the poetical works of Sidonius, which he afterwards condemned (l. ix. Epist. 16, p. 285), the fabulous deities are the principal actors. If Jerom was scourged by the angels for only reading Virgil, the bishop of Clermont, for such a vile imitation, deserved an additional whipping from the Muses.

as the fancy of shepherds might create, sportive, petulant, and lascivious; whose power was limited, and whose malice was inoffensive. A goat was the offering the best adapted to their character and attributes; the flesh of the victim was roasted on willow spits; and the riotous youths, who crowded to the feast, ran naked about the fields, with leather thongs in their hands, communicating, as it was supposed, the blessing of fecundity to the women whom they touched.[80] The altar of Pan was erected, perhaps by Evander the Arcadian, in a dark recess in the side of the Palatine hill, watered by a perpetual fountain, and shaded by a hanging grove. A tradition that, in the same place, Romulus and Remus were suckled by the wolf, rendered it still more sacred and venerable in the eyes of the Romans; and this sylvan spot was gradually surrounded by the stately edifices of the Forum.[81] After the conversion of the Imperial city, the Christians still continued, in the month of Feburary, the annual celebration of the Lupercalia; to which they ascribed a secret and mysterious influence on the genial powers of the animal and vegetable world. The bishops of Rome were solicitous to abolish a profane custom so repugnant to the spirit of Christianity; but their zeal was not supported by the authority of the civil magistrate: the inveterate abuse subsisted till the end of the fifth century, and pope Gelasius, who purified the capital from the last stain of idolatry, appeased, by a formal apology, the murmurs of the senate and people.[82]

In all his public declarations the emperor Leo assumes the authority, and professes the affection of a father for his son Anthemius, with whom he had divided the administration of the universe.[83] The situation, and perhaps the character, of Leo dissuaded him from exposing his person to the toils and dangers of an African war. But the powers of the Eastern empire were strenuously exerted to deliver Italy and the Mediterranean from the Vandals; and Genseric, who had so long oppressed both the land and sea, was threatened from every side with a

[80] Ovid (Fast. l. ii. 267-452) has given an amusing description of the follies of antiquity, which still inspired so much respect, that a grave magistrate, running naked through the streets, was not an object of astonishment or laughter.

[81] See Dionys. Halicarn. l. i. [c. 79] p. 25, 65, edit. Hudson. The Roman antiquaries, Donatus (l. ii. c. 18, p. 173, 174) and Nardini (p. 386, 387), have laboured to ascertain the true situation of the Lupercal.

[82] Baronius published, from the MSS. of the Vatican, this epistle of Pope Gelasius (A.D. 496, No. 28-45), which is entitled Adversus Andromachum Senatorem, cæterosque Romanos, qui Lupercalia secundum morem pristinum colenda constituebant. Gelasius always supposes that his adversaries are nominal Christians, and, that he may not yield to them is absurd prejudice, he imputes to this harmless festival all the calamities of the age.

[83] Itaque nos quibus totius mundi regimen commisit superna provisio. . . . Pius et triumphator semper Augustus filius noster Anthemius, licet Divina Majestas et nostra creatio pietati ejus plenam Imperii commiserit, potestatem, etc. . . . Such is the dignified style of Leo, whom Anthemius respectfully names Dominus et Pater meus Princeps sacratissimus Leo. See Novell. Anthem. tit. ii. iii. p. 38, ad calcem Cod. Theod.

formidable invasion. The campaign was opened by a bold and success-ful enterprise of the præfect Heraclius.[84] The troops of Egypt, Thebais, and Libya were embarked under this command: and the Arabs, with a train of horses and camels, opened the roads of the desert. Heraclius landed on the coast of Tripoli, surprised and subdued the cities of that province, and prepared, by a laborious march, which Cato had formerly executed,[85] to join the Imperial army under the walls of Carthage. The intelligence of this loss extorted from Genseric some insidious and ineffectual propositions of peace: but he was still more seriously alarmed by the reconciliation of Marcellinus with the two empires. The independent patrician had been persuaded to acknowl-edge the legitimate title of Anthemius, whom he accompanied in his journey to Rome; the Dalmatian fleet was received into the harbours of Italy; the active valour of Marcellinus expelled the Vandals from the island of Sardinia; and the languid efforts of the West added some weight to the immense preparations of the Eastern Romans. The expense of the naval armament which Leo sent against the Vandals has been distinctly ascertained; and the curious and instructive account displays the wealth of the declining empire. The Royal demesnes, or private patrimony of the prince, supplied seventeen thou-sand pounds of gold; forty-seven thousand pounds of gold, and seven hundred thousand of silver, were levied and paid into the treasury by the Prætorian præfects. But the cities were reduced to extreme pov-erty; and the diligent calculation of fines and forfeitures, as a valuable object of the revenue, does not suggest the idea of a just, or merciful administration. The whole expense, by whatsoever means it was de-frayed, of the African campaign, amounted to the sum of one hundred and thirty thousand pounds of gold, about five millions two hundred thousand pounds sterling, at a time when the value of money appears, from the comparative price of corn, to have been somewhat higher than in the present age.[86] The fleet that sailed from Constantinople to Car-

[84] The expedition of Heraclius is clouded with difficulties (Tillemont, Hist. des Empereurs, tom. vi. p. 640), and it requires some dexterity to use the cir-cumstances afforded by Theophanes, without injury to the more respectable evidence of Procopius.

[85] The march of Cato from Berenice, in the province of Cyrene, was much longer than that of Heraclius from Tripoli. He passed the deep sandy desert in thirty days, and it was found necessary to provide, besides the ordinary supplies, a great number of skins filled with water, and several *Psylli,* who were supposed to possess the art of sucking the wounds which had been made by the serpents of their native country. See Plutarch in Caton. Uticens. [c. 56] tom. iv. p. 275; Strabon. Geograph. l. xvii. p. 1193 [p. 836, ed. Casaub.].

[86] The principal sum is clearly expressed by Procopius (de Bell. Vandal. l. i. c. 6, p. 191 [tom. i. p. 335, ed. Bonn]) : the smaller constituent parts, which Tillemont (Hist. des Empereurs, tom. vi. p. 396) has laboriously collected from the Byzantine writers, are less certain and less important. The historian Malchus laments the public misery (Excerpt. ex Suida in Corp. Hist. Byzant. p. 58) ; but he is surely unjust when he charges Leo with hoarding the treasures which he extorted from the people [p. 270, ed. Bonn].

thage consisted of eleven hundred and thirteen ships, and the number of soldiers and mariners exceeded one hundred thousand men. Basiliscus, the brother of the empress Verina, was intrusted with this important command. His sister, the wife of Leo, had exaggerated the merit of his former exploits against the Scythians. But the discovery of his guilt, or incapacity, was reserved for the African war; and his friends could only save his military reputation by asserting that he had conspired with Aspar to spare Genseric, and to betray the last hope of the Western empire.

Experience has shown that the success of an invader most commonly depends on the vigour and celerity of his operations. The strength and sharpness of the first impression are blunted by delay; the health and spirit of the troops insensibly languish in a distant climate; the naval and military force, a mighty effort which perhaps can never be repeated, is silently consumed; and every hour that is wasted in negotiation accustoms the enemy to contemplate and examine those hostile terrors which, on their first appearance, he deemed irresistible. The formidable navy of Basiliscus pursued its prosperous navigation from the Thracian Bosphorus to the coast of Africa. He landed his troops at Cape Bona, or the promontory of Mercury, about forty miles from Carthage.[87] The army of Heraclius, and the fleet of Marcellinus, either joined or seconded the Imperial lieutenant; and the Vandals who opposed his progress by sea or land were successively vanquished.[88] If Basiliscus had seized the moment of consternation, and boldly advanced to the capital, Carthage must have surrendered, and the kingdom of the Vandals was extinguished. Genseric beheld the danger with firmness, and eluded it with his veteran dexterity. He protested, in the most respectful language, that he was ready to submit his person and his dominions to the will of the emperor; but he requested a truce of five days to regulate the terms of his submission; and it was universally believed that his secret liberality contributed to the success of this public negotiation. Instead of obstinately refusing whatever indulgence his enemy so earnestly solicited, the guilty, or the credulous, Basiliscus consented to the fatal truce; and his imprudent security seemed to proclaim that he already considered himself as the conqueror of Africa. During this short interval the wind became favourable to the designs

[John Lydus, in his work, De Magistratibus, estimates the expenditure at 65,000 pounds of gold and 700,000 pounds of silver, and regards this proceeding, the blame of which he lays on Basiliscus, as bringing about the shipwreck of the state. On this point Milman says, " From that time all the revenues of the empire were anticipated, and the finances fell into inextricable confusion."—O. S.]

[87] This promontory is forty miles from Carthage (Procop. l. i. c. 6, p. 192 [De Bell. Vandal. tom. i. p. 377, ed. Bonn]), and twenty leagues from Sicily (Shaw's Travels, p. 89). Scipio landed farther in the bay, at the fair promontory; see the animated description of Livy, xxix. 26, 27.

[88] Theophanes (p. 100 [tom. i. p. 179, ed. Bonn]) affirms that many ships of the Vandals were sunk. The assertion of Jornandes (de Successione Regn.), that Basiliscus attacked Carthage, must be understood in a very qualified sense.

of Genseric. He manned his largest ships of war with the bravest of the Moors and Vandals; and they towed after them many large barks filled with combustible materials. In the obscurity of the night, these destructive vessels were impelled against the unguarded and unsuspecting fleet of the Romans, who were awakened by the sense of their instant danger. Their close and crowded order assisted the progress of the fire, which was communicated with rapid and irresistible violence; and the noise of the wind, the crackling of the flames, the dissonant cries of the soldiers and mariners, who could neither command nor obey, increased the horror of the nocturnal tumult. Whilst they laboured to extricate themselves from the fire-ships, and to save at least a part of the navy, the galleys of Genseric assaulted them with temperate and disciplined valour; and many of the Romans, who escaped the fury of the flames, were destroyed or taken by the victorious Vandals. Among the events of that disastrous night, the heroic, or rather desperate, courage of John, one of the principal officers of Basiliscus, has rescued his name from oblivion. When the ship which he had bravely defended was almost consumed, he threw himself in his armour into the sea, disdainfully rejected the esteem and pity of Genso, the son of Genseric, who pressed him to accept honourable quarter, and sunk under the waves; exclaiming, with his last breath, that he would never fall alive into the hands of those impious dogs. Actuated by a far different spirit, Basiliscus, whose station was the most remote from danger, disgracefully fled in the beginning of the engagement, returned to Constantinople with the loss of more than half of his fleet and army, and sheltered his guilty head in the sanctuary of St. Sophia, till his sister, by her tears and entreaties, could obtain his pardon from the indignant emperor. Heraclius effected his retreat through the desert; Marcellinus retired to Sicily, where he was assassinated, perhaps at the instigation of Ricimer, by one of his own captains; and the king of the Vandals expressed his surprise and satisfaction that the Romans themselves should remove from the world his most formidable antagonists.[89] After the failure of this great expedition, Genseric again became the tyrant of the sea: the coasts of Italy, Greece, and Asia, were again exposed to his revenge and avarice; Tripoli and Sardinia returned to his obedience; he added Sicily to the number of his provinces; and, before he died, in the fulness of years and of glory, be beheld the final extinction of the empire of the West.[90]

[89] Damascius in Vit. Isidor. apud Phot. p. 1048 [p. 342, ed. Bekk.]. It will appear, by comparing the three short chronicles of the times, that Marcellinus had fought near Carthage, and was killed in Sicily.

[90] For the African war see Procopius (de Bell. Vandal. l. i. c. 6, p. 191, 192, 193 [tom. i. p. 335 sqq., ed. Bonn]), Theophanes (p. 99, 100, 101, [ed. Par.; tom. i. p. 179 sqq., ed. Bonn]), Cedrenus (p. 349, 350 [tom. i. p. 613, ed. Bonn]), and Zonaras (tom. ii. l. xiv. p. 50, 51). Montesquieu (Considérations sur la Grandeur, etc., c. xx. tom. iii. p. 497) has made a judicious observation on the failure of these great naval armaments.

During his long and active reign the African monarch had studiously cultivated the friendship of the barbarians of Europe, whose arms he might employ in a seasonable and effectual diversion against the two empires. After the death of Attila he renewed his alliance with the Visigoths of Gaul; and the sons of the elder Theodoric, who succes- sively reigned over that warlike nation, were easily persuaded, by the sense of interest, to forget the cruel affront which Genseric had inflicted on their sister.[91] The death of the emperor Majorian delivered Theo- doric the Second from the restraint of fear, and perhaps of honour; he violated his recent treaty with the Romans; and the ample territory of Narbonne, which he firmly united to his dominions, became the immediate reward of his perfidy. The selfish policy of Ricimer encour- aged him to invade the provinces which were in the possession of Ægidius, his rival; but the active count, by the defence of Arles and the victory of Orleans, saved Gaul, and checked during his lifetime the progress of the Visigoths. Their ambition was soon rekindled; and the design of extinguishing the Roman empire in Spain and Gaul was con- ceived and almost completed in the reign of Euric, who assassinated his brother Theodoric, and displayed, with a more savage temper, superior abilities both in peace and war. He passed the Pyrenees at the head of a numerous army, subdued the cities of Saragossa and Pampe- luna, vanquished in battle the martial nobles of the Tarragonese prov- ince, carried his victorious arms into the heart of Lusitania, and permitted the Suevi to hold the kingdom of Gallicia under the Gothic monarchy of Spain.[92] The efforts of Euric were not less vigorous or less successful in Gaul; and throughout the country that extends from the Pyrenees to the Rhône and the Loire, Berry and Auvergne were the only cities or dioceses which refused to acknowledge him as their master.[93] In the defence of Clermont, their principal town, the inhab- itants of Auvergne sustained with inflexible resolution the miseries of of war, pestilence, and famine; and the Visigoths, relinquishing the fruitless siege, suspended the hopes of that important conquest. The youth of the province were animated by the heroic and almost incredible valour of Ecdicius, the son of the emperor Avitus,[94] who made a desper- ate sally with only eighteen horsemen, boldly attacked the Gothic army, and, after maintaining a flying skirmish, retired safe and victorious

[91] Jornandes is our best guide through the reigns of Theodoric II. and Euric (de Rebus Geticis, c. 44, 45, 46, 47, p. 675-681). Idatius ends too soon, and Isidore is too sparing of the information which he might have given on the affairs of Spain. The events that relate to Gaul are laboriously illustrated in the third book of the Abbé Dubos, Hist. Critique, tom. i. p. 424-620.

[92] See Mariana, Hist. Hispan. tom. i. l. v. c. 5, p. 162.

[93] An imperfect, but original, picture of Gaul, more especially of Auvergne, is shown by Sidonius; who, as a senator and afterwards as a bishop, was deeply interested in the fate of his country. See l. v. [vii.] Epist. 1, 5, 9, etc.

[94] Sidonius, l. iii. Epist. 3, p. 65-68; Greg. Turon. l. ii. c. 24, in tom. ii. p. 174; Jornandes, c. 45, p. 679. Perhaps Ecdicius was only the son-in-law of Avitus, his wife's son by another husband.

within the walls of Clermont. His charity was equal to his courage: in a time of extreme scarcity four thousand poor were fed at his expense; and his private influence levied an army of Burgundians for the deliverance of Auvergne. From *his* virtues alone the faithful citizens of Gaul derived any hopes of safety or freedom; and even such virtues were insufficient to avert the impending ruin of their country, since they were anxious to learn, from his authority and example, whether they should prefer the alternative of exile or servitude.[95] The public confidence was lost; the resources of the state were exhausted; and the Gauls had too much reason to believe that Anthemius, who reigned in Italy, was incapable of protecting his distressed subjects beyond the Alps. The feeble emperor could only procure for their defence the service of twelve thousand British auxiliaries. Riothamus, one of the independent kings or chieftains of the island, was persuaded to transport his troops to the continent of Gaul: he sailed up the Loire, and established his quarters in Berry, where the people complained of these oppressive allies, till they were destroyed or dispersed by the arms of the Visigoths.[96]

One of the last acts of jurisdiction which the Roman senate exercised over their subjects of Gaul was the trial and condemnation of Arvandus, the Prætorian præfect. Sidonius, who rejoices that he lived under a reign in which he might pity and assist a state-criminal, has expressed, with tenderness and freedom, the faults of his indiscreet and unfortunate friend.[97] From the perils which he had escaped, Arvandus imbibed confidence rather than wisdom; and such was the various, though uniform, imprudence of his behaviour, that his prosperity must appear much more surprising than his downfall. The second præfecture, which he obtained within the term of five years, abolished the merit and popularity of his preceding administration. His easy temper was corrupted by flattery and exasperated by opposition; he was forced to satisfy his importunate creditors with the spoils of the province; his capricious insolence offended the nobles of Gaul; and he sunk under the weight of the public hatred. The mandate of his disgrace summoned him to justify his conduct before the senate; and he passed the sea of

---

[95] Si nullæ a republicâ vires, nulla præsidia, si nullæ, quantum rumor est, Anthemii principis opes, statuit, et auctore, nobilitas, seu patriam dimitere seu capillos (Sidon. l. ii. Epist. 1, p. 33). The last words (Sirmond, Not. p. 25) may likewise denote the clerical tonsure, which was indeed the choice of Sidonius himself.

[96] The history of these Britons may be traced in Jornandes (c. 45, p. 678), Sidonius (l. iii. Epistol. 9, p. 73, 74), and Gregory of Tours (l. ii. c. 18, in tom. ii. p. 170). Sidonius (who styles these mercenary troops argutos, armatos, tumultuosos, virtute, numero, contubernio, contumaces) addresses their general in a tone of friendship and familiarity.

[97] See Sidonius, l. i. Epist. 7, p. 15-20, with Sirmond's notes. This letter does honour to his heart as well as to his understanding. The prose of Sidonius, however vitiated by a false and affected taste, is much superior to his insipid verses.

Tuscany with a favourable wind, the presage, as he vainly imagined, of his future fortunes. A decent respect was still observed for the *Præfectorian* rank; and on his arrival at Rome Arvandus was committed to the hospitality, rather than to the custody, of Flavius Asellus, the count of the sacred largesses, who resided in the Capitol.[98] He was eagerly pursued by his accusers, the four deputies of Gaul, who were all distinguished by their birth, their dignities, or their eloquence. In the name of a great province, and according to the forms of Roman jurisprudence, they instituted a civil and criminal action, requiring such restitution as might compensate the losses of individuals, and such punishment as might satisfy the justice of the state. Their charges of corrupt oppression were numerous and weighty; but they placed their secret dependence on a letter which they had intercepted, and which they could prove, by the evidence of his secretary, to have been dictated by Arvandus himself. The author of this letter seemed to dissuade the king of the Goths from a peace with the *Greek* emperor: he suggested the attack of the Britons on the Loire; and he recommended a division of Gaul, according to the law of nations, between the Visigoths and the Burgundians.[99] These pernicious schemes, which a friend could only palliate by the reproaches of vanity and indiscretion, were susceptible of a treasonable interpretation; and the deputies had artfully resolved not to produce their most formidable weapons till the decisive moment of the contest. But their intentions were discovered by the zeal of Sidonius. He immediately apprised the unsuspecting criminal of his danger; and sincerely lamented, without any mixture of anger, the haughty presumption of Arvandus, who rejected, and even resented, the salutary advice of his friends. Ignorant of his real situation, Arvandus showed himself in the Capitol in the white robe of a candidate, accepted indiscriminate salutations and offers of service, examined the shops of the merchants, the silks, and gems, sometimes with the indifference of a spectator and sometimes with the attention of a purchaser; and complained of the times, of the senate, of the prince, and of the delays of justice. His complaints were soon removed. An early day was fixed for his trial; and Arvandus appeared, with his accusers, before a numerous assembly of the Roman senate. The mournful garb which they affected excited the compassion of the judges, who were scandalised by the gay and splendid dress of their adversary: and when the præfect Arvandus, with the first of the Gallic deputies, were directed to take their places on the senatorial benches, the same contrast of pride and

[98] When the Capitol ceased to be a temple, it was appropriated to the use of the civil magistrate; and it is still the residence of the Roman senator. The jewellers, etc., might be allowed to expose their precious wares in the porticoes.

[99] Hæc ad regem Gothorum, charta videbatur emitti pacem cum Græco Imperatore dissuadens, Britannos super Ligerim sitos impugnari oportere demonstrans, cum Burgundionibus jure gentium Gallias dividi debere confirmans.

modesty was observed in their behaviour. In this memorable judgment, which presented a lively image of the old republic, the Gauls exposed, with force and freedom, the grievances of the province; and as soon as the minds of the audience were sufficiently inflamed, they recited the fatal epistle. The obstinacy of Arvandus was founded on the strange supposition that a subject could not be convicted of treason, unless he had actually conspired to assume the purple. As the paper was read, he repeatedly, and with a loud voice, acknowledged it for his genuine composition; and his astonishment was equal to his dismay when the unanimous voice of the senate declared him guilty of a capital offence. By their decree he was degraded from the rank of a præfect to the obscure condition of a plebeian, and ignominiously dragged by servile hands to the public prison. After a fortnight's adjournment the senate was again convened to pronounce the sentence of his death: but while he expected, in the island of Æsculapius, the expiration of the thirty days allowed by an ancient law to the vilest malefactors,[100] his friends interposed, the emperor Anthemius relented, and the præfect of Gaul obtained the milder punishment of exile and confiscation. The faults of Arvandus might deserve compassion; but the impunity of Seronatus accused the justice of the republic, till he was condemned and executed on the complaint of the people of Auvergne. That flagitious minister, the Catiline of his age and country, held a secret correspondence with the Visigoths to betray the province which he oppressed: his industry was continually exercised in the discovery of new taxes and obsolete offences; and his extravagant vices would have inspired contempt if they had not excited fear and abhorrence.[101]

Such criminals were not beyond the reach of justice; but whatever might be the guilt of Ricimer, that powerful barbarian was able to contend or to negotiate with the prince whose alliance he had condescended to accept. The peaceful and prosperous reign which Anthemius had promised to the West was soon clouded by misfortune and discord. Ricimer, apprehensive or impatient of a superior, retired from Rome and fixed his residence at Milan; an advantageous situation, either to invite or to repel the warlike tribes that were seated between the Alps and the Danube.[102] Italy was gradually divided into two independent and hostile kingdoms; and the nobles of Liguria, who trembled at the

[100] *Senatûsconsultum Tiberianum* (Sirmond, Not. p. 17); but that law allowed only ten days between the sentence and execution; the remaining twenty were added in the reign of Theodosius.

[101] Catilina seculi nostri. Sidonius, l. ii. Epist. 1, p. 33; l. v. Epist. 13, p. 143; l. vii. Epist. 7, p. 185. He execrates the crimes and applauds the punishment of Seronatus, perhaps with the indignation of a virtuous citizen, perhaps with the resentment of a personal enemy.

[102] Ricimer, under the reign of Anthemius, defeated and slew in battle Beorgor, king of the Alani (Jornandes, c. 45, p. 678). His sister had married the king of the Burgundians, and he maintained an intimate connection with the Suevic colony established in Pannonia and Noricum.

near approach of a civil war, fell prostrate at the feet of the patrician, and conjured him to spare their unhappy country. " For my own part," replied Ricimer, in a tone of insolent moderation, " I am still inclined to embrace the friendship of the Galatian;[103] but who will undertake to appease his anger, or to mitigate the pride which always rises in proportion to our submission?" They informed him that Epiphanius, bishop of Pavia,[104] united the wisdom of the serpent with the innocence of the dove; and appeared confident that the eloquence of such an ambassador must prevail against the strongest opposition, either of interest or passion. Their recommendation was approved; and Epiphanius, assuming the benevolent office of mediation, proceeded without delay to Rome, where he was received with the honours due to his merit and reputation. The oration of a bishop in favour of peace may be easily supposed: he argued that, in all possible circumstances, the forgiveness of injuries must be an act of mercy, or magnanimity, or prudence; and he seriously admonished the emperor to avoid a contest with a fierce barbarian, which might be fatal to himself, and must be ruinous to his dominions. Anthemius acknowledged the truth of his maxims; but he deeply felt, with grief and indignation, the behaviour of Ricimer; and his passion gave eloquence and energy to his discourse. " What favours," he warmly exclaimed, " have we refused to this ungrateful man? What provocations have we not endured? Regardless of the majesty of the purple, I gave my daughter to a Goth; I sacrificed my own blood to the safety of the republic. The liberality which ought to have secured the eternal attachment of Ricimer has exasperated him against his benefactor. What wars has he not excited against the empire? How often has he instigated and assisted the fury of hostile nations? Shall I now accept his perfidious friendship? Can I hope that he will respect the engagements of a treaty, who has already violated the duties of a son? " But the anger of Anthemius evaporated in these passionate exclamations: he insensibly yielded to the proposals of Epiphanius; and the bishop returned to his diocese with the satisfaction of restoring the peace of Italy by a reconciliation,[105] of which the sincerity and continuance might be reasonably suspected. The clemency of the emperor was extorted from his weakness; and Ricimer suspended his ambitious

---

[103] Galatam concitatum. Sirmond (in his notes to Ennodius [tom. i. p. 659]) applies this appellation to Anthemius himself. The emperor was probably born in the province of Galatia, whose inhabitants, the Gallo-Grecians, were supposed to unite the vices of a savage and a corrupted people.

[104] Epiphanius was thirty years bishop of Pavia (A.D. 467-497; see Tillemont, Mém. Ecclés. tom. xvi. p. 788). His name and actions would have been unknown to posterity if Ennodius, one of his successors, had not written his Life (Sirmond, Opera, tom. i. p. 1647-1692) ; in which he represents him as one of the greatest characters of the age.

[105] Ennodius (p. 1659-1664) has related this embassy of Epiphanius; and his narrative, verbose and turgid as it must appear, illustrates some curious passages in the fall of the Western empire.

designs till he had secretly prepared the engines with which he resolved to subvert the throne of Anthemius. The mask of peace and moderation was then thrown aside. The army of Ricimer was fortified by a numerous reinforcement of Burgundians and Oriental Suevi: he disclaimed all allegiance to the Greek emperor, marched from Milan to the gates of Rome, and, fixing his camp on the banks of the Anio, impatiently expected the arrival of Olybrius, his Imperial candidate.

The senator Olybrius, of the Anician family, might esteem himself the lawful heir of the Western empire. He had married Placidia, the younger daughter of Valentinian, after she was restored by Genseric, who still detained her sister Eudoxia, as the wife, or rather as the captive, of his son. The king of the Vandals supported, by threats and solicitations, the fair pretensions of his Roman ally; and assigned, as one of the motives of the war, the refusal of the senate and people to acknowledge their lawful prince, and the unworthy preference which they had given to a stranger.[106] The friendship of the public enemy might render Olybrius still more unpopular to the Italians; but when Ricimer meditated the ruin of the emperor Anthemius, he tempted, with the offer of a diadem, the candidate who could justify his rebellion by an illustrious name and a royal alliance. The husband of Placidia, who, like most of his ancestors, had been invested with the consular dignity, might have continued to enjoy a secure and splendid fortune in the peaceful residence of Constantinople; nor does he appear to have been tormented by such a genius as cannot be amused or occupied unless by the administration of an empire. Yet Olybrius yielded to the importunities of his friends, perhaps of his wife; rashly plunged into the dangers and calamities of a civil war; and, with the secret connivance of the emperor Leo, accepted the Italian purple, which was bestowed, and resumed, at the capricious will of a barbarian. He landed without obstacle (for Genseric was master of the sea) either at Ravenna or the port of Ostia, and immediately proceeded to the camp of Ricimer, where he was received as the sovereign of the Western world.[107]

The patrician, who had extended his posts from the Anio to the Milvian bridge, already possessed two quarters of Rome, the Vatican and the Janiculum, which are separated by the Tiber from the rest of the city;[108] and it may be conjectured that an assembly of seceding

---

[106] Priscus Excerpt. Legation. p. 74 [p. 219, ed. Bonn]. Procopius de Bell. Vandal. l. i. c. 6, p. 191 [tom. i. p. 336, ed. Bonn]. Eudoxia and her daughter were restored after the death of Majorian. Perhaps the consulship of Olybrius (A.D. 464) was bestowed as a nuptial present.

[107] The hostile appearance of Olybrius is fixed (notwithstanding the opinion of Pagi) by the duration of his reign. The secret connivance of Leo is acknowledged by Theophanes and the Paschal Chronicle. We are ignorant of his motives; but in this obscure period our ignorance extends to the most public and important facts.

[108] Of the fourteen regions, or quarters, into which Rome was divided by Augustus, only *one*, the Janiculum, lay on the Tuscan side of the Tiber. But, in

senators imitated, in the choice of Olybrius, the forms of a legal election But the body of the senate and people firmly adhered to the cause of Anthemius; and the more effectual support of a Gothic army enabled him to prolong his reign, and the public distress, by a resistance of three months, which produced the concomitant evils of famine and pestilence. At length Ricimer made a furious assult on the bridge of Hadrian, or St. Angelo; and the narrow pass was defended with equal valour by the Goths till the death of Gilimer, their leader. The victorious troops, breaking down every barrier, rushed with irresistible violence into the heart of the city, and Rome (if we may use the language of a contemporary pope) was subverted by the civil fury of Anthemius and Ricimer.[109] The unfortunate Anthemius was dragged from his concealment and inhumanly massacred by the command of his son-in-law, who thus added a third, or perhaps a fourth, emperor to the number of his victims. The soldiers, who united the rage of factious citizens with the savage manners of barbarians, were indulged without control in the licence of rapine and murder: the crowd of slaves and plebeians, who were unconcerned in the event, could only gain by the indiscriminate pillage; and the face of the city exhibited the strange contrast of stern cruelty and dissolute intemperance.[110] Forty days after this calamitous event, the subject, not of glory, but of guilt, Italy was delivered, by a painful disease, from the tyrant Ricimer, who bequeathed the command of his army to his nephew Gundobald, one of the princes of the Burgundians. In the same year all the principal actors in this great revolution were removed from the stage; and the whole reign of Olybrius, whose death does not betray any symptoms of violence, is included within the term of seven months. He left one daughter, the offspring of his marriage with Placidia; and the family of the great Theodosius, transplanted from Spain to Constantinople, was propagated in the female line as far as the eighth generation.[111]

the fifth century, the Vatican suburb formed a considerable city; and in the ecclesiastical distribution, which had been recently made by Simplicius, the reigning pope, *two* of the *seven* regions or parishes of Rome depended on the church of St. Peter. See Nardini Roma Antica, p. 67. It would require a tedious dissertation to mark the circumstances in which I am inclined to depart from the topography of that learned Roman.

[109] Nuper Anthemii et Ricimeris civili furore subversa est. Gelasius (in Epist. ad Andromach. apud Baron. A.D. 496, No. 42), Sigonius (tom. i. l. xiv. de Occidentali Imperio, p. 542, 543), and Muratori (Annali d'Italia tom. iv. p. 308, 309), with the aid of a less imperfect MS. of the Historia Miscella, have illustrated this dark and bloody transaction.

[110] Such had been the sæva ac deformis urbe totâ facies, when Rome was assaulted and stormed by the troops of Vespasian (see Tacit. Hist. iii. 82, 83); and every cause of mischief had since acquired much additional energy. The revolution of ages may bring round the same calamities; but ages may revolve without producing a Tacitus to describe them.

[111] See Ducange, Familiæ Byzantin. p. 74, 75. Areobindus, who appears to have married the niece of the emperor Justinian, was the eighth descendant of the elder Theodosius.

Whilst the vacant throne of Italy was abandoned to lawless barbar‑ians,[112] the election of a new colleague was seriously agitated in the council of Leo. The empress Verina, studious to promote the greatness of her own family, had married one of her nieces to Julius Nepos, who succeeded his uncle Marcellinus in the sovereignty of Dalmatia, a more solid possession than the title which he was persuaded to accept of Emperor of the West. But the measures of the Byzantine court were so languid and irresolute, that many months elapsed after the death of Anthemius, and even of Olybrius, before their destined successor could show himself, with a respectable force, to his Italian subjects. During that interval, Glycerius, an obscure soldier, was invested with the purple by his patron Gundobald; but the Burgundian prince was unable or unwilling to support his nomination by a civil war: the pursuits of domestic ambition recalled him beyond the Alps,[113] and his client was permitted to exchange the Roman sceptre for the bishopric of Salona. After extinguishing such a competitor, the emperor Nepos was acknowl‑edged by the senate, by the Italians, and by the provincials of Gaul; his moral virtues and military talents were loudly celebrated; and those who derived any private benefit from his government announced in prophetic strains the restoration of the public felicity.[114] Their hopes (if such hopes had been entertained) were confounded within the term of a single year; and the treaty of peace, which ceded Auvergne to the Visigoths, is the only event of his short and inglorious reign. The most faithful subjects of Gaul were sacrificed by the Italian emperor to the hope of domestic security;[115] but his repose was soon invaded by a furious sedition of the barbarian confederates, who, under the command of Orestes, their general, were in full march from Rome to Ravenna. Nepos trembled at their approach; and, instead of placing a just con‑fidence in the strength of Ravenna, he hastily escaped to his ships, and retired to his Dalmation principality, on the opposite coast of the

---

[112] The last revolutions of the Western empire are faintly marked in Theo‑phanes (p. 102 [tom. i. p. 184, ed. Bonn]), Jornandes (c. 45, p. 679), the Chronicle of Marcellinus, and the Fragments of an anonymous writer, published by Valesius at the end of Ammianus (p. 716, 717 [tom. ii. p. 303 *sq.*, ed. Bipon.] If Photius had not been so wretchedly concise, we should derive much informa‑tion from the contemporary histories of Malchus and Candidus. See his Extracts, p. 172-179 [p. 54-56, ed. Bekk.].

[113] See Greg. Turon. l. ii. c. 28, in tom. ii. p. 175. Dubos, Hist. Critique, tom. i. p. 613. By the murder or death of his two brothers, Gundabald acquired the sole possession of the kingdom of Burgundy, whose ruin was hastened by their discord.

[114] Julius Nepos armis pariter summus Augustus ac moribus. Sidonius, l. v. Ep. 16, p. 146. Nepos had given to Ecdicius the title of Patrician, which An‑themius had promised, decessoris Anthemii fidem absolvit. See l. viii. Ep. 7, p. 224 [l. v. Ep. 16, p. 146].

[115] Epiphanius was sent ambassador from Nepos to the Visigoths for the purpose of ascertaining the *fines Imperii Italici* (Ennodius in Sirmond, tom. i. p. 1665-1669). His pathetic discourse concealed the disgraceful secret which soon excited the just and bitter complaints of the bishop of Clermont.

Hadriatic. By this shameful abdication he protracted his life about
five years, in a very ambiguous state between an emperor and an exile,
till he was assassinated at Salona by the ungrateful Glycerius, who was
translated, perhaps as the reward of his crime, to the archbishopric of
Milan.[116]

The nations who had asserted their independence after the death of
Attila were established, by the right of possession or conquest, in the
boundless countries to the north of the Danube; or in the Roman provinces between the river and the Alps. But the bravest of their youth enlisted in the army of *confederates*, who formed the defence and the terror
of Italy;[117] and in this promiscuous multitude, the names of the Heruli,
the Sciri, the Alani, the Turcilingi, and the Rugians, appear to have
predominated. The example of these warriors was imitated by Orestes,[118] the son of Tatullus, and the father of the last Roman emperor of
the West. Orestes, who has been already mentioned in this history,
had never deserted his country. His birth and fortunes rendered him
one of the most illustrious subjects of Pannonia. When that province
was ceded to the Huns, he entered into the service of Attila, his lawful sovereign, obtained the office of his secretary, and was repeatedly
sent ambassador to Constantinople, to represent the person and signify
the commands of the imperious monarch. The death of that conqueror
restored him to his freedom; and Orestes might honourably refuse either
to follow the sons of Attila into the Scythian desert, or to obey the Ostrogoths, who had usurped the dominion of Pannonia. He preferred the
service of the Italian princes, the successors of Valentinian; and, as
he possessed the qualifications of courage, industry, and experience, he
advanced with rapid steps in the military profession, till he was elevated,
by the favour of Nepos himself, to the dignities of patrician and master-
general of the troops. These troops had been long accustomed to

[116] Malchus, apud Phot. p. 172 [p. 54 b. ed. Bekk.]. Ennod. Epigram, lxxxii.
in Sirmond Oper. tom. i. p. 1879. Some doubt may however be raised on the
identity of the emperor and the archbishop.

[117] Our knowledge of these mercenaries who subverted the Western empire
is derived from Procopius (de Bell. Gothico. l. i. c. i. p. 308 [tom. ii. p. 6, ed.
Bonn]). The popular opinion and the recent historians represent Odoacer in
the false light of a *stranger* and a *king*, who invaded Italy with an army of
foreigners, his native subjects.

[Of these peoples who formed at once the defence and the terror of Italy,
nearly all originally came from the neighbourhood of the Baltic. The Heruli
appear again later on. The Turcilingi are probably the same tribe which are
described by Ptolemy (ii. 11, 14) under the corrupt form, Ρουτικλειοι, and are
stated to be dwelling on the Vistula. The Sciri or Scirri are also placed by
Pliny on the eastern side of the Vistula. The Rugii are first mentioned by
Tacitus in the Germania (Germ. c. 43), who places them on the Baltic, and are
perhaps the people of the gulf of Riga. Cf. Zeuss, *Die Deutschen und die
Nachbarstämme.*—O. S.]

[118] Orestes, qui eo tempore quando Attila ad Italiam venit, se illi junxit, et
ejus notarius factus fuerat. Anonym. Vales. p. 716 [Amm. Marc. tom. ii. p. 303,
ed. Bipon.] He is mistaken in the date; but we may credit his assertion that
the secretary of Attila was the father of Augustulus.

reverence the character and authority of Orestes, who affected their manners, conversed with them in their own language, and was intimately connected with their national chieftains by long habits of familiarity and friendship. At his solicitaton they rose in arms against the obscure Greek who presumed to claim their obedience; and when Orestes, from some secret motive, declined the purple, they consented, with the same facility, to acknowledge his son Augustulus as the emperor of the West. By the abdication of Nepos, Orestes had now attained the summit of his ambitious hopes; but he soon discovered, before the end of the first year, that the lessons of perjury and ingratitude which a rebel must inculcate will be retorted against himself, and that the precarious sovereign of Italy was only permitted to choose whether he would be the slave or the victim of his barbarian mercenaries. The dangerous alliance of these strangers had oppressed and insulted the last remains of Roman freedom and dignity. At each revolution their pay and privileges were augmented; but their insolence increased in a still more extravagant degree; they envied the fortune of their brethren in Gaul, Spain, and Africa, whose victorious arms had acquired an independent and perpetual inheritance; and they insisted on their peremptory demand that a *third* part of the lands of Italy should be immediately divided among them. Orestes, with a spirit which, in another situation, might be entitled to our esteem, chose rather to encounter the rage of an armed multitude than to subscribe the ruin of an innocent people. He rejected the audacious demand; and his refusal was favourable to the ambition of Odoacer, a bold barbarian, who assured his fellow-soldiers that, if they dared to associate under his command, they might soon extort the justice which had been denied to their dutiful petitions. From all the camps and garrisons of Italy the confederates, actuated by the same resentment and the same hopes, impatiently flocked to the standard of this popular leader; and the unfortunate patrician, overwhelmed by the torrent, hastily retreated to the strong city of Pavia, the episcopal seat of the holy Epiphanites. Pavia was immediately besieged, the fortifications were stormed, the town was pillaged; and although the bishop might labour, with much zeal and some success, to save the property of the church and the chastity of female captives, the tumult could only be appeased by the execution of Orestes.[119] His brother Paul was slain in an action near Ravenna; and the helpless Augustulus, who could no longer command the respect, was reduced to implore the clemency, of Odoacer.

That successful barbarian was the son of Edecon; who, in some remarkable transactions, particularly described in a preceding chapter, had been the colleague of Orestes himself. The honour of an ambassador should be exempt from suspicion; and Edecon had listened to a conspiracy against the life of his sovereign. But this apparent guilt was

---

[119] See Ennodius (in Vit. Epiphan. Sirmond, tom. i. p. 1669, 1670). He adds weight to the narrative of Procopius, though we may doubt whether the devil actually contrived the siege of Pavia to distress the bishop and his flock.

expiated by his merit or repentance: his rank was eminent and conspicuous; he enjoyed the favour of Attila; and the troops under his command, who guarded in their turn the royal village, consisted of a tribe of Sciri, his immediate and hereditary subjects. In the revolt of the nations they still adhered to the Huns; and, more than twelve years afterwards, the name of Edecon is honourably mentioned in their unequal contest with the Ostrogoths; which was terminated, after two bloody battles, by the defeat and dispersion of the Sciri.[120] Their gallant leader, who did not survive this national calamity, left two sons, Onulf and Odoacer, to struggle with adversity, and to maintain as they might, by rapine or service, the faithful followers of their exile. Onulf directed his steps towards Constantinople, where he sullied, by the assassination of a generous benefactor, the fame which he had acquired in arms. His brother Odoacer led a wandering life among the barbarians of Noricum, with a mind and a fortune suited to the most desperate adventures; and when he had fixed his choice, he piously visited the cell of Severinus, the popular saint of the country, to solicit his approbation and blessing. The lowness of the door would not admit the lofty stature of Odoacer: he was obliged to stoop; but in that humble attitude the saint could discern the symptoms of his future greatness; and addressing him in a prophetic tone, " Pursue (said he) your design; proceed to Italy, you will soon cast away this coarse garment of skins; and your wealth will be adequate to the liberality of your mind." [121] The barbarian, whose daring spirit accepted and ratified the prediction, was admitted into the service of the Western empire, and soon obtained an honourable rank in the guards. His manners were gradually polished, his military skill was improved, and the confederates of Italy would not have elected him for their general unless the exploits of Odoacer had established a high opinion of his courage and capacity.[122] Their military acclamations saluted him with the title of king; but he abstained during his whole reign from the use of the purple and diadem,[123] lest he should offend those princes whose

---

[120] Jornandes, c. 53, 54, p. 692-695. M. de Buat (Hist. des Peuples de l'Europe, tom. viii. p. 221-228) has clearly explained the origin and adventures of Odoacer. I am almost inclined to believe that he was the same who pillaged Angers, and commanded a fleet of Saxon pirates on the ocean. Greg. Turon. l. ii. c. 18, in tom. ii. p. 170.

[121] Vade ad Italiam, vade vilissimis nunc pellibus coopertus : sed multis cito plurima largiturus. Anonym. Vales. p. 717 [Amm. Marc. ii. p. 305, ed. Bipon.]. He quotes the Life of St. Severinus, which is extant, and contains much unknown and valuable history; it was composed by his disciple Eugippius (A.D. 511), thirty years after his death. See Tillemont, Mém. Ecclés. tom. xvi. p. 168-181.

[122] Theophanes, who calls him a Goth, affirms that he was educated, nursed (τράφεντος), in Italy (p. 102 [tom. i. p. 184, ed. Bonn]) ; and as this strong expression will not bear a literal interpretation, it must be explained by long service in the Imperial guards.

[123] Nomen regis Odoacer assumpsit, cum tamen neque purpurâ nec regalibus uteretur insignibus. Cassiodor. in Chron. A.D. 476. He seems to have assumed the abstract title of a king without applying it to any particular nation or country.

subjects, by their accidental mixture, had formed the victorious army which time and policy might insensibly unite into a great nation.

Royalty was familiar to the barbarians, and the submissive people of Italy was prepared to obey, without a murmur, the authority which he should condescend to exercise as the vice-gerent of the emperor of the West. But Odoacer had resolved to abolish that useless and expensive office; and such is the weight of antique prejudice, that it required some boldness and penetration to discover the extreme facility of the enterprise. The unfortunate Augustulus was made the instrument of his own disgrace; he signified his resignation to the senate; and that assembly, in their last act of obedience to a Roman prince, still affected the spirit of freedom and the forms of the constitution. An epistle was addressed, by their unanimous decree, to the emperor Zeno, the son-in-law and successor of Leo, who had lately been restored, after a short rebellion, to the Byzantine throne. They solemnly " disclaim the necessity, or even the wish, of continuing any longer the Imperial succession in Italy; since, in their opinion, the majesty of a sole monarch is sufficient to pervade and protect, at the same time, both the East and the West. In their own name, and in the name of the people, they consent that the seat of universal empire shall be transferred from Rome to Constantinople; and they basely renounce the right of choosing their master, the only vestige that yet remained of the authority which had given laws to the world. The republic (they repeat that name without a blush) might safely confide in the civil and military virtues of Odoacer; and they humbly request that the emperor would invest him with the title of Patrician, and the administration of the *diocese* of Italy." The deputies of the senate were received at Constantinople with some mark of displeasure and indignation: and when they were admitted to the audience of Zeno, he sternly reproached them with their treatment of the two emperors, Anthemius and Nepos, whom the East had successively granted to the prayers of Italy. " The first (continued he) you have murdered; the second you have expelled: but the second is still alive, and whilst he lives he is your lawful sovereign." But the prudent Zeno soon deserted the hopeless cause of his abdicated colleague. His vanity was gratified by the title of sole emperor, and by the statues erected to his honour in the several quarters of Rome; he entertained a friendly, though ambiguous, correspondence with the *patrician* Odoacer; and he gratefully accepted the Imperial ensigns, the sacred ornaments of the throne and palace, which the barbarian was not unwilling to remove from the sight of the people.[124]

In the space of twenty years since the death of Valentinian, nine emperors had successively disappeared; and the son of Orestes, a youth recommended only by his beauty, would be the least entitled to the notice

---

[124] Malchus, whose loss excites our regret, has preserved (in Excerpt. Legat. p. 93 [ed. Par.; p. 235, ed. Bonn]) this extraordinary embassy from the senate to Zeno. The anonymous fragment (p. 717) and the extract from Candidus (apud Phot. p. 176 [p. 55, ed. Bekk.]) are likewise of some use.

of posterity, if his reign, which was marked by the extinction of the
Roman empire in the West, did not leave a memorable era in the history
of mankind.[125] The patrician Orestes had married the daughter of Count
Romulus, of Petovio in Noricum: the name of *Augustus*, notwithstanding
the jealousy of power, was known at Aquileia as a familiar surname; and
the appellations of the two great founders, of the city and of the monarchy, were thus strangely united in the last of their successors.[126] The
son of Orestes assumed and disgraced the names of Romulus Augustus;
but the first was corrupted into Momyllus by the Greeks, and the second
has been changed by the Latins into the contemptible diminutive Augustulus. The life of this inoffensive youth was spared by the generous
clemency of Odoacer; who dismissed him, with his whole family, from
the Imperial palace, fixed his annual allowance at six thousand pieces of
gold, and assigned the castle of Lucullus, in Campania, for the place
of his exile or retirement.[127] As soon as the Romans breathed from the
toils of the Punic war, they were attracted by the beauties and the
pleasures of Campania; and the country-house of the elder Scipio at
Liternum exhibited a lasting model of their rustic simplicity.[128] The delicious shores of the bay of Naples were crowded with villas; and Sylla
applauded the masterly skill of his rival, who had seated himself on the
lofty promontory of Misenum, that commands, on every side, the sea
and land, as far as the boundaries of the horizon.[129] The villa of Marius was purchased within a few years, by Lucullus, and the price had

---

[125] The precise year in which the Western empire was extinguished is not
positively ascertained. The vulgar era of A.D. 476 *appears* to have the sanction
of authentic chronicles. But the two dates assigned by Jornandes (c. 46, p. 680)
would delay that great event to the year 479; and though M. de Buat has overlooked *his* evidence, he produces (tom. viii. p. 261-288) many collateral circumstances in support of the same opinion.

[126] See his medals in Ducange (Fam. Byzantin. p. 81), Priscus (Excerpt.
Legat. p. 57 [p. 185, ed. Bonn]). Maffei (Osservazioni Letterarie, tom. ii.
p. 314). We may allege a famous and similar case. The meanest subjects of the
Roman empire assumed the *illustrious* name of *Patricius*, which, by the conversion of Ireland, has been communicated to a whole nation.

[127] Ingrediens autem Ravennam deposuit Augustulum de regno, cujus in-
fantiam misertus concessit ei sanguinem; et quia pulcher erat, tamen donavit ei
reditum sex millia solidos, et misit eum intra Campaniam cum parentibus suis
libere vivere. Anonym. Vales. p. 716 [Amm. Marc. tom. ii. p. 303, ed. Bipon.].
Jornandes says (c. 46, p. 680), in Lucullano Campaniæ castello exsilii pœna
damnavit.

[128] See the eloquent Declamation of Seneca (Epist. lxxxvi.). The philosopher
might have recollected that all luxury is relative; and that the elder Scipio,
whose manners were polished by study and conversation, was himself accused
of that vice by his ruder contemporaries (Livy, xxix. 19).

[129] Sylla, in the language of a soldier, praised his *peritia castrametandi* (Plin.
Hist. Natur. xviii. 7). Phædrus, who makes its shady walks (*læta viridia*)
the scene of an insipid fable (ii. 5), has thus described the situation:—
Cæsar Tiberius quum petens Neapolim,
In Misenensem villam venisset suam,
Quæ monte summo posita Luculli manu
Prospectat Siculum et despicit Tuscum mare.

increased from two thousand five hundred, to more than fourscore thousand, pounds sterling.[130] It was adorned by the new proprietor with Grecian arts and Asiatic treasures; and the houses and gardens of Lucullus obtained a distinguished rank in the list of Imperial palaces.[131] When the Vandals became formidable to the sea-coast, the Lucullan villa, on the promontory of Misenum, gradually assumed the strength and appellation of a strong castle, the obscure retreat of the last emperor of the West. About twenty years after that great revolution it was converted into a church and monastery, to receive the bones of St. Severinus. They securely reposed, amidst the broken trophies of Cimbric and Armenian victories, till the beginning of the tenth century; when the fortifications, which might afford a dangerous shelter to the Saracens, were demolished by the people of Naples.[132]

Odoacer was the first barbarian who reigned in Italy, over a people who had once asserted their just superiority above the rest of mankind. The disgrace of the Romans still excites our respectful compassion, and we fondly sympathise with the imaginary grief and indignation of their degenerate posterity. But the calamities of Italy had gradually subdued the proud consciousness of freedom and glory. In the age of Roman virtue the provinces were subject to the arms, and the citizens to the laws, of the republic, till those laws were subverted by civil discord, and both the city and the provinces became the servile property of a tyrant. The forms of the constitution, which alleviated or disguised their abject slavery, were abolished by time and violence; the Italians alternately lamented the presence or the absence of the sovereigns whom they detested or despised; and the succession of five centuries inflicted the various evils of military licence, capricious despotism, and elaborate oppression. During the same period, the barbarians had emerged from obscurity and contempt, and the warriors of Germany and Scythia were introduced into the provinces, as the servants, the allies, and at length the masters, of the Romans, whom they insulted or protected. The hatred of the people was suppressed by fear; they respected the spirit and splendour of the martial chiefs who were invested with the honours of the empire; and the fate of Rome had long depended on the sword of those formidable strangers. The stern Ricimer, who trampled on the

[130] From seven myriads and a half to two hundred and fifty myriads of drachmæ. Yet even in the possession of Marius it was a luxurious retirement. The Romans derided his indolence; they soon bewailed his activity. See Plutarch in Mario [c. 34], tom. ii. p. 524.

[131] Lucullus had other villas of equal, though various, magnificence at Baiæ, Naples, Tusculum, etc. He boasted that he changed his climate with the storks and cranes. Plutarch, in Lucull. [c. 39] tom. iii. p. 193.

[132] Severinus died in Noricum, A.D. 482. Six years afterwards his body, which scattered miracles as it passed, was transported by his disciples into Italy. The devotion of a Neapolitan lady invited the saint to the Lucullan villa, in the place of Augustulus, who was probably no more. See Baronius (Annal. Eccles. A.D. 496, No. 50, 51) and Tillemont (Mém. Ecclés. tom. xvi. p. 178-181), from the original Life by Eugippius. The narrative of the last migration of Severinus to Naples is likewise an authentic piece.

ruins of Italy, had exercised the power, without assuming the title, of a king; and the patient Romans were insensibly prepared to acknowledge the royalty of Odoacer and his barbaric successors.

The king of Italy was not unworthy of the high station to which his valour and fortune had exalted him: his savage manners were polished by the habits of conversation; and he respected, though a conqueror and a barbarian, the institutions, and even the prejudices, of his subjects. After an interval of seven years, Odoacer restored the consulship of the West. For himself, he modestly, or proudly, declined an honour which was still accepted by the emperors of the East; but the curule chair was successively filled by eleven of the most illustrious senators;[133] and the list is adorned by the respectable name of Basilius, whose virtues claimed the friendship and grateful applause of Sidonius, his client.[134] The laws of the emperors were strictly enforced, and the civil administration of Italy was still exercised by the Prætorian præfect and his subordinate officers. Odoacer devolved on the Roman magistrates the odious and oppressive task of collecting the public revenue; but he reserved for himself the merit of seasonable and popular indulgence.[135] Like the rest of the barbarians, he had been instructed in the Arian heresy; but he revered the monastic and episcopal characters; and the silence of the catholics attests the toleration which they enjoyed. The peace of the city required the interposition of his præfect Basilius in the choice of a Roman pontiff: the decree which restrained the clergy from alienating their lands was ultimately designed for the benefit of the people, whose devotion would have been taxed to repair the dilapidations of the church.[136] Italy was protected by the arms of its conqueror; and its frontiers were respected by the barbarians of Gaul and Germany, who had so long insulted the feeble race of Theodosius. Odoacer passed the Hadriatic, to chastise the assassins of the emperor Nepos, and to acquire the maritime province of Dalmatia. He passed the Alps, to rescue the remains of Noricum from Fava, or Feletheus, king of the Rugians, who held his residence beyond the Danube. The king was vanquished in battle, and led away prisoner; a numerous colony of captives and subjects was transplanted into Italy; and Rome, after a long period of de-

---

[133] The consular Fasti may be found in Pagi or Muratori. The consuls named by Odoacer, or perhaps by the Roman senate, appear to have been acknowledged in the Eastern empire.

[134] Sidonius Apollinaris (l. i. Epist. 9, p. 22, edit. Sirmond) has compared the two leading senators of his time (A.D. 468), Gennadius Avienus and Cæcina Basilius. To the former he assigns the specious, to the latter the solid, virtues of public and private life. A Basilius junior, possibly his son, was consul in the year 480.

[135] Epiphanius interceded for the people of Pavia; and the king first granted an indulgence of five years, and afterwards relieved them from the oppression of Pelagius, the Prætorian præfect (Ennodius, in Vit. St. Epiphan, in Sirmond. Oper. tom. i. p. 1670-1672).

[136] See Baronius, Annal. Eccles. A.D. 483, No. 10-15. Sixteen years afterwards the irregular proceedings of Basilius were condemned by pope Symmachus in a Roman synod.

feat and disgrace, might claim the triumph of her barbarian master.[137]

Notwithstanding the prudence and success of Odoacer, his kingdom exhibited the sad prospect of misery and desolation. Since the age of Tiberius, the decay of agriculture had been felt in Italy; and it was a just subject of complaint that the life of the Roman people depended on the accidents of the winds and waves.[138] In the division and the decline of the empire, the tributary harvests of Egypt and Africa were withdrawn; the numbers of the inhabitants continually diminished with the means of subsistence; and the country was exhausted by the irretrievable losses of war, famine,[139] and pestilence. St. Ambrose has deplored the ruin of a populous district, which had been once adorned with the flourishing cities of Bologna, Modena, Rhegium, and Placentia.[140] Pope Gelasius was a subject of Odoacer; and he affirms, with strong exaggeration, that in Æmilia, Tuscany, and the adjacent provinces, the human species was almost extirpated.[141] The plebeians of Rome, who were fed by the hand of their master, perished or disappeared as soon as his liberality was suppressed; the decline of the arts reduced the industrious mechanic to idleness and want; and the senators, who might support with patience the ruin of their country, bewailed their private loss of wealth and luxury. One third of those ample estates, to which the ruin of Italy is originally imputed,[142] was extorted for the use of the conquerors. Injuries were aggravated by insults; the sense of actual sufferings was embittered by the fear of more dreadful evils; and as new lands were allotted to new swarms of barbarians, each senator was apprehensive lest the arbitrary surveyors should approach his favourite villa, or his most profitable farm. The least unfortunate were those who submitted without a murmur to the power which it was impossible to resist. Since they desired to live, they owed some gratitude to the tyrant who had spared their lives; and since he was the absolute master of their fortunes, the portion which he left must be accepted as his pure and

---

[137] The wars of Odoacer are concisely mentioned by Paul the Deacon (de Gest. Langobard. l. i. c. 19, p. 757, edit Grot.) and in the two Chronicles of Cassiodorus and Cuspinian. The Life of St. Severinus, by Eugippius, which the Count de Buat (Hist. des Peuples, etc., tom. viii. c. 1, 4, 8, 9) has diligently studied, illustrates the ruin of Noricum and the Bavarian antiquities.

[138] Tacit. Annal. iii. 53 [54]. The Recherches sur l'Administration des Terres chez les Romains (p. 351-361) clearly state the progress of internal decay.

[139] A famine, which afflicted Italy at the time of the irruption of Odoacer, king of the Heruli, is eloquently described in prose and verse by a French poet (Les Mois, tom. ii. p. 174, 206, edit. in 12mo.). I am ignorant from whence he derives his information; but I am well assured that he relates some facts incompatible with the truth of history.

[140] See the xxxixth epistle of St. Ambrose [tom. ii. p. 944, ed. Bened.] as it is quoted by Muratori, sopra le Antichità Italiane, tom. i. Dissert. xxi. p. 354.

[141] Æmilia, Tuscia, ceteræque provinciæ in quibus hominum prope nullus exsistit. Gelasius, Epist. ad Andromachum, ap. Baronium Annal. Eccles. A.D. 496, No. 36.

[142] Verumque confitentibus, latifundia perdidere Italiam. Plin. Hist. Natur. xviii. 7 [§ 31].

voluntary gift.[143]   The distress of Italy was mitigated by the prudence and humanity of Odoacer, who had bound himself, as the price of his elevation, to satisfy the demands of a licentious and turbulent multitude. The kings of the barbarians were frequently resisted, deposed, or murdered, by their *native* subjects; and the various bands of Italian mercenaries, who associated under the standard of an elective general, claimed a larger privilege of freedom and rapine.   A monarchy destitute of national union and hereditary right hastened to its dissolution.   After a reign of fourteen years Odoacer was oppressed by the superior genius of Theodoric, king of the Ostrogoths; a hero alike excellent in the arts of war and of government, who restored an age of peace and prosperity, and whose name still excites and deserves the attention of mankind.

CHAPTER XXXVII (305–712 A.D.)

Origin, Progress, and Effects of the Monastic Life—Conversion of the Barbarians to Christianity and Arianism—Persecution of the Vandals in Africa—Extinction of Arianism among the Barbarians

THE indissoluble connection of civil and ecclesiastical affairs has compelled and encouraged me to relate the progress, the persecutions, the establishment, the divisions, the final triumph, and the gradual corruption of Christianity.   I have purposely delayed the consideration of two religious events interesting in the study of human nature, and important in the decline and fall of the Roman empire.   I. The institution of the monastic life;[1] and II. The conversion of the northern barbarians.

I. Prosperity and peace introduced the distinction of the *vulgar* and the *Ascetic Christians*.[2]   The loose and imperfect practice of religion satisfied the conscience of the multitude.   The prince or magistrate, the soldier or merchant, reconciled their fervent zeal and implicit faith with the exercise of their profession, the pursuit of their interest, and the indulgence of their passions: but the Ascetics, who obeyed and abused the rigid precepts of the Gospel, were inspired by the savage enthusiasm which represents man as a criminal, and God as a tyrant.   They seriously renounced the business and the pleasures of the age; abjured the use

[143]Such are the topics of consolation, or rather of patience, which Cicero ad Familiares, lib. ix. Epist. 17) suggests to his friend Papirius Pætus, under the military despotism of Cæsar.   The argument, however, or "vivere pulcherrimum duxi," is more forcibly addressed to a Roman philosopher, who possessed the free alternative of life or death.

[1] The origin of the monastic institution has been laboriously discussed by Thomassin (Discipline de l'Eglise, tom. i. p. 1419-1426) and Helyot (Hist. des Ordres Monastiques, tom. i. p. 1-66).   These authors are very learned and tolerably honest, and their difference of opinion shows the subject in its full extent.   Yet the cautious Protestant, who distrusts *any* Popish guides, may consult the seventh book of Bingham's Christian Antiquities.

[2] See Euseb. Demonstrat. Evangel. (l. i. p. 20, 21, edit. Græc. Rob. Stephani, Paris, 1545).   In his Ecclesiastical History, published twelve years after the Demonstration, Eusebius (l. ii. c. 17) asserts the Christianity of the Therapeutæ; but he appears ignorant that a similar institution was actually revived in Egypt.

of wine, of flesh, and of marriage; chastised their body, mortified their affections, and embraced a life of misery, as the price of eternal happiness. In the reign of Constantine the Ascetics fled from a profane and degenerate world to perpetual solitude or religious society. Like the first Christians of Jerusalem,[3] they resigned the use or the property of their temporal possessions; established regular communities of the same sex and a similar disposition; and assumed the names of *Hermits, Monks,* and *Anachorets,* expressive of their lonely retreat in a natural or artificial desert. They soon acquired the respect of the world, which they despised; and the loudest applause was bestowed on this DIVINE PHILOSOPHY,[4] which surpassed, without the aid of science or reason, the laborious virtues of the Grecian schools. The monks might indeed contend with the Stoics in the contempt of fortune, of pain, and of death: the Pythagorean silence and submission were revived in their servile discipline; and they disdained as firmly as the Cynics themselves all the forms and decencies of civil society. But the votaries of this Divine Philosophy aspired to imitate a purer and more perfect model. They trod in the footsteps of the prophets, who had retired to the desert;[5] and they restored the devout and contemplative life, which had been instituted by the Essenians in Palestine and Egypt. The philosophic eye of Pliny had surveyed with astonishment a solitary people, who dwelt among the palm-trees near the Dead Sea; who subsisted without money; who were propagated without women; and who derived from the disgust and repentance of mankind a perpetual supply of voluntary associates.[6]

Egypt, the fruitful parent of superstition, afforded the first example of

[3] Cassian (Collat. xviii. 5 [Max. Bibl. Patr. t. vii. p. 208]) claims this origin for the institution of the *Cœnobites,* which gradually decayed till it was restored by Antony and his disciples.

[4] Ὠφελιμώτατον γάρ τι χρῆμα εἰς ἀνθρώπους ἐλθοῦσα παρὰ Θεοῦ ἡ τοιαύτη φιλοσοφία. These are the expressive words of Sozomen, who copiously and agreeably describes (l. i. c. 12, 13, 14) the origin and progress of this monkish philosophy (see Suicer. Thesaur. Eccles. tom. ii. p. 1441). Some modern writers, Lipsius (tom. iv. p. 448; Manuduct. ad Philosoph. Stoic. iii. 13) and La Mothe de Vayer (tom. ix. de la Vertu des Payens, p. 228-262), have compared the Carmelites to the Pythagoreans, and the Cynics to the Capucins.

[5] The Carmelites derive their pedigree in regular succession from the prophet Elijah (see the Theses of Beziers, A.D. 1682, in Bayle's Nouvelles de la République des Lettres, Œuvres, tom. i. p. 82, etc.; and the prolix irony of the Ordres Monastiques, an anonymous work, tom. i. p. 1-433; Berlin, 1751). Rome and the inquisition of Spain silenced the profane criticism of the Jesuits of Flanders (Helyot, Hist. des Ordres Monastiques, tom. i. p. 282-300), and the statue of Elijah the Carmelite has been erected in the church of St. Peter (Voyages du P. Labat, tom. iii. p. 87).

[6] Plin. Hist. Natur. v. 15. Gens sola, et in toto orbe præter ceteras mira, sine ullâ feminâ, omni venere abdicatâ, sine pecuniâ, socia palmarum. Ita per seculorum millia (incredibile dictu) gens æterna est in quâ nemo nascitur. Tam fecunda illis aliorum vitæ pœnitentia est. He places them just beyond the noxious influence of the lake, and names Engaddi and Masada as the nearest towns. The Laura and monastery of St. Sabas could not be far distant from this place. See Reland, Palestin. tom. i. p. 295; tom. ii. p. 763, 874, 880, 890.

the monastic life. Antony,[7] an illiterate [8] youth of the lower parts of Thebais, distributed his patrimony,[9] deserted his family and native home, and executed his *monastic* penance with original and intrepid fanaticism. After a long and painful novitiate among the tombs and in a ruined tower, he boldly advanced into the desert three days' journey to the eastward of the Nile; discovered a lonely spot, which possessed the advantages of shade and water; and fixed his last residence on Mount Colzim, near the Red Sea, where an ancient monastery still preserves the name and memory of the saint.[10] The curious devotion of the

[7] See Athanas. Op. tom. ii. p. 450-505 [tom. i. p. 793-866, ed. Bened. 1698], and the Vit. Patrum, p. 26-74, with Rosweyde's Annotations. The former is the Greek original; the latter, a very ancient Latin version by Evagrius, the friend of St. Jerom.

[8] Τράμματα μὲν μάθειν οὐκ ἠνέσχετο. Athanas. tom. ii. in Vit. St. Anton. p. 452 [p. 795, ed. Bened. 1698; cf. c. 72, p. 849], and the assertion of his total ignorance has been received by many of the ancients and moderns. But Tillemont (Mém. Ecclés. tom. vii. p. 666) shows, by some probable arguments, that Antony could read and write in the Coptic, his native tongue; and that he was only a stranger to the *Greek letters*. The philosopher Synesius (p. 51 [ed. Par. 1612]) acknowledges that the natural genius of Antony did not require the aid of learning.

[Athanasius, in his Life of Antony (chap. 47), boasts of the fact of the saint's holy horror of clean water, by which his feet at least had never been contaminated since his adoption of the holy rule, unless under the dire necessity of crossing a river or the like.—O. S.]

[9] *Aruræ* autem erant ei trecentæ uberes, et valde optimæ (Vit. Patr. l. v. [l. i.] p. 36). If the *Arura* be a square measure of an hundred Egyptian cubits (Rosweyde, Onomasticon ad Vit. Patrum, p. 1014, 1015 [p. 1009]), and the Egyptian cubit of all ages be equal to twenty-two English inches (Greaves, vol. i. p. 233), the arura will consist of about three-quarters of an English acre.

[10] The description of the monastery is given by Jerom (tom. i. p. 248, 249, in Vit. Hilarion [tom. ii. p. 31, ed. Vallars.]), and the P. Sicard (Missions du Levant, tom. v. p. 122-200). Their accounts cannot always be reconciled: the father painted from his fancy, and the Jesuit from his experience.

[For those desirous of studying the origin of monasticism, the earliest and perhaps, all things considered, the best authorities are Palladius, Rufinus, and Sozomen. The monastic system began with the isolated individuals who, like Antony, went out into the desert to live the life of meditation and prayer. Then came the "organized community," evolved by Pachomius, who had become convinced that life in a society of recluses was more accordant to the mind of the Founder of Christianity than the solitary existence of an anchorite. He developed a rigid system or rule for the brethren thus living together. At first the church was opposed to the idea, and both the bishops and the clergy persecuted the monks. The church, however, soon discovered that, if it desired to retain its influence with the people, it must not only refrain from hindering, but must reconcile itself to and patronise a movement which was striking its roots deep into the spiritual imagination of the community at large. For a long time the church merely stood aloof, refraining from persecuting. Then by a tactful move on the part of the Patriarch Athanasius, the reconciliation between the church and monachism was accomplished. Grutzmacher has aptly said that Athanasius's Life of St. Anthony is the seal which the church sets on its recognition of the new movement. Cf. Bury, vol. iv. Appendix 3, for a most valuable list of the authorities on monachism to which I am indebted; also, in German, Weingarten, Harnack, Mayer, and in French, Amelineau.— O. S.]

Christians pursued him to the desert; and when he was obliged to appear at Alexandria, in the face of mankind, he supported his fame with discretion and dignity. He enjoyed the friendship of Athanasius, whose doctrine he approved; and the Egyptian peasant respectfully declined a respectful invitation from the emperor Constantine. The venerable patriarch (for Antony attained the age of one hundred and five years) beheld the numerous progeny which had been formed by his example and his lessons. The prolific colonies of monks multiplied with rapid increase on the sands of Libya, upon the rocks of Thebais, and in the cities of the Nile. To the south of Alexandria, the mountain, and adjacent desert, of Nitria was peopled by five thousand anachorets; and the traveller may still investigate the ruins of fifty monasteries, which were planted in that barren soil by the disciples of Antony.[11]   In the Upper Thebais, the vacant island of Tabenne,[12] was occupied by Pachomius and fourteen hundred of his brethren.   That holy abbot successively founded nine monasteries of men, and one of women; and the festival of Easter sometimes collected fifty thousand religious persons, who followed his *angelic* rule of discipline.[13]   The stately and populous city of Oxyrinchus, the seat of Christian orthodoxy, had devoted the temples, the public edifices, and even the ramparts, to pious and charitable uses; and the bishop, who might preach in twelve churches, computed ten thousand females, and twenty thousand males, of the monastic profession.[14] The Egyptians, who gloried in this marvellous revolution, were disposed to hope, and to believe, that the number of the monks was equal to the remainder of the people;[15] and posterity might repeat the saying which had formerly been applied to the sacred animals of the same country, that in Egypt it was less difficult to find a god than a man.

Athanasius introduced into Rome the knowledge and practice of the monastic life; and a school of this new philosophy was opened by the disciples of Antony, who accompanied their primate to the holy thresh-

---

[11] Jerom, tom. i. p. 146, ad Eustochium [Ep. 22, p. 119, ed. Vall.]; Hist. Lausiac. c. 7, in Vit. Patrum, p. 712 [p. 982].   The P. Sicard (Missions du Levant, tom. ii. p. 29-79) visited and has described this desert, which now contains four monasteries, and twenty or thirty monks.   See D'Anville, Description de l'Egypte, p. 74.

[12] Tabenne is a small island in the Nile, in the diocese of Tentyra or Dendera, between the modern town of Girge and the ruins of ancient Thebes (D'Anville, p. 194).   M. de Tillemont doubts whether it was an isle; but I may conclude, from his own facts, that the primitive name was afterwards transferred to the great monastery of Bau or Pabau (Mém. Ecclés. tom. vii. p. 678, 688).

[13] See in the Codex Regularum (published by Lucas Holstenius, Rome, 1661) a preface of St. Jerom to his Latin version of the Rule of Pachomius, tom. i. p. 61 [tom. i. p. 25, ed. Augsb. 1759].

[14] Rufin. c. 5, in Vit. Patrum, p. 459.   He calls it civitas ampla valde et populosa, and reckons twelve churches.   Strabo (l. xvii. p. 1166 [p. 812, ed. Casaub.]) and Ammianus (xxii. 16) have made honourable mention of Oxyrinchus, whose inhabitants adored a small fish in a magnificent temple.

[15] Quanti populi habentur in urbibus, tantæ pene habentur in desertis multitudines monachorum. Rufin. c. 7, in Vit. Patrum, p. 461.   He congratulates the fortunate change.

old of the Vatican. The strange and savage appearance of these Egyptians excited, at first, horror and contempt, and, at length, applause and
zealous imitation. The senators, and more specially the matrons, transformed their palaces and villas into religious houses; and the narrow
institution of *six* Vestals was eclipsed by the frequent monasteries, which
were seated on the ruins of ancient temples and in the midst of the Roman
forum.[16] Inflamed by the example of Antony, a Syrian youth, whose
name was Hilarion,[17] fixed his dreary abode on a sandy beach between
the sea and a morass about seven miles from Gaza. The austere penance,
in which he persisted forty-eight years, diffused a similar enthusiasm;
and the holy man was followed by a train of two or three thousand anachorets, whenever he visited the innumerable monasteries of Palestine.
The fame of Basil[18] is immortal in the monastic history of the East.
With a mind that had tasted the learning and eloquence of Athens; with
an ambition scarcely to be satisfied by the archbishopric of Cæsarea,
Basil retired to a savage solitude in Pontus; and deigned, for a while,
to give laws to the spiritual colonies which he profusely scattered along
the coast of the Black Sea. In the West, Martin of Tours,[19] a soldier,
a hermit, a bishop, and a saint, established the monasteries of Gaul;
two thousand of his disciples followed him to the grave; and his eloquent historian challenges the deserts of Thebais to produce, in a more
favourable climate, a champion of equal virtue. The progress of the
monks was not less rapid or universal than that of Christianity itself.
Every province, and, at last, every city, of the empire was filled with their
increasing multitudes; and the bleak and barren isles, from Lerins to
Lipari, that arise out of the Tuscan Sea, were chosen by the anachorets
for the place of their voluntary exile. An easy and perpetual intercourse
by sea and land connected the provinces of the Roman world; and the
life of Hilarion displays the facility with which an indigent hermit of
Palestine might traverse Egypt, embark for Sicily, escape to Epirus, and
finally settle in the island of Cyprus.[20] The Latin Christians embraced

[16] The introduction of the monastic life into Rome and Italy is occasionally
mentioned by Jerom, tom. i. p. 119, 120, 199.

[17] See the Life of Hilarion, by St. Jerom (tom. i. p. 241, 252 [tom. ii. p. 15,
24, ed. Vall.]). The stories of Paul, Hilarion, and Malchus, by the same
author, are admirably told; and the only defect of these pleasing compositions
is the want of truth and common sense.

[18] His original retreat was in a small village on the banks of the Iris, not
far from Neo-Cæsarea. The ten or twelve years of his monastic life were
disturbed by long and frequent avocations. Some critics have disputed the
authenticity of his ascetic rules; but the external evidence is weighty, and
they can only prove that it is the work of a real or affected enthusiast. See
Tillemont, Mém. Ecclés. tom. ix. p. 636-644; Helyot, Hist. des Ordres
Monastiques, tom. i. p. 175-181.

[19] See his Life, and the three Dialogues by Sulpicius Severus, who asserts
(Dialog. i. 16) that the booksellers of Rome were delighted with the quick
and ready sale of his popular work.

[20] When Hilarion sailed from Parætonium to Cape Pachynus, he offered to
pay his passage with a book of the Gospels. Posthumian, a Gallic monk,
who had visited Egypt, found a merchant-ship bound from Alexandria to

the religious institutions of Rome. The pilgrims who visited Jerusalem eagerly copied, in the most distant climates of the earth, the faithful model of the monastic life. The disciples of Antony spread themselves beyond the tropic, over the Christian empire of Æthiopia.[21] The monastery of Banchor,[22] in Flintshire, which contained above two thousand brethren, dispersed a numerous colony among the barbarians of Ireland;[23] and Iona, one of the Hebrides, which was planted by the Irish monks, diffused over the northern regions a doubtful ray of science and superstition.[24]

These unhappy exiles from social life were impelled by the dark and impiacable genius of superstition. Their mutual resolution was supported by the example of millions, of either sex, of every age, and of every rank; and each proselyte who entered the gates of a monastery was persuaded that he trod the steep and thorny path of eternal happiness.[25] But the operation of these religious motives was variously determined by the temper and situation of mankind. Reason might subdue, or passion might suspend, their influence; but they acted most forcibly on the infirm minds of children and females; they were strengthened by secret remorse or accidental misfortune; and they might derive some aid from the temporal considerations of vanity or interest. It was naturally supposed that the pious and humble monks, who had renounced the world to accomplish the work of their salvation, were the best qualified for the spiritual government of the Christians. The reluctant hermit was torn from his cell, and seated, amidst the acclamations of the people, on the episcopal throne: the monasteries of Egypt, of Gaul, and of the

Marseilles, and performed the voyage in thirty days (Sulp. Sever. Dialog. i. 1). Athanasius, who addressed his Life of St. Antony to the foreign monks, was obliged to hasten the composition, that it might be ready for the sailing ot the fleets (tom. ii. p. 451 [tom. i. p. 794, ed. Bened. 1698]).

[21] See Jerom (tom. i. p. 126), Assemanni, Bibliot. Orient. tom. iv. p. 92, p. 857-919, and Geddes, Church History of Æthiopia, p. 29, 30, 31. The Abyssinian monks adhere very strictly to the primitive institution.

[22] Camden's Britannia, vol. i. p. 666, 667.

[23] All that learning can extract from the rubbish of the dark ages is copiously stated by Archbishop Usher in his Britannicarum Ecclesiarum Antiquitates, cap. xvi. p. 425-503.

[24] This small though not barren spot, Iona, Hy, or Columbkill, only two miles in length and one mile in breadth, has been distinguished—1. By the monastery of St. Columba, founded A.D. 566, whose abbot exercised an extraordinary jurisdiction over the bishops of Caledonia; 2. By a classic library, which afforded some hopes of an entire Livy; and, 3. By the tombs of sixty kings, Scots, Irish, and Norwegians, who reposed in holy ground. See Usher (p. 311, 360-370) and Buchanan (Rer. Scot. l. ii. p. 15, edit. Ruddiman).

[25] Chrysostom (in the first tome of the Benedictine edition) has consecrated three books to the praise and defence of the monastic life. He is encouraged, by the example of the ark, to presume that none but the elect (the monks) can possibly be saved (l. i. p. 55, 56). Elsewhere, indeed, he becomes more merciful (l. iii. p. 83, 84), and allows different degrees of glory, like the sun, moon, and stars. In his lively comparison of a king and a monk (l. iii. p. 116-121), he supposes (what is hardly fair) that the king will be more sparingly rewarded, and more rigorously punished.

East, supplied a regular succession of saints and bishops; and ambition soon discovered the secret road which led to the possession of wealth and honours.[26] The popular monks, whose reputation was connected with the fame and success of the order, assiduously laboured to multiply the number of their fellow-captives. They insinuated themselves into noble and opulent families; and the specious arts of flattery and seduction were employed to secure those proselytes who might bestow wealth or dignity on the monastic profession. The indignant father bewailed the loss, perhaps, of an only son;[27] the credulous maid was betrayed by vanity to violate the laws of nature; and the matron aspired to imaginary perfection by renouncing the virtues of domestic life. Paula yielded to the persuasive eloquence of Jerom;[28] and the profane title of mother-in-law of God [29] tempted that illustrious widow to consecrate the virginity of her daughter Eustochium. By the advice, and in the company, of her spiritual guide, Paula abandoned Rome and her infant son; retired to the holy village of Bethlem; founded an hospital and four monasteries; and acquired, by her alms and penance, an eminent and conspicuous station in the catholic church. Such rare and illustrious penitents were celebrated as the glory and example of their age; but the monasteries were filled by a crowd of obscure and abject plebeians,[30] who gained in the cloister much more than they had sacrificed in the world. Peasants, slaves, and mechanics might escape from poverty and contempt to a safe and honourable profession, whose apparent hardships were mitigated by custom, by popular applause, and by the secret relaxation of discipline.[31] The subjects of Rome, whose persons and fortunes were made

[26] Thomassin (Discipline de l'Eglise, tom. i. p. 1426-1469) and Mabillon (Œuvres Posthumes, tom. ii. p. 115-158). The monks were gradually adopted as a part of the ecclesiastical hierarchy.

[27] Dr. Middleton (vol. i. p. 110) liberally censures the conduct and writings of Chrysostom, one of the most eloquent and successful advocates for the monastic life.

[28] Jerom's devout ladies form a very considerable portion of his works: the particular treatise, which he styles the Epitaph of Paula (tom. i. p. 169-192 [Ep. 108, tom. i. p. 684, ed. Vallars.]), is an elaborate and extravagant panegyric. The exordium is ridiculously turgid:—"If all the members of my body were changed into tongues, and if all my limbs resounded with a human voice, yet should I be incapable," etc.

[29] Socrus Dei esse cœpisti (Jerom. tom. i. p. 140, ad Eustochium), Rufinus (in Hieronym. Op. tom. iv. p. 223), who was justly scandalised, asks his adversary, From what Pagan poet he had stolen an expression so impious and absurd?

[30] Nunc autem veniunt *plerumque* ad hanc professionem servitutis Dei, et ex conditione servili, vel etiam liberati, vel propter hoc a Dominis liberati sive liberandi; et ex vitâ rusticanâ, et ex opificum exercitatione, et plebeio labore. Augustin. de Oper. Monach. c. 22, ap. Thomassin, Discipline de l'Eglise, tom. iii. p. 1094. The Egyptian, who blamed Arsenius, owned that he led a more comfortable life as a monk than as a shepherd. See Tillemont, Mém. Ecclés. tom. xiv. p. 679.

[31] A Dominican friar (Voyages du P. Labat, tom. i. p. 10), who lodged at Cadiz in a convent of his brethren, soon understood that their repose was never interrupted by nocturnal devotion; "quoiqu'on ne laisse pas de sonner pour l'édification du peuple."

responsible for unequal and exorbitant tributes, retired from the oppression of the Imperial government; and the pusillanimous youth preferred the penance of a monastic, to the dangers of a military, life. The affrighted provincials of every rank, who fled before the barbarians, found shelter and subsistence; whole legions were buried in these religious sanctuaries; and the same cause which relieved the distress of individuals impaired the strength and fortitude of the empire.[32]

The monastic profession of the ancients [33] was an act of voluntary devotion. The inconstant fanatic was threatened with the eternal vengeance of the God whom he deserted; but the doors of the monastery were still open for repentance. Those monks whose conscience was fortified by reason or passion were at liberty to resume the character of men and citizens; and even the spouses of Christ might accept the legal embraces of an earthly lover.[34] The examples of scandal, and the progress of superstition, suggested the propriety of more forcible restraints. After a sufficient trial, the fidelity of the novice was secured by a solemn and perpetual vow; and his irrevocable engagement was ratified by the laws of the church and state. A guilty fugitive was pursued, arrested, and restored to his perpetual prison; and the interposition of the magistrate oppressed the freedom and merit which had alleviated, in some degree, the abject slavery of the monastic discipline.[35] The actions of a monk, his words, and even his thoughts, were determined by an inflexible rule [36] or a capricious superior: the slightest offences were corrected by disgrace or confinement, extraordinary fasts, or bloody flagellation; and disobedience, murmur, or delay were ranked in the catalogue of the most

[32] See a very sensible preface of Lucas Holstenius to the Codex Regularum. The emperors attempted to support the obligation of public and private duties; but the feeble dykes were swept away by the torrent of superstition; and Justinian surpassed the most sanguine wishes of the monks (Thomassin, tom. i. p. 1782-1799, and Bingham, l. vii. c. 3, p. 253).

[33] The monastic institutions, particularly those of Egypt, about the year 400, are described by four curious and devout travellers—Rufinus (Vit. Patrum, l. ii. iii. p. 424-536), Posthumian (Sulp. Sever. Dialog. i.), Palladius (Hist. Lausiac. in Vit. Patrum, p. 709-863 [783]), and Cassian (see in tom. vii. Bibliothec. Max. Patrum, his four first books of Institutes, and the twenty-four Collations or Conferences).

[34] The example of Malchus (Jerom. tom. i. p. 256 [tom. ii. p. 44, ed. Vallars.]), and the design of Cassian and his friend (Collation xxiv. 1), are incontestable proofs of their freedom, which is elegantly described by Erasmus in his Life of St. Jerom. See Chardon, Hist. des Sacremens, tom. vi. p. 279-300.

[35] See the Laws of Justinian (Novell. cxxiii. No. 42 [Auth. Coll. ix. tit. vii.]), and of Lewis the Pious (in the Historians of France, tom. vi. p. 427), and the actual jurisprudence of France, in Denissart (Decisions, etc., tom. iv. p. 855, etc.).

[36] The ancient Codex Regularum, collected by Benedict Anianinus, the reformer of the monks in the beginning of the ninth century, and published in the seventeenth by Lucas Holstenius, contains thirty different rules for men and women. Of these, seven were composed in Egypt, one in the East, one in Cappadocia, one in Italy, one in Africa, four in Spain, eight in Gaul or France, and one in England.

heinous sins.[37] A blind submission to the commands of the abbot, however absurd, or even criminal, they might seem, was the ruling principle,
the first virtue of the Egyptian monks; and their patience was frequently
exercised by the most extravagant trials. They were directed to remove an enormous rock; assiduously to water a barren staff that was
planted in the ground, till, at the end of three years, it should vegetate
and blossom like a tree; to walk into a fiery furnace; or to cast their
infant into a deep pond: and several saints, or madmen, have been immortalised in monastic story by their thoughtless and fearless obedience.[38] The freedom of the mind, the source of every generous and
rational sentiment, was destroyed by the habits of credulity and submission; and the monk, contracting the vices of a slave, devoutly
followed the faith and passions of his ecclesiastical tyrant. The peace
of the Eastern church was invaded by a swarm of fanatics, incapable of
fear, or reason, or humanity; and the Imperial troops acknowledged,
without shame, that they were much less apprehensive of an encounter
with the fiercest barbarians.[39]

Superstition has often framed and consecrated the fantastic garments
of the monks:[40] but their apparent singularity sometimes proceeds from
their uniform attachment to a simple and primitive model, which the
revolutions of fashion have made ridiculous in the eyes of mankind.
The father of the Benedictines expressly disclaims all idea of choice or
merit; and soberly exhorts his disciples to adopt the coarse and convenient dress of the countries which they may inhabit.[41] The monastic
habits of the ancients varied with the climate and their mode of life;
and they assumed, with the same indifference, the sheepskin of the
Egyptian peasants or the cloak of the Grecian philosophers. They

[37] The rule of Columbanus, so prevalent in the West inflicts one hundred
lashes for very slight offences (Cod. Reg. part ii. p. 174 [tom. i. p. 178, ed.
1759]). Before the time of Charlemagne the abbots indulged themselves
in mutilating their monks, or putting out their eyes—a punishment much
less cruel than the tremendous *vade* in *pace* (the subterraneous dungeon, or
sepulchre), which was afterwards invented. See an admirable discourse
of the learned Mabillon (Œuvres Posthumes, tom. ii. p. 321-336), who, on
this occasion, seems to be inspired by the genius of humanity. For such an
effort, I can forgive his defence of the holy tear of Vendome (p. 361-399).
[38] Sulp. Sever. Dialog. i. 12, 13, p. 532, etc. [ed. Lugd. B. 1647]; Cassian.
Institut. l. iv. c. 26, 27. " Præcipua ibi virtus et prima est obedientia." Among
the Verba seniorum (in Vit. Patrum, l. v. p. 617), the fourteenth libel or discourse is on the subject of obedience; and the Jesuit Rosweyde, who published that huge volume for the use of convents, has collected all the scattered
passages in his two copious indexes.
[39] Dr. Jortin (Remarks on Ecclesiastical History, vol. iv. p. 161) has observed the scandalous valour of the Cappadocian monks, which was exemplified
in the banishment of Chrysostom.
[40] Cassian has simply, though copiously, described the monastic habit of
Egypt (Institut. l. i.), to which Sozomen (l. iii. c. 14) attributes such allegorical meaning and virtue.
[41] Regul. Benedict. cap. 55, in Cod. Regul. part ii. p. 51 [tom. i. p. 130, ed.
Augsb. 1759].

allowed themselves the use of linen in Egypt, where it was a cheap and domestic manufacture; but in the West they rejected such an expensive article of foreign luxury.[42] It was the practice of the monks either to cut or shave their hair; they wrapped their heads in a cowl, to escape the sight of profane objects; their legs and feet were naked, except in the extreme cold of winter; and their slow and feeble steps were supported by a long staff. The aspect of a genuine anachoret was horrid and disgusting: every sensation that is offensive to man was thought acceptable to God; and the angelic rule of Tabenne condemned the salutary custom of bathing the limbs in water and of anointing them with oil.[43] The austere monks slept on the ground, on a hard mat or a rough blanket; and the same bundle of palm-leaves served them as a seat in the day and a pillow in the night. Their original cells were low narrow huts, built of the slightest materials; which formed, by the regular distribution of the streets, a large and populous village, enclosing, within the common wall, a church, a hospital, perhaps a library, some necessary offices, a garden, and a fountain or reservoir of fresh water. Thirty or forty brethren composed a family of separate discipline and diet; and the great monasteries of Egypt consisted of thirty or forty families.

Pleasure and guilt are synonymous terms in the language of the monks, and they had discovered, by experience, that rigid fasts and abstemious diet are the most effectual preservatives against the impure desires of the flesh.[44] The rules of abstinence which they imposed, or practised, were not uniform or perpetual: the cheerful festival of the Pentecost was balanced by the extraordinary mortification of Lent; the fervour of new monasteries was insensibly relaxed; and the voracious appetite of the Gauls could not imitate the patient and temperate virtue of the Egyptians.[45] The disciples of Antony and Pachomius

[42] See the Rule of Ferreolus, bishop of Usez (cap. 31, in Cod. Regul. part ii. p. 136 [tom. i. p. 162]), and of Isidore, bishop of Seville (cap. 13, in Cod. Regul. part ii. p. 214 [tom. i. p. 193]).

[43] Some partial indulgences were granted for the hands and feet. "Totum autem corpus nemo unguet nisi causâ infirmitatis, nec lavabitur aquâ nudo corpore, nisi languor perspicuus sit." (Regul. Pachom. xcii. part. i. p. 78 [tom. i. p. 31].)

[44] St. Jerom, in strong but indiscreet language, expresses the most important use of fasting and abstinence: "Non quod Deus universitatis Creator et Dominus, intestinorum nostrorum rugitû, et inanitate ventris, pulmonisque ardore delectetur, sed quod aliter pudicitia tuta esse non possit." (Op. tom. i. p. 137, ad Eustochium [Ep. 22, tom. i. p. 94, ed. Vallars.].) See the twelfth and twenty-second Collations of Cassian, de Castitate and de Illusionibus Nocturnis.

[45] Edacitas in Græcas gula est, in Gallis natura (Dialog. i. c. 4, p. 521). Cassian fairly owns that the perfect model of abstinence cannot be imitated in Gaul, on account of the aërum temperies, and the qualitas nostræ fragilitatis (Institut. iv. 11). Among the Western rules, that of Columbanus is the most austere: he had been educated amidst the poverty of Ireland, as rigid, perhaps, and inflexible as the abstemious virtue of Egypt. The rule of Isidore of Seville is the mildest: on holidays he allows the use of flesh.

were satisfied with their daily pittance [46] of twelve ounces of bread, or rather biscuit,[47] which they divided into two frugal repasts, of the after-noon and of the evening. It was esteemed a merit, and almost a duty, to abstain from the boiled vegetables which were provided for the re-fectory; but the extraordinary bounty of the abbot sometimes indulged them with the luxury of cheese, fruit, salad, and the small dried fish of the Nile.[48] A more ample latitude of sea and river fish was gradually allowed or assumed; but the use of flesh was long confined to the sick or travellers: and when it gradually prevailed in the less rigid monasteries of Europe, a singular distinction was introduced; as if birds, whether wild or domestic, had been less profane than the grosser animals of the field. Water was the pure and innocent beverage of the primitive monks; and the founder of the Benedictines regrets the daily portion of half a pint of wine which had been extorted from him by the intemperance of the age.[49] Such an allowance might be easily supplied by the vineyards of Italy; and his victorious disciples, who passed the Alps, the Rhine, and the Baltic, required, in the place of wine, an ade-quate compensation of strong beer or cider.

The candidate who aspired to the virtue of evangelical poverty, ab-jured, at his first entrance into a regular community, the idea, and even the name, of all separate or exclusive possession.[50] The brethren were supported by their manual labour; and the duty of labour was strenu-ously recommended as a penance, as an exercise, and as the most laud-able means of securing their daily subsistence.[51] The garden and fields,

[46] " Those who drink only water, and have no nutritious liquor, ought at least to have a pound and a half (*twenty-four ounces*) of bread every day." State of Prisons, p. 40, by Mr. Howard.

[47] See Cassian. Collat. ii. 19, 20, 21. The small loaves or biscuit of six ounces each had obtained the name of *Paximacia* (Rosweyde, Onomasticon, p. 1045 [1033]). Pachomius, however, allowed his monks some latitude in the quantity of their food; but he made them work in proportion as they ate (Pallad. in Hist. Lausiac. c. 38, 39, in Vit. Patrum, l. viii. p. 736, 737).

[48] See the banquet to which Cassian (Collation viii. 1) was invited by Serenus, an Egyptian abbot.

[49] See the Rule of St. Benedict, cap. 39, 40 (in Cod. Reg. part ii. p. 41, 42 [tom. i. p. 129, ed. 1759]). Licet legamus vinum omnino monachorum non esse, sed quia nostris temporibus id monachis persuaderi non potest; he allows them a Roman *hemina*, a measure which may be ascertained from Arbuthnot's Tables.

[50] Such expressions as *my* book, *my* cloak, *my* shoes (Cassian. Institut. l. iv. c. 13) were not less severely prohibited among the Western monks (Cod. Regul. part ii. p. 174 [tom. i. p. 178], 235, 288) ; and the Rule of Columbanus punished them with six lashes. The ironical author of the *Ordres Monastiques,* who laughs at the foolish nicety of modern convents, seems ignorant that the ancients were equally absurd.

[51] Two great masters of ecclesiastical science, the P. Thomassin (Disci-pline de l'Eglise, tom. iii. p. 1090-1139) and the P. Mabillon (Etudes Monas-tiques, tom. i. p. 116-155), have seriously examined the manual labour of the monks, which the former considers as a *merit,* and the latter as a *duty.*

which the industry of the monks had often rescued from the forest or the morass, were diligently cultivated by their hands. They performed, without reluctance, the menial offices of slaves and domestics; and the several trades that were necessary to provide their habits, their utensils, and their lodging, were exercised within the precincts of the great monasteries. The monastic studies have tended, for the most part, to darken, rather than to dispel, the cloud of superstition. Yet the curiosity or zeal of some learned solitaries has cultivated the ecclesiastical and even the profane sciences: and posterity must gratefully acknowledge that the monuments of Greek and Roman literature have been preserved and multiplied by their indefatigable pens.[52] But the more humble industry of the monks, especially in Egypt, was contented with the silent, sedentary occupation of making wooden sandals, or of twisting the leaves of the palm-tree into mats and baskets. The superfluous stock, which was not consumed in domestic use, supplied, by trade, the wants of the community: the boats of Tabenne, and the other monasteries of Thebais, descended the Nile as far as Alexandria; and, in a Christian market, the sanctity of the workmen might enhance the intrinsic value of the work.

But the necessity of manual labour was insensibly superseded. The novice was tempted to bestow his fortune on the saints in whose society he was resolved to spend the remainder of his life; and the pernicious indulgence of the laws permitted him to receive, for their use, any future accessions of legacy or inheritance.[53] Melania contributed her plate, three hundred pounds' weight of silver, and Paula contracted an immense debt for the relief of their favourite monks, who kindly imparted the merits of their prayers and penance to a rich and liberal sinner.[54] Time continually increased, and accidents could seldom diminish, the estates of the popular monasteries, which spread over the adjacent country and cities: and, in the first century of their institution, the infidel Zosimus has maliciously observed, that, for the benefit of the poor, the Christian monks had reduced a great part of mankind

[52] Mabillon (Etudes Monastiques, tom. i. p. 47-55) has collected many curious facts to justify the literary labours of his predecessors both in the East and West. Books were copied in the ancient monasteries of Egypt (Cassian. Institut. l. iv. c. 12), and by the disciples of St. Martin (Sulp. Sever. in Vit. Martin. c. 7, p. 473). Cassiodorus has allowed an ample scope for the studies of the monks; and *we* shall not be scandalised if their pen sometimes wandered from Chrysostom and Augustin to Homer and Virgil.

[53] Thomassin (Discipline de l'Eglise, tom. iii. p. 118, 145, 146, 171-179) has examined the revolution of the civil, canon, and common law. Modern France confirms the death which monks have inflicted on themselves, and justly deprives them of all right of inheritance.

[54] See Jerom (tom. i. p. 176, 183). The monk Pambo made a sublime answer to Melania, who wished to specify the value of her gift:—"Do you offer it to me, or to God? If to God, HE who suspends the mountains in a balance need not be informed of the weight of your plate." (Pallad. Hist. Lausiac. c. 10, in the Vit. Patrum, l. viii. p. 715.)

to a state of beggary.[55] As long as they maintained their original fervour, they approved themselves, however, the faithful and benevolent stewards of the charity which was intrusted to their care. But their discipline was corrupted by prosperity: they gradually assumed the pride of wealth, and at last indulged the luxury of expense. Their public luxury might be excused by the magnificence of religious worship, and the decent motive of erecting durable habitations for an immortal society. But every age of the church has accused the licentiousness of the degenerate monks; who no longer remembered the object of their institution, embraced the vain and sensual pleasures of the world which they had renounced,[56] and scandalously abused the riches which had been acquired by the austere virtues of their founders.[57] Their natural descent, from such painful and dangerous virtue, to the common vices of humanity, will not, perhaps, excite much grief or indignation in the mind of a philosopher.

The lives of the primitive monks were consumed in penance and solitude, undisturbed by the various occupations which fill the time, and exercise the faculties, of reasonable, active, and social beings. Whenever they were permitted to step beyond the precincts of the monastery, two jealous companions were the mutual guards and spies of each other's actions; and, after their return, they were condemned to forget, or, at least, to suppress, whatever they had seen or heard in the world. Strangers, who professed the orthodox faith, were hospitably entertained in a separate apartment; but their dangerous conversation was restricted to some chosen elders of approved discretion and fidelity. Except in their presence, the monastic slave might not receive the visits of his friends or kindred; and it was deemed highly meritorious, if he afflicted a tender sister, or an aged parent, by the obstinate refusal of a word or look.[58] The monks themselves passed their lives, without personal attachments, among a crowd which had been formed by accident, and was detained, in the same prison, by force or prejudice. Re-

---

[55] Τὸ πολὺ μέρος τῆς γῆς ὠκειώσαντο, προφάσει τοῦ μεταδιδόναι πάντων πτωχοῖς, πάντας (ὡς εἰπεῖν) πτωχοὺς καταστήσαντες. Zosim. l. v. [c. 23] p. 325. Yet the wealth of the Eastern monks was far surpassed by the princely greatness of the Benedictines.

[56] The sixth general council (the Quinisext in Trullo, Canon xlvii. in Beveridge, tom. i. p. 213) restrains women from passing the night in a male, or men in a female, monastery. The seventh general council (the second Nicene, Canon xx. in Beveridge, tom. i. p. 325) prohibits the erection of double or promiscuous monasteries of both sexes; but it appears from Balsamon that the prohibition was not effectual. On the irregular pleasures and expenses of the clergy and *monks,* see Thomassin, tom. iii. p. 1334-1368.

[57] I have somewhere heard or read the frank confession of a Benedictine abbot: "My vow of poverty has given me an hundred thousand crowns a year; my vow of obedience has raised me to the rank of a sovereign prince." I forget the consequences of his vow of chastity.

[58] Pior, an Egyptian monk, allowed his sister to see him; but he shut his eyes during the whole visit. See Vit Patrum, l. iii. p. 504. Many such examples might be added.

cluse fanatics have few ideas or sentiments to communicate: a special licence of the abbot regulated the time and duration of their familiar visits; and, at their silent meals, they were enveloped in their cowls, inaccessible, and almost invisible, to each other.[59]　Study is the resource of solitude; but education had not prepared and qualified for any liberal studies the mechanics and peasants who filled the monastic communities.　They might work; but the vanity of spiritual perfection was tempted to disdain the exercise of manual labour; and the industry must be faint and languid which is not excited by the sense of personal interest.

According to their faith and zeal, they might employ the day, which they passed in their cells, either in vocal or mental prayer: they assembled in the evening, and they were awakened in the night, for the public worship of the monastery.　The precise moment was determined by the stars, which are seldom clouded in the serene sky of Egypt; and a rustic horn, or trumpet, the signal of devotion, twice interrupted the vast silence of the desert.[60]　Even sleep, the last refuge of the unhappy, was rigorously measured: the vacant hours of the monk heavily rolled along, without business or pleasure; and, before the close of each day, he had repeatedly accused the tedious progress of the sun.[61]　In this comfortless state, superstition still pursued and tormented her wretched votaries.[62]　The repose which they had sought in the cloister was disturbed by tardy repentance, profane doubts, and guilty desires; and, while they considered each natural impulse as an unpardonable sin, they perpetually trembled on the edge of a flaming and bottomless abyss.　From the painful struggles of disease and despair, these unhappy victims were sometimes relieved by madness or death; and, in the sixth century, a hospital was founded at Jerusalem for a small portion of the austere penitents who were deprived of their senses.[63]　Their visions, before they attained this extreme and acknowledged term

---

[59] The 7th, 8th, 29th, 30th, 31st, 34th, 57th, 60th, 86th, and 95th articles of the Rule of Pachomius, impose most intolerable *laws* of silence and mortification.

[60] The diurnal and nocturnal prayers of the monks are copiously discussed by Cassian, in the third and fourth books of his Institutions; and he constantly prefers the liturgy which an angel had dictated to the monasteries of Tabennœ.

[61] Cassian, from his own experience, describes the *acedia*, or listlessness of mind and body, to which a monk was exposed when he sighed to find himself alone.　Sæpiusque egreditur et ingreditur cellam, et Solem velut ad occasum tardius properantem crebrius intuetur (Institut. x. 2).

[62] The temptations and sufferings of Stagirius were communicated by that unfortunate youth to his friend St. Chrysostom.　See Middleton's Works, vol. i. p. 107-110.　Something similar introduces the life of every saint; and the famous Inigo, or Ignatius, the founder of the Jesuits (Vida d'Inigo de Guiposcoa, tom. i. p. 29-38) may serve as a memorable example.

[63] Fleury, Hist. Ecclésiastique, tom. vii. p. 46.　I have read somewhere in the Vitæ Patrum, but I cannot recover the place, that *several*, I believe *many*, of the monks, who did not reveal their temptations to the abbot, became guilty of suicide.

of frenzy, have afforded ample materials of supernatural history. It was their firm persuasion that the air which they breathed was peopled with invisible enemies; with innumerable demons, who watched every occasion, and assumed every form, to terrify, and above all to tempt, their unguarded virtue. The imagination, and even the senses, were deceived by the illusions of distempered fanaticism; and the hermit, whose midnight prayer was oppressed by involuntary slumber, might easily confound the phantoms of horror or delight which had occupied his sleeping and his waking dreams.[64]

The monks were divided into two classes: the *Cœnobites,* who lived under a common and regular discipline; and the *Anachorets,* who indulged their unsocial, independent fanaticism.[65]   The most devout, or the most ambitious, of the spiritual brethren renounced the convent, as they had renounced the world. The fervent monasteries of Egypt, Palestine, and Syria were surrounded by a *Laura,*[66] a distant circle of solitary cells; and the extravagant penance of the Hermits was stimulated by applause and emulation.[67]   They sunk under the painful weight of crosses and chains; and their emaciated limbs were confined by collars, bracelets, gauntlets, and greaves of massy and rigid iron. All superfluous incumbrance of dress they contemptuously cast away; and some savage saints of both sexes have been admired, whose naked bodies were only covered by their long hair. They aspired to reduce themselves to the rude and miserable state in which the human brute is scarcely distinguished above his kindred animals; and the numerous sect of Anachorets derived their name from their humble practice of grazing in the fields of Mesopotamia with the common herd.[68]   They often usurped the den of some wild beast whom they affected to resemble; they buried themselves in some gloomy cavern, which art or nature had scooped out of the rock; and the marble quarries of

[64] See the seventh and eighth Collations of Cassian, who gravely examines why the dæmons were grown less active and numerous since the time of St. Antony.   Rosweyde's copious index to the Vitæ Patrum will point out a variety of infernal scenes.   The devils were most formidable in a female shape.

[65] For the distinction of the *Cœnobites* and the *Hermits,* especially in Egypt, see Jerom (tom. i. p. 45, ad Rusticum [Ep. 125, tom. i. p. 932, ed. Vallars.]), the first Dialogue of Sulpicius Severus, Rufinus (c. 22, in Vit. Patrum, l. ii. p. 478), Palladius (c. 7, 69, in Vit. Patrum, l. viii. p. 712, 758), and, above all, the eighteenth and nineteenth Collations of Cassian. These writers, who compare the common and solitary life, reveal the abuse and danger of the latter.

[66] Suicer. Thesaur. Ecclesiast. tom. ii. p. 205, 218.   Thomassin (Discipline de l'Eglise, tom. i. p. 1501, 1502) gives a good account of these cells. When Gerasimus founded his monastery, in the wilderness of Jordan, it was accompanied by a Laura of seventy cells.

[67] Theodoret, in a large volume (the Philotheus in Vit. Patrum, l. ix. p. 793-863) has collected the lives and miracles of thirty Anachorets.   Evagrius (l. i. c. 21) more briefly celebrates the monks and hermits of Palestine.

[68] Sozomen, l. vi. c. 33.   The great St. Ephrem composed a panegyric on these βόσκοι, or grazing monks (Tillemont, Mém. Ecclés. tom. viii. p. 292).

Thebais are still inscribed with the monuments of their penance.[69] The most perfect Hermits are supposed to have passed many days without food, many nights without sleep, and many years without speaking; and glorious was the *man* (I abuse that name) who contrived any cell, or seat, of a peculiar construction, which might expose him, in the most inconvenient posture, to the inclemency of the seasons.

Among these heroes of the monastic life, the name and genius of Simeon Stylites [70] have been immortalised by the singular invention of an aërial penance. At the age of thirteen the young Syrian deserted the profession of a shepherd, and threw himself into an austere monastery. After a long and painful novitiate, in which Simeon was repeatedly saved from pious suicide, he established his residence on a mountain, about thirty or forty miles to the east of Antioch. Within the space of a *mandra*, or circle of stones, to which he had attached himself by a ponderous chain, he ascended a column, which was successively raised from the height of nine, to that of sixty, feet from the ground.[71] In this last and lofty station, the Syrian Anachoret resisted the heat of thirty summers, and the cold of as many winters. Habit and exercise instructed him to maintain his dangerous situation without fear or giddiness, and successively to assume the different postures of devotion. He sometimes prayed in an erect attitude, with his outstretched arms in the figure of a cross; but his most familiar practice was that of bending his meagre skeleton from the forehead to the feet; and a curious spectator, after numbering twelve hundred and forty-four repetitions, at length desisted from the endless account. The progress of an ulcer in his thigh [72] might shorten, but it could not disturb, this *celestial* life; and the patient Hermit expired without descending from his column. A prince, who should capriciously inflict such tortures, would be deemed a tyrant; but it would surpass the power of a tyrant to impose a long and miserable existence on the reluctant victims of his cruelty. This voluntary martyrdom must have gradually destroyed the sensibility both of the mind and body; nor can it be presumed that the fanatics who torment themselves are susceptible of any lively affection for the

[69] The P. Sicard (Missions du Levant, tom. ii. p. 217-233) examined the caverns of the Lower Thebais with wonder and devotion. The inscriptions are in the old Syriac character, which was used by the Christians of Abyssinia.

[70] See Theodoret (in Vit. Patrum, l. ix. p. 848-854), Antony (in Vit. Patrum, l. i. p. 170-177), Cosmas (in Asseman. Bibliot. Oriental. tom. i. p. 239-253), Evagrius (l. i. c. 13, 14), and Tillemont (Mém Ecclés. tom. xv. p. 347-392).

[71] The narrow circumference of two cubits, or three feet, which Evagrius assigns for the summit of the column, is inconsistent with reason, with facts, and with the rules of architecture. The people who saw it from below might be easily deceived.

[72] I must not conceal a piece of ancient scandal concerning the origin of this ulcer. It has been reported that the Devil, assuming an angelic form, invited him to ascend, like Elijah, into a fiery chariot. The saint too hastily raised his foot, and Satan seized the moment of inflicting this chastisement on his vanity.

rest of mankind. A cruel, unfeeling temper has distinguished the monks of every age and country: their stern indifference, which is seldom mollified by personal friendship, is inflamed by religious hatred; and their merciless zeal has strenuously administered the holy office of the Inquisition.

The monastic saints, who excite only the contempt and pity of a philosopher, were respected and almost adored by the prince and people. Successive crowds of pilgrims from Gaul and India saluted the divine pillar of Simeon; the tribes of Saracens disputed in arms the honour of his benediction; the queens of Arabia and Persia gratefully confessed his supernatural virtue; and the angelic Hermit was consulted by the younger Theodosius in the most important concerns of the church and state. His remains were transported from the mountain of Telenissa, by a solemn procession of the patriarch, the master-general of the East, six bishops, twenty-one counts or tribunes, and six thousand soldiers; and Antioch revered his bones as her glorious ornament and impregnable defence. The fame of the apostles and martyrs was gradually eclipsed by these recent and popular Anachorets; the Christian world fell prostrate before their shrines; and the miracles ascribed to their relics exceeded, at least in number and duration, the spiritual exploits of their lives. But the golden legend of their lives [73] was embellished by the artful credulity of their interested brethren; and a believing age was easily persuaded that the slightest caprice of an Egyptian or a Syrian monk had been sufficient to interrupt the eternal laws of the universe. The favourites of Heaven were accustomed to cure inveterate diseases with a touch, a word, or a distant message; and to expel the most obstinate demons from the souls or bodies which they possessed. They familiarly accosted, or imperiously commanded, the lions and serpents of the desert; infused vegetation into a sapless trunk; suspended iron on the surface of the water; passed the Nile on the back of a crocodile; and refreshed themselves in a fiery furnace. These extravagant tales, which display the fiction, without the genius, of poetry, have seriously affected the reason, the faith, and the morals of the Christians. Their credulity debased and vitiated the faculties of the mind: they corrupted the evidence of history; and superstition gradually extinguished the hostile light of philosophy and science. Every mode of religious worship which had been practised by the saints, every mysterious doctrine which they believed, was fortified by the sanction of divine revelation, and all the manly virtues were oppressed by the servile and pusillanimous reign of the monks. If it be possible

---

[73] I know not how to select or specify the miracles contained in the *Vitæ Patrum* of Rosweyde, as the number very much exceeds the thousand pages of that voluminous work. An elegant specimen may be found in the Dialogues of Sulpicius Severus and his Life of St. Martin. He reveres the monks of Egypt; yet he insults them with the remark that *they* never raised the dead; whereas the bishop of Tours had restored *three* dead men to life.

to measure the interval between the philosophic writings of Cicero and the sacred legend of Theodoret, between the character of Cato and that of Simeon, we may appreciate the memorable revolution which was accomplished in the Roman empire within a period of five hundred years.

II. The progress of Christianity has been marked by two glorious and decisive victories: over the learned and luxurious citizens of the Roman empire; and over the warlike barbarians of Scythia and Germany, who subverted the empire and embraced the religion of the Romans. The Goths were the foremost of these savage proselytes; and the nation was indebted for its conversion to a countryman, or at least to a subject, worthy to be ranked among the inventors of useful arts who have deserved the remembrance and gratitude of posterity. A great number of Roman provincials had been led away into captivity by the Gothic bands who ravaged Asia in the time of Gallienus; and of these captives many were Christians, and several belonged to the ecclesiastical order. Those involuntary missionaries, dispersed as slaves in the villages of Dacia, successively laboured for the salvation of their masters. The seeds which they planted of the evangelic doctrine were gradually propagated; and before the end of a century the pious work was achieved by the labours of Ulphilas, whose ancestors had been transported beyond the Danube from a small town of Cappadocia.

Ulphilas, the bishop and apostle of the Goths,[74] acquired their love and reverence by his blameless life and indefatigable zeal, and they received with implicit confidence the doctrines of truth and virtue which he preached and practised. He executed the arduous task of translating the Scriptures into their native tongue, a dialect of the German or Teutonic language; but he prudently suppressed the four books of Kings, as they might tend to irritate the fierce and sanguinary spirit of the barbarians. The rude, imperfect idiom of soldiers and shepherds,

[74] On the subject of Ulphilas and the conversion of the Goths, see Sozomen, l. vi. c. 37; Socrates, l. iv. c. 33; Theodoret, l. iv. c. 37; Philostorg. l. ii. c. 5. The heresy of Philostorgius appears to have given him superior means of information.

[The alphabet which Ulphilas or Ulfilas was obliged to construct is the Mœso-Gothic, of which many of the letters are evidently formed from the Greek and Roman. St. Martin contends that it is impossible that some written alphabet had not been known long before among the Goths. He supposes that their former letters were those inscribed on the runes, which being inseparably connected with the old idolatrous superstitions were proscribed by the Christian missionaries. Everywhere the runes, so common among all German tribes, disappear after the propagation of Christianity. On this point Bury says, "The Goths before Ulfilas used the Runic alphabet, consisting of twenty-four signs. Ulfilas based his alphabet on the Greek, adopting the Greek order, and adapted it to the requirements of Gothic speech. But his alphabet has twenty-five letters, five of them being derived from the Runic, one from the Latin (S), and one is of uncertain origin. This uncertain letter has the value of Q, and corresponds in position in the alphabet to the Greek numeral sigma, between E and Z."—O. S.]

so ill qualified to communicate any spiritual ideas, was improved and modulated by his genius; and Ulphilas, before he could frame his version, was obliged to compose a new alphabet of twenty-four letters; four of which he invented to express the peculiar sounds that were unknown to the Greek and Latin pronunciation.[75] But the prosperous state of the Gothic church was soon afflicted by war and intestine discord, and the chieftains were divided by religion as well as by interest. Fritigern, the friend of the Romans, became the proselyte of Ulphilas; while the haughty soul of Athanaric disdained the yoke of the empire and of the Gospel. The faith of the new converts was tried by the persecution which he excited. A waggon, bearing aloft the shapeless image of Thor, perhaps, or of Woden, was conducted in solemn procession through the streets of the camp, and the rebels who refused to worship the god of their fathers were immediately burnt with their tents and families. The character of Ulphilas recommended him to the esteem of the Eastern court, where he twice appeared as the minister of peace; he pleaded the cause of the distressed Goths, who implored the protection of Valens; and the name of *Moses* was applied to this spiritual guide, who conducted his people through the deep waters of the Danube to the Land of Promise.[76] The devout shepherds, who were attached to his person and tractable to his voice, acquiesced in their settlement at the foot of the Mæsian mountains, in a country of woodlands and pastures, which supported their flocks and herds, and enabled them to purchase the corn and wine of the more plentiful provinces. These harmless barbarians multiplied in obscure peace and the profession of Christianity.[77]

[75] A mutilated copy of the four Gospels in the Gothic version was published A.D. 1665, and is esteemed the most ancient monument of the Teutonic language, though Wetstein attempts, by some frivolous conjectures, to deprive Ulphilas of the honour of the work. Two of the four additional letters express the *W* and our own *Th*. See Simon, Hist. Critique du Nouveau Testament, tom. ii. p. 219-223. Mill. Prolegom. p. 151, edit. Kuster. Wetstein, Prolegom. tom. i. p. 114.
[This mutilated copy of the Gospels is contained in a MS. called the Codex Argenteus, found at Werden in Westphalia in the sixteenth century, and now preserved at Upsal. It contains more than half of the four Gospels. In 1762 Knettel discovered and published from a palimpsest MS. four chapters of the Epistle to the Romans. They were reprinted at Upsal, 1763. There can be little doubt that Ulfilas made such a version, but it is considered by many critics extremely doubtful whether it is contained in the MS. at Upsal, or whether the language of the MS. is genuine Old Gothic. These critics maintain that its language is a century and a half later than the time of Ulfilas. Cf. Aschbach, *Geschichte der Westgothen*, p. 35 *seq.* With regard to the accounts in Sozomen and Socrates, these are largely derived from Philostorgius.—O. S.]
[76] Philostorgius erroneously places this passage under the reign of Constantine; but I am much inclined to believe that it preceded the great emigration.
[77] We are obliged to Jornandes (de Reb. Get. c. 51, p. 688) for a short and lively picture of these lesser Goths. Gothi minores, populus immensus, cum suo Pontifice ipsoque primate Wulfila. The last words, if they are not mere tautology, imply some temporal jurisdiction.

Their fiercer brethren, the formidable Visigoths, universally adopted the religion of the Romans, with whom they maintained a perpetual intercourse of war, of friendship, or of conquest. In their long and victorious march from the Danube to the Atlantic Ocean they converted their allies; they educated the rising generation; and the devotion which reigned in the camp of Alaric, or the court of Toulouse, might edify or disgrace the palaces of Rome and Constantinople.[78] During the same period Christianity was embraced by almost all the barbarians who established their kingdoms on the ruins of the Western empire; the Burgundians in Gaul, the Suevi in Spain, the Vandals in Africa, the Ostrogoths in Pannonia, and the various bands of mercenaries that raised Odoacer to the throne of Italy. The Franks and the Saxons still persevered in the errors of Paganism; but the Franks obtained the monarchy of Gaul by their submission to the example of Clovis; and the Saxon conquerors of Britain were reclaimed from their savage superstition by the missionaries of Rome. These barbarian proselytes displayed an ardent and successful zeal in the propagation of the faith. The Merovingian kings and their successors, Charlemagne and the Othos, extended by their laws and victories the dominion of the cross. England produced the apostle of Germany; and the evangelic light was gradually diffused from the neighbourhood of the Rhine to the nations of the Elbe, the Vistula, and the Baltic.[79]

The different motives which influenced the reason or the passions of the barbarian converts cannot easily be ascertained. They were often capricious and accidental; a dream, an omen, the report of a miracle, the example of some priest or hero, the charms of a believing wife, and, above all, the fortunate event of a prayer or vow which, in a moment of danger, they had addressed to the God of the Christians.[80] The early prejudices of education were insensibly erased by the habits of frequent and familiar society; the moral precepts of the Gospel were protected by the extravagant virtues of the monks; and a spiritual theology was supported by the visible power of relics, and the pomp of religious worship. But the rational and ingenious mode of persuasion which a Saxon bishop [81] suggested to a popular saint might sometimes be employed by the missionaries who laboured for the conversion of

[78] At non ita Gothi non ita Vandali; malis licet doctoribus instituti, meliores tamen etiam in hâc parte quam nostri. Salvian de Gubern. Dei, l. vii. p. 243 [ed. Par. 1608].

[79] Mosheim has slightly sketched the progress of Christianity in the North, from the fourth to the fourteenth century. The subject would afford materials for an ecclesiastical and even philosophical history.

[80] To such a cause has Socrates (l. vii. c. 30) ascribed the conversion of the Burgundians, whose Christian piety is celebrated by Orosius (l. vii. c. 19 [32]).

[81] See an original and curious epistle from Daniel, the first bishop of Winchester (Beda, Hist. Eccles. Anglorum, l. v. c. 18, p. 203, edit. Smith), to St. Boniface, who preached the Gospel among the savages of Hesse and Thuringia. Epistol. Bonifacii, lxvii. in the Maxima Bibliotheca Patrum, tom. xiii. p. 93.

infidels. "Admit," says the sagacious disputant, " whatever they are pleased to assert of the fabulous and carnal genealogy of their gods and goddesses, who are propagated from each other. From this principle deduce their imperfect nature and human infirmities, the assurance they were *born,* and the probability that they will *die.* At what time, by what means, from what cause, were the eldest of the gods or goddesses produced? Do they still continue, or have they ceased, to propagate? If they have ceased, summon your antagonist to declare the reason of this strange alteration. If they still continue, the number of the gods must become infinite; and shall we not risk, by the indiscreet worship of some impotent deity, to excite the resentment of his jealous superior? The visible heavens and earth, the whole system of the universe, which may be conceived by the mind, is it created or eternal? If created, how or where could the gods themselves exist before the creation? If eternal, how could they assume the empire of an independent and pre-existing world? Urge these arguments with temper and moderation; insinuate, at seasonable intervals, the truth and beauty of the Christian revelation; and endeavour to make the unbelievers ashamed without making them angry." This metaphysical reasoning, too refined perhaps for the barbarians of Germany, was fortified by the grosser weight of authority and popular consent. The advantage of temporal prosperity had deserted the Pagan cause and passed over to the service of Christianity. The Romans themselves, the most powerful and enlightened nation of the globe, had renounced their ancient superstition; and if the ruin of their empire seemed to accuse the efficacy of the new faith, the disgrace was already retrieved by the conversion of the victorious Goths. The valiant and fortunate barbarians who subdued the provinces of the West successively received and reflected the same edifying example. Before the age of Charlemagne, the Christian nations of Europe might exult in the exclusive possession of the temperate climates, of the fertile lands which produced corn, wine, and oil; while the savage idolaters and their helpless idols were confined to the extremities of the earth, the dark and frozen regions of the North.[82]

Christianity, which opened the gates of Heaven to the barbarians, introduced an important change in their moral and political condition. They received, at the same time, the use of letters, so essential to a religion whose doctrines are contained in a sacred book; and while they studied the divine truth, their minds were insensibly enlarged by the distant view of history, of nature, of the arts, and of society. The version of the Scriptures into their native tongue, which had facilitated their conversion, must excite, among their clergy, some curiosity to read the original text, to understand the sacred liturgy of the church, and

[82] The sword of Charlemagne added weight to the argument; but when Daniel wrote this epistle (A.D. 723), the Mahometans, who reigned from India to Spain, might have retorted it against the Christians.

to examine, in the writings of the fathers, the chain of ecclesiastical tradition. These spiritual gifts were preserved in the Greek and Latin languages, which concealed the inestimable monuments of ancient learning. The immortal productions of Virgil, Cicero, and Livy, which were accessible to the Christian barbarians, maintained a silent intercourse between the reign of Augustus and the times of Clovis and Charlemagne. The emulation of mankind was encouraged by the remembrance of a more perfect state; and the flame of science was secretly kept alive, to warm and enlighten the mature age of the Western world. In the most corrupt state of Christianity the barbarians might learn justice from the *law,* and mercy from the *gospel;* and if the knowledge of their duty was insufficient to guide their actions or to regulate their passions, they were sometimes restrained by conscience, and frequently punished by remorse. But the direct authority of religion was less effectual than the holy communion, which united them with their Christian brethren in spiritual friendship. The influence of these sentiments contributed to secure their fidelity in the service or the alliance of the Romans, to alleviate the horrors of war, to moderate the insolence of conquest, and to preserve, in the downfall of the empire, a permanent respect for the name and institutions of Rome. In the days of Paganism the priests of Gaul and Germany reigned over the people, and controlled the jurisdiction of the magistrates; and the zealous proselytes transferred an equal, or more ample, measure of devout obedience to the pontiffs of the Christian faith. The sacred character of the bishops was supported by their temporal possessions; they obtained an honourable seat in the legislative assemblies of soldiers and freemen; and it was their interest, as well as their duty, to mollify by peaceful counsels the fierce spirit of the barbarians. The perpetual correspondence of the Latin clergy, the frequent pilgrimages to Rome and Jerusalem, and the growing authority of the popes, cemented the union of the Christian republic, and gradually produced the similar manners and common jurisprudence which have distinguished from the rest of mankind the independent, and even hostile, nations of modern Europe.

But the operation of these causes was checked and retarded by the unfortunate accident which infused a deadly poison into the cup of salvation. Whatever might be the early sentiments of Ulphilas, his connections with the empire and the church were formed during the reign of Arianism. The apostle of the Goths subscribed the creed of Rimini; professed with freedom, and perhaps with sincerity, that the Son was not equal or consubstantial to the FATHER;[83] communicated these errors to the clergy and people; and infected the barbaric world

---

[83] The opinions of Ulphilas and the Goths inclined to semi-Arianism, since they would not say that the Son was a *creature,* though they held communion with those who maintained that heresy. Their apostle represented the whole controversy as a question of trifling moment which had been raised by the passions of the clergy. Theodoret, l. iv. c. 37.

with an heresy [84] which the great Theodosius proscribed and extinguished among the Romans. The temper and understanding of the new proselytes were not adapted to metaphysical subtleties; but they strenuously maintained what they had piously received as the pure and genuine doctrines of Christianity. The advantage of preaching and expounding the Scriptures in the Teutonic language promoted the apostolic labours of Ulphilas and his successors; and they ordained a competent number of bishops and presbyters for the instruction of the kindred tribes. The Ostrogoths, the Burgundians, the Suevi, and the Vandals, who had listened to the eloquence of the Latin clergy,[85] preferred the more intelligible lessons of their domestic teachers; and Arianism was adopted as the national faith of the warlike converts who were seated on the ruins of the Western empire. This irreconcilable difference of religion was a perpetual source of jealousy and hatred; and the reproach of *Barbarian* was embittered by the more odious epithet of *Heretic*. The heroes of the North, who had submitted with some reluctance to believe that all their ancestors were in hell,[86] were astonished and exasperated to learn that they themselves had only changed the mode of their eternal condemnation. Instead of the smooth applause which Christian kings are accustomed to expect from their loyal prelates, the orthodox bishops and their clergy were in a state of opposition to the Arian courts; and their indiscreet opposition frequently became criminal, and might sometimes be dangerous.[87] The pulpit, that safe and sacred organ of sedition, resounded with the names of Pharaoh and Holofernes;[88] the public discontent was inflamed by the hope or promise of a glorious deliverance; and the seditious saints were tempted to promote the accomplishment of their own predictions. Notwithstanding these provocations, the catholics of Gaul, Spain, and Italy enjoyed, under the reign of the Arians, the free and peaceful exercise of their religion. Their haughty masters respected the zeal of a

[84] The Arianism of the Goths has been imputed to the emperor Valens: " Itaque justo Dei judicio ipsi eum vivum incenderunt. qui propter eum etiam mortui, vitio erroris arsuri sunt." Orosius, l. vii. c. 33, p. 554. This cruel sentence is confirmed by Tillemont (Mém. Ecclés. tom. vi. p. 604-610), who coolly observes, "un seul homme entraina dans l'enfer un nombre infini de Septentrionaux," etc. Salvian (de Gubern. Dei, l. v. p. 150, 151) pities and excuses their involuntary error.

[85] Orosius affirms, in the year 416 (l. vii. c. 41, p. 580), that the churches of Christ (of the catholics) were filled with Huns, Suevi, Vandals, Burgundians.

[86] Radbod, king of the Frisons, was so much scandalised by this rash declaration of a missionary, that he drew back his foot after he had entered the baptismal font. See Fleury, Hist. Ecclés. tom. ix. p. 167.

[87] The epistles of Sidonius, bishop of Clermont under the Visigoths, and of Avitus, bishop of Vienne under the Burgundians, explain, sometimes in dark hints, the general dispositions of the catholics. The history of Clovis and Theodoric will suggest some particular facts.

[88] Genseric confessed the resemblance by the severity with which he punished such indiscreet allusions. Victor Vitensis, i. 7, p. 10.

numerous people, resolved to die at the foot of their altars, and the example of their devout constancy was admired and imitated by the barbarians themselves. The conquerors evaded, however, the disgraceful reproach or confession of fear, by attributing their toleration to the liberal motives of reason and humanity; and while they affected the language, they imperceptibly imbibed the spirit, of genuine Christianity.

The peace of the church was sometimes interrupted. The catholics were indiscreet, the barbarians were impatient; and the partial acts of severity or injustice, which had been recommended by the Arian clergy, were exaggerated by the orthodox writers. The guilt of persecution may be imputed to Euric, king of the Visigoths who suspended the exercise of ecclesiastical, or, at least, of episcopal functions, and punished the popular bishops of Aquitain with imprisonment, exile, and confiscation.[89] But the cruel and absurd enterprise of subduing the minds of a whole people was undertaken by the Vandals alone. Genseric himself, in his early youth, had renounced the orthodox communion; and the apostate could neither grant nor expect a sincere forgiveness. He was exasperated to find that the Africans, who had fled before him in the field, still presumed to dispute his will in synods and churches; and his ferocious mind was incapable of fear or of compassion. His catholic subjects were oppressed by intolerant laws and arbitrary punishments. The language of Genseric was furious and formidable; the knowledge of his intentions might justify the most unfavourable interpretation of his actions; and the Arians were reproached with the frequent executions which stained the palace and the dominions of the tyrant. Arms and ambition were, however, the ruling passions of the monarch of the sea. But Hunneric, his inglorious son, who seemed to inherit only his vices, tormented the catholics with the same unrelenting fury which had been fatal to his brother, his nephews, and the friends and favourites of his father; and even to the Arian patriarch, who was inhumanly burnt alive in the midst of Carthage. The religious war was preceded and prepared by an insidious truce; persecution was made the serious and important business of the Vandal court; and the loathsome disease which hastened the death of Hunneric revenged the injuries, without contributing to the deliverance, of the church. The throne of Africa was successively filled by the two nephews of Hunneric; by Gundamund, who reigned about twelve, and by Thrasimund, who governed the nation above twenty-seven, years. Their administration was hostile and oppressive to the orthodox party. Gundamund appeared to emulate, or even to surpass, the cruelty of his uncle; and if at length he relented, if he recalled the bishops, and restored the free-

---

[89] Such are the contemporary complaints of Sidonius, bishop of Clermont (1. vii. c. 6, p. 182, etc., edit. Sirmond). Gregory of Tours, who quotes this Epistle (1. ii. c. 25, in tom. ii. p. 174), extorts an unwarrantable assertion, that, of the nine vacancies in Aquitain, some had been produced by episcopal *martyrdoms*.

dom of Athanasian worship, a premature death intercepted the benefits of his tardy clemency. His brother, Thrasimund, was the greatest and most accomplished of the Vandal kings, whom he excelled in beauty, prudence, and magnanimity of soul. But this magnanimous character was degraded by his intolerant zeal and deceitful clemency. Instead of threats and tortures, he employed the gentle, but efficacious, powers of seduction. Wealth, dignity, and the royal favour were the liberal rewards of apostasy; the catholics who had violated the laws might purchase their pardon by the renunciation of their faith; and whenever Thrasimund mediated any rigorous measure, he patiently waited till the indiscretion of his adversaries furnished him with a specious opportunity. Bigotry was his last sentiment in the hour of death; and he exacted from his successor a solemn oath that he would never tolerate the sectaries of Athanasius. But his successor, Hilderic, the gentle son of the savage Hunneric, preferred the duties of humanity and justice to the vain obligation of an impious oath; and his accession was gloriously marked by the restoration of peace and universal freedom. The throne of that virtuous, though feeble, monarch was usurped by his cousin Gelimer, a zealous Arian: but the Vandal kingdom, before he could enjoy or abuse his power, was subverted by the arms of Belisarius; and the orthodox party retaliated the injuries which they had endured.[90]

The passionate declamations of the catholics, the sole historians of this persecution, cannot afford any distinct series of causes and events, any impartial view of characters or counsels; but the most remarkable circumstances that deserve either credit or notice may be referred to the following heads: I. In the original law, which is still extant,[91] Hunneric expressly declares, and the declaration appears to be correct, that he had faithfully transcribed the regulations and penalties of the Imperial edicts against the heretical congregations, the clergy, and the people, who dissented from the established religion. If the rights of conscience had been understood, the catholics must have condemned their past conduct, or acquiesced in their actual sufferings. But they still persisted to refuse the indulgence which they claimed. While they trembled under the lash of persecution, they praised the *laudable* sever-

---

[90] The original monuments of the Vandal persecution are preserved in the five books of the history of Victor Vitensis (de Persecutione Vandalicâ), a bishop who was exiled by Hunneric; in the Life of St. Fulgentius, who was distinguished in the persecution of Thrasimund (in Biblioth. Max. Patrum, tom. ix. p. 4-16); and in the first book of the Vandalic War, by the impartial Procopius (c. 7, 8, p. 196, 197, 198, 199 [ed. Paris; tom. i. p. 344 *sqq.*, ed, Bonn]). Dom. Ruinart, the last editor of Victor, has illustrated the whole subject with a copius and learned apparatus of notes and supplement. (Paris, 1694.)

[91] Victor, iv. 2, p. 65. Hunneric refuses the name of Catholics to the *Homoousians*. He describes, as the veri Divinæ Majestatis cultores, his own party, who professed the faith, confirmed by more than a thousand bishops, in the synods of Rimini and Seleucia.

ity of Hunneric himself, who burnt or banished great numbers of Manichæans;[92] and they rejected with horror the ignominious compromise
that the disciples of Arius and of Athanasius should enjoy a reciprocal
and similar toleration in the territories of the Romans and in those of
the Vandals.[93] II. The practice of a conference, which the catholics had
so frequently used to insult and punish their obstinate antagonists, was
retorted against themselves.[94] At the command of Hunneric, four hundred and sixty-six orthodox bishops assembled at Carthage; but when
they were admitted into the hall of audience, they had the mortification
of beholding the Arian Cyrila exalted on the patriarchal throne. The
disputants were separated, after the mutual and ordinary reproaches of
noise and silence, of delay and precipitation, of military force and of
popular clamour. One martyr and one confessor were selected among
the catholic bishops; twenty-eight escaped by flight, and eighty-eight
by conformity; forty-six were sent into Corsica to cut timber for the
royal navy; and three hundred and two were banished to the different
parts of Africa, exposed to the insults of their enemies, and carefully
deprived of all the temporal and spiritual comforts of life.[95] The hardships of ten years' exile must have reduced their numbers; and if
they had complied with the law of Thrasimund, which prohibited any
episcopal consecrations, the orthodox church of Africa must have expired with the lives of its actual members. They disobeyed; and their
disobedience was punished by a second exile of two hundred and twenty
bishops into Sardinia, where they languished fifteen years, till the accession of the gracious Hilderic.[96] The two islands were judiciously chosen
by the malice of their Arian tyrants. Seneca, from his own experience,
has deplored and exaggerated the miserable state of Corsica,[97] and the
plenty of Sardinia was overbalanced by the unwholesome quality of

[92] Victor, ii. 1, p. 21, 22, *Laudabilior* . . . videbatur. In the MSS. which
omit this word, the passage is unintelligible. See Ruinart, Not. p. 164.
[93] Victor, ii. 2, p. 22, 23 [21, 22]. The clergy of Carthage called these
conditions *periculosæ;* and they seem, indeed, to have been proposed as a snare
to entrap the catholic bishops.
[94] See the narrative of this conference and the treatment of the bishops
in Victor, ii. 13-18, p. 35-42, and the whole fourth book, p. 63-71. The third
book, p. 42-62, is entirely filled by their apology or confession of faith.
[95] See the list of the African bishops, in Victor, p. 117-140, and Ruinart's
notes, p. 215-397. The schismatic name of *Donatus* frequently occurs, and
they appear to have adopted (like our fanatics of the last age) the pious
appellations of *Deodatus, Deogratias, Quidvultdeus, Habetdeum,* etc.
[96] Fulgent. Vit. c. 16-29. Thrasimund affected the praise of moderation and
learning; and Fulgentius addressed three books of controversy to the Arian
tyrant, whom he styles *piissime Rex.* Biblioth. Maxim. Patrum, tom. ix. p. 4L
Only sixty bishops are mentioned as exiles in the Life of Fulgentius; they are
increased to one hundred and twenty by Victor Tunnunensis and Isidore; but
the number of two hundred and twenty is specified in the *Historia Miscella*
and a short authentic chronicle of the times. See Ruinart, p. 570, 571.
[97] See the base and insipid epigrams of the Stoic, who could not support
exile with more fortitude than Ovid. Corsica might not produce corn, wine,
or oil; but it could not be destitute of grass, water, and even fire.

the air.[98] III. The zeal of Genseric and his successors for the conversion of the catholics must have rendered them still more jealous to guard the purity of the Vandal faith. Before the churches were finally shut, it was a crime to appear in a barbarian dress; and those who presumed to neglect the royal mandate were rudely dragged backwards by their long hair.[99] The palatine officers, who refused to profess the religion of their prince, were ignominiously stripped of their honours and employments; banished to Sardinia and Sicily; or condemned to the servile labours of slaves and peasants in the fields of Utica. In the districts which had been peculiarly allotted to the Vandals, the exercise of the catholic worship was more strictly prohibited; and severe penalties were denounced against the guilt both of the missionary and the proselyte. By these arts the faith of the barbarians was preserved, and their zeal was inflamed: they discharged with devout fury the office of spies, informers, or executioners; and whenever their cavalry took the field, it was the favourite amusement of the march to defile the churches and to insult the clergy of the adverse faction.[100] IV. The citizens who had been educated in the luxury of the Roman province were delivered, with exquisite cruelty, to the Moors of the desert. A venerable train of bishops, presbyters, and deacons, with a faithful crowd of four thousand and ninety-six persons, whose guilt is not precisely ascertained, were torn from their native homes by the command of Hunneric. During the night they were confined, like a herd of cattle, amidst their own ordure: during the day they pursued their march over the burning sands; and if they fainted under the heat and fatigue, they were goaded or dragged along till they expired in the hands of their tormentors.[101] These unhappy exiles, when they reached the Moorish huts, might excite the compassion of a people whose native humanity was neither improved by reason nor corrupted by fanaticism: but if they escaped the dangers, they were condemned to share the distress, of a savage life. V. It is incumbent on the authors of persecution previously to reflect whether they are determined to support it in the last extreme. They excite the flame which they strive to extinguish; and it soon becomes necessary to chastise the contumacy, as well as the crime, of the offender. The fine, which is he unable or unwilling to discharge, exposes his person to the severity of the law; and his contempt of lighter penalties suggests the use and propriety of capital pun-

---

[98] Si ob gravitatem cœli interissent, *vile* damnum. Tacit. Annal. ii. 85. In this application Thrasimund would have adopted the reading of some critics, *utile* damnum.

[99] See these preludes of a *general* persecution, in Victor, ii. c. 3, 4, 7, and the two edicts of Hunneric, l. ii. p. 35, l. iv. p. 64.

[100] See Procopius de Bell. Vandal. l. i. c. 7 [c. 8], p. 197, 198 [tom. i. p. 344 *sqq.*, ed. Bonn]. A Moorish prince endeavoured to propitiate the God of the Christians by his diligence to erase the marks of the Vandal sacrilege.

[101] See this story in Victor, ii. 8-12, p. 30-34. Victor describes the distress of these confessors as an eye-witness.

ishment. Through the veil of fiction and declamation we may clearly perceive that the catholics, more especially under the reign of Hunneric, endured the most cruel and ignominious treatment.[102]   Respectable citizens, noble matrons, and consecrated virgins were stripped naked and raised in the air by pulleys, with a weight suspended at their feet. In this painful attitude their naked bodies were torn with scourges, or burnt in the most tender parts with red-hot plates of iron.   The amputation of the ears, the nose, the tongue, and the right hand was inflicted by the Arians; and although the precise number cannot be defined, it is evident that many persons, among whom a bishop,[103] and a proconsul,[104] may be named, were entitled to the crown of martyrdom.   The same honour has been ascribed to the memory of Count Sebastian, who professed the Nicene creed with unshaken constancy; and Genseric might detest as an heretic the brave and ambitious fugitive whom he dreaded as a rival.[105]   VI. A new mode of conversion, which might subdue the feeble and alarm the timorous, was employed by the Arian ministers.   They imposed, by fraud or violence, the rites of baptism; and punished the apostacy of the catholics, if they disclaimed this odious and profane ceremony, which scandalously violated the freedom of the will and the unity of the sacrament.[106]   The hostile sects had formerly allowed the validity of each other's baptism; and the innovation, so fiercely maintained by the Vandals, can be imputed only to the example and advice of the Donatists.   VII. The Arian clergy surpassed in religious cruelty the king and his Vandals; but they were incapable of cultivating the spiritual vineyard which they were so desirous to possess.   A patriarch [107] might seat himself on the throne of Carthage; some bishops, in the principal cities, might usurp the place of their rivals; but the smallness of their numbers, and their ignorance of the Latin language,[108] disqualified the barbarians for the ecclesiastical ministry of a great church; and the Africans, after the

---

[102] See the fifth book of Victor. His passionate complaints are confirmed by the sober testimony of Procopius and the public declaration of the emperor Justinian. Cod. l. i. tit. xxvii.

[103] Victor, ii. 18, p. 41.

[104] Victor, v. 4, p. 74, 75. His name was Victorianus, and he was a wealthy citizen of Adrumetum, who enjoyed the confidence of the king, by whose favour he had obtained the office, or at least the title, of proconsul of Africa.

[105] Victor, i. 6, p. 8, 9. After relating the firm resistance and dexterous reply of Count Sebastian, he adds, quare alio [alius] generis argumento postea bellicosum virum occidit.

[106] Victor, v. 12, 13. Tillemont, Mém. Ecclés. tom. vi. p. 609.

[107] *Primate* was more properly the title of the bishop of Carthage; but the name of *patriarch* was given by the sects and nations to their principal ecclesiastic. See Thomassin, Discipline de l'Eglise, tom. i. p. 155, 158.

[108] The patriarch Cyrila himself publicly declared that he did not understand Latin (Victor, ii. 18, p. 42): Nescio Latine; and he might converse with tolerable ease, without being capable of disputing or preaching in that language. His vandal clergy were still more ignorant; and small confidence could be placed in the Africans who had conformed.

*l*oss of their orthodox pastors, were deprived of the public exercise of Christianity. VIII. The emperors were the natural protectors of the Homoousian doctrine; and the faithful people of Africa, both as Romans and as catholics, preferred their lawful sovereignty to the usurpation of the barbarous heretics. During an interval of peace and friendship Hunneric restored the cathedral of Carthage, at the intercession of Zeno, who reigned in the East, and of Placidia, the daughter and relict of emperors and the sister of the queen of the Vandals.[109] But this decent regard was of short duration; and the haughty tyrant displayed his contempt for the religion of the empire by studiously arranging the bloody images of persecution in all the principal streets through which the Roman ambassador must pass in his way to the palace.[110] An oath was required from the bishops who were assembled at Carthage, that they would support the succession of his son Hilderic, and that they would renounce all foreign or *transmarine* correspondence. This engagement, consistent, as it should seem, with their moral and religious duties, was refused by the more sagacious members [111] of the assembly. Their refusal, faintly coloured by the pretence that it is unlawful for a Christian to swear, must provoke the suspicions of a jealous tyrant.

The catholics, oppressed by royal and military force, were far superior to their adversaries in numbers and learning. With the same weapons which the Greek [112] and Latin fathers had already provided for the Arian controversy, they repeatedly silenced or vanquished the fierce and illiterate successors of Ulphilas. The consciousness of their own superiority might have raised them above the arts and passions of religious warfare. Yet, instead of assuming such honourable pride, the orthodox theologians were tempted, by the assurance of impunity, to compose fictions which must be stigmatised with the epithets of fraud and forgery. They ascribed their own polemical works to the most venerable names of Christian antiquity; the characters of Athanasius and Augustin were awkwardly personated by Vigilius and his disciples;[113] and the famous creed, which so clearly expounds the mysteries of the

[109] Victor, ii. 1, 2, p. 22.
[110] Victor, v. 7, p. 77. He appeals to the ambassador himself, whose name was Uranius.
[111] *Astutiores,* Victor, iv. 4, p. 70. He plainly intimates that their quotation of the Gospel, " Non jurabitis in toto," was only meant to elude the obligation of an inconvenient oath. The forty-six bishops who refused were banished to Corsica; the three hundred and two who swore were distributed through the provinces of Africa.
[112] Fulgentius, bishop of Ruspæ, in the Byzacene province, was of a senatorial family and had received a liberal education. He could repeat all Homer and Menander before he was allowed to study Latin, his native tongue (Vit. Fulgent. c. 1). Many African bishops might understand Greek, and many Greek theologians were translated into Latin.
[113] Compare the two prefaces to the Dialogue of Vigilius of Thapsus (p. 118, 119, edit. Chiflet). He might amuse his learned reader with an innocent fiction; but the subject was too grave, and the Africans were too ignorant.

Trinity and the Incarnation, is deduced, with strong probability, from this African school.[114]   Even the Scriptures themselves were profaned by their rash and sacrilegious hands.   The memorable text which asserts the unity of the THREE who bear witness in heaven [115] is condemned by the universal silence of the orthodox fathers, ancient versions, and authentic manuscripts.[116]   It was first alleged by the catholic bishops whom Hunneric summoned to the conference of Carthage.[117]   An allegorical interpretation, in the form perhaps of a marginal note, invaded the text of the Latin Bibles which were renewed and corrected in a dark period of ten centuries.[118]   After the invention of printing,[119] the editors of the Greek Testament yielded to their own prejudices, or those of the times;[120] and the pious fraud, which was

[114] The P. Quesnel started this opinion, which has been favourably received. But the three following truths, however surprising they may seem, are *now* universally acknowledged (Gerard Vossius, tom. vi. p. 516-522; Tillemont, Mém. Ecclés. tom. viii. p. 667-671).   1. St. Athanasius is not the author of the creed which is so frequently read in our churches.   2. It does not appear to have existed within a century after his death.   3. It was originally composed in the Latin tongue, and, consequently, in the Western provinces. Gennadius, a patriarch of Constantinople, was so much amazed by this extraordinary composition, that he frankly pronounced it to be the work of a drunken man. Petav. Dogmat. Theologica, tom. ii. l. vii. c. 8, p. 687.

[115] 1 John v. 7.   See Simon, Hist. Critique du Nouveau Testament, part i. c. xviii. p. 203-218; and part ii. c. ix. p. 99-121; and the elaborate Prolegomena and Annotations of Dr. Mill and Wetstein to their editions of the Greek Testament.   In 1689, the papist Simon strove to be free; in 1707, the Protestant Mill wished to be a slave; in 1751, the Arminian Wetstein used the liberty of his times and of his sect.

[116] Of *all* the MSS. now extant, above fourscore in number, some of which are more than 1200 years old (Wetstein ad loc.).   The *orthodox* copies of the Vatican, of the Complutensian editors, of Robert Stephens, are become invisible; and the *two* MSS. of Dublin and Berlin are unworthy to form an exception. See Emyln's Works, vol. ii. p. 227-255, 269-299; and M. de Missy's four ingenious letters, in tom. viii. and ix. of the Journal Britannique.

[117] Or, more properly, by the *four* bishops who composed and published the profession of faith in the name of their brethren.   They styled this text luce clarius (Victor Vitensis de Persecut. Vandal. l. iii. c. 11, p. 54).   It is quoted soon afterwards by the African polemics Vigilius and Fulgentius.

[118] In the eleventh and twelfth centuries the Bibles were corrected by Lanfranc, archbishop of Canterbury, and by Nicolas, cardinal and librarian of the Roman church, secundum orthodoxam fidem (Wetstein, Prolegom. p. 84, 85). Notwithstanding these corrections, the passage is still wanting in twenty-five Latin MSS. (Wetstein ad loc.), the oldest and the fairest; two qualities seldom united, except in manuscripts.

[119] The art which the Germans had invented was applied in Italy to the profane writers of Rome and Greece.   The original Greek of the New Testament was published about the same time (A.D. 1514, 1516, 1520) by the industry of Erasmus and the munificence of Cardinal Ximenes.   The Complutensian Polyglot cost the cardinal 50,000 ducats.   See Mattaire, Annal. Typograph. tom. ii. p. 2-8, 125-133; and Wetstein, Prolegomena, p. 116-127.

[120] The three witnesses have been established in our Greek Testaments by the prudence of Erasmus; the honest bigotry of the Complutensian editors; the typographical fraud or error of Robert Stephens in the placing a crotchet; and the deliberate falsehood or strange misapprehension of Theodore Beza.

embraced with equal zeal at Rome and at Geneva, has been infinitely multiplied in every country and every language of modern Europe.

The example of fraud must excite suspicion: and the specious miracles by which the African catholics have defended the truth and justice of their cause may be ascribed, with more reason, to their own industry than to the visible protection of Heaven. Yet the historian who views this religious conflict with an impartial eye may condescend to mention *one* preternatural event, which will edify the devout and surprise the incredulous. Tipasa,[121] a maritime colony of Mauritania, sixteen miles to the east of Cæsarea, had been distinguished in every age by the orthodox zeal of its inhabitants. They had braved the fury of the Donatists;[122] they resisted or eluded the tyranny of the Arians. The town was deserted on the approach of an heretical bishop: most of the inhabitants who could procure ships passed over to the coast of Spain; and the unhappy remnant, refusing all communion with the usurper, still presumed to hold their pious, but illegal, assemblies. Their disobedience exasperated the cruelty of Hunneric. A military count was despatched from Carthage to Tipasa: he collected the catholics in the Forum, and, in the presence of the whole province, deprived the guilty of their right hands and their tongues. But the holy confessors continued to speak without tongues; and this miracle is attested by Victor, an African bishop, who published an history of the persecution within two years after the event.[123] " If any one," says Victor, " should doubt of the truth, let him repair to Constantinople, and listen to the clear and perfect language of Restitutus, the subdeacon, one of these glorious sufferers, who is now lodged in the palace of the emperor Zeno, and is respected by the devout empress." At Constantinople we are astonished to find a cool, a learned, and unexceptionable witness, without interest, and without passion. Æneas of Gaza, a Platonic philosopher, has accurately described his own observations on these African sufferers. " I saw them myself: I heard them speak: I diligently inquired by what means such an articulate voice could be formed without any organ of speech: I used my eyes to examine the report of my ears: I opened their mouth, and saw that the whole tongue had been completely torn away by the roots; an operation which the physicians generally suppose to be mortal." [124] The testimony of Æneas of Gaza

---

[121] Plin. Hist. Natural. v. 1; Itinerar. Wesseling, p. 15; Cellarius, Geograph Antiq. tom. ii. part ii. p. 127. This Tipasa (which must not be confounded with another in Numidia) was a town of some note, since Vespasian endowed it with the right of Latium.

[122] Optatus Milevitanus de Schism. Donatist. l. ii. p. 38.

[123] Victor Vitensis, v. 6. p. 76. Ruinart, p. 483-487.

[124] Æneas Gazæus in Theophrasto, in Biblioth. Patrum, tom. viii. p. 664, 665. He was a Christian, and composed this Dialogue (the Theophrastus) on the immortality of the soul and the resurrection of the body; besides twenty-five Epistles, still extant. See Cave (Hist. Litteraria, p. 297) and Fabricius (Biblioth. Græc. tom. i. p. 422).

might be confirmed by the superfluous evidence of the emperor Justinian, in a perpetual edict; of Count Marcellinus, in his Chronicle of the times; and of pope Gregory the First, who had resided at Constantinople as the minister of the Roman pontiff.[125]   They all lived within the compass of a century; and they all appeal to their personal knowledge or the public notoriety for the truth of a miracle which was repeated in several instances, displayed on the greatest theatre of the world, and submitted during a series of years to the calm examination of the senses.   This supernatural gift of the African confessors, who spoke without tongues, will command the assent of those, and of those only, who already believe that their language was pure and orthodox. But the stubborn mind of an infidel is guarded by secret, incurable suspicion; and the Arian, or Socinian, who has seriously rejected the doctrine of the Trinity, will not be shaken by the most plausible evidence of an Athanasian miracle.

The Vandals and the Ostrogoths persevered in the profession of Arianism till the final ruin of the kingdoms which they had founded in Africa and Italy.   The barbarians of Gaul submitted to the orthodox dominion of the Franks; and Spain was restored to the catholic church by the voluntary conversion of the Visigoths.

This salutary revolution [126] was hastened by the example of a royal martyr, whom our calmer reason may style an ungrateful rebel. Leovigild, the Gothic monarch of Spain, deserved the respect of his enemies and the love of his subjects: the catholics enjoyed a free toleration, and his Arian synods attempted, without much success, to reconcile their scruples by abolishing the unpopular rite of a *second* baptism.   His eldest son Hermenegild, who was invested by his father with the royal diadem and the fair principality of Bætica, contracted an honourable and orthodox alliance with a Merovingian princess, the daughter of Sigebert, king of Austrasia, and of the famous Brunechild.   The beauteous Ingundis, who was no more than thirteen years of age, was received, beloved, and persecuted in the Arian court of Toledo; and her religious constancy was alternately assaulted with blandishments and violence by Goisvintha, the Gothic queen, who abused the double claim

---

[125] Justinian. Codex, l. i. tit. xxvii. [leg. 1] ; Marcellin. in Chron. p. 45, in Thesaur. Temporum Scaliger ; Procopius, de Bell. Vandal. l. i. c. 8, p. 196 [ed. Par.; tom. i. p. 345, ed. Bonn] ; Gregor. Magnus, Dialog. iii. 32.   None of these witnesses have specified the number of the confessors, which is fixed at sixty in an old menology (apud Ruinart, p. 486).   Two of them lost their speech by fornication; but the miracle is enhanced by the singular instance of a boy who had *never* spoken before his tongue was cut out.

[126] See the two general historians of Spain, Mariana (Hist. de Rebus Hispaniæ, tom. i. l. v. c. 12-15, p. 182-194) and Ferreras (French translation tom. ii. p. 206-247).   Mariana almost forgets that he is a Jesuit, to assume the style and spirit of a Roman classic.   Ferreras, an industrious compiler, reviews his facts and rectifies his chronology.

of maternal authority.[127] Incensed by her resistance, Goisvintha seized the catholic princess by her long hair, inhumanly dashed her against the ground, kicked her till she was covered with blood, and at last gave orders that she should be stripped and thrown into a basin or fish-pond.[128] Love and honour might excite Hermenegild to resent this injurious treatment of his bride; and he was gradually persuaded that Ingundis suffered for the cause of divine truth. Her tender complaints, and the weighty arguments of Leander, archbishop of Seville, accomplished his conversion; and the heir of the Gothic monarchy was initiated in the Nicene faith by the solemn rites of confirmation.[129] The rash youth, inflamed by zeal, and perhaps by ambition, was tempted to violate the duties of a son and a subject; and the catholics of Spain, although they could not complain of persecution, applauded his pious rebellion against an heretical father. The civil war was protracted by the long and obstinate sieges of Merida, Cordova, and Seville, which had strenuously espoused the party of Hermenegild. He invited the orthodox barbarians, the Suevi and the Franks, to the destruction of his native land: he solicited the dangerous aid of the Romans, who possessed Africa and a part of the Spanish coast; and his holy ambassador, the archbishop Leander, effectually negotiated in person with the Byzantine court. But the hopes of the catholics were crushed by the active diligence of a monarch who commanded the troops and treasures of Spain; and the guilty Hermenegild, after his vain attempts to resist or to escape, was compelled to surrender himself into the hands of an incensed father. Leovigild was still mindful of that sacred character; and the rebel, despoiled of the regal ornaments, was still permitted, in a decent exile, to profess the catholic religion. His repeated and unsuccessful treasons at length provoked the indignation of the Gothic king; and the sentence of death, which he pronounced with apparent reluctance, was privately executed in the tower of Seville. The inflexible constancy with which he refused to accept the Arian communion, as the price of his safety, may excuse the honours that have been paid to the memory of St. Hermenegild. His wife and infant son were detained by the Romans in ignominious captivity; and this domestic misfortune tarnished the glories of Leovigild, and embittered the last moments of his life.

His son and successor, Recared, the first catholic king of Spain, had imbibed the faith of his unfortunate brother, which he supported with

---

[127] Goisvintha successively married two kings of the Visigoths: Athanigild, to whom she bore Brunechild, the mother of Ingundis; and Leovigild, whose two sons, Hermenegild and Recared, were the issue of a former marriage.

[128] Iracundiæ furore succensa, adprehensam per comam capitis puellam in terram conlidit, et diu calcibus verberatam, ac sanguine cruentatam, jussit exspoliari, et piscinæ immergi. Greg. Turon. l. v. c. 39, in tom. ii. p. 255. Gregory is one of our best originals for this portion of history.

[129] The catholics, who admitted the baptism of heretics, repeated the rite, or, as it was afterwards styled, the sacrament, of confirmation, to which they ascribed many mystic and marvellous prerogatives, both visible and invisible. See Chardon, Hist. des Sacremens, tom. i. p. 405-552.

more prudence and success. Instead of revolting against his father, Recared patiently expected the hour of his death. Instead of condemning his memory, he piously supposed that the dying monarch had abjured the errors of Arianism, and recommended to his son the conversion of the Gothic nation. To accomplish that salutary end, Recared convened an assembly of the Arian clergy and nobles, declared himself a catholic, and exhorted them to imitate the example of their prince. The laborious interpretation of doubtful texts, or the curious pursuit of metaphysical arguments, would have excited an endless controversy; and the monarch discreetly proposed to his illiterate audience two substantial and visible arguments—the testimony of Earth and of Heaven. The *Earth* had submitted to the Nicene synod: the Romans, the barbarians, and the inhabitants of Spain unanimously professed the same orthodox creed; and the Visigoths resisted, almost alone, the consent of the Christian world. A superstitious age was prepared to reverence, as the testimony of Heaven, the preternatural cures which were performed by the skill or virtue of the catholic clergy; the baptismal fonts of Osset in Bætica,[130] which were spontaneously replenished each year on the vigil of Easter;[131] and the miraculous shrine of St. Martin of Tours, which had already converted the Suevic prince and people of Gallicia.[132] The catholic king encountered some difficulties on this important change of the national religion. A conspiracy, secretly fomented by the queen-dowager, was formed against his life; and two counts excited a dangerous revolt in the Narbonnese Gaul. But Recared disarmed the conspirators, defeated the rebels, and executed severe justice, which the Arians, in their turn, might brand with the reproach of persecution. Eight bishops, whose names betray their barbaric origin, abjured their errors; and all the books of Arian theology were reduced to ashes, with the house in which they had been purposely collected. The whole body of the Visigoths and Suevi were allured or driven into the pale of the catholic communion; the faith, at least of the rising generation, was fervent and sincere; and the devout liberality of the barbarians enriched the churches and monasteries of Spain. Seventy bishops, assembled in the council of Toledo, received the submission of their conquerors; and the zeal of the Spaniards improved the Nicene creed, by declaring the procession of the Holy Ghost from the Son, as well as from the Father; a weighty point of doctrine, which produced, long afterwards, the schism of the

[130] Osset, or Julia Constantia, was opposite to Seville, on the northern side of the Bætis (Plin. Hist. Natur. iii. 3) : and the authentic reference of Gregory of Tours (Hist. Francor. l. vi. c. 43, p. 288) deserves more credit than the name of Lusitania (de Gloriâ Martyr. c. 24), which has been eagerly embraced by the vain and superstitious Portuguese (Ferreras, Hist. d'Espagne, tom. ii. p. 166.)

[131] This miracle was skilfully performed. An Arian king sealed the doors and dug a deep trench round the church without being able to intercept the Easter supply of baptismal water.

[132] Ferreras (tom. ii. p. 168-175, A.D. 550) has illustrated the difficulties which regard the time and circumstances of the conversion of the Suevi. They had been recently united by Leovigild to the Gothic monarchy of Spain.

Greek and Latin churches.[133]   The royal proselyte immediately saluted and consulted pope Gregory, surnamed the Great, a learned and holy prelate, whose reign was distinguished by the conversion of heretics and infidels. The ambassadors of Recared respectfully offered on the threshold of the Vatican his rich presents of gold and gems; they accepted, as a lucrative exchange, the hairs of St. John the Baptist; a cross which enclosed a small piece of the true wood; and a key that contained some particles of iron which had been scraped from the chains of St. Peter.[134]

The same Gregory, the spiritual conqueror of Britain, encouraged the pious Theodelinda, queen of the Lombards, to propagate the Nicene faith among the victorious savages, whose recent Christianity was polluted by the Arian heresy. Her devout labours still left room for the industry and success of future missionaries, and many cities of Italy were still disputed by hostile bishops. But the cause of Arianism was gradually suppressed by the weight of truth, of interest, and of example; and the controversy, which Egypt had derived from the Platonic school, was terminated, after a war of three hundred years, by the final conversion of the Lombards of Italy.[135]

The first missionaries who preached the Gospel to the barbarians appealed to the evidence of reason, and claimed the benefit of toleration.[136] But no sooner had they established their spiritual dominion than they exhorted the Christian kings to extirpate, without mercy, the remains of Roman or barbaric superstition. The successors of Clovis inflicted one hundred lashes on the peasants who refused to destroy their idols; the crime of sacrificing to the demons was punished by the Anglo-Saxon laws with the heavier penalties of imprisonment and confiscation; and even the wise Alfred adopted, as an indispensable duty, the extreme rigour of the Mosaic institutions.[137] But the punishment and the crime were gradually abolished among a Christian people; the theological disputes of the schools were suspended by propitious ignorance; and the intolerant spirit which could find neither idolaters nor heretics, was reduced to the persecution of the Jews. That exiled nation had founded some synagogues in the cities of Gaul; but Spain, since the time of

---

[133] This addition to the Nicene, or rather the Constantinopolitan creed, was first made in the eighth council of Toledo, A.D. 653; but it was expressive of the popular doctrine (Gerard Vossius, tom. vi. p. 527, de tribus Symbolis).

[134] See Gregor. Magn. l. vii. Epist. 126, apud Baronium, Annal. Eccles. A. D. 599, No. 25, 26 [l. ix. Ep. 122, tom. ii. p. 1031, ed. Bened.].

[135] Paul Warnefrid (de Gestis Langobard. l. iv. c. 44, p. 853, edit. Grot.) allows that Arianism still prevailed under the reign of Rotharis (A.D. 636-652). The pious *deacon* does not attempt to mark the precise era of the national conversion, which was accomplished, however, before the end of the seventh century.

[136] Quorum fidei et conversioni ita congratulatus esse rex perhibetur, ut nullum tamen cogeret ad Christianismum. . . . Didicerat enim a doctoribus auctoribusque suæ salutis, servitium Christi voluntarium non coactitium esse debere. Bedæ Hist. Ecclesiastic. l. i. c. 26, p. 62, edit. Smith.

[137] See the Historians of France, tom. iv. p. 114; and Wilkins, Leges Anglo-Saxonicæ, p. 11, 31. Siquis sacrificium immolaverit præter Deo soli morte moriatur.

Hadrian, was filled with their numerous colonies.[138]   The wealth which they accumulated by trade and the management of the finances invited the pious avarice of their masters; and they might be oppressed without danger, as they had lost the use, and even the remembrance, of arms. Sisebut, a Gothic king who reigned in the beginning of the seventh century, proceeded at once to the last extremes of persecution.[139]   Ninety thousand Jews were compelled to receive the sacrament of baptism; the fortunes of the obstinate infidels were confiscated, their bodies were tortured, and it seems doubtful whether they were permitted to abandon their native country.   The excessive zeal of the catholic king was moderated even by the clergy of Spain, who solemnly pronounced an inconsistent sentence: *that* the sacraments should not be forcibly imposed; but *that* the Jews who had been baptised should be constrained, for the honour of the church, to persevere in the external practice of a religion which they disbelieved and detested.   Their frequent relapses provoked one of the successors of Sisebut to banish the whole nation from his dominions; and a council of Toledo published a decree that every Gothic king should swear to maintain this salutary edict.   But the tyrants were unwilling to dismiss the victims whom they delighted to torture, or to deprive themselves of the industrious slaves over whom they might exercise a lucrative oppression.   The Jews still continued in Spain, under the weight of the civil and ecclesiastical laws, which in the same country have been faithfully transcribed in the Code of the Inquisition.   The Gothic kings and bishops at length discovered that injuries will produce hatred, and that hatred will find the opportunity of revenge.   A nation, the secret or professed enemies of Christianity, still multiplied in servitude and distress; and the intrigues of the Jews promoted the rapid success of the Arabian conquerors.[140]

As soon as the barbarians withdrew their powerful support, the unpopular heresy of Arius sunk into contempt and oblivion.   But the Greeks still retained their subtle and loquacious disposition: the establishment of an obscure doctrine suggested new questions and new disputes; and it was always in the power of an ambitious prelate or a fanatic monk to violate the peace of the church, and perhaps of the empire.   The historian of the empire may overlook those disputes which were confined to the obscurity of schools and synods.   The

---

[138] The Jews pretend that they were introduced into Spain by the fleets of Solomon and the arms of Nebuchadnezzar; that Hadrian transported forty thousand families of the tribe of Judah, and ten thousand of the tribe of Benjamin, etc.   Basnage, Hist. des Juifs, tom. vii. c. 9, p. 240-256.

[139] Isidore, at that time archbishop of Seville, mentions, disapproves, and congratulates, the zeal of Sisebut (Chron. Goth. p. 728 [ed. Grot.]).   Baronius (A.D. 614, No. 41) assigns the number on the evidence of Aimoin (l. iv. c. 22): but the evidence is weak, and I have not been able to verify the quotation (Historians of France, tom. iii. p. 127).

[140] Basnage (tom. viii. c. 13, p. 388-400) faithfully represents the state of the Jews: but he might have added, from the canons of the Spanish councils and the laws of the Visigoths, many curious circumstances essential to his subject, though they are foreign to mine.

Manichæans, who laboured to reconcile the religions of Christ and of Zoroaster, had secretly introduced themselves into the provinces: but these foreign sectaries were involved in the common disgrace of the Gnostics, and the Imperial laws were executed by the public hatred. The rational opinions of the Pelagians were propagated from Britain to Rome, Africa, and Palestine, and silently expired in a superstitious age. But the East was distracted by the Nestorian and Eutychian controversies, which attempted to explain the mystery of the incarnation, and hastened the ruin of Christianity in her native land. These controversies were first agitated under the reign of the younger Theodosius: but their important consequences extend far beyond the limits of the present volume. The metaphysical chain of argument, the contests of ecclesiastical ambition, and their political influence on the decline of the Byzantine empire, may afford an interesting and instructive series of history, from the general councils of Ephesus and Chalcedon to the conquest of the East by the successors of Mahomet.

CHAPTER XXXVIII (449-582 A.D.)

Reign and Conversion of Clovis—His Victories over the Alemanni, Burgundians, and Visigoths—Establishment of the French Monarchy in Gaul —Laws of the Barbarians—State of the Romans—The Visigoths of Spain —Conquest of Britain by the Saxons

THE Gauls,[1] who impatiently supported the Roman yoke, received a memorable lesson from one of the lieutenants of Vespasian, whose weighty sense has been refined and expressed by the genius of Tacitus.[2] "The protection of the republic has delivered Gaul from internal discord and foreign invasions. By the loss of national independence you have acquired the name and privileges of Roman citizens. You enjoy, in common with ourselves, the permanent benefits of civil government; and your remote situation is less exposed to the accidental mischiefs of tyranny. Instead of exercising the rights of conquest, we have been contented to impose such tributes as are requisite for your own preservation. Peace cannot be secured without armies, and armies must be supported at the expense of the people. It is for your sake, not for our own, that we guard the barrier of the Rhine against the ferocious Germans, who have so often attempted, and who will always desire, to

[1] In this chapter I shall draw my quotations from the Recueil des Historiens des Gaules et de la France, Paris, 1738-1767, in eleven volumes in folio. By the labour of Dom Bouquet and the other Benedictines, all the original testimonies, as far as A.D. 1060, are disposed in chronological order, and illustrated with learned notes. Such a national work, which will be continued to the year 1500, might provoke our emulation.

[2] Tacit. Hist. iv. 73, 74, in tom. i. p. 445. To abridge Tacitus would indeed be presumptuous; but I may select the general ideas which he applies to the present state and future revolutions of Gaul.

exchange the solitude of their woods and morasses for the wealth and fertility of Gaul. The fall of Rome would be fatal to the provinces, and you would be buried in the ruins of that mighty fabric which has been raised by the valour and wisdom of eight hundred years. Your imaginary freedom would be insulted and oppressed by a savage master, and the expulsion of the Romans would be succeeded by the eternal hostilities of the barbarian conquerors." [3] This salutary advice was accepted, and this strange prediction was accomplished. In the space of four hundred years the hardy Gauls, who had encountered the arms of Cæsar, were imperceptibly melted into the general mass of citizens and subjects: the Western empire was dissolved; and the Germans who had passed the Rhine fiercely contended for the possession of Gaul, and excited the contempt or abhorrence of its peaceful and polished inhabitants. With that conscious pride which the pre-eminence of knowledge and luxury seldom fails to inspire, they derided the hairy and gigantic savages of the North; their rustic manners, dissonant joy, voracious appetite, and their horrid appearance, equally disgusting to the sight and to the smell. The liberal studies were still cultivated in the schools of Autun and Bordeaux, and the language of Cicero and Virgil was familiar to the Gallic youth. Their ears were astonished by the harsh and unknown sounds of the Germanic dialect, and they ingeniously lamented that the trembling muses fled from the harmony of a Burgundian lyre. The Gauls were endowed with all the advantages of art and nature, but, as they wanted courage to defend them, they were justly condemned to obey, and even to flatter, the victorious barbarians by whose clemency they held their precarious fortunes and their lives. [4]

As soon as Odoacer had extinguished the Western empire, he sought the friendship of the most powerful of the barbarians. The new sovereign of Italy resigned to Euric, king of the Visigoths, all the Roman conquests beyond the Alps, as far as the Rhine and the Ocean; [5] and the senate might confirm this liberal gift with some ostentation of power, and without any real loss of revenue or dominion. The lawful pretensions of Euric were justified by ambition and success, and the Gothic nation might aspire under his command to the monarchy of Spain and Gaul. Arles and Marseilles surrendered to his arms: he oppressed the freedom of Auvergne, and the bishop condescended to purchase his recall from exile by a tribute of just but reluctant praise. Sidonius waited before the gates of the palace among a crowd of am-

[3] Eadem semper causa Germanis transcendendi in Gallias, libido atque avaritia, et mutandæ sedis amor; ut relictis paludibus et solitudinibus suis, fecundissimum hoc solum vosque ipsos possiderent. . . . Nam pulsis Romanis quid aliud quam bella omnium inter se gentium exsistent?

[4] Sidonius Apollinaris ridicules, with affected wit and pleasantry, the hardships of his situation (Carm. xii. in tom. i. p. 811).

[5] See Procopius de Bell. Gothico, l. i. c. 12, in tom. ii. p. 31 [tom. ii. p. 64, ed. Bonn]. The character of Grotius inclines me to believe that he has not substituted the *Rhine* for the *Rhône* (Hist. Gothorum, p. 175) without the authority of some MS.

bassadors and suppliants, and their various business at the court of
Bordeaux attested the power and the renown of the king of the Visigoths. The Heruli of the distant ocean, who painted their naked bodies
with its cærulean colour, implored his protection; and the Saxons respected the maritime provinces of a prince who was destitute of any
naval force. The tall Burgundians submitted to his authority; nor did
he restore the captive Franks till he had imposed on that fierce nation
the terms of an unequal peace. The Vandals of Africa cultivated his
useful friendship, and the Ostrogoths of Pannonia were supported by
his powerful aid against the oppression of the neighbouring Huns. The
North (such are the lofty strains of the poet) was agitated or appeased by the nod of Euric, the great king of Persia consulted the oracle
of the West, and the aged god of the Tiber was protected by the swelling genius of the Garonne.[6] The fortune of nations has often depended
on accidents; and France may ascribe her greatness to the premature
death of the Gothic king at a time when his son Alaric was a helpless
infant, and his adversary Clovis[7] an ambitious and valiant youth.

While Childeric, the father of Clovis, lived an exile in Germany, he
was hospitably entertained by the queen as well as by the king of the
Thuringians. After his restoration Bafina escaped from her husband's
bed to the arms of her lover, freely declaring that, if she had known
a man wiser, stronger, or more beautiful than Childeric, that man
should have been the object of her preference.[8] Clovis was the offspring of this voluntary union, and when he was no more than fifteen
years of age he succeeded, by his father's death, to the command of
the Salian tribe. The narrow limits of his kingdom[9] were confined
to the island of the Batavians, with the ancient dioceses of Tournay
and Arras;[10] and at the baptism of Clovis the number of his warriors

[6] Sidonius, l. viii. Epist. 3, 9, in tom. i. p. 800. Jornandes de Rebus Geticis
(c. 47, p. 680) justifies in some measure this portrait of the Gothic hero.
[7] I use the familiar appellation of *Clovis*, from the Latin *Chlodovechus* or
Chlodovæus. But the *Ch* expresses only the German aspiration; and the
true name is not different from *Luduin* or *Lewis* (Mém de l'Académie des
Inscriptions, tom. xx. p. 68).
[8] Greg. Turon. l. ii. c. 12, in tom. ii. p. 168. Bafina speaks the language of
nature: the Franks, who had seen her in their youth, might converse with
Gregory in their old age; and the bishop of Tours could not wish to defame
the mother of the first Christian king.
[9] The Abbé Dubos (Hist. Critique de l'Etablissement de la Monarchie
Françoise dans les Gaules, tom. i. p. 630-650) has the merit of defining the
primitive kingdom of Clovis, and of ascertaining the genuine number of his
subjects.
[The dominions of Clovis (or Chlodwig), Ragnachar, and Chararich, the
independent kings of the Merovingian race, over the tribes of Franks that
had seated themselves along the Belgian rivers, the Scheldt, Meuse, Moselle,
and Rhine, corresponded, according to Junghans, to Brabant, Hainault,
and Flanders.—O. S.]
[10] Ecclesiam incultam ac negligentiâ civium Paganorum prætermissam,
veprium densitate oppletam, etc. Vit. St. Vedasti, in tom. iii. p. 372. This
description supposes that Arras was possessed by the Pagans many years before the baptism of Clovis.

could not exceed five thousand. The kindred tribes of the Franks who had seated themselves along the Belgic rivers, the Scheldt, the Meuse, the Moselle, and the Rhine, were governed by their independent kings of the Merovingian race—the equals, the allies, and sometimes the enemies, of the Salic prince. But the Germans, who obeyed in peace the hereditary jurisdiction of their chiefs, were free to follow the standard of a popular and victorious general; and the superior merit of Clovis attracted the respect and allegiance of the national confederacy. When he first took the field, he had neither gold and silver in his coffers, nor wine and corn in his magazines;[11] but he imitated the example of Cæsar, who in the same country had acquired wealth by the sword, and purchased soldiers with the fruits of conquest. After each successful battle or expedition the spoils were accumulated in one common mass; every warrior received his proportionable share, and the royal prerogative submitted to the equal regulations of military law. The untamed spirit of the barbarians was taught to acknowledge the advantages of regular discipline.[12] At the annual review of the month of March their arms were diligently inspected, and when they traversed a peaceful territory they were prohibited from touching a blade of grass. The justice of Clovis was inexorable, and his careless or disobedient soldiers were punished with instant death. It would be superfluous to praise the valour of a Frank, but the valour of Clovis was directed by cool and consummate prudence.[13] In all his transactions with mankind he calculated the weight of interest, of passion, and of opinion; and his measures were sometimes adapted to the sanguinary manners of the Germans, and sometimes moderated by the milder genius of Rome and Christianity. He was intercepted in the career of victory, since he died in the forty-fifth year of his age: but he had already accomplished, in a reign of thirty years, the establishment of the French monarchy in Gaul.

The first exploit of Clovis was the defeat of Syagrius, the son of Ægidius, and the public quarrel might on this occasion be inflamed by private resentment. The glory of the father still insulted the Merovingian race; the power of the son might excite the jealous ambition of the king of the Franks. Syagrius inherited, as a patrimonial estate, the city and diocese of Soissons: the desolate remnant of the second Belgic, Rheims and Troyes, Beauvais and Amiens, would nat-

---

[11] Gregory of Tours (l. v. c. i. tom. ii. p. 232) contrasts the poverty of Clovis with the wealth of his grandsons. Yet Remigius (in tom. iv. p. 52) mentions his *paternas opes*, as sufficient for the redemption of captives.

[12] See Gregory (l. ii. c. 27, 37, in tom. iii. p. 175, 181, 182). The famous story of the vase of Soissons explains both the power and character of Clovis. As a point of controversy, it has been strangely tortured by Boulainvilliers, Dubos, and the other political antiquarians.

[13] The Duke of Nivernois, a noble statesman, who has managed weighty and delicate negotiations, ingeniously illustrates (Mém. de l'Acad. des Inscriptions, tom. xx. p. 147-184) the political system of Clovis.

urally submit to the count or patrician;[14] and after the dissolution of the Western empire he might reign with the title, or at least with the authority, of king of the Romans.[15] As a Roman, he had been educated in the liberal studies of rhetoric and jurisprudence; but he was engaged by accident and policy in the familiar use of the Germanic idiom. The independent barbarians resorted to the tribunal of a stranger who possessed the singular talent of explaining, in their native tongue, the dictates of reason and equity. The diligence and affability of their judge rendered him popular, the impartial wisdom of his decrees obtained their voluntary ·obedience, and the reign of Syagrius over the Franks and Burgundians seemed to revive the original institution of civil society.[16] In the midst of these peaceful occupations Syagrius received, and boldly accepted, the hostile defiance of Clovis, who challenged his rival in the spirit, and almost in the language of chivalry, to appoint the day and the field [17] of battle. In the time of Cæsar, Soissons would have poured forth a body of fifty thousand horse; and such an army might have been plentifully supplied with shields, cuirasses, and military engines from the three arsenals or manufactures of the city.[18] But the courage and numbers of the Gallic youth were long since exhausted, and the loose bands of volunteers or mercenaries who marched under the standard of Syagrius were incapable of contending with the national valour of the Franks. It would be ungenerous, without some more accurate knowledge of his strength and resources, to condemn the rapid flight of Syagrius, who escaped after the loss of a battle to the distant court of Toulouse. The feeble minority of Alaric could not assist or protect an unfortunate fugitive;

[14] M. Biet (in a Dissertation which deserved the prize of the Academy of Soissons, p. 178-226) has accurately defined the nature and extent of the kingdom of Syagrius, and his father; but he too readily allows the slight evidence of Dubos (tom. ii. p. 54-57) to deprive him of Beauvais and Amiens.

[The precise position of Syagrius in northern Gaul is thus succinctly stated by Bury: " His kingdom was bounded by the Somme, beyond which was the Salian territory under Chlodwig; by the territory of the Ripuarian Franks on the Lower Mosel; by the Burgundian kingdom, Auxerre being probably near the frontier, and by the Seine."—O. S.]

[15] I may observe that Fredegarius, in his epitome of Gregory of Tours (tom. ii. p. 398 [c. 15]), has prudently substituted the name of *Patricius* for the incredible title of *Rex Romanorum*.

[16] Sidonius (l. v. Epist. 5, in tom. i. p. 794), who styles him the Solon, the Amphion, of the barbarians, addresses this imaginary king in the tone of friendship and equality. From such offices of arbitration, the crafty Deioces had raised himself to the throne of the Medes (Herodot. l. i. c. 96-100).

[17] Campum sibi præparari jussit. M. Biet (p. 226-251) has diligently ascertained this field of battle at Nogent, a Benedictine abbey, about ten miles to the north of Soissons. The ground was marked by a circle of Pagan sepulchres; and Clovis bestowed the adjacent lands of Leuilly and Coucy on the church of Rheims.

[18] See Cæsar. Comment. de Bell. Gallic. ii. 4, in tom. i. p. 220, and the Notitiæ, tom. i. p. 126. The three *Fabricæ* of Soissons were, *Scutaria, Balistaria,* and *Clinabaria.* The last supplied the complete armour of the heavy cuirassiers.

the pusillanimous [19] Goths were intimidated by the menaces of Clovis: and the Roman *king*, after a short confinement, was delivered into the hands of the executioner. The Belgic cities surrendered to the king of the Franks, and his dominions were enlarged towards the east by the ample diocese of Tongres,[20] which Clovis subdued in the tenth year of his reign.

The name of the Alemanni has been absurdly derived from their imaginary settlement on the banks of the *Leman* lake.[21] That fortunate district, from the lake to Avenche and Mount Jura, was occupied by the Burgundians.[22] The northern parts of Helvetia had indeed been subdued by the ferocious Alemanni, who destroyed with their own hands the fruits of their conquest. A province, improved and adorned by the arts of Rome, was again reduced to a savage wilderness, and some vestige of the stately Vindonissa may still be discovered in the fertile and populous valley of the Aar.[23] From the source of the Rhine to its conflux with the Main and the Moselle, the formidable swarms of the Alemanni commanded either side of the river by the right of ancient possession or recent victory. They had spread themselves into Gaul over the modern provinces of Alsace and Lorraine; and their bold invasion of the kingdom of Cologne summoned the Salic prince to the defence of his Ripuarian allies. Clovis encountered the invaders of Gaul in the plain of Tolbiac, about twenty-four miles from Cologne, and the two fiercest nations of Germany were mutually animated by the memory of past exploits and the prospect of future

[19] The epithet must be confined to the circumstances; and history cannot justify the French prejudice of Gregory (l. ii. c. 27, in tom. ii. p. 175), ut Gothorum pavere *mos* est.

[20] Dubos has satisfied me (tom. i. p. 277-286) that Gregory of Tours, his transcribers or his readers, have repeatedly confounded the German kingdom of *Thuringia*, beyond the Rhine, and the Gallic *city* of *Tongria*, on the Meuse, which was more anciently the country of the Eburones, and more recently the diocese of Liege.

[21] Populi habitantes juxta *Lemannum* lacum, *Alemanni* dicuntur. Servius, ad Virgil. Georgic. iv. 278. Dom Bouquet (tom. i. p. 817) has only alleged the more recent and corrupt text of Isidore of Seville.

[22] Gregory of Tours sends St. Lupicinus inter illa Jurensis deserti secreta, quæ, inter Burgundiam Alamanniamque sita, Aventicæ adjacent civitati, in tom. i. p. 648. M. de Watteville (Hist. de la Confédération Helvétique, tom. i. p. 9, 10) has accurately defined the Helvetian limits of the duchy of Alemannia, and the Transjurane Burgundy. They were commensurate with the dioceses of Constance and Avenche, or Lausanne, and are still discriminated in modern Switzerland by the use of the German or French language.

[I agree with Prof. Bury that the statement by Gibbon in this note is in all probability near the truth. The Alemanni were certainly defeated, and some of the tribes in all likelihood settled in Rhætia under the protection of Theodoric.—O. S.]

[23] See Guilliman de Rebus Helveticis, l. i. c. 3, p. 11, 12. Within the ancient walls of Vindonissa, the castle of Hapsburg, the abbey of Königsfeld, and the town of Bruck, have successively arisen. The philosophic traveller may compare the monuments of Roman conquest, of feudal or Austrian tyranny, of monkish superstition, and of industrious freedom. If he be truly a philosopher, he will applaud the merit and happiness of his own times.

greatness. The Franks after an obstinate struggle gave way, and the Alemanni, raising a shout of victory, impetuously pressed their retreat. But the battle was restored by the valour, the conduct, and perhaps by the piety, of Clovis; and the event of the bloody day decided for ever the alternative of empire or servitude. The last king of the Alemanni was slain in the field, and his people were slaughtered and pursued till they threw down their arms and yielded to the mercy of the conqueror. Without discipline it was impossible for them to rally: they had contemptuously demolished the walls and fortifications which might have protected their distress; and they were followed into the the heart of their forests by an enemy not less active or intrepid than themselves. The great Theodoric congratulated the victory of Clovis, whose sister Albofleda the king of Italy had lately married; but he mildly interceded with his brother in favour of the suppliants and fugitives who had implored his protection. The Gallic territories which were possessed by the Alemanni became the prize of their conqueror; and the haughty nation, invincible or rebellious to the arms of Rome, acknowledged the sovereignty of the Merovingian kings, who graciously permitted them to enjoy their peculiar manners and institutions under the government of official, and, at length, of hereditary dukes. After the conquest of the Western provinces, the Franks alone maintained their ancient habitations beyond the Rhine. They gradually subdued and civilised the exhausted countries as far as the Elbe and the mountains of Bohemia, and the peace of Europe was secured by the obedience of Germany.[24]

Till the thirtieth year of his age Clovis continued to worship the gods of his ancestors.[25] His disbelief, or rather disregard of Christianity, might encourage him to pillage with less remorse the churches of an hostile territory: but his subjects of Gaul enjoyed the free exercise of religious worship, and the bishops entertained a more favourable hope of the idolater than of the heretics. The Merovingian prince had contracted a fortunate alliance with the fair Clotilda, the niece of the king of Burgundy, who in the midst of an Arian court was educated in the profession of the catholic faith. It was her interest as well as her duty to achieve the conversion [26] of a Pagan husband; and

[24] Gregory of Tours (l. ii. 30, 37, in tom. ii. p. 176, 177, 182), the Gesta Francorum (in tom. ii. p. 551), and the epistle of Theodoric (Cassiodor. Variar. l. ii. Ep. 41, in tom. iv. p. 4) represent the defeat of the Alemanni. Some of their tribes settled in Rhætia, under the protection of Theodoric, whose successors ceded the colony and their country to the grandson of Clovis. The state of the Alemanni under the Merovingian kings may be seen in Mascou (Hist. of the Ancient Germans, xi. 8, etc.; Annotation xxxvi.) and Guilliman (de Reb. Helvet. l. ii. c. 10-12, p. 72-80).

[25] Clotilda, or rather Gregory, supposes that Clovis worshipped the gods of Greece and Rome. The fact is incredible, and the mistake only shows how completely, in less than a century, the national religion of the Franks had been abolished, and even forgotten.

[26] Gregory of Tours relates the marriage and conversion of Clovis (l. ii. c. 28-31, in tom. ii. p. 175-178). Even Fredegarius, or the nameless Epitomiser

Clovis insensibly listened to the voice of love and religion. He consented (perhaps such terms had been previously stipulated) to the baptism of his eldest son; and though the sudden death of the infant excited some superstitious fears, he was persuaded a second time to repeat the dangerous experiment. In the distress of the battle of Tolbiac, Clovis loudly invoked the God of Clotilda and the Christians; and victory disposed him to hear with respectful gratitude the eloquent [27] Remigius,[28] bishop of Rheims, who forcibly displayed the temporal and spiritual advantages of his conversion. The king declared himself satisfied of the truth of the catholic faith; and the political reasons which might have suspended his public profession were removed by the devout or loyal acclamations of the Franks, who showed themselves alike prepared to follow their heroic leader to the field of battle or to the baptismal font. The important ceremony was performed in the cathedral of Rheims with every circumstance of magnificence and solemnity that could impress an awful sense of religion on the minds of its rude proselytes.[29] The new Constantine was immediately baptised with three thousand of his warlike subjects, and their example was imitated by the remainder of the *gentle barbarians,* who, in obedience to the victorious prelate, adored the cross which they had burnt, and burnt the idols which they had formerly adored.[30] The mind of Clovis was susceptible of transient fervour: he was exasperated by the pathetic tale of the passion and death of Christ; and instead of weighing the salutary consequences of that mysterious sacrifice, he exclaimed with indiscreet fury, " Had I been present at the head of my valiant Franks,

(in tom. ii. p. 398-400), the author of the Gesta Francorum (in tom. ii. p. 548-552), and Aimoin himself (l. i. c. 13-16, in tom. iii. p. 37-40), may be heard without disdain. Tradition might long preserve some curious circumstances of these important transactions.

[27] A traveller, who returned from Rheims to Auvergne, had stolen a copy of his Declamations from the secretary or bookseller of the modest archbishop (Sidonius Apollinar. l. ix. Epist. 7). Four epistles of Remigius, which are still extant (in tom. iv. p. 51, 52, 53), do not correspond with the splendid praise of Sidonius.

[28] Hincmar, one of the successors of Remigius (A.D. 845-882), has composed his Life (in tom. iii. p. 373-380). The authority of ancient MSS. of the church of Rheims might inspire some confidence, which is destroyed, however, by the selfish and audacious fictions of Hincmar. It is remarkable enough that Remigius, who was consecrated at the age of twenty-two (A.D. 457), filled the episcopal chair seventy-four years (Pagi Critica, in Baron. tom. ii. p. 384, 572).

[29] A vial (the *Sainte Ampoulle*) of holy or rather celestial oil was brought down by a white dove, for the baptism of Clovis; and it is still used and renewed in the coronation of the kings of France. Hincmar (he aspired to the primacy of Gaul) is the first author of this fable (in tom. iii. p. 377), whose slight foundations the Abbé de Vertot (Mémoires de l'Académie des Inscriptions, tom. ii. p. 619-633) has undermined with profound respect and consummate dexterity.

[30] Mitis depone colla, Sicamber: adora quod incendisti, incende quod adorasti. Greg. Turon. l. ii. c. 31. in tom. ii. p. 177.

I would have revenged his injuries." [31]   But the savage conqueror of
Gaul was incapable of examining the proofs of a religion which depends
on the laborious investigation of historic evidence and speculative theology.   He was still more incapable of feeling the mild influence of
the Gospel, which persuades and purifies the heart of a genuine convert.   His ambitious reign was a perpetual violation of moral and
Christian duties: his hands were stained with blood in peace as well as
in war; and, as soon as Clovis had dismissed a synod of the Gallician
church, he calmly assassinated *all* the princes of the Merovingian
race.[32]   Yet the king of the Franks might sincerely worship the Christian God as a Being more excellent and powerful than his national
deities; and the signal deliverance and victory of Tolbiac encouraged
Clovis to confide in the future protection of the Lord of Hosts.   Martin,
the most popular of the saints, had filled the Western world with the
fame of those miracles which were incessantly performed at his holy
sepulchre of Tours.   His visible or invisible aid promoted the cause
of a liberal and orthodox prince; and the profane remark of Clovis
himself, that St. Martin was an expensive friend,[33] need not be interpreted as the symptom of any permanent or rational scepticism.   But
earth as well as heaven rejoiced in the conversion of the Franks.   On
the memorable day when Clovis ascended from the baptismal font, he
alone in the Christian world deserved the name and prerogatives of a
catholic king.   The emperor Anastasius entertained some dangerous
errors concerning the nature of the divine incarnation; and the barbarians of Italy, Africa, Spain, and Gaul were involved in the Arian
heresy.   The eldest, or rather the only son of the church, was acknowledged by the clergy as their lawful sovereign or glorious deliverer; and
the arms of Clovis were strenuously supported by the zeal and favour
of the catholic faction.[34]

Under the Roman empire the wealth and jurisdiction of the bishops,
their sacred character and perpetual office, their numerous dependents,

[31] Si ego ibidem cum Francis meis fuissem, injurias ejus vindicassem.   This
rash expression, which Gregory has prudently concealed, is celebrated by
Fredegarius (Epitom. c. 21, in tom. ii. p. 400), Aimoin (l. i. c. 16, in tom. iii.
p. 40), and the Chroniques de St. Denys (l. i. c. 20, in tom. iii. p. 171), as an
admirable effusion of Christian zeal.

[32] Gregory (l. ii. c. 40-43, in tom. ii. p. 183-185), after coolly relating the
repeated crimes and affected remorse of Clovis, concludes, perhaps undesignedly, with a lesson which ambition will never hear—" His ita trans-
actis . . . obiit."

[33] After the Gothic victory, Clovis made rich offerings to St. Martin of
Tours.   He wished to redeem his war-horse by the gift of one hundred pieces
of gold, but the enchanted steed could not move from the stable till the price
of his redemption had been doubled.   This *miracle* provoked the king to exclaim, Vere B. Martinus est bonus in auxilio, sed carus in negotio. (Gesta
Francorum, in tom. ii. p. 554, 555.)

[34] See the epistle from Pope Anastasius to the royal convert (in tom. iv. p.
50, 51).   Avitus, bishop of Vienne, addressed Clovis on the same subject (p.
49); and many of the Latin bishops would assure him of their joy and
attachment.

popular eloquence, and provincial assemblies, had rendered them always respectable, and sometimes dangerous. Their influence was augmented with the progress of superstition; and the establishment of the French monarchy may, in some degree, be ascribed to the firm alliance of an hundred prelates, who reigned in the discontented or independent cities of Gaul. The slight foundations of the *Armorican* republic had been repeatedly shaken or overthrown; but the same people still guarded their domestic freedom; asserted the dignity of the Roman name; and bravely resisted the predatory inroads and regular attacks of Clovis. who laboured to extend his conquests from the Seine to the Loire. Their successful opposition introduced an equal and honourable union. The Franks esteemed the valour of the Armoricans;[35] and the Armoricans were reconciled by the religion of the Franks.   The military force which had been stationed for the defence of Gaul consisted of one hundred different bands of cavalry or infantry; and these troops, while they assumed the title and privileges of Roman soldiers, were renewed by an incessant supply of the barbarian youth.   The extreme fortifications and scattered fragments of the empire were still defended by their hopeless courage.   But their retreat was intercepted, and their communication was impracticable: they were abandoned by the Greek princes of Constantinople, and they piously disclaimed all connection with the Arian usurpers of Gaul.   They accepted, without shame or reluctance, the generous capitulation which was proposed by a catholic hero; and the spurious or legitimate progeny of the Roman legions was distinguished in the succeeding age by their arms, their ensigns, and their peculiar dress and institutions.   But the national strength was increased by these powerful and voluntary accessions; and the neighbouring kingdoms dreaded the numbers as well as the spirit of the Franks.   The reduction of the northern provinces of Gaul, instead of being decided by the chance of a single battle, appears to have been slowly effected by the gradual operation of war and treaty; and Clovis acquired each object of his ambition by such efforts or such concessions as were adequate to its real value.   *His* savage character and the virtues of Henry IV. suggest the most opposite ideas of human nature; yet some resemblance may be found in the situation of two princes who conquered France by their valour, their policy, and the merits of a seasonable conversion.[36]

[35] Instead of the Ἀρβόρυχοι, an unknown people, who now appear in the text of Procopius [Bell. Goth. l. i. c. 12], Hadrian de Valois has restored the proper name of the Ἀρμόρυχοι; and this easy correction has been almost universally approved.   Yet an unprejudiced reader would naturally suppose that Procopius means to describe a tribe of Germans in the alliance of Rome, and not a confederacy of Gallic cities which had revolted from the empire.

[36] This important digression of Procopius (de Bell. Gothic. l. i. c. 12, in tom. ii. p. 29-36 [tom. ii. p. 62, *sqq.,* ed. Bonn]) illustrates the origin of the French monarchy.   Yet I must observe, 1. That the Greek historian betrays an inexcusable ignorance of the geography of the West; 2. That these treaties and privileges, which should leave some lasting traces, are totally invisible in Gregory of Tours, the Salic laws. etc.

The kingdom of the Burgundians, which was defined by the course of two Gallic rivers, the Saone and the Rhône, extended from the forest of Vosges to the Alps and the sea of Marseilles.[37] The sceptre was in the hands of Gundobald. That valiant and ambitious prince had reduced the number of royal candidates by the death of two brothers, one of whom was the father of Clotilda;[38] but his imperfect prudence still permitted Godegesil, the youngest of his brothers, to possess the dependent principality of Geneva. The Arian monarch was justly alarmed by the satisfaction and the hopes which seemed to animate his clergy and people after the conversion of Clovis; and Gundobald convened at Lyons an assembly of his bishops, to reconcile, if it were possible, their religious and political discontents. A vain conference was agitated between the two factions. The Arians upbraided the catholics with the worship of three Gods: the catholics defended their cause by theological distinctions; and the usual arguments, objections, and replies were reverberated with obstinate clamour, till the king revealed his secret apprehensions by an abrupt but decisive question, which he addressed to the orthodox bishops: " If you truly profess the Christian religion, why do you not restrain the king of the Franks? He has declared war against me, and forms alliances with my enemies for my destruction. A sanguinary and covetous mind is not the symptom of a sincere conversion: let him show his faith by his works." The answer of Avitus, bishop of Vienne, who spoke in the name of his brethren, was delivered with the voice and countenance of an angel. " We are ignorant of the motives and intentions of the king of the Franks: but we are taught by Scripture that the kingdoms which abandon the divine laws are frequently subverted; and that enemies will arise on every side against those who have made God their enemy. Return, with thy people, to the law of God, and he will give peace and security to thy dominions." The king of Burgundy, who was not prepared to accept the condition which the catholics considered as essential to the treaty, delayed and dismissed the ecclesiastical conference, after reproaching his bishops, that Clovis, their friend and proselyte, had privately tempted the allegiance of his brother.[39]

[37] Regnum circa Rhodanum aut Ararium cum provinciâ Massiliensi retinebant. Greg. Turon. l. ii. c. 32, in tom. ii. p. 178. The province of Marseilles, as far as the Durance, was afterwards ceded to the Ostrogoths; and the signatures of twenty-five bishops are supposed to represent the kingdom of Burgundy, A.D. 519. (Concil. Epaon. in tom. iv. p. 104, 105.) Yet I would except Vindonissa. The bishop, who lived under the Pagan Alemanni, would naturally resort to the synods of the next Christian kingdom. Mascou (in his four first annotations) has explained many circumstances relative to the Burgundian monarchy.

[38] Mascou (Hist. of the Germans, xi. 10), who very reasonably distrusts the testimony of Gregory of Tours, has produced a passage from Avitus (Epist. v.) to prove that Gundobald affected to deplore the tragic event which his subjects affected to applaud.

[39] See the original conference (in tom. iv. p. 99-102). Avitus, the principal actor, and probably the secretary of the meeting, was bishop of Vienne. A

The allegiance of his brother was already seduced; and the obedience of Godegesil, who joined the royal standard with the troops of Geneva, more effectually promoted the success of the conspiracy. While the Franks and Burgundians contended with equal valour, his seasonable desertion decided the event of the battle; and as Gundobald was faintly supported by the disaffected Gauls, he yielded to the arms of Clovis, and hastily retreated from the field, which appears to have been situate between Langres and Dijon. He distrusted the strength of Dijon, a quadrangular fortress, encompassed by two rivers and by a wall thirty feet high and fifteen thick, with four gates and thirty-three towers:[40] he abandoned to the pursuit of Clovis the important cities of Lyons and Vienne; and Gundobald still fled with precipitation till he had reached Avignon, at the distance of two hundred and fifty miles from the field of battle. A long siege and an artful negotiation admonished the king of the Franks of the danger and difficulty of his enterprise. He imposed a tribute on the Burgundian prince, compelled him to pardon and reward his brother's treachery, and proudly returned to his own dominions with the spoils and captives of the southern provinces. This splendid triumph was soon clouded by the intelligence that Gundobald had violated his recent obligations, and that the unfortunate Godegesil, who was left at Vienne with a garrison of five thousand Franks,[41] had been besieged, surprised, and massacred by his inhuman brother. Such an outrage might have exasperated the patience of the most peaceful sovereign; yet the conqueror of Gaul dissembled the injury, released the tribute, and accepted the alliance and military service of the king of Burgundy. Clovis no longer possessed those advantages which had assured the success of the preceding war; and his rival, instructed by adversity, had found new resources in the affections of his people. The Gauls or Romans applauded the mild and impartial laws of Gundobald, which almost raised them to the same level with their conquerors. The bishops were reconciled and flattered by the hopes which he artfully suggested of his approaching conversion; and though he eluded their accomplishment to the last moment of his life, his moderation secured the peace and suspended the ruin of the kingdom of Burgundy.[42]

short account of his person and works may be found in Dupin (Bibliothèque Ecclésiastique, tom. v. p. 5-10).

[40] Gregory of Tours (l. iii. c. 19, in tom. ii. p. 197) indulges his genius, or rather transcribes some more eloquent writer, in the description of Dijon —a castle, which already deserved the title of a city. It depended on the bishops of Langres till the twelfth century, and afterwards became the capital of the dukes of Burgundy. Longuerue, Description de la France, part i. p. 280.

[41] The Epitomiser of Gregory of Tours (in tom. ii. p. 401) has supplied this number of Franks, but he rashly supposes that they were cut in pieces by Gundobald. The prudent Burgundian spared the soldiers of Clovis, and sent these captives to the king of the Visigoths, who settled them in the territory of Toulouse.

[42] In this Burgundian war I have followed Gregory of Tours (l. ii. c. 32, 33, in tom. ii. p. 178, 179), whose narrative *appears* so incompatible with that

I am impatient to pursue the final ruin of that kingdom, which was accomplished under the reign of Sigismond, the son of Gundobald. The catholic Sigismond has acquired the honours of a saint and martyr;[43] but the hands of the royal saint were stained with the blood of his innocent son, whom he inhumanly sacrificed to the pride and resentment of a stepmother. He soon discovered his error, and bewailed the irreparable loss. While Sigismond embraced the corpse of the unfortunate youth, he received a severe admonition from one of his attendants: " It is not his situation, O king ! it is thine which deserves pity and lamentation." The reproaches of a guilty conscience were alleviated, however, by his liberal donations to the monastery of Agaunum, or St. Maurice, in Vallais; which he himself had founded in honour of the imaginary martyrs of the Thebæan legion.[44] A full chorus of perpetual psalmody was instituted by the pious king; he assiduously practised the austere devotion of the monks; and it was his humble prayer that Heaven would inflict in this world the punishment of his sins, His prayer was heard: the avengers were at hand; and the provinces of Burgundy were overwhelmed by an army of victorious Franks. After the event of an unsuccessful battle, Sigismond, who wished to protract his life that he might prolong his penance, concealed himself in the desert in a religious habit till he was discovered and betrayed by his subjects, who solicited the favour of their new masters. The captive monarch, with his wife and two children, was transported to Orleans, and buried alive in a deep well by the stern command of the sons of Clovis, whose cruelty might derive some excuse from the maxims and examples of their barbarous age. Their ambition, which urged them to achieve the conquest of Burgundy, was inflamed or disguised by filial piety: and Clotilda, whose sanctity did not consist in the forgiveness of injuries, pressed them to revenge her father's death on the family of his assassin. The rebellious Burgundians, for they attempted to break their chains, were still permitted to enjoy their national laws under the obligation of tribute and military service; and the Merovingian princes peaceably reigned over a kingdom whose glory and greatness had been first overthrown by the arms of Clovis.[45]

of Procopius (de Bell. Goth. l. i. c. 12, in tom. ii. p. 31, 32 [tom. ii. p. 63, *sqq.,* ed. Bonn)], that some critics have supposed *two* different wars. The Abbé Dubos (Hist. Critique, etc., tom. ii. p. 126-162) has distinctly represented the causes and the events.

[43] See his Life or legend (in tom. iii. p. 402). A martyr! how strangely has that word been distorted from its original sense of a common witness! St. Sigismond was remarkable for the cure of fevers.

[44] Before the end of the fifth century, the church of St. Maurice, and his Thebæan legion, had rendered Agaunum a place of devout pilgrimage. A promiscuous community of both sexes had introduced some deeds of darkness, which were abolished (A.D. 515) by the regular monastery of Sigismond. Within fifty years, his *angels of light* made a nocturnal sally to murder their bishop and his clergy. See, in the Bibliothèque Raisonnée (tom. xxxvi. p. 435-438), the curious remarks of a learned librarian of Geneva.

[45] Marius, bishop of Avenche (Chron. in tom. ii. p. 15), has marked the authentic dates, and Gregory of Tours (l. iii. c. 5, 6, in tom. ii. p. 188, 189)

The first victory of Clovis had insulted the honour of the Goths. They viewed his rapid progress with jealousy and terror; and the youthful fame of Alaric was oppressed by the more potent genius of his rival. Some disputes inevitably arose on the edge of their contiguous dominions; and after the delays of fruitless negotiation a personal interview of the two kings was proposed and accepted. This conference of Clovis and Alaric was held in a small island of the Loire, near Amboise. They embraced, familiarly conversed, and feasted together; and separated with the warmest professions of peace and brotherly love. But their apparent confidence concealed a dark suspicion of hostile and treacherous designs; and their mutual complaints solicited, eluded, and disclaimed a final arbitration. At Paris, which he already considered as his royal seat, Clovis declared to an assembly of the princes and warriors the pretence and the motive of a Gothic war. " It grieves me to see that the Arians still possess the fairest portion of Gaul. Let us march against them with the aid of God; and, having vanquished the heretics, we will possess and divide their fertile provinces." [46] The Franks, who were inspired by hereditary valour and recent zeal, applauded the generous design of their monarch; expressed their resolution to conquer or die, since death and conquest would be equally profitable; and solemnly protested that they would never shave their beards till victory should absolve them from that inconvenient vow. The enterprise was promoted by the public or private exhortations of Clotilda. She reminded her husband how effectually some pious foundation would propitiate the Deity and his servants: and the Christian hero, darting his battle-axe with a skilful and nervous hand, " There (said he), on that spot where my *Francisca* [47] shall fall, will I erect a church in honour of the holy apostles." This ostentatious piety confirmed and justified the attachment of the catholics, with whom he secretly corresponded; and their devout wishes were gradually ripened into a formidable conspiracy. The people of Aquitain was alarmed by the indiscreet reproaches of their Gothic tyrants, who justly accused them of preferring the dominion of the Franks; and their zealous adherent Quintianus,

has expressed the principal facts, of the life of Sigismond and the conquest of Burgundy. Procopius (in tom. ii. p. 34 [tom. ii. p. 65, ed. Bonn]) and Agathias (in tom. ii. p. 49) show their remote and imperfect knowledge.

[46] Gregory of Tours (l. ii. c. 37, in tom. ii. p. 181) inserts the short but persuasive speech of Clovis. Valde moleste fero, quod hi Ariani partem teneant Galliarum (the author of the Gesta Francorum, in tom. ii. p. 553, adds the precious epithet of *optimam*), eamus cum Dei adjutorio, et, superatis eis, redigamus terram in ditionem nostram.

[47] Tunc rex projecit a se in directum Bipennem suam quod est *Francisca*, etc. (Gesta Franc. in tom. ii. p. 554.) The form and use of this weapon are clearly described by Procopius (in tom. ii. p. 37 [Bell. Goth. l. ii. c. 25, tom. ii. p. 247, 248, ed. Bonn]). Examples of its *national* appellation in Latin and French may be found in the Glossary of Ducange and the large Dictionnaire de Trevoux.

bishop of Rodez,[48] preached more forcibly in his exile than in his diocese. To resist these foreign and domestic enemies, who were fortified by the alliance of the Burgundians, Alaric collected his troops, far more numerous than the military powers of Clovis. The Visigoths resumed the exercise of arms, which they had neglected in a long and luxurious peace;[49] a select band of valiant and robust slaves attended their masters to the field;[50] and the cities of Gaul were compelled to furnish their doubtful and reluctant aid. Theodoric, king of the Ostrogoths, who reigned in Italy, had laboured to maintain the tranquillity of Gaul; and he assumed, or affected, for that purpose the impartial character of a mediator. But the sagacious monarch dreaded the rising empire of Clovis, and he was firmly engaged to support the national and religious cause of the Goths.

The accidental or artificial prodigies which adorned the expedition of Clovis were accepted, by a superstitious age, as the manifest declaration of the Divine favour. He marched from Paris; and as he proceeded with decent reverence through the holy diocese of Tours, his anxiety tempted him to consult the shrine of St. Martin, the sanctuary, and the oracle of Gaul. His messengers were instructed to remark the words of the Psalm which should happen to be chanted at the precise moment when they entered the church. Those words most fortunately expressed the valour and victory of the champions of Heaven, and the application was easily transferred to the new Joshua, the new Gideon, who went forth to battle against the enemies of the Lord.[51] Orleans secured to the Franks a bridge on the Loire; but, at the distance of forty miles from Poitiers, their progress was intercepted by an extraordinary swell of the river Vigenna or Vienne; and the opposite banks were covered by the encampment of the Visigoths. Delay must be always dangerous to barbarians, who consume the country through which they march; and had Clovis

---

[48] It is singular enough that some important and authentic facts should be found in a Life of Quintianus, composed in rhyme in the old *patois* of Rouergue (Dubos, Hist. Critique, etc., tom. ii. p. 179).

[49] Quamvis fortitudini vestræ confidentiam tribuat parentum vestrorum innumerabilis multitudo; quamvis Attilam potentem reminiscamini Visigotharum viribus inclinatum; tamen quia populorum ferocia corda longa pace mollescunt, cavete subito in aleam mittere, quos constat tantis temporibus exercitia non habere. Such was the salutary but fruitless advice of peace, of reason, and of Theodoric (Cassiodor. l. iii. Ep. 2 [ed. Rotom. 1679]).

[50] Montesquieu (Esprit des Loix, l. xv. c. 14) mentions and approves the law of the Visigoths (l. ix. tit. 2, in tom. iv. p. 425), which obliged all masters to arm and send or lead into the field a tenth of their slaves.

[51] This mode of divination, by accepting as an omen the first sacred words which in particular circumstances should be presented to the eye or ear, was derived from the Pagans; and the Psalter or Bible was substituted to the poems of Homer and Virgil. From the fourth to the fourteenth century, these *sortes sanctorum,* as they are styled, were repeatedly condemned by the decrees of councils, and repeatedly practised by kings, bishops, and saints. See a curious dissertation of the Abbé du Resnel, in the Mémoires de l'Académie, tom. xix. p. 287-310.

possessed leisure and materials, it might have been impracticable to construct a bridge, or to force a passage, in the face of a superior enemy. But the affectionate peasants, who were impatient to welcome their deliverer, could easily betray some unknown or unguarded ford: the merit of the discovery was enhanced by the useful interposition of fraud or fiction; and a white hart, of singular size and beauty, appeared to guide and animate the march of the catholic army. The counsels of the Visigoths were irresolute and distracted. A crowd of impatient warriors, presumptuous in their strength, and disdaining to fly before the robbers of Germany, excited Alaric to assert in arms the name and blood of the conqueror of Rome. The advice of the graver chieftains pressed him to elude the first ardour of the Franks; and to expect, in the southern provinces of Gaul, the veteran and victorious Ostrogoths, whom the king of Italy had already sent to his assistance. The decisive moments were wasted in idle deliberation; the Goths too hastily abandoned, perhaps, an advantageous post; and the opportunity of a secure retreat was lost by their slow and disorderly motions. After Clovis had passed the ford, as it is still named, of the *Hart,* he advanced with bold and hasty steps to prevent the escape of the enemy. His nocturnal march was directed by a flaming meteor suspended in the air above the cathedral of Poitiers; and this signal, which might be previously concerted with the orthodox successor of St. Hilary, was compared to the column of fire that guided the Israelites in the desert. At the third hour of the day, about ten miles beyond Poitiers, Clovis overtook, and instantly attacked, the Gothic army, whose defeat was already prepared by terror and confusion. Yet they rallied in their extreme distress, and the martial youths, who had clamorously demanded the battle, refused to survive the ignominy of flight. The two kings encountered each other in single combat. Alaric fell by the hand of his rival; and the victorious Frank was saved, by the goodness of his cuirass and the vigour of his horse, from the spears of two desperate Goths, who furiously rode against him to revenge the death of their sovereign. The vague expression of a mountain of the slain serves to indicate a cruel, though indefinite, slaughter; but Gregory has carefully observed that his valiant countryman Apollinaris, the son of Sidonius, lost his life at the head of the nobles of Auvergne. Perhaps these suspected catholics had been maliciously exposed to the blind assault of the enemy; and perhaps the influence of religion was superseded by personal attachment or military honour.[52]

[52] After correcting the text or excusing the mistake of Procopius, who places the defeat of Alaric near Carcassonne, we may conclude, from the evidence of Gregory, Fortunatus, and the author of the Gesta Francorum, that the battle was fought *in campo Vocladensi,* on the banks of the Clain, about ten miles to the south of Poitiers. Clovis overtook and attacked the Visigoths near Vivonne, and the victory was decided near a village still named Champagné St. Hilaire. See the Dissertations of the Abbé le Bœuf, tom. i. p. 304-331. [This statement by Gibbon regarding the battle, that it was fought *in campo Vocladensi,* on the banks of the Clain, is scarcely correct. It should be at Vouille, which is more than ten miles from the river.—O. S.]

Such is the empire of Fortune (if we may still disguise our ignorance under that popular name), that it is almost equally difficult to foresee the events of war, or to explain their various consequences. A bloody and complete victory has sometimes yielded no more than the possession of the field; and the loss of ten thousand men has sometimes been sufficient to destroy, in a single day, the work of ages. The decisive battle of Poitiers was followed by the conquest of Aquitain. Alaric had left behind him an infant son, a bastard competitor, factious nobles, and a disloyal people; and the remaining forces of the Goths were oppressed by the general consternation, or opposed to each other in civil discord. The victorious king of the Franks proceeded without delay to the siege of Angoulême. At the sound of his trumpets the walls of the city imitated the example of Jericho, and instantly fell to the ground; a splendid miracle, which may be reduced to the supposition that some clerical engineers had secretly undermined the foundations of the rampart.[53] At Bordeaux, which had submitted without resistance, Clovis established his winter quarters; and his prudent economy transported from Toulouse the royal treasures, which were depoisited in the capital of the monarchy. The conqueror penetrated as far as the confines of Spain;[54] restored the honours of the catholic church; fixed in Aquitain a colony of Franks;[55] and delegated to his lieutenants the easy task of subduing or extirpating the nation of the Visigoths. But the Visigoths were protected by the wise and powerful monarch of Italy. While the balance was still equal, Theodoric had perhaps delayed the march of the Ostrogoths; but their strenuous efforts successfully resisted the ambition of Clovis; and the army of the Franks, and their Burgundian allies, was compelled to raise the siege of Arles, with the loss, as it is said, of thirty thousand men. These vicissitudes inclined the fierce spirit of Clovis to acquiesce in an advantageous treaty of peace. The Visigoths were suffered to retain the possession of Septimania, a narrow tract of sea-coast, from the Rhône to the Pyrenees; but the ample province of Aquitain, from those mountains to the Loire, was indissolubly united to the kingdom of France.[56]

[53] Angoulême is in the road from Poitiers to Bordeaux, and, although Gregory delays the siege, I can more readily believe that he confounded the order of history than that Clovis neglected the rules of war.

[54] Pyrenæos montes usque Perpinianum subjecit, is the expression of Rorico, which betrays his recent date, since Perpignan did not exist before the tenth century (Marca Hispanica, p. 458). This florid and fabulous writer (perhaps a monk of Amiens—see the Abbé le Bœuf, Mém. de l'Académie, tom. xvii. p. 228-245) relates, in the *allegorical* character of a shepherd, the general history of his countrymen the Franks; but his narrative ends with the death of Clovis.

[55] The author of the Gesta Francorum positively affirms that Clovis fixed a body of Franks in the Saintonge and Bourdelois; and he is not injudiciously followed by Rorico, electos milites, atque fortissimos, cum parvulis, atque mulieribus. Yet it should seem that they soon mingled with the Romans of Aquitain, till Charlemagne introduced a more numerous and powerful colony (Dubos, Hist. Critique, tom. ii. p. 215).

[56] In the composition of the Gothic war I have used the following materials, with due regard to their unequal value:—Four epistles from Theodoric, king

After the success of the Gothic war, Clovis accepted the honours of the Roman consulship. The emperor Anastasius ambitiously bestowed on the most powerful rival of Theodoric the title and ensigns of that eminent dignity; yet, from some unknown cause, the name of Clovis has not been inscribed in the *Fasti* either of the East or West.[57] On the solemn day, the monarch of Gaul, placing a diadem on his head, was invested, in the church of St. Martin, with a purple and mantle. From thence he proceeded on horseback to the cathedral of Tours; and, as he passed through the streets, profusely scattered, with his own hand, a donative of gold and silver to the joyful multitude, who incessantly repeated their acclamations of *Consul* and *Augustus*. The actual or legal authority of Clovis could not receive any new accessions from the consular dignity. It was a name, a shadow, an empty pageant; and if the conqueror had been instructed to claim the ancient prerogatives of that high office, they must have expired with the period of its annual duration. But the Romans were disposed to revere, in the person of their master, that antique title which the emperors condescended to assume: the barbarian himself seemed to contract a sacred obligation to respect the majesty of the republic; and the successors of Theodosius, by soliciting his friendship, tacitly forgave, and almost ratified, the usurpation of Gaul.

of Italy (Cassiodor. l. iii. Epist. 1-4, in tom. iv. p. 3-5), Procopius (de Bell. Goth. l. i. c. 12, in tom. ii. p. 32, 33), Gregory of Tours (l. ii. c. 35, 36, 37, in tom. ii. p. 181-183), Jornandes (de Reb. Geticis, c. 58, in tom. ii. p. 28), Fortunatus (in Vit. St. Hilarii, in tom. iii. p. 380), Isidore (in Chron. Goth. in tom. ii. p. 702), the Epitome of Gregory of Tours (in tom. ii. p. 401), the author of the Gesta Francorum (in tom. ii. p. 553-555), the Fragments of Fredegarius (in tom. ii. p. 463), Aimoin (l. i. c. 20, in tom. iii. p. 41, 42), and Rorico (l. iv. in tom. iii. p. 14-19).

[57] The *Fasti* of Italy would naturally reject a consul, the enemy of their sovereign; but any ingenious hypothesis that might explain the silence of Constantinople and Egypt (the Chronicle of Marcellinus, and the Paschal) is overturned by the similar silence of Marius, bishop of Avenche, who composed his *Fasti* in the kingdom of Burgundy. If the evidence of Gregory of Tours were less weighty and positive (l. ii. c. 38, in tom. ii. p. 183), I could believe that Clovis, like Odoacer, received the lasting title and honours of *Patrician* (Pagi Critica, tom. ii. p. 474, 492).

[Dr. W. Smith in his edition says on the point whether or not Anastasius conferred the consulship on Clovis: "It can scarcely admit of doubt that Anastasius conferred the consulship on Clovis, and this fact has been employed by Dubos and other writers to prove what may be called the Roman origin of the French monarchy, since they suppose that it was mainly by the recognition of Clovis as their emperor that he was recognised as their sovereign by the provincials of Gaul." On the other side, Prof. Bury says: "There is not the least probability in the theory supported by Valesius that Chlodwig was made a Patrician: nor was he a consul. The solution of the difficulty is supplied by his title in the Prologue to the Lex Salica 'proconsolis regis Chlodovechi.' Thus Clovis received the title of proconsul. Perhaps he asked for the consulship and was refused." Gregory states "that the Emperor sent him a letter about the consulate (codicilios de consulata). It may have offered the name proconsul instead of consul. At the same time the consular insignia were conferred. But what of Gregory's *aut Augustus?* It is difficult to believe that Anastasius would have granted to Chlodwig the highest title of all, or that if he had it should not have appeared in the Lex Salica." See Note [1], p. 64.—O. S.]

Twenty-five years after the death of Clovis this important concession was more formally declared in a treaty between his sons and the emperor Justinian. The Ostrogoths of Italy, unable to defend their distant acquisitions, had resigned to the Franks the cities of Arles and Marseilles: of Arles, still adorned with the seat of a Prætorian præfect, and of Marseilles, enriched by the advantages of trade and navigation.[58] This transaction was confirmed by the Imperial authority; and Justinian, generously yielding to the Franks the sovereignty of the countries beyond the Alps, which they already possessed, absolved the provincials from their allegiance; and established on a more lawful, though not more solid, foundation, the throne of the Merovingians.[59] From that era they enjoyed the right of celebrating at Arles the games of the circus; and by a singular privilege, which was denied even to the Persian monarch, the *gold* coin, impressed with their name and image, obtained a legal currency in the empire.[60] A Greek historian of that age has praised the private and public virtues of the Franks, with a partial

[58] Under the Merovingian kings, Marseilles still imported from the East, paper, wine, oil, linen, silk, precious stones, spices, etc. The Gauls or Franks traded to Syria, and the Syrians were established in Gaul. See M. de Guignes, Mém. de l'Académie, tom. xxxvii. p. 471-475.

[59] Οὐ γάρ ποτε ὤοντο Γαλλίας ξὺν τῷ ἀσφαλεῖ κεκτῆοθαι Φράγγοι, μὴ τοῦ αὐτοκράτορος τὸ ἔργον ἐπισφραγίσαντος τοῦτό γε. This strong declaration of Procopius (de Bell. Gothic. l. iii. cap. 33, in tom. ii. p. 41 [tom. ii. p. 417, ed. Bonn]) would almost suffice to justify the Abbé Dubos.

[With regard to the remark by Gibbon in the above note, that the strong declaration of Procopius there quoted would almost suffice to justify the Abbé Dubos, it has been well observed by Hallam that it was merely a piece of Greek vanity in Procopius to pretend that the Franks never thought themselves secure of Gaul until they had obtained that sanction from the emperor. They had lately put to flight the armies of Justinian in Italy, and they had held possession of Gaul for the preceding sixty years. It may also be questioned whether Procopius ever meant to say that Justinian confirmed to the Frank sovereign his rights over the whole of Gaul. The word Γαλλίαι should probably be understood according to the general sense of the passage, which would limit its meaning to Provence, the recent acquisition of the Franks.—O. S.]

[60] The Franks, who probably used the mints of Trèves, Lyons, and Arles, imitated the coinage of the Roman emperors, of seventy-two *solidi*, or pieces, to the pound of gold. But as the Franks established only a decuple proportion of gold and silver, ten shillings will be a sufficient valuation of their solidus of gold. It was the common standard of the barbaric fines, and contained forty *denarii*, or silver threepences. Twelve of these denarii made a *solidus*, or *shilling*, the twentieth part of the ponderal and numeral *livre* or pound of silver, which has been so strangely reduced in modern France. See Le Blanc, Traité Historique des Monnoyes de France, p. 37-43, etc.

[In criticising this statement, that the gold coin of the Merovingian kings, which was denied to the Persian monarch, obtained a legal currency in the empire, Hallam says that this legal currency was not distinctly mentioned by Procopius, though he strongly asserts that it was not lawful (οὐ θεμὶς) for the king of Persia to coin gold with his own effigy, as if the θεμὶς of Constantinople were regarded at Seleucia. There is reason to believe that the Goths as well as the Franks coined gold which might possibly circulate in the empire without having, strictly speaking, a legal currency.—O. S.]

enthusiasm which cannot be sufficiently justified by their domestic annals.[61] He celebrates their politeness and urbanity, their regular government, and orthodox religion; and boldly asserts that these barbarians could be distinguished only by their dress and language from the subjects of Rome. Perhaps the Franks already displayed the social disposition, and lively graces, which, in every age, have disguised their vices, and sometimes concealed their intrinsic merit. Perhaps Agathias, and the Greeks, were dazzled by the rapid progress of their arms, and the splendour of their empire. Since the conquest of Burgundy, Gaul, except the Gothic province of Septimania, was subject, in its whole extent, to the sons of Clovis. They had extinguished the German kingdom of Thuringia, and their vague dominion penetrated beyond the Rhine, into the heart of their native forests. The Alemanni and Bavarians, who had occupied the Roman provinces of Rhætia and Noricum, to the south of the Danube, confessed themselves the humble vassals of the Franks; and the feeble barrier of the Alps was incapable of resisting their ambition. When the last survivor of the sons of Clovis united the inheritance and conquests of the Merovingians, his kingdom extended far beyond the limits of modern France. Yet modern France, such has been the progress of arts and policy, far surpasses, in wealth, populousness, and power, the spacious but savage realms of Clotaire or Dagobert.[62]

The Franks, or French, are the only people of Europe who can deduce a perpetual succession from the conquerors of the Western empire. But their conquest of Gaul was followed by ten centuries of anarchy and ignorance. On the revival of learning, the students who had been formed in the schools of Athens and Rome disdained their barbarian ancestors; and a long period elapsed before patient labour could provide the requisite materials to satisfy, or rather to excite, the curiosity of more enlightened times.[63] At length the eye of criticism and philosophy was directed to the antiquities of France; but even philosophers have been tainted by the contagion of prejudice and passion. The most extreme and exclusive systems, of the personal servitude of the Gauls, or of their voluntary

[61] Agathias, in tom. ii. p. 47 [p. 17, ed. Bonn]. Gregory of Tours exhibits a very different picture. Perhaps it would not be easy, within the same historical space, to find more vice and less virtue. We are continually shocked by the union of savage and corrupt manners.

[62] M. de Foncemagne has traced, in a correct and elegant dissertation (Mém. de l'Académie, tom. viii. p. 505-528), the extent and limits of the French monarchy.

[63] The Abbé Dubos (Histoire Critique, tom. i. p. 29-36) has truly and agreeably represented the slow progress of these studies; and he observes that Gregory of Tours was only once printed before the year 1560. According to the complaint of Heineccius (Opera, tom. iii. Sylloge iii. p. 248, etc.), Germany received with indifference and contempt the codes of barbaric laws which were published by Heroldus, Lindebrogius, etc. At present those laws (as far as they relate to Gaul), the history of Gregory of Tours, and all the monuments of the Merovingian race, appear in a pure and perfect state, in the first four volumes of the Historians of France.

and equal alliance with the Franks, have been rashly conceived, and obstinately defended; and the intemperate disputants have accused each other of conspiring against the prerogative of the crown, the dignity of the nobles, or the freedom of the people. Yet the sharp conflict has usefully exercised the adverse powers of learning and genius; and each antagonist, alternately vanquished and victorious, has extirpated some ancient errors, and established some interesting truths. An impartial stranger, instructed by their discoveries, their disputes, and even their faults, may describe, from the same original materials, the state of the Roman provincials, after Gaul had submitted to the arms and laws of the Merovingian kings.[64]

The rudest, or the most servile, condition of human society, is regulated however by some fixed and general rules. When Tacitus surveyed the primitive simplicity of the Germans, he discovered some permanent maxims, or customs, of public and private life, which were preserved by faithful tradition till the introduction of the art of writing, and of the Latin tongue.[65] Before the election of the Merovingian kings, the most powerful tribe, or nation, of the Franks, appointed four venerable chieftains to compose the *Salic* laws:[66] and their labours were examined

[64] In the space of [*about*] thirty years (1728-1765) this interesting subject has been agitated by the free spirit of the Count de Boulainvilliers (Mémoires Historiques sur l'Etat de la France, particularly tom. i. p. 15-49), the learned ingenuity of the Abbé Dubos (Histoire Critique de l'Etablissement de la Monarchie Françoise dans les Gaules, 2 vols. in 4to.), the comprehensive genius of the President de Montesquieu (Esprit des Loix, particularly l. xxviii. xxx. xxxi.), and the good sense and diligence of the Abbé de Mably (Observations sur l'Histoire de France, 2 vols. 12mo.).

[65] I have derived much instruction from two learned works of Heineccius —the *History* and the *Elements* of the Germanic law. In a judicious preface to the Elements, he considers, and tries to excuse, the defects of that barbarous jurisprudence.

[66] Latin appears to have been the original language of the Salic law. It was probably composed in the beginning of the fifth century, before the era (A.D. 421) of the real or fabulous Pharamond. The preface mentions the four cantons which produced the four legislators; and many provinces —Franconia, Saxony, Hanover, Brabant, etc.—have claimed them as their own. See an excellent Dissertation of Heineccius, de Lege Salicâ, tom. iii. Sylloge iii. p. 247-267.
[With regard to the Salic law, Hallam says: "The Salic law exists in two texts: one purely Latin, of which there are fifteen MSS.; the other mingled with German words, of which there are three. Most have considered the latter to be the original. The MSS. containing it are entitled, *Lex Salica antiquissima* or *vetustior:* the others generally run, *Lex Salica recentior* or *emendata*. This seems to create a presumption. But M. Wraida, who published a history of the Salic law in 1808, inclines to think the pure Latin older than the other, and M. Guizot adopts the same opinion. M. Wraida refers its original enactment to the period when the Franks were still on the left bank of the Rhine, *i. e.* before the reign of Clovis. . . . M. Guizot is of opinion that it bears marks of an age when the Franks had long been mingled with the Roman population." Hallam's *Middle Ages*, vol. i. p. 276. —O. S.]

and approved in three successive assemblies of the people. After the baptism of Clovis, he reformed several articles that appeared incompatible with Christianity: the Salic law was again amended by his sons; and at length, under the reign of Dagobert, the code was revised and promulgated in its actual form, one hundred years after the establishment of the French monarchy. Within the same period, the customs of the *Ripuarians* were transcribed and published; and Charlemagne himself, the legislator of his age and country, had accurately studied the *two* national laws which still prevailed among the Franks.[67] The same care was extended to their vassals; and the rude institutions of the *Alemanni* and *Bavarians* were diligently compiled and ratified by the supreme authority of the Merovingian kings. The *Visigoths* and *Burgundians,* whose conquests in Gaul preceded those of the Franks, showed less impatience to attain one of the principal benefits of civilised society. Euric was the first of the Gothic princes who expressed in writing the manners and customs of his people; and the composition of the Burgundian laws was a measure of policy rather than of justice, to alleviate the yoke and regain the affections of their Gallic subjects.[68] Thus, by a singular coincidence, the Germans framed their artless institutions at a time when the elaborate system of Roman jurisprudence was finally consummated. In the Salic laws, and the Pandects of Justinian, we may compare the first rudiments, and the full maturity, of civil wisdom; and whatever prejudices may be suggested in favour of barbarism, our calmer reflections will ascribe to the Romans the superior advantages, not only of science and reason, but of humanity and justice. Yet the laws of the barbarians were adapted to their wants and desires, their occupations and their capacity; and they all contributed to preserve the peace, and promote the improvements, of the society for whose use they were originally established. The Merovingians, instead of imposing a uniform rule of conduct on their various subjects, permitted each people, and each family, of their empire freely to enjoy their domestic institutions;[69] nor were the Romans excluded from the common benefits of this legal tol-

[67] Eginhard, in Vit. Caroli Magni, c. 29, in tom. v. p. 100. By these two laws most critics understand the Salic and the Ripuarian. The former extended from the Carbonarian forest to the Loire (tom. iv. p. 151 [Lex Sal. tit. L.]), and the latter might be obeyed from the same forest to the Rhine (tom. iv. p. 232).

[68] Consult the ancient and modern prefaces of the several codes, in the fourth volume of the Historians of France. The original prologue to the Salic law expresses (though in a foreign dialect) the genuine spirit of the Franks more forcibly than the ten books of Gregory of Tours.

[69] The Ripuarian law declares and defines this indulgence in favour of the plaintiff (tit. xxxi. in tom. iv. p. 240); and the same toleration is understood or expressed in all the codes except that of the Visigoths of Spain. Tanta diversitas legum (says Agobard in the ninth century) quanta non solum in [singulis] regionibus, aut civitatibus, sed etiam in multis domibus habetur. Nam plerumque contingit ut simul eant aut sedeant quinque homines, et nullus eorum communem legem cum altero habeat (in tom. vi. p. 356). He foolishly proposes to introduce an uniformity of law as well as of faith.

eration.[70]   The children embraced the *law* of their parents, the wife that
of her husband, the freedman that of his patron; and in all causes where
the parties were of different nations, the plaintiff or accuser was obliged
to follow the tribunal of the defendant, who may always plead a judicial
presumption of right or innocence.   A more ample latitude was allowed,
if every citizen, in the presence of the judge, might declare the law under
which he desired to live, and the national society to which he chose to
belong.   Such an indulgence would abolish the partial distinctions of
victory: and the Roman provincials might patiently acquiesce in the
hardships of their condition, since it depended on themselves to assume
the privilege, if they dared to assert the character, of free and warlike
barbarians.[71]

When justice inexorably requires the death of a murderer, each private
citizen is fortified by the assurance that the laws, the magistrate, and
the whole community, are the guardians of his personal safety.   But in
the loose society of the Germans, revenge was always honourable, and
often meritorious: the independent warrior chastised, or vindicated, with
his own hand, the injuries which he had offered or received; and he had
only to dread the resentment of the sons and kinsmen of the enemy whom
he had sacrificed to his selfish or angry passions.   The magistrate, conscious of his weakness, interposed, not to punish, but to reconcile; and
he was satisfied if he could persuade or compel the contending parties
to pay and to accept the moderate fine which had been ascertained as the
price of blood.[72]   The fierce spirit of the Franks would have opposed a
more rigorous sentence; the same fierceness despised these ineffectual restraints; and, when their simple manners had been corrupted
by the wealth of Gaul, the public peace was continually violated by
acts of hasty or deliberate guilt.   In every just government the same

[70] Inter Romanos negotia causarum Romanis legibus præcipimus terminari.
Such are the words of a general constitution promulgated by Clotaire, the son
of Clovis, and sole monarch of the Franks (in tom. iv. p. 116), about the
year 560.
[71] This liberty of choice has been aptly deduced (Esprit des Loix, l. xxviii.
2) from a constitution of Lothaire I. (Leg. Langobard. l. ii. tit. lvii. in Codex
Lindebrog. p. 664), though the example is too recent and partial.   From a
various reading in the Salic law (tit. xliv. not. xlv.), the Abbé de Mably
(tom. i. p. 290-293) has conjectured that at first a *barbarian* only, and afterwards any *man* (consequently a Roman), might live according to the law of
the Franks.   I am sorry to offend this ingenious conjecture by observing that
the stricter sense (*barbarum*) is expressed in the reformed copy of Charlemagne, which is confirmed by the Royal and Wolfenbüttel MSS.   The looser
interpretation (*hominem*) is authorised only by the MS. of Fulda, from
whence Heroldus published his edition.   See the four original texts of the
Salic law, in tom. iv. p. 147, 173, 196, 220.
[72] In the heroic times of Greece, the guilt of murder was expiated by a
pecuniary satisfaction to the family of the deceased (Feithius Antiquitat.
Homer. l. ii. c. 8).   Heineccius, in his preface to the Elements of Germanic
Law, favourably suggests that at Rome and Athens homicide was only punished
with exile.   It is true; but exile was a *capital* punishment for a citizen of Rome
or Athens.

penalty is inflicted, or at least is imposed, for the murder of a peasant or a prince. But the national inequality established by the Franks in their criminal proceedings was the last insult and abuse of conquest.[73] In the calm moments of legislation they solemnly pronounced that the life of a Roman was of smaller value than that of a barbarian. The *Antrustion*,[74] a name expressive of the most illustrious birth or dignity among the Franks, was appreciated at the sum of six hundred pieces of gold; while the noble provincial, who was admitted to the king's table, might be legally murdered at the expense of three hundred pieces. Two hundred were deemed sufficient for a Frank of ordinary condition; but the meaner Romans were exposed to disgrace and danger by a trifling compensation of one hundred, or even fifty, pieces of gold. Had these laws been regulated by any principle of equity or reason, the public protection should have supplied, in just proportion, the want of personal strength. But the legislator had weighed in the scale, not of justice, but of policy, the loss of a soldier against that of a slave: the head of an insolent and rapacious barbarian was guarded by a heavy fine; and the slightest aid was afforded to the most defenceless subjects. Time insensibly abated the pride of the conquerors, and the patience of the vanquished; and the boldest citizen was taught by experience that he might suffer more injuries than he could inflict. As the manners of the Franks became less ferocious, their laws were rendered more severe; and the Merovingian kings attempted to imitate the impartial rigour of the Visigoths and Burgundians.[75] Under the empire of Charlemagne murder was universally punished with death; and the use of capital punishments has been liberally multiplied in the jurisprudence of modern Europe.[76]

[73] This proportion is fixed by the Salic (tit. xliv. in tom. iv. p. 147) and the Ripuarian (tit. vii. xi. xxxvi. in tom. iv. p. 237, 241) laws; but the latter does not distinguish any difference of Romans. Yet the orders of the clergy are placed above the Franks themselves, and the Burgundians and Alemanni between the Franks and the Romans.

[74] The *Antrustiones, qui in truste Dominicâ sunt, leudi, fideles,* undoubtedly represent the first order of Franks; but it is a question whether their rank was personal or hereditary. The Abbé de Mably (tom. i. p. 334-347) is not displeased to mortify the pride of birth (Esprit, 1. xxx. c. 25) by dating the *origin* of French nobility from the reign of Clotaire II. (A.D. 615).

[75] See the Burgundian laws (tit. ii. in tom. iv. p. 257), the code of the Visigoths (l. vi. tit. v. in tom. iv. p. 383), and the constitution of *Childebert,* not of Paris, but most evidently of Austrasia (in tom. iv. p. 112). Their premature severity was sometimes rash and excessive. Childebert condemned not only murderers but robbers; quomodo sine lege involavit, sine lege moriatur; and even the negligent judge was involved in the same sentence. The Visigoths abandoned an unsuccessful surgeon to the family of his deceased patient, ut quod de eo facere voluerint habeant potestatem (1. xi. tit. i. in tom. iv. p. 435).

[76] See in the sixth volume of the works of Heineccius, the Elementa Juris Germanici, l. ii. p. ii. No. 261, 262, 280-283. Yet some vestiges of these pecuniary compositions for murder have been traced in Germany as late as the sixteenth century.

The civil and military professions, which had been separated by Constantine, were again united by the barbarians. The harsh sound of the Teutonic appellations was mollified into the Latin titles of Duke, of Count, or of Præfect; and the same officer assumed, within his district, the command of the troops and the administration of justice.[77] But the fierce and illiterate chieftain was seldom qualified to discharge the duties of a judge, which require all of the faculties of a philosophic mind, laboriously cultivated by experience and study; and his rude ignorance was compelled to embrace some simple and visible methods of ascertaining the cause of justice. In every religion the Deity has been invoked to confirm the truth, or to punish the falsehood, of human testimony; but this powerful instrument was misapplied and abused by the simplicity of the German legislators. The party accused might justify his innocence, by producing before their tribunal a number of friendly witnesses, who solemnly declared their belief or assurance that he was not guilty. According to the weight of the charge this legal number of *compurgators* was multiplied: seventy-two voices were required to absolve an incendiary or assassin; and when the chastity of a queen of France was suspected, three hundred gallant nobles swore, without hesitation, that the infant prince had been actually begotten by her deceased husband.[78] The sin and scandal of manifest and frequent perjuries engaged the magistrates to remove these dangerous temptations, and to supply the defects of human testimony by the famous experiments of fire and water. These extraordinary trials were so capriciously contrived, that in some cases guilt, and innocence in others, could not be proved without the interposition of a miracle. Such miracles were readily provided by fraud and credulity; the most intricate causes were determined by this easy and infallible method; and the turbulent barbarians, who might have disdained the sentence of the magistrate, submissively acquiesced in the judgment of God.[79]

But the trials by single combat gradually obtained superior credit

[77] The whole subject of the Germanic judges, and their jurisdiction, is copiously treated by Heineccius (Element. Jur. Germ. 1. iii. No. 1-72). I cannot find any proof that, under the Merovingian race, the *scabini,* or assessors, were chosen by the people.
[Gibbon, in his note on the Germanic judges, says he cannot find any proof that under the Merovingian race the *scabini,* or assessors, were chosen by the people. The whole question of the scabini is treated by Savigny, who questions the existence of the scabini before Charlemagne. Before that time the decision was by open court of the boni homines or freemen. In fact, as Bury says, " the name does not appear until Carolingian times."—O. S.]

[78] Gregor. Turon. 1. viii. c. 9, in tom. ii. p. 316. Montesquieu observes (Esprit des Loix, 1. xxviii. c. 13) that the Salic law did not admit these *negative proofs* so universally established in the barbaric codes. Yet this obscure concubine (Fredegundis), who became the wife of the grandson of Clovis, must have followed the Salic law.

[79] Muratori, in the Antiquities of Italy, has given two Dissertations (xxxviii. xxxix.) on the *judgments of God.* It was expected that *fire* would not burn the innocent, and that the pure element of *water* would not allow the guilty to sink into its bosom.

and authority among a warlike people, who could not believe that a brave man deserved to suffer, or that a coward deserved to live.[80] Both in civil and criminal proceedings, the plaintiff, or accuser, the defendant, or even the witness, were exposed to mortal challenge from the antagonist who was destitute of legal proofs; and it was incumbent on them either to desert their cause or publicly to maintain their honour in the lists of battle. They fought either on foot or on horseback, according to the custom of their nation;[81] and the decision of the sword or lance was ratified by the sanction of Heaven, of the judge, and of the people. This sanguinary law was introduced into Gaul by the Burgundians; and their legislator Gundobald[82] condescended to answer the complaints and objections of his subject Avitus. " Is it not true," said the king of Burgundy to the bishop, " that the event of national wars and private combats is directed by the judgment of God; and that his providence awards the victory to the juster cause? " By such prevailing arguments, the absurd and cruel practice of judicial duels, which had been peculiar to some tribes of Germany, was propagated and established in all the monarchies of Europe, from Sicily to the Baltic. At the end of ten centuries the reign of legal violence was not totally extinguished; and the ineffectual censures of saints, of popes, and of synods, may seem to prove that the influence of superstition is weakened by its unnatural alliance with reason and humanity. The tribunals were stained with the blood, perhaps, of innocent and respectable citizens; the law, which now favours the rich, then yielded to the strong; and the old, the feeble, and the infirm, were condemned either to renounce their fairest claims and possessions, to sustain the dangers of an unequal conflict,[83] or to trust the doubtful aid of a mercenary champion. This oppressive jurisprudence was imposed on the provincials of Gaul who complained of any injuries in their persons

[80] Montesquieu (Esprit des Loix, l. xxviii. c. 17) has condescended to explain and excuse " la manière de penser de nos pères " on the subject of judicial combats. He follows this strange institution from the age of Gundobald to that of St. Lewis; and the philosopher is sometimes lost in the legal antiquarian.

[81] In a memorable duel at Aix-la-Chapelle (A.D. 820), before the emperor Lewis the Pious, his biographer observes, secundum legem propriam, utpote quia uterque Gothus erat, equestri pugnâ [prœlio] congressus est (Vit. Lud. Pii. c. 33, in tom. vi. p. 103). Ermoldus Nigellus (l. iii. 543-628, in tom. vi. p. 48-50), who describes the duel, admires the ars nova of fighting on horseback, which was unknown to the Franks.

[82] In his original edict published at Lyons (A.D. 501), Gundobald establishes and justifies the use of judicial combat. (Leg. Burgund. tit. xlv. in tom. iii. p. 267, 268.) Three hundred years afterwards, Agobard, bishop of Lyons, solicited Lewis the Pious to abolish the law of an Arian tyrant (in tom. vi. p. 356-358). He relates the conversation of Gundobald and Avitus.

[83] " Accidit (says Agobard), ut non solum valentes viribus, sed etiam infirmi et senes lacessantur ad [certamen et] pugnam, etiam pro vilissimis rebus. Quibus feralibus certaminibus contingunt homicidia injusta, et crudeles ac perversi eventus judiciorum " [tom. vi. p. 357]. Like a prudent rhetorician, he suppresses the legal privilege of hiring champions.

and property. Whatever might be the strength or courage of individuals, the victorious barbarians excelled in the love and exercise of arms; and the vanquished Roman was unjustly summoned to repeat, in his own person, the bloody contest which had been already decided against his country.[84]

A devouring host of one hundred and twenty thousand Germans had formerly passed the Rhine under the command of Ariovistus. One-third part of the fertile lands of the Sequani was appropriated to their use; and the conqueror soon repeated his oppressive demand of another third, for the accommodation of a new colony of twenty-four thousand barbarians whom he had invited to share the rich harvest of Gaul.[85] At the distance of five hundred years the Visigoths and Burgundians, who revenged the defeat of Ariovistus, usurped the same unequal proportion of *two-thirds* of the subject lands. But this distribution, instead of spreading over the province, may be reasonably confined to the peculiar districts where the victorious people had been planted by their own choice or by the policy of their leader. In these districts each barbarian was connected by the ties of hospitality with some Roman provincial. To this unwelcome guest the proprietor was compelled to abandon two-thirds of his patrimony: but the German, a shepherd and a hunter, might sometimes content himself with a spacious range of wood and pasture, and resign the smallest, though most valuable, portion to the toil of the industrious husbandman.[86] The silence of ancient and authentic testimony has encouraged an opinion that the rapine of the *Franks* was not moderated or disguised by the forms of a legal division; that they dispersed themselves over the provinces of Gaul without order or control; and that each victorious robber, according to his wants, his avarice, and his strength, measured with his sword the extent of his new inheritance. At a distance from their sovereign the barbarians might indeed be tempted to exercise such arbitrary depredation; but the firm and artful policy of Clovis must curb a licentious spirit which would aggravate the misery of the vanquished whilst it

[84] Montesquieu (Esprit des Loix, xxviii. c. 14), who understands *why* the judicial combat was admitted by the Burgundians, Ripuarians, Alemanni, Bavarians, Lombards, Thuringians, Frisons, and Saxons, is satisfied (and Agobard seems to countenance the assertion) that it was not allowed by the Salic law. Yet the same custom, at least in cases of treason, is mentioned by Ermoldus Nigellus (l. iii. 543, in tom. vi. p. 48) and the anonymous biographer of Lewis the Pious (c. 46, in tom. vi. p. 112), as the "mos antiquus Francorum, more Francis solito," etc., expressions too general to exclude the noblest of their tribes.

[85] Cæsar de Bell. Gall. l. i. c. 31, in tom. i. p. 213.

[86] The obscure hints of a division of lands occasionally scattered in the laws of the Burgundians (tit. liv. No. 1, 2, in tom. iv. p. 271, 272) and Visigoths (l. x. tit. i. No. 8, 9, 16, in tom. iv. p. 428, 429, 430) are skilfully explained by the President Montesquieu (Esprit des Loix, l. xxx. c. 7, 8, 9). I shall only add that, among the Goths, the division seems to have been ascertained by the judgment of the neighbourhood; that the barbarians frequently usurped the remaining *third;* and that the Romans might recover their right, unless they were barred by a prescription of fifty years.

corrupted the union and discipline of the conquerors.[87] The memorable vase of Soissons is a monument and a pledge of the regular distribution of the Gallic spoils. It was the duty and the interest of Clovis to provide rewards for a successful army, and settlements for a numerous people, without inflicting any wanton or superfluous injuries on the loyal catholics of Gaul. The ample fund which he might lawfully acquire of the Imperial patrimony, vacant lands, and Gothic usurpations, would diminish the cruel necessity of seizure and confiscation, and the humble provincials would more patiently acquiesce in the equal and regular distribution of their loss.[88]

The wealth of the Merovingian princes consisted in their extensive domain. After the conquest of Gaul they still delighted in the rustic simplicity of their ancestors; the cities were abandoned to solitude and decay; and their coins, their charters, and their synods, are still inscribed with the names of the villas or rural palaces in which they successively resided. One hundred and sixty of these *palaces,* a title which need not excite any unseasonable ideas of art or luxury, were scattered through the provinces of their kingdom; and if some might claim the honours of a fortress, the far greater part could be esteemed only in the light of profitable farms. The mansion of the long-haired kings was surrounded with convenient yards and stables for the cattle and the poultry; the garden was planted with useful vegetables; the various trades, the labours of agriculture, and even the arts of hunting and fishing, were exercised by servile hands for the emolument of the sovereign; his magazines were filled with corn and wine, either for sale or consumption; and the whole administration was conducted by the strictest maxims of private economy.[89] This ample patrimony

[87] [Sismondi notes upon this question that the Franks were not a conquering people who had emigrated with their families, like the Goths or Burgundians. The women, the children, and the old had not followed Clovis. They remained on their ancient possessions on the Waal and the Rhine. The adventurers alone had formed the invading force, and they always considered themselves as an army, not as a colony. Hence their laws retain no traces of the partition of the Roman properties. *Histoire des Français,* vol. i. p. 197.— O. S.]

[88] It is singular enough that the President de Montesquieu (Esprit des Loix, l. xxx. c. 7) and the Abbé de Mably (Observations, tom. i. p. 21, 22) agree in this strange supposition of arbitrary and private rapine. The Count de Boulainvilliers (Etat de la France, tom. i. p. 22, 23) shows a strong understanding through a cloud of ignorance and prejudice.

[Sismondi supposes, regarding private rapine, that the barbarians, if a farm were conveniently situated, would show no great respect for the laws of property; but in general there would have been vacant land enough for the lots assigned to old and worn-out warriors. *Hist. des Français,* vol. ii. p. 196.—O. S.]

[89] See the rustic edict, or rather code, of Charlemagne, which contains seventy distinct and minute regulations of that great monarch (in tom. v. p. 652-657). He requires an account of the horns and skins of the goats, allows his fish to be sold, and carefully directs that the larger villas (*Capitaneæ*) shall maintain one hundred hens and thirty geese, and the smaller (*Mansionales*) fifty hens and twelve geese. Mabillon (de Re Diplomaticâ)

was appropriated to supply the hospitable plenty of Clovis and his successors, and to reward the fidelity of their brave companions, who, both in peace and war, were devoted to their personal service. Instead of a horse or a suit of armour, each companion, according to his rank, or merit, or favour, was invested with a *benefice*, the primitive name and most simple form of the feudal possessions. These gifts might be resumed at the pleasure of the sovereign; and his feeble prerogative derived some support from the influence of his liberality. But this dependent tenure was gradually abolished [90] by the independent and rapacious nobles of France, who established the perpetual property and hereditary succession of their benefices; a revolution salutary to the earth, which had been injured or neglected by its precarious masters.[91] Besides these royal and beneficiary estates, a large proportion had been assigned, in the division of Gaul, of *allodial* and *Salic* lands: they were exempt from tribute, and the Salic lands were equally shared among the male descendants of the Franks.[92]

In the bloody discord and silent decay of the Merovingian line a new order of tyrants arose in the provinces, who, under the appellation of *Seniors* or Lords, usurped a right to govern and a licence to oppress the subjects of their peculiar territory. Their ambition might be checked by the hostile resistance of an equal: but the laws were extinguished; and the sacrilegious barbarians, who dared to provoke the vengeance of a saint or bishop,[93] would seldom respect the landmarks of a profane and defenceless neighbour. The common or public rights of nature, such as they had always been deemed by the Roman juris-

has investigated the names, the number, and the situation of the Merovingian villas.

[90] From a passage of the Burgundian law (tit. i. No. 4 [3] in tom. iv. p. 257) it is evident that a deserving son might expect to hold the lands which his father had received from the royal bounty of Gundobald. The Burgundians would firmly maintain their privilege, and their example might encourage the beneficiaries of France.

[91] The revolutions of the benefices and fiefs are clearly fixed by the Abbé de Mably. His accurate distinction of *times* gives him a merit to which even Montesquieu is a stranger.

[92] See the Salic law (tit. lxii. in tom. iv. p. 156). The origin and nature of these Salic lands, which in times of ignorance were perfectly understood, now perplex our most learned and sagacious critics.

[No solution seems more probable than that the ancient law-givers of the Salic Franks prohibited females from inheriting lands assigned to the nation, upon its conquest of Gaul, both in compliance with their ancient usages and in order to secure the military service of every proprietor. But lands subsequently acquired by purchase or otherwise, though equally bound to the public defence, were relieved from the severity of this rule, and presumed not to belong to the class of Salic. Hallam's *Middle Ages*, vol. i. p. 146; cf. Sismondi, vol. i. p. 196.—O. S.]

[93] Many of the two hundred and six miracles of St. Martin (Greg. Turon. in Maximâ Bibliothecâ Patrum, tom. xi. p. 896-932) were repeatedly performed to punish sacrilege. Audite hæc omnes (exclaims the bishop of Tours) potestatem habentes, after relating how some horses ran mad that had been turned into a sacred meadow.

prudence,[94] were severely restrained by the German conquerors, whose amusement, or rather passion, was the exercise of hunting. The vague dominion which MAN has assumed over the wild inhabitants of the earth, the air, and the waters, was confined to some fortunate individuals of the human species. Gaul was again overspread with woods; and the animals, who were reserved for the use or pleasure of the lord, might ravage with impunity the fields of his industrious vassals. The chase was the sacred privilege of the nobles and their domestic servants. Plebeian transgressors were legally chastised with stripes and imprisonment;[95] but in an age which admitted a slight composition for the life of a citizen, it was a capital crime to destroy a stag or a wild bull within the precincts of the royal forests.[96]

According to the maxims of ancient war, the conqueror became the lawful master of the enemy whom he had subdued and spared:[97] and the fruitful cause of personal slavery, which had been almost suppressed by the peaceful sovereignty of Rome, was again revived and multiplied by the perpetual hostilities of the independent barbarians. The Goth, the Burgundian, or the Frank, who returned from a successful expedition, dragged after him a long train of sheep, of oxen, and of human captives, whom he treated with the same brutal contempt. The youths of an elegant form and ingenuous aspect were set apart for the domestic service; a doubtful situation, which alternately exposed them to the favourable or cruel impulse of passion. The useful mechanics and servants (smiths, carpenters, tailors, shoemakers, cooks, gardeners, dyers, and workmen in gold and silver, etc.) employed their skill for the use or profit of their master. But the Roman captives who were destitute of art, but capable of labour, were condemned, without regard to their former rank, to tend the cattle and cultivate the lands of the barbarians. The number of the hereditary bondsmen who were attached to the Gallic estates was continually increased by new supplies; and the servile people, according to the situation and temper of their lords, was sometimes raised by pre-

[94] Heinec. Element. Jur. German. 1. ii. p. 1, No. 8.

[95] Jonas, bishop of Orleans (A.D. 821-826; Cave, Hist. Litteraria, p. 443), censures the *legal* tyranny of the nobles. Pro feris, quas cura hominum non aluit, sed Deus in commune mortalibus ad utendum concessit, pauperes a potentioribus spoliantur, flagellantur, ergastulis detruduntur, et multa alia patiuntur. Hoc enim qui faciunt, *lege mundi* se facere juste posse contendunt. De Institutione Laicorum, 1. ii. c. 23, apud Thomassin, Discipline de l'Eglise, tom. iii. p. 1348.

[96] On a mere suspicion, Chundo, a chamberlain of Gontram, king of Burgundy, was stoned to death (Greg. Turon. 1. x. c. 10, in tom. ii. p. 369). John of Salisbury (Policrat. 1. i. c. 4) asserts the rights of nature, and exposes the cruel practice of the twelfth century. See Heineccius, Elem. Jur. Germ. 1. ii. p. 1, No. 51-57.

[97] The custom of enslaving prisoners of war was totally extinguished in the thirteenth century by the prevailing influence of Christianity; but it might be proved, from frequent passages of Gregory of Tours, etc., that it was practised without censure under the Merovingian race; and even Grotius himself (de Jure Belli et Pacis, 1. iii. c. 7), as well as his commentator Barbeyrac, have laboured to reconcile it with the laws of nature and reason.

carious indulgence, and more frequently depressed by capricious despotism.[98] An absolute power of life and death was exercised by these lords; and when they married their daughters, a train of useful servants, chained on the waggons to prevent their escape, was sent as a nuptial present into a distant country.[99] The majesty of the Roman laws protected the liberty of each citizen against the rash effects of his own distress or despair. But the subjects of the Merovingian kings might alienate their personal freedom; and this act of legal suicide, which was familiarly practised, is expressed in terms most disgraceful and afflicting to the dignity of human nature.[100] The example of the poor, who purchased life by the sacrifice of all that can render life desirable, was gradually imitated by the feeble and the devout, who, in times of public disorder, pusillanimously crowded to shelter themselves under the battlements of a powerful chief and around the shrine of a popular saint. Their submission was accepted by these temporal or spiritual patrons; and the hasty transaction irrecoverably fixed their own condition and that of their latest posterity. From the reign of Clovis, during five successive centuries, the laws and manners of Gaul uniformly tended to promote the increase, and to confirm the duration, of personal servitude. Time and violence almost obliterated the intermediate ranks of society, and left an obscure and narrow interval between the noble and the slave. This arbitrary and recent division has been transformed by pride and prejudice into a *national* distinction, universally established by the arms and the laws of the Merovingians. The nobles, who claimed their genuine or fabulous descent from the independent and victorious Franks, have asserted and abused the indefeasible right of conquest over a prostrate crowd of slaves and plebeians, to whom they imputed the imaginary disgrace of a Gallic or Roman extraction.

The general state and revolutions of *France,* a name which was imposed by the conquerors, may be illustrated by the particular example of a province, a diocese, or a senatorial family. Auvergne had formerly maintained a just pre-eminence among the independent states and cities of Gaul. The brave and numerous inhabitants displayed a singular trophy —the sword of Cæsar himself, which he had lost when he was repulsed

[98] The state, professions, etc., of the German, Italian, and Gallic slaves, during the middle ages, are explained by Heineccius (Element. Jur. Germ. l. i. No. 28-47), Muratori (Dissertat. xiv. xv.), Ducange (Gloss. sub voce *Servi*), and the Abbé de Mably (Observations, tom. ii. p. 3, etc., p. 237, etc.).

[99] Gregory of Tours (l. vi. c. 45, in tom. ii. p. 289) relates a memorable example, in which Chilperic only abused the private rights of a master. Many families, which belonged to his *domus fiscales* in the neighbourhood of Paris, were forcibly sent away into Spain.

[100] Licentiam habeatis mihi qualemcunque volueritis disciplinam ponere; vel venumdare, aut quod vobis placuerit de me facere. Marculf. Formul. l. ii. 28, in tom. iv. p. 497. The *Formula* of Lindenbrogius (p. 559), and that of Anjou (p. 565), are to the same effect. Gregory of Tours (l. vii. c. 45, in tom. ii. p. 311) speaks of many persons who sold themselves for bread in a great famine.

before the walls of Gergovia.[101] As the common offspring of Troy, they claimed a fraternal alliance with the Romans;[102] and if each province had imitated the courage and loyalty of Auvergne, the fall of the Western empire might have been prevented or delayed. They firmly maintained the fidelity which they had reluctantly sworn to the Visigoths; but when their bravest nobles had fallen in the battle of Poitiers, they accepted without resistance a victorious and catholic sovereign. This easy and valuable conquest was achieved and possessed by Theodoric, the eldest son of Clovis: but the remote province was separated from his Austrasian dominions by the intermediate kingdoms of Soissons, Paris, and Orleans, which formed, after their father's death, the inheritance of his three brothers. The king of Paris, Childebert, was tempted by the neighbourhood and beauty of Auvergne.[103] The upper country, which rises towards the south into the mountains of the Cevennes, presented a rich and various prospect of woods and pastures; the sides of the hills were clothed with vines; and each eminence was crowned with a villa or castle. In the Lower Auvergne, the river Allier flows through the fair and spacious plain of Limagne; and the inexhaustible fertility of the soil supplied, and still supplies, without any interval of repose, the constant repetition of the same harvests.[104] On the false report that their lawful sovereign had been slain in Germany, the city and diocese of Auvergne were betrayed by the grandson of Sidonius Apollinaris. Childebert enjoyed this clandestine victory; and the free subjects of Theodoric threatened to desert his standard if he indulged his private resentment while the nation was engaged in the Burgundian war. But the Franks of Austrasia soon yielded to the persuasive eloquence of their king. " Follow me," said Theodoric, " into Auvergne; I will lead you into a province where you may acquire gold, silver, slaves, cattle, and precious apparel, to the full extent of your wishes. I repeat my promise; I give you the people and their wealth as your prey; and you may transport them at pleasure into your own country." By the execution of this

---

[101] When Cæsar saw it, he laughed (Plutarch. in Cæsar. [c. 26] in tom. i. p. 409 [p. 720, ed. Frankf.]) ; yet he relates his unsuccessful siege of Gergovia with less frankness than we might expect from a great man to whom victory was familiar. He acknowledges, however, that in one attack he lost forty-six centurions and seven hundred men (de Bell. Gallico, l. vi. [vii.] c. 44-53, in tom. i. p. 270-272).

[102] Audebant se quondam fratres Latio dicere, et sanguine ab Iliaco populos computare (Sidon. Apollinar. l. vii. Epist. 7, in tom. i. p. 799). I am not informed of the degrees and circumstances of this fabulous pedigree.

[103] Either the first or second partition among the sons of Clovis had given Berry to Childebert (Greg. Turon. l. iii. c. 12, in tom. ii. p. 192). Velim (said he), Arvernam *Lemanem,* quæ tantæ jocunditatis gratiâ refulgere dicitur, oculis cernere (l. iii. c. 9, p. 191). The face of the country was concealed by a thick fog when the king of Paris made his entry into Clermont.

[104] For the description of Auvergne, see Sidonius (l. iv. Epist. 21, in tom. i. p. 793), with the notes of Savaron and Sirmond (p. 279 and 51 of their respective editions). Boulainvilliers (Etat de la France, tom. ii. p. 242-268), and the Abbé de la Longuerue (Description de la France, part i. p. 132-139).

promise Theodoric justly forfeited the allegiance of a people whom he devoted to destruction. His troops, reinforced by the fiercest barbarians of Germany,[105] spread desolation over the fruitful face of Auvergne; and two places only, a strong castle and a holy shrine, were saved or redeemed from their licentious fury. The castle of Meroliac [106] was seated on a lofty rock, which rose an hundred feet above the surface of the plain; and a large reservoir of fresh water was enclosed with some arable lands within the circle of its fortifications. The Franks beheld with envy and despair this impregnable fortress: but they surprised a party of fifty stragglers; and, as they were oppressed by the number of their captives, they fixed at a trifling ransom the alternative of life or death for these wretched victims, whom the cruel barbarians were prepared to massacre on the refusal of the garrison. Another detachment penetrated as far as Brivas, or Brioude, where the inhabitants, with their valuable effects, had taken refuge in the sanctuary of St. Julian. The doors of the church resisted the assault, but a daring soldier entered through a window of the choir and opened a passage to his companions. The clergy and people, the sacred and the profane spoils, were rudely torn from the altar; and the sacrilegious division was made at a small distance from the town of Brioude. But this act of impiety was severely chastised by the devout son of Clovis. He punished with death the most atrocious offenders; left their secret accomplices to the vengeance of St. Julian; released the captives; restored the plunder; and extended the rights of sanctuary five miles round the sepulchre of the holy martyr.[107]

Before the Austrasian army retreated from Auvergne, Theodoric exacted some pledges of the future loyalty of a people whose just hatred could be restrained only by their fear. A select band of noble youths, the sons of the principal senators, was delivered to the conqueror as the hostages of the faith of Childebert and of their countrymen. On the first rumour of war or conspiracy these guiltless youths were reduced to a state of servitude; and one of them, Attalus,[108]

[105] Furorem gentium, quæ de ulteriore Rheni amnis parte venerant, superare non poterat (Greg. Turon. l. iv. c. 50, in tom. ii. 229), was the excuse of another king of Austrasia (A.D. 574) for the ravages which his troops committed in the neighbourhood of Paris.

[106] From the name and situation, the Benedictine editors of Gregory of Tours (in tom. ii. p. 192) have fixed this fortress at a place named *Chastel Merliac*, two miles from Mauriac, in the Upper Auvergne. In this description I translate *infra* as if I read *intra;* the two prepositions are perpetually confounded by Gregory or his transcribers, and the sense must always decide.

[107] See these revolutions and wars of Auvergne in Gregory of Tours (l. ii. c. 37, in tom. ii. p. 183, and l. iii. c. 9, 12, 13, p. 191, 192, de Miraculis St. Julian. c. 13, in tom. ii. p. 466). He frequently betrays his extraordinary attention to his native country.

[108] The story of Attalus is related by Gregory of Tours (l. iii. c. 15, in tom. ii. p. 193-195). His editor, the P. Ruinart, confounds this Attalus, who was a youth (*puer*) in the year 532, with a friend of Sidonius of the same name, who was count of Autun fifty or sixty years before. Such an error, which cannot be imputed to ignorance, is excused in some degree by its own magnitude.

whose adventures are more particularly related, kept his master's horses in the diocese of Trèves. After a painful search he was discovered, in this unworthy occupation, by the emissaries of his grandfather, Gregory bishop of Langres; but his offers of ransom were sternly rejected by the avarice of the barbarian, who required an exorbitant sum of ten pounds of gold for the freedom of his noble captive. His deliverance was effected by the hardy stratagem of Leo, a slave belonging to the kitchens of the bishop of Langres.[109] An unknown agent easily introduced him into the same family. The barbarian purchased Leo for the price of twelve pieces of gold; and was pleased to learn that he was deeply skilled in the luxury of an episcopal table: "Next Sunday," said the Frank, "I shall invite my neighbours and kinsmen. Exert thy art, and force them to confess that they have never seen or tasted such an entertainment, even in the king's house." Leo assured him that, if he would provide a sufficient quantity of poultry, his wishes should be satisfied. The master, who already aspired to the merit of elegant hospitality, assumed as his own the praise which the voracious guests unanimously bestowed on his cook; and the dexterous Leo insensibly acquired the trust and management of his household. After the patient expectation of a whole year, he cautiously whispered his design to Attalus, and exhorted him to prepare for flight in the ensuing night. At the hour of midnight the intemperate guests retired from table, and the Frank's son-in-law, whom Leo attended to his apartment with a nocturnal potation, condescended to jest on the facility with which he might betray his trust. The intrepid slave, after sustaining this dangerous raillery, entered his master's bedchamber; removed his spear and shield; silently drew the fleetest horses from the stable; unbarred the ponderous gates; and excited Attalus to save his life and liberty by incessant diligence. Their apprehensions urged them to leave their horses on the banks of the Meuse;[110] they swam the river, wandered three days in the adjacent forest, and subsisted only by the accidental discovery of a wild plum-tree. As they lay concealed in a dark thicket, they heard the noise of horses; they were terrified by the angry countenance of their master, and they anxiously listened to his declaration that, if he could seize the guilty fugitives, one of them he would cut in pieces with his sword, and would expose the other on a gibbet. At length Attalus and his faithful

[109] This Gregory, the great-grandfather of Gregory of Tours (in tom. ii. p. 197, 490), lived ninety-two years, of which he passed forty as count of Autun, and thirty-two as bishop of Langres. According to the poet Fortunatus, he displayed equal merit in these different stations:—

> Nobilis antiquâ decurrens prole parentum,
> Nobilior gestis, nunc super astra manet.
> Arbiter ante ferox, dein pius ipse sacerdos,
> Quos domuit judex, fovit amore patris.

[110] As M. de Valois and the P. Ruinart are determined to change the *Mosella* of the text into *Mosa*, it becomes me to acquiesce in the alteration. Yet, after some examination of the topography, I could defend the common reading.

Leo reached the friendly habitation of a presbyter of Rheims, who recruited their fainting strength with bread and wine, concealed them from the search of their enemy, and safely conducted them beyond the limits of the Austrasian kingdom to the episcopal palace of Langres. Gregory embraced his grandson with tears of joy, gratefully delivered Leo with his whole family from the yoke of servitude, and bestowed on him the property of a farm, where he might end his days in happiness and freedom. Perhaps this singular adventure, which is marked with so many circumstances of truth and nature, was related by Attalus himself to his cousin or nephew, the first historian of the Franks. Gregory of Tours [111] was born about sixty years after the death of Sidonius Apollinaris; and their situation was almost similar, since each of them was a native of Auvergne, a senator, and a bishop. The difference of their style and sentiments may, therefore, express the decay of Gaul; and clearly ascertain how much, in so short a space, the human mind had lost of its energy and refinement. [112]

We are now qualified to despise the opposite, and perhaps artful, misrepresentations which have softened or exaggerated the oppression of the Romans of Gaul under the reign of the Merovingians. The conquerors never promulgated any *universal* edict of servitude or confiscation: but a degenerate people, who excused their weakness by the specious names of politeness and peace, was exposed to the arms and laws of the ferocious barbarians, who contemptuously insulted their possessions, their freedom, and their safety. Their personal injuries were partial and irregular; but the great body of the Romans survived the revolution, and still preserved the property and privileges of citizens. A large portion of their lands was exacted for the use of the Franks: but they enjoyed the remainder exempt from tribute; [113] and the same irresistible violence which swept away the arts and manufactures of Gaul destroyed the elaborate and expensive system of Imperial despotism. The provincials must frequently deplore the savage jurisprudence of the Salic or Ripuarian laws; but their private

[111] The parents of Gregory (Gregorius Florentius Georgius) were of noble extraction (*natalibus . . . illustres*), and they possessed large estates (*latifundia*) both in Auvergne and Burgundy. He was born in the year 539, was consecrated bishop of Tours in 573, and died in 593 or 595, soon after he had terminated his history. See his Life by Odo, abbot of Clugny (in tom. ii. p. 129-135), and a new Life in the Mémoires de l'Académie, etc., tom. xxvi. p. 598-637.

[112] Decedente atque immo potius pereunte ab urbibus Gallicanis liberalium culturâ literarum, etc. (in præfat. in tom. ii. p. 137), is the complaint of Gregory himself, which he fully verifies by his own work. His style is equally devoid of elegance and simplicity. In a conspicuous station he still remained a stranger to his own age and country; and in a prolix work (the five last books contain ten years) he has omitted almost everything that posterity desires to learn. I have tediously acquired, by a painful perusal, the right of pronouncing this unfavourable sentence.

[113] The Abbé de Mably (tom. i. p. 247-267) has diligently confirmed this opinion of the President de Montesquieu (Esprit des Loix, l. xxx. c. 13).

life, in the important concerns of marriage, testaments, or inheritance, was still regulated by the Theodosian Code; and a discontented Roman might freely aspire or descend to the title and character of a barbarian. The honours of the state were accessible to his ambition: the education and temper of the Romans more peculiarly qualified them for the offices of civil government; and as soon as emulation had rekindled their military ardour, they were permitted to march in the ranks, or even at the head, of the victorious Germans. I shall not attempt to enumerate the generals and magistrates whose names [114] attest the liberal policy of the Merovingians. The supreme command of Burgundy, with the title of Patrician, was successively intrusted to three Romans; and the last and most powerful, Mummolus,[115] who alternately saved and disturbed the monarchy, had supplanted his father in the station of count of Autun, and left a treasure of thirty talents of gold and two hundred and fifty talents of silver. The fierce and illiterate barbarians were excluded, during several generations, from the dignities, and even from the orders, of the church.[116] The clergy of Gaul consisted almost entirely of native provincials; the haughty Franks fell prostrate at the feet of their subjects who were dignified with the episcopal character; and the power and riches which had been lost in war were insensibly recovered by superstition.[117] In all temporal affairs the Theodosian Code was the universal law of the clergy; but the barbaric jurisprudence had liberally provided for their personal safety: a subdeacon was equivalent to two Franks; the *antrustion* and priest were held in similar estimation; and the life of a bishop was appreciated far above the common standard, at the price of nine hundred pieces of gold.[118] The Romans communicated to their conquerors the use of

[114] See Dubos, Hist. Critique de la Monarchie Françoise, tom. ii. 1. vi. c. 9, 10. The French antiquarians establish as a *principle* that the Romans and barbarians may be distinguished by their names. Their names undoubtedly form a reasonable *presumption;* yet, in reading Gregory of Tours, I have observed Gondulphus, of Senatorian or Roman extraction (1. vi. c. 11, in tom. ii. p. 273), and Claudius, a barbarian (1. vii. c. 29, p. 303).

[115] Eunius Mummolus is repeatedly mentioned by Gregory of Tours, from the fourth (c. 42, p. 224) to the seventh (c. 40, p. 310) book. The computation by talents is singular enough; but if Gregory attached any meaning to that obsolete word, the treasures of Mummolus must have exceeded £100,000 sterling.

[116] See Fleury, Discours iii. sur l'Histoire Ecclésiastique.

[117] The bishop of Tours himself has recorded the complaint of Chilperic, the grandson of Clovis. Ecce pauper remansit fiscus noster; ecce divitiæ nostræ ad ecclesias sunt translatæ: nulli penitus nisi soli Episcopi regnant (1. vi. c. 46, in tom. ii. p. 291).

[118] See the Ripuarian Code (tit. xxxvi. in tom. iv. p. 241). The Salic law does not provide for the safety of the clergy; and we might suppose, on the behalf of the more civilised tribe, that they had not foreseen such an impious act as the murder of a priest. Yet Prætextatus, archbishop of Rouen, was assassinated by the order of queen Fredegundis before the altar (Greg. Turon. 1. viii. c. 31, in tom. ii. p. 326).

the Christian religion and Latin language;[119] but their language and their religion had alike degenerated from the simple purity of the Augustan and Apostolic age. The progress of superstition and barbarism was rapid and universal: the worship of the saints concealed from vulgar eyes the God of the Christians, and the rustic dialect of peasants and soldiers was corrupted by a Teutonic idiom and pronunciation. Yet such intercourse of sacred and social communion eradicated the distinctions of birth and victory; and the nations of Gaul were gradually confounded under the name and government of the Franks.

The Franks, after they mingled with their Gallic subjects, might have imparted the most valuable of human gifts, a spirit and system of constitutional liberty. Under a king, hereditary but limited, the chiefs and counsellors might have debated at Paris in the palace of the Cæsars: the adjacent field, where the emperors reviewed their mercenary legions, would have admitted the legislative assembly of freemen and warriors; and the rude model which had been sketched in the woods of Germany [120] might have been polished and improved by the civil wisdom of the Romans. But the careless barbarians, secure of their personal independence, disdained the labour of government: the annual assemblies of the month of March were silently abolished, and the nation was separated and almost dissolved by the conquest of Gaul. [121] The monarchy was left without any regular establishment of justice, of arms, or of revenue. The successors of Clovis wanted resolution to assume, or strength to exercise, the legislative and executive powers which the people had abdicated: the royal prerogative was distinguished only by a more ample privilege of rapine and murder; and the love of freedom, so often invigorated and disgraced by private ambition, was reduced among the licentious Franks to the contempt of order and the desire of impunity. Seventy-five years after the death of Clovis, his grandson Gontran, king of Burgundy, sent an army to invade the Gothic possessions of Septimania, or Languedoc. The troops of Burgundy, Berry, Auvergne, and the adjacent territories were excited by the hopes of spoil. They marched without discipline under the banners of German or Gallic counts: their attack was feeble and unsuccessful, but the friendly and hostile provinces were desolated with indiscriminate rage. The cornfields, the villages, the churches themselves, were consumed by fire; the inhabitants were massacred or dragged into captivity; and, in the dis-

[119] M. Bonamy (Mém. de l'Académie des Inscriptions, tom. xxiv. p. 582-670) has ascertained the *Lingua Romana Rustica*, which, through the medium of the *Romance*, has gradually been polished into the actual form of the French language. Under the Carlovingian race the kings and nobles of France still understood the dialect of their German ancestors.

[120] Ce beau systême a été trouvé dans les bois. Montesquieu, Esprit des Loix, l. xi. c. 6.

[121] See the Abbé de Mably, Observations, etc., tom. i. p. 34-56. It should seem that the institution of national assemblies, which are coeval with the French nation, has never been congenial to its temper.

orderly retreat, five thousand of these inhuman savages were destroyed by hunger or intestine discord. When the pious Gontran reproached the guilt or neglect of their leaders, and threatened to inflict, not a legal sentence, but instant and arbitrary execution, they accused the universal and incurable corruption of the people. " No one, " they said, " any longer fears or respects his king, his duke, or his count. Each man loves to do evil, and freely indulges his criminal inclinations. The most gentle correction provokes an immediate tumult, and the rash magistrate who presumes to censure or restrain his seditious subjects seldom escapes alive from their revenge." [122] It has been reserved for the same nation to expose, by their intemperate vices, the most odious abuse of freedom, and to supply its loss by the spirit of honour and humanity which now alleviates and dignifies their obedience to an absolute sovereign.

The Visigoths had resigned to Clovis the greatest part of their Gallic possessions; but their loss was amply compensated by the easy conquest and secure enjoyment of the provinces of Spain. From the monarchy of the Goths, which soon involved the Suevic kingdom of Gallicia, the modern Spaniards still derive some national vanity, but the historian of the Roman empire is neither invited nor compelled to pursue the obscure and barren series of their annals.[123] The Goths of Spain were separated from the rest of mankind by the lofty ridge of the Pyrenæan mountains: their manners and institutions, as far as they were common to the Germanic tribes, have been already explained. I have anticipated in the preceding chapter the most important of their ecclesiastical events—the fall of Arianism and the persecution of the Jews: and it only remains to observe some interesting circumstances which relate to the civil and ecclesiastical constitution of the Spanish kingdom.

After their conversion from idolatry or heresy, the Franks and the Visigoths were disposed to embrace, with equal submission, the inherent evils and the accidental benefits of superstition. But the prelates of France, long before the extinction of the Merovingian race, had degenerated into fighting and hunting barbarians. They disdained the use of synods, forgot the laws of temperance and chastity, and preferred the indulgence of private ambition and luxury to the general interest of the sacerdotal profession.[124] The bishops of Spain respected themselves,

[122] Gregory of Tours (l. viii. c. 30, in tom. ii. p. 325-326) relates, with much indifference, the crimes, the reproof, and the apology. Nullus Regem metuit, nullus Ducem, nullus Comitem reveretur; et si fortassis alicui ista displicent, et ea, pro longævitate vitæ vestræ, emendare conatur, statim seditio in populo, statim tumultus exoritur, et in tantum unusquisque contra seniorem, sævâ intentione grassatur, ut vix se credat evadere, si tandem silere nequiverit.

[123] Spain in these dark ages has been peculiarly unfortunate. The Franks had a Gregory of Tours; the Saxons, or Angles, a Bede; the Lombards, a Paul Warnefrid, etc. But the history of the Visigoths is contained in the short and imperfect Chronicles of Isidore of Seville and John of Biclar.

[124] Such are the complaints of St. Boniface, the apostle of Germany and the reformer of Gaul (in tom. iv. p. 94). The fourscore years which he deplores of licence and corruption would seem to insinuate that the barbarians were admitted into the clergy about the year 660.

and were respected by the public: their indissoluble union disguised
their vices, and confirmed their authority; and the regular discipline of
the church introduced peace, order, and stability into the government
of the state. From the reign of Recared, the first catholic king, to that
of Witiza, the immediate predecessor of the unfortunate Roderic, sixteen
national councils were successively convened. The six metropolitans,
Toledo, Seville, Merida, Braga, Tarragona, and Narbonne, presided
according to their respective seniority; the assembly was composed of
their suffragan bishops, who appeared in person or by their proxies, and
a place was assigned to the most holy or opulent of the Spanish abbots.
During the first three days of the convocation, as long as they agitated
the ecclesiastical questions of doctrine and discipline, the profane laity
was excluded from their debates, which were conducted, however, with
decent solemnity. But on the morning of the fourth day the doors were
thrown open for the entrance of the great officers of the palace, the dukes
and counts of the provinces, the judges of the cities, and the Gothic
nobles; and the decrees of Heaven were ratified by the consent of the
people. The same rules were observed in the provincial assemblies, the
annual synods, which were empowered to hear complaints and to redress
grievances; and a legal government was supported by the prevailing influence of the Spanish clergy. The bishops, who in each revolution were
prepared to flatter the victorious and to insult the prostrate, laboured
with diligence and success to kindle the flames of persecution, and to exalt
the mitre above the crown. Yet the national councils of Toledo, in which
the free spirit of the barbarians was tempered and guided by episcopal
policy, have established some prudent laws for the common benefit of
the king and people. The vacancy of the throne was supplied by the
choice of the bishops and palatines; and after the failure of the line of
Alaric, the regal dignity was still limited to the pure and noble blood of
the Goths. The clergy, who anointed their lawful prince, always
recommended, and sometimes practised, the duty of allegiance: and the
spiritual censures were denounced on the heads of the impious subjects
who should resist his authority, conspire against his life, or violate by an
indecent union the chastity even of his widow. But the monarch himself,
when he ascended the throne, was bound by a reciprocal oath to God
and his people that he would faithfully execute his important trust. The
real or imaginary faults of his administration were subject to the control
of a powerful aristocracy; and the bishops and palatines were guarded by
a fundamental privilege that they should not be degraded, imprisoned,
tortured, nor punished with death, exile, or confiscation, unless by the
free and public judgment of their peers.[125]

[125] The acts of the councils of Toledo are still the most authentic records of
the church and constitution of Spain. The following passages are particularly
important:—iii. 17, 18; iv. 75; v. 2, 3, 4, 5, 8; vi. 11, 12, 13, 14, 17, 18; vii. 1; xiii.
2, 3, 6. I have found Mascou (Hist. of the Ancient Germans, xv. 29, and
Annotations, xxvi. and xxxiii.) and Ferreras (Hist. Générale de l'Espagne,
tom. ii.) very useful and accurate guides.

One of these legislative councils of Toledo examined and ratified the code of laws which had been compiled by a succession of Gothic kings, from the fierce Euric to the devout Egica. As long as the Visigoths themselves were satisfied with the rude customs of their ancestors, they indulged their subjects of Aquitain and Spain in the enjoyment of the Roman law. Their gradual improvement in arts, in policy, and at length in religion, encouraged them to imitate and to supersede these foreign institutions, and to compose a code of civil and criminal jurisprudence for the use of a great and united people. The same obligations and the same privileges were communicated to the nations of the Spanish monarchy; and the conquerors, insensibly renouncing the Teutonic idiom, submitted to the restraints of equity, and exalted the Romans to the participation of freedom. The merit of this impartial policy was enhanced by the situation of Spain under the reign of the Visigoths. The provincials were long separated from their Arian masters by the irreconcilable difference of religion. After the conversion of Recared had removed the prejudices of the catholics, the coasts both of the Ocean and Mediterranean were still possessed by the Eastern emperors, who secretly excited a discontented people to reject the yoke of the barbarians, and to assert the name and dignity of Roman citizens. The allegiance of doubtful subjects is indeed most effectually secured by their own persuasion that they hazard more in a revolt than they can hope to obtain by a revolution; but it has appeared so natural to oppress those whom we hate and fear, that the contrary system well deserves the praise of wisdom and moderation.[126]

While the kingdoms of the Franks and Visigoths were established in Gaul and Spain, the Saxons achieved the conquest of Britain, the third great diocese of the præfecture of the West. Since Britain was already separated from the Roman empire, I might without reproach decline a story familiar to the most illiterate, and obscure to the most learned, of my readers. The Saxons, who excelled in the use of the oar or the battle-axe, were ignorant of the art which could alone perpetuate the fame of their exploits; the provincials, relapsing into barbarism, neglected to describe the ruin of their country; and the doubtful tradition was almost extinguished before the missionaries of Rome restored the light of science and Christianity. The declamations of Gildas, the fragments or fables of Nennius, the obscure hints of the Saxon laws and chronicles, and the ecclesiastical tales of the venerable Bede,[127] have been illustrated

---

[126] The Code of the Visigoths, regularly divided into twelve books, has been correctly published by Dom Bouquet (in tom. iv. p. 283-460). It has been treated by the President De Montesquieu (Esprit des Loix, l. xxviii. c. 1) with excessive severity. I dislike the style; I detest the superstition; but I shall presume to think that the civil jurisprudence displays a more civilised and enlightened state of society than that of the Burgundians or even of the Lombards.

[127] See Gildas de Excidio Britanniæ, c. 11-25, p. 4-9, edit. Gale; Nennius, Hist. Britonum, c. 28, 35-65, p. 105-115, edit. Gale; Bede, Hist. Ecclesiast.

by the diligence, and sometimes embellished by the fancy, of succeeding writers, whose works I am not ambitious either to censure or to transcribe.[128] Yet the historian of the empire may be tempted to pursue the revolutions of a Roman province till it vanishes from his sight; and an Englishman may curiously trace the establishment of the barbarians from whom he derives his name, his laws, and perhaps his origin.

About forty years after the dissolution of the Roman government Vortigern appears to have obtained the supreme, though precarious, command of the princes and cities of Britain. That unfortunate monarch has been almost unanimously condemned for the weak and mischievous policy of inviting [129] a formidable stranger to repel the vexatious inroads of a domestic foe. His ambassadors are despatched by the gravest historians to the coast of Germany: they address a pathetic oration to the general assembly of the Saxons, and those warlike barbarians resolve to assist with a fleet and army the suppliants of a distant and unknown island. If Britain had indeed been unknown to the Saxons, the measure of its calamities would have been less complete. But the strength of the Roman government could not always guard the maritime province against the pirates of Germany: the independent and divided states were exposed to their attacks, and the Saxons might sometimes join the Scots and the Picts in a tacit or express confederacy of rapine and destruction. Vortigern could only balance the various perils which assaulted on every side his throne and his people; and his policy may deserve either praise or excuse if he preferred the alliance of *those* barbarians whose naval power rendered them the most dangerous enemies, and the most serviceable allies. Hengist and Horsa, as they ranged along the eastern coast with three ships, were engaged by the promise of an ample stipend to embrace the defence of Britain, and their intrepid valour soon delivered the country from the Caledonian invaders. The Isle of Thanet, a secure and fertile district, was allotted for the residence of these German auxiliaries, and they were supplied according to the treaty with a plentiful allowance of clothing and provisions. This favourable reception encouraged five thousand warriors to embark with their families in

Gentis Anglorum, l. i. c. 12-16, p. 49-53, c. 22, p. 58, edit. Smith; Chron. Saxonicum, p. 11-23, etc., edit. Gibson. The Anglo-Saxon laws were published by Wilkins, London, 1731, in folio; and the Leges Wallicæ, by Wotton and Clarke, London, 1730, in folio.

[128] The laborious Mr. Carte and the ingenious Mr. Whitaker are the two modern writers to whom I am principally indebted. The particular historian of Manchester embraces, under that obscure title, a subject almost as extensive as the general history of England.

[129] This *invitation,* which may derive some countenance from the loose expressions of Gildas and Bede, is framed into a regular story by Witikind, a Saxon monk of the tenth century (see Cousin, Hist. de l'Empire d'Occident, tom. ii. p. 356). Rapin, and even Hume, have too freely used this suspicious evidence without regarding the precise and probable testimony of Nennius: Interea venerunt tres Chiulæ à Germaniâ *in exilio pulsæ,* in quibus erant Hors et Hengist [c. 28].

seventeen vessels, and the infant power of Hengist was fortified by this strong and seasonable reinforcement. The crafty barbarian suggested to Vortigern the obvious advantage of fixing, in the neighbourhood of the Picts, a colony of faithful allies: a third fleet, of forty ships, under the command of his son and nephew, sailed from Germany, ravaged the Orkneys, and disembarked a new army on the coast of Northumberland or Lothian, at the opposite extremity of the devoted land. It was easy to foresee, but it was impossible to prevent, the impending evils. The two nations were soon divided and exasperated by mutual jealousies. The Saxons magnified all that they had done and suffered in the cause of an ungrateful people; while the Britons regretted the liberal rewards which could not satisfy the avarice of those haughty mercenaries. The causes of fear and hatred were inflamed into an irreconcilable quarrel. The Saxons flew to arms; and if they perpetrated a treacherous massacre during the security of a feast, they destroyed the reciprocal confidence which sustains the intercourse of peace and war.[130]

Hengist, who boldly aspired to the conquest of Britain, exhorted his countrymen to embrace the glorious opportunity: he painted in lively colours the fertility of the soil, the wealth of the cities, the pusillanimous temper of the natives, and the convenient situation of a spacious solitary island, accessible on all sides to the Saxon fleets. The successive colonies which issued in the period of a century from the mouths of the Elbe, the

[130] Nennius imputes to the Saxons the murder of three hundred British chiefs; a crime not unsuitable to their savage manners. But we are not obliged to believe (see Jeffrey of Monmouth, l. viii. c. 9-12) that Stonehenge is their monument, which the giants had formerly transported from Africa to Ireland, and which was removed to Britain by the order of Ambrosius and the art of Merlin.

[Macaulay remarks that "Hengist and Horsa, Vortigern and Rowena, Arthur and Mordred, are mythical persons whose very existence may be questioned, and whose adventures may be classed with those of Hercules and Romulus." *History of England,* vol. i. p. 6.

The details of the Saxon conquest are very obscure, there being no reliable account by any contemporary writer, and rest wholly on tradition. Yet, as Freeman well says, there is no absurdity in the familiar story that a British prince took Teutonic mercenaries into his pay, and that these dangerous allies took advantage of the weakness of their hosts to establish themselves as permanent possessors of part of the island. If the story in question be rejected, the general narrative of the conquest is not affected. The conquest of England by the Saxons began somewhere about 449 A.D., but it is a mistake to set a hard and fast date, for there is evidence that there were Saxons in England before that date, because in the Notitia Imperii, which was drawn up about A.D. 400, there is mentioned as an officer of state "Comes littoris Saxonici per Britannias," whose government extended along the coast from the neighbourhood of Portsmouth to the Wash. The Saxons ravaged the coast of Britain in their piratical expeditions as early as A.D. 287, and it may reasonably be supposed that not long after that date they began to form isolated settlements in the island. "The count of the Saxon shore" may either have taken his name from the shore exposed to the attacks of Saxon pirates, or from the shore peopled by Saxon colonists. Cf. Kemble, *The Saxons in England;* Freeman, *Norman Conquest;* Stubbs, *Constitutional History of England;* also Plummer's edition of Bede.—O. S.]

Weser, and the Rhine, were principally composed of three valiant tribes or nations of Germany; the *Jutes*, the *old Saxons*, and the *Angles*. The Jutes, who fought under the peculiar banner of Hengist, assumed the merit of leading their countrymen in the paths of glory, and of erecting in Kent the first independent kingdom. The fame of the enterprise was attributed to the primitive Saxons, and the common laws and language of the conquerors are described by the national appellation of a people which, at the end of four hundred years, produced the first monarchs of South Britain. The Angles were distinguished by their numbers and their success; and they claimed the honour of fixing a perpetual name on the country of which they occupied the most ample portion. The barbarians, who followed the hopes of rapine either on the land or sea, were insensibly blended with this triple confederacy; the *Frisians*, who had been tempted by their vicinity to the British shores, might balance during a short space the strength and reputation of the native Saxons; the *Danes*, the *Prussians*, the *Rugians*, are faintly described; and some adventurous *Huns*, who had wandered as far as the Baltic, might embark on board the German vessels for the conquest of a new world.[131] But this arduous achievement was not prepared or executed by the union of national powers. Each intrepid chieftain, according to the measure of his fame and fortunes, assembled his followers; equipped a fleet of three, or perhaps of sixty, vessels; chose the place of the attack, and conducted his subsequent operations according to the events of the war and the dictates of his private interest. In the invasion of Britain many heroes vanquished and fell; but only seven victorious leaders assumed, or at least maintained, the title of kings. Seven independent thrones, the Saxon Heptarchy, were founded by the conquerors; and seven families, one of which has been continued, by female succession, to our present sovereign, derived their equal and sacred lineage from Woden, the god of war. It has been pretended that this republic of kings was moderated by a general council and a supreme magistrate. But such an artificial scheme of policy is repugnant to the rude and turbulent spirit of the Saxons: their laws are silent, and their imperfect annals afford only a dark and bloody prospect of intestine discord.[132]

[131] All these tribes are expressly enumerated by Bede (l. i. c. 15, p. 52, l. v. c. 9, p. 190) ; and though I have considered Mr. Whitaker's remarks (Hist. of Manchester, vol. ii. p. 538-543), I do not perceive the absurdity of supposing that the Frisians, etc., were mingled with the Anglo-Saxons.

[132] Bede has enumerated seven kings—two Saxons, a Jute, and four Angles—who successively acquired in the heptarchy an indefinite supremacy of power and renown. But their reign was the effect, not of law, but of conquest; and he observes. in similar terms, that one of them subdued the Isles of Man and Anglesey; and that another imposed a tribute on the Scots and Picts (Hist. Eccles. l. ii. c. 5, p. 83).

[The term Heptarchy no longer has any significance in fact, and must be rejected as conveying an idea radically erroneous. At no period were there ever in Saxon England seven kingdoms independent of each other. Mr. Sharon Turner was the first to confute the old-established doctrine that Saxon England was heptarchical in character.—O. S.]

A monk, who in the profound ignorance of human life has presumed to exercise the office of historian, strangely disfigures the state of Britain at the time of its separation from the Western empire. Gildas [133] describes in florid language the improvements of agriculture, the foreign trade which flowed with every tide into the Thames and the Severn, the solid and lofty construction of public and private edifices: he accuses the sinful luxury of the British people; of a people, according to the same writer, ignorant of the most simple arts, and incapable, without the aid of the Romans, of providing walls of stone or weapons of iron for the defence of their native land.[134] Under the long dominion of the emperors, Britain had been insensibly moulded into the elegant and servile form of a Roman province, whose safety was intrusted to a foreign power. The subjects of Honorius contemplated their new freedom with surprise and terror; they were left destitute of any civil or military constitution; and their uncertain rulers wanted either skill, or courage, or authority to direct the public force against the common enemy. The introduction of the Saxons betrayed their internal weakness, and degraded the character both of the prince and people. Their consternation magnified the danger, the want of union diminished their resources, and the madness of civil factions was more solicitous to accuse than to remedy the evils which they imputed to the misconduct of their adversaries. Yet the Britons were not ignorant, they could not be ignorant, of the manufacture or the use of arms: the successive and disorderly attacks of the Saxons allowed them to recover from their amazement, and the prosperous or adverse events of the war added discipline and experience to their native valour.

While the continent of Europe and Africa yielded, without resistance, to the barbarians, the British island, alone and unaided, maintained a long, vigorous, though an unsuccessful, struggle, against the formidable pirates who, almost at the same instant, assaulted the northern, the eastern, and the southern coasts. The cities, which had been fortified with skill, were defended with resolution; the advantages of ground, hills, forests, and morasses, were diligently improved by the inhabitants; the conquest of each district was purchased with blood; and the defeats of the Saxons are strongly attested by the discreet silence of their annalist. Hengist might hope to achieve the conquest of Britain; but his ambition, in an active reign of thirty-five years, was confined to the possession of Kent; and the numerous colony which he had planted in the North was extirpated by the sword of the Britons. The monarchy of the West Saxons was laboriously founded by the persevering efforts of three martial generations. The life of Cerdic, one of the bravest of the children of Woden, was consumed in the conquest of Hampshire and the

[133] See Gildas de Excidio Britanniæ, c. i. p. 1, edit. Gale.
[134] Mr. Whitaker (History of Manchester, vol. ii. p. 503, 516) has smartly exposed this glaring absurdity, which had passed unnoticed by the general historians, as they were hastening to more interesting and important events.

Isle of Wight; and the loss which he sustained in the battle of Mount Badon reduced him to a state of inglorious repose. Kenric, his valiant son, advanced into Wiltshire; besieged Salisbury, at that time seated on a commanding eminence; and vanquished an army which advanced to the relief of the city. In the subsequent battle of Marlborough,[135] his British enemies displayed their military science. Their troops were formed in three lines; each line consisted of three distinct bodies; and the cavalry, the archers, and the pikemen were distributed according to the principles of Roman tactics. The Saxons charged in one weighty column, boldly encountered with their short swords the long lances of the Britons, and maintained an equal conflict till the approach of night. Two decisive victories, the death of three British kings, and the reduction of Ciren- cester, Bath, and Gloucester, established the fame and power of Ceaulin, the grandson of Cerdic, who carried his victorious arms to the banks of the Severn.

After a war of an hundred years the independent Britons still occupied the whole extent of the western coast, from the wall of Antoninus to the extreme promontory of Cornwall; and the principal cities of the inland country still opposed the arms of the barbarians. Resistance became more languid, as the number and boldness of the assailants continually increased. Winning their way by slow and painful efforts, the Saxons, the Angles, and their various confederates, advanced from the North, from the East, and from the South, till their victorious banners were united in the centre of the island. Beyond the Severn the Britons still asserted their national freedom, which survived the heptarchy, and even the monarchy, of the Saxons. The bravest warriors, who preferred exile to slavery, found a secure refuge in the mountains of Wales: the re- luctant submission of Cornwall was delayed for some ages;[136] and a band of fugitives acquired a settlement in Gaul, by their own valour, or the liberality of the Merovingian kings.[137] The western angle of Armorica

---

[135] At Beran-birig, or Barbury-castle, near Marlborough. The Saxon Chronicle assigns the name and date. Camden (Britannia, vol. i. p. 128) ascertains the place; and Henry of Huntingdon (Scriptores post Bedam, p. 314) relates the circumstances of this battle. They are probable and charac- teristic; and the historians of the twelfth century might consult some materials that no longer exist.

[136] Cornwall was finally subdued by Athelstan (A.D. 927-941), who planted an English colony at Exeter, and confined the Britons beyond the river Tamar. See William of Malmesbury, l. ii. in the Scriptores post Bedam, p. 50. The spirit of the Cornish knights was degraded by servitude: and it should seem, from the romance of Sir Tristram, that their cowardice was almost proverbial.

[137] The establishment of the Britons in Gaul is proved in the sixth century by Procopius [Bell. Goth. iv. 20], Gregory of Tours, the second council of Tours (A.D. 567), and the least suspicious of their chronicles and lives of saints. The subscription of a bishop of the Britons to the first council of Tours (A.D. 461, or rather 481), the army of Riothamus, and the loose declama- tion of Gildas (alii transmarinas petebant regiones, c. 25, p. 8), may counte- nance an emigration as early as the middle of the fifth century. Beyond that era the Britons of Armorica can be found only in romance; and I am sur-

acquired the new appellations of *Cornwall* and the *Lesser Britain;* and the vacant lands of the Osismii were filled by a strange people, who, under the authority of their counts and bishops, preserved the laws and language of their ancestors.   To the feeble descendants of Clovis and Charlemagne, the Britons of Armorica refused the customary tribute, subdued the neighbouring dioceses of Vannes, Rennes, and Nantes, and formed a powerful, though vassal, state, which has been united to the crown of France.[138]

In a century of perpetual, or at least implacable, war, much courage, and some skill, must have been exerted for the defence of Britain. Yet if the memory of its champions is almost buried in oblivion, we need not repine; since every age, however destitute of science or virtue, sufficiently abounds with acts of blood and military renown. The tomb of Vortimer, the son of Vortigern, was erected on the margin of the sea-shore, as a landmark formidable to the Saxons, whom he had thrice vanquished in the fields of Kent. Ambrosius Aurelian was descended from a noble family of Romans;[139] his modesty was equal to his valour, and his valour, till the last fatal action,[140] was crowned with splendid success.

prised that Mr. Whitaker (Genuine History of the Britons, p. 214-221) should so faithfully transcribe the gross ignorance of Carte, whose venial errors he has so rigorously chastised.

[Lappenberg asserts that as early as the usurpation of Maximus in Britain, there was a settlement in Armorica of a Roman military colony (*milites limitanei*), consisting of British warriors, which has given name as well as a distinctive character to Bretagne. See accounts in Gildas, c. 10; Nennius, c. 23. Bæda also gives the words of Gildas.—O. S.]

[138] The antiquities of *Bretagne*, which have been the subject even of political controversy, are illustrated by Hadrian Valesius (Notitia Galliarum, sub voce *Britannia Cismarina*, p. 98-100), M. d'Anville (Notice de l'Ancienne Gaule, *Corisopiti, Curiosolites, Osismii, Vorganium,* p. 248, 258, 508, 720, and Etats de l'Europe, p. 76-80), Longuerue (Description de la France, tom. i. p. 84-94), and the Abbé de Vertot (Hist. Critique de l'Etablissement des Bretons dans les Gaules, 2 vols. in 12mo. Paris 1720). I may assume the merit of examining the original evidence which they have produced.

[Bretagne unquestionably had an existence of its own much earlier than is commonly supposed. Milman says that after careful study of Gallet (*Mémoires sur la Bretagne*) and Daru (*Histoire de Bretagne*), these writers appear to him to establish the point of the independence of Bretagne at the time that the insular Britons took refuge in their country, and that the greater part landed as fugitives rather than conquerors.—O. S.]

[139] Bede, who in his chronicle (p. 28) places Ambrosius under the reign of Zeno (A.D. 474-491), observes that his parents had been "purpurâ induti;" which he explains, in his ecclesiastical history, by "regium nomen et insigne ferentibus" (l. i. c. 16, p. 53). The expression of Nennius (c. 44, p. 110, edit. Gale) is still more singular, "Unus de *consulibus* gentis Romanicæ est pater meus."

[140] By the unanimous, though doubtful, conjecture of our antiquarians, Ambrosius is confounded with Natanleod, who (A.D. 508) lost his own life and five thousand of his subjects in a battle against Cerdic, the West Saxon (Chron. Saxon. p. 17, 18).

But every British name is effaced by the illustrious name of ARTHUR,[141] the hereditary prince of the Silures, in South Wales, and the elective king or general of the nation. According to the most rational account, he defeated, in twelve successive battles, the Angles of the North and the Saxons of the West; but the declining age of the hero was embittered by popular ingratitude and domestic misfortunes. The events of his life are less interesting than the singular revolutions of his fame. During a period of five hundred years the tradition of his exploits was preserved, and rudely embellished, by the obscure bards of Wales and Armorica, who were odious to the Saxons, and unknown to the rest of mankind. The pride and curiosity of the Norman conquerors prompted them to inquire into the ancient history of Britain; they listened with fond credulity to the tale of Arthur, and eagerly applauded the merit of a prince who had triumphed over the Saxons, their common enemies. His romance, transcribed in the Latin of Jeffrey of Monmouth, and afterwards translated into the fashionable idiom of the times, was enriched with the various, though incoherent, ornaments which were familiar to the experience, the learning, or the fancy of the twelfth century. The progress of a Phrygian colony, from the Tiber to the Thames, was easily engrafted on the fable of the Æneid; and the royal ancestors of Arthur derived their origin from Troy, and claimed their alliance with the Cæsars. His trophies were decorated with captive provinces and Imperial titles; and his Danish victories avenged the recent injuries of his country. The gallantry and superstition of the British hero, his feasts and tournaments, and the memorable institution of his Knights of the *Round Table,* were faithfully copied from the reigning manners of chivalry; and the fabulous exploits of Uther's son appear less incredible than the adventures which were achieved by the enterprising valour of the Normans. Pilgrimage, and the holy wars, introduced into Europe the specious miracles of Arabian magic. Fairies and giants, flying dragons and enchanted palaces, were blended with the more simple fictions of the West; and the fate of Britain depended on the art, or the predictions, or Merlin. Every nation embraced and adorned the popular romance of Arthur and the Knights of the Round Table: their names were celebrated in Greece [142] and Italy; and the voluminous

[141] As I am a stranger to the Welsh bards, Myrdhin, Llomarch, and Taliessin, my faith in the existence and exploits of Arthur principally rests on the simple and circumstantial testimony of Nennius (Hist. Brit. c. 62, 63, p. 114). Mr. Whitaker (Hist. of Manchester, vol. ii. p. 31-71) has framed an interesting, and even probable, narrative of the wars of Arthur: though it is impossible to allow the reality of the round table.

[Gibbon quotes these names incorrectly. Myrdhin, Llomarch, and Taliessin are probably meant for Merlin, Llywarch Hen, or " The Aged," and Taliessin. See Sharon Turner's Essay on the Welsh Bards.—O. S.]

[142] [With reference to the Arthurian cycle of romance, as early as the twelfth century, a Greek epic poem, brought to light in the middle of the nineteenth century, was composed in celebration of Arthur and the Knights of the Round Table. It was first published by Von der Hagen in his *Denkmale des Mittelalters,* Berlin, 1824. It should be carefully studied.—O. S.]

tales of Sir Lancelot and Sir Tristram [143] were devoutly studied by the princes and nobles who disregarded the genuine heroes and historians of antiquity. At length the light of science and reason was rekindled; the talisman was broken; the visionary fabric melted into air; and by a natural, though unjust, reverse of the public opinion, the severity of the present age is inclined to question the *existence* of Arthur.[144]

Resistance, if it cannot avert, must increase the miseries of conquest; and conquest has never appeared more dreadful and destructive than in the hands of the Saxons, who hated the valour of their enemies, disdained the faith of treaties, and violated, without remorse, the most sacred objects of the Christian worship. The fields of battle might be traced, almost in every district, by monuments of bones; the fragments of falling towers were stained with blood; the last of the Britons, without distinction of age or sex, was massacred,[145] in the ruins of Anderida;[146] and the repetition of such calamities was frequent and familiar under the Saxon heptarchy. The arts and religion, the laws and language, which the Romans had so carefully planted in Britain, were extirpated by their barbarous successors. After the destruction of the principal churches, the bishops who had declined the crown of martyrdom retired with the holy relics into Wales and Armorica; the remains of their flocks were left destitute of any spiritual food; the practice, and even the remembrance, of Christianity were abolished; and the British clergy might obtain some comfort from the damnation of the idolatrous strangers. The kings of France maintained the privileges of their Roman subjects; but the ferocious Saxons trampled on the laws of Rome and of the emperors. The proceedings of civil and

[143] [Regarding the poems, " Tristram " and " Lancelot du Laik," the former may be said to have been brought to modern knowledge by Sir Walter Scott, whose edition, if now somewhat obsolete, is still full of interesting antiquarian information. " Lancelot " has been immortalised by Tennyson in his " Idylls of the King," but the orignal poem was edited in 1865 by Dr. W. W. Skeat for the Early English Text Society, and is entitled " Lancelot of the Laik," a Scottish metrical romance about 1490-1500, re-edited from a MS. in Cambridge University Library. A former edition has been edited by Mr. Joseph Stevenson in 1839 for the Maitland Club, but was full of errors, consequent upon the state of etymological and philological scholarship at the time. These two poems were the great metrical romances of the Middle Ages.—O. S.]

[144] The progress of romance and the state of learning in the middle ages are illustrated by Mr. Thomas Warton, with the taste of a poet and the minute diligence of an antiquarian. I have derived much instruction from the two learned dissertations prefixed to the first volume of his History of English Poetry.

[145] Hoc anno (490) Ælla et Cissa obsederunt Andredes-Ceaster; et interfecerunt omnes qui id incolerent; adeo ut ne unus Brito ibi superstes fuerit (Chron. Saxon. p. 15) ; an expression more dreadful in its simplicity than all the vague and tedious lamentations of the British Jeremiah.

[146] Andredes-Ceaster, or Anderida, is placed by Camden (Britannia, vol. i. p. 258) at Newenden, in the marshy grounds of Kent, which might be formerly covered by the sea, and on the edge of the great forest (Anderida) which overspread so large a portion of Hampshire and Sussex.

criminal jurisdiction, the titles of honour, the forms of office, the ranks of society, and even the domestic rights of marriage, testament, and inheritance, were finally suppressed; and the indiscriminate crowd of noble and plebeian slaves was governed by the traditionary customs which had been coarsely framed for the shepherds and pirates of Germany. The language of science, of business, and of conversation, which had been introduced by the Romans, was lost in the general desolation. A sufficient number of Latin or Celtic words might be assumed by the Germans to express their new wants and ideas;[147] but those *illiterate* Pagans preserved and established the use of their national dialect.[148] Almost every name, conspicuous either in the church or state, reveals its Teutonic origin;[149] and the geography of *England* was universally inscribed with foreign characters and appellations. The example of a revolution so rapid and so complete may not easily be found; but it will excite a probable suspicion that the arts of Rome were less deeply rooted in Britain than in Gaul or Spain; and that the native rudeness of the country and its inhabitants was covered by a thin varnish of Italian manners.

This strange alteration has persuaded historians, and even philosophers, that the provincials of Britain were totally exterminated; and that the vacant land was again peopled by the perpetual influx and rapid increase of the German colonies. Three hundred thousand Saxons are *said* to have obeyed the summons of Hengist;[150] the entire emigration of the Angles was attested, in the age of Bede, by the solitude of their native country;[151] and our experience has shown the free

[147] Dr. Johnson affirms that *few* English words are of British extraction. Mr. Whitaker, who understands the British language, has discovered more than *three thousand,* and actually produces a long and various catalogue (vol. ii. p. 235-329). It is possible, indeed, that many of these words may have been imported from the Latin or Saxon into the native idiom of Britain.

[Since Gibbon's time the science of Philology has been completely revolutionised, and the Keltic family of languages has now taken its place as one of branches of the great Indo-European group. It is now clear that the Anglo-Saxons adopted Keltic words to a far greater extent than was supposed. Many words denoting the daily processes of agriculture, domestic life, and generally those expressive of indoor and outdoor service, have been taken by us from the Keltic. Cf. Garnett, *Transactions Philological Society,* vol. i. p. 169; also *First Steps in English Accidence,* by Morris and Skeat.—O. S.]

[148] In the beginning of the seventh century the Franks and the Anglo-Saxons mutually understood each other's language, which was derived from the same Teutonic root (Bede. l. i. c. 25, p. 60).

[149] After the first generation of Italian or Scottish missionaries, the dignities of the church were filled with Saxon proselytes.

[150] Carte's History of England, vol. i. p. 195. He quotes the British historians; but I much fear that Jeffrey of Monmouth (l. vi. c. 15) is his only witness.

[151] Bede, Hist. Ecclesiast. l. i. c. 15, p. 52. The fact is probable and well attested: yet such was the loose intermixture of the German tribes, that we find, in a subsequent period, the law of the Angli and Warini of Germany (Lindenbrog. Codex, p. 479-486).

propagation of the human race, if they are cast on a fruitful wilderness, where their steps are unconfined, and their subsistence is plentiful. The Saxon kingdoms displayed the face of recent discovery and cultivation: the towns were small, the villages were distant; the husbandry was languid and unskilful; four sheep were equivalent to an acre of the best land;[152] an ample space of wood and morass was resigned to the vague dominion of nature; and the modern bishopric of Durham, the whole territory from the Tyne to the Tees, had returned to its primitive state of a savage and solitary forest.[153] Such imperfect population might have been supplied, in some generations, by the English colonies; but neither reason nor facts can justify the unnatural supposition that the Saxons of Britain remained alone in the desert which they had subdued. After the sanguinary barbarians had secured their dominion and gratified their revenge, it was their interest to preserve the peasants, as well as the cattle, of the unresisting country. In each successive revolution the patient herd becomes the property of its new masters; and the salutary compact of food and labour is silently ratified by their mutual necessities. Wilfrid, the apostle of Sussex,[154] accepted from his royal convert the gift of the peninsula of Selsey, near Chichester, with the persons and property of its inhabitants, who then amounted to eighty-seven families. He released them at once from spiritual and temporal bondage; and two hundred and fifty slaves of both sexes were baptised by their indulgent master. The kingdom of Sussex, which spread from the sea to the Thames, contained seven thousand families: twelve hundred were ascribed to the Isle of Wight; and, if we multiply this vague computation, it may seem probable that England was cultivated by a million of servants, or *villains*, who were attached to the estates of their arbitrary landlords. The indigent barbarians were often tempted to sell their children or themselves into perpetual, and even foreign, bondage;[155] yet the special exemptions which were granted to *national* slaves[156] sufficiently declare that they were much less numerous than the strangers and captives who had lost their liberty, or

[152] See Dr. Henry's useful and laborious History of Great Britain, vol. ii. p. 388.

[153] Quicquid (says John of Tinemouth) inter Tynam et Tesam fluvios extitit, sola eremi vastitudo tunc temporis fuit, et idcirco nullius ditioni servivit, eo quod sola indomitorum et silvestrium animalium spelunca et habitatio fuit (apud Carte, vol. i. p. 195). From Bishop Nicholson (English Historical Library, p. 65, 98) I understand that fair copies of John of Tinemouth's ample collections are preserved in the libraries of Oxford, Lambeth, etc.

[154] See the mission of Wilfrid, etc., in Bede, Hist. Eccles. l. iv. c. 13, 16, p. 155, 156, 159.

[155] From the concurrent testimony of Bede (l. ii. c. 1, p. 78) and William of Malmesbury (l. iii. p. 102), it appears that the Anglo-Saxons, from the first to the last age, persisted in this unnatural practice. Their youths were publicly sold in the market of Rome.

[156] According to the laws of Ina they could not be lawfully sold beyond the seas.

changed their masters, by the accidents of war. When time and religion had mitigated the fierce spirit of the Anglo-Saxons, the laws encouraged the frequent practice of manumission; and their subjects, of
Welsh or Cambrian extraction, assumed the respectable station of inferior freemen, possessed of lands, and entitled to the rights of civil
society.[157] Such gentle treatment might secure the allegiance of a fierce
people, who had been recently subdued on the confines of Wales and
Cornwall. The sage Ina, the legislator of Wessex, united the two nations in the bands of domestic alliance; and four British lords of
Somersetshire may be honourably distinguished in the court of a Saxon
monarch.[158]

The independent Britons appear to have relapsed into the state of
original barbarism from whence they had been imperfectly reclaimed.
Separated by their enemies from the rest of mankind, they soon became
an object of scandal and abhorrence to the catholic world.[159] Christianity was still professed in the mountains of Wales; but the rude
schismatics, in the *form* of the clerical tonsure, and in the *day* of the
celebration of Easter, obstinately resisted the imperious mandates of
the Roman pontiffs. The use of the Latin language was insensibly
abolished, and the Britons were deprived of the arts and learning which
Italy communicated to her Saxon proselytes. In Wales and Armorica,
the Celtic tongue, the native idiom of the West, was preserved and
propagated; and the *Bards*, who had been the companions of the Druids,
were still protected, in the sixteenth century, by the laws of Elizabeth.
Their chief, a respectable officer of the courts of Pengwern, or Aber-
fraw, or Caermarthen, accompanied the king's servants to war: the
monarchy of the Britons, which he sung in the front of battle, excited
their courage, and justified their depredations; and the songster claimed
for his legitimate prize the fairest heifer of the spoil. His subordinate
ministers, the masters and disciples of vocal and instrumental music,
visited, in their respective circuits, the royal, the noble, and the plebeian
houses; and the public poverty, almost exhausted by the clergy, was
oppressed by the importunate demands of the bards. Their rank and
merit were ascertained by solemn trials, and the strong belief of super-

---

[157] The life of a *Wallus*, or *Cambricus, homo,* who possessed a hyde of land,
is fixed at 120 shillings, by the same laws (of Ina, tit. xxxii. in Leg. Anglo-
Saxon. p. 20) which allowed 200 shillings for a free Saxon, and 1200 for a
Thane (see likewise Leg. Anglo-Saxon. p. 71). We may observe that these
legislators, the West-Saxons and Mercians, continued their British conquests
after they became Christians. The laws of the four kings of Kent do not
condescend to notice the existence of any subject Britons.

[158] See Carte's Hist. of England, vol. i. p. 278.

[159] At the conclusion of his history (A.D. 731), Bede describes the ecclesiastical state of the island, and censures the implacable, though impotent, hatred
of the Britons against the English nation and the catholic church (l. v. c. 23.
p. 219).

natural inspiration exalted the fancy of the poet and of his audience.[160] The last retreats of Celtic freedom, the extreme territories of Gaul and Britain, were less adapted to agriculture than to pasturage: the wealth of the Britons consisted in their flocks and herds; milk and flesh were their ordinary food; and bread was sometimes esteemed, or rejected, as a foreign luxury. Liberty had peopled the mountains of Wales and the morasses of Armorica: but their populousness has been maliciously ascribed to the loose practice of polygamy; and the houses of these licentious barbarians have been supposed to contain ten wives, and perhaps fifty children.[161] Their disposition was rash and choleric: they were bold in action and in speech;[162] and as they were ignorant of the arts of peace, they alternately indulged their passions in foreign and domestic war. The cavalry of Armorica, the spearmen of Gwent, and the archers of Merioneth, were equally formidable; but their poverty could seldom procure either shields or helmets; and the inconvenient weight would have retarded the speed and agility of their desultory operations. One of the greatest of the English monarchs was requested to satisfy the curiosity of a Greek emperor concerning the state of Britain; and Henry II. could assert, from his personal experience, that Wales was inhabited by a race of naked warriors, who encountered, without fear, the defensive armour of their enemies.[163]

By the revolution of Britain the limits of science as well as of empire were contracted. The dark cloud which had been cleared by the Phœnician discoveries, and finally dispelled by the arms of Cæsar, again settled on the shores of the Atlantic, and a Roman province was again lost among the fabulous Islands of the Ocean. One hundred and fifty years after the reign of Honorius the gravest historian of the times [164] describes the wonders of a remote isle, whose eastern and western parts

[160] Mr. Pennant's Tour in Wales (p. 426-449) has furnished me with a curious and interesting account of the Welsh bards. In the year 1568 a session was held at Caerwys by the special command of queen Elizabeth, and regular degrees in vocal and instrumental music were conferred on fifty-five minstrels. The prize (a silver harp) was adjudged by the Mostyn family.

[161] Regio longe lateque diffusa, milite, magis quam credibile sit, referta. Partibus equidem in illis miles unus quinquaginta generat, sortitus more barbaro denas aut amplius uxores. This reproach of William of Poitiers (in the Historians of France, tom. xi. p. 88) is disclaimed by the Benedictine editors.

[162] Giraldus Cambrensis confines this gift of bold and ready eloquence to the Romans, the French and the Britons. The malicious Welshman insinuates that the English taciturnity might possibly be the effect of their servitude under the Normans.

[163] The picture of Welsh and Armorican manners is drawn from Giraldus (Descript. Cambriæ, c. 6-15, inter Script. Camden. p. 886-891) and the authors quoted by the Abbé de Vertot (Hist. Critique, tom. ii. p. 259-266).

[164] See Procopius de Bell. Gothic. 1. iv. c. 20, p. 620-625 [ed. Paris; tom. ii. p. 559 *sqq.*, ed. Bonn]. The Greek historian is himself so confounded by the wonders which he relates, that he weakly attempts to distinguish the islands of *Brittia* and *Britain,* which he has identified by so many inseparable circumstances

are divided by an antique wall, the boundary of life and death, or, more properly, of truth and fiction. The east is a fair country, inhabited by a civilised people: the air is healthy, the waters are pure and plentiful, and the earth yields her regular and fruitful increase. In the west, beyond the wall, the air is infectious and mortal; the ground is covered with serpents; and this dreary solitude is the region of departed spirits, who are transported from the opposite shores in substantial boats and by living rowers. Some families of fishermen, the subjects of the Franks, are excused from tribute, in consideration of the mysterious office which is performed by these Charons of the ocean. Each in his turn is summoned, at the hour of midnight, to hear the voices, and even the names, of the ghosts: he is sensible of their weight, and he feels himself impelled by an unknown, but irresistible, power. After this dream of fancy, we read with astonishment that the name of this island is *Brittia;* that it lies in the ocean, against the mouth of the Rhine, and less than thirty miles from the continent; that it is possessed by three nations, the Frisians, the Angles, and the Britons; and that some Angles had appeared at Constantinople in the train of the French ambassadors. From these ambassadors Procopius might be informed of a singular, though not improbable, adventure, which announces the spirit, rather than the delicacy, of an English heroine. She had been betrothed to Radiger, king of the Varni, a tribe of Germans who touched the ocean and the Rhine; but the perfidious lover was tempted, by motives of policy, to prefer his father's widow, the sister of Theodebert, king of the Franks.[165] The forsaken princess of the Angles, instead of bewailing, revenged her disgrace. Her warlike subjects are *said* to have been ignorant of the use, and even of the form, of a horse; but she boldly sailed from Britain to the mouth of the Rhine, with a fleet of four hundred ships and an army of one hundred thousand men. After the loss of a battle, the captive Radiger implored the mercy of his victorious bride, who generously pardoned his offence, dismissed her rival, and compelled the king of the Varni to discharge with honour and fidelity the duties of a husband.[166] This gallant exploit appears to be the last naval enterprise of the Anglo-Saxons. The arts of navigation, by which they had acquired the empire of Britain and of the sea, were soon neglected by the indolent

[165] Theodebert, grandson of Clovis and king of Austrasia, was the most powerful and warlike prince of the age; and this remarkable adventure may be placed between the years 534 and 547, the extreme terms of his reign. His sister Theudechildis retired to Sens, where she founded monasteries and distributed alms (see the notes of the Benedictine editors, in tom. ii. p. 216). If we may credit the praises of Fortunatus (l. vi. carm. 5, in tom. ii. p. 507), Radiger was deprived of a most valuable wife.

[166] Perhaps she was the sister of one of the princes or chiefs of the Angles who landed, in 527 and the following years, between the Humber and the Thames, and gradually founded the kingdoms of East Anglia and Mercia. The English writers are ignorant of her name and existence; but Procopius may have suggested to Mr. Rowe the character and situation of Rodogune in the tragedy of the Royal Convert.

barbarians, who supinely renounced all the commercial advantages of their insular situation. Seven independent kingdoms were agitated by perpetual discord; and the *British world* was seldom connected, either in peace or war, with the nations of the continent.[167]

I have now accomplished the laborious narrative of the decline and fall of the Roman empire, from the fortunate age of Trajan and the Antonines to its total extinction in the West, about five centuries after the Christian era. At that unhappy period the Saxons fiercely struggled with the natives for the possession of Britain: Gaul and Spain were divided between the powerful monarchies of the Franks and Visigoths and the dependent kingdoms of the Suevi and Burgundians: Africa was exposed to the cruel persecution of the Vandals and the savage insults of the Moors: Rome and Italy, as far as the banks of the Danube, were afflicted by an army of barbarian mercenaries, whose lawless tyranny was succeeded by the reign of Theodoric the Ostrogoth. All the subjects of the empire, who, by the use of the Latin language, more particularly deserved the name and privileges of Romans, were oppressed by the disgrace and calamities of foreign conquest; and the victorious nations of Germany established a new system of manners and government in the western countries of Europe. The majesty of Rome was faintly represented by the princes of Constantinople, the feeble and imaginary successors of Augustus. Yet they continued to reign over the East, from the Danube to the Nile and Tigris; the Gothic and Vandal kingdoms of Italy and Africa were subverted by the arms of Justinian; and the history of the *Greek* emperors may still afford a long series of instructive lessons and interesting revolutions.

GENERAL OBSERVATIONS ON THE FALL OF THE ROMAN EMPIRE IN THE WEST

THE Greeks, after their country had been reduced into a province, imputed the triumphs of Rome, not to the merit, but to the FORTUNE, of the republic. The inconstant goddess who so blindly distributes and resumes her favours, had *now* consented (such was the language of envious flattery) to resign her wings, to descend from her globe, and to fix her firm and immutable throne on the banks of the Tiber.[1] A wiser Greek,

---

[167] In the copious history of Gregory of Tours we cannot find any traces of hostile or friendly intercourse between France and England, except in the marriage of the daughter of Caribert, king of Paris, quam in Cantia regis *cujusdam* filius matrimonio copulavit (l. ix. c. 26, in tom. ii. p. 348). The bishop of Tours ended his history and his life almost immediately before the conversion of Kent.

[1] Such are the figurative expressions of Plutarch (Opera, tom. ii. p. 318, edit. Wechel [Frankf. 1620]), to whom, on the faith of his son Lamprias (Fabricius, Bibliot. Græc. tom. iii. p. 341), I shall boldly impute the malicious declamation, περὶ τῆς Ρωμαίων τύχης. The same opinions had prevailed among the

who has composed, with a philosophic spirit, the memorable history of his own times, deprived his countrymen of this vain and delusive comfort, by opening to their view the deep foundations of the greatness of Rome.[2] The fidelity of the citizens to each other and to the state was confirmed by the habits of education and the prejudices of religion. Honour, as well as virtue, was the principle of the republic; the ambitious citizens laboured to deserve the solemn glories of a triumph; and the ardour of the Roman youth was kindled into active emulation as often as they beheld the domestic images of their ancestors.[3] The temperate struggles of the patricians and plebeians had finally established the firm and equal balance of the constitution, which united the freedom of popular assemblies with the authority and wisdom of a senate and the executive powers of a regal magistrate. When the consul displayed the standard of the republic, each citizen bound himself, by the obligation of an oath, to draw his sword in the cause of his country till he had discharged the sacred duty by a military service of ten years. This wise institution continually poured into the field the rising generations of freemen and soldiers; and their numbers were reinforced by the warlike and populous states of Italy, who, after a brave resistance, had yielded to the valour and embraced the alliance of the Romans. The sage historian, who excited the virtue of the younger Scipio and beheld the ruin of Carthage,[4] has accurately described their military system; their levies, arms, exercises, subordination, marches, encampments; and the invincible legion, superior in active strength to the Macedonian phalanx of Philip and Alexander. From these institutions of peace and war Polybius has deduced the spirit and success of a people incapable of fear and impatient of repose. The ambitious design of conquest, which might have been defeated by the seasonable conspiracy of mankind, was attempted and achieved; and the perpetual violation of justice was maintained by the political virtues of prudence and courage. The arms of the republic, sometimes vanquished in battle, always victorious in war, advanced with rapid steps to the Euphrates, the Danube, the Rhine, and the Ocean; and the images of gold, or silver, or brass, that might serve to

---

Greeks two hundred and fifty years before Plutarch; and to confute them is the professed intention of Polybius (Hist. l. i. [c. 63] p. 90, edit. Gronov. Amstel. 1670).

[2] See the inestimable remains of the sixth book of Polybius, and many other parts of his general history, particularly a digression in the seventeenth book [l. xviii. c. 12-15], in which he compares the phalanx and the legion.

[3] Sallust, de Bell. Jugurthin. c. 4. Such were the generous professions of P. Scipio and Q. Maximus. The Latin historian had read, and most probably transcribes, Polybius, their contemporary and friend.

[4] While Carthage was in flames Scipio repeated two lines of the Iliad, which express the destruction of Troy, acknowledging to Polybius, his friend and preceptor (Polyb. [Fragm. l. xxxix. *sub fin.*] in Excerpt. de Virtut. et Vit. tom. ii. p. 1455-1465), that while he recollected the vicissitudes of human affairs he inwardly applied them to the future calamities of Rome (Appian. in Libycis [l. viii. c. 132], p. 136, edit. Toll.).

represent the nations and their kings, were successively broken by the *iron* monarchy of Rome.[5]

The rise of a city, which swelled into an empire, may deserve, as a singular prodigy, the reflection of a philosophic mind. But the decline of Rome was the natural and inevitable effect of immoderate greatness. Prosperity ripened the principle of decay; the causes of destruction multiplied with the extent of conquest; and as soon as time or accident had removed the artificial supports, the stupendous fabric yielded to the pressure of its own weight. The story of its ruin is simple and obvious; and instead of inquiring *why* the Roman empire was destroyed, we should rather be surprised that it had subsisted so long. The victorious legions, who, in distant wars, acquired the vices of strangers and mercenaries, first oppressed the freedom of the republic, and afterwards violated the majesty of the purple. The emperors, anxious for their personal safety and the public peace, were reduced to the base expedient of corrupting the discipline which rendered them alike formidable to their sovereign and to the enemy; the vigour of the military government was relaxed and finally dissolved by the partial institutions of Constantine; and the Roman world was overwhelmed by a deluge of barbarians.

The decay of Rome has been frequently ascribed to the translation of the seat of empire; but this history has already shown that the powers of Government were *divided* rather than *removed*. The throne of Constantinople was erected in the East; while the West was still possessed by a series of emperors who held their residence in Italy, and claimed their equal inheritance of the legions and provinces. This dangerous novelty impaired the strength and fomented the vices of a double reign: the instruments of an oppressive and arbitrary system were multiplied; and a vain emulation of luxury, not of merit, was introduced and supported between the degenerate successors of Theodosius. Extreme distress, which unites the virtue of a free people, embitters the factions of a declining monarchy. The hostile favourites of Arcadius and Honorius betrayed the republic to its common enemies; and the Byzantine court beheld with indifference, perhaps with pleasure, the disgrace of Rome, the misfortunes of Italy, and the loss of the West. Under the succeeding reigns the alliance of the two empires was restored; but the aid of the Oriental Romans was tardy, doubtful, and ineffectual; and the national schism of the Greeks and Latins was enlarged by the perpetual difference of language and manners, of interests, and even of religion. Yet the salutary event approved in some measure the judgment of Constantine.

---

[5] See Daniel ii. 31-40. "And the fourth kingdom shall be strong as *iron;* forasmuch as iron breaketh in pieces and subdueth all things." The remainder of the prophecy (the mixture of iron and *clay*) was accomplished, according to St. Jerom, in his own time. Sicut enim in principio nihil Romano Imperio fortius et durius, ita in fine rerum nihil imbecillius: quum et in bellis civilibus et adversus diversas nationes, aliarum gentium barbararum auxilio indigemus (Opera, tom. v. p. 572).

During a long period of decay his impregnable city repelled the victorious armies of barbarians, protected the wealth of Asia, and commanded, both in peace and war, the important straits which connect the Euxine and Mediterranean seas. The foundation of Constantinople more essentially contributed to the preservation of the East than to the ruin of the West.

As the happiness of a *future* life is the great object of religion, we may hear without surprise or scandal that the introduction, or at least the abuse of Christianity, had some influence on the decline and fall of the Roman empire. The clergy successfully preached the doctrines of patience and pusillanimity; the active virtues of society were discouraged; and the last remains of military spirit were buried in the cloister: a large portion of public and private wealth was consecrated to the specious demands of charity and devotion; and the soldiers' pay was lavished on the useless multitudes of both sexes who could only plead the merits of abstinence and chastity. Faith, zeal, curiosity, and more earthly passions of malice and ambition, kindled the flame of theological discord; the church, and even the state, were distracted by religious factions, whose conflicts were sometimes bloody and always implacable; the attention of the emperors was diverted from camps to synods; the Roman world was oppressed by a new species of tyranny; and the persecuted sects became the secret enemies of their country. Yet party-spirit, however pernicious or absurd, is a principle of union as well as of dissension. The bishops, from eighteen hundred pulpits, inculcated the duty of passive obedience to a lawful and orthodox sovereign; their frequent assemblies and perpetual correspondence maintained the communion of distant churches; and the benevolent temper of the Gospel was strengthened, though confirmed, by the spiritual alliance of the catholics. The sacred indolence of the monks was devoutly embraced by a servile and effeminate age; but if superstition had not afforded a decent retreat, the same vices would have tempted the unworthy Romans to desert, from baser motives, the standard of the republic. Religious precepts are easily obeyed which indulge and sanctify the natural inclinations of their votaries; but the pure and genuine influence of Christianity may be traced in its beneficial, though imperfect, effects on the barbarian proselytes of the North. If the decline of the Roman empire was hastened by the conversion of Constantine, his victorious religion broke the violence of the fall, and mollified the ferocious temper of the conquerors.

This awful revolution may be usefully applied to the instruction of the present age. It is the duty of a patriot to prefer and promote the exclusive interest and glory of his native country: but a philosopher may be permitted to enlarge his views, and to consider Europe as one great republic, whose various inhabitants have attained almost the same level of politeness and cultivation. The balance of power will continue to fluctuate, and the prosperity of our own or the neighbouring kingdoms may be alternately exalted or depressed; but these partial events cannot essentially injure our general state of happiness, the system of arts, and laws, and manners, which so advantageously distinguish, above the rest of mankind, the Europeans and their colonies. The savage nations of the globe are the common enemies of civilised society; and we may inquire, with anxious curiosity, whether Europe is still threatened with a repetition of those calamities which formerly oppressed the arms and institutions of Rome. Perhaps the same reflections will illustrate the fall of that mighty empire, and explain the probable causes of our actual security.

I. The Romans were ignorant of the extent of their dangers and the number of their enemies. Beyond the Rhine and Danube the northern countries of Europe and Asia were filled with innumerable tribes of hunters and shepherds, poor, voracious, and turbulent; bold in arms, and impatient to ravish the fruits of industry. The barbarian world was agitated by the rapid impulse of war; and the peace of Gaul or Italy was shaken by the distant revolutions of China. The Huns, who fled before a victorious enemy, directed their march towards the West; and the torrent was swelled by the gradual accession of captives and allies. The flying tribes who yielded to the Huns assumed in *their* turn the spirit of conquest; the endless column of barbarians pressed on the Roman empire with accumulated weight; and, if the foremost were destroyed, the vacant space was instantly replenished by new assailants. Such formidable emigrations no longer issue from the North; and the long repose, which has been imputed to the decrease of population, is the happy consequence of the progress of arts and agriculture. Instead of some rude villages thinly scattered among its woods and morasses, Germany now produces a list of two thousand three hundred walled towns: the Christian kingdoms of Denmark, Sweden, and Poland have been successively established; and the Hanse merchants, with the Teutonic knights, have extended their colonies along the coast of the Baltic as far as the Gulf of Finland. From the Gulf of Finland to the Eastern Ocean, Russia now assumes the form of a powerful and civilised empire. The plough, the loom, and the forge are introduced on the banks of the Volga, the Oby, and the Lena; and the fiercest of the Tartar hordes have been taught to tremble and obey. The reign of independent barbarism is now contracted to a narrow span; and the remnant of Calmucks or Uzbecks, whose forces may be almost numbered, cannot seriously excite the apprehensions of the great republic of Europe.[6] Yet this apparent security

[6] The French and English editors of the Genealogical History of the Tartars have subjoined a curious, though imperfect, description of their present state. We might question the independence of the Calmucks, or Eluths, since they have been recently vanquished by the Chinese, who, in the year 1759, subdued the lesser Bucharia, and advanced into the country of Badakshan, near the sources of the Oxus (Mémoires sur les Chinois, tom. i. p. 325-400). But these conquests are precarious, nor will I venture to ensure the safety of the Chinese empire.

should not tempt us to forget that new enemies and unknown dangers may *possibly* arise from some obscure people, scarcely visible in the map of the world. The Arabs or Saracens, who spread their conquests from India to Spain, had languished in poverty and contempt till Mahomet breathed into those savage bodies the soul of enthusiasm.

II. The empire of Rome was firmly established by the singular and perfect coalition of its members. The subject nations, resigning the hope and even the wish of independence, embraced the character of Roman citizens; and the provinces of the West were reluctantly torn by the barbarians from the bosom of their mother country.[7] But this union was purchased by the loss of national freedom and military spirit; and the servile provinces, destitute of life and motion, expected their safety from the mercenary troops and governors who were directed by the orders of a distant court. The happiness of an hundred millions depended on the personal merit of one or two men, perhaps children, whose minds were corrupted by education, luxury, and despotic power. The deepest wounds were inflicted on the empire during the minorities of the sons and grandsons of Theodosius; and, after those incapable princes seemed to attain the age of manhood, they abandoned the church to the bishops, the state to the eunuchs, and the provinces to the barbarians. Europe is now divided into twelve powerful, though unequal kingdoms, three respectable commonwealths, and a variety of smaller, though independent states: the chances of royal and ministerial talent are multiplied, at least, with the number of its rulers; and a Julian, or Semiramis, may reign in the North, while Arcadius and Honorius again slumber on the thrones of the South. The abuses of tyranny are restrained by the mutual influence of fear and shame; republics have acquired order and stability; monarchies have imbibed the principles of freedom, or, at least, of moderation; and some sense of honour and justice is introduced into the most defective constitutions by the general manners of the times. In peace, the progress of knowledge and industry is accelerated by the emulation of so many active rivals: in war, the European forces are exercised by temperate and undecisive contests. If a savage conqueror should issue from the deserts of Tartary, he must repeatedly vanquish the robust peasants of Russia, the numerous armies of Germany, the gallant nobles of France, and the intrepid freemen of Britain; who, perhaps, might confederate for their common defence. Should the victorious barbarians carry slavery and desolation as far as the Atlantic Ocean, ten thousand vessels would transport beyond their pursuit the remains of civilised society; and Europe would revive and flourish in the American world, which is already filled with her colonies and institutions.[8]

---

[7] The prudent reader will determine how far this general proposition is weakened by the revolt of the Isaurians, the independence of Britain and Armorica, the Moorish tribes, or the Bagaudæ of Gaul and Spain (vol. i. p. 414, vol. iv. pp. 130, 178, 252).

[8] America now contains about six millions of European blood and descent:

III. Cold, poverty, and a life of danger and fatigue fortify the strength and courage of barbarians. In every age they have oppressed the polite and peaceful nations of China, India, and Persia, who neglected, and still neglect, to counterbalance these natural powers by the resources of military art. The warlike states of antiquity, Greece, Macedonia, and Rome, educated a race of soldiers; exercised their bodies, disciplined their courage, multiplied their forces by regular evolutions, and converted the iron which they possessed into strong and serviceable weapons. But this superiority insensibly declined with their laws and manners: and the feeble policy of Constantine and his successors armed and instructed, for the ruin of the empire, the rude valour of the barbarian mercenaries. The military art has been changed by the invention of gunpowder; which enables man to command the two most powerful agents of nature, air and fire. Mathematics, chemistry, mechanics, architecture, have been applied to the service of war; and the adverse parties oppose to each other the most elaborate modes of attack and of defence. Historians may indignantly observe that the preparations of a siege would found and maintain a flourishing colony;[9] yet we cannot be displeased that the subversion of a city should be a work of cost and difficulty; or that an industrious people should be protected by those arts which survive and supply the decay of military virtue. Cannon and fortifications now form an impregnable barrier against the Tartar horse; and Europe is secure from any future irruption of barbarians; since, before they can conquer, they must cease to be barbarous. Their gradual advances in the science of war would always be accompanied, as we may learn from the example of Russia, with a proportionable improvement in the arts of peace and civil policy; and they themselves must deserve a place among the polished nations whom they subdue.

Should these speculations be found doubtful or fallacious, there still remains a more humble source of comfort and hope. The discoveries of ancient and modern navigators, and the domestic history or tradition of the most enlightened nations, represent the *human savage* naked both in mind and body, and destitute of laws, of arts, of ideas, and almost of

and their numbers, at least in the North, are continually increasing. Whatever may be the changes of their political situation, they must preserve the manners of Europe: and we may reflect with some pleasure that the English language will probably be diffused over an immense and populous continent.

[9] On avoit fait venir (for the siege of Turin) 140 pièces de canon; et il est à remarquer que chaque gros canon monté revient à environ 2000 écus: il y avoit 100,000 boulets; 106,000 cartouches d'une façon, et 300,000 d'une autre; 21,000 bombes; 27,700 grenades, 15,000 sacs à terre, 30,000 instruments pour la pionnage; 1,200,000 livres de poudre. Ajoutez à ces munitions le plomb, le fer, et le fer-blanc, les cordages, tout ce qui sert aux mineurs, le souphre, le salpêtre, les outils de toute espèce. Il est certain que les frais de tous ces préparatifs de destruction suffiroient pour fonder et pour faire fleurir la plus nombreuse colonie. Voltaire, Siècle de Louis XIV. c. xx. in his Works, tom. xi. p. 391.

language.[10] From this abject condition, perhaps the primitive and universal state of man, he has gradually arisen to command the animals, to fertilise the earth, to traverse the ocean, and to measure the heavens. His progress in the improvement and exercise of his mental and corporeal faculties [11] has been irregular and various; infinitely slow in the beginning, and increasing by degrees with redoubled velocity: ages of laborious ascent have been followed by a moment of rapid downfall; and the several climates of the globe have felt the vicissitudes of light and darkness. Yet the experience of four thousand years should enlarge our hopes and diminish our apprehensions: we cannot determine to what height the human species may aspire in their advance towards perfection; but it may safely be presumed that no people, unless the face of nature is changed, will relapse into their original barbarism. The improvements of society may be viewed under a threefold aspect. 1. The poet or philosopher illustrates his age and country by the efforts of a *single* mind; but these superior powers of reason or fancy are rare and spontaneous productions; and the genius of Homer, or Cicero, or Newton, would excite less admiration if they could be created by the will of a prince or the lessons of a preceptor. 2. The benefits of law and policy, of trade and manufactures, of arts and sciences, are more solid and permanent; and *many* individuals may be qualified, by education and discipline, to promote, in their respective stations, the interest of the community. But this general order is the effect of skill and labour; and the complex machinery may be decayed by time, or injured by violence. 3. Fortunately for mankind, the more useful, or, at least, more necessary arts, can be performed without superior talents or national subordination; without powers of *one,* or the union of *many.* Each village, each family, each individual, must always possess both ability and inclination to perpetuate the use of fire [12] and of metals; the propagation and service of domestic animals; the methods of hunting and fishing; the rudiments of navigation; the imperfect cultivation of corn or other nutritive grain;

[10] It would be an easy, though tedious, task to produce the authorities of poets, philosophers, and historians. I shall therefore content myself with appealing to the decisive and authentic testimony of Diodorus Siculus (tom. i. l. i. p. 11, 12, l. iii. [c. 14 *sqq.*] p. 184, etc., edit. Wesseling). The Ichthyophagi, who in his time wandered along the shores of the Red Sea, can only be compared to the natives of New Holland (Dampier's Voyages, vol. i. p. 464-469). Fancy, or perhaps reason, may still suppose an extreme and absolute state of nature far below the level of these savages, who had acquired some arts and instruments.

[11] See the learned and rational work of the President Goguet, de l'Origine des Loix, des Arts, et des Sciences. He traces from facts or conjectures (tom. i. p. 147-337, edit. 12mo.) the first and most difficult steps of human invention.

[12] It is certain, however strange, that many nations have been ignorant of the use of fire. Even the ingenious natives of Otaheite, who are destitute of metals, have not invented any earthen vessels capable of sustaining the action of fire and of communicating the heat to the liquids which they contain.

and the simple practice of the mechanic trades. Private genius and
public industry may be extirpated, but these hardy plants survive the
tempest, and strike an everlasting root into the most unfavourable soil.
The splendid days of Augustus and Trajan were eclipsed by a cloud of
ignorance; and the barbarians subverted the laws and palaces of Rome.
But the scythe, the invention or emblem of Saturn,[13] still continued annually to mow the harvests of Italy; and the human feasts of the
Læstrigons[14] have never been renewed on the coast of Campania.

Since the first discovery of the arts, war, commerce, and religious zeal
have diffused among the savages of the Old and New World these inestimable gifts: they have been successively propagated; they can never
be lost. We may therefore acquiesce in the pleasing conclusion that
every age of the world has increased and still increases the real wealth,
the happiness, the knowledge, and perhaps the virtue, of the human
race.[15]

CHAPTER XXXIX (455-526 A.D.)

*Zeno and Anastasius, Emperors of the East—Birth, Education, and first Ex-
ploits of Theodoric the Ostrogoth—His Invasion and Conquest of Italy—
The Gothic Kingdom of Italy—State of the West—Military and Civil
Government—The Senator Boethius—Last Acts and Death of Theodoric*

AFTER the fall of the Roman empire in the West, an interval of fifty
years, till the memorable reign of Justinian, is faintly marked by the
obscure names and imperfect annals of Zeno, Anastasius, and Justin, who
successively ascended the throne of Constantinople. During the same
period, Italy revived and flourished under the government of a Gothic
king who might have deserved a statue among the best and bravest of
the ancient Romans.

Theodoric the Ostrogoth, the fourteenth in lineal descent of the royal

[13] Plutarch. Quæst. Rom. in tom. ii. p. 275 [tom. vii. p. 112, ed. Reiske].
Macrob. Saturnal. l. i. c. 7, p. 152, edit. London. The arrival of Saturn (of his
religious worship) in a ship may indicate that the savage coast of Latium was
first discovered and civilised by the Phœnicians.

[14] In the ninth and tenth books of the Odyssey, Homer has embellished the
tales of fearful and credulous sailors who transformed the cannibals of Italy
and Sicily into monstrous giants.

[15] The merit of discovery has too often been stained with avarice, cruelty, and
fanaticism; and the intercourse of nations has produced the communication
of disease and prejudice. A singular exception is due to the virtue of our
own times and country. The five great voyages, successively undertaken by
the command of his present Majesty, were inspired by the pure and generous
love of science and mankind. The same prince, adapting his benefactions to
the different stages of society, has founded a school of painting in his capital,
and has introduced into the islands of the South Sea the vegetables and animals
most useful to human life.

line of the Amali,[1] was born in the neighbourhood of Vienna [2] two years after the death of Attila. A recent victory had restored the independence of the Ostrogoths; and the three brothers, Walamir, Theodemir, and Widimir, who ruled that warlike nation with united counsels, had separately pitched their habitations in the fertile, though desolate, province of Pannonia.[3] The Huns still threatened their revolted subjects, but their hasty attack was repelled by the single forces of Walamir, and the news of his victory reached the distant camp of his brother in the same auspicious moment that the favourite concubine of Theodemir was delivered of a son and heir.[4] In the eighth year of his age, Theodoric was reluctantly yielded by his father to the public interest, as the pledge of an alliance which Leo, emperor of the East, had consented to purchase

[1] Jornandes (de Rebus Geticis, c. 13, 14, p. 629, 630, edit. Grot.) has drawn the pedigree of Theodoric from Gapt, one of the *Anses* or Demi-gods, who lived about the time of Domitian. Cassiodorus, the first who celebrates the royal race of the Amali (Variar. viii. 5, ix. 25, x. 2, xi. 1), reckons the grandson of Theodoric as the xviith in descent. Peringsciold (the Swedish commentator of Cochlœus, Vit. Theodoric. p. 271, etc., Stockholm, 1699) labours to connect this genealogy with the legends or traditions of his native country.
[Amala was a name of peculiar respect and honour among the Ostrogoths. It means "strength," and enters into many names, Amalaberg, Amalafred, Amalarich, etc. In the Nibelungen Lied the Ostrogoths are called the Amilungen.—O. S.]
[2] More correctly on the banks of the lake Pelso (Nieusiedler-see) near Carnuntum, almost on the same spot where Marcus Antoninus composed his Meditations (Jornandes, c. 52, p. 689. Severin. Pannonia Illustrata, p. 22. Cellarius, Geograph. Antiq. tom. i. p. 350).
[3] [The division of the Gothic kingdom as given by Hodgkin, *Italy and Her Invaders*, iii. p. 14. The portion of Walamer lay between the rivers Save and Drave, that of Widimer between the Save and the Plattensee, Theodemir's between the Plattensee and the Danube.—O. S.]
[4] Genealogical table of the family of Theodoric:—

Walamir.	Theodemir = Erelieva.			Widemir, ob. 473.
				Widimer.
Theudimundus =	THEODORIC = ob. 526.	Audefleda, sister or daughter of Clovis.	Amalafreda, m. Trasamundus, king of the Vandals.	
Theudegotha, m. Alaric, king of the Visigoths, ob. 507.	Ostrogotha, m. Sigismundus, king of the Burgundians, ob. 523.	Amala-suentha, ob. 534, m. Eutharicus.	Theoda-hadus, ob. 536.	Amala-berga, m. Hermen-fredus.
Amalaric, ob. 531.	Sigeric, ob. 522.	Athalaric, ob. 534.		

See Clinton. Fasti Romani, vol. ii. p. 143.—S.

by an annual subsidy of three hundred pounds of gold. The royal hostage was educated at Constantinople with care and tenderness. His body was formed to all the exercises of war, his mind was expanded by the habits of liberal conversation; he frequented the schools of the most skilful masters, but he disdained or neglected the arts of Greece; and so ignorant did he always remain of the first elements of science, that a rude mark was contrived to represent the signature of the illiterate king of Italy.[5] As soon as he had attained the age of eighteen he was restored to the wishes of the Ostrogoths, whom the emperor aspired to gain by liberality and confidence. Walamir had fallen in battle; the youngest of the brothers, Widimir, had led away into Italy and Gaul an army of barbarians; and the whole nation acknowledged for their king the father of Theodoric. His ferocious subjects admired the strength and stature of their young prince,[6] and he soon convinced them that he had not degenerated from the valour of his ancestors. At the head of six thousand volunteers he secretly left the camp in quest of adventures, descended the Danube as far as Singidunum or Belgrade, and soon returned to his father with the spoils of a Sarmatian king whom he had vanquished and slain. Such triumphs, however, were productive only of fame, and the invincible Ostrogoths were reduced to extreme distress by the want of clothing and food. They unanimously resolved to desert their Pannonian encampments, and boldly to advance into the warm and wealthy neighbourhood of the Byzantine court, which already maintained in pride and luxury so many bands of confederate Goths. After proving, by some acts of hostility, that they could be dangerous, or at least troublesome, enemies, the Ostrogoths sold at a high price their reconciliation and fidelity, accepted a donative of lands and money, and 'were intrusted with the defence of the lower Danube under the command of Theodoric, who succeeded after his father's death to the hereditary throne of the Amali.[7]

An hero, descended from a race of kings, must have despised the base Isaurian who was invested with the Roman purple, without any endowments of mind or body, without any advantages of royal birth or superior

---

[5] The four first letters of his name (ΘΕΟΔ) were inscribed on a gold plate, and when it was fixed on the paper the king drew his pen through the intervals (Anonym. Valesian. ad calcem Amm. Marcellin. p. 722 [tom. ii. p. 313, ed. Bipon.]). This authentic fact, with the testimony of Procopius, or at least of the contemporary Goths (Gothic. l. i. c. 2, p 312 [ed. Paris; tom. ii. p. 14, ed. Bonn]), far outweighs the vague praises of Ennodius (Sirmond. Opera, tom. i. p. 1596) and Theophanes (Chronograph. p. 112 [ed. Par.; p. 202, 203, ed. Bonn]).

[6] Statura est quæ resignet proceritate regnantem (Ennodius, p. 1614). The bishop of Pavia (I mean the ecclesiastic who wished to be a bishop) then proceeds to celebrate the complexion, eyes, hands, etc., of his sovereign.

[7] The state of the Ostrogoths and the first years of Theodoric are found in Jornandes (c. 52-56, p. 689-696) and Malchus (Excerpt. Legat. p. 78-80 [ed. Par.; p. 244-248, ed. Bonn]), who erroneously styles him the son of Walamir.

qualifications. After the failure of the Theodosian line, the choice of Pulcheria and of the senate might be justified in some measure by the characters of Marcian and Leo; but the latter of these princes confirmed and dishonoured his reign by the perfidious murder of Aspar and his sons, who too rigorously exacted the debt of gratitude and obedience. The inheritance of Leo and of the East was peaceably devolved on his infant grandson, the son of his daughter Ariadne; and her Isaurian husband, the fortunate Trascalisseus, exchanged that barbarous sound for the Grecian appellation of Zeno. After the decease of the elder Leo, he approached with unnatural respect the throne of his son, humbly received as a gift the second rank in the empire, and soon excited the public suspicion on the sudden and premature death of his young colleague, whose life could no longer promote the success of his ambition. But the palace of Constantinople was ruled by female influence, and agitated by female passions; and Verina, the widow of Leo, claiming his empire as her own, pronounced a sentence of deposition against the worthless and ungrateful servant on whom she alone had bestowed the sceptre of the East.[8] As soon as she sounded a revolt in the ears of Zeno, he fled with precipitation into the mountains of Isauria; and her brother Basiliscus, already infamous by his African expedition,[9] was unanimously proclaimed by the servile senate. But the reign of the usurper was short and turbulent. Basiliscus presumed to assassinate the lover of his sister; he dared to offend the lover of his wife, the vain and insolent Harmatius, who, in the midst of Asiatic luxury, affected the dress, the demeanour, and the surname of Achilles.[10] By the conspiracy of the malcontents, Zeno was recalled from exile; the armies, the capital, the person of Basiliscus, were betrayed; and his whole family was condemned to the long agony of cold and hunger by the inhuman conqueror, who wanted courage to encounter or to forgive his enemies. The haughty spirit of Verina was still incapable of submission or repose. She provoked the enmity of a favourite general, embraced his cause as soon as he was disgraced, created a new emperor in Syria and Egypt, raised an army of seventy thousand men, and persisted to the last moment of her life in a fruitless rebellion, which, according to the fashion of the age, had been predicted by Christian hermits and Pagan magicians. While the East was afflicted by the passions of Verina, her daughter Ariadne was distinguished by the female virtues of mildness and fidelity; she followed her husband in his exile, and after his restoration she implored his clemency in favour of her mother. On the decease of Zeno, Ariadne, the daughter, the mother, and the widow of an emperor, gave her hand and the Imperial

---

[8] Theophanes (p. 111 [p. 200, ed. Bonn]) inserts a copy of her *sacred* letters to the provinces; ἴστε ὅτι τὸ βασίλειον ἡμέτερόν ἐστι . . . καὶ ὅτι προχειρησάμεθα βασιλέα Τρασκαλλισαῖον, etc. Such female pretensions would have astonished the slaves of the *first* Cæsars.

[9] Vol. iv. p. 284, *seq.*

[10] Suidas, tom. i. p. 332, 333, edit. Kuster.

title to Anastasius, an aged domestic of the palace, who survived his
elevation above twenty-seven years, and whose character is attested by
the acclamation of the people, " Reign as you have lived!" [11]
Whatever fear or affection could bestow was profusely lavished by
Zeno on the king of the Ostrogoths; the rank of patrician and consul, the
command of the Palatine troops, an equestrian statue, a treasure in gold
and silver of many thousand pounds, the name of son, and the promise
of a rich and honourable wife. As long as Theodoric condescended to
serve, he supported with courage and fidelity the cause of his benefactor;
his rapid march contributed to the restoration of Zeno; and in the second
revolt, the *Walamirs,* as they were called, pursued and pressed the Asiatic
rebels, till they left an easy victory to the Imperial troops.[12] But the
faithful servant was suddenly converted into a formidable enemy, who
spread the flames of war from Constantinople to the Hadriatic; many
flourishing cities were reduced to ashes, and the agriculture of Thrace
was almost extirpated by the wanton cruelty of the Goths, who deprived
their captive peasants of the right hand that guided the plough.[13] On
such occasions Theodoric sustained the loud and specious reproach of
disloyalty, of ingratitude, and of insatiate avarice, which could be only
excused by the hard necessity of his situation. He reigned, not as the
monarch, but as the minister of a ferocious people, whose spirit was
unbroken by slavery, and impatient of real or imaginary insults. Their
poverty was incurable, since the most liberal donatives were soon dissipated in wasteful luxury, and the most fertile estates became barren in
their hands; they despised, but they envied, the laborious provincials;
and when their subsistence had failed, the Ostrogoths embraced the
familiar resources of war and rapine. It had been the wish of Theodoric
(such, at least, was his declaration) to lead a peaceful, obscure, obedient
life, on the confines of Scythia, till the Byzantine court, by splendid and
fallacious promises, seduced him to attack a confederate tribe of Goths,
who had been engaged in the party of Basiliscus. He marched from his
station in Mæsia, on the solemn assurance that before he reached Adri-

[11] The contemporary histories of Malchus and Candidus are lost; but some
extracts or fragments have been saved by Photius (lxxviii. lxxix. p. 100-102
[p. 54-56, ed. Bekk.]), Constantine Porphyrogenitus (Excerpt. Leg. p. 78-97),
and in various articles of the Lexicon of Suidas. The Chronicles of Marcellinus
(Imago Historiæ) are originals for the reigns of Zeno and Anastasius; and I
must acknowledge, almost for the last time, my obligations to the large and
accurate collections of Tillemont (Hist. des Emp. tom. vi. p. 472-652).

[12] In ipsis congressionis tuæ foribus cessit invasor, cum *profugo* per te
sceptra redderentur de salute dubitanti. Ennodius then proceeds (p. 1596,
1597, tom. i. Sirmond) to transport his hero (on a flying dragon?) into
Æthiopia, beyond the tropic of Cancer. The evidence of the Valesian Fragment (p. 717), Liberatus (Brev. Eutych. c. 25, p. 118), and Theophanes (p. 112
[p. 203, ed. Bonn]), is more sober and rational.

[13] This cruel practice is specially imputed to the *Triarian* Goths, less barbarous, as it should seem, than the *Walamirs*; but the son of Theodemir is
charged with the ruin of many Roman cities (Malchus, Excerpt. Leg. p 95
[ed. Par.; p. 238, ed. Bonn]).

anople he should meet a plentiful convoy of provisions, and a reinforcement of eight thousand horse and thirty thousand foot, while the legions of Asia were encamped at Heraclea to second his operations. These measures were disappointed by mutual jealousy. As he advanced into Thrace, the son of Theodemir found an inhospitable solitude, and his Gothic followers, with an heavy train of horses, of mules, and of waggons, were betrayed by their guides among the rocks and precipices of Mount Sondis, where he was assaulted by the arms and invectives of Theodoric, the son of Triarius. From a neighbouring height his artful rival harangued the camp of the *Walamirs,* and branded their leader with the opprobrious names of child, of madman, of perjured traitor, the enemy of his blood and nation. " Are you ignorant," exclaimed the son of Triarius, " that it is the constant policy of the Romans to destroy the Goths by each other's swords? Are you insensible that the victor in this unnatural contest will be exposed, and justly exposed, to their implacable revenge? Where are those warriors, my kinsmen and thy own, whose widows now lament that their lives were sacrificed to thy rash ambition? Where is the wealth which thy soldiers possessed when they were first allured from their native homes to enlist under thy standard? Each of them was then master of three or four horses; they now follow thee on foot like slaves, through the deserts of Thrace; those men who were tempted by the hope of measuring gold with a bushel, those brave men who are as free and as noble as thyself." A language so well suited to the temper of the Goths excited clamour and discontent; and the son of Theodemir, apprehensive of being left alone, was compelled to embrace his brethren, and to imitate the example of Roman perfidy.[14]

In every state of his fortune the prudence and firmness of Theodoric were equally conspicuous: whether he threatened Constantinople at the head of the confederate Goths, or retreated with a faithful band to the mountains and sea-coast of Epirus. At length the accidental death of the son of Triarius [15] destroyed the balance which the Romans had been so anxious to preserve, the whole nation acknowledged the supremacy of the Amali, and the Byzantine court subscribed an ignominious and oppressive treaty.[16] The senate had already declared that it was necessary to choose a party among the Goths, since the public was unequal to the support of their united forces. A subsidy of two thousand pounds of

[14] Jornandes (c. 56, 57, p. 696) displays the services of Theodoric, confesses his rewards, but dissembles his revolt, of which such curious details have been preserved by Malchus (Excerpt. Legat. p. 78-97 [p. 244 *sqq.,* ed. Bonn]). Marcellinus, a domestic of Justinian, under whose ivth consulship (A.D. 534) he composed his Chronicle (Scaliger, Thesaurus Temporum, P. ii. p. 34-57), betrays his prejudice and passion: in [apud] Græciam debacchantem . . . Zenonis munificentiâ pene pacatus . . . beneficiis nunquam satiatus, etc. [p. 368, 369, and 370, ed. Sirmond].

[15] As he was riding in his own camp an unruly horse threw him against the point of a spear which hung before a tent, or was fixed on a waggon (Marcellin. in Chron. Evagrius, l. iii. c. 25).

[16] See Malchus (p. 91 [ed. Par.; p. 268, ed. Bonn]) and Evagrius (l. iii. c. 35).

gold, with the ample pay of thirteen thousand men, were required for the least considerable of their armies;[17] and the Isaurians, who guarded not the empire but the emperor, enjoyed, besides the privilege of rapine, an annual pension of five thousand pounds. The sagacious mind of Theodoric soon perceived that he was odious to the Romans, and suspected by the barbarians; he understood the popular murmur, that his subjects were exposed in their frozen huts to intolerable hardships, while their king was dissolved in the luxury of Greece; and he prevented the painful alternative of encountering the Goths as the champion, or of leading them to the field as the enemy, of Zeno. Embracing an enterprise worthy of his courage and ambition, Theodoric addressed the emperor in the following words:—" Although your servant is maintained in affluence by your liberality, graciously listen to the wishes of my heart! Italy, the inheritance of your predecessors, and Rome itself, the head and mistress of the world, now fluctuate under the violence and oppression of Odoacer the mercenary. Direct me, with my national troops, to march against the tyrant. If I fall, you will be relieved from an expensive and troublesome friend: if, with the Divine permission, I succeed, I shall govern in your name, and to your glory, the Roman senate, and the part of the republic delivered from slavery by my victorious arms." The proposal of Theodoric was accepted, and perhaps had been suggested, by the Byzantine court. But the forms of the commission or grant appear to have been expressed with a prudent ambiguity, which might be explained by the event; and it was left doubtful whether the conqueror of Italy should reign as the lieutenant, the vassal, or the ally, of the emperor of the East.[18]

The reputation both of the leader and of the war diffused a universal ardour; the *Walamirs* were multiplied by the Gothic swarms already engaged in the service, or seated in the provinces, of the empire; and each bold barbarian who had heard of the wealth and beauty of Italy was impatient to seek, through the most perilous adventures, the possession of such enchanting objects. The march of Theodoric must be considered as the emigration of an entire people; the wives and children of the Goths, their aged parents, and most precious effects were carefully transported; and some idea may be formed of the heavy baggage that now followed the camp by the loss of two thousand waggons which had been sustained in a single action in the war of Epirus. For their subsistence, the Goths depended on the magazines of corn, which was ground in portable mills by the hands of their women, on the milk and flesh of their flocks and herds, on the casual produce of the chase, and upon the con-

---

[17] Malchus, p. 85 [p. 256, ed. Bonn]. In a single action, which was decided by the skill and discipline of Sabinian, Theodoric could lose 5000 men.
[18] Jornandes (c. 57, p. 696, 697) has abridged the great history of Cassiodorus. See, compare, and reconcile, Procopius (Gothic. 1. i. c. i.), the Valesian Fragment (p. 718 [ad Calcem Amm. Marc. tom. ii. p. 306, ed. Bip.]), Theophanes (p. 113 [p. 203, ed. Bonn]), and Marcellinus (in Chron.).

tributions which they might impose on all who should presume to dispute the passage or to refuse their friendly assistance.[19]   Notwithstanding these precautions, they were exposed to the danger, and almost to the distress, of famine, in a march of seven hundred miles, which had been undertaken in the depth of a rigorous winter.   Since the fall of the Roman power, Dacia and Pannonia no longer exhibited the rich prospect of populous cities, well-cultivated fields, and convenient highways: the reign of barbarism and desolation was restored; and the tribes of Bulgarians, Gepidæ, and Sarmatians, who had occupied the vacant province, were prompted by their native fierceness, or the solicitations of Odoacer, to resist the progress of his enemy.   In many obscure though bloody battles, Theodoric fought and vanquished: till at length, surmounting every obstacle by skilful conduct and persevering courage, he descended from the Julian Alps, and displayed his invincible banners on the confines of Italy.[20]

Odoacer, a rival not unworthy of his arms, had already occupied the advantageous and well-known post of the river Sontius, near the ruins of Aquileia, at the head of a powerful host, whose independent *kings* [21] or leaders disdained the duties of subordination, and the prudence of delays.   No sooner had Theodoric granted a short repose and refreshment to his wearied cavalry, than he boldly attacked the fortifications of the enemy; the Ostrogoths showed more ardour to acquire, than the mercenaries to defend, the lands of Italy, and the reward of the first victory was the possession of the Venetian province as far as the walls of Verona. In the neighbourhood of that city, on the steep banks of the rapid Adige, he was opposed by a new army, reinforced in its numbers, and not impaired in its courage: the contest was more obstinate, but the event was still more decisive; Odoacer fled to Ravenna, Theodoric advanced to Milan, and the vanquished troops saluted their conqueror with loud acclamations of respect and fidelity.   But their want either of constancy or of faith soon exposed him to the most imminent danger; his vanguard, with several Gothic counts, which had been rashly intrusted to a deserter, was betrayed and destroyed near Faenza by his double treachery; Odoacer again appeared master of the field, and the invader, strongly entrenched in his camp of Pavia, was reduced to solicit the aid of a kindred nation, the Visigoths of Gaul.   In the course of this history the most voracious appetite for war will be abundantly satiated; nor can I much lament that our dark and imperfect materials do not afford a more ample

[19] [Several attempts have been made to estimate the number of the fighting men relatively to the nation.   Hodgkin, in *Italy and its Invaders*, considers the former to have been about 40,000, the latter 200,000.—O. S.]

[20] Theodoric's march is supplied and illustrated by Ennodius (p. 1598-1602), when the bombast of the oration is translated into the language of common sense.

[21] Tot reges, etc. (Ennodius, p. 1602).   We must recollect how much the royal title was multiplied and degraded, and that the mercenaries of Italy were the fragments of many tribes and nations.

narrative of the distress of Italy, and of the fierce conflict which was finally decided by the abilities, experience, and valour of the Gothic king. Immediately before the battle of Verona he visited the tent of his mother [22] and sister, and requested that on a day, the most illustrious festival of his life, they would adorn him with the rich garments which they had worked with their own hands. " Our glory," said he, " is mutual and inseparable. You are known to the world as the mother of Theodoric, and it becomes me to prove that I am the genuine offspring of those heroes from whom I claim my descent." The wife or concubine of Theodemir was inspired with the spirit of the German matrons, who esteemed their sons' honour far above their safety; and it is reported that in a desperate action, when Theodoric himself was hurried along by the torrent of a flying crowd, she boldly met them at the entrance of the camp, and, by her generous reproaches, drove them back on the swords of the enemy.[23]

From the Alps to the extremity of Calabria, Theodoric reigned by the right of conquest: the Vandal ambassadors surrendered the island of Sicily as a lawful appendage of his kingdom, and he was accepted as the deliverer of Rome by the senate and people, who had shut their gates against the flying usurper.[24] Ravenna alone, secure in the fortifications of art and nature, still sustained a siege of almost three years, and the daring sallies of Odoacer carried slaughter and dismay into the Gothic camp. At length, destitute of provisions and hopeless of relief, that unfortunate monarch yielded to the groans of his subjects and the clamours of his soldiers. A treaty of peace was negotiated by the bishop of Ravenna; the Ostrogoths were admitted into the city; and the hostile kings consented, under the sanction of an oath, to rule with equal and undivided authority the provinces of Italy. The event of such an

---

[22] See Ennodius, p. 1603, 1604. Since the orator, in the king's presence, could mention and praise his mother, we may conclude that the magnanimity of Theodoric was not hurt by the vulgar reproaches of concubine and bastard.

[23] This anecdote is related on the modern but respectable authority of Sigonius (Op. tom. i. p. 580; De Occident. Imp. l. xv.) : his words are curious :— " Would you return?" etc. She presented and almost displayed the original recess.

[24] Hist. Miscell. l. xv., a Roman history from Janus to the ninth century, an Epitome of Eutropius, Paulus Diaconus, and Theophanes, which Muratori has published from a MS. in the Ambrosian library (Script. Rerum Italicarum, tom. i. p. 100).

[Prof. Bury cites the following account of the murder of Odoacer from a fragment of John of Antioch. " To a feast in the palace of the consul at the south-east corner of Ravenna on March 5, 493, Theodoric invited Odoacer, now 60 years of age. As the latter sat at table two men knelt before him with a petition and clasped his hands. Then soldiers who had been hidden in recesses on either side of the hall rushed out, but from some cause they could not bring themselves to strike the king. Theodoric himself stepped forward and raised his sword. ' Where is God?' cried Odoacer. ' Thus didst thou to my friends,' said Theodoric, and clave him from the collar bone to the loin. Surprised at his own stroke he exclaimed, ' The wretch can have had no bones in his body.' "—O. S.]

agreement may be easily foreseen. After some days had been devoted to the semblance of joy and friendship, Odoacer, in the midst of a solemn banquet, was stabbed by the hand, or at least by the command, of his rival. Secret and effectual orders had been previously despatched; the faithless and rapacious mercenaries at the same moment, and without resistance, were universally massacred; and the royalty of Theodoric was proclaimed by the Goths, with the tardy, reluctant, ambiguous consent of the emperor of the East. The design of a conspiracy was imputed, according to the usual forms, to the prostrate tyrant, but his innocence and the guilt of his conqueror [25] are sufficiently proved by the advantageous treaty which *force* would not sincerely have granted, nor *weakness* have rashly infringed. The jealousy of power, and the mischiefs of discord, may suggest a more decent apology, and a sentence less rigorous may be pronounced against a crime which was necessary to introduce into Italy a generation of public felicity. The living author of this felicity was audaciously praised in his own presence by sacred and profane orators; [26] but history (in his time she was mute and inglorious) has not left any just representation of the events which displayed, or of the defects which clouded, the virtues of Theodoric. [27] One record of his fame, the volume of public epistles composed by Cassiodorus in the royal name, is still extant, and has obtained more implicit credit than it seems to deserve. [28] They exhibit the forms, rather than the substance, of his government; and we should vainly search for the pure and spontaneous sentiments of the barbarian amidst the declamation and learning of a sophist, the wishes of a Roman senator, the precedents of office, and the vague professions which, in every court, and on every occasion, compose the language of discreet ministers. The

[25] Procopius (Gothic. l. i. c. i.) approves himself an impartial sceptic; φασὶ . . . δολερῷ τρόπῳ ἔκτεινε [tom. ii. p. 10, ed. Bonn]. Cassiodorus (in Chron.) and Ennodius (p. 1605) are loyal and credulous, and the testimony of the Valesian Fragment (p. 718 [Amm. tom. ii. p. 307, ed. Bip.]) may justify their belief. Marcellinus spits the venom of a Greek subject—perjuriis illectus, interfectusque est (in Chron. [anno 489]).

[26] The sonorous and servile oration of Ennodius was pronounced at Milan or Ravenna in the years 507 or 508 (Sirmond, tom. i. p. 1615). Two or three years afterwards the orator was rewarded with the bishopric of Pavia, which he held till his death in the year 521. (Dupin, Bibliot. Eccles. tom. v. p. 11-14. See Saxii Onomasticon, tom. ii. p. 12.)

[27] Our best materials are occasional hints from Procopius and the Valesian Fragment, which was discovered by Sirmond and is published at the end of Ammianus Marcellinus. The author's name is unknown, and his style is barbarous; but in his various facts he exhibits the knowledge, without the passions, of a contemporary. The President Montesquieu had formed the plan of a history of Theodoric, which at a distance might appear a rich and interesting subject.

[28] The best edition of the *Variarum Libri* xii. is that of Joh. Garretius (Rotomagi, 1679, in Opp. Cassiodor. 2 vols. in fol.); but they deserved and required such an editor as the Marquis Scipio Maffei, who thought of publishing them at Verona. The *Barbara Eleganza* (as it is ingeniously named by Tiraboschi) is never simple, and seldom perspicuous.

reputation of Theodoric may repose with more confidence on the visible peace and prosperity of a reign of thirty-three years, the unanimous esteem of his own times, and the memory of his wisdom and courage, his justice and humanity, which was deeply impressed on the minds of the Goths and Italians.

The partition of the lands of Italy, of which Theodoric assigned the third part to his soldiers, is *honourably* arraigned as the sole injustice of his life. And even this act may be fairly justified by the example of Odoacer, the rights of conquest, the true interest of the Italians, and the sacred duty of subsisting a whole people, who, on the faith of his promises, had transported themselves into a distant land.[29] Under the reign of Theodoric, and in the happy climate of Italy, the Goths soon multiplied to a formidable host of two hundred thousand men,[30] and the whole amount of their families may be computed by the ordinary addition of women and children. Their invasion of property, a part of which must have been already vacant, was disguised by the generous but improper name of *hospitality*; these unwelcome guests were irregularly dispersed over the face of Italy, and the lot of each barbarian was adequate to his birth and office, the number of his followers, and the rustic wealth which he possessed in slaves and cattle. The distinctions of noble and plebeian were acknowledged,[31] but the lands of every freeman were exempt from taxes, and he enjoyed the inestimable privilege of being subject only to the laws of his country.[32] Fashion, and even convenience, soon persuaded the conquerors to assume the more elegant dress of the natives, but they still persisted in the use of their mother tongue; and their contempt for the Latin schools was applauded by Theodoric himself, who gratified their prejudices, or his own, by declaring that the child who had trembled at a rod would never dare to look upon a sword.[33] Distress might sometimes provoke the indigent Roman to

[29] Procopius, Gothic. 1. i. c. i.; Variarum, ii. Maffei (Verona Illustrata, P. i. p. 228) exaggerates the injustice of the Goths, whom he hated as an Italian noble. The plebeian Muratori crouches under their oppression.
[With regard to the partition of the lands of Italy whereof Theodoric assigned a third part to his soldiers, Bury thinks that the process of distribution may have been in the main a transferring of the thirds of the men of Odoacer to the men of Theodoric. In this connection too (cf. Gibbon, vol. i. page 1302) it must be remembered that, as shown by Savigny, the Goths retained the land tax and the capitation tax of the Roman emperors. *Geschichte des Römischen Rechts,* vol. i. p. 332.—O. S.]
[30] Procopius, Goth. 1. iii. c. 4 and 21 [tom. ii. p. 295 and 366, ed. Bonn]. Ennodius describes (p. 1612, 1613) the military arts and increasing numbers of the Goths.
[31] When Theodoric gave his sister to the king of the Vandals, she sailed for Africa with a guard of 1000 noble Goths, each of whom was attended by five armed followers (Procop. Vandal. 1. i. c. 8 [tom. i. p. 346, ed. Bonn]). The Gothic nobility must have been as numerous as brave.
[32] See the acknowledgment of Gothic liberty (Var. v. 30).
[33] Procopius, Goth. 1. i. c. 2 [tom. ii. p. 14, ed. Bonn]. The Roman boys learnt the language (Var. viii. 21) of the Goths. Their general ignorance is not destroyed by the exceptions of Amalasuntha, a female, who might

assume the ferocious manners which were insensibly relinquished by the rich and luxurious barbarian;[34] but these mutual conversions were not encouraged by the policy of a monarch who perpetuated the separation of the Italians and Goths, reserving the former for the arts of peace, and the latter for the service of war. To accomplish this design, he studied to protect his industrious subjects, and to moderate the violence, without enervating the valour, of his soldiers, who were maintained for the public defence. They held their lands and benefices as a military stipend: at the sound of the trumpet they were prepared to march under the conduct of their provincial officers, and the whole extent of Italy was distributed into the several quarters of a well-regulated camp. The service of the palace and of the frontiers was performed by choice or by rotation, and each extraordinary fatigue was recompensed by an increase of pay and occasional donatives. Theodoric had convinced his brave companions that empire must be acquired and defended by the same arts. After his example, they strove to excel in the use not only of the lance and sword, the instruments of their victories, but of the missile weapons, which they were too much inclined to neglect: and the lively image of war was displayed in the daily exercise and annual reviews of the Gothic cavalry. A firm though gentle discipline imposed the habits of modesty, obedience, and temperance; and the Goths were instructed to spare the people, to reverence the laws, to understand the duties of civil society, and to disclaim the barbarous licence of judicial combat and private revenge.[35]

Among the barbarians of the West the victory of Theodoric had spread a general alarm. But as soon as it appeared that he was satisfied with conquest and desirous of peace, terror was changed into respect, and they submitted to a powerful mediation, which was uniformly employed for the best purposes of reconciling their quarrels and civilising their manners.[36] The ambassadors who resorted to Ravenna from the most distant countries of Europe admired his wisdom, magnificence,[37] and courtesy; and if he sometimes accepted either slaves or arms, white horses or strange animals, the gift of a sun-dial, a water-clock, or a

study without shame, or of Theodatus, whose learning provoked the indignation and contempt of his countrymen.

[34] A saying of Theodoric was founded on experience: "Romanus miser imitatur Gothum; et utilis (*dives*) Gothus imitatur Romanum." See the Fragment and Notes of Valesius, p. 719 [Amm. ii. p. 308, ed. Bip.]).

[35] The view of the military establishment of the Goths in Italy is collected from the Epistles of Cassiodorus (Var. i. 24, 40; iii. 3, 24, 48; iv. 13, 14; v. 26, 27; viii. 3, 4, 25). They are illustrated by the learned Mascou (Hist. of the Germans, l. xi. 40-44; Annotation xiv.).

[36] See the clearness and vigour of his negotiations in Ennodius (p. 1607) and Cassiodorus (Var. iii. 1, 2, 3, 4; iv. 13; v. 43, 44), who gives the different styles of friendship, counsel, expostulation, etc.

[37] Even of his table (Var. vi. 9) and palace (vii. 5). The admiration of strangers is represented as the most rational motive to justify these vain expenses, and to stimulate the diligence of the officers to whom these provinces were intrusted.

musician, admonished even the princes of Gaul of the superior art and industry of his Italian subjects.   His domestic alliances,[38] a wife, two daughters, a sister, and a niece, united the family of Theodoric with the kings of the Franks, the Burgundians, the Visigoths, the Vandals, and the Thuringians, and contributed to maintain the harmony, or at least the balance, of the great republic of the West.[39]   It is difficult in the dark forests of Germany and Poland to pursue the emigrations of the Heruli, a fierce people who disdained the use of armour, and who condemned their widows and aged parents not to survive the loss of their husbands or the decay of their strength.[40]   The king of these savage warriors solicited the friendship of Theodoric, and was elevated to the rank of his son, according to the barbaric rites of a military adoption.[41]   From the shores of the Baltic the Æstians or Livonians laid their offerings of native amber [42] at the feet of a prince whose fame had excited them to undertake an unknown and dangerous journey of fifteen hundred miles.   With the country [43] from whence the Gothic nation derived their origin he maintained a frequent and friendly correspondence: the Italians were clothed in the rich sables [44] of Sweden; and one

[38] See the public and private alliances of the Gothic monarch, with the Burgundians (Var. i. 45, 46), with the Franks (ii. 40), with the Thuringians (iv. 1), and with the Vandals (v. 1); each of these epistles affords some curious knowledge of the policy and manners of the barbarians.

[39] His political system may be observed in Cassiodorus (Var. iv. 1, ix. 1), Jornandes (c. 58, p. 698, 699), and the Valesian Fragment (p. 720, 721 [Amm. tom. ii. p. 311, ed. Bip.]).   Peace, honourable peace, was the constant aim of Theodoric.

[40] The curious reader may contemplate the Heruli of Procopius (Goth. l. ii. c. 14), and the patient reader may plunge into the dark and minute researches of M. de Buat (Hist. des Peuples Anciens, tom. ix. p. 348-396).

[The Heruli are first mentioned about the middle of the third century, when they accompany the Goths in their expeditions on the Euxine in the reigns of Claudius and Gallienus.   Hence it has been supposed they were Germans.   This is not conclusive, however, as Slavonic tribes appear to have taken part in these expeditions.   Cf. Zeuss *Die Deutschen und die Nachbarstämme.*—O. S.]

[41] Variarum, iv. 2.   The spirit and forms of this martial institution are noticed by Cassiodorus; but he seems to have only translated the sentiments of the Gothic king into the language of Roman eloquence.

[42] Cassiodorus, who quotes Tacitus to the Æstians, the unlettered savages of the Baltic (Var. v. 2), describes the amber for which their shores have ever been famous as the gum of a tree hardened by the sun and purified and wafted by the waves.   When that singular substance is analysed by the chemists, it yields a vegetable oil and a mineral acid.

[43] Scanzia, or Thule, is described by Jornandes (c. 3, p. 610-613) and Procopius (Goth. l. ii. c. 15).   Neither the Goth nor the Greek had visited the country: both had conversed with the natives in their exile at Ravenna or Constantinople.

[44] *Saphirinas pelles.*   In the time of Jornandes they inhabited *Suethans,* the proper Sweden; but that beautiful race of animals has gradually been driven into the eastern parts of Siberia.   See Buffon (Hist. Nat. tom. xiii. p. 309-313, quarto edition); Pennant (System of Quadrupeds, vol. i. p. 322-328); Gmelin (Hist. Gén. des Voyages, tom. xviii. p. 257, 258); and Levesque (Hist. de Russie, tom. v. p. 165, 166, 514, 515).

of its sovereigns, after a voluntary or reluctant abdication, found an hospitable retreat in the palace of Ravenna. He had reigned over one of the thirteen populous tribes who cultivated a small portion of the great island or peninsula of Scandinavia, to which the vague appellation of Thule has been sometimes applied. That northern region was peopled, or had been explored, as high as the sixty-eighth degree of latitude, where the natives of the polar circle enjoy and lose the presence of the sun at each summer and winter solstice during an equal period of forty days.[45] The long night of his absence or death was the mournful season of distress and anxiety, till the messengers, who had been sent to the mountain tops, descried the first rays of returning light, and proclaimed to the plain below the festival of his resurrection.[46]

The life of Theodoric represents the rare and meritorious example of a barbarian who sheathed his sword in the pride of victory and the vigour of his age. A reign of three and thirty years was consecrated to the duties of civil government, and the hostilities, in which he was sometimes involved, were speedily terminated by the conduct of his lieutenants, the discipline of his troops, the arms of his allies, and even by the terror of his name. He reduced, under a strong and regular government, the unprofitable countries of Rhætia, Noricum, Dalmatia, and Pannonia, from the source of the Danube and the territory of the Bavarians [47] to the petty kingdom erected by the Gepidæ on the ruins of Sirmium. His prudence could not safely intrust the bulwark of Italy to such feeble and turbulent neighbours; and his justice might claim the lands which they oppressed, either as a part of his kingdom, or as the inheritance of his father. The greatness of a servant, who was named perfidious because he was successful, awakened the jealousy of the emperor Anastasius; and a war was kindled on the Dacian frontier, by the protection which the Gothic king, in the vicissitude of human affairs, had granted to one of the descendants of Attila. Sabinian, a general illustrious by his own and father's merit, advanced at the head of ten thousand Romans; and the provisions and arms, which filled a long train

[45] In the system or romance of M. Bailly (Lettres sur les Sciences et sur l'Atlantide, tom. i. p. 249-256, tom. ii. p. 114-139), the phœnix of the Edda, and the annual death and revival of Adonis and Osiris, are the allegorical symbols of the absence and return of the sun in the Arctic regions. This ingenious writer is a worthy disciple of the great Buffon; nor is it easy for the coldest reason to withstand the magic of their philosophy.

[46] Αὕτη τε Θουλίταις ἡ μεγίστη τῶν ἑορτων ἔστι, says Procopius [tom. ii. p. 207, ed. Bonn]. At present a rude Manicheism (generous enough) prevails among the Samoyedes in Greenland and in Lapland (Hist. des Voyages, tom. xviii. p. 508, 509, tom. xix. p. 105, 106, 527, 528) ; yet, according to Grotius, Samojutæ cœlum atque astra adorant, numina haud aliis iniquiora (de Rebus Belgicis, l. iv. p. 338, folio edition); a sentence which Tacitus would not have disowned.

[47] See the Hist. des Peuples Anciens, etc., tom. ix. p. 255-273, 396-501. The Count de Buat was French minister at the court of Bavaria : a liberal curiosity prompted his inquiries into the antiquities of the country, and that curiosity was the *germ* of twelve respectable volumes.

of waggons, were distributed to the fiercest of the Bulgarian tribes. But in the fields of Margus the Eastern powers were defeated by the inferior forces of the Goths and Huns; the flower and even the hope of the Roman armies was irretrievably destroyed; and such was the temperance with which Theodoric had inspired his victorious troops, that, as their leader had not given the signal of pillage, the rich spoils of the enemy lay untouched at their feet.[48] Exasperated by this disgrace, the Byzantine court despatched two hundred ships and eight thousand men to plunder the sea-coast of Calabria and Apulia: they assaulted the ancient city of Tarentum, interrupted the trade and agriculture of a happy country, and sailed back to the Hellespont, proud of their piratical victory over a people whom they still presumed to consider as their *Roman* brethren.[49] Their retreat was possibly hastened by the activity of Theodoric; Italy was covered by a fleet of a thousand light vessels,[50] which he constructed with incredible despatch; and his firm moderation was soon rewarded by a solid and honourable peace. He maintained with a powerful hand the balance of the West, till it was at length overthrown by the ambition of Clovis; and although unable to assist his rash and unfortunate kinsman the king of the Visigoths, he saved the remains of his family and people, and checked the Franks in the midst of their victorious career. I am not desirous to prolong or repeat [51] this narrative of military events, the least interesting of the reign of Theodoric; and shall be content to add that the Alemanni were protected,[52] that an inroad of the Burgundians was severely chastised, and that the conquest of Arles and Marseilles opened a free communication with the Visigoths, who revered him both as their national protector, and as the guardian of his grandchild, the infant son of Alaric. Under this respectable character, the king of Italy restored the Prætorian præfecture of the Gauls, reformed some abuses in the civil government of Spain, and accepted the annual tribute and apparent submission of its military governor, who wisely refused to trust his person in the palace

[48] See the Gothic transactions on the Danube and in Illyricum, in Jornandes (c. 58, p. 699), Ennodius (p. 1607-1610), Marcellinus (in Chron. p. 44, 47, 48), and Cassiodorus (in Chron. and Var. iii. 23, 50; iv. 13; vii. 4, 24; viii. 9, 10, 11, 21; ix. 8, 9).

[49] I cannot forbear transcribing the liberal and classic style of Count Marcellinus: Romanus comes domesticorum, et Rusticus comes scholariorum cum centum armatis navibus, totidemque dromonibus, octo millia militum armatorum secum ferentibus, ad devastanda Italiæ littora processerunt, et usque ad Tarentum antiquissimam civitatem aggressi sunt; remensoque mari inhonestam victoriam quam piratico ausu Romani ex Romanis rapuerunt, Anastasio Cæsari reportarunt (in Chron. p. 48 [anno 508]). See Variar. i. 16, ii. 38.

[50] See the royal orders and instructions (Var. iv. 15; v. 16-20). These armed boats should be still smaller than the thousand vessels of Agamemnon at the siege of Troy [Manso, p. 121].

[51] Vol. iv. p. 357, *seq.*

[52] Ennodius (p. 1610) and Cassiodorus, in the royal name (Var. ii. 41), record his salutary protection of the Alemanni.

of Ravenna.[53]   The Gothic sovereignty was established from Sicily to the Danube, from Sirmium or Belgrade to the Atlantic Ocean; and the Greeks themselves have acknowledged that Theodoric reigned over the fairest portion of the Western empire.[54]

The union of the Goths and Romans might have fixed for ages the transient happiness of Italy; and the first of nations, a new people of free subjects and enlightened soldiers, might have gradually arisen from the mutual emulation of their respective virtues.   But the sublime merit of guiding or seconding such a revolution was not reserved for the reign of Theodoric: he wanted either the genius or the opportunities of a legislator;[55] and while he indulged the Goths in the enjoyment of rude liberty, he servilely copied the institutions, and even the abuses, of the political system which had been framed by Constantine and his successors.   From a tender regard to the expiring prejudices of Rome, the barbarian declined the name, the purple, and the diadem of the emperors; but he assumed, under the hereditary title of king, the whole substance and plentitude of Imperial prerogative.[56]   His addresses to the Eastern throne were respectful and ambiguous: he celebrated in pompous style the harmony of the two republics, applauded his own government as the perfect similitude of a sole and undivided empire, and claimed above the kings of the earth the same pre-eminence which he modestly allowed to the person or rank of Anastasius.   The alliance of the East and West was annually declared by the unanimous choice of two consuls; but it should seem that the Italian candidate, who was named by Theodoric, accepted a formal confirmation from the sovereign

[53] The Gothic transactions in Gaul and Spain are represented with some perplexity in Cassiodorus (Var. iii. 32, 38, 41, 43, 44; v. 39), Jornandes (c. 58, p. 698, 699), and Procopius (Goth. l. i. c. 12).   I will neither hear nor reconcile the long and contradictory arguments of the Abbé Dubos and the Count de Buat, about the wars of Burgundy.

[54] Theophanes, p. 113 [p. 203, ed. Bonn].

[55] Procopius affirms that no laws whatsoever were promulgated by Theodoric and the succeeding kings of Italy (Goth. l. ii. c. 6 [tom. ii. p. 170, ed. Bonn]). He must mean in the Gothic language.   A Latin edict of Theodoric is still extant, in one hundred and fifty-four articles.

[This Latin edict of Theodoric was promulgated in 500 A.D., and its articles were intended to apply to cases in which either the Romans or the Goths and Romans were concerned.   While the Goths retained the exclusive privilege of arms, it was the policy of Theodoric to unite them and the Romans in all their civil relations into one people.   In this respect the Ostrogothic kingdom was distinct from all the other German states founded upon the downfall of the empire, since in the latter each nation preserved its separate laws. Cf. Savigny.   In differences between Goth and Roman, a Roman jurisconsult acted as assessor to the Comes Gothorum, or the official dealing with the disputes between Goths themselves.   Of course there was a natural leaning at times to the side of the Goth.—O. S.]

[56] The image of Theodoric is engraved on his coins: his modest successors were satisfied with adding their own name to the head of the reigning emperor (Muratori, Antiquitat. Italiæ Medii Ævi, tom. ii. dissert. xxvii. p. 577-579. Giannone, Istoria Civile di Napoli, tom. i. p. 166).

of Constantinople.[57]   The Gothic palace of Ravenna reflected the image of the court of Theodosius or Valentinian.   The Prætorian præfect, the præfect of Rome, the quæstor, the master of the offices, with the public and patrimonial treasurers, whose functions are painted in gaudy colours by the rhetoric of Cassiodorus, still continued to act as the ministers of state.   And the subordinate care of justice and the revenue was delegated to seven consulars, three correctors, and five presidents, who governed the fifteen *regions* of Italy according to the principles, and even the forms, of Roman jurisprudence.[58]   The violence of the conquerors was abated or eluded by the slow artifice of judicial proceedings; the civil administration, with its honours and emoluments, was confined to the Italians; and the people still preserved their dress and language, their laws and customs, their personal freedom, and two-thirds of their landed property.   It had been the object of Augustus to conceal the introduction of monarchy; it was the policy of Theodoric to disguise the reign of a barbarian.[59]   If his subjects were sometimes awakened from this pleasing vision of a Roman government, they derived more substantial comfort from the character of a Gothic prince who had penetration to discern, and firmness to pursue, his own and the public interest.   Theodoric loved the virtues which he possessed, and the talents of which he was destitute.   Liberius was promoted to the office of Prætorian præfect for his unshaken fidelity to the unfortunate cause of Odoacer.   The ministers of Theodoric, Cassiodorus,[60] and Boethius,

[57] The alliance of the emperor and the king of Italy are represented by Cassiodorus (Var. i. 1; ii. 1, 2, 3; vi. 1) and Procopius (Goth. l. ii. c. 6; l. iii. c. 21 [tom. ii. p. 369, ed. Bonn]), who celebrate the friendship of Anastasius and Theodoric: but the figurative style of compliment was interpreted in a very different sense at Constantinople and Ravenna.

[58] To the seventeen provinces of the Notitia, Paul Warnefrid the deacon (De Reb. Longobard. l. ii. c. 14-22) has subjoined an eighteenth, the Apennine (Muratori, Script. Rerum Italicarum, tom. i. p. 431-433).   But of these, Sardinia and Corsica were possessed by the Vandals, and the two Rhætias, as well as the Cottian Alps, seem to have been abandoned to a military government. The state of the four provinces that now form the kingdom of Naples is laboured by Giannone (tom. i. p. 172, 178) with patriotic diligence.

[59] See the Gothic history of Procopius (l. i. c. 1, l. ii. c. 6), the Epistles of Cassiodorus (passim, but especially the fifth and sixth books [vi. and vii.], which contain the *formulæ*, or patents of offices), and the Civil History of Giannone (tom. i. l. ii. iii.).   The Gothic counts, which he places in every Italian city, are annihilated, however, by Maffei (Verona Illustrata, P. i. l. viii. p. 227); for those of Syracuse and Naples (Var. vi. 22, 23) were special and temporary commissions.

[60] Two Italians of the name of Cassiodorus, the father (Var. i. 24 [4], 40) and the son (ix. 24, 25), were successively employed in the administration of Theodoric.   The son was born in the year 479: his various epistles as quæstor, master of the offices, and Prætorian præfect, extend from 509 to 539, and he lived as a monk about thirty years.   (Tiraboschi, Storia della Letteratura Italiana, tom. iii. p. 7-24.   Fabricius, Biblioth. Lat. Med. Ævi. tom. i. p. 357, 358, edit. Mansi.)

[Cassiodorus was of an ancient and honourable family.   His grandfather had distinguished himself in the defence of Sicily against the ravages of

have reflected on his reign the lustre of their genius and learning. More prudent or more fortunate than his colleague, Cassiodorus preserved his own esteem without forfeiting the royal favour; and after passing thirty years in the honours of the world, he was blessed with an equal term of repose in the devout and studious solitude of Squillace.

As the patron of the republic, it was the interest and duty of the Gothic king to cultivate the affections of the senate [61] and people. The nobles of Rome were flattered by sonorous epithets and formal professions of respect, which had been more justly applied to the merit and authority of their ancestors. The people enjoyed, without fear or danger, the three blessings of a capital, order, plenty, and public amusements. A visible diminution of their numbers may be found even in the measure of liberality;[62] yet Apulia, Calabria, and Sicily poured their tribute of corn into the granaries of Rome; an allowance of bread and meat was distributed to the indigent citizens; and every office was deemed honourable which was consecrated to the care of their health and happiness. The public games, such as a Greek ambassador might politely applaud, exhibited a faint and feeble copy of the magnificence of the Cæsars: yet the musical, the gymnastic, and the pantomime arts, had not totally sunk in oblivion; the wild beasts of Africa still exercised in the amphitheatre the courage and dexterity of the hunters; and the indulgent Goth either patiently tolerated or gently restrained the blue and green factions, whose contests so often filled the circus with clamour, and even with blood.[63] In the seventh year of his peaceful reign, Theodoric visited the old capital of the world; the senate and people advanced in solemn procession to salute a second Trajan, a new Valentinian; and he nobly supported that character, by the assurance of a just and legal government,[64] in a discourse which he was not afraid to pronounce in public and to inscribe on a tablet of brass. Rome, in this august ceremony, shot a last ray of declining glory; and a saint, the

Genseric, while his father held a high rank at the court of Valentinian III. Cassiodorus was first the treasurer of the private expenditure to Odoacer, afterwards " Count of the Sacred Largesses." Yielding with the rest of the Romans to the dominion of Theodoric, he was instrumental in securing the peaceful submission of Sicily. He was successively governor of his native provinces of Bruttium and Lucania, quæstor, magister palatii, Prætorian Præfect, patrician, consul, private secretary, and, in fact, first minister to the king. He died in 575 at the great age of 95.—O. S.]

[61] See his regard for the senate in Cochlœus (Vit. Theod. viii. p. 72-80).

[62] No more than 120,000 *modii*, or four thousand quarters (Anonym. Valesian, p. 721 [Amm. ii. p. 310, ed. Bip.], and Var. i. 35, vi. 18, xi. 5, 39).

[63] See his regard and indulgence for the spectacles of the circus, the amphitheatre, and the theatre, in the Chronicle and Epistles of Cassiodorus (Var. i. 20, 27, 30, 31, 32, iii. 51, iv. 51, illustrated by the fourteenth Annotation of Mascou's History), who has contrived to sprinkle the subject with ostentatious, though agreeable, learning.

[64] Anonym. Vales. p. 721 [l. c. ed. Bip.]. Marius Aventicensis in Chron. In the scale of public and personal merit, the Gothic conqueror is at least as much *above* Valentinian as he may seem *inferior* to Trajan.

spectator of this pompous scene, could only hope, in his pious fancy, that it was excelled by the celestial splendour of the New Jerusalem.[65] During a residence of six months, the fame, the person, and the courteous demeanour of the Gothic king excited the admiration of the Romans, and he contemplated, with equal curiosity and surprise, the monuments that remained of their ancient greatness. He imprinted the footsteps of a conqueror on the Capitoline hill, and frankly confessed that each day he viewed with fresh wonder the forum of Trajan and his lofty column. The theatre of Pompey appeared, even in its decay, as a huge mountain, artificially hollowed and polished, and adorned by human industry; and he vaguely computed that a river of gold must have been drained to erect the colossal amphitheatre of Titus.[66] From the mouths of fourteen aqueducts a pure and copious stream was diffused into every part of the city; among these the Claudian water, which arose at the distance of thirty-eight miles in the Sabine mountains, was conveyed along a gentle though constant declivity of solid arches, till it descended on the summit of the Aventine hill. The long and spacious vaults which had been constructed for the purpose of common sewers subsisted after twelve centuries in their pristine strength; and these subterraneous channels have been preferred to all the visible wonders of Rome.[67] The Gothic kings, so injuriously accused of the ruin of antiquity, were anxious to preserve the monuments of the nation whom they had subdued.[68] The royal edicts were framed to prevent the abuses, the neglect, or the depredations of the citizens themselves; and a professed architect, the annual sum of two hundred pounds of gold, twenty-five thousand tiles, and the receipt of customs from the Lucrine port, were assigned for the ordinary repairs of the walls and public edifices. A similar care was extended to the statues of metal or marble of men or animals. The spirit of the horses which have given a modern name to the Quirinal was applauded by the barbarians;[69] the brazen elephants of the *Via sacra* were dili-

---

[65] Vit. Fulgentii in Baron. Annal. Eccles. A.D. 500, No. 10.

[66] Cassiodorus describes in his pompous style the Forum of Trajan (Var. vii. 6), the theatre of Marcellus (iv. 51), and the amphitheatre of Titus (v. 42) ; and his descriptions are not unworthy of the reader's perusal. According to the modern prices, the Abbé Barthelemy computes that the brickwork and masonry of the Coliseum would now cost twenty millions of French livres (Mém. de l'Académie des Inscriptions, tom. xxviii. p. 585, 586). How small a part of that stupendous fabric!

[67] For the aqueducts and cloacæ see Strabo (l. v. p. 360 [p. 235, ed. Casaub.]), Pliny (Hist. Nat. xxxvi. 24 [§ 3]), Cassiodorus (Var. iii. 30, 31, vi. 6), Procopius (Goth. l. i. c. 19), and Nardini (Roma Antica, p. 514-522). How such works could be executed by a king of Rome is yet a problem.

[68] For the Gothic care of the buildings and statues, see Cassiodorus (Var. i. 21, 25, ii. 34, iv. 30, vii. 6, 13, 15), and the Valesian Fragment (p. 721 [Amm. tom. ii. p. 310, ed. Bip.]).

[69] Var. vii. 15. These horses of Monte Cavallo had been transported from Alexandria to the baths of Constantine (Nardini, p. 188). Their sculpture is disdained by the Abbé Dubos (Réflexions sur la Poésie et sur la Peinture, tom. i. section 39), and admired by Winckelman (Hist. de l'Art, tom. ii. p. 159).

gently restored;[70] the famous heifer of Myron deceived the cattle, as they were driven through the forum of peace;[71] and an officer was created to protect those works of art, which Theodoric considered as the noblest ornament of his kingdom.

After the example of the last emperors, Theodoric preferred the residence of Ravenna, where he cultivated an orchard with his own hands.[72] As often as the peace of his kingdom was threatened (for it was never invaded) by the barbarians, he removed his court to Verona [73] on the northern frontier, and the image of his palace, still extant on a coin, represents the oldest and most authentic model of Gothic architecture. These two capitals, as well as Pavia, Spoleto, Naples, and the rest of the Italian cities, acquired under his reign the useful or splendid decorations of churches, aqueducts, baths, porticoes, and palaces.[74] But the happiness of the subject was more truly conspicuous in the busy scene of labour and luxury, in the rapid increase and bold enjoyment of national wealth. From the shades of Tibur and Præneste, the Roman senators still retired in the winter season to the warm sun and salubrious springs of Baiæ; and their villas, which advanced on solid moles into the bay of Naples, commanded the various prospect of the sky, the earth, and the water. On the eastern side of the Hadriatic a new Campania was formed in the fair and fruitful province of Istria, which communicated with the palace of Ravenna by an easy navigation of one hundred miles. The rich productions of Lucania and the adjacent provinces were exchanged at the Marcilian fountain, in a populous fair annually dedicated to trade, intemperance, and superstition. In the solitude of Comum, which had once been ani-

---

[70] Var. x. 30. They were probably a fragment of some triumphal car (Cuper de Elephantis, ii. 10).

[71] Procopius (Goth. 1. iv. c. 21 [tom. ii. p. 571, ed. Bonn]) relates a foolish story of Myron's cow, which is celebrated by the false wit of thirty-six Greek epigrams (Antholog. 1. iv. p. 302-306, edit. Hen. Steph.; Auson. Epigram. lviii.-lxviii.).

[72] See an epigram of Ennodius (ii. 3, p. 1893, 1894) on this garden and the royal gardener.

[73] His affection for that city is proved by the epithet of "Verona tua," and the legend of the hero; under the barbarous name of Dietrich of Bern (Peringsciold ad Cochlœum, p. 240), Maffei traces him with knowledge and pleasure in his native country (l. ix. p. 230-236).

[74] See Maffei (Verona Illustrata, Part. i. p. 231, 232, 308, etc.). He imputes Gothic architecture, like the corruption of language, writing, etc., not to the barbarians, but to the Italians themselves. Compare his sentiments with those of Tiraboschi (tom. iii. p. 61).

[With regard to Theodoric's architecture, Hallam states that the "image" of it is represented in Maffei, not from a coin, but from a seal. There is also an engraving from a mosaic in the church of St. Apollinaris in Ravenna representing a building ascribed to Theodoric in that city. Neither of these, as Hallam says, in the least approximates to the Gothic style. They are evidently the degenerate Roman architecture, and, as Milman says, more resemble the attempts of our English architects to get back from our national Gothic into a classical Greek style. One of them, adds Milman, calls to mind Inigo Jones's inner quadrangle in St. John's College, Oxford.—O. S.]

mated by the mild genius of Pliny, a transparent basin above sixty miles in length still reflected the rural seats which encompassed the margin of the Larian lake; and the gradual ascent of the hills was covered by a triple plantation of olives, of vines, and of chestnut-trees.[75] Agriculture revived under the shadow of peace, and the number of husbandmen was multiplied by the redemption of captives.[76] The iron-mines of Dalmatia, a gold-mine in Bruttium, were carefully explored, and the Pomptine marshes, as well as those of Spoleto, were drained and cultivated by private undertakers, whose distant reward must depend on the continuance of the public prosperity.[77] Whenever the seasons were less propitious, the doubtful precautions of forming magazines of corn, fixing the price, and prohibiting the exportation, attested at least the benevolence of the state; but such was the extraordinary plenty which an industrious people produced from a grateful soil, that a gallon of wine was sometimes sold in Italy for less than three farthings, and a quarter of wheat at about five shillings and sixpence.[78] A country possessed of so many valuable objects of exchange soon attracted the merchants of the world, whose beneficial traffic was encouraged and protected by the liberal spirit of Theodoric. The free intercourse of the provinces by land and water was restored and extended; the city gates were never shut either by day or by night; and the common saying, that a purse of gold might be safely left in the fields, was expressive of the conscious security of the inhabitants.

A difference of religion is always pernicious and often fatal to the harmony of the prince and people: the Gothic conqueror had been educated in the profession of Arianism, and Italy was devoutly attached to the Nicene faith. But the persuasion of Theodoric was not infected by zeal: and he piously adhered to the heresy of his fathers, without condescending to balance the subtile arguments of theological metaphysics. Satisfied with the private toleration of his Arian sectaries, he justly conceived himself to be the guardian of the public worship,

[75] The villas, climate, and landscape of Baiæ (Var. ix. 6; see Cluver. Italia Antiq. l. iv. c. 2, p. 1119, etc.), Istria (Var. xii. 22, 26), and Comum (Var. xi. 14, compare with Pliny's two villas, ix. 7), are agreeably painted in the epistles of Cassiodorus.

[76] In Liguria numerosa agricolarum progenies (Ennodius, p. 1678, 1679, 1680). St. Epiphanius of Pavia redeemed by prayer or ransom 6000 captives from the Burgundians of Lyons and Savoy. Such deeds are the best of miracles.

[77] The political economy of Theodoric (see Anonym. Vales. p. 721 [Amm. tom. ii. p. 311, ed. Bip.] and Cassiodorus, in Chron.) may be distinctly traced under the following heads: iron-mine (Var. iii. 25); gold-mine (ix. 3); Pomptine marshes (ii. 32, 33); Spoleto (ii. 21); corn (i. 34, x. 27, 28, xi. 11, 12); trade (vi. 7, vii. 9, 23); fair of Leucothoe or St. Cyprian in Lucania (viii. 33); plenty (xii. 4); the cursus, or public post (i. 29, ii. 31, iv. 47, v. 5, vi. 6, vii. 33); the Flaminian way (xii. 18).

[78] LX modii tritici in solidum ipsius tempore fuerunt, et vinum xxx amphoras in solidum (Fragment. Vales. [p. 311, ed. Bip.]). Corn was distributed from the granaries at xv or xxv modii for a piece of gold, and the price was still moderate.

and his external reverence for a superstition which he despised may have nourished in his mind the salutary indifference of a statesman or philosopher. The catholics of his dominions acknowledged, perhaps with reluctance, the peace of the church; their clergy, according to the degrees of rank or merit, were honourably entertained in the palace of Theodoric; he esteemed the living sanctity of Cæsarius [79] and Epiphanius,[80] the orthodox bishops of Arles and Pavia; and presented a decent offering on the tomb of St. Peter, without any scrupulous inquiry into the creed of the apostle.[81] His favourite Goths, and even his mother, were permitted to retain or embrace the Athanasian faith, and his long reign could not afford the example of an Italian catholic who, either from choice or compulsion, had deviated into the religion of the conqueror.[82] The people, and the barbarians themselves, were edified by the pomp and order of religious worship; the magistrates were instructed to defend the just immunities of ecclesiastical persons and possessions; the bishops held their synods, the metropolitans exercised their jurisdiction, and the privileges of sanctuary were maintained or moderated according to the spirit of the Roman jurisprudence.[83] With the protection, Theodoric assumed the legal supremacy, of the church; and his firm administration restored or extended some useful prerogatives which had been neglected by the feeble emperors of the West. He was not ignorant of the dignity and importance of the Roman pontiff, to whom the venerable name of POPE was now appropriated. The peace or the revolt of Italy might depend on the character of a wealthy and popular bishop, who claimed such ample dominion both in heaven and earth; who had been declared in a numerous synod to be pure from all sin, and exempt from all judgment.[84] When the chair

[79] See the Life of St. Cæsarius in Baronius (A.D. 508, No. 12, 13, 14). The king presented him with 300 gold solidi, and a discus of silver of the weight of sixty pounds.

[80] Ennodius in Vit. St. Epiphanii, in Sirmond Op. tom. i. p. 1672-1690. Theodoric bestowed some important favours on this bishop, whom he used as a counsellor in peace and war.

[81] Devotissimus ac si catholicus (Anonym. Vales. p. 720 [p. 310, ed. Bip.]); yet his offering was no more than two silver candlesticks (*cerostrata*) of the weight of seventy pounds, far inferior to the gold and gems of Constantinople and France (Anastasius in Vit. Pont. in Hormisda, p. 34, edit. Paris [tom. i. p. 93, ed. Rom. 1718]).

[82] The tolerating system of his reign (Ennodius, p. 1612, Anonym. Vales. p. 719 [p. 308, ed. Bip.], Procop. Goth. l. i. c. 1, l. ii. c. 6) may be studied in the Epistles of Cassiodorus, under the following heads: *bishops* (Var. i. 9, viii. 15, 24, xi. 23); *immunities* (i. 26, ii. 29, 30); *church lands* (iv. 17, 20); *sanctuaries* (ii. 11, iii. 47); *church plate* (xii. 20); *discipline* (iv. 44); which prove at the same time that he was the head of the church as well as of the state.

[83] We may reject a foolish tale of his beheading a catholic deacon who turned Arian (Theodor. Lector. No. 17). Why is Theodoric surnamed *Afer?* From *Vafer?* (Vales. ad loc.) A light conjecture.

[84] Ennodius, p. 1621, 1622, 1636, 1638. His *libel* was approved and registered (synodaliter) by a Roman council (Baronius, A.D. 503, No. 6. Franciscus Pagi in Breviar. Pont. Rom. tom. i. p. 242).

of St. Peter was disputed by Symmachus, and Laurence, they appeared at his summons before the tribunal of an Arian monarch, and he confirmed the election of the most worthy or the more obsequious candidate. At the end of his life, in a moment of jealousy and resentment, he prevented the choice of the Romans, by nominating a pope in the palace of Ravenna. The danger and furious contests of a schism were mildly restrained, and the last decree of the senate was enacted to extinguish, if it were possible, the scandalous venality of the papal elections.[85]

I have descanted with pleasure on the fortunate condition of Italy, but our fancy must not hastily conceive that the golden age of the poets, a race of men without vice or misery, was realised under the Gothic conquest. The fair prospect was sometimes overcast with clouds; the wisdom of Theodoric might be deceived, his power might be resisted, and the declining age of the monarch was sullied with popular hatred and patrician blood. In the first insolence of victory he had been tempted to deprive the whole party of Odoacer of the civil and even the natural rights of society;[86] a tax, unseasonably imposed after the calamities of war, would have crushed the rising agriculture of Liguria; a rigid pre-emption of corn, which was intended for the public relief, must have aggravated the distress of Campania. These dangerous projects were defeated by the virtue and eloquence of Epiphanius and Boethius, who, in the presence of Theodoric himself, successfully pleaded the cause of the people:[87] but, if the royal ear was open to the voice of truth, a saint and a philosopher are not always to be found at the ear of kings. The privileges of rank, or office, or favour were too frequently abused by Italian fraud and Gothic violence, and the avarice of the king's nephew was publicly exposed, at first by the usurpation, and afterwards by the restitution, of the estates which he had unjustly extorted from his Tuscan neighbours. Two hundred thousand barbarians, formidable even to their master, were seated in the heart of Italy; they indignantly supported the restraints of peace and discipline; the disorders of their march were always felt and sometimes compensated; and where it was dangerous to punish, it might be prudent to dissemble, the sallies of their native fierceness. When the indulgence of Theodoric had remitted two-thirds of the Ligurian

[85] See Cassiodorus (Var. viii. 15, ix. 15, 16), Anastasius (in Symmacho, p. 31 [p. 84, ed. Rom.]), and the seventeenth Annotation of Mascou. Baronius, Pagi, and most of the catholic doctors, confess, with an angry growl, this Gothic usurpation.
[86] He disabled them—a licentia testandi; and all Italy mourned—lamentabili justitio. I wish to believe that these penalties were enacted against the rebels who had violated their oath of allegiance; but the testimony of Ennodius (p. 1675-1678) is the more weighty, as he lived and died under the reign of Theodoric.
[87] Ennodius, in Vit. Epiphan. p. 1689, 1690. Boethius de Consolatione Philosophiæ, l. i. pros. iv. p. 45, 46, 47 [ed. Callyus, Par. 1680]. Respect, but weigh, the passions of the saint and the senator; and fortify or alleviate their complaints by the various hints of Cassiodorus (ii. 8, iv. 36, viii. 5).

tribute, he condescended to explain the difficulties of his situation, and to lament the heavy though inevitable burdens which he imposed on his subjects for their own defence.[88] These ungrateful subjects could never be cordially reconciled to the origin, the religion, or even the virtues of the Gothic conqueror; past calamities were forgotten, and the sense or suspicion of injuries was rendered still more exquisite by the present felicity of the times.

Even the religious toleration which Theodoric had the glory of introducing into the Christian world was painful and offensive to the orthodox zeal of the Italians. They respected the armed heresy of the Goths; but their pious rage was safely pointed against the rich and defenceless Jews, who had formed their establishments at Naples, Rome, Ravenna, Milan, and Genoa, for the benefit of trade and under the sanction of the laws.[89] Their persons were insulted, their effects were pillaged, and their synagogues were burnt by the mad populace of Ravenna and Rome, inflamed, as it should seem, by the most frivolous or extravagant pretences. The government which could neglect, would have deserved such an outrage. A legal inquiry was instantly directed; and, as the authors of the tumult had escaped in the crowd, the whole community was condemned to repair the damage, and the obstinate bigots, who refused their contributions, were whipped through the streets by the hand of the executioner. This simple act of justice exasperated the discontent of the catholics, who applauded the merit and patience of these holy confessors. Three hundred pulpits deplored the persecution of the church; and if the chapel of St. Stephen at Verona was demolished by the command of Theodoric, it is probable that some miracle hostile to his name and dignity had been performed on that sacred theatre. At the close of a glorious life, the king of Italy discovered that he had excited the hatred of a people whose happiness he had so assiduously laboured to promote; and his mind was soured by indignation, jealousy, and the bitterness of unrequited love. The Gothic conqueror condescended to disarm the unwarlike natives of Italy, interdicting all weapons of offence, and excepting only a small knife for domestic use. The deliverer of Rome was accused of conspiring with the vilest informers against the lives of senators whom he suspected of a secret and treasonable correspondence with the Byzantine court.[90] After the death of Anastasius, the diadem had been placed on the head of a feeble old man, but the powers of government were assumed by his nephew Justinian, who already meditated the extirpation of heresy and the conquest of Italy

[88] Immanium expensarum pondus . . . pro ipsorum salute, etc.; yet these are no more than words.

[89] The Jews were settled at Naples (Procopius, Goth. 1. i. c. 8 [tom. ii. p. 44, ed. Bonn]), at Genoa (Var. ii. 27, iv. 33), Milan (v. 37), Rome (iv. 43). See likewise Basnage, Hist. des Juifs, tom. viii. c. 7, p. 254.

[90] Rex avidus communis exitii, etc. (Boethius, 1. i. p. 55) : rex dolum Romanis tendebat (Anonym. Vales. p. 723). These are hard words: they speak the passions of the Italians, and those (I fear) of Theodoric himself.

and Africa. A rigorous law, which was published at Constantinople, to reduce the Arians, by the dread of punishment, within the pale of the church, awakened the just resentment of Theodoric, who claimed for his distressed brethren of the East the same indulgence which he had so long granted to the catholics of his dominions. At his stern command the Roman pontiff, with four *illustrious* senators, embarked on an embassy of which he must have alike dreaded the failure or the success. The singular veneration shown to the first pope who had visited Constantinople was punished as a crime by this jealous monarch; the artful or peremptory refusal of the Byzantine court might excuse an equal, and would provoke a larger, measure of retaliation; and a mandate was prepared in Italy to prohibit, after a stated day, the exercise of the catholic worship. By the bigotry of his subjects and enemies the most tolerant of princes was driven to the brink of persecution, and the life of Theodoric was too long, since he lived to condemn the virtue of Boethius and Symmachus.[91]

The senator Boethius[92] is the last of the Romans whom Cato or Tully could have acknowledged for their countrymen. As a wealthy orphan, he inherited the patrimony and honours of the Anician family, a name ambitiously assumed by the kings and emperors of the age, and the appellation of Manlius asserted his genuine or fabulous descent from a race of consuls and dictators who had repulsed the Gauls from the Capitol, and sacrificed their sons to the discipline of the republic. In the youth of a Boethius the studies of Rome were not totally abandoned; a Virgil[93] is now extant corrected by the hand of a consul; and the professors of grammar, rhetoric, and jurisprudence were maintained in their privileges and pensions by the liberality of the Goths. But the erudition of the Latin language was insufficient to satiate his ardent curiosity; and Boethius is said to have employed eighteen laborious years in the schools of Athens,[94] which were supported by

[91] I have laboured to extract a rational narrative from the dark, concise, and various hints of the Valesian Fragment (p. 722, 723, 724 [p. 313, *sqq.* ed. Bip.]), Theophanes (p. 145 [tom. i. p. 261, ed. Bonn]), Anastasius (in Johanne, p. 35 [p. 94, ed. Rom.]), and the Hist. Miscella (p. 103, edit. Muratori [Milan, 1723]). A gentle pressure and paraphrase of their words is no violence. Consult likewise Muratori (Annali d'Italia, tom. iv. p. 471-478), with the Annals and Breviary (tom. i. p. 259-263) of the two Pagis, the uncle and the nephew.

[92] Le Clerc has composed a critical and philosophical Life of Anicius Manlius Severinus Boethius (Bibliot. Choisie, tom. xvi. p. 168-275); and both Tiraboschi (tom. iii.) and Fabricius (Bibliot. Latin.) may be usefully consulted. The date of his birth may be placed about the year 470, and his death in 524, in a premature old age (Consol. Phil. Metrica, i. p. 5).

[93] For the age and value of this MS., now in the Medicean library at Florence, see the Cenotaphia Pisana (p. 430-447) of Cardinal Noris.

[94] The Athenian studies of Boethius are doubtful (Baronius, A.D. 510, No. 3, from a spurious tract, De Disciplina Scholarum), and the term of eighteen years is doubtless too long: but the simple fact of a visit to Athens is justified by much internal evidence (Brucker, Hist. Crit. Philosoph. tom. iii. p. 524-527), and by an expression (though vague and ambiguous) of his friend Cassiodorus (Var. i. 45), " longè positas Athenas introisti."

the zeal, the learning, and the diligence of Proclus and his disciples. The reason and piety of their Roman pupil were fortunately saved from the contagion of mystery and magic which polluted the groves of the Academy; but he imbibed the spirit, and imitated the method, of his dead and living masters, who attempted to reconcile the strong and subtle sense of Aristotle with the devout contemplation and sublime fancy of Plato. After his return to Rome, and his marriage with the daughter of his friend the patrician Symmachus, Boethius still continued, in a palace of ivory and marble, to prosecute the same studies.[95] The church was edified by his profound defence of the orthodox creed against the Arian, the Eutychian, and the Nestorian heresies; and the catholic unity was explained or exposed in a formal treatise by the *indifference* of three distinct though consubstantial persons. For the benefit of his Latin readers, his genius submitted to teach the first elements of the arts and sciences of Greece. The geometry of Euclid, the music of Pythagoras, the arithmetic of Nicomachus, the mechanics of Archimedes, the astronomy of Ptolemy, the theology of Plato, and the logic of Aristotle, with the commentary of Porphyry, were translated and illustrated by the indefatigable pen of the Roman senator. And he alone was esteemed capable of describing the wonders of art, a sundial, a water-clock, or a sphere which represented the motions of the planets. From these abstruse speculations Boethius stooped—or, to speak more truly, he rose—to the social duties of public and private life; the indigent were relieved by his liberality, and his eloquence, which flattery might compare to the voice of Demosthenes or Cicero, was uniformly exerted in the cause of innocence and humanity. Such conspicuous merit was felt and rewarded by a discerning prince: the dignity of Boethius was adorned with the titles of consul and patrician, and his talents were usefully employed in the important station of master of the offices. Notwithstanding the equal claims of the East and West, his two sons were created, in their tender youth, the consuls of the same year.[96] On the memorable day of their inauguration they proceeded in solemn pomp from their palace to the forum amidst the applause of the senate and people; and their joyful father, the true consul of Rome, after pronouncing an oration in the praise of his royal benefactor, distributed a triumphal largess in the games of the circus.

[95] Bibliothecæ comptos ebore ac vitro parietes, etc. (Consol. Phil. l. i. pros. v. p. 74). The Epistles of Ennodius (vi. 6, vii. 13, viii. 1, 31, 37, 40) and Cassiodorus (Var. i. 39, iv. 6, ix. 21) afford many proofs of the high reputation which he enjoyed in his own times. It is true that the bishop of Pavia wanted to purchase of him an old house at Milan, and praise might be tendered and accepted in part of payment.

[96] Pagi, Muratori, etc., are agreed that Boethius himself was consul in the year 510, his two sons in 522, and in 487, perhaps, his father. A desire of ascribing the last of these consulships to the philosopher had perplexed the chronology of his life. In his honours, alliances, children, he celebrates his own felicity—his past felicity (p. 109, 110).

Prosperous in his fame and fortunes, in his public honours and private alliances, in the cultivation of science and the consciousness of virtue, Boethius might have been styled happy, if that precarious epithet could be safely applied before the last term of the life of man.

A philosopher, liberal of his wealth and parsimonious of his time, might be insensible to the common allurements of ambition, the thirst of gold and employment. And some credit may be due to the asseveration of Boethius, that he had reluctantly obeyed the divine Plato, who enjoins every virtuous citizen to rescue the state from the usurpation of vice and ignorance. For the integriy of his public conduct he appeals to the memory of his country. His authority had restrained the pride and oppression of the royal officers, and his eloquence had delivered Paulianus from the dogs of the palace. He had always pitied, and often relieved, the distress of the provincials, whose fortunes were exhausted by public and private rapine; and Boethius alone had courage to oppose the tyranny of the barbarians, elated by conquest, excited by avarice, and, as he complains, encouraged by impunity. In these honourable contests his spirit soared above the consideration of danger, and perhaps of prudence; and we may learn from the example of Cato that a character of pure and inflexible virtue is the most apt to be misled by prejudice, to be heated by enthusiasm, and to confound private enmities with public justice. The disciple of Plato might exaggerate the infirmities of nature and the imperfections of society; and the mildest form of a Gothic kingdom, even the weight of allegiance and gratitude, must be insupportable to the free spirit of a Roman patriot. But the favour and fidelity of Boethius declined in just proportion with the public happiness, and an unworthy colleague was imposed to divide and control the power of the master of the offices. In the last gloomy season of Theodoric he indignantly felt that he was a slave; but as his master had only power over his life, he stood, without arms and without fear, against the face of an angry barbarian, who had been provoked to believe that the safety of the senate was incompatible with his own. The senator Albinus was accused and already convicted on the presumption of *hoping,* as it was said, the liberty of Rome. " If Albinus be criminal," exclaimed the orator, " the senate and myself are all guilty of the same crime. If we are innocent, Albinus is equally entitled to the protection of the laws." These laws might not have punished the simple and barren wish of an unattainable blessing; but they would have shown less indulgence to the rash confession of Boethius, that, had he known of a conspiracy, the tyrant never should.[97] The advocate of Albinus was soon involved in the danger and perhaps the guilt of his client; their signature (which they denied as a forgery) was affixed to the original address inviting the emperor to deliver Italy from the Goths; and

[97] Si ego scissem tu nescisses. Boethius adopts this answer (l. i. pros. 4, p. 53) of Julius Canus, whose philosophic death is described by Seneca (De Tranquillitate Animi, c. 14).

three witnesses of honourable rank, perhaps of infamous reputation, attested the treasonable designs of the Roman patrician.[98] Yet his innocence must be presumed, since he was deprived by Theodoric of the means of justification, and rigorously confined in the tower of Pavia, while the senate, at the distance of five hundred miles, pronounced a sentence of confiscation and death against the most illustrious of its members. At the command of the barbarians, the occult science of a philosopher was stigmatised with the names of sacrilege and magic.[99] A devout and dutiful attachment to the senate was condemned as criminal by the trembling voices of the senators themselves; and their ingratitude deserved the wish or prediction of Boethius, that, after him, none should be found guilty of the same offence.[100]

While Boethius, oppressed with fetters, expected each moment the sentence or the stroke of death, he composed in the tower of Pavia the *Consolation of Philosophy;* a golden volume not unworthy of the leisure of Plato or Tully, but which claims incomparable merit from the barbarism of the times and the situation of the author. The celestial guide whom he had so long invoked at Rome and Athens now condescended to illumine his dungeon, to revive his courage, and to pour into his wounds her salutary balm. She taught him to compare his long prosperity and his recent distress, and to conceive new hopes from the inconstancy of fortune. Reason had informed him of the precarious condition of her gifts; experience had satisfied him of their real value; he had enjoyed them without guilt, he might resign them without a sigh, and calmly disdain the impotent malice of his enemies, who had left him happiness, since they had left him virtue. From the earth Boethius ascended to heaven in search of the SUPREME GOOD; explored the metaphysical labyrinth of chance and destiny, of prescience and free-will, of time and eternity; and generously attempted to reconcile the perfect attributes of the Deity with the apparent disorders of his moral and physical government. Such topics of consolation, so obvious, so vague, or so abstruse, are ineffectual to subdue the feelings of human nature. Yet the sense of misfortune may be diverted by the labour of thought; and the sage who could artfully combine in the same work the various riches of philosophy, poetry,

[98] The characters of his two delators, Basilius (Var. ii. 10, 11, iv. 22) and Opilio (v. 41, viii. 16), are illustrated, not much to their honour, in the Epistles of Cassiodorus, which likewise mention Decoratus (v. 31), the worthless colleague of Boethius (l. iii. pros. 4, p. 193).

[99] A severe inquiry was instituted into the crime of magic (Var. iv. 22, 23, ix. 18); and it was believed that many necromancers had escaped by making their gaolers mad: for *mad,* I should read *drunk.*

[100] Boethius had composed his own Apology (p. 53), perhaps more interesting than his Consolation. We must be content with the general view of his honours, principles, persecution, etc. (l. i. pros. 4, p. 42-62), which may be compared with the short and weighty words of the Valesian Fragment (p. 723 [Amm. tom. ii. p. 314, ed. Bip.]). An anonymous writer [Sinner, Catalog. MSS. Bibliot. Bern. tom. i. p. 287) charges him home with honourable and patriotic treason.

and eloquence, must already have possessed the intrepid calmness which he affected to seek. Suspense, the worst of evils, was at length determined by the ministers of death, who executed, and perhaps exceeded, the inhuman mandate of Theodoric. A strong cord was fastened round the head of Boethius, and forcibly tightened till his eyes almost started from their sockets; and some mercy may be discovered in the milder torture of beating him with clubs till he expired.[101]   But his genius survived to diffuse a ray of knowledge over the darkest ages of the Latin world; the writings of the philosopher were translated by the most glorious of the English kings,[102] and the third emperor of the name of Otho removed to a more honourable tomb the bones of a catholic saint who, from his Arian persecutors, had acquired the honours of martyrdom and the fame of miracles.[103]   In the last hours of Boethius he derived some comfort from the safety of his two sons, of his wife, and of his father-in-law, the venerable Symmachus. But the grief of Symmachus was indiscreet, and perhaps disrespectful: he had presumed to lament, he might dare to revenge, the death of an injured friend. He was dragged in chains from Rome to the palace of Ravenna, and the suspicions of Theodoric could only be appeased by the blood of an innocent and aged senator.[104]

Humanity will be disposed to encourage any report which testifies the jurisdiction of conscience and the remorse of kings; and philosophy is not ignorant that the most horrid spectres are sometimes created by the powers of a disordered fancy, and the weakness of a distempered body. After a life of virtue and glory, Theodoric was now descending with shame and guilt into the grave: his mind was humbled by the contrast of the past, and justly alarmed by the invisible terrors of futurity. One evening, as it is related, when the head of a large fish

[101] He was executed in Agro Calventiano (Calvenzano, between Marignano and Pavia), Anonym. Vales. p. 723 [p. 315, ed. Bip.], by order of Eusebius count of Ticinum or Pavia. The place of his confinement is styled the *baptistery,* an edifice and name peculiar to cathedrals. It is claimed by the perpetual tradition of the church of Pavia. The tower of Boethius subsisted till the year 1584, and the draught is yet preserved (Tiraboschi, tom. iii. p. 47, 48).

[102] See the Biographia Britannica, ALFRED, tom. i. p. 80, 2nd edition. The work is still more honourable if performed under the learned eye of Alfred by his foreign and domestic doctors. For the reputation of Boethius in the middle ages consult Brucker (Hist. Crit. Philosoph. tom. iii. p. 565, 566).

[103] The inscription on his new tomb was composed by the preceptor of Otho the Third, the learned pope Silvester II., who, like Boethius himself, was styled a magician by the ignorance of the times. The catholic martyr had carried his head in his hands a considerable way (Baronius, A.D. 526, No. 17, 18); yet on a similar tale, a lady of my acquaintance once observed, "La distance n'y fait rien; il n'y a que le premier pas qui coûte."

[104] Boethius applauds the virtues of his father-in-law (l. i. pros. 4, p. 59, l. ii. pros. 4, p. 118). Procopius (Goth. l. i. c. i. [tom. ii. p. 11, ed. Bonn]), the Valesian Fragment (p. 724 [p. 316, ed. Bip.]), and the Historia Miscella (l. xv. p. 105 [103?]), agree in praising the superior innocence or sanctity of Symmachus; and in the estimation of the legend, the guilt of his murder is equal to the imprisonment of a pope.

was served on the royal table,[105] he suddenly exclaimed that he beheld the angry countenance of Symmachus, his eyes glaring fury and
revenge, and his mouth armed with long sharp teeth, which threatened to
devour him.   The monarch instantly retired to his chamber, and, as
he lay trembling with aguish cold under a weight of bed-clothes, he
expressed in broken murmurs to his physician Elpidius his deep repentance for the murders of Boethius and Symmachus.[106]   His malady
increased, and, after a dysentery which continued three days, he expired in the palace of Ravenna, in the thirty-third, or, if we compute
from the invasion of Italy, in the thirty-seventh year of his reign.
Conscious of his approaching end, he divided his treasures and provinces between his two grandsons, and fixed the Rhône as their common boundary.[107]   Amalaric was restored to the throne of Spain.
Italy, with all the conquests of the Ostrogoths, was bequeathed to
Athalaric, whose age did not exceed ten years, but who was cherished
as the last male offspring of the line of Amali, by the short-lived marriage of his mother Amalasuntha with a royal fugitive of the same
blood.[108]   In the presence of the dying monarch the Gothic chiefs and
Italian magistrates mutually engaged their faith and loyalty to the
young prince and to his guardian mother; and received, in the same
awful moment, his last salutary advice to maintain the laws, to love
the senate and people of Rome, and to cultivate with decent reverence
the friendship of the emperor.[109]   The monument of Theodoric was
erected by his daughter Amalasuntha in a conspicuous situation, which
commanded the city of Ravenna, the harbour, and the adjacent coast.
A chapel of a circular form, thirty feet in diameter, is crowned by a
dome of one entire piece of granite: from the centre of the dome four
columns arose, which supported in a vase of porphyry the remains of
the Gothic king, surrounded by the brazen statues of the twelve

[105] In the fanciful eloquence of Cassiodorus, the variety of sea and river
fish are an evidence of extensive dominion; and those of the Rhine, of Sicily,
and of the Danube, were served on the table of Theodoric (Var. xii. 44).
The monstrous turbot of Domitian (Juvenal, Satir. iv. 39) had been caught
on the shores of the Hadriatic.

[106] Procopius, Goth. l. i. c. 1 [tom. ii. p. 11, ed. Bonn].   But he might have
informed us whether he had received this curious anecdote from common
report, or from the mouth of the royal physician.

[107] Procopius, Goth. l. i. c. 1, 2, 12, 13.   This partition had been directed
by Theodoric, though it was not executed till after his death.   Regni heredi-
tatem superstes reliquit (Isidor. Chron. p. 721, edit. Grot.).

[108] Berimund, the third in descent from Hermanric, king of the Ostrogoths, had retired into Spain, where he lived and died in obscurity (Jornandes,
c. 33, p. 202, edit. Muratori).   See the discovery, nuptials, and death of his
grandson Eutharic (c. 58, p. 220).   His Roman games might render him
popular (Cassiodor. in Chron.), but Eutharic was asper in religione (Anonym.
Vales. p. 722, 723 [p. 313, ed. Bip.]).

[109] See the counsels of Theodoric, and the professions of his successor, in
Procopius (Goth. l. i. c. 1, 2), Jornandes (c. 59 [p. 700, 701, ed. Grot.]), and
Cassiodorus (Var. viii. 1-7).   These epistles are the triumph of his ministerial
eloquence.

apostles.¹¹⁰   His spirit, after some previous expiation, might have been permitted to mingle with the benefactors of mankind, if an Italian hermit had not been witness in a vision to the damnation of Theodoric,¹¹¹ whose soul was plunged by the ministers of divine vengeance into the volcano of Lipari, one of the flaming mouths of the infernal world.¹¹²

CHAPTER XL (482-565 A.D.)

Elevation of Justin the Elder—Reign of Justinian—I. The Empress Theodora —II. Factions of the Circus, and Sedition of Constantinople—III. Trade and Manufacture of Silk—IV. Finances and Taxes—V. Edifices of Justinian—Church of St. Sophia—Fortifications and Frontiers of the Eastern Empire—Abolition of the Schools of Athens and the Consulship of Rome

THE emperor Justinian was born¹ near the ruins of Sardica (the modern Sophia), of an obscure race² of barbarians,³ the inhabitants of a wild and desolate country, to which the names of Dardania, of Dacia, and of Bulgaria have been successively applied.⁴   His elevation was

¹¹⁰ Anonym. Vales. p. 724 [p. 316, ed. Bip.].   Agnellus de Vitis Pont. Raven. in Muratori Script. Rerum Ital. tom. ii. P. i. p. 67.   Alberti Descrizione d'Italia, p. 311.

¹¹¹ This legend is related by Gregory I. (Dialog. iv. 30 [tom. ii. p. 420, ed. Bened.]), and approved by Baronius (A.D. 526, No. 28); and both the pope and cardinal are grave doctors, sufficient to establish a *probable* opinion.

¹¹² Theodoric himself, or rather Cassiodorus, had described in tragic strains the volcanos of Lipari (Cluver. Sicilia, p. 406-410), and Vesuvius ([Var.] iv. 50).

¹ There is some difficulty in the date of his birth (Ludewig in Vit. Justiniani, p. 125); none in the place—the district Bederiana—the village Tauresium, which he afterwards decorated with his name and splendour (D'Anville, Hist. de l'Acad. etc., tom. xxxi. p. 287-292).

[The father of Justinian was named Sabatius, and he was the brother of Justin: while his mother's name was Bigleniza.—O. S.]

² The names of these Dardanian peasants are Gothic, and almost English: *Justinian* is a translation of *uprauda* (*upright*); his father *Sabatius* (in Græcobarbarous language *stipes*) was styled in his village *Istock* (*Stock*); his mother Bigleniza was softened into Vigilantia.

³ Ludewig (p. 127-135) attempts to justify the Anician name of Justinian and Theodora, and to connect them with a family from which the house of Austria has been derived.

⁴ The following table exhibits the most important persons of the family of Justinian:—

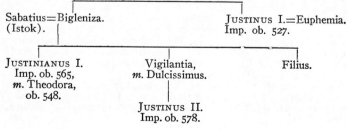

prepared by the adventurous spirit of his uncle Justin, who, with two other peasants of the same village, deserted for the profession of arms the more useful employment of husbandmen or shepherds.[5] On foot, with a scanty provision of biscuit in their knapsacks, the three youths followed the high road of Constantinople, and were soon enrolled, for their strength and stature, among the guards of the emperor Leo. Under the two succeeding reigns, the fortunate peasant emerged to wealth and honours; and his escape from some dangers which threatened his life was afterwards ascribed to the guardian angel who watches over the fate of kings. His long and laudable service in the Isaurian and Persian wars would not have preserved from oblivion the name of Justin; yet they might warrant the military promotion which, in the course of fifty years, he gradually obtained—the rank of tribune, of count, and of general, the dignity of senator, and the command of the guards, who obeyed him as their chief at the important crisis when the emperor Anastasius was removed from the world. The powerful kinsmen whom he had raised and enriched were excluded from the throne; and the eunuch Amantius, who reigned in the palace, had secretly resolved to fix the diadem on the head of the most obsequious of his creatures. A liberal donative, to conciliate the suffrage of the guards, was intrusted for that purpose in the hands of their commander. But these weighty arguments were treacherously employed by Justin in his own favour; and as no competitor presumed to appear, the Dacian peasant was invested with the purple by the unanimous consent of the soldiers, who knew him to be brave and gentle; of the clergy and people, who believed him to be orthodox; and of the provincials, who yielded a blind and implicit submission to the will of the capital. The elder Justin, as he is distinguished from another emperor of the same family and name, ascended the Byzantine throne at the age of sixty-eight years; and, had he been left to his own guidance, every moment of a nine-years' reign must have exposed to his subjects the impropriety of their choice. His ignorance was similar to that of Theodoric; and it is remarkable that, in an age not destitute of learning, two contemporary monarchs had never been instructed in the knowledge of the alphabet. But the genius of Justin was far inferior to that the Gothic king: the experience of a soldier had not qualified him for the government of an empire; and though personally brave, the consciousness of his own weakness was naturally attended with doubt, distrust, and political apprehension. But the official business of the state was diligently

Justinian had several other nephews besides Justin II., the children both of his sister Vigilantia, and of his brother, whose name is unknown. See the genealogical table by Alemannus (Procop. vol. iii. p. 417, ed. Bonn).

[5] See the Anecdotes of Procopius (c. 6) with the notes of N. Alemannus. The satirist would not have sunk, in the vague and decent appellation of γέωργος, the βούκολος and σύφορβος of Zonaras. Yet why are those names disgraceful?—and what German baron would not be proud to descend from the Eumæus of the Odyssey?

and faithfully transacted by the quæstor Proclus;[6] and the aged emperor adopted the talents and ambition of his nephew Justinian, an aspiring youth, whom his uncle had drawn from the rustic solitude of Dacia, and educated at Constantinople as the heir of his private fortune, and at length of the Eastern empire.

Since the eunuch Amantius had been defrauded of his money, it became necessary to deprive him of his life. The task was easily accomplished by the charge of a real or fictitious conspiracy; and the judges were informed, as an accumulation of guilt, that he was secretly addicted to the Manichæan heresy.[7] Amantius lost his head; three of his companions, the first domestics of the palace, were punished either with death or exile; and their unfortunate candidate for the purple was cast into a deep dungeon, overwhelmed with stones, and ignominiously thrown without burial into the sea. The ruin of Vitalian was a work of more difficulty and danger. That Gothic chief had rendered himself popular by the civil war which he boldly waged against Anastasius for the defence of the orthodox faith; and after the conclusion of an advantageous treaty, he still remained in the neighbourhood of Constantinople at the head of a formidable and victorious army of barbarians. By the frail security of oaths he was tempted to relinquish this advantageous situation, and to trust his person within the walls of a city whose inhabitants, particularly the *blue* faction, were artfully incensed against him by the remembrance even of his pious hostilities. The emperor and his nephew embraced him as the faithful and worthy champion of the church and state, and gratefully adorned their favourite with the titles of consul and general; but in the seventh month of his consulship Vitalian was stabbed with seventeen wounds at the royal banquet,[8] and Justinian, who inherited the spoil, was accused as the assassin of a spiritual brother, to whom he had recently pledged his faith in the participation of the Christian mysteries.[9] After the fall of his rival, he was promoted, without any claim of military service, to the office of master-general of the Eastern armies, whom it was his duty to lead into the field against the public enemy. But,

[6] His virtues are praised by Procopius (Persic. l. i. c. 11 [tom. i. p. 52, ed. Bonn]). The quæstor Proclus was the friend of Justinian and the enemy of every other adoption.

[7] Manichæan signifies Eutychian. Hear the furious acclamations of Constantinople and Tyre, the former no more than six days after the decease of Anastasius. *They* produced, the latter applauded, the eunuch's death (Baronius, A.D. 518, P. ii. No. 15; Fleury, Hist. Ecclés. tom. vii. p. 200, 205, from the Councils, tom. v. p. 182, 207).

[8] His power, character, and intentions are perfectly explained by the Count de Buat (tom. ix. p. 54-81). He was great-grandson of Aspar, hereditary prince in the Lesser Scythia, and count of the Gothic *fœderati* of Thrace. The Bessi, whom he could influence, are the minor Goths of Jornandes (c. 51).

[9] Justiniani patricii factione dicitur interfectus fuisse (Victor Tununensis Chron. in Thesaur. Temp. Scaliger, P. ii. p. 7). Procopius (Anecdot. c. 7 [c. 6, tom. iii. p. 46, ed. Bonn]) styles him a tyrant, but acknowledges the ἀδελφοπίστια, which is well explained by Alemannus.

in the pursuit of fame, Justinian might have lost his present dominion over the age and weakness of his uncle; and instead of acquiring by Scythian or Persian trophies the applause of his countrymen,[10] the prudent warrior solicited their favour in the churches, the circus, and the senate of Constantinople. The catholics were attached to the nephew of Justin, who, between the Nestorian and Eutychian heresies, trod the narrow path of inflexible and intolerant orthodoxy.[11] In the first days of the new reign he prompted and gratified the popular enthusiasm against the memory of the deceased emperor. After a schism of thirty-four years, he reconciled the proud and angry spirit of the Roman pontiff, and spread among the Latins a favourable report of his pious respect for the apostolic see. The thrones of the East were filled with catholic bishops devoted to his interest, the clergy and the monks were gained by his liberality, and the people were taught to pray for their future sovereign, the hope and pillar of the true religion. The magnificence of Justinian was displayed in the superior pomp of his public spectacles, an object not less sacred and important in the eyes of the multitude than the creed of Nice of Chalcedon: the expense of his consulship was esteemed at two hundred and eighty-eight thousand pieces of gold; twenty lions and thirty leopards were produced at the same time in the amphitheatre; and a numerous train of horses, with their rich trappings, was bestowed as an extraordinary gift on the victorious charioteers of the circus. While he indulged the people of Constantinople, and received the addresses of foreign kings, the nephew of Justin assiduously cultivated the friendship of the senate. That venerable name seemed to qualify its members to declare the sense of the nation, and to regulate the succession of the Imperial throne. The feeble Anastasius had permitted the vigour of government to degenerate into the form or substance of an aristocracy, and the military officers who had obtained the senatorial rank were followed by their domestic guards, a band of veterans whose arms or acclamations might fix in a tumultuous moment the diadem of the East. The treasures of the state were lavished to procure the voices of the senators, and their unanimous wish that he would be pleased to adopt Justinian for his colleague was communicated to the emperor. But this request, which too clearly admonished him of his approaching end, was unwelcome to the jealous temper of an aged monarch desirous to retain the power which he was incapable of exercising; and Justin, holding his purple with both his hands, advised them to prefer, since

---

[10] In his earliest youth (plane adolescens) he had passed some time as a hostage with Theodoric. For this curious fact Alemannus (ad Procop. Anecdot. c. 9, p. 34 [tom. iii. p. 383, ed. Bonn] of the first edition) quotes a MS. history of Justinian, by his preceptor Theophilus. Ludewig (p. 143) wishes to make him a soldier.

[11] The ecclesiastical history of Justinian will be shown hereafter. See Baronius, A.D. 518-521, and the copius article *Justinianus* in the index to the seventh volume of his Annals.

an election was so profitable, some older candidate. Notwithstanding this reproach, the senate proceeded to decorate Justinian with the royal epithet of *nobilissimus;* and their decree was ratified by the affection or the fears of his uncle. After some time the languor of mind and body to which he was reduced by an incurable wound in his thigh indispensably required the aid of a guardian. He summoned the patriarch and senators, and in their presence solemnly placed the diadem on the head of his nephew, who was conducted from the palace to the circus, and saluted by the loud and joyful applause of the people. The life of Justin was prolonged about four months; but from the instant of this ceremony he was considered as dead to the empire, which acknowledged Justinian in the forty-fifth year of his age, for the lawful sovereign of the East.[12]

From his elevation to his death, Justinian governed the Roman empire thirty-eight years, seven months, and thirteen days. The events of his reign, which excite our curious attention by their number, variety, and importance, are diligently related by the secretary of Belisarius, a rhetorician, whom eloquence had promoted to the rank of senator and præfect of Constantinople. According to the vicissitudes of courage or servitude, of favour or disgrace, Procopius [13] successively composed the *history,* the *panegyric,* and the *satire* of his own times. The eight books of the Persian, Vandalic, and Gothic wars,[14] which are continued in the five books of Agathias, deserve our esteem as a laborious and successful imitation of the Attic, or at least of the Asiatic, writers of ancient Greece. His facts are collected from the personal experience and free conversation of a soldier, a statesman, and a traveller; his style continually aspires, and often attains, to the merit of strength and elegance; his reflections, more especially in the speeches, which he too frequently inserts, contain a rich fund of political knowledge; and the historian, excited by the generous ambition of pleasing and instructing posterity, appears to disdain the prejudices of the

---

[12] The reign of the elder Justin may be found in the three Chronicles of Marcellinus, Victor, and John Malala (tom. ii. p. 130-150 [ed. Oxon.; l. xvii. p. 410-424, ed. Bonn]), the last of whom (in spite of Hody, Prolegom. No. 14, 39, edit. Oxon.) lived soon after Justinian (Jortin's Remarks, etc., vol. iv. p. 383); in the Ecclesiastical History of Evagrius (l. iv. c. 1, 2, 3, 9), and the Excerpta of Theodorus Lector (No. 37 [l. ii.]), and in Cedrenus (p. 363-366 [ed. Par.; tom. i. p. 636-642, ed. Bonn]) and Zonaras (l. xiv. p. 58-60), who may pass for an original.

[13] See the characters of Procopius and Agathias in La Mothe le Vayer (tom. viii. p. 144-174), Vossius (de Historicis Græcis, l. ii. c. 22), and Fabricius (Bibliot. Græc. l. v. c. 5, tom. vi. p. 248-278). Their religion, an honourable problem, betrays occasional conformity, with a secret attachment to Paganism and Philosophy.

[14] In the seven first books, two Persic, two Vandalic, and three Gothic, Procopius has borrowed from Appian the division of provinces and wars: the eighth book, though it bears the name of Gothic, is a miscellaneous and general supplement down to the spring of the year 553, from whence it is continued by Agathias till 559 (Pagi, Critica, A.D. 579. No. 5).

people and the flattery of courts.   The writings of Procopius [15] were read and applauded by his contemporaries: [16] but, although he respectfully laid them at the foot of the throne, the pride of Justinian must have been wounded by the praise of a hero who perpetually eclipses the glory of his inactive sovereign.   The conscious dignity of independence was subdued by the hopes and fears of a slave; and the secretary of Belisarius laboured for pardon and reward in the six books of the Imperial *edifices*.   He had dexterously chosen a subject of apparent splendour, in which he could loudly celebrate the genius, the magnificence, and the piety of a prince who, both as a conqueror and legislator, had surpassed the puerile virtues of Themistocles and Cyrus.[17] Disappointment might urge the flatterer to secret revenge; and the first glance of favour might again tempt him to suspend and suppress a libel [18] in which the Roman Cyrus is degraded into an odious and contemptible tyrant, in which both the emperor and his consort Theodora are seriously represented as two dæmons who had assumed a human form for the destruction of mankind.[19]   Such base inconsistency must doubtless sully the reputation, and detract from the credit, of Procopius: yet, after the venom of his malignity has been suffered to

[15] The literary fate of Procopius has been somewhat unlucky.   1. His books de Bello Gothico were stolen by Leonard Aretin, and published (Fulginii, 1470; Venet. 1471, apud Janson. Mattaire, Annal. Typograph. tom. i. edit. posterior, p. 290, 304, 279, 299) in his own name (see Vossius de Hist. Lat. 1. iii. c. 5, and the feeble defence of the Venice Giornale de' Letterati, tom. xix. p. 207).   2. His works were mutilated by the first Latin translators, Christopher Persona (Giornale, tom. xix. p. 340-348) and Raphael de Volaterra (Huet. de Claris Interpretibus, p. 166), who did not even consult the MS. of the Vatican library, of which they were præfects (Aleman. in Præfat. Anecdot.).   3. The Greek text was not printed till 1607, by Hoeschelius of Augsburg (Dictionnaire de Bayle, tom. ii. p. 782).   4. The Paris edition was imperfectly executed by Claude Maltret, a Jesuit of Toulouse (in 1663), far distant from the Louvre press and the Vatican MS., from which, however, he obtained some supplements.   His promised commentaries, etc., have never appeared.   The Agathias of Leyden (1594) has been wisely reprinted by the Paris editor, with the Latin version of Bonaventura Vulcanius, a learned interpreter (Huet., p. 176).

[16] Agathias in Præfat. p. 7, 8, l. iv. p. 136 [ed. Par.; p. 11, 264, ed. Bonn]; Evagrius, l. iv. c. 12.   See likewise Photius, cod. lxiii. p. 65 [p. 21, ed. Bekk.].

[17] Κύρου παιδεία (says he, Præfat. ad l. de Ædificiis περὶ κτισμάτων) is no more than Κύρου παιδία—a pun!   In these five books Procopius affects a Christian as well as a courtly style.

[18] Procopius discloses himself (Præfat. ad Anecdot. c. 1, 2, 5), and the anecdotes are reckoned as the ninth book by Suidas (tom. iii. p. 186, ed. Kuster).   The silence of Evagrius is a poor objection.   Baronius (A.D. 548, No. 24) regrets the loss of this secret history: it was then in the Vatican library, in his own custody, and was first published sixteen years after his death, with the learned but partial notes of Nicholas Alemannus (Lugd. 1623).

[19] Justinian an ass—the perfect likeness of Domitian—Anecdot. c. 8—Theodora's lovers driven from her bed by rival dæmons—her marriage foretold with a great dæmon—a monk saw the prince of the dæmons, instead of Justinian, on the throne—the servants who watched beheld a face without features, a body walking without a head, etc., etc.   Procopius declares his own and his friends' belief in these diabolical stories (c. 12).

exhale, the residue of the *anecdotes*, even the most disgraceful facts, some of which had been tenderly hinted in his public history, are established by their internal evidence, or the authentic monuments of the times.[20]   From these various materials I shall now proceed to describe the reign of Justinian, which will deserve and occupy an ample space.   The present chapter will explain the elevation and character of Theodora, the factions of the circus, and the peaceful administration of the sovereign of the East.   In the three succeeding chapters I shall relate the wars of Justinian, which achieved the conquest of Africa and Italy; and I shall follow the victories of Belisarius and Narses, without disguising the vanity of their triumphs, or the hostile virtue of the Persian and Gothic heroes.   The series of this volume will embrace the jurisprudence and theology of the emperor; the controversies and sects which still divide the Oriental church; the reformatioon of the Roman law which is obeyed or respected by the nations of modern Europe.

I.   In the exercise of supreme power, the first act of Justinian was to divide it with the woman whom he loved, the famous Theodora,[21] whose strange elevation cannot be applauded as the triumph of female virtue.   Under the reign of Anastasius, the care of the wild beasts maintained by the green faction at Constantinople was intrusted to Acacius, a native of the isle of Cyprus, who, from his employment, was surnamed the master of the bears.   This honourable office was given after his death to another candidate, notwithstanding the diligence of his widow, who had already provided a husband and a successor. Acacius had left three daughters, Comito,[22] THEODORA, and Anastasia, the eldest of whom did not then exceed the age of seven years.   On a solemn festival, these helpless orphans were sent by their distressed and indignant mother, in the garb of suppliants, into the midst of the theatre: the green faction received them with contempt, the blues with compassion; and this difference, which sunk deep into the mind of Theodora, was felt long afterwards in the administration of the empire.   As they improved in age and beauty, the three sisters were successively devoted to the public and private pleasures of the Byzantine people; and Theodora, after following Comito on the stage, in the dress of a slave, with a stool on her head, was at length permitted to exercise her independent talents.   She neither danced, nor sung, nor played on the flute; her skill was confined to the pantomime art; she excelled in buffoon characters; and as often as the comedian swelled her cheeks, and complained with a ridiculous tone and gesture of the

---

[20] Montesquieu (Considérations sur la Grandeur et la Décadence des Romains, c. xx.) gives credit to these anecdotes, as connected, 1, with the weakness of the empire, and, 2, with the instability of Justinian's laws.

[21] For the life and manners of the empress Theodora see the Anecdotes; more especially c. 1-5, 9, 10-15, 16, 17, with the learned notes of Alemannus —a reference which is always implied.

[22] Comito was afterwards married to Sittas duke of Armenia, the father, perhaps, at least she might be the mother, of the empress Sophia.   Two nephews of Theodora may be the sons of Anastasia (Aleman. p. 30, 31).

blows that were inflicted, the whole theatre of Constantinople resounded
with laughter and applause. The beauty of Theodora [23] was the subject of more flattering praise, and the source of more exquisite delight. Her features were delicate and regular; her complexion, though
somewhat pale, was tinged with a natural colour; every sensation was
instantly expressed by the vivacity of her eyes; her easy motions displayed the graces of a small but elegant figure; and either love or
adulation might proclaim that painting and poetry were incapable of
delineating the matchless excellence of her form. But this form was
degraded by the facility with which it was exposed to the public eye,
and prostituted to licentious desire. Her venal charms were abandoned to a promiscuous crowd of citizens and strangers, of every rank
and of every profession: the fortunate lover who had been promised
a night of enjoyment was often driven from her bed by a stronger or
more wealthy favourite; and when she passed through the streets, her
presence was avoided by all who wished to escape either the scandal
or the temptation. The satirical historian has not blushed [24] to describe the naked scenes which Theodora was not ashamed to exhibit in
the theatre.[25] After exhausting the arts of sensual pleasure,[26] she
most ungratefully murmured against the parsimony of Nature;[27] but
her murmurs, her pleasures, and her arts, must be veiled in the obscurity of a learned language. After reigning for some time the delight
and contempt of the capital, she condescended to accompany Ecebolus,
a native of Tyre, who had obtained the government of the African
Pentapolis. But this union was frail and transient; Ecebolus soon

[23] Her statue was raised at Constantinople on a porphyry column. See
Procopius (de Ædif. l. i. c. 11), who gives her portrait in the Anecdotes (c.
10 [tom. iii. p. 69, ed. Bonn]). Aleman. (p. 47) produces one from a
mosaic at Ravenna, loaded with pearls and jewels, and yet handsome.

[24] A fragment of the Anecdotes (c. 9), somewhat too naked, was suppressed
by Alemannus, though extant in the Vatican MS.; nor has the defect been
supplied in the Paris or Venice editions. La Mothe le Vayer (tom. viii. p. 155)
gave the first hint of this curious and genuine passage (Jortin's Remarks,
vol. iv. p. 366), which he had received from Rome, and it has been since
published in the Menagiana (tom. iii. p. 254-259), with a Latin version.

[25] After the mention of a narrow girdle (as none could appear stark naked
in the theatre), Procopius thus proceeds: ἀναπεπτωκυῖά τε ἐν τῷ ἐδάφει ὑπτία
ἔκειτο. Θῆτες δέ τινες . . . κριθὰς αὐτῇ ὑπερθεν τῶν αἰδοίων ἐρρίπτουν, ἃς δὴ οἱ
χῆνες, οἳ ἐς τοῦτο παρεσκευασμένοι ἐτύγχανον, τοῖς στόμασιν ἐνθένδε κατὰ
μίαν ἀνελόμενοι ἤσθιον. I have heard that a learned prelate, now deceased, was
fond of quoting this passage in conversation.

[26] Theodora surpassed the Crispa of Ausonius (Epigram lxxi.), who imitated the capitalis luxus of the females of Nola. See Quintilian Institut. viii.
6, and Torrentius ad Horat. Sermon. l. i. sat. 2, v. 101. At a memorable supper
thirty slaves waited round the table; ten young men feasted with Theodora
Her charity was *universal*.
            Et lassata viris, necdum satiata, recessit.

[27] Ἡ δε κἀκ τῶν τριῶν τρυπημάτων ἐργαζομένη ἐνεκάλει τῃ φύσει, δυσφορουμένη
ὅτι δὴ μὴ καὶ τοὺς τιτθοὺς αὐτῇ εὐρύτερον ἢ νῦν εἰσι τρυπῳη, ὅπως δυνατὴ εἴη καὶ
ἐκείνῃ ἐργάζεσθαι. She wished for a *fourth* altar on which she might pour
libations to the god of love.

rejected an expensive or faithless concubine; she was reduced at Alexandria to extreme distress; and in her laborious return to Constantinople, every city of the East admired and enjoyed the fair Cyprian, whose merit appeared to justify her descent from the peculiar island of Venus. The vague commerce of Theodora, and the most detestable precautions, preserved her from the danger which she feared; yet once, and once only, she became a mother. The infant was saved and educated in Arabia by his father, who imparted to him on his death-bed that he was the son of an empress. Filled with ambitious hopes, the unsuspecting youth immediately hastened to the palace of Constantinople, and was admitted to the presence of his mother. As he was never more seen, even after the decease of Theodora, she deserves the foul imputation of extinguishing with his life a secret so offensive to her imperial virtue.

In the most abject state of her fortune and reputation, some vision, either of sleep or of fancy, had whispered to Theodora the pleasing assurance that she was destined to become the spouse of a potent monarch. Conscious of her approaching greatness, she returned from Paphlagonia to Constantinople; assumed, like a skilful actress, a more decent character; relieved her poverty by the laudable industry of spinning wool; and affected a life of chastity and solitude in a small house, which she afterwards changed into a magnificent temple.[28] Her beauty, assisted by art or accident, soon attracted, captivated, and fixed, the patrician Justinian, who already reigned with absolute sway under the name of his uncle. Perhaps she contrived to enhance the value of a gift which she had so often lavished on the meanest of mankind; perhaps she inflamed, at first by modest delays, and at last by sensual allurements, the desires of a lover who, from nature or devotion, was addicted to long vigils and abstemious diet. When his first transports had subsided, she still maintained the same ascendant over his mind by the more solid merit of temper and understanding. Justinian delighted to ennoble and enrich the object of his affection: the treasures of the East were poured at her feet, and the nephew of Justin was determined, perhaps by religious scruples, to bestow on his concubine the sacred and legal character of a wife. But the laws of Rome expressly prohibited the marriage of a senator with any female who had been dishonoured by a servile origin or theatrical profession: the empress Lupicina or Euphemia, a barbarian of rustic manners, but of irreproachable virtue, refused to accept a prostitute for her niece; and even Vigilantia, the superstitious mother of Justinian, though she acknowledged the wit and beauty of Theodora, was seriously apprehensive lest the levity and arrogance of that artful paramour might corrupt the piety and happiness of her son. These obstacles were removed by the inflexible con-

[28] Anonym. de Antiquitat. C. P. l. iii. 132, in Banduri Imperium Orient. tom. i. p. 47. Ludewig (p. 154) argues sensibly that Theodora would not have immortalised a brothel: but I apply this fact to her second and chaster residence at Constantinople.

stancy of Justinian. He patiently expected the death of the empress; he despised the tears of his mother, who soon sunk under the weight of her affliction; and a law was promulgated, in the name of the emperor Justin, which abolished the rigid jurisprudence of antiquity. A glorious repentance (the words of the edict) was left open for the unhappy females who had prostituted their persons on the theatre, and they were permitted to contract a legal union with the most illustrious of the Romans.[29] This indulgence was speedily followed by the solemn nuptials of Justinian and Theodora; her dignity was gradually exalted with that of her lover; and, as soon as Justin had invested his nephew with the purple, the patriarch of Constantinople placed the diadem on the heads of the emperor and empress of the East. But the usual honours which the severity of Roman manners had allowed to the wives of princes could not satisfy either the ambition of Theodora or the fondness of Justinian. He seated her on the throne as an equal and independent colleague in the sovereignty of the empire, and an oath of allegiance was imposed on the governors of the provinces in the joint names of Justinian and Theodora.[30] The Eastern world fell prostrate before the genius and fortune of the daughter of Acacius. The prostitute who, in the presence of innumerable spectators, had polluted the theatre of Constantinople, was adored as a queen in the same city, by grave magistrates, orthodox bishops, victorious generals, and captive monarchs.[31]

Those who believe that the female mind is totally depraved by the loss of chastity will eagerly listen to all the invectives of private envy or popular resentment, which have dissembled the virtues of Theodora, exaggerated her vices, and condemned with rigour the venal or voluntary sins of the youthful harlot. From a motive of shame or contempt, she often declined the servile homage of the multitude, escaped from the odious light of the capital, and passed the greatest part of the year in the palaces and gardens which were pleasantly seated on the sea-coast of the Propontis and the Bosphorus. Her private hours were devoted to the prudent as well as grateful care of her beauty, the luxury of the bath and table, and the long slumber of the evening and the morning. Her secret apartments were occupied by the favourite women and eu-

[29] See the old law in Justinian's Code (l. v. tit. v. leg. 7, tit. xxvii. leg. 1) under the years 336 and 454. The new edict (about the year 521 or 522, Aleman. p. 38, 96) very awkwardly repeals no more than the clause of mulieres *scenicæ,* libertinæ, tabernariæ. See the novels 89 and 117, and a Greek rescript from Justinian to the bishops (Aleman. p. 41).

[30] I swear by the Father, etc., by the Virgin Mary, by the four Gospels, quæ in manibus teneo, and by the Holy Archangels Michael and Gabriel, puram conscientiam germanumque servitium me servaturum, sacratissimis DDNN. Justiniano et Theodoræ conjugi ejus (Novell. viii. tit. 3). Would the oath have been binding in favour of the widow? Communes tituli et triumphi, etc. (Aleman. p. 47, 48).

[31] " Let greatness own her, and she's mean no more," etc. Without Warburton's critical telescope, I should never have seen, in this general picture of triumphant vice, any personal allusion to Theodora.

nuchs, whose interests and passions she indulged at the expense of justice: the most illustrious personages of the state were crowded into a dark and sultry antechamber; and when at last, after tedious attendance, they were admitted to kiss the feet of Theodora, they experienced, as her humour might suggest, the silent arrogance of an empress or the capricious levity of a comedian. Her rapacious avarice to accumulate an immense treasure may be excused by the apprehension of her husband's death, which could leave no alternative between ruin and the throne; and fear as well as ambition might exasperate Theodora against two generals who, during a malady of the emperor, had rashly declared that they were not disposed to acquiesce in the choice of the capital. But the reproach of cruelty, so repugnant even to her softer vices, has left an indelible stain on the memory of Theodora. Her numerous spies observed and zealously reported every action, or word, or look, injurious to their royal mistress. Whomsoever they accused were cast into her peculiar prisons,[32] inaccessible to the inquiries of justice; and it was rumoured that the torture of the rack or scourge had been inflicted in the presence of a female tyrant, insensible to the voice of prayer or of pity.[33] Some of these unhappy victims perished in deep unwholesome dungeons, while others were permitted, after the loss of their limbs, their reason, or their fortune, to appear in the world, the living monuments of her vengeance, which was commonly extended to the children of those whom she had suspected or injured. The senator or bishop whose death or exile Theodora had pronounced, was delivered to a trusty messenger, and his diligence was quickened by a menace from her own mouth. " If you fail in the execution of my commands, I swear by him who liveth for ever that your skin shall be flayed from your body." [34]

If the creed of Theodora had not been tainted with heresy, her exemplary devotion might have atoned, in the opinion of her contemporaries, for pride, avarice, and cruelty; but if she employed her influence to assuage the intolerant fury of the emperor, the present age will allow some merit to her religion, and much indulgence to her speculative errors.[35] The name of Theodora was introduced, with equal honour, in all the pious and charitable foundations of Justinian; and the most benevolent institution of his reign may be ascribed to the sympathy of the empress for her less fortunate sisters, who had been seduced or compelled to embrace the trade of prostitution. A palace,

[32] Her prisons, a labyrinth, a Tartarus (Anecdot. c. 4), were under the palace. Darkness is propitious to cruelty, but it is likewise favourable to calumny and fiction.

[33] A more jocular whipping was inflicted on Saturninus, for presuming to say that his wife, a favourite of the empress, had not been found ἄτρητος (Anecdot. c. 17 [tom. iii. p. 104, ed. Bonn]).

[34] Per viventem in sæcula excoriari te faciam. Anastasius de Vitis Pont. Roman. in Vigilio, p. 40.

[35] Ludewig. p. 161-166. I give him credit for the charitable attempt, although he hath not much charity in his temper.

on the Asiatic side of the Bosphorus, was converted into a stately and spacious monastery, and a liberal maintenance was assigned to five hundred women who had been collected from the streets and brothels of Constantinople. In this safe and holy retreat they were devoted to perpetual confinement; and the despair of some, who threw themselves headlong into the sea, was lost in the gratitude of the penitents who had been delivered from sin and misery by their generous benefactress.[36] The prudence of Theodora is celebrated by Justinian himself; and his laws are attributed to the sage counsels of his most reverend wife, whom he had received as the gift of the Deity.[37] Her courage was displayed amidst the tumult of the people and the terrors of the court. Her chastity, from the moment of her union with Justinian, is founded on the silence of her implacable enemies; and although the daughter of Acacius might be satiated with love, yet some applause is due to the firmness of a mind which could sacrifice pleasure and habit to the stronger sense either of duty or interest. The wishes and prayers of Theodora could never obtain the blessing of a lawful son, and she buried an infant daughter, the sole offspring of her marriage.[38] Notwithstanding this disappointment, her dominion was permanent and absolute; she preserved, by art or merit, the affections of Justinian; and their seeming dissensions were always fatal to the courtiers who believed them to be sincere. Perhaps her health had been impaired by the licentiousness of her youth; but it was always delicate, and she was directed by her physicians to use the Pythian warm-baths. In this journey the empress was followed by the Prætorian præfect, the great treasurer, several counts and patricians, and a splendid train of four thousand attendants: the highways were repaired at her approach; a palace was erected for her reception; and as she passed through Bithynia she distributed liberal alms to the churches, the monasteries, and the hospitals, that they might implore Heaven for the restoration of her health.[39] At length, in the twenty-fourth year of her marriage, and the twenty-second of her reign, she was consumed by a cancer;[40] and the irreparable loss was deplored

[36] Compare the Anecdotes (c. 17) with the Edifices (1. i. c. 9). How differently may the same fact be stated! John Malala (tom. ii. p. 174, 175 [p. 440, 441, ed. Bonn]) observes, that on this, or a similar occasion, she released and clothed the girls whom she had purchased from the stews at five aurei apiece.

[37] Novel. viii. 1. An allusion to Theodora. Her enemies read the name Dæmonodora (Aleman. p. 66 [Procop. tom. iii. p. 415, ed. Bonn]).

[38] St. Sabas refused to pray for a son of Theodora, lest he should prove a heretic worse than Anastasius himself (Cyril in Vit. St. Sabæ, apud Aleman. p. 70, 109 [Procop. tom. iii. p. 421, 462, ed. Bonn]).

[39] See John Malala, tom. ii. p. 174 [p. 441, ed. Bonn]. Theophanes, p. 158 [tom. i. p. 286, ed. Bonn]. Procopius de Ædific. 1. v. c. 3.

[40] Theodora Chalcedonensis synodi inimica canceris plagâ toto corpore perfusa vitam prodigiose finivit (Victor Tununensis in Chron.). On such occasions an orthodox mind is steeled against pity. Alemannus (p. 12, 13) understands the εὐσεβῶς ἐκοιμήθη of Theophanes as civil language, which does not imply either piety or repentance; yet two years after her death St. Theodora is celebrated by Paul Silentiarius (in Proem. ver. 58-62).

by her husband, who, in the room of a theatrical prostitute, might have selected the purest and most noble virgin of the East.[41]

II. A material difference may be observed in the games of antiquity: the most eminent of the Greeks were actors, the Romans were merely spectators. The Olympic stadium was open to wealth, merit, and ambition; and if the candidates could depend on their personal skill and activity, they might pursue the footsteps of Diomede and Menelaus, and conduct their own horses in the rapid career.[42] Ten, twenty, forty chariots, were allowed to start at the same instant; a crown of leaves was the reward of the victor, and his fame, with that of his family and country, was chanted in lyric strains more durable than monuments of brass and marble. But a senator, or even a citizen, conscious of his dignity, would have blushed to expose his person or his horses in the circus of Rome. The games were exhibited at the expense of the republic, the magistrates, or the emperors; but the reins were abandoned to servile hands; and if the profits of a favourite charioteer sometimes exceeded those of an advocate, they must be considered as the effects of popular extravagance, and the high wages of a disgraceful profession. The race, in its first institution, was a simple contest of two chariots, whose drivers were distinguished by *white* and *red* liveries: two additional colours, a light *green* and a cærulean *blue*, were afterwards introduced; and, as the races were repeated twenty-five times, one hundred chariots contributed in the same day to the pomp of the circus. The four *factions* soon acquired a legal establishment and a mysterious origin, and their fanciful colours were derived from the various appearances of nature in the four seasons of the year; the red dog-star of summer, the snows of winter, the deep shades of autumn, and the cheerful verdure of the spring.[43] Another interpretation preferred the elements to the seasons, and the struggle of the green and blue was supposed to represent the conflict of the earth and sea. Their respective victories announced either a plentiful harvest or a prosperous navigation, and the hostility of the husbandmen and mariners was somewhat less absurd than the blind ardour of the Roman people, who devoted their lives and fortunes to the colour which they had espoused. Such folly was

[41] As she persecuted the popes, and rejected a council, Baronius exhausts the names of Eve, Dalila, Herodias, etc.; after which he has recourse to his infernal dictionary: civis inferni—alumna dæmonum—satanico agitata spiritû —œstro percita diabolico, etc. etc. (A.D. 548, No. 24).

[42] Read and feel the twenty-third book of the Iliad, a living picture of manners, passions, and the whole form and spirit of the chariot-race. West's Dissertation on the Olympic Games (sect. xii.-xvii.) affords much curious and authentic information.

[43] The four colours, *albati, russati, prasini, veneti,* represent the four seasons, according to Cassiodorus. (Var. iii. 51), who lavishes much wit and eloquence on this theatrical mystery. Of these colours, the three first may be fairly translated, *white, red,* and *green. Venetus* is explained by *cœruleus,* a word various and vague: it is properly the sky reflected in the sea; but custom and convenience may allow *blue* as an equivalent. (Robert. Stephan. sub voce. Spence's Polymetis, p. 228.)

disdained and indulged by the wisest princes; but the names of Caligula, Nero, Vitellius, Verus, Commodus, Caracalla, and Elagabalus, were enrolled in the blue or green factions of the circus: they frequented their stables, applauded their favourites, chastised their antagonists, and deserved the esteem of the populace by the natural or affected imitation of their manners. The bloody and tumultuous contest continued to disturb the public festivity till the last age of the spectacles of Rome; and Theodoric, from a motive of justice or affection, interposed his authority to protect the greens against the violence of a consul and a patrician who were passionately addicted to the blue faction of the circus.[44]

Constantinople adopted the follies, though not the virtues, of ancient Rome; and the same factions which had agitated the circus raged with redoubled fury in the hippodrome. Under the reign of Anastasius, this popular frenzy was inflamed by religious zeal; and the greens, who had treacherously concealed stones and daggers under baskets of fruit, massacred at a solemn festival three thousand of their blue adversaries.[45] From the capital this pestilence was diffused into the provinces and cities of the East, and the sportive distinction of two colours produced two strong and irreconcilable factions, which shook the foundations of a feeble government.[46] The popular dissensions, founded on the most serious interest or holy pretence, have scarcely equalled the obstinacy of this wanton discord, which invaded the peace of families, divided friends and brothers, and tempted the female sex, though seldom seen in the circus, to espouse the inclinations of their lovers, or to contradict the wishes of their husbands. Every law, either human or divine, was trampled under foot; and as long as the party was successful, its deluded followers appeared careless of private distress or public calamity. The licence, without the freedom, of democracy, was revived at Antioch and Constantinople, and the support of a faction became necessary to every candidate for civil or ecclesiastical honours. A secret attachment to the family or sect of Anastasius was imputed to the greens; the blues were zealously devoted to the cause of orthodoxy and Justinian,[47] and

[44] See Onuphrius Panvinius de Ludis Circensibus, l. i. c. 10, 11; the seventeenth Annotation on Mascou's History of the Germans; and Aleman. ad c. vii.

[45] Marcellin. in Chron. p. 47 [anno 501]. Instead of the vulgar word *veneta*, he uses the more exquisite terms of *cærulea* and *cærealis*. Baronius (A.D. 501, No. 4, 5, 6) is satisfied that the blues were orthodox; but Tillemont is angry at the supposition, and will not allow any martyrs in a playhouse (Hist. des Emp. tom. vi. p. 554).

[46] See Procopius (Persic. l. i. c. 24). In describing the vices of the factions and of the government, the *public* is not more favourable than the *secret* historian. Aleman. (p. 26 [tom. iii. p. 373, ed. Bonn]) has quoted a fine passage from Gregory Nazianzen, which proves the inveteracy of the evil.

[47] The partiality of Justinian for the blues (Anecdot. c. 7 [tom. iii. p. 53, ed. Bonn]) is attested by Evagrius (Hist. Eccles. l. iv. c. 32), John Malala (tom. ii. p. 138, 139 [p. 152, ed. Oxon.; lib. xviii. p. 425, ed. Bonn]), especially for Antioch, and Theophanes (p. 142 [p. 256, ed. Bonn]).

their grateful patron protected, above five years, the disorders of a faction whose seasonable tumults overawed the palace, the senate, and the capitals of the East. Insolent with royal favour, the blues affected to strike terror by a peculiar and barbaric dress—the long hair of the Huns, their close sleeves and ample garments, a lofty step, and a sonorous voice. In the day they concealed their two-edged poniards, but in the night they boldly assembled in arms and in numerous bands, prepared for every act of violence and rapine. Their adversaries of the green faction, or even inoffensive citizens, were stripped and often murdered by these nocturnal robbers, and it became dangerous to wear any gold buttons or girdles, or to appear at a late hour in the streets of a peaceful capital. A daring spirit, rising with impunity, proceeded to violate the safeguard of private houses; and fire was employed to facilitate the attack, or to conceal the crimes, of these factious rioters. No place was safe or sacred from their depredations; to gratify either avarice or revenge they profusely spilt the blood of the innocent; churches and altars were polluted by atrocious murders, and it was the boast of the assassins that their dexterity could always inflict a mortal wound with a single stroke of their dagger. The dissolute youth of Constantinople adopted the blue livery of disorder; the laws were silent, and the bonds of society were relaxed; creditors were compelled to resign their obligations; judges to reverse their sentence; masters to enfranchise their slaves; fathers to supply the extravagance of their children; noble matrons were prostituted to the lust of their servants; beautiful boys were torn from the arms of their parents; and wives, unless they preferred a voluntary death, were ravished in the presence of their husbands.[48] The despair of the greens, who were persecuted by their enemies and deserted by the magistrate, assumed the privilege of defence, perhaps of retaliation; but those who survived the combat were dragged to execution, and the unhappy fugitives, escaping to woods and caverns, preyed without mercy on the society from whence they were expelled. Those ministers of justice who had courage to punish the crimes and to brave the resentment of the blues became the victims of their indiscreet zeal: a præfect of Constantinople fled for refuge to the holy sepulchre, a count of the East was ignominiously whipped, and a governor of Cilicia was hanged, by the order of Theodora, on the tomb of two assassins whom he had condemned for the murder of his groom, and a daring attack upon his own life.[49] An aspiring candidate may be tempted to build his greatness on the public con-

[48] A wife (says Procopius) who was seized and almost ravished by a blue-coat, threw herself into the Bosphorus. The bishops of the second Syria (Aleman. p. 26 [tom. iii. p. 374, ed. Bonn]) deplore a similar suicide, the guilt or glory of female chastity, and name the heroine.

[49] The doubtful credit of Procopius (Anecdot. c. 17) is supported by the less partial Evagrius, who confirms the fact, and specifies the names. The tragic fate of the præfect of Constantinople is related by John Malala (tom. ii. p. 139 [p. 416, ed. Bonn]).

fusion, but it is the interest as well as duty of a sovereign to maintain the authority of the laws. The first edict of Justinian, which was often repeated and sometimes executed, announced his firm resolution to support the innocent, and to chastise the guilty, of every denomination and *colour*. Yet the balance of justice was still inclined in favour of the blue faction, by the secret affection, the habits, and the fears of the emperor; his equity, after an apparent struggle, submitted without reluctance to the implacable passions of Theodora, and the empress never forgot or forgave the injuries of the comedian. At the accession of the younger Justin, the proclamation of equal and rigorous justice indirectly condemned the partiality of the former reign. " Ye blues, Justinian is no more! ye greens, he is still alive! " [50]

A sedition, which almost laid Constantinople in ashes, was excited by the mutual hatred and momentary reconciliation of the two factions. In the fifth year of his reign Justinian celebrated the festival of the ides of January: the games were incessantly disturbed by the clamorous discontent of the greens; till the twenty-second race the emperor maintained his silent gravity; at length, yielding to his impatience, he condescended to hold, in abrupt sentences, and by the voice of a crier, the most singular dialogue [51] that ever passed between a prince and his subjects. Their first complaints were respectful and modest; they accused the subordinate ministers of oppression, and proclaimed their wishes for the long life and victory of the emperor. " Be patient and attentive, ye insolent railers! " exclaimed Justinian; " be mute, ye Jews, Samaritans, and Manichæans! " The greens still attempted to awaken his compassion. " We are poor, we are innocent, we are injured, we dare not pass through the streets: a general persecution is exercised against our name and colour. Let us die, O emperor! but let us die by your command, and for your service! " But the repetition of partial and passionate invectives degraded, in their eyes, the majesty of the purple; they renounced allegiance to the prince who refused justice to his people, lamented that the father of Justinian had been born, and branded his son with the opprobrious names of a homicide, an ass, and a perjured tyrant. " Do you despise your lives? " cried the indignant monarch. The blues rose with fury from their seats, their hostile clamours thundered in the hippodrome, and their adversaries, deserting the unequal contest, spread terror and despair through the streets of Constantinople. At this dangerous moment, seven notorious assassins of both factions, who had been condemned by the præfect, were carried round the city,

[50] See John Malala (tom. ii. p. 147 [p. 422, ed. Bonn]) ; yet he owns that Justinian was attached to the blues. The seeming discord of the emperor and Theodora is perhaps viewed with too much jealousy and refinement by Procopius (Anecdot. c. 10 [t. iii. p. 70, ed. Bonn]). See Aleman. Præfat. p. 6.
[51] This dialogue, which Theophanes has preserved, exhibits the popular language, as well as the manners, of Constantinople in the sixth century. Their Greek is mingled with many strange and barbarous words, for which Ducange cannot always find a meaning or etymology.

and afterwards transported to the place of execution in the suburb of Pera. Four were immediately beheaded; a fifth was hanged; but, when the same punishment was inflicted on the remaining two, the rope broke, they fell alive to the ground, the populace applauded their escape, and the monks of St. Conon, issuing from the neighbouring convent, conveyed them in a boat to the sanctuary of the church.[52] As one of these criminals was of the blue, and the other of the green, livery, the two factions were equally provoked by the cruelty of their oppressor or the ingratitude of their patron, and a short truce was concluded till they had delivered their prisoners and satisfied their revenge. The palace of the præfect, who withstood the seditious torrent, was instantly burnt, his officers and guards were massacred, the prisons were forced open, and freedom was restored to those who could only use it for the public destruction. A military force which had been despatched to the aid of the civil magistrate was fiercely encountered by an armed multitude, whose numbers and boldness continually increased: and the Heruli, the wildest barbarians in the service of the empire, overturned the priests and their relics, which, from a pious motive, had been rashly interposed to separate the bloody conflict. The tumult was exasperated by this sacrilege; the people fought with enthusiasm in the cause of God; the women, from the roofs and windows, showered stones on the heads of the soldiers, who darted firebrands against the houses; and the various flames, which had been kindled by the hands of citizens and strangers, spread without control over the face of the city. The conflagration involved the cathedral of St. Sophia, the baths of Zeuxippus, a part of the palace from the first entrance to the altar of Mars, and the long portico from the palace to the forum of Constantine: a large hospital, with the sick patients, was consumed; many churches and stately edifices were destroyed; and an immense treasure of gold and silver was either melted or lost. From such scenes of horror and distress the wise and wealthy citizens escaped over the Bosphorus to the Asiatic side, and during five days Constantinople was abandoned to the factions, whose watchword, NIKA, *vanquish!* has given a name to this memorable sedition.[53]

As long as the factions were divided, the triumphant blues and desponding greens appeared to behold with the same indifference the disorders of the state. They agreed to censure the corrupt management of justice and the finance; and the two responsible ministers, the artful Tribonian and the rapacious John of Cappadocia, were loudly arraigned as the authors of the public misery. The peaceful murmurs of the

---

[52] See this church and monastery in Ducange, C. P. Christiana, l. iv. p. 182.
[53] The history of the *Nika* sedition is extracted from Marcellinus (in Chron. [an. 532]), Procopius (Persic. l. i. c. 26 [c. 24, tom. i. p. 119, ed. Bonn]), John Malala (tom. ii. p. 213-218 [ed. Ox.; p. 473-477, ed. Bonn]), Chron. Paschal. (p. 336-340, tom. i. p. 620 *sqq.* [ed. Bonn]), Theophanes (Chronograph. p. 154-158 [ed. Par. tom. i. p. 278-286, ed. Bonn]), and Zonaras (l. xiv. p. 61-63).

people would have been disregarded: they were heard with respect when the city was in flames; the quæstor and the præfect were instantly removed, and their offices were filled by two senators of blameless integrity. After this popular concession Justinian proceeded to the hippodrome to confess his own errors, and to accept the repentance of his grateful subjects; but they distrusted his assurances, though solemnly pronounced in the presence of the holy gospels; and the emperor, alarmed by their distrust, retreated with precipitation to the strong fortress of the palace. The obstinacy of the tumult was now imputed to a secret and ambitious conspiracy, and a suspicion was entertained that the insurgents, more especially the green faction, had been supplied with arms and money by Hypatius and Pompey, two patricians who could neither forget with honour, nor remember with safety, that they were the nephews of the emperor Anastasius. Capriciously trusted, disgraced, and pardoned by the jealous levity of the monarch, they had appeared as loyal servants before the throne, and, during five days of the tumult, they were detained as important hostages; till at length, the fears of Justinian prevailing over his prudence, he viewed the two brothers in the light of spies, perhaps of assassins, and sternly commanded them to depart from the palace. After a fruitless representation that obedience might lead to involuntary treason, they retired to their houses, and in the morning of the sixth day Hypatius was surrounded and seized by the people, who, regardless of his virtuous resistance and the tears of his wife, transported their favourite to the forum of Constantine, and, instead of a diadem, placed a rich collar on his head. If the usurper, who afterwards pleaded the merit of his delay, had complied with the advice of his senate, and urged the fury of the multitude, their first irresistible effort might have oppressed or expelled his trembling competitor. The Byzantine palace enjoyed a free communication with the sea, vessels lay ready at the garden-stairs, and a secret resolution was already formed to convey the emperor with his family and treasures to a safe retreat at some distance from the capital.

Justinian was lost, if the prostitute whom he raised from the theatre had not renounced the timidity as well as the virtues of her sex. In the midst of a council where Belisarius was present, Theodora alone displayed the spirit of a hero, and she alone, without apprehending his future hatred, could save the emperor from the imminent danger and his unworthy fears. "If flight," said the consort of Justinian, "were the only means of safety, yet I should disdain to fly. Death is the condition of our birth, but they who have reigned should never survive the loss of dignity and dominion. I implore Heaven that I may never be seen, not a day, without my diadem and purple; that I may no longer behold the light when I cease to be saluted with the name of queen. If you resolve, O Cæsar! to fly, you have treasures; behold the sea, you have ships; but tremble lest the desire of life should expose you to wretched exile and ignominious death. For my own part, I adhere to the maxim of antiquity, that the throne is a glorious sepulchre." The firmness of a woman restored the courage to deliberate and act, and courage soon discovers the resources of the most desperate situation. It was an easy and a decisive measure to revive the animosity of the factions; the blues were astonished at their own guilt and folly, that a trifling injury should provoke them to conspire with their implacable enemies against a gracious and liberal benefactor; they again proclaimed the majesty of Justinian; and the greens, with their upstart emperor, were left alone in the hippodrome. The fidelity of the guards was doubtful; but the military force of Justinian consisted in three thousand veterans, who had been trained to valour and discipline in the Persian and Illyrian wars. Under the command of Belisarius and Mundus, they silently marched in two divisions from the palace, forced their obscure way through narrow passages, expiring flames, and falling edifices, and burst open at the same moment the two opposite gates of the hippodrome. In this narrow space the disorderly and affrighted crowd was incapable of resisting on either side a firm and regular attack; the blues signalised the fury of their repentance, and it is computed that above thirty thousand persons were slain in the merciless and promiscuous carnage of the day. Hypatius was dragged from his throne, and conducted with his brother Pompey to the feet of the emperor; they implored his clemency, but their crime was manifest, their innocence uncertain, and Justinian had been too much terrified to forgive. The next morning the two nephews of Anastasius, with eighteen *illustrious* accomplices, of patrician or consular rank, were privately executed by the soldiers, their bodies were thrown into the sea, their palaces razed, and their fortunes confiscated. The hippodrome itself was condemned, during several years, to a mournful silence; with the restoration of the games the same disorders revived, and the blue and green factions continued to afflict the reign of Justinian, and to disturb the tranquillity of the Eastern empire.[57]

III. That empire, after Rome was barbarous, still embraced the nations whom she had conquered beyond the Hadriatic, and as far as the frontiers of Æthiopia and Persia. Justinian reigned over sixty-four provinces and nine hundred and thirty-five cities;[58] his dominions were blessed by nature with the advantages of soil, situation, and climate, and the improvements of human art had been perpetually diffused along the coast of the Mediterranean and the banks of the Nile from ancient Troy to the Egyptian Thebes. Abraham[59] had been relieved by the

[57] Marcellinus says, in general terms, innumeris populis in circo trucidatis. Procopius numbers 30,000 victims [tom. i. p. 129, ed. Bonn]; and the 35,000 of Theophanes are swelled to 40,000 by the more recent Zonaras [tom. ii. p. 63]. Such is the usual progress of exaggeration.

[58] Hierocles, a contemporary of Justinian, composed his Συνέκδημος (Itineraria, p. 631), or review of the eastern provinces and cities, before the year 535 (Wesseling, in Præfat. and Not. ad p. 623, etc.).

[59] See the Book of Genesis (xii. 10), and the administration of Joseph. The annals of the Greeks and Hebrews agree in the early arts and plenty of Egypt: but this antiquity supposes a long series of improvement; and Warburton, who is almost stifled by the Hebrew, calls aloud for the Samaritan, chronology (Divine Legation, vol. iii. p. 29, etc.).

well-known plenty of Egypt; the same country, a small and populous tract, was still capable of exporting each year two hundred and sixty thousand quarters of wheat for the use of Constantinople;[60] and the capital of Justinian was supplied with the manufactures of Sidon fifteen centuries after they had been celebrated in the poems of Homer.[61] The annual powers of vegetation, instead of being exhausted by two thousand harvests, were renewed and invigorated by skilful husbandry, rich manure, and seasonable repose. The breed of domestic animals was infinitely multiplied. Plantations, buildings, and the instruments of labour and luxury, which are more durable than the term of human life, were accumulated by the care of successive generations. Tradition preserved, and experience simplified, the humble practice of the arts; society was enriched by the division of labour and the facility of exchange; and every Roman was lodged, clothed, and subsisted by the industry of a thousand hands. The invention of the loom and distaff has been piously ascribed to the gods. In every age a variety of animal and vegetable productions, hair, skins, wool, flax, cotton, and at length *silk*, have been skilfully manufactured to hide or adorn the human body; they were stained with an infusion of permanent colours, and the pencil was successfully employed to improve the labours of the loom. In the choice of those colours [62] which imitate the beauties of nature, the freedom of taste and fashion was indulged; but the deep purple [63] which the Phœnicians extracted from a shell-fish was restrained to the sacred person and palace of the emperor, and the penalties of treason were denounced against the ambitious subjects who dared to usurp the prerogative of the throne.[64]

[60] Eight millions of Roman modii, besides a contribution of 80,000 aurei for the expenses of water-carriage, from which the subject was graciously excused. See the thirteenth Edict of Justinian [c. viii.]; the numbers are checked and verified by the agreement of the Greek and Latin texts.

[61] Homer's Iliad, vi. 289. These veils, πέπλοι παμποίκιλοι, were the work of the Sidonian women. But this passage is more honourable to the manufactures than to the navigation of Phœnicia, from whence they had been imported to Troy in Phrygian bottoms.

[62] See in Ovid (de Arte Amandi, iii. 269, etc.) a poetical list of twelve colours borrowed from flowers, the elements, etc. But it is almost impossible to discriminate by words all the nice and various shades both of art and nature.

[63] By the discovery of cochineal, etc., we far surpass the colours of antiquity. Their royal purple had a strong smell, and a dark cast as deep as bull's blood—obscuritas rubens (says Cassiodorus, Var. l. 1, c. 2) nigredo sanguinea. The President Goguet (Origine des Loix et des Arts, part ii. l. ii. c. 2, p. 184-215) will amuse and satisfy the reader. I doubt whether his book, especially in England, is as well known as it deserves to be.

[64] Historical proofs of this jealousy have been occasionally introduced, and many more might have been added; but the arbitrary acts of despotism. were justified by the sober and general declarations of law (Codex Theodosian. l. x. tit. 21, leg. 3; Codex Justinian. l. xi. tit. 8, leg. 5). An inglorious permission, and necessary restriction, was applied to the *mimæ*, the female dancers (Cod. Theodos. l. xv. tit. 7, leg. 11).

I need not explain that *silk* [65] is originally spun from the bowels of a caterpillar, and that it composes the golden tomb from whence a worm emerges in the form of a butterfly. Till the reign of Justinian, the silk-worms who feed on the leaves of the white mulberry-tree were confined to China; those of the pine, the oak, and the ash were common in the forests both of Asia and Europe; but as their education is more difficult, and their produce more uncertain, they were generally neglected, except in the little island of Ceos, near the coast of Attica. A thin gauze was procured from their webs, and this Cean manufacture, the invention of a woman, for female use, was long admired both in the East and at Rome. Whatever suspicions may be raised by the garments of the Medes and Assyrians, Virgil is the most ancient writer who expressly mentions the soft wool which was combed from the trees of the Seres or Chinese;[66] and this natural error, less marvellous than the truth, was slowly corrected by the knowledge of a valuable insect, the first artificer of the luxury of nations. That rare and elegant luxury was censured, in the reign of Tiberius, by the gravest of the Romans; and Pliny, in affected though forcible language, has condemned the thirst of gain, which explored the last confines of the earth for the pernicious purpose of exposing to the public eye naked draperies and transparent matrons.[67] A dress which showed the turn of the limbs and colour of the skin might gratify vanity or provoke desire; the silks which had been closely woven in China were sometimes unravelled by the Phœnician women, and the precious materials were multiplied

[65] In the history of insects (far more wonderful than Ovid's Metamorphoses) the silkworm holds a conspicuous place. The bombyx of the isle of Ceos, as described by Pliny (Hist. Natur. xi. 26, 27, with the notes of the two learned Jesuits, Hardouin and Brotier), may be illustrated by a similar species in China (Mémoires sur les Chinois, tom. ii. p. 575-598) ; but our silkworm, as well as the white mulberry-tree, were unknown to Theophrastus and Pliny.

[The first ancient writer who gives any information respecting the use of silk is Aristotle (*Hist. Anim.* v. c. 19), whose account has been adopted with various modifications by Pliny, Clemens Alexandrinus, and Basil. Gibbon has fallen into one or two mistakes here. He has confounded the island of Ceos, near the coast of Attica, with the island of Cos, off the western coast of Asia Minor, the latter, and not Ceos, being celebrated for its transparent garments; and he has without authority supposed that a species of silkworm was bred in this island. But Aristotle, after describing the silkworm of the East, only says, " Pamphile, daughter of Plates, is reported to have first woven in Cos." It is therefore probable that the raw silk from the interior of Asia was brought to Cos, and there manufactured, in the same way, as we learn from Procopius, that it was brought some centuries later to be woven in the Phœnician cities of Tyre and Berytus.—O. S.]

[66] Georgic. ii. 121. Serica quando venerint in usum planissime non scio: suspicor tamen in Julii Cæsaris ævo, nam ante non invenio, says Justus Lipsius (Excursus i. ad Tacit. Annal. ii. 32). See Dion Cassius (l. xliii. [c. 24] p. 358, edit. Reimar), and Pausanias (l. vi. [c. 26, § 6-9] p. 519), the first who describes, however strangely, the Seric insect.

[67] Tam longinquo orbe petitur, ut in publico matrona transluceat . . . ut denudet fœminas vestis (Plin. vi. 20, xi. 26). Varro and Publius Syrus had already played on the Toga vitrea, ventus textilis, and nebula linea (Horat. Sermon. i. 2, 101, with the notes of Torrentius and Dacier).

by a looser texture, and the intermixture of linen threads.[68] Two hundred years after the age of Pliny the use of pure or even of mixed silks was confined to the female sex, till the opulent citizens of Rome and the provinces were insensibly familiarised with the example of Elagabalus, the first who, by this effeminate habit, had sullied the dignity of an emperor and a man. Aurelian complained that a pound of silk was sold at Rome for twelve ounces of gold; but the supply increased with the demand, and the price diminished with the supply. If accident or monopoly sometimes raised the value even above the standard of Aurelian, the manufacturers of Tyre and Berytus were sometimes compelled, by the operation of the same causes, to content themselves with a ninth part of that extravagant rate.[69] A law was thought necessary to discriminate the dress of comedians from that of senators, and of the silk exported from its native country the far greater part was consumed by the subjects of Justinian. They were still more intimately acquainted with a shell-fish of the Mediterranean, surnamed the silkworm of the sea: the fine wool or hair by which the mother-of-pearl affixes itself to the rock is now manufactured for curiosity rather than use; and a robe obtained from the same singular materials was the gift of the Roman emperor to the satraps of Armenia.[70]

A valuable merchandise of small bulk is capable of defraying the expense of land-carriage, and the caravans traversed the whole latitude of Asia in two hundred and forty-three days from the Chinese ocean to the sea-coast of Syria. Silk was immediately delivered to the Romans by the Persian merchants,[71] who frequented the fairs of Armenia and Nisibis; but this trade, which in the intervals of truce was oppressed by avarice and jealousy, was totally interrupted by the long wars of the rival monarchies. The Great King might proudly number Sogdiana, and even *Serica,* among the provinces of his empire, but his real dominion was bounded by the Oxus, and his useful intercourse with the Sogdoites, beyond the river, depended on the pleasure of their conquerors, the white Huns and the Turks, who successively reigned over that industrious people. Yet the most savage dominion has not extir-

---

[68] On the texture, colours, names, and use of the silk, half-silk, and linen garments of antiquity, see the profound, diffuse, and obscure researches of the great Salmasius (in Hist. August. p. 127, 309, 310, 339, 341, 342, 344, 388-391, 395, 513), who was ignorant of the most common trades of Dijon or Leyden.

[69] Flavius Vopiscus in Aurelian. c. 45, in Hist. August. p. 224. See Salmasius ad Hist. Aug. p. 392, and Plinian. Excercitat. in Solinum, p. 694, 695. The Anecdotes of Procopius (c. 25) state a partial and imperfect rate of the price of silk in the time of Justinian.

[70] Procopius de Ædif. l. iii. c. 1. These *pinnes de mer* are found near Smyrna, Sicily, Corsica, and Minorca; and a pair of gloves of their silk was presented to Pope Benedict XIV.

[71] Procopius, Persic. l. i. c. 20; l. ii. c. 25; Gothic. l. iv. c. 17. Menander in Excerpt. Legat. p. 107 [ed. Par.; p. 296, ed. Bonn]. Of the Parthian or Persian empire, Isidore of Charax (in Stathmis Parthicis, p. 7, 8, in Hudson, Geograph, Minor. tom. ii.) has marked the roads, and Ammianus Marcellinus (l. xxiii. c. 6, p. 400) has enumerated the provinces.

pated the seeds of agriculture and commerce in a region which is celebrated as one of the four gardens of Asia; the cities of Samarcand and
Bochara are advantageously seated for the exchange of its various
productions, and their merchants purchased from the Chinese [72] the
raw or manufactured silk which they transported into Persia for the
use of the Roman empire. In the vain capital of China the Sogdian
caravans were entertained as the suppliant embassies of tributary kingdoms, and, if they returned in safety, the bold adventure was rewarded
with exorbitant gain. But the difficult and perilous march from Samarcand to the first town of Shensi could not be performed in less than
sixty, eighty, or one hundred days; as soon as they had passed the
Jaxartes they entered the desert, and the wandering hordes, unless they
are restrained by armies and garrisons, have always considered the
citizen and the traveller as the objects of lawful rapine. To escape the
Tartar robbers and the tyrants of Persia, the silk-caravans explored a
more southern road: they traversed the mountains of Thibet, descended
the streams of the Ganges or the Indus, and patiently expected, in the
ports of Guzerat and Malabar, the annual fleets of the West. [73] But
the dangers of the desert were found less intolerable than toil, hunger,
and the loss of time; the attempt was seldom renewed, and the only
European who has passed that unfrequented way applauds his own
diligence that, in nine months after his departure from Pekin, he reached
the mouth of the Indus. The ocean, however, was open to the free
communication of mankind. From the great river to the tropic of
Cancer the provinces of China were subdued and civilised by the emperors of the North; they were filled about the time of the Christian
era with cities and men, mulberry-trees and their precious inhabitants;
and if the Chinese, with the knowledge of the compass, had possessed
the genius of the Greeks or Phœnicians, they might have spread their
discoveries over the southern hemisphere. I am not qualified to examine, and I am not disposed to believe, their distant voyages to the
Persian Gulf or the Cape of Good Hope; but their ancestors might
equal the labours and success of the present race, and the sphere of
their navigation might extend from the isles of Japan to the straits
of Malacca, the Pillars, if we may apply that name, of an Oriental

---

[72] The blind admiration of the Jesuits confounds the different periods of
the Chinese history. They are more critically distinguished by M. de Guignes
(Hist. des Huns, tom. i. part i. in the Tables, part ii. in the Geography.
Mémoires de l'Académie des Inscriptions, tom. xxxii. xxxvi. xlii. xliii.), who
discovers the gradual progress of the truth of the annals and the extent of
the monarchy, till the Christian era. He has searched with a curious eye the
connections of the Chinese with the nations of the West; but these connections
are slight, casual, and obscure; nor did the Romans entertain a suspicion that
the Seres or Sinæ possessed an empire not inferior to their own.

[73] The roads from China to Persia and Hindostan may be investigated in
the relations of Hackluyt and Thevenot (the ambassadors of Sharokh, Anthony
Jenkinson, the Père Greuber, etc. See likewise Hanway's Travels, vol. i.
p. 345-357). A communication through Thibet has been lately explored by
the English sovereigns of Bengal.

Hercules.[74] Without losing sight of land, they might sail along the coast to the extreme promontory of Achin, which is annually visited by ten or twelve ships laden with the productions, the manufactures, and even the artificers of China; the island of Sumatra and the opposite peninsula are faintly delineated [75] as the regions of gold and silver, and the trading cities named in the geography of Ptolemy may indicate that this wealth was not solely derived from the mines. The direct interval between Sumatra and Ceylon is about three hundred leagues; the Chinese and Indian navigators were conducted by the flight of birds and periodical winds, and the ocean might be securely traversed in square-built ships, which, instead of iron, were sewed together with the strong thread of the cocoanut. Ceylon, Serendib, or Taprobana was divided between two hostile princes, one of whom possessed the mountains, the elephants, and the luminous carbuncle, and the other enjoyed the more solid riches of domestic industry, foreign trade, and the capacious harbour of Trinquemale, which received and dismissed the fleets of the East and West. In this hospitable isle, at an equal distance (as it was computed) from their respective countries, the silk-merchants of China, who had collected in their voyages aloes, cloves, nutmeg, and sandal-wood, maintained a free and beneficial commerce with the inhabitants of the Persian Gulf. The subjects of the Great King exalted, without a rival, his power and magnificence; and the Roman, who confounded their vanity by comparing his paltry coin with a gold medal of the emperor Anastasius, had sailed to Ceylon, in an Æthiopian ship, as a simple passenger.[76]

As silk became of indispensable use, the emperor Justinian saw with concern that the Persians had occupied by land and sea the monopoly of this important supply, and that the wealth of his subjects was continually drained by a nation of enemies and idolators. An active government would have restored the trade of Egypt and the navigation of the Red Sea, which had decayed with the prosperity of the empire; and the Roman vessels might have sailed for the purchase of silk to the ports of Ceylon, of Malacca, or even of China. Justinian embraced

[74] For the Chinese navigation to Malacca and Achin, perhaps to Ceylon, see Renaudot (on the two Mahometan Travellers, p. 8-11, 13-17, 141-157), Dampier (vol. ii. p. 136), the Hist. Philosophique des deux Indes (tom. i. p. 98), and the Hist. Générale des Voyages (tom. vi. p. 201).

[75] The knowledge, or rather ignorance, of Strabo, Pliny, Ptolemy, Arrian, Marcian, etc., of the countries eastward of Cape Comorin, is finely illustrated by D'Anville (Antiquité Géographique de l'Inde, especially p. 161-198). Our geography of India is improved by commerce and conquest; and has been illustrated by the excellent maps and memoirs of Major Rennell. If he extends the sphere of his inquiries with the same critical knowledge and sagacity, he will succeed, and may surpass, the first of modern geographers.

[76] The Taprobane of Pliny (vi. 24), Solinus (c. 56), and Salmas. Plinianæ Exercitat. (p. 781, 782), and most of the ancients, who often confound the islands of Ceylon and Sumatra, is more clearly described by Cosmas Indicopleustes; yet even the Christian topographer has exaggerated its dimensions. His information on the Indian and Chinese trade is rare and curious (l. ii. p. 138, l. xi. p. 337, 338, edit. Montfaucon [Coll. Nova Patrum, tom. ii. Paris, 1706]).

a more humble expedient, and solicited the aid of his Christian allies, the Æthiopians of Abyssinia, who had recently acquired the arts of navigation, the spirit of trade, and the seaport of Adulis,[77] still decorated with the trophies of a Grecian conqueror. Along the African coast they penetrated to the equator in search of gold, emeralds, and aromatics; but they wisely declined an unequal competition, in which they must be always prevented by the vicinity of the Persians to the markets of India: and the emperor submitted to the disappointment till his wishes were gratified by an unexpected event. The Gospel had been preached to the Indians: a bishop already governed the Christians of St. Thomas on the pepper-coast of Malabar; a church was planted in Ceylon, and the missionaries pursued the footsteps of commerce to the extremities of Asia.[78] Two Persian monks had long resided in China, perhaps in the royal city of Nankin, the seat of a monarch addicted to foreign superstitions, and who actually received an embassy from the isle of Ceylon. Amidst their pious occupations they viewed with a curious eye the common dress of the Chinese, the manufactures of silk, and the myriads of silkworms, whose education (either on trees or in houses) had once been considered as the labour of queens.[79] They soon discovered that it was impracticable to transport the short-lived insect, but that in the eggs a numerous progeny might be preserved and multiplied in a distant climate. Religion or interest had more power over the Persian monks than the love of their country: after a long journey they arrived at Constantinople, imparted their project to the emperor, and were liberally encouraged by the gifts and promises of Justinian. To the historians of that prince a campaign at the foot of Mount Caucasus has seemed more deserving of a minute relation than the labours of these missionaries of commerce, who again entered China, deceived a jealous people by concealing the eggs of the silkworm in a hollow cane, and returned in triumph with the spoils of the East. Under their direction the eggs were hatched at the proper season by the artificial heat of dung; the worms were fed with mulberry-leaves; they lived and laboured in a foreign climate; a sufficient number of butterflies was saved to propagate the race, and trees were planted to supply the nourishment of the rising generations. Experience and reflection corrected the errors of a new attempt, and the Sogdoite ambassadors acknowledged in the succeeding reign that the Romans were not inferior to the natives of China in the education of the insects and the manufac-

---

[77] See Procopius, Persic. (l. ii. c. 20 [l. i. c. 19]). Cosmas affords some interesting knowledge of the port and inscription of Adulis (Topograph. Christ. l. ii. p. 139, 140-143), and of the trade of the Axumites along the African coast of Barbaria or Zingi (p. 138, 139), and as far as Taprobane (l. xi. p. 339).

[78] See the Christian missions in India, in Cosmas (l. iii. p. 178, 179, l. xi. p. 337), and consult Asseman. Bibliot. Orient. (tom. iv. p. 413-548).

[79] The invention, manufacture, and general use of silk in China, may be seen in Duhalde (Description Générale de la Chine, tom. ii. p. 165, 205-223). The province of Chekian is the most renowned both for quantity and quality.

tures of silk,[80] in which both China and Constantinople have been surpassed by the industry of modern Europe. I am not insensible of the
benefits of elegant luxury; yet I reflect with some pain that if the im-
porters of silk had introduced the art of printing, already practised by
the Chinese, the comedies of Menander and the entire decads of Livy
would have been perpetuated in the editions of the sixth century. A
larger view of the globe might at least have promoted the improvement
of speculative science; but the Christian geography was forcibly extracted from texts of Scripture, and the study of nature was the surest
symptom of an unbelieving mind. The orthodox faith confined the
habitable world to *one* temperate zone, and represented the earth as
an oblong surface, four hundred days' journey in length, two hundred
in breadth, encompassed by the ocean and covered by the solid crystal
of the firmament.[81]

IV. The subjects of Justinian were dissatisfied with the times and
with the government. Europe was overrun by the barbarians and Asia
by the monks: the poverty of the West discouraged the trade and manufactures of the East: the produce of labour was consumed by the unprofitable servants of the church, the state, and the army; and a rapid
decrease was felt in the fixed and circulating capitals which constitute
the national wealth. The public distress had been alleviated by the
economy of Anastasius, and that prudent emperor accumulated an immense treasure while he delivered his people from the most odious or
oppressive taxes. Their gratitude universally applauded the abolition
of the *gold of affliction,* a personal tribute on the industry of the poor,[82]

---

[80] Procopius, Bell. Gothic. iv. c. 17. Theophanes, Byzant. apud Phot. Cod.
lxxxiv. [lxiv.] p. 38 [ed. Hoeschel.; p. 26 a, ed. Bekk.]. Zonaras, tom. ii. l. xiv.
p. 69). Pagi (tom. ii. p. 602) assigns to the year 552 this memorable importation. Menander (in Excerpt. Legat. p. 107 [p. 295, 296, ed. Bonn.]) mentions
the admiration of the Sogdoites; and Theophylact Simocatta (l. vii. c. 9)
darkly represents the two rival kingdoms in (*China*) the country of silk.

[81] Cosmas, surnamed Indicopleustes, or the Indian navigator, performed
his voyage about the year 522, and composed at Alexandria, between 535
and 547, Christian Topography (Montfaucon, Præfat. c. i.), in which he
refutes the impious opinion that the earth is a globe; and Photius had read
this work (Cod. xxxvi. p. 9, 10 [p. 7, ed. Bekk.]), which displays the prejudices
of a monk, with the knowledge of a merchant: the most valuable part has
been given in French and in Greek by Melchisedec Thevenot (Relations Cu-
rieuses, part i.), and the whole is since published in a splendid edition by
Père Montfaucon (Collectio Nova Patrum, Paris, 1706, 2 vols. in fol. tom. ii.
p. 113-346). But the editor, a theologian, might blush at not discovering
the Nestorian heresy of Cosmas, which has been detected by La Croze (Christianisme des Indes, tom. i. p. 40-56).
[See the character of Anastasius in Joannes Lydus de Magistratibus, lib. iii
c. 45, 46. His economy is there said to have degenerated into parsimony.
He is accused of having taken away the levying of taxes and payment of the
troops from the municipal authorities (the decurionate) in the Eastern cities,
and entrusted it to an extortionate officer named Mannus. But he admits
that the Imperial revenue was enormously increased by this measure.—O. S.]

[82] Evagrius (l. iii. c. 39, 40) is minute and grateful, but angry with Zosimus
for calumniating the great Constantine. In collecting all the bonds and records
of the tax, the humanity of Anastasius was diligent and artful: fathers were

but more intolerable, as it should seem, in the form than in the substance, since the flourishing city of Edessa paid only one hundred and forty pounds of gold, which was collected in four years from ten thousand artificers.[83] Yet such was the parsimony which supported this liberal disposition, that, in a reign of twenty-seven years, Anastasius saved from his annual revenue the enormous sum of thirteen millions sterling, or three hundred and twenty thousand pounds of gold.[84] His example was neglected, and his treasure was abused, by the nephew of Justin. The riches of Justinian were speedily exhausted by alms and buildings, by ambitious wars and ignominious treaties. His revenues were found inadequate to his expenses. Every art was tried to extort from the people the gold and silver which he scattered with a lavish hand from Persia to France:[85] his reign was marked by the vicissitudes, or rather by the combat, of rapaciousness and avarice, of splendour and poverty; he lived with the reputation of hidden treasures,[86] and bequeathed to his successor the payment of his debts.[87] Such a character has been justly accused by the voice of the people and of posterity: but public discontent is credulous; private malice is bold; and a lover of truth will peruse with a suspicious eye the instructive anecdotes of Procopius. The secret historian represents only the vices of Justinian, and those vices are darkened by his malevolent pencil. Ambiguous actions are imputed to the worst motives: error is confounded with guilt, accident with design, and laws with abuses; the partial injustice of a moment is dexterously applied as the general maxim of a reign of thirty-two years: the emperor alone is made responsible for the faults of his officers, the disorders of the times, and the corruption of his subjects; and even the calamities of nature, plagues, earthquakes, and inundations, are imputed to the prince of the dæmons, who had mischievously assumed the form of Justinian.[88]

sometimes compelled to prostitute their daughters (Zosim. Hist. l. ii. c. 38, p. 165, 166, Lipsiæ, 1784 [p. 104, ed. Bonn]. Timotheus of Gaza chose such an event for the subject of a tragedy (Suidas, tom. iii. p. 475), which contributed to the abolition of the tax (Cedrenus, p. 357 [ed. Par.; tom. i. p. 627, ed. Bonn])—an happy instance (if it be true) of the use of the theatre.
[83] See Josua Stylites, in the Bibliotheca Orientalis of Asseman (tom. i. p. 268). This capitation-tax is slightly mentioned in the Chronicle of Edessa.
[84] Procopius (Anecdot. c. 19 [tom. iii. p. 113, ed. Bonn]) fixes this sum from the report of the treasurers themselves. Tiberius had *vicies ter millies;* but far different was his empire from that of Anastasius.
[85] Evagrius (l. iv. c. 30), in the next generation, was moderate and well informed; and Zonaras (l. xiv. c. 61), in the twelfth century, had read with care, and thought without prejudice: yet their colours are almost as black as those of the Anecdotes.
[86] Procopius (Anecdot. c. 30) relates the idle conjectures of the times. The death of Justinian, says the secret historian, will expose his wealth or poverty.
[87] See Corippus de Laudibus Justini Aug. l. ii. v. 260, etc., 389, etc.
"Plurima sunt vivo nimium neglecta parente,
Unde tot exhaustus contraxit debita fiscus."
Centenaries of gold were brought by strong arms into the Hippodrome:
"Debita persolvit genitoris, cauta recepit."
[88] The Anecdotes (c. 11-14, 18, 20-30) supply many facts and more complaints.

After this precaution I shall briefly relate the anecdotes of avarice and rapine under the following heads: I. Justinian was so profuse that he could not be liberal. The civil and military officers, when they were admitted into the service of the palace, obtained a humble rank and a moderate stipend; they ascended by seniority to a station of affluence and repose; the annual pensions, of which the most honourable class was abolished by Justinian, amounted to four hundred thousand pounds; and this domestic economy was deplored by the venal or indigent courtiers as the last outrage on the majesty of the empire. The posts, the salaries of physicians, and the nocturnal illuminations were objects of more general concern; and the cities might justly complain that he usurped the municipal revenues which had been appropriated to these useful institutions. Even the soldiers were injured; and such was the decay of military spirit, that they were injured with impunity. The emperor refused at the return of each fifth year the customary donative of five pieces of gold, reduced his veterans to beg their bread, and suffered unpaid armies to melt away in the wars of Italy and Persia. II. The humanity of his predecessors had always remitted, in some auspicious circumstance of their reign, the arrears of the public tribute, and they dexterously assumed the merit of resigning those claims which it was impracticable to enforce. " Justinian, in the space of thirty-two years, has never granted a similar indulgence; and many of his subjects have renounced the possession of those lands whose value is insufficient to satisfy the demands of the treasury. To the cities which had suffered by hostile inroads Anastasius promised a general exemption of seven years: the provinces of Justinian have been ravaged by the Persians and Arabs, the Huns and Sclavonians; but his vain and ridiculous dispensation of a single year has been confined to those places which were actually taken by the enemy." Such is the language of the secret historian, who expressly denies that *any* indulgence was granted to Palestine after the revolt of the Samaritans; a false and odious charge, confuted by the authentic record which attests a relief of thirteen centenaries of gold (fifty-two thousand pounds) obtained for that desolate province by the intercession of St. Sabas.[89] III. Procopius has not condescended to explain the system of taxation, which fell like a hailstorm upon the land, like a devouring pestilence on its inhabitants: but we should become the accomplices of his malignity if we imputed to Justinian alone the ancient, though rigorous principle, that a whole district should be condemned to sustain the partial loss of the persons or property of individuals. The *Annona,* or supply of corn for the use of the army and capital, was a grievous and arbitrary exaction, which exceeded, perhaps in a tenfold proportion, the ability of the farmer; and his distress was aggravated by the partial injustice of weights and measures, and the expense and labour of distant carriage. In a time of

---

[89] One to Scythopolis, capital of the second Palestine, and twelve for the rest of the province. Aleman. (p. 59 [Procop. tom. iii. p. 407, 408, ed. Bonn]) honestly produces this fact from a MS. Life of St. Sabas, by his disciple Cyril, in the Vatican library, and since published by Cotelerius.

scarcity an extraordinary requisition was made to the adjacent provinces of Thrace, Bithynia, and Phrygia: but the proprietors, after a wearisome journey and a perilous navigation, received so inadequate a compensation, that they would have chosen the alternative of delivering both the corn and price at the doors of their granaries. These precautions might indicate a tender solicitude for the welfare of the capital; yet Constantinople did not escape the rapacious despotism of Justinian. Till his reign the straits of the Bosphorus and Hellespont were open to the freedom of trade, and nothing was prohibited except the exportation of arms for the service of the barbarians. At each of these gates of the city a prætor was stationed, the minister of Imperial avarice; heavy customs were imposed on the vessels and their merchandise; the oppression was retaliated on the helpless consumer; the poor were afflicted by the artificial scarcity and exorbitant price of the market; and a people accustomed to depend on the liberality of their prince might sometimes complain of the deficiency of water and bread.[90] The *aërial* tribute, without a name, a law, or a definite object, was an annual gift of one hundred and twenty thousand pounds, which the emperor accepted from his Prætorian præfect; and the means of payment were abandoned to the discretion of that powerful magistrate. IV. Even such a tax was less intolerable than the privilege of monopolies, which checked the fair competition of industry, and, for the sake of a small and dishonest gain, imposed an arbitrary burden on the wants and luxury of the subject. "As soon (I transcribe the Anecdotes) as the exclusive sale of silk was usurped by the Imperial treasurer, a whole people, the manufacturers of Tyre and Berytus, was reduced to extreme misery, and either perished with hunger or fled to the hostile dominions of Persia." A province might suffer by the decay of its manufactures, but in this example of silk Procopius has partially overlooked the inestimable and lasting benefit which the empire received from the curiosity of Justinian. His addition of one-seventh to the ordinary price of copper-money may be interpreted with the same candour; and the alteration, which might be wise, appears to have been innocent; since he neither alloyed the purity nor enhanced the value of the gold coin,[91] the legal measure of public and private payments. V. The ample jurisdiction required by the farmers of the revenue to accomplish their engagements might be placed in an odious light, as if they had purchased from the emperor the lives and fortunes of their fellow-citizens. And a more direct sale of honours and offices was transacted in the palace, with the permission, or at least with the connivance, of Justinian and

[90] John Malala (tom. ii. p. 232 [p. 488, ed. Bonn]) mentions the want of bread, and Zonaras (l. xiv. p. 63) the leaden pipes, which Justinian, or his servants, stole from the aqueducts.

[91] For an aureus, one-sixth of an ounce of gold, instead of 210, he gave no more than 180 folles or ounces of copper. A disproportion of the mint, below the market price, must have soon produced a scarcity of small money. In England, *twelve* pence in copper would sell for no more than *seven* pence (Smith's Inquiry into the Wealth of Nations, vol. i. p. 49). For Justinian's gold coin, see Evagrius (l. iv. c. 30).

Theodora. The claims of merit, even those of favour, were disregarded, and it was almost reasonable to expect that the bold adventurer who had undertaken the trade of a magistrate should find a rich compensation for infamy, labour, danger, the debts which he had contracted, and the heavy interest which he paid. A sense of the disgrace and mischief of this venal practice at length awakened the slumbering virtue of Justinian; and he attempted, by the sanction of oaths [92] and penalties, to guard the integrity of his government: but at the end of a year of perjury his rigorous edict was suspended, and corruption licentiously abused her triumph over the impotence of the laws. VI. The testament of Eulalius, count of the domestics, declared the emperor his sole heir, on condition, however, that he should discharge his debts and legacies, allow to his three daughters a decent maintenance, and bestow each of them in marriage, with a portion of ten pounds of gold. But the splendid fortune of Eulalius had been consumed by fire, and the inventory of his goods did not exceed the trifling sum of five hundred and sixty-four pieces of gold. A similar instance in Grecian history admonished the emperor of the honourable part prescribed for his imitation. He checked the selfish murmurs of the treasury, applauded the confidence of his friend, discharged the legacies and debts, educated the three virgins under the eye of the empress Theodora, and doubled the marriage-portion which had satisfied the tenderness of their father.[93] The humanity of a prince (for princes cannot be generous) is entitled to some praise; yet even in this act of virtue we may discover the inveterate custom of supplanting the legal or natural heirs which Procopius imputes to the reign of Justinian. His charge is supported by eminent names and scandalous examples; neither widows nor orphans were spared; and the art of soliciting, or extorting, or supposing testaments, was beneficially practised by the agents of the palace. This base and mischievous tyranny invades the security of private life; and the monarch who has indulged an appetite for gain will soon be tempted to anticipate the moment of succession, to interpret wealth as an evidence of guilt, and to proceed, from the claim of inheritance, to the power of confiscation. VII. Among the forms of rapine a philosopher may be permitted to name the conversion of Pagan or heretical riches to the use of the faithful; but in the time of Justinian this holy plunder was condemned by the sectaries alone, who became the victims of his orthodox avarice.[94]

Dishonour might be ultimately reflected on the character of Justinian; but much of the guilt, and still more of the profit, was intercepted by

[92] The oath is conceived in the most formidable words (Novell. viii. tit. 3). The defaulters imprecate on themselves, quicquid habent telorum armamentaria cœli; the part of Judas, the leprosy of Giezi, the tremor of Cain, etc., besides all temporal pains.

[93] A similar or more generous act of friendship is related by Lucian of Eudamidas of Corinth (in Toxare, c. 22, 23, tom. ii. p. 530), and the story has produced an ingenious, though feeble, comedy of Fontenelle.

[94] John Malala, tom. ii. p. 101, 102, 103 [p. 171-173 ed. Oxon.; 439, 440, ed. Bonn].

the ministers, who were seldom promoted for their virtues, and not always selected for their talents.[95] The merits of Tribonian the quæstor will hereafter be weighed in the reformation of the Roman law; but the economy of the East was subordinate to the Prætorian præfect; and Procopius has justified his anecdotes by the portrait which he exposes, in his public history, of the notorious vices of John of Cappadocia.[96] His knowledge was not borrowed from the schools,[97] and his style was scarcely legible; but he excelled in the powers of native genius, to suggest the wisest counsels, and to find expedients in the most desperate situations. The corruption of his heart was equal to the vigour of his understanding. Although he was suspected of magic and Pagan superstition, he appeared insensible to the fear of God or the reproaches of man; and his aspiring fortune was raised on the death of thousands, the poverty of millions, the ruin of cities, and the desolation of provinces. From the dawn of light to the moment of dinner, he assiduously laboured to enrich his master and himself at the expense of the Roman world; the remainder of the day was spent in sensual and obscene pleasures, and the silent hours of the night were interrupted by the perpetual dread of the justice of an assassin. His abilities, perhaps his vices, recommended him to the lasting friendship of Justinian: the emperor yielded with reluctance to the fury of the people; his victory was displayed by the immediate restoration of their enemy; and they felt above ten years, under his oppressive administration, that he was stimulated to revenge rather than instructed by misfortune. Their murmurs served only to fortify the resolution of Justinian; but the præfect, in the insolence of favour, provoked the resentment of Theodora, disdained a power before which every knee was bent, and attempted to sow the seeds of discord between the emperor and his beloved consort. Even Theodora herself was constrained to dissemble, to wait a favourable moment, and, by an artful conspiracy, to render John of Cappadocia the accomplice of his own destruction. At a time when Belisarius, unless he had been a hero, must have shown himself a rebel, his wife Antonina, who enjoyed the secret confidence of the empress, communicated his feigned discontent to Euphemia, the daughter of the præfect; the credulous virgin imparted to her father the dangerous project; and John, who might have known the value of oaths and promises, was tempted to accept a nocturnal, and almost treasonable, interview with the wife of Belisarius. An ambuscade of guards and eunuchs had been

[95] One of these, Anatolius, perished in an earthquake—doubtless a judgment! The complaints and clamours of the people in Agathias (l. v. p. 146, 147 [ed. Par.; p. 284 sq., ed. Bonn]) are almost an echo of the anecdote. The aliena pecunia reddenda of Corippus (l. ii. 381, etc. [Laud. Just. Min.]) is not very honourable to Justinian's memory.

[96] See the history and character of John of Cappadocia in Procopius (Persic. l. i. c. 24, 25, l. ii. c. 30. Vandal. l. i. c. 13. Anecdot. c. 2, 17, 22). The agreement of the history and anecdotes is a mortal wound to the reputation of the præfect.

[97] Οὐ γὰρ ἄλλο οὐδὲν ἐς γραμματιστοῦ φοιτῶν ἔμαθεν, ὅτι μὴ γράμματα, καὶ ταῦτα κακὰ κακῶς γράψαι—a forcible expression [Pers. i. c. 24]

posted by the command of Theodora; they rushed with drawn swords
to seize or to punish the guilty minister: he was saved by the fidelity
of his attendants; but, instead of appealing to a gracious sovereign
who had privately warned him of his danger, he pusillanimously fled
to the sanctuary of the church. The favourite of Justinian was sacrificed
to conjugal tenderness or domestic tranquillity; the conversion of a
præfect into a priest extinguished his ambitious hopes; but the friendship of the emperor alleviated his disgrace, and he retained in the
mild exile of Cyzicus an ample portion of his riches. Such imperfect
revenge could not satisfy the unrelenting hatred of Theodora; the
murder of his old enemy, the bishop of Cyzicus, afforded a decent pretence; and John of Cappadocia, whose actions had deserved a thousand
deaths, was at last condemned for a crime of which he was innocent.
A great minister, who had been invested with the honours of consul and
patrician, was ignominiously scourged like the vilest of malefactors; a
tattered cloak was the sole remnant of his fortunes; he was transported
in a bark to the place of his banishment at Antinopolis in Upper Egypt,
and the præfect of the East begged his bread through the cities which
had trembled at his name. During an exile of seven years, his life was
protracted and threatened by the ingenious cruelty of Theodora; and
when her death permitted the emperor to recall a servant whom he
had abandoned with regret, the ambition of John of Cappadocia was
reduced to the humble duties of the sacerdotal profession. His successors convinced the subjects of Justinian that the arts of oppression
might still be improved by experience and industry; the frauds of a
Syrian banker were introduced into the administration of the finances;
and the example of the præfect was diligently copied by the quæstor,
the public and private treasurer, the governors of provinces, and the
principal magistrates of the Eastern empire.[98]

V. The *edifices* of Justinian were cemented with the blood and
treasure of his people; but those stately structures appeared to announce the prosperity of the empire, and actually displayed the skill
of their architects. Both the theory and practice of the arts which depend on mathematical science and mechanical power were cultivated
under the patronage of the emperors; the fame of Archimedes was
rivalled by Proclus and Anthemius; and if their *miracles* had been
related by intelligent spectators, they might now enlarge the speculations, instead of exciting the distrust, of philosophers. A tradition has
prevailed that the Roman fleet was reduced to ashes in the port of
Syracuse by the burning-glasses of Archimedes;[99] and it is asserted

[98] The chronology of Procopius is loose and obscure; but with the aid of
Pagi I can discern that John was appointed Prætorian præfect of the East
in the year 530; that he was removed in January, 532—restored before June,
533—banished in 541—and recalled between June, 548, and April 1, 549.
Aleman. (p. 96, 97 [Procop. tom. iii. p. 449, 450, ed. Bonn]) gives the list
of his ten successors—a rapid series in a part of a single reign.
[99] This conflagration is hinted by Lucian (in Hippia, c. 2) and Galen (l. iii.
de Temperamentis, tom. i. p. 81, edit. Basil) in the second century. A thousand
years afterwards it is positively affirmed by Zonaras (l. ix. p. 424) on the

that a similar expedient was employed by Proclus to destroy the Gothic vessels in the harbour of Constantinople, and to protect his benefactor Anastasius against the bold enterprise of Vitalian.[100] A machine was fixed on the walls of the city, consisting of a hexagon mirror of polished brass, with many smaller and movable polygons to receive and reflect the rays of the meridian sun; and a consuming flame was darted to the distance, perhaps, of two hundred feet.[101] The truth of these two extraordinary facts is invalidated by the silence of the most authentic historians; and the use of burning-glasses was never adopted in the attack or defence of places.[102] Yet the admirable experiments of a French philosopher [103] have demonstrated the possibility of such a mirror; and, since it is possible, I am more disposed to attribute the art to the greatest mathematicians of antiquity, than to give the merit of the fiction to the idle fancy of a monk or a sophist. According to another story, Proclus applied sulphur to the destruction of the Gothic fleet; [104] in a modern imagination, the name of sulphur is instantly connected with the suspicion of gunpowder, and that suspicion is propagated by the secret arts of his disciple Anthemius.[105] A citizen of Tralles in Asia had five sons, who were all distinguished in their respective professions by merit and success. Olympius excelled in the knowledge and practice of the Roman jurisprudence. Dioscorus and Alexander became learned physicians; but the skill of the former was exercised for the benefit of his fellow-citizens, while his more ambitious brother acquired wealth and reputation at Rome. The fame of Metrodorus the grammarian, and of Anthemius the mathematician and architect, reached the ears of the emperor Justinian, who invited them to Constantinople; and while the one instructed the rising generation in

faith of Dion Cassius, by Tzetzes (Chiliad ii. 119, etc.), Eustathius (ad Iliad, E. p. 338), and the scholiast of Lucian. See Fabricius (Biblioth. Græc. l. iii. c. 22, tom. ii. p. 551, 552 [ed. Hamb. 1716]), to whom I am more or less indebted for several of these quotations.

[100] Zonaras (l. xiv. p. 55) affirms the fact, without quoting any evidence.

[101] Tzetzes describes the artifice of these burning-glasses, which he had read, perhaps with no learned eyes, in a mathematical treatise of Anthemius. That treatise, περὶ παραδόξων μηχανημάτων, has been lately published, translated, and illustrated by M. Dupuys, a scholar and a mathematician (Mémoires de l'Académie des Inscriptions, tom. xlii. p. 392-451).

[102] In the siege of Syracuse, by the silence of Polybius, Plutarch, Livy; in the siege of Constantinople, by that of Marcellinus and all the contemporaries of the sixth century.

[103] Without any previous knowledge of Tzetzes or Anthemius, the immortal Buffon imagined and executed a set of burning-glasses, with which he could inflame planks at the distance of 200 feet (Supplément à l'Hist. Naturelle, tom. i. p. 399-483, quarto edition). What miracles would not his genius have performed for the public service, with royal expense, and in the strong sun of Constantinople or Syracuse!

[104] John Malala (tom. ii. p. 120-124 [p. 403-406, ed. Bonn]) relates the fact; but he seems to confound the names or persons of Proclus and Marinus.

[105] Agathias, l. v. p. 149-152 [ed. Par.; p. 289-294, ed. Bonn]. The merit of Anthemius as an architect is loudly praised by Procopius (de Ædif. l. i. c. 1 [tom. iii. p. 174, ed. Bonn]) and Paulus Silentiarius (part i. 134, etc. [p. 15, ed. Bonn]).

the schools of eloquence, the other filled the capital and provinces with more lasting monuments of his art. In a trifling dispute relative to the walls or windows of their contiguous houses, he had been vanquished by the eloquence of his neighbour Zeno; but the orator was defeated in his turn by the master of mechanics, whose malicious, though harmless, stratagems are darkly represented by the ignorance of Agathias. In a lower room, Anthemius arranged several vessels or caldrons of water, each of them covered by the wide bottom of a leathern tube, which rose to a narrow top, and was artificially conveyed among the joists and rafters of the adjacent building. A fire was kindled beneath the caldron; the steam of the boiling water ascended through the tubes; the house was shaken by the efforts of imprisoned air, and its trembling inhabitants might wonder that the city was unconscious of the earthquake which they had felt. At another time, the friends of Zeno, as they sat at table, were dazzled by the intolerable light which flashed in their eyes from the reflecting mirrors of Anthemius; they were astonished by the noise which he produced from the collision of certain minute and sonorous particles; and the orator declared in tragic style to the senate, that a mere mortal must yield to the power of an antagonist who shook the earth with the trident of Neptune, and imitated the thunder and lightning of Jove himself. The genius of Anthemius, and his colleague Isidore the Milesian, was excited and employed by a prince whose taste for architecture had degenerated into a mischievous and costly passion. His favourite architects submitted their designs and difficulties to Justinian, and discreetly confessed how much their laborious meditations were surpassed by the intuitive knowledge or celestial inspiration of an emperor whose views were always directed to the benefit of his people, the glory of his reign, and the salvation of his soul.[106]

The principal church, which was dedicated by the founder of Constantinople to Saint Sophia, or the eternal wisdom, had been twice destroyed by fire; after the exile of John Chrysostom and during the *Nika* of the blue and green factions. No sooner did the tumult subside than the Christian populace deplored their sacrilegious rashness; but they might have rejoiced in the calamity, had they foreseen the glory of the new temple, which at the end of forty days was strenuously undertaken by the piety of Justinian.[107] The ruins were cleared away, a

[106] See Procopius (de Ædificiis, l. i. c. 1, 2, l. ii. c. 3). He relates a coincidence of dreams which supposes some fraud in Justinian or his architect. They both saw, in a vision, the same plan for stopping an inundation at Dara. A stone-quarry near Jerusalem was revealed to the emperor (l. v. c. 6 [tom. iii. p. 323, ed. Bonn]): an angel was tricked into the perpetual custody of St. Sophia (Anonym. de Antiq. C. P. l. iv. p. 70).

[107] Among the crowd of ancients and moderns who have celebrated the edifice of St. Sophia, I shall distinguish and follow, 1. Four original spectators and historians: Procopius (de Ædific. l. i. c. 1), Agathias (l. v. p. 152, 153 [p. 296, 297, ed. Bonn]), Paul Silentiarius (in a poem of 1026 hexameters, ad calcem Annæ Comnen. Alexiad.), and Evagrius (l. iv. c. 31). 2. Two legendary Greeks of a later period: George Codinus (de Origin. C. P. p. 64-

more spacious plan was described, and, as it required the consent of some proprietors of ground, they obtained the most exorbitant terms from the eager desires and timorous conscience of the monarch. Anthemius formed the design, and his genius directed the hands of ten thousand workmen, whose payment in pieces of fine silver was never delayed beyond the evening. The emperor himself, clad in a linen tunic, surveyed each day their rapid progress, and encouraged their diligence by his familiarity, his zeal, and his rewards. The new cathedral of St. Sophia was consecrated by the patriarch, five years, eleven months, and ten days from the first foundation; and in the midst of the solemn festival Justinian exclaimed with devout vanity, " Glory be to God, who hath thought me worthy to accomplish so great a work; I have vanquished thee, O Solomon! " [108] But the pride of the Roman Solomon, before twenty years had elapsed, was humbled by an earthquake, which overthrew the eastern part of the dome. Its splendour was again restored by the perseverance of the same prince; and in the thirty-sixth year of his reign Justinian celebrated the second dedication of a temple which remains, after twelve centuries, a stately monument of his fame. The architecture of St. Sophia, which is now converted into the principal mosque, has been imitated by the Turkish sultans, and that venerable pile continues to excite the fond admiration of the Greeks, and the more rational curiosity of European travellers. The eye of the spectator is disappointed by an irregular prospect of half-domes and shelving roofs: the western front, the principal approach, is destitute of simplicity and magnificence; and the scale of dimensions has been much surpassed by several of the Latin cathedrals. But the architect who first erected an *aërial* cupola is entitled to the praise of bold design and skilful execution. The dome of St. Sophia, illuminated by four-and-twenty windows, is formed with so small a curve, that the depth is equal only to one-sixth of its diameter; the measure of that diameter is one hundred and fifteen feet, and the lofty centre, where a crescent has supplanted the cross, rises to the perpendicular height of one hundred and eighty feet above the pavement. The circle which encompasses the dome lightly reposes on four strong arches, and their weight is firmly supported by four massy piles, whose strength is assisted on the north-

74 [ed. Par.; p. 130-148, ed. Bonn]), and the anonymous writer of Banduri (Imp. Orient. tom. i. 1. iv. p. 65-80). 3. The great Byzantine antiquarian, Ducange (Comment. ad Paul Silentiar. p. 525-598, and C. P. Christ. l. iii. p. 5-78). 4. Two French travellers—the one, Peter Gyllius (de Topograph. C. P. l. ii. c. 3, 4) in the sixteenth; the other, Grelot (Voyage de C. P. p. 95-164, Paris, 1680, in 4to) : he has given plans, prospects, and inside views of St. Sophia; and his plans, though on a smaller scale, appear more correct than those of Ducange. I have adopted and reduced the measures of Grelot: but as no Christian can now ascend the dome, the height is borrowed from Evagrius, compared with Gyllius, Greaves, and the Oriental Geographer.

[108] Solomon's temple was surrounded with courts, porticoes, etc.; but the proper structure of the house of God was no more (if we take the Egyptian or Hebrew cubit at 22 inches) than 55 feet in height, 36⅔ in breadth, and 110 in length—a small parish church, says Prideaux (Connection, vol. i. p. 144, folio) ; but few sanctuaries could be valued at four or five millions sterling!

ern and southern sides by four columns of Egyptian granite. A Greek cross, inscribed in a quadrangle, represents the form of the edifice; the exact breadth is two hundred and forty-three feet, and two hundred and sixty-nine may be assigned for the extreme length, from the sanctuary in the east to the nine western doors which open into the vestibule, and from thence into the *narthex* or exterior portico. That portico was the humble station of the penitents. The nave or body of the church was filled by the congregation of the faithful; but the two sexes were prudently distinguished, and the upper and lower galleries were allotted for the more private devotion of the women. Beyond the northern and southern piles, a balustrade, terminated on either side by the thrones of the emperor and the patriarch, divided the nave from the choir; and the space, as far as the steps of the altar, was occupied by the clergy and singers. The altar itself, a name which insensibly became familiar to Christian ears, was placed in the eastern recess, artificially built in the form of a demicylinder; and this sanctuary communicated by several doors with the sacristy, the vestry, the baptistery, and the contiguous buildings, subservient either to the pomp of worship, or the private use of the ecclesiastical ministers. The memory of past calamities inspired Justinian with a wise resolution that no wood, except for the doors, should be admitted into the new edifice; and the choice of the materials was applied to the strength, the lightness, or the splendour of the respective parts. The solid piles which sustained the cupola were composed of huge blocks of freestone, hewn into squares and triangles, fortified by circles of iron, and firmly cemented by the infusion of lead and quicklime; but the weight of the cupola was diminished by the levity of its substance, which consists either of pumice-stone that floats in the water, or of bricks, from the isle of Rhodes, five times less ponderous than the ordinary sort. The whole frame of the edifice was constructed of brick; but those base materials were concealed by a crust of marble; and the inside of St. Sophia, the cupola, the two larger and the six smaller semidomes, the walls, the hundred columns, and the pavement, delight even the eyes of barbarians with a rich and variegated picture.

A poet,[109] who beheld the primitive lustre of St. Sophia, enumerates the colours, the shades, and the spots of ten or twelve marbles, jaspers, and porphyries, which nature had profusely diversified, and which were blended and contrasted as it were by a skilful painter. The tri-

---

[109] Paul Silentiarius, in dark and poetic language, describes the various stones and marbles that were employed in the edifice of St. Sophia (P. ii. ver. 129, 133, etc. etc. [p. 27 *sqq.,* ed. Bonn]) : 1. The *Carystian*—pale, with iron veins. 2. The *Phrygian*—of two sorts, both of a rosy hue; the one with a white shade, the other purple, with silver flowers. 3. The *Porphyry of Egypt* —with small stars. 4. The *green marble of Laconia.* 5. The *Carian*—from Mount Iassis, with oblique veins, white and red. 6. The *Lydian*—pale, with a red flower. 7. The *African,* or *Mauritanian*—of a gold or saffron hue. 8. The *Celtic*—black, with white veins. 9. The *Bosphoric*—white, with black edges. Besides the *Proconnesian,* which formed the pavement; the *Thessalian, Molossian,* etc., which are less distinctly painted.

umph of Christ was adorned with the last spoils of Paganism, but the greater part of these costly stones was extracted from the quarries of Asia Minor, the isles and continent of Greece, Egypt, Africa, and Gaul. Eight columns of porphyry, which Aurelian had placed in the Temple of the Sun, were offered by the piety of a Roman matron; eight others of green marble were presented by the ambitious zeal of the magistrates of Ephesus: both are admirable by their size and beauty, but every order of architecture disclaims their fantastic capitals. A variety of ornaments and figures was curiously expressed in mosaic; and the images of Christ, of the Virgin, of saints, and of angels, which have been defaced by Turkish fanaticism, were dangerously exposed to the superstition of the Greeks. According to the sanctity of each object, the precious metals were distributed in thin leaves or in solid masses. The balustrade of the choir, the capitals of the pillars, the ornaments of the doors and galleries, were of gilt bronze. The spectator was dazzled by the glittering aspect of the cupola. The sanctuary contained forty thousand pound weight of silver, and the holy vases and vestments of the altar were of the purest gold, enriched with inestimable gems. Before the structure of the church had arisen two cubits above the ground, forty-five thousand two hundred pounds were already consumed, and the whole expense amounted to three hundred and twenty thousand. Each reader, according to the measure of his belief, may estimate their value either in gold or silver; but the sum of one million sterling is the result of the lowest computation. A magnificent temple is a laudable monument of national taste and religion, and the enthusiast who entered the dome of St. Sophia might be tempted to suppose that it was the residence, or even the workmanship, of the Deity. Yet how dull is the artifice, how insignificant is the labour, if it be compared with the formation of the vilest insect that crawls upon the surface of the temple!

So minute a description of an edifice which time has respected may attest the truth and excuse the relation of the innumerable works, both in the capital and provinces, which Justinian constructed on a smaller scale and less durable foundations.[110] In Constantinople alone, and the adjacent suburbs, he dedicated twenty-five churches to the honour of Christ, the Virgin, and the saints. Most of these churches were decorated with marble and gold; and their various situation was skilfully chosen in a populous square or a pleasant grove, on the margin of the sea-shore or on some lofty eminence which overlooked the continents of Europe and Asia. The church of the Holy Apostles at Constantinople, and that of St. John at Ephesus, appear to have been framed on the same model: their domes aspired to imitate the cupolas

---

[110] The six books of the Edifices of Procopius are thus distributed: the *first* is confined to Constantinople; the *second* includes Mesopotamia and Syria; the *third*, Armenia and the Euxine; the *fourth*, Europe; the *fifth*, Asia Minor and Palestine; the *sixth*, Egypt and Africa. Italy is forgot by the emperor or the historian, who published this work of adulation before the date (A.D. 555) of its final conquest.

of St. Sophia, but the altar was more judiciously placed under the centre of the dome, at the junction of four stately porticoes, which more accurately expressed the figure of the Greek cross. The Virgin of Jerusalem might exult in the temple erected by her imperial votary on a most ungrateful spot, which afforded neither ground nor materials to the architect. A level was formed by raising part of a deep valley to the height of the mountain. The stones of a neighbouring quarry were hewn into regular forms; each block was fixed on a peculiar carriage drawn by forty of the strongest oxen, and the roads were widened for the passage of such enormous weights. Lebanon furnished her loftiest cedars for the timbers of the church; and the seasonable discovery of a vein of red marble supplied its beautiful columns, two of which, the supporters of the exterior portico, were esteemed the largest in the world. The pious munificence of the emperor was diffused over the Holy Land; and if reason should condemn the monasteries of both sexes which were built or restored by Justinian, yet charity must applaud the wells which he sunk, and the hospitals which he founded, for the relief of the weary pilgrims. The schismatical temper of Egypt was ill entitled to the royal bounty; but in Syria and Africa some remedies were applied to the disasters of wars and earthquakes, and both Carthage and Antioch, emerging from their ruins, might revere the name of their gracious benefactor.[111] Almost every saint in the calendar acquired the honours of a temple—almost every city of the empire obtained the solid advantages of bridges, hospitals, and aqueducts; but the severe liberality of the monarch disdained to indulge his subjects in the popular luxury of baths and theatres. While Justinian laboured for the public service, he was not unmindful of his own dignity and ease. The Byzantine palace, which had been damaged by the conflagration, was restored with new magnificence; and some notion may be conceived of the whole edifice by the vestibule or hall, which, from the doors perhaps, or the roof, was surnamed *chalce,* or the brazen. The dome of a spacious quadrangle was supported by massy pillars; the pavement and walls were incrusted with many-coloured marbles —the emerald green of Laconia, the fiery red, and the white Phrygian stone, intersected with veins of a sea-green hue. The mosaic paintings of the dome and sides represented the glories of the African and Italian triumphs. On the Asiatic shore of the Propontis, at a small distance to the east of Chalcedon, the costly palace and gardens of Heræum,[112] were prepared for the summer residence of Justinian, and more especially of Theodora. The poets of the age have celebrated the rare alliance of nature and art, the harmony of the nymphs of the groves,

---

[111] Justinian once gave forty-five centenaries of gold (£180,000) for the repairs of Antioch after the earthquake (John Malala, tom. ii. p. 146-149 [p. 422-424, ed. Bonn]).

[112] For the Heræum, the palace of Theodora, see Gyllius (de Bosphoro Thracio, l. iii. c. xi.), Aleman. (Not. ad Anec. p. 80, 81 [Procop. tom. iii. p. 431, 432, ed. Bonn], who quotes several epigrams of the Anthology) and Ducange (C. P. Christ. l. iv. e. 13, p. 175, 176).

the fountains and the waves; yet the crowd of attendants who followed the court complained of their inconvenient lodgings,[113] and the nymphs were too often alarmed by the famous Porphyrio, a whale of ten cubits in breadth and thirty in length, who was stranded at the mouth of the river Sangaris after he had infested more than half a century the seas of Constantinople.[114]

The fortifications of Europe and Asia were multiplied by Justinian; but the repetition of those timid and fruitless precautions exposes, to a philosophic eye, the debility of the empire.[115]   From Belgrade to the Euxine, from the conflux of the Save to the mouth of the Danube, a chain of above fourscore fortified places was extended along the banks of the great river. Single watch-towers were changed into spacious citadels; vacant walls, which the engineers contracted or enlarged according to the nature of the ground, were filled with colonies or garrisons; a strong fortress defended the ruins of Trajan's bridge;[116] and several military stations affected to spread beyond the Danube the pride of the Roman name. But that name was divested of its terrors; the barbarians, in their annual inroads, passed and contemptuously repassed before these useless bulwarks; and the inhabitants of the frontier, instead of reposing under the shadow of the general defence, were compelled to guard with incessant vigilance their separate habitations. The solitude of ancient cities was replenished; the new foundations of Justinian acquired, perhaps too hastily, the epithets of impregnable and populous; and the auspicious place of his own nativity attracted the grateful reverence of the vainest of princes. Under the name of *Justiniana prima,* the obscure village of Tauresium became the seat of an archbishop and a præfect, whose jurisdiction extended over seven warlike provinces of Illyricum;[117] and the corrupt appellation of

[113] Compare, in the Edifices (l. i. c. 11) and in the Anecdotes (c. 8, 15), the different styles of adulation and malevolence: stripped of the paint, or cleansed from the dirt, the object appears to be the same.

[114] Procopius, Goth. iii. 29; most probably a stranger and wanderer, as the Mediterranean does not breed whales. Balænæ quoque in nostra maria penetrant (Plin. Hist. Natur. ix. 2 [5]). Between the polar circle and the tropic, the cetaceous animals of the ocean grow to the length of 50, 80, or 100 feet.   (Hist. des Voyages, tom. xv. p. 289. Pennant's British Zoology, vol. iii. p. 35.)

[115] Montesquieu observes (tom. iii. p. 503, Considérations sur la Grandeur et la Décadence des Romains, c. xx.) that Justinian's empire was like France in the time of the Norman inroads—never so weak as when every village was fortified.

[116] Procopius affirms (l. iv. c. 6 [tom. iii. p. 289, ed. Bonn]) that the Danube was stopped by the ruins of the bridge. Had Apollodorus, the architect, left a description of his own work, the fabulous wonders of Dion Cassius (l. lxviii. [c. 13] p. 1129) would have been corrected by the genuine picture. Trajan's bridge consisted of twenty or twenty-two stone piles with wooden arches; the river is shallow, the current gentle, and the whole interval no more than 443 (Reimar ad Dion, from Marsigli) or 515 *toises* (D'Anville, Géographie Ancienne, tom. i. p. 305).

[117] Of the two Dacias, *Mediterranea* and *Ripensis,* Dardania, Prævalitana, the second Mæsia, and the second Macedonia. See Justinian (Novell. xi.

Giustendil still indicates, about twenty miles to the south of Sophia, the residence of a Turkish sanjak.[118] For the use of the emperor's countrymen, a cathedral, a palace, and an aqueduct were speedily constructed; the public and private edifices were adapted to the greatness of a royal city; and the strength of the walls resisted, during the lifetime of Justinian, the unskilful assaults of the Huns and Sclavonians. Their progress was sometimes retarded, and their hopes of rapine were disappointed, by the innumerable castles which, in the provinces of Dacia, Epirus, Thessaly, Macedonia, and Thrace, appeared to cover the whole face of the country. Six hundred of these forts were built or repaired by the emperor; but it seems reasonable to believe that the far greater part consisted only of a stone or brick tower in the midst of a square or circular area, which was surrounded by a wall and ditch, and afforded in a moment of danger some protection to the peasants and cattle of the neighbouring villages.[119] Yet these military works, which exhausted the public treasure, could not remove the just apprehensions of Justinian and his European subjects. The warm-baths of Anchialus, in Thrace, were rendered as safe as they were salutary; but the rich pastures of Thessalonica were foraged by the Scythian cavalry; the delicious vale of Tempe, three hundred miles from the Danube, was continually alarmed by the sound of war;[120] and no unfortified spot, however distant or solitary, could securely enjoy the blessings of peace. The straits of Thermopylæ, which seemed to protect, but which had so often betrayed, the safety of Greece, were diligently strengthened by the labours of Justinian. From the edge of the sea-shore, through the forests and valleys, and as far as the summit of the Thessalian mountains, a strong wall was continued which occupied every practicable entrance. Instead of a hasty crowd of peasants, a garrison of two thousand soldiers was stationed along the rampart, granaries of corn and reservoirs of water were provided for their use, and, by a precaution that inspired the cowardice which it foresaw, convenient fortresses were erected for their retreat. The walls of Corinth, overthrown by an earthquake, and the mouldering bulwarks of Athens and Platæa, were carefully restored; the barbarians were discouraged by the prospect of successive and painful sieges, and the naked cities of Peloponnesus were covered by the fortifications of the isthmus of Corinth. At the

[Præf.]), who speaks of his castles beyond the Danube, and of homines semper bellicis sudoribus inhærentes.

[118] See D'Anville (Mémoires de l'Académie, etc. tom. xxxi. p. 289, 290). Rycaut (Present State of the Turkish Empire, p. 97, 316), Marsigli (Stato Militare del Imperio Ottomano, p. 130). The sanjak of Guistendil is one of the twenty under the beglerbeg of Rumelia, and his district maintains 48 *zaims* and 588 *timariots*.

[119] These fortifications may be compared to the castles in Mingrelia (Chardin, Voyages en Perse, tom. i. p. 60, 131)—a natural picture.

[120] The valley of Tempe is situate along the river Peneus, between the hills of Ossa and Olympus: it is only five miles long, and in some places no more than 120 feet in breadth. Its verdant beauties are elegantly described by Pliny (Hist. Natur. l. iv. 15), and more diffusely by Ælian (Hist. Var. l. iii. c. i.).

extremity of Europe, another peninsula, the Thracian Chersonesus, runs three days' journey into the sea, to form, with the adjacent shores of Asia, the straits of the Hellespont. The intervals between eleven populous towns were filled by lofty woods, fair pastures, and arable lands; and the isthmus, of thirty-seven stadia or furlongs, had been fortified by a Spartan general nine hundred years before the reign of Justinian.[121] In an age of freedom and valour the slightest rampart may prevent a surprise; and Procopius appears insensible of the superiority of ancient times, while he praises the solid construction and double parapet of a wall whose long arms stretched on either side into the sea, but whose strength was deemed insufficient to guard the Chersonesus, if each city, and particularly Gallipoli and Sestus, had not been secured by their peculiar fortifications. The *long* wall, as it was emphatically styled, was a work as disgraceful in the object as it was respectable in the execution. The riches of a capital diffuse themselves over the neighbouring country, and the territory of Constantinople, a paradise of nature, was adorned with the luxurious gardens and villas of the senators and opulent citizens. But their wealth served only to attract the bold and rapacious barbarians; the noblest of the Romans, in the bosom of peaceful indolence, were led away into Scythian captivity; and their sovereign might view from his palace the hostile flames which were insolently spread to the gates of the Imperial city. At the distance only of forty miles, Anastasius was constrained to establish a last frontier; his long wall of sixty miles, from the Propontis to the Euxine, proclaimed the impotence of his arms; and as the danger became more imminent, new fortifications were added by the indefatigable prudence of Justinian.[122]

Asia Minor, after the submission of the Isaurians,[123] remained without enemies and without fortifications. Those bold savages, who had disdained to be the subjects of Gallienus, persisted two hundred and thirty years in a life of independence and rapine. The most successful princes respected the strength of the mountains and the despair of the natives: their fierce spirit was sometimes soothed with gifts, and sometimes restrained by terror; and a military count, with three legions, fixed his permanent and ignominious station in the heart of the Roman provinces.[124] But no sooner was the vigilance of power relaxed or diverted, than the light-armed squadrons descended from the

[121] Xenophon Hellenic. l. iii. c. 2. After a long and tedious conversation with the Byzantine declaimers, how refreshing is the truth, the simplicity, the elegance of an Attic writer!

[122] See the long wall in Evagrius (l. iv. [iii.] c. 38). This whole article is drawn from the fourth book of the Edifices, except Anchialus (l. iii. c. 7).

[123] Turn back to Vol. i. p. 244. In the course of this history I have sometimes mentioned, and much oftener slighted, the hasty inroads of the Isaurians, which were not attended with any consequences.

[124] Trebellius Pollio in Hist. August. p. 197 [Triginta Tyr. 25], who lived under Diocletian, or Constantine. See likewise Pancirolus ad Notit. Imp. Orient. c. 115, 141. See Cod. Theodos. l. ix. tit. 35, leg. 37 [7], with a copious collective Annotation of Godefroy, tom. iii. p. 256, 257.

hills, and invaded the peaceful plenty of Asia. Although the Isaurians were not remarkable for stature or bravery, want rendered them bold, and experience made them skilful in the exercise of predatory war. They advanced with secrecy and speed to the attack of villages and defenceless towns; their flying parties have sometimes touched the Hellespont, the Euxine, and the gates of Tarsus, Antioch, or Damascus;[125] and the spoil was lodged in their inaccessible mountains, before the Roman troops had received their orders, or the distant province had computed its loss. The guilt of rebellion and robbery excluded them from the rights of national enemies; and the magistrates were instructed by an edict, that the trial or punishment of an Isaurian, even on the festival of Easter, was a meritorious act of justice and piety.[126] If the captives were condemned to domestic slavery, they maintained, with their sword or dagger, the private quarrel of their masters; and it was found expedient for the public tranquillity to prohibit the service of such dangerous retainers. When their countryman Tarcalissæus or Zeno ascended the throne, he invited a faithful and formidable band of Isaurians, who insulted the court and city, and were rewarded by an annual tribute of five thousand pounds of gold. But the hopes of fortune depopulated the mountains, luxury enervated the hardiness of their minds and bodies, and, in proportion as they mixed with mankind, they became less qualified for the enjoyment of poor and solitary freedom. After the death of Zeno, his successor Anastasius suppressed their pensions, exposed their persons to the revenge of the people, banished them from Constantinople, and prepared to sustain a war which left only the alternative of victory or servitude. A brother of the last emperor usurped the title of Augustus; his cause was powerfully supported by the arms, the treasures, and the magazines collected by Zeno; and the native Isaurians must have formed the smallest portion of the hundred and fifty thousand barbarians under his standard, which was sanctified for the first time by the presence of a fighting bishop. Their disorderly numbers were vanquished in the plains of Phrygia by the valour and discipline of the Goths, but a war of six years almost exhausted the courage of the emperor.[127] The Isaurians retired to their mountains, their fortresses were successively besieged and ruined, their communication with the sea was intercepted, the bravest of their leaders died in arms, the surviving chiefs before their execution were dragged in chains through the hippodrome, a colony of their youth was transplanted into Thrace, and the remnant of the people submitted to the Roman govern-

---

[125] See the full and wide extent of their inroads in Philostorgius (Hist Eccles. l. xi. c. 8), with Godefroy's learned Dissertations.

[126] Cod. Justinian. l. ix. tit. 12, leg. 10. The punishments are severe—a fine of an hundred pounds of gold, degradation, and even death. The public peace might afford a pretence, but Zeno was desirous of monopolising the valour and service of the Isaurians.

[127] The Isaurian war and the triumph of Anastasius are briefly and darkly represented by John Malala (tom. ii. p. 106, 107 [p. 393, 394, ed. Bonn], Evagrius (l. iii. c. 35), Theophanes (p. 118-120 [ed. Par.; tom. i. p. 212-215, ed. Bonn]), and the Chronicle of Marcellinus.

ment. Yet some generations elapsed before their minds were reduced to the level of slavery. The populous villages of Mount Taurus were filled with horsemen and archers; they resisted the imposition of tributes, but they recruited the armies of Justinian; and his civil magistrates, the proconsul of Cappadocia, the count of Isauria, and the prætors of Lycaonia and Pisidia, were invested with military power to restrain the licentious practice of rapes and assassinations.[128]

If we extend our view from the tropic to the mouth of the Tanais, we may observe, on one hand, the precautions of Justinian to curb the savages of Æthiopia,[129] and, on the other, the long walls which he constructed in Crimæa for the protection of his friendly Goths, a colony of three thousand shepherds and warriors.[130]   From that peninsula to Trebizond the eastern curve of the Euxine was secured by forts, by alliance, or by religion; and the possession of *Lazica*, the Colchos of ancient, the Mingrelia of modern, geography, soon became the object of an important war.   Trebizond, in after times the seat of a romantic empire, was indebted to the liberality of Justinian for a church, an aqueduct, and a castle, whose ditches are hewn in the solid rock.   From that maritime city a frontier line of five hundred miles may be drawn to the fortress of Circesium, the last Roman station on the Euphrates.[131] Above Trebizond immediately, and five days' journey to the south, the country rises into dark forests and craggy mountains, as savage though not so lofty as the Alps and the Pyrenees.   In this rigorous climate,[132] where the snows seldom melt, the fruits are tardy and taste-

---

[128] Fortes ea regio (says Justinian) viros habet, nec in ullo differt ab Isauriâ, though Procopius (Persic. l. i. c. 18 [tom. i. p. 96, ed. Bonn]) marks an essential difference between their military character; yet in former times the Lycaonians and Pisidians had defended their liberty against the Great King (Xenophon. Anabasis, l. iii. c. 2).   Justinian introduces some false and ridiculous erudition of the ancient empire of the Pisidians, and of Lycaon, who, after visiting Rome (long before Æneas), gave a name and people to Lycaonia (Novell. 24, 25, 27, 30).

[129] See Procopius, Persic. l. i. c. 19.   The altar of national concord, of annual sacrifice and oaths, which Diocletian had erected in the Isle of Elephantine, was demolished by Justinian with less policy than zeal.

[130] Procopius de Ædificiis, l. iii. c. 7 [p. 262, ed. Bonn]; Bell. Goth. iv. c. 3, 4 [p. 469, *seq.*, ed. Bonn].   These unambitious Goths had refused to follow the standard of Theodoric.   As late as the fifteenth and sixteenth century the name and nation might be discovered between Caffa and the Straits of Azoph (D'Anville, Mémoires de l'Académie, tom. xxx. p. 240).   They well deserved the curiosity of Busbequius (p. 321-326); but seem to have vanished in the more recent account of the Missions du Levant (tom. i.), Tott, Peysonnel, etc.

[131] For the geography and architecture of this Armenian border see the Persian Wars and Edifices (l. ii. c. 4-7; l. iii. c. 2-7) of Procopius.

[132] The country is described by Tournefort (Voyage au Levant, tom. iii. lettre xvii. xviii.).   That skilful botanist soon discovered the plant that infects the honey (Plin. xxi. 44, 45): he observes that the soldiers of Lucullus might indeed be astonished at the cold, since, even in the plain of Erzerum, snow sometimes falls in June, and the harvest is seldom finished before September.   The hills of Armenia are below the fortieth degree of latitude; but in the mountainous country which I inhabit it is well known that an ascent of some hours carries the traveller from the climate of Languedoc

less; even honey is poisonous: the most industrious tillage would be confined to some pleasant valleys, and the pastoral tribes obtained a scanty sustenance from the flesh and milk of their cattle. The *Chaly-bians* [133] derived their name and temper from the iron quality of the soil; and, since the days of Cyrus, they might produce, under the various appellations of Chaldæans and Zanians, an uninterrupted prescription of war and rapine. Under the reign of Justinian they acknowledged the god and the emperor of the Romans, and seven fortresses were built in the most accessible passes to exclude the ambition of the Persian monarch. [134] The principal source of the Euphrates descends from the Chalybian mountains, and seems to flow towards the west and the Euxine: bending to the south-west, the river passes under the walls of Satala and Melitene (which were restored by Justinian as the bulwarks of the lesser Armenia), and gradually approaches the Mediterranean Sea, till at length, repelled by Mount Taurus, [135] the Euphrates inclines his long and flexible course to the south-east and the Gulf of Persia. Among the Roman cities beyond the Euphrates we distinguish two recent foundations, which were named from Theodosius and the relics of the martyrs, and two capitals, Amida and Edessa, which are celebrated in the history of every age. Their strength was proportioned by Justinian to the danger of their situation. A ditch and palisade might be sufficient to resist the artless force of the cavalry of Scythia, but more elaborate works were required to sustain a regular siege against the arms and treasures of the Great King. His skilful engineers understood the methods of conducting deep mines, and of raising platforms to the level of the rampart. He shook the strongest battlements with his military engines, and sometimes advanced to the assault with a line of movable turrets on the backs of elephants. In the great cities of the East the disadvantage of space, perhaps of position, was compensated by the zeal of the people, who seconded the garrison in the defence of their country and religion; and the fabulous promise of the Son of God, that Edessa should never be taken, filled the citizens with valiant confidence and chilled the besiegers with doubt and dismay. [136] The subordinate

to that of Norway; and a general theory has been introduced that, under the line, an elevation of 2400 *toises* is equivalent to the cold of the polar circle (Remond, Observations sur les Voyages de Coxe dans la Suisse, tom. ii. p. 104).

[133] The identity or proximity of the Chalybians, or Chaldæans, may be investigated in Strabo (l. xii. p. 825, 826 [p. 548, 549, ed. Casaub.]), Cellarius (Geograph. Antiq. tom. ii. p. 202-204), and Fréret (Mém. de l'Académie, tom. iv. p. 594). Xenophon supposes, in his romance (Cyropæd. l. iii. [c. 2]), the same barbarians against whom he had fought in his retreat (Anabasis, 1 iv. [c. 3]).

[134] Procopius, Persic. l. i. c. 15; De Ædific. l. iii. c. 6.

[135] Ni Tauros obstet in nostra maria venturus (Pomponius Mela, iii. 8). Pliny, a poet as well as a naturalist (v. 20), personifies the river and mountain and describes their combat. See the course of the Tigris and Euphrates in the excellent treatise of D'Anville.

[136] Procopius (Persic. l. ii. c. 12 [tom. i. p. 208, ed. Bonn]) tells the story with the tone, half sceptical, half superstitious, of Herodotus. The promise was not in the primitive lie of Eusebius, but dates at least from the year 400;

towns of Armenia and Mesopotamia were diligently strengthened, and the posts which appeared to have any command of ground or water were occupied by numerous forts substantially built of stone, or more hastily erected with the obvious materials of earth and brick. The eye of Justinian investigated every spot, and his cruel precautions might attract the war into some lonely vale, whose peaceful natives, connected by trade and marriage, were ignorant of national discord and the quarrels of princes. Westward of the Euphrates a sandy desert extends above six hundred miles to the Red Sea. Nature had interposed a vacant solitude between the ambition of two rival empires; the Arabians, till Mahomet arose, were formidable only as robbers; and in the proud security of peace the fortifications of Syria were neglected on the most vulnerable side.

But the national enmity, at least the effects of that enmity, had been suspended by a truce which continued above fourscore years. An ambassador from the emperor Zeno accompanied the rash and unfortunate Perozes in his expedition against the Nephthalites, or White Huns, whose conquests had been stretched from the Caspian to the heart of India, whose throne was enriched with emeralds,[137] and whose cavalry was supported by a line of two thousand elephants.[138] The Persians were twice circumvented, in a situation which made valour useless and flight impossible, and the double victory of the Huns was achieved by military stratagem. They dismissed their royal captive after he had submitted to adore the majesty of a barbarian, and the humiliation was poorly evaded by the casuistical subtlety of the Magi, who instructed Perozes to direct his attention to the rising sun. The indignant successor of Cyrus forgot his danger and his gratitude; he renewed the attack with headstrong fury, and lost both his army and his life.[139] The death of

and a third lie, the *Veronica,* was soon raised on the two former (Evagrius, l. iv. c. 27). As Edessa *has* been taken, Tillemont *must* disclaim the promise (Mém. Ecclés. tom. i. p. 362, 383, 617).

[137] They were purchased from the merchants of Adulis who traded to India (Cosmas, Topograph. Christ. l. xi. p. 339); yet, in the estimate of precious stones, the Scythian emerald was the first, the Bactrian the second, the Æthiopian only the third (Hill's Theophrastus, p. 61, etc., 92). The production, mines, etc., of emeralds, are involved in darkness; and it is doubtful whether we possess any of the twelve sorts known to the ancients (Goguet, Origine des Loix, etc., part ii. l. ii. c. 2, art. 3). In this war the Huns got, or at least Perozes lost, the finest pearl in the world, of which Procopius relates a ridiculous fable.

[138] The Indo-Scythæ continued to reign from the time of Augustus (Dionys. Perieget. 1088, with the Commentary of Eustathius, in Hudson, Geograph. Minor. tom. iv.) to that of the elder Justin (Cosmas, Topograph. Christ. l. xi. p. 338, 339). On their origin and conquests see D'Anville (sur l'Inde, p. 18, 45, etc., 69, 85, 89). In the second century they were masters of Larice or Guzerat.

[139] See the fate of Phirouz or Perozes and its consequences, in Procopius (Persic. l. i. c. 3-6), who may be compared with the fragments of Oriental history (D'Herbelot, Bibliot. Orient. p. 351, and Texeira, History of Persia, translated or abridged by Stephens, l. i. c. 32, p. 132-138). The chronology is ably ascertained by Asseman (Bibliot. Orient. tom. iii. p. 396-427).

Perozes abandoned Persia to her foreign and domestic enemies, and twelve years of confusion elapsed before his son Cabades or Kobad could embrace any designs of ambition or revenge. The unkind parsimony of Anastasius was the motive or pretence of a Roman war;[140] the Huns and Arabs marched under the Persian standard, and the fortifications of Armenia and Mesopotamia were at that time in a ruinous or imperfect condition. The emperor returned his thanks to the governor and people of Martyropolis for the prompt surrender of a city which could not be successfully defended, and the conflagration of Theodosiopolis might justify the conduct of their prudent neighbours. Amida sustained a long and destructive siege: at the end of three months the loss of fifty thousand of the soldiers of Cabades was not balanced by any prospect of success, and it was in vain that the Magi deduced a flattering prediction from the indecency of the women on the ramparts, who had revealed their most secret charms to the eyes of the assailants. At length, in a silent night, they ascended the most accessible tower, which was guarded only by some monks, oppressed, after the duties of a festival, with sleep and wine. Scaling-ladders were applied at the dawn of day; the presence of Cabades, his stern command, and his drawn sword, compelled the Persians to vanquish, and, before it was sheathed, fourscore thousand of the inhabitants had expiated the blood of their companions. After the siege of Amida the war continued three years, and the unhappy frontier tasted the full measure of its calamities. The gold of Anastasius was offered too late, the number of his troops was defeated by the number of their generals, the country was stripped of its inhabitants, and both the living and the dead were abandoned to the wild beasts of the desert. The resistance of Edessa and the deficiency of spoil inclined the mind of Cabades to peace; he sold his conquests for an exorbitant price; and the same line, though marked with slaughter and devastation, still separated the two empires. To avert the repetition of the same evils, Anastasius resolved to found a new colony, so strong that it should defy the power of the Persian, so far advanced towards Assyria that its stationary troops might defend the province by the menace or operation of offensive war. For this purpose the town of Dara,[141] fourteen miles from Nisibis, and four days' journey from the Tigris, was peopled and adorned: the hasty works of Anastasius were improved by the perseverance of Justinian, and, without insisting on places less important, the fortifications of Dara may represent the military architecture of the age. The city was surrounded

---

[140] The Persian war, under the reigns of Anastasius and Justin, may be collected from Procopius (Persic. l. i. c. 7, 8, 9), Theophanes (in Chronograph. p. 124-127 [ed. Par.; tom. i. p. 222-229, ed. Bonn]), Evagrius (l. iii. c. 37), Marcellinus (in Chron. p. 47 [p. 372, sq., ed. Sirmond.]), and Josua Stylites (apud Asseman. tom. i. p. 272-281).

[141] The description of Dara is amply and correctly given by Procopius (Persic. l. i. c. 10, l. ii. c. 13; De Ædific. l. ii. c. 1, 2, 3; l. iii. c. 5). See the situation in D'Anville (l'Euphrate et le Tigre, p. 53, 54, 55), though he seems to double the interval between Dara and Nisibis.

with two walls, and the interval between them, of fifty paces, afforded a retreat to the cattle of the besieged. The inner wall was a monument of strength and beauty: it measured sixty feet from the ground, and the height of the towers was one hundred feet; the loopholes, from whence an enemy might be annoyed with missile weapons, were small, but numerous; the soldiers were planted along the rampart, under the shelter of double galleries; and a third platform, spacious and secure, was raised on the summit of the towers. The exterior wall appears to have been less lofty, but more solid, and each tower was protected by a quadrangular bulwark. A hard rocky soil resisted the tools of the miners, and on the south-east, where the ground was more tractable, their approach was retarded by a new work, which advanced in the shape of a half-moon. The double and treble ditches were filled with a stream of water, and in the management of the river the most skilful labour was employed to supply the inhabitants, to distress the besiegers, and to prevent the mischiefs of a natural or artificial inundation. Dara continued more than sixty years to fulfil the wishes of its founders and to provoke the jealousy of the Persians, who incessantly complained that this impregnable fortress had been constructed in manifest violation of the treaty of peace between the two empires.

Between the Euxine and the Caspian the countries of Colchos, Iberia, and Albania are intersected in every direction by the branches of Mount Caucasus, and the two principal *gates*, or passes, from north to south, have been frequently confounded in the geography both of the ancients and moderns. The name of *Caspian* or *Albanian* gates is properly applied to Derbend,[142] which occupies a short declivity between the mountains and the sea; the city, if we give credit to local tradition, had been founded by the Greeks, and this dangerous entrance was fortified by the kings of Persia with a mole, double walls, and doors of iron. The *Iberian* gates [143] are formed by a narrow passage of six miles in Mount Caucasus, which opens from the northern side of Iberia or Georgia into the plain that reaches to the Tanais and the Volga. A fortress, designed by Alexander perhaps, or one of his successors, to command that important pass, had descended by right of conquest or inheritance to a prince of the Huns, who offered it for a moderate price to the emperor; but while Anastasius paused, while he timorously computed the cost and the distance, a more vigilant rival interposed, and Cabades forcibly occupied the straits of Caucasus. The Albanian and Iberian gates excluded the horsemen of Scythia from the shortest and most practicable

[142] For the city and pass of Derbend see D'Herbelot (Bibliot. Orient. p. 157, 291, 807), Petit de la Croix (Hist. de Gengiscan, 1. iv. c. 9), Histoire Généalogique des Tartars (tom. i. p. 120), Olearius (Voyage en Perse, p. 1039-1041), and Corneille le Bruyn (Voyages, tom. i. p. 146, 147) : his view may be compared with the plan of Olearius, who judges the wall to be of shells and gravel hardened by time.

[143] Procopius, though with some confusion, always denominates them Caspian (Persic. 1. i. c. 10). The pass is now styled Tatar-topa, the Tartar-gates (D'Anville, Géographie Ancienne, tom. ii. p. 119, 120).

roads, and the whole front of the mountains was covered by the rampart of Gog and Magog, the long wall which has excited the curiosity of an Arabian caliph [144] and a Russian conqueror.[145] According to a recent description, huge stones, seven feet thick, twenty-one feet in length or height, are artificially joined, without iron or cement, to compose a wall which runs above three hundred miles from the shores of Derbend, over the hills and through the valleys of Daghestan and Georgia. Without a vision such a work might be undertaken by the policy of Cabades; without a miracle it might be accomplished by his son, so formidable to the Romans under the name of Chosroes, so dear to the Orientals under the appellation of Nushirwan. The Persian monarch held in his hand the keys both of peace and war; but he stipulated in every treaty that Justinian should contribute to the expense of a common barrier which equally protected the two empires from the inroads of the Scythians.[146]

VII. Justinian suppressed the schools of Athens and the consulship of Rome, which had given so many sages and heroes to mankind. Both these institutions had long since degenerated from their primitive glory, yet some reproach may be justly inflicted on the avarice and jealousy of a prince by whose hand such venerable ruins were destroyed.

Athens, after her Persian triumphs, adopted the philosophy of Ionia and the rhetoric of Sicily; and these studies became the patrimony of a city whose inhabitants, about thirty thousand males, condensed, within the period of a single life, the genius of ages and millions. Our sense of the dignity of human nature is exalted by the simple recollection that Isocrates [147] was the companion of Plato and Xenophon; that he assisted, perhaps with the historian Thucydides, at the first representations of the Œdipus of Sophocles and the Iphigenia of Euripides; and that his pupils Æschines and Demosthenes contended for the crown of patriotism in the presence of Aristotle, the master of Theophrastus, who taught at Athens with the founders of the Stoic and Epicurean sects.[148]

---

[144] The imaginary rampart of Gog and Magog, which was seriously explored and believed by a caliph of the ninth century, appears to be derived from the gates of Mount Caucasus, and a vague report of the wall of China (Geograph. Nubiensis, p. 267-270; Mémoires de l'Académie, tom. xxxi. p. 210-219).

[145] See a learned dissertation of Baier, de muro Caucaseo, in Comment. Acad Petropol. ann. 1726, tom. i. p. 425-463; but it is destitute of a map or plan, When the Czar Peter I. became master of Derbend in the year 1722, the measure of the wall was found to be 3285 Russian orgyiæ, or fathom, each of seven feet English; in the whole somewhat more than four miles in length.

[146] See the fortifications and treaties of Chosroes or Nushirwan, in Procopius (Persic. l. i. c. 16, 22, l. ii.) and D'Herbelot (p. 682).

[147] The life of Isocrates extends from Olymp. lxxxvi. 1, to cx. 3 (ante Christ. 436-338). See Dionys. Halicarn. tom. ii. p. 149, 150, edit. Hudson. Plutarch (sive anonymus), in Vit. X. Oratorum, p. 1538-1543, edit. H. Steph. Phot. cod. cclix. p. 1453 [p. 486 b, ed. Bekk.].

[148] The schools of Athens are copiously though concisely represented in the Fortuna Attica of Meursius (c. viii. p. 59-73, in tom. i. Opp.). For the state and arts of the city, see the first book of Pausanias, and a small tract of Dicæarchus (in the second volume of Hudson's Geographers), who wrote about Olymp. cxvii. (Dodwell's Dissertat. sect. 4).

The ingenuous youth of Attica enjoyed the benefits of their domestic education, which was communicated without envy to the rival cities. Two thousand disciples heard the lessons of Theophrastus;[149] the schools of rhetoric must have been still more populous than those of philosophy; and a rapid succession of students diffused the fame of their teachers as far as the utmost limits of the Grecian language and name. Those limits were enlarged by the victories of Alexander; the arts of Athens survived her freedom and dominion; and the Greek colonies which the Macedonians planted in Egypt, and scattered over Asia, undertook long and frequent pilgrimages to worship the Muses in their favourite temple on the banks of the Ilissus. The Latin conquerors respectfully listened to the instructions of their subjects and captives; the names of Cicero and Horace were enrolled in the schools of Athens; and after the perfect settlement of the Roman empire, the natives of Italy, of Africa, and of Britain, conversed in the groves of the Academy with their fellow-students of the East. The studies of philosophy and eloquence are congenial to a popular state, which encourages the freedom of inquiry, and submits only to the force of persuasion. In the republics of Greece and Rome the art of speaking was the powerful engine of patriotism or ambition; and the schools of rhetoric poured forth a colony of statesmen and legislators. When the liberty of public debate was suppressed, the orator, in the honourable profession of an advocate, might plead the cause of innocence and justice; he might abuse his talents in the more profitable trade of panegyric; and the same precepts continued to dictate the fanciful declamations of the sophist, and the chaster beauties of historical composition. The systems which professed to unfold the nature of God, of man, and of the universe, entertained the curiosity of the philosophic student; and according to the temper of his mind, he might doubt with the Sceptics, or decide with the Stoics, sublimely speculate with Plato, or severely argue with Aristotle. The pride of the adverse sects had fixed an unattainable term of moral happiness and perfection: but the race was glorious and salutary; the disciples of Zeno, and even those of Epicurus, were taught both to act and to suffer; and the death of Petronius was not less effectual than that of Seneca to humble a tyrant by the discovery of his impotence. The light of science could not indeed be confined within the walls of Athens. Her incomparable writers address themselves to the human race; the living masters emigrated to Italy and Asia; Berytus, in later times, was devoted to the study of the law; astronomy and physic were cultivated in the museum of Alexandria; but the Attic schools of rhetoric and philosophy maintained their superior reputation from the Peloponnesian war to the reign of Justinian. Athens, though situate in a barren soil, possessed a pure air, a free navigation, and the monuments of ancient art. That sacred retirement was seldom disturbed by the business of trade or government; and the last of the Athenians were distinguished

[149] Diogen. Laert. de Vit. Philosoph. l. v. [c. 2] segm. 37, p. 289.

by their lively wit, the purity of their taste and language, their social manners, and some traces, at least in discourse, of the magnanimity of their fathers. In the suburbs of the city, the *Academy* of the Platonists, the *Lyceum* of the Peripatetics, the *Portico* of the Stoics, and the *Garden* of the Epicureans, were planted with trees and decorated with statues; and the philosophers, instead of being immured in a cloister, delivered their instructions in spacious and pleasant walks, which at different hours were consecrated to the exercises of the mind and body. The genius of the founders still lived in those venerable seats; the ambition of succeeding to the masters of human reason excited a generous emula-tion; and the merit of the candidates was determined, on each vacancy, by the free voices of an enlightened people. The Athenian professors were paid by their disciples: according to their mutual wants and abili-ties, the price appears to have varied from a mina to a talent; and Isocrates himself, who derides the avarice of the sophists, required, in his school of rhetoric, about thirty pounds from each of his hundred pupils. The wages of industry are just and honourable, yet the same Isocrates shed tears at the first receipt of a stipend: the Stoic might blush when he was hired to preach the contempt of money; and I should be sorry to discover that Aristotle or Plato so far degenerated from the example of Socrates as to exchange knowledge for gold. But some property of lands and houses was settled, by the permission of the laws, and the legacies of deceased friends, on the philosophic chairs of Athens. Epicurus bequeathed to his disciples the gardens which he had purchased for eighty minæ or two hundred and fifty pounds, with a fund sufficient for their frugal subsistence and monthly festivals;[150] and the patrimony of Plato afforded an annual rent, which, in eight centuries, was gradually increased from three to one thousand pieces of gold.[151] The schools of Athens were protected by the wisest and most virtuous of the Roman princes. The library, which Hadrian founded, was placed in a portico adorned with pictures, statues, and a roof of alabaster, and supported by one hundred columns of Phrygian marble. The public salaries were assigned by the generous spirit of the Antonines; and each professor, of politics, of rhetoric, of the Platonic, the Peripatetic, the Stoic, and the Epicurean philosophy, received an annual stipend of ten thousand drachmæ, or more than three hundred pounds sterling.[152] After the

[150] See the Testament of Epicurus in Diogen. Laert. l. x. [c. 1] segm. 16-20, p. 611, 612. A single epistle (ad Familiares, xiii. 1) displays the injustice of the Areopagus, the fidelity of the Epicureans, the dexterous politeness of Cicero, and the mixture of contempt and esteem with which the Roman sena-tors considered the philosophy and philosophers of Greece.

[151] Damascius, in Vit. Isidor. apud Photium, cod. ccxlii. p. 1057 [p. 346 a, ed. Bekk.].

[152] See Lucian (in Eunuch. tom. ii. [c. 3, *sqq.*] p. 350-359, edit Reitz), Philostratus (in Vit. Sophist. l. ii. c. 2), and Dion Cassius, or Xiphilin (l. lxxi. [c. 31] p. 1195), with their editors Du Soul, Olearius, and Reimar, and, above all, Salmasius (ad Hist. August. p. 72). A judicious philosopher (Smith's Wealth of Nations, vol. ii. p. 340-374) prefers the free contributions of the students to a fixed stipend for the professor.

death of Marcus, these liberal donations, and the privileges attached to the *thrones* of science, were abolished and revived, diminished and enlarged; but some vestige of royal bounty may be found under the successors of Constantine; and their arbitrary choice of an unworthy candidate might tempt the philosophers of Athens to regret the days of independence and poverty.[153] It is remarkable that the impartial favour of the Antonines was bestowed on the four adverse sects of philosophy, which they considered as equally useful, or at least as equally innocent. Socrates had formerly been the glory and the reproach of his country; and the first lessons of Epicurus so strangely scandalised the pious ears of the Athenians, that by his exile, and that of his antagonists, they silenced all vain disputes concerning the nature of the gods. But in the ensuing year they recalled the hasty decree, restored the liberty of the schools, and were convinced by the experience of ages that the moral character of philosophers is not affected by the diversity of their theological speculations.[154]

The Gothic arms were less fatal to the schools of Athens than the establishment of a new religion, whose ministers superseded the exercise of reason, resolved every question by an article of faith, and condemned the infidel or sceptic to eternal flame. In many a volume of laborious controversy they exposed the weakness of the understanding and the corruption of the heart, insulted human nature in the sages of antiquity, and proscribed the spirit of philosophical inquiry, so repugnant to the doctrine, or at least to the temper, of a humble believer. The surviving sect of the Platonists, whom Plato would have blushed to acknowledge, extravagantly mingled a sublime theory with the practice of superstition and magic; and as they remained alone in the midst of a Christian world, they indulged a secret rancour against the government of the church and state, whose severity was still suspended over their heads. About a century after the reign of Julian,[155] Proclus[156] was permitted to teach in the philosophic chair of the Academy; and such was his industry, that he frequently, in the same day, pronounced five lessons, and

---

[153] Brucker, Hist. Crit. Philosoph. tom. ii. p. 310, etc.

[154] The birth of Epicurus is fixed to the year 342 before Christ (Bayle), Olympiad cix. 3; and he opened his school at Athens, Olymp. cxviii. 3, 306 years before the same era. This intolerant law (Athenæus, l. xiii. p. 610; Diogen. Laertius, l. v. [c. 2] s. 38, p. 290; Julius Pollux, ix. 5) was enacted in the same or the succeeding year (Sigonius, Opp. tom. v. p. 62; Menagius, ad Diogen. Laert. p. 204; Corsini, Fasti Attici, tom. iv. p. 67, 68). Theophrastus, chief of the Peripatetics, and disciple of Aristotle, was involved in the same exile.

[155] This is no fanciful era: the Pagans reckoned their calamities from the reign of their hero. Proclus, whose nativity is marked by his horoscope (A.D. 412, February 8, at C. P.), died 124 years ἀπὸ Ἰουλιανοῦ βασιλέως, A.D. 485 (Marin. in Vitâ Procli, c. 36).

[156] The Life of Proclus, by Marinus, was published by Fabricius (Hamburg, 1700, et ad Calcem Biblioth. Latin. Lond. 1703). See Suidas (tom. iii. p. 185, 186), Fabricius (Biblioth. Græc. l. v. c. 26, p. 449-552), and Brucker (Hist. Crit. Philosoph. tom. ii. p. 319-326).

composed seven hundred lines. His sagacious mind explored the deepest questions of morals and metaphysics, and he ventured to urge eighteen arguments against the Christian doctrine of the creation of the world. But in the intervals of study he *personally* conversed with Pan, Æsculapius, and Minerva, in whose mysteries he was secretly initiated, and whose prostrate statues he adored; in the devout persuasion that the philosopher, who is a citizen of the universe, should be the priest of its various deities. An eclipse of the sun announced his approaching end; and his Life, with that of his scholar Isidore,[157] compiled by two of their most learned disciples, exhibits a deplorable picture of the second childhood of human reason. Yet the golden chain, as it was fondly styled, of the Platonic succession, continued forty-four years from the death of Proclus to the edict of Justinian,[158] which imposed a perpetual silence on the schools of Athens, and excited the grief and indignation of the few remaining votaries of Grecian science and super-stition. Seven friends and philosophers, Diogenes and Hermias, Eula-lius and Priscian, Damascius, Isidore, and Simplicius, who dissented from the religion of their sovereign, embraced the resolution of seeking in a foreign land the freedom which was denied in their native country. They had heard, and they credulously believed, that the republic of Plato was realised in the despotic government of Persia, and that a patriot king reigned over the happiest and most virtuous of nations. They were soon astonished by the natural discovery that Persia resembled the other countries of the globe; that Chosroes, who affected the name of a philosopher, was vain, cruel, and ambitious; that bigotry, and a spirit of intolerance, prevailed among the Magi; that the nobles were haughty, the courtiers servile, and the magistrates unjust; that the guilty sometimes escaped, and that the innocent were often oppressed. The disappointment of the philosophers provoked them to overlook the real virtues of the Persians; and they were scandalised, more deeply perhaps than became their profession, with the plurality of wives and concubines, the incestuous marriages, and the custom of exposing dead bodies to the dogs and vultures, instead of hiding them in the earth, or consuming them with fire. Their repentance was expressed by a precipitate return, and they loudly declared that they had rather die on the borders of the empire than enjoy the wealth and favour of the barbarian. From this journey, however, they derived a benefit which reflects the purest lustre on the character of Chosroes. He required that the seven sages who had visited the court of Persia should be exempted from the penal laws which Justinian enacted against his

---

[157] The Life of Isidore was composed by Damascius (apud Photium, cod. ccxlii. p. 1028-1076 [p. 335-353, ed. Bekk.]). See the last age of the Pagan philosophers in Brucker (tom. ii. p. 341-351).

[158] The suppression of the schools of Athens is recorded by John Malala (tom. ii. p. 187 [p. 451, ed. Bonn], sub Decio Cos. Sol.), and an anonymous Chronicle in the Vatican library (apud Aleman. p. 106 [Procop. tom. iii. p. 459, ed. Bonn]).

Pagan subjects; and this privilege, expressly stipulated in a treaty of peace, was guarded by the vigilance of a powerful mediator.[159]   Simplicius and his companions ended their lives in peace and obscurity; and as they left no disciples, they terminate the long list of Grecian philosophers, who may be justly praised, notwithstanding their defects, as the wisest and most virtuous of their contemporaries.   The writings of Simplicius are now extant.   His physical and metaphysical commentaries on Aristotle have passed away with the fashion of the times; but his moral interpretation of Epictetus is preserved in the library of nations, as a classic book, most excellently adapted to direct the will, to purify the heart, and to confirm the understanding, by a just confidence in the nature both of God and man.

About the same time that Pythagoras first invented the appellation of philosopher, liberty and the consulship were founded at Rome by the elder Brutus.   The revolutions of the consular office, which may be viewed in the successive lights of a substance, a shadow, and a name, have been occasionally mentioned in the present history.   The first magistrates of the republic had been chosen by the people, to exercise, in the senate and in the camp, the powers of peace and war, which were afterwards translated to the emperors.   But the tradition of ancient dignity was long revered by the Romans and barbarians.   A Gothic historian applauds the consulship of Theodoric as the height of all temporal glory and greatness;[160] the king of Italy himself congratulates those annual favourites of fortune who, without the cares, enjoyed the splendour of the throne; and at the end of a thousand years two consuls were created by the sovereigns of Rome and Constantinople for the sole purpose of giving a date to the year and a festival to the people.   But the expenses of this festival, in which the wealthy and the vain aspired to surpass their predecessors, insensibly arose to the enormous sum of fourscore thousand pounds; the wisest senators declined a useless honour which involved the certain ruin of their families, and to this reluctance I should impute the frequent chasms in the last age of the consular *Fasti*.   The predecessors of Justinian had assisted from the public treasures the dignity of the less opulent candidates; the avarice of that prince preferred the cheaper and more convenient method of advice and regulation.[161]   Seven *processions* or spectacles were the number to which his edict confined the horse and chariot races, the athletic sports, the music and pantomimes of the theatre, and the hunting of wild beasts; and small pieces of silver were discreetly substituted to the gold medals,

---

[159] Agathias (l. ii. p. 69, 70, 71 [ed. Par.; p. 130-136, ed. Bonn]) relates this curious story.   Chosroes ascended the throne in the year 531, and made his first peace with the Romans in the beginning of 533, a date most compatible with his *young* fame and the *old* age of Isidore (Asseman. Biblioth. Orient. tom. iii. p. 404; Pagi, tom. ii. p. 543, 550).

[160] Cassiodor. Variarum Epist. vi. 1. Jornandes, c. 57, p. 696, edit. Grot. Quod summum bonum primumque in mundo decus edicitur.

[161] See the regulations of Justinian (Novell. cv.), dated at Constantinople, July 5, and addressed to Strategius, treasurer of the empire.

which had always excited tumult and drunkenness when they were scattered with a profuse hand among the populace. Notwithstanding these precautions and his own example, the succession of consuls finally ceased in the thirteenth year of Justinian, whose despotic temper might be gratified by the silent extinction of a title which admonished the Romans of their ancient freedom.[162] Yet the annual consulship still lived in the minds of the people; they fondly expected its speedy restoration; they applauded the gracious condescension of successive princes, by whom it was assumed in the first year of their reign; and three centuries elapsed, after the death of Justinian, before that obsolete dignity, which had been suppressed by custom, could be abolished by law.[163] The imperfect mode of distinguishing each year by the name of a magistrate was usefully supplied by the date of a permanent era: the creation of the world, according to the Septuagint version, was adopted by the Greeks;[164] and the Latins, since the age of Charlemagne, have computed their time from the birth of Christ.[165]

[162] Procopius, in Anecdot. c. 26 [tom. iii. p. 144, ed. Bonn]. Aleman. p. 106 [p. 459, ed. Bonn]. In the eighteenth year after the consulship of Basilius, according to the reckoning of Marcellinus, Victor, Marius, etc., the secret history was composed, and, in the eyes of Procopius, the consulship was finally abolished.

[163] By Leo, the philosopher (Novell. xciv. A.D. 886-911). See Pagi (Dissertat. Hypatica, p. 325-362) and Ducange (Gloss. Græc. p. 1635, 1636.) Even the title was vilified: consulatus codicilli . . . vilescunt, says the emperor himself.

[164] According to Julius Africanus, etc., the world was created the first of September, 5508 years, three months, and twenty-five days before the birth of Christ (see Pezron, Antiquité des Tems défendue, p. 20-28) ; and this era has been used by the Greeks, the Oriental Christians, and even by the Russians, till the reign of Peter I. The period, however arbitrary, is clear and convenient. Of the 7296 years which are supposed to elapse since the creation, we shall find 3000 of ignorance and darkness; 2000 either fabulous or doubtful; 1000 of ancient history, commencing with the Persian empire and the republics of Rome and Athens; 1000 from the fall of the Roman empire in the West to the discovery of America; and the remaining 296 will almost complete three centuries of the modern state of Europe and mankind. I regret this chronology, so far preferable to our double and perplexed method of counting backwards and forwards the years before and after the Christian era.

[165] The era of the world has prevailed in the East since the sixth general council (A.D. 681). In the West the Christian era was first invented in the sixth century: it was propagated in the eighth by the authority and writings of venerable Bede; but it was not till the tenth that the use became legal and popular. See l'Art de vérifier les Dates, Dissert. Préliminaire, p. iii. xii.; Dictionnaire Diplomatique, tom. i. p. 329-337 : the works of a laborious society of Benedictine monks.

CHAPTER XLI (522-620 A.D.)

Conquests of Justinian in the West—Character and first Campaigns of Belisarius—He invades and subdues the Vandal Kingdom of Africa—His Triumph—The Gothic War—He recovers Sicily, Naples, and Rome—Siege of Rome by the Goths—Their Retreat and Losses—Surrender of Ravenna—Glory of Belisarius—His domestic Shame and Misfortunes

WHEN Justinian ascended the throne, about fifty years after the fall of the Western Empire, the kingdoms of the Goths and Vandals had obtained a solid, and, as it might seem, a legal establishment both in Europe and Africa.   The titles which Roman victory had inscribed were erased with equal justice by the sword of the barbarians; and their successful rapine derived a more venerable sanction from time, from treaties, and from the oaths of fidelity, already repeated by a second or third generation of obedient subjects.   Experience and Christianity had refuted the superstitious hope that Rome was founded by the gods to reign for ever over the nations of the earth.   But the proud claim of perpetual and indefeasible dominion, which her soldiers could no longer maintain, was firmly asserted by her statesmen and lawyers, whose opinions have been sometimes revived and propagated in the modern schools of jurisprudence.   After Rome herself had been stripped of the Imperial purple, the princes of Constantinople assumed the sole and sacred sceptre of the monarchy; demanded, as their rightful inheritance, the provinces which had been subdued by the consuls or possessed by the Cæsars; and feebly aspired to deliver their faithful subjects of the West from the usurpation of heretics and barbarians.   The execution of this splendid design was in some degree reserved for Justinian.   During the five first years of his reign he reluctantly waged a costly and unprofitable war against the Persians, till his pride submitted to his ambition, and he purchased, at the price of four hundred and forty thousand pounds sterling, the benefit of a precarious truce, which, in the language of both nations, was dignified with the appellation of the *endless* peace.   The safety of the East enabled the emperor to employ his forces against the Vandals; and the internal state of Africa afforded an honourable motive, and promised a powerful support to the Roman arms.[1]

According to the testament of the founder, the African kingdom had

[1] The complete series of the Vandal war is related by Procopius in a regular and elegant narrative (l. i. c. 9-25, l. ii. c. 1-13) ; and happy would be my lot, could I always tread in the footsteps of such a guide.   From the entire and diligent perusal of the Greek text I have a right to pronounce that the Latin and French versions of Grotius and Cousin may not be implicitly trusted; yet the President Cousin has been often praised, and Hugo Grotius was the first scholar of a learned age.

lineally descended to Hilderic, the eldest of the Vandal princes. A mild disposition inclined the son of a tyrant, the grandson of a conqueror, to prefer the counsels of clemency and peace, and his accession was marked by the salutary edict which restored two hundred bishops to their churches, and allowed the free profession of the Athanasian creed.[2] But the catholics accepted with cold and transient gratitude a favour so inadequate to their pretensions, and the virtues of Hilderic offended the prejudices of his countrymen. The Arian clergy presumed to insinuate that he had renounced his faith, and the soldiers more loudly complained that he had degenerated from the courage, of his ancestors. His ambassadors were suspected of a secret and disgraceful negotiation in the Byzantine court; and his general, the Achilles,[3] as he was named, of the Vandals, lost a battle against the naked and disorderly Moors. The public discontent was exasperated by Gelimer, whose age, descent, and military fame gave him an apparent title to the succession: he assumed, with the consent of the nation, the reins of government, and his unfortunate sovereign sunk without a struggle from the throne to a dungeon, where he was strictly guarded with a faithful counsellor, and his unpopular nephew the Achilles of the Vandals. But the indulgence which Hilderic had shown to his catholic subjects had powerfully recommended him to the favour of Justinian, who, for the benefit of his own sect, could acknowledge the use and justice of religious toleration: their alliance, while the nephew of Justin remained in a private station, was cemented by the mutual exchange of gifts and letters, and the emperor Justinian asserted the cause of royalty and friendship. In two successive embassies he admonished the usurper to repent of his treason, or to abstain, at least, from any further violence which might provoke the displeasure of God and of the Romans, to reverence the laws of kindred and succession, and to suffer an infirm old man peaceably to end his days either on the throne of Carthage or in the palace of Constantinople. The passions or even the prudence of Gelimer compelled him to reject these requests, which were urged in the haughty tone of menace and command; and he justified his ambition in a language rarely spoken in the Byzantine court, by alleging the right of a free people to remove or punish their chief magistrate who had failed in the execution of the kingly office. After this fruitless expostulation, the captive monarch

[2] See Ruinart, Hist. Persecut. Vandal. c. xii. p. 589 [ed. Par. 1694]. His best evidence is drawn from the Life of St. Fulgentius, composed by one of his disciples, transcribed in a great measure in the Annals of Baronius, and printed in several great collections (Catalog. Bibliot. Bunavianæ, tom. i. vol. ii. p. 1258).

[3] For what quality of the mind or body? For speed, or beauty, or valour?—In what language did the Vandals read Homer?—Did he speak German?—The Latins had four versions (Fabric. tom. i. 1. ii. c. 3, p. 297) : yet, in spite of the praises of Seneca (Consol. [ad Polyb.] c. 26), they appear to have been more successful in imitating than in translating the Greek poets. But the name of Achilles might be famous and popular, even among the illiterate barbarians.

was more rigorously treated, his nephew was deprived of his eyes, and the cruel Vandal, confident in his strength and distance, derided the vain threats and slow preparations of the emperor of the East. Justinian resolved to deliver or revenge his friend, Gelimer to maintain his usurpation; and the war was preceded, according to the practice of civilised nations, by the most solemn protestations that each party was sincerely desirous of peace.

The report of an African war was grateful only to the vain and idle populace of Constantinople, whose poverty exempted them from tribute, and whose cowardice was seldom exposed to military service. But the wiser citizens, who judged of the future by the past, revolved in their memory the immense loss, both of men and money, which the empire had sustained in the expedition of Basiliscus. The troops, which, after five laborious campaigns, had been recalled from the Persian frontier, dreaded the sea, the climate, and the arms of an unknown enemy. The ministers of the finances computed, as far as they might compute, the demands of an African war, the taxes which must be found and levied to supply those insatiate demands, and the danger lest their own lives, or at least their lucrative employments, should be made responsible for the deficiency of the supply. Inspired by such selfish motives (for we may not suspect him of any zeal for the public good), John of Cappadocia ventured to oppose in full council the inclinations of his master. He confessed that a victory of such importance could not be too dearly purchased; but he represented in a grave discourse the certain difficulties and the uncertain event. " You undertake," said the præfect, " to besiege Carthage: by land the distance is not less than one hundred and forty days' journey; on the sea, a whole year [4] must elapse before you can receive any intelligence from your fleet. If Africa should be reduced, it cannot be preserved without the additional conquest of Sicily and Italy. Success will impose the obligation of new labours; a single misfortune will attract the barbarians into the heart of your exhausted empire." Justinian felt the weight of this salutary advice; he was confounded by the unwonted freedom of an obsequious servant; and the design of the war would perhaps have been relinquished, if his courage had not been revived by a voice which silenced the doubts of profane reason. " I have seen a vision," cried an artful or fanatic bishop of the East. " It is the will of heaven, O emperor! that you should not abandon your holy enterprise for the deliverance of the African church. The God of battles will march before your standard, and disperse your enemies, who are the enemies of his Son." The emperor might be tempted, and his counsellors were constrained, to give credit to this seasonable revelation; but they derived more rational hope from the revolt which the adherents of Hilderic or Athanasius had already

---

[4] *A year*—absurd exaggeration! The conquest of Africa may be dated A.D. 533, September 14. It is celebrated by Justinian in the preface to his Institutes, which were published November 21 of the same year. Including the voyage and return, such a computation might be truly applied to *our* Indian empire.

excited on the borders of the Vandal monarchy. Pudentius, an African subject, had privately signified his loyal intentions, and a small military aid restored the province of Tripoli to the obedience of the Romans. The government of Sardinia had been intrusted to Godas, a valiant barbarian: he suspended the payment of tribute, disclaimed his allegiance to the usurper, and gave audience to the emissaries of Justinian, who found him master of that fruitful island, at the head of his guards, and proudly invested with the ensigns of royalty. The forces of the Vandals were diminished by discord and suspicion; the Roman armies were animated by the spirit of Belisarius, one of those heroic names which are familiar to every age and to every nation.[5]

The Africanus of new Rome was born, and perhaps educated, among the Thracian peasants,[6] without any of those advantages which had formed the virtues of the elder and younger Scipio—a noble origin, liberal studies, and the emulation of a free state. The silence of a loquacious secretary may be admitted to prove that the youth of Belisarius could not afford any subject of praise: he served, most assuredly with valour and reputation, among the private guards of Justinian; and when his patron became emperor, the domestic was promoted to military command. After a bold inroad into Persarmenia, in which his glory was shared by a colleague, and his progress was checked by an enemy, Belisarius repaired to the important station of Dara, where he first accepted the service of Procopius, the faithful companion, and diligent historian, of his exploits.[7] The Mirranes of Persia advanced with forty thousand of her best troops, to raze the fortifications of Dara; and signified the day and the hour on which the citizens should prepare a bath for his refreshment after the toils of victory. He encountered an adversary equal to himself, by the new title of General of the East; his superior

[5] [Stilicho, Aëtius, Boniface, Belisarius, were the quartette of great soldiers who hurled back the hordes of barbarians, and of these unquestionably the first and the last were the greatest and best. See Lord Mahon's *Life of Belisarius* (London, 1848, second ed.).—O. S.]

[6] Ὥρμητο δὲ ὁ Βελισάριος ἐκ Γερμανίας, ἥ Θρακῶντε καί Ἰλλυρῶν μεταξὺ κεῖται (Procop. Vandal. l. i. c. 11 [tom. i. p. 361, ed. Bonn]). Aleman. (Not. ad Anecdot. p. 5), an Italian, could easily reject the German vanity of Giphanius and Velserus, who wished to claim the hero; but his Germania, a metropolis of Thrace, I cannot find in any civil or ecclesiastical lists of the provinces and cities.

[Lord Mahon expresses surprise that Gibbon cannot find the town of Germania in any civil or ecclesiastical lists, and says that it is mentioned by Procopius (de Ædific. lib. iv. c. 1) as near Sardica. In that passage it is called Γερμάνη. It is also mentioned by Constant. Porphyrog. de Themat. l. ii. under Δυρραχιον θέμα 9, Banduri Imp. Orient. i. p. 26, where it is placed in the eparchia of Dacia); and by the grammarian Hierocles in the same work (p. 36), where it is called Γερμαη. Von Hammer, in a review of Lord Mahon's book in the *Jahrbücher der Literatur* of Vienna, in 1832, observes that Germania may be identified with the present Tschirmien or Tschermen, a town near the line of road between Constantinople and Adrianople, and about one day's journey from the latter.—O. S.]

[7] The two first Persian campaigns of Belisarius are fairly and copiously related by his secretary (Persic. l. i. c. 12-18).

in the science of war, but much inferior in the number and quality of his troops, which amounted only to twenty-five thousand Romans and strangers, relaxed in their discipline, and humbled by recent disasters. As the level plain of Dara refused all shelter to stratagem and ambush, Belisarius protected his front with a deep trench, which was prolonged at first in perpendicular, and afterwards in parallel, lines, to cover the wings of cavalry advantageously posted to command the flanks and rear of the enemy. When the Roman centre was shaken, their well-timed and rapid charge decided the conflict: the standard of Persia fell; the *immortals* fled; the infantry threw away their bucklers, and eight thousand of the vanquished were left on the field of battle. In the next campaign Syria was invaded on the side of the desert; and Belisarius, with twenty thousand men, hastened from Dara to the relief of the province. During the whole summer the designs of the enemy were baffled by his skilful dispositions:[8] he pressed their retreat, occupied each night their camp of the preceding day, and would have secured a bloodless victory, if he could have resisted the impatience of his own troops. Their valiant promise was faintly supported in the hour of battle; the right wing was exposed by the treacherous or cowardly desertion of the Christian Arabs; the Huns, a veteran band of eight hundred warriors, were oppressed by superior numbers; the flight of the Isaurians was intercepted; but the Roman infantry stood firm on the left; for Belisarius himself, dismounting from his horse, showed them that intrepid despair was their only safety. They turned their backs to the Euphrates, and their faces to the enemy: innumerable arrows glanced without effect from the compact and shelving order of their bucklers; an impenetrable line of pikes was opposed to the repeated assaults of the Persian cavalry; and after a resistance of many hours, the remaining troops were skilfully embarked under the shadow of the night. The Persian commander retired with disorder and disgrace, to answer a strict account of the lives of so many soldiers which he had consumed in a barren victory. But the fame of Belisarius was not sullied by a defeat in which he alone had saved his army from the consequences of their own rashness: the approach of peace relieved him from the guard of the eastern frontier, and his conduct in the sedition of Constantinople amply discharged his obligations to the emperor. When the African war became the topic of popular discourse and secret deliberation, each of the Roman generals was apprehensive, rather than ambitious, of the dangerous honour; but as soon as Justinian had declared his preference of superior merit, their envy was rekindled by the unanimous applause which was given to the choice of Belisarius. The temper of the Byzantine court may encourage a suspicion that the hero was darkly assisted by the intrigues of his wife, the fair and subtle Antonina, who alternately enjoyed the confidence, and incurred the

---

[8] [The statement that during the whole summer the designs of the Persians were baffled by the skilful dispositions of Belisarius is also incorrect, because, as Lord Mahon says, the decisive battle of Callinicum was fought on Easter Sunday (April 19).—O. S.]

hatred, of the empress Theodora. The birth of Antonina was ignoble; she descended from a family of charioteers; and her chastity has been stained with the foulest reproach. Yet she reigned with long and absolute power over the mind of her illustrious husband; and if Antonina disdained the merit of conjugal fidelity, she expressed a manly friendship to Belisarius, whom she accompanied with undaunted resolution in all the hardships and dangers of a military life.[9]

The preparations for the African war were not unworthy of the last contest between Rome and Carthage. The pride and flower of the army consisted of the guards of Belisarius, who, according to the pernicious indulgence of the times, devoted themselves, by a particular oath of fidelity, to the service of their patrons. Their strength and stature, for which they had been curiously selected, the goodness of their horses and armour, and the assiduous practice of all the exercises of war, enabled them to act whatever their courage might prompt; and their courage was exalted by the social honour of their rank, and the personal ambition of favour and fortune. Four hundred of the bravest of the Heruli marched under the banner of the faithful and active Pharas; their untractable valour was more highly prized than the tame submission of the Greeks and Syrians; and of such importance was it deemed to procure a reinforcement of six hundred Massagetæ, or Huns, that they were allured by fraud and deceit to engage in a naval expedition. Five thousand horse and ten thousand foot were embarked at Constantinople for the conquest of Africa; but the infantry, for the most part levied in Thrace and Isauria, yielded to the more prevailing use and reputation of the cavalry; and the Scythian bow was the weapon on which the armies of Rome were now reduced to place their principal dependence. From a laudable desire to assert the dignity of his theme, Procopius defends the soldiers of his own time against the morose critics, who confined that respectable name to the heavy-armed warriors of antiquity, and maliciously observed that the word *archer* is introduced by Homer[10] as a term of contempt. " Such contempt might perhaps be due to the naked youths who appeared on foot in the fields of Troy, and, lurking behind a tombstone, or the shield of a friend, drew the bowstring to their breast,[11] and dismissed a feeble and lifeless arrow. But our archers (pursues the historian) are mounted on horses, which they manage with admirable skill; their head and shoulders are protected by a casque or buckler; they wear greaves of iron on their

[9] See the birth and character of Antonina, in the Anecdotes, c. 1, and the notes of Alemannus, p. 3.

[10] See the preface of Procopius [Bell. Pers. c. 1]. The enemies of archery might quote the reproaches of Diomede (Iliad, Δ, 385, etc.) and the permittere vulnera ventis of Lucan (viii. 383) : yet the Romans could not despise the arrows of the Parthians; and in the siege of Troy, Pandarus, Paris, and Teucer pierced those haughty warriors who insulted them as women or children.

[11] Νευρὴν μὲν μαζῷ πέλασεν, τόξῳ δὲ σίδηρον (Iliad, Δ, 123). How concise—how just—how beautiful is the whole picture! I see the attitudes of the archer—I hear the twanging of the bow :—

Λίγξε βιὸς, νευρῆ δὲ μέγ' ἴαχεν, ἆλτο δ' ὀϊστός.

legs, and their bodies are guarded by a coat of mail. On their right side
hangs a quiver, a sword on their left, and their hand is accustomed to
wield a lance or javelin in closer combat. Their bows are strong and
weighty; they shoot in every possible direction, advancing, retreating,
to the front, to the rear, or to either flank; and as they are taught to
draw the bowstring not to the breast, but to the right ear, firm indeed
must be the armour that can resist the rapid violence of their shaft."
Five hundred transports, navigated by twenty thousand mariners of
Egypt, Cilicia, and Ionia, were collected in the harbour of Constantinople. The smallest of these vessels may be computed at thirty, the
largest at five hundred, tons; and the fair average will supply an
allowance, liberal, but not profuse, of about one hundred thousand
tons,[12] for the reception of thirty-five thousand soldiers and sailors, of
five thousand horses, of arms, engines, and military stores, and of a
sufficient stock of water and provisions for a voyage, perhaps, of three
months. The proud galleys which in former ages swept the Mediterranean with so many hundred oars had long since disappeared; and the
fleet of Justinian was escorted only by ninety-two light brigantines,
covered from the missile weapons of the enemy, and rowed by two
thousand of the brave and robust youth of Constantinople. Twenty-
two generals are named, most of whom were afterwards distinguished
in the wars of Africa and Italy; but the supreme command, both by
land and sea, was delegated to Belisarius alone, with a boundless power
of acting according to his discretion, as if the emperor himself were
present. The separation of the naval and military professions is at once
the effect and the cause of the modern improvements in the science of
navigation and maritime war.

In the seventh year of the reign of Justinian, and about the time
of the summer solstice, the whole fleet of six hundred ships was ranged
in martial pomp before the gardens of the palace. The patriarch pronounced his benediction, the emperor signified his last commands, the
general's trumpet gave the signal of departure, and every heart, according to its fears or wishes, explored with anxious curiosity the omens of
misfortune and success. The first halt was made at Perinthus or Heraclea, where Belisarius waited five days to receive some Thracian horses,
a military gift of his sovereign. From thence the fleet pursued their
course through the midst of the Propontis; but as they struggled to
pass the Straits of the Hellespont, an unfavourable wind detained them
four days at Abydus, where the general exhibited a memorable lesson

[12] The text appears to allow for the largest vessels 50,000 medimni, or 3000
tons (since the *medimnus* weighed 160 Roman, or 120 avoirdupois, pounds). I
have given a more rational interpretation, by supposing that the Attic style of
Procopius conceals the legal and popular *modius,* a sixth part of the *medimnus*
(Hooper's Ancient Measures, p. 152, etc.). A contrary, and indeed a stranger,
mistake has crept into an oration of Dinarchus (contra Demosthenem, in
Reiske Orator. Græc. tom. iv. P. ii. p. 34). By reducing the *number* of ships
from 500 to 50, and translating μεδίμνοι by *mines,* or pounds, Cousin has generously allowed 500 tons for the whole of the Imperial fleet?—Did he never
think?

of firmness and severity. Two of the Huns, who in a drunken quarrel had slain one of their fellow-soldiers, were instantly shown to the army suspended on a lofty gibbet. The national indignity was resented by their countrymen, who disclaimed the servile laws of the empire, and asserted the free privilege of Scythia, where a small fine was allowed to expiate the hasty sallies of intemperance and anger. Their complaints were specious, their clamours were loud, and the Romans were not averse to the example of disorder and impunity. But the rising sedition was appeased by the authority and eloquence of the general, and he represented to the assembled troops the obligation of justice, the importance of discipline, the rewards of piety and virtue, and the unpardonable guilt of murder, which, in his apprehension, was aggravated rather than excused by the vice of intoxication.[13] In the navigation from the Hellespont to Peloponnesus, which the Greeks after the siege of Troy had performed in four days,[14] the fleet of Belisarius was guided in their course by his master-galley, conspicuous in the day by the redness of the sails, and in the night by the torches blazing from the mast-head. It was the duty of the pilots, as they steered between the islands and turned the capes of Malea and Tænarium, to preserve the just order and regular intervals of such a multitude of ships; as the wind was fair and moderate, their labours were not unsuccessful, and the troops were safely disembarked at Methone on the Messenian coast, to repose themselves for awhile after the fatigues of the sea. In this place they experienced how avarice, invested with authority, may sport with the lives of thousands which are bravely exposed for the public service. According to military practice, the bread or biscuit of the Romans was twice prepared in the oven, and the diminution of one-fourth was cheerfully allowed for the loss of weight. To gain this miserable profit, and to save the expense of wood, the præfect, John of Cappadocia, had given orders that the flour should be slightly baked by the same fire which warmed the baths of Constantinople; and when the sacks were opened, a soft and mouldy paste was distributed to the army. Such unwholesome food, assisted by the heat of the climate and season, soon produced an epidemical disease which swept away five hundred soldiers. Their health was restored by the diligence of Belisarius, who provided fresh bread at Methone, and boldly expressed his just and humane indignation: the emperor heard his complaint; the general was praised, but the minister was not punished. From the port of Methone the pilots steered along the western coast of Peloponnesus, as far as the isle of Zacynthus or Zante, before they undertook the

[13] I have read of a Greek legislator who inflicted a *double* penalty on the crimes committed in a state of intoxication; but it seems agreed that this was rather a political than a moral law.

[14] Or even in three days, since they anchored the first evening in the neighbouring isle of Tenedos: the second day they sailed to Lesbos, the third to the promontory of Eubœa, and on the fourth they reached Argos (Homer. Odyss. Γ 130-183; Wood's Essay on Homer, p. 40-46). A pirate sailed from the Hellespont to the seaport of Sparta in three days (Xenophon. Hellen. l. ii. c. 1).

voyage (in their eyes a most arduous voyage) of one hundred leagues over the Ionian Sea. As the fleet was surprised by a calm, sixteen days were consumed in the slow navigation; and even the general would have suffered the intolerable hardship of thirst, if the ingenuity of Antonina had not preserved the water in glass bottles, which she buried deep in the sand in a part of the ship impervious to the rays of the sun. At length the harbour of Caucana,[15] on the southern side of Sicily, afforded a secure and hospitable shelter. The Gothic officers, who governed the island in the name of the daughter and grandson of Theodoric, obeyed their imprudent orders to receive the troops of Justinian like friends and allies; provisions were liberally supplied, the cavalry was remounted,[16] and Procopius soon returned from Syracuse with correct information of the state and designs of the Vandals. His intelligence determined Belisarius to hasten his operations, and his wise impatience was seconded by the winds. The fleet lost sight of Sicily, passed before the isle of Malta, discovered the capes of Africa, ran along the coast with a strong gale from the north-east, and finally cast anchor at the promontory of Caput Vada, about five days' journey to the south of Carthage.[17]

If Gelimer had been informed of the approach of the enemy, he must have delayed the conquest of Sardinia for the immediate defence of his person and kingdom.[18] A detachment of five thousand soldiers and one hundred and twenty galleys would have joined the remaining forces of the Vandals; and the descendant of Genseric might have surprised and oppressed a fleet of deep-laden transports incapable of action, and of light brigantines that seem only qualified for flight.[19] Belisarius had secretly trembled when he overheard his soldiers in the passage emboldening each other to confess their apprehensions. If they were once on shore, they hoped to maintain the honour of their arms; but if they should be attacked at sea, they did not blush to acknowledge that they wanted courage to contend at the same time with the winds, the waves,

---

[15] Caucana, near Camarina, is at least 50 miles (350 or 400 stadia) from Syracuse (Cluver. Sicilia Antiqua, p. 191).

[16] Procopius, Gothic. l. i. c. 3. Tibi tollit hinnitum apta quadrigis equa, in the Sicilian pastures of Grosphus (Horat. Carm. ii. 16). Acragas . . . magnanimûm quondam generator equorum (Virg. Æneid. iii. 704). Thero's horses, whose victories are immortalised by Pindar, were bred in this country.

[17] The Caput Vada of Procopius (where Justinian afterwards founded a city—De Ædific. l. vi. c. 6) is the promontory of Ammon in Strabo, the Brachodes of Ptolemy, the Capaudia of the moderns, a long narrow slip that runs into the sea (Shaw's Travels, p. 111).
[Procopius suggests that the reason why Belisarius chose Caput Vada as the place for disembarking his troops was doubtless because the province of Tripolitana had revolted against the Vandals (Procop. Bell. Vandal. l. i. c. 10, p. 337). In case of a reverse by land or by sea, Belisarius would be able to retreat to the imperial provinces of Cyrenaïca and Egypt.—O. S.]

[18] [Lord Mahon, in his *Life of Belisarius,* suggests that in place of "Cauable to retreat to the imperial provinces of Cyrenaïca and Egypt.—O. S.]

[19] [Lord Mahon, in his *Life of Belisarius,* says that the proposal, rejected by Belisarius, was not to sail into the port of Carthage, but into a haven 40 stadia from Carthage, viz., the present Lake of Tunis.—O. S.]

and the barbarians.[20] The knowledge of their sentiments decided Belisarius to seize the first opportunity of landing them on the coast of Africa; and he prudently rejected, in a council of war, the proposal of sailing with the fleet and army into the port of Carthage. Three months after their departure from Constantinople, the men and horses, the arms and military stores, were safely disembarked; and five soldiers were left as a guard on board each of the ships, which were disposed in the form of a semicircle. The remainder of the troops occupied a camp on the sea-shore, which they fortified, according to ancient discipline, with a ditch and rampart; and the discovery of a source of fresh water, while it allayed the thirst, excited the superstitious confidence of the Romans. The next morning some of the neighbouring gardens were pillaged; and Belisarius, after chastising the offenders, embraced the slight occasion, but the decisive moment, of inculcating the maxims of justice, moderation, and genuine policy. " When I first accepted the commission of subduing Africa, I depended much less," said the general, " on the numbers, or even the bravery of my troops, than upon the friendly disposition of the natives, and their immortal hatred to the Vandals. You alone can deprive me of this hope: if you continue to extort by rapine what might be purchased for a little money, such acts of violence will reconcile these implacable enemies, and unite them in a just and holy league against the invaders of their country." These exhortations were enforced by a rigid discipline, of which the soldiers themselves soon felt and praised the salutary effects. The inhabitants, instead of deserting their houses or hiding their corn, supplied the Romans with a fair and liberal market, the civil officers of the province continued to exercise their functions in the name of Justinian, and the clergy, from motives of conscience and interest, assiduously laboured to promote the cause of a catholic emperor. The small town of Sullecte,[21] one day's journey from the camp, had the honour of being foremost to open her gates and to resume her ancient allegiance; the larger cities of Leptis and Adrumetum imitated the example of loyalty as soon as Belisarius appeared; and he advanced without opposition as far as Grasse, a palace of the Vandal kings, at the distance of fifty miles from Carthage. The weary Romans indulged themselves in the refreshment of shady groves, cool fountains, and delicious fruits; and the preference

---

[20] A centurion of Mark Antony expressed, though in a more manly strain, the same dislike to the sea and to naval combats (Plutarch in Antonio, p. 1730, edit. Hen. Steph.).

[21] Sullecte is perhaps the Turris Hannibalis, an old building, now as large as the Tower of London. The march of Belisarius to Leptis, Adrumetum, etc., is illustrated by the campaign of Cæsar (Hirtius de Bello Africano, with the Analyse of Guichardt), and Shaw's Travels (p. 105-113) in the same country.
[The name of Sullecte is still preserved in that of Salekto, a small town on the coast, situate about eight French leagues from Capaudia (Caput Vada). Leptis is now called Lenta, also Lamba, Adrumetum is Soussa, and Grasse is conjectured to be the town previously called Aphrodisium, now Faradise. —O. S.]

which Procopius allows to these gardens over any that he had seen, either in the East or West, may be ascribed either to the taste or the fatigue of the historian. In three generations prosperity and a warm climate had dissolved the hardy virtue of the Vandals, who insensibly became the most luxurious of mankind. In their villas and gardens, which might deserve the Persian name of *Paradise*,[22] they enjoyed a cool and elegant repose; and, after the daily use of the bath, the barbarians were seated at a table profusely spread with the delicacies of the land and sea. Their silken robes, loosely flowing after the fashion of the Medes, were embroidered with gold; love and hunting were the labours of their life, and their vacant hours were amused by pantomimes, chariot-races, and the music and dances of the theatre.

In a march of ten or twelve days the vigilance of Belisarius was constantly awake and active against his unseen enemies, by whom, in every place and at every hour, he might be suddenly attacked. An officer of confidence and merit, John the Armenian, led the vanguard of three hundred horse, six hundred Massagetæ covered at a certain distance the left flank, and the whole fleet, steering along the coast, seldom lost sight of the army, which moved each day about twelve miles, and lodged in the evening in strong camps or in friendly towns. The near approach of the Romans to Carthage filled the mind of Gelimer with anxiety and terror. He prudently wished to protract the war till his brother, with his veteran troops, should return from the conquest of Sardinia; and he now lamented the rash policy of his ancestors, who, by destroying the fortifications of Africa, had left him only the dangerous resource of risking a battle in the neighbourhood of his capital. The Vandal conquerors, from their original number of fifty thousand, were multiplied, without including their women and children, to one hundred and sixty thousand fighting men; and such forces, animated with valour and union, might have crushed at their first landing the feeble and exhausted bands of the Roman general. But the friends of the captive king were more inclined to accept the invitations than to resist the progress of Belisarius; and many a proud barbarian disguised his aversion to war under the more specious name of his hatred to the usurper. Yet the authority and promises of Gelimer collected a formidable army, and his plans were concerted with some degree of military skill. An order was despatched to his brother Ammatas to collect all the forces of Carthage, and to encounter the van of the Roman army at the distance of ten miles from the city: his nephew Gibamund with two thousand horse was destined to attack their left, when the monarch himself, who silently followed, should charge their rear in a situation which excluded them from the aid or even the view of their fleet. But the rashness of Ammatas was fatal to himself and his country. He anticipated the hour of the attack, outstripped his tardy

---

[22] Παράδεισος κάλλιστος ἁπάντων ὧν ἡμεῖς ἴσμεν. The paradises, a name and fashion adopted from Persia, may be represented by the royal garden of Ispahan (Voyage d'Olearius, p. 774). See, in the Greek romances, their most perfect model (Longus, Pastoral. l. iv. p. 99-101; Achilles Tatius, l. i. p. 22, 23).

followers, and was pierced with a mortal wound after he had slain with his own hand twelve of his boldest antagonists. His Vandals fled to Carthage; the highway, almost ten miles, was strewed with dead bodies; and it seemed incredible that such multitudes could be slaughtered by the swords of three hundred Romans. The nephew of Gelimer was defeated, after a slight combat, by the six hundred Massagetæ: they did not equal the third part of his numbers, but each Scythian was fired by the example of his chief, who gloriously exercised the privilege of his family by riding foremost and alone to shoot the first arrow against the enemy. In the meanwhile Gelimer himself, ignorant of the event, and misguided by the windings of the hills, inadvertently passed the Roman army, and reached the scene of action where Ammatas had fallen. He wept the fate of his brother and of Carthage, charged with irresistible fury the advancing squadrons, and might have pursued, and perhaps decided the victory, if he had not wasted those inestimable moments in the discharge of a vain though pious duty to the dead. While his spirit was broken by this mournful office, he heard the trumpet of Belisarius, who, leaving Antonina and his infantry in the camp, pressed forwards with his guards and the remainder of the cavalry to rally his flying troops, and to restore the fortune of the day. Much room could not be found in this disorderly battle for the talents of a general; but the king fled before the hero, and the Vandals, accustomed only to a Moorish enemy, were incapable of withstanding the arms and discipline of the Romans. Gelimer retired with hasty steps towards the desert of Numidia; but he had soon the consolation of learning that his private orders for the execution of Hilderic and his captive friends had been faithfully obeyed. The tyrant's revenge was useful only to his enemies. The death of a lawful prince excited the compassion of his people; his life might have perplexed the victorious Romans; and the lieutenant of Justinian, by a crime of which he was innocent, was relieved from the painful alternative of forfeiting his honour or relinquishing his conquests.

As soon as the tumult had subsided, the several parts of the army informed each other of the accidents of the day; and Belisarius pitched his camp on the field of victory, to which the tenth mile-stone from Carthage had applied the Latin appellation of *Decimus*. From a wise suspicion of the stratagems and resources of the Vandals, he marched the next day in order of battle, halted in the evening before the gates of Carthage, and allowed a night of repose, that he might not in darkness and disorder expose the city to the licence of the soldiers, or the soldiers themselves to the secret ambush of the city. But as the fears of Belisarius were the result of calm and intrepid reason, he was soon satisfied that he might confide, without danger, in the peaceful and friendly aspect of the capital. Carthage blazed, with innumerable torches, the signals of the public joy; the chain was removed that guarded the entrance of the port, the gates were thrown open, and the people with acclamations of gratitude hailed and invited their Roman deliverers. The defeat of the Vandals and the freedom of Africa were

announced to the city on the eve of St. Cyprian, when the churches were
already adorned and illuminated for the festival of the martyr, whom
three centuries of superstition had almost raised to a local deity. The
Arians, conscious that their reign had expired, resigned the temple to
the catholics, who rescued their saint from profane hands, performed
the holy rites, and loudly proclaimed the creed of Athanasius and
Justinian. One awful hour reversed the fortunes of the contending
parties. The suppliant Vandals, who had so lately indulged the vices
of conquerors, sought an humble refuge in the sanctuary of the church;
while the merchants of the East were delivered from the deepest
dungeon of the palace by their affrighted keeper, who implored the protection of his captives, and showed them, through an aperture in the
wall, the sails of the Roman fleet. After their separation from the army,
the naval commanders had proceeded with slow caution along the coast
till they reached the Hermæan promontory, and obtained the first intelligence of the victory of Belisarius. Faithful to his instructions, they
would have cast anchor about twenty miles from Carthage, if the more
skilful seamen had not represented the perils of the shore and the signs
of an impending tempest. Still ignorant of the revolution, they declined, however, the rash attempt of forcing the chain of the port;
and the adjacent harbour and suburb of Mandracium were insulted
only by the rapine of a private officer who disobeyed and deserted his
leaders. But the imperial fleet, advancing with a fair wind, steered
through the narrow entrance of the Goletta, and occupied in the deep
and capacious lake of Tunis a secure station about five miles from the
capital.[23] No sooner was Belisarius informed of their arrival than he
despatched orders that the greatest part of the mariners should be immediately landed, to join the triumph, and to swell the apparent numbers of the Romans. Before he allowed them to enter the gates of
Carthage, he exhorted them, in a discourse worthy of himself and the
occasion, not to disgrace the glory of their arms; and to remember that
the Vandals had been the tyrants, but that *they* were the deliverers,
of the Africans, who must now be respected as the voluntary and affectionate subjects of their common sovereign. The Romans marched
through the streets in close ranks, prepared for battle if an enemy
had appeared: the strict order maintained by the general imprinted on
their minds the duty of obedience; and in an age in which custom and
impunity almost sanctified the abuse of conquest, the genius of one
man repressed the passions of a victorious army. The voice of menace
and complaint was silent; the trade of Carthage was not interrupted;
while Africa changed her master and her government, the shops con-

---

[23] The neighbourhood of Carthage, the sea, the land, and the rivers, are
changed almost as much as the works of man. The isthmus, or neck, of
the city is now confounded with the continent; the harbour is a dry plain;
and the lake, or stagnum, no more than a morass, with six or seven feet water
in the mid-channel. See D'Anville (Géographie Ancienne, tom. iii. p. 82),
Shaw (Travels, p. 77-84), Marmol (Description de l'Afrique, tom. ii. p. 465),
and Thuanus (lviii. 12. tom. iii. p. 334).

tinued open and busy; and the soldiers, after sufficient guards had been posted, modestly departed to the houses which were allotted for their reception. Belisarius fixed his residence in the palace, seated himself on the throne of Genseric, accepted and distributed the barbaric spoil, granted their lives to the suppliant Vandals, and laboured to repair the damage which the suburb of Mandracium had sustained in the preceding night. At supper he entertained his principal officers with the form and magnificence of a royal banquet.[24] The victor was respectfully served by the captive officers of the household; and in the moments of festivity, when the impartial spectators applauded the fortune and merit of Belisarius, his envious flatterers secretly shed their venom on every word and gesture which might alarm the suspicions of a jealous monarch. One day was given to these pompous scenes, which may not be despised as useless if they attracted the popular veneration; but the active mind of Belisarius, which in the pride of victory could suppose a defeat, had already resolved that the Roman empire in Africa should not depend on the chance of arms or the favour of the people. The fortifications of Carthage had alone been exempted from the general proscription; but in the reign of ninety-five years they were suffered to decay by the thoughtless and indolent Vandals. A wiser conqueror restored, with incredible despatch, the walls and ditches of the city. His liberality encouraged the workmen; the soldiers, the mariners, and the citizens vied with each other in the salutary labour; and Gelimer, who had feared to trust his person in an open town, beheld with astonishment and despair the rising strength of an impregnable fortress.

That unfortunate monarch, after the loss of his capital, applied himself to collect the remains of an army scattered, rather than destroyed, by the preceding battle, and the hopes of pillage attracted some Moorish bands to the standard of Gelimer. He encamped in the fields of Bulla, four days' journey from Carthage; insulted the capital, which he deprived of the use of an aqueduct; proposed a high reward for the head of every Roman; affected to spare the persons and property of his African subjects; and secretly negotiated with the Arian sectaries and the confederate Huns. Under these circumstances the conquest of Sardinia served only to aggravate his distress: he reflected, with the deepest anguish, that he had wasted in that useless enterprise five thousand of his bravest troops, and he read, with grief and shame, the victorious letters of his brother Zano, who expressed a sanguine confidence that the king, after the example of their ancestors, had already chastised the rashness of the Roman invader. " Alas! my brother," replied Gelimer, " Heaven has declared against our unhappy nation. While you have subdued Sardinia, we have lost Africa. No sooner did Belisarius appear with a handful of soldiers, than courage and prosperity

---

[24] From Delphi, the name of Delphicum was given, both in Greek and Latin, to a tripod; and, by an easy analogy, the same appellation was extended at Rome, Constantinople, and Carthage to the royal banqueting-room. (Procopius. Vandal. l. i. c. 21. Ducange, Gloss. Græc. p. 277. Δελφικον, ad Alexiad. 412.)

deserted the cause of the Vandals. Your nephew Gibamund, your brother Ammatas, have been betrayed to death by the cowardice of their followers. Our horses, our ships, Carthage itself, and all Africa, are in the power of the enemy. Yet the Vandals still prefer an ignominious repose, at the expense of their wives and children, their wealth and liberty. Nothing now remains except the field of Bulla, and the hope of your valour. Abandon Sardinia; fly to our relief; restore our empire, or perish by our side." On the receipt of this epistle Zano imparted his grief to the principal Vandals, but the intelligence was prudently concealed from the natives of the island. The troops embarked in one hundred and twenty galleys at the port of Cagliari, cast anchor the third day on the confines of Mauritania, and hastily pursued their march to join the royal standard in the camp of Bulla. Mournful was the interview: the two brothers embraced; they wept in silence; no questions were asked of the Sardinian victory; no inquiries were made of the African misfortunes: they saw before their eyes the whole extent of their calamities, and the absence of their wives and children afforded a melancholy proof that either death or captivity had been their lot. The languid spirit of the Vandals was at length awakened and united by the entreaties of their king, the example of Zano, and the instant danger which threatened their monarchy and religion. The military strength of the nation advanced to battle, and such was the rapid increase, that, before their army reached Tricameron, about twenty miles from Carthage, they might boast, perhaps with some exaggeration, that they surpassed, in a tenfold proportion, the diminutive powers of the Romans. But these powers were under the command of Belisarius, and, as he was conscious of their superior merit, he permitted the barbarians to surprise him at an unseasonable hour. The Romans were instantly under arms; a rivulet covered their front; the cavalry formed the first line, which Belisarius supported in the centre at the head of five hundred guards; the infantry, at some distance, was posted in the second line; and the vigilance of the general watched the separate station and ambiguous faith of the Massagetæ, who secretly reserved their aid for the conquerors. The historian has inserted, and the reader may easily supply, the speeches [25] of the commanders, who, by arguments the most opposite to their situation, inculcated the importance of victory and the contempt of life. Zano, with the troops which had followed him to the conquest of Sardinia, was placed in the centre, and the throne of Genseric might have stood, if the multitude of Vandals had imitated their intrepid resolution. Casting away their lances and missile weapons, they drew their swords and expected the charge; the Roman cavalry thrice passed the rivulet, they were thrice repulsed, and the conflict was firmly maintained till Zano fell and the standard of Belisarius was displayed. Gelimer retreated to his camp, the Huns joined the pursuit, and the victors despoiled the bodies of the slain. Yet no more than fifty

---

[25] These orations always express the sense of the times, and sometimes of the actors. I have condensed that sense, and thrown away declamation.

Romans and eight hundred Vandals were found on the field of battle; so inconsiderable was the carnage of a day which extinguished a nation and transferred the empire of Africa. In the evening Belisarius led his infantry to the attack of the camp, and the pusillanimous flight of Gelimer exposed the vanity of his recent declarations, that to the vanquished death was a relief, life a burden, and infamy the only object of terror. His departure was secret, but, as soon as the Vandals discovered that their king had deserted them, they hastily dispersed, anxious only for their personal safety, and careless of every object that is dear or valuable to mankind. The Romans entered the camp without resistance, and the wildest scenes of disorder were veiled in the darkness and confusion of the night. Every barbarian who met their swords was inhumanly massacred: their widows and daughters, as rich heirs or beautiful concubines, were embraced by the licentious soldiers; and avarice itself was almost satiated with the treasures of gold and silver, the accumulated fruits of conquest or economy in a long period of prosperity and peace. In this frantic search the troops, even of Belisarius, forgot their caution and respect. Intoxicated with lust and rapine, they explored, in small parties or alone, the adjacent fields, the woods, the rocks, and the caverns that might possibly conceal any desirable prize; laden with booty, they deserted their ranks, and wandered, without a guide, on the high road to Carthage, and, if the flying enemies had dared to return, very few of the conquerors would have escaped. Deeply sensible of the disgrace and danger, Belisarius passed an apprehensive night on the field of victory; at the dawn of day he planted his standard on a hill, recalled his guards and veterans, and gradually restored the modesty and obedience of the camp. It was equally the concern of the Roman general to subdue the hostile, and to save the prostrate, barbarian; and the suppliant Vandals, who could be found only in churches, were protected by his authority, disarmed, and separately confined, that they might neither disturb the public peace nor become the victims of popular revenge. After despatching a light detachment to tread the footsteps of Gelimer, he advanced, with his whole army, about ten days' march, as far as Hippo Regius, which no longer possessed the relics of St. Augustin.[26] The season, and the certain intelligence that the Vandal had fled to the inaccessible country of the Moors, determined Belisarius to relinquish the vain pursuit, and to fix his winter quarters at Carthage. From thence he despatched his

[26] The relics of St. Augustin were carried by the African bishops to their Sardinian exile (A.D. 500); and it was believed, in the eighth century, that Liutprand, king of the Lombards, transported them (A.D. 721) from Sardinia to Pavia. In the year 1695 the Augustin friars of that city *found* a brick arch, marble coffin, silver case, silk wrapper, bones, blood, etc., and perhaps an inscription of Agostino in Gothic letters. But this useful discovery has been disputed by reason and jealousy. (Baronius, Annal. A.D. 725, No. 2-9. Tillemont, Mém. Ecclés. tom. xiii. p. 944. Montfaucon, Diarium Ital. p. 26-30. Muratori, Antiq. Ital. Medii Ævi. tom. v. dissert. lviii. p. 9, who had composed a separate treatise before the decree of the bishop of Pavia, and pope Benedict XIII.)

principal lieutenant to inform the emperor that in the space of three months he had achieved the conquest of Africa.

Belisarius spoke the language of truth. The surviving Vandals yielded, without resistance, their arms and their freedom; the neighbourhood of Carthage submitted to his presence, and the more distant provinces were successively subdued by the report of his victory. Tripoli was confirmed in her voluntary allegiance; Sardinia and Corsica surrendered to an officer who carried instead of a sword the head of the valiant Zano; and the isles of Majorca, Minorca, and Yvica consented to remain an humble appendage of the African kingdom. Cæsarea, a royal city, which in looser geography may be confounded with the modern Algiers, was situate thirty days' march to the westward of Carthage; by land the road was infested by the Moors, but the sea was open, and the Romans were now masters of the sea. An active and discreet tribune sailed as far as the Straits, where he occupied Septem or Ceuta,[27] which rises opposite to Gibraltar on the African coast; that remote place was afterwards adorned and fortified by Justinian, and he seems to have indulged the vain ambition of extending his empire to the Columns of Hercules. He received the messengers of victory at the time when he was preparing to publish the Pandects of the Roman law, and the devout or jealous emperor celebrated the divine goodness, and confessed in silence the merit of his successful general.[28] Impatient to abolish the temporal and spiritual tyranny of the Vandals, he proceeded without delay to the full establishment of the catholic church. Her jurisdiction, wealth, and immunities, perhaps the most essential part of episcopal religion, were restored and amplified with a liberal hand; the Arian worship was suppressed, the Donatist meetings were proscribed,[29] and the synod of Carthage, by the voice of two hundred and seventeen bishops,[30] applauded the just measure of pious retaliation. On such an occasion it may not be presumed that many orthodox prelates were absent; but the comparative smallness of their number, which in ancient councils had been twice or even thrice multiplied, most clearly indicates the decay both of the church and state. While Justinian approved himself the defender of the faith, he entertained an ambitious hope that his victorious lieutenant would speedily enlarge the narrow

---

[27] Τὰ τῆς πολιτείας προοίμια, is the expression of Procopius (de Ædific. l. vi. c. 7). Ceuta, which has been defaced by the Portuguese, flourished in nobles and palaces, in agriculture and manufactures, under the more prosperous reign of the Arabs (l'Afrique de Marmol, tom. ii. p. 236).

[28] See the second and third preambles to the Digest, or Pandects, promulgated A.D. 533, December 16. To the titles of *Vandalicus* and *Africanus,* Justinian, or rather Belisarius, had acquired a just claim; *Gothicus* was premature, and *Francicus* false, and offensive to a great nation.

[29] See the original acts in Baronius (A.D. 535, No. 21-54). The emperor applauds his own clemency to the heretics, cum sifficiat eis vivere.

[30] Dupin (Geograph. Sacra Africana, p. lix. ad Optat. Milev.) observes and bewails this episcopal decay. In the more prosperous age of the church, he had noticed 690 bishoprics; but however minute were the dioceses, it is not probable that they all existed at the same time.

limits of his dominion to the space which they occupied before the invasion of the Moors and Vandals; and Belisarius was instructed to establish five *dukes* or commanders in the convenient stations of Tripoli, Leptis, Cirta, Cæsarea, and Sardinia, and to compute the military force of *palatines* or *borderers* that might be sufficient for the defence of Africa. The kingdom of the Vandals was not unworthy of the presence of a Prætorian præfect; and four consulars, three presidents, were appointed to administer the seven provinces under his civil jurisdiction. The number of their subordinate officers, clerks, messengers, or assistants, was minutely expressed: three hundred and ninety-six for the præfect himself, fifty for each of his vicegerents; and the rigid definition of their fees and salaries was more effectual to confirm the right than to prevent the abuse. These magistrates might be oppressive, but they were not idle, and the subtle questions of justice and revenue were infinitely propagated under the new government, which professed to revive the freedom and equity of the Roman republic. The conqueror was solicitous to extract a prompt and plentiful supply from his African subjects, and he allowed them to claim, even in the third degree and from the collateral line, the houses and lands of which their families had been unjustly despoiled by the Vandals. After the departure of Belisarius, who acted by a high and special commission, no ordinary provision was made for a master-general of the forces; but the office of Prætorian præfect was intrusted to a soldier; the civil and military powers were united, according to the practice of Justinian, in the chief governor; and the representative of the emperor in Africa, as well as in Italy, was soon distinguished by the appellation of Exarch.[31]

Yet the conquest of Africa was imperfect till her former sovereign was delivered, either alive or dead, into the hands of the Romans. Doubtful of the event, Gelimer had given secret orders that a part of his treasure should be transported to Spain, where he hoped to find a secure refuge at the court of the king of the Visigoths. But these intentions were disappointed by accident, treachery, and the indefatigable pursuit of his enemies, who intercepted his flight from the sea-shore, and chased the unfortunate monarch, with some faithful followers, to the inaccessible mountain of Papua,[32] in the inland country of Numidia. He was immediately besieged by Pharas, an officer whose truth and sobriety were the more applauded, as such qualities could seldom be found among the Heruli, the most corrupt of the barbarian tribes. To his vigilance Belisarius had intrusted this important charge; and, after a bold attempt to scale the mountain, in which he lost an hundred and ten soldiers, Pharas expected, during a winter siege, the operation of distress and famine on the mind of the Vandal king. From the softest

---

[31] The African laws of Justinian are illustrated by his German biographer (Cod. l. i. tit. 27. Novell. 36, 37, 131. Vit. Justinian. p. 349-377).

[32] Mount Papua is placed by D'Anville (tom. iii. p. 92, and Tabul. Imp. Rom. Occident.) near Hippo Regius and the sea; yet this situation ill agrees with the long pursuit beyond Hippo, and the words of Procopius (l. ii. c. 4 [tom. i. p. 427, ed. Bonn]), ἐν τοῖς Νουμιδίας ἐσχάτοις.

habits of pleasure, from the unbounded command of industry and wealth, he was reduced to share the poverty of the Moors,[33] supportable only to themselves by their ignorance of a happier condition. In their rude hovels of mud and hurdles, which confined the smoke and excluded the light, they promiscuously slept on the ground, perhaps on a sheepskin, with their wives, their children, and their cattle. Sordid and scanty were their garments; the use of bread and wine was unknown, and their oaten or barley cakes, imperfectly baked in the ashes, were devoured almost in a crude state by the hungry savages. The health of Gelimer must have sunk under these strange and unwonted hardships, from whatsoever cause they had been endured; but his actual misery was embittered by the recollection of past greatness, the daily insolence of his protectors, and the just apprehension that the light and venal Moors might be tempted to betray the rights of hospitality. The knowledge of his situation dictated the humane and friendly epistle of Pharas. "Like yourself," said the chief of the Heruli, "I am an illiterate barbarian, but I speak the language of plain sense and an honest heart. Why will you persist in hopeless obstinacy? Why will you ruin yourself, your family, and nation? The love of freedom and abhorrence of slavery? Alas! my dearest Gelimer, are you not already the worst of slaves, the slave of the vile nation of the Moors? Would it not be preferable to sustain at Constantinople a life of poverty and servitude, rather than to reign the undoubted monarch of the mountain of Papua? Do you think it a disgrace to be the subject of Justinian? Belisarius is his subject, and we ourselves, whose birth is not inferior to your own, are not ashamed of our obedience to the Roman emperor. That generous prince will grant you a rich inheritance of lands, a place in the senate, and the dignity of patrician: such are his gracious intentions, and you may depend with full assurance on the word of Belisarius. So long as Heaven has condemned us to suffer, patience is a virtue; but. if we reject the proffered deliverance, it degenerates into blind and stupid despair." "I am not insensible," replied the king of the Vandals, "how kind and rational is your advice. But I cannot persuade myself to become the slave of an unjust enemy, who has deserved my implacable hatred. *Him* I had never injured either by word or deed; yet he has sent against me, I know not from whence, a certain Belisarius, who has cast me headlong from the throne into this abyss of misery. Justinian is a man; he is a prince; does he not dread for himself a similar reverse of fortune? I can write no more; my grief oppresses me. Send me, I beseech you, my dear Pharas, send me a lyre,[34] a sponge, and a loaf of bread." From the Vandal messenger, Pharas was informed of the

[33] Shaw (Travels, p. 220) most accurately represents the manners of the Bedoweens and Kabyles, the last of whom, by their language, are the remnant of the Moors; yet how changed—how civilised are these modern savages!—provisions are plenty among them, and bread is common.

[34] By Procopius it is styled a *lyre;* perhaps *harp* would have been more national. The instruments of music are thus distinguished by Venantius Fortunatus:—

Romanusque *lyrâ* tibi plaudat, Barbarus *harpâ.*

motives of this singular request. It was long since the king of Africa
had tasted bread, a defluxion had fallen on his eyes, the effect of fatigue
or incessant weeping, and he wished to solace the melancholy hours by
singing to the lyre the sad story of his own misfortunes. The humanity
of Pharas was moved: he sent the three extraordinary gifts; but even
his humanity prompted him to redouble the vigilance of his guard, that
he might sooner compel his prisoner to embrace a resolution advantageous to the Romans, but salutary to himself. The obstinacy of
Gelimer at length yielded to reason and necessity; the solemn assurances of safety and honourable treatment were ratified in the emperor's
name by the ambassador of Belisarius, and the king of the Vandals descended from the mountain. The first public interview was in one of
the suburbs of Carthage; and when the royal captive accosted his
conqueror, he burst into a fit of laughter. The crowd might naturally
believe that extreme grief had deprived Gelimer of his senses; but in
this mournful state unseasonable mirth insinuated to more intelligent
observers that the vain and transitory scenes of human greatness are
unworthy of a serious thought.[35]

Their contempt was soon justified by a new example of a vulgar
truth—that flattery adheres to power, and envy to superior merit. The
chiefs of the Roman army presumed to think themselves the rivals of
an hero. Their private despatches maliciously affirmed that the conqueror of Africa, strong in his reputation and the public love, conspired
to seat himself on the throne of the Vandals. Justinian listened with
too patient an ear; and his silence was the result of jealousy rather than
of confidence. An honourable alternative, of remaining in the province
or of returning to the capital, was indeed submitted to the discretion of
Belisarius; but he wisely concluded, from intercepted letters and the
knowledge of his sovereign's temper, that he must either resign his head,
erect his standard, or confound his enemies by his presence and submission. Innocence and courage decided his choice: his guards, captives, and treasures were diligently embarked; and so prosperous was
the navigation, that his arrival at Constantinople preceded any certain
account of his departure from the port of Carthage. Such unsuspecting
loyalty removed the apprehensions of Justinian: envy was silenced and
inflamed by the public gratitude; and the third Africanus obtained the
honours of a triumph, a ceremony which the city of Constantine had
never seen, and which ancient Rome, since the reign of Tiberius, had
reserved for the *auspicious* arms of the Cæsars.[36] From the palace of

[35] Herodotus elegantly describes the strange effects of grief in another royal
captive, Psammetichus [Psammenitus] of Egypt, who wept at the lesser and
was silent at the greatest of his calamities (l. iii. c. 14). In the interview
of Paulus Æmilius and Perses, Belisarius might study his part: but it is
probable that he never read either Livy or Plutarch; and it is certain that
his generosity did not need a tutor.

[36] After the title of *imperator* had lost the old military sense, and the Roman
auspices were abolished by Christianity (see La Blèterie, Mém. de l'Académie,
tom. xxi. p. 302-332), a triumph might be given with less inconsistency to a
private general.

Belisarius the procession was conducted through the principal streets to the hippodrome; and this memorable day seemed to avenge the injuries of Genseric and to expiate the shame of the Romans. The wealth of nations was displayed, the trophies of martial or effeminate luxury; rich armour, golden thrones, and the chariots of state which had been used by the Vandal queen; the massy furniture of the royal banquet, the splendour of precious stones, the elegant forms of statues and vases, the more substantial treasure of gold, and the holy vessels of the Jewish temple, which, after their long peregrination, were respectfully deposited in the Christian church of Jerusalem. A long train of the noblest Vandals reluctantly exposed their lofty stature and manly countenance. Gelimer slowly advanced: he was clad in a purple robe, and still maintained the majesty of a king. Not a tear escaped from his eyes, not a sigh was heard; but his pride or piety derived some secret consolation from the words of Solomon,[37] which he repeatedly pronounced, VANITY! VANITY! ALL IS VANITY! Instead of ascending a triumphal car drawn by four horses or elephants, the modest conqueror marched on foot at the head of his brave companions: his prudence might decline an honour too conspicuous for a subject; and his magnanimity might justly disdain what had been so often sullied by the vilest of tyrants. The glorious procession entered the gate of the hippodrome; was saluted by the acclamations of the senate and people; and halted before the throne where Justinian and Theodora were seated to receive the homage of the captive monarch and the victorious hero. They both performed the customary adoration; and falling prostrate on the ground, respectfully touched the footstool of a prince who had not unsheathed his sword, and of a prostitute who had danced on the theatre: some gentle violence was used to bend the stubborn spirit of the grandson of Genseric; and however trained to servitude, the genius of Belisarius must have secretly rebelled. He was immediately declared consul for the ensuing year, and the day of his inauguration resembled the pomp of a second triumph: his curule chair was borne aloft on the shoulders of captive Vandals; and the spoils of war, gold cups, and rich girdles, were profusely scattered among the populace.

But the purest reward of Belisarius was in the faithful execution of a treaty for which his honour had been pledged to the king of the Vandals. The religious scruples of Gelimer, who adhered to the Arian heresy, were incompatible with the dignity of senator or patrician: but he received from the emperor an ample estate in the province of Galatia, where the abdicated monarch retired, with his family and friends, to a life of peace, of affluence, and perhaps of content.[38] The daughters

[37] If the Ecclesiastes be truly a work of Solomon, and not, like Prior's poem, a pious and moral composition of more recent times, in his name, and on the subject of his repentance. The latter is the opinion of the learned and free-spirited Grotius (Opp. Theolog. tom. i. p. 258); and indeed the Ecclesiastes and Proverbs display a larger compass of thought and experience than seem to belong either to a Jew or a king.

[38] In the Bélisaire of Marmontel the king and the conqueror of Africa meet, sup, and converse, without recollecting each other. It is surely a fault

of Hilderic were entertained with the respectful tenderness due to their age and misfortune; and Justinian and Theodora accepted the honour of educating and enriching the female descendants of the great Theodosius. The bravest of the Vandal youth were distributed into five squadrons of cavalry, which adopted the name of their benefactor, and supported in the Persian wars the glory of their ancestors. But these rare exceptions, the reward of birth or valour, are insufficient to explain the fate of a nation whose numbers, before a short and bloodless war, amounted to more than six hundred thousand persons. After the exile of their king and nobles, the servile crowd might purchase their safety by adjuring their character, religion, and language; and their degenerate posterity would be insensibly mingled with the common herd of African subjects. Yet even in the present age, and in the heart of the Moorish tribes, a curious traveller has discovered the white complexion and long flaxen hair of a northern race;[39] and it was formerly believed that the boldest of the Vandals fled beyond the power, or even the knowledge, of the Romans, to enjoy their solitary freedom on the shores of the Atlantic ocean.[40] Africa had been their empire, it became their prison; nor could they entertain a hope, or even a wish, of returning to the banks of the Elbe, where their brethren, of a spirit less adventurous, still wandered in their native forests. It was impossible for cowards to surmount the barriers of unknown seas and hostile barbarians; it was impossible for brave men to expose their nakedness and defeat before the eyes of their countrymen, to describe the kingdoms which they had lost, and to claim a share of the humble inheritance which, in a happier hour, they had almost unanimously renounced.[41] In the country between the Elbe and the Oder several populous villages of Lusatia are inhabited by the Vandals: they still preserve their language, their customs, and the purity of their blood; support, with some impatience, the Saxon or Prussian yoke; and serve, with secret and voluntary allegiance, the descendant of their ancient kings, who in his garb and present fortune is confounded with the meanest of his vassals.[42] The name and

of that romance, that not only the hero, but all to whom he had been so conspicuously known, appear to have lost their eyes or their memory.

[39] Shaw, p. 59. Yet since Procopius (l. ii. c. 13 [tom. i. p. 466, ed. Bonn]) speaks of a people of Mount Atlas, as already distinguished by white bodies and yellow hair, the phenomenon (which is likewise visible in the Andes of Peru, Buffon, tom. iii. p. 504) may naturally be ascribed to the elevation of the ground and the temperature of the air.

[40] The geographer of Ravenna (l. iii. c. xi. p. 129, 130, 131; Paris, 1688) describes the Mauritania *Gaditana* (opposite to Cadiz), ubi gens Vandalorum, a Belisario devicta in Africâ, fugit, et nunquam comparuit.

[41] A single voice had protested, and Genseric dismissed, without a formal answer, the Vandals of Germany: but those of Africa derided his prudence, and affected to despise the poverty of their forests (Procopius, Vandal. l. i. c. 22).

[42] From the mouth of the great Elector (in 1687) Tollius describes the secret royalty and rebellious spirit of the Vandals of Brandenburgh, who could muster five or six thousand soldiers, who had procured some cannon, etc. (Itinerar. Hungar. p. 42, apud Dubos, Hist. de la Monarchie Françoise,

situation of this unhappy people might indicate their descent from one common stock with the conquerors of Africa. But the use of a Sclavonian dialect more clearly represents them as the last remnant of the new colonies who succeeded to the genuine Vandals, already scattered or destroyed in the age of Procopius.[43]

If Belisarius had been tempted to hesitate in his allegiance, he might have urged, even against the emperor himself, the indispensable duty of saving Africa from an enemy more barbarous than the Vandals. The origin of the Moors is involved in darkness: they were ignorant of the use of letters.[44] Their limits cannot be precisely defined; a boundless continent was open to the Libyan shepherds; the change of seasons and pastures regulated their motions; and their rude huts and slender furniture were transported with the same ease as their arms, their families, and their cattle, which consisted of sheep, oxen, and camels.[45] During the vigour of the Roman power they observed a respectful distance from Carthage and the sea-shore; under the feeble reign of the Vandals they invaded the cities of Numidia, occupied the sea-coast from Tangier to Cæsarea, and pitched their camps, with impunity, in the fertile province of Pyzacium. The formidable strength and artful conduct of Belisarius secured the neutrality of the Moorish princes, whose vanity aspired to receive in the emperor's name the ensigns of their regal dignity.[46] They were astonished by the rapid event, and trembled in the presence of their conqueror. But his approaching departure soon relieved the apprehensions of a savage and superstitious people; the number of their wives allowed them to disregard the safety of their infant hostages; and when the Roman general hoisted sail in the port of Carthage, he heard the cries and almost beheld the flames of the desolated province. Yet he persisted in his resolution; and leaving only a part of his guards to reinforce the feeble garrisons, he intrusted the command of Africa to the eunuch Solomon,[47] who proved himself not unworthy to be the

tom. i. p. 182, 183). The veracity, not of the elector, but of Tollius himself, may justly be suspected.

[43] Procopius (l. i. c. 22 [tom. i. p. 400, ed. Bonn]) was in total darkness— οὔτε μνήμη τις οὔτε ὄνομα ἐς ἐμὲ σωζέται. Under the reign of Dagobert (A.D. 630) the Sclavonian tribes of the Sorbi and Venedi already bordered on Thuringia (Mascou, Hist. of the Germans, xv. 3, 4, 5).

[44] Sallust represents the Moors as a remnant of the army of Heracles (de Bell. Jugurth. c. 21 [18], and Procopius (Vandal. l. ii. c. 10 [tom. ii. p. 450, ed. Bonn]) as the posterity of the Cananæans who fled from the robber Joshua (λῃστής). He quotes two columns, with a Phœnician inscription. I believe in the columns—I doubt the inscription—and I reject the pedigree.

[45] Virgil (Georgic. iii. 339) and Pomponius Mela (i. 8) describe the wandering life of the African shepherds, similar to that of the Arabs and Tartars; and Shaw (p. 222) is the best commentator on the poet and the geographer.

[46] The customary gifts were a sceptre, a crown or cap, a white cloak, a figured tunic, and shoes, all adorned with gold and silver; nor were these precious metals less acceptable in the shape of coin (Procop. Vandal. l. i. c. 25).

[47] See the African government and warfare of Solomon in Procopius (Vandal. l. ii. c. 10, 11, 12, 13, 19, 20). He was recalled and again restored; and

successor of Belisarius. In the first invasion some detachments, with two officers of merit, were surprised and intercepted; but Solomon speedily assembled his troops, marched from Carthage into the heart of the country, and in two great battles destroyed sixty thousand of the barbarians. The Moors depended on their multitude, their swiftness, and their inaccessible mountains; and the aspect and smell of their camels are said to have produced some confusion in the Roman cav. alry.[48] But as soon as they were commanded to dismount, they derided this contemptible obstacle: as soon as the columns ascended the hills, the naked and disorderly crowd was dazzled by glittering arms and regular evolutions; and the menace of their female prophets was repeatedly fulfilled, that the Moors should be discomfited by a *beardless* antagonist. The victorious eunuch advanced thirteen days' journey from Carthage to besiege Mount Aurasius,[49] the citadel, and at the same time the garden, of Numidia. That range of hills, a branch of the great Atlas, contains, within a circumference of one hundred and twenty miles, a rare variety of soil and climate; the intermediate valleys and elevated plains abound with rich pastures, perpetual streams, and fruits of a delicious taste and uncommon magnitude. This fair solitude is decorated with the ruins of Lambesa, a Roman city, once the seat of a legion, and the residence of forty thousand inhabitants. The Ionic temple of Æsculapius is encompassed with Moorish huts; and the cattle now graze in the midst of an amphitheatre, under the shade of Corinthian columns. A sharp perpendicular rock rises above the level of the mountain, where the African princes deposited their wives and treasure; and a proverb is familiar to the Arabs, that the man may eat fire who dares to attack the craggy cliffs and inhospitable natives of Mount Aurasius. This hardy enterprise was twice attempted by the eunuch Solomon: from the first, he retreated with some disgrace; and in the second, his patience and provisions were almost exhausted; and he must again have retired, if he had not yielded to the impetuous courage of his troops, who audaciously scaled, to the astonishment of the Moors, the mountain, the hostile camp, and the summit of the Geminian rock. A citadel was erected to secure this important conquest, and to remind the barbarians of their defeat; and as Solomon pursued his march to the west,

---

his last victory dates in the thirteenth year of Justinian (A.D. 539). An accident in his childhood had rendered him an eunuch (l. i. c. 11): the other Roman generals were amply furnished with beards, πώγωνος ἐμπιπλάμενοι (l. ii c. 8).

[48] This natural antipathy of the horse for the camel is affirmed by the ancients (Xenophon. Cyropæd. l. vi. [c. 2.] p. 438; l. vii. [c. 1] p. 483, 492, edit. Hutchinson; Polyæn. Stratagem. vii. 6 [§ 6]; Plin. Hist. Nat. viii. 26; Ælian de Natur. Animal. l. iii. c. 7) ; but it is disproved by daily experience, and derided by the best judges, the Orientals (Voyage d'Olearius, p. 553).

[49] Procopius is the first who describes Mount Aurasius (Vandal. l. ii. c. 13; De Ædific. l. vi. c. 7). He may be compared with Leo Africanus (dell' Africa, parte v. in Ramusio, tom. i. fol. 77, recto), Marmol (tom. ii. p. 430), and Shaw (p. 56-59).

the long-lost province of Mauritanian Sitifi was again annexed to the Roman empire. The Moorish war continued several years after the departure of Belisarius; but the laurels which he resigned to a faithful lieutenant may be justly ascribed to his own triumph.

The experience of past faults, which may sometimes correct the mature age of an individual, is seldom profitable to the successive generations of mankind. The nations of antiquity, careless of each other's safety, were separately vanquished and enslaved by the Romans. This awful lesson might have instructed the barbarians of the West to oppose, with timely counsels and confederate arms, the unbounded ambition of Justinian. Yet the same error was repeated, the same consequences were felt, and the Goths, both of Italy and Spain, insensible of their approaching danger, beheld with indifference, and even with joy, the rapid downfall of the Vandals. After the failure of the royal line, Theudes, a valiant and powerful chief, ascended the throne of Spain, which he had formerly administered in the name of Theodoric and his infant grandson. Under his command the Visigoths besieged the fortress of Ceuta, on the African coast; but, while they spent the Sabbath-day in peace and devotion, the pious security of their camp was invaded by a sally from the town, and the king himself, with some difficulty and danger, escaped from the hands of a sacrilegious enemy.[50] It was not long before his pride and resentment were gratified by a suppliant embassy from the unfortunate Gelimer, who implored, in his distress, the aid of the Spanish monarch. But instead of sacrificing these unworthy passions to the dictates of generosity and prudence, Theudes amused the ambassadors till he was secretly informed of the loss of Carthage, and then dismissed them, with obscure and contemptuous advice, to seek in their native country a true knowledge of the state of the Vandals.[51] The long continuance of the Italian war delayed the punishment of the Visigoths, and the eyes of Theudes were closed before they tasted the fruits of his mistaken policy. After his death the sceptre of Spain was disputed by a civil war. The weaker candidate solicited the protection of Justinian, and ambitiously subscribed a treaty of alliance which deeply wounded the independence and happiness of his country. Several cities, both on the ocean and the Mediterranean, were ceded to the Roman troops, who afterwards refused to evacuate those pledges, as it should seem, either of safety or payment; and as they were fortified by perpetual supplies from Africa, they maintained their impregnable stations for the mischievous purpose of inflaming the civil and religious factions of the barbarians. Seventy years elapsed before this painful thorn could be extirpated from the bosom of the monarchy; and as long as the emperors retained any share of these remote and useless

---

[50] Isidor. Chron. p. 722, edit. Grot. Mariana, Hist. Hispan. l. v. c. 8, p. 173. Yet, according to Isidore, the siege of Ceuta and the death of Theudes happened, A. Æ. H. 586-A.D. 548; and the place was defended, not by the Vandals, but by the Romans.

[51] Procopius, Vandal. l. i. c. 24.

possessions, their vanity might number Spain in the list of their provinces, and the successors of Alaric in the rank of their vassals.[52]

The error of the Goths who reigned in Italy was less excusable than that of their Spanish brethren, and their punishment was still more immediate and terrible. From a motive of private revenge, they enabled their most dangerous enemy to destroy their most valuable ally. A sister of the great Theodoric had been given in marriage to Thrasimond the African king:[53] on this occasion the fortress of Lilybæum,[54] in Sicily, was resigned to the Vandals, and the princess Amalafrida was attended by a martial train of one thousand nobles and five thousand Gothic soldiers, who signalised their valour in the Moorish wars. Their merit was over-rated by themselves, and perhaps neglected by the Vandals: they viewed the country with envy, and the conquerors with disdain; but their real or fictitious conspiracy was prevented by a massacre; the Goths were oppressed, and the captivity of Amalafrida was soon followed by her secret and suspicious death. The eloquent pen of Cassiodorus was employed to reproach the Vandal court with the cruel violation of every social and public duty; but the vengeance which he threatened in the name of his sovereign might be derided with impunity as long as Africa was protected by the sea, and the Goths were destitute of a navy. In the blind impotence of grief and indignation they joyfully saluted the approach of the Romans, entertained the fleet of Belisarius in the ports of Sicily, and were speedily delighted or alarmed by the surprising intelligence that their revenge was executed beyond the measure of their hopes, or perhaps of their wishes. To their friendship the emperor was indebted for the kingdom of Africa, and the Goths might reasonably think that they were entitled to resume the possession of a barren rock, so recently separated as a nuptial gift from the island of Sicily. They were soon undeceived by the haughty mandate of Belisarius, which excited their tardy and unavailing repentance. " The city and promontory of Lilybæum," said the Roman general, " belonged to the Vandals, and I claim them by the right of conquest. Your submission may deserve the favour of the emperor; your obstinacy will provoke his displeasure, and must kindle a war that can terminate only in your utter ruin. If you compel us to take up arms, we shall contend, not to regain the possession of a single city, but to deprive you of all the provinces which you unjustly withhold from their lawful sovereign." A nation of two hundred thousand soldiers

[52] See the original Chronicle of Isidore and the fifth and sixth books of the History of Spain by Mariana. The Romans were finally expelled by Suintila king of the Visigoths (A.D. 621-626), after their re-union to the catholic church.

[53] See the marriage and fate of Amalafrida in Procopius (Vandal. l. i. c. 8, 9), and in Cassiodorus (Var. ix. 1) the expostulation of her royal brother. Compare likewise the Chronicle of Victor Tunnunensis.

[54] Lilybæum was built by the Carthaginians, Olymp. xcv. 4; and in the first Punic war a strong situation and excellent harbour rendered that place an important object to both nations.

might have smiled at the vain menace of Justinian and his lieutenant; but a spirit of discord and disaffection prevailed in Italy, and the Goths supported with reluctance the indignity of a female reign.[55]

The birth of Amalasontha, the regent and queen of Italy,[56] united the two most illustrious families of the barbarians. Her mother, the sister of Clovis, was descended from the long-haired kings of the *Merovingian* race,[57] and the regal succession of the *Amali* was illustrated in the eleventh generation by her father, the great Theodoric, whose merit might have ennobled a plebeian origin. The sex of his daughter excluded her from the Gothic throne; but his vigilant tenderness for his family and his people discovered the last heir of the royal line, whose ancestors had taken refuge in Spain, and the fortunate Eutharic was suddenly exalted to the rank of a consul and a prince. He enjoyed only a short time the charms of Amalasontha and the hopes of the succession; and his widow, after the death of her husband and father, was left the guardian of her son Athalaric and the kingdom of Italy. At the age of about twenty-eight years, the endowments of her mind and person had attained their perfect maturity. Her beauty, which, in the apprehension of Theodora herself, might have disputed the conquest of an emperor, was animated by manly sense, activity, and resolution. Education and experience had cultivated her talents; her philosophic studies were exempt from vanity; and, though she expressed herself with equal elegance and ease in the Greek, the Latin, and the Gothic tongue, the daughter of Theodoric maintained in her counsels a discreet and impenetrable silence. By a faithful imitation of the virtues, she revived the prosperity of his reign; while she strove, with pious care, to expiate the faults and to obliterate the darker memory of his declining age. The children of Boethius and Symmachus were restored to their paternal inheritance; her extreme lenity never consented to inflict any corporal or pecuniary penalties on her Roman subjects; and she generously despised the clamours of the Goths, who, at the end of forty years, still considered the people of Italy as their slaves or their enemies. Her salutary measures were directed by the wisdom and celebrated by the eloquence of Cassiodorus; she solicited and deserved the friendship of the emperor; and the kingdoms of Europe respected, both in peace and war, the majesty of the Gothic throne. But the future happiness of the queen of Italy depended on the education of her son, who was destined, by his birth, to support the different and almost incompatible

[55] Compare the different passages of Procopius (Vandal. 1. ii. c. 5; Gothic. l. i. c. 3).

[56] For the reign and character of Amalasontha see Procopius (Gothic. 1. i. c. 2, 3, 4, and Anecdot. c. 16, with the Notes of Alemannus), Cassiodorus (Var. viii. ix. x. and xi. 1), and Jornandes (de Rebus Geticis, c. 59, and De Successione Regnorum, in Muratori, tom. i. p. 241).

[57] The marriage of Theodoric with Audefleda, the sister of Clovis, may be placed in the year 495, soon after the conquest of Italy (De Buat, Hist. des Peuples, tom. ix. p. 213). The nuptials of Eutharic and Amalasontha were celebrated in 515 (Cassiodor. in Chron. p. 453 [tom. i. p. 395, ed. Rotom.]).

characters of the chief of a barbarian camp and the first magistrate of a civilised nation. From the age of ten years [58] Athalaric was diligently instructed in the arts and sciences either useful or ornamental for a Roman prince, and three venerable Goths were chosen to instil the principles of honour and virtue into the mind of their young king. But the pupil who is insensible of the benefits must abhor the restraints of education; and the solicitude of the queen, which affection rendered anxious and severe, offended the untractable nature of her son and his subjects. On a solemn festival, when the Goths were assembled in the palace of Ravenna, the royal youth escaped from his mother's apartment, and, with tears of pride and anger, complained of a blow which his stubborn disobedience had provoked her to inflict. The barbarians resented the indignity which had been offered to their king, accused the regent of conspiring against his life and crown, and imperiously demanded that the grandson of Theodoric should be rescued from the dastardly discipline of women and pedants, and educated, like a valiant Goth, in the society of his equals and the glorious ignorance of his ancestors. To this rude clamour, importunately urged as the voice of the nation, Amalasontha was compelled to yield her reason and the dearest wishes of her heart. The king of Italy was abandoned to wine, to women, and to rustic sports; and the indiscreet contempt of the ungrateful youth betrayed the mischievous designs of his favourites and her enemies. Encompassed with domestic foes, she entered into a secret negotiation with the emperor Justinian, obtained the assurance of a friendly reception, and had actually deposited at Dyrrachium, in Epirus, a treasure of forty thousand pounds of gold. Happy would it have been for her fame and safety if she had calmly retired from barbarous faction to the peace and splendour of Constantinople. But the mind of Amalasontha was inflamed by ambition and revenge; and while her ships lay at anchor in the port, she waited for the success of a crime which her passions excused or applauded as an act of justice. Three of the most dangerous malcontents had been separately removed, under the pretence of trust and command, to the frontiers of Italy: they were assassinated by her private emissaries; and the blood of these noble Goths rendered the queen-mother absolute in the court of Ravenna, and justly odious to a free people. But if she had lamented the disorders of her son, she soon wept his irreparable loss; and the death of Athalaric, who, at the age of sixteen, was consumed by premature intemperance, left her destitute of any firm support or legal authority. Instead of submitting to the laws of her country, which held as a fundamental maxim that the succession could never pass from the lance to the distaff, the daughter of Theodoric conceived the impracticable design of sharing, with one of her cousins, the regal title, and of

[58] At the death of Theodoric his grandson Athalaric is described by Procopius as a boy about eight years old—ὀκτὼ γεγονὼς ἔτη. Cassiodorus, with authority and reason, adds two years to his age—infantulum adhuc vix decennem.

reserving in her own hands the substance of supreme power. He received the proposal with profound respect and affected gratitude; and the eloquent Cassiodorus announced to the senate and the emperor that Amalasontha and Theodatus had ascended the throne of Italy. His birth (for his mother was the sister of Theodoric) might be considered as an imperfect title; and the choice of Amalasontha was more strongly directed by her contempt of his avarice and pusillanimity, which had deprived him of the love of the Italians and the esteem of the barbarians. But Theodatus was exasperated by the contempt which he deserved: her justice had repressed and reproached the oppression which he exercised against his Tuscan neighbours; and the principal Goths, united by common guilt and resentment, conspired to instigate his slow and timid disposition. The letters of congratulation were scarcely dispatched before the queen of Italy was imprisoned in a small island of the lake of Bolsena,[59] where, after a short confinement, she was strangled in the bath, by the order or with the connivance of the new king, who instructed his turbulent subjects to shed the blood of their sovereigns.

Justinian beheld with joy the dissensions of the Goths, and the mediation of an ally concealed and promoted the ambitious views of the conqueror. His ambassadors, in their public audience, demanded the fortress of Lilybæum, ten barbarian fugitives, and a just compensation for the pillage of a small town on the Illyrian borders; but they secretly negotiated with Theodatus to betray the province of Tuscany, and tempted Amalasontha to extricate herself from danger and perplexity by a free surrender of the kingdom of Italy. A false and servile epistle was subscribed by the reluctant hand of the captive queen; but the confession of the Roman senators who were sent to Constantinople revealed the truth of her deplorable situation, and Justinian, by the voice of a new ambassador, most powerfully interceded for her life and liberty. Yet the secret instructions of the same minister were adapted to serve the cruel jealousy of Theodora, who dreaded the presence and superior charms of a rival: he prompted, with artful and ambiguous hints, the execution of a crime so useful to the Romans,[60] received the intelligence of her death with grief and indignation, and denounced, in his master's name, immortal war against the perfidious assassin. In Italy, as well as in Africa, the guilt of a usurper appeared to justify the arms of Justinian; but the forces which he prepared were insuffi-

---

[59] The lake, from the neighbouring towns of Etruria, was styled either Vulsiniensis (now of Bolsena) or Tarquiniensis. It is surrounded with white rocks, and stored with fish and wild-fowl. The younger Pliny (Epist. ii. 96 [95]) celebrates two woody islands that floated on its waters: if a fable, how credulous the ancients! If a fact, how careless the moderns! Yet, since Pliny, the island may have been fixed by new and gradual accessions.

[60] Yet Procopius discredits his own evidence (Anecdot. c. 16), by confessing that in his public history he had not spoken the truth. See the Epistles from queen Gundelina to the empress Theodora (Var. x. 20, 21, 23, and observe a suspicious word, de illâ personâ, etc.), with the elaborate Commentary of Buat (tom, x. p. 177-185).

cient for the subversion of a mighty kingdom, if their feeble numbers
had not been multiplied by the name, the spirit, and the conduct of a
hero. A chosen troop of guards, who served on horseback and were
armed with lances and bucklers, attended the person of Belisarius;
his cavalry was composed of two hundred Huns, three hundred Moors,
and four thousand *confederates,* and the infantry consisted only of
three thousand Isaurians. Steering the same course as in his former
expedition, the Roman consul cast anchor before Catana, in Sicily, to
survey the strength of the island, and to decide whether he should
attempt the conquest or peaceably pursue his voyage for the African
coast. He found a fruitful land and a friendly people. Notwithstanding the decay of agriculture, Sicily still supplied the granaries of Rome;
the farmers were graciously exempted from the oppression of military
quarters; and the Goths, who trusted the defence of the island to the
inhabitants, had some reason to complain that their confidence was
ungratefully betrayed. Instead of soliciting and expecting the aid of
the king of Italy, they yielded to the first summons a cheerful obedience; and this province, the first fruits of the Punic wars, was again,
after a long separation, united to the Roman empire.[61] The Gothic
garrison of Palermo, which alone attempted to resist, was reduced, after
a short siege, by a singular stratagem. Belisarius introduced his ships
into the deepest recess of the harbour; their boats were laboriously
hoisted with ropes and pulleys to the top-mast head, and he filled them
with archers, who, from that superior station, commanded the ramparts of the city. After this easy though successful campaign, the conqueror entered Syracuse in triumph, at the head of his victorious bands,
distributing gold medals to the people, on the day which so gloriously
terminated the year of the consulship. He passed the winter season in
the palace of ancient kings, amidst the ruins of a Grecian colony which
once extended to a circumference of two-and-twenty miles;[62] but in the
spring, about the festival of Easter, the prosecution of his designs was
interrupted by a dangerous revolt of the African forces. Carthage
was saved by the presence of Belisarius, who suddenly landed with a
thousand guards. Two thousand soldiers of doubtful faith returned
to the standard of their old commander, and he marched, without hesitation, above fifty miles, to seek an enemy whom he affected to pity
and despise. Eight thousand rebels trembled at his approach; they
were routed at the first onset by the dexterity of their master, and this
ignoble victory would have restored the peace of Africa, if the conqueror
had not been hastily recalled to Sicily to appease a sedition which was

[61] For the conquest of Sicily compare the narrative of Procopius with the
complaints of Totila (Gothic. l. i. c. 5; l. iii. c. 16). The Gothic queen had
lately relieved that thankless island (Var. ix. 10, 11).
[62] The ancient magnitude and splendour of the five quarters of Syracuse
are delineated by Cicero (in Varrem, actio ii. l. iv. c. 52, 53), Strabo (l. vi.
p. 415 [p. 270, ed. Casaub.]), and D'Orville Sicula (tom. ii. p. 174-202). The
new city, restored by Augustus, shrunk towards the island.

kindled during his absence in his own camp.[63] Disorder and disobedience were the common malady of the times: the genius to command and
the virtue to obey resided only in the mind of Belisarius.

Although Theodatus descended from a race of heroes, he was ignorant
of the art and averse to the dangers of war. Although he had studied
the writings of Plato and Tully, philosophy was incapable of purifying
his mind from the basest passions, avarice and fear. He had purchased
a sceptre by ingratitude and murder: at the first menace of an enemy
he degraded his own majesty, and that of a nation which already disdained their unworthy sovereign. Astonished by the recent example
of Gelimer, he saw himself dragged in chains through the streets of
Constantinople: the terrors which Belisarius inspired were heightened
by the eloquence of Peter, the Byzantine ambassador; and that bold
and subtle advocate persuaded him to sign a treaty too ignominious to
become the foundation of a lasting peace. It was stipulated that in
the acclamations of the Roman people the name of the emperor should
be always proclaimed before that of the Gothic king; and that, as often
as the statue of Theodatus was erected in brass or marble, the divine
image of Justinian should be placed on its right hand. Instead of con-
ferring, the king of Italy was reduced to solicit, the honours of the
senate; and the consent of the emperor was made indispensable before
he could execute, against a priest or senator, the sentence either of death
or confiscation. The feeble monarch resigned the possession of Sicily;
offered, as the annual mark of his dependence, a crown of gold of the
weight of three hundred pounds; and promised to supply, at the requisition of his sovereign, three thousand Gothic auxiliaries for the service of
the empire. Satisfied with these extraordinary concessions, the successful agent of Justinian hastened his journey to Constantinople; but
no sooner had he reached the Alban villa [64] than he was recalled by the
anxiety of Theodatus; and the dialogue which passed between the king
and the ambassador deserves to be represented in its original simplicity. "Are you of opinion that the emperor will ratify this treaty?
Perhaps. If he refuses, what consequence will ensue? *War.* Will such
a war be just or reasonable? *Most assuredly: every one should act
according to his character.* What is your meaning? *You are a philosopher—Justinian is emperor of the Romans: it would ill become the
disciple of Plato to shed the blood of thousands in his private quarrel:
the successor of Augustus should vindicate his rights, and recover by
arms the ancient provinces of his empire.*" This reasoning might not

---

[63] Procopius (Vandal. l. ii. c. 14, 15) so clearly relates the return of Belisarius into Sicily (p. 146, edit. Hoeschelii [tom. i. p. 481, ed. Bonn]), that I
am astonished at the strange misapprehension and reproaches of a learned
critic (Œuvres de la Mothe le Vayer, tom. viii. p. 162, 163).

[64] The ancient Alba was ruined in the first age of Rome. On the same
spot, or at least in the neighbourhood, successively arose, 1. The villa of
Pompey, etc. 2. A camp of the Prætorian cohorts. 3. The modern episcopal
city of Albanum or Albano (Procop. Goth. l. ii. c. 4. Cluver. Ital. Antiq.
tom. ii. p. 914).

convince, but it was sufficient to alarm and subdue the weakness of Theodatus; and he soon descended to his last offer, that for the poor equivalent of a pension of forty-eight thousand pounds sterling he would resign the kingdom of the Goths and Italians, and spend the remainder of his days in the innocent pleasures of philosophy and agriculture. Both treaties were intrusted to the hands of the ambassador, on the frail security of an oath not to produce the second till the first had been positively rejected. The event may be easily foreseen: Justinian required and accepted the abdication of the Gothic king. His indefatigable agent returned from Constantinople to Ravenna with ample instructions, and a fair epistle, which praised the wisdom and generosity of the royal philosopher, granted his pension, with the assurance of such honours as a subject and a catholic might enjoy, and wisely referred the final execution of the treaty to the presence and authority of Belisarius. But in the interval of suspense two Roman generals, who had entered the province of Dalmatia, were defeated and slain by the Gothic troops. From blind and abject despair, Theodatus capriciously rose to groundless and fatal presumption,[65] and dared to receive, with menace and contempt, the ambassador of Justinian, who claimed his promise, solicited the allegiance of his subjects, and boldly asserted the inviolable privilege of his own character. The march of Belisarius dispelled this visionary pride; and as the first campaign[66] was employed in the reduction of Sicily, the invasion of Italy is applied by Procopius to the second year of the GOTHIC WAR.[67]

After Belisarius had left sufficient garrisons in Palermo and Syracuse, he embarked his troops at Messina, and landed them, without resistance, on the opposite shores of Rhegium. A Gothic prince, who had married the daughter of Theodatus, was stationed with an army to guard the entrance of Italy; but he imitated without scruple the example of a sovereign faithless to his public and private duties. The perfidious Ebermor deserted with his followers to the Roman camp, and was dismissed to enjoy the servile honours of the Byzantine court.[68] From

---

[65] A Sibylline oracle was ready to pronounce—Africâ captâ *mundus* cum nato peribit; a sentence of portentous ambiguity (Gothic. l. i. c. 7), which has been published in unknown characters by Opsopæus, an editor of the oracles. The Père Maltret has promised a commentary; but all his promises have been vain and fruitless.

[66] In his chronology, imitated in some degree from Thucydides, Procopius begins each spring the years of Justinian and of the Gothic war; and his first era coincides with the first of April, 535, and not 536, according to the Annals of Baronius (Pagi Crit. tom. ii. p. 555, who is followed by Muratori and the editors of Sigonius). Yet in some passages we are at a loss to reconcile the dates of Procopius with himself, and with the Chronicle of Marcellinus.

[67] The series of the first Gothic war is represented by Procopius (l. i. c. 5-29, l. ii. c. 1-30, l. iii. c. 1) till the captivity of Vitiges. With the aid of Sigonius (Opp. tom. i. de Imp. Occident. l. xvii., xviii.) and Muratori (Annali d'Italia, tom. v.), I have gleaned some few additional facts.

[68] Iornandes, de Rebus Geticis, c. 60, p. 702, edit. Grot., and tom. i. p. 221, Muratori. de Success. Regn. [ib.] p. 241.

Rhegium to Naples the fleet and army of Belisarius, almost always in view of each other, advanced near three hundred miles along the sea-coast. The people of Bruttium, Lucania, and Campania, who abhorred the name and religion of the Goths, embraced the specious excuse that their ruined walls were incapable of defence: the soldiers paid a just equivalent for a plentiful market; and curiosity alone interrupted the peaceful occupations of the husbandman or artificer. Naples, which has swelled to a great and populous capital, long cherished the language and manners of a Grecian colony;[69] and the choice of Virgil had ennobled this elegant retreat, which attracted the lovers of repose and study from the noise, the smoke, and the laborious opulence of Rome.[70] As soon as the place was invested by sea and land, Belisarius gave audience to the deputies of the people, who exhorted him to disregard a conquest unworthy of his arms, to seek the Gothic king in a field of battle, and, after his victory, to claim, as the sovereign of Rome, the allegiance of the dependent cities. " When I treat with my enemies," replied the Roman chief with a haughty smile, " I am more accustomed to give than to receive counsel; but I hold in one hand inevitable ruin, and in the other peace and freedom, such as Sicily now enjoys." The impatience of delay urged him to grant the most liberal terms; his honour secured their performance: but Naples was divided into two factions; and the Greek democracy was inflamed by their orators, who with much spirit and some truth represented to the multitude that the Goths would punish their defection, and that Belisarius himself must esteem their loyalty and valour. Their deliberations, however, were not perfectly free: the city was commanded by eight hundred barbarians, whose wives and children were detained at Ravenna as the pledge of their fidelity; and even the Jews, who were rich and numerous, resisted, with desperate enthusiasm, the intolerant laws of Justinian. In a much later period the circumference of Naples [71] measured only two thousand three hundred and sixty-three paces:[72] the fortifications were defended by precipices or the sea; when the aqueducts were inter-

---

[69] Nero (says Tacitus, Annal. xv. 33) Neapolim quasi Græcum urbem delegit. One hundred and fifty years afterwards, in the time of Septimius Severus, the *Hellenism* of the Neapolitans is praised by Philostratus: γένος "Ελληνες καὶ ἀστυκοί, ὅθεν καὶ τὰς σπουδὰς τῶν λόγων Ἑλληνικοί εἰσι (Icon. 1. i. p. 763, edit. Olear.).

[70] The otium of Naples is praised by the Roman poets, by Virgil, Horace, Silius Italicus, and Statius (Cluver. Ital. Ant. l. iv. p. 1149, 1150). In an elegant epistle (Silv. l. iii. 5. p. 94-98, edit. Markland) Statius undertakes the difficult task of drawing his wife from the pleasures of Rome to that calm retreat.

[71] This measure was taken by Roger I. after the conquest of Naples (A.D. 1139), which he made the capital of his new kingdom (Giannone, Istoria Civile, tom. ii. p. 169). That city, the third in Christian Europe, is now at least twelve miles in circumference (Jul. Cæsar. Capaccii Hist. Neapol. l. i. p. 47), and contains more inhabitants (350,000) in a given space than any other spot in the known world.

[72] Not geometrical, but common, paces or steps, of 22 French inches (D'Anville, Mesures Itinéraires, p. 7, 8) : the 2363 do not make an English mile.

cepted, a supply of water might be drawn from wells and fountains; and the stock of provisions was sufficient to consume the patience of the besiegers. At the end of twenty days that of Belisarius was almost exhausted, and he had reconciled himself to the disgrace of abandoning the siege, that he might march, before the winter season, against Rome and the Gothic king. But his anxiety was relieved by the bold curiosity of an Isaurian, who explored the dry channel of an aqueduct, and secretly reported that a passage might be perforated to introduce a file of armed soldiers into the heart of the city. When the work had been silently executed, the humane general risked the discovery of his secret by a last and fruitless admonition of the impending danger. In the darkness of the night four hundred Romans entered the aqueduct, raised themselves by a rope, which they fastened to an olive-tree, into the house or garden of a solitary matron, sounded their trumpets, surprised the sentinels, and gave admittance to their companions, who on all sides scaled the walls and burst open the gates of the city. Every crime which is punished by social justice was practised as the rights of war: the Huns were distinguished by cruelty and sacrilege, and Belisarius alone appeared in the streets and churches of Naples to moderate the calamities which he predicted. " The gold and silver," he repeatedly exclaimed, " are the just rewards of your valour. But spare the inhabitants; they are Christians, they are suppliants, they are now your fellow-subjects. Restore the children to their parents, the wives to their husbands; and show them by your generosity of what friends they have obstinately deprived themselves." The city was saved by the virtue and authority of its conqueror;[73] and when the Neapolitans returned to their houses, they found some consolation in the secret enjoyment of their hidden treasures. The barbarian garrison enlisted in the service of the emperor; Apulia and Calabria, delivered from the odious presence of the Goths, acknowledged his dominion; and the tusks of the Calydonian boar, which were still shown at Beneventum, are curiously described by the historian of Belisarius.[74]

The faithful soldiers and citizens of Naples had expected their deliverance from a prince who remained the inactive and almost indifferent spectator of their ruin. Theodatus secured his person within the walls of Rome, while his cavalry advanced forty miles on the Appian way, and encamped in the Pomptine marshes; which, by a canal of nineteen miles in length, had been recently drained and converted into excellent pastures.[75] But the principal forces of the Goths were dispersed in

[73] Belisarius was reproved by pope Sylverius for the massacre. He repeopled Naples, and imported colonies of African captives into Sicily, Calabria, and Apulia (Hist. Miscell. l. xvi. in Muratori, tom. i. p. 106, 107).

[74] Beneventum was built by Diomede, the nephew of Meleager (Cluver. tom. ii. p. 1195, 1196). The Calydonian hunt is a picture of savage life (Ovid, Metamorph. l. viii.). Thirty or forty heroes were leagued against a hog: the brutes (not the hog) quarrelled with a lady for the head.

[75] The *Decennovium* is strangely confounded by Cluverius (tom. ii. p. 1007) with the river Ufens. It was in truth a canal of nineteen miles, from Forum

Dalmatia, Venetia, and Gaul; and the feeble mind of their king was confounded by the unsuccessful event of a divination which seemed to presage the downfall of his empire.[76] The most abject slaves have arraigned the guilt or weakness of an unfortunate master. The character of Theodatus was rigorously scrutinised by a free and idle camp of barbarians, conscious of their privilege and power: he was declared unworthy of his race, his nation, and his throne; and their general Vitiges, whose valour had been signalised in the Illyrian war, was raised with unanimous applause on the bucklers of his companions. On the first rumour the abdicated monarch fled from the justice of his country, but he was pursued by private revenge. A Goth, whom he had injured in his love, overtook Theodatus on the Flaminian way, and, regardless of his unmanly cries, slaughtered him as he lay prostrate on the ground, like a victim (says the historian) at the foot of the altar. The choice of the people is the best and purest title to reign over them: yet such is the prejudice of every age, that Vitiges impatiently wished to return to Ravenna, where he might seize, with the reluctant hand of the daughter of Amalasontha, some faint shadow of hereditary right. A national council was immediately held, and the new monarch reconciled the impatient spirit of the barbarians to a measure of disgrace which the misconduct of his predecessor rendered wise and indispensable. The Goths consented to retreat in the presence of a victorious enemy, to delay till the next spring the operations of offensive war, to summon their scattered forces, to relinquish their distant possessions, and to trust even Rome itself to the faith of its inhabitants. Leuderis, an aged warrior, was left in the capital with four thousand soldiers; a feeble garrison, which might have seconded the zeal, though it was incapable of opposing the wishes, of the Romans. But a momentary enthusiasm of religion and patriotism was kindled in their minds. They furiously exclaimed that the apostolic throne should no longer be profaned by the triumph or toleration of Arianism; that the tombs of the Cæsars should no longer be trampled by the savages of the North; and, without reflecting that Italy must sink into a province of Constantinople, they fondly hailed the restoration of a Roman emperor as a new era of freedom and prosperity. The deputies of the pope and clergy, of the senate and people, invited the lieutenant of Justinian to accept their voluntary allegiance, and to enter the city, whose gates would be thrown open for his reception. As soon as Belisarius had fortified his new conquests, Naples and Cumæ, he advanced about twenty miles to the banks of the Vulturnus, contemplated the

Appii to Terracina, on which Horace embarked in the night. The Decennovium which is mentioned by Lucan, Dion Cassius, and Cassiodorus, has been successively ruined, restored, and obliterated (D'Anville, Analyse de l'Italie, p. 185, etc.).

[76] A Jew gratified his contempt and hatred for *all* the Christians, by enclosing three bands, each of ten hogs, and discriminated by the names of Goths, Greeks, and Romans. Of the first, almost all were found dead— almost all of the second were alive—of the third, half died, and the rest lost their bristles. No unsuitable emblem of the event.

decayed grandeur of Capua, and halted at the separation of the Latin and Appian ways. The work of the censor, after the incessant use of nine centuries, still preserved its primæval beauty, and not a flaw could be discovered in the large polished stones of which that solid though narrow road was so firmly compacted.[77] Belisarius, however, preferred the Latin way, which, at a distance from the sea and the marshes, skirted in a space of one hundred and twenty miles along the foot of the mountains. His enemies had disappeared: when he made his entrance through the Asinarian gate the garrison departed without molestation along the Flaminian way; and the city, after sixty years' servitude, was delivered from the yoke of the barbarians. Leuderis alone, from a motive of pride or discontent, refused to accompany the fugitives; and the Gothic chief, himself a trophy of the victory, was sent with the keys of Rome to the throne of the emperor Justinian.[78]

The first days, which coincided with the old Saturnalia, were devoted to mutual congratulations and the public joy; and the catholics prepared to celebrate without a rival the approaching festival of the nativity of Christ. In the familiar conversation of a hero the Romans acquired some notion of the virtues which history ascribed to their ancestors; they were edified by the apparent respect of Belisarius for the successor of St. Peter, and his rigid discipline secured in the midst of war the blessings of tranquillity and justice. They applauded the rapid success of his arms, which overran the adjacent country as far as Narni, Perusia, and Spoleto; but they trembled, the senate, the clergy, and the unwarlike people, as soon as they understood that he had resolved, and would speedily be reduced, to sustain a siege against the powers of the Gothic monarchy. The designs of Vitiges were executed during the winter season with diligence and effect. From their rustic habitations, from their distant garrisons, the Goths assembled at Ravenna for the defence of their country; and such were their numbers, that, after an army had been detached for the relief of Dalmatia, one hundred and fifty thousand fighting men marched under the royal standard. According to the degrees of rank or merit, the Gothic king distributed arms and horses, rich gifts, and liberal promises: he moved along the Flaminian way, declined the useless sieges of Perusia and Spoleto, respected the impregnable rock of Narni, and arrived within two miles of Rome at the foot of the Milvian bridge. The narrow passage was fortified with a tower, and Belisarius had computed the value of the twenty days which must be lost in the construction of another bridge.

[77] Bergier (Hist. des Grands Chemins des Romains, tom. i. p. 221-228, 440-444) examines the structure and materials, while D'Anville (Analyse de l'Italie, p. 200-213) defines the geographical line.

[78] Of the first recovery of Rome, the *year* (536) is certain, from the series of events, rather than from the corrupt, or interpolated, text of Procopius: the *month* (December) is ascertained by Evagrius (l. iv. c. 19); and the *day* (the *tenth*) may be admitted on the slight evidence of Nicephorus Callistus (l. xvii. c. 13). For this accurate chronology we are indebted to the diligence and judgment of Pagi (tom. ii. p. 559, 560).

But the consternation of the soldiers of the tower, who either fled or deserted, disappointed his hopes, and betrayed his person into the most imminent danger. At the head of one thousand horse the Roman general sallied from the Flaminian gate to mark the ground of an advantageous position, and to survey the camp of the barbarians; but while he still believed them on the other side of the Tiber, he was suddently encompassed and assaulted by their innumerable squadrons. The fate of Italy depended on his life; and the deserters pointed to the conspicuous horse, a bay [79] with a white face, which he rode on that memorable day. " Aim at the bay horse," was the universal cry. Every bow was bent, every javelin was directed, against that fatal object, and the command was repeated and obeyed by thousands who were ignorant of its real motive. The bolder barbarians advanced to the more honourable combat of swords and spears; and the praise of an enemy has graced the fall of Visandus, the standard-bearer,[80] who maintained his foremost station, till he was pierced with thirteen wounds, perhaps by the hand of Belisarius himself. The Roman general was strong, active, and dexterous: on every side he discharged his weighty and mortal strokes: his faithful guards imitated his valour and defended his person; and the Goths, after the loss of a thousand men, fled before the arms of a hero. They were rashly pursued to their camp; and the Romans, oppressed by multitudes, made a gradual and at length a precipitate retreat to the gates of the city: the gates were shut against the fugitives; and the public terror was increased by the report that Belisarius was slain. His countenance was indeed disfigured by sweat, dust, and blood; his voice was hoarse, his strength was almost exhausted; but his unconquerable spirit still remained; he imparted that spirit to his desponding companions; and their last desperate charge was felt by the flying barbarians as if a new army, vigorous and entire, had been poured from the city. The Flaminian gate was thrown open to a *real* triumph; but it was not before Belisarius had visited every post and provided for the public safety that he could be persuaded by his wife and friends to taste the needful refreshments of food and sleep. In the more improved state of the art of war a general is seldom required, or even permitted, to display the personal prowess of a soldier, and the example of Belisarius may be added to the rare examples of Henry IV., of Pyrrhus, and of Alexander.

After this first and unsuccessful trial of their enemies, the whole army of the Goths passed the Tiber, and formed the siege of the city, which

---

[79] A horse of a bay or red colour was styled φάλιος by the Greeks, balan by the barbarians, and spadix by the Romans. Honesti spadices, says Virgil (Georgic. l. iii. 81, with the Observations of Martin and Heyne). Σπαδίξ, or βαίον, signifies a branch of the palm-tree, whose name, φοινίξ, is synonymous to *red* (Aulus Gellius, ii. 26).

[80] I interpret βανδαλάριος, not as a proper name, but an office, standard-bearer, from *bandum* (vexillum), a barbaric word adopted by the Greeks and Romans (Paul Diacon. l. i. c. 20, p. 760). Grot. Nomina Gothica, p. 575. (Ducange, Gloss. Latin. tom. i. p. 539, 540.)

continued above a year, till their final departure. Whatever fancy may conceive, the severe compass of the geographer defines the circumference of Rome within a line of twelve miles and three hundred and forty-five paces; and that circumference, except in the Vatican, has invariably been the same from the triumph of Aurelian to the peaceful but obscure reign of the modern popes.[81] But in the day of her greatness the space within her walls was crowded with habitations and inhabitants, and the populous suburbs, that stretched along the public roads, were darted like so many rays from one common centre. Adversity swept away these extraneous ornaments, and left naked and desolate a considerable part even of the seven hills. Yet Rome in its present state could send into the field above thirty thousand males of a military age;[82] and, notwithstanding the want of discipline and exercise, the far greater part, inured to the hardships of poverty, might be capable of bearing arms for the defence of their country and religion. The prudence of Belisarius did not neglect this important resource. His soldiers were relieved by the zeal and diligence of the people, who watched while *they* slept, and laboured while *they* reposed: he accepted the voluntary service of the bravest and most indigent of the Roman youth; and the companies of townsmen sometimes represented in a vacant post the presence of the troops which had been drawn away to more essential duties. But his just confidence was placed in the veterans who had fought under his banner in the Persian and African wars; and although that gallant band was reduced to five thousand men, he undertook, with such contemptible numbers, to defend a circle of twelve miles against an army of one hundred and fifty thousand barbarians. In the walls of Rome, which Belisarius constructed or restored, the materials of ancient architecture may be discerned;[83] and the whole fortification was completed, except in a chasm still extant between the Pincian and Flaminian gates, which the prejudices of the Goths and Romans left under the effectual guard of St. Peter the apostle.[84]

The battlements or bastions were shaped in sharp angles; a ditch, broad and deep, protected the foot of the rampart; and the archers on the rampart were assisted by military engines; the *balista,* a powerful

[81] M. D'Anville has given, in the Memoirs of the Academy for the year 1756 (tom. xxx. p. 198-236), a plan of Rome on a smaller scale, but far more accurate, than that which he had delineated in 1738 for Rollin's history. Experience had improved his knowledge; and instead of Rossi's topography he used the new and excellent map of Nolli. Pliny's old measure of xiii must be reduced to viii miles. It is easier to alter a text than to remove hills or buildings.

[82] In the year 1709 Labat (Voyages en Italie, tom. iii. p. 218) reckoned 138,568 Christian souls, besides 8000 or 10,000 Jews—without souls?—In the year 1763 the numbers exceeded 160,000.

[83] The accurate eye of Nardini (Roma Antica, 1. i. c. viii. p. 31) could distinguish the tumultuarie opere di Belisario.

[84] The fissure and leaning in the upper part of the wall, which Procopius observed (Goth. 1. i. c. 14 [tom. ii. p. 76, ed. Bonn]), is visible to the present hour (Donat. Roma Vetus, 1. i. c. 17, p. 53, 54).

cross-bow, which darted short but massy arrows; the *onagri*, or wild asses, which, on the principle of a sling, threw stones and bullets of an enormous size.[85] A chain was drawn across the Tiber; the arches of the aqueducts were made impervious, and the mole or sepulchre of Hadrian [86] was converted, for the first time, to the uses of a citadel. That venerable structure, which contained the ashes of the Antonines, was a circular turret rising from a quadrangular basis: it was covered with the white marble of Paros, and decorated by the statues of gods and heroes; and the lover of the arts must read with a sigh that the works of Praxiteles or Lysippus were torn from their lofty pedestals, and hurled into the ditch on the heads of the besiegers.[87]   To each of his lieutenants Belisarius assigned the defence of a gate, with the wise and peremptory instruction that, whatever might be the alarm, they should steadily adhere to their respective posts, and trust their general for the safety of Rome.   The formidable host of the Goths was insufficient to embrace the ample measure of the city: of the fourteen gates, seven only were invested from the Prænestine to the Flaminian way; and Vitiges divided his troops into six camps, each of which was fortified with a ditch and rampart.   On the Tuscan side of the river a seventh encampment was formed in the field or circus of the Vatican, for the important purpose of commanding the Milvian bridge and the course of the Tiber; but they approached with devotion the adjacent church of St. Peter; and the threshold of the holy apostles was respected during the siege by a Christian enemy.   In the ages of victory, as often as the senate decreed some distant conquest, the consul denounced hostilities by unbarring, in solemn pomp, the gates of the temple of Janus.[88] Domestic war now rendered the admonition superfluous, and the ceremony was superseded by the establishment of a new religion.   But the brazen temple of Janus was left standing in the forum; of a size sufficient only to contain the statue of the god, five cubits in height, of a

[85] Lipsius (Opp. tom. iii. Poliorcet. l. iii.) was ignorant of this clear and conspicuous passage of Procopius (Goth. l. i. c. 21 [p. 104, ed. Bonn]).   The engine was named ὄναγρος, the wild ass, a calcitrando (Hen. Steph. Thesaur. Linguæ Græc. tom. ii. p. 1340, 1341, tom. iii. p. 877).   I have seen an ingenious model, contrived and executed by General Melville, which imitates or surpasses the art of antiquity.

[86] The description of this mausoleum, or mole, in Procopius (l. i. c. 22 [tom. i. p. 106, ed. Bonn]), is the first and best.   The height above the walls σχεδόν τι ἐς λίθου βολὴν.   On Nolli's great plan, the sides measure 260 English feet.

[87] Praxiteles excelled in Fauns, and that of Athens was his own masterpiece.   Rome now contains above thirty of the same character.   When the ditch of St. Angelo was cleansed under Urban VIII. the workmen found the sleeping Faun of the Barberini palace; but a leg, a thigh, and the right arm had been broken from that beautiful statue (Winckelman, Hist. de l'Art, tom. ii. p. 52, 53, tom. iii. p. 265).

[88] Procopius has given the best description of the temple of Janus [Goth. l. i. c. 25], a national deity of Latium (Heyne, Excurs. v. ad l. vii. Æneid). It was once a gate in the primitive city of Romulus and Numa (Nardini, p. 13, 256, 329).   Virgil has described the ancient rite like a poet and an antiquarian.

human form, but with two faces directed to the east and west. The double gates were likewise of brass; and a fruitless effort to turn them on their rusty hinges revealed the scandalous secret that some Romans were still attached to the superstition of their ancestors.

Eighteen days were employed by the besiegers to provide for all the instruments of attack which antiquity had invented. Fascines were prepared to fill the ditches, scaling-ladders to ascend the walls. The largest trees of the forest supplied the timbers of four battering-rams: their heads were armed with iron; they were suspended by ropes, and each of them was worked by the labour of fifty men. The lofty wooden turrets moved on wheels or rollers, and formed a spacious platform of the level of the rampart. On the morning of the nineteenth day a general attack was made from the Prænestine gate to the Vatican: seven Gothic columns, with their military engines, advanced to the assault; and the Romans, who lined the ramparts, listened with doubt and anxiety to the cheerful assurances of their commander. As soon as the enemy approached the ditch, Belisarius himself drew the first arrow; and such was his strength and dexterity, that he transfixed the foremost of the barbarian leaders.

A shout of applause and victory was re-echoed along the wall. He drew a second arrow, and the stroke was followed with the same success and the same acclamation. The Roman general then gave the word that the archers should aim at the teams of oxen; they were instantly covered with mortal wounds; the towers which they drew remained useless and immovable, and a single moment disconcerted the laborious projects of the king of the Goths. After this disappointment Vitiges still continued, or feigned to continue, the assault of the Salarian gate, that he might divert the attention of his adversary, while his principal forces more strenuously attacked the Prænestine gate and the sepulchre of Hadrian, at the distance of three miles from each other. Near the former, the double walls of the Vivarium [89] were low or broken; the fortifications of the latter were feebly guarded: the vigour of the Goths was excited by the hope of victory and spoil; and if a single post had given way, the Romans, and Rome itself, were irrecoverably lost. This perilous day was the most glorious in the life of Belisarius. Amidst tumult and dismay, the whole plan of the attack and defence was distinctly present to his mind; he observed the changes of each instant, weighed every possible advantage, transported his person to the scenes of danger, and communicated his spirit in calm and decisive orders. The contest was fiercely maintained from the morning to the evening; the Goths were repulsed on all sides; and each Roman might boast that he had vanquished thirty barbarians, if the strange disproportion of numbers were not counterbalanced by the merit of one man. Thirty thousand Goths, according to the confession of their own chiefs, perished

[89] *Vivarium* was an angle in the new wall enclosed for wild beasts (Procopius, Goth. l. i. c. 23 [tom. ii. p. 111, ed. Bonn]). The spot is still visible in Nardini (l. iv. c. 2, p. 159, 160) and Nolli's great plan of Rome.

in this bloody action; and the multitude of the wounded was equal to that of the slain. When they advanced to the assault, their close disorder suffered not a javelin to fall without effect; and as they retired, the populace of the city joined the pursuit, and slaughtered, with impunity, the backs of their flying enemies. Belisarius instantly sallied from the gates; and while the soldiers chanted his name and victory, the hostile engines of war were reduced to ashes. Such was the loss and consternation of the Goths, that from this day the siege of Rome degenerated into a tedious and indolent blockade; and they were incessantly harassed by the Roman general, who, in frequent skirmishes, destroyed above five thousand of their bravest troops. Their cavalry was unpractised in the use of the bow; their archers served on foot; and this divided force was incapable of contending with their adversaries, whose lances and arrows, at a distance or at hand, were alike formidable. The consummate skill of Belisarius embraced the favourable opportunities; and as he chose the ground and the moment, as he pressed the charge or sounded the retreat,[90] the squadrons which he detached were seldom unsuccessful. These partial advantages diffused an impatient ardour among the soldiers and people, who began to feel the hardships of a siege, and to disregard the dangers of a general engagement. Each plebeian conceived himself to be a hero, and the infantry, who, since the decay of discipline, were rejected from the line of battle, aspired to the ancient honours of the Roman legion. Belisarius praised the spirit of his troops, condemned their presumption, yielded to their clamours, and prepared the remedies of a defeat, the possiblity of which he alone had courage to suspect. In the quarter of the Vatican the Romans prevailed; and if the irreparable moments had not been wasted in the pillage of the camp, they might have occupied the Milvian bridge, and charged in the rear of the Gothic host. On the other side of the Tiber, Belisarius advanced from the Pincian and Salarian gates. But his army, four thousand soldiers perhaps, was lost in a spacious plain; they were encompassed and oppressed by fresh multitudes, who continually relieved the broken ranks of the barbarians. The valiant leaders of the infantry were unskilled to conquer; they died: the retreat (a hasty retreat) was covered by the prudence of the general, and the victors started back with affright from the formidable aspect of an armed rampart. The reputation of Belisarius was unsullied by a defeat; and the vain confidence of the Goths was not less serviceable to his designs than the repentance and modesty of the Roman troops.

From the moment that Belisarius had determined to sustain a siege, his assiduous care provided Rome against the danger of famine, more dreadful than the Gothic arms. An extraordinary supply of corn was imported from Sicily: the harvests of Campania and Tuscany were

---

[90] For the Roman trumpet and its various notes, consult Lipsius, de Militiâ Romanâ (Opp. tom. iii. l. iv. dialog. x. p. 125-129). A mode of distinguishing the *charge* by the horse-trumpet of solid brass, and the *retreat* by the foot-trumpet of leather and light wood, was recommended by Procopius, and adopted by Belisarius (Goth. l. ii. c. 23 [tom. ii. p. 241, ed. Bonn]).

forcibly swept for the use of the city; and the rights of private property were infringed by the strong plea of the public safety. It might easily be foreseen that the enemy would intercept the aqueducts; and the cessation of the water-mills was the first inconvenience, which was speedily removed by mooring large vessels, and fixing mill-stones in the current of the river. The stream was soon embarrassed by the trunks of trees, and polluted with dead bodies; yet so effectual were the precautions of the Roman general, that the waters of the Tiber still continued to give motion to the mills and drink to the inhabitants: the more distant quarters were supplied from domestic wells; and a besieged city might support, without impatience, the privation of her public baths. A large portion of Rome, from the Prænestine gate to the church of St. Paul, was never invested by the Goths; their excursions were restrained by the activity of the Moorish troops: the navigation of the Tiber, and the Latin, Appian, and Ostian ways, were left free and unmolested for the introduction of corn and cattle, or the retreat of the inhabitants who sought a refuge in Campania or Sicily. Anxious to relieve himself from a useless and devouring multitude, Belisarius issued his peremptory orders for the instant departure of the women, the children, and slaves; required his soldiers to dismiss their male and female attendants; and regulated their allowance that one moiety should be given in provisions and the other in money. His foresight was justified by the increase of the public distress as soon as the Goths had occupied two important posts in the neighbourhood of Rome. By the loss of the port, or, as it is now called, the city of Porto, he was deprived of the country on the right of the Tiber and the best communication with the sea; and he reflected with grief and anger that three hundred men, could he have spared such a feeble band, might have defended its impregnable works. Seven miles from the capital, between the Appian and the Latin ways, two principal aqueducts crossing, and again crossing each other, enclosed within their solid and lofty arches a fortified space,[91] where Vitiges established a camp of seven thousand Goths to intercept the convoys of Sicily and Campania. The granaries of Rome were insensibly exhausted; the adjacent country had been wasted with fire and sword; such scanty supplies as might yet be obtained by hasty excursions were the reward of valour and the purchase of wealth; the forage of the horses and the bread of the soldiers never failed; but in the last months of the siege the people was exposed to the miseries of scarcity, unwholesome food,[92] and contagious disorders. Belisarius saw and pitied their

[91] Procopius (Goth. l. ii. c. 3 [p. 154, ed. Bonn]) has forgot to name these aqueducts; nor can such a double intersection, at such a distance from Rome, be clearly ascertained from the writings of Frontinus, Fabretti, and Eschinard, de Aquis and de Agro Romano, or from the local maps of Lameti and Cingolani. Seven or eight miles from the city (50 stadia), on the road to Albano, between the Latin and Appian ways, I discern the remains of an aqueduct (probably the Septimian), a series (630 paces) of arches twenty-five feet high (ὑψηλὼ ἐς ἄγαν).

[92] They made sausages, ἀλλᾶντας, of mule's flesh: unwholesome, if the animals had died of the plague. Otherwise the famous Bologna sausages are said to be made of ass-flesh (Voyages de Labat, tom. ii. p. 218).

sufferings; but he had foreseen, and he watched, the decay of their loyalty and the progress of their discontent. Adversity had awakened the Romans from the dreams of grandeur and freedom, and taught them the humiliating lesson that it was of small moment to the real happiness whether the name of their master was derived from the Gothic or the Latin language. The lieutenant of Justinian listened to their just complaints, but he rejected with disdain the idea of flight or capitulation; repressed their clamorous impatience for battle; amused them with the prospect of sure and speedy relief; and secured himself and the city from the effects of their despair or treachery. Twice in each month he changed the station of the officers to whom custody of the gates was committed: the various precautions of patrols, watch-words, lights, and music, were repeatedly employed to discover whatever passed on the ramparts; out-guards were posted beyond the ditch, and the trusty vigilance of dogs supplied the more doubtful fidelity of mankind. A letter was intercepted which assured the king of the Goths that the Asinarian gate, adjoining to the Lateran church, should be secretly opened to his troops. On the proof or suspicion of treason several senators were banished, and the pope Sylverius was summoned to attend the representative of his sovereign at his headquarters in the Pincian palace.[93] The ecclesiastics, who followed their bishop, were detained in the first or second apartment,[94] and he alone was admitted to the presence of Belisarius. The conqueror of Rome and Carthage was modestly seated at the feet of Antonina, who reclined on a stately couch: the general was silent, but the voice of reproach and menace issued from the mouth of his imperious wife. Accused by credible witnesses, and the evidence of his own subscription, the successor of St. Peter was despoiled of his pontifical ornaments, clad in the mean habit of a monk, and embarked, without delay, for a distant exile in the East. At the emperor's command, the clergy of Rome proceeded to the choice of a new bishop, and, after a solemn invocation of the Holy Ghost, elected the deacon Vigilius, who had purchased the papal throne by a bribe of two hundred pounds of gold. The profit, and consequently the guilt, of this simony was imputed to Belisarius: but the hero obeyed the orders of his wife; Antonina served the passions of the empress; and Theodora lavished her treasures in the vain hope of obtaining a pontiff hostile or indifferent to the council of Chalcedon.[95]

[93] The name of the palace, the hill, and the adjoining gate were all derived from the senator Pincius. Some recent vestiges of temples and churches are now smoothed in the garden of the Minims of the Trinità del Monte (Nardini, l. iv. c. 7, p. 196; Eschinard, p. 209, 210; the old plan of Buffalino; and the great plan of Nolli). Belisarius had fixed his station between the *Pincian* and Salarian gates (Procop. Goth. l. i. c. 19 [tom. ii. p. 97, ed. Bonn]).

[94] From the mention of the primum et secundum velum, it should seem that Belisarius, even in a siege, represented the emperor, and maintained the proud ceremonial of the Byzantine palace.

[95] Of this act of sacrilege, Procopius (Goth. l. i. c. 25 [tom. ii. p. 121, ed. Bonn]) is a dry and reluctant witness. The narratives of Liberatus (Breviarium, c. 22), and Anastasius (de Vit. Pont. p. 39 [ap. Murat. tom. iii. p. 130])

The epistle of Belisarius to the emperor announced his victory, his danger, and his resolution. "According to your commands, we have entered the dominions of the Goths, and reduced to your obedience Sicily, Campania, and the city of Rome; but the loss of these conquests will be more disgraceful than their acquisition was glorious. Hitherto we have successfuly fought against the multitudes of the barbarians, but their multitudes may finally prevail. Victory is the gift of Providence, but the reputation of kings and generals depends on the success or the failure of their designs. Permit me to speak with freedom: if you wish that we should live, send us subsistence; if you desire that we should conquer, send us arms, horses, and men. The Romans have received us as friends and deliverers: but in our present distress, *they* will be either betrayed by their confidence, or we shall be oppressed by *their* treachery and hatred. For myself, my life is consecrated to your service: it is yours to reflect whether my death in this situation will contribute to the glory and prosperity of your reign." Perhaps that reign would have been equally prosperous if the peaceful master of the East had abstained from the conquest of Africa and Italy: but as Justinian was ambitious of fame, he made some efforts, they were feeble and languid, to support and rescue his victorious general. A reinforcement of sixteen hundred Sclavonians and Huns was led by Martin and Valerian; and as they had reposed during the winter season in the harbours of Greece, the strength of the men and horses was not impaired by the fatigues of a sea-voyage; and they distinguished their valour in the first sally against the besiegers. About the time of the summer solstice, Euthalius landed at Terracina with large sums of money for the payment of the troops: he cautiously proceeded along the Appian way, and this convoy entered Rome through the gate Capena,[96] while Belisarius, on the other side, diverted the attention of the Goths by a vigorous and successful skirmish. These seasonable aids, the use and reputation of which were dexterously managed by the Roman general, revived the courage, or at least the hopes, of the soldiers and people. The historian Procopius was despatched with an important commission to collect the troops and provisions which Campania could furnish or Constantinople had sent; and the secretary of Belisarius was soon followed by Antonina herself,[97] who boldly traversed the posts of the enemy, and returned with the Oriental succours to the relief of her husband and the besieged city. A fleet of three thousand Isaurians

are characteristic, but passionate. Hear the execrations of Cardinal Baronius (A.D. 536, No. 123; A.D. 538, No. 4-20) : portentum, facinus omni execratione dignum.

[96] The old Capena was removed by Aurelian to, or near, the modern gate of St. Sebastian (see Nolli's plan). That memorable spot has been consecrated by the Egerian grove, the memory of Numa, triumphal arches, the sepulchres of the Scipios, Metelli, etc.

[97] The expression of Procopius has an invidious cast—τύχην ἐκ τοῦ ἀσφῆλους τὴν σφίσι ξυμβησομένην καραδοκεῖν (Goth. l. ii. c. 4 [tom. ii. p. 160, ed. Bonn]). Yet he is speaking of a woman.

cast anchor in the bay of Naples, and afterwards at Ostia. Above two thousand horse, of whom a part were Thracians, landed at Tarentum; and, after the junction of five hundred soldiers of Campania, and a train of waggons laden with wine and flour, they directed their march on the Appian way from Capua to the neighbourhood of Rome. The forces that arrived by land and sea were united at the mouth of the Tiber. Antonina convened a council of war: it was resolved to surmount, with sails and oars, the adverse stream of the river; and the Goths were apprehensive of disturbing, by any rash hostilities, the negotiation to which Belisarius had craftily listened. They credulously believed that they saw no more than the vanguard of a fleet and army which already covered the Ionian Sea and the plains of Campania; and the illusion was supported by the haughty language of the Roman general when he gave audience to the ambassadors of Vitiges. After a specious discourse to vindicate the justice of his cause, they declared that, for the sake of peace, they were disposed to renounce the possession of Sicily. "The emperor is not less generous," replied his lieutenant, with a disdainful smile; "in return for a gift which you no longer possess, he presents you with an ancient province of the empire; he resigns to the Goths the sovereignty of the British island." Belisarius rejected with equal firmness and contempt the offer of a tribute; but he allowed the Gothic ambassadors to seek their fate from the mouth of Justinian himself, and consented, with seeming reluctance, to a truce of three months, from the winter solstice to the equinox of spring. Prudence might not safely trust either the oaths or hostages of the barbarians, but the conscious superiority of the Roman chief was expressed in the distribution of his troops. As soon as fear or hunger compelled the Goths to evacuate Alba, Porto, and Centumcellæ, their place was instantly supplied; the garrisons of Narni, Spoleto, and Perusia were reinforced, and the seven camps of the besiegers were gradually encompassed with the calamities of a siege. The prayers and pilgrimage of Datius, bishop of Milan, were not without effect; and he obtained one thousand Thracians and Isaurians to assist the revolt of Liguria against her Arian tyrant. At the same time, John the Sanguinary,[98] the nephew of Vitalian, was detached with two thousand chosen horse, first to Alba on the Fucine lake, and afterwards to the frontiers of Picenum on the Hadriatic Sea. "In that province," said Belisarius, "the Goths have deposited their families and treasures, without a guard or the suspicion of danger. Doubtless they will violate the truce: let them feel your presence before they hear of your motions. Spare the Italians; suffer not any fortified places to remain hostile in your rear; and faithfully reserve the spoil for an equal and common partition. It would not be reasonable," he added, with a laugh, "that, whilst we are toiling to the destruction of the drones, our more fortunate brethren should rifle and enjoy the honey."

[98] Anastasius (p. 40 [tom. iii. p. 130, ed. Murat.]) has preserved this epithet of *Sanguinarius,* which might do honour to a tiger.

The whole nation of the Ostrogoths had been assembled for the attack, and was almost entirely consumed in the siege of Rome. If any credit be due to an intelligent spectator, one-third at least of their enormous host was destroyed in frequent and bloody combats under the walls of the city. The bad fame and pernicious qualities of the summer air might already be imputed to the decay of agriculture and population, and the evils of famine and pestilence were aggravated by their own licentiousness and the unfriendly disposition of the country. While Vitiges struggled with his fortune, while he hesitated between shame and ruin, his retreat was hastened by domestic alarms. The king of the Goths was informed by trembling messengers that John the Sanguinary spread the devastations of war from the Apennine to the Hadriatic; that the rich spoils and innumerable captives of Picenum were lodged in the fortifications of Rimini; and that this formidable chief had defeated his uncle, insulted his capital, and seduced, by secret correspondence, the fidelity of his wife, the imperious daughter of Amalasontha. Yet, before he retired, Vitiges made a last effort either to storm or to surprise the city. A secret passage was discovered in one of the aqueducts; two citizens of the Vatican were tempted by bribes to intoxicate the guards of the Aurelian gate; an attack was meditated on the walls beyond the Tiber, in a place which was not fortified with towers; and the barbarians advanced, with torches and scaling-ladders, to the assault of the Pincian gate. But every attempt was defeated by the intrepid vigilance of Belisarius and his band of veterans, who, in the most perilous moments, did not regret the absence of their companions; and the Goths, alike destitute of hope and subsistence, clamorously urged their departure before the truce should expire, and the Roman cavalry should again be united. One year and nine days after the commencement of the siege, an army so lately strong and triumphant burnt their tents, and tumultuously repassed the Milvian bridge. They repassed not with impunity; their thronging multitudes, oppressed in a narrow passage, were driven headlong into the Tiber by their own fears and the pursuit of the enemy, and the Roman general, sallying from the Pincian gate, inflicted a severe and disgraceful wound on their retreat. The slow length of a sickly and desponding host was heavily dragged along the Flaminian way, from whence the barbarians were sometimes compelled to deviate, lest they should encounter the hostile garrisons that guarded the high road to Rimini and Ravenna. Yet so powerful was this flying army, that Vitiges spared ten thousand men for the defence of the cities which he was most solicitous to preserve, and detached his nephew Uraias, with an adequate force, for the chastisement of rebellious Milan. At the head of his principal army he besieged Rimini, only thirty-three miles distant from the Gothic capital. A feeble rampart and a shallow ditch were maintained by the skill and valour of John the Sanquinary, who shared the danger and fatigue of the meanest soldier, and emulated, on a theatre less illustrious, the military virtues of his great commander. The towers and battering-engines of the barbarians were rendered useless, their attacks were repulsed, and the tedious blockade, which reduced the garrison to the last extremity of hunger, afforded time for the union and march of the Roman forces. A fleet, which had surprised Ancona, sailed along the coast of the Hadriatic to the relief of the besieged city. The eunuch Narses landed in Picenum with two thousand Heruli and five thousand of the bravest troops of the East. The rock of the Apennine was forced, ten thousand veterans moved round the foot of the mountains, under the command of Belisarius himself, and a new army, whose encampment blazed with innumerable lights, *appeared* to advance along the Flaminian way. Overwhelmed with astonishment and despair, the Goths abandoned the siege of Rimini, their tents, their standards, and their leaders; and Vitiges, who gave or followed the example of flight, never halted till he found a shelter within the walls and morasses of Ravenna.

To these walls, and to some fortresses destitute of any mutual support, the Gothic monarchy was now reduced. The provinces of Italy had embraced the party of the emperor, and his army, gradually recruited to the number of twenty thousand men, must have achieved an easy and rapid conquest if their invincible powers had not been weakened by the discord of the Roman chiefs. Before the end of the siege, an act of blood, ambiguous and indiscreet, sullied the fair fame of Belisarius. Presidius, a loyal Italian, as he fled from Ravenna to Rome, was rudely stopped by Constantine, the military governor of Spoleto, and despoiled, even in a church, of two daggers, richly inlaid with gold and precious stones. As soon as the public danger had subsided, Presidius complained of the loss and injury; his complaint was heard, but the order of restitution was disobeyed by the pride and avarice of the offender. Exasperated by the delay, Presidius boldly arrested the general's horse as he passed through the forum, and, with the spirit of a citizen, demanded the common benefit of the Roman laws. The honour of Belisarius was engaged: he summoned a council, claimed the obedience of his subordinate officer, and was provoked, by an insolent reply, to call hastily for the presence of his guards. Constantine, viewing their entrance as the signal of death, drew his sword, and rushed on the general, who nimbly eluded the stroke and was protected by his friends, while the desperate assassin was disarmed, dragged into a neighbouring chamber, and executed, or rather murdered, by the guards, at the arbitrary command of Belisarius.[99] In this hasty act of violence the guilt of Constantine was no longer remembered; the despair and death of that valiant officer were secretly imputed to the revenge of An-

---

[99] This transaction is related in the public history (Goth. l. ii. c. 8 [p. 180, ed. Bonn]) with candour or caution; in the Anecdotes (c. 7 [c. i. p. 16, ed. Bonn]) with malevolence or freedom; but Marcellinus, or rather his continuator (in Chron.), casts a shade of premeditated assassination over the death of Constantine. He had performed good service at Rome and Spoleto (Procop. Goth. l. i. c. 7, 16 [tom. ii. p. 81, ed. Bonn]); but Alemannus confounds him with a Constantianus comes stabuli.

tonina; and each of his colleagues, conscious of the same rapine, was apprehensive of the same fate. The fear of a common enemy suspended the effects of their envy and discontent, but, in the confidence of approaching victory, they instigated a powerful rival to oppose the conqueror of Rome and Africa. From the domestic service of the palace and the administration of the private revenue, Narses the eunuch was suddenly exalted to the head of an army, and the spirit of a hero, who afterwards equalled the merit and glory of Belisarius, served only to perplex the operations of the Gothic war. To his prudent counsels the relief of Rimini was ascribed by the leaders of the discontented faction, who exhorted Narses to assume an independent and separate command. The epistle of Justinian had indeed enjoined his obedience to the general, but the dangerous exception, " as far as may be advantageous to the public service," reserved some freedom of judgment to the discreet favourite, who had so lately departed from the *sacred* and familiar conversation of his sovereign. In the exercise of this doubtful right the eunuch perpetually dissented from the opinions of Belisarius, and, after yielding with reluctance to the siege of Urbino, he deserted his colleague in the night, and marched away to the conquest of the Æmilian province. The fierce and formidable bands of the Heruli were attached to the person of Narses;[100] ten thousand Romans and confederates were persuaded to march under his banners; every malcontent embraced the fair opportunity of revenging his private or imaginary wrongs; and the remaining troops of Belisarius were divided and dispersed from the garrisons of Sicily to the shores of the Hadriatic. His skill and perseverance overcame every obstacle: Urbino was taken, the sieges of Fæsulæ, Orvieto, and Auximum were undertaken, and vigorously prosecuted, and the eunuch Narses was at length recalled to the domestic cares of the palace. All dissensions were healed, and all opposition was subdued, by the temperate authority of the Roman general, to whom his enemies could not refuse their esteem; and Belisarius inculcated the salutary lesson that the forces of the state should compose one body and be animated by one soul. But in the interval of discord the Goths were permitted to breathe; an important season was lost, Milan was destroyed, and the northern provinces of Italy were afflicted by an inundation of the Franks.

When Justinian first meditated the conquest of Italy, he sent ambassadors to the kings of the Franks, and adjured them, by the common ties of alliance and religion, to join in the holy enterprise against the Arians. The Goths, as their wants were more urgent, employed a more effectual mode of persuasion, and vainly strove, by the gift of lands and money, to purchase the friendship, or at least the neutrality, of a

---

[100] They refused to serve after his departure; sold their captives and cattle to the Goths; and swore never to fight against them. Procopius introduces a curious digression on the manners and adventures of this wandering nation, a part of whom finally emigrated to Thule or Scandinavia (Goth. l. ii. c. 14, 15).

light and perfidious nation.[101]   But the arms of Belisarius and the ᴅe-
volt of the Italians had no sooner shaken the Gothic monarchy, than
Theodebert of Austrasia, the most powerful and warlike of the Merovingian kings, was persuaded to succour their distress by an indirect
and seasonable aid. Without expecting the consent of their sovereign,
ten thousand Burgundians, his recent subjects, descended from the
Alps, and joined the troops which Vitiges had sent to chastise the revolt
of Milan. After an obstinate siege the capital of Liguria was reduced
by famine, but no capitulation could be obtained, except for the safe
retreat of the Roman garrison. Datius, the orthodox bishop, who had
seduced his countrymen to rebellion [102] and ruin, escaped to the luxury
and honours of the Byzantine court;[103] but the clergy, perhaps the
Arian clergy, were slaughtered at the foot of their own altars by the
defenders of the catholic faith. Three hundred thousand males were
reported to be slain;[104] the female sex and the more precious spoil was
resigned to the Burgundians; and the houses, or at least the walls, of
Milan were levelled with the ground. The Goths, in their last moments,
were revenged by the destruction of a city second only to Rome in size
and opulence, in the splendour of its buildings, or the number of its inhabitants, and Belisarius sympathised alone in the fate of his deserted
and devoted friends. Encouraged by this successful inroad, Theodebert
himself, in the ensuing spring, invaded the plains of Italy with an army
of one hundred thousand barbarians.[105] The king and some chosen
followers were mounted on horseback and armed with lances; the infantry, without bows or spears, were satisfied with a shield, a sword, and
a double-edged battleaxe, which in their hands became a deadly and
unerring weapon. Italy trembled at the march of the Franks, and both
the Gothic prince and the Roman general, alike ignorant of their designs, solicited with hope and terror the friendship of these dangerous
allies. Till he had secured the passage of the Po on the bridge of

[101] This national reproach of perfidy (Procop. Goth. l. ii. c. 25 [tom. ii.
p. 247, ed. Bonn]) offends the ear of La Mothe le Vayer (tom. viii. p. 163-
165), who criticises, as if he had not read, the Greek historian.
[102] Baronius applauds his treason, and justifies the catholic bishops—qui
ne sub heretico principe degant omnem lapidem movent—a useful caution.
The more rational Muratori (Annali d'Italia, tom. v. p. 54) hints at the guilt
of perjury, and blames at least the *imprudence* of Datius.
[103] St. Datius was more successful against devils than against barbarians.
He travelled with a numerous retinue, and occupied at Corinth a large house
(Baronius, A.D. 538, No. 89; A.D. 539, No. 20).
[104] Μυριάδες τριάκοντα (compare Procopius, Goth. l. ii. c. 7, 21 [tom. ii. p. 234,
ed. Bonn]). Yet such population is incredible; and the second or third
city of Italy need not repine if we only decimate the numbers of the present
text. Both Milan and Genoa revived in less than thirty years (Paul Diacon.
de Gestis Langobard. l. ii. c. 38 [16 or 22?]).
[105] Besides Procopius, perhaps too Roman, see the Chronicles of Marius
and Marcellinus, Jornandes (in Success. Regn. in Muratori, tom. i. p. 241),
and Gregory of Tours (l. iii. c. 32, in tom. ii. of the Historians of France).
Gregory supposes a defeat of Belisarius, who, in Aimoin (de Gestis Franc.
l. ii. c. 23, in tom. iii. p. 59), is slain by the Franks.

Pavia, the grandson of Clovis dissembled his intentions, which he at length declared by assaulting, almost at the same instant, the hostile camps of the Romans and Goths. Instead of uniting their arms, they fled with equal precipitation, and the fertile though desolate provinces of Liguria and Æmilia were abandoned to a licentious host of barbarians, whose rage was not mitigated by any thoughts of settlement or conquest. Among the cities which they ruined, Genoa, not yet constructed of marble, is particularly enumerated; and the deaths of thousands, according to the regular practice of war, appear to have excited less horror than some idolatrous sacrifices of women and children which were performed with impunity in the camp of the most Christian king. If it were not a melancholy truth that the first and most cruel sufferings must be the lot of the innocent and helpless, history might exult in the misery of the conquerors, who, in the midst of riches, were left destitute of bread or wine, reduced to drink the waters of the Po, and to feed on the flesh of distempered cattle. The dysentery swept away one-third of their army, and the clamours of his subjects, who were impatient to pass the Alps, disposed Theodebert to listen with respect to the mild exhortations of Belisarius. The memory of this inglorious and destructive warfare was perpetuated on the medals of Gaul, and Justinian, without unsheathing his sword, assumed the title of conqueror of the Franks. The Merovingian prince was offended by the vanity of the emperor; he affected to pity the fallen fortunes of the Goths; and his insidious offer of a fœderal union was fortified by the promise or menace of descending from the Alps at the head of five hundred thousand men. His plans of conquest were boundless, and perhaps chimerical. The king of Austrasia threatened to chastise Justinian, and to march to the gates of Constantinople;[106] he was overthrown and slain[107] by a wild bull,[108] as he hunted in the Belgic or German forests.

As soon as Belisarius was delivered from his foreign and domestic enemies, he seriously applied his forces to the final reduction of Italy. In the siege of Osimo the general was nearly transpierced with an arrow, if the mortal stroke had not been intercepted by one of his guards, who lost in that pious office the use of his hand. The Goths of Osimo, four thousand warriors, with those of Fæsulæ and the Cottian Alps, were among the last who maintained their independence; and their gallant resistance, which almost tired the patience, deserved

[106] Agathias, 1. i. [c. 4], p. 14, 15 [ed. Par.; p. 20, 21, ed. Bonn]. Could he have seduced or subdued the Gepidæ or Lombards of Pannonia, the Greek historian is confident that he must have been destroyed in Thrace.

[107] The king pointed his spear—the bull overturned a tree on his head—he expired the same day. Such is the story of Agathias; but the original historians of France (tom. ii. p. 202, 403, 558, 667) impute his death to a fever.

[108] Without losing myself in a labyrinth of species and names—the aurochs, urus, bisons, bubalus, bonasus, buffalo, etc. (Buffon. Hist. Nat. tom. xi. and Supplement, tom. iii. vi.), it is certain that in the sixth century a large wild species of horned cattle was hunted in the great forests of the Vosges in Lorraine, and the Ardennes (Greg. Turon. tom. ii. 1. x. c. 10, p. 369).

the esteem, of the conqueror. His prudence refused to subscribe the safe-conduct which they asked to join their brethren of Ravenna: but they saved, by an honourable capitulation, one moïety at least of their wealth, with the free alternative of retiring peaceably to their estates or enlisting to serve the emperor in his Persian wars. The multitudes which yet adhered to the standard of Vitiges far surpassed the number of the Roman troops, but neither prayers nor defiance, nor the extreme danger of his most faithful subjects, could tempt the Gothic king beyond the fortifications of Ravenna. These fortifications were indeed impregnable to the assaults of art or violence, and when Belisarius invested the capital he was soon convinced that famine only could tame the stubborn spirit of the barbarians. The sea, the land, and the channels of the Po were guarded by the vigilance of the Roman general; and his morality extended the rights of war to the practice of poisoning the waters [109] and secretly firing the granaries [110] of a besieged city.[111]   While he pressed the blockade of Ravenna, he was surprised by the arrival of two ambassadors from Constantinople, with a treaty of peace, which Justinian had imprudently signed without deigning to consult the author of his victory. By this disgraceful and precarious agreement, Italy and the Gothic treasure were divided, and the provinces beyond the Po were left with the regal title to the successor of Theodoric. The ambassadors were eager to accomplish their salutary commission; the captive Vitiges accepted with transport the unexpected offer of a crown; honour was less prevalent among the Goths than the want and appetite of food; and the Roman chiefs, who murmured at the continuance of the war, professed implicit submission to the commands of the emperor. If Belisarius had possessed only the courage of a soldier, the laurel would have been snatched from his hand by timid and envious counsels; but in this decisive moment he resolved, with the magnanimity of a statesman, to sustain alone the danger and merit of generous disobedience. Each of his officers gave a written opinion that the siege of Ravenna was impracticable and hopeless; the

[109] In the siege of Auximum, he first laboured to demolish an old aqueduct, and then cast into the stream, 1. dead bodies; 2. mischievous herbs; and 3. quick lime, which is named (says Procopius, l. ii. c. 27) τίτανος by the ancients; by the moderns ἄσβεστος. Yet both words are used as synonymous in Galen, Dioscorides, and Lucian (Hen. Steph. Thesaur. Ling. Græc. tom. iii. p. 748).

[110] The Goths suspected Mathasuenta as an accomplice in the mischief, which perhaps was occasioned by accidental lightning.

[111] In strict philosophy, a limitation of the rights of war seems to imply nonsense and contradiction. Grotius himself is lost in an idle distinction between the jus naturæ and the jus gentium, between poison and infection. He balances in one scale the passages of Homer (Odyss. A, 259, etc.) and Florus (l. ii. c. 20, No. 7, ult.); and in the other, the examples of Solon (Pausanias, l. x. c. 37) and Belisarius. See his great work De Jure Belli et Pacis (l. iii. c. 4, s. 15, 16, 17, and in Barbeyrac's version, tom. ii. p. 257, etc.). Yet I can understand the benefit and validity of an agreement, tacit or express, mutually to abstain from certain modes of hostility. See the Amphictyonic oath in Æschines, de Falsâ Legatione.

general then rejected the treaty of partition, and declared his own
resolution of leading Vitiges in chains to the feet of Justinian. The
Goths retired with doubt and dismay; this peremptory refusal deprived
them of the only signature which they could trust, and filled their
minds with a just apprehension that a sagacious enemy had discovered
the full extent of their deplorable state. They compared the fame and
fortune of Belisarius with the weakness of their ill-fated king, and the
comparison suggested an extraordinary project, to which Vitiges, with
apparent resignation, was compelled to acquiesce. Partition would
ruin the strength, exile would disgrace the honour, of the nation; but
they offered their arms, their treasures, and the fortifications of Ravenna, if Belisarius would disclaim the authority of a master, accept
the choice of the Goths, and assume, as he had deserved, the kingdom
of Italy. If the false lustre of a diadem could have tempted the
loyalty of a faithful subject, his prudence must have foreseen the inconstancy of the barbarians, and his rational ambition would prefer
the safe and honourable station of a Roman general. Even the
patience and seeming satisfaction with which he entertained a proposal of treason might be susceptible of a malignant interpretation.
But the lieutenant of Justinian was conscious of his own rectitude; he
entered into a dark and crooked path, as it might lead to the voluntary
submission of the Goths; and his dexterous policy persuaded them that
he was disposed to comply with their wishes, without engaging an oath
or a promise for the performance of a treaty which he secretly abhorred. The day of the surrender of Ravenna was stipulated by the
Gothic ambassadors; a fleet, laden with provisions, sailed as a welcome
guest into the deepest recess of the harbour, the gates were opened
to the fancied king of Italy, and Belisarius, without meeting an enemy,
triumphantly marched through the streets of an impregnable city.[112]
The Romans were astonished by their success; the multitudes of tall
and robust barbarians were confounded by the image of their own
patience; and the masculine females, spitting in the faces of their
sons and husbands, most bitterly reproached them for betraying their
dominion and freedom to these pigmies of the south, contemptible in
their numbers, diminutive in their stature. Before the Goths could
recover from the first surprise and claim the accomplishment of their
doubtful hopes, the victor established his power in Ravenna beyond
the danger of repentance and revolt. Vitiges, who perhaps had attempted to escape, was honourably guarded in his palace;[113] the

---

[112] Ravenna was taken, not in the year 540, but in the latter end of 539;
and Pagi (tom. ii. p. 569) is rectified by Muratori (Annali d'Italia, tom. v.
p. 62), who proves, from an original act on papyrus (Antiquit. Italiæ Medii
Ævi, tom. ii. dissert. xxxii. p. 999-1007; Maffei, Istoria Diplomat. p. 155-160),
that before the third of January, 540, peace and free correspondence were
restored between Ravenna and Faenza.

[113] He was seized by John the Sanguinary, but an oath or sacrament was
pledged for his safety in the Basilica Julii (Hist. Miscell. l. xvi. in Muratori,
tom. i. p. 107). Anastasius (in Vit. Pont. p. 40 [t iii. p. 130, ed. Murat.])

flower of the Gothic youth was selected for the service of the emperor; the remainder of the people was dismissed to their peaceful habitations in the southern provinces, and a colony of Italians was invited to replenish the depopulated city. The submission of the capital was imitated in the towns and villages of Italy which had not been subdued or even visited by the Romans; and the independent Goths, who remained in arms at Pavia and Verona, were ambitious only to become the subjects of Belisarius. But his inflexible loyalty rejected, except as the substitute of Justinian, their oaths of allegiance, and he was not offended by the reproach of their deputies that he rather chose to be a slave than a king.

After the second victory of Belisarius, envy again whispered, Justinian listened, and the hero was recalled. " The remnant of the Gothic war was no longer worthy of his presence: a gracious sovereign was impatient to reward his services and to consult his wisdom; and he alone was capable of defending the East against the innumerable armies of Persia." Belisarius understood the suspicion, accepted the excuse, embarked at Ravenna his spoils and trophies, and proved by his ready obedience that such an abrupt removal from the government of Italy was not less unjust than it might have been indiscreet. The emperor received with honourable courtesy both Vitiges and his more noble consort; and as the king of the Goths conformed to the Athanasian faith, he obtained, with a rich inheritance of lands in Asia, the rank of senator and patrician.[114] Every spectator admired, without peril, the strength and stature of the young barbarians: they adored the majesty of the throne, and promised to shed their blood in the service of their benefactor. Justinian deposited in the Byzantine palace the treasures of the Gothic monarchy. A flattering senate was sometimes admitted to gaze on the magnificent spectacle, but it was enviously secluded from the public view; and the conqueror of Italy renounced without a murmur, perhaps without a sigh, the well-earned honours of a second triumph. His glory was, indeed, exalted above all external pomp; and the faint and hollow praises of the court were supplied, even in a servile age, by the respect and admiration of his country. Whenever he appeared in the streets and public places of Constantinople, Belisarius attracted and satisfied the eyes of the people. His lofty stature and majestic countenance fulfilled their expectations of a hero, the meanest of his fellow-citizens were emboldened by his gentle and gracious demeanour, and the martial train which attended his footsteps left his person more accessible than in a day of battle.

---

gives a dark but probable account. Montfaucon is quoted by Mascou (Hist. of the Germans, xii. 21) for a votive shield representing the captivity of Vitiges, and now in the collection of Signor Landi at Rome.

[114] Vitiges lived two years at Constantinople, and imperatoris in affectû *convictus* (or conjunctus) rebus excessit humanis. His widow, *Mathasuenta*, the wife and mother of the patricians, the elder and younger Germanus, united the streams of Anician and Amali blood. (Jornandes, c. 60, p. 221, in Muratori, tom. i.)

Seven thousand horsemen, matchless for beauty and valour, were maintained in the service, and at the private expense, of the general.[115] Their prowess was always conspicuous in single combats or in foremost ranks, and both parties confessed that in the siege of Rome the guards of Belisarius had alone vanquished the barbarian host. Their numbers were continually augmented by the bravest and most faithful of the enemy; and his fortunate captives, the Vandals, the Moors, and the Goths, emulated the attachment of his domestic followers. By the union of liberality and justice he acquired the love of the soldiers, without alienating the affections of the people. The sick and wounded were relieved with medicines and money, and still more efficaciously by the healing visits and smiles of their commander. The loss of a weapon or a horse was instantly repaired, and each deed of valour was rewarded by the rich and honourable gifts of a bracelet or a collar, which were rendered more precious by the judgment of Belisarius. He was endeared to the husbandmen by the peace and plenty which they enjoyed under the shadow of his standard. Instead of being injured, the country was enriched by the march of the Roman armies; and such was the rigid discipline of their camp, that not an apple was gathered from the tree, not a path could be traced in the fields of corn. Belisarius was chaste and sober. In the licence of a military life, none could boast that they had seen him intoxicated with wine; the most beautiful captives of Gothic or Vandal race were offered to his embraces, but he turned aside from their charms, and the husband of Antonina was never suspected of violating the laws of conjugal fidelity. The spectator and historian of his exploits has observed that amidst the perils of war he was daring without rashness, prudent without fear, slow or rapid according to the exigencies of the moment; that in the deepest distress he was animated by real or apparent hope, but that he was modest and humble in the most prosperous fortune. By these virtues he equalled or excelled the ancient masters of the military art. Victory, by sea and land, attended his arms. He subdued Africa, Italy, and the adjacent islands; led away captives the successors of Genseric and Theodoric; filled Constantinople with the spoils of their palaces; and in the space of six years recovered half the provinces of the Western empire. In his fame and merit, in wealth and power, he remained without a rival, the first of the Roman subjects: the voice of envy could only magnify his dangerous importance, and the emperor might applaud his own discerning spirit, which had discovered and raised the genius of Belisarius.

It was the custom of the Roman triumphs that a slave should be placed behind the chariot, to remind the conqueror of the instability of fortune and the infirmities of human nature. Procopius, in his An-

[115] Procopius, Goth. l. iii. c. 1 [p. 283, ed. Bonn]. Aimoin, a French monk of the eleventh century, who had obtained, and has disfigured, some authentic information of Belisarius, mentions, in his name, 12,000 *pueri* or slaves— quos propriis alimus stipendiis—besides 18,000 soldiers (Historians of France, tom. iii. De Gestis Franc. l. ii. c. 6, p. 48).

ecdotes, has assumed that servile and ungrateful office. The generous reader may cast away the libel, but the evidence of facts will adhere to his memory; and he will reluctantly confess that the fame and even the virtue of Belisarius were polluted by the lust and cruelty of his wife, and that the hero deserved an appellation which may not drop from the pen of the decent historian. The mother of Antonina [116] was a theatrical prostitute, and both her father and grandfather exercised, at Thessalonica and Constantinople, the vile though lucrative profession of charioteers. In the various situations of their fortune she became the companion, the enemy, the servant, and the favourite of the empress Theodora: these loose and ambitious females had been connected by similar pleasures; they were separated by the jealousy of vice, and at length reconciled by the partnership of guilt. Before her marriage with Belisarius, Antonina had one husband and many lovers; Photius, the son of her former nuptials, was of an age to distinguish himself at the siege of Naples; and it was not till the autumn of her age and beauty [117] that she indulged a scandalous attachment to a Thracian youth. Theodosius had been educated in the Eunomian heresy; the African voyage was consecrated by the baptism and auspicious name of the first soldier who embarked, and the proselyte was adopted into the family of his spiritual parents, [118] Belisarius and Antonina. Before they touched the shores of Africa, this holy kindred degenerated into sensual love; and as Antonina soon overleaped the bounds of modesty and caution, the Roman general was alone ignorant of his own dishonour. During their residence at Carthage he surprised the two lovers in a subterraneous chamber, solitary, warm, and almost naked. Anger flashed from his eyes. " With the help of this young man," said the unblushing Antonina, " I was secreting our most precious effects from the knowledge of Justinian." The youth resumed his garments, and the pious husband consented to disbelieve the evidence of his own senses. From this pleasing and perhaps voluntary delusion, Belisarius was awakened at Syracuse by the officious information of Macedonia; and that female attendant, after requiring an oath for her security, produced two chamberlains who like herself had often beheld the adulteries of Antonina. A hasty flight into Asia saved Theodosius from the justice of an injured husband, who had signified to one of his guards the order of his death; but the tears of Antonina and her artful seductions

---

[116] The diligence of Alemannus could add but little to the four first and most curious chapters of the Anecdotes. Of these strange Anecdotes, a part may be true, because probable; and a part true, because improbable. Procopius must have *known* the former, and the latter he could scarcely *invent*.

[117] Procopius insinuates (Anecdot. c. 4 [tom. iii. p. 35, ed. Bonn]), that, when Belisarius returned to Italy (A.D. 543), Antonina was sixty years of age. A forced, but more polite construction, which refers that date to the moment when he was writing (A.D. 559), would be compatible with the manhood of Photius (Gothic. l. i. c. 10) in 536.

[118] Compare the Vandalic War (l. i. c. 12) with the Anecdotes (c. i. [tom. iii. p. 14, ed. Bonn]) and Alemannus (p. 2, 3). This mode of baptismal adoption was revived by Leo the philosopher

assured the credulous hero of her innocence, and he stooped, against his faith and judgment, to abandon those imprudent friends who had presumed to accuse or doubt the chastity of his wife. The revenge of a guilty woman is implacable and bloody: the unfortunate Macedonia, with the two witnesses, were secretly arrested by the minister of her cruelty; their tongues were cut out, their bodies were hacked into small pieces, and their remains were cast into the sea of Syracuse. A rash though judicious saying of Constantine, " I would sooner have punished the adulteress than the boy," was deeply remembered by Antonina; and two years afterwards, when despair had armed that officer against his general, her sanguinary advice decided and hastened his execution. Even the indignation of Photius was not forgiven by his mother; the exile of her son prepared the recall of her lover, and Theodosius condescended to accept the pressing and humble invitation of the conqueror of Italy. In the absolute direction of his household, and in the important commissions of peace and war,[119] the favourite youth most rapidly acquired a fortune of four hundred thousand pounds sterling; and after their return to Constantinople the passion of Antonina at least continued ardent and unabated. But fear, devotion, and lassitude perhaps, inspired Theodosius with more serious thoughts. He dreaded the busy scandal of the capital, and the indiscreet fondness of the wife of Belisarius, escaped from her embraces, and, retiring to Ephesus, shaved his head and took refuge in the sanctuary of a monastic life. The despair of the new Ariadne could scarcely have been excused by the death of her husband. She wept, she tore her hair, she filled the palace with her cries; " she had lost the dearest of friends, a tender, a faithful, a laborious friend!" But her warm entreaties, fortified by the prayers of Belisarius, were insufficient to draw the holy monk from the solitude of Ephesus. It was not till the general moved forward for the Persian war that Theodosius could be tempted to returr to Constantin·ple, and the short interval before the departure of Antonina herself was boldly devoted to love and pleasure.

A philosopher may pity and forgive the infirmities of female nature from which he receives no real injury; but contemptible is the husband who feels, and yet endures, his own infamy in that of his wife. Antonina pursued her son with implacable hatred, and the gallant Photius [120] was exposed to her secret persecutions in the camp beyond the Tigris. Enraged by his own wrongs and by the dishonour of his blood, he cast away in his turn the sentiments of nature, and revealed to Belisarius the turpitude of a woman who had violated all the duties of

---

[119] In November, 537, Photius arrested the pope (Liberat. Brev. c. 22; Pagi, tom. ii. p. 562). About the end of 539 Belisarius sent Theodosius— τὸν τῇ οἰκίᾳ τῃ αὐτοῦ ἐφέστωτα—on an important and lucrative commission to Ravenna (Goth. l. ii. c. 28 [tom. ii. p. 261, ed. Bonn]).

[120] Theophanes (Chronograph. p. 204 [ed. Par.; tom. i. p. 373, ed. Bonn]) styles him *Photinus*, the son-in-law of Belisarius; and he is copied by the Historia Miscella and Anastasius.

a mother and a wife. From the surprise and indignation of the Roman general, his former credulity appears to have been sincere: he embraced the knees of the son of Antonina, adjured him to remember his obligations rather than his birth, and confirmed at the altar their holy vows of revenge and mutual defence. The dominion of Antonina was impaired by absence; and when she met her husband on his return from the Persian confines, Belisarius, in his first and transient emotions, confined her person and threatened her life. Photius was more resolved to punish, and less prompt to pardon; he flew to Ephesus, extorted from a trusty eunuch of his mother the full confession of her guilt, arrested Theodosius and his treasures in the church of St. John the Apostle, and concealed his captives, whose execution was only delayed, in a secure and sequestered fortress of Cilicia. Such a daring outrage against public justice could not pass with impunity, and the cause of Antonina was espoused by the empress, whose favour she had deserved by the recent services of the disgrace of a præfect, and the exile and murder of a pope. At the end of the campaign Belisarius was recalled; he complied as usual with the Imperial mandate. His mind was not prepared for rebellion: his obedience, however adverse to the dictates of honour, was consonant to the wishes of his heart; and when he embraced his wife, at the command and perhaps in the presence of the empress, the tender husband was disposed to forgive or to be forgiven. The bounty of Theodora reserved for her companion a more precious favour. " I have found," she said, " my dearest patrician, a pearl of inestimable value; it has not yet been viewed by any mortal eye, but the sight and the possession of this jewel are destined for my friend." As soon as the curiosity and impatience of Antonina were kindled, the door of a bedchamber was thrown open, and she beheld her lover, whom the diligence of the eunuchs had discovered in his secret prison. Her silent wonder burst into passionate exclamations of gratitude and joy, and she named Theodora her queen, her benefactress, and her saviour. The monk of Ephesus was nourished in the palace with luxury and ambition; but instead of assuming, as he was promised, the command of the Roman armies, Theodosius expired in the first fatigues of an amorous interview. The grief of Antonina could only be assuaged by the sufferings of her son. A youth of consular rank and a sickly constitution was punished without a trial, like a malefactor and a slave; yet such was the constancy of his mind, that Photius sustained the tortures of the scourge and the rack without violating the faith which he had sworn to Belisarius. After this fruitless cruelty the son of Antonina, while his mother feasted with the empress, was buried in her subterraneous prisons, which admitted not the distinction of night and day. He twice escaped to the most venerable sanctuaries of Constantinople, the church of St. Sophia and of the Virgin; but his tyrants were insensible of religion as of pity, and the helpless youth, amidst the clamours of the clergy and people, was twice dragged from the altar to the dungeon. His third attempt was more successful. At the end of three years the prophet Zachariah, or some mortal friend, indicated the means of an escape: he eluded the spies and guards of the empress, reached the holy sepulchre of Jerusalem, embraced the profession of a monk, and the abbot Photius was employed, after the death of Justinian, to reconcile and regulate the churches of Egypt. The son of Antonina suffered all that an enemy can inflict; her patient husband imposed on himself the more exquisite misery of violating his promise and deserting his friend.

In the succeeding campaign Belisarius was again sent against the Persians: he saved the East, but he offended Theodora, and perhaps the emperor himself. The malady of Justinian had countenanced the rumour of his death; and the Roman general, on the supposition of that probable event, spoke the free language of a citizen and a soldier. His colleague Buzes, who concurred in the same sentiments, lost his rank, his liberty, and his health by the persecution of the empress; but the disgrace of Belisarius was alleviated by the dignity of his own character and the influence of his wife, who might wish to humble, but could not desire to ruin, the partner of her fortunes. Even his removal was coloured by the assurance that the sinking state of Italy would be retrieved by the single presence of its conqueror. But no sooner had he returned, alone and defenceless, than a hostile commission was sent to the East to seize his treasures and criminate his actions; the guards and veterans who followed his private banner were distributed among the chiefs of the army, and even the eunuchs presumed to cast lots for the partition of his martial domestics. When he passed with a small and sordid retinue through the streets of Constantinople, his forlorn appearance excited the amazement and compassion of the people. Justinian and Theodora received him with cold ingratitude, the servile crowd with insolence and contempt; and in the evening he retired with trembling steps to his deserted palace. An indisposition, feigned or real, had confined Antonina to her apartment; and she walked disdainfully silent in the adjacent portico, while Belisarius threw himself on his bed, and expected, in an agony of grief and terror, the death which he had so often braved under the walls of Rome. Long after sunset a messenger was announced from the empress: he opened with anxious curiosity the letter which contained the sentence of his fate. "You cannot be ignorant how much you have deserved my displeasure. I am not insensible of the services of Antonina. To her merits and intercession I have granted your life, and permit you to retain a part of your treasures, which might be justly forfeited to the state. Let your gratitude where it is due be displayed, not in words, but in your future behaviour." I know not how to believe or to relate the transports with which the hero is said to have received this ignominious pardon. He fell prostrate before his wife, he kissed the feet of his saviour, and he devoutly promised to live the grateful and submissive slave of Antonina. A fine of one hundred and twenty thousand pounds sterling was levied on the fortunes of Belisarius; and with the office of count, or master of the royal stables, he accepted the conduct of the Italian war. At his departure from Constantinople, his friends, and even the public, were persuaded that as soon as he regained his freedom he would renounce his dissimulation; and that his wife, Theodora, and perhaps the emperor himself, would be sacrificed to the just revenge of a virtuous rebel. Their hopes were deceived; and the unconquerable patience and loyalty of Belisarius appear either *below* or *above* the character of a MAN.[1]

CHAPTER XLII (500-582 A.D.)

State of the Barbaric World—Establishment of the Lombards on the Danube —Tribes and Inroads of the Sclavonians—Origin, Empire, and Embassies of the Turks—The Flight of the Avars—Chosroes I., or Nushirvan, King of Persia—His prosperous Reign and Wars with the Romans—The Colchian or Lazic War—The Æthiopians

OUR estimate of personal merit is relative to the common faculties of mankind. The aspiring efforts of genius or virtue, either in active or speculative life, are measured not so much by their real elevation as by the height to which they ascend above the level of their age or country; and the same stature which in a people of giants would pass unnoticed, must appear conspicuous in a race of pigmies. Leonidas and his three hundred companions devoted their lives at Thermopylæ; but the education of the infant, the boy, and the man, had prepared and almost ensured this memorable sacrifice; and each Spartan would approve, rather than admire, an act of duty, of which himself and eight thousand of his fellow-citizens were equally capable.[2] The great Pompey might inscribe on his trophies that he had defeated in battle two millions of enemies, and reduced fifteen hundred cities from the lake Mæotis to the Red Sea;[3] but the fortune of Rome flew before his eagles; the nations were oppressed by their own fears; and the invincible legions which he commanded had been formed by the habits of conquest and the discipline of ages. In this view the character of Belisarius may be deservedly placed above the heroes of the ancient republics. His imperfections flowed from the contagion of the times; his virtues were his own, the free gift of nature or reflection; he raised himself without a master or a

[1] The continuator of the Chronicle of Marcellinus gives, in a few decent words, the substance of the Anecdotes: Belisarius de Oriente evocatus, in offensam periculumque incurrens grave, et invidiæ subjacens rursus remittitur in Italiam (p. 54).
[2] It will be a pleasure, not a task, to read Herodotus (l. vii. c. 104, 134, p. 550, 615). The conversation of Xerxes and Demaratus at Thermopylæ is one of the most interesting and moral scenes in history. It was the torture of the royal Spartan to behold, with anguish and remorse, the virtue of his country.
[3] See this proud inscription in Pliny (Hist. Natur. vii. 27). Few men have more exquisitely tasted of glory and disgrace; nor could Juvenal (Satir. x.) produce a more striking example of the vicissitudes of fortune, and the vanity of human wishes.

rival; and so inadequate were the arms committed to his hand, that his sole advantage was derived from the pride and presumption of his adversaries. Under his command, the subjects of Justinian often deserved to be called Romans; but the unwarlike appellation of Greeks was imposed as a term of reproach by the haughty Goths, who affected to blush that they must dispute the kingdom of Italy with a nation of tragedians, pantomimes, and pirates.[4] The climate of Asia has indeed been found less congenial than that of Europe to military spirit: those populous countries were enervated by luxury, despotism, and superstition, and the monks were more expensive and more numerous than the soldiers of the East. The regular force of the empire had once amounted to six hundred and forty-five thousand men: it was reduced, in the time of Justinian, to one hundred and fifty thousand; and this number, large as it may seem, was thinly scattered over the sea and land—in Spain and Italy, in Africa and Egypt, on the banks of the Danube, the coast of the Euxine, and the frontiers of Persia. The citizen was exhausted, yet the soldier was unpaid; his poverty was mischievously soothed by the privilege of rapine and indolence, and the tardy payments were detained and intercepted by the fraud of those agents who usurp, without courage or danger, the emoluments of war. Public and private distress recruited the armies of the state; but in the field, and still more in the presence of the enemy, their numbers were always defective. The want of national spirit was supplied by the precarious faith and disorderly service of barbarian mercenaries. Even military honour, which has often survived the loss of virtue and freedom, was almost totally extinct. The generals, who were multiplied beyond the example of former times, laboured only to prevent the success or to sully the reputation of their colleagues; and they had been taught by experience that, if merit sometimes provoked the jealousy, error, or even guilt, would obtain the indulgence, of a gracious emperor.[5] In such an age the triumphs of Belisarius, and afterwards of Narses, shine with incomparable lustre; but they are encompassed with the darkest shades of disgrace and calamity. While the lieutenant of Justinian subdued the kingdoms of the Goths and Vandals, the emperor,[6] timid, though ambitious, balanced the forces of the barbarians, fomented their divisions by flattery and falsehood, and invited by his patience and liberality the repetition of injuries.[7] The keys of Carthage, Rome, and

---

[4] Γραικοὺς . . . ἐξ ὧν τὰ πρότερα οὐδένα ἐς Ἰταλίαν ἥκοντα εἶδον, ὅτι μὴ τραγῳδοὺς, καὶ ναύτας λωποδύτας [Goth. i. 18, tom. ii. p. 93, ed. Bonn]. This last epithet of Procopius is too nobly translated by pirates; naval thieves is the proper word: strippers of garments, either for injury or insult (Demosthenes contra Conon. in Reiske, Orator. Græc. tom. ii. p. 1264).

[5] See the third and fourth books of the Gothic War: the writer of the Anecdotes cannot aggravate these abuses.

[6] Agathias, l. v. [c. 14] p. 157, 158 [p. 306, ed. Bonn]. He confines this weakness of the emperor and the empire to the old age of Justinian; but, alas! he was never young.

[7] This mischievous policy, which Procopius (Anecdot. c. 19 [tom. iii. p. 113, ed. Bonn]) imputes to the emperor, is revealed in his epistle to a Scythian

Ravenna were presented to their conqueror, while Antioch was destroyed by the Persians, and Justinian trembled for the safety of Constantinople.

Even the Gothic victories of Belisarius were prejudicial to the state, since they abolished the important barrier of the Upper Danube, which had been so faithfully guarded by Theodoric and his daughter. For the defence of Italy, the Goths evacuated Pannonia and Noricum, which they left in a peaceful and flourishing condition: the sovereignty was claimed by the emperor of the Romans; the actual possession was abandoned to the boldness of the first invader. On the opposite banks of the Danube, the plains of Upper Hungary and the Transylvanian hills were possessed, since the death of Attila, by the tribes of the Gepidæ, who respected the Gothic arms, and despised, not indeed the gold of the Romans, but the secret motive of their annual subsidies. The vacant fortifications of the river were instantly occupied by these barbarians; their standards were planted on the walls of Sirmium and Belgrade; and the ironical tone of their apology aggravated this insult on the majesty of the empire: " So extensive, O Cæsar, are your dominions, so numerous are your cities, that you are continually seeking for nations to whom, either in peace or war, you may relinquish these useless possessions. The Gepidæ are your brave and faithful allies, and, if they have anticipated your gifts, they have shown a just confidence in your bounty." Their presumption was excused by the mode of revenge which Justinian embraced. Instead of asserting the rights of a sovereign for the protection of his subjects, the emperor invited a strange people to invade and possess the Roman provinces between the Danube and the Alps; and the ambition of the Gepidæ was checked by the rising power and fame of the LOMBARDS.[8] This corrupt appellation has been diffused in the thirteenth century by the merchants and bankers, the Italian posterity of these savage warriors;

---

prince who was capable of understanding it. Ἄγαν προμηθῆ καὶ ἀγχινούστατον, says Agathias (l. v. [c. 5] p. 170, 171 [p. 331, ed. Bonn]).

[8] Gens Germanâ feritate ferocior, says Velleius Paterculus of the Lombards (ii. 106). Langobardos paucitas nobilitat. Plurimis ac valentissimis nationibus cincti non per obsequium, sed prœliis et periclitando, tuti sunt (Tacit. de Moribus German. c. 40). See likewise Strabo (l. vii. p. 446 [p. 290, 291, ed. Casaub.]). The best geographers place them beyond the Elbe, in the bishopric of Magdeburg and the middle march of Brandenburg; and their situation will agree with the patriotic remark of the Count de Hertzeberg, that most of the barbarian conquerors issued from the same countries which still produce the armies of Prussia.

[The etymology of the word Lombards, from Langobards, so called from the peculiar length and fashion of their beards, has been called in question, and it is now believed that the name Langobardi should be derived from the district they inhabited on the banks of the Elbe, where Börde (or Bord) still signifies a fertile plain by the side of a river, and a district near Magdeburg is still called the " lange börde." According to this view langobardi would mean " inhabitants of the long bord of the river ; " and traces of their name are still supposed to occur in such words as Bardengau and Bardewick in the neighbourhood of the Elbe.—O. S.]

but the original name of *Langobards* is expressive only of the peculiar length and fashion of their beards. I am not disposed either to question or to justify their Scandinavian origin,[9] nor to pursue the migrations of the Lombards through unknown regions and marvellous adventures. About the time of Augustus and Trajan, a ray of historic light breaks on the darkness of their antiquities, and they are discovered, for the first time, between the Elbe and the Oder. Fierce, beyond the example of the Germans, they delighted to propagate the tremendous belief that their heads were formed like the heads of dogs, and that they drank the blood of their enemies whom they vanquished in battle. The smallness of their numbers was recruited by the adoption of their bravest slaves; and alone, amidst their powerful neighbours, they defended by arms their high-spirited independence. In the tempests of the north, which overwhelmed so many names and nations, this little bark of the Lombards still floated on the surface; they gradually descended towards the south and the Danube, and at the end of four hundred years they again appear with their ancient valour and renown. Their manners were not less ferocious. The assassination of a royal guest was executed in the presence and by the command of the king's daughter, who had been provoked by some words of insult, and disappointed by his diminutive stature; and a tribute, the price of blood, was imposed on the Lombards by his brother, the king of the Heruli. Adversity revived a sense of moderation and justice, and the insolence of conquest was chastised by the signal defeat and irreparable dispersion of the Heruli, who were seated in the southern provinces of Poland.[10] The victories of the Lombards recommended them to the friendship of the emperors; and, at the solicitation of Justinian, they passed the Danube to reduce, according to their treaty, the cities of Noricum and the fortresses of Pannonia. But the spirit of rapine soon tempted them beyond these ample limits; they wandered along the coast of the Hadriatic as far as Dyrrachium, and presumed, with familiar rudeness, to enter the towns and houses of their Roman allies, and to seize the captives who had escaped from their audacious hands, These acts of hostility, the sallies, as it might be pretended, of some loose adventurers, were disowned by the nation, and excused by the emperor; but the arms of the Lombards were more seriously engaged by a contest of thirty years, which was terminated only by the extirpation of the Gepidæ. The hostile nations often pleaded their cause before the throne of Constantinople; and the crafty Justinian, to whom the barbarians were almost equally odious, pronounced a partial and

---

[9] The Scandinavian origin of the Goths and Lombards, as stated by Paul Warnefrid [l. i. c. 2], surnamed the Deacon, is attacked by Cluverius (Germania Antiq. l. iii. c. 26, p. 102, etc.), a native of Prussia, and defended by Grotius (Prolegom. ad Hist. Goth. p. 28, etc.), the Swedish ambassador.

[10] Two facts in the narrative of Paul Diaconus (l. i. c. 20) are expressive of national manners: 1. Dum *ad tabulam* luderet—while he played at draughts. 2. Camporum viridantia *lina*. The cultivation of flax supposes property, commerce, agriculture, and manufactures.

ambiguous sentence, and dexterously protracted the war by slow and ineffectual succours. Their strength was formidable, since the Lombards, who sent into the field several *myriads* of soldiers, still claimed, as the weaker side, the protection of the Romans. Their spirit was intrepid; yet such is the uncertainty of courage, that the two armies were suddenly struck with a panic: they fled from each other, and the rival kings remained with their guards in the midst of an empty plain. A short truce was obtained; but their mutual resentment again kindled, and the remembrance of their shame rendered the next encounter more desperate and bloody. Forty thousand of the barbarians perished in the decisive battle which broke the power of the Gepidæ, transferred the fears and wishes of Justinian, and first displayed the character of Alboin, the youthful prince of the Lombards, and the future conqueror of Italy.[11]

The wild people who dwelt or wandered in the plains of Russia, Lithuania, and Poland, might be reduced, in the age of Justinian, under the two great families of the BULGARIANS[12] and the SCLAVO-NIANS. According to the Greek writers, the former, who touched the Euxine and the lake Mæotis, derived from the Huns their name or

[11] I have used, without undertaking to reconcile, the facts in Procopius (Goth. l. ii. c. 14, l. iii. c. 33, 34, l. iv. c. 18, 25), Paul Diaconus (de Gestis Langobard. l. i. c. 1-23, in Muratori, Script. Rerum Italicarum, tom. i. p. 405-419), and Jornandes (de Success. Regnorum, p. 242). The patient reader may draw some light from Mascou (Hist. of the Germans, and Annotat. xxiii.) and De Buat (Hist. des Peuples, etc., tom. ix. x. xi.).

[12] I adopt the appellation of Bulgarians from Ennodius (in Panegyr. Theodorici, Opp. Sirmond, tom. i. p. 1598, 1599), Jornandes (de Rebus Geticis, c. 5, p. 194, et de Regn. Successione, p. 242), Theophanes (p. 185 [tom. i. p. 338, ed. Bonn]), and the Chronicles of Cassiodorus and Marcellinus. The name of Huns is too vague; the tribes of the Cutturgurians and Utturgurians are too minute and too harsh.

[The Bulgarians unquestionably derived their descent from a Hunnish source. Procopius and Agathias explain that the Kotrigurs inhabiting "this side of the Mæotic Lake," and the Uturgurs or Utigurs beyond that on the east of the Cimmerian Bosphorus, the river Don dividing their territories, were also of Hunnish extraction. Therefore Kotrigurs, Uturgurs, and Bulgarians were all closely allied to the Huns of Attila and spoke a cognate language. But the modern Bulgarian exhibits far more features of affinity to the Slav than to the Hun.

The Slavonians or Sarmatians are believed to be the ancestors of the various modern Slav families of nations. For convenience sake it may be stated briefly that the ancient Sarmatians or Slavonians inhabited that part of modern Europe which lies between the Vistula, the Carpathian Mountains, the Volga, and the Black Sea. They were akin to the ancient Scythians, and were therefore Iranians, probably of Median descent. The Sarmatians almost exterminated the Scythians, and were in turn conquered by the Goths, to become in time the ancestors of the modern Slavs. These are divided into an Eastern and a Western branch, the Eastern including the various types of Russians, including the Red and White Russians, some of the modern Bulgarians, the Serbo-Croats, the Montenegrins and Slovenzi; while the Western branch comprehended the Poles, the Czechs, the Moravians, the Slovaks, and the Lusatian Wends.—O. S.]

descent; and it is needless to renew the simple and well-known picture of Tartar manners. They were bold and dexterous archers, who drank the milk and feasted on the flesh of their fleet and indefatigable horses; whose flocks and herds followed, or rather guided, the motions of their roving camps; to whose inroads no country was remote or impervious, and who were practised in flight, though incapable of fear. The nation was divided into two powerful and hostile tribes, who pursued each other with fraternal hatred. They eagerly disputed the friendship or rather the gifts of the emperor; and the distinction which nature had fixed between the faithful dog and the rapacious wolf was applied by an ambassador who received only verbal instructions from the mouth of his illiterate prince.[13] The Bulgarians, of whatsoever species, were equally attracted by Roman wealth: they assumed a vague dominion over the Sclavonian name, and their rapid marches could only be stopped by the Baltic Sea, or the extreme cold and poverty of the north. But the same race of Sclavonians appears to have maintained, in every age, the possession of the same countries. Their numerous tribes, however distant or adverse, used one common language (it was harsh and irregular), and were known by the resemblance of their form, which deviated from the swarthy Tartar, and approached withou'. attaining the lofty stature and fair complexion of the German. Four thousand six hundred villages [14] were scattered over the provinces of Russia and Poland, and their huts were hastily built of rough timber, in a country deficient both in stone and iron. Erected, or rather concealed, in the depth of forests, on the banks of rivers, or the edge of morasses, we may not perhaps, without flattery, compare them to the architecture of the beaver, which they resembled in a double issue, to the land and water, for the escape of the savage inhabitant, an animal less cleanly, less diligent, and less social, than that marvellous quadruped. The fertility of the soil, rather than the labour of the natives, supplied the rustic plenty of the Sclavonians. Their sheep and horned cattle were large and numerous, and the fields which they sowed with millet and panic [15] afforded, in the place of bread, a coarse and less nutritive food. The incessant rapine of their neighbours compelled them to bury this treasure in the earth; but on the appearance of a stranger it was freely imparted by a people whose unfavourable character is qualified by the epithets of chaste, patient, and hospitable. As their

[13] Procopius (Goth. l. iv. c. 19 [tom. ii. p. 556, ed. Bonn]). His verbal message (he owns himself an illiterate barbarian) is delivered as an epistle. The style is savage, figurative, and original.

[14] This sum is the result of a particular list, in a curious MS. fragment of the year 550, found in the library of Milan. The obscure geography of the times provokes and exercises the patience of the Count de Buat (tom. xi. p. 69-189). The French minister often loses himself in a wilderness which requires a Saxon and Polish guide.

[15] *Panicum, milium.* See Columella, l. ii. c. 9, p. 430, edit. Gesner. Plin. Hist. Natur. xviii. 24, 25. The Sarmatians made a pap of millet, mingled with mare's milk or blood. In the wealth of modern husbandry, our millet feeds poultry, and not heroes. See the dictionaries of Bomare and Miller.

supreme god, they adored an invisible master of the thunder. The rivers and the nymphs obtained their subordinate honours, and the popular worship was expressed in vows and sacrifice. The Sclavonians disdained to obey a despot, a prince, or even a magistrate; but their experience was too narrow, their passions too headstrong, to compose a system of equal law or general defence. Some voluntary respect was yielded to age and valour; but each tribe or village existed as a separate republic, and all must be persuaded where none could be compelled. They fought on foot, almost naked, and, except an unwieldy shield, without any defensive armour: their weapons of offence were a bow, a quiver of small poisoned arrows, and a long rope, which they dexterously threw from a distance, and entangled their enemy in a running noose. In the field, the Sclavonian infantry was dangerous by their speed, agility, and hardiness: they swam, they dived, they remained under water, drawing their breath through a hollow cane; and a river or lake was often the scene of their unsuspected ambuscade. But these were the achievements of spies or stragglers: the military art was unknown to the Sclavonians; their name was obscure, and their conquests were inglorious.[16]

I have marked the faint and general outline of the Sclavonians and Bulgarians, without attempting to define their intermediate boundaries, which were not accurately known or respected by the barbarians themselves. Their importance was measured by their vicinity to the empire; and the level country of Moldavia and Wallachia was occupied by the Antes,[17] a Sclavonian tribe, which swelled the titles of Justinian with an epithet of conquest.[18] Against the Antes he erected the fortifications of the Lower Danube, and laboured to secure the alliance of a people seated in the direct channel of northern inundation, an interval of two hundred miles between the mountains of Transylvania and the Euxine Sea. But the Antes wanted power and inclination to stem the fury of the torrent: and the light-armed Sclavonians from a hundred tribes pursued with almost equal speed the footsteps of the Bulgarian horse.

[16] For the name and nation, the situation and manners, of the Sclavonians, see the original evidence of the sixth century, in Procopius (Goth. l. ii. c. 26, l. iii. c. 14), and the emperor Mauritius or Maurice (Stratagemat. l. xi. c. 5, apud Mascou, Annotat. xxxi.). The Stratagems of Maurice have been printed only, as I understand, at the end of Scheffer's edition of Arrian's Tactics, at Upsal, 1664 (Fabric. Bibliot. Græc. l. iv. c. 8, tom. iii. p. 278), a scarce, and hitherto, to me, an inaccessible book.
[The *Stategikon* (or the Stratagems) is a scarce work of the sixth century, but it is not by Maurice.—O. S.]
[17] Antes eorum fortissimi . . . Taysis [Tausis] qui rapidus et verticosus in Histri fluenta furens devolvitur (Jornandes, c. 5, p. 194, edit. Murator. Procopius, Goth. l. iii. c. 14, et de Ædific. l. iv. c. 7). Yet the same Procopius mentions the Goths and Huns as neighbours, γειτονοῦντα, to the Danube (de Ædific. l. iv. c. 1).
[18] The national title of *Anticus,* in the laws and inscriptions of Justinian, was adopted by his successors, and is justified by the pious Ludewig (in Vit. Justinian. p. 515). It had strangely puzzled the civilians of the middle age.

The payment of one piece of gold for each soldier procured a safe and easy retreat through the country of the Gepidæ, who commanded the passage of the Upper Danube.[19]   The hopes or fears of the barbarians, their intestine union or discord, the accident of a frozen or shallow stream, the prospect of harvest or vintage, the prosperity or distress of the Romans, were the causes which produced the uniform repetition of annual visits,[20] tedious in the narrative, and destructive in the event.   The same year, and possibly the same month, in which Ravenna surrendered, was marked by an invasion of the Huns or Bulgarians, so dreadful that it almost effaced the memory of their past inroads.   They spread from the suburbs of Constantinople to the Ionian Gulf, destroyed thirty-two cities or castles, erased Potidæa, which Athens had built and Philip had besieged, and repassed the Danube, dragging at their horses' heels one hundred and twenty thousand of the subjects of Justinian.   In a subsequent inroad they pierced the wall of the Thracian Chersonesus, extirpated the habitations and the inhabitants, boldly traversed the Hellespont, and returned to their companions laden with the spoils of Asia.   Another party, which seemed a multitude in the eyes of the Romans, penetrated without opposition from the straits of Thermopylæ to the isthmus of Corinth; and the last ruin of Greece has appeared an object too minute for the attention of history.   The works which the emperor raised for the protection, but at the expense of his subjects, served only to disclose the weakness of some neglected part; and the walls, which by flattery had been deemed impregnable, were either deserted by the garrison or scaled by the barbarians.   Three thousand Sclavonians, who insolently divided themselves into two bands, discovered the weakness and misery of a triumphant reign.   They passed the Danube and the Hebrus, vanquished the Roman generals who dared to oppose their progress, and plundered with impunity the cities of Illyricum and Thrace, each of which had arms and numbers to overwhelm their contemptible assailants.   Whatever praise the boldness of the Sclavonians may deserve, it is sullied by the wanton and deliberate cruelty which they are accused of exercising on their prisoners.   Without distinction of rank or age or sex, the captives were impaled or flayed alive, or suspended between four posts and beaten with clubs till they expired, or enclosed in some spacious building and left to perish in the flames with the spoil and cattle which might impede the march of these savage victors.[21]   Perhaps a more impartial narrative would reduce the number and qualify the nature of these horrid acts, and they might sometimes

[19] Procopius, Goth. l. iv. c. 25 [tom. ii. p. 592, ed. Bonn].
[20] An inroad of the Huns is connected by Procopius with a comet; perhaps that of 531 (Persic. l. ii. c. 4).   Agathias (l. v. [c. 11] p. 154, 155 [p. 300, ed. Bonn]) borrows from his predecessor some early facts.
[21] The cruelties of the Sclavonians are related or magnified by Procopius (Goth. l. iii. c. 29, 38).   For their mild and liberal behaviour to their prisoners we may appeal to the authority, somewhat more recent, of the emperor Maurice (Stratagem. l. xi. c. 5 [p. 272, sqq.]).

be excused by the cruel laws of retaliation. In the siege of Topirus,[22] whose obstinate defence had enraged the Sclavonians, they massacred fifteen thousand males, but they spared the women and children; the most valuable captives were always reserved for labour or ransom; the servitude was not rigorous, and the terms of their deliverance were speedy and moderate. But the subject, or the historian of Justinian, exhaled his just indignation in the language of complaint and reproach; and Procopius has confidently affirmed that in a reign of thirty-two years each *annual* inroad of the barbarians consumed two hundred thousand of the inhabitants of the Roman empire. The entire population of Turkish Europe, which nearly corresponds with the provinces of Justinian, would perhaps be incapable of supplying six millions of persons, the result of this incredible estimate.[23]

In the midst of these obscure calamities, Europe felt the shock of a revolution, which first revealed to the world the name and nation of the TURKS. Like Romulus, the founder of that martial people was suckled by a she-wolf, who afterwards made him the father of a numerous progeny; and the representation of that animal in the banners of the Turks preserved the memory, or rather suggested the idea, of a fable which was invented, without any mutual intercourse, by the shepherds of Latium and those of Scythia. At the equal distance of two thousand miles from the Caspian, the Icy, the Chinese, and the Bengal seas, a ridge of mountains is conspicuous, the centre, and perhaps the summit, of Asia, which, in the language of different nations, has been styled Imaus, and Caf,[24] and Altai, and the Golden Mountains,

---

[22] Topirus was situate near Philippi in Thrace, or Macedonia, opposite to the isle of Thasos, twelve days' journey from Constantinople (Cellarius, tom. i. p. 676, 840).

[23] According to the malevolent testimony of the Anecdotes (c. 18 [tom. iii. p. 108, ed. Bonn] these inroads had reduced the provinces south of the Danube to the state of a Scythian wilderness.

[The Turks were essentially an Eastern Asiatic race, coming from the neighbourhood of Lake Baikal (see Note, vol. i. p. 917, for divisions thereof). A branch of these dwelling on Mount Altai were styled Thu-kiu by Chinese writers, and are regarded as the same people as the Hiongnu of earlier times. The name of Thu-kiu first appears at the beginning of the fifth century in the Chinese writers, who relate that 500 families of the Hiongnu, under their leader Assena, when the major part of their tribe was crushed by the Tungusic Tartars, fled west from their abodes in Pe-leang to the territory of the Geougen, settling at the foot of a helmet-shaped mountain "terk," whence they derived their name. They were employed by the Geougen or Jeugen as iron workers. The seat of the Turkish power, about the sixth century was near the eastern frontier of the Chinese province of to-day Kansuh. This, in fact, was where they had been working for over 200 years for the Geougen. The Turks became very powerful under their leader Tumere, who, after conquering the Geougen, invited under his sway all the Turkish tribes in Central and Northern Asia, and assumed the title of Chagan or Khan, A.D. 546.—O. S.]

[24] From Caf to Caf; which a more rational geography would interpret, from Imaus, perhaps, to Mount Atlas. According to the religious philosophy of the Mahometans the basis of Mount Caf is an emerald, whose reflection produces the azure of the sky. The mountain is endowed with a sensitive action in its

and the Girdle of the Earth.   The sides of the hills were productive of minerals; and the iron-forges,[25] for the purpose of war, were exercised by the Turks, the most despised portion of the slaves of the great khan of the Geougen.   But their servitude could only last till a leader, bold and eloquent, should arise to persuade his countrymen that the same arms which they forged for their masters might become in their own hands the instruments of freedom and victory.   They sallied from the mountain;[26] a sceptre was the reward of his advice; and the annual ceremony, in which a piece of iron was heated in the fire, and a smith's hammer was successively handled, by the prince and his nobles, recorded for ages the humble profession and rational pride of the Turkish nation. Bertezena, their first leader, signalised their valour and his own in successful combats against the neighbouring tribes; but when he presumed to ask in marriage the daughter of the great khan, the insolent demand of a slave and a mechanic was contemptuously rejected. The disgrace was expiated by a more noble alliance with a princess of China; and the decisive battle which almost extirpated the nation of the Geougen established in Tartary the new and more powerful empire of the Turks.   They reigned over the north; but they confessed the vanity of conquest by their faithful attachment to the mountain of their fathers.   The royal encampment seldom lost sight of Mount Altai, from whence the river Irtish descends to water the rich pastures of the Calmucks,[27] which nourish the largest sheep and oxen in the world.   The soil is fruitful, and the climate mild and temperate: the happy region was ignorant of earthquake and pestilence; the emperor's throne was turned towards the east, and a golden wolf on the top of a spear seemed to guard the entrance of his tent.   One of the successors of Bertezena was tempted by the luxury and superstition of China; but his design of building cities and temples was defeated by the simple wisdom of a barbarian counsellor.   " The Turks," he said, " are not equal in number to one hundredth part of the inhabitants of China. If we balance their power, and elude their armies, it is because we

roots or nerves; and their vibration, at the command of God, is the cause of earthquakes (D'Herbelot, p. 230, 231).

[25] The Siberian iron is the best and most plentiful in the world: and in the southern parts above sixty mines are now worked by the industry of the Russians (Strahlenberg, Hist. of Siberia, p. 342, 387; Voyage en Sibérie, par l'Abbé Chappe d'Auteroche, p. 603-608, edit. in 12mo. Amsterdam, 1770). The Turks offered iron for sale; yet the Roman ambassadors, with strange obstinacy, persisted in believing that it was all a trick, and that their country produced none (Menander in Excerpt. Leg. p. 152 [ed. Par.; p. 380, ed Bonn]).

[26] Of Irgana-kon (Abulghazi Khan, Hist. Généalogique des Tatars, P. ii. c. 5, p. 71-77, c. 15, p. 155). The tradition of the Moguls, of the 450 years which they passed in the mountains, agrees with the Chinese periods of the history of the Huns and Turks (De Guignes, tom. i. part ii. p. 376), and the twenty generations from their restoration to Zingis.

[27] The country of the Turks, now of the Calmucks, is well described in the Genealogical History, p. 521-562. The curious notes of the French translator are enlarged and digested in the second volume of the English version.

wander without any fixed habitations in the exercise of war and hunting. Are we strong? we advance and conquer: are we feeble? we retire
and are concealed. Should the Turks confine themselves within the
walls of cities, the loss of a battle would be the destruction of their
empire. The bonzes preach only patience, humility, and the renunciation of the world. Such, O king! is not the religion of heroes." They
entertained with less reluctance the doctrines of Zoroaster; but the
greatest part of the nation acquiesced without inquiry in the opinions,
or rather in the practice, of their ancestors. The honours of sacrifice
were reserved for the supreme deity; they acknowledged in rude hymns
their obligations to the air, the fire, the water, and the earth; and their
priests derived some profit from the art of divination. Their unwritten
laws were rigorous and impartial: theft was punished by a tenfold
restitution; adultery, treason, and murder with death; and no chastisement could be inflicted too severe for the rare and inexpiable guilt of
cowardice. As the subject nations marched under the standard of the
Turks, their cavalry, both men and horses, were proudly computed by
millions; one of their effective armies consisted of four hundred thousand soldiers, and in less than fifty years they were connected in peace
and war with the Romans, the Persians, and the Chinese. In their
northern limits some vestige may be discovered of the form and situation of Kamtchatka, of a people of hunters and fishermen, whose
sledges were drawn by dogs, and whose habitations were buried in the
earth. The Turks were ignorant of astronomy; but the observation
taken by some learned Chinese, with a gnomon of eight feet, fixes the
royal camp in the latitude of forty-nine degrees, and marks their
extreme progress within three, or at least ten degrees of the polar
circle.[28] Among their southern conquests the most splendid was that
of the Nephthalites or White Huns, a polite and warlike people, who
possessed the commercial cities of Bochara and Samarcand, who had
vanquished the Persian monarch, and carried their victorious arms along
the banks and perhaps to the mouth of the Indus. On the side of the
west the Turkish cavalry advanced to the lake Mæotis. They passed
that lake on the ice. The khan, who dwelt at the foot of Mount Altai,
issued his commands for the siege of Bosphorus,[29] a city the voluntary
subject of Rome, and whose princes had formerly been the friends of
Athens.[30] To the east the Turks invaded China, as often as the vigour
of the government was relaxed: and I am taught to read in the history
of the times that they mowed down their patient enemies like hemp or

[28] Visdelou, p. 141, 151. The fact, though it strictly belongs to a subordinate
and successive tribe, may be introduced here.
[29] Procopius (Persic. l. i. c. 12, l. ii. c. 3; Peyssonel, Observations sur les
Peuples Barbares, p. 99, 100) defines the distance between Caffa and the
old Bosphorus at xvi long Tartar leagues.
[30] See, in a Mémoire of M. de Boze (Mém. de l'Académie des Inscriptions,
tom. vi. p. 549-565), the ancient kings and medals of the Cimmerian Bosphorus;
and the gratitude of Athens, in the Oration of Demosthenes against Leptines
(in Reiske, Orator. Græc. tom. i. p. 466, 467).

grass, and that the mandarins applauded the wisdom of an emperor who repulsed these barbarians with golden lances. This extent of savage empire compelled the Turkish monarch to establish three subordinate princes of his own blood, who soon forgot their gratitude and allegiance. The conquerors were enervated by luxury, which is always fatal except to an industrious people; the policy of China solicited the vanquished nations to resume their independence; and the power of the Turks was limited to a period of two hundred years. The revival of their name and dominion in the southern countries of Asia are the events of a later age; and the dynasties which succeeded to their native realms may sleep in oblivion, since *their* history bears no relation to the decline and fall of the Roman empire.[31]

In the rapid career of conquest the Turks attacked and subdued the nation of the Ogors or Varchonites on the banks of the river Til, which derived the epithet of Black from its dark water or gloomy forests.[32] The khan of the Ogors was slain with three hundred thousand of his subjects, and their bodies were scattered over the space of four days' journey: their surviving countrymen acknowledged the strength and mercy of the Turks; and a small portion, about twenty thousand warriors, preferred exile to servitude. They followed the well-known road of the Volga, cherished the error of the nations who confounded them with the AVARS, and spread the terror of that false, though famous appellation, which had not, however, saved its lawful proprietors from the yoke of the Turks.[33] After a long and victorious march the new Avars arrived at the foot of Mount Caucasus, in the country of the Alani[34] and Circassians, where they first heard of the

[31] For the origin and revolutions of the first Turkish empire, the Chinese details are borrowed from De Guignes (Hist. des Huns, tom. i. P. ii. p. 367-462) and Visdelou (Supplément à la Bibliothèque Orient. d'Herbelot, p. 82-114). The Greek or Roman hints are gathered in Menander (p. 108-164 [p. 298, 404, ed. Bonn]), and Theophylact Simocatta (l. vii. c. 7, 8).

[32] The river Til, or Tula, according to the geography of De Guignes (tom. i. part ii. p. lviii. and 352), is a small, though grateful, stream of the desert, that falls into the Orhon, Selinga, etc. See Bell, Journey from Petersburg to Pekin (vol. ii. p. 124) ; yet his own description of the Keat, down which he sailed into the Oby, represents the name and attributes of the *black river* (p. 139).

[The river is supposed to be an eastern affluent of the Volga, the Kama, which, from the colour of its waters, may be called black. The Volga, however, is called Atel or Etel by all the Turkish tribes.—O. S.]

[33] Theophylact, l. vii. c. 7, 8. And yet his *true* Avars are invisible even to the eyes of M. de Guignes; and what can be more illustrious than the *false?* The right of the fugitive Ogors to that national appellation is confessed by the Turks themselves (Menander, p. 108).

[The Avars, like the Huns, belonged to the Turkish stock. Their chiefs bear the Turkish or Mongolian titles of Chagan or Khan. They are first mentioned after the downfall of the empire of the Huns, between 461-465, as devastating the lands of the tribes on the Mæotic Lake and Caspian Sea.—O. S.]

[34] The Alani are still found in the Genealogical History of the Tartars (p. 617), and in D'Anville's maps. They opposed the march of the generals

splendour and weakness of the Roman empire. They humbly requested their confederate, the prince of the Alani, to lead them to this source of riches; and their ambassador, with the permission of the governor of Lazica, was transported by the Euxine Sea to Constantinople. The whole city was poured forth to behold with curiosity and terror the aspect of a strange people; their long hair, which hung in tresses down their backs, was gracefully bound with ribands, but the rest of their habit appeared to imitate the fashion of the Huns. When they were admitted to the audience of Justinian, Candish, the first of the ambassadors, addressed the Roman emperor in these terms: " You see before you, O mighty prince, the representatives of the strongest and most populous of nations, the invincible, the irresistible Avars. We are willing to devote ourselves to your service: we are able to vanquish and destroy all the enemies who now disturb your repose. But we expect, as the price of our alliance, as the reward of our valour, precious gifts, annual subsidies, and fruitful possessions." At the time of this embassy Justinian had reigned above thirty, he had lived above seventy-five years: his mind, as well as his body, was feeble and languid; and the conqueror of Africa and Italy, careless of the permanent interest of his people, aspired only to end his days in the bosom even of inglorious peace. In a studied oration, he imparted to the senate his resolution to dissemble the insult and to purchase the friendship of the Avars; and the whole senate, like the mandarins of China, applauded the incomparable wisdom and foresight of their sovereign. The instruments of luxury were immediately prepared to captivate the barbarians; silken garments, soft and splendid beds, and chains and collars incrusted with gold. The ambassadors, content with such liberal reception, departed from Constantinople, and Valentin, one of the emperor's guards, was sent with a similar character to their camp at the foot of Mount Caucasus. As their destruction or their success must be alike advantageous to the empire, he persuaded them to invade the enemies of Rome; and they were easily tempted, by gifts and promises, to gratify their ruling inclinations. These fugitives, who fled before the Turkish arms, passed the Tanais and Borysthenes, and boldly advanced into the heart of Poland and Germany, violating the law of nations and abusing the rights of victory. Before ten years had elapsed their camps were seated on the Danube and the Elbe, many Bulgarian and Sclavonian names were obliterated from the earth, and the remainder of their tribes are found, as tributaries and vassals, under the standard of the Avars. The chagan, the peculiar title of their king, still affected to cultivate the friendship of the emperor; and Justinian entertained some thoughts of fixing them in Pannonia, to balance the prevailing power of the Lombards. But the virtue or treachery of an Avar betrayed the secret enmity and ambitious designs of their countrymen; and they loudly complained of the timid, though jealous policy, of detaining

of Zingis round the Caspian Sea, and were overthrown in a great battle (Hist. de Gengiscan, l. iv. c. 9, p. 447).

their ambassadors and denying the arms which they had been allowed to purchase in the capital of the empire.[35]

Perhaps the apparent change in the dispositions of the emperors may be ascribed to the embassy which was received from the conquerors of the Avars.[36] The immense distance which eluded their arms could not extinguish their resentment: the Turkish ambassadors pursued the footsteps of the vanquished to the Jaik, the Volga, Mount Caucasus, the Euxine, and Constantinople, and at length appeared before the successor of Constantine, to request that he would not espouse the cause of rebels and fugitives. Even commerce had some share in this remarkable negotiation: and the Sogdoites, who were now the tributaries of the Turks, embraced the fair occasion of opening, by the north of the Caspian, a new road for the importation of Chinese silk into the Roman empire. The Persian, who preferred the navigation of Ceylon, had stopped the caravans of Bochara and Samarcand: their silk was contemptuously burnt: some Turkish ambassadors died in Persia, with a suspicion of poison; and the great khan permitted his faithful vassal Maniach, the prince of the Sogdoites, to propose, at the Byzantine court, a treaty of alliance against their common enemies. Their splendid apparel and rich presents, the fruit of Oriental luxury, distinguished Maniach and his colleagues from the rude savages of the North: their letters, in the Scythian character and language, announced a people who had attained the rudiments of science:[37] they enumerated the conquests, they offered the friendship and military aid, of the Turks; and their sincerity was attested by direful imprecations (if they were guilty of falsehood) against their own head and the head of Disabul their master. The Greek prince entertained with hospitable regard the ambassadors of a remote and powerful monarch: the sight of silkworms and looms disappointed the hopes of the Sogdoites; the emperor renounced, or seemed to renounce, the fugitive Avars, but he accepted the alliance of the Turks; and the ratification of the treaty was carried by a Roman minister to the foot of Mount Altai. Under the successors of Justinian the friendship of the two nations was cultivated by frequent and cordial

[35] The embassies and first conquests of the Avars may be read in Menander (Excerpt. Legat. p. 99, 100, 101, 154, 155 [p. 282-287, 385-388, ed. Bonn]), Theophanes (p. 196 [tom. i. p. 359, ed. Bonn]), the Historia Miscella (l. xvi. p. 109), and Gregory of Tours (l. iv. c. 23, 29, in the Historians of France, tom. ii. p. 214, 217).

[36] Theophanes (Chron. p. 204) and the Hist. Miscella (l. xvi. p. 110), as understood by De Guignes (tom. i. part ii. p. 354), appear to speak of a Turkish embassy to Justinian himself; but that of Maniach, in the fourth year of his successor Justin, is positively the first that reached Constantinople (Menander, p. 108).

[37] The Russians have found characters, rude hieroglyphics, on the Irtish and Yenisei, on medals, tombs, idols, rocks, obelisks, etc. (Strahlenberg, Hist. of Siberia, p. 324, 346, 406, 429). Dr. Hyde (de Religione Veterum Persarum, p. 521, etc.) has given two alphabets of Thibet and of the Eygours. I have long harboured a suspicion that all the Scythian, and some, perhaps much, of the Indian science, was derived from the Greeks of Bactriana.

intercourse; the most favoured vassals were permitted to imitate the example of the great khan; and one hundred and six Turks, who on various occasions had visited Constantinople, departed at the same time for their native country. The duration and length of the journey from the Byzantine court to Mount Altai are not specified: it might have been difficult to mark a road through the nameless deserts, the mountains, rivers, and morasses of Tartary; but a curious account has been preserved of the reception of the Roman ambassadors at the royal camp. After they had been purified with fire and incense, according to a rite still practised under the sons of Zingis, they were introduced to the presence of Disabul. In a valley of the Golden Mountain they found the great khan in his tent, seated in a chair with wheels, to which a horse might be occasionally harnessed. As soon as they had delivered their presents, which were received by the proper officers, they exposed in a florid oration the wishes of the Roman emperor that victory might attend the arms of the Turks, that their reign might be long and prosperous, and that a strict alliance, without envy or deceit, might for ever be maintained between the two most powerful nations of the earth. The answer of Disabul corresponded with these friendly professions, and the ambassadors were seated by his side at a banquet which lasted the greatest part of the day: the tent was surrounded with silk hangings, and a Tartar liquor was served on the table which possessed at least the intoxicating qualities of wine. The entertainment of the succeeding day was more sumptuous; the silk hangings of the second tent were embroidered in various figures; and the royal seat, the cups, and the vases were of gold. A third pavilion was supported by columns of gilt wood; a bed of pure and massy gold was raised on four peacocks of the same metal: and before the entrance of the tent, dishes, basins, and statues of solid silver and admirable art were ostentatiously piled in waggons, the monuments of valour rather than of industry. When Disabul led his armies against the frontiers of Persia, his Roman allies followed many days the march of the Turkish camp, nor were they dismissed till they had enjoyed their precedency over the envoy of the Great King, whose loud and intemperate clamours interrupted the silence of the royal banquet. The power and ambition of Chosroes cemented the union of the Turks and Romans, who touched his dominions on either side: but those distant nations, regardless of each other, consulted the dictates of interest, without recollecting the obligations of oaths and treaties. While the successor of Disabul celebrated his father's obsequies, he was saluted by the ambassadors of the emperor Tiberius, who proposed an invasion of Persia, and sustained with firmness the angry and perhaps the just reproaches of that haughty barbarian. " You see my ten fingers," said the great khan, and he applied them to his mouth. " You Romans speak with as many tongues, but they are tongues of deceit and perjury. To me you hold one language, to my subjects another; and the nations are successively deluded by your perfidious eloquence. You precipitate your allies into war and danger, you enjoy their labours, and you neglect your benefactors. Hasten your return, inform your master that a Turk is incapable of uttering or forgiving falsehood, and that he shall speedily meet the punishment which he deserves. While he solicits my friendship with flattering and hollow words, he is sunk to a confederate of my fugitive Varchonites. If I condescend to march against those contemptible slaves, they will tremble at the sound of our whips; they will be trampled, like a nest of ants, under the feet of my innumerable cavalry. I am not ignorant of the road which they have followed to invade your empire; nor can I be deceived by the vain pretence that Mount Cau· casus is the impregnable barrier of the Romans. I know the course of the Dniester, the Danube, and the Hebrus; the most warlike nations have yielded to the arms of the Turks; and from the rising to the setting sun the earth is my inheritance." Notwithstanding this menace, a sense of mutual advantage soon renewed the alliance of the Turks and Romans: but the pride of the great khan survived his re· sentment; and when he announced an important conquest to his friend the emperor Maurice, he styled himself the master of the seven races and the lord of the seven climates of the world.[38]

Disputes have often arisen between the sovereigns of Asia for the title of king of the world, while the contest has proved that it could not belong to either of the competitors. The kingdom of the Turks was bounded by the Oxus or Gihon; and *Touran* was separated by that great river from the rival monarchy of *Iran,* or Persia, which in a smaller compass contained perhaps a larger measure of power and population. The Persians, who alternately invaded and repulsed the Turks and the Romans, were still ruled by the house of Sassan, which ascended the throne three hundred years before the accession of Justinian. His contemporary, Cabades, or Kobad, had been successful in war against the emperor Anastasius; but the reign of that prince was distracted by civil and religious troubles. A prisoner in the hands of his subjects, an exile among the enemies of Persia, he recovered his liberty by prostituting the honour of his wife, and regained his kingdom with the dangerous and mercenary aid of the barbarians who had slain his father. His nobles were suspicious that Kobad never forgave the authors of his expulsion, or even those of his restoration. The people was deluded and inflamed by the fanaticism of Mazdak,[39] who asserted

---

[38] All the details of these Turkish and Roman embassies, so curious in the history of human manners, are drawn from the Extracts of Menander p. 106-110, 151-154, 161-164 [295-303, 380-385, 397-405, ed. Bonn]), in which we often regret the want of order and connection.

[39] See D'Herbelot (Bibliot. Orient. p. 568, 929); Hyde (de Religione Vet. Persarum, c. 21, p. 290, 291); Pocock (Specimen Hist. Arab. p. 70, 71); Eutychius (Annal. tom. ii. p. 176); Texeira (in Stevens, Hist. of Persia, l. i. c. 34).

[Mazdak was an Archimagus born at Nischapour in Khorassan. His father's name was Bamdadan. He announced himself as a reformer of Zoroastrianism, and carried the doctrine of the two principles to a much greater height. He

the community of women [40] and the equality of mankind, whilst he appropriated the richest lands and most beautiful females to the use of his sectaries. The view of these disorders, which had been fomented by his laws and example,[41] embittered the declining age of the Persian monarch; and his fears were increased by the consciousness of his design to reverse the natural and customary order of succession in favour of his third and most favoured son, so famous under the names of Chosroes and Nushirvan. To render the youth more illustrious in the eyes of the nations, Kobad was desirous that he should be adopted by the emperor Justin: the hope of peace inclined the Byzantine court to accept this singular proposal; and Chosroes might have acquired a specious claim to the inheritance of his Roman parent. But the future mischief was diverted by the advice of the quæstor Proclus: a difficulty was started, whether the adoption should be performed as a civil or military rite;[42] the treaty was abruptly dissolved; and the sense of this indignity sunk deep into the mind of Chosroes, who had already advanced to the Tigris on his road to Constantinople. His father did not long survive the disappointment of his wishes: the testament of their deceased sovereign was read in the assembly of the nobles; and a powerful faction, prepared for the event, and regardless of the priority of age, exalted Chosroes to the throne of Persia. He filled that throne during a prosperous period of forty-eight years;[43] and the JUSTICE of Nushirvan is celebrated as the theme of immortal praise by the nations of the East.

taught the absolute indifference of human action, perfect equality of rank, community of property and women, marriages between the nearest kindred, but he interdicted animal food and enforced a vegetable diet. Prof. Bury says, "Its religious character distinguished Mazdakism from all modern socialistic theories. His doctrines were embraced by the ancient Gnostics, and Mazdak was enrolled by them with Thoth, Saturn, Zoroaster, Pythagoras, Epicurus, John, and Christ as the teachers of the true Gnostic doctrines."—O. S.]

[40] The fame of the new law for the community of women was soon propagated in Syria (Asseman. Biblioth. Orient. tom. iii. p. 402) and Greece (Procop. Persic. l. i. c. 5).

[41] He offered his own wife and sister to the prophet; but the prayers of Nushirvan saved his mother, and the indignant monarch never forgave the humiliation to which his filial piety had stooped: pedes tuos deosculatus (said he to Mazdak) cujus fœtor adhuc nares occupat (Pocock, Specimen Hist. Arab. p. 71).

[42] Procopius, Persic. l. i. c. 11. Was not Proclus over-wise? Was not the danger imaginary?—The excuse, at least, was injurious to a nation not ignorant of letters: οὐ γράμμασιν οἱ βάρβαροι τοὺς παῖδας ποιοῦνται ἀλλ' ὅπλων σκευῇ. Whether any mode of adoption was practised in Persia I much doubt.

[43] From Procopius and Agathias, Pagi (tom. ii. p. 543, 626) has proved that Chosroes Nushirvan ascended the throne in the fifth year of Justinian (A.D. 531, April 1—A.D. 532, April 1). But the true chronology, which harmonises with the Greeks and Orientals, is ascertained by John Malala (tom. ii. 211 [ed. Oxon.; p. 471, ed. Bonn]). Cabades, or Kobad, after a reign of forty-three years and two months, sickened the 8th, and died the 13th of September, A.D. 531, aged eighty-two years. According to the Annals of Eutychius, Nushirvan reigned forty-seven years and six months; and his death must consequently be placed in March, A.D. 579.

But the justice of kings is understood by themselves, and even by their subjects, with an ample indulgence for the gratification of passion and interest. The virtue of Chosroes was that of a conqueror who, in the measures of peace and war, is excited by ambition and restrained by prudence; who confounds the greatness with the happiness of a nation, and calmly devotes the lives of thousands to the fame, or even the amusement, of a single man. In his domestic administration the just Nushirvan would merit in our feelings the appellation of a tyrant. His two elder brothers had been deprived of their fair expectations of the diadem: their future life, between the supreme rank and the condition of subjects, was anxious to themselves and formidable to their master: fear, as well as revenge, might tempt them to rebel; the slightest evidence of a conspiracy satisfied the author of their wrongs; and the repose of Chosroes was secured by the death of these unhappy princes, with their families and adherents. One guiltless youth was saved and dismissed by the compassion of a veteran general; and this act of humanity, which was revealed by his son, overbalanced the merit of reducing twelve nations to the obedience of Persia. The zeal and prudence of Mebodes had fixed the diadem on the head of Chosroes himself; but he delayed to attend the royal summons till he had performed the duties of a military review: he was instantly commanded to repair to the iron tripod which stood before the gate of the palace,[44] where it was death to relieve or approach the victim; and Mebodes languished several days before his sentence was pronounced by the inflexible pride and calm ingratitude of the son of Kobad. But the people, more especially in the East, is disposed to forgive, and even to applaud, the cruelty which strikes at the loftiest heads—at the slaves of ambition, whose voluntary choice has exposed them to live in the smiles, and to perish by the frown, of a capricious monarch. In the execution of the laws which he had no temptation to violate; in the punishment of crimes which attacked his own dignity, as well as the happiness of individuals; Nushirvan, or Chosroes, deserved the appellation of *just*. His government was firm, rigorous, and impartial. It was the first labour of his reign to abolish the dangerous theory of common or equal possessions: the lands and women which the sectaries of Mazdak had usurped were restored to their lawful owners; and the temperate chastisement of the fanatics or impostors confirmed the domestic rights of society. Instead of listening with blind confidence to a favourite minister, he established four viziers over the four great provinces of his empire—Assyria, Media, Persia, and Bactriana. In the choice of judges, præfects, and counsellors, he strove to remove the mask which is always worn in the presence of kings: he wished to substitute the natural order of talents for the accidental distinctions of birth and fortune; he professed, in specious language, his intention to prefer those men who carried the poor

---

[44] Procopius, Persic. 1. i. c. 23 [tom. i. p. 118, ed. Bonn]. Brisson de Regn. Pers. p. 494. The gate of the palace of Ispahan is, or was, the fatal scene of disgrace or death (Chardin, Voyage en Perse, tom. iv. p. 312, 313).

in their bosoms, and to banish corruption from the seat of justice, as dogs were excluded from the temples of the Magi. The code of laws of the first Artaxerxes was revived and published as the rule of the magistrates; but the assurance of speedy punishment was the best security of their virtue. Their behaviour was inspected by a thousand eyes, their words were overheard by a thousand ears, the secret or public agents of the throne; and the provinces, from the Indian to the Arabian confines, were enlightened by the frequent visits of a sovereign who affected to emulate his celestial brother in his rapid and salutary career. Education and agriculture he viewed as the two objects most deserving of his care. In every city of Persia, orphans and the children of the poor were maintained and instructed at the public expense; the daughters were given in marriage to the richest citizens of their own rank, and the sons, according to their different talents, were employed in mechanic trades or promoted to more honourable service. The deserted villages were relieved by his bounty; to the peasants and farmers who were found incapable of cultivating their lands he distributed cattle, seed, and the instruments of husbandry; and the rare and inestimable treasure of fresh water was parsimoniously managed, and skilfully dispersed over the arid territory of Persia.[45] The prosperity of that kingdom was the effect and the evidence of his virtues; his vices are those of Oriental despotism; but in the long competition between Chosroes and Justinian, the advantage, both of merit and fortune, is almost always on the side of the barbarian.[46]

To the praise of justice Nushirvan united the reputation of knowledge; and the seven Greek philosophers who visited his court were invited and deceived by the strange assurance that a disciple of Plato was seated on the Persian throne. Did they expect that a prince, strenuously exercised in the toils of war and government, should agitate, with dexterity like their own, the abstruse and profound questions which amused the leisure of the schools of Athens? Could they hope that the precepts of philosophy should direct the life and control the passions of a despot whose infancy had been taught to consider *his* absolute and fluctuating will as the only rule of moral obligation? [47]

[45] In Persia the prince of the waters is an officer of state. The number of wells and subterraneous channels is much diminished, and with it the fertility of the soil: 400 wells have been recently lost near Tauris, and 42,000 were once reckoned in the province of Khorasan (Chardin, tom. iii. p. 99, 100; Tavernier, tom. i. p. 416).

[46] The character and government of Nushirvan is represented sometimes ir the words of D'Herbelot (Bibliot. Orient. p. 680, etc., from Khondemir), Eutychius (Annal. tom. ii. p. 179, 180—very rich), Abulpharagius (Dynast. vii. p. 94, 95—very poor), Tarikh Schikard (p. 144-150), Texeira (in Stevens, l. i. c. 35), Asseman (Bibliot. Orient. tom. iii. p. 404-410), and the Abbé Fourmont (Hist. de l'Acad. des Inscriptions, tom. vii. p. 325-334), who has translated a spurious or genuine testament of Nushirvan.

[47] A thousand years before his birth, the judges of Persia had given a solemn opinion—τῷ βασιλεύοντι Περσέων ἐξεῖναι ποιέειν τὸ ἂν βούληται (Herodot. l. iii. c. 31, p. 210, edit. Wesseling.). Nor had this constitutional maxim been neglected as a useless and barren theory.

The studies of Chosroes were ostentatious and superficial; but his example awakened the curiosity of an ingenious people, and the light of science was diffused over the dominions of Persia.[48] At Gondi Sapor, in the neighbourhood of the royal city of Susa, an academy of physic was founded, which insensibly became a liberal school of poetry, philosophy, and rhetoric.[49] The annals of the monarchy[50] were composed; and while recent and authentic history might afford some useful lessons both to the prince and people, the darkness of the first ages was embellished by the giants, the dragons, and the fabulous heroes of Oriental romance.[51] Every learned or confident stranger was enriched by the bounty and flattered by the conversation of the monarch: he nobly rewarded a Greek physician[52] by the deliverance of three thousand captives; and the sophists, who contended for his favour, were exasperated by the wealth and insolence of Uranius, their more successful rival. Nushirvan believed, or at least respected, the religion of the Magi; and some traces of persecution may be discovered in his reign.[53] Yet he allowed himself freely to compare the tenets of the various sects; and the theological disputes, in which he frequently presided, diminished the authority of the priest and enlightened the minds of the people. At his command the most celebrated writers of Greece and India were translated into the Persian language—a smooth and elegant idiom, recommended by Mahomet to the use of paradise, though it is branded with the epithets of savage and unmusical by the ignorance and presumption of Agathias.[54] Yet the Greek historian

[48] On the literary state of Persia, the Greek versions, philosophers, sophists, the learning or ignorance of Chosroes, Agathias (l. ii. [c. 28 sq.] p. 66-71 [p. 126 sqq., ed. Bonn]) displays much information and strong prejudices.

[49] Asseman. Bibliot. Orient. tom. iv. p. DCCXLV. vi. vii.

[50] The Shah Nameh, or Book of Kings, is perhaps the original record of history which was translated into Greek by the interpreter Sergius (Agathias, l. iv. [c. 30] p. 141 [p. 273, ed. Bonn]), preserved after the Mahometan conquest, and versified, in the year 994, by the national poet Ferdoussi. See D'Anquetil (Mém. de l'Académie, tom. xxxi. p. 379) and Sir William Jones (Hist. of Nadir Shah, p. 161).

[51] In the fifth century, the name of Restom, or Rostam, a hero who equalled the strength of twelve [one hundred and twenty—S.] elephants, was familiar to the Armenians (Moses Chorenensis, Hist. Armen. l. ii. c. 7, p. 96, edit. Whiston). In the beginning of the seventh, the Persian romance of Rostam and Isfendiar was applauded at Mecca (Sale's Koran, c. xxxi. p. 335). Yet this exposition of ludicrum novæ historiæ is not given by Maracci (Refutat. Alcoran. p. 544-548).

[52] Procop. (Goth. l. iv. c. 10 [tom. ii. p. 505, ed. Bonn]). Kobad had a favourite Greek physician, Stephen of Edessa (Persic. l. ii. c. 26 [tom. i. p. 271, ed. Bonn]). The practice was ancient; and Herodotus relates the adventures of Democedes of Crotona (l. iii. c. 125-137).

[53] See Pagi, tom. ii. p. 626. In one of the treaties an honourable article was inserted for the toleration and burial of the catholics (Menander, in Excerpt. Legat. p. 142 [p. 363 sq., ed. Bonn]). Nushizad, a son of Nushirvan, was a Christian, a rebel, and—a martyr? (D'Herbelot, p. 681.)

[54] On the Persian language, and its three dialects, consult D'Anquetil (p. 339-343) and Jones (p. 153-185): ἀγρίᾳ τινὶ γλώττῃ καὶ ἀμουσοτάτῃ, is the

might reasonably wonder that it should be found possible to execute an entire version of Plato and Aristotle in a foreign dialect, which had not been framed to express the spirit of freedom and the subtleties of philosophic disquisition. And, if the reason of the Stagyrite might be equally dark or equally intelligible in every tongue, the dramatic art and verbal argumentation of the disciple of Socrates [55] appear to be indissolubly mingled with the grace and perfection of his Attic style. In the search of universal knowledge, Nushirvan was informed that the moral and political fables of Pilpay, an ancient Brahman, were preserved with jealous reverence among the treasures of the kings of India. The physician Perozes was secretly despatched to the banks of the Ganges, with instructions to procure, at any price, the communication of this valuable work. His dexterity obtained a transcript, his learned diligence accomplished the translation; and the fables of Pilpay [56] were read and admired in the assembly of Nushirvan and his nobles. The Indian original and the Persian copy have long since disappeared; but this venerable monument has been saved by the curiosity cf the Arabian caliphs, revived in the modern Persic, the Turkish, the Syriac, the Hebrew, and the Greek idioms, and transfused through successive versions into the modern languages of Europe. In their present form, the peculiar character, the manners and religion of the Hindoos, are completely obliterated; and the intrinsic merit of the fables of Pilpay is far inferior to the concise elegance of Phædrus and the native graces of La Fontaine. Fifteen moral and political sentences are illustrated in a series of apologies; but the composition is intricate, the narrative prolix, and the precept obvious and barren. Yet the Brahman may assume the merit of *inventing* a pleasing fiction, which adorns the nakedness of truth, and alleviates, perhaps, to a royal ear, the harshness of instruction. With a similar design, to admonish kings that they

character which Agathias (l. ii. [c. 28] p. 67 [p. 126, ed. Bonn]) ascribes to an idiom renowned in the East for poetical softness.

[55] Agathias [l. c.] specifies the Gorgias, Phædon, Parmenides, and Timæus. Renaudot (Fabricius, Biblioth. Græc. tom. xii. p. 246-261) does not mention this barbaric version of Aristotle.

[56] Of these fables I have seen three copies in three different languages: 1. In *Greek*, translated by Simeon Seth (A.D. 1100) from the Arabic, and published by Starck at Berlin in 1697, in 12mo. 2. In *Latin*, a version from the Greek, Sapientia Indorum, inserted by Père Poussin at the end of his edition of Pachymer (p. 547-620, edit. Roman.). 3. In *French*, from the Turkish, dedicated, in 1540, to Sultan Soliman. Contes et Fables Indiennes de Bidpai et de Lokman, par MM. Galland et Cardonne, Paris, 1778, 3 vols. in 12mo. Mr. Warton (History of English Poetry, vol. i. p. 129-131) takes a larger scope.

[The oldest Indian collection is the Panchatantra—literally, the five collections—which were translated into Pehlevi in the reign of Nushirvan, from which the Arabic translation, executed by Abdolla Ibn Mokaffa in the eighth century, and styled " Kalila and Dimnah, or the Fables of Pilpay (or Bidpai)," was taken. They were rendered from Sanscrit into German in 1859 by Theodore Benfey, whose masterly introduction to the first volume of his " Pantschatantra " is the source whence much of our knowledge regarding this specific branch of Indian literature is drawn.—O. S.]

are strong only in the strength of their subjects, the same Indians invented the game of chess, which was likewise introduced into Persia under the reign of Nushirvan.[57]

The son of Kobad found his kingdom involved in a war with the successor of Constantine; and the anxiety of his domestic situation inclined him to grant the suspension of arms which Justinian was impatient to purchase. Chosroes saw the Roman ambassadors at his feet. He accepted eleven thousand pounds of gold as the price of an *endless* or indefinite peace;[58] some mutual exchanges were regulated; the Persian assumed the guard of the gates of Caucasus, and the demolition of Dara was suspended on condition that it should never be made the residence of the general of the East. This interval of repose had been solicited and was diligently improved by the ambition of the emperor: his African conquests were the first fruits of the Persian treaty; and the avarice of Chosroes was soothed by a large portion of the spoils of Carthage, which his ambassadors required in a tone of pleasantry and under the colour of friendship.[59] But the trophies of Belisarius disturbed the slumbers of the Great King; and he heard with astonishment, envy, and fear that Sicily, Italy, and Rome itself had been reduced in three rapid campaigns to the obedience of Justinian. Unpractised in the art of violating treaties, he secretly excited his bold and subtle vassal Almondar. That prince of the Saracens, who resided at Hira,[60] had not been included in the general peace, and still waged an obscure war against his rival Arethas, the chief of the tribe of Gassan, and confederate of the empire. The subject of their dispute was an extensive sheep-walk in the desert to the south of Palmyra. An immemorial tribute for the licence of pasture appeared to attest the rights of Almondar, while the Gassanite appealed to the Latin name of strata, a paved road, as an unquestionable evidence of the sovereignty and labours of the Romans.[61] The two monarchs supported the cause of their respective vassals; and the Persian Arab, without expecting the event of a slow and doubtful arbitration, enriched his flying camp with the spoil and captives of Syria. Instead of repelling the arms,

[57] See the Historia Shahiludii of Dr. Hyde (Syntagm. Dissertat. tom. ii. p. 61-69).

[58] The endless peace (Procopius, Persic. l. i. c. 22 [tom. i. p. 114, ed. Bonn]) was concluded or ratified in the sixth year, and third consulship, of Justinian (A.D. 533, between January 1 and April 1; Pagi, tom. ii. p. 550). Marcellinus, in his Chronicle, uses the style of Medes and Persians.

[59] Procopius, Persic. l. i. c. 26 [p. 137, ed. Bonn].

[60] Almondar, king of Hira, was deposed by Kobad, and restored by Nushirvan. His mother, from her beauty, was surnamed *Celestial Water,* an appellation which became hereditary, and was extended for a more noble cause (liberality in famine) to the Arab princes of Syria (Pocock, Specimen Hist. Arab. p. 69, 70).

[61] Procopius, Persic. l. ii. c. 1 [tom. i. p. 154, ed. Bonn]. We are ignorant of the origin and object of this *strata,* a paved road of ten days' journey from Auranitis to Babylonia. (See a Latin note in Delisle's Map Imp. Orient.) Wesseling and D'Anville are silent.

Justinian attempted to seduce the fidelity of Almondar, while he called from the extremities of the earth the nations of Æthiopia and Scythia to invade the dominions of his rival. But the aid of such allies was distant and precarious, and the discovery of this hostile correspondence justified the complaints of the Goths and Armenians, who implored, almost at the same time, the protection of Chosroes. The descendants of Arsaces, who were still numerous in Armenia, had been provoked to assert the last relics of national freedom and hereditary rank; and the ambassadors of Vitiges had secretly traversed the empire to expose the instant, and almost inevitable, danger of the kingdom of Italy. Their representations were uniform, weighty, and effectual. " We stand before your throne, the advocates of your interest as well as of our own. The ambitious and faithless Justinian aspires to be the sole master of the world. Since the endless peace, which betrayed the common freedom of mankind, that prince, your ally in words, your enemy in actions, has alike insulted his friends and foes, and has filled the earth with blood and confusion. Has he not violated the privileges of Armenia, the independence of Colchis, and the wild liberty of the Tzanian mountains? Has he not usurped, with equal avidity, the city of Bosphorus on the frozen Mæotis, and the vale of palm-trees on the shores of the Red Sea? The Moors, the Vandals, the Goths, have been successively oppressed, and each nation has calmly remained the spectator of their neighbour's ruin. Embrace, O king! the favourable moment; the East is left without defence, while the armies of Justinian and his renowned general are detained in the distant regions of the West. If you hesitate and delay, Belisarius and his victorious troops will soon return from the Tiber to the Tigris, and Persia may enjoy the wretched consolation of being the last devoured." [62]   By such arguments, Chosroes was easily persuaded to imitate the example which he condemned; but the Persian, ambitious of military fame, disdained the inactive warfare of a rival who issued his sanguinary commands from the secure station of the Byzantine palace.

Whatever might be the provocations of Chosroes, he abused the confidence of treaties; and the just reproaches of dissimulation and falsehood could only be concealed by the lustre of his victories.[63]   The Persian army, which had been assembled in the plains of Babylon, prudently declined the strong cities of Mesopotamia, and followed the western bank of the Euphrates, till the small though populous town

[62] I have blended, in a short speech, the two orations of the Arsacides of Armenia and the Gothic ambassadors. Procopius, in his public history, feels, and makes us feel, that Justinian was the true author of the war (Persic. l. ii. c. 2, 3).

[63] The invasion of Syria, the ruin of Antioch, etc., are related in a full and regular series by Procopius (Persic. l. ii. c. 5-14). Small collateral aid can be drawn from the Orientals: yet not they, but D'Herbelot himself (p. 680), should blush, when he blames them for making Justinian and Nushirvan contemporaries. On the geography of the seat of war, D'Anville (l'Euphrate et le Tigre) is sufficient and satisfactory.

of Dura presumed to arrest the progress of the Great King. The gates
of Dura, by treachery and surprise, were burst open; and as soon as
Chosroes had stained his scimitar with the blood of the inhabitants,
he dismissed the ambassador of Justinian to inform his master in what
place he had left the enemy of the Romans. The conqueror still
affected the praise of humanity and justice; and as he beheld a noble
matron with her infant rudely dragged along the ground, he sighed,
he wept, and implored the divine justice to punish the author of these
calamities. Yet the herd of twelve thousand captives was ransomed
for two hundred pounds of gold; the neighbouring bishop of Sergiopolis
pledged his faith for the payment, and in the subsequent year the
unfeeling avarice of Chosroes exacted the penalty of an obligation
which it was generous to contract and impossible to discharge. He
advanced into the heart of Syria; but a feeble enemy, who vanished
at his approach, disappointed him of the honour of victory; and as he
could not hope to establish his dominion, the Persian king displayed
in this inroad the mean and rapacious vices of a robber. Hierapolis,
Berrhœa or Aleppo, Apamea and Chalcis, were successively besieged:
they redeemed their safety by a ransom of gold or silver proportioned
to their respective strength and opulence, and their new master enforced
without observing the terms of capitulation. Educated in the religion
of the Magi, he exercised, without remorse, the lucrative trade of
sacrilege; and, after stripping of its gold and gems a piece of the true
cross, he generously restored the naked relic to the devotion of the
Christians of Apamea. No more than fourteen years had elapsed since
Antioch was ruined by an earthquake; but the queen of the East, the
new Theopolis, had been raised from the ground by the liberality of
Justinian; and the increasing greatness of the buildings and the people
already erased the memory of this recent disaster. On one side the
city was defended by the mountain, on the other by the river Orontes;
but the most accessible part was commanded by a superior eminence:
the proper remedies were rejected, from the despicable fear of discovering its weakness to the enemy; and Germanus, the emperor's nephew,
refused to trust his person and dignity within the walls of a besieged
city. The people of Antioch had inherited the vain and satirical genius
of their ancestors: they were elated by a sudden reinforcement of six
thousand soldiers; they disdained the offers of an easy capitulation,
and their intemperate clamours insulted from the ramparts the majesty
of the Great King. Under his eye the Persian myriads mounted with
scaling-ladders to the assault; the Roman mercenaries fled through the
opposite gate of Daphne; and the generous assistance of the youth of
Antioch served only to aggravate the miseries of their country. As
Chosroes, attended by the ambassadors of Justinian, was descending
from the mountain, he affected, in a plaintive voice, to deplore the obstinacy and ruin of that unhappy people; but the slaughter still raged
with unrelenting fury, and the city, at the command of a barbarian,
was delivered to the flames. The cathedral of Antioch was indeed

preserved by the avarice, not the piety, of the conqueror: a more honourable exemption was granted to the church of St. Julian and the quarter of the town where the ambassadors resided; some distant streets were saved by the shifting of the wind, and the walls still subsisted to protect, and soon to betray, their new inhabitants. Fanaticism had defaced the ornaments of Daphne; but Chosroes breathed a purer air amidst her groves and fountains, and some idolaters in his train might sacrifice with impunity to the nymphs of that elegant retreat. Eighteen miles below Antioch the river Orontes falls into the Mediterranean. The haughty Persian visited the term of his conquests, and, after bathing alone in the sea, he offered a solemn sacrifice of thanksgiving to the sun, or rather to the Creator of the sun, whom the Magi adored. If this act of superstition offended the prejudices of the Syrians, they were pleased by the courteous and even eager attention with which he assisted at the games of the circus; and as Chosroes had heard that the *blue* faction was espoused by the emperor, his peremptory command secured the victory of the *green* charioteer. From the discipline of his camp, the people derived more solid consolation, and they interceded in vain for the life of a soldier who had too faithfully copied the rapine of the just Nushirvan. At length, fatigued though unsatiated with the spoil of Syria, he slowly moved to the Euphrates, formed a temporary bridge in the neighbourhood of Barbalissus, and defined the space of three days for the entire passage of his numerous host. After his return he founded, at the distance of one day's journey from the palace of Ctesiphon, a new city, which perpetuated the joint names of Chosroes and of Antioch. The Syrian captives recognised the form and situation of their native abodes; baths and a stately circus were constructed for their use; and a colony of musicians and charioteers revived in Assyria the pleasures of a Greek capital. By the munificence of the royal founder, a liberal allowance was assigned to these fortunate exiles, and they enjoyed the singular privilege of bestowing freedom on the slaves whom they acknowledged as their kinsmen. Palestine and the holy wealth of Jerusalem were the next objects that attracted the ambition, or rather the avarice, of Chosroes. Constantinople and the palace of the Cæsars no longer appeared impregnable or remote; and his aspiring fancy already covered Asia Minor with the troops, and the Black Sea with the navies, of Persia.

These hopes might have been realised, if the conqueror of Italy had not been seasonably recalled to the defence of the East.[64] While Chosroes pursued his ambitious designs on the coast of the Euxine, Belisarius, at the head of an army without pay or discipline, encamped beyond the Euphrates, within six miles of Nisibis. He meditated, by a skilful operation, to draw the Persians from their impregnable citadel,

---

[64] In the public history of Procopius (Persic. l. ii. c. 16, 18, 19, 20, 21, 24, 25, 26, 27, 28) ; and with some slight exceptions, we may reasonably shut our ears against the malevolent whisper of the Anecdotes (c. 2, 3, with the Notes, as usual, of Alemannus).

and, improving his advantage in the field, either to intercept their retreat, or perhaps to enter the gates with the flying barbarians. He advanced one day's journey on the territories of Persia, reduced the fortress of Sisaurane, and sent the governor, with eight hundred chosen horsemen, to serve the emperor in his Italian wars. He detached Arethas and his Arabs, supported by twelve hundred Romans, to pass the Tigris, and to ravage the harvests of Assyria, a fruitful province, long exempt from the calamities of war. But the plans of Belisarius were disconcerted by the untractable spirit of Arethas, who neither returned to the camp, nor sent any intelligence of his motions. The Roman general was fixed in anxious expectation to the same spot; the time of action elapsed; the ardent sun of Mesopotamia inflamed with fevers the blood of his European soldiers; and the stationary troops and officers of Syria affected to tremble for the safety of their defenceless cities. Yet this diversion had already succeeded in forcing Chosroes to return with loss and precipitation; and if the skill of Belisarius had been seconded by discipline and valour, his success might have satisfied the sanguine wishes of the public, who required at his hands the conquest of Ctesiphon and the deliverance of the captives of Antioch. At the end of the campaign, he was recalled to Constantinople by an ungrateful court, but the dangers of the ensuing spring restored his confidence and command; and the hero, almost alone, was despatched, with the speed of post-horses, to repel, by his name and presence, the invasion of Syria. He found the Roman generals, among whom was a nephew of Justinian, imprisoned by their fears in the fortifications of Hierapolis. But instead of listening to their timid counsels, Belisarius commanded them to follow him to Europus, where he had resolved to collect his forces, and to execute whatever God should inspire him to achieve against the enemy. His firm attitude on the banks of the Euphrates restrained Chosroes from advancing towards Palestine; and he received with art and dignity the ambassadors, or rather spies, of the Persian monarch. The plain between Hierapolis and the river was covered with the squadrons of cavalry, six thousand hunters, tall and robust, who pursued their game without the apprehension of an enemy. On the opposite bank the ambassadors descried a thousand Armenian horse, who appeared to guard the passage of the Euphrates. The tent of Belisarius was of the coarsest linen, the simple equipage of a warrior who disdained the luxury of the East. Around his tent the nations who marched under his standard were arranged with skilful confusion. The Thracians and Illyrians were posted in the front, the Heruli and Goths in the centre; the prospect was closed by the Moors and Vandals, and their loose array seemed to multiply their numbers. Their dress was light and active; one soldier carried a whip, another a sword, a third a bow, a fourth, perhaps, a battle-axe, and the whole picture exhibited the intrepidity of the troops and the vigilance of the general. Chosroes was deluded by the address, and awed by the genius, of the lieutenant of Justinian. Conscious of the merit, and ignorant of the force, of his antagonist, he dreaded a decisive battle in a distant country, from whence not a Persian might return to relate the melancholy tale. The Great King hastened to repass the Euphrates; and Belisarius pressed his retreat, by affecting to oppose a measure so salutary to the empire, and which could scarcely have been prevented by an army of a hundred thousand men. Envy might suggest to ignorance and pride that the public enemy had been suffered to escape; but the African and Gothic triumphs are less glorious than this safe and bloodless victory, in which neither fortune, nor the valour of the soldiers, can subtract any part of the general's renown. The second removal of Belisarius from the Persian to the Italian war revealed the extent of his personal merit, which had corrected or supplied the want of discipline and courage. Fifteen generals, without concert or skill, led through the mountains of Armenia an army of thirty thousand Romans, inattentive to their signals, their ranks, and their ensigns. Four thousand Persians, entrenched in the camp of Dubis, vanquished, almost without a combat, this disorderly multitude; their useless arms were scattered along the road, and their horses sunk under the fatigue of their rapid flight. But the Arabs of the Roman party prevailed over their brethren; the Armenians returned to their allegiance; the cities of Dara and Edessa resisted a sudden assault and a regular siege, and the calamities of war were suspended by those of pestilence. A tacit or formal agreement between the two sovereigns protected the tranquillity of the Eastern frontier; and the arms of Chosroes were confined to the Colchian or Lazic war, which has been too minutely described by the historians of the times.[65]

The extreme length of the Euxine Sea,[66] from Constantinople to the mouth of the Phasis, may be computed as a voyage of nine days, and a measure of seven hundred miles. From the Iberian Caucasus, the most lofty and craggy mountains of Asia, that river descends with such oblique vehemence, that in a short space it is traversed by one hundred and twenty bridges. Nor does the stream become placid and navigable till it reaches the town of Sarapana, five days' journey from the Cyrus,

[65] The Lazic war, the contest of Rome and Persia on the Phasis, is tediously spun through many a page of Procopius (Persic. l. ii. c. 15, 17, 28, 29, 30; Gothic. l. iv. c. 7-16) and Agathias (l. ii., iii., and iv. p. 55-132, 141).
[66] The *Periplus*, or circumnavigation of the Euxine Sea, was described in Latin by Sallust, and in Greek by Arrian: 1. The former work, which no longer exists, has been restored by the *singular* diligence of M. de Brosses, first president of the parliament of Dijon (Hist. de la République Romaine, tom. ii. l. iii. p. 199-298), who ventures to assume the character of the Roman historian. His description of the Euxine is ingeniously formed of *all* the fragments of the original, and of *all* the Greeks and Latins whom Sallust might copy, or by whom he might be copied; and the merit of the execution atones for the whimsical design. 2. The Periplus of Arrian is addressed to the emperor Hadrian (in Geograph. Minor. Hudson, tom. i.), and contains whatever the governor of Pontus had seen from Trebizond to Dioscurias; whatever he had heard from Dioscurias to the Danube; and whatever he knew from the Danube to Trebizond.

which flows from the same hills, but in a contrary direction to the Caspian lake. The proximity of these rivers has suggested the practice, or at least the idea, of wafting the precious merchandise of India down the Oxus, over the Caspian, up the Cyrus, and with the current of the Phasis into the Euxine and Mediterranean seas. As it successively collects the streams of the plain of Colchis, the Phasis moves with diminished speed, though accumulated weight. At the mouth it is sixty fathoms deep and half a league broad, but a small woody island is interposed in the midst of the channel: the water, so soon as it has deposited an earthy or metallic sediment, floats on the surface of the waves, and is no longer susceptible of corruption. In a course of one hundred miles, forty of which are navigable for large vessels, the Phasis divides the celebrated region of Colchis,[67] or Mingrelia,[68] which, on three sides, is fortified by the Iberian and Armenian mountains, and whose maritime coast extends about two hundred miles from the neighbourhood of Trebizond to Dioscurias and the confines of Circassia. Both the soil and climate are relaxed by excessive moisture: twenty-eight rivers, besides the Phasis and his dependent streams, convey their waters to the sea; and the hollowness of the ground appears to indicate the subterraneous channels between the Euxine and the Caspian. In the fields where wheat or barley is sown, the earth is too soft to sustain the action of the plough; but the *gom,* a small grain, not unlike the millet or coriander seed, supplies the ordinary food of the people; and the use of bread is confined to the prince and his nobles. Yet the vintage is more plentiful than the harvest; and the bulk of the stems, as well as the quality of the wine, display the unassisted powers of nature. The same powers continually tend to overshadow the face of the country with thick forests: the timber of the hills, and the flax of the plains, contribute to the abundance of naval stores; the wild and tame animals, the horse, the ox, and the hog, are remarkably prolific, and the name of the pheasant is expressive of his native habitation on the banks of the Phasis. The gold-mines to the south of Trebizond, which are still worked with sufficient profit, were a subject of national dispute between Justinian and Chosroes; and it is not unreasonable to believe that a vein of precious metal may be equally

[67] Besides the many occasional hints from the poets, historians, etc., of antiquity, we may consult the geographical descriptions of Colchis by Strabo (l. xi. p. 760-765 [p. 497-501, ed. Casaub.]) and Pliny (Hist. Natur. vi. 5, 19, etc.).
[68] I shall quote, and have used, three modern descriptions of Mingrelia and the adjacent countries. 1. Of the Père Archangeli Lamberti (Relations de Thevenot, part i. p. 31-52, with a map), who has all the knowledge and prejudices of a missionary. 2. Of Chardin (Voyages en Perse, tom. i. p. 54, 68-168) : his observations are judicious; and his own adventures in the country are still more instructive than his observations. 3. Of Peyssonel (Observations sur les Peuples Barbares, p. 49, 50, 51, 58, 62, 64, 65, 71, etc., and a more recent treatise, Sur le Commerce de la Mer Noire, tom. ii. p. 1-53) : he had long resided at Caffa, as consul of France; and his erudition is less valuable than his experience.

diffused through the circle of the hills, although these secret treasures are neglected by the laziness, or concealed by the prudence, of the Mingrelians. The waters, impregnated with particles of gold, are carefully strained through sheepskins or fleeces; but this expedient, the groundwork perhaps of a marvellous fable, affords a faint image of the wealth extracted from a virgin earth by the power and industry of ancient kings. Their silver palaces and golden chambers surpass our belief; but the fame of their riches is said to have excited the enterprising avarice of the Argonauts.[69]   Tradition has affirmed, with some colour of reason, that Egypt planted on the Phasis a learned and polite colony,[70] which manufactured linen, built navies, and invented geographical maps. The ingenuity of the moderns has peopled with flourishing cities and nations the isthmus between the Euxine and the Caspian;[71] and a lively writer, observing the resemblance of climate, and, in his apprehension, of trade, has not hesitated to pronounce Colchis the Holland of antiquity.[72]

But the riches of Colchis shine only through the darkness of conjecture or tradition; and its genuine history presents a uniform scene of rudeness and poverty.   If one hundred and thirty languages were spoken in the market of Dioscurias,[73] they were the imperfect idioms of so many savage tribes or families, sequestered from each other in the valleys of Mount Caucasus; and their separation, which diminished the importance, must have multiplied the number of their rustic capitals.   In the present state of Mingrelia, a village is an assemblage of huts within a wooden fence; the fortresses are seated in the depth of forests; the princely town of Cyta, or Cotatis, consists of two hundred houses, and a stone edifice appertains only to the magnificence of kings.   Twelve ships from Constantinople, and about sixty barks, laden with the fruits of industry, annually cast anchor on the coast; and the list of Colchian exports is much increased, since the natives had only slaves and hides to offer in exchange for the corn and salt which they purchased from the subjects of Justinian.   Not a vestige can be found of the art, the knowledge, or the navigation of the ancient

---

[69] Pliny, Hist. Natur. l. xxxiii. 15.   The gold and silver mines of Colchis attracted the Argonauts (Strab. l. i. p. 77 [p. 45, ed. Casaub.]).   The sagacious Chardin could find no gold in mines, rivers, or elsewhere.   Yet a Mingrelian lost his hand and foot for showing some specimens at Constantinople of native gold.

[70] Herodot. l. ii. c. 104, 105, p. 150, 151; Diodor. Sicul. l. i. [c. 28] p. 33, edit. Wesseling; Dionys. Perieget. 689; and Eustath. ad loc Scholiast. ad Apollonium Argonaut. l. iv. 282-291.

[71] Montesquieu, Esprit des Loix, l. xxi. c. 6.   L'Isthme . . . couvert de villes et nations qui ne sont plus.

[72] Bougainville, Mémoires de l'Académie des Inscriptions, tom. xxvi. p. 33, on the African voyage of Hanno and the commerce of antiquity.

[73] A Greek historian, Timosthenes, had affirmed, in eam ccc nationes dissimilibus linguis descendere; and the modest Pliny is content to add, et postea a nostris cxxx interpretibus negotia ibi gesta (vi. 5) : but the words nunc deserta cover a multitude of past fictions.

Colchians: few Greeks desired or dared to pursue the footsteps of the Argonauts; and even the marks of an Egyptian colony are lost on a nearer approach. The rite of circumcision is practised only by the Mahometans of the Euxine; and the curled hair and swarthy complexion of Africa no longer disfigure the most perfect of the human race. It is in the adjacent climates of Georgia, Mingrelia, and Circassia, that nature has placed, at least to our eyes, the model of beauty, in the shape of the limbs, the colour of the skin, the symmetry of the features, and the expression of the countenance.[74] According to the destination of the two sexes, the men seem formed for action, the women for love; and the perpetual supply of females from Mount Caucasus has purified the blood, and improved the breed, of the southern nations of Asia. The proper district of Mingrelia, a portion only of the ancient Colchis, has long sustained an exportation of twelve thousand slaves. The number of prisoners or criminals would be inadequate to the annual demand; but the common people are in a state of servitude to their lords; the exercise of fraud or rapine is unpunished in a lawless community; and the market is continually replenished by the abuse of civil and paternal authority. Such a trade,[75] which reduces the human species to the level of cattle, may tend to encourage marriage and population, since the multitude of children enriches their sordid and inhuman parent. But this source of impure wealth must inevitably poison the national manners, obliterate the sense of honour and virtue, and almost extinguish the instincts of nature: the *Christians* of Georgia and Mingrelia are the most dissolute of mankind; and their children, who, in a tender age, are sold into foreign slavery, have already learned to imitate the rapine of the father and the prostitution of the mother. Yet, amidst the rudest ignorance, the untaught natives discover a singular dexterity both of mind and hand; and although the want of union and discipline exposes them to their more powerful neighbours, a bold and intrepid spirit has animated the Colchians of every age. In the host of Xerxes they served on foot; and their arms were a dagger or a javelin, a wooden casque, and a buckler of raw hides. But in their own country the use of cavalry has more generally prevailed: the meanest of the peasants disdain to walk; the martial nobles are possessed, perhaps, of two hundred horses; and above five thousand are numbered in the train of the prince of Mingrelia. The Colchian government has been always a pure and hereditary kingdom; and the authority of the sovereign is only restrained by the turbulence of his subjects. Whenever

[74] Buffon (Hist. Nat. tom. iii. p. 433-437) collects the unanimous suffrage of naturalists and travellers. If, in the time of Herodotus, they were in truth μελάγχροes and οὐλότριχεs (and he had observed them with care), this precious fact is an example of the influence of climate on a foreign colony.

[75] The Mingrelian ambassador arrived at Constantinople with two hundred persons; but he ate (*sold*) them day by day, till his retinue was diminished to a secretary and two valets (Tavernier, tom. i. p. 365). To purchase his mistress, a Mingrelian gentleman sold twelve priests and his wife to the Turks (Chardin, tom. i. p. 66).

they were obedient, he could lead a numerous army into the field; but some faith is requisite to believe that the single tribe of the Suanians was composed of two hundred thousand soldiers, or that the population of Mingrelia now amounts to four millions of inhabitants.[76]

It was the boast of the Colchians that their ancestors had checked the victories of Sesostris; and the defeat of the Egyptian is less incredible than his successful progress as far as the foot of Mount Caucasus. They sunk without any memorable effort under the arms of Cyrus, followed in distant wars the standard of the Great King, and presented him every fifth year with one hundred boys and as many virgins, the fairest produce of the land.[77] Yet he accepted this *gift* like the gold and ebony of India, the frankincense of the Arabs, or the negroes and ivory of Æthiopia: the Colchians were not subject to the dominion of a satrap, and they continued to enjoy the name as well as substance of national independence.[78] After the fall of the Persian empire, Mithridates, king of Pontus, added Colchis to the wide circle of his dominions on the Euxine; and when the natives presumed to request that his son might reign over them, he bound the ambitious youth in chains of gold, and delegated a servant in his place. In pursuit of Mithridates, the Romans advanced to the banks of the Phasis, and their galleys ascended the river till they reached the camp of Pompey and his legions.[79] But the senate, and afterwards the emperors, disdained to reduce that distant and useless conquest into the form of a province. The family of a Greek rhetorician was permitted to reign in Colchis and the adjacent kingdoms from the time of Mark Antony to that of Nero; and after the race of Polemo [80] was extinct, the eastern Pontus, which preserved his name, extended no farther than the neighbourhood of Trebizond. Beyond these limits the fortifications of Hyssus, of Apsarus, of the Phasis, of Dioscurias or Sebastopolis, and

---

[76] Strabo, l. xi. p. 763 [p. 499, ed. Casaub.]. Lamberti, Relation de la Mingrelie. Yet we must avoid the contrary extreme of Chardin, who allows no more than 20,000 inhabitants to supply an annual exportation of 12,000 slaves; an absurdity unworthy of that judicious traveller.

[77] Herodot. l. iii. c. 97. See, in l. vii. c. 79, their arms and service in the expedition of Xerxes against Greece.

[78] Xenophon, who had encountered the Colchians in his retreat (Anabasis, l. iv. [c. 8] p. 320, 343, 348, edit. Hutchinson; and Foster's Dissertation, p. liii.-lviii., in Spelman's English version, vol. ii.), styles them αὐτόνομοι. Before the conquest of Mithridates they are named by Appian ἔθνος ἀρειμανὲς (de Bell. Mithridatico, c. 15, tom. i. p. 661, of the last and best edition, by John Schweighæuser, Lipsiæ, 1785, 3 vols. large octavo).

[79] The conquest of Colchis by Mithridates and Pompey is marked by Appian (de Bell. Mithridat. [l. c.]) and Plutarch (in Vit. Pomp. [c. 30, 34]).

[80] We may trace the rise and fall of the family of Polemo, in Strabo (l. xi. p. 755; l. xii. p. 867 [p. 493 and 578, ed. Casaub.]), Dion Cassius or Xiphilin (p. 588, 593, 601, 719, 754, 915, 946, edit. Reimar [l. xlix. c. 25, 33, 44; l. liii. c. 25; l. liv. c. 24; l. lix. c. 12; l. lx. c. 8]), Suetonius (in Neron. c. 18, in Vespasian. c. 8), Eutropius (vii. 14 [9], Josephus (Antiq. Judaic. l. xx. c. 6, p. 970, edit. Havercamp), and Eusebius (Chron. with Scaliger, Animadvers. p. 196).

of Pityus, were guarded by sufficient detachments of horse and foot; and six princes of Colchis received their diadems from the lieutenants of Cæsar. One of these lieutenants, the eloquent and philosophic Arrian, surveyed and has described the Euxine coast under the reign of Hadrian. The garrison which he reviewed at the mouth of the Phasis consisted of four hundred chosen legionaries; the brick walls and towers, the double ditch, and the military engines on the rampart, rendered this place inaccessible to the barbarians; but the new suburbs which had been built by the merchants and veterans required in the opinion of Arrian some external defence.[81] As the strength of the empire was gradually impaired, the Romans stationed on the Phasis were either withdrawn or expelled; and the tribe of the Lazi,[82] whose posterity speak a foreign dialect and inhabit the sea-coast of Trezibond, imposed their name and dominion on the ancient kingdom of Colchis. Their independence was soon invaded by a formidable neighbour, who had acquired by arms and treaties the sovereignty of Iberia. The dependent king of Lazica received his sceptre at the hands of the Persian monarch, and the successors of Constantine acquiesced in this injurious claim, which was proudly urged as a right of immemorial prescription. In the beginning of the sixth century their influence was restored by the introduction of Christianity, which the Mingrelians still profess with becoming zeal, without understanding the doctrines or observing the precepts of their religion. After the decease of his father, Zathus was exalted to the regal dignity by the favour of the Great King; but the pious youth abhorred the ceremonies of the Magi, and sought in the palace of Constantinople an orthodox baptism, a noble wife, and the alliance of the emperor Justin. The king of Lazica was solemnly invested with the diadem, and his cloak and tunic of white silk, with a gold border, displayed in rich embroidery the figure of his new patron, who soothed the jealousy of the Persian court, and excused the revolt of Colchis, by the venerable names of hospitality and religion. The common interest of both empires imposed on the Colchians the duty of guarding the passes of Mount Caucasus, where a wall of sixty miles is now defended by the monthly service of the musketeers of Mingrelia.[83]

[81] In the time of Procopius there were no Roman forts on the Phasis. Pityus and Sebastopolis were evacuated on the rumour of the Persians (Goth. 1. iv. c. 4); but the latter was afterwards restored by Justinian (de Ædif. 1. iii. c. 7 [tom. iii. p. 261, ed. Bonn]).

[82] In the time of Pliny, Arrian, and Ptolemy, the Lazi were a particular tribe on the northern skirts of Colchis (Cellarius, Geograph. Antiq. tom. ii. p. 222). In the age of Justinian they spread, or at least reigned, over the whole country. At present they have migrated along the coast towards Trebizond, and compose a rude seafaring people, with a peculiar language (Chardin, p. 149; Peyssonel, p. 64).

[83] John Malala, Chron. tom. ii. p. 134-137 [ed. Oxon.; p. 412-414, ed. Bonn]; Theophanes, p. 144 [tom. i. p. 259, ed Bonn]; Hist. Miscell. 1. xv. p. 103. The fact is authentic, but the date seems too recent. In speaking of their Persian alliance, the Lazi contemporaries of Justinian employ the most obsolete words—

But this honourable connection was soon corrupted by the avarice and ambition of the Romans. Degraded from the rank of allies, the Lazi were incessantly reminded by words and actions of their dependent state. At the distance of a day's journey beyond the Apsarus they beheld the rising fortress of Petra,[84] which commanded the maritime country to the south of the Phasis. Instead of being protected by the valour, Colchis was insulted by the licentiousness, of foreign mercenaries; the benefits of commerce were converted into base and vexatious monopoly; and Gubazes, the native prince, was reduced to a pageant of royalty by the superior influence of the officers of Justinian. Disappointed in their expectations of Christian virtue, the indignant Lazi reposed some confidence in the justice of an unbeliever. After a private assurance that their ambassadors should not be delivered to the Romans, they publicly solicited the friendship and aid of Chosroes. The sagacious monarch instantly discerned the use and importance of Colchis, and meditated a plan of conquest which was renewed at the end of a thousand years by Shah Abbas, the wisest and most powerful of his successors.[85] His ambition was fired by the hope of launching a Persian navy from the Phasis, of commanding the trade and navigation of the Euxine Sea, of desolating the coast of Pontus and Bithynia, of distressing, perhaps of attacking, Constantinople, and of persuading the barbarians of Europe to second his arms and counsels against the common enemy of mankind. Under the pretence of a Scythian war he silently led his troops to the frontiers of Iberia; the Colchian guides were prepared to conduct them through the woods and along the precipices of Mount Caucasus, and a narrow path was laboriously formed into a safe and spacious highway for the march of cavalry, and even of elephants. Gubazes laid his person and diadem at the feet of the king of Persia, his Colchians imitated the submission of their prince; and after the walls of Petra had been shaken, the Roman garrison prevented by a capitulation the impending fury of the last assault. But the Lazi soon discovered that their impatience had urged them to choose an evil more intolerable than the calamities which they strove to escape. The monopoly of salt and corn was effectually removed by the loss of those valuable commodities. The authority of a Roman legislator was succeeded by the pride of an Oriental despot, who beheld with equal disdain the slaves whom he had exalted, and the kings whom he had humbled before the footstool of his throne.

ἐν γράμμασι μνημεῖα, πρόγονοι, etc. Could they belong to a connection which had not been dissolved above twenty years?

[84] The sole vestige of Petra subsists in the writings of Procopius and Agathias. Most of the towns and castles of Lazica may be found by comparing their names and position with the map of Mingrelia, in Lamberti.

[85] See the amusing letters of Pietro della Valle, the Roman traveller (Viaggi, tom. ii. 207, 209, 213, 215, 266, 286, 300; tom. iii. p. 54, 127). In the years 1618, 1619, and 1620, he conversed with Shah Abbas, and strongly encouraged a design which might have united Persia and Europe against their common enemy the Turk.

The adoration of fire was introduced into Colchis by the zeal of the Magi, their intolerant spirit provoked the fervour of a Christian people, and the prejudice of nature or education was wounded by the impious practice of exposing the dead bodies of their parents on the summit of a lofty tower to the crows and vultures of the air.[86] Conscious of the increasing hatred which retarded the execution of his great designs, the just Nushirvan had secretly given orders to assassinate the king of the Lazi, to transplant the people into some distant land, and to fix a faithful and warlike colony on the banks of the Phasis. The watchful jealousy of the Colchians foresaw and averted the approaching ruin. Their repentance was accepted at Constantinople by the prudence, rather than the clemency, of Justinian; and he commanded Dagisteus, with seven thousand Romans and one thousand of the Zani, to expel the Persians from the coast of the Euxine.

The siege of Petra, which the Roman general with the aid of the Lazi immediately undertook, is one of the most remarkable actions of the age. The city was seated on a craggy rock, which hung over the sea, and communicated by a steep and narrow path with the land. Since the approach was difficult, the attack might be deemed impossible; the Persian conqueror had strengthened the fortifications of Justinian, and the places least inaccessible were covered by additional bulwarks. In this important fortress the vigilance of Chosroes had deposited a magazine of offensive and defensive arms sufficient for five times the number, not only of the garrison, but of the besiegers themselves. The stock of flour and salt provisions was adequate to the consumption of five years; the want of wine was supplied by vinegar, and grain from whence a strong liquor was extracted; and a triple aqueduct eluded the diligence and even the suspicions of the enemy. But the firmest defence of Petra was placed in the valour of fifteen hundred Persians, who resisted the assaults of the Romans, whilst in a softer vein of earth a mine was secretly perforated. The wall, supported by slender and temporary props, hung tottering in the air; but Dagisteus delayed the attack till he had secured a specific recompense, and the town was relieved before the return of his messenger from Constantinople. The Persian garrison was reduced to four hundred men, of whom no more than fifty were exempt from sickness or wounds; yet such had been their inflexible perseverance, that they concealed their losses from the enemy by enduring without a murmur the sight and putrefying stench of the dead bodies of their eleven hundred companions. After their deliverance the breaches were hastily stopped with sandbags, the mine was replen-

---

[86] See Herodotus (l. i. c. 140, p. 69), who speaks with diffidence, Lacher tom. i. p. 399-401; Notes sur Herodote), Procopius (Persic. l. i. c. 11 [tom. i. p. 56, ed. Bonn]), and Agathias (l. ii. p. 61, 62 [ed. Par.; p. 113 *sq.*, ed. Bonn]). This practice, agreeable to the Zendavesta (Hyde, de Relig. Pers. c. 34, p. 414-421), demonstrates that the burial of the Persian kings (Xenophon, Cyropæd. l. viii. [c. 7] p. 658), τί γὰρ τούτου μακαρίωτερον τοῦ τῇ γῇ μιχθῆναι, is a Greek fiction, and that their tombs could be no more than cenotaphs.

ished with earth, a new wall was erected on a frame of substantial timber, and a fresh garrison of three thousand men was stationed at Petra to sustain the labours of a second siege. The operations, both of the attack and defence, were conducted with skilful obstinacy; and each party derived useful lessons from the experience of their past faults. A battering-ram was invented, of light construction and powerful effect; it was transported and worked by the hands of forty soldiers; and as the stones were loosened by its repeated strokes, they were torn with long iron hooks from the wall. From those walls a shower of darts was incessantly poured on the heads of the assailants, but they were most dangerously annoyed by a fiery composition of sulphur and bitumen, which in Colchis might with some propriety be named the oil of Medea. Of six thousand Romans who mounted the scaling-ladders, their general Besas was first, a gallant veteran of seventy years of age: the courage of their leader, his fall, and extreme danger, animated the irresistible effort of his troops, and their prevailing numbers oppressed the strength, without subduing the spirit, of the Persian garrison. The fate of these valiant men deserves to be more distinctly noticed. Seven hundred had perished in the siege, two thousand three hundred survived to defend the breach. One thousand and seventy were destroyed with fire and sword in the last assault; and if seven hundred and thirty were made prisoners, only eighteen among them were found without the marks of honourable wounds. The remaining five hundred escaped into the citadel, which they maintained without any hopes of relief, rejecting the fairest terms of capitulation and service till they were lost in the flames. They died in obedience to the commands of their prince, and such examples of loyalty and valour might excite their countrymen to deeds of equal despair and more prosperous event. The instant demolition of the works of Petra confessed the astonishment and apprehension of the conqueror.

A Spartan would have praised and pitied the virtue of these heroic slaves; but the tedious warfare and alternate success of the Roman and Persian arms cannot detain the attention of posterity at the foot of Mount Caucasus. The advantages obtained by the troops of Justinian were more frequent and splendid; but the forces of the Great King were continually supplied till they amounted to eight elephants and seventy thousand men, including twelve thousand Scythian allies and above three thousand Dilemites, who descended by their free choice from the hills of Hyrcania, and were equally formidable in close or in distant combat. The siege of Archæopolis, a name imposed or corrupted by the Greeks, was raised with some loss and precipitation, but the Persians occupied the passes of Iberia. Colchis was enslaved by their forts and garrisons, they devoured the scanty sustenance of the people, and the prince of the Lazi fled into the mountains. In the Roman camp faith and discipline were unknown, and the independent leaders, who were invested with equal power, disputed with each other the pre-eminence of vice and corruption. The Persians followed without a murmur the commands of a single chief, who implicitly obeyed the instructions of their supreme lord. Their general was distinguished among the heroes of the East by his wisdom in council and his valour in the field. The advanced age of Mermeroes, and the lameness of both his feet, could not diminish the activity of his mind or even of his body; and, whilst he was carried in a litter in the front of battle, he inspired terror to the enemy, and a just confidence to the troops, who under his banners were always successful. After his death the command devolved to Nacoragan, a proud satrap who, in a conference with the Imperial chiefs, had presumed to declare that he disposed of victory as absolutely as of the ring on his finger. Such presumption was the natural cause and forerunner of a shameful defeat. The Romans had been gradually repulsed to the edge of the sea-shore; and their last camp, on the ruins of the Grecian colony of Phasis, was defended on all sides by strong entrenchments, the river, the Euxine, and a fleet of galleys. Despair united their counsels and invigorated their arms; they withstood the assault of the Persians, and the flight of Nacoragan preceded or followed the slaughter of ten thousand of his bravest soldiers. He escaped from the Romans to fall into the hands of an unforgiving master, who severely chastised the error of his own choice: the unfortunate general was flayed alive, and his skin, stuffed into the human form, was exposed on a mountain—a dreadful warning to those who might hereafter be intrusted with the fame and fortune of Persia.[87] Yet the prudence of Chosroes insensibly relinquished the prosecution of the Colchian war, in the just persuasion that it is impossible to reduce, or at least to hold, a distant country against the wishes and efforts of its inhabitants. The fidelity of Gubazes sustained the most rigorous trials. He patiently endured the hardships of a savage life, and rejected with disdain the specious temptations of the Persian court. The king of the Lazi had been educated in the Christian religion; his mother was the daughter of a senator; during his youth he had served ten years a silentiary of the Byzantine palace,[88] and the arrears of an unpaid salary were a motive of attachment as well as of complaint. But the long continuance of his sufferings extorted from him a naked representation of the truth, and truth was an unpardonable libel on the lieutenants of Justinian, who, amidst the delays of a ruinous war, had spared his enemies and trampled on his allies. Their malicious information persuaded the emperor that his faithless vassal already meditated a second defection: an order was surprised to send him prisoner to Constantinople; a treacherous clause was inserted that he might be lawfully killed

---

[87] The punishment of flaying alive could not be introduced into Persia by Sapor (Brisson, de Regn. Pers. 1. ii. p. 578), nor could it be copied from the foolish tale of Marsyas the Phrygian piper, most foolishly quoted as a precedent by Agathias (l. iv. p. 132, 133).

[88] In the palace of Constantinople there were thirty silentiaries, who are styled hastati ante fores cubiculi, τῆς [ἀμφὶ τὸν βασιλέα] σιγῆς ἐπιστάται, an honourable title which conferred the rank, without imposing the duties, of a senator (Cod. Theodos. l. vi. tit. 23; Gothofred. Comment. tom. ii. p. 129).

in case of resistance; and Gubazes, without arms or suspicion of danger, was stabbed in the security of a friendly interview. In the first moments of rage and despair, the Colchians would have sacrificed their country and religion to the gratification of revenge. But the authority and eloquence of the wiser few obtained a salutary pause: the victory of the Phasis restored the terror of the Roman arms, and the emperor was solicitous to absolve his own name from the imputation of so foul a murder. A judge of senatorial rank was commissioned to inquire into the conduct and death of the king of the Lazi. He ascended a stately tribunal, encompassed by the ministers of justice and punishment: in the presence of both nations this extraordinary cause was pleaded according to the forms of civil jurisprudence, and some satisfaction was granted to an injured people by the sentence and execution of the meaner criminals.[89]

In peace the king of Persia continually sought the pretences of a rupture, but no sooner had he taken up arms than he expressed his desire of a safe and honourable treaty. During the fiercest hostilities the two monarchs entertained a deceitful negotiation: and such was the superiority of Chosroes, that, whilst he treated the Roman ministers with insolence and contempt, he obtained the most unprecedented honours for his own ambassadors at the Imperial court. The successor of Cyrus assumed the majesty of the Eastern sun, and graciously permitted his younger brother Justinian to reign over the West with the pale and reflected splendour of the moon. This gigantic style was supported by the pomp and eloquence of Isdigune, one of the royal chamberlains. His wife and daughters, with a train of eunuchs and camels, attended the march of the ambassador; two satraps with golden diadems were numbered among his followers; he was guarded by five hundred horse, the most valiant of the Persians, and the Roman governor of Dara wisely refused to admit more than twenty of this martial and hostile caravan. When Isdigune had saluted the emperor and delivered his presents, he passed ten months at Constantinople without discussing any serious affairs. Instead of being confined in his palace, and receiving food and water from the hands of his keepers, the Persian ambassador, without spies or guards, was allowed to visit the capital, and the freedom of conversation and trade enjoyed by his domestics offended the prejudices of an age which rigorously practised the law of nations without confidence or courtesy.[90] By an unexampled indulgence, his interpreter, a servant below the notice of a Roman magistrate, was

---

[89] On these judicial orations Agathias (l. iii. p. 81-89; l. iv. p. 108-119 [p. 155-170, 206-230, ed. Bonn]) lavishes eighteen or twenty pages of false and florid rhetoric. His ignorance or carelessness overlooks the strongest argument against the king of Lazica—his former revolt.

[90] Procopius represents the practice of the Gothic court of Ravenna (Goth. l. i. c. 7 [tom. ii. p. 34, ed. Bonn]); and foreign ambassadors have been treated with the same jealousy and rigour in Turkey (Busbequius, Epist. iii. p. 149, 242, etc.), Russia (Voyage d'Olearius), and China (Narrative of M. de Lange, in Bell's Travels, vol. ii. p. 189-311).

seated at the table of Justinian by the side of his master, and one thousand pounds of gold might be assigned for the expense of his journey and entertainment. Yet the repeated labours of Isdigune could procure only a partial and imperfect truce, which was always purchased with the treasures, and renewed at the solicitation, of the Byzantine court. Many years of fruitless desolation elapsed before Justinian and Chosroes were compelled by mutual lassitude to consult the repose of their declining age. At a conference held on the frontier, each party, without expecting to gain credit, displayed the power, the justice, and the pacific intentions of their respective sovereigns; but necessity and interest dictated the treaty of peace, which was concluded for a term of fifty years, diligently composed in the Greek and Persian languages, and attested by the seals of twelve interpreters. The liberty of commerce and religion was fixed and defined, the allies of the emperor and the Great King were included in the same benefits and obligations, and the most scrupulous precautions were provided to prevent or determine the accidental disputes that might arise on the confines of two hostile nations. After twenty years of destructive though feeble war, the limits still remained without alteration, and Chosroes was persuaded to renounce his dangerous claim to the possession or sovereignty of Colchis and its dependent states. Rich in the accumulated treasures of the East, he extorted from the Romans an annual payment of thirty thousand pieces of gold; and the smallness of the sum revealed the disgrace of a tribute in its naked deformity. In a previous debate, the chariot of Sesostris and the wheel of fortune were applied by one of the Ministers of Justinian, who observed that the reduction of Antioch and some Syrian cities had elevated beyond measure the vain and ambitious spirit of the barbarian. " You are mistaken," replied the modest Persian; " the king of kings, the lord of mankind, looks down with contempt on such petty acquisitions; and of the ten nations vanquished by his invincible arms, he esteems the Romans as the least formidable." [91] According to the Orientals, the empire of Nushirvan extended from Ferganah, in Transoxiana, to Yemen, or Arabia Felix. He subdued the rebels of Hyrcania, reduced the provinces of Cabul and Zablestan on the banks of the Indus, broke the power of the Euthalites, terminated by an honourable treaty the Turkish war, and admitted the daughter of the great khan into the number of his lawful wives. Victorious and respected among the princes of Asia, he gave audience, in his palace of Madain or Ctesiphon, to the ambassadors of the world. Their gifts or tributes, arms, rich garments, gems, slaves, or aromatics, were humbly presented at the foot of his throne; and he condescended to accept from the king of India ten quintals of the wood of aloes, a

---

[91] The negotiations and treaties between Justinian and Chosroes are copiously explained by Procopius (Persic. l. ii. c. 10, 13, 26, 27, 28; Gothic. l. ii. c. 11, 15; Agathias, l. iv. p. 141, 142 [ed. Par.; p. 274 sqq., ed. Bonn]), and Menander (in Excerpt. Legat. p. 132-147 [p. 346 sqq., ed. Bonn]). Consult Barbeyrac, Hist. des Anciens Traités, tom. ii. p. 154, 181-184, 193-200.

maid seven cubits in height, and a carpet softer than silk, the skin, as it was reported, of an extraordinary serpent.[92]

Justinian had been reproached for his alliance with the Æthiopians, as if he attempted to introduce a people of savage negroes into the system of civilised society. But the friends of the Roman empire, the Axumites or Abyssinians, may be always distinguished from the original natives of Africa.[93] The hand of nature has flattened the noses of the negroes, covered their heads with shaggy wool, and tinged their skin with inherent and indelible blackness. But the olive complexion of the Abyssinians, their hair, shape, and features, distinctly mark them as a colony of Arabs, and this descent is confirmed by the resemblance of language and manners, the report of an ancient emigration, and the narrow interval between the shores of the Red Sea. Christianity had raised that nation above the level of African barbarism;[94] their intercourse with Egypt and the successors of Constantine [95] had communicated the rudiments of the arts and sciences: their vessels traded to the isle of Ceylon,[96] and seven kingdoms obeyed the Negus or supreme prince of Abyssinia. The independence of the Homerites,[97]

[92] D'Herbelot, Biblioth. Orient. p. 680, 681, 294, 295.
[93] See Buffon, Hist. Naturelle, tom. iii. p. 449. This Arab cast of features and complexion, which has continued 3400 years (Ludolph. Hist. et Comment. Æthiopic. l. i. c. 4) in the colony of Abyssinia, will justify the suspicion that race, as well as climate, must have contributed to form the negroes of the adjacent and similar regions.
[94] The Portuguese missionaries, Alvarez (Ramusio, tom. i. fol. 204, rect. 274, vers.), Bermudez (Purchas's Pilgrims, vol. ii. l. v. c. 7, p. 1149-1188), Lobo (Relation, etc., par M. le Grand, with xv Dissertations, Paris, 1728), and Tellez (Relations de Thevenot, part iv.), could only relate of modern Abyssinia what they had seen or invented. The erudition of Ludolphus (Hist. Æthiopica, Francofurt. 1681; Commentarius, 1691; Appendix, 1694), in twenty-five languages, could add little concerning its ancient history. Yet the fame of Caled, or Ellisthæus, the conqueror of Yemen, is celebrated in national songs and legends.
[95] The negotiations of Justinian with the Axumites, or Æthiopians, are recorded by Procopius (Persic. l. i. c. 19, 20) and John Malala (tom. ii. p. 163-165, 193-196 [p. 433, 434-457, 459, ed. Bonn]). The historian of Antioch quotes the original narrative of the ambassador Nonnosus, of which Photius (Biblioth. Cod. iii.) has preserved a curious extract.
[96] The trade of the Axumites to the coast of India and Africa and the isle of Ceylon is curiously represented by Cosmas Indicopleustes (Topograph. Christian. l. ii. p. 132, 138, 139, 140; l. xi. p. 338, 339).
[97] [The Axumites and the Hemyarites or Homerites were closely allied peoples. The Homerites hailed from Yemen in Arabia, and were largely engaged in the overland carrying trade between East and West, before the sea-route by the Cape of Good Hope was discovered by Vasco da Gama. These Homerites had crossed the Red Sea to Abyssinia, on the western side. The chief city of that state was called Axum, and the people were often termed Axumites. The Homerites succeeded in overcoming the Axumites at first, but eventually both states remained watchful rivals of each other until, in the fourth century, we find that the king of Axum had brought the Homerites under his authority. Both nations were originally adherents of the old Sabæan faith, but about the middle of the fourth century Christianity was introduced into Abyssinia, while the conversion of the Homerites was begun

who reigned in the rich and happy Arabia, was first violated by an Æthiopian conqueror: he drew his hereditary claim from the Queen of Sheba,[98] and his ambition was sanctified by religious zeal. The Jews, powerful and active in exile, had seduced the mind of Dunaan, prince of the Homerites. They urged him to retaliate the persecution inflicted by the Imperial laws on their unfortunate brethren; some Roman merchants were injuriously treated, and several Christians of Negra [99] were honoured with the crown of martyrdom.[100] The churches of Arabia implored the protection of the Abyssinian monarch. The Negus passed the Red Sea with a fleet and army, deprived the Jewish proselyte of his kingdom and life, and extinguished a race of princes who had ruled above two thousand years the sequestered region of myrrh and frankincense. The conqueror immediately announced the victory of the Gospel, requested an orthodox patriarch, and so warmly professed his friendship to the Roman empire, that Justinian was flattered by the hope of diverting the silk trade through the channel of Abyssinia, and of exciting the forces of Arabia against the Persian king. Nonnosus, descended from a family of ambassadors, was named by the emperor to execute this important commission. He wisely declined the shorter but more dangerous road through the sandy deserts of Nubia, ascended the Nile, embarked on the Red Sea, and safely landed at the African port of Adulis. From Adulis to the royal city of Axume is no more than fifty leagues in a direct line, but the winding passes of the mountains detained the ambassador fifteen days, and as he traversed the forests he saw, and vaguely computed, about five thousand wild elephants. The capital, according to his report, was large and populous; and the *village* of Axume is still conspicuous by the regal coronations, by the ruins of a Christian temple, and by sixteen or seventeen obelisks inscribed with Grecian characters.[101] But the Negus gave audience

in the reign of the emperor Constantius, but it was not until about the beginning of the sixth century that the faith of Christ began to spread in both districts. But later in the same century the Homerites and Axumites were at war, and religious matters suffered somewhat until peace was restored. Those interested in this subject should read Bury's *Later Roman Empire* or Appendix 17, vol. iv. of his edition of Gibbon.—O. S.]

[98] Ludolph. Hist. et Comment. Æthiop. l. ii. c. 3.

[99] The city of Negra, or Nag'ran, in Yemen, is surrounded with palm-trees, and stands in the high road between Saana, the capital, and Mecca; from the former ten, from the latter twenty days' journey of a caravan of camels (Abulfeda, Descript. Arabiæ, p. 52).

[100] The martyrdom of St. Arethas, prince of Negra, and his three hundred and forty companions, is embellished in the legends of Metaphrastes and Nicephorus Callistus, copied by Baronius (A.D. 522, No. 22-66; A.D. 523, No. 16-29), and refuted, with obscure diligence, by Basnage (Hist. des Juifs, tom. xii. l. viii. c. ii. p. 333-348), who investigates the state of the Jews in Arabia and Æthiopia.

[101] Alvarez (in Ramusio, tom. i. fol. 219, vers. 221, vers.) saw the flourishing state of Axume in the year 1520—luogo molto buono e grande. It was ruined in the same century by the Turkish invasion. No more than one hundred houses remain; but the memory of its past greatness is preserved by the regal coronation (Ludolph. Hist. et Comment. l. ii. c. 11)

in the open field, seated on a lofty chariot, which was drawn by four elephants superbly caparisoned, and surrounded by his nobles and musicians. He was clad in a linen garment and cap, holding in his hand two javelins and a light shield; and, although his nakedness was imperfectly covered, he displayed the barbaric pomp of gold chains, collars, and bracelets, richly adorned with pearls and precious stones. The ambassador of Justinian knelt: the Negus raised him from the ground, embraced Nonnosus, kissed the seal, perused the letter, accepted the Roman alliance, and, brandishing his weapons, denounced implacable war against the worshippers of fire. But the proposal of the silk-trade was eluded; and notwithstanding the assurances, and perhaps the wishes, of the Abyssinians, these hostile menaces evaporated without effect. The Homerites were unwilling to abandon their aromatic groves, to explore a sandy desert, and to encounter, after all their fatigues, a formidable nation from whom they had never received any personal injuries. Instead of enlarging his conquests, the king of Æthiopia was incapable of defending his possessions. Abrahah, the slave of a Roman merchant of Adulis, assumed the sceptre of the Homerites; the troops of Africa were seduced by the luxury of the climate; and Justinian solicited the friendship of the usurper, who honoured with a slight tribute the supremacy of his prince. After a long series of prosperity the power of Abrahah was overthrown before the gates of Mecca, his children were despoiled by the Persian conqueror, and the Æthiopians were finally expelled from the continent of Asia. This narrative of obscure and remote events is not foreign to the decline and fall of the Roman empire. If a Christian power had been maintained in Arabia, Mahomet must have been crushed in his cradle, and Abyssinia would have prevented a revolution which has changed the civil and religious state of the world.[102]

[102] The revolutions of Yemen in the sixth century must be collected from Procopius (Persic. l. i. c. 19, 20), Theophanes Byzant. (apud Phot. cod. lxiv. p. 80 [p. 26, ed. Bekk.]), St. Theophanes (in Chronograph. p. 144, 145, 188, 189, 206, 207 [tom. i. p. 259, 260, 377, 378, ed. Bonn], who is full of strange blunders), Pocock (Specimen Hist. Arab. p. 62, 65), D'Herbelot (Bibliot. Orientale, p. 12, 477), and Sale's Preliminary Discourse and Koran (c. 105). The revolt of Abrahah is mentioned by Procopius; and his fall, though clouded with miracles, is an historical fact.

CHAPTER XLIII (531-594 A.D.)

Rebellions of Africa—Restoration of the Gothic Kingdom by Totila—Loss and Recovery of Rome—Final Conquest of Italy by Narses—Extinction of the Ostrogoths—Defeat of the Franks and Alemanni—Last Victory, Disgrace, and Death of Belisarius—Death and Character of Justinian—Comet, Earthquakes, and Plague

THE review of the nations from the Danube to the Nile has exposed, on every side, the weakness of the Romans; and our wonder is reasonably excited that they should presume to enlarge an empire whose ancient limits they were incapable of defending. But the wars, the conquests, and the triumphs of Justinian, are the feeble and pernicious efforts of old age, which exhaust the remains of strength and accelerate the decay of the powers of life. He exulted in the glorious act of restoring Africa and Italy to the republic; but the calamities which followed the departure of Belisarius betrayed the impotence of the conqueror, and accomplished the ruin of those unfortunate countries.

From his new acquisitions Justinian expected that his avarice, as well as his pride, should be richly gratified. A rapacious minister of the finances closely pursued the footsteps of Belisarius; and, as the old registers of tribute had been burnt by the Vandals, he indulged his fancy in a liberal calculation and arbitrary assessment of the wealth of Africa.[1] The increase of taxes, which were drawn away by a distant sovereign, and a general resumption of the patrimony of crown lands, soon dispelled the intoxication of the public joy: but the emperor was insensible to the modest complaints of the people till he was awakened and alarmed by the clamours of military discontent. Many of the Roman soldiers had married the widows and daughters of the Vandals. As their own, by the double right of conquest and inheritance, they claimed the estates which Genseric had assigned to his victorious troops. They heard with disdain the cold and selfish representations of their officers, that the liberality of Justinian had raised them from a savage or servile condition; that they were already enriched by the spoils of Africa, the treasure, the slaves, and the movables of the vanquished barbarians; and that the ancient and lawful patrimony of the emperors would be applied only to the support of that government on which their own safety and reward must ultimately depend. The mutiny

---

[1] For the troubles of Africa I neither have nor desire another guide than Procopius, whose eye contemplated the image, and whose ear collected the reports, of the memorable events of his own times. In the second book of the Vandalic War he relates the revolt of Stoza (c. 14-24), the return of Belisarius (c. 15), the victory of Germanus (c. 16, 17, 18), the second administration of Solomon (c. 19, 20, 21), the government of Sergius (c. 22, 23), of Areobindus (c. 24), the tyranny and death of Gontharis (c. 25, 26, 27, 28); nor can I discern any symptoms of flattery or malevolence in his various portraits.

was secretly inflamed by a thousand soldiers, for the most part Heruli, who had imbibed the doctrines, and were instigated by the clergy, of the Arian sect; and the cause of perjury and rebellion was sanctified by the dispensing powers of fanaticism. The Arians deplored the ruin of their church, triumphant above a century in Africa; and they were justly provoked by the laws of the conqueror which interdicted the baptism of their children and the exercise of all religious worship. Of the Vandals chosen by Belisarius, the far greater part, in the honours of the Eastern service, forgot their country and religion. But a generous band of four hundred obliged the mariners, when they were in sight of the isle of Lesbos, to alter their course: they touched on Peloponnesus, ran ashore on a desert coast of Africa, and boldly erected on Mount Aurasius the standard of independence and revolt. While the troops of the province disclaimed the commands of their superiors, a conspiracy was formed at Carthage against the life of Solomon, who filled with honour the place of Belisarius; and the Arians had piously resolved to sacrifice the tyrant at the foot of the altar during the awful mysteries of the festival of Easter. Fear or remorse restrained the daggers of the assassins, but the patience of Solomon emboldened their discontent, and at the end of ten days a furious sedition was kindled in the circus, which desolated Africa above ten years. The pillage of the city, and the indiscriminate slaughter of its inhabitants, were suspended only by darkness, sleep, and intoxication. The governor, with seven companions, among whom was the historian Procopius, escaped to Sicily. Two-thirds of the army were involved in the guilt of treason; and eight thousand insurgents, assembling in the field of Bulla, elected Stoza for their chief, a private soldier, who possessed in a superior degree the virtues of a rebel. Under the mask of freedom, his eloquence could lead, or at least impel, the passions of his equals. He raised himself to a level with Belisarius and the nephew of the emperor, by daring to encounter them in the field; and the victorious generals were compelled to acknowledge that Stoza deserved a purer cause and a more legitimate command. Vanquished in battle, he dexterously employed the arts of negotiation; a Roman army was seduced from their allegiance, and the chiefs who had trusted to his faithless promise were murdered by his order in a church of Numidia. When every resource, either of force or perfidy, was exhausted, Stoza, with some desperate Vandals, retired to the wilds of Mauritania, obtained the daughter of a barbarian prince, and eluded the pursuit of his enemies by the report of his death. The personal weight of Belisarius, the rank, the spirit, and the temper of Germanus, the emperor's nephew, and the vigour and success of the second administration of the eunuch Solomon, restored the modesty of the camp, and maintained for a while the tranquillity of Africa. But the vices of the Byzantine court were felt in that distant province; the troops complained that they were neither paid nor relieved; and as soon as the public disorders were sufficiently mature, Stoza was again alive, in arms, and at the gates of Carthage. He fell in a single combat, but he smiled in the agonies of death when he was informed that his own javelin had reached the heart of his antagonist.[2] The example of Stoza, and the assurance that a fortunate soldier had been the first king, encouraged the ambition of Gontharis, and he promised, by a private treaty, to divide Africa with the Moors, if, with their dangerous aid, he should ascend the throne of Carthage. The feeble Areobindus, unskilled in the affairs of peace and war, was raised by his marriage with the niece of Justinian to the office of exarch. He was suddenly oppressed by a sedition of the guards, and his abject supplications, which provoked the contempt, could not move the pity, of the inexorable tyrant. After a reign of thirty days, Gontharis himself was stabbed at a banquet by the hand of Artaban; and it is singular enough that an Armenian prince of the royal family of Arsaces should re-establish at Carthage the authority of the Roman empire. In the conspiracy which unsheathed the dagger of Brutus against the life of Cæsar, every circumstance is curious and important to the eyes of posterity; but the guilt or merit of these loyal or rebellious assassins could interest only the contemporaries of Procopius, who, by their hopes and fears, their friendship or resentment, were personally engaged in the revolutions of Africa.[3]

That country was rapidly sinking into the state of barbarism from whence it had been raised by the Phœnician colonies and Roman laws; and every step of intestine discord was marked by some deplorable victory of savage man over civilised society. The Moors,[4] though ignorant of justice, were impatient of oppression: their vagrant life and boundless wilderness disappointed the arms and eluded the chains of a conqueror; and experience had shown that neither oaths nor obligations could secure the fidelity of their attachment. The victory of Mount Auras had awed them into momentary submission; but if they respected the character of Solomon, they hated and despised the pride and luxury of his two nephews, Cyrus and Sergius, on whom their uncle had imprudently bestowed the provincial governments of Tripoli and Pentapolis. A Moorish tribe encamped under the walls of Leptis, to renew their alliance and receive from the governor the customary

---

[2] [Corippus relates the death of Stoza as occurring somewhat differently. He was transfixed by an arrow from the hand of John, the son of Sisiniolus —not the hero of his poem (the Johannidos, book iv. l. 211). All the other authorities confirm Gibbon's account of the death of John by the hand of Stoza. Stoza repented (says the poet) of his treasonous rebellion before his death, but anticipated eternal torments as his punishment. Cf. Corippus, *Johannidos*, iv. 211.—O. S.]

[3] Yet I must not refuse him the merit of painting, in lively colours, the murder of Gontharis. One of the assassins uttered a sentiment not unworthy of a Roman patriot: "If I fail," says Artasires, "in the first stroke, kill me on the spot, lest the rack should extort a discovery of my accomplices." [Vand. ii. 28, tom. i. p. 529, ed. Bonn.]

[4] The Moorish wars are occasionally introduced into the narrative of Procopius (Vandal. l. ii. c. 19-23, 25, 27, 28; Gothic. l. iv. c. 17); and Theophanes adds some prosperous and adverse events in the last years of Justinian.

gifts. Fourscore of their deputies were introduced as friends into the city; but, on the dark suspicion of a conspiracy, they were massacred at the table of Sergius, and the clamour of arms and revenge was re-echoed through the valleys of Mount Atlas from both the Syrtes to the Atlantic Ocean. A personal injury, the unjust execution or murder of his brother, rendered Antalas the enemy of the Romans. The defeat of the Vandals had formerly signalised his valour; the rudiments of justice and prudence were still more conspicuous in a Moor; and, while he laid Adrumetum in ashes, he calmly admonished the emperor that the peace of Africa might be secured by the recall of Solomon and his unworthy nephews. The exarch led forth his troops from Carthage; but, at the distance of six days' journey, in the neighbourhood of Tebeste,[5] he was astonished by the superior numbers and fierce aspect of the barbarians. He proposed a treaty, solicited a reconciliation, and offered to bind himself by the most solemn oaths. " By what oaths can he bind himself? " interrupted the indignant Moors. " Will he swear by the Gospels, the divine books of the Christians? It was on those books that the faith of his nephew Sergius was pledged to eighty of our innocent and unfortunate brethren. Before we trust them a second time, let us try their efficacy in the chastisement of perjury and the vindication of their own honour." Their honour was vindicated in the field of Tebeste by the death of Solomon and the total loss of his army.[6] The arrival of fresh troops and more skilful commanders soon checked the insolence of the Moors; seventeen of their princes were slain in the same battle; and the doubtful and transient submission of their tribes was celebrated with lavish applause by the people of Constantinople. Successive inroads had reduced the province of Africa to one-third of the measure of Italy; yet the Roman emperors continued to reign above a century over Carthage and the fruitful coast of the Mediterranean. But the victories and the losses of Justinian were alike pernicious to mankind; and such was the desolation of Africa, that in many parts a stranger might wander whole days without meeting the face either of a friend or an enemy. The nation of the Vandals had disappeared: they once amounted to a hundred and sixty thousand warriors, without including the children, the women, or the slaves. Their numbers were infinitely surpassed by the number of the Moorish families extirpated in a relentless war; and the same destruction was retaliated on the Romans and their allies, who perished by the

[5] Now Tibesh, in the kingdom of Algiers. It is watered by a river, the Sujerass, which falls into the Mejerda (*Bagradas*). Tibesh is still remarkable for its walls of large stones (like the Coliseum of Rome), a fountain, and a grove of walnut-trees: the country is fruitful, and the neighbouring Bereberes are warlike. It appears from an inscription, that, under the reign of Hadrian, the road from Carthage to Tebeste was constructed by the third legion (Marmol, Description de l'Afrique, tom. ii. p. 442, 443; Shaw's Travels, p. 64, 65, 66).

[6] [The defeat and death of Solomon are described at length in Corippus (*Johannidos*, book iii. 417-441) with historic fidelity.—O. S.]

climate, their mutual quarrels, and the rage of the barbarians. When Procopius first landed, he admired the populousness of the cities and country, strenuously exercised in the labours of commerce and agriculture. In less than twenty years that busy scene was converted into a silent solitude; the wealthy citizens escaped to Sicily and Constantinople; and the secret historian has confidently affirmed that five millions of Africans were consumed by the wars and government of the emperor Justinian.[7]

The jealousy of the Byzantine court had not permitted Belisarius to achieve the conquest of Italy; and his abrupt departure revived the courage of the Goths,[8] who respected his genius, his virtue, and even the laudable motive which had urged the servant of Justinian to deceive and reject them. They had lost their king (an inconsiderable loss), their capital, their treasures, the provinces from Sicily to the Alps, and the military force of two hundred thousand barbarians, magnificently equipped with horses and arms. Yet all was not lost as long as Pavia was defended by one thousand Goths, inspired by a sense of honour, the love of freedom, and the memory of their past greatness. The supreme command was unanimously offered to the brave Uraias; and it was in his eyes alone that the disgrace of his uncle Vitiges could appear as a reason of exclusion. His voice inclined the election in favour of Hildibald, whose personal merit was recommended by the vain hope that his kinsman Theudes, the Spanish monarch, would support the common interest of the Gothic nation. The success of his arms in Liguria and Venetia seemed to justify their choice; but he soon declared to the world that he was incapable of forgiving or commanding his benefactor. The consort of Hildibald was deeply wounded by the beauty, the riches, and the pride of the wife of Uraias; and the death of that virtuous patriot excited the indignation of a free people. A bold assassin executed their sentence by striking off the head of Hildibald in the midst of a banquet; the Rugians, a foreign tribe, assumed the privilege of election; and Totila, the nephew of the late king, was tempted by revenge to deliver himself and the garrison of Trevigo into the hands of the Romans. But the gallant and accomplished youth was easily persuaded to prefer the Gothic throne before the service of Justinian; and, as soon as the palace of Pavia had been purified from the Rugian usurper, he reviewed the national force of five thousand soldiers, and generously undertook the restoration of the kingdom of Italy.

The successors of Belisarius, eleven generals of equal rank, neglected

---

[7] Procopius, Anecdot. c. 18 [tom. iii. p. 107, ed. Bonn]. The series of the African history attests this melancholy truth.

[8] In the second (c. 30) and third books (c. 1-40), Procopius continues the history of the Gothic war from the fifth to the fifteenth year of Justinian. As the events are less interesting than in the former period, he allots only half the space to double the time. Jornandes, and the Chronicle of Marcellinus, afford some collateral hints. Sigonius, Pagi, Muratori, Mascou, and De Buat are useful, and have been used.

to crush the feeble and disunited Goths, till they were roused to action
by the progress of Totila and the reproaches of Justinian. The gates
of Verona were secretly opened to Artabazus, at the head of one hundred
Persians in the service of the empire.[9] The Goths fled from the city.
At the distance of sixty furlongs the Roman generals halted to regulate
the division of the spoil. While they disputed, the enemy discovered
the real number of the victors: the Persians were instantly overpowered,
and it was by leaping from the wall that Artabazus preserved a life
which he lost in a few days by the lance of a barbarian who had defied
him to single combat. Twenty thousand Romans encountered the
forces of Totila near Faenza, and on the hills of Mugello of the Florentine territory. The ardour of freedmen who fought to regain their
country was opposed to the languid temper of mercenary troops, who
were even destitute of the merits of strong and well-disciplined servitude. On the first attack they abandoned their ensigns, threw down
their arms, and dispersed on all sides with an active speed which abated
the loss, whilst it aggravated the shame, of their defeat. The king of
the Goths, who blushed for the baseness of his enemies, pursued with
rapid steps the path of honour and victory. Totila passed the Po,
traversed the Apennine, suspended the important conquest of Ravenna,
Florence, and Rome, and marched through the heart of Italy to form
the siege, or rather the blockade, of Naples. The Roman chiefs, imprisoned in their respective cities and accusing each other of the common disgrace, did not presume to disturb his enterprise. But the
emperor, alarmed by the distress and danger of his Italian conquests,
despatched to the relief of Naples a fleet of galleys and a body of
Thracian and Armenian soldiers. They landed in Sicily, which yielded
its copious stores of provisions; but the delays of the new commander,
an unwarlike magistrate, protracted the sufferings of the besieged;
and the succours which he dropped with a timid and tardy hand were
successively intercepted by the armed vessels stationed by Totila in
the Bay of Naples. The principal officer of the Romans was dragged,
with a rope round his neck, to the foot of the wall, from whence, with
a trembling voice, he exhorted the citizens to implore, like himself, the
mercy of the conqueror. They requested a truce, with a promise of
surrendering the city if no effectual relief should appear at the end of
thirty days. Instead of *one* month, the audacious barbarian granted
them *three,* in the just confidence that famine would anticipate the term
of their capitulation. After the reduction of Naples and Cumæ, the
provinces of Lucania, Apulia, and Calabria submitted to the king of
the Goths. Totila led his army to the gates of Rome, pitched his camp
at Tibur or Tivoli, within twenty miles of the capital, and calmly exhorted the senate and people to compare the tyranny of the Greeks
with the blessings of the Gothic reign.

    [9] ["At the head of one hundred Persians"—this did not imply that "one
hundred" was the total number of the army, but that he had "one hundred
picked men from the army."—O. S.]

The rapid success of Totila may be partly ascribed to the revolution which three years' experience had produced in the sentiments of the Italians. At the command, or at least in the name, of a catholic emperor, the pope,[10] their spiritual father, had been torn from the Roman church, and either starved or murdered on a desolate island.[11] The virtues of Belisarius were replaced by the various or uniform vices of eleven chiefs at Rome, Ravenna, Florence, Perugia, Spoleto, etc., who abused their authority for the indulgence of lust or avarice. The improvement of the revenue was committed to Alexander, a subtle scribe, long practised in the fraud and oppression of the Byzantine schools, and whose name of *Psalliction*, the *scissars*,[12] was drawn from the dexterous artifice with which he reduced the size, without defacing the figure, of the gold coin. Instead of expecting the restoration of peace and industry, he imposed a heavy assessment on the fortunes of the Italians. Yet his present or future demands were less odious than a prosecution of arbitrary rigour against the persons and property of all those who, under the Gothic kings, had been concerned in the receipt and expenditure of the public money. The subjects of Justinian who escaped these partial vexations were oppressed by the irregular maintenance of the soldiers, whom Alexander defrauded and despised, and their hasty sallies in quest of wealth or subsistence provoked the inhabitants of the country to await or implore their deliverance from the virtues of a barbarian. Totila [13] was chaste and temperate, and none were deceived, either friends or enemies, who depended on his faith or his clemency. To the husbandmen of Italy the Gothic king issued a welcome proclamation, enjoining them to pursue their important labours, and to rest assured that, on the payment of the ordinary taxes, they should be defended by his valour and discipline from the injuries of war. The strong towns he successively attacked, and, as soon as they had yielded to his arms, he demolished the fortifications, to save the people from the calamities of a future siege, to deprive the Romans of the arts of defence, and to decide the tedious quarrel of the two nations by an equal and honourable conflict in the field of battle. The Roman captives and deserters were tempted to enlist in the service of a liberal and courteous adversary, the slaves were attracted by the firm and faithful promise that they should never be delivered to their

[10] Sylverius, bishop of Rome, was first transported to Patara, in Lycia, and at length starved (sub eorum custodiâ inedia confectus) in the isle of Palmaria, A.D. 538, June 20 (Liberat. in Breviar. c. 22; Anastasius, in Sylverio; Baronius, A.D. 540, No. 2, 3; Pagi, in Vit. Pont. tom. i. p. 285, 286). Procopius (Anecdot. c. 1) accuses only the empress and Antonina.

[11] Palmaria, a small island, opposite to Terracina and the coast of the Volsci (Cluver. Ital. Antiq. l. iii. c. 7, p. 1014).

[12] As the Logothete Alexander, and most of his civil and military colleagues, were either disgraced or despised, the ink of the Anecdotes (c. 4, 5, 18) is scarcely blacker than that of the Gothic History (l. iii. c. 1, 3, 4, 9, 20, 21, etc.).

[13] Procopius (l. iii. c. 2, 8, etc.) does ample and willing justice to the merit of Totila. The Roman historians, from Sallust and Tacitus, were happy to forget the vices of their countrymen in the contemplation of barbaric virtue.

masters; and from the thousand warriors of Pavia a new people, under the same appellation of Goths, was insensibly formed in the camp of Totila. He sincerely accomplished the articles of capitulation, without seeking or accepting any sinister advantage from ambiguous expressions or unforeseen events: the garrison of Naples had stipulated that they should be transported by sea; the obstinacy of the winds prevented their voyage, but they were generously supplied with horses, provisions, and a safe-conduct to the gates of Rome. The wives of the senators who had been surprised in the villas of Campania were restored without a ransom to their husbands; the violation of female chastity was inexorably chastised with death; and in the salutary regulation of the diet of the famished Neapolitans, the conqueror assumed the office of a humane and attentive physician. The virtues of Totila are equally laudable, whether they proceeded from true policy, religious principle, or the instinct of humanity. He often harangued his troops; and it was his constant theme that national vice and ruin are inseparably connected; that victory is the fruit of moral as well as military virtue; and that the prince, and even the people, are responsible for the crimes which they neglect to punish.

The return of Belisarius to save the country which he had subdued was pressed with equal vehemence by his friends and enemies, and the Gothic war was imposed as a trust or an exile on the veteran commander. A hero on the banks of the Euphrates, a slave in the palace of Constantinople, he accepted with reluctance the painful task of supporting his own reputation and retrieving the faults of his successors. The sea was open to the Romans; the ships and soldiers were assembled at Salona, near the palace of Diocletian; he refreshed and reviewed his troops at Pola in Istria, coasted round the head of the Hadriatic, entered the port of Ravenna, and despatched orders rather than supplies to the subordinate cities. His first public oration was addressed to the Goths and Romans, in the name of the emperor, who had suspended for a while the conquest of Persia and listened to the prayers of his Italian subjects. He gently touched on the causes and the authors of the recent disasters, striving to remove the fear of punishment for the past, and the hope of impunity for the future, and labouring with more zeal than success to unite all the members of his government in a firm league of affection and obedience. Justinian, his gracious master, was inclined to pardon and reward, and it was their interest, as well as duty, to reclaim their deluded brethren, who had been seduced by the arts of the usurper. Not a man was tempted to desert the standard of the Gothic king. Belisarius soon discovered that he was sent to remain the idle and impotent spectator of the glory of a young barbarian, and his own epistle exhibits a genuine and lively picture of the distress of a noble mind. " Most excellent prince, we are arrived in Italy, destitute of all the necessary implements of war—men, horses, arms, and money. In our late circuit through the villages of Thrace and Illyricum, we have collected with extreme difficulty about four thousand recruits, naked and unskilled in the use of weapons and the exercises of the camp. The soldiers already stationed in the province are discontented, fearful, and dismayed; at the sound of an enemy they dismiss their horses, and cast their arms on the ground. No taxes can be raised, since Italy is in the hands of the barbarians: the failure of payment has deprived us of the right of command, or even of admonition. Be assured, dread Sir, that the greater part of your troops have already deserted to the Goths. If the war could be achieved by the presence of Belisarius alone, your wishes are satisfied; Belisarius is in the midst of Italy. But if you desire to conquer, far other preparations are requisite: without a military force the title of general is an empty name. It would be expedient to restore to my service my own veterans and domestic guards. Before I can take the field I must receive an adequate supply of light and heavy armed troops, and it is only with ready money that you can procure the indispensable aid of a powerful body of the cavalry of the Huns." [14] An officer in whom Belisarius confided was sent from Ravenna to hasten and conduct the succours, but the message was neglected, and the messenger was detained at Constantinople by an advantageous marriage. After his patience had been exhausted by delay and disappointment, the Roman general repassed the Hadriatic, and expected at Dyrrachium the arrival of the troops, which were slowly assembled among the subjects and allies of the empire. His powers were still inadequate to the deliverance of Rome, which was closely besieged by the Gothic king. The Appian way, a march of forty days, was covered by the barbarians; and as the prudence of Belisarius declined a battle, he preferred the safe and speedy navigation of five days from the coast of Epirus to the mouth of the Tiber.

After reducing, by force or treaty, the towns of inferior note in the midland provinces of Italy, Totila proceeded, not to assault, but to encompass and starve, the ancient capital. Rome was afflicted by the avarice, and guarded by the valour, of Bessas, a veteran chief of Gothic extraction, who filled, with a garrison of three thousand soldiers, the spacious circle of her venerable walls. From the distress of the people he extracted a profitable trade, and secretly rejoiced in the continuance of the siege. It was for his use that the granaries had been replenished; the charity of Pope Vigilius had purchased and embarked an ample supply of Sicilian corn, but the vessels which escaped the barbarians were seized by a rapacious governor, who imparted a scanty sustenance to the soldiers, and sold the remainder to the wealthy Romans. The medimnus, or fifth part of the quarter of wheat, was exchanged for seven pieces of gold; fifty pieces were given for an ox, a rare and accidental prize; the progress of famine enhanced this exorbitant value, and the mercenaries were tempted to deprive themselves of the allowance which was scarcely sufficient for the support of life.

[14] Procopius, l. iii. c. 12. The soul of a hero is deeply impressed on the letter; nor can we confound such genuine and original acts with the elaborate and often empty speeches of the Byzantine historians.

A tasteless and unwholesome mixture, in which the bran thrice exceeded the quantity of flour, appeased the hunger of the poor; they were gradually reduced to feed on dead horses, dogs, cats, and mice, and eagerly to snatch the grass and even the nettles which grew among the ruins of the city. A crowd of spectres, pale and emaciated, their bodies oppressed with disease and their minds with despair, surrounded the palace of the governor, urged, with unavailing truth, that it was the duty of a master to maintain his slaves, and humbly requested that he would provide for their subsistence, permit their flight, or command their immediate execution. Bessas replied, with unfeeling tranquillity, that it was impossible to feed, unsafe to dismiss, and unlawful to kill, the subjects of the emperor. Yet the example of a private citizen might have shown his countrymen that a tyrant cannot withhold the privilege of death. Pierced by the cries of five children, who vainly called on their father for bread, he ordered them to follow his steps, advanced with calm and silent despair to one of the bridges of the Tiber, and, covering his face, threw himself headlong into the stream, in the presence of his family and the Roman people. To the rich and pusillanimous, Bessas sold the permission of departure; but the greatest part of the fugitives expired on the public highways, or were intercepted by the flying parties of barbarians.[15] In the meanwhile the artful governor soothed the discontent, and revived the hopes, of the Romans, by the vague reports of the fleets and armies which were hastening to their relief from the extremities of the East. They derived more rational comfort from the assurance that Belisarius had landed at the *port;* and, without numbering his forces, they firmly relied on the humanity, the courage, and the skill of their great deliverer.

The foresight of Totila had raised obstacles worthy of such an antagonist. Ninety furlongs below the city, in the narrowest part of the river, he joined the two banks by strong and solid timbers in the form of a bridge, on which he erected two lofty towers, manned by the bravest of his Goths, and profusely stored with missile weapons and engines of offence. The approach of the bridge and towers was covered by a strong and massy chain of iron, and the chain, at either end, on the opposite sides of the Tiber, was defended by a numerous and chosen detachment of archers. But the enterprise of forcing these barriers and relieving the capital displays a shining example of the boldness and conduct of Belisarius. His cavalry advanced from the port along the public road to awe the motions and distract the attention of the enemy. His infantry and provisions were distributed in two hundred large boats, and each boat was shielded by a high rampart of

---

[15] The avarice of Bessas is not dissembled by Procopius (l. iii. c. 17, 20). He expiated the loss of Rome by the glorious conquest of Petræa (Goth. l. iv. c. 12); but the same vices followed him from the Tiber to the Phasis (c. 13); and the historian is equally true to the merits and defects of his character. The chastisement which the author of the romance of *Belisaire* has inflicted on the oppressor of Rome is more agreeable to justice than to history.

thick planks, pierced with many small holes for the discharge of missile weapons. In the front, two large vessels were linked together to sustain a floating castle, which commanded the towers of the bridge, and contained a magazine of fire, sulphur, and bitumen. The whole fleet, which the general led in person, was laboriously moved against the current of the river. The chain yielded to their weight, and the enemies who guarded the banks were either slain or scattered. As soon as they touched the principal barrier, the fireship was instantly grappled to the bridge; one of the towers, with two hundred Goths, was consumed by the flames, the assailants shouted victory, and Rome was saved, if the wisdom of Belisarius had not been defeated by the misconduct of his officers. He had previously sent orders to Bessas to second his operations by a timely sally from the town, and he had fixed his lieutenant, Isaac, by a peremptory command, to the station of the port. But avarice rendered Bessas immovable, while the youthful ardour of Isaac delivered him into the hands of a superior enemy. The exaggerated rumour of his defeat was hastily carried to the ears of Belisarius: he paused, betrayed in that single moment of his life some emotions of surprise and perplexity, and reluctantly sounded a retreat to save his wife Antonina, his treasures, and the only harbour which he possessed on the Tuscan coast. The vexation of his mind produced an ardent and almost mortal fever, and Rome was left without protection to the mercy or indignation of Totila. The continuance of hostilities had embittered the national hatred; the Arian clergy was ignominiously driven from Rome; Pelagius, the archdeacon, returned without success from an embassy to the Gothic camp; and a Sicilian bishop, the envoy or nuncio of the pope, was deprived of both his hands for daring to utter falsehoods in the service of the church and state.

Famine had relaxed the strength and discipline of the garrison of Rome. They could derive no effectual service from a dying people; and the inhuman avarice of the merchant at length absorbed the vigilance of the governor. Four Isaurian sentinels, while their companions slept and their officers were absent, descended by a rope from the wall, and secretly proposed to the Gothic king to introduce his troops into the city. The offer was entertained with coldness and suspicion; they returned in safety; they twice repeated their visit: the place was twice examined; the conspiracy was known and disregarded; and no sooner had Totila consented to the attempt, than they unbarred the Asinarian gate and gave admittance to the Goths. Till the dawn of day they halted in order of battle, apprehensive of treachery or ambush; but the troops of Bessas, with their leader, had already escaped; and when the king was pressed to disturb their retreat, he prudently replied that no sight could be more grateful than that of a flying enemy. The patricians who were still possessed of horses, Decius, Basilius, etc., accompanied the governor; their brethren, among whom Olybrius, Orestes, and Maximus are named by the historian, took refuge in the church of St. Peter: but the assertion that only five hundred persons remained in the capital inspires some doubt of the fidelity either of his narrative or of his text. As soon as daylight had displayed the entire victory of the Goths, their monarch devoutly visited the tomb of the prince of the apostles; but while he prayed at the altar, twenty-five soldiers and sixty citizens were put to the sword in the vestibule of the temple. The archdeacon Pelagius [16] stood before him, with the Gospels in his hand. " O Lord, be merciful to your servant." " Pelagius," said Totila with an insulting smile, " your pride now condescends to become a suppliant." " I *am* a suppliant," replied the prudent archdeacon; " God has now made us your subjects, and, as your subjects, we are entitled to your clemency." At his humble prayer the lives of the Romans were spared; and the chastity of the maids and matrons was preserved inviolate from the passions of the hungry soldiers. But they were rewarded by the freedom of pillage, after the most precious spoils had been reserved for the royal treasury. The houses of the senators were plentifully stored with gold and silver; and the avarice of Bessas had laboured with so much guilt and shame for the benefit of the conqueror. In this revolution the sons and daughters of Roman consuls tasted the misery which they had spurned or relieved, wandered in tattered garments through the streets of the city, and begged their bread, perhaps without success, before the gates of their hereditary mansions. The riches of Rusticiana, the daughter of Symmachus and widow of Boethius, had been generously devoted to alleviate the calamities of famine. But the barbarians were exasperated by the report that she had prompted the people to overthrow the statues of the great Theodoric; and the life of that venerable matron would have been sacrificed to his memory, if Totila had not respected her birth, her virtues, and even the pious motive of her revenge. The next day he pronounced two orations, to congratulate and admonish his victorious Goths, and to reproach the senate, as the vilest of slaves, with their perjury, folly, and ingratitude; sternly declaring that their estates and honours were justly forfeited to the companions of his arms. Yet he consented to forgive their revolt; and the senators repaid his clemency by despatching circular letters to their tenants and vassals in the provinces of Italy, strictly to enjoin them to desert the standard of the Greeks, to cultivate their lands in peace, and to learn from their masters the duty of obedience to a Gothic sovereign. Against the city which had so long delayed the course of his victories he appeared inexorable: one-third of the walls, in different parts, were demolished by his command; fire and engines prepared to consume or subvert the most stately works of antiquity; and the world was astonished by

---

[16] During the long exile, and after the death of Vigilius, the Roman church was governed, at first by the archdeacon, and at length (A.D. 555) by the pope Pelagius, who was not thought guiltless of the sufferings of his predecessor. See the original Lives of the popes under the name of Anastasius (Muratori, Script. Rer. Italicarum, tom. iii. P. i. p. 130, 131), who relates several curious incidents of the sieges of Rome and the wars of Italy.

the fatal decree that Rome should be changed into a pasture for cattle. The firm and temperate remonstrance of Belisarius suspended the execution; he warned the barbarian not to sully his fame by the destruction of those monuments which were the glory of the dead and the delight of the living; and Totila was persuaded, by the advice of an enemy, to preserve Rome as the ornament of his kingdom, or the fairest pledge of peace and reconciliation. When he had signified to the ambassadors of Belisarius his intention of sparing the city, he stationed an army at the distance of one hundred and twenty furlongs, to observe the motions of the Roman general. With the remainder of his forces he marched into Lucania and Apulia, and occupied on the summit of Mount Garganus [17] one of the camps of Hannibal.[18] The senators were dragged in his train, and afterwards confined in the fortresses of Campania; the citizens, with their wives and children, were dispersed in exile; and during forty days Rome was abandoned to desolate and dreary solitude.[19]

The loss of Rome was speedily retrieved by an action to which, according to the event, the public opinion would apply the names of rashness or heroism. After the departure of Totila, the Roman general sallied from the port at the head of a thousand horse, cut in pieces the enemy who opposed his progress, and visited with pity and reverence the vacant space of the *eternal* city. Resolved to maintain a station so conspicuous in the eyes of mankind, he summoned the greatest part of his troops to the standard which he erected on the Capitol: the old inhabitants were recalled by the love of their country and the hopes of food; and the keys of Rome were sent a second time to the emperor Justinian. The walls, as far as they had been demolished by the Goths, were repaired with rude and dissimilar materials; the ditch was restored; iron spikes [20] were profusely scattered in the highways to annoy the feet of the horses; and as new gates could not suddenly be procured, the entrance was guarded by a Spartan rampart of his bravest

[17] Mount Garganus, now Monte St. Angelo, in the kingdom of Naples, runs three hundred stadia into the Hadriatic Sea (Strab. l. vi. p. 436 [p. 284, ed. Casaub.]), and in the darker ages was illustrated by the apparition, miracles, and church of St. Michael the archangel. Horace, a native of Apulia or Lucania, had seen the elms and oaks of Garganus labouring and bellowing with the north wind that blew on that lofty coast (Carm. ii. 9; Epist. ii. i. 202).

[18] I cannot ascertain this particular camp of Hannibal; but the Punic quarters were long and often in the neighbourhood of Arpi (T. Liv. xxii. 9, 12; xxiv. 3, etc.).

[19] Totila . . . Romam ingreditur . . . ac evertit muros, domos aliquantas igni comburens, ac omnes Romanorum res in prædam accepit, hos ipsos Romanos in Campaniam captivos abduxit. Post quam devastationem, xl aut amplius dies, Roma fuit ita desolata, ut nemo ibi hominum, nisi (*nullæ?*) bestiæ morarentur (Marcellin. in Chron. p. 54).

[20] The *tribuli* are small engines with four spikes, one fixed in the ground the three others erect or adverse (Procopius, Gothic. l. iii. c. 24 [tom. ii. p. 379, ed. Bonn]; Just. Lipsius, Poliorcetων, l. v. c. 3). The metaphor was borrowed from the tribuli (*land-caltrops*), an herb with a prickly fruit, common in Italy (Martin, ad Virgil. Georgic. i. 153, vol. ii. p. 33).

soldiers. At the expiration of twenty-five days Totila returned by hasty marches from Apulia to avenge the injury and disgrace. Belisarius expected his approach. The Goths were thrice repulsed in three general assaults; they lost the flower of their troops; the royal standard had almost fallen into the hands of the enemy, and the fame of Totila sunk, as it had risen, with the fortune of his arms. Whatever skill and courage could achieve had been performed by the Roman general: it remained only that Justinian should terminate, by a strong and seasonable effort, the war which he had ambitiously undertaken. The indolence, perhaps the impotence, of a prince who despised his enemies and envied his servants, protracted the calamities of Italy. After a long silence Belisarius was commanded to leave a sufficient garrison at Rome, and to transport himself into the province of Lucania, whose inhabitants, inflamed by catholic zeal, had cast away the yoke of their Arian conquerors. In this ignoble warfare the hero, invincible against the power of the barbarians, was basely vanquished by the delay, the disobedience, and the cowardice of his own officers. He reposed in his winter quarters of Crotona, in the full assurance that the two passes of the Lucanian hills were guarded by his cavalry. They were betrayed by treachery or weakness; and the rapid march of the Goths scarcely allowed time for the escape of Belisarius to the coast of Sicily. At length a fleet and army were assembled for the relief of Ruscianum, or Rossano,[21] a fortress sixty furlongs from the ruins of Sybaris, where the nobles of Lucania had taken refuge. In the first attempt the Roman forces were dissipated by a storm. In the second, they approached the shore; but they saw the hills covered with archers, the landing-place defended by a line of spears, and the king of the Goths impatient for battle. The conqueror of Italy retired with a sigh, and continued to languish, inglorious and inactive, till Antonina, who had been sent to Constantinople to solicit succours, obtained, after the death of the empress, the permission of his return.

The five last campaigns of Belisarius might abate the envy of his competitors, whose eyes had been dazzled and wounded by the blaze of his former glory. Instead of delivering Italy from the Goths, he had wandered like a fugitive along the coast, without daring to march into the country, or to accept the bold and repeated challenge of Totila. Yet in the judgment of the few who could discriminate counsels from events, and compare the instruments with the execution, he appeared a more consummate master of the art of war than in the season of his prosperity, when he presented two captive kings before the throne of Justinian. The valour of Belisarius was not chilled by age: his prudence was matured by experience; but the moral virtues of humanity and justice seem to have yielded to the hard necessity of the times. The

[21] Ruscia, the *navale Thuriorum,* was transferred to the distance of sixty stadia to Ruscianum, Rossano, an archbishopric without suffragans. The republic of Sybaris is now the estate of the Duke of Corigliano (Riedesel, Travels into Magna Græcia and Sicily, p. 166-171).

parsimony or poverty of the emperor compelled him to deviate from the rule of conduct which had deserved the love and confidence of the Italians. The war was maintained by the oppression of Ravenna, Sicily, and all the faithful subjects of the empire; and the rigorous prosecution of Herodian provoked that injured or guilty officer to deliver Spoleto into the hands of the enemy. The avarice of Antonina, which had been sometimes diverted by love, now reigned without a rival in her breast. Belisarius himself had always understood that riches, in a corrupt age, are the support and ornament of personal merit. And it cannot be presumed that he should stain his honour for the public service, without applying a part of the spoil to his private emolument. The hero had escaped the sword of the barbarians, but the dagger of conspiracy [22] awaited his return. In the midst of wealth and honours, Artaban, who had chastised the African tyrant, complained of the ingratitude of courts. He aspired to Præjecta, the emperor's niece, who wished to reward her deliverer; but the impediment of his previous marriage was asserted by the piety of Theodora. The pride of royal descent was irritated by flattery; and the service in which he gloried had proved him capable of bold and sanguinary deeds. The death of Justinian was resolved, but the conspirators delayed the execution till they could surprise Belisarius, disarmed and naked, in the palace of Constantinople. Not a hope could be entertained of shaking his long-tried fidelity; and they justly dreaded the revenge, or rather justice, of the veteran general, who might speedily assemble an army in Thrace to punish the assassins, and perhaps to enjoy the fruits of their crime. Delay afforded time for rash communications and honest confessions: Artaban and his accomplices were condemned by the senate, but the extreme clemency of Justinian detained them in the gentle confinement of the palace, till he pardoned their flagitious attempt against his throne and life. If the emperor forgave his enemies, he must cordially embrace a friend whose victories were alone remembered, and who was endeared to his prince by the recent circumstance of their common danger. Belisarius reposed from his toils, in the high station of general of the East and count of the domestics; and the older consuls and patricians respectfully yielded the precedency of rank to the peerless merit of the first of the Romans.[23] The first of the Romans still submitted to be the slave of his wife; but the servitude of habit and affection became less disgraceful when the

---

[22] This conspiracy is related by Procopius (Gothic. l. iii. c. 31, 32) with such freedom and candour that the liberty of the Anecdotes gives him nothing to add.

[Spoleto was betrayed by Herodian in 545 A.D. It was recovered by the empire in 547; was lost once more about 549 A.D., and was recovered finally in 552.—O. S.]

[23] The honours of Belisarius are gladly commemorated by his secretary (Procop. Goth. l. iii. c. 35; l. iv. c. 21). The title of Στράτηγος is ill translated, at least in this instance, by præfectus prætorio; and to a military character, magister militum is more proper and applicable (Ducange, Gloss. Græc. p. 1458, 1459).

death of Theodora had removed the baser influence of fear. Joannina their daughter, and the sole heiress of their fortunes, was betrothed to Anastasius, the grandson, or rather the nephew, of the empress,[24] whose kind interposition forwarded the consummation of their youthful loves. But the power of Theodora expired, the parents of Joannina returned, and her honour, perhaps her happiness, were sacrificed to the revenge of an unfeeling mother, who dissolved the imperfect nuptials before they had been ratified by the ceremonies of the church.[25]

Before the departure of Belisarius, Perusia was besieged, and few cities were impregnable to the Gothic arms. Ravenna, Ancona, and Crotona still resisted the barbarians; and when Totila asked in marriage one of the daughters of France, he was stung by the just reproach that the king of Italy was unworthy of his title till it was acknowledged by the Roman people. Three thousand of the bravest soldiers had been left to defend the capital. On the suspicion of a monopoly, they massacred the governor, and announced to Justinian, by a deputation of the clergy, that, unless their offence was pardoned, and their arrears were satisfied, they should instantly accept the tempting offers of Totila. But the officer who succeeded to the command (his name was Diogenes) deserved their esteem and confidence; and the Goths, instead of finding an easy conquest, encountered a vigorous resistance from the sodiers and people, who patiently endured the loss of the port and of all maritime supplies. The siege of Rome would perhaps have been raised, if the liberality of Totila to the Isaurians had not encouraged some of their venal countrymen to copy the example of treason. In a dark night, while the Gothic trumpets sounded on another side, they silently opened the gate of St. Paul: the barbarians rushed into the city; and the flying garrison was intercepted before they could reach the harbour of Centumcellæ. A soldier trained in the school of Belisarius, Paul of Cilicia, retired with four hundred men to the mole of Hadrian. They repelled the Goths; but they felt the approach of famine; and their aversion to the taste of horse-flesh confirmed their resolution to risk the event of a desperate and decisive sally. But their spirit insensibly stooped to the offers of capitulation: they retrieved their arrears of pay, and preserved

[24] Alemannus (ad Hist. Arcanam, p. 68 [tom. iii. p. 418, ed. Bonn]), Ducange (Familiæ Byzant. p. 98), and Heineccius (Hist. Juris Civilis, p. 434), all three represent Anastasius as the son of the daughter of Theodora; and their opinion firmly reposes on the unambiguous testimony of Procopius (Anecdot. c. 4, 5—θυγατρίδῳ twice repeated). And yet I will remark, 1. That in the year 547 Theodora could scarcely have a grandson at the age of puberty; 2. That we are totally ignorant of this daughter and her husband; and, 3. That Theodora concealed her bastards, and that her grandson by Justinian would have been heir-apparent of the empire.

[25] The ἁμαρτήματα, or sins, of the hero in Italy and after his return, are manifested ἀπαρακαλύπτως, and most probably swelled, by the author of the Anecdotes (c. 4, 5). The designs of Antonina were favoured by the fluctuating jurisprudence of Justinian. On the law of marriage and divorce, that emperor was trocho versatilior (Heineccius, Element. Juris Civil. ad Ordinem Pandect. P. iv. No. 233).

their arms and horses, by enlisting in the service of Totila; their chiefs, who pleaded a laudable attachment to their wives and children in the East, were dismissed with honour; and above four hundred enemies, who had taken refuge in the sanctuaries, were saved by the clemency of the victor. He no longer entertained a wish of destroying the edifices of Rome,[26] which he now respected as the seat of the Gothic kingdom: the senate and people were restored to their country; the means of subsistence were liberally provided; and Totila, in the robe of peace, exhibited the equestrian games of the circus. Whilst he amused the eyes of the multitude, four hundred vessels were prepared for the embarkation of his troops. The cities of Rhegium and Tarentum were reduced; he passed into Sicily, the object of his implacable resentment; and the island was stripped of its gold and silver, of the fruits of the earth, and of an infinite number of horses, sheep, and oxen. Sardinia and Corsica obeyed the fortune of Italy; and the sea-coast of Greece was visited by a fleet of three hundred galleys.[27] The Goths were landed in Corcyra and the ancient continent of Epirus; they advanced as far as Nicopolis, the trophy of Augustus, and Dodona,[28] once famous by the oracle of Jove. In every step of his victories the wise barbarian repeated to Justinian his desire of peace, applauded the concord of their predecessors, and offered to employ the Gothic arms in the service of the empire.

Justinian was deaf to the voice of peace, but he neglected the prosecution of war; and the indolence of his temper disappointed, in some degree, the obstinacy of his passions. From this salutary slumber the emperor was awakened by the pope Vigilius and the patrician Cethegus, who appeared before his throne, and adjured him, in the name of God and the people, to resume the conquest and deliverance of Italy. In the choice of the generals, caprice, as well as judgment, was shown. A fleet and army sailed for the relief of Sicily, under the conduct of Liberius; but his want of youth and experience were afterwards discovered, and before he touched the shores of the island he was overtaken

[26] The Romans were still attached to the monuments of their ancestors; and according to Procopius (Goth. l. iv. c. 22 [tom. ii. p. 573, ed. Bonn]), the galley of Æneas, of a single rank of oars, 25 feet in breadth, 120 in length, was preserved entire in the *navalia*, near Monte Testaceo, at the foot of the Aventine (Nardini, Roma Antica, l. vii. c. 9, p. 466; Donatus, Roma Antiqua, l. iv. c. 13, p. 334). But all antiquity is ignorant of this relic.

[27] In these seas Procopius searched without success for the isle of Calypso. He was shown, at Phæacia or Corcyra, the petrified ship of Ulysses (Odyss. xiii. 163); but he found it a recent fabric of many stones, dedicated by a merchant to Jupiter Casius (l. iv. c. 22 [tom. ii. p. 575, ed. Bonn]). Eustathius had supposed it to be the fanciful likeness of a rock.

[28] M. D'Anville (Mémoires de l'Acad. tom. xxxii. p. 513-528) illustrates the gulf of Ambracia; but he cannot ascertain the situation of Dodona. A country in sight of Italy is less known than the wilds of America.

[" Dodona once famous by the oracle of Jove." The site of this once famous place cannot now be fixed with accuracy, though strong presumption exists that the fertile valley of Joannina was the territory of Dodona, and that the ruins upon the hill of Kastritza at the southern end of the lake of Joannina are those of the ancient city.—O. S.]

by his successor. In the place of Liberius the conspirator Artaban was raised from a prison to military honours, in the pious presumption that gratitude would animate his valour and fortify his allegiance. Belisarius reposed in the shade of his laurels, but the command of the principal army was reserved for Germanus,[29] the emperor's nephew, whose rank and merit had been long depressed by the jealousy of the court. Theodora had injured him in the rights of a private citizen, the marriage of his children, and the testament of his brother; and although his conduct was pure and blameless, Justinian was displeased that he should be thought worthy of the confidence of the malcontents. The life of Germanus was a lesson of implicit obedience: he nobly refused to prostitute his name and character in the factions of the circus; the gravity of his manners was tempered by innocent cheerfulness; and his riches were lent without interest to indigent or deserving friends. His valour had formerly triumphed over the Sclavonians of the Danube and the rebels of Africa: the first report of his promotion revived the hopes of the Italians; and he was privately assured that a crowd of Roman deserters would abandon, on his approach, the standard of Totila. His second marriage with Malasontha, the grand-daughter of Theodoric, endeared Germanus to the Goths themselves; and they marched with reluctance against the father of a royal infant, the last offspring of the line of Amali.[30] A splendid allowance was assigned by the emperor: the general contributed his private fortune; his two sons were popular and active; and he surpassed, in the promptitude and success of his levies, the expectation of mankind. He was permitted to select some squadrons of Thracian cavalry: the veterans, as well as the youth of Constantinople and Europe, engaged their voluntary service; and as far as the heart of Germany, his fame and liberality attracted the aid of the barbarians. The Romans advanced to Sardica; an army of Sclavonians fled before their march; but within two days of their final departure the designs of Germanus were terminated by his malady and death. Yet the impulse which he had given to the Italian war still continued to act with energy and effect. The maritime towns, Ancona, Crotona, Centumcellæ, resisted the assaults of Totila. Sicily was reduced by the zeal of Artaban, and the Gothic navy was defeated near the coast of the Hadriatic. The two fleets were almost equal, forty-seven to fifty galleys: the victory was decided by the knowledge and dexterity of the Greeks; but the ships were so closely grappled that only twelve of the Goths escaped from this unfortunate conflict. They affected to depreciate an element in which they were unskilled; but their

---

[29] See the acts of Germanus in the public (Vandal. l. ii. c. 16, 17, 18; Goth. l. iii. c. 31, 32) and private history (Anecdot. c. 5), and those of his son Justin, in Agathias (l. iv. p. 130, 131 [p. 250 *sq.*, ed. Bonn]). Notwithstanding an ambiguous expression of Jornandes, fratri suo, Alemannus has proved that he was the son of the emperor's brother.

[30] Conjuncta Aniciorum gens cum Amalâ stirpe spem adhuc utriusque generis promittit (Jornandes, c. 60, p. 703). He wrote at Ravenna before the death of Totila.

own experience confirmed the truth of a maxim, that the master of the sea will always acquire the dominion of the land.[31]

After the loss of Germanus, the nations were provoked to smile by the strange intelligence that the command of the Roman armies was given to a eunuch. But the eunuch Narses[32] is ranked among the few who have rescued that unhappy name from the contempt and hatred of mankind. A feeble, diminutive body concealed the soul of a statesman and a warrior. His youth had been employed in the management of the loom and distaff, in the cares of the household, and the service of female luxury; but while his hands were busy, he secretly exercised the faculties of a vigorous and discerning mind. A stranger to the schools and the camp, he studied in the palace to dissemble, to flatter, and to persuade; and as soon as he approached the person of the emperor, Justinian listened with surprise and pleasure to the manly counsels of his chamberlain and private treasurer.[33] The talents of Narses were tried and improved in frequent embassies: he led an army into Italy, acquired a practical knowledge of the war and the country, and presumed to strive with the genius of Belisarius. Twelve years after his return the eunuch was chosen to achieve the conquests which had been left imperfect by the first of the Roman generals. Instead of being dazzled by vanity or emulation, he seriously declared that, unless he were armed with an adequate force, he would never consent to risk his own glory and that of his sovereign. Justinian granted to the favourite what he might have denied to the hero: the Gothic war was rekindled from its ashes, and the preparations were not unworthy of the ancient majesty of the empire. The key of the public treasure was put into his hand to collect magazines, to levy soldiers, to purchase arms and horses, to discharge the arrears of pay, and to tempt the fidelity of the fugitives and deserters. The troops of Germanus were still in arms; they halted at Salona in the expectation of a new leader, and

[31] The third book of Procopius is terminated by the death of Germanus (Add. l. iv. c. 23, 24, 25, 26).

[32] Procopius relates the whole series of this second Gothic war and the victory of Narses (l. iv. c. 21, 26-35). A splendid scene! Among the six subjects of epic poetry which Tasso revolved in his mind, he hesitated between the conquests of Italy by Belisarius and by Narses (Hayley's Works, vol. iv. p. 70).

[33] The country of Narses is unknown, since he must not be confounded with the Persarmenian. Procopius styles him (Goth. l. ii. c. 13 [tom. ii. p. 199, ed. Bonn]) βασιλικῶν χρημάτων ταμίας; Paul Warnefrid (l. ii. c. 3, p. 776), Chartularius: Marcellinus adds the name of Cubicularius. In an inscription on the Salarian bridge he is entitled Ex-consul, Ex-præpositus, Cubiculi Patricius (Mascou, Hist. of the Germans, l. xiii. c. 25). The law of Theodosius against eunuchs was obsolete or abolished (Annotation xx.), but the foolish prophecy of the Romans subsisted in full vigour (Procop. l. iv. c. 21 [tom. ii. p. 571, ed. Bonn]).

[There were two Persarmenians of the name of Narses, of whom one deserted to the Romans and the other received the deserter. The latter, who is called ὁβασιλέως ταμίας, the imperial treasurer, is, as Procopius says, the individual in whom we are interested.—O. S.]

legions of subjects and allies were created by the well-known liberality
of the eunuch Narses.   The king of the Lombards [34] satisfied or surpassed the obligations of a treaty, by lending two thousand two hundred
of his bravest warriors, who were followed by three thousand of their
martial attendants.   Three thousand Heruli fought on horseback under
Philemuth, their native chief; and the noble Aratus, who adopted the
manners and discipline of Rome, conducted a band of veterans of the
same nation.   Dagistheus was released from prison to command the
Huns; and Kobad, the grandson and nephew of the Great King, was
conspicuous by the regal tiara at the head of his faithful Persians, who
had devoted themselves to the fortunes of their prince.[35]   Absolute in
the exercise of his authority, more absolute in the affection of his troops,
Narses led a numerous and gallant army from Philippopolis to Salona,
from whence he coasted the eastern side of the Hadriatic as far as the
confines of Italy.   His progress was checked.   The East could not supply
vessels capable of transporting such multitudes of men and horses.   The
Franks, who in the general confusion had usurped the greater part of
the Venetian province, refused a free passage to the friends of the
Lombards.   The station of Verona was occupied by Teias with the flower
of the Gothic forces; and that skilful commander had overspread the
adjacent country with the fall of woods and the inundation of waters.[36]
In this perplexity an officer of experience proposed a measure, secure
by the appearance of rashness, that the Roman army should cautiously
advance along the sea-shore, while the fleet preceded their march, and
successively cast a bridge of boats over the mouths of the rivers, the
Timavus, the Brenta, the Adige, and the Po, that fall into the Hadriatic
to the north of Ravenna.   Nine days he reposed in the city, collected
the fragments of the Italian army, and marched towards Rimini to
meet the defiance of an insulting enemy.

The prudence of Narses impelled him to speedy and decisive action.
His powers were the last effort of the state; the cost of each day accumulated the enormous account, and the nations, untrained to discipline

[34] Paul Warnefrid, the Lombard, records with complacency the succour,
service, and honourable dismission of his countrymen—Romanæ reipublicæ
adversum æmulos adjutores fuerunt (l. ii. c. i. p. 774, edit. Grot.).   I am surprised that Alboin, their martial king, did not lead his subjects in person.
[Gibbon here is in error.   He has followed translators in place of the Greek
of the original.   Πεντακοσίους τε καὶ δισχιλίους reads Procopius (*Goth. Bell.*
lib. iv. c. 26), but Gibbon prefers to follow the Latin translation of Maltretus,
which by some unaccountable oversight translates the above phrase bis mille
ducentos, or, in other words, two thousand two hundred.—O. S.]
[35] He was, if not an impostor, the sun of the blind Zames, saved by compassion and educated in the Byzantine court by the various motives of policy,
pride, and generosity (Procop. Persic. l. i. c. 23 [tom. i. p. 115, ed. Bonn]).
[36] In the time of Augustus and in the middle ages the whole waste from
Aquileia to Ravenna was covered with woods, lakes, and morasses.   Man has
subdued nature, and the land has been cultivated, since the waters are confined
and embanked.   See the learned researches of Muratori (Antiquitat. Italiæ
Medii Ævi, tom. i. dissert. xxi. p. 253, 254), from Vitruvius, Strabo, Herodian,
old charters, and local knowledge.

or fatigue, might be rashly provoked to turn their arms against each other, or against their benefactor. The same considerations might have tempered the ardour of Totila. But he was conscious that the clergy and people of Italy aspired to a second revolution: he felt or suspected the rapid progress of treason, and he resolved to risk the Gothic kingdom on the chance of a day, in which the valiant would be animated by instant danger, and the disaffected might be awed by mutual ignorance. In his march from Ravenna the Roman general chastised the garrison of Rimini, traversed in a direct line the hills of Urbino, and re-entered the Flaminian way, nine miles beyond the perforated rock, an obstacle of art and nature which might have stopped or retarded his progress.[37] The Goths were assembled in the neighbourhood of Rome, they advanced without delay to seek a superior enemy, and the two armies approached each other at the distance of one hundred furlongs, between Tagina [38] and the sepulchres of the Gauls.[39] The haughty message of Narses was an offer not of peace, but of pardon. The answer of the Gothic king declared his resolution to die or conquer. " What day," said the messenger, " will you fix for the combat? " " The eighth day," replied Totila; but early the next morning he attempted to surprise a foe suspicious of deceit and prepared for battle. Ten thousand Heruli and Lombards, of approved valour and doubtful faith, were placed in the centre. Each of the wings was composed of eight thousand Romans; the right was guarded by the cavalry of the Huns, the left was covered by fifteen hundred chosen horse, destined, according to the emergencies of action, to sustain the retreat of their friends, or to encompass the flank of the enemy. From his proper station at the head of the right wing, the eunuch rode along the line, expressing by his voice and countenance the assurance of victory, exciting the soldiers of the emperor to punish the guilt and madness of a band of robbers, and exposing to their view gold chains, collars, and bracelets, the rewards of military

[37] The Flaminian way, as it is corrected from the Itineraries, and the best modern maps, by D'Anville (Analyse de l'Italie, p. 147-162), may be thus stated: ROME to Narni, 51 Roman miles; Terni, 57; Spoleto, 75; Foligno, 88; Nocera, 103; Cagli, 142; Intercisa, 157; Fossombrone, 160; Fano, 176; Pesaro, 184; RIMINI, 208—about 189 English miles. He takes no notice of the death of Totila; but Wesseling (Itinerar. p. 614) exchanges, for the field of *Taginas,* the unknown appellation of *Ptanias,* eight miles from Nocera.

[38] Taginæ, or rather Tadinæ, is mentioned by Pliny [iii. 19]; but the bishopric of that obscure town, a mile from Gualdo, in the plain, was united, in the year 1007, with that of Nocera. The signs of antiquity are preserved in the local appellations, *Fossato,* the camp; *Capraia,* Caprea; *Bastia,* Busta Gallorum. See Cluverius (Italia Antiqua. l. ii. c. 6, p. 615, 616, 617), Lucas Holstenius (Annotat. ad Cluver. p. 85, 86), Guazzesi (Dissertat. p. 177-217, a professed inquiry), and the maps of the ecclesiastical state and the march of Ancona, by Le Maire and Magini.

[39] The battle was fought in the year of Rome 458; and the consul Decius, by devoting his own life, assured the triumph of his country and his colleague Fabius (T. Liv. x. 28, 29). Procopius ascribes to Camillus the victory of the *Busta Gallorum* [tom. ii. p. 610, ed. Bonn]; and his error is branded by Cluverius with the national reproach of Græcorum nugamenta.

virtue. From the event of a single combat they drew an omen of success; and they beheld with pleasure the courage of fifty archers, who maintained a small eminence against three successive attacks of the Gothic cavalry. At the distance only of two bow-shots the armies spent the morning in dreadful suspense, and the Romans tasted some necessary food without unloosening the cuirass from their breast or the bridle from their horses. Narses awaited the charge; and it was delayed by Totila till he had received his last succours of two thousand Goths. While he consumed the hours in fruitless treaty, the king exhibited in a narrow space the strength and agility of a warrior. His armour was enchased with gold; his purple banner floated with the wind: he cast his lance into the air, caught it with the right hand, shifted it to the left, threw himself backwards, recovered his seat, and managed a fiery steed in all the paces and evolutions of the equestrian school. As soon as the succours had arrived, he retired to his tent, assumed the dress and arms of a private soldier, and gave the signal of battle. The first line of cavalry advanced with more courage than discretion, and left behind them the infantry of the second line. They were soon engaged between the horns of a crescent, into which the adverse wings had been insensibly curved, and were saluted from either side by the volleys of four thousand archers. Their ardour, and even their distress, drove them forwards to a close and unequal conflict, in which they could only use their lances against an enemy equally skilled in all the instruments of war. A generous emulation inspired the Romans and their barbarian allies; and Narses, who calmly viewed and directed their efforts, doubted to whom he should adjudge the prize of superior bravery. The Gothic cavalry was astonished and disordered, pressed and broken; and the line of infantry, instead of presenting their spears or opening their intervals, were trampled under the feat of the flying horse. Six thousand of the Goths were slaughtered without mercy in the field of Tagina. Their prince, with five attendants, was overtaken by Asbad, of the race of the Gepidæ: " Spare the king of Italy," cried a loyal voice, and Asbad struck his lance through the body of Totila. The blow was instantly revenged by the faithful Goths: they transported their dying monarch seven miles beyond the scene of his disgrace, and his last moments were not embittered by the presence of an enemy. Compassion afforded him the shelter of an obscure tomb; but the Romans were not satisfied of their victory till they beheld the corpse of the Gothic king. His hat, enriched with gems, and his bloody robe, were presented to Justinian by the messengers of triumph.[40]

As soon as Narses had paid his devotions to the Author of victory and the blessed Virgin, his peculiar patroness,[41] he praised, rewarded,

---

[40] Theophanes, Chron. p. 193 [tom. i. p. 354, ed. Bonn]. Hist. Miscell. l. xvi. p. 108.

[41] Evagrius, l. iv. c. 24. The inspiration of the Virgin revealed to Narses the day, and the word. of battle (Paul Diacon. l. ii. c. 3, p. 776).

and dismissed the Lombards. The villages had been reduced to ashes by these valiant savages: they ravished matrons and virgins on the altar; their retreat was diligently watched by a strong detachment of regular forces, who prevented a repetition of the like disorders. The victorious eunuch pursued his march through Tuscany, accepted the submission of the Goths, heard the acclamations and often the complaints of the Italians, and encompassed the walls of Rome with the remainder of his formidable host. Round the wide circumference Narses assigned to himself and to each of his lieutenants a real or a feigned attack, while he silently marked the place of easy and unguarded entrance. Neither the fortifications of Hadrian's mole, nor of the port, could long delay the progress of the conqueror; and Justinian once more received the keys of Rome, which, under his reign, had been *five* times taken and recovered.[42] But the deliverance of Rome was the last calamity of the Roman people. The barbarian allies of Narses too frequently confounded the privileges of peace and war. The despair of the flying Goths found some consolation in sanguinary revenge; and three hundred youths of the noblest families, who had been sent as hostages beyond the Po, were inhumanly slain by the successor of Totila. The fate of the senate suggests an awful lesson of the vicissitude of human affairs. Of the senators whom Totila had banished from their country, some were rescued by an officer of Belisarius and transported from Campania to Sicily, while others were too guilty to confide in the clemency of Justinian, or too poor to provide horses for their escape to the sea-shore. Their brethren languished five years in a state of indigence and exile: the victory of Narses revived their hopes; but their premature return to the metropolis was prevented by the furious Goths, and all the fortresses of Campania were stained with patrician [43] blood. After a period of thirteen centuries the institution of Romulus expired; and if the nobles of Rome still assumed the title of senators, few subsequent traces can be discovered of a public council or constitutional order. Ascend six hundred years, and contemplate the kings of the earth soliciting an audience, as the slaves or freedmen of the Roman senate! [44]

The Gothic war was yet alive. The bravest of the nation retired beyond the Po, and Teias was unanimously chosen to succeed and re-

[42] Ἐπὶ τούτου βασιλεύοντος τὸ πέμπτον ἑάλω. [Procop. Goth. lib. iv. c. 33; tom. ii. p. 632, ed. Bonn.] In the year 536 by Belisarius, in 546 by Totila, in 547 by Belisarius, in 549 by Totila, and in 552 by Narses. Maltretus had inadvertently translated *sextum*; a mistake which he afterwards retracts: but the mischief was done; and Cousin, with a train of French and Latin readers, have fallen into the snare.

[43] Compare two passages of Procopius (l. iii. c. 26, l. iv. c. 34 [tom. ii. p. 389 and 633, ed. Bonn]), which, with some collateral hints from Marcellinus and Jornandes, illustrate the state of the expiring senate.

[44] See, in the example of Prusias, as it is delivered in the fragments of Polybius (Excerpt. Legat. xcvii. p. 927, 928), a curious picture of a royal slave.

venge their departed hero. The new king immediately sent ambassadors to implore, or rather to purchase, the aid of the Franks, and nobly lavished for the public safety the riches which had been deposited in the palace of Pavia. The residue of the royal treasure was guarded by his brother Aligern, at Cumæ in Campania; but the strong castle which Totila had fortified was closely besieged by the arms of Narses. From the Alps to the foot of Mount Vesuvius, the Gothic king by rapid and secret marches advanced to the relief of his brother, eluded the vigilance of the Roman chiefs, and pitched his camp on the banks of the Sarnus or *Draco*,[45] which flows from Nuceria into the bay of Naples. The river separated the two armies; sixty days were consumed in distant and fruitless combats, and Teias maintained this important post till he was deserted by his fleet and the hope of subsistence. With reluctant steps he ascended the *Lactarian* mount, where the physicians of Rome since the time of Galen had sent their patients for the benefit of the air and the milk.[46] But the Goths soon embraced a more generous resolution—to descend the hill, to dismiss their horses, and to die in arms and in the possession of freedom. The king marched at their head, bearing in his right hand a lance, and an ample buckler in his left: with the one he struck dead the foremost of the assailants, with the other he received the weapons which every hand was ambitious to aim against his life. After a combat of many hours, his left arm was fatigued by the weight of twelve javelins which hung from his shield. Without moving from his ground or suspending his blows, the hero called aloud on his attendants for a fresh buckler, but in the moment while his side was uncovered, it was pierced by a mortal dart. He fell; and his head, exalted on a spear, proclaimed to the nations that the Gothic kingdom was no more. But the example of his death served only to animate the companions who had sworn to perish with their leader. They fought till darkness descended on the earth. They reposed on their arms. The combat was renewed with the return of light, and maintained with unabated vigour till the evening of the second day. The repose of a second night, the want of water, and the loss of their bravest champions, determined the surviving Goths to accept the fair capitulation which the prudence of Narses was inclined to propose. They embraced the alternative of residing in Italy as the subjects and soldiers of Justinian, or departing with a portion of their private wealth in

---

[45] The Δράκων of Procopius (Goth. l. iv. c. 35) is evidently the Sarnus. The text is accused or altered by the rash violence of Cluverius (l. iv. c. 3, p. 1156): but Camillo Pellegrini of Naples (Discorsi sopra la Campania Felice, p. 330, 331) has proved from old records that as early as the year 822 that river was called the Dracontio, or Draconcello.

[46] Galen (de Method. Medendi, l. v. apud Cluver. l. iv. c. 3, p. 1159, 1160) describes the lofty site, pure air, and rich milk of Mount Lactarius, whose medicinal benefits were equally known and sought in the time of Symmachus (l. vi. Epist. 18 [17?]), and Cassiodorus (Var. xi. 10). Nothing is now left except the name of the town of *Lettere*.

search of some independent country.[47] Yet the oath of fidelity or exile was alike rejected by one thousand Goths, who broke away before the treaty was signed, and boldly effected their retreat to the walls of Pavia. The spirit as well as the situation of Aligern prompted him to imitate rather than to bewail his brother: a strong and dexterous archer, he transpierced with a single arrow the armour and breast of his antagonist, and his military conduct defended Cumæ[48] above a year against the forces of the Romans.   Their industry had scooped the Sibyl's cave[49] into a prodigious mine; combustible materials were introduced to consume the temporary props: the wall and the gate of Cumæ sunk into the cavern, but the ruins formed a deep and inaccessible precipice. On the fragment of a rock Aligern stood alone and unshaken, till he calmly surveyed the hopeless condition of his country, and judged it more honourable to be the friend of Narses than the slave of the Franks. After the death of Teias the Roman general separated his troops to reduce the cities of Italy; Lucca sustained a long and vigorous siege, and such was the humanity or the prudence of Narses, that the repeated perfidy of the inhabitants could not provoke him to exact the forfeit lives of their hostages. These hostages were dismissed in safety, and their grateful zeal at length subdued the obstinacy of their countrymen.[50]

Before Lucca had surrendered, Italy was overwhelmed by a new deluge of barbarians. A feeble youth, the grandson of Clovis, reigned over the Austrasians or Oriental Franks. The guardians of Theodebald entertained with coldness and reluctance the magnificent promises of the Gothic ambassadors. But the spirit of a martial people outstripped the timid counsels of the court: two brothers, Lothaire and Buccelin,[51] the dukes of the Alamanni, stood forth as the leaders of the Italian war, and seventy-five thousand Germans descended in the autumn from

[47] Buat (tom. xi. p. 2, etc.) conveys to his favourite Bavaria this remnant of Goths, who by others are buried in the mountains of Uri, or restored to their native isle of Gothland (Mascou, Annot. xxi.).

[48] I leave Scaliger (Animadvers. in Euseb. p. 59) and Salmasius (Exercitat. Plinian. p. 51, 52) to quarrel about the origin of Cumæ, the oldest of the Greek colonies in Italy (Strab. l. v. p. 372 [p. 243, ed. Casaub.]; Velleius Paterculus, l. i. c. 4), already vacant in Juvenal's time (Satir. iii. [v. 2]), and now in ruins.

[49] Agathias (l. i. p. 21 [c. 10, p. 34, ed. Bonn]) settles the Sibyl's cave under the wall of Cumæ: he agrees with Servius (ad l. vi. Æneid.); nor can I perceive why their opinion should be rejected by Heyne, the excellent editor of Virgil (tom. ii. p. 650, 651). In urbe mediâ secreta religio! But Cumæ was not yet built; and the lines (l. vi. 96, 97) would become ridiculous if Æneas were actually in a Greek city.

[50] There is some difficulty in connecting the 35th chapter of the fourth book of the Gothic War of Procopius with the first book of the history of Agathias. We must now relinquish a statesman and soldier to attend the footsteps of a poet and rhetorician (l. i. p. 11, l. ii. p. 51, edit. Louvre).

[51] Among the fabulous exploits of Buccelin, he discomfited and slew Belisarius, subdued Italy and *Sicily*, etc. See in the Historians of France, Gregory of Tours (tom. ii. l. iii. c. 32, p. 201), and Aimoin (tom. iii. l. ii. de Gestis Francorum, c. 23, p. 59).

the Rhætian Alps into the plain of Milan. The vanguard of the Roman army was stationed near the Po under the conduct of Fulcaris, a bold Herulian, who rashly conceived that personal bravery was the sole duty and merit of a commander. As he marched without order or precaution along the Æmilian way, an ambuscade of Franks suddenly rose from the amphitheatre of Parma; his troops were surprised and routed, but their leader refused to fly, declaring to the last moment that death was less terrible than the angry countenance of Narses. The death of Fulcaris, and the retreat of the surviving chiefs, decided the fluctuating and rebellious temper of the Goths; they flew to the standard of their deliverers, and admitted them into the cities which still resisted the arms of the Roman general. The conqueror of Italy opened a free passage to the irresistible torrent of barbarians. They passed under the walls of Cesena, and answered by threats and reproaches the advice of Aligern, that the Gothic treasures could no longer repay the labour of an invasion. Two thousand Franks were destroyed by the skill and valour of Narses himself, who sallied from Rimini at the head of three hundred horse to chastise the licentious rapine of their march. On the confines of Samnium the two brothers divided their forces. With the right wing Buccelin assumed the spoil of Campania, Lucania, and Bruttium; with the left, Lothaire accepted the plunder of Apulia and Calabria. They followed the coast of the Mediterranean and the Hadriatic as far as Rhegium and Otranto, and the extreme lands of Italy were the term of their destructive progress. The Franks, who were Christians and catholics, contented themselves with simple pillage and occasional murder. But the churches which their piety had spared were stripped by the sacrilegious hands of the Alamanni, who sacrificed horses' heads to their native deities of the woods and rivers;[52] they melted or profaned the consecrated vessels, and the ruins of shrines and altars were stained with the blood of the faithful. Buccelin was actuated by ambition, and Lothaire by avarice. The former aspired to restore the Gothic kingdom; the latter, after a promise to his brother of speedy succours, returned by the same road to deposit his treasure beyond the Alps. The strength of their armies was already wasted by the change of climate and contagion of disease; the Germans revelled in the vintage of Italy, and their own intemperance avenged in some degree the miseries of a defenceless people.

At the entrance of the spring the Imperial troops who had guarded the cities assembled, to the number of eighteen thousand men, in the neighbourhood of Rome. Their winter hours had not been consumed in idleness. By the command and after the example of Narses, they repeated each day their military exercise on foot and on horseback,

---

[52] Agathias notices their superstition in a philosophic tone (1. i. p. 18 [c. 28, sq., ed. Bonn]). At Zug, in Switzerland, idolatry still prevailed in the year 613: St. Columban and St. Gall were the apostles of that rude country; and the latter founded an hermitage, which has swelled into an ecclesiastical principality and a populous city, the seat of freedom and commerce.

accustomed their ear to obey the sound of the trumpet, and practised the steps and evolutions of the Pyrrhic dance. From the straits of Sicily, Buccelin with thirty thousand Franks and Alamanni slowly moved towards Capua, occupied with a wooden tower the bridge of Casilinum, covered his right by the stream of the Vulturnus, and secured the rest of his encampment by a rampart of sharp stakes, and a circle of waggons whose wheels were buried in the earth. He impatiently expected the return of Lothaire; ignorant, alas! that his brother could never return, and that the chief and his army had been swept away by a strange disease [53] on the banks of the lake Benacus, between Trent and Verona. The banners of Narses soon approached the Vulturnus, and the eyes of Italy were anxiously fixed on the event of this final contest. Perhaps the talents of the Roman general were most conspicuous in the calm operations which precede the tumult of a battle. His skilful movements intercepted the subsistence of the barbarian, deprived him of the advantage of the bridge and river, and in the choice of the ground and moment of action reduced him to comply with the inclination of his enemy. On the morning of the important day, when the ranks were already formed, a servant for some trivial fault was killed by his master, one of the leaders of the Heruli. The justice or passion of Narses was awakened: he summoned the offender to his presence, and without listening to his excuses gave the signal to the minister of death. If the cruel master had not infringed the laws of his nation, this arbitrary execution was not less unjust than it appears to have been imprudent. The Heruli felt the indignity; they halted: but the Roman general, without soothing their rage or expecting their resolution, called aloud, as the trumpets sounded, that, unless they hastened to occupy their place, they would lose the honour of the victory. His troops were disposed [54] in a long front; the cavalry on the wings; in the centre the heavy-armed foot; the archers and slingers in the rear. The Germans advanced in a sharp-pointed column of the form of a triangle or solid wedge. They pierced the feeble centre of Narses, who received them with a smile into the fatal snare, and directed his wings of cavalry insensibly to wheel on their flanks and encompass their rear. The host of the Franks and Alamanni consisted of infantry: a sword and buckler hung by their side, and they used as their weapons of offence a weighty hatchet and a hooked javelin,

[53] See the death of Lothaire in Agathias (l. ii. p. 38 [p. 70, ed. Bonn]) and Paul Warnefrid, surnamed Diaconus (l. ii. c. 2, p. 775). The Greek makes him rave and tear his flesh. He had plundered churches.

[A body of Lothaire's troops was defeated near Fano: some were driven down precipices into the sea, others fled to the camp: many prisoners seized the opportunity of making their escape; and the barbarians lost much of their booty in their precipitate retreat.—O. S.]

[54] Père Daniel (Hist. de la Milice Françoise, tom. i. p. 17-21) has exhibited a fanciful representation of this battle, somewhat in the manner of the Chevalier Folard, the once famous editor of Polybius, who fashioned to his own habits and opinions all the military operations of antiquity.

which were only formidable in close combat or at a short distance. The flower of the Roman archers, on horseback and in complete armour, skirmished without peril round this immovable phalanx, supplied by active speed the deficiency of number, and aimed their arrows against a crowd of barbarians who, instead of a cuirass and helmet, were covered by a loose garment of fur or linen. They paused, they trembled, their ranks were confounded, and in the decisive moment the Heruli, preferring glory to revenge, charged with rapid violence the head of the column. Their leader Sindbal, and Aligern the Gothic prince, deserved the prize of superior valour; and their example incited the victorious troops to achieve with swords and spears the destruction of the enemy. Buccelin and the greatest part of his army perished on the field of battle, in the waters of the Vulturnus, or by the hands of the enraged peasants; but it may seem incredible that a victory[55] which no more than five of the Alamanni survived could be purchased with the loss of fourscore Romans. Seven thousand Goths, the relics of the war, defended the fortress of Campsa till the ensuing spring; and every messenger of Narses announced the reduction of the Italian cities, whose names were corrupted by the ignorance or vanity of the Greeks.[56] After the battle of Casilinum Narses entered the capital; the arms and treasures of the Goths, the Franks, and the Alamanni were displayed; his soldiers, with garlands in their hands, chanted the praises of the conqueror; and Rome for the last time beheld the semblance of a triumph.

After a reign of sixty years the throne of the Gothic kings was filled by the exarchs of Ravenna, the representatives in peace and war of the emperor of the Romans. Their jurisdiction was soon reduced to the limits of a narrow province; but Narses himself, the first and most powerful of the exarchs, administered above fifteen years the entire kingdom of Italy. Like Belisarius, he had deserved the honours of envy, calumny, and disgrace: but the favourite eunuch still enjoyed the confidence of Justinian; or the leader of a victorious army awed and repressed the ingratitude of a timid court. Yet it was not by weak and mischievous indulgence that Narses secured the attachment of his troops. Forgetful of the past, and regardless of the future, they abused the present hour of prosperity and peace. The cities of Italy resounded with the noise of drinking and dancing: the spoils of victory were wasted in sensual pleasures; and nothing (says Agathias) remained unless to exchange their shields and helmets for the soft lute and the capacious hogshead.[57] In a manly oration, not unworthy of a Roman censor,

[55] Agathias (l. ii. p. 47 [p. 87, ed. Bonn]) has produced a Greek epigram of six lines on this victory of Narses, which is favourably compared to the battles of Marathon and Platæa. The chief difference is indeed in their consequences—so trivial in the former instance—so permanent and glorious in the latter.

[56] The Beroïa and Brincas of Theophanes or his transcriber (p. 201 [tom. i. p. 367, ed. Bonn]) must be read or understood Verona and Brixia.

[57] Ἐλείπετο γὰρ, οἶμαι, αὐτοῖς ὑπὸ ἀβελτερίας τὰς ἀσπίδας τυχὸν καὶ τὰ κράνη

the eunuch reproved these disorderly vices, which sullied their fame, and endangered their safety. The soldiers blushed, and obeyed; discipline was confirmed; the fortifications were restored; a *duke* was stationed for the defence and military command of each of the principal cities;[58] and the eye of Narses pervaded the ample prospect from Calabria to the Alps. The remains of the Gothic nation evacuated the country, or mingled with the people: the Franks, instead of revenging the death of Buccelin, abandoned, without a struggle, their Italian conquests; and the rebellious Sindbal, chief of the Heruli, was subdued, taken, and hung on a lofty gallows, by the inflexible justice of the exarch.[59] The civil state of Italy, after the agitation of a long tempest, was fixed by a pragmatic sanction, which the emperor promulgated at the request of the pope. Justinian introduced his own jurisprudence into the schools and tribunals of the West: he ratified the acts of Theodoric and his immediate successors, but every deed was rescinded and abolished which force had extorted or fear had subscribed under the usurpation of Totila. A moderate theory was framed to reconcile the rights of property with the safety of prescription, the claims of the state with the poverty of the people, and the pardon of offences with the interest of virtue and order of society. Under the exarchs of Ravenna, Rome was degraded to the second rank. Yet the senators were gratified by the permission of visiting their estates in Italy, and of approaching without obstacle the throne of Constantinople: the regulation of weights and measures was delegated to the pope and senate; and the salaries of lawyers and physicians, of orators and grammarians, were destined to preserve or rekindle the light of science in the ancient capital. Justinian might dictate benevolent edicts,[60] and Narses might second his wishes by the restoration of cities, and more especially of churches. But the power of kings is most effectual to destroy: and the twenty years of the Gothic war had consummated the distress and depopulation of Italy. As early as the fourth campaign, under the discipline of Belisarius himself, fifty thousand labourers died of hun-

---

ἀμφορέως οἴνου ἢ καὶ βαρβίτου ἀποδόσθαι (Agathias, l. ii. [c. 11] p. 48 [p. 88, ed. Bonn]). In the first scene of Richard III. our English poet has beautifully enlarged on this idea, for which, however, he was not indebted to the Byzantine historian.

[58] Maffei has proved (Verona Illustrata, P. i. l. x. p. 257, 289), against the common opinion, that the dukes of Italy were instituted before the conquest of the Lombards, by Narses himself. In the Pragmatic Sanction (No. 23) Justinian restrains the judices militares.

[59] See Paulus Diaconus, l. iii. c. 3, p. 776. Menander (in Excerpt. Legat. p. 133 [p. 345, ed. Bonn]) mentions some risings in Italy by the Franks, and Theophanes (p. 201 [tom. i. p. 367, ed. Bonn]) hints at some Gothic rebellions.

[60] The Pragmatic Sanction of Justinian, which restores and regulates the civil state of Italy, consists of xxvii. articles: it is dated August 15, A.D. 554; is addressed to Narses, V. J. Præpositus Sacri Cubiculi, and to Antiochus Præfectus Prætorio Italiæ; and has been preserved by Julian Antecessor, and in the Corpus Juris Civilis, after the novels and edicts of Justinian, Justin, and Tiberius.

ger [61] in the narrow region of Picenum; [62] and a strict interpretation of the evidence of Procopius would swell the loss of Italy above the total sum of her present inhabitants. [63]

I desire to believe, but I dare not affirm, that Belisarius sincerely rejoiced in the triumph of Narses. Yet the consciousness of his own exploits might teach him to esteem, without jealousy, the merit of a rival; and the repose of the aged warrior was crowned by a last victory, which saved the emperor and the capital. The barbarians, who annually visited the provinces of Europe, were less discouraged by some accidental defeats than they were excited by the double hope of spoil and of subsidy. In the thirty-second winter of Justinian's reign the Danube was deeply frozen; Zabergan led the cavalry of the Bulgarians, and his standard was followed by a promiscuous multitude of Sclavonians. The savage chief passed, without opposition, the river and the mountains, spread his troops over Macedonia and Thrace, and advanced with no more than seven thousand horse to the long walls which should have defended the territory of Constantinople. But the works of man are impotent against the assaults of nature: a recent earthquake had shaken the foundations of the walls; and the forces of the empire were employed on the distant frontiers of Italy, Africa, and Persia. The seven *schools*, [64] or companies, of the guards or domestic troops had been augmented to the number of five thousand five hundred men, whose ordinary station was in the peaceful cities of Asia. But the places of the brave Armenians were insensibly supplied by lazy citizens, who purchased an exemption from the duties of civil life without being exposed to the dangers of military service. Of such soldiers few could be tempted to sally from the gates; and none could be persuaded to remain in the field, unless they wanted strength and speed to escape from the Bulgarians. The report of the fugitives exaggerated the numbers and fierceness of an enemy who had polluted holy virgins and abandoned newborn infants to the dogs and vultures; a crowd of rustics, imploring food and protection, increased the consternation of the city; and the tents of Zabergan were pitched at the distance of twenty miles, [65] on

[61] A still greater number was consumed by famine in the southern provinces, without (ἐκτὸς) the Ionian Gulf. Acorns were used in the place of bread. Procopius had seen a deserted orphan suckled by a she-goat [Goth. ii. c. 17]. Seventeen passengers were lodged, murdered, and eaten, by two women, who were detected and slain by the eighteenth, etc.

[62] Quinta regio Piceni est; quondam uberrimæ multitudinis, ccclx millia Picentium in fidem P. R. venere (Plin. Hist. Natur. iii. 18). In the time of Vespasian this ancient population was already diminished.

[63] Perhaps fifteen or sixteen millions. Procopius (Anecdot. c. 18) computes that Africa lost five millions, that Italy was thrice as extensive, and that the depopulation was in a larger proportion. But his reckoning is inflamed by passion, and clouded with uncertainty.

[64] In the decay of these military schools, the satire of Procopius (Anecdot. c. 24 [tom. iii. p. 135, ed. Bonn]; Aleman. p. 102, 103) is confirmed and illustrated by Agathias (l. v. p. 159 [p. 310, ed. Bonn]), who cannot be rejected as an hostile witness.

[65] The distance from Constantinople to Melanthias, Villa Cæsariana (Am-

the banks of a small river which encircles Melanthias and afterwards falls into the Propontis.[66]   Justinian trembled: and those who had only seen the emperor in his old age were pleased to suppose that he had *lost* the alacrity and vigour of his youth.   By his command the vessels of gold and silver were removed from the churches in the neighbourhood, and even the suburbs, of Constantinople: the ramparts were lined with trembling spectators; the golden gate was crowded with useless generals and tribunes; and the senate shared the fatigues and the apprehensions of the populace.

But the eyes of the prince and people were directed to a feeble veteran, who was compelled by the public danger to resume the armour in which he had entered Carthage and defended Rome.   The horses of the royal stables, of private citizens, and even of the circus, were hastily collected; the emulation of the old and young was roused by the name of Belisarius, and his first encampment was in the presence of a victorious enemy.   His prudence, and the labour of the friendly peasants, secured, with a ditch and rampart, the repose of the night; innumerable fires and clouds of dust were artfully contrived to magnify the opinion of his strength; his soldiers suddenly passed from despondency to presumption; and, while ten thousand voices demanded the battle, Belisarius dissembled his knowledge that in the hour of trial he must depend on the firmness of three hundred veterans.   The next morning the Bulgarian cavalry advanced to the charge.   But they heard the shouts of multitudes, they beheld the arms and discipline of the front; they were assaulted on the flanks by two ambuscades which rose from the woods; their foremost warriors fell by the hand of the aged hero and his guards; and the swiftness of their evolutions was rendered useless by the close attack and rapid pursuit of the Romans.   In this action (so speedy was their flight) the Bulgarians lost only four hundred horse: but Constantinople was saved; and Zabergan, who felt the hand of a master, withdrew to a respectful distance.   But his friends were numerous in the councils of the emperor, and Belisarius obeyed with reluctance the commands of envy and Justinian, which forbade him to achieve the deliverance of his country.   On his return to the city, the people, still conscious of their danger, accompanied his triumph with acclamations of joy and gratitude, which were imputed as a crime to the victorious general.   But when he entered the palace the courtiers were silent, and the emperor, after a cold and thankless embrace, dismissed him to mingle with the train of slaves.   Yet so

mian. Marcellin. xxxi. 11), is variously fixed at 120 or 140 stadia (Suidas, tom. ii. p. 522, 523; Agathias, l. v. [c. 14] p. 158 [p. 308, ed. Bonn]), or xviii or xix miles (Itineraria, p. 138, 230, 323, 332, and Wesseling's Observations). The first xii miles, as far as Rhegium, were paved by Justinian, who built a bridge over a morass or gullet between a lake and the sea (Procop. de Ædif. l. iv. c. 8).

[66] The Atyras (Pompon. Mela, l. ii. c. 2, p. 169, edit. Voss.).   At the river's mouth a town or castle of the same name was fortified by Justinian (Procop. de Ædif. l. iv. c. 2; Itinerar. p. 570; and Wesseling).

deep was the impression of his glory on the minds of men, that Justinian, in the seventy-seventh year of his age, was encouraged to advance near forty miles from the capital, and to inspect in person the restoration of the long wall.   The Bulgarians wasted the summer in the plains of Thrace; but they were inclined to peace by the failure of their rash attempts on Greece and the Chersonesus. A menace of killing their prisoners quickened the payment of heavy ransoms; and the departure of Zabergan was hastened by the report that double-prowed vessels were built on the Danube to intercept his passage.   The danger was soon forgotten; and a vain question, whether their sovereign had shown more wisdom or weakness, amused the idleness of the city.[67]

About two years after the last victory of Belisarius, the emperor returned from a Thracian journey of health, or business, or devotion. Justinian was afflicted by a pain in his head; and his private entry countenanced the rumour of his death.   Before the third hour of the day, the bakers' shops were plundered of their bread, the houses were shut, and every citizen, with hope or terror, prepared for the impending tumult.   The senators themselves, fearful and suspicious, were convened at the ninth hour; and the præfect received their commands to visit every quarter of the city and proclaim a general illumination for the recovery of the emperor's health.   The ferment subsided; but every accident betrayed the impotence of the government and the factious temper of the people: the guards were disposed to mutiny as often as their quarters were changed, or their pay was withheld: the frequent calamities of fires and earthquakes afforded the opportunities of disorder; the disputes of the blues and greens, of the orthodox and heretics, degenerated into bloody battles; and, in the presence of the Persian ambassador, Justinian blushed for himself and for his subjects.   Capricious pardon and arbitrary punishment embittered the irksomeness and discontent of a long reign: a conspiracy was formed in the palace; and, unless we are deceived by the names of Marcellus and Sergius, the most virtuous and the most profligate of the courtiers were associated in the same designs. They had fixed the time of the execution; their rank gave them access to the royal banquet; and their black slaves [68] were stationed in the vestibule and porticoes to announce the death of the tyrant, and to excite a sedition in the capital. But the indiscretion of an accomplice saved the poor remnant of the days of Justinian. The conspirators were detected and seized with daggers hidden under

---

[67] The Bulgarian war, and the last victory of Belisarius, are imperfectly represented in the prolix declamation of Agathias (l. v. p. 154-174 [p. 299 sqq., ed. Bonn]) and the dry Chronicle of Theophanes (p. 197, 198 [tom. i. p. 360 sq., ed. Bonn]).

[68] Ἰνδούς.   They could scarcely be real Indians; and the Æthiopians, sometimes known by that name, were never used by the ancients as guards or followers: they were the trifling, though costly, objects of female and royal luxury (Terent. Eunuch. act i. scene ii. [v. 88]; Sueton. in August. c. 83, with a good note of Casaubon, in Caligulâ, c. 57).

their garments; Marcellus died by his own hand, and Sergius was dragged from the sanctuary.[69] Pressed by remorse, or tempted by the hopes of safety, he accused two officers of the household of Belisarius, and torture forced them to declare that they had acted according to the secret instructions of their patron.[70] Posterity will not hastily believe that a hero who in the vigour of life had disdained the fairest offers of ambition and revenge should stoop to the murder of his prince, whom he could not long expect to survive. His followers were impatient to fly; but flight must have been supported by rebellion, and he had lived enough for nature and for glory. Belisarius appeared before the council with less fear than indignation: after forty years' service the emperor had prejudged his guilt; and injustice was sanctified by the presence and authority of the patriarch. The life of Belisarius was graciously spared, but his fortunes were sequestered; and, from December to July, he was guarded as a prisoner in his own palace. At length his innocence was acknowledged; his freedom and honours were restored; and death, which might be hastened by resentment and grief, removed him from the world about eight months after his deliverance. The name of Belisarius can never die: but, instead of the funeral, the monuments, the statues, so justly due to his memory, I only read that his treasures, the spoils of the Goths and Vandals, were immediately confiscated by the emperor. Some decent portion was reserved, however, for the use of his widow: and as Antonina had much to repent, she devoted the last remains of her life and fortune to the foundation of a convent. Such is the simple and genuine narrative of the fall of Belisarius and the ingratitude of Justinian.[71] That he was deprived

---

[69] The Sergius (Vandal. l. ii. c. 21, 22, Anecdot. c. 5) and Marcellus (Goth. l. iii. c. 32) are mentioned by Procopius. See Theophanes, p. 197, 201 [tom. i. p. 360, 367, ed. Bonn].

[70] Alemannus (p. 3) quotes an old Byzantine MS., which has been printed in the Imperium Orientale of Banduri [tom. iii. p. 349, ed. Bonn].

[71] Of the disgrace and restoration of Belisarius, the genuine original record is preserved in the Fragment of John Malala (tom. ii. p. 234-243 [p. 494 *sq.*, ed. Bonn]) and the exact Chronicle of Theophanes (p. 194-204 [tom. i. p. 368 *sqq.*, ed. Bonn]). Cedrenus (Compend. p. 387, 388 [tom. i. p. 680, ed. Bonn]) and Zonaras (tom. ii. l. xiv. [c. 9] p. 69) seem to hesitate between the obsolete truth and the growing falsehood.

[John Tzetzes was not a monk, and he relates the story of the blindness and the beggary of Belisarius in his Cheliads, iii. No. 88, 339-348. But the story is to be found earlier than he, viz., in the Πάτρια τῆς πόλεως of Codinus compiled in the time of Basil II. The earliest writer who mentions the disgrace of Belisarius is Theophanes, who lived in the ninth century, and he expressly adds that Belisarius was restored to his freedom and honours. Two theories have been started to account for the origin of the story of Belisarius. The first is that of Le Beau, who supposes that Belisarius was confounded with his contemporary John of Cappadocia, who was reduced to such poverty that he begged his bread from province to province. The second is that of Mr. Finlay, who suggests that the story took its rise from the fate of Symbatius and Peganes, who, having formed a conspiracy against Michael III. in the ninth century, were deprived of their sight and exposed as common beggars in Constantinople. (See Finlay, *Hist. of Byzantine Empire*.)—O. S.]

of his eyes, and reduced by envy to beg his bread, " Give a penny to Belisarius the general!" is a fiction of later times,[72] which has obtained credit, or rather favour, as a strange example of the vicissitudes of fortune.[73]

If the emperor could rejoice in the death of Belisarius, he enjoyed the base satisfaction only eight months, the last period of a reign of thirty-eight and a life of eighty-three years. It would be difficult to trace the character of a prince who is not the most conspicuous object of his own times: but the confessions of an enemy may be received as the safest evidence of his virtues. The resemblance of Justinian to the bust of Domitian is maliciously urged,[74] with the acknowledgment, however, of a well-proportioned figure, a ruddy complexion, and a pleasing countenance. The emperor was easy of access, patient of hearing, courteous and affable in discourse, and a master of the angry passions which rage with such destructive violence in the breast of a despot. Procopius praises his temper, to reproach him with calm and deliberate cruelty: but in the conspiracies which attacked his authority and person, a more candid judge will approve the justice, or admire the clemency, of Justinian. He excelled in the private virtues of chastity and temperance; but the impartial love of beauty would have been less mischievous than his conjugal tenderness for Theodora; and his abstemious diet was regulated, not by the prudence of a philosopher, but the superstition of a monk. His repasts were short and frugal: on solemn fasts he contented himself with water and vegetables; and such was his strength as well as fervour, that he frequently passed two

---

[72] The source of this idle fable may be derived from a miscellaneous work of the twelfth century, the Chiliads of John Tzetzes, a monk (Basil. 1546, ad calcem Lycophront. Colon. Allobrog. 1614, in Corp. Poet. Græc.). He relates the blindness and beggary of Belisarius in ten vulgar or *political* verses (Chiliad iii. No. 88, 339-348, in Corp. Poet. Græc. tom. ii. p. 311).

Ἔκπωμα ξύλινον κρατῶν, ἐβόα τῷ μιλίῳ,
Βελισαρίῳ ὀβολὸν δότε τῷ στρατηλάτῃ
Ὃν τύχη μὲν ἐδόξασεν, ἀποτυφλοῖ δ' ὁ φθόνος.

This moral or romantic tale was imported into Italy with the language and manuscripts of Greece; repeated before the end of the fifteenth century by Crinitus, Pontanus, and Volaterranus; attacked by Alciat, for the honour of the law; and defended by Baronius (A.D. 561, No. 2, etc.), for the honour of the church. Yet Tzetzes himself had read in *other* chronicles that Belisarius did not lose his sight, and that he recovered his fame and fortunes.

[73] The statue in the villa Borghese at Rome, in a sitting posture, with an open hand, which is vulgarly given to Belisarius, may be ascribed with more dignity to Augustus in the act of propitiating Nemesis (Winckelman, Hist. de l'Art, tom. iii. p. 266). Ex nocturno visû etiam stipem, quotannis, die certo, emendicabat a populo, cavam manum asses porrigentibus præbens (Sueton. in August. c. 91, with an excellent note of Casaubon).
[It should be noted that the statue formerly in the villa Borghese at Rome is now in the Louvre.—O. S.]

[74] The *rubor* of Domitian is stigmatised, quaintly enough, by the pen of Tacitus (in Vit. Agricol. c. 45), and has been likewise noticed by the younger Pliny (Panegyr. c. 48) and Suetonius (in Domitian, c. 18, and Casaubon ad locum). Procopius (Anecdot. c. 8 [tom. iii. p. 55, ed. Bonn]) foolishly believes that only *one* bust of Domitian had reached the sixth century.

days, and as many nights, without tasting any food. The measure of his sleep was not less rigorous: after the repose of a single hour, the body was awakened by the soul, and, to the astonishment of his chamberlains, Justinian walked or studied till the morning light. Such restless application prolonged his time for the acquisition of knowledge [75] and the despatch of business; and he might seriously deserve the reproach of confounding, by minute and preposterous diligence, the general order of his administration. The emperor professed himself a musician and architect, a poet and philosopher, a lawyer and theologian; and if he failed in the enterprise of reconciling the Christian sects, the review of the Roman jurisprudence is a noble monument of his spirit and industry. In the government of the empire he was less wise, or less successful: the age was unfortunate; the people was oppressed and discontented; Theodora abused her power; a succession of bad ministers disgraced his judgment; and Justinian was neither beloved in his life nor regretted at his death. The love of fame was deeply implanted in his breast, but he condescended to the poor ambition of titles, honours, and contemporary praise; and while he laboured to fix the admiration, he forfeited the esteem and affection, of the Romans. The design of the African and Italian wars was boldly conceived and executed; and his penetration discovered the talents of Belisarius in the camp, of Narses in the palace. But the name of the emperor is eclipsed by the names of his victorious generals; and Belisarius still lives to upbraid the envy and ingratitude of his sovereign. The partial favour of mankind applauds the genius of a conqueror who leads and directs his subjects in the exercise of arms. The characters of Philip the Second and of Justinian are distinguished by the cold ambition which delights in war, and declines the dangers of the field. Yet a colossal statue of bronze represented the emperor on horseback, preparing to march against the Persians in the habit and armour of Achilles. In the great square before the church of St. Sophia, this monument was raised on a brass column and a stone pedestal of seven steps; and the pillar of Theodosius, which weighed seven thousand four hundred pounds of silver, was removed from the same place by the avarice and vanity of Justinian. Future princes were more just or indulgent to *his* memory; the elder Andronicus, in the beginning of the fourteenth century, repaired and beautified his equestrian statue: since the fall of the empire it has been melted into cannon by the victorious Turks.[76]

I shall conclude this chapter with the comets, the earthquakes, and the plague, which astonished or afflicted the age of Justinian.

[75] The studies and science of Justinian are attested by the confession (Anecdot. c. 8, 13), still more than by the praises (Gothic. l. iii. c. 31, de Ædific. l. i. Proem. c. 7) of Procopius. Consult the copious index of Alemannus, and read the Life of Justinian by Ludewig (p. 135-142).

[76] See in the C. P. Christiana of Ducange (l. i. c. 24, No. 1) a chain of original testimonies, from Procopius in the sixth, to Gyllius in the sixteenth century.

I. In the fifth year of his reign, and in the month of September, a comet [77] was seen during twenty days in the western quarter of the heavens, and which shot its rays into the north. Eight years afterwards, while the sun was in Capricorn, another comet appeared to follow in the Sagittary: the size was gradually increasing; the head was in the east, the tail in the west, and it remained visible above forty days. The nations, who gazed with astonishment, expected wars and calamities from their baleful influence; and these expectations were abundantly fulfilled. The astronomers dissembled their ignorance of the nature of these blazing stars, which they affected to represent as the floating meteors of the air; and few among them embraced the simple notion of Seneca and the Chaldæans, that they are only planets of a longer period and more eccentric motion.[78] Time and science have justified the conjectures and predictions of the Roman sage: the telescope has opened new worlds to the eyes of astronomers;[79] and, in the narrow space of history and fable, one and the same comet is already found to have visited the earth in *seven* equal revolutions of five hundred and seventy-five years. The *first*,[80] which ascends beyond the Christian era one thousand seven hundred and sixty-seven years, is coëval with Ogyges, the father of Grecian antiquity. And this appearance explains the tradition which Varro has preserved, that under his reign the planet Venus changed her colour, size, figure, and course; a prodigy without example either in past or succeeding ages.[81] The *second* visit, in the year eleven hundred and ninety-three, is darkly implied in the fable of Electra, the seventh of the Pleiads, who have been reduced to six since the time of the Trojan war. That nymph, the wife of Dardanus,

[77] The first comet is mentioned by John Malala (tom. ii. p. 190, 219 [p. 454, 477, ed. Bonn]) and Theophanes (p. 154 [tom. i. p. 278, ed. Bonn]) ; the second by Procopius (Persic. l. ii. c. 4). Yet I strongly suspect their identity. The paleness of the sun (Vandal. l. ii. c. 14) is applied by Theophanes (p. 158) to a different year.

[78] Seneca's seventh book of Natural Questions displays in the theory of comets a philosophic mind. Yet should we not too candidly confound a vague prediction, a venient tempus, etc., with the merit of real discoveries.

[79] Astronomers may study Newton and Halley. I draw my humble science from the article COMÈTE, in the French Encyclopédie, by M. d'Alembert.

[The identity of the comet of A.D. 1680, with the comets of A.D. 1106, A.D. 531, B.C. 44, etc., was an ingenious speculation of Halley. The observations made upon the eccentricity of a comet's orbit, whether it was a parabola or an ellipse with great eccentricity, have recently been made with such accuracy as to warrant almost exact conclusions being obtained. Cf. John Williams, *Observations of Comets from Chinese Annals.*—O. S.]

[80] Whiston, the honest, pious, visionary Whiston, had fancied, for the era of Noah's flood (2242 years before Christ), a prior apparition of the same comet which drowned the earth with its tail.

[81] A dissertation of Fréret (Mémoires de l'Académie des Inscriptions, tom. x. p. 357-377) affords a happy union of philosophy and erudition. The phenomenon in the time of Ogyges was preserved by Varro (apud Augustin. de Civitate Dei, xxi. 8), who quotes Castor, Dion of Naples, and Adrastus of Cyzicus—nobiles mathematici. The two subsequent periods are preserved by the Greek mythologists and the spurious books of Sibylline verses.

was unable to support the ruin of her country: she abandoned the dances of her sister orbs, fled from the zodiac to the north pole, and obtained, from her dishevelled locks, the name of the *comet*. The *third* period expires in the year six hundred and eighteen, a date that exactly agrees with the tremendous comet of the Sibyl, and perhaps of Pliny, which arose in the West two generations before the reign of Cyrus. The *fourth* apparition, forty-four years before the birth of Christ, is of all others the most splendid and important. After the death of Cæsar, a long-haired star was conspicuous to Rome and to the nations during the games which were exhibited by young Octavian in honour of Venus and his uncle. The vulgar opinion, that it conveyed to heaven the divine soul of the dictator, was cherished and consecrated by the piety of a statesman; while his secret superstition referred the comet to the glory of his own times.[82] The *fifth* visit has been already ascribed to the fifth year of Justinian, which coincides with the five hundred and thirty-first of the Christian era. And it may deserve notice, that in this, as in the preceding instance, the comet was followed, though at a longer interval, by a remarkable paleness of the sun. The *sixth* return, in the year eleven hundred and six, is recorded by the chronicles of Europe and China: and in the first fervour of the Crusades, the Chris- tians and the Mahometans might surmise, with equal reason, that it portended the destruction of the Infidels. The *seventh* phenomenon, or one thousand six hundred and eighty, was presented to the eyes of an enlightened age.[83] The philosophy of Bayle dispelled a prejudice which Milton's muse had so recently adorned, that the comet, " from its horrid hair shakes pestilence and war." [84] Its road in the heavens was observed with exquisite skill by Flamsteed and Cassini: and the mathematical science of Bernoulli, Newton, and Halley investigated the laws of its revolutions. At the *eighth* period, in the year two thousand three hundred and fifty-five, their calculations may perhaps be verified by the astronomers of some future capital in the Siberian or American wilderness.

II. The near approach of a comet may injure or destroy the globe

---

[82] Pliny (Hist. Nat. ii. 23) has transcribed the original memorial of Augustus. Mairan, in his most ingenious letters to the P. Parennin, missionary in China, removes the games and the comet of September from the year 44 to the year 43 before the Christian era; but I am not totally subdued by the criticism of the astronomer (Opuscules, p. 275-351).

[83] This last comet was visible in the month of December, 1680. Bayle, who began his Pensées sur la Comète in January, 1681 (Œuvres, tom. iii.), was forced to argue that a *supernatural* comet would have confirmed the ancients in their idolatry. Bernoulli (see his *Eloge*, in Fontenelle, tom. v. p. 99) was forced to allow that the tail, though not the head, was a *sign* of the wrath of God.

[84] Paradise Lost was published in the year 1667; and the famous lines (l. ii. 708, etc.), which startled the licenser, may allude to the recent comet of 1664, observed by Cassini at Rome in the presence of queen Christina (Fontenelle, in his *Eloge*, tom. v. p. 338). Had Charles II. betrayed any symptoms of curiosity or fear?

which we inhabit; but the changes on its surface have been hitherto produced by the action of volcanoes and earthquakes.[85] The nature of the soil may indicate the countries most exposed to these formidable concussions, since they are caused by subterraneous fires, and such fires are kindled by the union and fermentation of iron and sulphur. But their times and effects appear to lie beyond the reach of human curiosity; and the philosopher will discreetly abstain from the prediction of earthquakes, till he has counted the drops of water that silently filtrate on the inflammable mineral, and measured the caverns which increase by resistance the explosion of the imprisoned air. Without assigning the cause, history will distinguish the periods in which these calamitous events have been rare or frequent, and will observe that this fever of the earth raged with uncommon violence during the reign of Justinian.[86] Each year is marked by the repetition of earthquakes, of such duration that Constantinople has been shaken above forty days; of such extent that the shock has been communicated to the whole surface of the globe, or at least of the Roman empire. An impulsive or vibratory motion was felt, enormous chasms were opened, huge and heavy bodies were discharged into the air, the sea alternately advanced and retreated beyond its ordinary bounds, and a mountain was torn from Libanus[87] and cast into the waves, where it protected, as a mole, the new harbour of Botrys[88] in Phœnicia. The stroke that agitates an ant-hill may crush the insect-myriads in the dust; yet truth must extort a confession that man has industriously laboured for his own destruction. The institution of great cities, which include a nation within the limits of a wall, almost realises the wish of Caligula that the Roman people had but one neck. Two hundred and fifty thousand persons are said to have perished in the earthquake of Antioch, whose domestic multitudes were swelled by the conflux of strangers to the festival of the Ascension. The loss of Berytus[89] was of smaller account, but of much greater value. That

[85] For the cause of earthquakes see Buffon (tom. i. p. 502-536; Supplément à l'Hist. Naturelle, tom. v. p. 382-390, edition in 4to), Valmont de Bomare (Dictionnaire d'Histoire Naturelle, *Tremblemens de Terre, Pyrites*), Watson (Chemical Essays, tom. i. p. 181-209).

[86] The earthquakes that shook the Roman world in the reign of Justinian are described or mentioned by Procopius (Goth. l. iv. c. 25 [tom. ii. p. 594, ed. Bonn]; Anecdot. c. 18), Agathias (l. ii. p. 52, 53, 54; l. v. p. 145-152 [p. 96-101, 281-294, ed. Bonn]), John Malala (Chron. tom. ii. p. 140-146, 176, 177, 183, 193, 220, 229, 231, 233, 234 [p. 419, *sq.*, 442 *sq.*, 448, 456, 478, 485 *sq.*, 488 *sq.*, ed. Bonn]), and Theophanes (p. 151, 183 189, 191-196 [tom. i. p. 272, 336, 347, 350, 357, ed. Bonn]).

[87] An abrupt height, a perpendicular cape, between Aradus and Botrys, named by the Greeks θεῶν πρόσωπον, and εὐπρόσωπον or λιθοπρόσωπον by the scrupulous Christians (Polyb. l. v. [c. 68] p. 411; Pompon. Mela, l. i. c. 12, p. 87, cum Isaac Voss. Observat. Maundrell, Journey, p. 32, 33; Pocock's Description, vol. ii. p. 99).

[88] Botrys was founded (ann. ante Christ. 935-903) by Ithobal, king of Tyre (Marsham, Canon Chron. p. 387, 388). Its poor representative, the village of Patrone, is now destitute of an harbour.

[89] The university, splendour, and ruin of Berytus, are celebrated by Heineccius (p. 351-356) as an essential part of the history of the Roman law.

city, on the coast of Phœnicia, was illustrated by the study of the civil law, which opened the surest road to wealth and dignity: the schools of Berytus were filled with the rising spirits of the age, and many a youth was lost in the earthquake who might have lived to be the scourge or the guardian of his country. In these disasters the architect becomes the enemy of mankind. The hut of a savage, or the tent of an Arab, may be thrown down without injury to the inhabitant; and the Peruvians had reason to deride the folly of their Spanish conquerors, who with so much cost and labour erected their own sepulchres. The rich marbles of a patrician are dashed on his own head; a whole people is buried under the ruins of public and private edifices; and the conflagration is kindled and propagated by the innumerable fires which are necessary for the subsistence and manufactures of a great city. Instead of the mutual sympathy which might comfort and assist the distressed, they dreadfully experience the vices and passions which are released from the fear of punishment; the tottering houses are pillaged by intrepid avarice; revenge embraces the moment and selects the victim; and the earth often swallows the assassin, or the ravisher, in the consummation of their crimes. Superstition involves the present danger with invisible terrors; and if the image of death may sometimes be subservient to the virtue or repentance of individuals, an affrighted people is more forcibly moved to expect the end of the world, or to deprecate with servile homage the wrath of an avenging Deity.

III. Æthiopia and Egypt have been stigmatised in every age as the original source and seminary of the plague.[90] In a damp, hot, stagnating air, this African fever is generated from the putrefaction of animal substances, and especially from the swarms of locusts, not less destructive to mankind in their death than in their lives. The fatal disease which depopulated the earth in the time of Justinian and his successors[91] first appeared in the neighbourhood of Pelusium, between the Serbonian bog and the eastern channel of the Nile. From thence, tracing as it were a double path, it spread to the East, over Syria, Persia, and the Indies, and penetrated to the West, along the coast of Africa and over the continent of Europe. In the spring of the second year Constantinople, during three or four months, was visited by the pestilence; and Procopius, who observed its progress and symptoms

It was overthrown in the twenty-fifth year of Justinian, A.D. 551, July 9 (Theophanes, p. 192); but Agathias (l. ii. p. 51, 52 [p. 95 sq., ed. Bonn]) suspends the earthquake till he has achieved the Italian war.

[90] I have read with pleasure Mead's short, but elegant, treatise concerning Pestilential Disorders, the seventh edition, London, 1722.

[91] The great plague which raged in 542 and the following years (Pagi, Critica, tom. ii. p. 518) must be traced in Procopius (Persic. l. ii. c. 22, 23), Agathias (l. v. p. 153, 154 [p. 297 sq., ed. Bonn]), Evagrius (l. iv. c. 29), Paul Diaconus (l. ii. c. 4, p. 776, 777), Gregory of Tours (tom. ii. l. iv. c. 5, p. 205), who styles it Lues Inguinaria, and the Chronicles of Victor Tunnunensis (p. 9 in Thesaur. Temporum), of Marcellinus (p. 54), and of Theophanes (p. 153).

with the eyes of a physician,[92] has emulated the skill and diligence of Thucydides in the description of the plague of Athens.[93] The infection was sometimes announced by the visions of a distempered fancy, and the victim despaired as soon as he had heard the menace and felt the stroke of an invisible spectre. But the greater number, in their beds, in the streets, in their usual occupation, were surprised by a slight fever; so slight, indeed, that neither the pulse nor the colour of the patient gave any signs of the approaching danger. The same, the next, or the succeeding day, it was declared by the swelling of the glands, particularly those of the groin, of the armpits, and under the ear; and when these buboes or tumours were opened, they were found to contain a *coal*, or black substance, of the size of a lentil. If they came to a just swelling and suppuration, the patient was saved by this kind and natural discharge of the morbid humour; but if they continued hard and dry, a mortification quickly ensued, and the fifth day was commonly the term of his life. The fever was often accompanied with lethargy or delirium; the bodies of the sick were covered with black pustules or carbuncles, the symptoms of immediate death; and in the constitutions too feeble to produce an eruption, the vomiting of blood was followed by a mortification of the bowels. To pregnant women the plague was generally mortal; yet one infant was drawn alive from his dead mother, and three mothers survived the loss of their infected fœtus. Youth was the most perilous season, and the female sex was less susceptible than the male; but every rank and profession was attacked with indiscriminate rage, and many of those who escaped were deprived of the use of their speech, without being secure from a return of the disorder.[94] The physicians of Constantinople were zealous and skilful; but their art was baffled by the various symptoms and pertinacious vehemence of the disease: the same remedies were productive of contrary effects, and the event capriciously disappointed their prognostics of death or recovery. The order of funerals and the right of sepulchres were confounded; those who were left without friends or servants lay unburied in the streets, or in their desolate houses; and a magistrate

[92] Dr. Friend (Hist. Medicin. in Opp. p. 416-420, Lond. 1733) is satisfied that Procopius must have studied physic, from his knowledge and use of the technical words. Yet many words that are now scientific were common and popular in the Greek idiom.

[93] See Thucydides, l. ii. c. 47-54, p. 127-133, edit. Duker, and the poetical description of the same plague by Lucretius (l. vi. 1136-1284). I was indebted to Dr. Hunter for an elaborate commentary on this part of Thucydides, a quarto of 600 pages (Venet. 1603, apud Juntas), which was pronounced in St. Mark's library by Fabius Paullinus Utinensis, a physician and philosopher.

[94] Thucydides (c. 51) affirms that the infection could only be once taken; but Evagrius, who had family experience of the plague, observes that some persons, who had escaped the first, sunk under the second attack; and this repetition is confirmed by Fabius Paullinus (p. 588). I observe that on this head physicians are divided; and the nature and operation of the disease may not always be similar.

was authorised to collect the promiscuous heaps of dead bodies, to transport them by land or water, and to inter them in deep pits beyond the precincts of the city. Their own danger and the prospect of public distress awakened some remorse in the minds of the most vicious of mankind: the confidence of health again revived their passions and habits; but philosophy must disdain the observation of Procopius, that the lives of such men were guarded by the peculiar favour of fortune or Providence. He forgot, or perhaps he secretly recollected, that the plague had touched the person of Justinian himself; but the abstemious diet of the emperor may suggest, as in the case of Socrates, a more rational and honourable cause for his recovery.[95] During his sickness the public consternation was expressed in the habits of the citizens; and their idleness and despondence occasioned a general scarcity in the capital of the East.

Contagion is the inseparable symptom of the plague; which, by mutual respiration, is transfused from the infected persons to the lungs and stomach of those who approach them. While philosophers believe and tremble, it is singular that the existence of a real danger should have been denied by a people most prone to vain and imaginary terrors.[96] Yet the fellow-citizens of Procopius were satisfied, by some short and partial experience, that the infection could not be gained by the closest conversation;[97] and this persuasion might support the assiduity of friends or physicians in the care of the sick, whom inhuman prudence would have condemned to solitude and despair. But the fatal security, like the predestination of the Turks, must have aided the progress of the contagion; and those salutary precautions to which Europe is indebted for her safety were unknown to the government of Justinian. No restraints were imposed on the free and frequent intercourse of the Roman provinces: from Persia to France the nations were mingled and infected by wars and emigrations; and the pestilential odour which lurks for years in a bale of cotton was imported, by the abuse of trade, into the most distant regions. The mode of its propagation is explained by the remark of Procopius himself, that it always spread from the seacoast to the inland country: the most sequestered islands and mountains were successively visited; the places which had escaped the fury of its

[95] It was thus that Socrates had been saved by his temperance, in the plague of Athens (Aul. Gellius, Noct. Attic. ii. 1). Dr. Mead accounts for the peculiar salubrity of religious houses by the two advantages of seclusion and abstinence (p. 18, 19).

[96] Mead proves that the plague is contagious, from Thucydides, Lucretius, Aristotle, Galen, and common experience (p. 10-20); and he refutes (Preface, p. ii.-xiii.) the contrary opinion of the French physicians who visited Marseilles in the year 1720. Yet these were the recent and enlightened spectators of a plague which, in a few months, swept away 50,000 inhabitants (sur la Peste de Marseille, Paris, 1786), of a city that, in the present hour of prosperity and trade, contains no more than 90,000 souls (Necker, sur les Finances, tom. i. p. 231).

[97] The strong assertions of Procopius—οὔτε γὰρ ἰατρῷ οὔτε ἰδιώτῃ—are overthrown by the subsequent experience of Evagrius.

first passage were alone exposed to the contagion of the ensuing year. The winds might diffuse that subtle venom; but unless the atmosphere be previously disposed for its reception, the plague would soon expire in the cold or temperate climates of the earth. Such was the universal corruption of the air, that the pestilence which burst forth in the fifteenth year of Justinian was not checked or alleviated by any difference of the seasons. In time its first malignity was abated and dispersed; the disease alternately languished and revived; but it was not till the end of a calamitous period of fifty-two years that mankind recovered their health, or the air resumed its pure and salubrious quality. No facts have been preserved to sustain an account, or even a conjecture, of the numbers that perished in this extraordinary mortality. I only find that, during three months, five and at length ten thousand persons died each day at Constantinople; that many cities of the East were left vacant; and that in several districts of Italy the harvest and the vintage withered on the ground. The triple scourge of war, pestilence, and famine afflicted the subjects of Justinian; and his reign is disgraced by a visible decrease of the human species, which has never been repaired in some of the fairest countries of the globe.[98]

CHAPTER XLIV (527-565 A.D.)

Idea of the Roman Jurisprudence—The Laws of the Kings—The Twelve Tables of the Decemvirs—The Laws of the People—The Decrees of the Senate—The Edicts of the Magistrates and Emperors—Authority of the Civilians—Code, Pandects, Novels, and Institutes of Justinian:—I. Rights of Persons—II. Rights of Things—III. Private Injuries and Actions— IV. Crimes and Punishments

THE vain titles of the victories of Justinian are crumbled into dust, but the name of the legislator is inscribed on a fair and everlasting monument. Under his reign, and by his care, the civil jurisprudence was digested in the immortal works of the CODE, the PANDECTS, and the INSTITUTES:[1] the public reason of the Romans has been silently or

---

[98] After some figures of rhetoric, the sands of the sea, etc., Procopius (Anecdot. c. 18) attempts a more definite account; that μυριάδας μυριάδων μυριάς had been exterminated under the reign of the Imperial demon. The expression is obscure in grammar and arithmetic; and a literal interpretation would produce several millions of millions. Alemannus (p. 80) and Cousin (tom. iii. p. 178) translate this passage "two hundred millions;" but I am ignorant of their motives. If we drop the μυριάδας, the remaining μυριάδων μυριάς, a myriad of myriads, would furnish one hundred millions, a number not wholly inadmissible.

[1] The civilians of the darker ages have established an absurd and incomprehensible mode of quotation, which is supported by authority and custom. In their references to the Code, the Pandects, and the Institutes, they mention the number, not of the *book*, but only of the *law;* and content themselves with reciting the first words of the *title* to which it belongs; and of these

studiously transfused into the domestic institutions of Europe,[2] and the laws of Justinian still command the respect or obedience of independent nations. Wise or fortunate is the prince who connects his own reputation with the honour and interest of a perpetual order of men. The defence of their founder is the first cause which in every age has exercised the zeal and industry of the civilians. They piously commemorate his virtues, dissemble or deny his failings, and fiercely chastise the guilt or folly of the rebels who presume to sully the majesty of the purple. The idolatry of love has provoked, as it usually happens, the rancour of opposition; the character of Justinian has been exposed to the blind vehemence of flattery and invective; and the injustice of a sect (the *Anti-Tribonians*) has refused all praise and merit to the prince, his ministers, and his laws.[3] Attached to no party, interested only for the truth and candour of history, and directed by the most temperate and skilful guides,[4] I enter with just diffidence on the subject of civil law, which has exhausted so many learned lives and clothed the walls of such spacious libraries. In a single, if possible in a short, chapter, I shall trace the Roman jurisprudence from Romulus to Justinian,[5] appreciate the labours of that emperor, and pause to contemplate the principles of a science so important to the peace and happiness of society. The laws of a nation form the most instructive portion of its history; and, although I have devoted myself to write the annals of a declining monarchy, I shall embrace the occasion to breathe the pure and invigorating air of the republic.

titles there are more than a thousand. Ludewig (Vit. Justiniani, p. 268) wishes to shake off this pedantic yoke; and I have dared to adopt the simple and rational method of numbering the book, the title, and the law.

[2] Germany, Bohemia, Hungary, Poland, and Scotland, have received them as common law or reason; in France, Italy, etc., they possess a direct or indirect influence; and they were respected in England from Stephen to Edward I., our national Justinian (Duck. de Usû et Auctoritate Juris Civilis, l. ii. c. 1, 8-15; Heineccius, Hist. Juris Germanici, c. 3, 4, No. 55-124, and the legal historians of each country).

[3] Francis Hottoman, a learned and acute lawyer of the sixteenth century, wished to mortify Cujacius and to please the Chancellor de l'Hôpital. His Anti-Tribonianus (which I have never been able to procure) was published in French in 1609; and his sect was propagated in Germany (Heineccius, Op. tom. iii. sylloge iii. p. 171-183).

[4] At the head of these guides I shall respectfully place the learned and perspicuous Heineccius, a German professor, who died at Halle in the year 1741 (see his Eloge in the Nouvelle Bibliothèque Germanique, tom. ii. p. 51-64). His ample works have been collected in eight volumes in 4to, Geneva, 1743-1748. The treatises which I have separately used are, 1. Historia Juris Romani et Germanici, Lugd. Batav. 1740, in 8vo. 2. Syntagma Antiquitatum Romanum Jurisprudentiam illustrantum, 2 vols. in 8vo. Traject. ad Rhenum. 3. Elementa Juris Civilis secundum Ordinem Institutionum, Lugd. Bat. 1751, in 8vo. 4. Elementa J. C. secundum Ordinem Pandectarum, Traject. 1772, in 8vo, 2 vols.

[5] Our original text is a fragment de Origine Juris (Pandect. l. i. tit. ii.) of Pomponius, a Roman lawyer, who lived under the Antonines (Heinecc. tom. iii. syl. iii. p. 66-126). It has been abridged, and probably corrupted, by Tribonian, and since restored by Bynkershoek (Opp. tom. i. p. 279-304).

The primitive government of Rome [6] was composed with some political skill of an elective king, a council of nobles, and a general assembly of the people. War and religion were administered by the supreme magistrate, and he alone proposed the laws which were debated in the senate, and finally ratified or rejected by a majority of votes in the thirty *curiæ* or parishes of the city. Romulus, Numa, and Servius Tullius are celebrated as the most ancient legislators; and each of them claims his peculiar part in the threefold division of jurisprudence.[7] The laws of marriage, the education of children, and the authority of parents, which may seem to draw their origin from *nature* itself, are ascribed to the untutored wisdom of Romulus. The law of *nations* and of religious worship, which Numa introduced, was derived from his nocturnal converse with the nymph Egeria. The *civil* law is attributed to the experience of Servius; he balanced the rights and fortunes of the seven classes of citizens, and guarded by fifty new regulations the observance of contracts and the punishment of crimes. The state, which he had inclined towards a democracy, was changed by the last Tarquin into lawless despotism; and when the kingly office was abolished, the patricians engrossed the benefits of freedom. The royal laws became odious or obsolete, the mysterious deposit was silently preserved by the priests and nobles, and at the end of sixty years the citizens of Rome still complained that they were ruled by the arbitrary sentence of the magistrates. Yet the positive institutions of the kings had blended themselves with the public and private manners of the city; some fragments of that venerable jurisprudence [8] were compiled by the diligence

[6] The constitutional history of the kings of Rome may be studied in the first book of Livy, and more copiously in Dionysius Halicarnassensis (l. ii. [c. 4-25] p. 80-96, 119-130 [c. 57-70]; l. iv. [c. 15, etc.] p. 198-220), who sometimes betrays the character of a rhetorician and a Greek.

[7] This threefold division of the law was applied to the three Roman kings by Justus Lipsius (Opp. tom. iv. p. 279); is adopted by Gravina (Origines Juris Civilis, p. 28, edit. Lips. 1737); and is reluctantly admitted by Mascou, his German editor.

[8] The most ancient Code or Digest was styled *Jus Papirianum*, from the first compiler, Papirius, who flourished somewhat before or after the *Regifugium* (Pandect. l. i. tit. ii.). The best judicial critics, even Bynkershoek (tom. i. p. 284, 285) and Heineccius (Hist. J. C. R. l. i. c. 16, 17, and Opp. tom. iii. sylloge iv. p. 1-8), give credit to this tale of Pomponius, without sufficiently adverting to the value and rarity of such a monument of the third century of the *illiterate* city. I much suspect that the Caius Papirius, the Pontifex Maximus, who revived the laws of Numa (Dionys. Hal. l. iii. [c. 36] p. 171), left only an oral tradition; and that the Jus Papirianum of Granius Flaccus (Pandect. l. l. tit. xvi. leg. 144) was not a commentary, but an original work, compiled in the time of Cæsar (Censorin. de Die Natali, c. iii. p. 13; Duker de Latinitate J. C. p. 157).
[Much has been written since the time of Gibbon respecting this compilation of Papirius, but nothing certain is known, and all conjecture is fruitless. The name of the compiler given is not quite certain, as he is variously called Caius, Sextus, and Publius. Dionysius says (iii. 36) that Caius Papirius, the Pontifex Maximus, made a collection of the religious ordinances of Numa, after the expulsion of the last Tarquin, viz., Tarquinius Superbus; and Pomponius *(Pandects,* lib. i. tit. ii. leg. 2, § 2, 36) states that Sextus or Publius Papirius

of antiquarians;[9] and above twenty texts still speak the rudeness of the Pelasgic idiom of the Latins.[10]

I shall not repeat the well-known story of the Decemvirs,[11] who sullied by their actions the honour of inscribing on brass, or wood, or ivory, the TWELVE TABLES of the Roman laws.[12] They were dictated by the rigid and jealous spirit of an aristocracy which had yielded with reluctance to the just demands of the people. But the substance of the Twelve Tables was adapted to the state of the city, and the Romans had emerged from barbarism, since they were capable of studying and embracing the institutions of their more enlightened neighbours. A wise Ephesian was driven by envy from his native country: before he could reach the shores of Latium, he had observed the various forms of human nature and civil society; he imparted his knowledge to the legislators of Rome, and a statue was erected in the forum to the perpetual memory of Hermodorus.[13] The names and divisions of the copper money, the sole coin of the infant state, were of Dorian origin;[14] the

made a compilation of all the Leges Regiæ. Cf. Dircksen, *Versuchen zur Kritik und Auslegung der Quellen des Römischen Rechts;* Zimmern, *Geschichte des Römischen Privatrechts.*—O. S.]

[9] A pompous, though feeble, attempt to restore the original, is made in the Histoire de la Jurisprudence Romaine of Terrasson, p. 22-72; Paris, 1750, in folio; a work of more promise than performance.

[10] In the year 1444 seven or eight tables of brass were dug up between Cortona and Gubbio. A part of these, for the rest is Etruscan, represents the primitive state of the Pelasgic letters and language, which are ascribed by Herodotus to that district of Italy (l. i. c. 56, 57, 58); though this difficult passage may be explained of a Crestona in Thrace (Notes de Larcher, tom. i. p. 256-261). The savage dialect of the Eugubine Tables has exercised, and may still elude, the divination of criticism; but the root is undoubtedly Latin, of the same age and character as the Saliare Carmen, which, in the time of Horace, none could understand. The Roman idiom, by an infusion of Doric and Æolic Greek, was gradually ripened into the style of the twelve tables, of the Duilian column, of Ennius, of Terence, and of Cicero (Gruter. Inscript. tom. i. p. cxlii.; Scipion Maffei, Istoria Diplomatica, p. 241-258; Bibliothèque Italique, tom. iii. p. 30-41, 174-205, tom. xiv. p. 1-52).

[The language of the Eugubine Tables, which contain four inscriptions in Etruscan characters, two in Latin, and one partially in Etruscan and partially in Latin, has recently been the subject of study. The best modern scholars are agreed that the language which is here found is Umbrian, who are represented by all ancient writers as nationally distinct from both the Etruscan and Sabellian races.—O. S.]

[11] Compare Livy (l. iii. c. 31-59) with Dionysius Halicarnassensis (l. x. [c. 55] p. 644—xi. [c. 1, *sqq.*] p. 691). How concise and animated is the Roman —how prolix and lifeless the Greek! Yet he has admirably judged the masters, and defined the rules, of historical composition.

[12] From the historians, Heineccius (Hist. J. R. l. i. No. 26) maintains that the twelve tables were of brass—*æreas:* in the text of Pomponius we read *eboreas;* for which Scaliger has substituted *roboreas* (Bynkershoek, p. 286). Wood, brass, and ivory, might be successively employed.

[13] His exile is mentioned by Cicero (Tusculan. Quæstion. v. 36); his statue by Pliny (Hist. Nat. xxxiv. 11). The letter, dream, and prophecy of Heraclitus are alike spurious (Epistolæ Græc. Divers. p. 337).

[14] This intricate subject of the Sicilian and Roman money is ably discussed by Dr. Bentley (Dissertation on the Epistles of Phalaris, p. 427-479), whose powers in this controversy were called forth by honour and resentment.

harvests of Campania and Sicily relieved the wants of a people whose agriculture was often interrupted by war and faction; and since the trade was established,[15] the deputies who sailed from the Tiber might return from the same harbours with a more precious cargo of political wisdom. The colonies of Great Greece had transported and improved the arts of their mother-country. Cumæ and Rhegium, Crotona and Tarentum, Agrigentum and Syracuse, were in the rank of the most flourishing cities. The disciples of Pythagoras applied philosophy to the use of government, the unwritten laws of Charondas accepted the aid of poetry and music,[16] and Zaleucus framed the republic of the Locrians, which stood without alteration above two hundred years.[17] From a similar motive of national pride, both Livy and Dionysius are willing to believe that the deputies of Rome visited Athens under the wise and splendid administration of Pericles, and the laws of Solon were transfused into the Twelve Tables. If such an embassy had indeed been received from the barbarians of Hesperia, the Roman name would have been familiar to the Greeks before the reign of Alexander,[18] and the faintest evidence would have been explored and celebrated by the curiosity of succeeding times. But the Athenian monuments are silent, nor will it seem credible that the patricians should undertake a long and perilous navigation to copy the purest model of a democracy. In

---

[15] The Romans, or their allies, sailed as far as the fair promontory of Africa (Polyb. l. iii. [c. 22] p. 177, edit. Casaubon, in folio). Their voyages to Cumæ, etc., are noticed by Livy and Dionysius.

[16] This circumstance would alone prove the antiquity of Charondas, the legislator of Rhegium and Catana, who, by a strange error of Diodorus Siculus (tom. i. l. xii. [c. 11 sq.] p. 485-492), is celebrated long afterwards as the author of the policy of Thurium.

[17] Zaleucus, whose existence has been rashly attacked, had the merit and glory of converting a band of outlaws (the Locrians) into the most virtuous and orderly of the Greek republics. (See two Mémoires of the Baron de St. Croix, sur la Législation de la Grande Grèce; Mém. de l'Académie, tom. xlii. p. 276-333.) But the laws of Zaleucus and Charondas, which imposed on Diodorus and Strobæus, are the spurious composition of a Pythagorean sophist, whose fraud has been detected by the critical sagacity of Bentley, p. 335-377.

[18] I seize the opportunity of tracing the progress of this national intercourse: 1. Herodotus and Thucydides (A.U.C. 300-350) appear ignorant of the name and existence of Rome (Joseph. contra Apion. tom. ii. l. i. c. 12, p. 444, edit. Havercamp.). 2. Theopompus (A.U.C. 400, Plin. iii. 9) mentions the invasion of the Gauls, which is noticed in looser terms by Heraclides Ponticus (Plutarch in Camillo [c. 15], p. 292, edit. H. Stephan.). 3. The real or fabulous embassy of the Romans to Alexander (A.U.C. 430) is attested by Clitarchus (Plin. iii. 9), by Aristus and Asclepiades (Arrian, l. vii. [c. 15] p. 294, 295), and by Memnon of Heraclea (apud Photium, cod. ccxxiv. p. 725 [p. 229, ed. Bekker]), though tacitly denied by Livy. 4. Theophrastus (A.U.C. 440) primus externorum aliqua de Romanis diligentius scripsit (Plin. iii. 9). 5. Lycophron (A.U.C. 480-500) scattered the first seed of a Trojan colony and the fable of the Æneid (Cassandra, 1226-1280):

Γῆς καὶ θαλάσσης σκῆπτρα καὶ μοναρχίαν
Λαβόντες.

A bold prediction before the end of the first Punic war.

the comparison of the tables of Solon with those of the Decemvirs, some casual resemblance may be found; some rules which nature and reason have revealed to every society; some proofs of a common descent from Egypt or Phœnicia.[19] But in all the great lines of public and private jurisprudence the legislators of Rome and Athens appear to be strangers or adverse to each other.

Whatever might be the origin or the merit of the Twelve Tables,[20] they obtained among the Romans that blind and partial reverence which the lawyers of every country delight to bestow on their municipal institutions. The study is recommended by Cicero [21] as equally pleasant and instructive. " They amuse the mind by the remembrance of old words, and the portrait of ancient manners; they inculcate the soundest principles of government and morals; and I am not afraid to affirm that the brief composition of the Decemvirs surpasses in genuine value the libraries of Grecian philosophy. How admirable," says Tully, with honest or affected prejudice, " is the wisdom of our ancestors! We alone are the masters of civil prudence, and our superiority is the more conspicuous if we deign to cast our eyes on the rude and almost ridiculous jurisprudence of Draco, of Solon, and of Lycurgus." The Twelve Tables were committed to the memory of the young and the meditation of the old; they were transcribed and illustrated with learned diligence: they had escaped the flames of the Gauls, they subsisted in the age of Justinian, and their subsequent loss has been imperfectly restored by the labours of modern critics.[22] But although these venerable monuments were considered as the rule of right and the fountain of justice,[23] they were overwhelmed by the weight and variety of new laws which, at the end of five centuries, became a grievance more intolerable than the vices of the city.[24] Three thousand brass plates, the acts of the senate and

---

[19] The tenth table, de modo sepulturæ, was borrowed from Solon (Cicero de Legibus, ii. 23-26) : the furtum per lancem et licium conceptum is derived by Heineccius from the manners of Athens (Antiquitat. Rom. tom. ii. p. 167-175). The right of killing a nocturnal thief was declared by Moses, Solon, and the Decemvirs (Exodus xxii. 2; Demosthenes contra Timocratem, tom. i. p. 736, edit. Reiske; Macrob. Saturnalia, l. i. c. 4; Collatio Legum Mosaicarum et Romanarum, tit. vii. No. i. p. 218, edit. Cannegieter [Lugd. Bat. 1774]).

[20] Βραχέως καὶ ἀπερίττως is the praise of Diodorus (tom. i. l. xii. [c. 26] p. 494), which may be fairly translated by the eleganti atque absolutâ brevitate verborum of Aulus Gellius (Noct. Attic. xx. 1).

[21] Listen to Cicero (de Legibus, ii. 23) and his representative Crassus (de Oratore, i. 43, 44).

[22] See Heineccius (Hist. J. R. No. 29-33). I have followed the restoration of the twelve tables by Gravina (Origines J. C. p. 280-307) and Terrasson (Hist. de la Jurisprudence Romaine, p. 94-205).

[23] Finis æqui juris (Tacit. Annal. iii. 27). Fons omnis publici et privati juris (T. Liv. iii. 34).

[24] De principiis juris, et quibus modis ad hanc multitudinem infinitam ac varietatem legum perventum sit altius disseram (Tacit. Annal. iii. 25). This deep disquisition fills only two pages, but they are the pages of Tacitus. With equal sense, but with less energy, Livy (iii. 34) had complained, in hoc immenso aliarum super alias acervatarum legum cumulo, etc.

people, were deposited in the Capitol;[25] and some of the acts, as the Julian law against extortion, surpassed the number of a hundred chapters.[26] The Decemvirs had neglected to import the sanction of Zaleucus, which so long maintained the integrity of his republic. A Locrian who proposed any new law stood forth in the assembly of the people with a cord round his neck, and if the law was rejected the innovator was instantly strangled.

The Decemvirs had been named, and their tables were approved, by an assembly of the *centuries*, in which riches preponderated against numbers. To the first class of Romans, the proprietors of one hundred thousand pounds of copper,[27] ninety-eight votes were assigned, and only ninety-five were left for the six inferior classes, distributed according to their substance by the artful policy of Servius. But the tribunes soon established a more specious and popular maxim, that every citizen has an equal right to enact the laws which he is bound to obey. Instead of the *centuries*, they convened the *tribes*; and the patricians, after an impotent struggle, submitted to the decrees of an assembly in which their votes were confounded with those of the meanest plebeians. Yet as long as the tribes successively passed over narrow *bridges*,[28] and gave their voices aloud, the conduct of each citizen was exposed to the eyes and ears of his friends and countrymen. The insolvent debtor consulted the wishes of his creditor, the client would have blushed to oppose the views of his patron, the general was followed by his veterans, and the aspect of a grave magistrate was a living lesson to the multitude. A new method of secret ballot abolished the influence of fear and shame, of honour and interest; and the abuse of freedom accelerated the progress of anarchy and despotism.[29] The Romans had aspired to be equal,

[25] Suetonius in Vespasiano, c. 8.

[26] Cicero ad Familiares, viii. 8.

[27] Dionysius, with Arbuthnot, and most of the moderns (except Eisenschmidt de Ponderibus, etc., p. 137-140), represent the 100,000 *asses* by 10,000 Attic drachmæ, or somewhat more than 300 pounds sterling. But their calculation can apply only to the later times, when the *as* was diminished to 1-24th of its ancient weight: nor can I believe that in the first ages, however destitute of the precious metals, a single ounce of silver could have been exchangd for seventy pounds of copper or brass. A more simple and rational method is to value the copper itself according to the present rate, and, after comparing the mint and the market-price, the Roman and avoirdupois weight, the primitive *as* or Roman pound of copper may be appreciated at one English shilling, and the 100,000 *asses* of the first class amounted to 5000 pounds sterling. It will appear from the same reckoning that an ox was sold at Rome for five pounds, a sheep for ten shillings, and a quarter of wheat for one pound ten shillings (Festus, p. 330, edit. Dacier; Plin. Hist. Natur. xviii. 4) : nor do I see any reason to reject these consequences, which moderate our ideas of the poverty of the first Romans.

[28] Consult the common writers on the Roman Comitia, especially Sigonius and Beaufort. Spanheim (de Præstantiâ et Usû Numismatum, tom. ii. dissert. x. p. 192, 193) shows, on a curious medal, the Cista, Pontes, Septa, Diribitor, etc.

[29] Cicero (de Legibus, iii. 16, 17, 18) debates this constitutional question, and assigns to his brother Quintus the most unpopular side.

they were levelled by the equality of servitude, and the dictates of Augustus were patiently ratified by the formal consent of the tribes or centuries. Once, and once only, he experienced a sincere and strenuous opposition. His subjects had resigned all political liberty; they defended the freedom of domestic life. A law which enforced the obligation and strengthened the bonds of marriage was clamorously rejected; Propertius, in the arms of Delia, applauded the victory of licentious love; and the project of reform was suspended till a new and more tractable generation had arisen in the world.[30] Such an example was not necessary to instruct a prudent usurper of the mischief of popular assemblies; and their abolition, whichAugustus had silently prepared, was accomplished without resistance, and almost without notice, on the accession of his successor.[31] Sixty thousand plebeian legislators, whom numbers made formidable and poverty secure, were supplanted by six hundred senators, who held their honours, their fortunes, and their lives by the clemency of the emperor. The loss of executive power was alleviated by the gift of legislative authority; and Ulpian might assert, after the practice of two hundred years, that the decrees of the senate obtained the force and validity of laws. In the times of freedom the resolves of the people had often been dictated by the passion or error of the moment: the Cornelian, Pompeian, and Julian laws were adapted by a single hand to the prevailing disorders; but the senate, under the reign of the Cæsars, was composed of magistrates and lawyers, and in questions of private jurisprudence the integrity of their judgment was seldom perverted by fear or interest.[32]

The silence or ambiguity of the laws was supplied by the occasional EDICTS of those magistrates who were invested with the *honours* of the state.[33] This ancient prerogative of the Roman kings was transferred

---

[30] Præ tumultu recusantium perferre non potuit (Sueton. in August. c. 34). See Propertius, l. ii. eleg. 6 [or 7]. Heineccius, in a separate history, has exhausted the whole subject of the Julian and Papian-Poppæan laws (Opp. tom. vii. P. i. p. 1-479).

[31] Tacit. Annal. i. 15; Lipsius, Excursus E, in Tacitum.

[32] Non ambigitur senatum jus facere posse, is the decision of Ulpian (l. xvi. ad Edict. in Pandect. l. i. tit. iii. leg. 9). Pomponius taxes the *comitia* of the people as a turba hominum (Pandect. l. i. tit. ii. leg. 9).

[Gibbon adopts the opinion that under the emperors alone the senate had a share in the legislative power. They had nevertheless participated in it under the republic, since *senatus-consulta* relating to civil rights have been preserved which are much earlier than the reigns of Augustus or Tiberius. It is true that under the emperors the senate exercised this right more frequently, and that the assemblies of the people had become much more rare, though in law they were still permitted in the time of Ulpian. (See the Fragments of Ulpian.) Bach has clearly shown that the senate had the same power in the time of the republic. It is natural that the senatus-consulta should be more frequent under the emperors, because they employed those means of flattering the pride of the senators by granting them the right of deliberating on all affairs which did not trench on the imperial power.—O. S.]

[33] The jus honorarium of the prætors and other magistrates is strictly defined in the Latin text of the Institutes (l. i. tit. ii. No. 7), and more loosely ex-

in their respective offices to the consuls and dictators, the censors and prætors; and a similar right was assumed by the tribunes of the people, the ædiles, and the proconsuls. At Rome, and in the provinces, the duties of the subject and the intentions of the governor were proclaimed; and the civil jurisprudence was reformed by the annual edicts of the supreme judge, the prætor of the city. As soon as he ascended his tribunal, he announced by the voice of the crier, and afterwards inscribed on a white wall, the rules which he proposed to follow in the decision of doubtful cases, and the relief which his equity would afford from the precise rigour of ancient statutes. A principle of discretion more congenial to monarchy was introduced into the republic: the art of respecting the name and eluding the efficacy of the laws was improved by successive prætors; subtleties and fictions were invented to defeat the plainest meaning of the Decemvirs; and where the end was salutary, the means were frequently absurd. The secret or probable wish of the dead was suffered to prevail over the order of succession and the forms of testaments; and the claimant, who was excluded from the character of heir, accepted with equal pleasure from an indulgent prætor the possession of the goods of his late kinsman or benefactor. In the redress of private wrongs, compensations and fines were substituted to the obsolete rigour of the Twelve Tables; time and space were annihilated by fanciful suppositions; and the plea of youth, or fraud, or violence, annulled the obligation or excused the performance of an inconvenient contract. A jurisdiction thus vague and arbitrary was exposed to the most dangerous abuse; the substance, as well as the form of justice, were often sacrificed to the prejudices of virtue, the bias of laudable affection, and the grosser seductions of interest or resentment. But the errors or vices of each prætor expired with his annual office; such maxims alone as had been approved by reason and practice were

plained in the Greek paraphrase of Theophilus (p. 33-38, edit. Reitz), who drops the important word *honorarium.*

[In his note upon the *jus honorarium,* Gibbon here follows the opinion of Heineccius, who, following his master Thomasius, was unwilling to suppose that magistrates exercising a judicial function could share in the legislative power. Heineccius was opposed by the learned Ritter, Professor at Wittenberg, and was followed by the celebrated Bach. But the most light on this question has been thrown by M. Hugo (*History of Roman Law*), who contended that the edicts of the prætors were the true organs of public opinion, and that their edicts furnished the salutary means of perpetually harmonising the legislation with the spirit of the times. It was not according to their caprice that they framed their regulations, but according to the manners and to the opinions of the great civil lawyers of the day who were invited by the prætor to assist in framing this annual law, which, according to its principle, was only a declaration which the prætor made to the public to announce the way in which he was to judge, and to guard against every charge of partiality. The prætor was responsible for all the faults he committed. He was strictly bound to follow the regulation published by him at the commencement of his year of office. Cf. the brief but admirable sketch of the growth of Roman jurisprudence, etc., in the first chapter of Savigny's *Geschichte des Römischen Rechts im Mittelalter.*—O. S.]

copied by succeeding judges; the rule of proceeding was defined by the solution of new cases; and the temptations of injustice were removed by the Cornelian law, which compelled the prætor of the year to adhere to the letter and spirit of his first proclamation.[34] It was reserved for the curiosity and learning of Hadrian to accomplish the design which had been conceived by the genius of Cæsar; and the prætorship of Salvius Julian, an eminent lawyer, was immortalised by the composition of the PERPETUAL EDICT. This well-digested code was ratified by the emperor and the senate; the long divorce of law and equity was at length reconciled; and, instead of the Twelve Tables, the Perpetual Edict was fixed as the invariable standard of civil jurisprudence.[35]

From Augustus to Trajan, the modest Cæsars were content to promulgate their edicts in the various characters of a Roman magistrate; and in the decrees of the senate the *epistles* and *orations* of the prince were respectfully inserted. Hadrian [36] appears to have been the first who assumed without disguise the plenitude of legislative power. And this innovation, so agreeable to his active mind, was countenanced by the patience of the times and his long absence from the seat of government. The same policy was embraced by succeeding monarchs, and, according to the harsh metaphor of Tertullian, " the gloomy and intricate forest of ancient laws was cleared away by the axe of royal mandates and *constitutions*." [37] During four centuries, from Hadrian to Justinian, the public and private jurisprudence was moulded by the will of the sovereign, and few institutions, either human or divine, were permitted to stand on their former basis. The origin of Imperial legislation was concealed by the darkness of ages and the terrors of armed despotism; and a double fiction was propagated by the servility, or perhaps the ignorance, of the civilians who basked in the sunshine of the Roman and Byzantine courts. i. To the prayer of the ancient Cæsars the people or the senate had sometimes granted a personal exemption from

[34] Dion Cassius (tom. i. l. xxxvi. [c. 23] p. 100) fixes the perpetual edicts in the year of Rome 686. Their institution, however, is ascribed to the year 585 in the Acta Diurna, which have been published from the papers of Ludovicus Vives. Their authenticity is supported or allowed by Pighius (Annal. Roman. tom. ii. p. 377, 378), Grævius (ad Sueton. p. 778), Dodwell (Prælection. Cambden, p. 665), and Heineccius: but a single word, Scutum *Cimbricum*, detects the forgery (Moyle's Works, vol. i. p. 303).

[35] The history of edicts is composed, and the text of the perpetual edict is restored, by the master-hand of Heineccius (Opp. tom. vii. P. ii. p. 1-564); in whose researches I might safely acquiesce. In the Academy of Inscriptions, M. Bouchaud has given a series of memoirs to this interesting subject of law and literature.

[36] His laws are the first in the Code. See Dodwell (Prælect. Cambden, p. 319-340), who wanders from the subject in confused reading and feeble paradox.

[37] Totam illam veterem et squalentem silvam legum novis principalium rescriptorum et edictorum securibus truncatis et cæditis (Apologet. c. 4, p. 50, edit. Havercamp.). He proceeds to praise the recent firmness of Severus, who repealed the useless or pernicious laws, without any regard to their age or authority.

the obligation and penalty of particular statutes, and each indulgence was an act of jurisdiction exercised by the republic over the first of her citizens. His humble privilege was at length transformed into the prerogative of a tyrant; and the Latin expression of " released from the laws " [38] was supposed to exalt the emperor above *all* human restraints, and to leave his conscience and reason as the sacred measure of his conduct. 2. A similar dependence was implied in the decrees of the senate, which in every reign defined the titles and powers of an elective magistrate. But it was not before the ideas and even the language of the Romans had been corrupted that a *royal* law,[39] and an irrevocable gift of the people, were created by the fancy of Ulpian, or more probably of Tribonian himself;[40] and the origin of Imperial power, though false in fact and slavish in its consequence, was supported on a principle of freedom and justice. " The pleasure of the emperor has the vigour and effect of law, since the Roman people, by the royal law, have transferred to their prince the full extent of their own power and sovereignty." [41] The will of a single man, of a child, perhaps, was allowed to prevail over the wisdom of ages and the inclinations of millions, and the degenerate Greeks were proud to declare that in his hands alone the arbitrary exercise of legislation could be safely deposited. " What interest or passion," exclaims Theophilus in the court of Justinian, " can reach the calm and sublime elevation of the monarch? he is already master of the lives and fortunes of his subjects, and those who have incurred his displeasure are already numbered with the dead." [42] Disdaining the language of flattery, the historian may confess that in questions of private jurisprudence the absolute sovereign of a great empire can seldom be influenced by any personal considerations. Virtue, or even reason, will suggest to his impartial mind that he is the guardian of peace and equity, and that the interest of society is inseparably connected with his own. Under the weakest and most vicious reign, the

[38] The constitutional style of *Legibus solutus* is misinterpreted by the art or ignorance of Dion Cassius (tom. i. 1. liii. [c. 18] p. 713). On this occasion his editor, Reimar, joins the universal censure which freedom and criticism have pronounced against that slavish historian.

[39] The *word* (*Lex Regia*) was still more recent than the *thing*. The slaves of Commodus or Caracalla would have started at the name of royalty.

[40] See Gravina (Opp. p. 501-512) and Beaufort (République Romaine, tom. i. p. 255-274). He has made a proper use of two dissertations by John Frederick Gronovius and Noodt, both translated, with valuable notes, by Barbeyrac, 2 vols. in 12mo, 1731.

[41] Institut. 1. i. tit. ii. No. 6; Pandect. 1. i. tit. iv. leg. 1; Cod. Justinian. 1. i. tit. xvii. leg. 1, No. 7. In his Antiquities and Elements, Heineccius has amply treated de constitutionibus principum, which are illustrated by Godefroy (Comment ad. Cod. Theodos. 1. i. tit. i. ii. iii.) and Gravina (p. 87-90).

[Imperial authority and legislative power were conferred even upon the early emperors by a law called " Lex Imperii" or " Lex de Imperio." Hence Gaius says, " Cum Imperator ipse per legem imperium accipiat."—O. S.]

[42] Theophilus, in Paraphras. Græc. Institut. p. 33, 34, edit. Reitz. For his person, time, writings, see the Theophilus of J. H. Mylius, Excurs. iii. p. 1034-1073.

seat of justice was filled by the wisdom and integrity of Papinian and Ulpian,[43] and the purest materials of the Code and Pandects are inscribed with the names of Caracalla and his ministers.[44] The tyrant of Rome was sometimes the benefactor of the provinces. A dagger terminated the crimes of Domitian; but the prudence of Nerva confirmed his acts, which, in the joy of their deliverance, had been rescinded by an indignant senate.[45] Yet in the *rescripts*,[46] replies to the consultations of the magistrates, the wisest of princes might be deceived by a partial exposition of the case. And this abuse, which placed their hasty decisions on the same level with mature and deliberate acts of legislation, was ineffectually condemned by the sense and example of Trajan. The *rescripts* of the emperor, his *grants* and *decrees*, his *edicts* and *pragmatic sanctions*, were subscribed in purple ink,[47] and transmitted to the provinces as general or special laws, which the magistrates were bound to execute and the people to obey. But as their number continually multiplied, the rule of obedience became each day more doubtful and obscure, till the will of the sovereign was fixed and ascertained in the Gregorian, the Hermogenian, and the Theodosian codes. The two first, of which some fragments have escaped, were framed by two private lawyers to preserve the constitutions of the Pagan emperors from Hadrian to Constantine. The third, which is still extant, was digested in sixteen books by the order of the younger Theodosius to consecrate the laws of the Christian princes from Constantine to his own reign.

[43] There is more envy than reason in the complaint of Macrinus (Jul. Capitolin. c. 13). Nefas esse leges videri Commodi et Caracallæ et hominum imperitorum voluntates. Commodus was made a Divus by Severus (Dodwell, Prælect. viii. p. 324, 325). Yet he occurs only twice in the Pandects.

[44] Of Antoninus Caracalla alone 200 constitutions are extant in the Code, and with his father 160. These two princes are quoted fifty times in the Pandects and eight in the Institutes (Terrasson, p. 265).

[45] Plin. Secund. Epistol. x. 66; Sueton. in Domitian, c. 23.

[46] It was a maxim of Constantine, contra jus rescripta non valeant (Cod. Theodos. l. i. tit. ii. leg. 1). The emperors reluctantly allow some scrutiny into the law and the fact, some delay, petition, etc.; but these insufficient remedies are too much in the discretion and at the peril of the judge.

[47] A compound of vermilion and cinnabar, which marks the Imperial diplomas from Leo I. (A.D. 470) to the fall of the Greek empire (Bibliothèque Raisonnée de la Diplomatique, tom. i. p. 509-514; Lami, de Eruditione Apostolorum, tom. ii. p. 720-726).

[Savigny states the following as the authorities for the Roman law at the beginning of the fifth century:—

1. The writings of the jurists according to the regulations of the constitution of Valentinian III., first promulgated in the West, but by its introduction into the Theodosian code established likewise in the East. This constitution established the authority of the five great jurists, Papinian, Paulus, Caius, Ulpian, and Modestinus, as interpreters of the ancient law. In case of difference of opinion among these five, a majority decided the case; when they were equal, the opinion of Papinian; when he was silent, the judge.

2. The Gregorian and Hermogenian Collection of Imperial Rescripts.

3. The Code of Theodosius II.

4. The particular Novellæ, as additions and supplements to this Code.— O. S.]

But the three codes obtained an equal authority in the tribunals, and any act which was not included in the sacred deposit might be disregarded by the judge as spurious or obsolete.[48]

Among savage nations the want of letters is imperfectly supplied by the use of visible signs, which awaken attention and perpetuate the remembrance of any public or private transaction. The jurisprudence of the first Romans exhibited the scenes of a pantomime; the words were adapted to the gestures, and the slightest error or neglect in the *forms* of proceeding was sufficient to annul the *substance* of the fairest claim. The communion of the marriage-life was denoted by the necessary elements of fire and water;[49] and the divorced wife resigned the bunch of keys, by the delivery of which she had been invested with the government of the family. The manumission of a son or a slave was performed by turning him round with a gentle blow on the cheek; a work was prohibited by the casting of a stone; prescription was interrupted by the breaking of a branch; the clenched fist was the symbol of a pledge or deposit; the right hand was the gift of faith and confidence. The indenture of covenants was a broken straw; weights and scales were introduced into every payment; and the heir who accepted a testament was sometimes obliged to snap his fingers, to cast away his garments, and to leap and dance with real or affected transport.[50] If a citizen pursued any stolen goods into a neighbour's house, he concealed his nakedness with a linen towel, and hid his face with a mask or basin, lest he should encounter the eyes of a virgin or a matron.[51] In a civil action, the plaintiff touched the ear of his witness, seized his reluctant adversary by the neck, and implored, in solemn lamentation, the aid of his fellow-citizens. The two competitors grasped each other's hand as if they stood prepared for combat before the tribunal of the prætor; he commanded them to produce the object of the dispute; they went, they returned with measured steps, and a clod of earth was cast at his feet to represent the field for which they contended. This occult science of the words and actions of law was the inheritance of the pontiffs and patricians. Like the Chaldæan astrologers, they announced to their clients the days of business and repose;

[48] Schulting, Jurisprudentia Ante-Justinianea, p. 681-718. Cujacius assigned to Gregory the reigns from Hadrian to Gallienus, and the continuation to his fellow-labourer Hermogenes. This general division may be just, but they often trespassed on each other's ground.

[49] Scævola, most probably Q. Cervidius Scævola, the master of Papinian, considers this acceptance of fire and water as the essence of marriage (Pandect. l. xxiv. tit. 1, leg. 66. See Heineccius, Hist. J. R. No. 317).

[50] Cicero (de Officiis, iii. 19) may state an ideal case, but St. Ambrose (de Officiis, iii. 2) appeals to the practice of his own times, which he understood as a lawyer and a magistrate (Schulting ad Ulpian. Fragment. tit. xxii. No. 28, p. 643, 644 [Jurispr. Ante-Justin.]).

[51] The furtum lance licioque conceptum was no longer understood in the time of the Antonines (Aulus Gellius, xvi. 10). The Attic derivation of Heineccius (Antiquitat. Rom. l. iv. tit. i. No. 13-21) is supported by the evidence of Aristophanes, his scholiast, and Pollux.

these important trifles were interwoven with the religion of Numa, and after the publication of the Twelve Tables the Roman people was still enslaved by the ignorance of judicial proceedings. The treachery of some plebeian officers at length revealed the profitable mystery; in a more enlightened age the legal actions were derided and observed, and the same antiquity which sanctified the practice, obliterated the use and meaning, of this primitive language.[52]

A more liberal art was cultivated, however, by the sages of Rome, who, in a stricter sense, may be considered as the authors of the civil law. The alteration of the idiom and manners of the Romans rendered the style of the Twelve Tables less familiar to each rising generation, and the doubtful passages were imperfectly explained by the study of legal antiquarians. To define the ambiguities, to circumscribe the latitude, to apply the principles, to extend the consequences, to reconcile the real or apparent contradictions, was a much nobler and more important task; and the province of legislation was silently invaded by the expounders of ancient statutes. Their subtle interpretations concurred with the equity of the prætor to reform the tyranny of the darker ages; however strange or intricate the means, it was the aim of artificial jurisprudence to restore the simple dictates of nature and reason, and the skill of private citizens was usefully employed to undermine the public institutions of their country. The revolution of almost one thousand years, from the Twelve Tables to the reign of Justinian, may be divided into three periods almost equal in duration, and distinguished from each other by the mode of instruction and the character of the civilians.[53] Pride and ignorance contributed, during the first period, to confine within narrow limits the science of the Roman law. On the public days of market or assembly the masters of the art were seen walking in the forum, ready to impart the needful advice to the meanest of their fellow-citizens, from whose votes, on a future occasion, they might solicit a grateful return. As their years and honours increased, they seated themselves at home on a chair or throne, to expect, with patient gravity, the visits of their clients, who at the dawn of

[52] In his Oration for Murena (c. 9-13) Cicero turns into ridicule the forms and mysteries of the civilians, which are represented with more candour by Aulus Gellius (Noct. Attic. xx. 10), Gravina (Opp. p. 265, 266, 267), and Heineccius, Antiquitat. l. iv. tit. vi.).

[53] The series of the civil lawyers is deduced by Pomponius (de Origine Juris Pandect. l. i. tit. ii. [§ 35 sqq.]). The moderns have discussed, with learning and criticism, this branch of literary history; and among these I have chiefly been guided by Gravina (p. 41-79) and Heineccius (Hist. J. R. No. 113-351). Cicero, more especially in his books de Oratore, de Claris Oratoribus, de Legibus, and the Clavis Ciceroniana of Ernesti (under the names of *Mucius*, etc.), afford much genuine and pleasing information. Horace often alludes to the morning labours of the civilians (Serm. I. i. 10, Epist. II. i. 103, etc.).

Agricolam laudat juris legumque peritus,
Sub galli cantum consultor ubi ostia pulsat.

Romæ dulce diu fuit et solemne, reclusâ
Mane domo vigilare, clienti promere jura.

day, from the town and country, began to thunder at their door. The duties of social life and the incidents of judicial proceeding were the ordinary subject of these consultations, and the verbal or written opinion of the *juris-consults* was framed according to the rules of prudence and law. The youths of their own order and family were permitted to listen; their children enjoyed the benefit of more private lessons, and the Mucian race was long renowned for the hereditary knowledge of the civil law. The second period, the learned and splendid age of jurisprudence, may be extended from the birth of Cicero to the reign of Severus Alexander. A system was formed, schools were instituted, books were composed, and both the living and the dead became subservient to the instruction of the student. The *tripartite* of Ælius Pætus, surnamed Catus, or the Cunning, was preserved as the oldest work of jurisprudence. Cato the censor derived some additional fame from his legal studies and those of his son; the kindred appellation of Mucius Scævola was illustrated by three sages of the law, but the perfection of the science was ascribed to Servius Sulpicius, their disciple, and the friend of Tully; and the long succession, which shone with equal lustre under the republic and under the Cæsars, is finally closed by the respectable characters of Papinian, of Paul, and of Ulpian. Their names, and the various titles of their productions, have been minutely preserved, and the example of Labeo may suggest some idea of their diligence and fecundity. That eminent lawyer of the Augustan age divided the year between the city and country, between business and composition, and four hundred books are enumerated as the fruit of his retirement. Of the collections of his rival Capito, the two hundred and fifty-ninth book is expressly quoted, and few teachers could deliver their opinions in less than a century of volumes. In the third period, between the reigns of Alexander and Justinian, the oracles of jurisprudence were almost mute. The measure of curiosity had been filled; the throne was occupied by tyrants and barbarians; the active spirits were diverted by religious disputes; and the professors of Rome, Constantinople, and Berytus, were humbly content to repeat the lessons of their more enlightened predecessors. From the slow advances and rapid decay of these legal studies, it may be inferred that they require a state of peace and refinement. From the multitude of voluminous civilians who fill the intermediate space, it is evident that such studies may be pursued, and such works may be performed, with a common share of judgment, experience, and industry. The genius of Cicero and Virgil was more sensibly felt, as each revolving age had been found incapable of producing a similar or a second; but the most eminent teachers of the law were assured of leaving disciples equal or superior to themselves in merit and reputation.

The jurisprudence which had been grossly adapted to the wants of the first Romans was polished and improved in the seventh century of the city by the alliance of Grecian philosophy. The Scævolas had been taught by use and experience; but Servius Sulpicius was the first civilian who established his art on a certain and general theory.[54] For the discernment of truth and falsehood he applied, as an infallible rule, the logic of Aristotle and the stoics, reduced particular cases to general principles, and diffused over the shapeless mass the light of order and eloquence. Cicero, his contemporary and friend, declined the reputation of a professed lawyer; but the jurisprudence of his country was adorned by his incomparable genius, which converts into gold every object that it touches. After the example of Plato, he composed a republic; and, for the use of his republic, a treatise of laws, in which he labours to deduce from a celestial origin the wisdom and justice of the Roman constitution. The whole universe, according to his sublime hypothesis, forms one immense commonwealth: gods and men, who participate of the same essence, are members of the same community; reason prescribes the law of nature and nations; and all positive institutions, however modified by accident or custom, are drawn from the rule of right, which the Deity has inscribed on every virtuous mind. From these philosophical mysteries he mildly excludes the sceptics who refuse to believe, and the epicureans who are unwilling to act. The latter disdain the care of the republic: he advises them to slumber in their shady gardens. But he humbly entreats that the new Academy would be silent, since her bold objections would too soon destroy the fair and well-ordered structure of his lofty system.[55] Plato, Aristotle, and Zeno he represents as the only teachers who arm and instruct a citizen for the duties of social life. Of these, the armour of the stoics[56] was found to be of the firmest temper; and it was chiefly worn, both for use and ornament, in the schools of jurisprudence. From the Portico the Roman civilians learned to live, to reason, and to die: but they imbibed in some degree the prejudices of the sect; the love of paradox, the pertinacious habits of dispute, and a minute attachment to words and verbal distinctions. The superiority of *form* to *matter* was introduced to ascertain the right of property: and the equality of crimes

[54] Crassus, or rather Cicero himself, proposes (de Oratore, i. 41, 42) an idea of the art or science of jurisprudence, which the eloquent, but illiterate, Antonius (i. 58) affects to deride. It was partly executed by Servius Sulpicius (in Bruto, c. 41), whose praises are elegantly varied in the classic Latinity of the Roman Gravina (p. 60).
[With regard to the Institutes of Justinian, M. Hugo, in his *Histoire du Droit Romain,* vol. ii. p. 119, thinks that the ingenious system of the Institutes adopted by a great many of the ancient lawyers and by Justinian himself dates from Servius Sulpicius.—O. S.]
[55] Perturbatricem autem omnium harum rerum Academiam, hanc ab Arcesila et Carneade recentem, exoremus ut sileat, nam si invaserit in hæc, quæ satis scite instructa et composita videntur, nimias edet ruinas, quam quidem ego placare cupio, submovere non audeo (de Legibus, i. 13). From this passage alone, Bentley (Remarks on Freethinking, p. 250) might have learned how firmly Cicero believed in the specious doctrines which he has adorned.
[56] The stoic philosophy was first taught at Rome by Panætius, the friend of the younger Scipio (see his Life in the Mém. de l'Académie des Inscriptions, tom. x. p. 75-89).

is countenanced by an opinion of Trebatius,[57] that he who touches the
ear touches the whole body; and that he who steals from a heap of corn
or a hogshead of wine, is guilty of the entire theft.[58]

Arms, eloquence, and the study of the civil law promoted a citizen
to the honours of the Roman state; and the three professions were sometimes more conspicuous by their union in the same character. In the
composition of the edict a learned prætor gave a sanction and preference
to his private sentiments; the opinion of a censor or a consul was entertained with respect; and a doubtful interpretation of the laws might
be supported by the virtues or triumphs of the civilian. The patrician
arts were long protected by the veil of mystery; and in more enlightened
times the freedom of inquiry established the general principles of jurisprudence. Subtle and intricate cases were elucidated by the disputes
of the forum; rules, axioms, and definitions [59] were admitted as the
genuine dictates of reason; and the consent of the legal professors was
interwoven into the practice of the tribunals. But these interpreters
could neither enact nor execute the laws of the republic; and the judges
might disregard the authority of the Scævolas themselves, which was
often overthrown by the eloquence or sophistry of an ingenious
pleader.[60] Augustus and Tiberius were the first to adopt, as a useful
engine, the science of the civilians; and their servile labours accommodated the old system to the spirit and views of despotism. Under the
fair pretence of securing the dignity of the art, the privilege of subscribing legal and valid opinions was confined to the sages of senatorian
or equestrian rank, who had been previously approved by the judgment of the prince; and this monopoly prevailed till Hadrian restored
the freedom of the profession to every citizen conscious of his abilities
and knowledge. The discretion of the prætor was now governed by the
lessons of his teachers; the judges were enjoined to obey the comment
as well as the text of the law; and the use of codicils was a memorable
innovation, which Augustus ratified by the advice of the civilians.[61]

The most absolute mandate could only require that the judges should
agree with the civilians, if the civilians agreed among themselves. But

[57] As he is quoted by Ulpian (leg. 40 ad Sabinum in Pandect. l. xlvii. tit. ii.
leg. 21). Yet Trebatius, after he was a leading civilian, qui [quod] familiam
duxit, became an epicurean (Cicero ad Fam. vii. 5). Perhaps he was not
constant or sincere in his new sect.

[58] See Gravina (p. 45-51) and the ineffectual cavils of Mascou. Heineccius
(Hist. J. R. No. 125) quotes and approves a dissertation of Everard Otto, de
Stoicâ Jurisconsultorum Philosophiâ.

[59] We have heard of the Catonion rule, the Aquilian stipulation, and the
Manilian forms, of 211 maxims, and of 247 definitions (Pandect. l. L. tit. xvi.
xvii.).

[60] Read Cicero, l. i. de Oratore, Topica, pro Murena.

[61] See Pomponius (de Origine Juris Pandect. l. i. tit. ii. leg. 2, No. 47),
Heineccius (ad Institut. l. i. tit. ii. No. 8, l. ii. tit. xxv. in Element. et Antiquitat.), and Gravina (p. 41-45). Yet the monopoly of Augustus, a harsh
measure, would appear with some softening in contemporary evidence; and it
was probably veiled by a decree of the senate.

positive institutions are often the result of custom and prejudice; laws and language are ambiguous and arbitrary; where reason is incapable of pronouncing, the love of argument is inflamed by the envy of rivals, the vanity of masters, the blind attachment of their disciples; and the Roman jurisprudence was divided by the once famous sects of the *Proculians* and *Sabinians*.[62] Two sages of the law, Ateius Capito and Antistius Labeo,[63] adorned the peace of the Augustan age: the former distinguished by the favour of his sovereign; the latter more illustrious by his contempt of that favour, and his stern though harmless opposition to the tyrant of Rome. Their legal studies were influenced by the various colours of their temper and principles. Labeo was attached to the form of the old republic; his rival embraced the more profitable substance of the rising monarchy. But the disposition of a courtier is tame and submissive; and Capito seldom presumed to deviate from the sentiments, or at least from the words, of his predecessors; while the bold republican pursued his independent ideas without fear of paradox or innovations. The freedom of Labeo was enslaved, however, by the rigour of his own conclusions, and he decided, according to the letter of the law, the same questions which his indulgent competitor resolved with a latitude of equity more suitable to the common sense and feelings of mankind. If a fair exchange had been substituted to the payment of money, Capito still considered the transaction as a legal sale;[64] and he consulted nature for the age of puberty, without confining his definition to the precise period of twelve or fourteen years.[65] This opposition of sentiments was propagated in the writings and lessons of the two founders; the schools of Capito and Labeo maintained their inveterate conflict from the age of Augustus to that of Hadrian;[66] and

[62] I have perused the Diatribe of Gotfridus Mascovius, the learned Mascou, de Sectis Jurisconsultorum (Lipsiæ, 1728, in 12mo. p. 276), a learned treatise on a narrow and barren ground.

[63] See the character of Antistius Labeo in Tacitus (Annal. iii. 75) and in an epistle of Ateius Capito (Aul. Gellius, xiii. 12), who accuses his rival of libertas nimia et *vecors*. Yet Horace would not have lashed a virtuous and respectable senator; and I must adopt the emendation of Bentley, who reads *Labieno* insanior (Serm. I. iii. 82). See Mascou, de Sectis (c. i. p. 1-24).

[64] Justinian (Institut. l. iii. tit. 23, and Theophil. Vers. Græc. p. 677, 680) has commemorated this weighty dispute, and the verses of Homer that were alleged on either side as legal authorities. It was decided by Paul (leg. 33, ad Edict. in Pandect. l. xviii. tit. i. leg. 1), since, in a simple exchange, the buyer could not be discriminated from the seller.

[65] This controversy was likewise given for the Proculians, to supersede the indecency of a search, and to comply with the aphorism of Hippocrates, who was attached to the septenary number of two weeks of years, or 700 of days (Institut. l. i. tit. xxii.). Plutarch and the Stoics (de Placit. Philosoph. l. v. c. 24) assign a more natural reason. Fourteen years is the age—περὶ ἣν ὁ σπερματικὸς κρίνεται ἁρρός. See the *vestigia* of the sects in Mascou, c. ix. p. 145-276.

[66] The series and conclusion of the sects are described by Mascou (c. ii.-vii. p. 24-120); and it would be almost ridiculous to praise his equal justice to these obsolete sects.

[The work of Gaius subsequent to Hadrian's time furnishes us with some

the two sects derived their appellations from Sabinus and Proculus, their most celebrated teachers. The names of *Cassians* and *Pegasians* were likewise applied to the same parties; but, by a strange reverse, the popular cause was in the hands of Pegasus,[67] a timid slave of Domitian, while the favourite of the Cæsars was represented by Cassius,[68] who gloried in his descent from the patriotic assassin. By the perpetual edict the controversies of the sects were in a great measure determined. For that important work the emperor Hadrian preferred the chief of the Sabinians: the friends of monarchy prevailed; but the moderation of Salvius Julian insensibly reconciled the victors and the vanquished. Like the contemporary philosophers, the lawyers of the age of the Antonines disclaimed the authority of a master, and adopted from every system the most probable doctrines.[69] But their writings would have been less voluminous, had their choice been more unanimous. The conscience of the judge was perplexed by the number and weight of discordant testimonies, and every sentence that his passion or interest might pronounce was justified by the sanction of some venerable name. An indulgent edict of the younger Theodosius excused him from the labour of comparing and weighing their arguments. Five civilians, Caius, Papinian, Paul, Ulpian, and Modestinus, were established as the oracles of jurisprudence: a majority was decisive; but if their opinions were equally divided, a casting vote was ascribed to the superior wisdom of Papinian.[70]

information about the rival legal schools of Capito and Labeo. The disputes which arose between them have been very numerous. Gaius avows himself a disciple of Sabinus and of Caius, though on controverted points he not infrequently follows the opinion of the opposite school.—O. S.]

[67] At the first summons he flies to the turbot-council; yet Juvenal (Satir. iv. 75-81) styles the præfect or *bailiff* of Rome sanctissimus legum interpres. From his science, says the old scholiast, he was called, not a man, but a book. He derived the singular name of Pegasus from the galley which his father commanded.

[68] Tacit. Annal. xvi. 7.   Sueton. in Nerone, c. xxxvii.

[69] Mascou, de Sectis, c. viii. p. 120-144, de Herciscundis, a legal term which was applied to these eclectic lawyers: *herciscere* is synonymous to dividere.

[70] See the Theodosian Code, l. i. tit. iv. with Godefroy's Commentary, tom. i. p. 31-35. This decree might give occasion to Jesuitical disputes like those in the Lettres Provinciales, whether a judge was obliged to follow the opinion of Papinian, or of a majority, against his judgment, against his conscience, etc. Yet a legislator might give that opinion, however false, the validity, not of truth, but of law.

[We possess since 1824 (says Milman) some interesting information as to the framing of the Theodosian Code and its ratification at Rome in the year 438. M. Closius, late professor at Dorpat in Russia, and M. Peyron, member of the Academy at Turin, discovered the one at Milan, the other at Turin, a great part of the first five books of the Code, which were wanting, and besides this the reports (gesta) of the sitting of the senate at Rome in which the Code was published, in the year after the marriage of Valentinian III. From this we gather that Theodosius designed a great reform in the legislation; to add to the Gregorian and Hermogenian codes all the new constitutions from Constantine to his own day; and to frame a second code for common use, with extracts from the three codes, and from the works of the civil lawyers. All

When Justinian ascended the throne, the reformation of the Roman jurisprudence was an arduous but indispensable task. In the space of ten centuries the infinite variety of laws and legal opinions had filled many thousand volumes, which no fortune could purchase and no capacity could digest. Books could not easily be found; and the judges, poor in the midst of riches, were reduced to the exercise of their illiterate discretion. The subjects of the Greek provinces were ignorant of the language that disposed of their lives and properties; and the *barbarous* dialect of the Latins was imperfectly studied in the academies of Berytus and Constantinople. As an Illyrian soldier, that idiom was familiar to the infancy of Justinian; his youth had been instructed by the lessons of jurisprudence, and his Imperial choice selected the most learned civilians of the East, to labour with their sovereign in the work of reformation.[71] The theory of professors was assisted by the practice of advocates and the experience of magistrates; and the whole undertaking was animated by the spirit of Tribonian.[72] This extraordinary man, the object of so much praise and censure, was a native of Side in Pamphilia; and his genius, like that of Bacon, embraced, as his own, all the business and knowledge of the age. Tribonian composed, both in prose and verse, on a strange diversity of curious and abstruse subjects:[73] a double panegyric of Justinian and the Life of the philosopher Theodotus; the nature of happiness and the duties of government; Homer's catalogue and the four-and-twenty sorts of metre; the astronomical canon of Ptolemy; the changes of the months; the houses of the planets; and the harmonic system of the world. To the literature of Greece he added the use of the Latin tongue; the Roman civilians were deposited in his library and in his mind; and he most assiduously cultivated those arts which opened the road of wealth and preferment. From the bar of the prætorian præfects he raised himself to the honours of quæstor, of consul, and of master of the offices: the council of Justinian listened to his eloquence and wisdom; and envy was mitigated by the gentleness and affability of his manners. The reproaches of

laws either abrogated or fallen into disuse were to be noted under their proper heads.—O. S.]

[71] For the legal labours of Justinian, I have studied the Preface to the Institutes; the 1st, 2nd, and 3rd Prefaces to the Pandects; the 1st and 2nd Preface to the Code; and the Code itself (l. i. tit. xvii. de Veteri Jure enucleando). After these original testimonies, I have consulted, among the moderns, Heineccius (Hist. J. R. No. 383-404), Terrasson (Hist. de la Jurisprudence Romaine, p. 295-356), Gravina (Opp. p. 93-100), and Ludewig, in his Life of Justinian (p. 19-123, 318-321; for the Code and Novels, p. 209-261; for the Digest or Pandects, p. 262-317).

[72] For the character of Tribonian, see the testimonies of Procopius (Persic. l. i. c. 23, 24 [24, 25]; Anecdot. c. 13, 20 [and Suidas (tom. iii. p. 501, edit. Kuster). Ludewig (in Vit. Justinian. p. 175-209) works hard, very hard, to whitewash—the blackamoor.

[73] I apply the two passages of Suidas to the same man; every circumstance so exactly tallies. Yet the lawyers appear ignorant; and Fabricius is inclined to separate the two characters (Biblioth. Græc. tom. i. p. 341, ii. p. 518, iii. p. 418, xii. p. 346, 353, 474).

impiety and avarice have stained the virtues or the reputation of Tribonian. In a bigoted and persecuting court, the principal minister was accused of a secret aversion to the Christian faith, and was supposed to entertain the sentiments of an Atheist and a Pagan, which have been imputed, inconsistently enough, to the last philosophers of Greece. His avarice was more clearly proved and more sensibly felt. If he were swayed by gifts in the administration of justice, the example of Bacon will again occur; nor can the merit of Tribonian atone for his baseness, if he degraded the sanctity of his profession, and if laws were every day enacted, modified, or repealed, for the base consideration of his private emolument. In the sedition of Constantinople, his removal was granted to the clamours, perhaps to the just indignation, of the people: but the quæstor was speedily restored, and, till the hour of his death, he possessed, above twenty years, the favour and confidence of the emperor. His passive and dutiful submission has been honoured with the praise of Justinian himself, whose vanity was incapable of discerning how often that submission degenerated into the grossest adulation. Tribonian adored the virtues of his gracious master: the earth was unworthy of such a prince; and he affected a pious fear, that Justinian, like Elijah or Romulus, would be snatched into the air, and translated alive to the mansions of celestial glory.[74]

If Cæsar had achieved the reformation of the Roman law, his creative genius, enlightened by reflection and study, would have given to the world a pure and original system of jurisprudence. Whatever flattery might suggest, the emperor of the East was afraid to establish his private judgment as the standard of equity: in the possession of legislative power, he borrowed the aid of time and opinion; and his laborious compilations are guarded by the sages and legislators of past times. Instead of a statue cast in a simple mould by the hand of an artist, the works of Justinian represent a tesselated pavement of antique and costly, but too often of incoherent, fragments. In the first year of his reign, he directed the faithful Tribonian, and nine learned associates, to revise the ordinances of his predecessors, as they were contained, since the time of Hadrian, in the Gregorian, Hermogenian, and Theodosian codes; to purge the errors and contradictions, to retrench whatever was obsolete or superfluous, and to select the wise and salutary laws best adapted to the practice of the tribunals and the use of his subjects. The work was accomplished in fourteen months; and the twelve books or *tables,* which the new decemvirs produced, might be designed to imitate the

---

[74] This story is related by Hesychius (de Viris Illustribus), Procopius (Anecdot. c. 13 [tom. iii. p. 84, ed. Bonn]), and Suidas (tom. iii. p. 501). Such flattery is incredible!

—— Nihil est quod credere de se
Non possit, cum laudatur Diis æqua potestas.

Fontenelle (tom. i. p. 32-39) has ridiculed the impudence of the modest Virgil. But the same Fontenelle places his king above the divine Augustus; and the sage Boileau has not blushed to say, " Le destin à ses yeux n'oseroit balancer." Yet neither Augustus nor Louis XIV. were fools.

labours of their Roman predecessors. The new CODE of Justinian was honoured with his name, and confirmed by his royal signature: authentic transcripts were multiplied by the pens of notaries and scribes; they were transmitted to the magistrates of the European, the Asiatic, and afterwards the African provinces; and the law of the empire was proclaimed on solemn festivals at the doors of churches. A more arduous operation was still behind—to extract the spirit of jurisprudence from the decisions and conjectures, the questions and disputes, of the Roman civilians. Seventeen lawyers, with Tribonian at their head, were appointed by the emperor to exercise an absolute jurisdiction over the works of their predecessors. If they had obeyed his commands in ten years, Justinian would have been satisfied with their diligence; and the rapid composition of the DIGEST or PANDECTS [75] in three years will deserve praise or censure according to the merit of the execution. From the library of Tribonian they chose forty, the most eminent civilians of former times: [76] two thousand treatises were comprised in an abridgment of fifty books; and it has been carefully recorded that three millions of lines or sentences [77] were reduced, in this abstract, to the moderate number of one hundred and fifty thousand. The edition of this great work was delayed a month after that of the INSTITUTES; and it seemed reasonable that the elements should precede the digest of the Roman law. As soon as the emperor had approved their labours, he ratified, by his legislative power, the speculations of these private citizens: their commentaries on the Twelve Tables, the Perpetual Edict, the laws of the people, and the decrees of the senate, succeeded to the authority of the text; and the text was abandoned, as a useless, though venerable, relic of antiquity. The *Code*, the *Pandects*, and the *Institutes* were declared to be the legitimate system of civil jurisprudence; they alone were admitted in the tribunals, and they alone were taught in the academies, of Rome, Constantinople, and Berytus. Justinian addressed to the senate and provinces his *eternal oracles*: and his pride,

---

[75] Πάνδεκται (general receivers) was a common title of the Greek miscellanies (Plin. Præfat. ad Hist. Natur.). The *Digesta* of Scævola, Marcellinus, Celsus, were already familiar to the civilians: but Justinian was in the wrong when he used the two appellations as synonymous. Is the word *Pandects* Greek or Latin—masculine or feminine? The diligent Brenckman will not presume to decide these momentous controversies (Hist. Pandect. Florentin. p. 300-304).

[76] Angelus Politianus (l. v. Epist. ult.) reckons thirty-seven (p. 192-200) civilians quoted in the Pandects—a learned, and for his times, an extraordinary list. The Greek index to the Pandects enumerates thirty-nine, and forty are produced by the indefatigable Fabricius (Biblioth. Græc. tom. iii. p. 488-502). Antoninus Augustus [Antonius Augustinus] (de Nominibus Propriis Pandect. apud Ludewig, p. 283) is said to have added fifty-four names; but they must be vague or secondhand references.

[77] The Στιχοί of the ancient MSS. may be strictly defined as sentences or periods of a complete sense, which, on the breadth of the parchment rolls or volumes, composed as many lines of unequal length. The number of Στιχοί in each book served as a check on the errors of the scribes (Ludewig, p. 211-215; and his original author Suicer. Thesaur. Ecclesiast. tom. i. p. 1021-1036).

under the mask of piety, ascribed the consummation of this great design to the support and inspiration of the Deity.

Since the emperor declined the fame and envy of original composition, we can only require at his hands method, choice, and fidelity—the humble, though indispensable, virtues of a compiler. Among the various combinations of ideas it is difficult to assign any reasonable preference; but, as the order of Justinian is different in his three works, it is possible that all may be wrong, and it is certain that two cannot be right. In the selection of ancient laws he seems to have viewed his predecessors without jealousy and with equal regard: the series could not ascend above the reign of Hadrian, and the narrow distinction of Paganism and Christianity, introduced by the superstition of Theodosius, had been abolished by the consent of mankind. But the jurisprudence of the Pandects is circumscribed within a period of a hundred years, from the Perpetual Edict to the death of Severus Alexander: the civilians who lived under the first Cæsars are seldom permitted to speak, and only three names can be attributed to the age of the republic. The favourite of Justinian (it has been fiercely urged) was fearful of encountering the light of freedom and the gravity of Roman sages. Tribonian condemned to oblivion the genuine and native wisdom of Cato, the Scævolas, and Sulpicius; while he invoked spirits more congenial to his own, the Syrians, Greeks, and Africans, who flocked to the Imperial court to study Latin as a foreign tongue, and jurisprudence as a lucrative profession. But the ministers of Justinian [78] were instructed to labour not for the curiosity of antiquarians, but for the immediate benefit of his subjects. It was their duty to select the useful and practical parts of the Roman law; and the writings of the old republicans, however curious or excellent, were no longer suited to the new system of manners, religion, and Government. Perhaps, if the preceptors and friends of Cicero were still alive, our candour would acknowledge that, except in purity of language,[79] their intrinsic merit was excelled by the school of Papinian and Ulpian. The science of the laws is the slow growth of time and experience, and the advantage both of method and materials

[78] An ingenious and learned oration of Schultingius (Jurisprudentia Ante-Justinianea, p. 883-907) justifies the choice of Tribonian against the passionate charges of Francis Hottoman and his sectaries.

[79] Strip away the crust of Tribonian, and allow for the use of technical words, and the Latin of the Pandects will be found not unworthy of the *silver* age. It has been vehemently attacked by Laurentius Valla, a fastidious grammarian of the fifteenth century, and by his apologist Floridus Sabinus. It has been defended by Alciat, and a nameless advocate (most probably James Capellus). Their various treatises are collected by Duker (Opuscula de Latinitate veterum Jurisconsultorum, Lugd. Bat. 1721, in 12mo).

[Gibbon is wrong here with respect to Valla, who, though he inveighs against the barbarous style of the civilians of his day, lavishes high praise on the admirable purity of the language of the ancient writers on civil law. M. Warnkönig quotes a long passage of Valla in justification of this observation. Since his time this truth has been recognised by men of high eminence, such as Erasmus, David Hume, and Ruhnkenius.—O. S.]

is naturally assumed by the most recent authors. The civilians of the reign of the Antonines had studied the works of their predecessors: their philosophic spirit had mitigated the rigour of antiquity, simplified the forms of proceeding, and emerged from the jealousy and prejudice of the rival sects. The choice of the authorities that compose the Pandects depended on the judgment of Tribonian; but the power of his sovereign could not absolve him from the sacred obligations of truth and fidelity. As the legislator of the empire, Justinian might repeal the acts of the Antonines, or condemn as seditious the free principles which were maintained by the last of the *Roman* lawyers.[80] But the existence of past facts is placed beyond the reach of despotism; and the emperor was guilty of fraud and forgery when he corrupted the integrity of their text, inscribed with their venerable names the words and ideas of his servile reign,[81] and suppressed by the hand of power the pure and authentic copies of their sentiments. The changes and interpolations of Tribonian and his colleagues are excused by the pretence of uniformity: but their cares have been insufficient, and the *antinomies*, or contradictions, of the Code and Pandects, still exercise the patience and subtlety of modern civilians.[82]

A rumour, devoid of evidence, has been propagated by the enemies of Justinian, that the jurisprudence of ancient Rome was reduced to ashes by the author of the Pandects, from the vain persuasion that it was now either false or superfluous. Without usurping an office so invidious, the emperor might safely commit to ignorance and time the accomplishment of this destructive wish. Before the invention of printing and paper, the labour and the materials of writing could be purchased only by the rich; and it may reasonably be computed that the price of books was a hundred-fold their present value.[83] Copies were slowly multiplied and cautiously renewed: the hopes of profit tempted the sacrilegious scribes to erase the characters of antiquity, and Sophocles or Tacitus were obliged to resign the parchment to missals, homilies, and the golden legend.[84] If such was the fate of the most beautiful

---

[80] Nomina quidem veteribus servavimus, legum autem veritatem nostram fecimus. Itaque siquid erat in illis *seditiosum,* multa autem talia erant ibi reposita, hoc decisum est et definitum, et in perspicuum finem deducta est quæque lex (Cod. Justinian. l. i. tit. xvii. leg. 3, No. 10). A frank confession!

[81] The number of these *emblemata* (a polite name for forgeries) is much reduced by Bynkershoek (in the four last books of his Observations), who poorly maintains the right of Justinian and the duty of Tribonian.

[82] The *antinomies*, or opposite laws of the Code and Pandects, are sometimes the cause, and often the excuse, of the glorious uncertainty of the civil law which so often affords what Montaigne calls "Questions pour l'Ami." See a fine passage of Franciscus Balduinus in Justinian (l. ii. p. 259, etc., apud Ludewig, p. 305, 306).

[83] When Fust, or Faustus, sold at Paris his first printed Bibles as manuscripts, the price of a parchment copy was reduced from four or five hundred to sixty, fifty, and forty crowns. The public was at first pleased with the cheapness, and at length provoked by the discovery of the fraud (Mattaire, Annal. Typograph. tom. i. p. 12; first edition).

[84] This execrable practice prevailed from the eighth, and more especially

compositions of genius, what stability could be expected for the dull and barren works of an obsolete science? The books of jurisprudence were interesting to few and entertaining to none; their value was connected with present use, and they sunk for ever as soon as that use was superseded by the innovations of fashion, superior merit, or public authority. In the age of peace and learning, between Cicero and the last of the Antonines, many losses had been already sustained, and some luminaries of the school or forum were known only to the curious by tradition and report. Three hundred and sixty years of disorder and decay accelerated the progress of oblivion; and it may fairly be presumed that, of the writings which Justinian is accused of neglecting, many were no longer to be found in the libraries of the East.[85] The copies of Papinian or Ulpian, which the reformer had proscribed, were deemed unworthy of future notice; the Twelve Tables and prætorian edict insensibly vanished; and the monuments of ancient Rome were neglected or destroyed by the envy and ignorance of the Greeks. Even the Pandects themselves have escaped with difficulty and danger from the common shipwreck, and criticism has pronounced that *all* the editions and manuscripts of the West are derived from one original.[86] It was transcribed at Constantinople in the beginning of the seventh century,[87] was successively transported by the accidents of war and commerce to Amalphi,[88] Pisa,[89] and Florence,[90] and is

from the twelfth century, when it became almost universal (Montfaucon, in the Mémoires de l'Académie, tom. vi. p. 606, etc.; Bibliothèque Raisonnée de la Diplomatique, tom. i. p. 176).

[85] Pomponius (Pandect. l. i. tit. ii. leg. 2 [§ 39]) observes, that of the three founders of the civil law, Mucius, Brutus, and Manilius, extant volumina, [in-] scripta Manilii monumenta; that of some old republican lawyers, hæc versantur eorum scripta inter manus hominum. Eight of the Augustan sages were reduced to a compendium: of Cascellius, scripta non extant sed unus liber, etc. [§ 45]; of Trebatius, minus frequentatur [ib.]; of Tubero, libri parum grati sunt [§ 46]. Many quotations in the Pandects are derived from books which Tribonian never saw; and, in the long period from the seventh to the thirteenth century of Rome, the *apparent* reading of the moderns successively depends on the knowledge and veracity of their predecessors.

[86] *All*, in several instances, repeat the errors of the scribe and the transpositions of some leaves in the Florentine Pandects. This fact, if it be true, is decisive. Yet the Pandects are quoted by Ivo of Chartres (who died in 1117), by Theobald, archbishop of Canterbury, and by Vacarius, our first professor, in the year 1140 (Selden ad Fletam, c. 7, tom. ii. p. 1080-1085). Have our British MSS. of the Pandects been collated?

[87] See the description of this original in Brenckman (Hist. Pandect. Florent. l. i. c. 2, 3, p. 4-17, and l. ii.). Politian, an enthusiast, revered it as the authentic standard of Justinian himself (p. 407, 408); but this paradox is refuted by the abbreviations of the Florentine MS. (l. ii. c. 3, p. 117-130). It is composed of two quarto volumes, with large margins, on a thin parchment, and the Latin characters betray the hand of a Greek scribe.

[88] Brenckman, at the end of his history, has inserted two dissertations on the republic of Amalphi, and the Pisan war in the year 1135, etc.

[89] The discovery of the Pandects at Amalphi (A.D. 1137) is first noticed (in 1501) by Ludovicus Bologninus (Brenckman, l. i. c. 11, p. 73, 74; l. iv. c. 2, p. 417-425), on the faith of a Pisan chronicle (p. 409, 410) without a name or a date. The whole story, though unknown to the twelfth century,

now deposited as a sacred relic [91] in the ancient palace of the republic.[92]

It is the first care of a reformer to prevent any future reformation. To maintain the text of the Pandects, the Institutes, and the Code, the use of ciphers and abbreviations was rigorously proscribed; and as Justinian recollected that the Perpetual Edict had been buried under the weight of commentators, he denounced the punishment of forgery against the rash civilians who should presume to interpret or pervert the will of their sovereign. The scholars of Accursius, of Bartolus, of Cujacius, should blush for their accumulated guilt, unless they dare to dispute his right of binding the authority of his successors and the native freedom of the mind. But the emperor was unable to fix his own inconstancy; and, while he boasted of renewing the exchange of Diomede, of transmuting brass into gold,[93] he discovered the necessity of purifying his gold from the mixture of baser alloy. Six years had not elapsed from the publication of the Code before he condemned the imperfect attempt by a new and more accurate edition of the same work, which he enriched with two hundred of his own laws and fifty decisions of the darkest and most intricate points of jurisprudence. Every year, or, according to Procopius, each day, of his long reign was marked by some legal innovation. Many of his acts were rescinded by himself; many were rejected by his successors; many have been obliterated by time; but the number of sixteen EDICTS, and one hundred and sixty-eight NOVELS,[94] has been admitted into the authentic body of the civil jurisprudence. In the opinion of a philosopher superior

embellished by ignorant ages, and suspected by rigid criticism, is not, however, destitute of much internal probability (l. i. c. 4-8, p. 17-50). The Liber Pandectarum of Pisa was undoubtedly consulted in the fourteenth century by the great Bartolus (p. 406, 407. See l. i. c. 9, p. 50-62).

[90] Pisa was taken by the Florentines in the year 1406; and in 1411 the Pandects were transported to the capital. These events are authentic and famous.

[91] They were new bound in purple, deposited in a rich casket, and shown to curious travellers by the monks and magistrates bare-headed, and with lighted tapers (Brenckman, l. i. c. 10, 11, 12, p. 62-93).

[92] After the collations of Politian, Bologninus, and Antoninus Augustinus, and the splendid edition of the Pandects by Taurellus (in 1551), Henry Brenckman, a Dutchman, undertook a pilgrimage to Florence, where he employed several years in the study of a single manuscript. His Historia Pandectarum Florentinorum (Utrecht, 1722, in 4to), though a monument of industry, is a small portion of his original design.

[Two mistakes must be corrected in this note. The edition of the Pandects was edited by Taurellius, not Taurellus, and in 1553, not 1551. Also the name of the third collator should be Antonius Augustinus, not Antoninus.—O. S.]

[93] Χρύσεα χαλκείων, ἐκατόμβοι ἐννεαβοίων, apud Homerum patrem omnis virtutis (1st Præfat. ad Pandect.). A line of Milton or Tasso would surprise us in an act of parliament. Quæ omnia obtinere sancimus in omne ævum. Of the first Code he says (2nd Præfat.) in æternum valiturum. Man and for ever!

[94] Novellæ is a classic adjective, but a barbarous substantive (Ludewig, p. 245). Justinian never collected them himself; the nine collations, the legal standard of modern tribunals, consists of ninety-eight Novels; but the number was increased by the diligence of Julian, Haloander, and Contius (Ludewig, p. 249, 258; Aleman. Not. in Anecdot. p. 98).

to the prejudices of his profession, these incessant, and for the most
part trifling alterations, can be only explained by the venal spirit of a
prince who sold without shame his judgments and his laws.[95]   The
charge of the secret historian is indeed explicit and vehement; but the
sole instance which he produces may be ascribed to the devotion as well
as to the avarice of Justinian. A wealthy bigot had bequeathed his
inheritance to the church of Emesa, and its value was enhanced by the
dexterity of an artist, who subscribed confessions of debt and promises
of payment with the names of the richest Syrians. They pleaded the
established prescription of thirty or forty years; but their defence was
overruled by a retrospective edict, which extended the claims of the
church to the term of a century—an edict so pregnant with injustice and
disorder, that, after serving this occasional purpose, it was prudently
abolished in the same reign.[96] If candour will acquit the emperor himself, and transfer the corruption to his wife and favourites, the suspicion
of so foul a vice must still degrade the majesty of his laws; and the
advocates of Justinian may acknowledge that such levity, whatsoever
be the motive, is unworthy of a legislator and a man.

Monarchs seldom condescend to become the preceptors of their subjects; and some praise is due to Justinian, by whose command an ample
system was reduced to a short and elementary treatise. Among the
various institutes of the Roman law,[97] those of Caius [98] were the most
popular in the East and West; and their use may be considered as an
evidence of their merit. They were selected by the Imperial delegates,
Tribonian, Theophilus, and Dorotheus; and the freedom and purity of
the Antonines was incrusted with the coarser materials of a degenerate
age. The same volume which introduced the youth of Rome, Constantinople, and Berytus to the gradual study of the Code and Pandects, is
still precious to the historian, the philosopher, and the magistrate. The

[95] Montesquieu, Considérations sur la Grandeur et la Décadence des Romains,
c. 20, tom. iii. p. 501, in 4to. On this occasion he throws aside the gown and
cap of a President à Mortier.
[96] Procopius, Anecdot. c. 28 [tom. iii. p. 155, ed. Bonn]. A similar privilege
was granted to the church of Rome (Novel. ix.). For the general repeal of
these mischievous indulgences, see Novel. cxi. and Edict. v.
[97] Lactantius, in his Institutes of Christianity, an elegant and specious work,
proposes to imitate the title and method of the civilians. Quidam prudentes
et arbitri æquitatis Institutiones Civilis Juris compositas ediderunt (Institut.
Divin. l. i. c. 1). Such as Ulpian, Paul, Florentinus, Marcian.
[98] The emperor Justinian calls him *suum,* though he died before the end of
the second century. His Institutes are quoted by Servius, Boethius, Priscian,
etc.; and the Epitome by Arrian is still extant. (See the Prolegomena and
notes to the edition of Schulting, in the Jurisprudentia Ante-Justinianea, Lugd.
Bat. 1717; Heineccius, Hist. J. R. No. 313; Ludewig, in Vit. Just. p. 199.)
[The three great works in Roman jurisprudence prior to Justinian are
(*a*) Ulpian's Fragments discovered in 1544; (*b*) the Institutes or Commentaries of Gaius or Caius were found by Niebuhr in 1816 in a palimpsest MS.,
preserved in the Cathedral Library of Verona, and was first published by
Goeschen in 1821; (*c*) the Sententiæ of Paulus, preserved as a portion of the
Visigothic Breviarium of Alaric II.—O. S.]

INSTITUTES of Justinian are divided into four books: they proceed, with no contemptible method, from, I. *Persons,* to, II. *Things,* and from things to, III. *Actions;* and the article IV., of *Private Wrongs,* is terminated by the principles of *Criminal Law.*

The distinction of ranks and *persons* is the firmest basis of a mixed and limited government. In France the remains of liberty are kept alive by the spirit, the honours, and even the prejudices of fifty thousand nobles.[99] Two hundred families supply, in lineal descent, the second branch of the English legislature, which maintains, between the king and commons, the balance of the constitution. A gradation of patricians and plebeians, of strangers and subjects, has supported the aristocracy of Genoa, Venice, and ancient Rome. The perfect equality of men is the point in which the extremes of democracy and despotism are confounded; since the majesty of the prince or people would be offended if any heads were exalted above the level of their fellow-slaves or fellow-citizens. In the decline of the Roman empire, the proud distinctions of the republic were gradually abolished, and the reason or instinct of Justinian completed the simple form of an absolute monarchy. The emperor could not eradicate the popular reverence which always waits on the possession of hereditary wealth or the memory of famous ancestors. He delighted to honour with titles and emoluments his generals, magistrates, and senators; and his precarious indulgence communicated some rays of their glory to the persons of their wives and children. But in the eye of the law all Roman citizens were equal, and all subjects of the empire were citizens of Rome. That inestimable character was degraded to an obsolete and empty name. The voice of a Roman could no longer enact his laws, or create the annual ministers of his power: his constitutional rights might have checked the arbitrary will of a master; and the bold adventurer from Germany or Arabia was admitted, with equal favour, to the civil and military command, which the citizen alone had been once entitled to assume over the conquests of his fathers. The first Cæsars had scrupulously guarded the distinction of *ingenuous* and *servile* birth, which was decided by the condition of the mother; and the candour of the laws was satisfied if *her* freedom could be ascertained, during a single moment, between the conception and the delivery. The slaves who were liberated by a generous master immediately entered into the middle class of *libertines* or freedmen; but they could never be enfranchised from the duties of obedience and gratitude: whatever were the fruits of their industry, their patron and his family inherited the third part; or even the whole of their fortune if they died without children and without a testament. Justinian respected the rights of patrons; but his indulgence removed the badge

[99] See the Annales Politiques de l'Abbé de St. Pierre, tom. i. p. 25, who dates in the year 1735. The most ancient families claim the immemorial possession of arms and fiefs. Since the Crusades, some, the most truly respectable, have been created by the king for merit and services. The recent and vulgar crowd is derived from the multitude of venal offices, without trust or dignity, which continually ennoble the wealthy plebeians.

of disgrace from the two inferior orders of freedmen: whoever ceased to be a slave obtained, without reserve or delay, the station of a citizen; and at length the dignity of an ingenuous birth, which nature had refused, was created, or supposed, by the omnipotence of the emperor. Whatever restraints of age, or forms, or numbers, had been formerly introduced to check the abuse of manumissions and the too rapid increase of vile and indigent Romans, he finally abolished; and the spirit of his laws promoted the extinction of domestic servitude.   Yet the eastern provinces were filled, in the time of Justinian, with multitudes of slaves, either born or purchased for the use of their masters; and the price, from ten to seventy pieces of gold, was determined by their age, their strength, and their education.[100]   But the hardships of this dependent state were continually diminished by the influence of government and religion; and the pride of a subject was no longer elated by his absolute dominion over the life and happiness of his bondsman.[101]

The law of nature instructs most animals to cherish and educate their infant progeny. The law of reason inculcates to the human species the returns of filial piety. But the exclusive, absolute, and perpetual dominion of the father over his children is peculiar to the Roman jurisprudence,[102] and seems to be coeval with the foundation of the city.[103] The paternal power was instituted or confirmed by Romulus himself; and, after the practice of three centuries, it was inscribed on the fourth

[100] If the option of a slave was bequeathed to several legatees, they drew lots, and the losers were entitled to their share of his value: ten pieces of gold for a common servant or maid under ten years; if above that age, twenty; if they knew a trade, thirty; notaries or writers, fifty; midwives or *physicians*, sixty; eunuchs under ten years, thirty pieces; above, fifty; if tradesmen, seventy (Cod. l. vi. tit. xliii. leg. 3).   These legal prices are generally below those of the market.

[101] For the state of slaves and freedmen see Institutes, l. i. tit. iii.-viii., l. ii. tit. ix., l. iii. tit. viii. ix. [vii. viii.] ; Pandects or Digest, l. i. tit. v. vi., l. xxxviii. tit. i.-iv., and the whole of the fortieth book; Code, l. vi. tit. iv. v., l. vii. tit. i.-xxiii.   Be it henceforward understood that, with the original text of the Institutes and Pandects, the correspondent articles in the Antiquities and Elements of Heineccius are implicitly quoted; and with the twenty-seven first books of the Pandects, the learned and rational Commentaries of Gerard Noodt (Opera, tom. ii. p. 1-590, the end, Lugd. Bat. 1724).

[102] See the patria potestas in the Institutes (l. i. tit. ix.), the Pandects (l. i. tit. vi. vii.), and the Code (l. viii. tit. xlvii. xlviii. xlix. [tit. xlvi. xlvii. xlviii.]).   Jus potestatis quod in liberos habemus proprium est civium Romanorum.   Nulli enim alii sunt homines, qui talem in liberos habeant potestatem qualem nos habemus.

[Gaius in his Institutes asserts that the absolute dominion of the father over his children supposed to be peculiar to the Roman law was also possessed by the Galatians, i. 55, while Cæsar (Bell. Gall. vi. 19) states that it also existed in Gaul.—O. S.]

[103] Dionysius Hal. l. ii. [c. 26] p. 94, 95.   Gravina (Opp. p. 286) produces the words of the twelve tables.   Papinian (in Collatione Legum Roman. et Mosaicarum, tit. iv. p. 204 [ed. Cannegieter, 1774]) styles this patria potestas, lex regia: Ulpian (ad Sabin. l. xxvi. in Pandect. l. i. tit. vi. leg. 8) says, jus potestatis moribus receptum; and furiosus filium in potestate habebit.   How sacred—or rather, how absurd!

table of the Decemvirs. In the forum, the senate, or the camp, the adult son of a Roman citizen enjoyed the public and private rights of a *person:* in his father's house he was a mere *thing;* confounded by the laws with the movables, the cattle, and the slaves, whom the capricious master might alienate or destroy without being responsible to any earthly tribunal. The hand which bestowed the daily sustenance might resume the voluntary gift, and whatever was acquired by the labour or fortune of the son was immediately lost in the property of the father. His stolen goods (his oxen or his children) might be recovered by the same action of theft;[104] and if either had been guilty of a trespass, it was in his own option to compensate the damage, or resign to the injured party the obnoxious animal. At the call of indigence or avarice, the master of a family could dispose of his children or his slaves. But the condition of the slave was far more advantageous, since he regained, by the first manumission, his alienated freedom: the son was again restored to his unnatural father; he might be condemned to servitude a second and a third time, and it was not till after the third sale and deliverance[105] that he was enfranchised from the domestic power which had been so repeatedly abused. According to his discretion, a father might chastise the real or imaginary faults of his children by stripes, by imprisonment, by exile, by sending them to the country to work in chains among the meanest of his servants. The majesty of a parent was armed with the power of life and death;[106] and the examples of such bloody executions, which were sometimes praised and never punished, may be traced in the annals of Rome, beyond the times of Pompey and Augustus. Neither age, nor rank, nor the consular office, nor the honours of a triumph, could exempt the most illustrious citizen from the bonds of filial subjection:[107] his own descendants were included in the family of their common ancestor; and the claims of adoption were not less sacred or less rigorous than those of nature. Without fear, though not without danger of abuse, the Roman legislators had reposed an unbounded confidence in the sentiments of paternal love; and the oppression was tempered by the assurance that each generation must succeed in its turn to the awful dignity of parent and master.

[104] Pandect. l. xlvii. tit. ii. leg. 14, No. 13, leg. 38, No. 1. Such was the decision of Ulpian and Paul.

[105] The trina mancipatio is most clearly defined by Ulpian (Fragment. x. p. 591, 592, edit. Schulting) ; and best illustrated in the Antiquities of Heineccius.

[106] By Justinian, the old law, the jus necis of the Roman father (Institut. l. iv. tit. ix. [viii.] No. 7), is reported and reprobated. Some legal vestiges are left in the Pandects (l. xliii. tit. xxix. leg. 3, No. 4) and the Collatio Legum Romanarum et Mosaicarum (tit. ii. No. 3, p. 189).

[107] Except on public occasions and in the actual exercise of his office. In publicis locis atque muneribus, atque actionibus patrum, jura cum filiorum qui in magistratu sunt, potestatibus collata interquiescere paullulum et connivere, etc. (Aul. Gellius, Noctes Atticæ, ii. 2). The Lessons of the philosopher Taurus were justified by the old and memorable example of Fabius; and we may contemplate the same story in the style of Livy (xxiv. 44) and the homely idiom of Claudius Quadrigarius the annalist.

The first limitation of paternal power is ascribed to the justice and humanity of Numa; and the maid who, with *his* father's consent, had espoused a freeman, was protected from the disgrace of becoming the wife of a slave. In the first ages, when the city was pressed and often famished by her Latin and Tuscan neighbours, the sale of children might be a frequent practice; but as a Roman could not legally purchase the liberty of his fellow-citizen, the market must gradually fail, and the trade would be destroyed by the conquests of the republic. An imperfect right of property was at length communicated to sons; and the threefold distinction of *projectitious, adventitious,* and *professional* was ascertained by the jurisprudence of the Code and Pandects.[108] Of all that proceeded from the father he imparted only the use, and reserved the absolute dominion; yet, if his goods were sold, the filial portion was excepted, by a favourable interpretation, from the demands of the creditors. In whatever accrued by marriage, gift, or collateral succession, the property was secured to the son; but the father, unless he had been specially excluded, enjoyed the usufruct during his life. As a just and prudent reward of military virtue, the spoils of the enemy were acquired, possessed, and bequeathed by the soldier alone; and the fair analogy was extended to the emoluments of any liberal profession, the salary of public service, and the sacred liberality of the emperor or the empress. The life of a citizen was less exposed than his fortune to the abuse of paternal power. Yet his life might be adverse to the interest or passions of an unworthy father: the same crimes that flowed from the corruption, were more sensibly felt by the humanity of the Augustan age; and the cruel Erixo, who whipped his son till he expired, was saved by the emperor from the just fury of the multitude.[109] The Roman father, from the licence of servile dominion, was reduced to the gravity and moderation of a judge. The presence and opinion of Augustus confirmed the sentence of exile pronounced against an intentional parricide by the domestic tribunal of Arius. Hadrian transported to an island the jealous parent, who, like a robber, had seized the opportunity of hunting to assassinate a youth, the incestuous lover of his stepmother.[110] A private jurisdiction is repugnant to the spirit of monarchy; the parent was again reduced from a judge to an accuser; and the magistrates were enjoined by Severus Alexander to hear his complaints and execute his sentence. He could no longer take the life of a son without incurring the guilt and punishment of murder; and the pains of parricide, from which he had been excepted by the Pompeian law, were finally inflicted by the

[108] See the gradual enlargement and security of the filial *peculium* in the Institutes (l. ii. tit. ix.), the Pandects (l. xv. tit. i., l. xli. tit. i.), and the Code (l. iv. tit. xxvi. xxvii.).

[109] The examples of Erixo and Arius are related by Seneca (de Clementia. i. 14, 15), the former with horror, the latter with applause.

[110] Quod latronis magis quam patris jure eum interfecisset, nam patria potestas in pietate debet non in atrocitate consistere (Marcian, Institut. l. xiv. in Pandect. l. xlviii. tit. ix. leg. 5).

justice of Constantine.[111] The same protection was due to every period of existence; and reason must applaud the humanity of Paulus for imputing the crime of murder to the father who strangles, or starves, or abandons his new-born infant, or exposes him in a public place to find the mercy which he himself had denied. But the exposition of children was the prevailing and stubborn vice of antiquity: it was sometimes prescribed, often permitted, almost always practised with impunity by the nations who never entertained the Roman ideas of paternal power; and the dramatic poets, who appeal to the human heart, represent with indifference a popular custom which was palliated by the motives of economy and compassion.[112] If the father could subdue his own feelings, he might escape, though not the censure, at least the chastisement, of the laws; and the Roman empire was stained with the blood of infants, till such murders were included by Valentinian and his colleagues in the letter and spirit of the Cornelian law. The lessons of jurisprudence [113] and Christianity had been insufficient to eradicate this inhuman practice, till their gentle influence was fortified by the terrors of capital punishment.[114]

Experience has proved that savages are the tyrants of the female sex, and that the condition of women is usually softened by the refinements of social life. In the hope of a robust progeny, Lycurgus had delayed the season of marriage: it was fixed by Numa at the tender age of twelve years, that the Roman husband might educate to his will a pure and obedient virgin.[115] According to the custom of antiquity, he bought his bride of her parents, and she fulfilled the *coemption* by

---

[111] The Pompeian and Cornelian laws de *sicariis* and *parricidis*, are repeated, or rather abridged, with the last supplements of Alexander Severus, Constantine, and Valentinian, in the Pandects (1. xlviii. tit. viii. ix.), and Code (1. ix. tit. xvi. xvii.). See likewise the Theodosian Code (1. ix. tit. xiv. xv.), with Godefroy's Commentary (tom. iii. p. 84-113), who pours a flood of ancient and modern learning over these penal laws.

[112] When the Chremes of Terence reproaches his wife for not obeying his orders and exposing their infant, he speaks like a father and a master, and silences the scruples of a foolish woman. See Apuleius (Metamorph. 1. x. p. 337, edit. Delphin.).

[113] The opinion of the lawyers, and the discretion of the magistrates, had introduced in the time of Tacitus some legal restraints, which might support his contrast of the boni mores of the Germans to the bonæ leges alibi—that is to say, at Rome (de Moribus Germanorum, c. 19). Tertullian (ad Nationes, 1. i. c. 15) refutes his own charges, and those of his brethren, against the heathen jurisprudence.

[114] The wise and humane sentence of the civilian Paul (1. ii. Sententiarum in Pandect. 1. xxv. tit. iii. leg. 4) is represented as a mere moral precept by Gerard Noodt (Opp. tom. i. in Julius Paulus, p. 567-588, and Amica Responsio, p. 591-606), who maintains the opinion of Justus Lipsius (Opp. tom. ii. p. 409, ad Belgas, cent. i. epist. 85), and as a positive binding law by Bynkershoek (de Jure occidendi Liberos, Opp. tom. i. p. 318-340; Curæ Secundæ, p. 391-427). In a learned but angry controversy the two friends deviated into the opposite extremes.

[115] Dionys. Hal. 1. ii. p. 92, 93; Plutarch, in Numa, p. 140, 141. Τὸ σῶμα καὶ τὸ ἦθος κάθαρον καὶ ἄθικτον ἐπὶ τῷ γαμοῦντι γένεσθαι. [Comp. Lycurg. cum Numâ, tom. i. p. 310, ed. Reiske.]

purchasing, with three pieces of copper, a just introduction to his house and household deities. A sacrifice of fruits was offered by the pontiffs in the presence of ten witnesses; the contracting parties were seated on the same sheepskin; they tasted a salt cake of *far,* or rice; and this ιonfarreation,[116] which denoted the ancient food of Italy, served as an emblem of their mystic union of mind and body. But this union on the side of the woman was rigorous and unequal; and she renounced the name and worship of her father's house, to embrace a new servitude, decorated only by the title of adoption: a fiction of the law, neither rational nor elegant, bestowed on the mother of a family [117] (her proper appellation) the strange characters of sister to her own children and of daughter to her husband or master, who was invested with the plenitude of paternal power. By his judgment or caprice her behaviour was approved, or censured, or chastised; he exercised the jurisdiction of life and death; and it was allowed that in the cases of adultery or drunkenness [118] the sentence might be properly inflicted. She acquired and inherited for the sole profit of her lord; and so clearly was woman defined, not as a *person,* but as a *thing,* that, if the original title were deficient, she might be claimed, like other movables, by the *use* and possession of an entire year. The inclination of the Roman husband discharged or withheld the conjugal debt, so scrupulously exacted by the Athenian and Jewish laws:[119] but as polygamy was unknown, he could never admit to his bed a fairer or more favoured partner.

After the Punic triumphs the matrons of Rome aspired to the common benefits of a free and opulent republic; their wishes were gratified by the indulgence of fathers and lovers, and their ambition was unsuccessfully resisted by the gravity of Cato the Censor.[120] They declined

[116] Among the winter *frumenta,* the *triticum,* or bearded wheat; the *siligo,* or the unbearded; the *far, adorea, oryza,* whose description perfectly tallies with the rice of Spain and Italy. I adopt this identity on the credit of M. Paucton in his useful and laborious Métrologie (p. 517-529).

[117] Aulus Gellius (Noctes Atticæ, xviii. 6) gives a ridiculous definition of Ælius Melissus, Matrona, quæ semel, *materfamilias* quæ sæpius peperit, as porcetra, and scropha in the sow kind. He then adds the genuine meaning, quæ in matrimonium vel in manum convenisset.

[By marriage a female passed wholly into the power of her husband, and this state was called *manas.* By this authority he had complete jurisdiction over her actions, yet he could only divorce her on the grounds of drunkenness, adultery, and carrying false keys.—O. S.]

[118] It was enough to have tasted wine, or to have stolen the key of the cellar (Plin. Hist. Nat. xiv. 14).

[119] Solon requires three payments per month. By the Misna, a daily debt was imposed on an idle, vigorous, young husband; twice a week on a citizen; once on a peasant; once in thirty days on a camel-driver; once in six months on a seaman. But the student or doctor was free from tribute; and *no* wife, if she received a *weekly* sustenance, could sue for a divorce; for one week a vow of abstinence was allowed. Polygamy divided, without multiplying, the duties of the husband (Selden, Uxor Ebraica, l. iii. c. 6, in his works, vol. ii. p. 717-720).

[120] On the Oppian law we may hear the mitigating speech of Valerius Flaccus and the severe censorial oration of the elder Cato (Liv. xxxiv. 1-8). But

the solemnities of the old nuptials, defeated the annual prescription by an absence of three days, and, without losing their name or independence, subscribed the liberal and definite terms of a marriage contract. Of their private fortunes, they communicated the use and secured the property: the estates of a wife could neither be alienated nor mortgaged by a prodigal husband; their mutual gifts were prohibited by the jealousy of the laws; and the misconduct of either party might afford, under another name, a future subject for an action of theft. To this loose and voluntary compact religious and civil rites were no longer essential, and between persons of a similar rank the apparent community of life was allowed as sufficient evidence of their nuptials. The dignity of marriage was restored by the Christians, who derived all spiritual grace from the prayers of the faithful and the benediction of the priest or bishop. The origin, validity, and duties of the holy institution were regulated by the tradition of the synagogue, the precepts of the Gospel, and the canons of general or provincial synods;[121] and the conscience of the Christians was awed by the decrees and censures of their ecclesiastical rulers. Yet the magistrates of Justinian were not subject to the authority of the church; the emperor consulted the unbelieving civilians of antiquity; and the choice of matrimonial laws in the Code and Pandects is directed by the earthly motives of justice, policy, and the natural freedom of both sexes.[122]

Besides the agreement of the parties, the essence of every rational contract, the Roman marriage required the previous approbation of the parents. A father might be forced by some recent laws to supply the wants of a mature daughter, but even his insanity was not generally allowed to supersede the necessity of his consent. The causes of the dissolution of matrimony have varied among the Romans;[123] but the most solemn sacrament, the confarreation itself, might always be done away by rites of a contrary tendency. In the first ages the father of a family might sell his children, and his wife was reckoned in the number of his children: the domestic judge might pronounce the death of the

we shall rather hear the polished historian of the eighth, than the rough orators of the sixth, century of Rome. The principles, and even the style, of Cato are more accurately preserved by Aulus Gellius (x. 23).

[121] For the system of Jewish and Catholic matrimony, see Selden (Uxor Ebraica, Opp. vol. ii. p. 529-860), Bingham (Christian Antiquities, l. xxii.), and Chardon (Hist. des Sacremens, tom. vi.).

[122] The civil laws of marriage are exposed in the Institutes (l. i. tit. x.), the Pandects (l. xxiii. xxiv. xxv.), and the Code (l. v.); but as the title de ritû nuptiarum is yet imperfect, we are obliged to explore the fragments of Ulpian (tit. ix. p. 590, 591), and the Collatio Legum Mosaicarum (tit. xvi. p. 790, 791) with the notes of Pithæus and Schulting [Jurispr. Ante-Justin.]. They find, in the Commentary of Servius (on the 1st Georgic and the 4th Æneid), two curious passages.

[123] According to Plutarch (p. 57 [Rom. c. 22]) Romulus allowed only three grounds of a divorce—drunkenness, adultery, and false keys. Otherwise, the husband who abused his supremacy forfeited half his goods to the wife, and half to the goddess Ceres, and offered a sacrifice (with the remainder?) to the terrestrial deities. This strange law was either imaginary or transient.

offender, or his mercy might expel her from his bed and house; but the slavery of the wretched female was hopeless and perpetual, unless he asserted for his own convenience the manly prerogative of divorce. The warmest applause has been lavished on the virtue of the Romans, who abstained from the exercise of this tempting privilege above five hundred years;[124] but the same fact evinces the unequal terms of a connection in which the slave was unable to renounce her tyrant, and the tyrant was unwilling to relinquish his slave. When the Roman matrons became the equal and voluntary companions of their lords, a new jurisprudence was introduced, that marriage, like other partnerships, might be dissolved by the abdication of one of the associates. In three centuries of prosperity and corruption, this principle was enlarged to frequent practice and pernicious abuse. Passion, interest, or caprice suggested daily motives for the dissolution of marriage; a word, a sign, a message, a letter, the mandate of a freedman, declared the separation; the most tender of human connections was degraded to a transient society of profit or pleasure. According to the various conditions of life, both sexes alternately felt the disgrace and injury: an inconstant spouse transferred her wealth to a new family, abandoning a numerous, perhaps a spurious, progeny to the paternal authority and care of her late husband; a beautiful virgin might be dismissed to the world, old, indigent, and friendless; but the reluctance of the Romans, when they were pressed to marriage by Augustus, sufficiently marks that the prevailing institutions were least favourable to the males. A specious theory is confuted by this free and perfect experiment, which demonstrates that the liberty of divorce does not contribute to happiness and virtue. The facility of separation would destroy all mutual confidence, and inflame every trifling dispute: the minute difference between a husband and a stranger, which might so easily be removed, might still more easily be forgotten; and the matron who in five years can submit to the embraces of eight husbands must cease to reverence the chastity of her own person.[125]

Insufficient remedies followed with distant and tardy steps the rapid progress of the evil. The ancient worship of the Romans afforded a peculiar goddess to hear and reconcile the complaints of a married life;

[124] In the year of Rome 523, Spurius Cavilius Ruga repudiated a fair, a good, but a barren wife (Dionysius Hal. l. ii. [c. 25] p. 93; Plutarch, in Numa [comp. Lycurg. cum Numâ, c. 3], p. 141; Valerius Maximus, l. ii. c. 1 [§ 4]; Aulus Gellius, iv. 3). He was questioned by the censors, and hated by the people; but his divorce stood unimpeached in law.

[125]   —— Sic fiunt octo mariti
                Quinque per autumnos.   (Juvenal, Satir. vi. 229.)
A rapid succession, which may yet be credible, as well as the non consulum numero, sed maritorum annos suos computant, of Seneca (de Beneficiis, iii. 16). Jerom saw at Rome a triumphant husband bury his twenty-first wife, who had interred twenty-two of his less sturdy predecessors (Opp. tom. i. p. 90, ad Gerontiam). But the ten husbands in a month of the poet Martial is an extravagant hyperbole (l. vi. epigram 7).

but her epithet of *Viriplaca*,[126] the appeaser of husbands, too clearly indicates on which side submission and repentance were always expected. Every act of a citizen was subject to the judgment of the *censors;* the first who used the privilege of divorce assigned at their command the motives of his conduct;[127] and a senator was expelled for dismissing his virgin spouse without the knowledge or advice of his friends. Whenever an action was instituted for the recovery of a marriage-portion, the *prætor*, as the guardian of equity, examined the cause and the characters, and gently inclined the scale in favour of the guiltless and injured party. Augustus, who united the powers of both magistrates, adopted their different modes of repressing or chastising the licence of divorce.[128] The presence of seven Roman witnesses was required for the validity of this solemn and deliberate act: if any adequate provocation had been given by the husband, instead of the delay of two years, he was compelled to refund immediately or in the space of six months; but if he could arraign the manners of his wife, her guilt or levity was expiated by the loss of the sixth or eighth part of her marriage-portion. The Christian princes were the first who specified the just causes of a private divorce; their institutions, from Constantine to Justinian, appear to fluctuate between the custom of the empire and the wishes of the church;[129] and the author of the Novels too frequently reforms the jurisprudence of the Code and Pandects. In the most rigorous laws a wife was condemned to support a gamester, a drunkard, or a libertine, unless he were guilty of homicide, poison, or sacrilege; in which cases the marriage, as it should seem, might have been dissolved by the hand of the executioner. But the sacred right of the husband was invariably maintained to deliver his name and family from the disgrace of adultery; the list of *mortal* sins, either male or female, was curtailed and enlarged by successive regulations, and the obstacles of incurable impotence, long absence, and monastic profession, were allowed to rescind the matrimonial obligation. Whoever transgressed the permission of the law was subject to various and heavy penalties. The woman was stripped of her wealth and ornaments, without excepting the bodkin of her hair; if the man introduced a new bride into his bed, *her* fortune might be lawfully seized by the vengeance of his exiled wife. Forfeiture was sometimes commuted to a fine; the fine was sometimes aggravated by transportation to an island, or imprisonment in a monastery; the injured party was released from the bonds of marriage, but

---

[126] Sacellum Viriplacæ (Valerius Maximus, l. ii. c. 1 [§ 6]), in the Palatine region, appears in the time of Theodosius, in the description of Rome by Publius Victor.

[127] Valerius Maximus, l. ii. c. 9 [§ 2]. With some propriety he judges divorce more criminal than celibacy: illo namque conjugalia sacra spreta tantum, hoc etiam injuriose tractata.

[128] See the laws of Augustus and his successors, in Heineccius, ad Legem Papiam-Poppæam, c. 19, in Opp. tom. vi. P. i. p. 323-333.

[129] Aliæ sunt leges Cæsarum, aliæ Christi; aliud Papinianus, aliud Paulus *noster* præcipit (Jerom, tom. i. p. 198; Selden, Uxor Ebraica, l. iii. c. 31, p. 847-853).

the offender, during life or a term of years, was disabled from the repetition of nuptials. The successor of Justinian yielded to the prayers of his unhappy subjects, and restored the liberty of divorce by mutual consent; the civilians were unanimous,[130] the theologians were divided,[131] and the ambiguous word which contains the precept of Christ is flexible to any interpretation that the wisdom of a legislator can demand.

The freedom of love and marriage was restrained among the Romans by natural and civil impediments. An instinct, almost innate and universal, appears to prohibit the incestuous commerce[132] of parents and children in the infinite series of ascending and descending generations. Concerning the oblique and collateral branches nature is indifferent, reason mute, and custom various and arbitrary. In Egypt the marriage of brothers and sisters was admitted without scruple or exception: a Spartan might espouse the daughter of his father; an Athenian, that of his mother; and the nuptials of an uncle with his niece were applauded at Athens as a happy union of the dearest relations. The profane lawgivers of Rome were never tempted by interest or superstition to multiply the forbidden degrees; but they inflexibly condemned the marriage of sisters and brothers, hesitated whether first-cousins should be touched by the same interdict, revered the parental character of aunts and uncles, and treated affinity and adoption as a just imitation of the ties of blood. According to the proud maxims of the republic, a legal marriage could only be contracted by free citizens; an honourable, at least an ingenuous, birth was required for the spouse of a senator: but the blood of kings could never mingle in legitimate nuptials with the blood of a Roman; and the name of Stranger degraded Cleo-

---

[130] The Institutes are silent; but we may consult the Codes of Theodosius (l. iii. tit. xvi. with Godefroy's Commentary, tom. i. p. 311-313) and Justinian (l. v. tit. xvii.), the Pandects (l. xxiv. tit. ii.) and the Novels (xxii. cxvii. cxxvii. cxxxiv. cxl.). Justinian fluctuated to the last between civil and ecclesiastical law.

[131] In pure Greek, πορνεία is not a common word; nor can the proper meaning, fornication, be strictly applied to matrimonial sin. In a figurative sense, how far, and to what offences, may it be extended? Did Christ speak the Rabbinical or Syriac tongue? Of what original word is πορνεία the translation? How variously is that Greek word translated in the versions ancient and modern! There are two (Mark x. 11, Luke xvi. 18) to one (Matthew xix. 9) that such ground of divorce was not excepted by Jesus. Some critics have presumed to think, by an evasive answer, he avoided the giving offence either to the school of Sammai or to that of Hillel (Selden, Uxor Ebraica, l. iii. c. 18-22, 28, 31).

[132] The principles of the Roman jurisprudence are exposed by Justinian (Institut. l. i. tit. x.); and the laws and manners of the different nations of antiquity concerning forbidden degrees, etc., are copiously explained by Dr. Taylor in his Elements of Civil Law (p. 108, 314-339), a work of amusing though various reading, but which cannot be praised for philosophical precision.

[In consequence of the marriage of the emperor Claudius with his niece Agrippina, the daughter of his brother Germanicus, it became lawful for a man to marry the daughter of his brother, but it was unlawful for him to marry the daughter of his sister.—O. S.]

patra and Berenice [133] to live the *concubines* of Mark Antony and Titus.[134] This appellation, indeed, so injurious to the majesty, cannot without indulgence be applied to the manners, of these Oriental queens. A concubine, in the strict sense of the civilians, was a woman of servile or plebeian extraction, the sole and faithful companion of a Roman citizen, who continued in a state of celibacy. Her modest station, below the honours of a wife, above the infamy of a prostitute, was acknowledged and approved by the laws: from the age of Augustus to the tenth century the use of this secondary marriage prevailed both in the West and East; and the humble virtues of a concubine were often preferred to the pomp and insolence of a noble matron. In this connection the two Antonines, the best of princes and of men, enjoyed the comforts of domestic love; the example was imitated by many citizens impatient of celibacy, but regardful of their families. If at any time they desired to legitimate their natural children, the conversion was instantly performed by the celebration of their nuptials with a partner whose fruitfulness and fidelity they had already tried.[135] By this epithet of *natural* the offspring of the concubine were distinguished from the spurious brood of adultery, prostitution, and incest, to whom Justinian reluctantly grants the necessary aliments of life; and these natural children alone were capable of succeeding to a sixth part of the inheritance of their reputed father. According to the rigour of law, bastards were entitled only to the name and condition of their mother, from whom they might derive the character of a slave, a stranger, or a citizen. The outcasts of every family were adopted, without reproach, as the children of the state.[136]

[133] When her father Agrippa died (A.D. 44), Berenice was sixteen years of age (Joseph. tom. i. Antiquit. Judaic. l. xix. c. 9, p. 952, edit. Havercamp.). She was therefore above fifty years old when Titus (A.D. 79) invitus invitam invisit. This date would not have adorned the tragedy or pastoral of the tender Racine.

[134] The *Ægyptia conjux* of Virgil (Æneid, viii. 688) seems to be numbered among the monsters who warred with Mark Antony against Augustus, the senate, and the gods of Italy.

[135] [The edict of Constantine first conferred this right of marriage after trial and experience of fecundity; for Augustus had prohibited the taking as a concubine the woman who might afterwards be taken as a wife: if marriage took place afterwards, this made no difference in the rights of the children born before it: recourse was then had to adoption, properly called arrogation.—O. S.]

[136] The humble but legal rights of concubines and natural children are stated in the Institutes (l. i. tit. x.), the Pandects (l. i. tit. vii.), the Code (l. v. tit. xxv.), and the Novels (lxxiv. lxxxix.). The researches of Heineccius and Giannone (ad Legem Juliam et Papiam-Poppæam, c. iv. p. 164-175, Opere Posthume, p. 108-158) illustrate this interesting and domestic subject.

[By the first law of Constantine the legitimate offspring could alone inherit: where there were no near legitimate relatives, the inheritance went to the fiscus. By the second law, all persons, even of the highest rank, senators, perfectissimi, decemvirs, were to be declared infamous, and out of the protection of the Roman law if born ex ancillâ vel ancillæ filiâ, vel libertâ, vel libertæ filiâ, sive Romanâ factâ, seu Latinâ, vel scænicæ filiâ, etc. Whatever a fond father had conferred on such children was revoked, and either restored to the legitimate children or confiscated to the state.—O. S.]

The relation of guardian and ward, or, in Roman words, of *tutor* and *pupil,* which covers so many titles of the Institutes and Pandects,[137] is of a very simple and uniform nature. The person and property of an orphan must always be trusted to the custody of some discreet friend. If the deceased father had not signified his choice, the *agnats,* or paternal kindred of the nearest degree, were compelled to act as the natural guardians: the Athenians were apprehensive of exposing the infant to the power of those most interested in his death; but an axiom of Roman jurisprudence has pronounced that the charge of tutelage should constantly attend the emolument of succession. If the choice of the father and the line of consanguinity afforded no efficient guardian, the failure was supplied by the nomination of the prætor of the city or the president of the province; but the person whom they named to this *public* office might be legally excused by insanity or blindness, by ignorance or inability, by previous enmity or adverse interest, by the number of children or guardianships with which he was already burthened, and by the immunities which were granted to the useful labours of magistrates, lawyers, physicians, and professors. Till the infant could speak and think, he was represented by the tutor,[138] whose authority was finally determined by the age of puberty. Without his consent, no act of the pupil could bind himself to his own prejudice, though it might oblige others for his personal benefit. It is needless to observe that the tutor often gave security, and always rendered an account; and that the want of diligence or integrity exposed him to a civil and almost criminal action for the violation of his sacred trust. The age of puberty had been rashly fixed by the civilians at fourteen;[139] but, as the fac-

---

[137] See the article of guardians and wards in the Institutes (l. i. tit. xiii.-xxvi.), the Pandects (l. xxvi. xxvii.), and the Code (l. v. tit. xxviii.-lxx.).

[138] [Gibbon's theory of pupillage does not seem correct according to Dr. W. Smith. The tutor did not represent the "pupillus." His office is always described as "augere auctoritatem, interponere, auctor fieri," *i.e.,* to fill out or complete the defective legal personality of the ward. All formal words essential to a legal transaction had to be pronounced by the ward himself, and then the tutor, by his assent, added the *animus,* or intention, of which the child was not capable.—O. S.]

[139] ["The civilians had rashly fixed the age of puberty at fourteen," but it is probable that the doctrine attributed generally to the civilians was quite unknown to the older law. As the "pupillus" was in theory a defectus paterfamilias, it is more than likely that the tutelage ceased at the epoch of actual physical manhood. We learn from Gaius (l. i. § 196) and Ulpian (Reg. ii. 28) that the Sabinians still maintained this view, while the Proculeians were in favour of the age of puberty being fixed at fourteen. It was not until the legislation of Justinian that the question was finally settled in favour of the latter opinion. In the case of females, the age of puberty was fixed at twelve from the earliest times.

As regards the function of the curator, there has been considerable dispute, but the following seems to be the most consistent account of the matter: The law of the "Twelve Tables" provided for the appointment of curators in the case of madmen and prodigals, but did not make any provision for the protection of young persons who had attained the age of puberty. The first enactment on the subject of which we have any knowledge is the *Lex Plætoria* (not *Lætoria* as often written), passed before the time of Plautus, which,

ulties of the mind ripen more slowly than those of the body, a *curator* was interposed to guard the fortunes of a Roman youth from his own inexperience and headstrong passions. Such a trustee had been first instituted by the prætor to save the family from the blind havoc of a prodigal or madman; and the minor was compelled by the laws to solicit the same protection to give validity to his acts till he accomplished the full period of twenty-five years. Women were condemned to the perpetual tutelage of parents, husbands, or guardians; a sex created to please and obey was never supposed to have attained the age of reason and experience. Such at least was the stern and haughty spirit of the ancient law, which had been insensibly mollified before the time of Justinian.

II. The original right of property can only be justified by the accident or merit of prior occupancy; and on this foundation it is wisely established by the philosophy of the civilians.[140] The savage who hollows a tree, inserts a sharp stone into a wooden handle, or applies a string to an elastic branch, becomes in a state of nature the just proprietor of the canoe, the bow, or the hatchet. The materials were common to all; the new form, the produce of his time and simple industry, belongs solely to himself. His hungry brethren cannot, without a sense of their own injustice, extort from the hunter the game of the forest overtaken or slain by his personal strength and dexterity. If his provident care preserves and multiplies the tame animals, whose nature is tractable to the arts of education, he acquires a perpetual title to the use and service of their numerous progeny, which derives its existence from him alone. If he encloses and cultivates a field for their sustenance and his own, a barren waste is converted into a fertile soil; the seed, the manure, the labour, create a new value, and the rewards of harvest are painfully earned by the fatigues of the revolving year. In the successive states of society, the hunter, the shepherd, the husbandman, may defend their possessions by two reasons which forcibly appeal to the feelings of the human mind: that whatever they enjoy is the fruit of their own industry; and that every man who envies their felicity may purchase similar acquisitions by the exercise of similar

fixing the age of the perfecta ætas at twenty-five years, provided that any one defrauding a person under that age should be liable to a criminal prosecution and to infamy (Cicero de Natura Deorum, iii. 30; de Officiis, iii. 15); and probably permitted the appointment of curators in cases where a good reason for the appointment was given. The prætor subsequently provided a remedy which was a great protection to persons under twenty-five years of age who came before him, by directing in all cases a *restitutio in integrum:* viz., that the applicant should be placed exactly in the position in which he would have been had not the fraud been practised against him. Finally, Marcus Antoninus ordered that curators should be given in all cases without inquiry on the application of the pubes. Cf. Julius Capitolinus, in Vita Marc. Aurel. Anton. c. 10. —O. S.]

[140] Institut. l. ii. tit. i. ii. Compare the pure and precise reasoning of Caius and Heineccius (l. ii. tit. i. p. 69-91) with the loose prolixity of Theophilus (p. 207-265). The opinions of Ulpian are preserved in the Pandects (l. i. tit. viii. leg. 41, No. 1).

diligence. Such, in truth, may be the freedom and plenty of a small colony cast on a fruitful island. But the colony multiplies, while the space still continues the same; the common rights, the equal inheritance of mankind, are engrossed by the bold and crafty; each field and forest is circumscribed by the landmarks of a jealous master; and it is the peculiar praise of the Roman jurisprudence that it asserts the claim of the first occupant to the wild animals of the earth, the air, and the waters. In the progress from primitive equity to final injustice, the steps are silent, the shades are almost imperceptible, and the absolute monopoly is guarded by positive laws and artificial reason. The active, insatiate principle of self-love can alone supply the arts of life and the wages of industry; and as soon as civil government and exclusive property have been introduced, they become necessary to the existence of the human race. Except in the singular institutions of Sparta, the wisest legislators have disapproved an agrarian law as a false and dangerous innovation. Among the Romans, the enormous disproportion of wealth surmounted the ideal restraints of a doubtful tradition and an obsolete statute—a tradition that the poorest follower of Romulus had been endowed with the perpetual inheritance of two *jugera;*[141] a statute which confined the richest citizen to the measure of five hundred jugera, or three hundred and twelve acres of land. The original territory of Rome consisted only of some miles of wood and meadow along the banks of the Tiber; and domestic exchange could add nothing to the national stock. But the goods of an alien or enemy were lawfully exposed to the first hostile occupier; the city was enriched by the profitable trade of war; and the blood of her sons was the only price that was paid for the Volscian sheep, the slaves of Britain, or the gems and gold of Asiatic kingdoms. In the language of ancient jurisprudence, which was corrupted and forgotten before the age of Justinian, these spoils were distinguished by the name of *manceps* or *mancipium,* taken with the hand; and whenever they were sold or *emancipated,* the purchaser required some assurance that they had been the property of an enemy, and not of a fellow-citizen.[142] A citizen could only forfeit his rights by apparent dereliction, and such dereliction of a valuable interest could not easily be presumed. Yet, according to the Twelve Tables, a prescription of one year for movables, and of two years for immov-

---

[141] The *heredium* of the first Romans is defined by Varro (de Re Rusticâ, 1. i. c. ii. p. 141, c. x. p. 160, 161, edit. Gesner), and clouded by Pliny's declamation (Hist. Natur. xviii. 2). A just and learned comment is given in the Administration des Terres chez les Romains (p. 12-66).

[142] The *res mancipi* is explained from faint and remote lights by Ulpian (Fragment. tit. xviii. [xix.] p. 618, 619) and Bynkershoek (Opp. tom. i. p. 306-315). The definition is somewhat arbitrary; and as none except myself have assigned a reason, I am diffident of my own.

[Since the time of Gibbon it has been proved incontestably that the agrarian laws of Rome related only to the Ager Publicus, or domains of the state, and that the laws of Lucinius and of Gracchus limited a Roman citizen to the possession of 500 jugera of such land, but that he might become the proprietor of any amount of private land.—O. S.]

ables, abolished the claim of the ancient master, if the actual possessor had acquired them by a fair transaction from the person whom he believed to be the lawful proprietor.[143] Such conscientious injustice, without any mixture of fraud or force, could seldom injure the members of a small republic; but the various periods of three, of ten, or of twenty years, determined by Justinian, are more suitable to the latitude of a great empire. It is only in the term of prescription that the distinction of real and personal fortune has been remarked by the civilians; and their general idea of property is that of simple, uniform, and absolute dominion. The subordinate exceptions of *use,* of *usufruct,*[144] of *servitudes,*[145] imposed for the benefit of a neighbour on lands and houses, are abundantly explained by the professors of jurisprudence. The claims of property, as far as they are altered by the mixture, the division, or the transformation of substances, are investigated with metaphysical subtlety by the same civilians.

The personal title of the first proprietor must be determined by his death; but the possession, without any appearance of change, is peaceably continued in his children, the associates of his toil, and the partners of his wealth. This natural inheritance has been protected by the legislators of every climate and age, and the father is encouraged to persevere in slow and distant improvements, by the tender hope that a long posterity will enjoy the fruits of his labour. The *principle* of hereditary succession is universal; but the *order* has been variously established by convenience or caprice, by the spirit of national institutions, or by some partial example which was originally decided by fraud or violence. The jurisprudence of the Romans appears to have deviated from the equality of nature much less than the Jewish,[146] the Athenian,[147] or the English institutions.[148] On the death of a citizen, all his

[143] From this short prescription, Hume (Essays, vol. i. p. 423) infers that there could not *then* be more order and settlement in Italy than *now* amongst the Tartars. By the civilian of his adversary Wallace he is reproached, and not without reason, for overlooking the conditions (Institut. l. ii. tit. vi.).

[144] See the Institutes (l. i. [ii.] tit. iv. v.) and the Pandects (l. vii.). Noodt has composed a learned and distinct treatise *de Usufructû* (Opp. tom. i. p. 387-478).

[145] The questions *de Servitutibus* are discussed in the Institutes (l. ii. tit. iii.) and Pandects (l. viii.). Cicero (pro Murenâ, c. 9) and Lactantius (Institut. Divin. l. i. c. i.) affect to laugh at the insignificant doctrine, de aquâ pluviâ arcendâ, etc. Yet it might be of frequent use among litigious neighbours, both in town and country.

[146] Among the patriarchs, the first-born enjoyed a mystic and spiritual primogeniture (Genesis xxv. 31). In the land of Canaan he was entitled to a double portion of inheritance (Deuteronomy xxi. 17, with Le Clerc's judicious Commentary).

[147] At Athens the sons were equal; but the poor daughters were endowed at the discretion of their brothers. See the κληρικοί pleadings of Isæus (in the seventh volume of the Greek Orators), illustrated by the version and comment of Sir William Jones, a scholar, a lawyer, and a man of genius.

[148] In England, the eldest son alone inherits *all* the land; a law, says the orthodox Judge Blackstone (Commentaries on the Laws of England, vol. ii. p. 215), unjust only in the opinion of younger brothers. It may be of some political use in sharpening their industry.

descendants, unless they were already freed from his paternal power, were called to the inheritance of his possessions. The insolent prerogative of primogeniture was unknown; the two sexes were placed on a just level; all the sons and daughters were entitled to an equal portion of the patrimonial estate; and if any of the sons had been intercepted by a premature death, his person was represented, and his share was divided, by his surviving children. On the failure of the direct line, the right of succession must diverge to the collateral branches. The degrees of kindred [149] are numbered by the civilians, ascending from the last possessor to a common parent, and descending from the common parent to the next heir: my father stands in the first degree, my brother in the second, his children in the third, and the remainder of the series may be conceived by fancy, or pictured in a genealogical table. In this computation a distinction was made, essential to the laws and even the constitution of Rome: the *agnats,* or persons connected by a line of males, were called, as they stood in the nearest degree, to an equal partition; but a female was incapable of transmitting any legal claims; and the *cognats* of every rank, without excepting the dear relation of a mother and a son, were disinherited by the Twelve Tables, as strangers and aliens. Among the Romans a *gens* or lineage was united by a common *name* and domestic rites; the various *cognomens* or *surnames* of Scipio or Marcellus distinguished from each other the subordinate branches or families of the Cornelian or Claudian race: the default of the *agnats* of the same surname was supplied by the larger denomination of *gentiles;* and the vigilance of the laws maintained, in the same name, the perpetual descent of religion and property. A similar principle dictated the Voconian law,[150] which abolished the right of female inheritance. As long as virgins were given or sold in marriage, the adoption of the wife extinguished the hopes of the daughter. But the equal succession of independent matrons supported their pride and luxury, and might transport into a foreign house the riches of their fathers. While the maxims of Cato [151] were revered, they tended to perpetuate in each family a just and virtuous mediocrity: till female blandishments insensibly triumphed, and every salutary restraint was lost in the dissolute greatness of the republic. The rigour of the decemvirs was tempered by the equity of the prætors. Their edicts restored

[149] Blackstone's Tables (vol. ii. p. 202) represent and compare the decrees of the civil with those of the canon and common law. A separate tract of Julius Paulus, de gradibus et affinibus, is inserted or abridged in the Pandects (1. xxxviii. tit. x. [leg. 10]). In the seventh degrees he computes (No. 18) 1024 persons.

[150] The Voconian law was enacted in the year of Rome 584. The younger Scipio, who was then 17 years of age (Freinsheimius, Supplement. Livian. xlvi. 44), found an occasion of exercising his generosity to his mother, sisters, etc. (Polybius, tom. ii. 1. xxxi. p. 1453-1464, edit. Gronov. [xxxii. 12], a domestic witness.)

[151] Legem Voconiam (Ernesti, Clavis Ciceroniana) voce magnâ bonis lateribus (at sixty-five years of age) suasissem, says old Cato (de Senectute, c. 5). Aulus Gellius (vii. 13,.xvii. 6) has saved some passages.

emancipated and posthumous children to the rights of nature; and upon the failure of the *agnats,* they preferred the blood of the *cognats* to the name of the gentiles, whose title and character were insensibly covered with oblivion. The reciprocal inheritance of mothers and sons was established in the Tertullian and Orphitian decrees by the humanity of the senate. A new and more impartial order was introduced by the novels of Justinian, who affected to revive the jurisprudence of the Twelve Tables. The lines of masculine and female kindred were confounded: the descending, ascending, and collateral series was accurately defined; and each degree, according to the proximity of blood and affection, succeeded to the vacant possessions of a Roman citizen.[152]

The order of succession is regulated by nature, or at least by the general and permanent reason of the lawgiver; but this order is frequently violated by the arbitrary and partial *wills,* which prolong the dominion of the testator beyond the grave.[153] In the simple state of society this last use or abuse of the right of property is seldom indulged; it was introduced at Athens by the laws of Solon, and the private testaments of the father of a family are authorised by the Twelve Tables. Before the time of the decemvirs,[154] a Roman citizen exposed his wishes and motives to the assembly of the thirty curiæ or parishes, and the general law of inheritance was suspended by an occasional act of the legislature. After the permission of the decemvirs, each private lawgiver promulgated his verbal or written testament in the presence of five citizens, who represented the five classes of the Roman people; a sixth witness attested their concurrence; a seventh weighed the copper money, which was paid by an imaginary purchaser, and the estate was emancipated by a fictitious sale and immediate release. This singular ceremony,[155] which excited the wonder of the Greeks, was still practised in the age of Severus; but the prætors had already approved a more simple testament, for which they required the seals and signatures of seven witnesses, free from all legal exception, and purposely

---

[152] See the law of succession in the Institutes of Caius (1. ii. tit. viii. p. 130-144, [Schulting, Jurispr. Ante-Justin. Lips. 1737]) and Justinian (1. iii. tit. i.-vi. with the Greek version of Theophilus, p. 515-575, 588-600), the Pandects (1. xxxviii. tit. vi-xvii.), the Code (1. vi. tit. lv.-lx.), and the Novels (cxviii.).

[153] That succession was the *rule,* testament the *exception,* is proved by Taylor (Elements of Civil Law, p. 519-527), a learned, rambling, spirited writer. In the second and third books the method of the Institutes is doubtless preposterous; and the chancellor Daguesseau (Œuvres, tom. i. p. 275) wishes his countryman Domat in the place of Tribonian. Yet *covenants* before *successions* is not surely *the natural order of the civil laws.*

[154] Prior examples of testaments are perhaps fabulous. At Athens a *childless* father only could make a will (Plutarch. in Solone, tom. i. [c. 21] p. 164. See Isæus and Jones).

[155] The testament of Augustus is specified by Suetonius (in August. c. 101, in Neron. c. 4), who may be studied as a code of Roman antiquities. Plutarch (Opuscul. tom. ii. p. 976) is surprised ὅταν δὲ διαθήκας γράθωσιν, ἑτέρους μὲν ἀπολείπουσι κληρονόμους, ἕτεροι δὲ πωλοῦσι τὰς οὐσίας. The language of Ulpian (Fragment. tit. xx. [§ 2] p. 627, edit. Schulting) is almost too exclusive—solum in usû est.

summoned for the execution of that important act. A domestic monarch, who reigned over the lives and fortunes of his children, might
distribute their respective shares according to the degrees of their merit
or his affection; his arbitrary displeasure chastised an unworthy son
by the loss of his inheritance, and the mortifying preference of a
stranger. But the experience of unnatural parents recommended some
limitations of their testamentary powers. A son, or, by the laws of
Justinian, even a daughter, could no longer be disinherited by their
silence: they were compelled to name the criminal, and to specify the
offence; and the justice of the emperor enumerated the sole causes that
could justify such a violation of the first principles of nature and society.[156] Unless a legitimate portion, a fourth part, had been reserved
for the children, they were entitled to institute an action or complaint
of *inofficious* testament—to suppose that their father's understanding
was impaired by sickness or age, and respectfully to appeal from his
rigorous sentence to the deliberate wisdom of the magistrate. In the
Roman jurisprudence an essential distinction was admitted between the
inheritance and the legacies. The heirs who succeeded to the entire
unity, or to any of the twelve fractions of the substance of the testator,
represented his civil and religious character, asserted his rights, fulfilled
his obligations, and discharged the gifts of friendship or liberality which
his last will had bequeathed under the name of legacies. But as the
imprudence or prodigality of a dying man might exhaust the inheritance, and leave only risk and labour to his successor, he was empowered to retain the *Falcidian* portion; to deduct, before the payment of
the legacies, a clear fourth for his own emolument. A reasonable time
was allowed to examine the proportion between the debts and the estate,
to decide whether he should accept or refuse the testament; and if he
used the benefit of an inventory, the demands of the creditors could not
exceed the valuation of the effects. The last will of a citizen might be
altered during his life, or rescinded after his death: the persons whom
he named might die before him, or reject the inheritance, or be exposed
to some legal disqualification. In the contemplation of these events, he
was permitted to substitute second and third heirs, to replace each other
according to the order of the testament; and the incapacity of a madman or an infant to bequeath his property might be supplied by a
similar substitution.[157] But the power of the testator expired with the
acceptance of the testament: each Roman of mature age and discretion
acquired the absolute dominion of his inheritance, and the simplicity of

---

[156] Justinian (Novell. cxv. c. 3, 4) enumerates only the public and private
crimes, for which a son might likewise disinherit his father.

[157] The *substitutions fidei-commissaires* of the modern civil law is a feudal
idea grafted on the Roman Jurisprudence, and bears scarcely any resemblance
to the ancient fidei-commissa (Institutions du Droit François, tom. i. p. 347-
383; Denissart, Décisions de Jurisprudence, tom. iv. p. 577-604). They were
stretched to the fourth degree by an abuse of the clixth Novel; a partial,
perplexed, declamatory law.

the civil law was never clouded by the long and intricate entails which confine the happiness and freedom of unborn generations.

Conquest and the formalities of law established the use of *codicils*. If a Roman was surprised by death in a remote province of the empire, he addressed a short epistle to his legitimate or testamentary heir, who fulfilled with honour, or neglected with impunity, this last request, which the judges before the age of Augustus were not authorised to enforce. A codicil might be expressed in any mode or in any language, but the subscription of five witnesses must declare that it was the genuine composition of the author. His intention, however laudable, was sometimes illegal, and the invention of *fidei-commissa*, or trusts, arose from the struggle between natural justice and positive jurisprudence. A stranger of Greece or Africa might be the friend or benefactor of a childless Roman, but none, except a fellow-citizen, could act as his heir. The Voconian law, which abolished female succession, restrained the legacy or inheritance of a woman to the sum of one hundred thousand sesterces;[158] and an only daughter was condemned almost as an alien in her father's house. The zeal of friendship and parental affection suggested a liberal artifice: a qualified citizen was named in the testament, with a prayer or injunction that he would restore the inheritance to the person for whom it was truly intended. Various was the conduct of the trustees in this painful situation; they had sworn to observe the laws of their country, but honour prompted them to violate their oath; and, if they preferred their interest under the mask of patriotism, they forfeited the esteem of every virtuous mind. The declaration of Augustus relieved their doubts, gave a legal sanction to confidential testaments and codicils, and gently unravelled the forms and restraints of the republican jurisprudence.[159] But as the new practice of trusts degenerated into some abuse, the trustee was enabled, by the Trebellian and Pegasian decrees, to reserve one fourth of the estate, or to transfer on the head of the real heir all the debts and actions of the succession. The interpretation of testaments was strict and literal; but the language of *trusts* and codicils was delivered from the minute and technical accuracy of the civilians.[160]

III. The general duties of mankind are imposed by their public and private relations, but their specific *obligations* to each other can only be the effect of, 1, a promise; 2, a benefit; or 3, an injury; and when these obligations are ratified by law, the interested party may compel the performance by a judicial *action*. On this principle the civilians of

---

[158] Dion Cassius (tom. ii. l. lvi. [c. 10] p. 814, with Reimar's Notes) specifies in Greek money the sum of 25,000 drachms.

[159] The revolutions of the Roman laws of inheritance are finely, though sometimes fancifully, deduced by Montesquieu (Esprit des Loix, l. xxvii.).

[160] Of the civil jurisprudence of successions, testaments, codicils, legacies, and trusts, the principals are ascertained in the Institutes of Caius (l. ii. tit. ii.-viii. p. 91-144), Justinian (l. ii. tit. x.-xxv.), and Theophilus (p. 328, 514); and the immense detail occupies twelve books (xxviii.-xxxix.) of the Pandects.

every country have erected a similar jurisprudence, the fair conclusion of universal reason and justice.[161]

1. The goddess of *faith* (of human and social faith) was worshipped, not only in her temples, but in the lives of the Romans; and if that nation was deficient in the more amiable qualities of benevolence and generosity, they astonished the Greeks by their sincere and simple performance of the most burdensome engagements.[162] Yet among the same people, according to the rigid maxims of the patricians and decemvirs, a *naked pact*, a promise, or even an oath, did not create any civil obligation, unless it was confirmed by the legal form of a *stipulation*. Whatever might be the etymology of the Latin word, it conveyed the idea of a firm and irrevocable contract, which was always expressed in the mode of a question and answer. Do you promise to pay me one hundred pieces of gold? was the solemn interrogation of Seius. I do promise —was the reply of Sempronius. The friends of Sempronius, who answered for his ability and inclination, might be separately sued at the option of Seius; and the benefit of partition, or order of reciprocal actions, insensibly deviated from the strict theory of stipulation. The most cautious and deliberate consent was justly required to sustain the validity of a gratuitous promise, and the citizen who might have obtained a legal security incurred the suspicion of fraud, and paid the forfeit of his neglect. But the ingenuity of the civilians successfully laboured to convert simple engagements into the form of solemn stipulations. The prætors, as the guardians of social faith, admitted every rational evidence of a voluntary and deliberate act, which in their tribunal produced an equitable obligation, and for which they gave an action and a remedy.[163]

2. The obligations of the second class, as they were contracted by the delivery of a thing, are marked by the civilians with the epithet of real.[164] A grateful return is due to the author of a benefit; and whoever is intrusted with the property of another has bound himself to the sacred duty of restitution. In the case of a friendly loan, the merit of generosity is on the side of the lender only; in a deposit, on the side

---

[161] The Institutes of Caius (l. ii. tit. ix. x. p. 144-214), of Justinian (l. iii. tit. xiv.-xxx. [xiii.-xxix.] l. iv. tit. i.-vi.), and of Theophilus (p. 616-837), distinguish four sorts of obligations—aut *re*, aut *verbis*, aut *literis*, aut *consensû*: but I confess myself partial to my own divison.

[162] How much is the cool, rational evidence of Polybius (l. vi. [c. 56] p. 693, l. xxxi. p. 1459, 1460) superior to vague, indiscriminate applause—omnium maxime et præcipue fidem coluit (A. Gellius, xx. 1 [tom. ii. p. 289, ed. Bipont.]).

[163] The Jus Prætorium de Pactis et Transactionibus is a separate and satisfactory treatise of Gerard Noodt (Opp. tom. i. p. 483-564). And I will here observe that the universities of Holland and Brandenburg, in the beginning of the present century, appear to have studied the civil law on the most just and liberal principles.

[164] The nice and various subject of contracts by consent is spread over four books (xvii.-xx.) of the Pandects, and is one of the parts best deserving of the attention of an English student.

of the receiver; but in a *pledge,* and the rest of the selfish commerce of ordinary life, the benefit is compensated by an equivalent, and the obligation to restore is variously modified by the nature of the transaction. The Latin language very happily expresses the fundamental difference between the *commodatum* and the *mutuum,* which our poverty is reduced to confound under the vague and common appellation of a loan. In the former, the borrower was obliged to restore the same individual thing with which he had been *accommodated* for the temporary supply of his wants; in the latter, it was destined for his use and consumption, and he discharged this *mutual* engagement by substituting the same specific value according to a just estimation of number, of weight, and of measure. In the contract of *sale,* the absolute dominion is transferred to the purchaser, and he repays the benefit with an adequate sum of gold or silver, the price and universal standard of all earthly possessions. The obligation of another contract, that of *location,* is of a more complicated kind. Lands or houses, labour or talents, may be hired for a definite term; at the expiration of the time, the thing itself must be restored to the owner with an additional reward for the beneficial occupation and employment. In these lucrative contracts, to which may be added those of partnership and commissions, the civilians sometimes imagine the delivery of the object, and sometimes presume the consent of the parties. The substantial pledge has been refined into the invisible rights of a mortgage or *hypotheca;* and the agreement of sale for a certain price imputes, from that moment, the chances of gain or loss to the account of the purchaser. It may be fairly supposed that every man will obey the dictates of his interest; and if he accepts the benefit, he is obliged to sustain the expense, of the transaction. In this boundless subject, the historian will observe the *location* of land and money, the rent of the one and the interest of the other, as they materially affect the prosperity of agriculture and commerce. The landlord was often obliged to advance the stock and instruments of husbandry, and to content himself with a partition of the fruits. If the feeble tenant was oppressed by accident, contagion, or hostile violence, he claimed a proportionable relief from the equity of the laws: five years were the customary term, and no solid or costly improvements could be expected from a farmer who, at each moment, might be ejected by the sale of the estate.[165] Usury,[166] the inveterate

---

[165] The covenants of rent are defined in the Pandects (1. xix.) and the Code (1. iv. tit. lxv.). The quinquennium, or term of five years, appears to have been a custom rather than a law; but in France all leases of land were determined in nine years. This limitation was removed only in the year 1775 (Encyclopédie Méthodique, tom. i. de la Jurisprudence, p. 668, 669); and I am sorry to observe that it yet prevails in the beauteous and happy country where I am permitted to reside.

[166] I might implicitly acquiesce in the sense and learning of the three books of G. Noodt, de fœnore et usuris (Opp. tom. i. p. 175-268). The interpretation of the *asses* or *centesimæ usuræ* at twelve, the *unciariæ* at one per cent., is maintained by the best critics and civilians: Noodt (1. ii. c. 2, p. 207), Gravina (Opp. p. 205, etc., 210), Heineccius (Antiquitat. ad Institut. 1. iii. tit. xv.),

grievance of the city, had been discouraged by the Twelve Tables,[167] and abolished by the clamours of the people. It was revived by their wants and idleness, tolerated by the discretion of the prætors, and finally determined by the Code of Justinian. Persons of illustrious rank were confined to the moderate profit of *four per cent.;* six was pronounced to be the ordinary and legal standard of interest; eight was allowed for the convenience of manufacturers and merchants; twelve was granted to nautical insurance, which the wiser ancients had not attempted to define; but, except in this perilous adventure, the practice of exorbitant usury was severely restrained.[168] The most simple interest was condemned by the clergy of the East and West;[169] but the sense of mutual benefit, which had triumphed over the laws of the republic, has resisted with equal firmness the decrees of the church, and even the prejudices of mankind.[170]

3. Nature and society impose the strict obligation of repairing an injury; and the sufferer by private injustice acquires a personal right and a legitimate action. It the property of another be intrusted to our care, the requisite degree of care may rise and fall according to the benefit which we derive from such temporary possession; we are seldom made responsible for inevitable accident, but the consequences of a voluntary fault must always be imputed to the author.[171] A Roman pursued and recovered his stolen goods by a civil action of theft; they might pass through a succession of pure and innocent hands, but nothing less than a prescription of thirty years could extinguish his original

Montesquieu (Esprit des Loix, l. xxii. c. 22, tom. ii. p. 36; Défense de l'Esprit des Loix, tom. iii. p. 478, etc.), and above all John Frederic Gronovius (de Pecunia Veteri, l. iii. c. 13, p. 213-227, and his three Antexegeses, p. 455-655), the founder, or at least the champion, of this probable opinion, which is, however, perplexed with some difficulties.

[167] Primo xii Tabulis sancitum est ne quis unciario fœnore amplius exerceret (Tacit. Annal. vi. 16). Pour peu (says Montesquieu, Esprit des Loix, l. xxii. c. 22) qu'on soit versé dans l'histoire de Rome, on verra qu'une pareille loi ne devoit pas être l'ouvrage des décemvirs. Was Tacitus ignorant—or stupid? But the wiser and more virtuous patricians might sacrifice their avarice to their ambition, and might attempt to check the odious practice by such interest as no lender would accept, and such penalties as no debtor would incur.

[168] Justinian has not condescended to give usury a place in his Institutes; but the necessary rules and restrictions are inserted in the Pandects (l. xxii. tit. i. ii.) and the Code (l. iv. tit. xxxii. xxxiii.).

[169] The fathers are unanimous (Barbeyrac, Morale des Pères, p. 144, etc.): Cyprian, Lactantius, Basil, Chrysostom (see his frivolous arguments in Noodt, l. i. c. 7, p. 188), Gregory of Nyssa, Ambrose, Jerom, Augustin, and a host of councils and casuists.

[170] Cato, Seneca, Plutarch, have loudly condemned the practice or abuse of usury. According to the etymology of *fœnus* and τόκος, the principal is supposed to *generate* the interest: a breed of barren metal, exclaims Shakspeare—and the stage is the echo of the public voice.

[171] Sir William Jones has given an ingenious and rational Essay on the Law of Bailment (London, 1781, p. 127, in 8vo.). He is perhaps the only lawyer equally conversant with the year-books of Westminster, the Commentaries of Ulpian, the Attic pleadings of Isæus, and the sentences of Arabian and Persian cadhis.

claim. They were restored by the sentence of the prætor, and the injury was compensated by double, or three-fold, or even quadruple damages, as the deed had been perpetrated by secret fraud or open rapine, as the robber had been surprised in the fact or detected by a subsequent research. The Aquilian law [172] defended the living property of a citizen, his slaves and cattle, from the stroke of malice or negligence: the highest price was allowed that could be ascribed to the domestic animal at any moment of the year preceding his death; a similar latitude of thirty days was granted on the destruction of any other valuable effects. A personal injury is blunted or sharpened by the manners of the times and the sensibility of the individual: the pain or the disgrace of a word or blow cannot easily be appreciated by a pecuniary equivalent. The rude jurisprudence of the decemvirs had confounded all hasty insults, which did not amount to the fracture of a limb, by condemning the aggressor to the common penalty of twenty-five *asses*. But the same denomination of money was reduced, in three centuries, from a pound to the weight of half an ounce; and the insolence of a wealthy Roman indulged himself in the cheap amusement of breaking and satisfying the law of the Twelve Tables. Veratius ran through the streets striking on the face the inoffensive passengers, and his attendant pursebearer immediately silenced their clamours by the legal tender of twenty-five pieces of copper, about the value of one shilling.[173] The equity of the prætors examined and estimated the distinct merits of each particular complaint. In the adjudication of civil damages, the magistrate assumed a right to consider the various circumstances of time and place, of age and dignity, which may aggravate the shame and sufferings of the injured person; but if he admitted the idea of a fine, a punishment, an example, he invaded the province, though perhaps he supplied the defects, of the criminal law.

The execution of the Alban dictator, who was dismembered by eight horses, is represented by Livy as the first and last instance of Roman cruelty in the punishment of the most atrocious crimes.[174] But this act of justice or revenge was inflicted on a foreign enemy in the heat of victory, and at the command of a single man. The Twelve Tables afford a more decisive proof of the national spirit, since they were framed by the wisest of the senate and accepted by the free voices of the people; yet these laws, like the statutes of Draco,[175] are written in

---

[172] Noodt (Opp. tom. i. p. 137-172) has composed a separate treatise, ad Legem Aquiliam (Pandect. l. ix. tit. ii.).

[173] Aulus Gellius (Noct. Attic. xx. 1 [tom. ii. p. 284]) borrowed this story from the Commentaries of Q. Labeo on the twelve tables.

[174] The narrative of Livy (i. 28) is weighty and solemn. At tu dictis, Albane, maneres, is a harsh reflection, unworthy of Virgil's humanity (Æneid. viii. 643). Heyne, with his usual good taste, observes that the subject was too horrid for the shield of Æneas (tom. iii. p. 229).

[175] The age of Draco (Olympiad xxxix. 1) is fixed by Sir John Marsham (Canon Chronicus, p. 593-596) and Corsini (Fasti Attici, tom. iii. p. 62). For his laws, see the writers on the government of Athens, Sigonius, Meursius, Potter, etc.

characters of blood.[176]   They approve the inhuman and unequal principle of retaliation; and the forfeit of an eye for an eye, a tooth for a tooth, a limb for a limb, is rigorously exacted, unless the offender can redeem his pardon by a fine of three hundred pounds of copper. The decemvirs distributed with much liberality the slighter chastisements of flagellation and servitude; and nine crimes of a very different complexion are adjudged worthy of death.   1. Any act of *treason* against the state, or of correspondence with the public enemy. The mode of execution was painful and ignominious: the head of the degenerate Roman was shrouded in a veil, his hands were tied behind his back, and, after he had been scourged by the lictor, he was suspended in the midst of the forum on a cross, or inauspicious tree.   2. Nocturnal meetings in the city, whatever might be the pretence—of pleasure, or religion, or the public good.   3. The murder of a citizen; for which the common feelings of mankind demand the blood of the murderer. Poison is still more odious than the sword or dagger; and we are surprised to discover, in two flagitious events, how early such subtle wickedness had infected the simplicity of the republic and the chaste virtues of the Roman matrons.[177]   The parricide, who violated the duties of nature and gratitude, was cast into the river or the sea, enclosed in a sack; and a cock, a viper, a dog, and a monkey, were successively added as the most suitable companions.[178]   Italy produces no monkeys; but the want could never be felt till the middle of the sixth century first revealed the guilt of a parricide.[179]   4. The malice of an *incendiary*. After the previous ceremony of whipping, he himself was delivered to the flames; and in this example alone our reason is tempted to applaud the justice of retaliation.   5. *Judicial perjury*. The corrupt or malicious witness was thrown headlong from the Tarpeian rock to expiate his falsehood, which was rendered still more fatal by the severity of the

[176] The seventh, de delictis, of the twelve tables is delineated by Gravina (Opp. p. 292, 293, with a commentary, p. 214-230). Aulus Gellius (xx. 1) and the Collatio Legum Mosaicarum et Romanarum afford much original information.

[177] Livy mentions two remarkable and flagitious eras, of 3000 persons accused, and of 190 noble matrons convicted, of the crime of poisoning (xl. 43, viii. 18). Mr. Hume discriminates the ages of private and public virtue (Essays, vol. i. p. 22, 23). I would rather say that such ebullitions of mischief (as in France in the year 1680) are accidents and prodigies which leave no marks on the manners of a nation.

[178] The twelve tables and Cicero (pro Roscio Amerino, c. 25, 26) are content with the sack; Seneca (Excerpt. Controvers. v. 4) adorns it with serpents; Juvenal pities the guiltless monkey (innoxia simia—Satir. xiii. 156). Adrian (apud Dositheum Magistrum, l. iii. c. 16, p. 874-876, with Schulting's Note), Modestinus (Pandect. xlviii. tit. ix. leg. 9), Constantine (Cod. l. ix. tit. xvii.), and Justinian (Institut. l. iv. tit. xviii.), enumerate all the companions of the parricide. But this fanciful execution was simplified in practice. Hodie tamen vivi exuruntur vel ad bestias dantur (Paul. Sentent. Recept. l. v. tit. xxiv. p. 512, edit. Schulting [Jurispr. Ante-Justin.]).

[179] The first parricide at Rome was L. Ostius, after the second Punic war (Plutarch in Romulo [c. 22], tom. i. p. 57). During the Cimbric, P. Malleolus was guilty of the first matricide (Liv. Epitom. l. lxviii.).

penal laws and the deficiency of written evidence. 6. The corruption of a judge, who accepted bribes to pronounce an iniquitous sentence. 7. Libels and satires, whose rude strains sometimes disturbed the peace of an illiterate city. The author was beaten with clubs, a worthy chastisement; but it is not certain that he was left to expire under the blows of the executioner.[180] 8. The nocturnal mischief of damaging or destroying a neighbour's corn. The criminal was suspended as a grateful victim to Ceres. But the sylvan deities were less implacable, and the extirpation of a more valuable tree was compensated by the moderate fine of twenty-five pounds of copper. 9. Magical incantations; which had power, in the opinion of the Latian shepherds, to exhaust the strength of an enemy, to extinguish his life, and to remove from their seats his deep-rooted plantations. The cruelty of the Twelve Tables against insolvent debtors still remains to be told; and I shall dare to prefer the literal sense of antiquity to the specious refinements of modern criticism.[181] After the judicial proof or confession of the debt, thirty days of grace were allowed before a Roman was delivered into the power of his fellow-citizen. In this private prison twelve ounces of rice were his daily food; he might be bound with a chain of fifteen pounds weight; and his misery was thrice exposed in the market-place, to solicit the compassion of his friends and countrymen. At the expiration of sixty days the debt was discharged by the loss of liberty or life; the insolvent debtor was either put to death or sold in foreign slavery beyond the Tiber: but, if several creditors were alike obstinate and unrelenting, they might legally dismember his body, and satiate their revenge by this horrid partition. The advocates for this savage law have insisted that it must strongly operate in deterring idleness and fraud from contracting debts which they were unable to discharge; but experience would dissipate this salutary terror, by proving that no creditor could be found to exact this unprofitable penalty of life or limb. As the manners of Rome were insensibly polished, the criminal code of the decemvirs was abolished by the humanity of accusers, witnesses, and judges; and impunity became the consequence of immoderate rigour. The Porcian and Valerian laws prohibited the magistrates from inflicting on a free citizen any capital, or even corporal, punishment; and the obsolete statutes of blood were artfully, and perhaps truly, ascribed to the spirit, not of patrician, but of regal, tyranny.

In the absence of penal laws and the insufficiency of civil actions, the peace and justice of the city were imperfectly maintained by the

---

[180] Horace talks of the formidine fustis (l. ii. Epist. i. 154), but Cicero (de Republicâ, l. iv. apud Augustin. de Civitat. Dei, ix. 6, in Fragment. Philosoph. tom. iii. p. 393, edit. Olivet) affirms that the decemvirs made libels a capital offence: cum perpaucas res capite sanxissent—*perpaucas!*

[181] Bynkershoek (Observat. Juris Rom. l. i. c. 1, in Opp. tom. i. p. 9, 10, 11) labours to prove that the creditors divided not the *body*, but the *price*, of the insolvent debtor. Yet his interpretation is one perpetual harsh metaphor; nor can he surmount the Roman authorities of Quintilian, Cæcilius, Favonius, and Tertullian. See Aulus Gellius, Noct. Attic. xx. 1 [tom. ii. p. 285].

private jurisdiction of the citizens. The malefactors who replenish our gaols are the outcasts of society, and the crimes for which they suffer may be commonly ascribed to ignorance, poverty, and brutal appetite. For the perpetration of similar enormities, a vile plebeian might claim and abuse the sacred character of a member of the republic; but on the proof or suspicion of guilt the slave or the stranger was nailed to a cross, and this strict and summary justice might be exercised without restraint over the greatest part of the populace of Rome. Each family contained a domestic tribunal, which was not confined, like that of the prætor, to the cognisance of external actions: virtuous principles and habits were inculcated by the discipline of education, and the Roman father was accountable to the state for the manners of his children, since he disposed without appeal of their life, their liberty, and their inheritance. In some pressing emergencies, the citizen was authorised to avenge his private or public wrongs. The consent of the Jewish, the Athenian, and the Roman laws, approved the slaughter of the nocturnal thief; though in open daylight a robber could not be slain without some previous evidence of danger and complaint. Whoever surprised an adulterer in his nuptial bed might freely exercise his revenge;[182] the most bloody or wanton outrage was excused by the provocation;[183] nor was it before the reign of Augustus that the husband was reduced to weigh the rank of the offender, or that the parent was condemned to sacrifice his daughter with her guilty seducer. After the expulsion of the kings, the ambitious Roman who should dare to assume their title or imitate their tyranny was devoted to the infernal gods: each of his fellow-citizens was armed with the sword of justice; and the act of Brutus, however repugnant to gratitude or prudence, had been already sanctified by the judgment of his country.[184] The barbarous practice of wearing arms in the midst of peace,[185] and the bloody maxims of honour, were unknown to the Romans; and during the two purest ages, from the establishment of equal freedom to the end of the Punic wars, the city was never disturbed by sedition, and rarely polluted with atrocious crimes. The failure of penal laws was more sensibly felt when

---

[182] The first speech of Lysias (Reiske, Orator. Græc. tom. v. p. 2-48) is in defence of a husband who had killed the adulterer. The rights of husbands and fathers at Rome and Athens are discussed with much learning by Dr. Taylor (Lectiones Lysiacæ, c. xi. in Reiske, tom. vi. p. 301-308).

[183] See Casaubon ad Athenæum, l. i. c. 5, p. 19. Percurrent raphanique mugilesque (Catull. [xv. 18] p. 41, 42, edit. Vossian.). Hunc mugilis intrat (Juvenal. Satir. x. 317). Hunc perminxere calones (Horat. 1. i. Satir. ii. 44). Familiæ stuprandum dedit [objecit] . . . fraudi non fuit (Val. Maxim. 1. vi. c. 1, No. 13).

[184] This law is noticed by Livy (ii. 8) and Plutarch (in Publicola [c. 12], tom. i. p. 187), and it fully justifies the public opinion on the death of Cæsar, which Suetonius could publish under the Imperial government. Jure cæsus existimatur (in Julio, c. 76). Read the letters that passed between Cicero and Matius a few months after the ides of March (ad Fam. xi. 27, 28).

[185] Πρῶτοι δὲ Ἀθηναῖοι τόν τε σίδηρον κατέθεντο. Thucydid. 1. i. c. 6. The historian who considers this circumstance as the test of civilisation would disdain the barbarism of a European court.

every vice was inflamed by faction at home and dominion abroad. In the time of Cicero each private citizen enjoyed the privilege of anarchy —each minister of the republic was exalted to the temptations of regal power, and their virtues are entitled to the warmest praise as the spontaneous fruits of nature or philosophy. After a triennial indulgence of lust, rapine, and cruelty, Verres, the tyrant of Sicily, could only be sued for the pecuniary restitution of three hundred thousand pounds sterling; and such was the temper of the laws, the judges, and perhaps the accuser himself,[186] that, on refunding a thirteenth part of his plunder, Verres could retire to an easy and luxurious exile.[187]

The first imperfect attempt to restore the proportion of crimes and punishments was made by the dictator Sylla, who, in the midst of his sanguinary triumph, aspired to restrain the licence rather than to oppress the liberty of the Romans. He gloried in the arbitrary proscription of four thousand seven hundred citizens.[188] But, in the character of a legislator, he respected the prejudices of the times; and instead of pronouncing a sentence of death against the robber or assassin, the general who betrayed an army or the magistrate who ruined a province, Sylla was content to aggravate the pecuniary damages by the penalty of exile, or, in more constitutional language, by the interdiction of fire and water. The Cornelian, and afterwards the Pompeian and Julian laws, introduced a new system of criminal jurisprudence;[189] and the emperors, from Augustus to Justinian, disguised their increasing rigour under the names of the original authors. But the invention and frequent use of *extraordinary pains* proceeded from the desire to extend and conceal the progress of despotism. In the condemnation of illustrious Romans, the senate was always prepared to confound, at the will of their masters, the judicial and legislative powers. It was the duty of the governors to maintain the peace of their province by the arbitrary and rigid administration of justice; the freedom of the city evaporated in the extent of empire, and the Spanish malefactor who claimed the

---

[186] He first rated at *millies* (£800,000) the damages of Sicily (Divinatio in Cæcilium, c. 5), which he afterwards reduced to *quadringenties* (£320,000— I Actio in Verrem, c. 18), and was finally content with *tricies* (£24,000). Plutarch (in Ciceron. [c. 8] tom. iii. p. 1584) has not dissembled the popular suspicion and report.

[187] Verres lived near thirty years after his trial, till the second triumvirate, when he was proscribed by the taste of Mark Antony for the sake of his Corinthian plate (Plin. Hist. Natur. xxxiv. 3).

[188] Such is the number assigned by Valerius Maximus (l. ix. c. 2, No. 1). Florus (iii. 21) distinguishes 2000 senators and knights. Appian (de Bell. Civil. l. i. c. 95, tom. ii. p. 133, edit. Schweighäuser) more accurately computes 40 victims of the senatorial rank and 1600 of the equestrian census or order.

[189] For the penal laws (Leges Corneliæ, Pompeiæ, Juliæ, of Sylla, Pompey, and the Cæsars), see the sentences of Paulus (l. iv. tit. xviii.-xxx. p. 497-528, edit. Schulting), the Gregorian Code (Fragment. l. xix. p. 705, 706, in Schulting), the Collatio Legum Mosaicarum et Romanarum (tit. i.-xv.), the Theodosian Code (l. ix.), the Code of Justinian (l. ix.), the Pandects (xlviii.), the Institutes (l. iv. tit. xviii.), and the Greek version of Theophilus (p. 917-926).

privilege of a Roman was elevated by the command of Galba on a fairer and more lofty cross.[190]   Occasional rescripts issued from the throne to decide the questions which, by their novelty or importance, appeared to surpass the authority and discernment of a proconsul. Transportation and beheading were reserved for honourable persons; meaner criminals were either hanged, or burnt, or buried in the mines, or exposed to the wild beasts of the amphitheatre.   Armed robbers were pursued and extirpated as the enemies of society; the driving away horses or cattle was made a capital offence;[191] but simple theft was uniformly considered as a mere civil and private injury.   The degrees of guilt and the modes of punishment were too often determined by the discretion of the rulers, and the subject was left in ignorance of the legal danger which he might incur by every action of his life.

A sin, a vice, a crime, are the objects of theology, ethics, and jurisprudence.   Whenever their judgments agree, they corroborate each other; but as often as they differ, a prudent legislator appreciates the guilt and punishment according to the measure of social injury.   On this principle the most daring attack on the life and property of a private citizen is judged less atrocious than the crime of treason or rebellion, which invades the *majesty* of the republic: the obsequious civilians unanimously pronounced that the republic is contained in the person of its chief, and the edge of the Julian law was sharpened by the incessant diligence of the emperors.   The licentious commerce of the sexes may be tolerated as an impulse of nature, or forbidden as a source of disorder and corruption; but the fame, the fortunes, the family of the husband, are seriously injured by the adultery of the wife.   The wisdom of Augustus, after curbing the freedom of revenge, applied to this domestic offence the animadversion of the laws; and the guilty parties, after the payment of heavy forfeitures and fines, were condemned to long or perpetual exile in two separate islands.[192]   Religion pronounces an equal censure against the infidelity of the husband, but, as it is not accompanied by the same civil effects, the wife was never permitted to vindicate her wrongs;[193] and the distinction of simple

---

[190] It was a guardian who had poisoned his ward.   The crime was atrocious: yet the punishment is reckoned by Suetonius (c. 9) among the acts in which Galba showed himself acer, vehemens, et in delictis coercendis immodicus.

[191] The abactores or abigeatores, who drove one horse, or two mares or oxen, or five hogs, or ten goats, were subject to capital punishment (Paul. Sentent. Recept. l. iv. tit. xviii. p. 497, 498).   Hadrian (ad Concil. Bæticæ), most severe where the offence was most frequent, condemns the criminals, ad gladium, ludi damnationem (Ulpian, de Officio Proconsulis, l. viii. in Collatione Legum Mosaic. et Rom. tit. xi. p. 236 [ed. Cannegieter, 1774]).

[192] Till the publication of the Julius Paulus of Schulting (l. ii. tit. xxvi. p. 317-323), it was affirmed and believed that the Julian laws punished adultery with death; and the mistake arose from the fraud or error of Tribonian.   Yet Lipsius had suspected the truth from the narratives of Tacitus (Annal. ii. 50, iii. 24, iv. 42), and even from the practice of Augustus, who distinguished the *treasonable* frailties of his female kindred.

[193] In cases of adultery Severus confined to the husband the right of public accusation (Cod. Justinian. l. ix. tit. ix. leg. 1).   Nor is this privilege unjust—so different are the effects of male or female infidelity.

or double adultery, so familiar and so important in the canon law, is unknown to the jurisprudence of the Code and Pandects. I touch with reluctance, and despatch with impatience, a more odious vice, of which modesty rejects the name, and nature abominates the idea. The primitive Romans were infected by the example of the Etruscans [194] and Greeks;[195] in the mad abuse of prosperity and power every pleasure that is innocent was deemed insipid; and the Scatinian law,[196] which had been extorted by an act of violence, was insensibly abolished by the lapse of time and the multitude of criminals. By this law the rape, perhaps the seduction, of an ingenuous youth was compensated as a personal injury by the poor damages of ten thousand sesterces, or fourscore pounds; the ravisher might be slain by the resistance or revenge of chastity; and I wish to believe that at Rome, as in Athens, the voluntary and effeminate deserter of his sex was degraded from the honours and the rights of a citizen.[197] But the practice of vice was not discouraged by the severity of opinion: the indelible stain of manhood was confounded with the more venial transgressions of fornication and adultery; nor was the licentious lover exposed to the same dishonour which he impressed on the male or female partner of his guilt. From Catullus to Juvenal,[198] the poets accuse and celebrate the degeneracy of the times; and the reformation of manners was feebly attempted by the reason and authority of the civilians, till the most virtuous of the Cæsars proscribed the sin against nature as a crime against society.[199]

A new spirit of legislation, respectable even in its error, arose in the empire with the religion of Constantine.[200] The laws of Moses were

---

[194] Timon [Timæus] (1. i.) and Theopompus (1. xliii. apud Athenæum, l. xii. p. 517 [c. 14, tom. iv. p. 422, ed. Schweigh.]) describe the luxury and lust of the Etruscans: πολὺ μέν τοι γε χαίρουσι συνόντες τοῖς παισὶ καὶ τοῖς μειρακίοις. About the same period (A. U. C. 445) the Roman youth studied in Etruria (liv. ix. 36).

[195] The Persians had been corrupted in the same school: ἀπ' Ἑλλήνων μαθόντες παισὶ μίσγονται (Herodot. l. i. c. 135). A curious dissertation might be formed on the introduction of pæderasty after the time of Homer, its progress among the Greeks of Asia and Europe, the vehemence of their passions, and the thin device of virtue and friendship which amused the philosophers of Athens. But, scelera ostendi oportet dum puniuntur, abscondi flagitia.

[196] The name, the date, and the provisions of this law are equally doubtful (Gravina, Opp. p. 432, 433; Heineccius, Hist. Jur. Rom. No. 108; Ernesti, Clav. Ciceron. in Indice Legum). But I will observe that the nefanda Venus of the honest German is styled aversa by the more polite Italian.

[197] See the oration of Æschines against the catamite Timarchus (in Reiske, Orator. Græc. tom. iii. p. 21-184).

[198] A crowd of disgraceful passages will force themselves on the memory of the classic reader: I will only remind him of the cool declaration of Ovid:—
Odi concubitus qui non utrumque resolvunt.
Hoc est quod puerûm tangar amore minus.

[199] Ælius Lampridius, in Vit. Heliogabal. in Hist. August. p. 112. Aurelius Victor, in Philippo [de Cæsar. c. 28], Codex Theodos. l. ix. tit. vii. leg. 6, and Godefroy's Commentary, tom. iii. p. 63. Theodosius abolished the subterraneous brothels of Rome, in which the prostitution of both sexes was acted with impunity.

[200] See the laws of Constantine and his successors against adultery, sodomy,

received as the divine original of justice, and the Christian princes adapted their penal statutes to the degrees of moral and religious turpitude. Adultery was first declared to be a capital offence: the frailty of the sexes was assimilated to poison or assassination, to sorcery or parricide; the same penalties were inflicted on the passive and active guilt of pæderasty; and all criminals, of free or servile condition, were either drowned, or beheaded, or cast alive into the avenging flames. The adulterers were spared by the common sympathy of mankind; but the lovers of their own sex were pursued by general and pious indignation: the impure manners of Greece still prevailed in the cities of Asia, and every vice was fomented by the celibacy of the monks and clergy. Justinian relaxed the punishment at least of female infidelity: the guilty spouse was only condemned to solitude and penance, and at the end of two years might be recalled to the arms of a forgiving husband. But the same emperor declared himself the implacable enemy of unmanly lust, and the cruelty of his persecution can scarcely be excused by the purity of his motives.[201] In defiance of every principle of justice, he stretched to past as well as future offences the operations of his edicts, with the previous allowance of a short respite for confession and pardon. A painful death was inflicted by the amputation of the sinful instrument, or the insertion of sharp reeds into the pores and tubes of most exquisite sensibility; and Justinian defended the propriety of the execution, since the criminals would have lost their hands had they been convicted of sacrilege. In this state of disgrace and agony two bishops, Isaiah of Rhodes and Alexander of Diospolis, were dragged through the streets of Constantinople, while their brethren were admonished by the voice of a crier to observe this awful lesson, and not to pollute the sanctity of their character. Perhaps these prelates were innocent. A sentence of death and infamy was often founded on the slight and suspicious evidence of a child or a servant: the guilt of the green faction, of the rich, and of the enemies of Theodora, was presumed by the judges, and pæderasty became the crime of those to whom no crime could be imputed. A French philosopher [202] has dared to remark that whatever is secret must be doubtful, and that our natural horror of vice may be abused as an engine of tyranny. But the favourable persuasion of the same writer, that a legislator may confide in the taste and reason of

etc., in the Theodosian (l. ix. tit. vii. leg. 7, l. xi. tit. xxxvi. leg. 1, 4) and Justinian Codes (l. ix. tit. ix. leg. 30, 31). These princes speak the language of passion as well as of justice, and fraudulently ascribe their own severity to the first Cæsars.

[201] Justinian, Novel. lxxvii. cxxxiv. cxli.; Procopius in Anecdot. c. 11, 16 [tom. iii. p. 76, 99, ed. Bonn], with the notes of Alemannus; Theophanes, p. 151 [ed. Par.; tom. i. p. 271, ed. Bonn]; Cedrenus, p. 368 [ed. Par.; tom. i. p. 645, ed. Bonn]; Zonaras, l. xiv. [c. 7] p. 64.

[202] Montesquieu, Esprit des Loix, l. xii. c. 6. That eloquent philosopher conciliates the rights of liberty and of nature, which should never be placed in opposition to each other.

mankind, is impeached by the unwelcome discovery of the antiquity and extent of the disease.[203]

The free citizens of Athens and Rome enjoyed in all criminal cases the invaluable privilege of being tried by their country.[204] 1. The administration of justice is the most ancient office of a prince: it was exercised by the Roman kings, and abused by Tarquin, who alone, without law or council, pronounced his arbitrary judgments. The first consuls succeeded to this regal prerogative; but the sacred right of appeal soon abolished the jurisdiction of the magistrates, and all public causes were decided by the supreme tribunal of the people. But a wild democracy, superior to the forms, too often disdains the essential principles, of justice; the pride of despotism was envenomed by plebeian envy; and the heroes of Athens might sometimes applaud the happiness of the Persian, whose fate depended on the caprice of a *single* tyrant. Some salutary restraints, imposed by the people on their own passions, were at once the cause and effect of the gravity and temperance of the Romans. The right of accusation was confined to the magistrates. A vote of the thirty-five tribes could inflict a fine; but the cognisance of all capital crimes was reserved by a fundamental law to the assembly of the centuries, in which the weight of influence and property was sure to preponderate. Repeated proclamations and adjournments were interposed, to allow time for prejudice and resentment to subside; the whole proceeding might be annulled by a seasonable omen or the opposition of a tribune, and such popular trials were commonly less formidable to innocence than they were favourable to guilt. But this union of the judicial and legislative powers left it doubtful whether the accused party was pardoned or acquitted; and, in the defence of an illustrious client, the orators of Rome and Athens address their arguments to the policy and benevolence, as well as to the justice, of their sovereign. 2. The task of convening the citizens for the trial of each offender became more difficult, as the citizens and the offenders continually multiplied, and the ready expedient was adopted of delegating the jurisdiction of the people to the ordinary magistrates or to extraordinary *inquisitors*.

[203] For the corruption of Palestine, 2000 years before the Christian era, see the history and laws of Moses. Ancient Gaul is stigmatised by Diodorus Siculus (tom. i. l. v. [c. 32] p. 356), China by the Mahometan and Christian travellers (Ancient Relations of India and China, p. 34, translated by Renaudot, and his bitter critic the Père Premare, Lettres Édifiantes, tom. xix. p. 435), and native America by the Spanish historians (Garcilasso de la Vega, l. iii. c. 13, Rycaut's translation; and Dictionnaire de Bayle, tom. iii. p. 88). I believe, and hope, that the negroes, in their own country, were exempt from this moral pestilence.

[204] The important subject of the public questions and judgments at Rome is explained with much learning, and in a classic style, by Charles Sigonius (l. iii. de Judiciis, in Opp. tom. iii. p. 679-864); and a good abridgment may be found in the République Romaine of Beaufort (tom. ii. l. v. p. 1-121). Those who wish for more abstruse law may study Noodt (de Jurisdictione et Imperio Libri duo, tom. i. p. 93-134), Heineccius (ad Pandect. l. i. et ii. ad Institut. l. iv. tit. xvii. Element. ad Antiquitat.), and Gravina (Opp. 230-251).

In the first ages these questions were rare and occasional. In the beginning of the seventh century of Rome they were made perpetual: four prætors were annually empowered to sit in judgment on the state offences of treason, extortion, peculation, and bribery; and Sylla added new prætors and new questions for those crimes which more directly injure the safety of individuals. By these *inquisitors* the trial was prepared and directed; but they could only pronounce the sentence of the majority of *judges*, who, with some truth and more prejudice, have been compared to the English juries.[205] To discharge this important though burdensome office, an annual list of ancient and respectable citizens was formed by the prætor. After many constitutional struggles, they were chosen in equal numbers from the senate, the equestrian order, and the people; four hundred and fifty were appointed for single questions, and the various rolls or *decuries* of judges must have contained the names of some thousand Romans, who represented the judicial authority of the state. In each particular cause a sufficient number was drawn from the urn; their integrity was guarded by an oath; the mode of ballot secured their independence; the suspicion of partiality was removed by the mutual challenges of the accuser and defendant; and the judges of Milo, by the retrenchment of fifteen on each side, were reduced to fifty-one voices or tablets, of acquittal, of condemnation, or of favourable doubt.[206] 3. In his civil jurisdiction the prætor of the city was truly a judge, and almost a legislator; but, as soon as he had prescribed the action of law, he often referred to a delegate the determination of the fact. With the increase of legal proceedings, the tribunal of the centumvirs, in which he presided, acquired more weight and reputation. But whether he acted alone or with the advice of his council, the most absolute powers might be trusted to a magistrate who was annually chosen by the votes of the people. The rules and precautions of freedom have required some explanation; the order of despotism is simple and inanimate. Before the age of Justinian, or perhaps of Diocletian, the decuries of Roman judges had sunk to an empty title; the humble advice of the assessors might be accepted or despised; and in each tribunal the civil and criminal jurisdiction was administered by a single magistrate, who was raised and disgraced by the will of the emperor.

A Roman accused of any capital crime might prevent the sentence of the law by voluntary exile or death. Till his guilt had been legally proved, his innocence was presumed and his person was free; till the votes of the last *century* had been counted and declared, he might peace-

[205] The office, both at Rome and in England, must be considered as an occasional duty, and not a magistracy or profession. But the obligation of a unanimous verdict is peculiar to our laws, which condemn the juryman to undergo the torture from whence they have exempted the criminal.

[206] We are indebted for this interesting fact to a fragment of Asconius Pedianus, who flourished under the reign of Tiberius. The loss of his Commentaries on the Orations of Cicero has deprived us of a valuable fund of historical and legal knowledge.

ably secede to any of the allied cities of Italy, or Greece, or Asia.[207] His fame and fortunes were preserved, at least to his children, by this civil death; and he might still be happy in every rational and sensual enjoyment, if a mind accustomed to the ambitious tumult of Rome could support the uniformity and silence of Rhodes or Athens. A bolder effort was required to escape from the tyranny of the Cæsars; but this effort was rendered familiar by the maxims of the Stoics, the example of the bravest Romans, and the legal encouragements of suicide. The bodies of condemned criminals were exposed to public ignominy, and their children, a more serious evil, were reduced to poverty by the confiscation of their fortunes. But, if the victims of Tiberius and Nero anticipated the decree of the prince or senate, their courage and despatch were recompensed by the applause of the public, the decent honours of burial, and the validity of their testaments.[208] The exquisite avarice and cruelty of Domitian appears to have deprived the unfortunate of this last consolation, and it was still denied even by the clemency of the Antonines. A voluntary death, which, in the case of a capital offence, intervened between the accusation and the sentence, was admitted as a confession of guilt, and the spoils of the deceased were seized by the inhuman claims of the treasury.[209] Yet the civilians have always respected the natural right of a citizen to dispose of his life; and the posthumous disgrace invented by Tarquin[210] to check the despair of his subjects was never revived or imitated by succeeding tyrants. The powers of this world have indeed lost their dominion over him who is resolved on death, and his arm can only be restrained by the religious apprehension of a future state. Suicides are enumerated by Virgil among the unfortunate, rather than the guilty,[211] and the poetical fables of the infernal shades could not seriously influence the faith or practice of mankind. But the precepts of the Gospel or the church have at length imposed a pious servitude on the minds of Christians, and condemn them to expect, without a murmur, the last stroke of disease or the executioner.

The penal statutes form a very small proportion of the sixty-two

[207] Polyb. 1. vi. [c. 14] p. 643. The extension of the empire and *city* of Rome obliged the exile to seek a more distant place of retirement.

[208] Qui de se statuebant, humabantur corpora, manebant testamenta; pretium festinandi. Tacit. Annal. vi. 29, with the Notes of Lipsius.

[209] Julius Paulus (Sentent. Recept. l. v. tit. xii. p. 476), the Pandects (l. xlviii. tit. xxi.), the Code (l. ix. tit. L.), Bynkershoek (tom. i. p. 59, Observat. J. C. R. iv. 4), and Montesquieu (Esprit des Loix, l. xxix. c. 9), define the civil limitations of the liberty and privileges of suicide. The criminal penalties are the production of a later and darker age.

[210] Plin. Hist. Natur. xxxvi. 24. When he fatigued his subjects in building the Capitol, many of the labourers were provoked to despatch themselves: he nailed their dead bodies to crosses.

[211] The sole resemblance of a violent and premature death has engaged Virgil (Æneid. vi. 434-439) to confound suicides with infants, lovers, and persons unjustly condemned. Heyne, the best of his editors, is at a loss to deduce the idea, or ascertain the jurisprudence, of the Roman poet.

books of the Code and Pandects, and in all judicial proceeding the life or death of a citizen is determined with less caution and delay than the most ordinary question of covenant or inheritance. This singular distinction, though something may be allowed for the urgent necessity of defending the peace of society, is derived from the nature of criminal and civil jurisprudence. Our duties to the state are simple and uniform; the law by which he is condemned is inscribed not only on brass or marble, but on the conscience of the offender, and his guilt is commonly proved by the testimony of a single fact. But our relations to each other are various and infinite; our obligations are created, annulled, and modified by injuries, benefits, and promises; and the interpretation of voluntary contracts and testaments, which are often dictated by fraud or ignorance, affords a long and laborious exercise to the sagacity of the judge. The business of life is multiplied by the extent of commerce and dominion, and the residence of the parties in the distant provinces of an empire is productive of doubt, delay, and inevitable appeals from the local to the supreme magistrate. Justinian, the Greek emperor of Constantinople and the East, was the legal successor of the Latian shepherd who had planted a colony on the banks of the Tiber. In a period of thirteen hundred years the laws had reluctantly followed the changes of government and manners; and the laudable desire of conciliating ancient names with recent institutions destroyed the harmony, and swelled the magnitude, of the obscure and irregular system. The laws which excuse on any occasions the ignorance of their subjects, confess their own imperfections; the civil jurisprudence, as it was abridged by Justinian, still continued a mysterious science and a profitable trade, and the innate perplexity of the study was involved in tenfold darkness by the private industry of the practitioners. The expense of the pursuit sometimes exceeded the value of the prize, and the fairest rights were abandoned by the poverty or prudence of the claimants. Such costly justice might tend to abate the spirit of litigation, but the unequal pressure serves only to increase the influence of the rich, and to aggravate the misery of the poor. By these dilatory and expensive proceedings the wealthy pleader obtains a more certain advantage than he could hope from the accidental corruption of his judge. The experience of an abuse from which our own age and country are not perfectly exempt may sometimes provoke a generous indignation, and extort the hasty wish of exchanging our elaborate jurisprudence for the simple and summary decrees of a Turkish cadhi. Our calmer reflection will suggest that such forms and delays are necessary to guard the person and property of the citizen; that the discretion of the judge is the first engine of tyranny; and that the laws of a free people should foresee and determine every question that may probably arise in the exercise of power and the transactions of industry. But the government of Justinian united the evils of liberty and servitude, and the Romans were oppressed at the same time by the multiplicity of their laws and the arbitrary will of their master.

CHAPTER XLV (565-643 A.D.)

Reign of the younger Justin—Embassy of the Avars—Their Settlement on the Danube—Conquest of Italy by the Lombards—Adoption and Reign of Tiberius—Of Maurice—State of Italy under the Lombards and the Exarchs—Of Ravenna—Distress of Rome—Character and Pontificate of Gregory the First

DURING the last years of Justinian, his infirm mind was devoted to heavenly contemplation, and he neglected the business of the lowei world. His subjects were impatient of the long continuance of his life and reign: yet all who were capable of reflection apprehended the moment of his death, which might involve the capital in tumult and the empire in civil war. Seven nephews[1] of the childless monarch, the sons or grandsons of his brother and sister, had been educated in the splendour of a princely fortune; they had been shown in high commands to the provinces and armies; their characters were known, their followers were zealous, and, as the jealousy of age postponed the declaration of a successor, they might expect with equal hopes the inheritance of their uncle. He expired in his palace, after a reign of thirty-eight years; and the decisive opportunity was embraced by the friends of Justin, the son of Vigilantia.[2] At the hour of midnight his domestics were awakened by an importunate crowd, who thundered at his door, and obtained admittance by revealing themselves to be the principal members of the senate. These welcome deputies announced the recent and momentous secret of the emperor's decease; reported, or perhaps invented, his dying choice of the best beloved and most deserving of his nephews; and conjured Justin to prevent the disorders of the multitude, if they should perceive, with the return of light, that they were left without a master. After composing his countenance to surprise, sorrow, and decent modesty, Justin, by the advice of his wife Sophia, submitted to the authority of the senate. He was conducted with speed and silence to the palace; the guards saluted their new sovereign; and the martial and religious rites of his coronation were diligently accomplished. By the hands of the proper officers he was invested with the Imperial garments, the red buskins, white tunic, and purple robe. A fortunate soldier, whom he instantly promoted to the rank of tribune, encircled his neck with a military collar; four robust youths exalted him on a shield; he stood firm and erect to receive the adoration of his

[1] See the family of Justin and Justinian in the Familiæ Byzantinæ of Du cange, p. 89-101. The devout civilians, Ludewig (in Vit. Justinian. p. 131) and Heineccius (Hist. Juris Roman. p. 374) have since illustrated the genealogy of their favourite prince.

[2] In the story of Justin's elevation I have translated into simple and concise prose the eight hundred verses of the two first books of Corippus, De Laudibus Justini, Appendix Hist. Byzant. p. 401-416, Rome, 1777 [p. 166-187, ed. Bonn].

subjects; and their choice was sanctified by the benediction of the patri-arch, who imposed the diadem on the head of an orthodox prince. The hippodrome was already filled with innumerable multitudes; and no sooner did the emperor appear on his throne than the voices of the blue and the green factions were confounded in the same loyal acclama-tions. In the speeches which Justin addressed to the senate and people he promised to correct the abuses which had disgraced the age of his predecessor, displayed the maxims of a just and beneficent government, and declared that, on the approaching calends of January,[3] he would revive in his own person the name and liberality of a Roman consul. The immediate discharge of his uncle's debts exhibited a solid pledge of his faith and generosity: a train of porters, laden with bags of gold, advanced into the midst of the hippodrome, and the hopeless creditors of Justinian accepted this equitable payment as a voluntary gift. Before the end of three years his example was imitated and surpassed by the empress Sophia, who delivered many indigent citizens from the weight of debt and usury: an act of benevolence the best entitled to gratitude, since it relieves the most intolerable distress; but in which the bounty of a prince is the most liable to be abused by the claims of prodigality and fraud.[4]

On the seventh day of his reign Justin gave audience to the ambassa-dors of the Avars, and the scene was decorated to impress the barbarians with astonishment, veneration, and terror. From the palace gate, the spacious courts and long porticoes were lined with the lofty crests and gilt bucklers of the guards, who presented their spears and axes with more confidence than they would have shown in a field of battle. The officers who exercised the power, or attended the person, of the prince, were attired in their richest habits, and arranged according to the mili-tary and civil order of the hierarchy. When the veil of the sanctuary was withdrawn, the ambassadors beheld the emperor of the East on his throne, beneath a canopy, or dome, which was supported by four columns, and crowned with a winged figure of Victory. In the first emo-tions of surprise, they submitted to the servile adoration of the Byzan-tine court; but, as soon as they rose from the ground, Targetius, the chief of the embassy, expressed the freedom and pride of a barbarian. He extolled, by the tongue of his interpreter, the greatness of the chagan, by whose clemency the kingdoms of the South were permitted to exist, whose victorious subjects had traversed the frozen rivers of Scythia, and who now covered the banks of the Danube with innumerable tents. The late emperor had cultivated, with annual and costly gifts, the friend-ship of a grateful monarch, and the enemies of Rome had respected

[3] It is surprising how Pagi (Critica, in Annal. Baron. tom. ii. p. 639) could be tempted by any chronicles to contradict the plain and decisive text of Corippus (vicina dona, l. ii. 354, vicina dies, l. iv. 1), and to postpone, till A.D. 567, the consulship of Justin.

[4] Theophan. Chronograph. p. 205 [tom. i. p. 374, ed. Bonn]. Whenever Cedrenus or Zonaras are mere transcribers, it is superfluous to allege their testimony.

the allies of the Avars. The same prudence would instruct the nephew of Justinian to imitate the liberality of his uncle, and to purchase the blessings of peace from an invincible people, who delighted and excelled in the exercise of war. The reply of the emperor was delivered in the same strain of haughty defiance, and he derived his confidence from the God of the Christians, the ancient glory of Rome, and the recent triumphs of Justinian. " The empire," said he, " abounds with men and horses, and arms sufficient to defend our frontiers and to chastise the barbarians. You offer aid, you threaten hostilities: we despise your enmity and your aid. The conquerors of the Avars solicit our alliance; shall we dread their fugitives and exiles? [5] The bounty of our uncle was granted to your misery, to your humble prayers. From us you shall receive a more important obligation, the knowledge of your own weakness. Retire from our presence; the lives of ambassadors are safe; and, if you return to implore our pardon, perhaps you will taste of our benevolence." [6] On the report of his ambassadors, the chagan was awed by the apparent firmness of a Roman emperor of whose character and resources he was ignorant. Instead of executing his threats against the Eastern empire, he marched into the poor and savage countries of Germany, which were subject to the dominion of the Franks. After two doubtful battles he consented to retire, and the Austrasian king relieved the distress of his camp with an immediate supply of corn and cattle.[7] Such repeated disappointments had chilled the spirit of the Avars, and their power would have dissolved away in the Sarmatian desert, if the alliance of Alboin, king of the Lombards, had not given a new object to their arms, and a lasting settlement to their wearied fortunes.

While Alboin served under his father's standard, he encountered in battle, and transpierced with his lance, the rival prince of the Gepidæ. The Lombards, who applauded such early prowess, requested his father, with unanimous acclamations, that the heroic youth, who had shared the dangers of the field, might be admitted to the feast of victory.

[5] Corippus, l. iii. 390. The unquestionable sense relates to the Turks, the conquerors of the Avars; but the word *scultor* has no apparent meaning, and the sole MS. of Corippus, from whence the first edition (1581, apud Plantin) was printed, is no longer visible. The last editor, Foggini of Rome, has inserted the conjectural emendation of *soldan:* but the proofs of Ducange (Joinville, Dissert. xvi. p. 238-240), for the early use of this title among the Turks and Persians, are weak or ambiguous. And I must incline to the authority of D'Herbelot (Bibliothèque Orient. p. 825), who ascribes the word to the Arabic and Chaldæan tongues, and the date to the beginning of the eleventh century, when it was bestowed by the khalif of Bagdad on Mahmud, prince of Gazna, and conqueror of India.

[6] For these characteristic speeches, compare the verse of Corippus (l. iii. 266-401) with the prose of Menander (Excerpt. Legation. p. 102, 103 [ed Par.; p. 287 *sq.*, ed. Bonn]). Their diversity proves that they did not copy each other; their resemblance, that they drew from a common original.

[7] For the Austrasian war, see Menander (Excerpt. Legat. p. 110 [c. 11, p. 303, ed. Bonn]), Gregory of Tours (Hist. Franc. l. iv. c. 29), and Paul the Deacon (de Gest. Langobard. l. ii. c. 10).

" You are not unmindful," replied the inflexible Audoin, " of the wise
customs of our ancestors. Whatever may be his merit, a prince is
incapable of sitting at table with his father till he has received his arms
from a foreign and royal hand." Alboin bowed with reverence to the
institutions of his country, selected forty companions, and boldly visited the court of Turisund, king of the Gepidæ, who embraced and
entertained, according to the laws of hospitality, the murderer of his
son. At the banquet, whilst Alboin occupied the seat of the youth
whom he had slain, a tender remembrance arose in the mind of Turisund. " How dear is that place—how hateful is that person! " were
the words that escaped, with a sigh, from the indignant father. His
grief exasperated the national resentment of the Gepidæ; and Cunimund, his surviving son, was provoked by wine, or fraternal affection, to
the desire of vengeance. " The Lombards," said the rude barbarian,
" resemble, in figure and in smell, the mares of our Sarmatian plains."
And this insult was a coarse allusion to the white bands which enveloped
their legs. " Add another resemblance," replied an audacious Lombard; " you have felt how strongly they kick. Visit the plain of Asfeld,
and seek for the bones of thy brother: they are mingled with those of
the vilest animals." The Gepidæ, a nation of warriors, started from
their seats, and the fearless Alboin, with his forty companions, laid
their hands on their swords. The tumult was appeased by the venerable
interposition of Turisund. He saved his own honour, and the life of
his guest; and, after the solemn rites of investiture, dismissed the
stranger in the bloody arms of his son, the gift of a weeping parent.
Alboin returned in triumph; and the Lombards, who celebrated his
matchless intrepidity, were compelled to praise the virtues of an enemy.[8]
In this extraordinary visit he had probably seen the daughter of Cunimund, who soon after ascended the throne of the Gepidæ. Her name
was Rosamond, an appellation expressive of female beauty, and which
our own history or romance has consecrated to amorous tales. The king
of the Lombards (the father of Alboin no longer lived) was contracted
to the grand-daughter of Clovis; but the restraints of faith and policy
soon yielded to the hope of possessing the fair Rosamond, and of insulting her family and nation. The arts of persuasion were tried without
success; and the impatient lover, by force and stratagem, obtained the
object of his desires. War was the consequence which he foresaw and
solicited; but the Lombards could not long withstand the furious assault
of the Gepidæ, who were sustained by a Roman army. And, as the
offer of marriage was rejected with contempt, Alboin was compelled
to relinquish his prey, and to partake of the disgrace which he had
inflicted on the house of Cunimund.[9]

[8] Paul Warnefrid, the deacon of Friuli, de Gest. Langobard. l. i. c. 23, 24.
His pictures of national manners, though rudely sketched, are more lively and
faithful than those of Bede or Gregory of Tours.
[9] The story is told by an impostor (Theophylact. Simocat. l. vi. c. 10 [p. 261,
ed. Bonn]) ; but he had art enough to build his fictions on public and notorious
facts.

When a public quarrel is envenomed by private injuries, a blow that is not mortal or decisive can be productive only of a short truce, which allows the unsuccessful combatant to sharpen his arms for a new encounter. The strength of Alboin had been found unequal to the gratification of his love, ambition, and revenge: he condescended to implore the formidable aid of the chagan; and the arguments that he employed are expressive of the art and policy of the barbarians. In the attack of the Gepidæ he had been prompted by the just desire of extirpating a people whom their alliance with the Roman empire had rendered the common enemies of the nations, and the personal adversaries of the chagan. If the forces of the Avars and the Lombards should unite in this glorious quarrel, the victory was secure and the reward inestimable: the Danube, the Hebrus, Italy, and Constantinople would be exposed, without a barrier, to their invincible arms. But, if they hesitated or delayed to prevent the malice of the Romans, the same spirit which had insulted would pursue the Avars to the extremity of the earth. These specious reasons were heard by the chagan with coldness and disdain: he detained the Lombard ambassadors in his camp, protracted the negotiation, and by turns alleged his want of inclination, or his want of ability, to undertake this important enterprise. At length he signified the ultimate price of his alliance, that the Lombards should immediately present him with the tithe of their cattle; that the spoils and captives should be equally divided; but that the lands of the Gepidæ should become the sole patrimony of the Avars. Such hard conditions were eagerly accepted by the passions of Alboin; and, as the Romans were dissatisfied with the ingratitude and perfidy of the Gepidæ, Justin abandoned that incorrigible people to their fate, and remained the tranquil spectator of this unequal conflict. The despair of Cunimund was active and dangerous. He was informed that the Avars had entered his confines; but, on the strong assurance that after the defeat of the Lombards these foreign invaders would easily be repelled, he rushed forwards to encounter the implacable enemy of his name and family. But the courage of the Gepidæ could secure them no more than an honourable death. The bravest of the nation fell in the field of battle: the king of the Lombards contemplated with delight the head of Cunimund, and his skull was fashioned into a cup to satiate the hatred of the conqueror, or perhaps to comply with the savage custom of his country.[10] After this victory no farther obstacle could impede the progress of the confederates, and they faithfully executed the terms of their agreement.[11] The fair countries of Wallachia, Moldavia,

[10] It appears from Strabo [l. vii.], Pliny [l. vii. c. 11] and Ammianus Marcellinus [l. xxvii.], that the same practice was common among the Scythian tribes (Muratori, Scriptores Rer. Italic. tom. i. p. 424). The *scalps* of North America are likewise trophies of valour. The skull of Cunimund was preserved above two hundred years among the Lombards; and Paul himself was one of the guests to whom Duke Ratchis exhibited this cup on a high festival (l. ii. c. 28).

[11] Paul, l. i. c. 27. Menander, in Excerpt. Legat. p. 110, 111 [p. 303, 304, ed. Bonn].

Transylvania, and the parts of Hungary beyond the Danube, were occupied without resistance by a new colony of Scythians; and the Dacian empire of the chagans subsisted with splendour above two hundred and thirty years. The nation of the Gepidæ was dissolved; but, in the distribution of the captives, the slaves of the Avars were less fortunate than the companions of the Lombards, whose generosity adopted a valiant foe, and whose freedom was incompatible with cool and deliberate tyranny. One moiety of the spoil introduced into the camp of Alboin more wealth than a barbarian could readily compute. The fair Rosamond was persuaded or compelled to acknowledge the rights of her victorious lover; and the daughter of Cunimund appeared to forgive those crimes which might be imputed to her own irresistible charms.

The destruction of a mighty kingdom established the fame of Alboin. In the days of Charlemagne the Bavarians, the Saxons, and the other tribes of the Teutonic language, still repeated the songs which described the heroic virtues, the valour, liberality, and fortune of the king of the Lombards.[12] But his ambition was yet unsatisfied; and the conqueror of the Gepidæ turned his eyes from the Danube to the richer banks of the Po and the Tiber. Fifteen years had not elapsed since his subjects, the confederates of Narses, had visited the pleasant climate of Italy; the mountains, the rivers, the highways, were familiar to their memory; the report of their success, perhaps the view of their spoils, had kindled in the rising generation the flame of emulation and enterprise. Their hopes were encouraged by the spirit and eloquence of Alboin; and it is affirmed that he spoke to their senses by producing at the royal feast the fairest and most exquisite fruits that grew spontaneously in the garden of the world. No sooner had he erected his standard than the native strength of the Lombards was multiplied by the adventurous youth of Germany and Scythia. The robust peasantry of Noricum and Pannonia had resumed the manners of barbarians; and the names of the Gepidæ, Bulgarians, Sarmatians, and Bavarians may be distinctly traced in the provinces of Italy.[13] Of the Saxons, the old allies of the Lombards, twenty thousand warriors, with their wives and children, accepted the invitation of Alboin. Their bravery contributed to his success; but the accession or the absence of their numbers was not sensibly felt in the magnitude of his host. Every mode of

[12] Ut hactenus etiam tam apud Bajoariorum gentem, quam et Saxonum, sed et alios ejusdem linguæ homines . . . in eorum carminibus celebretur. Paul. l. i. c. 27. He died A.D. 799 (Muratori, in Præfat. tom. i. p. 397). These German songs, some of which might be as old as Tacitus (de Moribus Germ. c. 2), were compiled and transcribed by Charlemagne. Barbara et antiquissima carmina, quibus veterum regum actus et bella canebantur scripsit memoriæque mandavit (Eginard, in Vit. Carol. Magn. c. 29, p. 130, 131). The poems, which Goldast commends (Animadvers. ad Eginard. p. 207), appear to be recent and contemptible romances.

[13] The other nations are rehearsed by Paul (l. ii. c. 6, 26). Muratori (Antichità Italiane, tom. i. dissert. i. p. 4) has discovered the village of the Bavarians, three miles from Modena.

religion was freely practised by its respective votaries. The king of the Lombards had been educated in the Arian heresy, but the catholics in their public worship were allowed to pray for his conversion; while the more stubborn barbarians sacrificed a she-goat, or perhaps a captive, to the gods of their fathers.[14] The Lombards and their confederates were united by their common attachment to a chief who excelled in all the virtues and vices of a savage hero; and the vigilance of Alboin provided an ample magazine of offensive and defensive arms for the use of the expedition. The portable wealth of the Lombards attended the march; their lands they cheerfully relinquished to the Avars, on the solemn promise, which was made and accepted without a smile, that if they failed in the conquest of Italy these voluntary exiles should be reinstated in their former possessions.

They might have failed if Narses had been the antagonist of the Lombards; and the veteran warriors, the associates of his Gothic victory, would have encountered with reluctance an enemy whom they dreaded and esteemed. But the weakness of the Byzantine court was subservient to the barbarian cause; and it was for the ruin of Italy that the emperor once listened to the complaints of his subjects. The virtues of Narses were stained with avarice; and in his provincial reign of fifteen years he accumulated a treasure of gold and silver which surpassed the modesty of a private fortune. His government was oppressive or unpopular, and the general discontent was expressed with freedom by the deputies of Rome. Before the throne of Justin they boldly declared that their Gothic servitude had been more tolerable than the despotism of a Greek eunuch; and that, unless their tyrant were instantly removed, they would consult their own happiness in the choice of a master. The apprehension of a revolt was urged by the voice of envy and detraction, which had so recently triumphed over the merit of Belisarius. A new exarch, Longinus, was appointed to supersede the conqueror of Italy; and the base motives of his recall were revealed in the insulting mandate of the empress Sophia, " that he should leave to *men* the exercise of arms, and return to his proper station among the maidens of the palace, where a distaff should be again placed in the hand of the eunuch." " I will spin her such a thread as she shall not easily unravel! " is said to have been the reply which indignation and conscious virtue extorted from the hero. Instead of attending, a slave and a victim, at the gate of the Byzantine palace, he retired to Naples, from whence (if any credit is due to the belief of the times) Narses invited the Lombards to chastise the ingratitude of the prince and people.[15] But the passions of the people are furious and change-

[14] Gregory the Roman (Dialog. l. iii. c. 27, 28, apud Baron. Annal. Eccles. A.D. 579, No. 10) supposes that they likewise adored this she-goat. I know but of one religion in which the god and the victim are the same.

[15] The charge of the deacon against Narses (l. ii. c. 5) may be groundless; but the weak apology of the cardinal (Baron. Annal. Eccles. A.D. 567, No. 8-12) is rejected by the best critics—Pagi (tom. ii. p. 639, 640), Muratori (Annali d'Italia, tom. v. p. 160-163), and the last editors, Horatius Blancus (Script.

able, and the Romans soon recollected the merits, or dreaded the resentment, of their victorious general. By the mediation of the pope, who undertook a special pilgrimage to Naples, their repentance was accepted; and Narses, assuming a milder aspect and a more dutiful language, consented to fix his residence in the Capitol. His death,[16] though in the extreme period of old age, was unseasonable and premature, since *his* genius alone could have repaired the last and fatal error of his life. The reality, or the suspicion, of a conspiracy disarmed and disunited the Italians. The soldiers resented the disgrace, and bewailed the loss, of their general. They were ignorant of their new exarch; and Longinus was himself ignorant of the state of the army and the province. In the preceding years Italy had been desolated by pestilence and famine, and a disaffected people ascribed the calamities of nature to the guilt or folly of their rulers.[17]

Whatever might be the grounds of his security, Alboin neither expected nor encountered a Roman army in the field. He ascended the Julian Alps, and looked down with contempt and desire on the fruitful plains to which his victory communicated the perpetual appellation of LOMBARDY. A faithful chieftain and a select band were stationed at Forum Julii, the modern Friuli, to guard the passes of the mountains. The Lombards respected the strength of Pavia, and listened to the prayers of the Trevisans: their slow and heavy multitudes proceeded to occupy the palace and city of Verona; and Milan, now rising from her ashes, was invested by the powers of Alboin five months after his departure from Pannonia. Terror preceded his march: he found everywhere, or he left, a dreary solitude; and the pusillanimous Italians presumed, without a trial, that the stranger was invincible. Escaping to lakes, or rocks, or morasses, the affrighted crowds concealed some fragments of their wealth, and delayed the moment of their servitude. Paulinus, the patriarch of Aquileia, removed his treasures, sacred and profane, to the isle of Grado,[18] and his successors were adopted by the infant republic of Venice, which was continually enriched by the public

---

Rerum Italic. tom. i. p. 427, 428) and Philip Argelatus (Sigon. Opera, tom. ii. p. 11, 12). The Narses who assisted at the coronation of Justin (Corippus, 1 iii. 221) is clearly understood to be a different person.

[16] The death of Narses is mentioned by Paul, l. ii. c. 11. Anastas. in Vit. Johan. iii. p. 43. Agnellus, Liber Pontifical. Raven. [c. 3 *fin*] in Script. Rer. Italicarum, tom. ii. part i. p. 114, 124. Yet I cannot believe with Agnellus that Narses was ninety-five years of age. Is it probable that all his exploits were performed at fourscore?

[17] The designs of Narses and of the Lombards for the invasion of Italy are exposed in the last chapter of the first book, and the seven first chapters of the second book, of Paul the Deacon.

[18] Which from this translation was called New Aquileia (Chron. Venet. p. 3). The patriarch of Grado soon became the first citizen of the republic (p. 9, etc.), but his seat was not removed to Venice till the year 1450. He is now decorated with titles and honours; but the genius of the church has bowed to that of the state, and the government of a catholic city is strictly presbyterian. Thomassin, Discipline de l'Eglise, tom. i. p. 156, 157, 161-165. Amelot de la Houssaye, Gouvernement de Venise, tom. i. p. 256-261.

calamities. Honoratus, who filled the chair of St. Ambrose, had credulously accepted the faithless offers of a capitulation; and the archbishop, with the clergy and nobles of Milan, were driven by the perfidy
of Alboin to seek a refuge in the less accessible ramparts of Genoa.
Along the maritime coast the courage of the inhabitants was supported
by the facility of supply, the hopes of relief, and the power of escape;
but, from the Trentine hills to the gates of Ravenna and Rome, the
inland regions of Italy became, without a battle or a siege, the lasting patrimony of the Lombards. The submission of the people invited
the barbarian to assume the character of a lawful sovereign, and the
helpless exarch was confined to the office of announcing to the emperor
Justin the rapid and irretrievable loss of his provinces and cities.[19]
One city, which had been diligently fortified by the Goths, resisted the
arms of a new invader; and, while Italy was subdued by the flying
detachments of the Lombards, the royal camp was fixed above three
years before the western gate of Ticinum, or Pavia. The same courage
which obtains the esteem of a civilised enemy provokes the fury of a
savage; and the impatient besieger had bound himself by a tremendous
oath that age, and sex, and dignity should be confounded in a general
massacre. The aid of famine at length enabled him to execute his
bloody vow; but as Alboin entered the gate his horse stumbled, fell, and
could not be raised from the ground. One of his attendants was
prompted by compassion, or piety, to interpret this miraculous sign of
the wrath of Heaven: the conqueror paused and relented; he sheathed
his sword, and, peacefully reposing himself in the palace of Theodoric,
proclaimed to the trembling multitude that they should live and obey.
Delighted with the situation of a city which was endeared to his pride
by the difficulty of the purchase, the prince of the Lombards disdained
the ancient glories of Milan; and Pavia during some ages was respected
as the capital of the kingdom of Italy.[20]

The reign of the founder was splendid and transient; and, before
he could regulate his new conquests, Alboin fell a sacrifice to domestic
treason and female revenge. In a palace near Verona, which had not
been erected for the barbarians, he feasted the companions of his arms;
intoxication was the reward of valour, and the king himself was tempted
by appetite or vanity to exceed the ordinary measure of his intemperance. After draining many capacious bowls of Rhætian or Falernian
wine he called for the skull of Cunimund, the noblest and most precious
ornament of his sideboard. The cup of victory was accepted with horrid applause by the circle of the Lombard chiefs. " Fill it again with

[19] Paul has given a description of Italy, as it was then divided, into eighteen
regions (l. ii. c. 14-24). The Dissertatio Chorographica de Italia Medii Ævi,
by Father Beretti, a Benedictine monk, and regius professor at Pavia, has been
usefully consulted.
[20] For the conquest of Italy, see the original materials of Paul (l. ii. c. 7-10,
12, 14, 25, 26, 27), the eloquent narrative of Sigonius (tom. ii. de Regno Italiæ,
l. i. p. 13-19), and the correct and critical review of Muratori (Annali d'Italia,
tom. v. p. 164-180).

wine!" exclaimed the inhuman conqueror, " fill it to the brim! carry this goblet to the queen, and request in my name that she would rejoice with her father." In an agony of grief and rage, Rosamond had strength to utter, " Let the will of my lord be obeyed!" and, touching it with her lips, pronounced a silent imprecation that the insult should be washed away in the blood of Alboin. Some indulgence might be due to the resentment of a daughter, if she had not already violated the duties of a wife. Implacable in her enmity, or inconstant in her love, the queen of Italy had stooped from the throne to the arms of a subject, and Helmichis, the king's armour-bearer, was the secret minister of her pleasure and revenge. Against the proposal of the murder he could no longer urge the scruples of fidelity or gratitude; but Helmichis trembled when he revolved the danger as well as the guilt, when he recollected the matchless strength and intrepidity of a warrior whom he had so often attended in the field of battle. He pressed, and obtained, that one of the bravest champions of the Lombards should be associated to the enterprise; but no more than a promise of secrecy could be drawn from the gallant Peredeus, and the mode of seduction employed by Rosamond betrays her shameless insensibility both to honour and love. She supplied the place of one of her female attendants who was beloved by Peredeus, and contrived some excuse for darkness and silence till she could inform her companion that he had enjoyed the queen of the Lombards, and that his own death or the death of Alboin must be the consequence of such treasonable adultery. In this alternative he chose rather to be the accomplice than the victim of Rosamond,[21] whose undaunted spirit was incapable of fear or remorse. She expected and soon found a favourable moment, when the king, oppressed with wine, had retired from the table to his afternoon slumbers. His faithless spouse was anxious for his health and repose; the gates of the palace were shut, the arms removed, the attendants dismissed, and Rosamond, after lulling him to rest by her tender caresses, unbolted the chamber-door and urged the reluctant conspirators to the instant execution of the deed. On the first alarm the warrior started from his couch: his sword, which he attempted to draw, had been fastened to the scabbard by the hand of Rosamond; and a small stool, his only weapon, could not long protect him from the spears of the assassins. The daughter of Cunimund smiled in his fall: his body was buried under the staircase of the palace; and the grateful posterity of the Lombards revered the tomb and the memory of their victorious leader.

The ambitious Rosamond aspired to reign in the name of her lover; the city and palace of Verona were awed by her power; and a faithful band of her native Gepidæ was prepared to applaud the revenge and to

[21] The classical reader will recollect the wife and murder of Candaules, so agreeably told in the first book of Herodotus [c. 8, *sqq.*]. The choice of Gyges, αἱρέεται αὐτὸς περιεῖναι, may serve as the excuse of Precedeus; and this soft insinuation of an odious idea has been imitated by the best writers of antiquity (Grævius, ad Ciceron. Orat. pro Milone, c. 10).

second the wishes of their sovereign. But the Lombard chiefs, who fled in the first moments of consternation and disorder, had resumed their courage and collected their powers; and the nation, instead of submitting to her reign, demanded with unanimous cries that justice should be executed on the guilty spouse and the murderers of their king. She sought a refuge among the enemies of her country, and a criminal who deserved the abhorrence of mankind was protected by the selfish policy of the exarch. With her daughter, the heiress of the Lombard throne, her two lovers, her trusty Gepidæ, and the spoils of the palace of Verona, Rosamond descended the Adige and the Po, and was transported by a Greek vessel to the safe harbour of Ravenna. Longinus beheld with delight the charms and the treasures of the widow of Alboin: her situation and her past conduct might justify the most licentious proposals, and she readily listened to the passion of a minister who, even in the decline of the empire, was respected as the equal of kings. The death of a jealous lover was an easy and grateful sacrifice, and as Helmichis issued from the bath he received the deadly potion from the hand of his mistress. The taste of the liquor, its speedy operation, and his experience of the character of Rosamond, convinced him that he was poisoned; he pointed his dagger to her breast, compelled her to drain the remainder of the cup, and expired in a few minutes with the consolation that she could not survive to enjoy the fruits of her wickedness. The daughter of Alboin and Rosamond, with the richest spoils of the Lombards, was embarked for Constantinople: the surprising strength of Peredeus amused and terrified the Imperial court; his blindness and revenge exhibited an imperfect copy of the adventures of Samson. By the free suffrage of the nation in the assembly of Pavia, Clepho, one of their noblest chiefs, was elected as the successor of Alboin. Before the end of eighteen months the throne was polluted by a second murder: Clepho was stabbed by the hand of a domestic; the regal office was suspended above ten years during the minority of his son Autharis, and Italy was divided and oppressed by a ducal aristocracy of thirty tyrants.[22]

When the nephew of Justinian ascended the throne, he proclaimed a new era of happiness and glory. The annals of the second Justin [23] are marked with disgrace abroad and misery at home. In the West the Roman empire was afflicted by the loss of Italy, the desolation of Africa, and the conquests of the Persians. Injustice prevailed both in the capital and the provinces: the rich trembled for their property, the poor for their safety; the ordinary magistrates were ignorant or venal, the occasional remedies appear to have been arbitrary and violent, and

---

[22] See the history of Paul, l. ii. c. 28-32. I have borrowed some interesting circumstances from the Liber Pontificalis of Agnellus [c. 4] in Script. Rer. Ital. tom ii. p. 124. Of all chronological guides Muratori is the safest.

[23] The original authors for the reign of Justin the younger are Evagrius, Hist. Eccles. l. v. c. 1-12; Theophanes, in Chronograph. p. 204-210 [tom. i. p. 373, *sqq.*, ed. Bonn]; Zonaras, tom. ii. l. xiv. [c. 10] p. 70-72; Cedrenus, in Compend. p. 388-392 [tom. i. p. 680-688, ed. Bonn].

the complaints of the people could no longer be silenced by the splendid names of a legislator and a conqueror. The opinion which imputes to the prince all the calamities of his times may be countenanced by the historian as a serious truth or a salutary prejudice. Yet a candid suspicion will arise that the sentiments of Justin were pure and benevolent, and that he might have filled his station without reproach if the faculties of his mind had not been impaired by disease, which deprived the emperor of the use of his feet and confined him to the palace, a stranger to the complaints of the people and the vices of the government. The tardy knowledge of his own impotence determined him to lay down the weight of the diadem, and in the choice of a worthy substitute he showed some symptoms of a discerning and even magnanimous spirit. The only son of Justin and Sophia died in his infancy; their daughter Arabia was the wife of Baduarius,[23a] superintendent of the palace, and afterwards commander of the Italian armies, who vainly aspired to confirm the rights of marriage by those of adoption. While the empire appeared an object of desire, Justin was accustomed to behold with jealousy and hatred his brothers and cousins, the rivals of his hopes; nor could he depend on the gratitude of those who would accept the purple as a restitution rather than a gift. Of these competitors one had been removed by exile, and afterwards by death; and the emperor himself had inflicted such cruel insults on another, that he must either dread his resentment or despise his patience. This domestic animosity was refined into a generous resolution of seeking a successor, not in his family, but in the republic; and the artful Sophia recommended Tiberius,[24] his faithful captain of the guards, whose virtues and fortune the emperor might cherish as the fruit of his judicious choice. The ceremony of his elevation to the rank of Cæsar or Augustus was performed in the portico of the palace in the presence of the patriarch and the senate. Justin collected the remaining strength of his mind and body; but the popular belief that his speech was inspired by the Deity betrays a very humble opinion both of the man and of the times.[25] " You behold," said the emperor, " the ensigns of

[23a] Dispositor que novus sacræ Baduarius aulæ.
  Successor soceri mox factus Cura-palati.—Corippus.
Baduarius is enumerated among the descendants and allies of the house of Justinian. A family of noble Venetians (Casa *Badoero*) built churches and gave dukes to the republic as early as the ninth century; and, if their descent be admitted, no kings in Europe can produce a pedigree so ancient and illustrious. Ducange, Fam. Byzantin. p. 99. Amelot de la Houssaye, Gouvernement de Venise, tom. ii. p. 555.

[24] The praise bestowed on princes before their elevation is the purest and most weighty. Corippus has celebrated Tiberius at the time of the accession of Justin (l. i. 212-222). Yet even a captain of the guards might attract the flattery of an African exile.

[25] Evagrius (l. v. c. 13) has added the reproach to his ministers. He applies this speech to the ceremony when Tiberius was invested with the rank of Cæsar. The loose expression, rather than the positive error, of Theophanes, etc., has delayed it to his *Augustan* investiture, immediately before the death of Justin.

supreme power. You are about to receive them, not from my hand, but from the hand of God. Honour them, and from them you will derive honour. Respect the empress your mother; you are now her son; before, you were her servant. Delight not in blood; abstain from revenge; avoid those actions by which I have incurred the public hatred; and consult the experience, rather than the example, of your predecessor. As a man, I have sinned; as a sinner, even in this life, I have been severely punished: but these servants (and he pointed to his ministers), who have abused my confidence and inflamed my passions, will appear with me before the tribunal of Christ. I have been dazzled by the splendour of the diadem: be thou wise and modest; remember what you have been, remember what you are. You see around us your slaves and your children; with the authority, assume the tenderness of a parent. Love your people like yourself; cultivate the affections, maintain the discipline, of the army; protect the fortunes of the rich, relieve the necessities of the poor." [26] The assembly, in silence and in tears, applauded the counsels and sympathised with the repentance of their prince; the patriarch rehearsed the prayers of the church; Tiberius received the diadem on his knees; and Justin, who in his abdication appeared most worthy to reign, addressed the new monarch in the following words:—"If you consent, I live; if you command, I die: may the God of heaven and earth infuse into your heart whatever I have neglected or forgotten." The four last years of the emperor Justin were passed in tranquil obscurity: his conscience was no longer tormented by the remembrance of those duties which he was incapable of discharging, and his choice was justified by the filial reverence and gratitude of Tiberius.

Among the virtues of Tiberius,[27] his beauty (he was one of the tallest and most comely of the Romans) might introduce him to the favour of Sophia; and the widow of Justin was persuaded that she should preserve her station and influence under the reign of a second and more youthful husband. But if the ambitious candidate had been tempted to flatter and dissemble, it was no longer in his power to fulfil her expectations or his own promise. The factions of the hippodrome demanded with some impatience the name of their new empress; both the people and Sophia were astonished by the proclamation of Anastasia, the secret though lawful wife of the emperor Tiberius. Whatever could alleviate the disappointment of Sophia, imperial honours, a stately palace, a numerous household, was liberally bestowed by the piety of

[26] Theophylact Simocatta (l. iii. c. 11 [p. 136, ed. Bonn]) declares that he shall give to posterity the speech of Justin as it was pronounced, without attempting to correct the imperfections of language or rhetoric. Perhaps the vain sophist would have been incapable of producing such sentiments.

[27] For the character and reign of Tiberius see Evagrius, l. v. c. 13; Theophylact. l. iii. c. 12, etc.; Theophanes, in Chron. p. 210-213 [ed. Par.; tom. i. p. 382-388, ed. Bonn]; Zonaras, tom. ii. l. xiv. [c. 11] p. 72; Cedrenus, p. 392 [tom. i. p. 688, ed. Bonn]; Paul Warnefrid, de Gestis Langobard. l. iii. c. 11, 12. The deacon of Forum Julii appears to have possessed some curious and authentic facts.

her adopted son; on solemn occasions he attended and consulted the widow of his benefactor, but her ambition disdained the vain semblance of royalty, and the respectful appellation of mother served to exasperate rather than appease the rage of an injured woman. While she accepted and repaid with a courtly smile the fair expressions of regard and confidence, a secret alliance was concluded between the dowager empress and her ancient enemies; and Justinian, the son of Germanus, was employed as the instrument of her revenge. The pride of the reigning house supported with reluctance the dominion of a stranger: the youth was deservedly popular, his name after the death of Justin had been mentioned by a tumultuous faction, and his own submissive offer of his head, with a treasure of sixty thousand pounds, might be interpreted as an evidence of guilt, or at least of fear. Justinian received a free pardon and the command of the eastern army. The Persian monarch fled before his arms, and the acclamations which accompanied his triumph declared him worthy of the purple. His artful patroness had chosen the month of the vintage, while the emperor in a rural solitude was permitted to enjoy the pleasures of a subject. On the first intelligence of her designs he returned to Constantinople, and the conspiracy was suppressed by his presence and firmness. From the pomp and honours which she had abused, Sophia was reduced to a modest allowance; Tiberius dismissed her train, intercepted her correspondence, and committed to a faithful guard the custody of her person. But the services of Justinian were not considered by that excellent prince as an aggravation of his offences: after a mild reproof his treason and ingratitude were forgiven, and it was commonly believed that the emperor entertained some thoughts of contracting a double alliance with the rival of his throne. The voice of an angel (such a fable was propagated) might reveal to the emperor that he should always triumph over his domestic foes, but Tiberius derived a firmer assurance from the innocence and generosity of his own mind.

With the odious name of Tiberius he assumed the more popular appellation of Constantine, and imitated the purer virtues of the Antonines. After recording the vice or folly of so many Roman princes, it is pleasing to repose for a moment on a character conspicuous by the qualities of humanity, justice, temperance, and fortitude; to contemplate a sovereign affable in his palace, pious in the church, impartial on the seat of judgment, and victorious, at least by his generals, in the Persian war. The most glorious trophy of his victory consisted in a multitude of captives, whom Tiberius entertained, redeemed, and dismissed to their native homes with the charitable spirit of a Christian hero. The merit or misfortunes of his own subjects had a dearer claim to his beneficence, and he measured his bounty not so much by their expectations as by his own dignity. This maxim, however dangerous in a trustee of the public wealth, was balanced by a principle of humanity and justice, which taught him to abhor, as of the basest alloy, the gold that was extracted from the tears of the people. For their relief, as often as they had suffered by natural or hostile calamities, he was impatient to remit the arrears of the past or the demands of future taxes: he sternly rejected the servile offerings of his ministers, which were compensated by tenfold oppression; and the wise and equitable laws of Tiberius excited the praise and regret of succeeding times. Constantinople believed that the emperor had discovered a treasure; but his genuine treasure consisted in the practice of liberal economy, and the contempt of all vain and superfluous expense. The Romans of the East would have been happy if the best gift of heaven, a patriot king, had been confirmed as a proper and permanent blessing. But in less than four years after the death of Justin, his worthy successor sunk into a mortal disease, which left him only sufficient time to restore the diadem, according to the tenure by which he held it, to the most deserving of his fellow-citizens. He selected Maurice from the crowd —a judgment more precious than the purple itself: the patriarch and senate were summoned to the bed of the dying prince; he bestowed his daughter and the empire, and his last advice was solemnly delivered by the voice of the quæstor. Tiberius expressed his hope that the virtues of his son and successor would erect the noblest mausoleum to his memory. His memory was embalmed by the public affliction; but the most sincere grief evaporates in the tumult of a new reign, and the eyes and acclamations of mankind were speedily directed to the rising sun.

The emperor Maurice derived his origin from ancient Rome;[28] but his immediate parents were settled at Arabissus in Cappadocia, and their singular felicity preserved them alive to behold and partake the fortune of their *august* son. The youth of Maurice was spent in the profession of arms: Tiberius promoted him to the command of a new and favourite legion of twelve thousand confederates; his valour and conduct were signalised in the Persian war; and he returned to Constantinople to accept, as his just reward, the inheritance of the empire. Maurice ascended the throne at the mature age of forty-three years; and he reigned above twenty years over the East and over himself;[29] expelling from his mind the wild democracy of passions, and establishing (according to the quaint expression of Evagrius) a perfect aristocracy of reason and virtue. Some suspicion will degrade the testimony of a subject, though he protests that his secret praise should never reach the ear of his sovereign,[30] and some failings seem to place the character

[28] It is therefore singular enough that Paul (1. iii. c. 15) should distinguish him as the first Greek emperor—primus ex Græcorum genere in Imperio constitutus [confirmatus]. His immediate predecessors had indeed been born in the Latin provinces of Europe: and a various reading, in Græcorum Imperio, would apply the expression to the empire rather than the prince.

[29] Consult, for the character and reign of Maurice, the fifth and sixth books of Evagrius, particularly l. vi. c. 1; the eight books of his prolix and florid history by Theophylact Sîmocatta; Theophanes, p. 213, etc. [tom. i. p. 288, *sqq.*, ed. Bonn]; Zonaras, tom. ii. l. xiv. [c. 12] p. 73; Cedrenus, p. 394 [tom. i. p. 691, ed. Bonn].

[30] Αὐτοκράτωρ ὄντως γενόμενος τὴν μὲν ὀχλοκρατείαν τῶν παθῶν ἐκ τῆς οἰκείας

of Maurice below the purer merit of his predecessor. His cold and reserved demeanour might be imputed to arrogance; his justice was not
always exempt from cruelty, nor his clemency from weakness; and his
rigid economy too often exposed him to the reproach of avarice. But
the rational wishes of an absolute monarch must tend to the happiness
of his people: Maurice was endowed with sense and courage to promote that happiness, and his administration was directed by the principles and example of Tiberius. The pusillanimity of the Greeks had
introduced so complete a separation between the offices of king and of
general, that a private soldier, who had deserved and obtained the
purple, seldom or never appeared at the head of his armies. Yet the
emperor Maurice enjoyed the glory of restoring the Persian monarch
to his throne; his lieutenants waged a doubtful war against the Avars
of the Danube; and he cast an eye of pity, of ineffectual pity, on the
abject and distressful state of his Italian provinces.

From Italy the emperors were incessantly tormented by tales of
misery and demands of succour, which extorted the humiliating confession of their own weakness. The expiring dignity of Rome was only
marked by the freedom and energy of her complaints: " If you are
incapable," she said, " of delivering us from the sword of the Lombards,
save us at least from the calamity of famine." Tiberius forgave the
reproach, and relieved the distress: a supply of corn was transported
from Egypt to the Tiber; and the Roman people, invoking the name,
not of Camillus, but of St. Peter, repulsed the barbarians from their
walls. But the relief was accidental, the danger was perpetual and
pressing; and the clergy and senate, collecting the remains of their
ancient opulence, a sum of three thousand pounds of gold, despatched
the patrician Pamphronius to lay their gifts and their complaints at
the foot of the Byzantine throne. The attention of the court, and the
forces of the East, were diverted by the Persian war; but the justice
of Tiberius applied the subsidy to the defence of the city; and he dismissed the patrician with his best advice, either to bribe the Lombard
chiefs, or to purchase the aid of the kings of France. Notwithstanding
this weak invention, Italy was still afflicted, Rome was again besieged,
and the suburb of Classe, only three miles from Ravenna, was pillaged
and occupied by the troops of a simple duke of Spoleto. Maurice gave
audience to a second deputation of priests and senators: the duties and
the menaces of religion were forcibly urged in the letters of the Roman
pontiff; and his nuncio, the deacon Gregory, was alike qualified to solicit
the powers either of heaven or of the earth. The emperor adopted, with
stronger effect, the measures of his predecessor: some formidable chiefs
were persuaded to embrace the friendship of the Romans; and one of
them, a mild and faithful barbarian, lived and died in the service of

ἐξενηλάτησε ψυχῆς· ἀριστοκρατείαν δὲ ἐν τοῖς ἑαυτοῦ λογισμοῖς καταστησάμενος [1.
vi. c. 1]. Evagrius composed his history in the twelfth year of Maurice; and
he had been so wisely indiscreet that the emperor knew and rewarded his
favourable opinion (1. vi. c. 24).

the exarch: the passes of the Alps were delivered to the Franks; and the pope encouraged them to violate, without scruple, their oaths and engagements to the misbelievers. Childebert, the great-grandson of Clovis, was persuaded to invade Italy by the payment of fifty thousand pieces; but, as he had viewed with delight some Byzantine coin of the weight of one pound of gold, the king of Austrasia might stipulate that the gift should be rendered more worthy of his acceptance by a proper mixture of these respectable medals. The dukes of the Lombards had provoked by frequent inroads their powerful neighbours of Gaul. As soon as they were apprehensive of a just retaliation, they renounced their feeble and disorderly independence: the advantages of regal government, union, secrecy, and vigour, were unanimously confessed; and Autharis, the son of Clepho, had already attained the strength and reputation of a warrior. Under the standard of their new king, the conquerors of Italy withstood three successive invasions, one of which was led by Childebert himself, the last of the Merovingian race who descended from the Alps. The first expedition was defeated by the jealous animosity of the Franks and Alemanni. In the second they were vanquished in a bloody battle, with more loss and dishonour than they had sustained since the foundation of their monarchy. Impatient for revenge, they returned a third time with accumulated force, and Autharis yielded to the fury of the torrent. The troops and treasures of the Lombards were distributed in the walled towns between the Alps and the Apennine. A nation, less sensible of danger than of fatigue and delay, soon murmured against the folly of their twenty commanders; and the hot vapours of an Italian sun infected with disease those tramontane bodies which had already suffered the vicissitudes of intemperance and famine. The powers that were inadequate to the conquest, were more than sufficient for the desolation, of the country; nor could the trembling natives distinguish between their enemies and their deliverers. If the junction of the Merovingian and Imperial forces had been effected in the neighbourhood of Milan, perhaps they might have subverted the throne of the Lombards; but the Franks expected six days the signal of a flaming village, and the arms of the Greeks were idly employed in the reduction of Modena and Parma, which were torn from them after the retreat of their transalpine allies. The victorious Autharis asserted his claim to the dominion of Italy. At the foot of the Rhætian Alps, he subdued the resistance, and rifled the hidden treasures, of a sequestered island in the lake of Comum. At the extreme point of Calabria, he touched with his spear a column on the sea-shore of Rhegium,[31] proclaiming that ancient landmark to stand the immovable boundary of his kingdom.[32]

[31] The Columna Rhegina, in the narrowest part of the Faro of Messina, one hundred stadia from Rhegium itself, is frequently mentioned in ancient geography. Cluver. Ital. Antiq. tom. ii. p. 1295; Lucas Holsten. Annotat. ad Cluver. p. 301; Wesseling, Itinerar. p. 106.

[32] The Greek historians afford some faint hints of the wars of Italy (Menander, in Excerpt. Legat. p. 124, 126 [p. 327, 331, ed. Bonn]; Theophylact, l. iii,

During a period of two hundred years Italy was unequally divided between the kingdom of the Lombards and the exarchate of Ravenna. The offices and professions which the jealousy of Constantine had separated were united by the indulgence of Justinian; and eighteen successive exarchs were invested, in the decline of the empire, with the full remains of civil, of military, and even of ecclesiastical power. Their immediate jurisdiction, which was afterwards consecrated as the patrimony of St. Peter, extended over the modern Romagna, the marshes or valleys of Ferrara and Commachio,[33] five maritime cities from Rimini to Ancona, and a second inland Pentapolis, between the Hadriatic coast and the hills of the Apennine. Three subordinate provinces, of Rome, of Venice, and of Naples, which were divided by hostile lands from the palace of Ravenna, acknowledged, both in peace and war, the supremacy of the exarch. The duchy of Rome appears to have included the Tuscan, Sabine, and Latin conquests of the first four hundred years of the city, and the limits may be distinctly traced along the coast, from Civita Vecchia to Terracina, and with the course of the Tiber from Ameria and Narni to the port of Ostia. The numerous islands from Grado to Chiozza composed the infant dominion of Venice; but the more accessible towns on the continent were overthrown by the Lombards, who beheld with impotent fury a new capital rising from the waves. The power of the dukes of Naples was circumscribed by the bay and the adjacent isles, by the hostile territory of Capua, and by the Roman colony of Amalphi,[34] whose industrious citizens, by the invention of the mariner's compass, have unveiled the face of the globe. The three islands of Sardinia, Corsica, and Sicily still adhered to the empire; and the acquisition of the farther Calabria removed the landmark of Autharis from the shore of Rhegium to the isthmus of Consentia. In Sardinia the savage mountaineers preserved the liberty and religion of their ancestors; but the husbandmen of Sicily were chained to their rich and cultivated soil. Rome was oppressed by the iron sceptre of the exarchs, and a Greek, perhaps a eunuch, insulted with impunity the ruins of the Capitol. But Naples soon acquired the privilege of electing her own dukes:[35] the independence of Amalphi was the fruit of commerce; and the voluntary attachment of Venice was finally ennobled by an equal alliance with the Eastern empire. On the map of Italy the measure of the exarchate occupies a very inadequate space,

c. 4 [p. 120, ed. Bonn]). The Latins are more satisfactory; and especially Paul Warnefrid (l. iii. c. 13-34), who had read the more ancient histories of Secundus and Gregory of Tours. Baronius produces some letters of the popes, etc.; and the times are measured by the accurate scale of Pagi and Muratori.

[33] The papal advocates, Zacagni and Fontanini, might justly claim the valley or morass of Commachio as a part of the exarchate. But the ambition of including Modena, Reggio, Parma, and Placentia, has darkened a geographical question somewhat doubtful and obscure. Even Muratori, as the servant of the house of Este, is not free from partiality and prejudice.

[34] See Brenckman, Dissert. Ima. de Republicâ Amalphitanâ, p. 1-42, ad calcem Hist. Pandect. Florent.

[35] Gregor. Magn. l. iii. Epist 23, 25, 26, 27.

but it included an ample proportion of wealth, industry, and population. The most faithful and valuable subjects escaped from the barbarian yoke; and the banners of Pavia and Verona, of Milan and Padua, were displayed in their respective quarters by the new inhabitants of Ravenna. The remainder of Italy was possessed by the Lombards; and from Pavia, the royal seat, their kingdom was extended to the east, the north, and the west, as far as the confines of the Avars, the Bavarians, and the Franks of Austrasia and Burgundy. In the language of modern geography, it is now represented by the Terra Firma of the Venetian republic, Tyrol, the Milanese, Piedmont, the coast of Genoa, Mantua, Parma, and Modena, the grand duchy of Tuscany, and a large portion of the ecclesiastical state from Perugia to the Hadriatic. The dukes, and at length the princes, of Beneventum, survived the monarchy, and propagated the name of the Lombards. From Capua to Tarentum, they reigned near five hundred years over the greatest part of the present kingdom of Naples.[36]

In comparing the proportion of the victorious and the vanquished people, the change of language will afford the most probable inference. According to this standard it will appear that the Lombards of Italy, and the Visigoths of Spain, were less numerous than the Franks or Burgundians; and the conquerors of Gaul must yield, in their turn, to the multitude of Saxons and Angles who almost eradicated the idioms of Britain. The modern Italian has been insensibly formed by the mixture of nations: the awkwardness of the barbarians in the nice management of declensions and conjugations reduced them to the use of articles and auxiliary verbs; and many new ideas have been expressed by Teutonic appellations. Yet the principal stock of technical and familiar words is found to be of Latin derivation;[37] and, if we were sufficiently conversant with the obsolete, the rustic, and the municipal dialects of ancient Italy, we should trace the origin of many terms which might, perhaps, be rejected by the classic purity of Rome. A numerous army constitutes but a small nation, and the powers of the Lombards were soon diminished by the retreat of twenty thousand Saxons, who scorned a dependent situation, and returned, after many bold and perilous adventures, to their native country.[38] The camp of Alboin was of formidable extent, but the extent of a camp would be easily circumscribed within the limits of a city; and its martial inhabitants must be thinly scattered over the face of a large country. When Alboin descended from

[36] I have described the state of Italy from the excellent Dissertation of Beretti. Giannone (Istoria Civile, tom. i. p. 374-387) has followed the learned Camillo Pellegrini in the geography of the kingdom of Naples. After the loss of the true Calabria the vanity of the Greeks substituted that name instead of the more ignoble appellation of Bruttium; and the change appears to have taken place before the time of Charlemagne (Eginard, p. 75 [c. 15]).

[37] Maffei (Verona Illustrata, part i. p. 310-321) and Muratori (Antichità Italiane, tom. ii. Dissertazione xxxii. xxxiii. p. 71-365) have asserted the native claims of the Italian idiom: the former with enthusiasm, the latter with discretion: both with learning, ingenuity, and truth.

[38] Paul, de Gest. Langobard. l. iii. c. 5, 6, 7.

the Alps, he invested his nephew, the first duke of Friuli, with the command of the province and the people: but the prudent Gisulf would have declined the dangerous office, unless he had been permitted to choose, among the nobles of the Lombards, a sufficient number of families [39] to form a perpetual colony of soldiers and subjects. In the progress of conquest, the same option could not be granted to the dukes of Brescia or Bergamo, of Pavia or Turin, of Spoleto or Beneventum; but each of these, and each of their colleagues, settled in his appointed district with a band of followers who resorted to his standard in war and his tribunal in peace. Their attachment was free and honourable: resigning the gifts and benefits which they had accepted, they might emigrate with their families into the jurisdiction of another duke; but their absence from the kingdom was punished with death, as a crime of military desertion.[40] The posterity of the first conquerors struck a deeper root into the soil, which, by every motive of interest and honour, they were bound to defend. A Lombard was born the soldier of his king and his duke; and the civil assemblies of the nation displayed the banners, and assumed the appellation, of a regular army. Of this army the pay and the rewards were drawn from the conquered provinces; and the distribution, which was not effected till after the death of Alboin, is disgraced by the foul marks of injustice and rapine. Many of the most wealthy Italians were slain or banished; the remainder were divided among the strangers, and a tributary obligation was imposed (under the name of hospitality) of paying to the Lombards a third part of the fruits of the earth. Within less than seventy years this artificial system was abolished by a more simple and solid tenure.[41] Either the Roman landlord was expelled by his strong and insolent guest, or the annual payment, a third of the produce, was exchanged by a more equitable transaction for an adequate proportion of landed property. Under these foreign masters, the business of agriculture, in the cultivation of corn, vines, and olives, was exercised with degenerate skill and industry by the labour of the slaves and natives. But the occupations of a pastoral life were more pleasing to the idleness of the barbarians. In the rich meadows of Venetia they restored and improved the breed of horses, for which that province had once been illustrious; [42] and the Italians beheld with astonishment a foreign race

[39] Paul, l. ii. c. 9. He calls these families or generations by the Teutonic name of *Faras*, which is likewise used in the Lombard laws. The humble deacon was not insensible of the nobility of his own race. See l. iv. c. 39.

[40] Compare No. 3 and 177 of the Laws of Rotharis.

[41] Paul, l. ii. c. 31, 32, l. iii. c. 16. The Laws of Rotharis, promulgated A.D. 643, do not contain the smallest vestige of this payment of thirds; but they preserve many curious circumstances of the state of Italy and the manners of the Lombards.

[42] The studs of Dionysius of Syracuse, and his frequent victories in the Olympic games, had diffused among the Greeks the fame of the Venetian horses; but the breed was extinct in the time of Strabo (l. v. p. 325 [p. 212, ed. Casaub.]). Gisulf obtained from his uncle generosarum equarum greges. Paul, l. ii. c. 9. The Lombards afterwards introduced caballi silvatici—wild horses. Paul, l. iv. c. 11.

of oxen or buffaloes.[43] The depopulation of Lombardy, and the increase of forests, afforded an ample range for the pleasures of the chase.[44] That marvellous art which teaches the birds of the air to acknowledge the voice, and execute the commands, of their master had been unknown to the ingenuity of the Greeks and Romans.[45] Scandinavia and Scythia produce the boldest and most tractable falcons:[46] they were tamed and educated by the roving inhabitants, always on horseback and in the field. This favourite amusement of our ancestors was introduced by the barbarians into the Roman provinces: and the laws of Italy esteem the sword and the hawk as of equal dignity and importance in the hands of a noble Lombard.[47]

So rapid was the influence of climate and example, that the Lombards of the fourth generation surveyed with curiosity and affright the portraits of their savage forefathers.[48] Their heads were shaven behind, but the shaggy locks hung over their eyes and mouth, and a long beard represented the name and character of the nation. Their dress consisted of loose linen garments, after the fashion of the Anglo-Saxons, which were decorated, in their opinion, with broad stripes of variegated colours. The legs and feet were clothed in long hose and open sandals, and even in the security of peace a trusty sword was constantly girt

[43] Tunc (A.D. 596) primum, *bubali* in Italiam delati Italiæ populis miracula fuere (Paul Warnefrid, l. iv. c. 11). The buffaloes, whose native climate appears to be Africa and India, are unknown to Europe, except in Italy, where they are numerous and useful. The ancients were ignorant of these animals, unless Aristotle (Hist. Anim. l. ii. c. 1, p. 58, Paris, 1783) has described them as the wild oxen of Arachosia. See Buffon, Hist. Naturelle, tom. xi. and Supplement, tom. vi. Hist. Générale des Voyages, tom. i. p. 7, 481, ii. 105, iii. 291, iv. 234, 461, v. 193, vi. 491, viii. 400, x. 666; Pennant's Quadrupedes, p. 24; Dictionnaire d'Hist. Naturelle, par Valmont de Bomare, tom. ii. p. 74. Yet I must not conceal the suspicion that Paul, by a vulgar error, may have applied the name of *bubalus* to the aurochs, or wild bull, of ancient Germany.

[44] Consult the twenty-first Dissertation of Muratori.

[45] Their ignorance is proved by the silence even of those who professedly treat of the arts of hunting and the history of animals. Aristotle (Hist. Animal. l. ix. c. 36, tom. i. p. 586, and the Notes of his last editor, M. Camus, tom. ii. p. 314), Pliny (Hist. Natur. l. x. c. 10), Ælian (de Natur. Animal. l. ii. c. 42), and perhaps Homer (Odyss. xxii. 302-306), describe with astonishment a tacit league and common chase between the hawks and the Thracian fowlers.

[46] Particularly the gerfaut, or gyrfalcon, of the size of a small eagle. See the animated description of M. de Buffon, Hist. Naturelle, tom. xvi. p. 239, etc.

[47] Script. Rerum Italicarum, tom. i. part ii. p. 129. This is the sixteenth law of the emperor Lewis the Pious. His father Charlemagne had falconers in his household as well as huntsmen (Mémoires sur l'Ancienne Chevalerie, par M. de St. Palaye, tom. iii. p. 175). I observe in the Laws of Rotharis a more early mention of the art of hawking (No. 322); and in Gaul, in the fifth century, it is celebrated by Sidonius Apollinaris among the talents of Avitus (202-207).

[48] The epitaph of Droctulf (Paul, l. iii. c. 19) may be applied to many of his countrymen:—

> Terribilis visu facies, sed mente benignus
> Longaque robusto pectore barba fuit.

The portraits of the old Lombards might still be seen in the palace of Monza twelve miles from Milan, which had been founded or restored by queen Theudelinda (l. iv. 22, 23). See Muratori, tom. i. dissertaz. xxiii. p. 300.

to their side. Yet this strange apparel and horrid aspect often concealed a gentle and generous disposition; and as soon as the rage of battle had subsided, the captives and subjects were sometimes surprised by the humanity of the victor. The vices of the Lombards were the effect of passion, of ignorance, of intoxication; their virtues are the more laudable, as they were not affected by the hypocrisy of social manners, nor imposed by the rigid constraint of laws and education. I should not be apprehensive of deviating from my subject, if it were in my power to delineate the private life of the conquerors of Italy; and I shall relate with pleasure the adventurous gallantry of Autharis, which breathes the true spirit of chivalry and romance.[49] After the loss of his promised bride, a Merovingian princess, he sought in marriage the daughter of the king of Bavaria, and Garibald accepted the alliance of the Italian monarch. Impatient of the slow progress of negotiation, the ardent lover escaped from his palace and visited the court of Bavaria in the train of his own embassy. At the public audience the unknown stranger advanced to the throne, and informed Garibald that the ambassador was indeed the minister of state, but that he alone was the friend of Autharis, who had trusted him with the delicate commission of making a faithful report of the charms of his spouse. Theudelinda was summoned to undergo this important examination, and, after a pause of silent rapture, he hailed her as the queen of Italy, and humbly requested that, according to the custom of the nation, she would present a cup of wine to the first of her new subjects. By the command of her father she obeyed: Autharis received the cup in his turn, and, in restoring it to the princess, he secretly touched her hand, and drew his own finger over his face and lips. In the evening Theudelinda imparted to her nurse the indiscreet familiarity of the stranger, and was comforted by the assurance that such boldness could proceed only from the king her husband, who, by his beauty and courage, appeared worthy of her love. The ambassadors were dismissed: no sooner did they reach the confines of Italy than Autharis, raising himself on his horse, darted his battle-axe against a tree with incomparable strength and dexterity: " Such," said he to the astonished Bavarians, " such are the strokes of the king of the Lombards." On the approach of a French army, Garibald and his daughter took refuge in the dominions of their ally, and the marriage was consummated in the palace of Verona. At the end of one year it was dissolved by the death of Autharis; but the virtues of Theudelinda [50] had endeared her to the nation, and she was permitted to bestow, with her hand, the sceptre of the Italian kingdom.

[49] The story of Autharis and Theudelinda is related by Paul, l. iii. c. 29, 34; and any fragment of Bavarian antiquity excites the indefatigable diligence of the Count de Buat, Hist. des Peuples de l'Europe, tom. xi. p. 595-635, tom. xii. p. 1-53.

[50] Giannone (Istoria Civile di Napoli, tom. i. p. 263) has justly censured the impertinence of Boccaccio (Gio. iii. Novel. 2), who, without right, or truth, or pretence, has given the pious queen Theudelinda to the arms of a muleteer.

From this fact, as well as from similar events,[51] it is certain that the Lombards possessed freedom to elect their sovereign, and sense to decline the frequent use of that dangerous privilege. The public revenue arose from the produce of land and the profits of justice. When the independent dukes agreed that Autharis should ascend the throne of his father, they endowed the regal office with a fair moiety of their respective domains. The proudest nobles aspired to the honours of servitude near the person of their prince; he rewarded the fidelity of his vassals by the precarious gift of pensions and *benefices,* and atoned for the injuries of war by the rich foundation of monasteries and churches. In peace a judge, a leader in war, he never usurped the powers of a sole and absolute legislator. The king of Italy convened the national assemblies in the palace, or more probably in the fields, of Pavia; his great council was composed of the persons most eminent by their birth and dignities; but the validity, as well as the execution, of their decrees depended on the approbation of the *faithful* people, the *fortunate* army of the Lombards. About fourscore years after the conquest of Italy their traditional customs were transcribed in Teutonic Latin,[52] and ratified by the consent of the prince and people; some new regulations were introduced, more suitable to their present condition; the example of Rotharis was imitated by the wisest of his successors: and the laws of the Lombards have been esteemed the least imperfect of the barbaric codes.[53] Secure by their courage in the possession of liberty, these rude and hasty legislators were incapable of balancing the powers of the constitution, or of discussing the nice theory of political government. Such crimes as threatened the life of the sovereign or the safety of the state were adjudged worthy of death; but their attention was principally confined to the defence of the person and property of the subject. According to the strange jurisprudence of the times, the guilt of blood might be redeemed by a fine; yet the high price of nine hundred pieces of gold declares a just sense of the value of a simple citizen. Less atrocious injuries, a wound, a fracture, a blow, an opprobious word, were measured with scrupulous and almost ridiculous diligence; and the prudence of the legislator encouraged the ignoble practice of bartering honour and revenge for a pecuniary compensation. The ignorance of the Lombards in the state of Paganism or Christianity gave implicit credit to the malice and mischief of witchcraft: but the judges of the seventeenth century might have been instructed and confounded by the wisdom of Rotharis, who

---

[51] Paul, l. iii. c. 16. The first dissertations of Muratori, and the first volume of Giannone's history, may be consulted for the state of the kingdom of Italy.

[52] The most accurate edition of the Laws of the Lombards is to be found in the Scriptores Rerum Italicarum, tom. i. part ii. p. 1-181, collated from the most ancient MSS., and illustrated by the critical notes of Muratori.

[53] Montesquieu, Esprit des Loix, l. xxviii. c. 1. Les loix des Bourguignons sont assez judicieuses; celles de Rotharis et des autres princes Lombards le sont encore plus.

derides the absurd superstition, and protects the wretched victims of popular or judicial cruelty.[54]   The same spirit of a legislator superior to his age and country may be ascribed to Liutprand, who condemns while he tolerates the impious and inveterate abuse of duels,[55] observing, from his own experience, that the juster cause had often been oppressed by successful violence.   Whatever merit may be discovered in the laws of the Lombards, they are the genuine fruit of the reason of the barbarians, who never admitted the bishops of Italy to a seat in their legislative councils.   But the succession of their kings is marked with virtue and ability; the troubled series of their annals is adorned with fair intervals of peace, order, and domestic happiness; and the Italians enjoyed a milder and more equitable government than any of the other kingdoms which had been founded on the ruins of the Western empire.[56]

Amidst the arms of the Lombards, and under the depotism of the Greeks, we again inquire into the fate of Rome,[57] which had reached, about the close of the sixth century, the lowest period of her depression.   By the removal of the seat of empire and the successive loss of the provinces, the sources of public and private opulence were exhausted: the lofty tree, under whose shade the nations of the earth had reposed, was deprived of its leaves and branches, and the sapless trunk was left to wither on the ground.   The ministers of command and the messengers of victory no longer met on the Appian or Flaminian way, and the hostile approach of the Lombards was often felt and continually feared.   The inhabitants of a potent and peaceful capital, who visit without an anxious thought the garden of the adjacent country, will faintly picture in their fancy the distress of the Romans: they shut or opened their gates with a trembling hand, beheld from the walls the flames of their houses, and heard the lamentations of their brethren, who were coupled together like dogs, and dragged away into distant slavery beyond the sea and the mountains.   Such incessant alarms must annihilate the pleasures and interrupt the labours of a rural life; and the Campagna of Rome was speedily reduced to the state of a dreary wilderness, in which the land is barren, the waters are impure, and the air is infectious.   Curiosity and ambition no longer

[54] See Leges Rotharis, No. 379, p. 47.   Striga is used as the name of a witch. It is of the purest classic origin (Horat. epod. v. 20; Petron. c. 134); and from the words of Petronius (quæ striges comederunt nervos tuos?) it may be inferred that the prejudice was of Italian rather than barbaric extraction.

[55] Quia incerti sumas de judicio Dei, et multos audivimus per pugnam sine justâ causâ suam causam perdere.   Sed propter consuetudinem gentem nostram Langobardorum legem impiam vetare non possumus.   See p. 74, No. 65, of the Laws of Liutprand, promulgated A.D. 724.

[56] Read the history of Paul Warnefrid; particularly 1. iii. c. 16.   Baronius rejects the praise, which appears to contradict the invectives, of pope Gregory the Great; but Muratori (Annali d'Italia, tom. v. p. 217) presumes to insinuate that the saint may have magnified the faults of Arians and enemies.

[57] The passages of the homilies of Gregory which represent the miserable state of the city and country are transcribed in the Annals of Baronius, A.D. 590, No. 16, A.D. 595, No. 2, etc. etc.

attracted the nations to the capital of the world; but, if chance or necessity directed the steps of a wandering stranger, he contemplated with horror the vacancy and solitude of the city, and might be tempted to ask, where is the senate, and where are the people? In a season of excessive rains the Tiber swelled above its banks, and rushed with irresistible violence into the valleys of the seven hills. A pestilential disease arose from the stagnation of the deluge, and so rapid was the contagion that fourscore persons expired in an hour in the midst of a solemn procession which implored the mercy of Heaven.[58] A society in which marriage is encouraged and industry prevails soon repairs the accidental losses of pestilence and war; but, as the far greater part of the Romans was condemned to hopeless indigence and celibacy, the depopulation was constant and visible, and the gloomy enthusiasts might expect the approaching failure of the human race.[59] Yet the number of citizens still exceeded the measure of subsistence: their precarious food was supplied from the harvests of Sicily or Egypt, and the frequent repetition of famine betrays the inattention of the emperor to a distant province. The edifices of Rome were exposed to the same ruin and decay; the mouldering fabrics were easily overthrown by inundations, tempests, and earthquakes; and the monks, who had occupied the most advantageous stations, exulted in their base triumph over the ruins of antiquity.[60] It is commonly believed that pope Gregory the First attacked the temples and mutilated the statues of the city; that, by the command of the barbarian, the Palatine library was reduced to ashes, and that the history of Livy was the peculiar mark of his absurd and mischievous fanaticism. The writings of Gregory himself reveal his implacable aversion to the monuments of classic genius, and he points his severest censure against the profane learning of a bishop who taught the art of grammar, studied the Latin poets, and pronounced with the same voice the praises of Jupiter and those of Christ. But the evidence of his destructive rage is doubtful and recent: the Temple of Peace or the Theatre of Marcellus have been demolished by the slow operation of ages, and a formal proscription would have multiplied the copies of Virgil and Livy in the countries which were not subject to the ecclesiastical dictator.[61]

[58] The inundation and plague were reported by a deacon, whom his bishop, Gregory of Tours, had despatched to Rome for some relics. The ingenious messenger embellished his tale and the river with a great dragon and a train of little serpents (Greg. Turon. l. x. c. 1).

[59] Gregory of Rome (Dialog. l. ii. c. 15) relates a memorable prediction of St. Benedict. Roma à Gentilibus [gentibus] non exterminabitur sed tempestatibus, coruscis turbinibus ac terræ motû [fatigata] in semetipsa marcescet. Such a prophecy melts into true history, and becomes the evidence of the fact after which it was invented.

[60] Quia in uno se ore cum Jovis laudibus, Christi laudes non capiunt, et quam grave nefandumque sit episcopis canere quod nec laico religioso conveniat, ipse considera (l. ix. Ep. 4). The writings of Gregory himself attest his innocence of any classic taste or literature.

[61] Bayle (Dictionnaire Critique, tom. ii. p. 598, 599), in a very good article of *Grégoire* I., has quoted, for the buildings and statues, Platina in Gregorio I.;

Like Thebes, or Babylon, or Carthage, the name of Rome might have been erased from the earth, if the city had not been animated by a vital principle, which again restored her to honour and dominion. A vague tradition was embraced, that two Jewish teachers, a tent-maker and a fisherman, had formerly been executed in the circus of Nero, and at the end of five hundred years their genuine or fictitious relics were adored as the Palladium of Christian Rome. The pilgrims of the East and West resorted to the holy threshold; but the shrines of the apostles were guarded by miracles and invisible terrors, and it was not without fear that the pious catholic approached the object of his worship. It was fatal to touch, it was dangerous to behold, the bodies of the saints; and those who, from the purest motives, presumed to disturb the repose of the sanctuary were affrighted by visions or punished with sudden death. The unreasonable request of an empress, who wished to deprive the Romans of their sacred treasure, the head of St. Paul, was rejected with the deepest abhorrence; and the pope asserted, most probably with truth, that a linen which had been sanctified in the neighbourhood of his body, or the filings of his chain, which it was sometimes easy and sometimes impossible to obtain, possessed an equal degree of miraculous virtue.[62]   But the power as well as virtue of the apostles resided with living energy in the breast of their successors: and the chair of St. Peter was filled under the reign of Maurice by the first and greatest of the name of Gregory.[63]   His grandfather Felix had himself been pope, and, as the bishops were already bound by the law of celibacy, his consecration must have been preceded by the death of his wife. The parents of Gregory, Sylvia and Gordian, were the noblest of the senate and the most pious of the church of Rome; his female relations were numbered among the saints and virgins, and his own figure, with those of his father and mother, were represented near three

for the Palatine library, John of Salisbury (de Nugis Curialium, l. ii. c. 26); and for Livy, Antoninus of Florence: the oldest of the three lived in the twelfth century.

[62] Gregor. l. iii. Epist. 24, Indict. 12, etc. [l. iv. Ep. 30, ed. Bened.]. From the Epistles of Gregory, and the eighth volume of the Annals of Baronius, the pious reader may collect the particles of holy iron which were inserted in keys or crosses of gold, and distributed in Britain, Gaul, Spain, Africa, Constantinople, and Egypt.   The pontifical smith who handled the file must have understood the miracles which it was in his own power to operate or withhold; a circumstance which abates the superstition of Gregory at the expense of his veracity.

[63] Besides the Epistles of Gregory himself, which are methodised by Dupin (Bibliothèque Ecclés. tom. v. p. 103-126), we have three Lives of the pope; the two first written in the eighth and ninth centuries (de Triplici Vita St. Greg. Preface to the fourth volume of the Benedictine edition) by the deacons Paul (p. 1-18) and John (p. 19-188), and containing much original, though doubtful, evidence; the third, a long and laboured compilation by the Benedictine editors (p. 199-305). The Annals of Baronius are a copious but partial history. His papal prejudices are tempered by the good sense of Fleury (Hist. Ecclés. tom. viii.), and his chronology has been rectified by the criticism of Pagi and Muratori.

hundred years in a family portrait [64] which he offered to the monastery of St. Andrew. The design and colouring of this picture afford an honourable testimony that the art of painting was cultivated by the Italians of the sixth century; but the most abject ideas must be entertained of their taste and learning, since the epistles of Gregory, his sermons, and his dialogues, are the work of a man who was second in erudition to none of his contemporaries:[65] his birth and abilities had raised him to the office of præfect of the city, and he enjoyed the merit of renouncing the pomp and vanities of this world. His ample patrimony was dedicated to the foundation of seven monasteries,[66] one in Rome [67] and six in Sicily; and it was the wish of Gregory that he might be unknown in this life and glorious only in the next. Yet his devotion, and it might be sincere, pursued the path which would have been chosen by a crafty and ambitious statesman. The talents of Gregory, and the splendour which accompanied his retreat, rendered him dear and useful to the church, and implicit obedience has been always inculcated as the first duty of a monk. As soon as he had received the character of deacon, Gregory was sent to reside at the Byzantine court, the nuncio or minister of the apostolic see; and he boldly assumed, in the name of St. Peter, a tone of independent dignity which would have been criminal and dangerous in the most illustrious layman of the empire. He returned to Rome with a just increase of reputation, and, after a short exercise of the monastic virtues, he was dragged from the cloister to the papal throne by the unanimous voice of the clergy, the senate, and the people. He alone resisted, or seemed to resist, his own elevation; and his humble petition that Maurice would be pleased to reject the choice of the Romans could only serve to exalt his character in the eyes of the emperor and the public. When the fatal mandate was pro-

[64] John the deacon has described them like an eye-witness (l. iv. c. 83, 84) ; and his description is illustrated by Angelo Rocca, a Roman antiquary (St. Greg. Opera, tom. iv. p. 312-326), who observes that some mosaics of the popes of the seventh century are still preserved in the old churches of Rome (p. 321-323). The same walls which represented Gregory's family are now decorated with the martyrdom of St. Andrew, the noble contest of Domenichino and Guido.

[65] Disciplinis vero liberalibus, hoc est grammaticâ, rhetoricâ, dialecticâ ita a puero est institutus, ut quamvis eo tempore florerent adhuc Romæ studia literarum, tamen nulli in urbe ipsâ secundus putaretur. Paul. Diacon. in Vit. S. Gregor. c. 2.

[66] The Benedictines (Vit. Greg. l. i. p. 205-208) labour to reduce the monasteries of Gregory within the rule of their own order; but, as the question is confessed to be doubtful, it is clear that these powerful monks are in the wrong. See Butler's Lives of the Saints, vol. iii. p. 145; a work of merit: the sense and learning belong to the author—his prejudices are those of his profession.

[67] Monasterium Gregorianum in ejusdem Beati Gregorii ædibus ad clivum Scauri prope ecclesiam SS. Johannis et Pauli in honorem St. Andreæ (John, in Vit. Greg. l. i. c. 6; Greg. l. vii. Epist. 13). This house and monastery were situate on the side of the Cælian hill which fronts the Palatine; they are now occupied by the Camaldoli: San Gregorio triumphs, and St. Andrew has retired to a small chapel. Nardini, Roma Antica, l. iii. c. 6, p. 100; Descrizione di Roma, tom. i. p. 442-446.

claimed, Gregory solicited the aid of some friendly merchants to convey him in a basket beyond the gates of Rome, and modestly concealed himself some days among the woods and mountains, till his retreat was discovered, as it is said, by a celestial light.

The pontificate of Gregory the *Great*, which lasted thirteen years, six months, and ten days, is one of the most edifying periods of the history of the church. His virtues, and even his faults, a singular mixture of simplicity and cunning, of pride and humility, of sense and superstition, were happily suited to his station and to the temper of the times. In his rival, the patriarch of Constantinople, he condemned the antichristian title of universal bishop, which the successor of St. Peter was too haughty to concede and too feeble to assume; and the ecclesiastical jurisdiction of Gregory was confined to the triple character of Bishop of Rome, Primate of Italy, and Apostle of the West. He frequently ascended the pulpit, and kindled, by his rude though pathetic eloquence, the congenial passions of his audience: the language of the Jewish prophets was interpreted and applied; and the minds of a people depressed by their present calamities were directed to the hopes and fears of the invisible world. His precepts and example defined the model of the Roman liturgy;[68] the distribution of the parishes, the calendar of festivals, the order of processions, the service of the priests and deacons, the variety and change of sacerdotal garments. Till the last days of his life he officiated in the canon of the mass, which continued above three hours: the Gregorian chant[69] has preserved the vocal and instrumental music of the theatre, and the rough voices of the barbarians attempted to imitate the melody of the Roman school.[70] Experience had shown him the efficacy of these solemn and pompous rites to soothe the distress, to confirm the faith, to mitigate the fierceness, and to dispel the dark enthusiasm of the vulgar, and he readily forgave their tendency to promote the reign of priesthood and superstition. The bishops of Italy and the adjacent islands acknowledged the Roman pontiff as their special metropolitan. Even the

[68] The Lord's prayer consists of half a dozen lines; the Sacramentarius and Antiphonarius of Gregory fill 880 folio pages (tom. iii. P. i. p. 1-880); yet these only constitute a part of the *Ordo Romanus*, which Mabillon has illustrated and Fleury has abridged (Hist. Ecclés. tom. viii. p. 139-152).

[69] I learn from the Abbé Dubos (Réflexions sur la Poésie et la Peinture, tom. iii. p. 174, 175) that the simplicity of the Ambrosian chant was confined to four *modes*, while the more perfect harmony of the Gregorian comprised the eight modes or fifteen chords of the ancient music. He observes (p. 332) that the connoisseurs admire the preface and many passages of the Gregorian office.

[70] John the deacon (in Vit. Greg. l. ii. c. 7) expresses the early contempt of the Italians for tramontane singing. Alpina scilicet corpora vocum suarum tonitruis altisone perstrepentia, susceptæ modulationis dulcedinem proprie non resultant: quia bibuli gutturis barbara feritas dum inflexionibus et repercussionibus mitem nititur edere cantilenam, naturali quodam fragore, quasi plaustra per gradus confuse sonantia, rigidas voces jactat, etc. In the time of Charlemagne, the Franks, though with some reluctance, admitted the justice of the reproach. Muratori, Dissert. xxv.

existence, the union, or the translation of episcopal seats was decided by his absolute discretion: and his successful inroads into the provinces of Greece, of Spain, and of Gaul, might countenance the more lofty pretensions of succeeding popes. He interposed to prevent the abuses of popular elections; his jealous care maintained the purity of faith and discipline; and the apostolic shepherd assiduously watched over the faith and discipline of the subordinate pastors. Under his reign the Arians of Italy and Spain were reconciled to the catholic church, and the conquest of Britain reflects less glory on the name of Cæsar than on that of Gregory the First. Instead of six legions, forty monks were embarked for that distant island, and the pontiff lamented the austere duties which forbade him to partake the perils of their spiritual warfare. In less than two years he could announce to the archbishop of Alexandria that they had baptised the king of Kent with ten thousand of his Anglo-Saxons; and that the Roman missionaries, like those of the primitive church, were armed only with spiritual and supernatural powers. The credulity or the prudence of Gregory was always disposed to confirm the truths of religion by the evidence of ghosts, miracles, and resurrections;[71] and posterity has paid to *his* memory the same tribute which he freely granted to the virtue of his own or the preceding generation. The celestial honours have been liberally bestowed by the authority of the popes, but Gregory is the last of their own order whom they have presumed to inscribe in the calendar of saints.

Their temporal power insensibly arose from the calamities of the times; and the Roman bishops, who have deluged Europe and Asia with blood, were compelled to reign as the ministers of charity and peace. I. The church of Rome, as it has been formerly observed, was endowed with ample possessions in Italy, Sicily, and the more distant provinces; and her agents, who were commonly subdeacons, had acquired a civil and even criminal jurisdiction over their tenants and husbandmen. The successor of St. Peter administered his patrimony with the temper of a vigilant and moderate landlord;[72] and the epistles of Gregory are filled with salutary instructions to abstain from doubtful or vexatious lawsuits, to preserve the integrity of weights and measures, to grant every reasonable delay, and to reduce the capitation of the slaves of the glebe, who purchased the right of marriage by the payment of an

[71] A French critic (Petrus Gussanvillus, Opera, tom. ii. p. 105-112) has vindicated the right of Gregory to the entire nonsense of the Dialogues. Dupin (tom. v. p. 138) does not think that any one will vouch for the truth of all these miracles: I should like to know *how many* of them he believed himself.

[72] Baronius is unwilling to expatiate on the care of the patrimonies, lest he should betray that they consisted not of *kingdoms* but *farms*. The French writers, the Benedictine editors (tom. iv. l. iii. p. 272, etc.), and Fleury (tom. viii. p. 29, etc.), are not afraid of entering into these humble, though useful, details; and the humanity of Fleury dwells on the social virtues of Gregory.

arbitrary fine.[73]   The rent or the produce of these estates was transported to the mouth of the Tiber, at the risk and expense of the pope: in the use of wealth he acted like a faithful steward of the church and the poor, and liberally applied to their wants the inexhaustible resources of abstinence and order.   The voluminous account of his receipts and disbursements was kept above three hundred years in the Lateran, as the model of Christian economy.   On the four great festivals he divided their quarterly allowance to the clergy, to his domestics, to the monasteries, the churches, the places of burial, the almshouses, and the hospitals of Rome, and the rest of the diocese.   On the first day of every month he distributed to the poor, according to the season, their stated portion of corn, wine, cheese, vegetables, oil, fish, fresh provisions, clothes, and money; and his treasurers were continually summoned to satisfy, in his name, the extraordinary demands of indigence and merit.   The instant distress of the sick and helpless, of strangers and pilgrims, was relieved by the bounty of each day and of every hour; nor would the pontiff indulge himself in a frugal repast till he had sent the dishes from his own table to some objects deserving of his compassion.   The misery of the times had reduced the nobles and matrons of Rome to accept, without a blush, the benevolence of the church: three thousand virgins received their food and raiment from the hand of their benefactor; and many bishops of Italy escaped from the barbarians to the hospitable threshold of the Vatican.   Gregory might justly be styled the Father of his country; and such was the extreme sensibility of his conscience, that, for the death of a beggar who had perished in the streets, he interdicted himself during several days from the exercise of sacerdotal functions.   II. The misfortunes of Rome involved the apostolical pastor in the business of peace and war; and it might be doubtful to himself whether piety or ambition prompted him to supply the place of his absent sovereign.   Gregory awakened the emperor from a long slumber; exposed the guilt or incapacity of the exarch and his inferior ministers; complained that the veterans were withdrawn from Rome for the defence of Spoleto; encouraged the Italians to guard their cities and altars; and condescended, in the crisis of danger, to name the tribunes and to direct the operations of the provincial troops.   But the martial spirit of the pope was checked by the scruples of humanity and religion: the imposition of tribute, though it was employed in the Italian war, he freely condemned as odious and oppressive; whilst he protected, against the Imperial edicts, the pious cowardice of the soldiers who deserted a military for a monastic life. If we may credit his own declarations, it would have been easy for Gregory to exterminate the Lombards by their domestic factions, without leaving a king, a duke, or a count, to save that unfortunate nation

[73] I much suspect that this pecuniary fine on the marriages of villains produced the famous, and often fabulous, right, de cuissage, de marquette, etc. With the consent of her husband, a handsome bride might commute the payment in the arms of a young landlord, and the mutual favour might afford a precedent of local rather than legal tyranny.

from the vengeance of their foes. As a Christian bishop, he preferred the salutary offices of peace; his mediation appeased the tumult of arms; but he was too conscious of the arts of the Greeks and the passions of the Lombards to engage his sacred promise for the observance of the truce. Disappointed in the hope of a general and lasting treaty, he presumed to save his country without the consent of the emperor or the exarch. The sword of the enemy was suspended over Rome; it was averted by the mild eloquence and seasonable gifts of the pontiff, who commanded the respect of heretics and barbarians. The merits of Gregory were treated by the Byzantine court with reproach and insult; but in the attachment of a grateful people he found the purest reward of a citizen, and the best right of a sovereign.[74]

CHAPTER XLVI (570-642 A.D.)

Revolutions of Persia after the Death of Chosroes or Nushirvan—His Son Hormouz, a Tyrant, is deposed—Usurpation of Bahram—Flight and Restoration of Chosroes II.—His Gratitude to the Romans—The Chagan of the Avars—Revolt of the Army against Maurice—His Death—Tyranny of Phocas—Elevation of Heraclius—The Persian War—Chosroes subdues Syria, Egypt, and Asia Minor—Siege of Constantinople by the Persians and Avars—Persian Expeditions—Victories and Triumph of Heraclius

THE conflict of Rome and Persia was prolonged from the death of Crassus to the reign of Heraclius. An experience of seven hundred years might convince the rival nations of the impossibility of maintaining their conquests beyond the fatal limits of the Tigris and Euphrates. Yet the emulation of Trajan and Julian was awakened by the trophies of Alexander, and the sovereigns of Persia indulged the ambitious hope of restoring the empire of Cyrus.[1] Such extraordinary efforts of power and courage will always command the attention of posterity; but the events by which the fate of nations is not materially changed leave a faint impression on the page of history, and the patience of the reader would be exhausted by the repetition of the same hostilities, undertaken without cause, prosecuted without glory, and terminated without effect. The arts of negotiation, unknown to the simple greatness of the senate and the Cæsars, were assiduously cultivated by the Byzantine princes; and the memorials of their perpetual embassies[2] repeat, with the same uniform prolixity, the language of falsehood and declamation, the insolence of the barbarians, and the servile

[74] The temporal reign of Gregory I. is ably exposed by Sigonius in the first book, de Regno Italiæ. See his works, tom. ii. p. 44-75.
[1] Missisqui . . . reposcerent . . . veteres Persarum ac Macedonum terminos, seque invasurum possessa Cyro et post Alexandro, per vaniloquentiam ac minas jaciebat. Tacit. Annal. vi. 31. Such was the language of the *Arsacides:* I have repeatedly marked the lofty claims of the *Sassanians.*
[2] See the embassies of Menander, extracted and preserved in the tenth century by the order of Constantine Porphyrogenitus.

temper of the tributary Greeks.   Lamenting the barren superfluity of
materials, I have studied to compress the narrative of these uninterest-
ing transactions: but the just Nushirvan is still applauded as the model
of Oriental kings, and the ambition of his grandson Chosroes prepared
the revolution of the East, which was speedily accomplished by the
arms and the religion of the successors of Mohammed.

    In the useless altercations that precede and justify the quarrels of
princes, the Greeks and the barbarians accused each other of violating
the peace which had been concluded between the two empires about
four years before the death of Justinian.   The sovereign of Persia and
India aspired to reduce under his obedience the province of Yemen,
or Arabia [3] Felix; the distant land of myrrh and frankincense, which
had escaped, rather than opposed, the conquerors of the East.   After
the defeat of Abrahah under the walls of Mecca, the discord of his
sons and brothers gave an easy entrance to the Persians: they chased
the strangers of Abyssinia beyond the Red Sea; and a native prince
of the ancient Homerites was restored to the throne as the vassal or
viceroy of the great Nushirvan.[4]   But the nephew of Justinian declared
his resolution to avenge the injuries of his Christian ally the prince of
Abyssinia, as they suggested a decent pretence to discontinue the annual *tribute,* which was poorly disguised by the name of pension.   The
churches of Persarmenia were oppressed by the intolerant spirit of the
Magi;[5] they secretly invoked the protector of the Christians, and, after

[3] The general independence of the Arabs, which cannot be admitted without
many limitations, is blindly asserted in a separate dissertation of the authors
of the Universal History, vol. xx. p. 196-250.   A perpetual miracle is supposed
to have guarded the prophecy in favour of the posterity of Ishmael; and
these learned bigots are not afraid to risk the truth of Christianity on this
frail and slippery foundation.

[It certainly seems difficult, as Milman says, to extract a prediction of the
perpetual independence of the Arabs from the text in Genesis, which would
have received an ample fulfilment during centuries of uninvaded freedom.
But the disputants appear to forget the inseparable connection, in the prediction of the wild, the Bedoween habits of the Ishmaelites, with their national
independence.   The stationary and civilised descendant of Ishmael, forfeited,
as it were, his birthright, and ceased to be a genuine son of the "wild man."
The phrase, "dwelling in the presence of his brethren," is interpreted by
Rosenmüller (in loc.) and others, according to the Hebrew geography, "to
the east" of his brethren, the legitimate descendants of Abraham.—O. S.]

[4] D'Herbelot, Biblioth. Orient. p. 477; Pocock, Specimen Hist. Arabum, p. 64,
65.   Father Pagi (Critica, tom. ii. p. 646) has proved that, after ten years'
peace, the Persian war, which continued twenty years, was renewed A.D. 571.
Mahomet was born A.D. 569, in the year of the elephant, or the defeat of
Abrahah (Gagnier, Vie de Mahomet, tom. i. p. 89, 90, 98); and this account
allows two years for the conquest of Yemen.

[Clinton has conclusively proved, with regard to the renewal of the Persian
war, that it was resumed in the seventh year of Justin's reign = 572 A.D.
Abrahah is said to have been succeeded by his son Taksoum, who reigned
seventeen years; his brother Mascouh, who was slain in battle against the
Persians, twelve; but this chronology is irreconcilable with the Arabian conquests of Nushirvan the Great.   Either Seif, or his son Maadi Karb, was the
native prince placed on the throne by the Persians.—O. S.]

[5] [Persarmenia was long maintained in peace by the tolerant administration

the pious murder of their satraps, the rebels were avowed and supported as the brethren and subjects of the Roman emperor. The complaints of Nushirvan were disregarded by the Byzantine court; Justin yielded to the importunities of the Turks, who offered an alliance against the common enemy; and the Persian monarchy was threatened at the same instant by the united forces of Europe, of Æthiopia, and of Scythia. At the age of fourscore the sovereign of the East would perhaps have chosen the peaceful enjoyment of his glory and greatness; but as soon as war became inevitable he took the field with the alacrity of youth, whilst the aggressor trembled in the palace of Constantinople. Nushirvan or Chosroes conducted in person the siege of Dara; and although that important fortress had been left destitute of troops and magazines, the valour of the inhabitants resisted above five months the archers, the elephants, and the military engines of the Great King. In the meanwhile his general Adarman advanced from Babylon, traversed the desert, passed the Euhprates, insulted the suburbs of Antioch, reduced to ashes the city of Apamea, and laid the spoils of Syria at the feet of his master, whose perseverance in the midst of winter at length subverted the bulwark of the East. But these losses, which astonished the provinces and the court, produced a salutary effect in the repentance and abdication of the emperor Justin: a new spirit arose in the Byzantine councils; and a truce of three years was obtained by the prudence of Tiberius. That seasonable interval was employed in the preparations of war; and the voice of rumour proclaimed to the world that from the distant countries of the Alps and the Rhine, from Scythia, Mæsia, Pannonia, Illyricum, and Isauria, the strength of the Imperial cavalry was reinforced with one hundred and fifty thousand soldiers. Yet the king of Persia, without fear or without faith, resolved to prevent the attack of the enemy; again passed the Euphrates, and, dismissing the ambassadors of Tiberius, arrogantly commanded them to await his arrival at Cæsarea, the metropolis of the Cappadocian provinces. The two armies encountered each other in the battle of Melitene: the barbarians, who darkened the air with a cloud of arrows, prolonged their line and extended their wings across the plain; while the Romans, in deep and solid bodies, expected to prevail in closer action by the weight of their swords and lances. A Scythian chief, who commanded their right wing, suddenly turned the

of Mejej, prince of the Gnounians. On his death he was succeeded by a persecutor, a Persian, named Ten-Schahpour, who attempted to propagate Zoroastrianism by violence. Nushirvan, on an appeal to the throne by the Armenian clergy, replaced Ten-Schahpour, in 552, by Veschnas-Vahram. The new governor was instructed to repress the bigoted Magi in their persecutions of the Armenians, but the Persian converts to Christianity underwent great sufferings. The most distinguished of them, Izdbouzid, was crucified at Dovin in the presence of a vast multitude. The fame of the martyr spread to the West. Armenia remained long at peace under Veschnas-Vahram and his successor Varazdat. The tyranny of his successor Surena led to the rising under Vartan, who revenged the death of his brother on Surena, and put the whole Magian party in Dovin to the sword.—O. S.]

flank of the enemy, attacked their rear-guard in the presence of Chos-roes, penetrated to the midst of the camp, pillaged the royal tent, pro-faned the eternal fire, loaded a train of camels with the spoils of Asia, cut his way through the Persian host, and returned with songs of vic-tory to his friends, who had consumed the day in single combats or ineffectual skirmishes. The darkness of the night and the separation of the Romans afforded the Persian monarch an opportunity of re-venge; and one of their camps was swept away by a rapid and impetu-ous assault. But the review of his loss and the consciousness of his danger determined Chosroes to a speedy retreat: he burnt in his pas-sage the vacant town of Melitene; and, without consulting the safety of his troops, boldly swam the Euphrates on the back of an elephant. After this unsuccessful campaign, the want of magazines, and perhaps some inroad of the Turks, obliged him to disband or divide his forces; the Romans were left masters of the field, and their general Justinian, advancing to the relief of the Persarmenian rebels, erected his standard on the banks of the Araxes. The great Pompey had formerly halted within three days' march of the Caspian:[6] that inland sea was explored for the first time by a hostile fleet,[7] and seventy thousand captives were transplanted from Hyrcania to the isle of Cyprus. On the return of spring Justinian descended into the fertile plains of Assyria; the flames of war approached the residence of Nushirvan; the indignant monarch sunk into the grave; and his last edict restrained his successors from exposing their person in a battle against the Romans. Yet the memory of this transient affront was lost in the glories of a long reign; and his formidable enemies, after indulging their dream of conquest, again solicited a short respite from the calamities of war.[8]

The throne of Chosroes Nushirvan was filled by Hormouz, or Hor-misdas, the eldest or the most favoured of his sons. With the king-doms of Persia and India, he inherited the reputation and example of his father, the service, in every rank, of his wise and valiant officers, and a general system of administration harmonised by time and political wisdom to promote the happiness of the prince and people. But the royal youth enjoyed a still more valuable blessing, the friendship of a

[6] He had vanquished the Albanians, who brought into the field 12,000 horse and 60,000 foot; but he dreaded the multitude of venomous reptiles, whose existence may admit of some doubt, as well as that of the neighbouring Amazons. Plutarch, in Pompeio [c. 36], tom. ii. p. 1165, 1166.

[7] In the history of the world I can only perceive two navies on the Caspian: 1. Of the Macedonians, when Patrocles, the admiral of the kings of Syria, Seleucus and Antiochus, descended most probably the river Oxus, from the confines of India (Plin. Hist. Natur. vi. 21). 2. Of the Russians, when Peter the First conducted a fleet and army from the neighbourhood of Moscow to the coast of Persia (Bell's Travels, vol. ii. p. 325-352). He justly observes that such martial pomp had never been displayed on the Volga.

[8] For these Persian wars and treaties, see Menander, in Excerpt. Legat. p. 113-125 [p. 311-331, ed. Bonn]; Theophanes Byzant. apud Photium, cod. lxiv. p. 77, 80, 81 [p. 26, 27, ed. Bekk.]; Evagrius, l. v. c. 7-15; Theophylact, l. iii. c. 9-16; Agathias, l. iv. [c. 29] p. 140 [p. 271, ed. Bonn].

sage who had presided over his education, and who always preferred the honour to the interest of his pupil, his interest to his inclination. In a dispute with the Greek and Indian philosophers, Buzurg [9] had once maintained that the most grievous misfortune of life is old age without the remembrance of virtue; and our candour will presume that the same principle compelled him during three years to direct the councils of the Persian empire. His zeal was rewarded by the gratitude and docility of Hormouz, who acknowledged himself more indebted to his preceptor than to his parent: but when age and labour had impaired the strength, and perhaps the faculties, of this prudent counsellor, he retired from court and abandoned the youthful monarch to his own passions and those of his favourites. By the fatal vicissitude of human affairs the same scenes were renewed at Ctesiphon which had been exhibited in Rome after the death of Marcus Antoninus. The ministers of flattery and corruption, who had been banished by the father, were recalled and cherished by the son; the disgrace and exile of the friends of Nushirvan established their tyranny; and virtue was driven by degrees from the mind of Hormouz, from his palace, and from the government of the state. The faithful agents, the eyes and ears of the king, informed him of the progress of disorder, that the provincial governors flew to their prey with the fierceness of lions and eagles, and that their rapine and injustice would teach the most loyal of his subjects to abhor the name and authority of their sovereign. The sincerity of this advice was punished with death; the murmurs of the cities were despised, their tumults were quelled by military execution; the intermediate powers between the throne and the people were abolished; and the childish vanity of Hormouz, who affected the daily use of the tiara, was fond of declaring that he alone would be the judge as well as the master of his kingdom. In every word and in every action the son of Nushirvan degenerated from the virtues of his father. His avarice defrauded the troops; his jealous caprice degraded the satraps; the palace, the tribunals, the waters of the Tigris, were stained with the blood of the innocent, and the tyrant exulted in the sufferings and execution of thirteen thousand victims. As the excuse of his cruelty, he sometimes condescended to observe that the fears of the Persians would be productive of hatred, and that their hatred must terminate in rebellion; but he forgot that his own guilt and folly had inspired the sentiments which he deplored, and prepared the event which he so justly apprehended. Exasperated by long and hopeless oppression, the provinces of Babylon, Susa, and Carmania erected the standard of revolt; and the princes of Arabia,

---

[9] Buzurg Mihir may be considered, in his character and station, as the Seneca of the East; but his virtues, and perhaps his faults, are less known than those of the Roman, who appears to have been much more loquacious. The Persian sage was the person who imported from India the game of chess and the fables of Pilpay. Such has been the fame of his wisdom and virtues, that the Christians claim him as a believer in the Gospel; and the Mohammedans revere Buzurg as a premature Musulman. D'Herbelot, Bibliothèque Orientale, p. 218.

India, and Scythia refused the customary tribute to the unworthy successor of Nushirvan. The arms of the Romans, in slow sieges and frequent inroads, afflicted the frontiers of Mesopotamia and Assyria: one of their generals professed himself the disciple of Scipio; and the soldiers were animated by a miraculous image of Christ, whose mild aspect should never have been displayed in the front of battle.[10] At the same time the eastern provinces of Persia were invaded by the great khan, who passed the Oxus at the head of three or four hundred thousand Turks. The imprudent Hormouz accepted their perfidious and formidable aid; the cities of Khorassan or Bactriana were commanded to open their gates; the march of the barbarians towards the mountains of Hyrcania revealed the correspondence of the Turkish and Roman arms; and their union must have subverted the throne of the house of Sassan.

Persia had been lost by a king; it was saved by a hero. After his revolt, Varanes or Bahram is stigmatised by the son of Hormouz as an ungrateful slave: the proud and ambiguous reproach of despotism, since he was truly descended from the ancient princes of Rei,[11] one of the seven families whose splendid, as well as substantial, prerogatives exalted them above the heads of the Persian nobility.[12] At the siege of Dara the valour of Bahram was signalised under the eyes of Nushirvan, and both the father and son successively promoted him to the command of armies, the government of Media, and the superintendence of the palace. The popular prediction which marked him as the deliverer of Persia might be inspired by his past victories and extraordinary figure: the epithet *Giubin* is expressive of the quality of *dry wood*; he had the strength and stature of a giant; and his savage countenance was fancifully compared to that of a wild cat. While the nation trembled, while

[10] See the imitation of Scipio in Theophylact, 1. i. c. 14; the image of Christ, 1. ii. c. 3. Hereafter I shall speak more amply of the Christian *images*—I had almost said *idols*. This, if I am not mistaken, is the oldest ἀχειροποίητος of divine manufacture; but in the next thousand years, many others issued from the same workshop.

[11] Ragæ, or Rei, is mentioned in the apocryphal book of Tobit as already flourishing 700 years before Christ, under the Assyrian empire. Under the foreign names of Europus and Arsacia, this city, 500 stadia to the south of the Caspian gates, was successively embellished by the Macedonians and Parthians (Strabo, 1. xi. p. 796 [p. 524, ed. Casaub.]). Its grandeur and populousness in the ninth century is exaggerated beyond the bounds of credibility; but Rei has been since ruined by wars and the unwholesomeness of the air. Chardin, Voyage en Perse, tom. i. p. 279, 280; D'Herbelot, Biblioth. Oriental. p. 714.

[12] Theophylact, 1. iii. c. 18 [p. 153, ed. Bonn]. The story of the seven Persians is told in the third book of Herodotus; and their noble descendants are often mentioned, especially in the fragments of Ctesias. Yet the independence of Otanes (Herodot. 1. iii. c. 83, 84) is hostile to the spirit of despotism, and it may not seem probable that the seven families could survive the revolutions of eleven hundred years. They might however be represented by the seven ministers (Brisson, de Regno Persico, 1. i. p. 190); and some Persian nobles, like the kings of Pontus (Polyb. 1. v. [c. 43] p. 540) and Cappadocia (Diodor. Sicul. 1. xxxi. [c. 19] tom. ii. p. 517), might claim their descent from the bold companions of Darius.

Hormouz disguised his terror by the name of suspicion, and his servants concealed their disloyalty under the mask of fear, Bahram alone displayed his undaunted courage and apparent fidelity: and as soon as he found that no more than twelve thousand soldiers would follow him against the enemy, he prudently declared that to this fatal number Heaven had reserved the honours of the triumph. The steep and narrow descent of the Pule Rudbar,[13] or Hyrcanian rock, is the only pass through which an army can penetrate into the territory of Rei and the plains of Media. From the commanding heights a band of resolute men might overwhelm with stones and darts the myriads of the Turkish host: their emperor and his son were transpierced with arrows; and the fugitives were left, without counsel or provisions, to the revenge of an injured people. The patriotism of the Persian general was stimulated by his affection for the city of his forefathers; in the hour of victory every peasant became a soldier, and every soldier a hero; and their ardour was kindled by the gorgeous spectacle of beds, and thrones, and tables of massy gold, the spoils of Asia and the luxury of the hostile camp. A prince of a less malignant temper could not easily have forgiven his benefactor; and the secret hatred of Hormouz was envenomed by a malicious report that Bahram had privately retained the most precious fruits of his Turkish victory. But the approach of a Roman army on the side of the Araxes compelled the implacable tyrant to smile and to applaud; and the toils of Bahram were rewarded with the permission of encountring a new enemy, by their skill and discipline more formidable than a Scythian multitude. Elated by his recent success, he despatched a herald with a bold defiance to the camp of the Romans, requesting them to fix a day of battle, and to choose whether they would pass the river themselves, or allow a free passage to the arms of the Great King. The lieutenant of the emperor Maurice preferred the safer alternative; and this local circumstance, which would have enhanced the victory of the Persians, rendered their defeat more bloody and their escape more difficult. But the loss of his subjects, and the danger of his kingdom, were overbalanced in the mind of Hormouz by the disgrace of his personal enemy; and no sooner had Bahram collected and reviewed his forces than he received from a royal messenger the insulting gift of a distaff, a spinning-wheel, and a complete suit of female apparel. Obedient to the will of his sovereign, he showed himself to the soldiers in this unworthy disguise: they resented his ignominy and their own; a shout of rebellion ran through the ranks; and the general accepted their oath of fidelity and vows of revenge. A second messenger, who had been commanded to bring the rebel in chains, was trampled under the feet of an elephant, and manifestos were diligently circulated, exhorting the Persians to assert their freedom against an odious and contemptible tyrant. The defection was rapid and universal; his loyal

[13] See an accurate description of this mountain by Olearius (Voyage en Perse, p. 997, 998), who ascended it with much difficulty and danger in his return from Ispahan to the Caspian Sea.

slaves were sacrificed to the public fury; the troops deserted to the standard of Bahram; and the provinces again saluted the deliverer of his country.

As the passes were faithfully guarded, Hormouz could only compute the number of his enemies by the testimony of a guilty conscience, and the daily defection of those who, in the hour of his distress, avenged their wrongs or forgot their obligations. He proudly displayed the ensigns of royalty; but the city and palace of Modain had already escaped from the hand of the tyrant. Among the victims of his cruelty, Bindoes, a Sassanian prince, had been cast into a dungeon: his fetters were broken by the zeal and courage of a brother; and he stood before the king at the head of those trusty guards who had been chosen as the ministers of his confinement, and perhaps of his death. Alarmed by the hasty intrusion and bold reproaches of the captive, Hormouz looked round, but in vain, for advice or assistance; discovered that his strength consisted in the obedience of others; and patiently yielded to the single arm of Bindoes, who dragged him from the throne to the same dungeon in which he himself had been so lately confined. At the first tumult, Chosroes, the eldest of the sons of Hormouz, escaped from the city; he was persuaded to return by the pressing and friendly invitation of Bindoes, who promised to seat him on his father's throne, and who expected to reign under the name of an inexperienced youth. In the just assurance that his accomplices could neither forgive nor hope to be forgiven, and that every Persian might be trusted as the judge and enemy of the tyrant, he instituted a public trial without a precedent and without a copy in the annals of the East. The son of Nushirvan, who had requested to plead in his own defence, was introduced as a criminal into the full assembly of the nobles and satraps.[14] He was heard with decent attention as long as he expatiated on the advantages of order and obedience, the danger of innovation, and the inevitable discord of those who had encouraged each other to trample on their lawful and hereditary sovereign. By a pathetic appeal to their humanity he extorted that pity which is seldom refused to the fallen fortunes of a king; and while they beheld the abject posture and squalid appearance of the prisoner, his tears, his chains, and the marks of ignominious stripes, it was impossible to forget how recently they had adored the divine splendour of his diadem and purple. But an angry murmur arose in the assembly as soon as he presumed to vindicate his conduct, and to applaud the victories of his reign. He defined the duties of a king, and the Persian nobles listened with a smile of contempt; they were fired with indignation when he dared to vilify the character of Chosroes; and by the indiscreet offer of resigning the sceptre to the second of his sons, he subscribed his own condemnation and sacrificed the life of his innocent favourite. The mangled bodies of the boy and his mother were exposed

[14] The Orientals suppose that Bahram convened this assembly and proclaimed Chosroes; but Theophylact is, in this instance, more distinct and credible.

to the people; the eyes of Hormouz were pierced with a hot needle; and the punishment of the father was succeeded by the coronation of his eldest son. Chosroes had ascended the throne without guilt, and his piety strove to alleviate the misery of the abdicated monarch; from the dungeon he removed Hormouz to an apartment of the palace, supplied with liberality the consolations of sensual enjoyment, and patiently endured the furious sallies of his resentment and despair. He might despise the resentment of a blind and unpopular tyrant, but the tiara was trembling on his head, till he could subvert the power, or acquire the friendship, of the great Bahram, who sternly denied the justice of a revolution in which himself and his soldiers, the true representatives of Persia, had never been consulted. The offer of a general amnesty, and of the second rank in his kingdom, was answered by an epistle from Bahram, friend of the gods, conqueror of men, and enemy of tyrants, the satrap of satraps, general of the Persian armies, and a prince adorned with the title of eleven virtues.[15] He commands Chosroes, the son of Hormouz, to shun the example and fate of his father, to confine the traitors who had been released from their chains, to deposit in some holy place the diadem which he had usurped, and to accept from his gracious benefactor the pardon of his faults and the government of a province. The rebel might not be proud, and the king most assuredly was not humble; but the one was conscious of his strength, the other was sensible of his weakness; and even the modest language of his reply still left room for treaty and reconciliation. Chosroes led into the field the slaves of the palace and the populace of the capital: they beheld with terror the banners of a veteran army; they were encompassed and surprised by the evolutions of the general; and the satraps who had deposed Hormouz received the punishment of their revolt, or expiated their first treason by a second and more criminal act of disloyalty. The life and liberty of Chosroes were saved, but he was reduced to the necessity of imploring aid or refuge in some foreign land; and the implacable Bindoes, anxious to secure an unquestionable title, hastily returned to the palace, and ended, with a bow-string, the wretched existence of the son of Nushirvan.[16]

While Chosroes despatched the preparations of his retreat, he deliberated with his remaining friends [17] whether he should lurk in the val-

---

[15] See the words of Theophylact, l. iv. c. 7 [p. 173, ed. Bonn]. Βαράμ φίλος τοῖς θεοῖς, νικητής, ἐπιφανής, τυράννων ἐχθρός, σατράπης μεγιστάνων τῆς Περσικῆς ἄρχων δυνάμεως, etc. In his answer Chosroes styles himself τῇ νυκτὶ χαριζόμενος ὄμματα . . . ὁ τοὺς ἥΑσωνας (the genii) μισθούμενος [p. 175]. This is genuine Oriental bombast.

[16] Theophylact (l. iv. c. 7 [p. 173, ed. Bonn]) imputes the death of Hormouz to his son, by whose command he was beaten to death with clubs. I have followed the milder account of Khondemir and Eutychius, and shall always be content with the slightest evidence to extenuate the crime of parricide.

[17] After the battle of Pharsalia, the Pompey of Lucan (l. viii. 256-455) holds a similar debate. He was himself desirous of seeking the Parthians: but his companions abhorred the unnatural alliance; and the adverse prejudices might operate as forcibly on Chosroes and his companions, who could

leys of Mount Caucasus, or fly to the tents of the Turks, or solicit the protection of the emperor. The long emulation of the successors of Artaxerxes and Constantine increased his reluctance to appear as a suppliant in a rival court; but he weighed the forces of the Romans, and prudently considered that the neighbourhood of Syria would render his escape more easy and their succours more effectual. Attended only by his concubines and a troop of thirty guards, he secretly departed from the capital, followed the banks of the Euphrates, traversed the desert, and halted at the distance of ten miles from Circesium. About the third watch of the night the Roman præfect was informed of his approach, and he introduced the royal stranger to the fortress at the dawn of day. From thence the king of Persia was conducted to the more honourable residence of Hierapolis; and Maurice dissembled his pride, and displayed his benevolence, at the reception of the letters and ambassadors of the grandson of Nushirvan. They humbly represented the vicissitudes of fortune and the common interest of princes, exaggerated the ingratitude of Bahram, the agent of the evil principle, and urged, with specious argument, that it was for the advantage of the Romans themselves to support the two monarchies which balance the world, the two great luminaries by whose salutary influence it is vivified and adorned. The anxiety of Chosroes was soon relieved by the assurance that the emperor had espoused the cause of justice and royalty; but Maurice prudently declined the expense and delay of his useless visit to Constantinople. In the name of his generous benefactor, a rich diadem was presented to the fugitive prince, with an inestimable gift of jewels and gold; a powerful army was assembled on the frontiers of Syria and Armenia, under the command of the valiant and faithful Narses;[18] and this general, of his own nation, and his own choice, was directed to pass the Tigris, and never to sheathe his sword till he had restored Chosroes to the throne of his ancestors. The enterprise, however splendid, was less arduous than it might appear. Persia had already repented of her fatal rashness, which betrayed the heir of the house of Sassan to the ambition of a rebellious subject: and the bold refusal of the Magi to consecrate his usurpation compelled Bahram to assume the sceptre, regardless of the laws and prejudices of the nation. The palace was soon distracted with conspiracy, the city with tumult, the provinces with insurrection; and the cruel execution of the guilty and the suspected served to irritate rather than subdue the public discontent. No sooner did the grandson of Nushirvan display his own and

describe, with the same vehemence, the contrast of laws, religion, and manners, between the East and West.

[18] In this age there were three warriors of the name of *Narses,* who have been often confounded (Pagi, Critica, tom. ii. p. 640); 1. A Persarmenian, the brother of Isaac and Armatius, who, after a successful action against Belisarius, deserted from his Persian sovereign, and afterwards served in the Italian war. 2. The eunuch who conquered Italy. 3. The restorer of Chosroes, who is celebrated in the poem of Corippus (l. iii. 220-227) as excelsus super omnia vertice agmina . . . habitu modestus . . . morum probitate placens, virtute verendus: fulmineus, cautus, vigilans. etc

the Roman banners beyond the Tigris, than he was joined, each day, by the increasing multitudes of the nobility and people; and as he advanced, he received from every side the grateful offerings of the keys of his cities and the heads of his enemies. As soon as Modain was freed from the presence of the usurper, the loyal inhabitants obeyed the first summons of Mebodes at the head of only two thousand horse, and Chosroes accepted the sacred and precious ornaments of the palace as the pledge of their truth and a presage of his approaching success. After the junction of the Imperial troops, which Bahram vainly struggled to prevent, the contest was decided by two battles on the banks of the Zab and the confines of Media. The Romans, with the faithful subjects of Persia, amounted to sixty thousand, while the whole force of the usurper did not exceed forty thousand men: the two generals signalised their valour and ability; but the victory was finally determined by the prevalence of numbers and discipline. With the remnant of a broken army, Bahram fled towards the eastern provinces of the Oxus: the enmity of Persia reconciled him to the Turks; but his days were shortened by poison, perhaps the most incurable of poisons, the stings of remorse and despair, and the bitter remembrance of lost glory. Yet the modern Persians still commemorate the exploits of Bahram; and some excellent laws have prolonged the duration of his troubled and transitory reign.[18]

The restoration of Chosroes was celebrated with feasts and executions; and the music of the royal banquet was often disturbed by the groans of dying or mutilated criminals. A general pardon might have diffused comfort and tranquillity through a country which had been shaken by the late revolutions; yet, before the sanguinary temper of Chosroes is blamed, we should learn whether the Persians had not been accustomed either to dread the rigour or to despise the weakness of their sovereign. The revolt of Bahram and the conspiracy of the satraps were impartially punished by the revenge or justice of the conqueror; the merits of Bindoes himself could not purify his hand from the guilt of royal blood; and the son of Hormouz was desirous to assert his own innocence and to vindicate the sanctity of kings. During the vigour of the Roman power several princes were seated on the throne of Persia by the arms and the authority of the first Cæsars. But their new subjects were soon disgusted with the vices or virtues which they had imbibed in a foreign land; the instability of their dominion gave birth to a vulgar observation, that the choice of Rome was solicited and rejected with equal ardour by the capricious levity of Oriental slaves.[20]

[19] [According to Mirkhond and the Oriental writers, Bahram received the daughter of the Khakan in marriage, and commanded a body of Turks in an invasion of Persia. Some say that he was assassinated; Malcolm adopts the opinion that he was poisoned. His sister Gourdieh, the companion of his flight, is celebrated in the Shah Nameh. She was afterwards one of the wives of Chosroes.—O. S.]

[20] Experimentis cognitum est barbaros malle Româ petere reges quam habere. These experiments are admirably represented in the invitation and expulsion of Vonones (Annal. ii. 1-3), Tiridates (Annal. vi. 32-44), and Meherdates (Annal. xi. 10, xii. 10-14). The eye of Tacitus seems to have transpierced the camp of the Parthians and the walls of the harem.

But the glory of Maurice was conspicuous in the long and fortunate reign of his *son* and his ally. A band of a thousand Romans, who continued to guard the person of Chosroes, proclaimed his confidence in the fidelity of the strangers; his growing strength enabled him to dismiss this unpopular aid, but he steadily professed the same gratitude and reverence to his adopted father; and, till the death of Maurice, the peace and alliance of the two empires were faithfully maintained. Yet the mercenary friendship of the Roman prince had been purchased with costly and important gifts; the strong cities of Martyropolis and Dara were restored, and the Persarmenians became the willing subjects of an empire whose eastern limit was extended, beyond the example of former times, as far as the banks of the Araxes and the neighbourhood of the Caspian. A pious hope was indulged that the church as well as the state might triumph in this revolution: but if Chosroes had sincerely listened to the Christian bishops, the impression was erased by the zeal and eloquence of the Magi; if he was armed with philosophic indifference, he accommodated his belief, or rather his professions, to the various circumstances of an exile and a sovereign. The imaginary conversion of the king of Persia was reduced to a local and superstitious veneration for Sergius,[21] one of the saints of Antioch, who heard his prayers and appeared to him in dreams; he enriched the shrine with offerings of gold and silver, and ascribed to this invisible patron the success of his arms, and the pregnancy of Sira, a devout Christian and the best beloved of his wives.[22] The beauty of Sira, or Schirin,[23] her wit, her musical talents, are still famous in the history, or rather in the romances, of the East: her own name is expressive, in the Persian tongue, of sweetness and grace; and the epithet of *Parviz* alludes to the charms of her royal lover. Yet Sira never shared the passion which she inspired, and the bliss of Chosroes was tortured by a jealous doubt, that while he possessed her person she had bestowed her affections on a meaner favourite.[24]

[21] Sergius and his companion Bacchus, who are said to have suffered in the persecution of Maximian, obtained divine honour in France, Italy, Constantinople, and the East. Their tomb at Rasaphe was famous for miracles, and that Syrian town acquired the more honourable name of Sergiopolis. Tillemont, Mém. Ecclés. tom. v. p. 491-496; Butler's Saints, vol. x. p. 155.

[22] Evagrius (l. vi. c. 21) and Theophylact (l. v. c. 13, 14 [p. 230, *sqq.*, ed. Bonn]) have preserved the original letters of Chosroes, written in Greek, signed with his own hand, and afterwards inscribed on crosses and tables of gold, which were deposited in the church of Sergiopolis. They had been sent to the bishop of Antioch, as primate of Syria.

[23] The Greeks only describe her as a Roman by birth, a Christian by religion; but she is represented as the daughter of the emperor Maurice in the Persian and Turkish romances which celebrate the love of Khosrou for Schirin, of Schirin for Ferhad, the most beautiful youth of the East. D'Herbelot, Biblioth. Orient. p. 789, 997, 998.

[24] The whole series of the tyranny of Hormouz, the revolt of Bahram, and the flight and restoration of Chosroes, is related by two contemporary Greeks —more concisely by Evagrius (l. vi. c. 16, 17, 18, 19), and most diffusely by Theophylact Simocatta (l. iii. c. 6-18, l. iv. c. 1-16, l. v. c. 1-15) : succeeding compilers, Zonaras and Cedrenus, can only transcribe and abridge. The

While the majesty of the Roman name was revived in the East, the prospect of Europe is less pleasing and less glorious. By the departure of the Lombards and the ruin of the Gepidæ the balance of power was destroyed on the Danube; and the Avars spread their permanent dominion from the foot of the Alps to the sea-coast of the Euxine. The reign of Baian is the brightest era of their monarchy; their chagan, who occupied the rustic palace of Attila, appears to have imitated his character and policy;[25] but as the same scenes were repeated in a smaller circle, a minute representation of the copy would be devoid of the greatness and novelty of the original. The pride of the second Justin, of Tiberius, and Maurice was humbled by a proud barbarian, more prompt to inflict than exposed to suffer the injuries of war; and as often as Asia was threatened by the Persian arms, Europe was oppressed by the dangerous inroads or costly friendship of the Avars. When the Roman envoys approached the presence of the chagan, they were commanded to wait at the door of his tent till, at the end perhaps of ten or twelve days, he condescended to admit them. If the substance or the style of their message was offensive to his ear, he insulted, with real or affected fury, their own dignity and that of their prince; their baggage was plundered, and their lives were only saved by the promise of a richer present and a more respectful address. But *his* sacred ambassadors enjoyed and abused an unbounded licence in the midst of Constantinople: they urged, with importunate clamours, the increase of tribute, or the restitution of captives and deserters: and the majesty of the empire was almost equally degraded by a base compliance, or by the false and fearful excuses with which they eluded such insolent demands. The chagan had never seen an elephant; and his curiosity was excited by the strange, and perhaps fabulous, portrait of that wonderful animal. At his command, one of the largest elephants of the Imperial stables was equipped with stately caparisons, and conducted by a numerous train to the royal village in the plains of Hungary. He surveyed the enormous beast with surprise, with disgust, and possibly with terror;

Christian Arabs, Eutychius (Annal. tom. ii. p. 200-208) and Abulpharagius (Dynast. p. 96-98), appear to have consulted some particular memoirs. The great Persian historians of the fifteenth century, Mirkhond and Khondemir, are only known to me by the imperfect extracts of Schikard (Tarikh, p. 150-155), Texeira, or rather Stevens (Hist. of Persia, p. 182-186), a Turkish MS. translated by the Abbé Fourmont (Hist. de l'Académie des Inscriptions, tom. vii. p. 325-334), and D'Herbelot (aux mots, *Hormouz*, p. 457-459; Bahram, p. 174; Khosrou Parviz, p. 996). Were I perfectly satisfied of their authority, I could wish these Oriental materials had been more copious.

[25] A general idea of the pride and power of the chagan may be taken from Menander (Excerpt. Legat. p. 113, etc. [p. 308, *sq.*, ed. Bonn]), and Theophylact (l. i. c. 3, l, vii. c. 15), whose eight books are much more honourable to the Avar than to the Roman prince. The predecessors of Baian had tasted the liberality of Rome, and *he* survived the reign of Maurice (Buat, Hist. des Peuples Barbares, tom. xi. p. 545). The chagan who invaded Italy A.D. 611 (Muratori, Annali, tom. v. p. 305) was then juvenili ætate florentem (Paul Warnefrid, de Gest. Langobard. l. iv. c. 38), the son, perhaps, or the grandson. of Baian.

and smiled at the vain industry of the Romans, who in search of such useless rarities could explore the limits of the land and sea. He wished, at the expense of the emperor, to repose in a golden bed. The wealth of Constantinople, and the skilful diligence of her artists, were instantly devoted to the gratification of his caprice; but when the work was finished, he rejected with scorn a present so unworthy the majesty of a great king.[26] These were the casual sallies of his pride; but the avarice of the chagan was a more steady and tractable passion: a rich and regular supply of silk apparel, furniture, and plate introduced the rudiments of art and luxury among the tents of the Scythians; their appetite was stimulated by the pepper and cinnamon of India;[27] the annual subsidy or tribute was raised from fourscore to one hundred and twenty thousand pieces of gold; and, after each hostile interruption, the payment of the arrears, with exorbitant interest, was always made the first condition of the new treaty. In the language of a barbarian, without guile, the prince of the Avars affected to complain of the insincerity of the Greeks;[28] yet he was not inferior to the most civilised nations in the refinements of dissimulation and perfidy. As the successor of the Lombards, the chagan asserted his claim to the important city of Sirmium, the ancient bulwark of the Illyrian provinces.[29] The plains of the Lower Hungary were covered with the Avar horse; and a fleet of large boats was built in the Hercynian wood, to descend the Danube, and to transport into the Save the materials of a bridge. But as the strong garrison of Singidunum, which commanded the conflux of the two rivers, might have stopped their passage and baffled his designs, he dispelled their apprehensions by a solemn oath that his views were not hostile to the empire. He swore by his sword, the symbol of the god of war, that he did not, as the enemy of Rome, construct a bridge upon the Save. " If I violate my oath," pursued the intrepid Baian, " may I myself, and the last of my nation, perish by the sword! May the heavens, and fire, the deity of the heavens, fall upon our heads! May the forests and mountains bury us in their ruins; and the Save, returning, against the laws of nature, to his source, overwhelm us in his angry waters!" After this barbarous imprecation he calmly inquired what oath was most sacred and venerable among the Christians; what guilt of perjury it was most dangerous to incur. The bishop of Singidunum presented the

---

[26] Theophylact, l. i. c. 5, 6.

[27] Even in the field the chagan delighted in the use of these aromatics. He solicited, as a gift, Ἰνδικὰς καρυκείας, and received πέπερι καὶ φύλλον Ἰνδῶν, κασίαν τε καὶ τόν λεγόμενον κόστον. Theophylact, l. vii. c. 13 [p. 294, ed. Bonn]. The Europeans of the ruder ages consumed more spices in their meat and drink than is compatible with the delicacy of a modern palate. Vie Privée des François, tom. ii. p. 162, 163.

[28] Theophylact, l. vi. c. 6, l. vii. c. 15 [p. 251, 299, ed. Bonn]. The Greek historian confesses the truth and justice of his reproach.

[29] Menander (in Excerpt. Legat. p. 126-132, 174, 175 [p. 332-342, 424, 425, ed. Bonn]) describes the perjury of Baian and the surrender of Sirmium. We have lost his account of the siege, which is commended by Theophylact, l. i. c. 3. Τὸ δ' ὅπως Μενάνδρῳ τῷ περιφανεῖ σαφῶς διηγόρευται [p. 38, ed. Bonn]).

Gospel, which the chagan received with devout reverence. "I swear," said he, "by the God who has spoken in this holy book, that I have neither falsehood on my tongue nor treachery in my heart." As soon as he rose from his knees he accelerated the labour of the bridge, and despatched an envoy to proclaim what he no longer wished to conceal. "Inform the emperor," said the perfidious Baian, "that Sirmium is invested on every side. Advise his prudence to withdraw the citizens and their effects, and to resign a city which it is now impossible to relieve or defend." Without the hope of relief, the defence of Sirmium was prolonged above three years: the walls were still untouched; but famine was enclosed within the walls, till a merciful capitulation allowed the escape of the naked and hungry inhabitants. Singidunum, at the distance of fifty miles, experienced a more cruel fate: the buildings were razed, and the vanquished people was condemned to servitude and exile. Yet the ruins of Sirmium are no longer visible; the advantageous situation of Singidunum soon attracted a new colony of Sclavonians; and the conflux of the Save and Danube is still guarded by the fortifications of Belgrade, or the *White City*, so often and so obstinately disputed by the Christian and Turkish arms.[30] From Belgrade to the walls of Constantinople a line may be measured of six hundred miles: that line was marked with flames and with blood; the horses of the Avars were alternately bathed in the Euxine and the Hadriatic; and the Roman pontiff, alarmed by the approach of a more savage enemy,[31] was reduced to cherish the Lombards as the protectors of Italy. The despair of a captive whom his country refused to ransom disclosed to the Avars the invention and practice of military engines.[32] But in the first attempts they were rudely framed and awkwardly managed; and the resistance of Diocletianopolis and Berœa, of Philippopolis and Adrianople, soon exhausted the skill and patience of the besiegers. The warfare of Baian was that of a Tartar; yet his mind was susceptible of a humane and generous sentiment: he spared Anchialus, whose salutary waters had restored the health of the best beloved of his wives; and the Romans confess that their starving army was fed and dismissed by the liberality of a foe. His empire extended over Hungary, Poland, and Prussia, from the mouth of the Danube to that of the Oder;[33] and his new subjects

---

[30] See D'Anville, in the Mémoires de l'Acad. des Inscriptions, tom. xxviii. p. 412-443. The Sclavonic name of *Belgrade* is mentioned in the tenth century by Constantine Porphyrogenitus: the Latin appellation of *Alba Græca* is used by the Franks in the beginning of the ninth (p. 414).

[31] Baron. Annal. Eccles. A.D. 600, No. 1. Paul Warnefrid (l. iv. c. 38) relates their irruption into Friuli, and (c. 39) the captivity of his ancestors, about A.D. 632. The Sclavi traversed the Hadriatic cum multitudine navium, and made a descent in the territory of Sipontum (c. 47).

[32] Even the helepolis, or movable turret. Theophylact, l. ii. 16, 17.

[33] The arms and alliances of the chagan reached to the neighbourhood of a western sea, fifteen months' journey from Constantinople. The emperor Maurice conversed with some itinerant harpers from that remote country, and only seems to have mistaken a trade for a nation. Theophylact, l. vi. c. 2 [p. 243, *sq.*, ed. Bonn].

were divided and transplanted by the jealous policy of the conquerer.[34] The eastern regions of Germany, which had been left vacant by the emigration of the Vandals, were replenished with Sclavonian colonists; the same tribes are discovered in the neighbourhood of the Hadriatic and of the Baltic; and with the name of Baian himself, the Illyrian cities of Neyss and Lissa are again found in the heart of Silesia. In the disposition both of his troops and provinces the chagan exposed the vassals, whose lives he disregarded,[35] to the first assault; and the swords of the enemy were blunted before they encountered the native valour of the Avars.

The Persian alliance restored the troops of the East to the defence of Europe; and Maurice, who had supported ten years the insolence of the chagan, declared his resolution to march in person against the barbarians. In the space of two centuries none of the successors of Theodosius had appeared in the field; their lives were supinely spent in the palace of Constantinople; and the Greeks could no longer understand that the name of *emperor*, in its primitive sense, denoted the chief of the armies of the republic. The martial ardour of Maurice was opposed by the grave flattery of the senate, the timid superstition of the patriarch, and the tears of the empress Constantina; and they all conjured him to devolve on some meaner general the fatigues and perils of a Scythian campaign. Deaf to their advice and entreaty, the emperor boldly advanced [36] seven miles from the capital; the sacred ensign of the cross was displayed in the front, and Maurice reviewed with conscious pride the arms and numbers of the veterans who had fought and conquered beyond the Tigris. Anchialus was the last term of his progress by sea and land; he solicited without success a miraculous answer to his nocturnal prayers; his mind was confounded by the death of a favourite horse, the encounter of a wild boar, a storm of wind and rain, and the birth of a monstrous child; and he forgot that the best of omens is to unsheathe our sword in the defence of our country.[37] Under the pretence of receiving the ambassadors of Persia, the emperor returned to Constantinople, exchanged the thoughts of war for those of devotion, and disappointed the public hope by his absence and the choice of his lieutenants. The blind par-

[34] This is one of the most probable and luminous conjectures of the learned Count de Buat (Hist. des Peuples Barbares, tom. xi. p. 546-568). The Tzechi and Serbi are found together near Mount Caucasus, in Illyricum, and on the lower Elbe. Even the wildest traditions of the Bohemians, etc., afford some colour to his hypothesis.

[35] See Fredegarius, in the Historians of France, tom. ii. p. 432. Baian did not conceal his proud insensibility. Ὅτι τοιουτοὺς (not τοσουτους, according to a foolish emendation) ἐπαφήσω τῇ Ῥωμαϊκῇ, ὡς εἰ καὶ συμβαίη γε σφισί θανατῷ ἀλῶναι, ἀλλ᾿ ἐμοί γε μὴ γένεσθαι συναίσθησιν.

[36] See the march and return of Maurice, in Theophylact, 1. v. c. 16, 1. vi. c. 1, 2, 3. If he were a writer of taste or genius, we might suspect him of an elegant irony; but Theophylact is surely harmless.

[37] Εἷς οἰωνὸς ἄριστος ἀμύνεσθαι περὶ πάτρης. Iliad, xii. 243. This noble verse, which unites the spirit of a hero with the reason of a sage, may prove that Homer was in every light superior to his age and country.

tiality of fraternal love might excuse the promotion of his brother Peter, who fled with equal disgrace from the barbarians, from his own soldiers, and from the inhabitants of a Roman city. That city, if we may credit the resemblance of name and character, was the famous Azimuntium,[38] which had alone repelled the tempest of Attila. The example of her warlike youth was propagated to succeeding generations; and they obtained, from the first or the second Justin, an honourable privilege that their valour should be always reserved for the defence of their native country. The brother of Maurice attempted to violate this privilege, and to mingle a patriot band with the mercenaries of his camp; they retired to the church; he was not awed by the sanctity of the place; the people rose in their cause, the gates were shut, the ramparts were manned; and the cowardice of Peter was found equal to his arrogance and injustice. The military fame of Commentiolus[39] is the object of satire or comedy rather than of serious history, since he was even deficient in the vile and vulgar qualification of personal courage. His solemn counsels, strange evolutions, and secret orders, always supplied an apology for flight or delay. If he marched against the enemy, the pleasant valleys of Mount Hæmus opposed an insuperable barrier; but in his retreat he explored with fearless curiosity the most difficult and obsolete paths, which had almost escaped the memory of the oldest native. The only blood which he lost was drawn, in a real or affected malady, by the lancet of a surgeon; and his health, which felt with exquisite sensibility the approach of the barbarians, was uniformly restored by the repose and safety of the winter season. A prince who could promote and support this unworthy favourite must derive no glory from the accidental merit of his colleague Priscus.[40] In five successive battles, which seem to have been conducted with skill and resolution, seventeen thousand two hundred barbarians were made prisoners: near sixty thousand, with four sons of the chagan, were slain: the Roman general surprised a peaceful district of the Gepidæ, who slept under the protection of the Avars; and his last trophies were erected on the banks of the Danube and the Theiss. Since the death of Trajan the arms of the empire had not penetrated so deeply into the old Dacia; yet the success of Priscus was transient and barren, and he was soon recalled by the apprehension that Baian, with dauntless spirit and recruited forces, was preparing to avenge his defeat under the walls of Constantinople.[41]

[38] Theophylact, l. vii. c. 3 [p. 274, ed. Bonn]. On the evidence of this fact, which had not occurred to my memory, the candid reader will correct and excuse a note in Chapter XXXIV., vol. i. p. 1213, of this History, which hastens the decay of Asimus, or Azimuntium: another century of patriotism and valour is cheaply purchased by such a confession.

[39] See the shameful conduct of Commentiolus, in Theophylact, l. ii. c. 10-15, l. vii. c. 13, 14, l. viii. c. 2, 4.

[40] See the exploits of Priscus, l. viii. c. 2, 3.

[41] The general detail of the war against the Avars may be traced in the first, second, sixth, seventh, and eighth books of the History of the Emperor Maurice, by Theophylact Simocatta. As he wrote in the reign of Heraclius,

The theory of war was not more familiar to the camps of Cæsar and Trajan than to those of Justinian and Maurice.[42] The iron of Tuscany or Pontus still received the keenest temper from the skill of the Byzantine workmen. The magazines were plentifully stored with every species of offensive and defensive arms. In the construction and use of ships, engines, and fortifications, the barbarians admired the superior ingenuity of a people whom they so often vanquished in the field. The science of tactics, the order, evolutions, and stratagems of antiquity, was transcribed and studied in the books of the Greeks and Romans. But the solitude or degeneracy of the provinces could no longer supply a race of men to handle those weapons, to guard those walls, to navigate those ships, and to reduce the theory of war into bold and successful practice. The genius of Belisarius and Narses had been formed without a master, and expired without a disciple. Neither honour, nor patriotism, nor generous superstition, could animate the lifeless bodies of slaves and strangers who had succeeded to the honours of the legions: it was in the camp alone that the emperor should have exercised a despotic command; it was only in the camps that his authority was disobeyed and insulted: he appeased and inflamed with gold the licentiousness of the troops; but their vices were inherent, their victories were accidental, and their costly maintenance exhausted the substance of a state which they were unable to defend. After a long and pernicious indulgence, the cure of this inveterate evil was undertaken by Maurice; but the rash attempt, which drew destruction on his own head, tended only to aggravate the disease. A reformer should be exempt from the suspicion of interest, and he must possess the confidence and esteem of those whom he proposes to reclaim. The troops of Maurice might listen to the voice of a victorious leader; they disdained the admonitions of statesmen and sophists; and when they received an edict which deducted from their pay the price of their arms and clothing, they execrated the avarice of a prince insensible of the dangers and fatigues from which he had escaped. The camps both of Asia and Europe were agitated with frequent and furious seditions;[43] the enraged soldiers of Edessa pursued with reproaches, with threats, with wounds, their trembling generals; they overturned the statues of the emperor, cast stones against the miraculous image of Christ, and either rejected the yoke of all civil and military laws, or instituted a dangerous model of voluntary subordination. The monarch, always distant and often deceived, was incapable of yielding or persisting, according to the exigence of the moment. But the fear of a general revolt induced him too readily to accept any act

he had no temptation to flatter; but his want of judgment renders him diffuse in trifles, and concise in the most interesting facts.

[42] Maurice himself composed twelve books on the military art, which are still extant, and have been published (Upsal, 1664) by John Scheffer, at the end of the Tactics of Arrian (Fabricius, Biblioth. Græca, l. iv. c. 8, tom. iii. p. 278), who promises to speak more fully of his work in its proper place.

[43] See the mutinies under the reign of Maurice, in Theophylact, l. iii. c. 1-4, l. vi. c. 7, 8, 10, l. vii. c. 1, l. viii. c. 6, etc.

of valour, or any expression of loyalty, as an atonement for the popular offence; the new reform was abolished as hastily as it had been announced; and the troops, instead of punishment and restraint, were agreeably surprised by a gracious proclamation of immunities and rewards. But the soldiers accepted without gratitude the tardy and reluctant gifts of the emperor: their insolence was elated by the discovery of his weakness and their own strength, and their mutual hatred was inflamed beyond the desire of forgiveness or the hope of reconciliation. The historians of the times adopt the vulgar suspicion that Maurice conspired to destroy the troops whom he had laboured to reform; the misconduct and favour of Commentiolus are imputed to this malevolent design; and every age must condemn the inhumanity or avarice [44] of a prince who, by the trifling ransom of six thousand pieces of gold, might have prevented the massacre of twelve thousand prisoners in the hands of the chagan. In the just fervour of indignation, an order was signified to the army of the Danube that they should spare the magazines of the province, and establish their winter quarters in the hostile country of the Avars. The measure of their grievances was full: they pronounced Maurice unworthy to reign, expelled or slaughtered his faithful adherents, and under the command of Phocas, a simple centurion, returned by hasty marches to the neighbourhood of Constantinople. After a long series of legal succession, the military disorders of the third century were again revived; yet such was the novelty of the enterprise that the insurgents were awed by their own rashness. They hesitated to invest their favourite with the vacant purple; and while they rejected all treaty with Maurice himself, they held a friendly correspondence with his son Theodosius and with Germanus, the father-in-law of the royal youth. So obscure had been the former condition of Phocas, that the emperor was ignorant of the name and character of his rival; but as soon as he learned that the centurion, though bold in sedition, was timid in the face of danger, " Alas! " cried the desponding prince, " if he is a coward, he will surely be a murderer."

Yet if Constantinople had been firm and faithful, the murderer might have spent his fury against the walls; and the rebel army would have been gradually consumed or reconciled by the prudence of the emperor. In the games of the circus, which he repeated with unusual pomp, Maurice disguised with smiles of confidence the anxiety of his heart, condescended to solicit the applause of the *factions*, and flattered their pride by accepting from their respective tribunes a list of nine hundred *blues* and fifteen hundred *greens*, whom he affected to esteem as the solid pillars of his throne. Their treacherous or languid support betrayed his weakness and hastened his fall: the green faction were the

[44] Theophylact and Theophanes seem ignorant of the conspiracy and avarice of Maurice. These charges, so unfavourable to the memory of that emperor, are first mentioned by the author of the Paschal Chronicle (p. 379, 380 [ed. Par.; tom. i. p. 695, ed. Bonn]); from whence Zonaras (tom. ii. l. xiv. [c. 13] p. 77, 78) has transcribed them. Cedrenus (p. 399 [tom. i. p. 700, ed. Bonn]) has followed another computation of the ransom.

secret accomplices of the rebels, and the blues recommended lenity and moderation in a contest with their Roman brethren. The rigid and parsimonious virtues of Maurice had long since alienated the hearts of his subjects: as he walked barefoot in a religious procession he was rudely assaulted with stones, and his guards were compelled to present their iron maces in the defence of his person. A fanatic monk ran through the streets with a drawn sword, denouncing against him the wrath and the sentence of God; and a vile plebeian, who represented his countenance and apparel, was seated on an ass and pursued by the imprecations of the multitude.[45] The emperor suspected the popularity of Germanus with the soldiers and citizens: he feared, he threatened, but he delayed to strike; the patrician fled to the sanctuary of the church; the people rose in his defence, the walls were deserted by the guards, and the lawless city was abandoned to the flames and rapine of a nocturnal tumult. In a small bark the unfortunate Maurice, with his wife and nine children, escaped to the Asiatic shore, but the violence of the wind compelled him to land at the church of St. Autonomus,[46] near Chalcedon, from whence he despatched Theodosius, his eldest son, to implore the gratitude and friendship of the Persian monarch. For himself, he refused to fly: his body was tortured with sciatic pains,[47] his mind was enfeebled by superstition; he patiently awaited the event of the revolution, and addressed a fervent and public prayer to the Almighty, that the punishment of his sins might be inflicted in this world rather than in a future life. After the abdication of Maurice, the two factions disputed the choice of an emperor; but the favourite of the blues was rejected by the jealousy of their antagonists, and Germanus himself was hurried along by the crowds who rushed to the palace of Hebdomon, seven miles from the city, to adore the majesty of Phocas the centurion. A modest wish of resigning the purple to the rank and merit of Germanus was opposed by *his* resolution, more obstinate and equally sincere; the senate and clergy obeyed his summons; and as soon as the patriarch was assured of his orthodox belief, he consecrated the successful usurper in the church of St. John the Baptist. On the third day, amidst the acclamations of a thoughtless people, Phocas made

[45] In their clamours against Maurice the people of Constantinople branded him with the name of Marcionite or Marcionist: a heresy (says Theophylact, l. viii. c. 9 [p. 331, ed. Bonn]) μετά τινος μωρᾶς εὐλαβείας, εὐήθης τε καὶ καταγέλαστος. Did they only cast out a vague reproach—or had the emperor really listened to some obscure teacher of those ancient Gnostics?

[46] The church of St. Autonomus (whom I have not the honour to know) was 150 stadia from Constantinople (Theophylact, l. viii. c. 9). The port of Eutropius, where Maurice and his children were murdered, is described by Gyllius (de Bosphoro Thracio, l. iii. c. xi) as one of the two harbours of Chalcedon.

[47] The inhabitants of Constantinople were generally subject to the νόσοι ἀρθρίτιδες; and Theophylact insinuates (l. viii. c. 9 [p. 332, ed. Bonn], that, if it were consistent with the rules of history, he could assign the medical cause. Yet such a digression would not have been more impertinent than his inquiry (l. vii. c. 16, 17) into the annual inundations of the Nile, and all the opinions of the Greek philosophers on that subject.

his public entry in a chariot drawn by four white horses: the revolt of the troops was rewarded by a lavish donative, and the new sovereign, after visiting the palace, beheld from his throne the games of the hippodrome. In a dispute of precedency between the two factions, his partial judgment inclined in favour of the greens. " Remember that Maurice is still alive " resounded from the opposite side; and the indiscreet clamour of the blues admonished and stimulated the cruelty of the tyrant. The ministers of death were despatched to Chalcedon: they dragged the emperor from his sanctuary, and the five sons of Maurice were successively murdered before the eyes of their agonising parent. At each stroke, which he felt in his heart, he found strength to rehearse a pious ejaculation: " Thou art just, O Lord! and thy judgments are righteous." And such in the last moments was his rigid attachment to truth and justice, that he revealed to the soldiers the pious falsehood of a nurse who presented her own child in the place of a royal infant.[48] The tragic scene was finally closed by the execution of the emperor himself, in the twentieth year of his reign, and the sixty-third of his age. The bodies of the father and his five sons were cast into the sea; their heads were exposed at Constantinople to the insults or pity of the multitude; and it was not till some signs of putrefaction had appeared that Phocas connived at the private burial of these venerable remains. In that grave the faults and errors of Maurice were kindly interred. His fate alone was remembered; and at the end of twenty years, in the recital of the history of Theophylact, the mournful tale was interrupted by the tears of the audience.[49]

Such tears must have flowed in secret, and such compassion would have been criminal, under the reign of Phocas, who was peaceably acknowledged in the provinces of the East and West. The images of the emperor and his wife Leontia were exposed in the Lateran to the veneration of the clergy and senate of Rome, and afterwards deposited in the palace of the Cæsars, between those of Constantine and Theodosius. As a subject and a Christian, it was the duty of Gregory to acquiesce in the established government; but the joyful applause with which he salutes the fortune of the assassin has sullied, with indelible disgrace, the character of the saint. The successor of the apostles might have inculcated with decent firmness the guilt of blood and the necessity of repentance; he is content to celebrate the deliverance of the people and the fall of the oppressor; to rejoice that the piety and

[48] From this generous attempt Corneille has deduced the intricate web of his tragedy of *Heraclius*, which requires more than one representation to be clearly understood (Corneille de Voltaire, tom. v. p. 300); and which, after an interval of some years, is said to have puzzled the author himself (Anecdotes Dramatiques, tom. i. p. 422).

[49] The revolt of Phocas and death of Maurice are told by Theophylact Simocatta (1. viii. c. 7-12), the Paschal Chronicle (p. 379, 380 [tom. i. p. 694, sq., ed. Bonn]), Theophanes (Chronograph. p. 238-244 [tom. i. p. 432-448, ed. Bonn]), Zonaras (tom. ii. 1. xiv. [c. 13, 14] p. 77-80), and Cedrenus (p. 399-404 [tom. i. p. 700-708, ed. Bonn]).

benignity of Phocas have been raised by Providence to the Imperial throne; to pray that his hands may be strengthened against all his enemies; and to express a wish, perhaps a prophecy, that, after a long and triumphant reign, he may be transferred from a temporal to an everlasting kingdom.[50] I have already traced the steps of a revolution so pleasing, in Gregory's opinion, both to heaven and earth; and Phocas does not appear less hateful in the exercise than in the acquisition of power. The pencil of an impartial historial has delineated the portrait of a monster;[51] his diminutive and deformed person, the closeness of his shaggy eyebrows, his red hair, his beardless chin, and his cheek disfigured and discoloured by a formidable scar. Ignorant of letters, of laws, and even of arms, he indulged in the supreme rank a more ample privilege of lust and drunkenness, and his brutal pleasures were either injurious to his subjects or disgraceful to himself. Without assuming the office of a prince, he renounced the profession of a soldier, and the reign of Phocas afflicted Europe with ignominious peace and Asia with desolating war. His savage temper was inflamed by passion, hardened by fear, exasperated by resistance or reproach. The flight of Theodosius to the Persian court had been intercepted by a rapid pursuit or a deceitful message: he was beheaded at Nice, and the last hours of the young prince were soothed by the comforts of religion and the consciousness of innocence. Yet his phantom disturbed the repose of the usurper; a whisper was circulated through the East that the son of Maurice was still alive; the people expected their avenger, and the widow and daughters of the late emperor would have adopted as their son and brother the vilest of mankind. In the massacre of the Imperial family,[52] the mercy, or rather the discretion, of Phocas had spared these unhappy females, and they were decently confined to a private house. But the spirit of the empress Constantina, still mindful of her father, her husband, and her sons, aspired to freedom and revenge. At the dead of night she escaped to the sanctuary of St. Sophia, but her tears and the gold of her associate Germanus were insufficient to provoke an insurrection. Her life was forfeited to revenge, and even to justice; but the patriarch obtained and pledged an oath for her safety, a monastery was allotted

---

[50] Gregor. 1. xi. Epist. 38 [1. xiii. Ep. 31, ed. Bened.] indict. vi. Benignitatem vestræ pietatis ad Imperiale fastigium pervenisse gaudemus. Lætentur cœli et evultet terra, et de vestris benignis actibus universæ reipublicæ populus nunc usque vehementer afflictus hilarescat, etc. This base flattery, the topic of Protestant invective, is justly censured by the philosopher Bayle (Dictionnaire Critique, Grégoire I. Not. H. tom. ii. p. 597, 598). Cardinal Baronius justifies the pope at the expense of the fallen emperor.

[51] The images of Phocas were destroyed; but even the malice of his enemies would suffer one copy of such a portrait or caricature (Cedrenus, p. 404 [tom. i. p. 708, ed. Bonn]) to escape the flames.

[52] The family of Maurice is represented by Ducange (Familiæ Byzantinæ, p. 106, 107, 108): his eldest son Theodosius had been crowned emperor when he was no more than four years and a half old, and he is always joined with his father in the salutations of Gregory. With the Christian daughters, Anastasia and Theocteste, I am surprised to find the Pagan name of Cleopatra.

for her prison, and the widow of Maurice accepted and abused the lenity of his assassin. The discovery or the suspicion of a second conspiracy dissolved the engagements, and rekindled the fury, of Phocas. A matron who commanded the respect and pity of mankind, the daughter, wife, and mother of emperors, was tortured like the vilest malefactor, to force a confession of her designs and associates; and the empress Constantina, with her three innocent daughters, was beheaded at Chalcedon, on the same ground which had been stained with the blood of her husband and five sons. After such an example, it would be superfluous to enumerate the names and sufferings of meaner victims. Their condemnation was seldom preceded by the forms of trial, and their punishment was embittered by the refinements of cruelty: their eyes were pierced, their tongues were torn from the root, the hands and feet were amputated; some expired under the lash, others in the flames, others again were transfixed with arrows, and a simple speedy death was mercy which they could rarely obtain. The hippodrome, the sacred asylum of the pleasures and the liberty of the Romans, was polluted with heads and limbs and mangled bodies; and the companions of Phocas were the most sensible that neither his favour nor their services could protect them from a tyrant, the worthy rival of the Caligulas and Domitians of the first age of the empire.[53]

A daughter of Phocas, his only child, was given in marriage to the patrician Crispus,[54] and the *royal* images of the bride and bridegroom were indiscreetly placed in the circus by the side of the emperor. The father must desire that his posterity should inherit the fruit of his crimes, but the monarch was offended by this premature and popular association; the tribunes of the green faction, who accused the officious error of their sculptors, were condemned to instant death; their lives were granted to the prayers of the people, but Crispus might reasonably doubt whether a jealous usurper could forget and pardon his involuntary competition. The green faction was alienated by the ingratitude of Phocas and the loss of their privileges: every province of the empire was ripe for rebellion; and Heraclius, exarch of Africa, persisted above two years in refusing all tribute and obedience to the centurion who disgraced the throne of Constantinople. By the secret emissaries of Crispus and the senate, the independent exarch was solicited to save and to govern his country: but his ambition was chilled by age, and he resigned the dangerous enterprise to his son Heraclius, and to Nicetas, the son of Gregory, his friend and lieutenant. The powers of Africa were armed by the two adventurous youths: they agreed that the one

---

[53] Some of the cruelties of Phocas are marked by Theophylact, l. viii. c. 13, 14, 15. George of Pisidia, the poet of Heraclius, styles him (Bell. Abaricum, p. 46, Rome, 1777) τῆς τυραννίδος ὁ δυσκάθεκτος καὶ βιοφθόρος δράκων [v. 49]. The latter epithet is just—but the corrupter of life was easily vanquished.

[54] In the writers, and in the copies of those writers, there is such hesitation between the names of *Priscus* and *Crispus* (Ducange, Fam. Byzant. p. 111), that I have been tempted to identify the son-in-law of Phocas with the hero five times victorious over the Avars.

should navigate the fleet from Carthage to Constantinople, that the other should lead an army through Egypt and Asia, and that the Imperial purple should be the reward of diligence and success. A faint rumour of their undertaking was conveyed to the ears of Phocas, and the wife and mother of the younger Heraclius were secured as the hostages of his faith; but the treacherous heart of Crispus extenuated the distant peril, the means of defence were neglected or delayed, and the tyrant supinely slept till the African navy cast anchor in the Hellespont. Their standard was joined at Abydus by the fugitives and exiles who thirsted for revenge: the ships of Heraclius, whose lofty masts were adorned with the holy symbols of religion,[55] steered their triumphant course through the Propontis; and Phocas beheld from the windows of the palace his approaching and inevitable fate. The green faction was tempted, by gifts and promises, to oppose a feeble and fruitless resistance to the landing of the Africans; but the people, and even the guards, were determined by the well-timed defection of Crispus, and the tyrant was seized by a private enemy, who boldly invaded the solitude of the palace. Stripped of the diadem and purple, clothed in a vile habit, and loaded with chains, he was transported in a small boat to the Imperial galley of Heraclius, who reproached him with the crimes of his abominable reign. " Wilt thou govern better? " were the last words of the despair of Phocas. After suffering each variety of insult and torture, his head was severed from his body, the mangled trunk was cast into the flames, and the same treatment was inflicted on the statues of the vain usurper and the seditious banner of the green faction. The voice of the clergy, the senate, and the people invited Heraclius to ascend the throne which he had purified from guilt and ignominy; after some graceful hesitation he yielded to their entreaties. His coronation was accompanied by that of his wife Eudoxia, and their posterity, till the fourth generation, continued to reign over the empire of the East.[56] The voyage of Heraclius had been easy and prosperous; the tedious march of Nicetas was not accomplished before the decision of the contest, but he submitted without a murmur to the fortune of his friend, and his laudable intentions were rewarded with an equestrian statue and a daughter of the emperor. It was more difficult to trust the fidelity of Crispus, whose recent services were recompensed by the command of the Cappadocian army. His arrogance soon provoked, and seemed to excuse, the ingratitude of his new sovereign. In the presence of the senate, the son-in-law of Phocas was condemned to embrace the

---

[55] According to Theophanes [tom. i. p. 459, ed. Bonn], κιβώτια and εἰκόνας [τῆς] θεομήτορος. Cedrenus adds an ἀχειροποίητον εἴκονα τοῦ κυρίου, which Heraclius bore as a banner in the first Persian expedition [tom. i. p. 719]. See George Pisid. Acroas. i. 140. The manufacture seems to have flourished, but Foggini, the Roman editor (p. 26), is at a loss to determine whether this picture was an original or a copy.

[56] The following is the genealogical table of the family of Heraclius:—

monastic life; and the sentence was justified by the weighty observation of Heraclius, that the man who had betrayed his father could never be faithful to his friend.[57]

Even after his death the republic was afflicted by the crimes of Phocas, which armed with a pious cause the most formidable of her enemies. According to the friendly and equal forms of the Byzantine and Persian courts, he announced his exaltation to the throne; and his ambassador Lilius, who had presented him with the heads of Maurice and his sons, was the best qualified to describe the circumstances of the tragic scene.[58] However it might be varnished by fiction or sophistry, Chosroes turned with horror from the assassin, imprisoned the pretended envoy, disclaimed the usurper, and declared himself the avenger of his father and benefactor. The sentiments of grief and resentment, which humanity would feel and honour would dictate, promoted on this occasion the interest of the Persian king, and his interest was

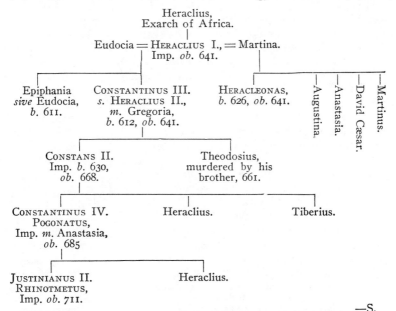

—S.

[57] See the tyranny of Phocas and the elevation of Heraclius, in Chron. Paschal. p. 380-383 [tom. i. p. 694-701, ed. Bonn] ; Theophanes, p. 242-250 [tom. i. p. 446-459, ed. Bonn] ; Nicephorus, p. 3-7 [ed. Par. 1648] ; Cedrenus, p. 404-407 [tom. i. p. 708-714, ed. Bonn] ; Zonaras, tom. ii. l. xiv. [c. 14, 15] p. 80-82.

[58] Theophylact, l. viii. c. 15 [p. 346, ed. Bonn]. The Life of Maurice was composed about the year 628 (l. viii. c. 13) by Theophylact Simocatta, expræfect, a native of Egypt. Photius, who gives an ample extract of the work (cod. lxv. p. 81-100 [p. 27-33, ed. Bekk.]), gently reproves the affectation and allegory of the style. His preface is a dialogue between Philosophy and History; they seat themselves under a plane-tree, and the latter touches her lyre.

powerfully magnified by the national and religious prejudices of the Magi and satraps. In a strain of artful adulation, which assumed the language of freedom, they presumed to censure the excess of his gratitude and friendship for the Greeks, a nation with whom it was dangerous to conclude either peace or alliance, whose superstition was devoid of truth and justice, and who must be incapable of any virtue since they could perpetrate the most atrocious of crimes, the impious murder of their sovereign.[59] For the crime of an ambitious centurion the nation which he oppressed was chastised with the calamities of war, and the same calamities, at the end of twenty years, were retaliated and redoubled on the heads of the Persians.[60] The general who had restored Chosroes to the throne still commanded in the East, and the name of Narses was the formidable sound with which the Assyrian mothers were accustomed to terrify their infants. It is not improbable that a native subject of Persia should encourage his master and his friend to deliver and possess the provinces of Asia. It is still more probable that Chosroes should animate his troops by the assurance that the sword which they dreaded the most would remain in its scabbard or be drawn in their favour. The hero could not depend on the faith of a tyrant, and the tyrant was conscious how little he deserved the obedience of a hero. Narses was removed from his military command; he reared an independent standard at Hierapolis, in Syria; he was betrayed by fallacious promises, and burnt alive in the market-place of Constantinople. Deprived of the only chief whom they could fear or esteem, the bands which he had led to victory were twice broken by the cavalry, trampled by the elephants, and pierced by the arrows of the barbarians; and a great number of the captives were beheaded on the field of battle by the sentence of the victor, who might justly condemn these seditious mercenaries as the authors or accomplices of the death of Maurice. Under the reign of Phocas, the fortifications of Merdin, Dara, Amida, and Edessa were successively besieged, reduced, and destroyed by the Persian monarch; he passed the Euphrates, occupied the Syrian cities, Hierapolis, Chalcis, and Berrhœa or Aleppo, and soon encompassed the walls of Antioch with his irresistible arms. The rapid tide of success discloses the decay of the empire, the incapacity of Phocas, and the disaffection of his subjects; and Chosrœs provided a decent apology

---

[59] Christianis nec pactum esse, nec fidem nec fœdus . . . quod si ulla ipsis fides fuisset, regem suum non occidissent. Eutych. Annales, tom. ii. p. 211, vers. Pocock.

[60] We must now, for some ages, take our leave of contemporary historians, and descend, if it be a descent, from the affectation of rhetoric to the rude simplicity of chronicles and abridgments. Those of Theophanes (Chronograph. p. 244-279 [tom. i. p. 449-516, ed. Bonn] and Nicephorus (p. 3-16) supply a regular, but imperfect, series of the Persian war; and for any additional facts I quote my special authorities. Theophanes, a courtier who became a monk, was born A.D. 748; Nicephorus, patriarch of Constantinople, who died A.D. 829, was somewhat younger: they both suffered in the cause of images. Hankius, de Scriptoribus Byzantinis, p. 200-246.

for their submission or revolt by an impostor who attended his camp as the son of Maurice [61] and the lawful heir of the monarchy.

The first intelligence from the East which Heraclius received [62] was that of the loss of Antioch; but the aged metropolis, so often overturned by earthquakes and pillaged by the enemy, could supply but a small and languid stream of treasure and blood. The Persians were equally successful and more fortunate in the sack of Cæsarea, the capital of Cappadocia; and as they advanced beyond the ramparts of the frontier, the boundary of ancient war, they found a less obstinate resistance and a more plentiful harvest. The pleasant vale of Damascus has been adorned in every age with a royal city: her obscure felicity has hitherto escaped the historian of the Roman empire: but Chosroes reposed his troops in the paradise of Damascus before he ascended the hills of Libanus or invaded the cities of the Phœnician coast. The conquest of Jerusalem,[63] which had been meditated by Nushirvan, was achieved by the zeal and avarice of his grandson; the ruin of the proudest monument of Christianity was vehemently urged by the intolerant spirit of the Magi; and he could enlist for this holy warfare an army of six-and-twenty thousand Jews, whose furious bigotry might compensate in some degree for the want of valour and discipline. After the reduction of Galilee and the region beyond the Jordan, whose resistance appears to have delayed the fate of the capital, Jerusalem itself was taken by assault. The sepulchre of Christ and the stately churches of Helena and Constantine were consumed, or at least damaged, by the flames; the devout offerings of three hundred years were rifled in one sacrilegious day; the patriarch Zachariah and the *true cross* were transported into Persia; and the massacre of ninety thousand Christians is imputed to the Jews and Arabs, who swelled the disorder of the Persian march. The fugitives of Palestine were entertained at Alexandria by the charity of John the archbishop, who is distinguished among a crowd of saints by the epithet of *almsgiver:* [64] and the revenues

[61] The Persian historians have been themselves deceived; but Theophanes (p. 244 [tom. i. p. 449, ed. Bonn]) accuses Chosroes of the fraud and falsehood; and Eutychius believes (Annal. tom. ii. p. 211) that the son of Maurice, who was saved from the assassins, lived and died a monk on Mount Sinai.

[62] Eutychius dates all the losses of the empire under the reign of Phocas; an error which saves the honour of Heraclius, whom he brings not from Carthage, but Salonica, with a fleet laden with vegetables for the relief of Constantinople (Annal. tom. ii. p. 223, 224). The other Christians of the East, Barhebræus (apud Asseman, Bibliothec. Oriental. tom. iii. p. 412, 413), Elmacin (Hist. Saracen. p. 13-16), Abulpharagius (Dynast. p. 98, 99), are more sincere and accurate. The years of the Persian war are disposed in the chronology of Pagi.

[63] On the conquest of Jerusalem, an event so interesting to the church, see the Annals of Eutychius (tom. ii. p. 212-223), and the lamentations of the monk Antiochus (apud Baronium, Annal. Eccles. A.D. 614, No. 16-26), whose one hundred and twenty-nine homilies are still extant, if what no one reads may be said to be extant.

[64] The Life of this worthy saint is composed by Leontius, a contemporary bishop; and I find in Baronius (Annal. Eccles. A.D. 610, No. 10, etc.) and Fleury (tom. viii. p. 235-242) sufficient extracts of this edifying work.

of the church, with a treasure of three hundred thousand pounds, were restored to the true proprietors, the poor of every country and every denomination. But Egypt itself, the only province which had been exempt since the time of Diocletian from foreign and domestic war, was again subdued by the successors of Cyrus. Pelusium, the key of that impervious country, was surprised by the cavalry of the Persians: they passed with impunity the innumerable channels of the Delta, and explored the long valley of the Nile from the pyramids of Memphis to the confines of Æthiopia. Alexandria might have been relieved by a naval force, but the archbishop and the præfect embarked for Cyprus; and Chosroes entered the second city of the empire, which still preserved a wealthy remnant of industry and commerce.[65] His western trophy was erected, not on the walls of Carthage,[66] but in the neighbourhood of Tripoli: the Greek colonies of Cyrene were finally extirpated; and the conqueror, treading in the footsteps of Alexander, returned in triumph through the sands of the Libyan desert. In the same campaign another army advanced from the Euphrates to the Thracian Bosphorus; Chalcedon surrendered after a long siege, and a Persian camp was maintained above ten years in the presence of Constantinople. The sea-coast of Pontus, the city of Ancyra, and the isle of Rhodes are enumerated among the last conquests of the Great King; and if Chosroes had possessed any maritime power, his boundless ambition would have spread slavery and desolation over the provinces of Europe.

From the long-disputed banks of the Tigris and Euphrates, the reign of the grandson of Nushirvan was suddenly extended to the Hellespont and the Nile, the ancient limits of the Persian monarchy. But the provinces, which had been fashioned by the habits of six hundred years to the virtues and vices of the Roman government, supported with reluctance the yoke of the barbarians. The idea of a republic was kept alive by the institutions, or at least by the writings, of the Greeks and Romans, and the subjects of Heraclius had been educated to pronounce the words of liberty and law. But it has always been the pride and policy of Oriental princes to display the titles and attributes of their omnipotence; to upbraid a nation of slaves with their true name and abject condition; and to enforce, by cruel and insolent threats, the rigour of their absolute commands. The Christians of the East were scandalised by the worship of fire and the impious doctrine of the two principles: the Magi were not less intolerant than the bishops; and the martyrdom of some native Persians who had deserted the religion of Zoroaster [67] was conceived to be the prelude of a

---

[65] [Theophanes gives the date of the conquest of Egypt as A.M. 6107 = A.D. 615.—O. S.]

[66] The error of Baronius, and many others who have carried the arms of Chosroes to Carthage instead of Chalcedon, is founded on the near resemblance of the Greek words Καλχηδόνα and Καρχηδόνα, in the text of Theophanes, etc., which have been sometimes confounded by transcribers, and sometimes by critics.

[67] The *genuine* acts of St. Anastasius are published in those of the seventh

fierce and general persecution. By the oppressive laws of Justinian the adversaries of the church were made the enemies of the state; the alliance of the Jews, Nestorians, and Jacobites had contributed to the success of Chosroes, and his partial favour to the sectaries provoked the hatred and fears of the catholic clergy. Conscious of their fear and hatred, the Persian conqueror governed his new subjects with an iron sceptre; and, as if he suspected the stability of his dominion, he exhausted their wealth by exorbitant tributes and licentious rapine; despoiled or demolished the temples of the East; and transported to his hereditary realms the gold, the silver, the precious marbles, the arts, and the artists of the Asiatic cities. In the obscure picture of the calamities of the empire [68] it is not easy to discern the figure of Chosroes himself, to separate his actions from those of his lieutenants, or to ascertain his personal merit in the general blaze of glory and magnificence. He enjoyed with ostentation the fruits of victory, and frequently retired from the hardships of war to the luxury of the palace. But, in the space of twenty-four years, he was deterred by superstition or resentment from approaching the gates of Ctesiphon: and his favourite residence of Artemita, or Dastagerd, was situate beyond the Tigris, about sixty miles to the north of the capital.[69] The adjacent pastures were covered with flocks and herds: the paradise or park was replenished with pheasants, peacocks, ostriches, roebucks, and wild boars; and the noble game of lions and tigers was sometimes turned loose for the bolder pleasures of the chase. Nine hundred and sixty elephants were maintained for the use or splendour of the Great King; his tents and baggage were carried into the field by twelve thousand great camels and eight thousand of a smaller size;[70] and the royal stables were filled with six thousand mules and horses, among whom the names of Shebdiz and Barid are renowned for their speed or beauty. Six thousand guards successively mounted before the palace gate; the service of the interior apartments was performed by twelve thousand slaves; and in the number of three thousand virgins, the fairest of Asia, some happy concubine might console her master for the age or the indifference of Sira. The various treasures of gold, silver, gems, silk, and aromatics were deposited in a hundred subterraneous vaults; and the chamber *Badaverd* denoted the accidental gift of the winds which had wafted the spoils of Heraclius into one of the Syrian harbours of his rival. The voice of

general council, from whence Baronius (Annal. Eccles. A.D. 614, 626, 627) and Butler (Lives of the Saints, vol. i. p. 242-248) have taken their accounts. The holy martyr deserted from the Persian to the Roman army, became a monk at Jerusalem, and insulted the worship of the Magi, which was then established at Cæsarea in Palestine.

[68] Abulpharagius, Dynast. p. 99; Elmacin, Hist. Saracen. p. 14.

[69] D'Anville, Mém. de l'Académie des Inscriptions, tom. xxxii. p. 568-571.

[70] The difference between the two races consists in one or two humps; the dromedary has only one; the size of the proper camel is larger; the country he comes from, Turkistan or Bactriana; the dromedary is confined to Arabia and Africa. Buffon, Hist. Naturelle, tom. xi. p. 211. etc.; Aristot. Hist. Animal. tom. i. l. ii. c. 1, tom. ii. p. 185.

flattery, and perhaps of fiction, is not ashamed to compute the thirty thousand rich hangings that adorned the walls; the forty thousand col- umns of silver, or more probably of marble, and plated wood, that supported the roof; and the thousand globes of gold suspended in the dome, to imitate the motions of the planets and the constellations of the zodiac.[71] While the Persian monarch contemplated the wonders of his art and power, he received an epistle from an obscure citizen of Mecca, inviting him to acknowledge Mohammed as the apostle of God. He rejected the invitation, and tore the epistle. "It is thus," ex- claimed the Arabian prophet, "that God will tear the kingdom and reject the supplications of Chosroes."[72] Placed on the verge of the two great empires of the East, Mohammed observed with secret joy the progress of their mutual destruction; and in the midst of the Persian triumphs he ventured to foretell that, before many years should elapse, victory would again return to the banners of the Romans.[73]

At the time when this prediction is said to have been delivered, no prophecy could be more distant from its accomplishment, since the first twelve years of Heraclius announced the approaching dissolution of the empire. If the motives of Chosroes had been pure and honourable, he must have ended the quarrel with the death of Phocas, and he would have embraced, as his best ally, the fortunate African who had so generously avenged the injuries of his benefactor Maurice. The prose- cution of the war revealed the true character of the barbarian; and the suppliant embassies of Heraclius to beseech his clemency, that he would spare the innocent, accept a tribute, and give peace to the world, were rejected with contemptuous silence or insolent menace. Syria, Egypt, and the provinces of Asia were subdued by the Persian arms; while Europe, from the confines of Istria to the long wall of Thrace, was oppressed by the Avars, unsatiated with the blood and rapine of the Italian war. They had coolly massacred their male captives in the

[71] Theophanes, Chronograph. p. 268 [tom. i. p. 494, ed. Bonn]. D'Her- belot, Bibliothèque Orientale, p. 997. The Greeks describe the decay, the Persians the splendour, of Dastagerd; but the former speak from the modest witness of the eye, the latter from the vague report of the ear.

[72] The historians of Mohammed, Abulfeda (in Vit. Mohammed, p. 92, 93) and Gagnier (Vie de Mohammed, tom. ii. p. 247), date this embassy in the seventh year of the Hegira, which commences A.D. 628, May 11. Their chro- nology is erroneous, since Chosroes died in the month of February of the same year (Pagi, Critica, tom. ii. p. 779). The Count de Boulainvilliers (Vie de Mahomed, p. 327, 328) places this embassy about A.D. 615, soon after the conquest of Palestine. Yet Mohammed would scarcely have ventured so soon on so bold a step.

[Chosroes (Khoosroo Purveez) was encamped on the banks of the Karasoo river when he received the letter, which he tore up and threw into the Karasoo. For this action to this day, as Sir John Malcolm records, he is regarded as an outcast by all pious Mohammedans.—O. S.]

[73] See the thirtieth chapter of the Koran, entitled *the Greeks*. Our honest and learned translator, Sale (p. 330, 331), fairly states this conjecture, guess, wager, of Mohammed; but Boulainvilliers (p. 329-344), with wicked intentions, labours to establish this evident prophecy of a future event, which must, in his opinion, embarrass the Christian polemics.

sacred field of Pannonia; the women and children were reduced to servitude, and the noblest virgins were abandoned to the promiscuous lust of the barbarians. The amorous matron who opened the gates of Friuli passed a short night in the arms of her royal lover; the next evening Romilda was condemned to the embraces of twelve Avars; and, the third day, the Lombard princess was impaled in the sight of the camp, while the chagan observed, with a cruel smile, that such a husband was the fit recompense of her lewdness and perfidy.[74] By these implacable enemies Heraclius, on either side, was insulted and besieged: and the Roman empire was reduced to the walls of Constantinople, with the remnant of Greece, Italy, and Africa, and some maritime cities, from Tyre to Trebizond, of the Asiatic coast. After the loss of Egypt the capital was afflicted by famine and pestilence; and the emperor, incapable of resistance and hopeless of relief, had resolved to transfer his person and government to the more secure residence of Carthage. His ships were already laden with the treasures of the palace; but his flight was arrested by the patriarch, who armed the powers of religion in the defence of his country, led Heraclius to the altar of St. Sophia, and extorted a solemn oath that he would live and die with the people whom God had intrusted to his care. The chagan was encamped in the plains of Thrace; but he dissembled his perfidious designs, and solicited an interview with the emperor near the town of Heraclea. Their reconciliation was celebrated with equestrian games; the senate and people, in their gayest apparel, resorted to the festival of peace; and the Avars beheld, with envy and desire, the spectacle of Roman luxury. On a sudden the hippodrome was encompassed by the Scythian cavalry, who had pressed their secret and nocturnal march: the tremendous sound of the chagan's whip gave the signal of the assault; and Heraclius, wrapping his diadem round his arm, was saved, with extreme hazard, by the fleetness of his horse. So rapid was the pursuit, that the Avars almost entered the golden gate of Constantinople with the flying crowds:[75] but the plunder of the suburbs rewarded their treason, and they transported beyond the Danube two hundred and seventy thousand captives. On the shore of Chalcedon the emperor held a safer conference with a more honourable foe, who, before Heraclius descended from his galley, saluted with reverence and pity the majesty of the purple. The friendly offer of Sain, the Persian general, to conduct an embassy to the presence of the Great King was accepted with the warmest gratitude; and the prayer for pardon and

---

[74] Paul Warnefrid, de Gestis Langobardorum, l. iv. c. 38, 42; Muratori, Annali d'Italia, tom. v. p. 305, etc.

[75] The Paschal Chronicle, which sometimes introduces fragments of history into a barren list of names and dates, gives the best account of the treason of the Avars, p. 389, 390 [tom. i. p. 712 *sq.*, ed. Bonn]. The number of captives is added by Nicephorus.

[Theophanes dates the attack of the Avars on Constantinople as 619 A.D., while others place it at 623. It was during this campaign that the clothing of the Holy Virgin was discovered at Blachern.—O. S.]

peace was humbly presented by the prætorian præfect, the præfect of the city, and one of the first ecclesiastics of the patriarchal church.[76] But the lieutenant of Chosroes had fatally mistaken the intentions of his master. "It was not an embassy," said the tyrant of Asia, "it was the person of Heraclius, bound in chains, that he should have brought to the foot of my throne. I will never give peace to the emperor of Rome till he has abjured his crucified God and embraced the worship of the sun." Sain was flayed alive, according to the inhuman practice of his country; and the separate and rigorous confinement of the ambassadors violated the law of nations and the faith of an express stipulation. Yet the experience of six years at length persuaded the Persian monarch to renounce the conquest of Constantinople, and to specify the annual tribute or ransom of the Roman empire: a thousand talents of gold, a thousand talents of silver, a thousand silk robes, a thousand horses, and a thousand virgins. Heraclius subscribed these ignominious terms; but the time and space which he obtained to collect such treasures from the poverty of the East was industriously employed in the preparations of a bold and desperate attack.

Of the characters conspicuous in history, that of Heraclius is one of the most extraordinary and inconsistent. In the first and the last years of a long reign the emperor appears to be the slave of sloth, of pleasure, or of superstition; the careless and impotent spectator of the public calamities. But the languid mists of the morning and evening are separated by the brightness of the meridian sun: the Arcadius of the palace arose the Cæsar of the camp; and the honour of Rome and Heraclius was gloriously retrieved by the exploits and trophies of six adventurous campaigns. It was the duty of the Byzantine historians to have revealed the causes of his slumber and vigilance. At this distance we can only conjecture that he was endowed with more personal courage than political resolution; that he was detained by the charms, and perhaps the arts, of his niece Martina, with whom, after the death of Eudocia, he contracted an incestuous marriage;[77] and that he yielded to the base advice of the counsellors who urged, as a fundamental law, that the life of the emperor should never be exposed in the field.[78] Perhaps he was awakened by the last insolent demand of the Persian conqueror; but at the moment when Heraclius assumed the spirit of a

[76] Some original pieces, such as the speech or letter of the Roman ambassadors (p. 386-388 [ed. Par.; tom. i. p. 707-709, ed. Bonn]), likewise constitute the merit of the Paschal Chronicle, which was composed, perhaps at Alexandria, under the reign of Heraclius.

[77] Nicephorus (p. 10, 11), who brands this marriage with the names of ἄθεσμον and ἀθέμιτον, is happy to observe, that of two sons, its incestuous fruit, the elder was marked by Providence with a stiff neck, the younger with the loss of hearing.

[78] George of Pisidia (Acroas. i. 112-125, p. 5), who states the opinions, acquits the pusillanimous counsellors of any sinister views. Would he have excused the proud and contemptuous admonition of Crispus? Ἐπιθωπτάζων οὐκ ἔξον βασιλεῖ ἔφασκε καταλιμπάνειν βασίλεια, καὶ τοῖς πόρρω ἐπιχωριάζειν δυνάμεσιν.

hero, the only hopes of the Romans were drawn from the vicissitudes cf fortune, which might threaten the proud prosperity of Chosroes, and must be favourable to those who had attained the lowest period of depression.[79] To provide for the expenses of war was the first care of the emperor; and for the purpose of collecting the tribute he was allowed to solicit the benevolence of the Eastern provinces. But the revenue no longer flowed in the usual channels; the credit of an arbitrary prince is annihilated by his power; and the courage of Heraclius was first displayed in daring to borrow the consecrated wealth of churches, under the solemn vow of restoring, with usury, whatever he had been compelled to employ in the service of religion and of the empire. The clergy themselves appear to have sympathised with the public distress; and the discreet patriarch of Alexandria, without admitting the precedent of sacrilege, assisted his sovereign by the miraculous or seasonable revelation of a secret treasure.[80] Of the soldiers who had conspired with Phocas, only two were found to have survived the stroke of time and of the barbarians;[81] the loss even of these seditious veterans was imperfectly supplied by the new levies of Heraclius; and the gold of the sanctuary united, in the same camp, the names, and arms, and languages of the East and West. He would have been content with the neutrality of the Avars; and his friendly entreaty that the chagan would act not as the enemy, but as the guardian of the empire, was accompanied with a more persuasive donative of two hundred thousand pieces of gold. Two days after the festival of Easter, the emperor, exchanging his purple for the simple garb of a penitent and warrior,[82] gave the signal of his departure. To the faith of the people Heraclius recommended his children; the civil and military powers were vested in the most deserving hands; and the discretion of the patriarch and senate was authorised to save or surrender the city, if they should be oppressed in his absence by the superior forces of the enemy.

[79] Εἰ τὰς ἐπ' ἄκρον ἡρμένας εὐεξίας
'Εσφαλμένας λέγουσιν οὐκ ἀπεικότως,
Κείσθω τὸ λοιπὸν ἐν κακοῖς τὰ Πέρσιδος,
'Αντιστρόψως δὲ, etc.
George Pisid. Acroas. i. 51, etc., p. 4.
The Orientals are not less fond of remarking this strange vicissitude; and I remember some story of Khosrou Parviz, not very unlike the ring of Polycrates of Samos.

[80] Baronius gravely relates this discovery, or rather transmutation, of barrels, not of honey, but of gold (Annal. Eccles. A.D. 620, No. 3, etc.). Yet the loan was arbitrary, since it was collected by soldiers, who were ordered to leave the patriarch of Alexandria no more than one hundred pounds of gold. Nicephorus (p. 11), two hundred years afterwards, speaks with ill-humour of this contribution, which the church of Constantinople might still feel.

[81] Theophylact Simocatta, l. viii. c. 12 [p. 340, ed. Bonn]. This circumstance need not excite our surprise. The muster-roll of a regiment, even in time of peace, is renewed in less than twenty or twenty-five years.

[82] He changed his *purple*, for *black*, buskins, and dyed them *red* in the blood of the Persians (George. Pisid. Acroas. iii. 118, 121, 122. See the Notes of Foggini, p. 35).

The neighbouring heights of Chalcedon were covered with tents and arms; but if the new levies of Heraclius had been rashly led to the attack, the victory of the Persians in the sight of Constantinople might have been the last day of the Roman empire. As imprudent would it have been to advance into the provinces of Asia, leaving their innumerable cavalry to intercept his convoys, and continually to hang on the lassitude and disorder of his rear. But the Greeks were still masters of the sea; a fleet of galleys, transports, and store-ships was assembled in the harbour; the barbarians consented to embark; a steady wind carried them through the Hellespont; the western and southern coast of Asia Minor lay on their left hand; the spirit of their chief was first displayed in a storm; and even the eunuchs of his train were excited to suffer and to work by the example of their master. He landed his troops on the confines of Syria and Cilicia, in the gulf of Scanderoon, where the coast suddenly turns to the south;[83] and his discernment was expressed in the choice of this important post.[84] From all sides the scattered garrisons of the maritime cities and the mountains might repair with speed and safety to his Imperial standard. The natural fortifications of Cilicia protected and even concealed the camp of Heraclius, which was pitched near Issus, on the same ground where Alexander had vanquished the host of Darius. The angle which the emperor occupied was deeply indented into a vast semicircle of the Asiatic, Armenian, and Syrian provinces; and to whatsoever point of the circumference he should direct his attack, it was easy for him to dissemble his own motions, and to prevent those of the enemy. In the camp of Issus the Roman general reformed the sloth and disorder of the veterans, and educated the new recruits in the knowledge and practice of military virtue. Unfolding the miraculous image of Christ, he urged them to *revenge* the holy altars which had been profaned by the worshippers of fire; addressing them by the endearing appellations of sons and brethren, he deplored

---

[83] George of Pisidia (Acroas. ii. 10, p. 8) has fixed this important point of the Syrian and Cicilian gates. They are elegantly described by Xenophon, who marched through them a thousand years before. A narrow pass of three stadia, between steep high rocks ($\pi\acute{\epsilon}\tau\rho\alpha\iota$ $\mathring{\eta}\lambda\acute{\iota}\beta\alpha\tau o\iota$) and the Mediterranean, was closed at each end by strong gates, impregnable to the land ($\pi\alpha\rho\epsilon\lambda\theta\epsilon\widehat{\iota}\nu$ $o\mathring{v}\kappa$ $\mathring{\eta}\nu$ $\beta\acute{\iota}\alpha$), accessible by sea (Anabasis, l. i. [c. 4] p. 35, 36, with Hutchinson's Geographical Dissertation, p. vi.). The gates were thirty-five parasangs, or leagues, from Tarsus (Anabasis, l. i. [c. 4] p. 33, 34), and eight or ten from Antioch. Compare Itinerar. Wesseling. p. 580, 581; Schultens, Index Geograph. ad calcem Vit. Saladin. p. 9; Voyage en Turquie et en Perse, par M. Otter, tom. i. p. 78, 79.
[This place where Heraclius pitched his camp has been called the Π$\acute{v}$λαι by George of Pisidia, and translated as well as identified as "the Cicilian Gates." But Tafel has shown that this identification is not correct, and that the locality indicated is Pylæ on the southern side of the Nicomedian Bay, which Heraclius had reached by sailing round the cape of Heræum.—O. S.]
[84] Heraclius might write to a friend in the modest words of Cicero: "Castra habuimus ea ipsa quæ contra Darium habuerat apud Issum Alexander, imperator haud paulo melior quam aut tu aut ego." Ad Atticum, v. 20. Issus, a rich and flourishing city in the time of Xenophon, was ruined by the prosperity of Alexandria or Scanderoon, on the other side of the bay.

the public and private wrongs of the republic. The subjects of a monarch were persuaded that they fought in the cause of freedom, and a similar enthusiasm was communicated to the foreign mercenaries, who must have viewed with equal indifference the interest of Rome and of Persia. Heraclius himself, with the skill and patience of a centurion, inculcated the lessons of the school of tactics, and the soldiers were assiduously trained in the use of their weapons and the exercises and evolutions of the field. The cavalry and infantry, in light or heavy armour, were divided into two parties; the trumpets were fixed in the centre, and their signals directed the march, the charge, the retreat or pursuit, the direct or oblique order, the deep or extended phalanx, to represent in fictitious combat the operations of genuine war. Whatever hardship the emperor imposed on the troops, he inflicted with equal severity on himself; their labour, their diet, their sleep, were measured by the inflexible rules of discipline; and, without despising the enemy, they were taught to repose an implicit confidence in their own valour and the wisdom of their leader. Cilicia was soon encompassed with the Persian arms, but their cavalry hesitated to enter the defiles of Mount Taurus till they were circumvented by the evolutions of Heraclius, who insensibly gained their rear, whilst he appeared to present his front in order of battle. By a false motion, which seemed to threaten Armenia, he drew them against their wishes to a general action. They were tempted by the artful disorder of his camp; but when they advanced to combat, the ground, the sun, and the expectation of both armies were unpropitious to the barbarians: the Romans successfully repeated their tactics in a field of battle,[85] and the event of the day declared to the world that the Persians were not invincible, and that a hero was invested with the purple. Strong in victory and fame, Heraclius boldly ascended the heights of Mount Taurus, directed his march through the plains of Cappadocia, and established his troops for the winter season in safe and plentiful quarters on the banks of the river Halys.[86] His soul was superior to the vanity of entertaining Constantinople with an imperfect triumph; but the presence of the emperor was indispensably required to soothe the restless and rapacious spirit of the Avars.

Since the days of Scipio and Hannibal, no bolder enterprise has been attempted than that which Heraclius achieved for the deliverance of the empire.[87] He permitted the Persians to oppress for awhile the

[85] Foggini (Annotat. p. 31) suspects that the Persians were deceived by the φάλαγξ πεπληγμένη of Ælian (Tactic. c. 48), an intricate spiral motion of the army. He observes (p. 28) that the military descriptions of George of Pisidia are transcribed in the Tactics of the emperor Leo.

[86] George of Pisidia, an eye-witness (Acroas. ii. 122, etc.), described, in three acroaseis or cantos, the first expedition of Heraclius. The poem has been lately (1777) published at Rome; but such vague and declamatory praise is far from corresponding with the sanguine hopes of Pagi, D'Anville, etc.

[87] Theophanes (p. 256) carries Heraclius swiftly (κατά ταχὸς) into Armenia. Nicephorus (p. 11), though he confounds the two expeditions, defines the province of Lazica. Eutychius (Annal. tom. ii. p. 231) has given the 5000 men with the more probable station of Trebizond.

provinces, and to insult with impunity the capital of the East, while the Roman emperor explored his perilous way through the Black Sea [88] and the mountains of Armenia, penetrated into the heart of Persia,[89] and recalled the armies of the Great King to the defense of their bleeding country.

With a select band of five thousand soldiers, Heraclius sailed from Constantinople to Trebizond; assembled his forces which had wintered in the Pontic regions; and from the mouth of the Phasis to the Caspian Sea, encouraged his subjects and allies to march with the successor of Constantine under the faithful and victorious banner of the cross. When the legions of Lucullus and Pompey first passed the Euphrates, they blushed at their easy victory over the natives of Armenia. But the long experience of war had hardened the minds and bodies of that effeminate people; their zeal and bravery were approved in the service of a declining empire; they abhorred and feared the usurpation of the house of Sassan, and the memory of persecution envenomed their pious hatred of the enemies of Christ. The limits of Armenia, as it had been ceded to the emperor Maurice, extended as far as the Araxes: the river submitted to the indignity of a bridge,[90] and Heraclius, in the footsteps of Mark Antony, advanced towards the city of Tauris or Gandzaca,[91] the ancient and modern capital of one of the provinces of Media. At the head of forty thousand men, Chosroes himself had returned from some distant expedition to oppose the progress of the Roman arms; but he retreated on the approach of Heraclius, declining the generous alternative of peace or battle. Instead of half a million of inhabitants, which have been ascribed to Tauris under the reign of the Sophys, the city contained no more than three thousand houses; but the value of the royal treasures was enhanced by a tradition that they were the spoils of Crœsus, which

[88] From Constantinople to Trebizond, with a fair wind, four or five days; from thence to Erzerom, five; to Erivan, twelve; to Tauris, ten: in all, thirty-two. Such is the Itinerary of Tavernier (Voyages, tom. i. p. 12-56), who was perfectly conversant with the roads of Asia. Tournefort, who travelled with a pasha, spent ten or twelve days between Trebizond and Erzerom (Voyage du Levant, tom. iii. lettre xviii.); and Chardin (Voyages, tom. i. p. 249-254) gives the more correct distance of fifty-three parasangs, each of 5000 paces (what paces?), between Erivan and Tauris.

[89] The expedition of Heraclius into Persia is finely illustrated by M. D'Anville (Mémoires de l'Académie des Inscriptions, tom. xxviii. p. 559-573). He discovers the situation of Gandzaca, Thebarma, Dastagerd, etc., with admirable skill and learning; but the obscure campaign of 624 he passes over in silence.

[90] Et pontem indignatus Araxes.—Virgil, Æneid, viii. 728. The river Araxes is noisy, rapid, vehement, and, with the melting of the snows, irresistible: the strongest and most massy bridges are swept away by the current; and its *indignation* is attested by the ruins of many arches near the old town of Zulfa. Voyages de Chardin, tom. i. p. 252.

[91] Chardin, tom. i. p. 255-259. With the Orientals (D'Herbelot, Biblioth. Orient. p. 834), he ascribes the foundation of Tauris, or Tebris, to Zobeide, the wife of the famous Khalif Haroun Alrashid; but it appears to have been more ancient; and the names of Gandzaca, Gazaca, Gaza, are expressive of the royal treasure. The number of 550,000 inhabitants is reduced by Chardin from 1,100,000, the popular estimate.

had been transported by Cyrus from the citadel of Sardes. The rapid conquests of Heraclius were suspended only by the winter season; a motive of prudence or superstition [92] determined his retreat into the province of Albania, along the shores of the Caspian; and his tents were most probably pitched in the plains of Mogan,[93] the favourite encampment of Oriental princes. In the course of this successful inroad he signalised the zeal and revenge of a Christian emperor: at his command the soldiers extinguished the fire, and destroyed the temples, of the Magi; the statues of Chosroes, who aspired to divine honours, were abandoned to the flames; and the ruin of Thebarma or Ormia,[94] which had given birth to Zoroaster himself, made some atonement for the injuries of the holy sepulchre. A purer spirit of religion was shown in the relief and deliverance of fifty thousand captives. Heraclius was rewarded by their tears and grateful acclamations; but this wise measure, which spread the fame of his benevolence, diffused the murmurs of the Persians against the pride and obstinacy of their own sovereign.

Admidst the glories of the succeeding campaign, Heraclius is almost lost to our eyes, and to those of the Byzantine historians.[95] From the spacious and fruitful plains of Albania, the emperor appears to follow the chain of Hyrcanian mountains, to descend into the province of Media or Irak, and to carry his victorious arms as far as the royal cities of Casbin and Ispahan, which had never been approached by a Roman conqueror. Alarmed by the danger of his kingdom, the powers of Chosroes were already recalled from the Nile and the Bosphorus, and three formidable armies surrounded, in a distant and hostile land, the camp of the emperor. The Colchian allies prepared to desert his standard; and the fears of the bravest veterans were expressed, rather than concealed, by their desponding silence. " Be not terrified," said the intrepid Heraclius, " by the multitude of your foes. With the aid of Heaven, one Roman may triumph over a thousand barbarians. But

[92] He opened the Gospel and applied or interpreted the first casual passage to the name and situation of Albania. Theophanes, p. 258 [tom. i. p. 474, ed. Bonn].

[93] The heath of Mogan, between the Cyrus and the Araxes, is sixty parasangs in length and twenty in breadth (Olearius, p. 1023, 1024), abounding in waters and fruitful pastures (Hist. de Nadir Shah, translated by Mr. Jones from a Persian MS. part ii. p. 2, 3). See the encampments of Timur (Hist. par Sherefeddin Ali, l. v. c. 37, l. vi. c. 13) and the coronation of Nadir Shah (Hist. Persanne, p. 3-13, and the English Life by Mr. Jones, p. 64, 65).

[94] Thebarma and Ormia, near the lake Spauta, are proved to be the same city by D'Anville (Mémoires de l'Académie, tom. xxviii. p. 564, 565). It is honoured as the birthplace of Zoroaster, according to the Persians (Schultens, Index Geograph. p. 48) ; and their tradition is fortified by M. Perron d'Anquetil (Mém. de l'Acad. des Inscript. tom. xxxi. p. 375), with some texts from his, or their, Zendavesta.

[95] I cannot find, and (what is much more) M. D'Anville does not attempt to seek, the Salban, Tarantum, territory of the Huns, etc., mentioned by Theophanes (p. 260-262). Eutychius (Annal. tom. ii. p. 231, 232), an insufficient author, names Asphahan; and Casbin is most probably the city of Sapor. Ispahan is twenty-four days' journey from Tauris, and Casbin half way between them (Voyages de Tavernier, tom. i. p. 63-82).

if we devote our lives for the salvation of our brethren, we shall obtain the crown of martyrdom, and our immortal reward will be liberally paid by God and posterity." These magnanimous sentiments were supported by the vigour of his actions. He repelled the threefold attack of the Persians, improved the divisions of their chiefs, and, by a well-concerted train of marches, retreats, and successful actions, finally chased them from the field into the fortified cities of Media and Assyria. In the severity of the winter season, Sarbaraza deemed himself secure in the walls of Salban: he was surprised by the activity of Heraclius, who divided his troops, and performed a laborious march in the silence of the night. The flat roofs of the houses were defended with useless valour against the darts and torches of the Romans: the satraps and nobles of Persia, with their wives and children, and the flower of their martial youth, were either slain or made prisoners. The general escaped by a precipitate flight, but his golden armour was the prize of the conqueror; and the soldiers of Heraclius enjoyed the wealth and repose which they had so nobly deserved. On the return of spring, the emperor traversed in seven days the mountains of Curdistan, and passed without resistance the rapid stream of the Tigris. Oppressed by the weight of their spoils and captives, the Roman army halted under the walls of Amida; and Heraclius informed the senate of Constantinople of his safety and success, which they had already felt by the retreat of the besiegers. The bridges of the Euphrates were destroyed by the Persians; but as soon as the emperor had discovered a ford, they hastily retired to defend the banks of the Sarus,[96] in Cilicia. That river, an impetuous torrent, was about three hundred feet broad; the bridge was fortified with strong turrets; and the banks were lined with barbarian archers. After a bloody conflict, which continued till the evening, the Romans prevailed in the assault; and a Persian of gigantic size was slain and thrown into the Sarus by the hand of the emperor himself. The enemies were dispersed and dismayed; Heraclius pursued his march to Sebaste in Cappadocia; and at the expiration of three years, the same coast of the Euxine applauded his return from a long and victorious expedition.[97]

Instead of skirmishing on the frontier, the two monarchs who disputed the empire of the East aimed their desperate strokes at the heart of their rival. The military force of Persia was wasted by the marches and combats of twenty years, and many of the veterans, who had survived the perils of the sword and the climate, were still detained in the fortresses of Egypt and Syria. But the revenge and ambition of Chosroes exhausted his kingdom; and the new levies of subjects, strangers, and slaves, were divided into three formidable bodies.[98] The first army of

[96] At ten parasangs from Tarsus the army of the younger Cyrus passed the Sarus, three plethra in breadth: the Pyramus, a stadium in breadth, ran five parasangs farther to the east (Xenophon, Anabas. l. i. p. 33, 34 [c. 4 *init*.]).
[97] George of Pisidia (Bell. Abaricum, 246-265, p. 49) celebrates with truth the persevering courage of the three campaigns (τρεις περιδρόμους) against the Persians.
[98] Petavius (Annotationes ad Nicephorum, p. 62, 63, 64) discriminates the

fifty thousand men, illustrious by the ornament and title of the *golden spears,* was destined to march against Heraclius; the second was stationed to prevent his junction with the troops of his brother Theodorus; and the third was commanded to besiege Constantinople, and to second the operations of the chagan, with whom the Persian king had ratified a treaty of alliance and partition. Sarbar, the general of the third army, penetrated through the provinces of Asia to the well-known camp of Chalcedon, and amused himself with the destruction of the sacred and profane buildings of the Asiatic suburbs, while he impatiently waited the arrival of his Scythian friends on the opposite side of the Bosphorus. On the twenty-ninth of June, thirty thousand barbarians, the vanguard of the Avars, forced the long wall, and drove into the capital a promiscuous crowd of peasants, citizens, and soldiers. Fourscore thousand [99] of his native subjects, and of the vassal tribes of Gepidæ, Russians, Bulgarians, and Sclavonians, advanced under the standard of the chagan; a month was spent in marches and negotiations, but the whole city was invested on the thirty-first of July, from the suburbs of Pera and Galata to the Blachernæ and seven towers; and the inhabitants descried with terror the flaming signals of the European and Asiatic shores. In the meanwhile the magistrates of Constantinople repeatedly strove to purchase the retreat of the chagan; but their deputies were rejected and insulted; and he suffered the patricians to stand before his throne, while the Persian envoys, in silk robes, were seated by his side. " You see," said the haughty barbarian, " the proofs of my perfect union with the Great King; and his lieutenant is ready to send into my camp a select band of three thousand warriors. Presume no longer to tempt your master with a partial and inadequate ransom: your wealth and your city are the only presents worthy of my acceptance. For yourselves, I shall permit you to depart, each with an undergarment and a shirt; and, at my entreaty, my friend Sarbar will not refuse a passage through his lines. Your absent prince, even now a captive or a fugitive, has left Constantinople to its fate; nor can you escape the arms of the Avars and Persians, unless you could soar into air like birds, unless like fishes you could dive into the waves." [100] During ten successive days the capital was assaulted by the Avars, who had made some progress in the science of attack: they advanced to sap or batter the

names and actions of five Persian generals who were successively sent against Heraclius.

[99] This number of eight myriads is specified by George of Pisidia (Bell. Abar. 219). The poet (50-88) clearly indicates that the old chagan lived till the reign of Heraclius, and that his son and successor was born of a foreign mother. Yet Foggini (Annotat. p. 57) has given another interpretation to this passage.

[100] A bird, a frog, a mouse, and five arrows, had been the present of the Scythian king to Darius (Herodot. l. iv. c. 131, 132). Substituez une lettre à ces signes (says Rousseau, with much good taste), plus elle sera menaçante moins elle effrayera: ce ne sera qu'une fanfaronnade dont Darius n'eut fait que rire (Emile, tom. iii. p. 146). Yet I much question whether the senate and people of Constantinople *laughed* at this message of the chagan.

wall, under the cover of the impenetrable tortoise; their engines discharged a perpetual volley of stones and darts; and twelve lofty towers of wood exalted the combatants to the height of the neighbouring ramparts. But the senate and people were animated by the spirit of Heraclius, who had detached to their relief a body of twelve thousand cuirassiers; the powers of fire and mechanics were used with superior art and success in the defence of Constantinople; and the galleys, with two and three ranks of oars, commanded the Bosphorus, and rendered the Persians the idle spectators of the defeat of their allies. The Avars were repulsed; a fleet of Sclavonian canoes was destroyed in the harbour; the vassals of the chagan threatened to desert, his provisions were exhausted, and, after burning his engines, he gave the signal of a slow and formidable retreat. The devotion of the Romans ascribed this signal deliverance to the Virgin Mary; but the mother of Christ would surely have condemned their inhuman murder of the Persian envoys, who were entitled to the rights of humanity, if they were not protected by the laws of nations.[101]

After the division of his army, Heraclius prudently retired to the banks of the Phasis, from whence he maintained a defensive war against the fifty thousand gold spears of Persia. His anxiety was relieved by the deliverance of Constantinople; his hopes were confirmed by a victory of his brother Theodorus; and to the hostile league of Chosroes with the Avars, the Roman emperor opposed the useful and honourable alliance of the Turks. At his liberal invitation, the horde of Chozars [102] transported their tents from the plains of the Volga to the mountains of Georgia; Heraclius received them in the neighbourhood of Teflis, and the khan with his nobles dismounted from their horses, if we may credit the Greeks, and fell prostrate on the ground to adore the purple of the Cæsar. Such voluntary homage and important aid were entitled to the warmest acknowledgments, and the emperor, taking off his own diadem, placed it on the head of the Turkish prince, whom he saluted with a tender embrace and the appellation of son. After a sumptuous banquet he presented Ziebel with the plate and ornaments, the gold, the gems, and the silk which had been used at the Imperial table, and, with his own hand, distributed rich jewels and earrings to his new allies. In a secret interview he produced the portrait of his daughter Eudocia,[103]

[101] The Paschal Chronicle (p. 392-397 [tom. i. p. 716-726, ed. Bonn]) gives a minute and authentic narrative of the siege and deliverance of Constantinople. Theophanes (p. 264) adds some circumstances; and a faint light may be obtained from the smoke of George of Pisidia, who has composed a poem (de Bello Abarico, p. 45-54) to commemorate this auspicious event.

[102] The power of the Chozars prevailed in the seventh, eighth, and ninth centuries. They were known to the Greeks, the Arabs, and, under the name of *Kosa*, to the Chinese themselves. De Guignes, Hist. des Huns, tom. ii. part ii. p. 507-509.

[103] Epiphania, or Eudocia, the only daughter of Heraclius and his first wife Eudocia, was born at Constantinople on the 7th of July A.D. 611, baptised the 15th of August, and crowned (in the oratory of St. Stephen in the palace) the 4th of October of the same year. At this time she was about fifteen.

condescended to flatter the barbarian with the promise of a fair and *august* bride, obtained an immediate succour of forty thousand horse, and negotiated a strong diversion of the Turkish arms on the side of the Oxus.[104] The Persians, in their turn, retreated with precipitation; in the camp of Edessa Heraclius reviewed an army of seventy thousand Romans and strangers; and some months were successfully employed in the recovery of the cities of Syria, Mesopotamia, and Armenia, whose fortifications had been imperfectly restored. Sarbar still maintained the important station of Chalcedon, but the jealousy of Chosroes, or the artifice of Heraclius, soon alienated the mind of that powerful satrap from the service of his king and country. A messenger was intercepted with a real or fictitious mandate to the cadarigan, or second in command, directing him to send, without delay, to the throne the head of a guilty or unfortunate general. The despatches were transmitted to Sarbar himself, and, as soon as he read the sentence of his own death, he dexterously inserted the names of four hundred officers, assembled a military council, and asked the *cadarigan* whether he was prepared to execute the commands of their tyrant? The Persians unanimously declared that Chosroes had forfeited the sceptre; a separate treaty was concluded with the government of Constantinople; and if some considerations of honour or policy restrained Sarbar from joining the standard of Heraclius, the emperor was assured that he might prosecute without interruption his designs of victory and peace.

Deprived of his firmest support, and doubtful of the fidelity of his subjects, the greatness of Chosroes was still conspicuous in its ruins. The number of five hundred thousand may be interpreted as an Oriental metaphor to describe the men and arms, the horses and elephants, that covered Media and Assyria against the invasion of Heraclius. Yet the Romans boldly advanced from the Araxes to the Tigris, and the timid prudence of Rhazates was content to follow them by forced marches through a desolate country, till he received a peremptory mandate to risk the fate of Persia in a decisive battle. Eastward of the Tigris, at the end of the bridge of Mosul, the great Nineveh had formerly been erected:[105] the city, and even the ruins of the city, had long since dis-

---

Eudocia was afterwards sent to her Turkish husband, but the news of his death stopped her journey, and prevented the consummation (Ducange, Familiæ Byzantin. p. 118).

[104] Elmacin (Hist. Saracen. p. 13-16) gives some curious and probable facts: but his numbers are rather too high—300,000 Romans assembled at Edessa—500,000 Persians killed at Nineveh. The abatement of a cipher is scarcely enough to restore his sanity.

[105] Ctesias (apud Diodor. Sicul. tom. i. l. ii. [c. 3] p. 115, edit. Wesseling) assigns 480 stadia (perhaps only 32 miles) for the circumference of Nineveh. Jonas talks of three days' journey: the 120,000 persons described by the prophet as incapable of discerning their right hand from their left may afford about 700,000 persons of all ages for the inhabitants of that ancient capital (Goguet, Origines des Loix, etc., tom. iii. part i. p. 92, 93), which ceased to exist 600 years before Christ. The western suburb still subsisted, and is mentioned under the name of Mosul, in the first age of the Arabian khalifs.

appeared;[106] the vacant space afforded a spacious field for the operations of the two armies. But these operations are neglected by the Byzantine historians, and, like the authors of epic poetry and romance, they ascribe the victory, not to the military conduct, but to the personal valour, of their favourite hero. On this memorable day Heraclius, on his horse Phallas, surpassed the bravest of his warriors; his lip was pierced with a spear, the steed was wounded in the thigh, but he carried his master safe and victorious through the triple phalanx of the barbarians. In the heat of the action three valiant chiefs were successively slain by the sword and lance of the emperor: among these was Rhazates himself; he fell like a soldier, but the sight of his head scattered grief and despair through the fainting ranks of the Persians. His armour of pure and massy gold, the shield of one hundred and twenty plates, the sword and belt, the saddle and cuirass, adorned the triumph of Heraclius; and if he had not been faithful to Christ and his mother, the champion of Rome might have offered the fourth *opime* spoils to the Jupiter of the Capitol.[107] In the battle of Nineveh, which was fiercely fought from daybreak to the eleventh hour, twenty-eight standards, besides those which might be broken or torn, were taken from the Persians; the greatest part of their army was cut in pieces; and the victors, concealing their own loss, passed the night on the field. They acknowledge that, on this occasion, it was less difficult to kill than to discomfit the soldiers of Chosroes; amidst the bodies of their friends, no more than two bow-shot from the enemy, the remnant of the Persian cavalry stood firm till the seventh hour of the night; about the eighth hour they retired to their unrifled camp, collected their baggage, and dispersed on all sides from the want of orders rather than of resolution. The diligence of Heraclius was not less admirable in the use of victory; by a march of forty-eight miles in four-and-twenty hours his vanguard occupied the bridges of the great and the lesser Zab, and the cities and palaces of Assyria were open for the first time to the Romans. By a just gradation of magnificent scenes they penetrated to the royal seat of Dastagerd, and, though much of the treasure had been removed and much had been expended, the remaining wealth appears to have exceeded their hopes, and even to have satiated their avarice. Whatever could not be easily transported they consumed with fire, that Chosroes might feel the anguish of those wounds which he had so often inflicted on the provinces of the empire; and justice might allow the excuse, if the

---

[106] Niebuhr (Voyage en Arabie, etc., tom. ii. p. 286) passed over Nineveh without perceiving it. He mistook for a ridge of hills the old rampart of brick or earth. It is said to have been 100 feet high, flanked with 1500 towers, each of the height of 200 feet.

[107] Rex regia arma fero (says Romulus, in the first consecration) . . . bina postea (continues Livy, i. 10) inter tot bella, opima parta sunt spolia, adeo rara ejus fortuna decoris. If Varro (apud Pomp. Festum, p. 306, edit. Dacier) could justify his liberality in granting the *opime* spoils even to a common soldier who had slain the king or general of the enemy, the honour would have been much more cheap and common.

desolation had been confined to the works of regal luxury—if national hatred, military licence, and religious zeal had not wasted with equal rage the habitations and the temples of the guiltless subject. The recovery of three hundred Roman standards and the deliverance of the numerous captives of Edessa and Alexandria reflect a purer glory on the arms of Heraclius. From the palace of Dastagerd he pursued his march within a few miles of Modain or Ctesiphon, till he was stopped, on the banks of the Arba, by the difficulty of the passage, the rigour of the season, and perhaps the fame of an impregnable capital. The return of the emperor is marked by the modern name of the city of Sherhzour: he fortunately passed Mount Zara before the snow, which fell incessantly thirty-four days; and the citizens of Gandzaca, or Tauris, were compelled to entertain his soldiers and their horses with an hospitable reception.[108]

When the ambition of Chosroes was reduced to the defence of his hereditary kingdom, the love of glory, or even the sense of shame, should have urged him to meet his rival in the field. In the battle of Nineveh his courage might have taught the Persians to vanquish, or he might have fallen with honour by the lance of a Roman emperor. The successor of Cyrus chose rather, at a secure distance, to expect the event, to assemble the relics of the defeat, and to retire by measured steps before the march of Heraclius, till he beheld with a sigh the once loved mansions of Dastagerd. Both his friends and enemies were persuaded that it was the intention of Chosroes to bury himself under the ruins of the city and palace: and as both might have been equally adverse to his flight, the monarch of Asia, with Sira and three concubines, escaped through a hole in the wall nine days before the arrival of the Romans. The slow and stately procession in which he showed himself to the prostrate crowd was changed to a rapid and secret journey; the first evening he lodged in the cottage of a peasant, whose humble door would scarcely give admittance to the Great King.[109] His superstition was subdued by fear: on the third day he entered with joy the fortifications of Ctesiphon; yet he still doubted of his safety till he had opposed the river Tigris to the pursuit of the Romans. The discovery of his flight agitated with terror and tumult the palace, the city, and the camp of Dastagerd: the satraps hesitated whether they had most to fear from their sovereign or the enemy; and the females of the harem were astonished and pleased by the sight of mankind, till the jealous husband

---

[108] In describing this last expedition of Heraclius, the facts, the places, and the dates of Theophanes (p. 265-271 [tom. i. p. 487-502, ed. Bonn]) are so accurate and authentic, that he must have followed the original letters of the emperor, of which the Paschal Chronicle has preserved (p. 398-402 [tom. i. p. 727-734, ed. Bonn]) a very curious specimen.

[109] The words of Theophanes are remarkable: εἰσῆλθεν Χοσρόης εἰς οἶκον γεωργοῦ μεδαμινοῦ μεῖναι, μόλις χωρηθεὶς ἐν τῇ τούτου θύρᾳ, ἣν ἰδὼν ἔσχατον Ἡράκλειος ἐθαύμασεν (p. 269 [p. 496, ed. Bonn]). Young princes who discover a propensity to war should repeatedly transcribe and translate such salutary texts.

of three thousand wives again confined them to a more distant castle. At his command the army of Dastagerd retreated to a new camp: the front was covered by the Arba and a line of two hundred elephants; the troops of the more distant provinces successively arrived; and the vilest domestics of the king and satraps were enrolled for the last defence of the throne. It was still in the power of Chosroes to obtain a reasonable peace; and he was repeatedly pressed by the messengers of Heraclius to spare the blood of his subjects, and to relieve a humane conqueror from the painful duty of carrying fire and sword through the fairest countries of Asia. But the pride of the Persian had not yet sunk to the level of his fortune; he derived a momentary confidence from the retreat of the emperor; he wept with impotent rage over the ruins of his Assyrian palaces; and disregarded too long the rising murmurs of the nation, who complained that their lives and fortunes were sacrificed to the obstinacy of an old man. That unhappy old man was himself tortured with the sharpest pains both of mind and body; and, in the consciousness of his approaching end, he resolved to fix the tiara on the head of Merdaza, the most favoured of his sons. But the will of Chosroes was no longer revered, and Siroes, who gloried in the rank and merit of his mother Sira, had conspired with the malcontents to assert and anticipate the rights of primogeniture.[110] Twenty-two satraps, they styled themselves patriots, were tempted by the wealth and honours of a new reign: to the soldiers the heir of Chosroes promised an increase of pay; to the Christians, the free exercise of their religion; to the captives, liberty and rewards; and to the nation, instant peace and the reduction of taxes. It was determined by the conspirators that Siroes, with the ensigns of royalty, should appear in the camp; and if the enterprise should fail, his escape was contrived to the Imperial court. But the new monarch was saluted with unanimous acclamations; the flight of Chosroes (yet where could he have fled?) was rudely arrested, eighteen sons were massacred before his face, and he was thrown into a dungeon, where he expired on the fifth day. The Greeks and modern Persians minutely described how Chosroes was insulted, and famished, and tortured, by the command of an inhuman son, who so far surpassed the example of his father; but at the time of his death what tongue would relate the story of the parricide? what eye could penetrate into the *tower of darkness?* According to the faith and mercy of his Christian enemies, he sunk without hope into a still deeper abyss,[111] and it will not be denied that

---

[110] The authentic narrative of the fall of Chosroes is contained in the letter of Heraclius (Chron. Paschal. p. 398 [tom. i. p. 727, ed. Bonn]) and the history of Theophanes (p. 271 [tom. i. p. 500, *sq.*, ed. Bonn]).

[111] On the first rumour of the death of Chosroes, an Heracliad in two cantos was instantly published at Constantinople by George of Pisidia (p. 97-105). A priest and a poet might very properly exult in the damnation of the public enemy (ἐμπεσὼν τῷ Ταρτάρῳ, v. 56) : but such mean revenge is unworthy of a king and a conqueror; and I am sorry to find so much black superstition (θεομάχος Χοσρόης ἔπεσεν καὶ ἐππωματίσθη εἰς τὰ καταχθονια . . . εἰς τὸ πῦρ τὸ ἀκατάσβεστον, etc.) in the letter of Heraclius [Chron. Pasch. p. 728 *sq.*, ed.

tryants of every age and sect are the best entitled to such infernal abodes. The glory of the house of Sassan ended with the life of Chosroes; his unnatural son enjoyed only eight months the fruit of his crimes; and in the space of four years the regal title was assumed by nine candidates, who disputed, with the sword or dagger, the fragments of an exhausted monarchy. Every province and each city of Persia was the scene of independence, of discord, and of blood; and the state of anarchy prevailed about eight years longer, till the factions were silenced and united under the common yoke of the Arabian caliphs.[112]

As soon as the mountains became passable the emperor received the welcome news of the success of the conspiracy, the death of Chosroes, and the elevation of his eldest son to the throne of Persia. The authors of the revolution, eager to display their merits in the court or camp of Tauris, preceded the ambassadors of Siroes, who delivered the letters of their master to his *brother* the emperor of the Romans.[113] In the language of the usurpers of every age, he imputes his own crimes to the Deity, and, without degrading his equal majesty, he offers to reconcile the long discord of the two nations by a treaty of peace and alliance more durable than brass or iron. The conditions of the treaty were easily defined and faithfully executed. In the recovery of the standards and prisoners which had fallen into the hands of the Persians, the emperor imitated the example of Augustus; their care of the national dignity was celebrated by the poets of the times, but the decay of genius may be measured by the distance between Horace and George of Pisidia; the subjects and brethren of Heraclius were redeemed from persecution, slavery, and exile; but, instead of the Roman eagles, the true wood of the holy cross was restored to the importunate demands of the successor of Constantine. The victor was not ambitious of enlarging the weakness of the empire; the son of Chosroes abandoned without regret the conquests of his father; the Persians who evacuated the cities of Syria and Egypt were honourably conducted to the frontier; and a war which had wounded the vitals of the two monarchies produced no change in their external and relative situation. The return of Heraclius from Tauris to Constantinople was a perpetual triumph, and after the exploits of six glorious campaigns he peaceably enjoyed the sabbath of his toils. After a long impatience, the senate, the clergy, and the people went forth to meet their hero with tears and acclamations, with olive-branches and innumerable lamps; he entered the capital in a chariot drawn by four elephants, and, as soon as the emperor could disengage himself from

Bonn] : he almost applauds the parricide of Siroes as an act of piety and justice.

[112] The best Oriental accounts of this last period of the Sassanian kings are found in Eutychius (Annal. tom. ii. p. 251-256), who dissembles the parricide of Siroes, D'Herbelot (Bibliothèque Orientale, p. 789), and Assemanni (Bibliothec. Oriental. tom. iii. p. 415-420).

[113] The letter of Siroes in the Paschal Chronicle (p. 402 [tom. i. p. 735, ed. Bonn]) unfortunately ends before he proceeds to business. The treaty appears in its execution in the histories of Theophanes and Nicephorus.

the tumult of public joy, he tasted more genuine satisfaction in the embraces of his mother and his sons.[114]

The succeeding year was illustrated by a triumph of a very different kind, the restitution of the true cross to the holy sepulchre. Heraclius performed in person the pilgrimage of Jerusalem: the identity of the relic was verified by the discreet patriarch,[115] and this august ceremony has been commemorated by the annual festival of the exaltation of the cross. Before the emperor presumed to tread the consecrated ground he was instructed to strip himself of the diadem and purple, the pomp and vanity of the world; but in the judgment of his clergy, the persecution of the Jews was more easily reconciled with the precepts of the Gospel. He again ascended his throne to receive the congratulations of the ambassadors of France and India; and the fame of Moses, Alexander, and Hercules [116] was eclipsed, in the popular estimation, by the superior merit and glory of the great Heraclius. Yet the deliverer of the East was indigent and feeble. Of the Persian spoils the most valuable portion had been expended in the war, distributed to the soldiers, or buried, by an unlucky tempest, in the waves of the Euxine. The conscience of the emperor was oppressed by the obligation of restoring the wealth of the clergy, which he had borrowed for their own defence: a perpetual fund was required to satisfy these inexorable creditors; the provinces, already wasted by the arms and avarice of the Persians, were compelled to a second payment of the same taxes; and the arrears of a simple citizen, the treasurer of Damascus, were commuted to a fine of one hundred thousand pieces of gold. The loss of two hundred thousand soldiers,[117] who had fallen by the sword, was of less fatal importance than the decay of arts, agriculture, and population in this long and destructive war; and although a victorious army had been formed under the standard of Heraclius, the unnatural effort appears to have exhausted rather than exercised their strength. While the emperor triumphed at Constantinople or Jerusalem, an obscure town on the confines of Syria was

[114] The burthen of Corneille's song,

"Montrez Heraclius au peuple qui l'attend,"

is much better suited to the present occasion. See his triumph in Theophanes (p. 272, 273 [tom. i. p. 503 *sq.*, ed. Bonn]) and Nicephorus (p. 15, 16). The life of the mother and tenderness of the son are attested by George of Pisidia (Bell. Abar. 255, etc. p. 49). The metaphor of the Sabbath is used, somewhat profanely, by these Byzantine Christians.

[115] See Baronius (Annal. Eccles. A.D. 628, No. 1-4), Eutychius (Annal. tom. ii. p. 240-248), Nicephorus (Brev. p. 15). The seals of the case had never been broken; and this preservation of the cross is ascribed (under God) to the devotion of queen Sira.

[116] George of Pisidia, Acroas. iii. de Expedit. contra Persas, 415, etc. [p. 21], and Heracliad. Acroas. i. 65-138. I neglect the meaner parallels of Daniel, Timotheus, etc.; Chosroes and the chagan were of course compared to Belshazzar, Pharaoh, the old serpent, etc.

[117] Suidas (in Excerpt. Hist. Byzant. p. 46) gives this number; but either the *Persian* must be read for the *Isaurian* war, or this passage does not belong to the *emperor* Heraclius.

pillaged by the Saracens, and they cut in pieces some troops who advanced to its relief; an ordinary and trifling occurrence, had it not been the prelude of a mighty revolution. These robbers were the apostles of Mohammed; their fanatic valour had emerged from the desert; and in the last eight years of his reign Heraclius lost to the Arabs the same provinces which he had rescued from the Persians.

CHAPTER XLVII (412-1632 A.D.)

Theological History of the Doctrine of the Incarnation—The Human and Divine Nature of Christ—Enmity of the Patriarchs of Alexandria and Constantinople—St. Cyril and Nestorius—Third General Council of Ephesus—Heresy of Eutyches—Fourth General Council of Chalcedon— Civil and Ecclesiastical Discord—Intolerance of Justinian—The Three Chapters—The Monothelite Controversy—State of the Oriental Sects— I. The Nestorians—II. The Jacobites—III. The Maronites—IV. The Armenians—V. The Copts and Abyssinians

AFTER the extinction of paganism, the Christians in peace and piety might have enjoyed their solitary triumph. But the principle of discord was alive in their bosom, and they were more solicitous to explore the nature, than to practise the laws, of their founder. I have already observed that the disputes of the TRINITY were succeeded by those of the INCARNATION; alike scandalous to the church, alike pernicious to the state, still more minute in their origin, still more durable in their effects. It is my design to comprise in the present chapter a religious war of two hundred and fifty years, to represent the ecclesiastical and political schism of the Oriental sects, and to introduce their clamorous or sanguinary contests by a modest inquiry into the doctrines of the primitive church.[1]

[1] By what means shall I authenticate this previous inquiry, which I have studied to circumscribe and compress?—If I persist in supporting each fact or reflection by its proper and special evidence, every line would demand a string of testimonies, and every note would swell to a critical dissertation. But the numberless passages of antiquity which I have seen with my own eyes are compiled, digested, and illustrated by *Petavius* and *Le Clerc,* by *Beausobre,* and *Mosheim.* I shall be content to fortify my narrative by the names and characters of these respectable guides; and in the contemplation of a minute or remote object, I am not ashamed to borrow the aid of the strongest glasses:—I. The *Dogmata Theologica* of Petavius are a work of incredible labour and compass; the volumes which relate solely to the Incarnation (two folios, fifth and sixth, of 837 pages) are divided into sixteen books—the first of history, the remainder of controversy and doctrine. The Jesuit's learning is copious and correct; his Latinity is pure, his method clear, his argument profound and well connected; but he is the slave of the fathers, the scourge of heretics, and the enemy of truth and candour, as often as *they* are inimical to the Catholic cause. 2. The Armenian Le Clerc, who has composed in a quarto volume (Amsterdam, 1716) the ecclesiastical history of the two first centuries, was free both in his temper and situation; his sense is clear, but his thoughts are narrow; he reduces the reason or folly of ages to the standard of his private judgment, and his impartiality is sometimes quickened.

I. A laudable regard for the honour of the first proselytes has countenanced the belief, the hope, the wish, that the Ebionites, or at least the
Nazarenes, were distinguished only by their obstinate perseverance in
the practise of the Mosaic rites. Their churches have disappeared, their
books are obliterated: their obscure freedom might allow a latitude of
faith, and the softness of their infant creed would be variously moulded
by the zeal or prudence of three hundred years. Yet the most charitable
criticism must refuse these sectaries any knowledge of the pure and
proper divinity of Christ. Educated in the school of Jewish prophecy
and prejudice, they had never been taught to elevate their hopes above
a human and temporal Messiah.[2] If they had courage to hail their king
when he appeared in a plebeian garb, their grosser apprehensions were
incapable of discerning their God, who had studiously disguised his
celestial character under the name and person of a mortal.[3] The familiar companions of Jesus of Nazareth conversed with their friend and
countryman, who, in all the actions of rational and animal life, appeared
of the same species with themselves. His progress from infancy to youth
and manhood was marked by a regular increase in stature and wisdom;
and after a painful agony of mind and body, he expired on the cross.
He lived and died for the service of mankind: but the life and death
of Socrates had likewise been devoted to the cause of religion and
justice; and although the stoic or the hero may disdain the humble
virtues of Jesus, the tears which he shed over his friend and country
may be esteemed the purest evidence of his humanity. The miracles
of the gospel could not astonish a people who held with intrepid faith

and sometimes tainted, by his opposition to the fathers. See the heretics
(Cerinthians, lxxx.; Ebionites, ciii.; Carpocratians, cxx.; Valentinians, cxxi.;
Basilidians, cxxiii.; Marcionites, cxli., etc.) under their proper dates. 3. The
Histoire Critique du Manichéisme (Amsterdam, 1734, 1739, in two vols. in
4to, with a posthumous dissertation sur les Nazarènes, Lausanne, 1745) of
M. de Beausobre, is a treasure of ancient philosophy and theology. The
learned historian spins with incomparable art the systematic thread of opinion,
and transforms himself by turns into the person of a saint, a sage, or an
heretic. Yet his refinement is sometimes excessive: he betrays an amiable
partiality in favour of the weaker side, and, while he guards against calumny,
he does not allow sufficient scope for superstition and fanaticism. A copious
table of contents will direct the reader to any point that he wishes to examine.
4. Less profound than Petavius, less independent than Le Clerc, less ingenious
than Beausobre, the historian Mosheim is full, rational, correct, and moderate.
In his learned work, De Rebus Christianis ante Constantinum (Helmstadt,
1753, in 4to), see the *Nazarenes* and *Ebionites*, p. 172-179, 328-332; the
Gnostics in general, p. 179, etc.; *Cerinthus*, p. 196-202; Basilides, p. 352-361;
Carpocrates, p. 363-367; Valentinus, p. 371-389; Marcion, p. 404-410; the
Manichæans, p. 829-837, etc.

[2] Καὶ γὰρ πάντες ἡμεῖς τὸν Χριστὸν ἄνθρωπον ἐξ ἀνθρώπων προσδοκῶμεν
γενήσεσθαι, says the Jew Tryphon (Justin. Dialog. p. 207 [p. 142, ed. Jebb]),
in the name of his countrymen; and the modern Jews, the few who divert
their thoughts from money to religion, still hold the same language, and allege
the literal sense of the prophets.

[3] Chrysostom (Basnage, Hist. des Juifs, tom. v. c. 9, p. 183) and Athanasius
(Petav. Dogmat. Theolog. tom. v. l. i. c. 2, p. 3) are obliged to confess that
the divinity of Christ is rarely mentioned by himself or his apostles.

the more splendid prodigies of the Mosaic law. The prophets of ancient days had cured diseases, raised the dead, divided the sea, stopped the sun, and ascended to heaven in a fiery chariot. And the metaphorical style of the Hebrews might ascribe to a saint and martyr the adoptive title of SON OF GOD.

Yet in the insufficient creed of the Nazarenes and the Ebionites a distinction is faintly noticed between the heretics, who confounded the generation of Christ in the common order of nature, and the less guilty schismatics, who revered the virginity of his mother and excluded the aid of an earthly father. The incredulity of the former was countenanced by the visible circumstances of his birth, the legal marriage of his reputed parents, Joseph and Mary, and his lineal claim to the kingdom of David and the inheritance of Judah. But the secret and authentic history has been recorded in several copies of the Gospel according to St. Matthew,[4] which these sectaries long preserved in the original Hebrew,[5] as the sole evidence of their faith. The natural suspicions of the husband, conscious of his own chastity, were dispelled by the assurance (in a dream) that his wife was pregnant of the Holy Ghost: and as this distant and domestic prodigy could not fall under the personal observation of the historian, he must have listened to the same voice which dictated to Isaiah the future conception of a virgin. The son of a virgin, generated by the ineffable operation of the Holy Spirit, was a creature without example or resemblance, superior in every attribute of mind and body to the children of Adam. Since the introduction of the Greek or Chaldean philosophy,[6] the Jews [7] were persuaded of the pre-existence, transmigration, and immortality of souls; and Providence was justified by a supposition that they were confined in their earthly prisons to expiate the stains which they had contracted

[4] The two first chapters of St. Matthew did not exist in the Ebionite copies (Epiphan. Hæres. xxx. 13) ; and the miraculous conception is one of the last articles which Dr. Priestley has curtailed from his scanty creed.

[5] It is probable enough that the first of the gospels for the use of the Jewish converts was composed in the Hebrew or Syriac idiom : the fact is attested by a chain of fathers—Papias, Irenæus, Origen, Jerom, etc. It is devoutly believed by the Catholics, and admitted by Casaubon, Grotius, and Isaac Vossius, among the Protestant critics. But this Hebrew Gospel of St. Matthew is most unaccountably lost; and we may accuse the diligence or fidelity of the primitive churches, who have preferred the unauthorized version of some nameless Greek. Erasmus and his followers, who respect our Greek text as the original gospel, deprived themselves of the evidence which declares it to be the work of an apostle. See Simon, Hist. Critique, etc., tom. iii. c. 5-9, p. 47-101, and the Prolegomena of Mill and Wetstein to the New Testament.

[6] The metaphysics of the soul are disengaged by Cicero (Tusculan. 1. i.) and Maximus of Tyre (Dissertat. xvi.) from the intricacies of dialogue, which sometimes amuse, and often perplex, the readers of the *Phædrus,* the *Phædon,* and the *Laws* of Plato.

[7] The disciples of Jesus were persuaded that a man might have sinned before he was born (John ix. 2), and the Pharisees held the transmigration of virtuous souls (Joseph. de Bell. Judaico, 1. ii. c. 7 [c. 8, § 14]) ; and a modern Rabbi is modestly assured that Hermes, Pythagoras, Plato, etc., derived their metaphysics from his illustrious countrymen.

in a former state.[8] But the degrees of purity and corruption are almost immeasurable. It might be fairly presumed that the most sublime and virtuous of human spirits was infused into the offspring of Mary and the Holy Ghost;[9] that his abasement was the result of his voluntary choice; and that the object of his mission was to purify, not his own, but the sins of the world. On his return to his native skies he received the immense reward of his obedience: the everlasting kingdom of the Messiah, which had been darkly foretold by the prophets, under the carnal images of peace, of conquest, and of dominion. Omnipotence could enlarge the human faculties of Christ to the extent of his celestial office. In the language of antiquity, the title of God has not been severely confined to the first parent; and his incomparable minister, his only begotten Son, might claim, without presumption, the religious, though secondary, worship of a subject world.

II. The seeds of the faith, which had slowly arisen in the rocky and ungrateful soil of Judea, were transplanted, in full maturity, to the happier climes of the Gentiles; and the strangers of Rome or Asia, who never beheld the manhood, were the more readily disposed to embrace the divinity, of Christ. The polytheist and the philosopher, the Greek and the barbarian, were alike accustomed to conceive a long succession, an infinite chain of angels, or demons, or deities, or æons, or emanations, issuing from the throne of light. Nor could it seem strange or incredible that the first of these æons, the *Logos,* or Word of God, of the same substance with the Father, should descend upon earth, to deliver the human race from vice and error, and to conduct them in the paths of life and immortality. But the prevailing doctrine of the eternity and inherent pravity of matter infected the primitive churches of the East. Many among the Gentile proselytes refused to believe that a celestial spirit, an undivided portion of the first essence, had been personally united with a mass of impure and contaminated flesh; and, in their zeal for the divinity, they piously abjured the humanity, of Christ. While his blood was still recent on Mount Calvary,[10] the *Docetes,* a numerous

[8] Four different opinions have been entertained concerning the origin of human souls. 1. That they are external and divine. 2. That they were created, in a separate state of existence, before their union with the body. 3. That they have been propagated from the original stock of Adam, who contained in himself the mental as well as the corporeal seed of his posterity. 4. That each soul is occasionally created and embodied in the moment of conception. —The last of these sentiments appears to have prevailed among the moderns; and our spiritual history is grown less sublime, without becoming more intelligible.

[9] Ὅτι ἡ τοῦ Σωτῆρος ψυχὴ, ἡ τοῦ Ἀδὰμ ἦν, was one of the fifteen heresies imputed to Origen, and denied by his apologist (Photius, Bibliothec. cod. cxvii. p. 296 [p. 92, ed. Bekk.]). Some of the Rabbis attribute one and the same soul to the persons of Adam, David, and the Messiah.

[10] Apostolis adhuc in seculo superstitibus, apud Judæam Christi sanguine recente, PHANTASMA domini corpus asserebatur. Hieronym. advers. Lucifer. c. 8. The epistle of Ignatius to the Smyrnæans, and even the Gospel according to St. John, are levelled against the growing error of the Docetes, who had obtained too much credit in the world (1 John iv. 1-5).

and learned sect of Asiatics, invented the *phantastic* system which was afterwards propagated by the Marcionites, the Manichæans, and the various names of the Gnostic heresy.[11]   They denied the truth and authenticity of the gospels, as far as they relate the conception of Mary, the birth of Christ, and the thirty years that preceded the exercise of his ministry.   He first appeared on the banks of the Jordan in the form of perfect manhood; but it was a form only, and not a substance; a human figure created by the hand of Omnipotence to imitate the faculties and actions of a man, and to impose a perpetual illusion on the senses of his friends and enemies.   Articulate sounds vibrated on the ears of the disciples; but the image which was impressed on their optic nerve eluded the more stubborn evidence of the touch; and they enjoyed the spiritual, not the corporeal, presence of the Son of God.   The rage of the Jews was idly wasted against an impassive phantom; and the mystic scenes of the passion and death, the resurrection and ascension of Christ, were represented on the theatre of Jerusalem for the benefit of mankind.   If it were urged that such ideal mimicry, such incessant deception, was unworthy of the God of truth, the Docetes agreed with too many of their othodox brethren in the justification of pious falsehood. In the system of the Gnostics the Jehovah of Israel, the Creator of this lower world, was a rebellious, or at least an ignorant, spirit.   The Son of God descended upon earth to abolish his temple and his law; and, for the accomplishment of this salutary end, he dexterously transferred to his own person the hope and prediction of a temporal Messiah.

One of the most subtle disputants of the Manichæan school has pressed the danger and indecency of supposing that the God of the Christians, in the state of a human fœtus, emerged at the end of nine months from a female womb.   The pious horror of his antagonists provoked them to disclaim all sensual circumstances of conception and delivery; to maintain that the divinity passed through Mary like a sunbeam through a plate of glass; and to assert that the seal of her virginity remained unbroken even at the moment when she became the mother of Christ. But the rashness of these concessions has encouraged a milder sentiment of those Docetes who taught, not that Christ was a phantom, but that he was clothed with an impassible and incorruptible body.   Such, indeed, in the more orthodox system, he has acquired since his resurrection, and such he must have always possessed, if it were capable of pervading, without resistance or injury, the density of intermediate matter.   Devoid of its most essential properties, it might be exempt from the attributes and infirmities of the flesh.   A fœtus that could increase from an invisible point to its full maturity; a child that could attain the stature of perfect manhood, without deriving any nourishment from the

---

[11] About the year 200 of the Christian era, Irenæus and Hippolytus refuted the thirty-two sects, τῆς ψευδωνύμου γνωσέως, which had multiplied to fourscore in the time of Epiphanius (Phot. Biblioth. cod. cxx. cxxi. cxxii.).   The five books of Irenæus exist only in barbarous Latin; but the original might perhaps be found in some monastery of Greece.

ordinary sources, might continue to exist without repairing a daily waste by a daily supply of external matter. Jesus might share the repasts of his disciples without being subject to the calls of thirst or hunger; and his virgin purity was never sullied by the involuntary stains of sensual concupiscence. Of a body thus singularly constituted, a question would arise, by what means and of what materials it was originally framed; and our sounder theology is startled by an answer which was not peculiar to the Gnostics, that both the form and the substance proceeded from the divine essence. The idea of pure and absolute spirit is a refinement of modern philosophy: the incorporeal essence, ascribed by the ancients to human souls, celestial beings, and even the Deity himself, does not exclude the notion of extended space; and their imagination was satisfied with a subtle nature of air, or fire, or ether, incomparably more perfect than the grossness of the material world. If we define the place, we must describe the figure, of the Deity. Our experience, perhaps our vanity, represents the powers of reason and virtue under a human form. The Anthropomorphites, who swarmed among the monks of Egypt and the Catholics of Africa, could produce the express declaration of Scripture, that man was made after the image of his Creator.[12] The venerable Serapion, one of the saints of the Nitrian desert, relinquished, with many a tear, his darling prejudice; and bewailed, like an infant, his unlucky conversion, which had stolen away his God, and left his mind without any visible object of faith or devotion.[13]

III. Such were the fleeting shadows of the Docetes. A more substantial, though less simple hypothesis, was contrived by Cerinthus of Asia,[14] who dared to oppose the last of the apostles. Placed on the confines of the Jewish and Gentile world, he laboured to reconcile the

[12] The pilgrim Cassian, who visited Egypt in the beginning of the fifth century, observes and laments the reign of anthropomorphism among the monks, who were not conscious that they embraced the system of Epicurus (Cicero, de Nat. Deorum, i. 18, 49). Ab universo propemodum genere monarchorum, qui per totam provinciam Egypti morabantur, pro simplicitatis errore susceptum est, ut e contrario memoratum pontificem (*Theophilus*) velut hæresi gravissimâ depravatum, pars maxima seniorum ab universo fraternitatis corpore decerneret detestandum (Cassian. Collation. x. 1). As long as St. Augustin remained a Manichæan, he was scandalised by the anthropomorphism of the vulgar Catholics.

[13] Ita est in oratione senex mente confusus, eo quod illam ἀνθρωπόμορφον imaginem Deitatis, quam proponere sibi in oratione consueverat, aboleri de suo corde sentiret, ut in amarissimos fletus, crebrosque singultus repente prorumpens, in terram prostratus, cum ejulatû validissimo proclamaret; "Heu me miserum! tulerunt a me Deum meum, et quem nunc teneam non habeo, vel quem adorem, aut interpellam jam nescio." Cassian, Collat. x. 2.

[14] St. John and Cerinthus (A.D. 80, Cleric. Hist. Eccles. p. 493) accidentally met in the public bath of Ephesus; but the apostle fled from the heretic lest the building should tumble on their heads. This foolish story, reprobated by Dr. Middleton (Miscellaneous Works, vol. ii.), is related however by Irenæus (iii. 3), on the evidence of Polycarp, and was probably suited to the time and residence of Cerinthus. The obsolete, yet probably the true, reading of 1 John iv. 3—ὃ λύει τὸν Ἰησοῦν—alludes to the double nature of that primitive heretic

Gnostic with the Ebionite, by confessing in the same Messiah the supernatural union of a man and a God; and this mystic doctrine was adopted with many fanciful improvements by Carpocrates, Basilides, and Valentine,[15] the heretics of the Egyptian school. In their eyes JESUS of Nazareth was a mere mortal, the legitimate son of Joseph and Mary: but he was the best and wisest of the human race, selected as the worthy instrument to restore upon earth the worship of the true and supreme Deity. When he was baptised in the Jordan, the CHRIST, the first of the æons, the Son of God himself, descended on Jesus in the form of a dove, to inhabit his mind and direct his actions during the allotted period of his ministry. When the Messiah was delivered into the hands of the Jews, the Christ, an immortal and impassible being, forsook his earthly tabernacle, flew back to the *pleroma* or world of spirits, and left the solitary Jesus to suffer, to complain, and to expire. But the justice and generosity of such a desertion are strongly questionable; and the fate of an innocent martyr, at first impelled, and at length abandoned, by his divine companion, might provoke the pity and indignation of the profane. Their murmurs were variously silenced by the sectaries who espoused and modified the double system of Cerinthus. It was alleged that, when Jesus was nailed to the cross, he was endowed with a miraculous apathy of mind and body, which rendered him insensible of his apparent sufferings. It was affirmed that these momentary, though real pangs, would be abundantly repaid by the temporal reign of a thousand years reserved for the Messiah in his kingdom of the new Jerusalem. It was insinuated that if he suffered, he deserved to suffer; that human nature is never absolutely perfect; and that the cross and passion might serve to expiate the venial transgressions of the son of Joseph, before his mysterious union with the Son of God.[16]

IV. All those who believe the immateriality of the soul, a specious and noble tenet, must confess, from their present experience, the incomprehensible union of mind and matter. A similar union is not inconsistent with a much higher, or even with the highest, degree of mental faculties; and the incarnation of an æon or archangel, the most perfect of created spirits, does not involve any positive contradiction or absurdity. In the age of religious freedom, which was determined

---

[15] The Valentinians embraced a complex and almost incoherent system. 1. Both Christ and Jesus were æons, though of different degrees; the one acting as the rational soul, the other as the divine spirit of the Saviour. 2. At the time of the passion they both retired, and left only a sensitive soul and a human body. 3. Even that body was ethereal, and perhaps apparent.—Such are the laborious conclusions of Mosheim. But I much doubt whether the Latin translator understood Irenæus, and whether Irenæus and the Valentinians understood themselves.

[16] The heretics abused the passionate exclamations of "My God, my God, why hast thou *forsaken* me?" Rousseau, who has drawn an eloquent but indecent parallel between Christ and Socrates, forgets that not a word of impatience or despair escaped from the mouth of the dying philosopher. In the Messiah such sentiments could be only apparent; and such ill-sounding words are properly explained as the application of a psalm and prophecy.

by the council of Nice, the dignity of Christ was measured by private judgment according to the indefinite rule of Scripture, or reason, or tradition. But when his pure and proper divinity had been established on the ruins of Arianism, the faith of the Catholics trembled on the edge of a precipice where it was impossible to recede, dangerous to stand, dreadful to fall; and the manifold inconveniences of their creed were aggravated by the sublime character of their theology. They hesitated to pronounce—*that* God himself, the second person of an equal and consubstantial trinity, was manifested in the flesh;[17] *that* a being who pervades the universe had been confined in the womb of Mary; *that* his eternal duration had been marked by the days, and months, and years of human existence; *that* the Almighty had been scourged and crucified; *that* his impassible essence had felt pain and anguish; *that* his omniscience was not exempt from ignorance; and *that* the source of life and immortality expired on Mount Calvary. These alarming consequences were affirmed with unblushing simplicity by Apollinaris,[18] bishop of Laodicea, and one of the luminaries of the church. The son of a learned grammarian, he was skilled in all the sciences of Greece; eloquence, erudition, and philosophy, conspicuous in the volumes of Apollinaris, were humbly devoted to the service of religion. The worthy friend of Athanasius, the worthy antagonist of Julian, he bravely wrestled with the Arians and Polytheists, and, though he affected the rigour of geometrical demonstration, his commentaries revealed the literal and allegorical sense of the Scriptures. A mystery which had long floated in the looseness of popular belief was defined by his perverse diligence in a technical form; and he first proclaimed the memorable words, " One incarnate nature of Christ," which are still re-echoed with hostile clamours in the churches of Asia, Egypt, and Æthiopia. He taught that the Godhead was united or mingled with the body of a man; and that the *Logos,* the eternal wisdom, supplied in the flesh the place and office of a human soul. Yet, as the profound doctor had been terrified at his own rashness, Apollinaris was heard to mutter some faint accents of excuse and explanation. He acquiesced in the old distinction of the Greek philosophers between the rational and sensi-

---

[17] This strong expression might be justified by the language of St. Paul (1 Tim. iii. 16) ; but we are deceived by our modern Bibles. The word ὃ (*which*) was altered to θεὸς (*God*) at Constantinople in the beginning of the sixth century: the true reading, which is visible in the Latin and Syriac versions, still exists in the reasoning of the Greek as well as of the Latin fathers; and this fraud, with that of the *three witnesses of St. John,* is admirably detected by Sir Isaac Newton. (See his two letters translated by M. de Missy, in the Journal Britannique, tom. xv. p. 148-190, 351-390.) I have weighed the arguments, and may yield to the authority of the first of philosophers, who was deeply skilled in critical and theological studies.

[18] For Apollinaris and his sect, see Socrates, l. ii. c. 46, l. iii. c. 16; Sozomen, l. v. c. 18, l. vi. c. 25, 27; Theodoret, l. v. 3, 10, 11; Tillemont, Mémoires Ecclésiastiques, tom. vii. p. 602-638; Not., p. 789-794, in 4to, Venice, 1732. The contemporary saints always mention the bishop of Laodicea as a friend and brother. The style of the more recent historians is harsh and hostile; yet Philostorgius compares him (l. viii. c. 11-15) to Basil and Gregory.

tive soul of man; that he might reserve the *Logos* for intellectual functions, and employ the subordinate human principle in the meaner actions
of animal life. With the moderate Docetes he revered Mary as the spiritual, rather than as the carnal, mother of Christ, whose body either came
from heaven, impassible and incorruptible, or was absorbed, and as it
were transformed, into the essence of the Deity. The system of Apollinaris was strenuously encountered by the Asiatic and Syrian divines,
whose schools are honoured by the names of Basil, Gregory, and Chrysostom, and tainted by those of Diodorus, Theodore, and Nestorius. But
the person of the aged bishop of Laodicea, his character and dignity,
remained inviolate; and his rivals, since we may not suspect them of
the weakness of toleration, were astonished, perhaps, by the novelty of
the argument, and diffident of the final sentence of the Catholic church.
Her judgment at length inclined in their favour; the heresy of Apollinaris was condemned, and the separate congregations of his disciples
were proscribed by the Imperial laws. But his principles were secretly
entertained in the monasteries of Egypt, and his enemies felt the hatred
of Theophilus and Cyril, the successive patriarchs of Alexandria.

V. The grovelling Ebionite and the fantastic Docetes were rejected
and forgotten: the recent zeal against the errors of Apollinaris reduced
the Catholics to a seeming agreement with the double nature of Cerinthus. But instead of a temporary and occasional alliance, *they* established, and *we* still embrace, the substantial, indissoluble, and everlasting
union of a perfect God with a perfect man, of the second person of the
trinity with a reasonable soul and human flesh. In the beginning of the
fifth century the *unity* of the *two natures* was the prevailing doctrine of
the church. On all sides it was confessed that the mode of their co-
existence could neither be represented by our ideas nor expressed by
our language. Yet a secret and incurable discord was cherished between
those who were most apprehensive of confounding, and those who were
most fearful of separating, the divinity and the humanity of Christ.
Impelled by religious frenzy, they fled with adverse haste from the
error which they mutually deemed most destructive of truth and salvation. On either hand they were anxious to guard, they were jealous to
defend, the union and the distinction of the two natures, and to invent
such forms of speech, such symbols of doctrine, as were least susceptible
of doubt or ambiguity. The poverty of ideas and language tempted
them to ransack art and nature for every possible comparison, and each
comparison misled their fancy in the explanation of an incomparable
mystery. In the polemic microscope an atom is enlarged to a monster,
and each party was skilful to exaggerate the absurd or impious conclusions that might be extorted from the principles of their adversaries.
To escape from each other they wandered through many a dark and
devious thicket, till they were astonished by the horrid phantoms of
Cerinthus and Apollinaris, who guarded the opposite issues of the theological labyrinth. As soon as they beheld the twilight of sense and
heresy, they started, measured back their steps, and were again involved

in the gloom of impenetrable orthodoxy. To purge themselves from the guilt or reproach of damnable error, they disavowed their consequences, explained their principles, excused their indiscretions, and unanimously pronounced the sounds of concord and faith. Yet a latent and almost invisible spark still lurked among the embers of controversy: by the breath of prejudice and passion it was quickly kindled to a mighty flame, and the verbal disputes [19] of the Oriental sects have shaken the pillars of the church and state.

The name of CYRIL of Alexandria is famous in controversial story, and the title of *saint* is a mark that his opinions and his party have finally prevailed. In the house of his uncle, the archbishop Theophilus, he imbibed the orthodox lessons of zeal and dominion, and five years of his youth were profitably spent in the adjacent monasteries of Nitria. Under the tuition of the abbot Serapion, he applied himself to ecclesiastical studies with such indefatigable ardour, that in the course of *one* sleepless night he has perused the four gospels, the catholic epistles, and the epistle to the Romans. Origen he detested; but the writings of Clemens and Dionysius, of Athanasius and Basil, were continually in his hands: by the theory and practice of dispute, his faith was confirmed and his wit was sharpened; he extended round his cell the cobwebs of scholastic theology, and meditated the works of allegory and metaphysics, whose remains, in seven verbose folios, now peaceably slumber by the side of their rivals.[20] Cyril prayed and fasted in the desert, but his thoughts (it is the reproach of a friend [21]) were still fixed on the world; and the call of Theophilus, who summoned him to the tumult of cities and synods, was too readily obeyed by the aspiring hermit. With the approbation of his uncle he assumed the office and acquired the fame of a popular preacher. His comely person adorned the pulpit; the harmony of his voice resounded in the cathedral; his friends were stationed to lead or second the applause of the congregation;[22] and the hasty notes of the scribes preserved his discourses, which,

[19] I appeal to the confession of two Oriental prelates, Gregory Abulpharagius the Jacobite primate of the East, and Elias the Nestorian metropolitan of Damascus (see Asseman, Bibliothec. Oriental. tom. ii. p. 291; tom. iii. p. 514, etc.), that the Melchites, Jacobites, Nestorians, etc., agree in the *doctrine,* and differ only in the *expression.* Our most learned and rational divines—Basnage, Le Clerc, Beausobre, La Croze, Mosheim, Jablonski—are inclined to favour this charitable judgment; but the zeal of Petavius is loud and angry, and the moderation of Dupin is conveyed in a whisper.

[20] La Croze (Hist. du Christianisme des Indes, tom. i. p. 24) avows his contempt for the genius and writings of Cyril—De tous les ouvrages des anciens, il y en a peu qu'on lise avec moins d'utilité: and Dupin (Bibliothèque Ecclésiastique, tom. iv. p. 42-52), in words of respect, teaches us to despise them.

[21] Of Isidore of Pelusium (l. i. Epist. 25, p. 8). As the letter is not of the most creditable sort, Tillemont, less sincere than the Bollandists, affects a doubt whether *this* Cyril is the nephew of Theophilus (Mém. Ecclés. tom. xiv. p. 268).

[22] A grammarian is named by Socrates (l. vii. c. 13) διάπυρος δὲ ἀκροατὴς τοῦ ἐπισκόπου Κυρίλλου καθεστὼς, καὶ περὶ τὸ κρότους ἐν ταῖς διδασκαλίαις αὐτοῦ ἐγείρειν ἦν σπουδαιότατος.

in their effect, though not in their composition, might be compared with those of the Athenian orators. The death of Theophilus expanded and realised the hopes of his nephew. The clergy of Alexandria was divided; the soldiers and their general supported the claims of the archdeacon; but a resistless multitude, with voices and with hands, asserted the cause of their favourite; and after a period of thirty-nine years Cyril was seated on the throne of Athanasius.[23]

The prize was not unworthy of his ambition. At a distance from the court, and at the head of an immense capital, the patriarch, as he was now styled, of Alexandria had gradually usurped the state and authority of a civil magistrate. The public and private charities of the city were managed by his discretion; his voice inflamed or appeased the passions of the multitude; his commands were blindly obeyed by his numerous and fanatic *parabolani*,[24] familiarised in their daily office with scenes of death; and the præfects of Egypt were awed or provoked by the temporal power of these Christian pontiffs. Ardent in the prosecution of heresy, Cyril auspiciously opened his reign by oppressing the Novatians, the most innocent and harmless of the sectaries. The interdiction of their religious worship appeared in his eyes a just and meritorious act; and he confiscated their holy vessels, without apprehending the guilt of sacrilege. The toleration, and even the privileges of the Jews, who had multiplied to the number of forty thousand, were secured by the laws of the Cæsars and Ptolemies, and a long prescription of seven hundred years since the foundation of Alexandria. Without any legal sentence, without any royal mandate, the patriarch, at the dawn of day, led a seditious multitude to the attack of the synagogues. Unarmed and unprepared, the Jews were incapable of resistance; their houses of prayer were levelled with the ground, and the episcopal warrior, after rewarding his troops with the plunder of their goods, expelled from the city the remnant of the unbelieving nation. Perhaps he might plead the insolence of their prosperity, and their deadly hatred of the Christians, whose blood they had recently shed in a malicious or accidental tumult. Such crimes would have deserved the animadversion of the magistrate; but in this promiscuous outrage the innocent were confounded with the guilty, and Alexandria was impoverished by the loss of a wealthy and industrious colony. The zeal of Cyril exposed him to

[23] See the youth and promotion of Cyril, in Socrates (l. vii. c. 7) and Renaudot (Hist. Patriarch. Alexandrin. p. 106, 108). The Abbé Renaudot drew his materials from the Arabic history of Severus, bishop of Hermopolis Magna, or Ashmunein, in the tenth century, who can never be trusted, unless our assent is extorted by the internal evidence of facts.

[24] The *Parabolani* of Alexandria were a charitable corporation, instituted during the plague of Gallienus, to visit the sick and to bury the dead. They gradually enlarged, abused, and sold the privileges of their order. Their outrageous conduct during the reign of Cyril provoked the emperor to deprive the patriarch of their nomination, and to restrain their number to five or six hundred. But these restraints were transient and ineffectual. See the Theodosian Code, l. xvi. tit. ii. [leg. 42], and Tillemont, Mém. Ecclés. tom. xiv. p. 276-278.

the penalties of the Julian law; but in a feeble government and a super-stitious age he was secure of impunity, and even of praise. Orestes com-plained; but his just complaints were too quickly forgotten by the min-isters of Theodosius, and too deeply remembered by a priest who affected to pardon, and continued to hate, the præfect of Egypt. As he passed through the streets his chariot was assaulted by a band of five hundred of the Nitrian monks; his guards fled from the wild beasts of the desert; his protestations that he was a Christian and a Catholic were answered by a volley of stones, and the face of Orestes was covered with blood. The loyal citizens of Alexandria hastened to his rescue; he in-stantly satisfied his justice and revenge against the monk by whose hand he had been wounded, and Ammonius expired under the rod of the lictor. At the command of Cyril his body was raised from the ground, and transported in solemn procession to the cathedral; the name of Ammonius was changed to that of Thaumasius, the *wonderful;* his tomb was decorated with the trophies of martyrdom; and the patriarch ascended the pulpit to celebrate the magnanimity of an assassin and a rebel. Such honours might incite the faithful to combat and die under the banners of the saint; and he soon prompted, or accepted, the sacri-fice of a virgin, who professed the religion of the Greeks, and cultivated the friendship of Orestes. Hypatia, the daughter of Theon the mathe-matician,[25] was initiated in her father's studies; her learned comments have elucidated the geometry of Apollonius and Diophantus; and she publicly taught, both at Athens and Alexandria, the philosophy of Plato and Aristotle. In the bloom of beauty, and in the maturity of wisdom, the modest maid refused her lovers and instructed her disciples; the persons most illustrious for their rank or merit were impatient to visit the female philosopher; and Cyril beheld with a jealous eye the gorgeous train of horses and slaves who crowded the door of her academy. A rumour was spread among the Christians that the daughter of Theon was the only obstacle to the reconciliation of the præfect and the arch-bishop; and that obstacle was speedily removed. On a fatal day, in the holy season of Lent, Hypatia was torn from her chariot, stripped naked, dragged to the church, and inhumanly butchered by the hands of Peter the reader and a troop of savage and merciless fanatics: her flesh was scraped from her bones with sharp oyster-shells,[26] and her quivering limbs were delivered to the flames. The just progress of inquiry and

---

[25] For Theon and his daughter Hypatia, see Fabricius, Bibliothec. tom. viii. p. 210, 211. Her article in the Lexicon of Suidas is curious and original. Hesychius (Meursii Opera, tom. vii. p. 295, 296) observes that she was perse-cuted διὰ τὴν ὑπερβάλλουσαν σοφίαν; and an epigram in the Greek Anthology (l. i. c. 76, p. 159, edit. Brodæi) celebrates her knowledge and eloquence. She is honourably mentioned (Epist. 10, 15, 16, 33-80, 124, 135, 153) by her friend and disciple the philosophic bishop Synesius.

[26] Ὀστράκοις ἀνεῖλον, καὶ μεληδὸν διασπάσαντες, etc. Oyster-shells were plenti-fully strewed on the sea-beach before the Cæsareum. I may therefore prefer the literal sense without rejecting the metaphorical version of *tegulæ,* tiles, which is used by M. de Valois. I am ignorant, and the assassins were prob-ably regardless, whether their victim was yet alive.

punishment was stopped by seasonable gifts; but the murder of Hypatia has imprinted an indelible stain on the character and religion of Cyril of Alexandria.[27]

Superstition, perhaps, would more gently expiate the blood of a virgin than the banishment of a saint; and Cyril had accompanied his uncle to the iniquitous synod of the Oak. When the memory of Chrysostom was restored and consecrated, the nephew of Theophilus, at the head of a dying faction, still maintained the justice of his sentence; nor was it till after a tedious delay and an obstinate resistance that he yielded to the consent of the Catholic world.[28] His enmity to the Byzantine pontiffs [29] was a sense of interest, not a sally of passion: he envied their fortunate station in the sunshine of the Imperial court; and he dreaded their upstart ambition, which oppressed the metropolitans of Europe and Asia, invaded the provinces of Antioch and Alexandria, and measured their diocese by the limits of the empire. The long moderation of Atticus, the mild usurper of the throne of Chrysostom, suspended the animosities of the Eastern patriarchs; but Cyril was at length awakened by the exaltation of a rival more worthy of his esteem and hatred. After the short and troubled reign of Sisinnius, bishop of Constantinople, the factions of the clergy and people were appeased by the choice of the emperor, who, on this occasion, consulted the voice of fame, and invited the merit of a stranger. Nestorius,[30] a native of Germanicia and a monk of Antioch, was recommended by the austerity of his life and the eloquence of his sermons; but the first homily which he preached before the devout Theodosius betrayed the acrimony and impatience of his zeal. " Give me, O Cæsar! " he exclaimed, " give me the earth purged of heretics, and I will give you in exchange the kingdom of heaven. Exterminate with me the heretics, and with you I will exterminate the Persians." On the fifth day, as if the treaty had been already signed, the patriarch of Constantinople discovered, surprised, and attacked a secret conventicle of the Arians; they preferred death to submission; the flames that were kindled by their despair soon spread to the neighbouring houses, and the triumph of Nestorius was clouded by the name of *incendiary*. On either side of the Hellespont his episcopal

[27] These exploits of St. Cyril are recorded by Socrates (l. vii. c. 13, 14, 15); and the most reluctant bigotry is compelled to copy an historian who coolly styles the murderers of Hypatia ἄνδρες τὸ φρόνημα ἔνθερμοι. At the mention of that injured name, I am pleased to observe a blush even on the cheek of Baronius (A.D. 415, No. 48).
[28] He was deaf to the entreaties of Atticus of Constantinople, and of Isidore of Pelusium, and yielded only (if we may believe Nicephorus, l. xiv. c. 18) to the personal intercession of the Virgin. Yet in his last years he still muttered that John Chrysostom had been justly condemned (Tillemont, Mém. Ecclés. tom. xiv. p. 278-282; Baronius, Annal. Eccles. A.D. 412, No. 46-64).
[29] See their characters in the history of Socrates (l. vii. c. 25-28); their power and pretensions in the huge compilation of Thomassin (Discipline de l'Eglise, tom. i. p. 80-91).
[30] His elevation and conduct are described by Socrates (l. vii. c. 29, 31); and Marcellinus seems to have applied the eloquentiæ satis, sapientiæ parum, of Sallust.

vigour imposed a rigid formulary of faith and discipline—a chronological error concerning the festival of Easter was punished as an offence against the church and state. Lydia and Caria, Sardes and Miletus, were purified with the blood of the obstinate Quartodecimans; and the edict of the emperor, or rather of the patriarch, enumerates three-and-twenty degrees and denominations in the guilt and punishment of heresy.[31] But the sword of persecution which Nestorius so furiously wielded was soon turned against his own breast. Religion was the pretence; but, in the judgment of a contemporary saint, ambition was the genuine motive of episcopal warfare.[32]

In the Syrian school Nestorius had been taught to abhor the confusion of the two natures, and nicely to discriminate the humanity of his *master* Christ from the divinity of the *Lord* Jesus.[33]   The Blessed Virgin he revered as the mother of Christ, but his ears were offended with the rash and recent title of mother of God,[34] which had been insensibly adopted since the origin of the Arian controversy. From the pulpit of Constantinople, a friend of the patriarch, and afterwards the patriarch himself, repeatedly preached against the use, or the abuse, of a word [35] unknown to the apostles, unauthorised by the church, and which could only tend to alarm the timorous, to mislead the simple, to amuse the profane, and to justify, by a seeming resemblance, the old genealogy of Olympus.[36]   In his calmer moments Nestorius confessed that it might be tolerated or excused by the union of the two natures,

[31] Cod. Theodos. l. xvi. tit. v. leg. 65; with the illustrations of Baronius (A.D. 428, No. 25, etc.), Godefroy (ad locum), and Pagi Critica, tom. ii. p. 208.
[32] Isidore of Pelusium (l. iv. Epist. 57).   His words are strong and scandalous—τί θαυμάζεις, εἰ καὶ νῦν περὶ πρᾶγμα θεῖον καὶ λόγου κρεῖττον διαφωνεῖν προσποιοῦνται ὑπὸ φιλαρχίας ἐκβακχευόμενοι.   Isidore is a saint, but he never became a bishop; and I half suspect that the pride of Diogenes trampled on the pride of Plato.
[33] La Croze (Christianisme des Indes, tom. i. p. 44-53; Thesaurus Epistolicus La Crozianus, tom. iii. p. 276-280) has detected the use of ὁ δεσπότης and ὁ κύριος Ἰησοῦς, which, in the fourth, fifth, and sixth centuries, discriminates the school of Diodorus of Tarsus and his Nestorian disciples.
[34] Θεοτόκος—*Deipara*: as in zoology we familiarly speak of oviparous and viviparous animals.   It is not easy to fix the invention of this word, which La Croze (Christianisme des Indes, tom. i. p. 16) ascribes to Eusebius of Cæsarea and the Arians.   The orthodox testimonies are produced by Cyril and Petavius (Dogmat. Theolog. tom. v. l. v. c. 15, p. 254, etc.) ; but the veracity of the saint is questionable, and the epithet of θεοτόκος so easily slides from the margin to the text of a Catholic MS.
[35] Basnage, in the Histoire de l'Eglise, a work of controversy (tom. i. p. 505), justifies the mother, by the blood, of God (Acts xx. 28, with Mill's various readings).   But the Greek MSS. are far from unanimous; and the primitive style of the blood of Christ is preserved in the Syriac version, even in those copies which were used by the Christians of St. Thomas on the coast of Malabar (La Croze, Christianisme des Indes, tom. i. p. 347).   The jealousy of the Nestorians and Monophysites has guarded the purity of their text.
[36] The pagans of Egypt already laughed at the new Cybele of the Christians (Isidor. l. i. Epist. 54) ; a letter was forged in the name of Hypatia, to ridicule the theology of her assassin (Synodicon, c. 216, in iv. tom. Concil. p. 484). In the article of Nestorius, Bayle has scattered some loose philosophy on the worship of the Virgin Mary.

and the communication of their *idioms:*[37] but he was exasperated by contradiction to disclaim the worship of a new-born, an infant Deity, to draw his inadequate similes from the conjugal or civil partnerships of life, and to describe the manhood of Christ as the robe, the instrument, the tabernacle of his Godhead. At these blasphemous sounds the pillars of the sanctuary were shaken. The unsuccessful competitors of Nestorius indulged their pious or personal resentment, the Byzantine clergy was secretly displeased with the intrusion of a stranger: whatever is superstitious or absurd might claim the protection of the monks; and the people was interested in the glory of their virgin patroness.[38] The sermons of the archbishop, and the service of the altar, were disturbed by seditious clamour; his authority and doctrine were renounced by separate congregations; every wind scattered round the empire the leaves of controversy; and the voice of the combatants on a sonorous theatre re-echoed in the cells of Palestine and Egypt. It was the duty of Cyril to enlighten the zeal and ignorance of his innumerable monks: in the school of Alexandria he had imbibed and professed the incarnation of one nature; and the successor of Athanasius consulted his pride and ambition when he rose in arms against another Arius, more formidable and more guilty, on the second throne of the hierarchy. After a short correspondence, in which the rival prelates disguised their hatred in the hollow language of respect and charity, the patriarch of Alexandria denounced to the prince and people, to the East and to the West, the damnable errors of the Byzantine pontiff. From the East, more especially from Antioch, he obtained the ambiguous counsels of toleration and silence, which were addressed to both parties while they favoured the cause of Nestorius. But the Vatican received with open arms the messengers of Egypt. The vanity of Celestine was flattered by the appeal; and the partial version of a monk decided the faith of the pope, who, with his Latin clergy, was ignorant of the language, the arts, and the theology of the Greeks. At the head of an Italian synod, Celestine weighed the merits of the cause, approved the creed of Cyril, condemned the sentiments and person of Nestorius, degraded the heretic from his episcopal dignity, allowed a respite of ten days for recantation and penance, and delegated to his enemy the execution of this rash and illegal sentence. But the patriarch of Alexandria, whilst he darted the thunders of a god, exposed the errors and passions of a mortal; and his twelve anathemas [39] still torture the orthodox slaves who adore the memory of a saint without forfeiting their allegiance to the synod of

[37] The ἀντίδοσις of the Greeks, a mutual loan or transfer of the idioms or properties of each nature to the other—of infinity to man, passibility to God, etc. Twelve rules on this nicest of subjects compose the Theological Grammar of Petavius (Dogmata Theolog. tom. v. l. iv. c. 14, 15, p. 209, etc.).

[38] See Ducange, C. P. Christiana, l. i. p. 30, etc.

[39] Concil. tom. iii. p. 943. They have never been *directly* approved by the church (Tillemont. Mém. Ecclés. tom. xiv. p. 368-372). I almost pity the agony of rage and sophistry with which Petavius seems to be agitated in the sixth book of his Dogmata Theologica.

Chalcedon. These bold assertions are indelibly tinged with the colours of the Apollinarian heresy; but the serious, and perhaps the sincere, professions of Nestorius have satisfied the wiser and less partial theologians of the present times.[40]

Yet neither the emperor nor the primate of the East were disposed to obey the mandate of an Italian priest; and a synod of the Catholic, or rather of the Greek, church was unanimously demanded as the sole remedy that could appease or decide this ecclesiastical quarrel.[41] Ephesus, on all sides accessible by sea and land, was chosen for the place, the festival of Pentecost for the day, of the meeting; a writ of summons was despatched to each metropolitan, and a guard was stationed to protect and confine the fathers till they should settle the mysteries of heaven and the faith of the earth. Nestorius appeared not as a criminal, but as a judge; he depended on the weight rather than the number of his prelates, and his sturdy slaves from the baths of Zeuxippus were armed for every service of injury or defence. But his adversary Cyril was more powerful in the weapons both of the flesh and of the spirit. Disobedient to the letter, or at least to the meaning, of the royal summons, he was attended by fifty Egyptian bishops, who expected from their patriarch's nod the inspiration of the Holy Ghost. He had contracted an intimate alliance with Memnon bishop of Ephesus. The despotic primate of Asia disposed of the ready succours of thirty or forty episcopal votes: a crowd of peasants, the slaves of the church, was poured into the city to support with blows and clamours a metaphysical argument; and the people zealously asserted the honour of the Virgin, whose body reposed within the walls of Ephesus.[42] The fleet which had transported Cyril from Alexandria was laden with the riches of Egypt; and he disembarked a numerous body of mariners, slaves, and fanatics, enlisted with blind obedience under the banner of St. Mark

[40] Such as the rational Basnage (ad tom. i.; Variar. Lection. Canisii in Præfat. c. 2, p. 11-23) and La Croze, the universal scholar (Christianisme des Indes, tom. i. p. 16-20; De l'Ethiopie, p. 26, 27; Thesaur. Epist. p. 176, etc., 283, 285). His free sentence is confirmed by that of his friends Jablonski (Thesaur. Epist. tom. i. p. 193-201) and Mosheim (idem, p. 304: Nestorium crimine caruisse est et mea sententia); and three more respectable judges will not easily be found. Asseman, a learned and modest slave, can *hardly* discern (Bibliothec. Orient. tom. iv. p. 190-224) the guilt and error of the Nestorians.

[41] The origin and progress of the Nestorian controversy, till the synod of Ephesus, may be found in Socrates (l. vii. c. 32), Evagrius (l. i. c. 1, 2), Liberatus (Brev. c. 1-4), the original Acts (Concil. tom. iii. p. 551-991, edit. Venice, 1728), the Annals of Baronius and Pagi, and the faithful collections of Tillemont (Mém. Ecclés. tom. xiv. p. 283-377).

[42] The Christians of the four first centuries were ignorant of the death and burial of Mary. The tradition of Ephesus is affirmed by the synod (ἔνθα ὁ θεολόγος Ἰωάννης, καὶ ἡ θεοτόκος παρθένος ἡ ἁγία Μαρία—Concil. tom. iii. p. 1102); yet it has been superseded by the claim of Jerusalem; and her *empty* sepulchre, as it was shown to the pilgrims, produced the fable of her resurrection and assumption, in which the Greek and Latin churches have piously acquiesced. See Baronius (Annal. Eccles. A.D. 48, No. 6, etc.) and Tillemont (Mém. Ecclés. tom. i. p. 467-477).

and the mother of God. The fathers, and even the guards, of the council were awed by this martial array; the adversaries of Cyril and Mary were insulted in the streets or threatened in their houses; his eloquence and liberality made a daily increase in the number of his adherents; and the Egyptian soon computed that he might command the attendance and the voices of two hundred bishops.[43] But the author of the twelve anathemas foresaw and dreaded the opposition of John of Antioch, who, with a small though respectable train of metropolitans and divines, was advancing by slow journeys from the distant capital of the East. Impatient of a delay which he stigmatised as voluntary and culpable,[44] Cyril announced the opening of the synod sixteen days after the festival of Pentecost. Nestorius, who depended on the near approach of his Eastern friends, persisted, like his predecessor Chrysostom, to disclaim the jurisdiction, and to disobey the summons, of his enemies: they hastened his trial, and his accuser presided in the seat of judgment. Sixty-eight bishops, twenty-two of metropolitan rank, defended his cause by a modest and temperate protest: they were excluded from the councils of their brethren. Candidian, in the emperor's name, requested a delay of four days; the profane magistrate was driven with outrage and insult from the assembly of the saints. The whole of this momentous transaction was crowded into the compass of a summer's day: the bishops delivered their separate opinions; but the uniformity of style reveals the influence or the hand of a master, who has been accused of corrupting the public evidence of their acts and subscriptions.[45] Without a dissenting voice they recognised in the epistles of Cyril the Nicene creed and the doctrine of the fathers: but the partial extracts from the letters and homilies of Nestorius were interrupted by curses and anathemas; and the heretic was degraded from his episcopal and ecclesiastical dignity. The sentence, maliciously inscribed to the new Judas, was affixed and proclaimed in the streets of Ephesus: the weary prelates, as they issued from the church of the mother of God, were saluted as her champions; and her victory was celebrated by the illuminations, the songs, and the tumult of the night.

[43] The Acts of Chalcedon (Concil. tom. iv. p. 1405, 1408) exhibit a lively picture of the blind, obstinate servitude of the bishops of Egypt to their patriarch.

[44] Civil or ecclesiastical business detained the bishops at Antioch till the 18th of May. Ephesus was at the distance of thirty days' journey; and ten days more may be fairly allowed for accidents and repose. The march of Xenophon over the same ground enumerates above 260 parasangs or leagues; and this measure might be illustrated from ancient and modern itineraries, if I knew how to compare the speed of an army, a synod, and a caravan. John of Antioch is reluctantly acquitted by Tillemont himself (Mém. Ecclés. tom. xiv. p. 386-389).

[45] Μεμφόμενον μὴ κατὰ τὸ δέον τὰ ἐν Ἐφέσῳ συντεθῆναι ὑπομνήματα, πανουργίᾳ δὲ καί τινι ἀθέσμῳ καινοτομίᾳ Κυρίλλου τεχνάζοντος. Evagrius, l. i. c. 7. The same imputation was urged by Count Irenæus (tom. iii. p. 1249) ; and the orthodox critics do not find it an easy task to defend the purity of the Greek or Latin copies of the Acts.

On the fifth day the triumph was clouded by the arrival and indignation of the Eastern bishops. In a chamber of the inn, before he had wiped the dust from his shoes, John of Antioch gave audience to Candidian the Imperial minister, who related his ineffectual efforts to prevent or to annul the hasty violence of the Egyptian. With equal haste and violence the Oriental synod of fifty bishops degraded Cyril and Memnon from their episcopal honours; condemned, in the twelve anathemas, the purest venom of the Apollinarian heresy; and described the Alexandrian primate as a monster, born and educated for the destruction of the church.[46] *His* throne was distant and inaccessible; but they instantly resolved to bestow on the flock of Ephesus the blessing of a faithful shepherd. By the vigilance of Memnon the churches were shut against them, and a strong garrison was thrown into the cathedral. The troops, under the command of Candidian, advanced to the assault; the outguards were routed and put to the sword, but the place was impregnable: the besiegers retired; their retreat was pursued by a vigorous sally; they lost their horses, and many of the soldiers were dangerously wounded with clubs and stones. Ephesus, the city of the Virgin, was defiled with rage and clamour, with sedition and blood; the rival synods darted anathemas and excommunications from their spiritual engines; and the court of Theodosius was perplexed by the adverse and contradictory narratives of the Syrian and Egyptian factions. During a busy period of three months the emperor tried every method, except the most effectual means of indifference and contempt, to reconcile this theological quarrel. He attempted to remove or intimidate the leaders by a common sentence of acquittal or condemnation; he invested his representatives at Ephesus with ample power and military force; he summoned from either party eight chosen deputies to a free and candid conference in the neighbourhood of the capital, far from the contagion of popular frenzy. But the Orientals refused to yield, and the Catholics, proud of their numbers and of their Latin allies, rejected all terms of union or toleration. The patience of the meek Theodosius was provoked, and he dissolved in anger this episcopal tumult, which at the distance of thirteen centuries assumes the venerable aspect of the third œcumenical council.[47] " God is my witness," said the pious prince, " that I am not the author of this confusion. His providence will discern and punish the guilty. Return to your provinces, and may your private virtues repair the mischief and scandal of your meeting." They returned to their provinces;

---

[46] Ὁ δὲ ἐπ' ὀλέθρῳ τῶν ἐκκλησιῶν τεχθεὶς καὶ τραφείς. After the coalition of John and Cyril these invectives were mutually forgotten. The style of declamation must never be confounded with the genuine sense which respectable enemies entertain of each other's merit (Concil. tom. iii. p. 1244).

[47] See the Acts of the Synod of Ephesus in the original Greek, and a Latin version almost contemporary (Concil. tom. iii. p. 991-1339, with the Synodicon adversus Tragœdiam Irenæi, tom. iv. p. 235-497), the Ecclesiastical Histories of Socrates (l. vii. c. 34) and Evagrius (l. i. c. 3, 4, 5), and the Breviary of Liberatus (in Concil. tom. vi. p. 419-459, c. 5, 6), and the Mémoires Ecclés. of Tillemont (tom. xiv. p. 377-487).

but the same passions which had distracted the synod of Ephesus were diffused over the Eastern world. After three obstinate and equal campaigns, John of Antioch and Cyril of Alexandria condescended to explain and embrace: but their seeming re-union must be imputed rather to prudence than to reason, to the mutual lassitude rather than to the Christian charity of the patriarchs.

The Byzantine pontiff had instilled into the royal ear a baleful prejudice against the character and conduct of his Egyptian rival. An epistle of menace and invective,[48] which accompanied the summons, accused him as a busy, insolent, and envious priest, who perplexed the simplicity of the faith, violated the peace of the church and state, and, by his artful and separate addresses to the wife and sister of Theodosius, presumed to suppose, or to scatter, the seeds of discord in the Imperial family. At the stern command of his sovereign, Cyril had repaired to Ephesus, where he was resisted, threatened, and confined, by the magistrates in the interest of Nestorius and the Orientals, who assembled the troops of Lydia and Ionia to suppress the fanatic and disorderly train of the patriarch. Without expecting the royal licence, he escaped from his guards, precipitately embarked, deserted the imperfect synod, and retired to his episcopal fortress of safety and independence. But his artful emissaries, both in the court and city, successfully laboured to appease the resentment, and to conciliate the favour, of the emperor. The feeble son of Arcadius was alternately swayed by his wife and sister, by the eunuchs and women of the palace: superstition and avarice were their ruling passions; and the orthodox chiefs were assiduous in their endeavours to alarm the former and to gratify the latter. Constantinople and the suburbs were sanctified with frequent monasteries, and the holy abbots, Dalmatius and Eutyches,[49] had devoted their zeal and fidelity to the cause of Cyril, the worship of Mary, and the unity of Christ. From the first moment of their monastic life they had never mingled with the world, or trod the profane ground of the city. But in-this awful moment of the danger of the church, their vow was superseded by a more sublime and indispensable duty. At the head of a long order of monks and hermits, who carried burning tapers in their hands, and chanted litanies to the mother of God, they proceeded from their monasteries to the palace. The people was edified and inflamed by this extraordinary spectacle, and the trembling monarch

---

[48] Ταραχὴν (says the emperor in pointed language) τὸ γε ἐπὶ σαυτῷ καὶ χωρισμὸν ταῖς ἐκκλησίαις ἐμβέβληκας . . . . ὡς θρασυτέρας ὁρμῆς πρεπούσης μᾶλλον ἢ ἀκριβείας . . . . καὶ ποικιλίας μᾶλλον τούτων ἡμῖν ἀρκούσης ἤπερ ἁπλότητος . . . . παντὸς μᾶλλον ἢ ἱέρεως. . . . τά τε τῶν ἐκκλησιῶν, τά τε τῶν βασιλέων μέλλειν χωρίζειν βούλεσθαι, ὡς οὐκ οὔσης ἀφορμῆς ἑτέρας εὐδοκιμήσεως. I should be curious to know how much Nestorius paid for these expressions, so mortifying to his rival.

[49] Eutyches, the heresiarch Eutyches, is honourably named by Cyril as a friend, a saint, and the strenuous defender of the faith. His brother, the abbot Dalmatius, is likewise employed to bind the emperor and all his chamberlains terribili conjuratione. Synodicon, c. 203, in Concil. tom. iv. p. 467.

listened to the prayers and adjurations of the saints, who boldly pronounced that none could hope for salvation unless they embraced the person and the creed of the orthodox successor of Athanasius. At the same time every avenue of the throne was assaulted with gold. Under the decent names of *eulogies* and *benedictions*, the courtiers of both sexes were bribed according to the measure of their power and rapaciousness. But their incessant demands despoiled the sanctuaries of Constantinople and Alexandria; and the authority of the patriarch was unable to silence the just murmur of his clergy, that a debt of sixty thousand pounds had already been contracted to support the expense of this scandalous corruption.[50] Pulcheria, who relieved her brother from the weight of an empire, was the firmest pillar of orthodoxy; and so intimate was the alliance between the thunders of the synod and the whispers of the court, that Cyril was assured of success if he could displace one eunuch, and substitute another in the favour of Theodosius. Yet the Egyptian could not boast of a glorious or decisive victory. The emperor, with unaccustomed firmness, adhered to his promise of protecting the innocence of the Oriental bishops; and Cyril softened his anathemas, and confessed, with ambiguity and reluctance, a twofold nature of Christ, before he was permitted to satiate his revenge against the unfortunate Nestorius.[51]

The rash and obstinate Nestorius, before the end of the synod, was oppressed by Cyril, betrayed by the court, and faintly supported by his Eastern friends. A sentiment of fear or indignation prompted him, while it was yet time, to affect the glory of a voluntary abdication:[52] his wish, or at least his request, was readily granted; he was conducted with honour from Ephesus to his old monastery of Antioch; and, after a short pause, his successors, Maximian and Proclus, were acknowledged as the lawful bishops of Constantinople. But in the silence of his cell the degraded patriarch could no longer resume the innocence and security of a private monk. The past he regretted, he was discontented

---

[50] Clerici qui hic sunt contristantur, quod ecclesia Alexandrina nudata sit hujus causâ turbelæ: et debet præter illa quæ hinc transmissa sint *auri libras mille quingentas.* Et nunc ei scriptum est ut præstet; sed de tuâ ecclesiâ præsta avaritiæ quorum nosti, etc. This curious and original letter, from Cyril's archdeacon to his creature the new bishop of Constantinople, has been unaccountably preserved in an old Latin version (Synodicon, c. 203, Concil. tom. iv. p. 465-468). The mask is almost dropped, and the saints speak the honest language of interest and confederacy.

[51] The tedious negotiations that succeeded the synod of Ephesus are diffusely related in the original Acts (Concil. tom. iii. p. 1339-1771) ad fin. vol. and the Synodicon, in tom. iv.), Socrates (l. vii. c. 28, 35, 40, 41), Evagrius (l. i. c. 6, 7, 8, 12), Liberatus (c. 7-10), Tillemont (Mém. Eccles. tom. xiv. p. 487-676). The most patient reader will thank me for compressing so much nonsense and falsehood in a few lines.

[52] Αὐτοῦ τε αὖ δεηθέντος, ἐπετράπη κατὰ τὸ οἰκεῖον ἐπαναζεῦξαι μοναστήριον. Evagrius, l. i. c. 7. The original letters in the Synodicon (c. 15, 24, 25, 26) justify the *appearance* of a voluntary resignation, which is asserted by Ebed-Jesu, a Nestorian writer, apud Asseman. Biblioth. Oriental. tom. iii. p. 299, 302.

with the present, and the future he had reason to dread: the Oriental bishops successively disengaged their cause from his unpopular name, and each day decreased the number of the schismatics who revered Nestorius as the confessor of the faith. After a residence at Antioch of four years, the hand of Theodosius subscribed an edict [53] which ranked him with Simon the magician, proscribed his opinions and followers, condemned his writings to the flames, and banished his person first to Petra in Arabia, and at length to Oasis, one of the *islands* of the Libyan desert.[54] Secluded from the church and from the world, the exile was still pursued by the rage of bigotry and war. A wandering tribe of the Blemmyes or Nubians invaded his solitary prison: in their retreat they dismissed a crowd of useless captives; but no sooner had Nestorius reached the banks of the Nile, than he would gladly have escaped from a Roman and orthodox city to the milder servitude of the savages. His flight was punished as a new crime: the soul of the patriarch inspired the civil and ecclesiastical powers of Egypt; the magistrates, the soldiers, the monks, devoutly tortured the enemy of Christ and St. Cyril; and, as far as the confines of Æthiopia, the heretic was alternately dragged and recalled, till his aged body was broken by the hardships and accidents of these reiterated journeys. Yet his mind was still independent and erect; the president of Thebais was awed by his pastoral letters; he survived the Catholic tyrant of Alexandria, and, after sixteen years' banishment, the synod of Chalcedon would perhaps have restored him to the honours, or at least to the communion, of the church. The death of Nestorius prevented his obedience to their welcome summons;[55] and his disease might afford some colour to the scandalous report, that his tongue, the organ of blasphemy, had been eaten by the worms. He was buried in a city of Upper Egypt, known by the names of Chemnis, or

[53] See the Imperial letters in the Acts of the Synod of Ephesus (Concil. tom. iii. p. 1730-1735). The odious name of *Simonians*, which was affixed to the disciples of this τερατώδους διδασκαλίας, was designed ὡς ἂν ὀνείδεσι προβληθέντες αἰώνιον ὑπομένοιεν τιμωρίαν τῶν ἁμαρτημάτων, καὶ μήτε ζῶντας τιμωρίας, μήτε θανόντας ἀτιμίας ἐκτὸς ὑπάρχειν. Yet these were Christians! who differed only in names and in shadows.

[54] The metaphor of islands is applied by the grave civilians (Pandect. l. xlviii. tit. 22, leg. 7 [§ 5]) to those happy spots which are discriminated by water and verdure from the Libyan sands. Three of these under the common name of Oasis, or Alvahat: 1. The temple of Jupiter Ammon. 2. The middle Oasis, three days' journey to the west of Lycopolis. 3. The southern, where Nestorius was banished, in the first climate, and only three days' journey from the confines of Nubia. See a learned Note of Michaelis (ad Descript. Ægypt. Abulfedæ, p. 21-34).

[55] The invitation of Nestorius to the synod of Chalcedon is related by Zacharias, bishop of Melitene (Evagrius, l. ii. c. 2; Asseman. Biblioth. Orient. tom. ii. p. 55), and the famous Xenaias or Philoxenus, bishop of Hierapolis (Asseman. Biblioth. Orient. tom. ii. p. 40, etc.), denied by Evagrius and Asseman, and stoutly maintained by La Croze (Thesaur. Epistol. tom. iii. p. 181, etc.). The fact is not improbable; yet it was the interest of the Monophysites to spread the invidious report; and Eutychius (tom. ii. p. 12) affirms that Nestorius died after an exile of seven years, and consequently ten years before the synod of Chalcedon.

Panopolis, or Akmim;[56] but the immortal malice of the Jacobites has persevered for ages to cast stones against his sepulchre, and to propagate the foolish tradition that it was never watered by the rain of heaven, which equally descends on the righteous and the ungodly.[57] Humanity may drop a tear on the fate of Nestorius; yet justice must observe that he suffered the persecution which he had approved and inflicted.[58]

The death of the Alexandrian primate, after a reign of thirty-two years, abandoned the Catholics to the intemperance of zeal and the abuse of victory.[59] The *monophysite* doctrine (one incarnate nature) was rigorously preached in the churches of Egypt and the monasteries of the East; the primitive creed of Apollinaris was protected by the sanctity of Cyril; and the name of EUTYCHES, his venerable friend, has been applied to the sect most adverse to the Syrian heresy of Nestorius. His rival Eutyches was the abbot, or archimandrite, or superior of three hundred monks; but the opinions of a simple and illiterate recluse might have expired in a cell where he had slept above seventy years if the resentment or indiscretion of Flavian, the Byzantine pontiff, had not exposed the scandal to the eyes of the Christian world. His domestic synod was instantly convened, their proceedings were sullied with clamour and artifice, and the aged heretic was surprised into a seeming confession that Christ had not derived his body from the substance of the Virgin Mary. From their partial decree Eutyches appealed to a general council; and his cause was vigorously asserted by his godson Chrysaphius, the reigning eunuch of the palace,. and his accomplice Dioscorus, who had succeeded to the throne, the creed, the talents, and the vices of the nephew of Theophilus. By the special summons of Theodosius, the second synod of Ephesus was judiciously composed of ten metropolitans and ten bishops from each of the six dioceses of the Eastern empire: some exceptions of favour or merit enlarged the number to one hundred and thirty-five; and the Syrian Barsumas, as the chief and representative of the monks, was invited to sit and vote with the successors of the apostles. But the despotism of

[56] Consult D'Anville (Mémoire sur l'Egypt, p. 191), Pocock (Description of the East, vol. i. p. 76) Abulfeda (Descript. Ægypt. p. 14), and his commentator Michaelis (Not. p. 78-83), and the Nubian Geographer (p. 42), who mentions, in the twelfth century, the ruins and the sugar-canes of Akmim.
[57] Eutychius (Annal. tom. ii. p. 12) and Gregory Bar-Hebræus, or Abulpharagius (Asseman. tom. ii. p. 316), represent the credulity of the tenth and thirteenth centuries.
[58] We are obliged to Evagrius (l. i. c. 7) for some extracts from the letters of Nestorius; but the lively picture of his sufferings is treated with insult by the hard and stupid fanatic.
[59] Dixi Cyrillum dum viveret, auctoritate suâ effecisse, ne Eutychianismus et Monophysitarum error in nervum erumperet: idque verum puto . . . aliquo . . . honesto modo παλινῳδίαν cecinerat. The learned but cautious Jablonski did not always speak the whole truth. Cum Cyrillo lenius omnino egi, quam si tecum aut cum aliis rei hujus probe gnaris et æquis rerum æstimatoribus sermones privatos conferrum (Thesaur. Epistol. La Crozian. tom. i. p. 197, 198); an excellent key to his dissertations on the Nestorian controversy!

the Alexandrian patriarch again oppressed the freedom of debate; the same spiritual and carnal weapons were again drawn from the arsenals of Egypt; the Asiatic veterans, a band of archers, served under the orders of Dioscorus; and the more formidable monks, whose minds were inaccessible to reason or mercy, besieged the doors of the cathedral. The general and, as it should seem, the unconstrained voice of the fathers accepted the faith and even the anathemas of Cyril; and the heresy of the two natures was formally condemned in the persons and writings of the most learned Orientals. " May those who divide Christ be divided with the sword, may they be hewn in pieces, may they be burned alive! " were the charitable wishes of a Christian synod.[60] The innocence and sanctity of Eutyches were acknowledged without hesitation; but the prelates, more especially those of Thrace and Asia, were unwilling to depose their patriarch for the use or even the abuse of his lawful jurisdiction. They embraced the knees of Dioscorus, as he stood with a threatening aspect on the footstool of his throne, and conjured him to forgive the offences and to respect the dignity of his brother. " Do you mean to raise a sedition? " exclaimed the relentless tyrant. " Where are the officers? " At these words a furious multitude of monks and soldiers, with stakes, and swords, and chains, burst into the church: the trembling bishops hid themselves behind the altar or under the benches; and as they were not inspired with the zeal of martyrdom they successively subscribed a blank paper, which was afterwards filled with the condemnation of the Byzantine pontiff. Flavian was instantly delivered to the wild beasts of this spiritual amphitheatre: the monks were stimulated by the voice and example of Barsumas to avenge the injuries of Christ: it is said that the patriarch of Alexandria reviled, and buffeted, and kicked, and trampled his brother of Constantinople:[61] it is certain that the victim, before he could reach the place of his exile, expired on the third day of the wounds and bruises which he had received at Ephesus. This second synod has been justly branded as a gang of robbers and assassins; yet the accusers of Dioscorus would magnify his violence, to alleviate the cowardice and inconstancy of their own behaviour.

The faith of Egypt had prevailed: but the vanquished party was sup-

[60] Ἡ ἁγία σύνοδος εἶπεν, ἆρον, καῦσον Εὐσέβιον, οὗτος ζῶν καῇ, οὗτος εἰς δύο γένηται, ὡς ἐμέρισε, μερισθῇ . . . . εἴ τις λέγει δύο, ἀνάθεμα. At the request of Dioscorus, those who were not able to roar (βοῆσαι), stretched out their hands. At Chalcedon, the Orientals disclaimed these exclamations: but the Egyptians more consistently declared ταῦτα καὶ τότε εἴπομεν καὶ νῦν λέγομεν. (Concil. tom. iv. p. 1012.)

[61] Ἔλεγε δὲ (Eusebius, bishop of Dorylæum) τὸν Φλαβιανόν τε δειλαίως ἀναιρεθῆναι πρὸς Διοσκόρου ὠθούμενόν τε καὶ λακτιζόμενον: and this testimony of Evagrius (l. ii. c. 2) is amplified by the historian Zonaras (tom. ii. l. xiii. [c. 23] p. 44), who affirms that Dioscorus kicked like a wild ass. But the language of Liberatus (Brev. c. 12, in Concil. tom. vi. p. 438) is more cautious; and the Acts of Chalcedon, which lavish the names of homicide, Cain, etc., do not justify so pointed a charge. The monk Barsumas is more particularly accused—ἔσφαξε τὸν μακάριον Φλαυιανόν· αὐτὸς ἔστηκε καὶ ἔλεγε, σφάξον. (Concil. tom. iv. p. 1413.)

ported by the same pope who encountered without fear the hostile rage of Attila and Genseric. The theology of Leo, his famous *tome* or epistle on the mystery of the incarnation, had been disregarded by the synod of Ephesus: his authority, and that of the Latin church, was insulted in his legates, who escaped from slavery and death to relate the melancholy tale of the tyranny of Dioscorus and the martyrdom of Flavian. His provincial synod annulled the irregular proceedings of Ephesus; but as this step was itself irregular, he solicited the convocation of a general council in the free and orthodox provinces of Italy. From his independent throne the Roman bishop spoke and acted without danger as the head of the Christians, and his dictates were obsequiously transcribed by Placidia and her son Valentinian, who addressed their Eastern colleague to restore the peace and unity of the church. But the pageant of Oriental royalty was moved with equal dexterity by the hand of the eunuch; and Theodosius could pronounce, without hesitation, that the church was already peaceful and triumphant, and that the recent flame had been extinguished by the just punishment of the Nestorians. Perhaps the Greeks would be still involved in the heresy of the Monophysites, if the emperor's horse had not fortunately stumbled; Theodosius expired; his orthodox sister, Pulcheria, with a nominal husband, succeeded to the throne; Chrysaphius was burnt, Dioscorus was disgraced, the exiles were recalled, and the *tome* of Leo was subscribed by the Oriental bishops. Yet the pope was disappointed in his favourite project of a Latin council: he disdained to preside in the Greek synod which was speedily assembled at Nice in Bithynia; his legates required in a peremptory tone the presence of the emperor; and the weary fathers were transported to Chalcedon under the immediate eye of Marcian and the senate of Constantinople. A quarter of a mile from the Thracian Bosphorus the church of St. Euphemia was built on the summit of a gentle though lofty ascent: the triple structure was celebrated as a prodigy of art, and the boundless prospect of the land and sea might have raised the mind of a sectary to the contemplation of the God of the universe. Six hundred and thirty bishops were ranged in order in the nave of the church; but the patriarchs of the East were preceded by the legates, of whom the third was a simple priest; and the place of honour was reserved for twenty laymen of consular or senatorian rank. The gospel was ostentatiously displayed in the centre, but the rule of faith was defined by the papal and imperial ministers, who moderated the thirteen sessions of the council of Chalcedon.[62]   Their partial interposition

---

[62] The acts of the Council of Chalcedon (Concil. tom. iv. p. 761-2071) comprehend those of Ephesus (p. 890-1189), which again comprise the synod of Constantinople under Flavian (p. 930-1072); and it requires some attention to disengage this double involution. The whole business of Eutyches, Flavian, and Dioscorus, is related by Evagrius (l. i. c. 9-12, and l. ii. c. 1, 2, 3, 4) and Liberatus (Brev. c. 11, 12, 13, 14). Once more, and almost for the last time, I appeal to the diligence of Tillemont (Mém. Ecclés. tom. xv. p. 479-719). The annals of Baronius and Pagi will accompany me much further on my long and laborious journey.

silenced the intemperate shouts and execrations which degraded the episcopal gravity; but, on the formal accusation of the legates, Dioscorus was compelled to descend from his throne to the rank of a criminal, already condemned in the opinion of his judges. The Orientals, less adverse to Nestorius than to Cyril, accepted the Romans as their deliverers: Thrace, and Pontus, and Asia, were exasperated against the murderer of Flavian, and the new patriarchs of Constantinople and Antioch secured their places by the sacrifice of their benefactor. The bishops of Palestine, Macedonia, and Greece were attached to the faith of Cyril; but in the face of the synod, in the heat of the battle, the leaders, with their obsequious train, passed from the right to the left wing, and decided the victory by this seasonable desertion. Of the seventeen suffragans who sailed from Alexandria, four were tempted from their allegiance, and the thirteen, falling prostrate on the ground, implored the mercy of the council, with sighs and tears, and a pathetic declaration, that, if they yielded, they should be massacred, on their return to Egypt, by the indignant people. A tardy repentance was allowed to expiate the guilt or error of the accomplices of Dioscorus: but their sins were accumulated on his head; he neither asked nor hoped for pardon, and the moderation of those who pleaded for a general amnesty was drowned in the prevailing cry of victory and revenge. To save the reputation of his late adherents, some *personal* offences were skilfully detected; his rash and illegal excommunication of the pope, and his contumacious refusal (while he was detained a prisoner) to attend the summons of the synod. Witnesses were introduced to prove the special facts of his pride, avarice, and cruelty; and the fathers heard with abhorrence that the alms of the church were lavished on the female dancers, that his palace, and even his bath, was open to the prostitutes of Alexandria, and that the infamous Pansophia, or Irene, was publicly entertained as the concubine of the patriarch.[63]

For these scandalous offences Dioscorus was deposed by the synod and banished by the emperor; but the purity of his faith was declared in the presence, and with the tacit approbation, of the fathers. Their prudence supposed rather than pronounced the heresy of Eutyches, who was never summoned before their tribunal; and they sat silent and

---

[63] Μάλιστα ἡ περιβόητος Πανσοφία, ἡ καλουμένη Ὀρεινὴ (perhaps Εἰρηνὴ), περὶ ἧς καὶ ὁ πολυάνθρωπος τῆς Ἀλεξανδρέων δῆμος ἀφῆκε φωνήν, αὐτῆς τε καὶ τοῦ ἐραστοῦ μεμνημένος (Concil. tom. iv. p. 1276). A specimen of the wit and malice of the people is preserved in the Greek Anthology (l. ii. c. 5, p. 188, edit. Wechel), although the application was unknown to the editor Brodæus. The nameless epigrammatist raises a tolerable pun, by confounding the episcopal salutation of "Peace be to all!" with the genuine or corrupted name of the bishop's concubine:—

Εἰρήνη πάντεσσιν, ἐπίσκοπος εἶπεν ἐπελθών.
Πῶς δύναται πᾶσιν, ἥν μόνος ἔνδον ἔχει;

I am ignorant whether the patriarch, who seems to have been a jealous lover, is the Cimon of a preceding epigram, whose πεὸς ἐστηκός was viewed with envy and wonder by Priapus himself.

abashed when a bold Monophysite, casting at their feet a volume of Cyril, challenged them to anathematise in his person the doctrine of the saint. If we fairly peruse the acts of Chalcedon as they are recorded by the orthodox party,[64] we shall find that a great majority of the bishops embraced the simple unity of Christ; and the ambiguous concession that he was formed OF or FROM two natures might imply either their previous existence, or their subsequent confusion, or some dangerous interval between the conception of the man and the assumption of the God. The Roman theology, more positive and precise, adopted the term most offensive to the ears of the Egyptians, that Christ existed IN two natures; and this momentous particle [65] (which the memory, rather than the understanding, must retain) had almost produced a schism among the Catholic bishops. The *tome* of Leo had been respectfully, perhaps sincerely, subscribed; but they protested, in two successive debates, that it was neither expedient nor lawful to transgress the sacred landmarks which had been fixed at Nice, Constantinople, and Ephesus, according to the rule of Scripture and tradition. At length they yielded to the importunities of their masters, but their infallible decree, after it had been ratified with deliberate votes and vehement acclamations, was overturned in the next session by the opposition of the legates and their Oriental friends. It was in vain that a multitude of episcopal voices repeated in chorus, " The definition of the fathers is orthodox and immutable! The heretics are now discovered! Anathema to the Nestorians! Let them depart from the synod! Let them repair to Rome." [66] The legates threatened, the emperor was absolute, and a committee of eighteen bishops prepared a new decree, which was imposed on the reluctant assembly. In the name of the fourth general council, the Christ in one person, but *in* two natures, was announced to the Catholic world: an invisible line was drawn between the heresy of Apollinaris and the faith of St. Cyril; and the road to paradise, a bridge as sharp as a razor, was suspended over the abyss by the master-hand of the theological artist. During

[64] Those who reverence the infallibility of synods may try to ascertain their sense. The leading bishops were attended by partial or careless scribes, who dispersed their copies round the world. Our Greek MSS. are sullied with the false and proscribed reading of ἐκ τῶν φυσέων (Concil. tom. iii. p. 1460) : the authentic translation of Pope Leo I. does not seem to have been executed, and the old Latin versions materially differ from the present Vulgate, which was revised (A.D. 550) by Rusticus, a Roman priest, from the best MSS. of the Ἀκοίμητοι at Constantinople (Ducange, C. P. Christiana, l. iv. p. 151), a famous monastery of Latins, Greeks, and Syrians. See Concil. tom. iv. p. 1959-2049, and Pagi, Critica, tom. ii. p. 326, etc.

[65] It is darkly represented in the microscope of Petavius (tom. v. l. iii. c. 5) ; yet the subtle theologian is himself afraid—ne quis fortasse supervacaneam, et nimis anxiam putet hujusmodi vocularum inquisitionem, et ab instituti theologici gravitate alienam (p. 124).

[66] Ἐβόησαν, ἢ ὁ ὅρος κρατείτω, ἢ ἀπερχόμεθα . . . . οἱ ἀντιλέγοντες φανεροὶ γένωνται, οἱ ἀντιλέγοντες Νεστοριανοὶ εἰσιν, οἱ ἀντιλέγοντες εἰς Ῥώμην ἀπέλθωσιν (Concil. tom. iv. p. 1449). Evagrius and Liberatus present only the placid face of the synod, and discreetly slide over these embers, suppositos cineri doloso.

ten centuries of blindness and servitude Europe received her religious opinions from the oracle of the Vatican; and the same doctrine, already varnished with the rust of antiquity, was admitted without dispute into the creed of the reformers, who disclaimed the supremacy of the Roman pontiff. The synod of Chalcedon still triumphs in the Protestant churches; but the ferment of controversy has subsided, and the most pious Christians of the present day are ignorant, or careless, of their own belief concerning the mystery of the incarnation.

Far different was the temper of the Greeks and Egyptians under the orthodox reigns of Leo and Marcian. Those pious emperors enforced with arms and edicts the symbol of their faith; [67] and it was declared by the conscience or honour of five hundred bishops, that the decrees of the synod of Chalcedon might be lawfully supported, even with blood. The Catholics observed with satisfaction that the same synod was odious both to the Nestorians and the Monophysites; [68] but the Nestorians were less angry, or less powerful, and the East was distracted by the obstinate and sanguinary zeal of the Monophysites. Jerusalem was occupied by an army of monks; in the name of the one incarnate nature, they pillaged, they burnt, they murdered; the sepulchre of Christ was defiled with blood; and the gates of the city were guarded in tumultuous rebellion against the troops of the emperor. After the disgrace and exile of Dioscorus, the Egyptians still regretted their spiritual father, and detested the usurpation of his successor, who was introduced by the fathers of Chalcedon. The throne of Proterius was supported by a guard of two thousand soldiers; he waged a five years' war against the people of Alexandria; and on the first intelligence of the death of Marcian, he became the victim of their zeal. On the third day before the festival of Easter the patriarch was besieged in the cathedral, and murdered in the baptistery. The remains of his mangled corpse were delivered to the flames, and his ashes to the wind: and the deed was inspired by the vision of a pretended angel; an ambitious monk who, under the name of Timothy the Cat,[69] succeeded to the place and opinions of Dioscorus. This

---

[67] See, in the Appendix to the Acts of Chalcedon, the confirmation of the synod by Marcian (Concil. tom. iv. p. 1781, 1783); his letters to the monks of Alexandria (p. 1791), of Mount Sinai (p. 1793), of Jerusalem and Palestine (p. 1798); his laws against the Eutychians (p. 1809, 1811, 1831); the correspondence of Leo with the provincial synods on the revolution of Alexandria (p. 1835-1930).

[68] Photius (or rather Eulogius of Alexandria) confesses, in a fine passage, the specious colour of this double charge against pope Leo and his synod of Chalcedon (Biblioth. cod. ccxxv. p. 768 [p. 243, ed. Bekk.]). He waged a double war against the enemies of the church, and wounded either foe with the darts of his adversary—καταλλήλοις βέλεσι τοὺς ἀντιπάλους ἐτίτρωσκε. Against Nestorius he seemed to introduce the σύγχυσις of the Monophysites; against Eutyches he appeared to countenance the ὑποστασέων διάφορα of the Nestorians. The apologist claims a charitable interpretation for the saints: if the same had been extended to the heretics, the *sound* of the controversy would have been lost in the air.

[69] Αἴλουρος, from his nocturnal expeditions. In darkness and disguise he

deadly superstition was inflamed on either side by the principle and the practice of retaliation: in the pursuit of a metyphysical quarrel many thousands [70] were slain, and the Christians of every degree were deprived of the substantial enjoyments of social life, and of the invisible gifts of baptism and the holy communion. Perhaps an extravagant fable of the times may conceal an allegorical picture of these fanatics, who tortured each other and themselves. " Under the consulship of Venantius and Celer," says a grave bishop, " the people of Alexandria, and all Egypt, were seized with a strange and diabolical frenzy: great and small, slaves and freedmen, monks and clergy, the natives of the land, who opposed the synod of Chalcedon, lost their speech and reason, barked like dogs, and tore, with their own teeth, the flesh from their hands and arms." [71]

The disorders of thirty years at length produced the famous HENOT-ICON [72] of the emperor Zeno, which in his reign, and in that of Anastasius, was signed by all the bishops of the East, under the penalty of degradation and exile if they rejected or infringed this salutary and fundamental law. The clergy may smile or groan at the presumption of a layman who defines the articles of faith; yet, if he stoops to the humiliating task, his mind is less infected by prejudice or interest, and the authority of the magistrate can only be maintained by the concord of the people. It is in ecclesiastical story that Zeno appears least contemptible; and I am not able to discern any Manichæan or Eutychian guilt in the generous saying of Anastasius, That it was unworthy of an emperor to persecute the worshippers of Christ and the citizens of Rome. The Henoticon was most pleasing to the Egyptians; yet the smallest blemish has not been descried by the jealous and even jaundiced eyes of our orthodox schoolmen, and it accurately represents the Catholic faith of the incarnation, without adopting or disclaiming the peculiar terms or tenets of the hostile sects. A solemn anathema is pronounced against Nestorius and Eutyches; against all heretics by whom Christ is divided, or confounded, or reduced to a phantom. Without defining the number or the article of the word *nature*, the pure system of St. Cyril, the faith of Nice, Constantinople, and Ephesus, is respectfully confirmed; but, instead of bowing at the name of the fourth council, the subject is dismissed by the censure of all contrary doctrines, *if* any such have been taught

crept round the cells of the monastery, and whispered the revelation to his slumbering brethren (Theodor. Lector. l. i. [c. 8]).

[70] Φόνους τε τολμηθῆναι μυρίους, [καὶ] αἱμάτων πλήθει μολυνθῆναι μὴ μόνον τὴν γῆν ἀλλὰ καὶ αὐτὸν τὸν ὄερα. Such is the hyperbolic language of the Henoticon.

[71] See the Chronicle of Victor Tunnunensis, in the Lectiones Antiquæ of Canisius, republished by Basnage, tom. i. p. 326.

[72] The Henoticon is transcribed by Evagrius (l. iii. c. 13 [14]), and translated by Liberatus (Brev. c. 18). Pagi (Critica, tom. ii. p. 411) and Asseman (Biblioth. Orient. tom. i. p. 343) are satisfied that it is free from heresy; but Petavius (Dogmat. Theolog. tom. v. l. i. c. 13, p. 40) most unaccountably affirms Chalcedonensem ascivit. An adversary would prove that he had never read the Henoticon.

either elsewhere or at Chalcedon. Under this ambiguous expression the friends and the enemies of the last synod might unite in a silent embrace. The most reasonable Christians acquiesced in this mode of toleration; but their reason was feeble and inconstant, and their obedi- ence was despised as timid and servile by the vehement spirit of their brethren. On a subject which engrossed the thoughts and discourses of men, it was difficult to preserve an exact neutrality; a book, a sermon, a prayer, rekindled the flame of controversy; and the bonds of communion were alternately broken and renewed by the private ani- mosity of the bishops. The space between Nestorius and Eutyches was filled by a thousand shades of language and opinion; the *aceph- ali* [73] of Egypt, and the Roman pontiffs, of equal valour, though of unequal strength, may be found at the two extremities of the theo- logical scale. The acephali, without a king or a bishop, were separated above three hundred years from the patriarchs of Alexandria, who had accepted the communion of Constantinople, without exacting a formal condemnation of the synod of Chalcedon. For accepting the communion of Alexandria, without a formal approbation of the same synod, the patriarchs of Constantinople were anathematised by the popes. Their inflexible despotism involved the most orthodox of the Greek churches in this spiritual contagion, denied or doubted the validity of their sacraments,[74] and fomented, thirty-five years, the schism of the East and West, till they finally abolished the memory of four Byzantine pontiffs who had dared to oppose the supremacy of St. Peter.[75] Before that period the precarious truce of Constantinople and Egypt had been violated by the zeal of the rival prelates. Mace- donius, who was suspected of the Nestorian heresy, asserted, in disgrace and exile, the synod of Chalcedon, while the successor of Cyril would have purchased its overthrow with a bribe of two thousand pounds of gold.

In the fever of the times the sense, or rather the sound of a syllable,

[73] See Renaudot (Hist. Patriarch. Alex. p. 123, 131, 145, 195, 247). They were reconciled by the care of Mark I. (A.D. 799-819) : he promoted their chiefs to the bishoprics of Athribis and Talba (perhaps Tava : see D'Anville, p. 82), and supplied the sacraments, which had failed for want of an episcopal ordination.

[74] De his quos baptizavit, quos ordinavit Acacius, majorum traditione con- fectam et veram, præcipue religiosæ solicitudini congruam præbemus sine dif- ficultate medicinam (Galasius, in Epist. i. ad Euphemium, Concil. tom. v. p. 286). The offer of a medicine proves the disease, and numbers must have perished before the arrival of the Roman physician. Tillemont himself (Mém. Ecclés. tom. xvi. p. 372, 642, etc.) is shocked at the proud, uncharitable temper of the popes : they are now glad, says he, to invoke St. Flavian of Antioch, St. Elias of Jerusalem, etc., to whom they refused communion whilst upon earth. But Cardinal Baronius is firm and hard as the rock of St. Peter.

[75] Their names were erased from the diptych of the church : ex venerabili diptycho, in quo piæ memoriæ transitum ad cœlum habentium episcoporum vocabula continentur (Concil. tom. iv. p. 1846). This ecclesiastical record was therefore equivalent to the book of life.

was sufficient to disturb the peace of an empire. The TRISAGION [76] (thrice holy), " Holy, holy, holy, Lord God of Hosts! " is supposed by the Greeks to be the identical hymn which the angels and cherubim eternally repeat before the throne of God, and which, about the middle of the fifth century, was miraculously revealed to the church of Constantinople. The devotion of Antioch soon added, " who was crucified for us!" and this grateful address, either to Christ alone, or to the whole Trinity, may be justified by the rules of theology, and has been gradually adopted by the Catholics of the East and West. But it had been imagined by a Monophysite bishop; [77] the gift of an enemy was at first rejected as a dire and dangerous blasphemy, and the rash innovation had nearly cost the emperor Anastasius his throne and his life.[78] The people of Constantinople was devoid of any rational principles of freedom; but they held, as a lawful cause of rebellion, the colour of a livery in the races, or the colour of a mystery in the schools. The Trisagion, with and without this obnoxious addition, was chanted in the cathedral by two adverse choirs, and, when their lungs were exhausted, they had recourse to the more solid arguments of sticks and stones; the aggressors were punished by the emperor, and defended by the patriarch; and the crown and mitre were staked on the event of this momentous quarrel. The streets were instantly crowded with innumerable swarms of men, women, and children; the legions of monks, in regular array, marched, and shouted, and fought at their head. " Christians! this is the day of martyrdom: let us not desert our spiritual father; anathema to the Manichæan tyrant! he is unworthy to reign." Such was the Catholic cry; and the galleys of Anastasius lay upon their oars before the palace, till the patriarch had pardoned his penitent, and hushed the waves of the troubled multitude. The triumph of Macedonius was checked by a speedy exile; but the zeal of his flock was again exasperated by the same question, " Whether one of the Trinity had been crucified? " On this momentous occasion the blue and green factions of Constantinople suspended their discord, and the civil and military powers were annihilated in their presence. The keys of the city, and the standards of the guards, were deposited in the forum of Constantine, the principal station and camp of the faithful. Day and night they were inces-

[76] Petavius (Dogmat. Theolog. tom. v. l. v. c. 2, 3, 4, p. 217-225) and Tillemont (Mém. Ecclés. tom. xiv. p. 713, etc., 799) represent the history and doctrine of the Trisagion. In the twelve centuries between Isaiah and St. Proclus's boy, who was taken up into heaven before the bishop and people of Constantinople, the song was considerably improved. The boy heard the angels sing, " Holy God! Holy strong! Holy immortal! "

[77] Peter Gnapheus, the *fuller* (a trade which he had exercised in his monastery), patriarch of Antioch. His tedious story is discussed in the Annals of Pagi (A.D. 477-490) and a dissertation of M. de Valois at the end of his Evagrius.

[78] The troubles under the reign of Anastasius must be gathered from the Chronicles of Victor, Marcellinus, and Theophanes. As the last was not published in the time of Baronius, his critic Pagi is more copious, as well as more correct.

santly busied either in singing hymns to the honour of their God, or in pillaging and murdering the servants of their prince. The head of his favourite monk, the friend, as they styled him, of the enemy of the Holy Trinity, was borne aloft on a spear; and the fire-brands, which had been darted against heretical structures, diffused the undistinguishing flames over the most orthodox buildings. The statues of the emperor were broken, and his person was concealed in a suburb, till, at the end of three days, he dared to implore the mercy of his subjects. Without his diadem, and in the posture of a suppliant, Anastasius appeared on the throne of the circus. The Catholics, before his face, rehearsed their genuine Trisagion; they exulted in the offer which he proclaimed by the voice of a herald of abdicating the purple; they listened to the admonition, that, since *all* could not reign, they should previously agree in the choice of a sovereign: and they accepted the blood of two unpopular ministers, whom their master without hesitation condemned to the lions. These furious but transient seditions were encouraged by the success of Vitalian, who, with an army of Huns and Bulgarians, for the most part idolaters, declared himself the champion of the Catholic faith. In this pious rebellion he depopulated Thrace, besieged Constantinople, exterminated sixty-five thousand of his fellow-Christians, till he obtained the recall of the bishops, the satisfaction of the pope, and the establishment of the council of Chalcedon, an orthodox treaty, reluctantly signed by the dying Anastasius, and more faithfully performed by the uncle of Justinian. And such was the event of the *first* of the religious wars which have been waged in the name and by the disciples of the God of Peace.[79]

Justinian has been already seen in the various lights of a prince, a conqueror, and a lawgiver: the theologian [80] still remains, and it affords an unfavourable prejudice that his theology should form a very prominent feature of his portrait. The sovereign sympathised with his subjects in their superstitious reverence for living and departed saints: his Code, and more especially his Novels, confirm and enlarge the privileges of the clergy; and in every dispute between a monk and a layman, the partial judge was inclined to pronounce that truth and

[79] The general history, from the council of Chalcedon to the death of Anastasius, may be found in the Breviary of Liberatus (c. 14-19), the second and third books of Evagrius, the abstract of the two books of Theodore the Reader, the Acts of the Synods, and the Epistles of the Popes (Concil. tom. v.). The series is continued with some disorder in the fifteenth and sixteenth tomes of the Mémoires Ecclésiastiques of Tillemont. And here I must take leave for ever of that incomparable guide, whose bigotry is overbalanced by the merits of erudition, diligence, veracity, and scrupulous minuteness. He was prevented by death from completing, as he designed, the sixth century of the church and empire.

[80] The strain of the Anecdotes of Procopius (c. 11, 13, 18, 27, 28) with the learned remarks of Alemannus is confirmed, rather than contradicted, by the Acts of the Councils, the fourth book of Evagrius, and the complaints of the African Facundus, in his twelfth book—de tribus capitulis, "cum videri doctus appetit importune . . . spontaneis quæstionibus ecclesiam turbat." See Procop. de Bell. Goth. l. iii. c. 35 [tom. ii. p. 429, ed. Bonn].

innocence and justice were always on the side of the church. In his
public and private devotions the emperor was assiduous and exemplary;
his prayers, vigils, and fasts displayed the austere penance of a monk;
his fancy was amused by the hope or belief of personal inspiration;
he had secured the patronage of the Virgin and St. Michael the archangel; and his recovery from a dangerous disease was ascribed to the
miraculous succour of the holy martyrs Cosmas and Damian. The
capital and the provinces of the East were decorated with the monuments of his religion; [81] and though the far greater part of these
costly structures may be attributed to his taste or ostentation, the
zeal of the royal architect was probably quickened by a genuine sense
of love and gratitude towards his invisible benefactors. Among the
titles of Imperial greatness the name of *Pious* was most pleasing to his
ear; to promote the temporal and spiritual interest of the church was
the serious business of his life; and the duty of father of his country
was often sacrificed to that of defender of the faith. The controversies
of the times were congenial to his temper and understanding; and the
theological professors must inwardly deride the diligence of a stranger
who cultivated their art and neglected his own. " What can ye fear,"
said a bold conspirator to his associates, " from your bigoted tyrant?
Sleepless and unarmed he sits whole nights in his closet debating with
reverend greybeards, and turning over the pages of ecclesiastical volumes." [82]   The fruits of these lucubrations were displayed in many
a conference, where Justinian might shine as the loudest and most
subtle of the disputants; in many a sermon which, under the name of
edicts and epistles, proclaimed to the empire the theology of their master.
While the barbarians invaded the provinces, while the victorious legions
marched under the banners of Belisarius and Narses, the successor of
Trajan, unknown to the camp, was content to vanquish at the head of
a synod. Had he invited to these synods a disinterested and rational
spectator, Justinian might have learned " *that* religious controversy is
the offspring of arrogance and folly; *that* true piety is most laudably
expressed by silence and submission; *that* man, ignorant of his own
nature, should not presume to scrutinise the nature of his God; and *that*
it is sufficient for us to know that power and benevolence are the perfect
attributes of the Deity." [83]
Toleration was not the virtue of the times, and indulgence to rebels
has seldom been the virtue of princes.   But when the prince descends

[81] Procop. de Ædificiis, l. i. c. 6, 7, etc., passim.
[82] Ὃς δὴ κάθηται ἀφύλακτος ἐς ἀεὶ ἐπὶ λέσχης τινὸς ἀωρὶ νυκτῶν, ὁμοῦ τοῖς τῶν
ἱερέων ἔσχατον γέρουσιν [ἐσχατογέρουσιν] ἀνακυκλεῖν τὰ Χριστιανῶν λόγια σπουδὴν
ἔχων.   Procop. de Bell. Goth. l. iii. c. 32 [tom. ii. p. 409, ed. Bonn].   In the
Life of St. Eutychius (apud Aleman. ad Procop. Arcan. c. 18 [tom. iii. p. 439,
ed. Bonn]) the same character is given with a design to praise Justinian.
[83] For these wise and moderate sentiments Procopius (de Bell. Goth. l. i.
c. 3) is scourged in the preface of Alemannus, who ranks him among the
political Christians—sed longe verius hæresium omnium sentinas, prorsusque
Atheos—abominable Atheists, who preached the imitation of God's mercy to
man (ad Hist. Arcan. c. 13).

to the narrow and peevish character of a disputant, he is easily provoked to supply the defect of argument by the plenitude of power, and to chastise without mercy the perverse blindness of those who wilfully shut their eyes against the light of demonstration. The reign of Justinian was a uniform yet various scene of persecution; and he appears to have surpassed his indolent predecessors, both in the contrivance of his laws and the rigour of their execution. The insufficient term of three months was assigned for the conversion or exile of all heretics;[84] and if he still connived at their precarious stay, they were deprived, under his iron yoke, not only of the benefits of society, but of the common birthright of men and Christians.

At the end of four hundred years the Montanists of Phrygia [85] still breathed the wild enthusiasm of perfection and prophecy which they had imbibed from their male and female apostles, the special organs of the Paraclete. On the approach of the Catholic priests and soldiers, they grasped with alacrity the crown of martyrdom; the conventicle and the congregation perished in the flames, but these primitive fanatics were not extinguished three hundred years after the death of their tyrant. Under the protection of the Gothic confederates, the church of the Arians at Constantinople had braved the severity of the laws: their clergy equalled the wealth and magnificence of the senate; and the gold and silver which were seized by the rapacious hand of Justinian might perhaps be claimed as the spoils of the provinces and the trophies of the barbarians. A secret remnant of pagans, who still lurked in the most refined and most rustic conditions of mankind, excited the indignation of the Christians, who were perhaps unwilling that any strangers should be the witnesses of their intestine quarrels. A bishop was named as the inquisitor of the faith, and his diligence soon discovered, in the court and city, the magistrates, lawyers, physicians, and sophists, who still cherished the superstition of the Greeks. They were sternly informed that they must choose without delay between the displeasure of Jupiter or Justinian, and that their aversion to the gospel could no longer be disguised under the scandalous mask of indifference or impiety. The patrician Photius perhaps alone was resolved to live and to die like his ancestors: he enfranchised himself with the stroke of a dagger, and left his tyrant the poor consolation of exposing with ignominy the lifeless corpse of the fugitive. His weaker brethren submitted to their earthly monarch, underwent the ceremony of baptism, and laboured, by their extraordinary zeal, to erase the suspicion, or to

[84] This alternative, a precious circumstance, is preserved by John Malala (tom. ii. p. 63, edit. Venet. 1733 [p. 449, ed. Bonn]), who deserves more credit as he draws towards his end. After numbering the heretics, Nestorians, Eutychians, etc., ne expectent, says Justinian, ut digni veniâ judicentur: jubemus enim ut . . . convicti et aperti hæretici justæ et idoneæ animadversioni subjiciantur. Baronius copies and applauds this edict of the Code (A.D. 527, No. 39, 40).
[85] See the character and principles of the Montanists, in Mosheim, de Rebus Christ. ante Constantinum. p. 410-424.

expiate the guilt, of idolatry. The native country of Homer, and the theatre of the Trojan war, still retained the last sparks of his mythology: by the care of the same bishop, seventy thousand pagans were detected and converted in Asia, Phrygia, Lydia, and Caria; ninety-six churches were built for the new proselytes; and linen vestments, bibles and liturgies, and vases of gold and silver, were supplied by the pious munificence of Justinian.[86] The Jews, who had been gradually stripped of their immunities, were oppressed by a vexatious law, which compelled them to observe the festival of Easter the same day on which it was celebrated by the Christians.[87] And they might complain with the more reason, since the Catholics themselves did not agree with the astronomical calculations of their sovereign: the people of Constantinople delayed the beginning of their Lent a whole week after it had been ordained by authority; and they had the pleasure of fasting seven days, while meat was exposed for sale by the command of the emperor. The Samaritans of Palestine [88] were a motley race, an ambiguous sect, rejected as Jews by the pagans, by the Jews as schismatics, and by the Christians as idolators. The abomination of the cross had already been planted on their holy mount of Garizim,[89] but the persecution of Justinian offered only the alternative of baptism or rebellion. They chose the latter: under the standard of a desperate leader they rose in arms, and retaliated their wrongs on the lives, the property, and the temples of a denfenceless people. The Samaritans were finally subdued by the regular forces of the East: twenty thousand were slain, twenty thousand were sold by the Arabs to the infidels of Persia and India, and the remains of that unhappy nation atoned for the crime of treason by the sin of hypocrisy. It has been computed that one hundred thousand Roman subjects were extirpated in the Samaritan war,[90] which converted

[86] Theophan. Chron. p. 153 [tom. i. p. 276, ed. Bonn]. John, the Monophysite bishop of Asia, is a more authentic witness of this transaction, in which he was himself employed by the emperor (Asseman. Bib. Orient. tom. ii. p. 85).

[87] Compare Procopius (Hist. Arcan. c. 28 [tom. iii. p. 156, ed. Bonn] and Aleman's Notes) with Theophanes (Chron. p. 190 [tom. i. p. 340, ed. Bonn]). The council of Nice has intrusted the patriarch, or rather the astronomers, of Alexandria, with the annual proclamation of Easter; and we still read, or rather we do not read, many of the Paschal epistles of St. Cyril. Since the reign of Monophytism in Egypt, the Catholics were perplexed by such a foolish prejudice as that which so long opposed, among the Protestants, the reception of the Gregorian style.

[88] For the religion and history of the Samaritans, consult Basnage, Histoire des Juifs, a learned and impartial work.

[89] Sichem, Neapolis, Naplous, the ancient and modern seat of the Samaritans, is situate in a valley between the barren Ebal, the mountain of cursing to the north, and the fruitful *Garizim*, or mountain of cursing to the south, ten or eleven hours' travel from Jerusalem. See Maundrell, Journey from Aleppo, etc., p. 59-63.

[90] Procop. Anecdot. c. 11 [p. 75, ed. Bonn]; Theophan. Chron. p. 122 [vol. i. p. 274, ed. Bonn]; John Malala, Chron. tom. ii. p. 62 [p. 447, ed. Bonn]. I remember an observation, half philosophical, half superstitious, that the province which had been ruined by the bigotry of Justinian was the same through which the Mohammedans penetrated into the empire.

the once fruitful province into a desolate and smoking wilderness. But in the creed of Justinian the guilt of murder could not be applied to the slaughter of unbelievers; and he piously laboured to establish with fire and sword the unity of the Christian faith.[91]

With these sentiments, it was incumbent on him, at least, to be always in the right. In the first years of his administration he signalised his zeal as the disciple and patron of orthodoxy: the reconciliation of the Greeks and Latins established the *tome* of St. Leo as the creed of the emperor and the empire; the Nestorians and Eutychians were exposed, on either side, to the double edge of persecution; and the four synods, of Nice, Constantinople, Ephesus, and *Chalcedon*, were ratified by the code of a Catholic law-giver.[92] But while Justinian strove to maintain the uniformity of faith and worship, his wife Theodora, whose vices were not incompatible with devotion, had listened to the Monophysite teachers; and the open or clandestine enemies of the church revived and multiplied at the smile of their gracious patroness. The capital, the palace, the nuptial bed, were torn by spiritual discord; yet so doubtful was the sincerity of the royal consorts, that their seeming disagreement was imputed by many to a secret and mischievous confederacy against the religion and happiness of their people.[93] The famous dispute of the THREE CHAPTERS,[94] which has filled more volumes than it deserves lines, is deeply marked with this subtle and disingenuous spirit. It was now three hundred years since the body of Origen [95] had been eaten by the worms: his soul, of which he held the pre-existence, was in the hands of its Creator; but his writings were eagerly perused by the monks of Palestine. In these writings the piercing eye of Justinian descried

[91] The expression of Procopius is remarkable: οὐ γὰρ οἱ ἐδόκει φόνος ἀνθρώπων εἶναι, ἥν γε μὴ τῆς αὑτοῦ δόξης οἱ τελευτῶντες τύχοιεν ὄντες. Anecdot. c. 13 [p. 84, ed. Bonn].

[92] See the Chronicle of Victor, p. 328, and the original evidence of the laws of Justinian. During the first years of his reign, Baronius himself is in extreme good humour with the emperor, who courted the popes, till he got them into his power.

[93] Procopius, Anecdot. c. 13; Evagrius, l. iv. c. 10. If the ecclesiastical never read the secret historian, their common suspicion proves at least the general hatred.

[94] On the subject of the three chapters, the original acts of the fifth general council of Constantinople supply much useless though authentic knowledge (Concil. tom. vi. p. 1-419). The *Greek* Evagrius is less copious and correct (l. iv. c. 38) than the three zealous *Africans,* Facundus (in his twelve books, de tribus capitulis, which are most correctly published by Sirmond), Liberatus (in his Breviarium, c. 22, 23, 24), and Victor Tununensis in his Chronicle (in tom. i. Antiq. Lect. Canisii, p. 330-334). The Liber Pontificalis, or Anastasius (in Vigilio, Pelagio, etc.), is original *Italian* evidence. The modern reader will derive some information from Dupin (Biblioth. Ecclés. tom. v. p. 189-207) and Basnage (Hist. de l'Eglise, tom. i. p. 519-541); yet the latter is too firmly resolved to depreciate the authority and character of the popes.

[95] Origen had indeed too great a propensity to imitate the πλάνη and δυσσέβεια of the old philosophers (Justinian, ad Mennam, in Concil. tom. vi. p. 356). His moderate opinions were too repugnant to the zeal of the church, and he was found guilty of the heresy of reason.

more than ten metaphysical errors; and the primitive doctor, in the company of Pythagoras and Plato, was devoted by the clergy to the *eternity* of hell-fire, which he had presumed to deny.   Under the cover of this precedent a treacherous blow was aimed at the council of Chalcedon. The fathers had listened without impatience to the praise of Theodore of Mopsuestia;[96] and their justice or indulgence had restored both Theodoret of Cyrrhus and Ibas of Edessa to the communion of the church.   But the characters of these Oriental bishops were tainted with the reproach of heresy; the first had been the master, the two others were the friends, of Nestorius: their most suspicious passages were accused under the title of the *three chapters;* and the condemnation of their memory must involve the honour of a synod whose name was pronounced with sincere or affected reverence by the Catholic world. If these bishops, whether innocent or guilty, were annihilated in the sleep of death, they would not probably be awakened by the clamour which, after a hundred years, was raised over their grave.   If they were already in the fangs of the demon, their torments could neither be aggravated nor assuaged by human industry.   If in the company of saints and angels they enjoyed the rewards of piety, they must have smiled at the idle fury of the theological insects who still crawled on the surface of the earth.   The foremost of these insects, the emperor of the Romans, darted his sting, and distilled his venom, perhaps without discerning the true motives of Theodora and her eccesiastical faction.   The victims were no longer subject to his power, and the vehement style of his edicts could only proclaim their damnation, and invite the clergy of the East to join in a full chorus of curses and anathemas.   The East, with some hesitation, consented to the voice of her sovereign: the fifth general council, of three patriarchs and one hundred and sixty-five bishops, was held at Constantinople; and the authors, as well as the defenders of the three chapters, were separated from the communion of the saints, and solemnly delivered to the prince of darkness.   But the Latin churches were more jealous of the honour of Leo and the synod of Chalcedon; and if they had fought as they usually did under the standard of Rome, they might have prevailed in the cause of reason and humanity.   But their chief was a prisoner in the hands of the enemy; the throne of St. Peter, which had been disgraced by the simony, was betrayed by the cowardice, of Vigilius, who yielded, after a long and inconsistent struggle, to the despotism of Justinian and the sophistry of the Greeks.   His apostasy provoked the indignation of the Latins, and no more than two bishops could be found who would impose their hands on his deacon and successor Pelagius.   Yet the perseverance of

---

[96] Basnage (Præfat. p. 11-14, ad tom. i. Antiq. Lect. Canis.) has fairly weighed the guilt and innocence of Theodore of Mopsuestia.   If he composed 10,000 volumes, as many errors would be a charitable allowance.   In all the subsequent catalogues of heresiarchs, he alone, without his two brethren, is included; and it is the duty of Asseman (Biblioth. Orient. tom. iv. p. 203-207) to justify the sentence.

the popes insensibly transferred to their adversaries the appellation of schismatics; the Illyrian, African, and Italian churches were oppressed by the civil and ecclesiastical powers, not without some effort of military force;[97] the distant barbarians transcribed the creed of the Vatican, and, in the period of a century, the schism of the three chapters expired in an obscure angle of the Venetian province.[98] But the religious discontent of the Italians had already promoted the conquests of the Lombards, and the Romans themselves were accustomed to suspect the faith, and to detest the government, of their Byzantine tyrant.

Justinian was neither steady nor consistent in the nice process of fixing his volatile opinions and those of his subjects. In his youth he was offended by the slightest deviation from the orthodox line; in his old age he transgressed the measure of temperate heresy, and the Jacobites, not less than the Catholics, were scandalised by his declaration that the body of Christ was incorruptible, and that his manhood was never subject to any wants and infirmities, the inheritance of our mortal flesh. This *fantastic* opinion was announced in the last edicts of Justinian; and at the moment of his seasonable departure, the clergy had refused to subscribe, the prince was prepared to persecute, and the people were resolved to suffer or resist. A bishop of Trèves, secure beyond the limits of his power, addressed the monarch of the East in the language of authority and affection. " Most gracious Justinian, remember your baptism and your creed. Let not your grey hairs be defiled with heresy. Recall your fathers from exile, and your followers from perdition. You cannot be ignorant that Italy and Gaul, Spain and Africa, already deplore your fall and anathematise your name. Unless, without delay, you destroy what you have taught; unless you exclaim with a loud voice, I have erred, I have sinned, anathema to Nestorius, anathema to Eutyches, you deliver your soul to the same flames in which *they* will eternally burn." He died and made no sign.[99] His death restored in some degree the peace of the church, and the reigns of his four successors, Justin, Tiberius, Maurice, and Phocas, are distinguished

---

[97] See the complaints of Liberatus and Victor, and the exhortations of pope Pelagius to the conqueror and exarch of Italy. Schisma . . . per potestates publicas opprimatur, etc. (Concil. tom. vi. p. 467, etc.). An army was detained to suppress the sedition of an Illyrian city. See Procopius (de Bell. Goth. l. iv. c. 25 [tom. iii. p. 594, ed. Bonn]) : ὧνπερ ἕνεκα σφίσιν αὐτοῖς οἱ Χριστιανοὶ διαμάχονται. He seems to promise an ecclesiastical history. It would have been curious and impartial.

[98] The bishops of the patriarchate of Aquileia were reconciled by pope Honorius A.D. 638 (Muratori, Annali d'Italia, tom. v. p. 376) ; but they again relapsed, and the schism was not finally extinguished till 698. Fourteen years before, the church of Spain had overlooked the fifth general council with contemptuous silence (xiii. Concil. Toletan. in Concil. tom. vii. p. 487-494).

[99] Nicetius, bishop of Trèves (Concil. tom. vi. p. 511-513) : he himself, like most of the Gallican prelates (Gregor. Epist. l. vii. Ep. 5, in Concil. tom. vi. p. 1007), was separated from the communion of the four patriarchs by his refusal to condemn the three chapters. Baronius almost pronounces the damnation of Justinian (A.D. 565, No. 6).

by a rare, though fortunate, vacancy in the ecclesiastical history of the East.[100]

The faculties of sense and reason are least capable of acting on themselves; the eye is most inaccessible to the sight, the soul to the thought; yet we think, and even feel, that *one will*, a sole principle of action, is essential to a rational and conscious being. When Heraclius returned from the Persian war, the orthodox hero consulted his bishops whether the Christ whom he adored, of one person but of two natures, was actuated by a single or a double will. They replied in the singular, and the emperor was encouraged to hope that the Jacobites of Egypt and Syria might be reconciled by the profession of a doctrine most certainly harmless and most probably true, since it was taught even by the Nestorians themselves.[101] The experiment was tried without effect, and the timid or vehement Catholics condemned even the semblance of a retreat in the presence of a subtle and audacious enemy. The orthodox (the prevailing) party devised new modes of speech, and argument, and interpretation: to either nature of Christ they speciously applied a proper and distinct energy; but the difference was no longer visible when they allowed that the human and the divine will were invariably the same.[102] The disease was attended with the customary symptoms; but the Greek clergy, as if satiate with the endless controversy of the incarnation, instilled a healing counsel into the ear of the prince and people. They declared themselves MONOTHELITES (asserters of the unity of will), but they treated the words as new, the questions as superfluous; and recommended a religious silence as the most agreeable to the prudence and charity of the gospel. This law of silence was successively imposed by the *ecthesis* or exposition of Heraclius, the *type* or model of his grandson Constans;[103] and the Imperial edicts were subscribed with alacrity or reluctance by the four patriarchs of Rome,

---

[100] After relating the last heresy of Justinian (l. iv. c. 39, 40, 41) and the edict of his successor (l. v. c. 3 [4]), the remainder of the history of Evagrius is filled with civil, instead of ecclesiastical, events.

[101] This extraordinary, and perhaps inconsistent, doctrine of the Nestorians, had been observed by La Croze (Christianisme des Indes, tom. i. p. 19, 20), and is more fully exposed by Abulpharagius (Biblioth. Orient. tom. ii. p. 292; Hist. Dynast. p. 91, vers. Latin. Pocock), and Asseman himself (tom. iv. p. 218). They seem ignorant that they might allege the positive authority of the ecthesis. Ὁ μίαρος Νεστόριος καίπερ διαίρων τὴν θείαν τοῦ Κυρίου ἐνανθρώπησιν, καὶ δύο εἰσάγων υἱοὺς (the common reproach of the Monophysites), δύο θελήματα τούτων εἴπειν οὐκ ἐτόλμησε, τουνάντιον δὲ τοῦτο βουλίαν τῶν . . . . δύο πρόσωπων ἐδόξασε (Concil. tom. vii. p. 205).

[102] See the orthodox faith in Petavius (Dogmata Theolog. tom. v. l. ix. c. 6-10, p. 433-447): all the depths of this controversy are sounded in the Greek dialogue between Maximus and Pyrrhus (ad calcem, tom. viii. Anna.. Baron. p. 755-794), which relates a real conference, and produced as a short-lived conversion.

[103] Impiissimam ecthesim . . . scelerosum typum (Concil. tom. vii. p. 366) diabolicæ operationis genimina (fors. *germina,* or else the Greek γενήματα, in the original—Concil. p. 363, 364) are the expressions of the eighteenth anathema. The epistle of pope Martin to Amandus, a Gallican bishop, stigmatises the Monothelites and their heresy with equal virulence (p. 392).

Constantinople, Alexandria, and Antioch. But the bishop and monks of Jerusalem sounded the alarm: in the language, or even in the silence, of the Greeks, the Latin churches detected a latent heresy; and the obedience of pope Honorius to the commands of his sovereign was retracted and censured by the bolder ignorance of his successors. They condemned the execrable and abominable heresy of the Monothelites, who revived the errors of Manes, Apollinaris, Eutyches, etc.; they signed the sentence of excommunication on the tomb of St. Peter; the ink was mingled with the sacramental wine, the blood of Christ; and no ceremony was omitted that could fill the superstitious mind with horror and affright. As the representative of the Western church, pope Martin and his Lateran synod anathematised the perfidious and guilty silence of the Greeks: one hundred and five bishops of Italy, for the most part the subjects of Constans, presumed to reprobate his wicked *type* and the impious *ecthesis* of his grandfather; and to confound the authors and their adherents with the twenty-one notorious heretics, the apostates from the church and the organs of the devil. Such an insult under the tamest reign could not pass with impunity. Pope Martin ended his days on the inhospitable shore of the Tauric Chersonesus, and his oracle, the abbot Maximus, was inhumanly chastised by the amputation of his tongue and his right hand.[104] But the same invincible spirit survived in their successors; and the triumph of the Latins avenged their recent defeat and obliterated the disgrace of the three chapters. The synods of Rome were confirmed by the sixth general council of Constantinople, in the palace and the presence of a new Constantine, a descendant of Heraclius. The royal convert converted the Byzantine pontiff and a majority of the bishops;[105] the dissenters, with their chief, Macarius of Antioch, were condemned to the spiritual and temporal pains of heresy; the East condescended to accept the lessons of the West; and the creed was finally settled which teaches the Catholics of every age that two wills or energies are harmonised in the person of Christ. The majesty of the pope and the Roman synod was represented by two priests, one deacon, and three bishops; but these obscure Latins had neither arms to compel, nor treasures to bribe, nor language to persuade; and I am ignorant by what arts they could determine the lofty emperor of the Greeks to abjure the catechism of his infancy, and to persecute the religion of his fathers. Perhaps the monks and people of Constantinople[106] were favourable to the Lateran creed, which is indeed the least

---

[104] The sufferings of Martin and Maximus are described with pathetic simplicity in their original letters and acts (Concil. tom. vii. p. 63-78; Baron. Annal. Eccles. A.D. 656, No. 2, et annos subsequent.). Yet the chastisement of their disobedience, ἐξόρια and σώματος αἴκισμος, had been previously announced in the Type of Constans (Concil. tom. vii. p. 240).

[105] Eutychius (Annal. tom. ii. p. 348) most erroneously supposes that the 124 bishops of the Roman synod transported themselves to Constantinople; and by adding them to the 168 Greeks, thus composes the sixth council of 292 fathers.

[106] The Monothelite Constans was hated by all, διὰ τοι ταῦτα (says Theophanes, Chron. p. 292 [ed. Par.; tom. i. p. 538, ed. Bonn]) ἐμισήθη σφόδρως παρ᾽

reasonable of the two: and the suspicion is countenanced by the unnatural moderation of the Greek clergy, who appear in this quarrel to be conscious of their weakness. While the synod debated, a fanatic proposed a more summary decision, by raising a dead man to life: the prelates assisted at the trial; but the acknowledged failure may serve to indicate that the passions and prejudices of the multitude were not enlisted on the side of the Monothelites. In the next generation, when the son of Constantine was deposed and slain by the disciple of Macarius, they tasted the feast of revenge and dominion; the image or monument of the sixth council was defaced, and the original acts were committed to the flames. But in the second year their patron was cast headlong from the throne, the bishops of the East were released from their occasional conformity, the Roman faith was more firmly replanted by the orthodox successors of Bardanes, and the fine problems of the incarnation were forgotten in the more popular and visible quarrel of the worship of images.[107]

Before the end of the seventh century the creed of the incarnation, which had been defined at Rome and Constantinople, was uniformly preached in the remote islands of Britain and Ireland;[108] the same ideas were entertained, or rather the same words were repeated, by all the Christians whose liturgy was performed in the Greek or the Latin tongue. Their numbers and visible splendour bestowed an imperfect claim to the appellation of Catholics: but in the East they were marked with the

πάντων. When the Monothelite monk failed in his miracle, the people shouted, ὁ λαὸς ἀνεβόησε (Concil. tom. vii. p. 1032). But this was a natural and transient emotion; and I much fear that the latter is an anticipation of orthodoxy in the good people of Constantinople.

[107] The history of Monothelitism may be found in the Acts of the Synods of Rome (tom. vii. p. 77-395, 601-608) and Constantinople (p. 609-1429). Baronius extracted some original documents from the Vatican library; and his chronology is rectified by the diligence of Pagi. Even Dupin (Bibliothèque Ecclés. tom. vi. p. 57-71) and Basnage (Hist. de l'Eglise, tom. i. p. 541-555) afford a tolerable abridgment.

[108] In the Lateran synod of 679, Wilfrid, an Anglo-Saxon bishop, subscribed pro omni Aquilonari parte Britanniæ et Hiberniæ, quæ ab Anglorum et Brittonum, necnon Scotorum et Pictorum gentibus colebantur (Eddius, in Vit. St. Wilfrid, c. 31, apud Pagi, Critica, tom. iii. p. 88). Theodore (magnæ insulæ Britanniæ archiepiscopus et philosophus) was long expected at Rome (Concil. tom. vii. p. 714), but he contented himself with holding (A.D. 680) his provincial synod of Hatfield, in which he received the decrees of pope Martin and the first Lateran council against the Monothelites (Concil. tom. vii. p. 597, etc.). Theodore, a monk of Tarsus in Cilicia, had been named to the primacy of Britain by pope Vitalian (A.D. 668, see Baronius and Pagi), whose esteem for his learning and piety was tainted by some distrust of his national character—ne quid contrarium veritati fidei, Græcorum more, in ecclesiam cui præesset introduceret. The Cilician was sent from Rome to Canterbury under the tuition of an African guide (Bedæ Hist. Eccles. Anglorum, l. iv. c. 1). He adhered to the Roman doctrine; and the same creed of the incarnation has been uniformly transmitted from Theodore to the modern primates, whose sound understanding is perhaps seldom engaged with that abstruse mystery.

less honourable name of *Melchites,* or Royalists;[109] of men whose faith, instead of resting on the basis of Scripture, reason, or tradition, had been established, and was still maintained, by the arbitrary power of a temporal monarch. Their adversaries might allege the words of the fathers of Constantinople, who profess themselves the slaves of the king; and they might relate, with malicious joy, how the decrees of Chalcedon had been inspired and reformed by the emperor Marcian and his virgin bride. The prevailing faction will naturally inculcate the duty of submission, nor is it less natural that dissenters should feel and assert the principles of freedom. Under the rod of persecution the Nestorians and Monophysites degenerated into rebels and fugitives; and the most ancient and useful allies of Rome were taught to consider the emperor not as the chief but as the enemy of the Christians. Language, the leading principle which unites or separates the tribes of mankind, soon discriminated the sectaries of the East by a peculiar and perpetual badge which abolished the means of intercourse and the hope of reconciliation. The long dominion of the Greeks, their colonies, and above all their eloquence, had propagated a language doubtless the most perfect that has been contrived by the art of man. Yet the body of the people, both in Syria and Egypt, still persevered in the use of their national idioms; with this difference, however, that the Coptic was confined to the rude and illiterate peasants of the Nile, while the Syriac,[110] from the mountains of Assyria to the Red Sea, was adapted to the higher topics of poetry and argument. Armenia and Abyssinia were infected by the speech or learning of the Greeks; and their barbaric tongues, which have been revived in the studies of modern Europe, were unintelligible to the inhabitants of the Roman empire. The Syriac and the Coptic, the Armenian and the Æthiopic, are consecrated in the service of their respective churches; and their theology is enriched by domestic versions [111] both of the scriptures and of the most popular fathers. After a period of

---

[109] This name, unknown till the tenth century, appears to be of Syriac origin. It was invented by the Jacobites, and eagerly adopted by the Nestorians and Mahometans; but it was accepted without shame by the Catholics, and is frequently used in the Annals of Eutychius (Asseman. Biblioth. Orient. tom. ii. p. 507, etc., tom. iii. p. 355; Renaudot, Hist. Patriarch. Alexandrin. p. 119). Ἡμεῖς δοῦλοι τοῦ Βασιλέως, was the acclamation of the fathers of Constantinople (Concil. tom. vii. p. 765).

[110] The Syriac, which the natives revere as the primitive language, was divided into three dialects. 1. The *Aramœan,* as it was refined at Edessa and the cities of Mesopotamia; 2. The *Palestine,* which was used in Jerusalem, Damascus, and the rest of Syria; 3. The *Nabathœan,* the rustic idiom of the mountains of Assyria and the villages of Irak (Gregor. Abulpharag. Hist Dynast. p. 11). On the Syriac, see Ebed-Jesu (Asseman. tom. iii. p. 326, etc.), whose prejudice alone could prefer it to the Arabic.

[111] I shall not enrich my ignorance with the spoils of Simon, Walton, Mill, Wetstein, Assemannus, Ludolphus, La Croze, whom I have consulted with some care. It appears, 1. *That,* of all the versions which are celebrated by the fathers, it is doubtful whether any are now extant in their pristine integrity. 2. *That* the Syriac has the best claim, and that the consent of the Oriental sects is a proof that it is more ancient than their schism.

thirteen hundred and sixty years, the spark of controversy, first kindled by a sermon of Nestorius, still burns in the bosom of the East, and the hostile communions still maintain the faith and discipline of their founders.   In the most abject state of ignorance, poverty, and servitude, the Nestorians and Monophysites reject the spiritual supremacy of Rome, and cherish the toleration of their Turkish masters, which allows them to anathematise, on one hand, St. Cyril and the synod of Ephesus; on the other, pope Leo and the council of Chalcedon.   The weight which they cast into the downfall of the Eastern empire demands our notice, and the reader may be amused with the various prospect of, I. The Nestorians; II. The Jacobites;[112] III. The Maronites; IV. The Armenians; V. The Copts; and VI. The Abyssinians.   To the three former the Syriac is common; but of the latter, each is discriminated by the use of a national idiom.   Yet the modern natives of Armenia and Abyssinia would be incapable of conversing with their ancestors; and the Christians of Egypt and Syria, who reject the religion, have adopted the language, of the Arabians.   The lapse of time has seconded the sacerdotal arts; and in the East as well as in the West the Deity is addressed in an obsolete tongue unknown to the majority of the congregation.

I. Both in his native and his episcopal province the heresy of the unfortunate Nestorius was speedily obliterated.   The Oriental bishops, who at Ephesus had resisted to his face the arrogance of Cyril, were mollified by his tardy concessions.   The same prelates, or their successors, subscribed, not without a murmur, the decrees of Chalcedon; the power of the Monophysites reconciled them with the Catholics in the conformity of passion, of interest, and, insensibly, of belief; and their last reluctant sigh was breathed in the defence of the three chapters. Their dissenting brethren, less moderate or more sincere, were crushed by the penal laws; and, as early as the reign of Justinian, it became difficult to find a church of Nestorians within the limits of the Roman empire.   Beyond those limits they had discovered a new world in which they might hope for liberty and aspire to conquest.   In Persia, notwithstanding the resistance of the Magi, Christianity had struck a deep root, and the nations of the East reposed under its salutary shade.   The *catholic,* or primate, resided in the capital: in *his* synods, and in *their* dioceses, his metropolitans, bishops, and clergy represented the pomp and order of a regular hierarchy: they rejoiced in the increase of proselytes, who were converted from the Zendavesta to the Gospel, from the secular to the monastic life; and their zeal was stimulated by the

---

[112] In the account of the Monophysites and Nestorians I am deeply indebted to the Bibliotheca Orientalis Clementino-Vaticana of Joseph Simon Assemannus.   That learned Maronite was despatched in the year 1715 by pope Clement XI. to visit the monasteries of Egypt and Syria, in search of MSS. His four folio volumes, published at Rome 1719-1728, contain a part only, though perhaps the most valuable, of his extensive project.   As a native and as a scholar, he possessed the Syriac literature; and, though a dependent of Rome, he wishes to be moderate and candid.

presence of an artful and formidable enemy. The Persian church had been founded by the missionaries of Syria; and their language, discipline, and doctrine were closely interwoven with its original frame. The *catholics* were elected and ordained by their own suffragans; but their filial dependence on the patriarchs of Antioch is attested by the canons of the Oriental church.[113] In the Persian school of Edessa,[114] the rising generations of the faithful imbibed their theological idiom: they studied in the Syriac version the ten thousand volumes of Theodore of Mopsuestia; and they revered the apostolic faith and holy martyrdom of his disciple Nestorius, whose person and language were equally unknown to the nations beyond the Tigris. The first indelible lesson of Ibas, bishop of Edessa, taught them to execrate the *Egyptians*, who, in the synod of Ephesus, had impiously confounded the two natures of Christ. The flight of the masters and scholars, who were twice expelled from the Athens of Syria, dispersed a crowd of missionaries inflamed by the double zeal of religion and revenge. And the rigid unity of the Monophysites, who, under the reigns of Zeno and Anastasius, had invaded the thrones of the East, provoked their antagonists in a land of freedom to avow a moral, rather than a physical, union of the two persons of Christ. Since the first preaching of the gospel the Sassanian kings beheld with an eye of suspicion a race of aliens and apostates who had embraced the religion, and who might favour the cause, of the hereditary foes of their country. The royal edicts had often prohibited their dangerous correspondence with the Syrian clergy: the progress of the schism was grateful to the jealous pride of Perozes, and he listened to the eloquence of an artful prelate, who painted Nestorius as the friend of Persia, and urged him to secure the fidelity of his Christian subjects by granting a just preference to the victims and enemies of the Roman tyrant. The Nestorians composed a large majority of the clergy and people: they were encouraged by the smile, and armed with the sword, of despotism; yet many of their weaker brethren were startled at the thought of breaking loose from the communion of the Christian world, and the blood of seven thousand seven hundred Monophysites or Catholics confirmed the uniformity of faith and discipline in the churches

[113] See the Arabic canons of Nice in the translation of Abraham Ecchelensis, No. 37, 38, 39, 40. Concil. tom. ii. p. 335, 336, edit. Venet. These vulgar titles, *Nicene* and *Arabic*, are both apocryphal. The council of Nice enacted no more than twenty canons (Theodoret, Hist. Eccles. l. i. c. 8); and the remainder, seventy or eighty, were collected from the synods of the Greek church. The Syriac edition of Maruthas is no longer extant (Asseman. Biblioth. Oriental. tom. i. p. 195, tom. iii. p. 74), and the Arabic version is marked with many recent interpolations. Yet this Code contains many curious relics of ecclesiastical discipline; and since it is equally revered by all the Eastern communions, it was probably finished before the schism of the Nestorians and Jacobites (Fabric. Biblioth. Græc. tom. xi. p. 363-367).

[114] Theodore the Reader (l. ii. c. 5, 49, ad calcem Hist. Eccles.) has noticed this Persian school of Edessa. Its ancient splendour and the two eras of its downfall (A.D. 431 and 489) are clearly discussed by Assemanni (Biblioth. Orient. tom. ii. p. 402, iii. p. 376, 378, iv. p. 70, 924).

of Persia.[115] Their ecclesiastical institutions are distinguished by a liberal principle of reason, or at least of policy: the austerity of the cloister was relaxed and gradually forgotten: houses of charity were endowed for the education of orphans and foundlings; the law of celibacy, so forcibly recommended to the Greeks and Latins, was disregarded by the Persian clergy; and the number of the elect was multiplied by the public and reiterated nuptials of the priests, the bishops, and even the patriarch himself. To this standard of natural and religious freedom myriads of fugitives resorted from all the provinces of the Eastern empire; the narrow bigotry of Justinian was punished by the emigration of his most industrious subjects; they transported into Persia the arts both of peace and war: and those who deserved the favour were promoted in the service of a discerning monarch. The arms of Nushirvan, and his fiercer grandson, were assisted with advice, and money, and troops, by the desperate sectaries who still lurked in their native cities of the East: their zeal was rewarded with the gift of the Catholic churches; but when those cities and churches were recovered by Heraclius, their open profession of treason and heresy compelled them to seek a refuge in the realm of their foreign ally. But the seeming tranquillity of the Nestorians was often endangered and sometimes overthrown. They were involved in the common evils of Oriental despotism: their enmity to Rome could not always atone for their attachment to the gospel: and a colony of three hundred thousand Jacobites, the captives of Apamea and Antioch, was permitted to erect a hostile altar in the face of the *catholic* and in the sunshine of the court. In his last treaty Justinian introduced some conditions which tended to enlarge and fortify the toleration of Christianity in Persia. The emperor, ignorant of the rights of conscience, was incapable of pity or esteem for the heretics who denied the authority of the holy synods: but he flattered himself that they would gradually perceive the temporal benefits of union with the empire and the Church of Rome; and if he failed in exciting their gratitude, he might hope to provoke the jealousy of their sovereign. In a later age the Lutherans have been burnt at Paris and protected in Germany, by the superstition and policy of the most Christian king.

The desire of gaining souls for God and subjects for the church has excited in every age the diligence of the Christian priests. From the conquest of Persia, they carried their spiritual arms to the north, the east, and the south; and the simplicity of the gospel was fashioned and painted with the colours of the Syriac theology. In the sixth century, according to the report of a Nestorian traveller,[116] Christianity was

---

[115] A dissertation on the state of the Nestorians has swelled in the hands of Assemanni to a folio volume of 950 pages, and his learned researches are digested in the most lucid order. Besides this fourth volume of the *Bibliotheca Orientalis*, the extracts in the three preceding tomes (tom. i. p. 203, ii. p. 321-463, iii. 64-70, 378-395, etc., 403-408, 580-589) may be usefully consulted.

[116] See the Topographia Christiana of Cosmos, surnamed Indicopleustes, or the Indian navigator. l. iii. p. 178, 179; l. xi. q. 337. The entire work, of

successfully preached to the Bactrians, the Huns, the Persians, the Indians, the Persarmenians, the Medes, and the Elamites: the barbaric churches, from the Gulf of Persia to the Caspian Sea, were almost infinite; and their recent faith was conspicuous in the number and sanctity of their monks and martyrs. The pepper coast of Malabar and the isles of the ocean, Socotora and Ceylon, were peopled with an increasing multitude of Christians; and the bishops and clergy of those sequestered regions derived their ordination from the catholic of Babylon. In a subsequent age the zeal of the Nestorians overleaped the limits which had confined the ambition and curiosity both of the Greeks and Persians. The missionaries of Balch and Samarcand pursued without fear the footsteps of the roving Tartar, and insinuated themselves into the camps of the valleys of Imaus and the banks of the Selinga. They exposed a metaphysical creed to those illiterate shepherds: to those sanguinary warriors they recommended humanity and repose. Yet a khan, whose power they vainly magnified, is said to have received at their hands the rites of baptism and even of ordination; and the fame of *Prester* or *Presbyter* John [117] has long amused the credulity of Europe. The royal convert was indulged in the use of a portable altar; but he despatched an embassy to the patriarch to inquire how, in the season of Lent, he should abstain from animal food, and how he might celebrate the Eucharist in a desert that produced neither corn nor wine. In their progress by sea and land the Nestorians entered China by the port of Canton and the northern residence of Sigan. Unlike the senators of Rome, who assumed with a smile the characters of priests and augurs, the mandarins, who affect in public the reason of philosophers, are devoted in private to every mode of popular superstition. They cherished and they confounded the gods of Palestine and of India; but the propagation of Christianity awakened the jealousy of the state, and, after a short vicissitude of favour and persecution, the foreign sect ex-

which some curious extracts may be found in Photius (cod. xxxvi. p. 9, 10, edit. Hoeschel), Thevenot (in the 1st part of his Relation des Voyages, etc.), and Fabricius (Biblioth. Græc. l. iii. c. 25, tom. ii. p. 603-617), has been published by Father Montfaucon at Paris, 1707, in the Nova Collectio Patrum (tom. ii. p. 113-346). It was the design of the author to confute the impious heresy of those who maintained that the earth is a globe, and not a flat oblong table, as it is represented in the Scriptures (l. ii. p. 138 [125, *sq.*]). But the nonsense of the monk is mingled with the practical knowledge of the traveller, who performed his voyage, A.D. 522, and published his book at Alexandria, A.D. 547 (l. ii. p. 140, 141; Montfaucon, Præfat. c. 1). The Nestorianism of Cosmas, unknown to his learned editor, was detected by La Croze (Christianisme des Indes, tom. i. p. 40-55), and is confirmed by Assemanni (Biblioth. Orient. tom. iv. p. 605, 606).

[117] In its long progress to Mosul, Jerusalem, Rome, etc., the story of Prester John evaporated in a monstrous fable, of which some features have been borrowed from the Lama of Thibet (Hist. Généalogique des Tatares, P. ii. p. 42; Hist. de Gengiscan, p. 31, etc.), and were ignorantly transferred by the Portuguese to the emperor of Abyssinia (Ludolph. Hist. Æthiop. Comment. l. ii. c. 1). Yet it is probable that in the eleventh and twelfth centuries Nestorian Christianity was professed in the horde of the Keraites (D'Herbelot, p. 256, 915, 959; Assemanni, tom. iv. p. 468-504).

pired in ignorance and oblivion.[118] Under the reign of the caliphs the Nestorian church was diffused from China to Jerusalem and Cyprus; and their numbers, with those of the Jacobites, were computed to surpass the Greek and Latin communions.[119] Twenty-five metropolitans or archbishops composed their hierarchy; but several of these were dispensed, by the distance and danger of the way, from the duty of personal attendance, on the easy condition that every six years they should testify their faith and obedience to the *catholic* or patriarch of Babylon, a vague appellation which has been successively applied to the royal seats of Seleucia, Ctesiphon, and Bagdad. These remote branches are long since withered; and the old patriarchal trunk [120] is now divided by the *Elijahs* of Mosul, the representatives almost in lineal descent of the genuine and primitive succession; the *Josephs* of Amida, who are reconciled to the church of Rome;[121] and the *Simeons* of Van or Ormia, whose revolt, at the head of forty thousand families, was promoted in the sixteenth century by the Sophis of Persia. The number of three hundred thousand is allowed for the whole body of the Nestorians, who, under the name of Chaldæans or Assyrians, are confounded with the most learned or the most powerful nation of Eastern antiquity.

According to the legend of antiquity, the gospel was preached in India by St. Thomas.[122] At the end of the ninth century his shrine, perhaps

[118] The Christianity of China, between the seventh and the thirteenth century, is invincibly proved by the consent of Chinese, Arabian, Syriac, and Latin evidence (Assemanni. Biblioth. Orient. tom. iv. p. 502-552; Mém. de l'Académie des Inscript. tom. xxx. p. 802-819). The inscription of Siganfu, which describes the fortunes of the Nestorian church, from the first mission, A.D. 636, to the current year 781, is accused of forgery by La Croze, Voltaire, etc., who become the dupes of their own cunning, while they are afraid of a Jesuitical fraud.
[The inscription of Siganfu, which is Nestorian in character, was stigmatised as a forgery by Voltaire, Julian, Renan, and others, but competent specialists, both European and Chinese, now recognise it as a genuine document of the eighth century. It was discovered by a Jesuit missionary, Alvarez Semedo, at Singanfu, the old capital of the Tang dynasty, in 1623. It was raised by Iezdbouzid, priest and chorepiscopus of Chumdan, that is the capital of the Chinese empire. Cf. St. Martin, vol. i. p. 69.—O. S.]
[119] Jacobitæ et Nestorianæ plures quam Græci et Latini. Jacob a Vitriaco, Hist. Hierosol. l. ii. c. 76, p. 1093, in the Gesta Dei per Francos. The numbers are given by Thomassin, Discipline de l'Eglise, tom. i. p. 172.
[120] The division of the patriarchate may be traced in the Bibliotheca Orient. of Assemanni, tom. i. p. 523-549, tom. ii. p. 457, etc., tom. iii. p. 603, 621-623, tom. iv. p. 164-169, 423, 622-629, etc.
[121] The pompous language of Rome, on the submission of a Nestorian patriarch, is elegantly represented in the seventh book of Fra-Paolo, Babylon, Nineveh, Arbela, and the trophies of Alexander, Tauris and Ecbatana, the Tigris and Indus.
[122] The Indian missionary, St. Thomas, an apostle, a Manichæan, or an Armenian merchant (La Croze, Christianisme des Indes, tom. i. p. 57-70), was famous, however, as early as the time of Jerom (ad Marcellam, Epist. 148 [Ep. 59, p. 328, ed., Vallars.]). Marco Polo was informed on the spot that he suffered martyrdom in the city of Maabar, or Meliapour, a league only from Madras (D'Anville, Eclaircissimens sur l'Inde, p. 125), where the Portuguese founded an episcopal church under the name of St. Thomé, and

in the neighbourhood of Madras, was devoutly visited by the ambassadors of Alfred; and their return with a cargo of pearls and spices rewarded the zeal of the English monarch, who entertained the largest projects of trade and discovery.[123] When the Portuguese first opened the navigation of India, the Christians of St. Thomas had been seated for ages on the coast of Malabar, and the difference of their character and colour attested the mixture of a foreign race. In arms, in arts, and possibly in virtue, they excelled the natives of Hindostan; the husbandmen cultivated the palm tree, the merchants were enriched by the pepper trade, the soldiers preceded the *nairs* or nobles of Malabar, and their hereditary privileges were respected by the gratitude or the fear of the king of Cochin and the Zamorin himself. They acknowledged a Gentoo sovereign, but they were governed, even in temporal concerns, by the bishop of Angamala. He still asserted his ancient title of metropolitan of India, but his real jurisdiction was exercised in fourteen hundred churches, and he was intrusted with the care of two hundred thousand souls. Their religion would have rendered them the firmest and most cordial allies of the Portuguese; but the inquisitors soon discerned in the Christians of St. Thomas the unpardonable guilt of heresy and schism. Instead of owning themselves the subjects of the Roman pontiff, the spiritual and temporal monarch of the globe, they adhered, like their ancestors, to the communion of the Nestorian patriarch; and the bishops whom he ordained at Mosul traversed the dangers of the sea and land to reach their diocese on the coast of Malabar. In their Syriac liturgy the names of Theodore and Nestorius were piously commemorated: they united their adoration of the two persons of Christ; the title of Mother of God was offensive to their ear; and they measured with scrupulous avarice the honours of the Virgin Mary, whom the superstition of the Latins had *almost* exalted to the rank of a goddess. When her image was first presented to the disciples of St. Thomas they indignantly exclaimed, "We are Christians, not idolators!" and their simple devotion was content with the veneration of the cross. Their separation from the Western world had left them in ignorance of the improvements or corruptions of a thousand years; and their conformity with the faith and practice of the fifth century would equally disappoint the prejudices of a Papist or a Protestant. It was the first care of the ministers of Rome to intercept all correspondence with the Nestorian patriarch, and several of his bishops expired in the prisons of the holy

where the saint performed an annual miracle, till he was silenced by the profane neighbourhood of the English (La Croze, tom. ii. p. 7-16).

[123] Neither the author of the Saxon Chronicle (A.D. 883) nor William of Malmesbury (de Gestis Regum Angliæ, l. ii. c. 4, p. 44) were capable, in the twelfth century, of inventing this extraordinary fact; they are incapable of explaining the motives and measures of Alfred, and their hasty notice serves only to provoke our curiosity. William of Malmesbury feels the difficulties of the enterprise, quod quivis in hoc sæculo miretur; and I almost suspect that the English ambassadors collected their cargo and legend in Egypt. The royal author has not enriched his Orosius (see Barrington's Miscellanies) with an Indian as well as a Scandinavian voyage.

office. The flock, without a shepherd, was assaulted by the power of the Portuguese, the arts of the Jesuits, and the zeal of Alexis de Menezes, archbishop of Goa, in his personal visitation of the coast of Malabar. The synod of Diamper, at which he presided, consummated the pious work of the re-union, and rigorously imposed the doctrine and discipline of the Roman church, without forgetting auricular confession, the strongest engine of ecclesiastical torture. The memory of Theodore and Nestorius was condemned, and Malabar was reduced under the dominion of the pope, of the primate, and of the Jesuits who invaded the see of Angamala or Cranganor. Sixty years of servitude and hypocrisy were patiently endured; but as soon as the Portuguese empire was shaken by the courage and industry of the Dutch, the Nestorians asserted with vigour and effect the religion of their fathers. The Jesuits were incapable of defending the power which they had abused; the arms of forty thousand Christians were pointed against their falling tyrants; and the Indian archdeacon assumed the character of bishop till a fresh supply of episcopal gifts and Syriac missionaries could be obtained from the patriarch of Babylon. Since the expulsion of the Portuguese the Nestorian creed is freely professed on the coast of Malabar. The trading companies of Holland and England are the friends of toleration; but if oppression be less mortifying than contempt, the Christians of St. Thomas have reason to complain of the cold and silent indifference of their brethren of Europe.[124]

II. The history of the Monophysites is less copious and interesting than that of the Nestorians. Under the reigns of Zeno and Anastasius their artful leaders surprised the ear of the prince, usurped the thrones of the East, and crushed on its native soil the school of the Syrians. The rule of the Monophysite faith was defined with exquisite discretion by Severus, patriarch of Antioch; he condemned, in the style of the Henoticon, the adverse heresies of Nestorius and Eutyches; maintained against the latter the reality of the body of Christ; and constrained the Greeks to allow that he was a liar who spoke truth.[125] But the approximation of ideas could not abate the vehemence of passion; each party was the more astonished that their blind antagonist could dispute on so trifling a difference; the tyrant of Syria enforced the belief of his creed, and his

---

[124] Concerning the Christians of St. Thomas, see Assemann. Biblioth. Orient. tom. iv. p. 391-407, 435-451; Geddes's Church History of Malabar; and, above all, La Croze, Histoire du Christianisme des Indes, in two vols. 12mo, La Haye, 1758—a learned and agreeable work. They have drawn from the same source the Portuguese and Italian narratives; and the prejudices of the Jesuits are sufficiently corrected by those of the Protestants.

[125] Οἷον εἰπεῖν ψευδαλήθης is the expression of Theodore, in his Treatise of the Incarnation, p. 245, 247, as he is quoted by La Croze (Hist. du Christianisme d'Ethiopie et d'Arménie, p. 35), who exclaims, perhaps too hastily, "Quel pitoyable raisonnement!" Renaudot has touched (Hist. Patriarch. Alex. p. 127-138) the Oriental accounts of Severus; and his authentic creed may be found in the epistle of John the Jacobite patriarch of Antioch, in the tenth century, to his brother Mennas of Alexandria (Asseman. Biblioth. Orient. tom. ii. p. 132-141).

reign was polluted with the blood of three hundred and fifty monks, who were slain, not perhaps without provocation or resistance, under the walls of Apamea.[126] The successor of Anastasius replanted the orthodox standard in the East; Severus fled into Egypt; and his friend, the eloquent Xenaias,[127] who had escaped from the Nestorians of Persia, was suffocated in his exile by the Melchites of Paphlagonia. Fifty-four bishops were swept from their thrones, eight hundred ecclesiastics were cast into prison,[128] and, notwithstanding the ambiguous favour of Theodora, the Oriental flocks, deprived of their shepherds, must insensibly have been either famished or poisoned. In this spiritual distress the expiring faction was revived, and united, and perpetuated by the labours of a monk; and the name of James Baradæus [129] has been preserved in the appellation of *Jacobites,* a familiar sound which may startle the ear of an English reader. From the holy confessors in their prison of Constantinople he received the powers of bishop of Edessa and apostle of the East, and the ordination of fourscore thousand bishops, priests, and deacons, is derived from the same inexhaustible source. The speed of the zealous missionary was promoted by the fleetest dromedaries of a devout chief of the Arabs; the doctrine and discipline of the Jacobites were secretly established in the dominions of Justinian; and each Jacobite was compelled to violate the laws and to hate the Roman legislator. The successors of Severus, while they lurked in convents or villages, while they sheltered their proscribed heads in the caverns of hermits or the tents of the Saracens, still asserted, as they now assert, their indefeasible right to the title, the rank, and the prerogatives of patriarch of Antioch: under the milder yoke of the infidels they reside about a league from Merdin, in the pleasant monastery of Zapharan, which they have embellished with cells, aqueducts, and plantations. The secondary, though honourable, place is filled by the *maphrian,* who, in his station at Mosul itself, defies the Nestorian *catholic* with whom he

---

[126] Epist. Archimandritarum et Monachorum Syriæ Secundæ ad Papam Hormisdam, Concil. tom. v. p. 598-602. The courage of St. Sabas, ut leo animosus, will justify the suspicion that the arms of these monks were not always spiritual or defensive (Baronius, A.D. 513, No. 7, etc.).

[127] Assemanni (Biblioth. Orient. tom. ii. p. 10-46) and La Croze (Christianisme d'Ethiopie, p. 36-40) will supply the history of Xenaias, or Philoxenus, bishop of Mabug, or Hierapolis, in Syria. He was a perfect master of the Syriac language, and the author or editor of a version of the New Testament.

[128] The names and titles of fifty-four bishops who were exiled by Justin are preserved in the Chronicle of Dionysius (apud Asseman. tom. ii. p. 54). Severus was personally summoned to Constantinople—for his trial, says Liberatus (Brev. c. 19)—that his tongue might be cut out, says Evagrius (l. iv. c. 4). The prudent patriarch did not stay to examine the difference. This ecclesiastical revolution is fixed by Pagi to the month of September of the year 518 (Critica, tom. ii. p. 506).

[129] The obscure history of James, or Jacobus Baradæus, or Zanzalus, may be gathered from Eutychius (Annal. tom. ii. p. 144, 147), Renaudot (Hist. Patriarch. Alex. p. 133), and Assemannus (Biblioth. Orient. tom. i. p. 424: tom. ii. p. 62-69, 324-332, 414; tom. iii. p. 385-388). He seems to be unknown to the Greeks. The Jacobites themselves had rather deduce their name and pedigree from St. James the apostle.

contests the primacy of the East. Under the patriarch and the maphrian one hundred and fifty archbishops and bishops have been counted in the different ages of the Jacobite church; but the order of the hierarchy is relaxed or dissolved, and the greater part of their dioceses is confined to the neighbourhood of the Euphrates and the Tigris. The cities of Aleppo and Amida, which are often visited by the patriarch, contain some wealthy merchants and industrious mechanics, but the multitude derive their scanty sustenance from their daily labour: and poverty, as well as superstition, may impose their excessive fasts—five annual lents, during which both the clergy and laity abstain not only from flesh or eggs, but even from the taste of wine, of oil, and of fish. Their present numbers are esteemed from fifty to fourscore thousand souls, the remnant of a populous church, which has gradually decreased under the oppression of twelve centuries. Yet in that long period some strangers of merit have been converted to the Monophysite faith, and a Jew was the father of Abulpharagius,[130] primate of the East, so truly eminent both in his life and death. In his life he was an elegant writer of the Syriac and Arabic tongues, a poet, physician, and historian, a subtle philosopher, and a moderate divine. In his death his funeral was attended by his rival the Nestorian patriarch, with a train of Greeks and Armenians, who forgot their disputes, and mingled their tears over the grave of an enemy. The sect which was honoured by the virtues of Abulpharagius appears, however, to sink below the level of their Nestorian brethren. The superstition of the Jacobites is more abject, their fasts more rigid,[131] their intestine divisions are more numerous, and their doctors (as far as I can measure the degrees of nonsense) are more remote from the precincts of reason. Something may possibly be allowed for the rigour of the Monophysite theology, much more for the superior influence of the monastic order. In Syria, in Egypt, in Æthiopia, the Jacobite monks have ever been distinguished by the austerity of their penance and the absurdity of their legends. Alive or dead, they are worshipped as the favourites of the Deity; the crosier of bishop and patriarch is reserved for their venerable hands; and they assume the government of men while they are yet reeking with the habits and prejudices of the cloister.[132]

III. In the style of the Oriental Christians, the Monothelites of every

---

[130] The account of his person and writings is perhaps the most curious article in the Bibliotheca of Assemannus (tom. ii. p. 244-321, under the name of *Gregorius Bar-Hebræus*). La Croze (Christianisme d'Ethiopie, p. 53-63) ridicules the prejudice of the Spaniards against the Jewish blood which secretly defiles their church and state.

[131] This *excessive* abstinence is censured by La Croze (p. 352), and even by the Syrian Assemannus (tom. i. p. 226; tom. ii. p. 304, 305).

[132] The state of the Monophysites is excellently illustrated in a dissertation at the beginning of the second volume of Assemannus, which contains 142 pages. The Syriac Chronicle of Gregory Bar-Hebræus, or Abulpharagius (Biblioth. Orient. tom. ii. p. 321-463), pursues the double series of the Nestorian *Catholics* and the *Maphrians* of the Jacobites.

age are described under the appellation of *Maronites*,[133] a name which has been insensibly transferred from a hermit to a monastery, from a monastery to a nation. Maron, a saint or savage of the fifth century, displayed his religious madness in Syria; the rival cities of Apamea and Emesa disputed his relics, a stately church was erected on his tomb, and six hundred of his disciples united their solitary cells on the banks of the Orontes. In the controversies of the incarnation they nicely threaded the orthodox line between the sects of Nestorius and Eutyches; but the unfortunate question of *one will* or operation in the two natures of Christ was generated by their curious leisure. Their proselyte, the emperor Heraclius, was rejected as a Maronite from the walls of Emesa; he found a refuge in the monastery of his brethren; and their theological lessons were repaid with the gift of a spacious and wealthy domain. The name and doctrine of this venerable school were propagated among the Greeks and Syrians, and their zeal is expressed by Macarius, patriarch of Antioch, who declared before the synod of Constantinople, that, sooner than subscribe the *two wills* of Christ, he would submit to be hewn piecemeal and cast into the sea.[134] A similar or a less cruel mode of persecution soon converted the unresisting subjects of the plain, while the glorious title of *Mardaites*,[135] or rebels, was bravely maintained by the hardy natives of Mount Libanus. John Maron, one of the most learned and popular of the monks, assumed the character of patriarch of Antioch; his nephew, Abraham, at the head of the Maronites, defended their civil and religious freedom against the tyrants of the East. The son of the orthodox Constantine pursued with pious hatred a people of soldiers, who might have stood the bulwark of his empire against the common foes of Christ and of Rome. An army of Greeks invaded Syria; the monastery of St. Maron was destroyed with fire; the bravest chieftains were betrayed and murdered, and twelve thousand of their followers were transplanted to the distant frontiers of Armenia and Thrace. Yet the humble nation of the Maronites has survived the empire of Constantinople, and they still enjoy, under their Turkish masters, a free religion and a mitigated servitude. Their domestic governors are chosen among the ancient nobility: the patriarch, in his monastery of Canobin, still fancies himself on the throne of Antioch; nine bishops compose

---

[133] The synonymous use of the two words may be proved from Eutychius (Annal. tom. ii. p. 191, 267, 332), and many similar passages which may be found in the methodical table of Pocock. He was not actuated by any prejudice against the Maronites of the tenth century; and we may believe a Melchite, whose testimony is confirmed by the Jacobites and Latins.

[134] Concil. tom. vii. p. 780. The Monothelite cause was supported with firmness and subtlety by Constantine, a *Syrian* priest of Apamea (p. 1040, etc.).

[135] Theophanes (Chron. p. 295, 296, 300, 302, 306 [tom. i. p. 542 *sq.*, 552, 555, 561, ed. Bonn]) and Cedrenus (p. 437, 440 (ed. Par.; tom. i. p. 765 *sqq.*, ed. Bonn]) relate the exploits of the Mardaites: the name (*Mard*, in Syriac *rebellavit*) is explained by La Roque (Voyage de la Syrie, tom. ii. p. 53); the dates are fixed by Pagi (A.D. 676, No. 4-14; A.D. 685, No. 3, 4); and even the obscure story of the patriarch John Maron (Asseman. Biblioth. Orient. tom. i. p. 496-520) illustrates, from the year 686 to 707, the troubles of Mount Libanus.

his synod, and one hundred and fifty priests, who retain the liberty of marriage, are intrusted with the care of one hundred thousand souls. Their country extends from the ridge of Mount Libanus to the shores of Tripoli; and the gradual descent affords, in a narrow space, each variety of soil and climate, from the Holy Cedars, erect under the weight of snow,[136] to the vine, the mulberry, and the olive trees of the fruitful valley. In the twelfth century the Maronites, abjuring the Monothelite error, were reconciled to the Latin churches of Antioch and Rome,[137] and the same alliance has been frequently renewed by the ambition of the popes and the distress of the Syrians. But it may reasonably be questioned whether their union has ever been perfect or sincere; and the learned Maronites of the college of Rome have vainly laboured to absolve their ancestors from the guilt of heresy and schism.[138]

IV. Since the age of Constantine, the ARMENIANS[139] had signalised their attachment to the religion and empire of the Christians. The disorders of their country, and their ignorance of the Greek tongue, prevented their clergy from assisting at the synod of Chalcedon, and they floated eighty-four years[140] in a state of indifference or suspense, till their vacant faith was finally occupied by the missionaries of Julian of Halicarnassus,[141] who in Egypt, their common exile, had been van-

[136] In the last century twenty large cedars still remained (Voyage de La Roque, tom. i. p. 68-76) ; at present they are reduced to four or five (Volney, tom. i. p. 264). These trees, so famous in Scripture, were guarded by excommunication: the wood was sparingly borrowed for small crosses, etc.; an annual mass was chanted under their shade; and they were endowed by the Syrians with a sensitive power of erecting their branches to repel the snow, to which Mount Libanus is less faithful than it is painted by Tacitus: inter ardores opacum fidumque nivibus—a daring metaphor (Hist. v. 6).

[137] The evidence of William of Tyre (Hist. in Gestis Dei per Francos, l. xxii. c. 8, p. 1022 [fol. Hanov. 1611]) is copied or confirmed by Jacques de Vitra (Hist. Hierosolym. l. ii. c. 77, p. 1093, 1094). But this unnatural league expired with the power of the Franks; and Abulpharagius (who died in 1286) considers the Maronites as a sect of Monothelites (Biblioth. Orient. tom. ii. p. 292).

[138] I find a description and history of the Maronites in the Voyage de la Syrie et du Mont Liban par La Roque (2 vols. in 12mo, Amsterdam, 1723; particularly tom. i. p. 42-47, 174-184, tom. ii. p. 10-120). In the ancient part he copies the prejudices of Nairon and the other Maronites of Rome, which Assemannus is afraid to renounce and ashamed to support. Jablonski (Institut. Hist. Christ. tom. iii. p. 186), Niebuhr (Voyage de l'Arabie, etc., tom. ii. p. 346, 370-381), and, above all, the judicious Volney (Voyage en Egypte et en Syrie, tom. ii. p. 8-31, Paris, 1787), may be consulted.

[139] The religion of the Armenians is briefly described by La Croze (Hist. du Christ. de l'Ethiopie et de l'Arménie, p. 269-402). He refers to the great Armenian History of Galanus (3 vols. in fol. Rome, 1650-1661), and commends the state of Armenia in the third volume of the Nouveaux Mémoires des Missions du Levant. The work of a Jesuit must have sterling merit when it is praised by La Croze.

[140] The schism of the Armenians is placed eighty-four years after the council of Chalcedon (Pagi, Critica, ad A.D. 535). It was consummated at the end of seventeen years; and it is from the year of Christ 552 that we date the era of the Armenians (l'Art de vérifier les Dates, p. xxxv.).

[141] The sentiments and success of Julian of Halicarnassus may be seen in

quished by the arguments or the influence of his rival Severus, the Monophysite patriarch of Antioch. The Armenians alone are the pure disciples of Eutyches, an unfortunate parent, who has been renounced by the greater part of his spiritual progeny. They alone persevere in the opinion that the manhood of Christ was created, or existed without creation, of a divine and incorruptible substance. Their adversaries reproach them with the adoration of a phantom; and they retort the accusation, by deriding or execrating the blasphemy of the Jacobites, who impute to the Godhead the vile infirmities of the flesh, even the natural effects of nutrition and digestion. The religion of Armenia could not derive much glory from the learning or the power of its inhabitants. The royalty expired with the origin of their schism; and their Christian kings, who arose and fell in the thirteenth century on the confines of Cilicia, were the clients of the Latins and the vassals of the Turkish sultan of Iconium. The helpless nation has seldom been permitted to enjoy the tranquillity of servitude. From the earliest period to the present hour Armenia has been the theatre of perpetual war: the lands between Tauris and Erivan were dispeopled by the cruel policy of the Sophis; and myriads of Christian families were transplanted, to perish or to propagate in the distant provinces of Persia. Under the rod of oppression, the zeal of the Armenians is fervent and intrepid; they have often preferred the crown of martyrdom to the white turban of Mohammed; they devoutly hate the error and idolatry of the Greeks; and their transient union with the Latins is not less devoid of truth than the thousand bishops whom their patriarch offered at the feet of the Roman pontiff.[142] The *catholic,* or patriarch, of the Armenians resides in the monastery of Ekmiasin, three leagues from Erivan. Forty-seven archbishops, each of whom may claim the obedience of four or five suffragans, are consecrated by his hand; but the far greater part are only titular prelates, who dignify with their presence and service the simplicity of his court. As soon as they have performed the liturgy, they cultivate the garden; and our bishops will hear with surprise that the austerity of their life increases in just proportion to the elevation of their rank. In the fourscore thousand towns or villages of his spiritual empire, the patriarch receives a small and voluntary tax from each person above the age of fifteen; but the annual amount of six hundred thousand crowns is insufficient to supply the incessant demands of charity and tribute. Since the beginning of the last century the Armenians have obtained a large and lucrative share of the commerce of the East: in their return from Europe, the caravan usually halts in the neighbourhood of Erivan, the altars are enriched with the fruits of their

Liberatus (Brev. c. 19), Renaudot (Hist. Patriarch. Alex. p. 132, 303), and Assemannus (Biblioth. Orient. tom. ii. Dissertat. de Monophysitis, p. viii. p. 286).
[142] See a remarkable fact of the twelfth century in the History of Nicetas Choniates (p. 258). Yet three hundred years before, Photius (Epistol. ii. p. 49, edit. Montacut.) had gloried in the conversion of the Armenians— λατρεύει σήμερον ὀρθοδόξως [τὴν χριστιάνων λατρείαν].

patient industry; and the faith of Eutyches is preached in their recent congregations of Barbary and Poland.[143]

V. In the rest of the Roman empire the despotism of the prince might eradicate or silence the sectaries of an obnoxious creed. But the stubborn temper of the Egyptians maintained their opposition to the synod of Chalcedon, and the policy of Justinian condescended to expect and to seize the opportunity of discord. The Monophysite church of Alexandria [144] was torn by the disputes of the *corruptibles* and *incorruptibles,* and on the death of the patriarch the two factions upheld their respective candidates.[145] Gaian was the disciple of Julian, Theodosius had been the pupil of Severus: the claims of the former were supported by the consent of the monks and senators, the city and the province; the latter depended on the priority of his ordination, the favour of the empress Theodora, and the arms of the eunuch Narses, which might have been used in more honourable warfare. The exile of the popular candidate to Carthage and Sardinia inflamed the ferment of Alexandria; and after a schism of one hundred and seventy years, the *Gaianites* still revered the memory and doctrine of their founder. The strength of numbers and of discipline was tried in a desperate and bloody conflict; the streets were filled with the dead bodies of citizens and soldiers; the pious women, ascending the roofs of their houses, showered down every sharp or ponderous utensil on the heads of the enemy; and the final victory of Narses was owing to the flames with which he wasted the third capital of the Roman world. But the lieutenant of Justinian had not conquered in the cause of a heretic; Theodosius himself was speedily, though gently, removed; and Paul of Tanis, an orthodox monk, was raised to the throne of Athanasius. The powers of government were strained in his support; he might appoint or displace the dukes and tribunes of Egypt; the allowance of bread, which Diocletian had granted, was suppressed, the churches were shut, and a nation of schismatics was deprived at once of their spiritual and carnal food. In his turn, the tyrant was excommunicated by the zeal and revenge of the people; and none except his servile Melchites would salute him as a man, a Christian, or a bishop. Yet such is the blindness of ambition, that, when Paul was expelled on a charge of murder, he solicited, with a bribe of seven hundred pounds of gold, his restoration to the same station of hatred and ignomy. His successor Apollinaris entered the hostile city in military array, alike qualified for prayer or for battle. His troops, under

---

[143] The travelling Armenians are in the way of every traveller, and their mother church is on the high road between Constantinople and Ispahan: for their present state, see Fabricius (Lux Evangelii, etc., c. xxxviii. p. 40-51), Olearius (l. iv. c. 40), Chardin (vol. ii. p. 232), Tournefort (lettre xx.), and, above all, Tavernier (tom. i. p. 28-37, 510-518), that rambling jeweller, who had read nothing, but had seen so much and so well.

[144] The history of the Alexandrian patriarchs, from Dioscorus to Benjamin, is taken from Renaudot (p. 114-164), and the second tome of the Annals of Eutychius.

[145] Liberat. Brev. c. 20, 23; Victor. Chron. p. 329, 330; Procop. Anecdot. c. 26, 27.

arms, were distributed through the streets; the gates of the cathedral were guarded, and a chosen band was stationed in the choir to defend the person of their chief. He stood erect on his throne, and, throwing aside the upper garment of a warrior, suddenly appeared before the eyes of the multitude in the robes of patriarch of Alexandria. Astonishment held them mute; but no sooner had Apollinaris begun to read the tome of St. Leo, than a volley of curses, and invectives, and stones assaulted the odious minister of the emperor and the synod. A charge was instantly sounded by the successor of the apostles; the soldiers waded to their knees in blood; and two hundred thousand Christians are said to have fallen by the sword: an incredible account, even if it be extended from the slaughter of a day to the eighteen years of the reign of Apollinaris. Two succeeding patriarchs, Eulogius [146] and John,[147] laboured in the conversion of heretics with arms and arguments more worthy of their evangelical profession. The theological knowledge of Eulogius was displayed in many a volume, which magnified the errors of Eutyches and Severus, and attempted to reconcile the ambiguous language of St. Cyril with the orthodox creed of pope Leo and the fathers of Chalcedon. The bounteous alms of John the Eleemosynary were dictated by superstition, or benevolence, or policy. Seven thousand five hundred poor were maintained at his expense; on his accession he found eight thousand pounds of gold in the treasury of the church; he collected ten thousand from the liberality of the faithful; yet the primate could boast in his testament that he left behind him no more than the third part of the smallest of the silver coins. The churches of Alexandria were delivered to the Catholics, the religion of the Monophysites was proscribed in Egypt, and a law was revived which excluded the natives from the honours and emoluments of the state.

A more important conquest still remained, of the patriarch, the oracle and leader of the Egyptian church. Theodosius had resisted the threats and promises of Justinian with the spirit of an apostle or an enthusiast. " Such," replied the patriarch, " were the offers of the tempter when he showed the kingdoms of the earth. But my soul is far dearer to me than life or dominion. The churches are in the hands of a prince who can kill the body; but my conscience is my own; and in exile, poverty, or chains, I will steadfastly adhere to the faith of my

---

[146] Eulogius, who had been a monk of Antioch, was more conspicuous for subtlety than eloquence. He proves that the enemies of the faith, the Gaianites and Theodosians, ought not to be reconciled; that the same proposition may be orthodox in the mouth of St. Cyril, heretical in that of Severus; that the opposite assertions of St. Leo are equally true, etc. His writings are no longer extant, except in the Extracts of Photius, who had perused them with care and satisfaction, cod. ccviii., ccxxv., ccxxvi., ccxxvii., ccxxx., cclxxx.

[147] See the Life of John the Eleemosynary by his contemporary Leontius, bishop of Neapolis in Cyprus, whose Greek text, either lost or hidden, is reflected in the Latin version of Baronius (A.D. 610, No. 9, A.D. 620, No. 8). Pagi (Critica, tom. ii. p. 763) and Fabricius (l. v. c. 11, tom. vii. p. 454) have made some critical observations.

holy predecessors, Athanasius, Cyril, and Dioscorus. Anathema to the tome of Leo and the synod of Chalcedon! Anathema to all who embrace their creed! Anathema to them now and for evermore! Naked came I out of my mother's womb, naked shall I descend into the grave. Let those who love God follow me and seek their salvation." After comforting his brethren, he embarked for Constantinople, and sustained, in six successive interviews, the almost irresistible weight of the royal presence. His opinions were favourably entertained in the palace and the city; the influence of Theodora assured him a safe-conduct and honourable dismission; and he ended his days, though not on the throne, yet in the bosom of his native country. On the news of his death, Apollinaris indecently feasted the nobles and the clergy; but his joy was checked by the intelligence of a new election; and while he enjoyed the wealth of Alexandria, his rivals reigned in the monasteries of Thebais, and were maintained by the voluntary oblations of the people. A perpetual succession of patriarchs arose from the ashes of Theodosius; and the Monophysite churches of Syria and Egypt were united by the name of Jacobites and the communion of the faith. But the same faith, which has been confined to a narrow sect of the Syrians, was diffused over the mass of the Egyptian or Coptic nation, who almost unanimously rejected the decrees of the synod of Chalcedon. A thousand years were now elapsed since Egypt had ceased to be a kingdom, since the conquerors of Asia and Europe had trampled on the ready necks of a people whose ancient wisdom and power ascends beyond the records of history. The conflict of zeal and persecution rekindled some sparks of their national spirit. They abjured, with a foreign heresy, the manners and language of the Greeks: every Melchite, in their eyes, was a stranger, every Jacobite a citizen; the alliance of marriage, the offices of humanity, were condemned as a deadly sin; the natives renounced all allegiance to the emperor; and his orders, at a distance from Alexandria, were obeyed only under the pressure of military force. A generous effort might have redeemed the religion and liberty of Egypt, and her six hundred monasteries might have poured forth their myriads of holy warriors, for whom death should have no terrors, since life had no comfort or delight. But experience has proved the distinction of active and passive courage; the fanatic who endures without a groan the torture of the rack or the stake, would tremble and fly before the face of an armed enemy. The pusillanimous temper of the Egyptians could only hope for a change of masters; the arms of Chosroes depopulated the land, yet under his reign the Jacobites enjoyed a short and precarious respite. The victory of Heraclius renewed and aggravated the persecution, and the patriarch again escaped from Alexandria to the desert. In his flight, Benjamin was encouraged by a voice which bade him expect, at the end of ten years, the aid of a foreign nation, marked like the Egyptians themselves with the ancient rite of circumcision. The character of these deliverers, and the nature of the deliverance, will be hereafter explained; and I shall step over the interval of eleven centuries to observe the present misery of the

Jacobites of Egypt. The populous city of Cairo affords a residence, or rather a shelter, for their indigent patriarch and a remnant of ten bishops; forty monasteries have survived the inroads of the Arabs; and the progress of servitude and apostacy has reduced the Coptic nation to the despicable number of twenty-five or thirty thousand families;[148] a race of illiterate beggars, whose only consolation is derived from the superior wretchedness of the Greek patriarch and his diminutive congregation.[149]

VI. The Coptic patriarch, a rebel to the Cæsars, or a slave to the Caliphs, still gloried in the filial obedience of the kings of Nubia and Æthiopia. He repaid their homage by magnifying their greatness; and it was boldly asserted that they could bring into the field a hundred thousand horse, with an equal number of camels;[150] that their hand could pour or restrain the waters of the Nile;[151] and the peace and plenty of Egypt was obtained, even in this world, by the intercession of the patriarch. In exile at Constantinople, Theodosius recommended to his patroness the conversion of the black nations of Nubia, from the tropic of Cancer to the confines of Abyssinia.[152] Her design was suspected and emulated by the more orthodox emperor. The rival mis-

[148] This number is taken from the curious Recherches sur les Egyptiens et les Chinois (tom. ii. p. 192, 193); and appears more probable than the 600,000 ancient or 15,000 modern Copts of Gemelli Carreri. Cyril Lucar, the Protestant patriarch of Constantinople, laments that those heretics were ten times more numerous than his orthodox Greeks, ingeniously applying the πολλαί κεν δεκάδες δενοίατο οἰνοχόοιο of Homer (Iliad. ii. 128), the most perfect expression of contempt (Fabric. Lux Evangelii, 740).

[149] The history of the Copts, their religion, manners, etc., may be found in the Abbé Renaudot's motley work, neither a translation nor an original; the Chronicon Orientale of Peter, a Jacobite; in the two versions of Abraham Ecchellensis, Paris, 1651; and John Simon Asseman, Venet. 1729. These annals descend no lower than the thirteenth century. The more recent accounts must be searched for in the travellers into Egypt, and the Nouveaux Mémoires des Missions du Levant. In the last century Joseph Abudacnus, a native of Cairo, published at Oxford, in thirty pages, a slight Historia Jacobitarum, 147, post. 150.

[150] About the year 737. See Renaudot, Hist. Patriarch. Alex. p. 221, 222; Elmacin, Hist. Saracen, p. 99.

[151] Ludolph. Hist. Æthiopic. et Comment. l. i. c. 8; Renaudot, Hist. Patriarch. Alex. p. 480, etc. This opinion, introduced into Egypt and Europe by the artifice of the Copts, the pride of the Abyssinians, the fear and ignorance of the Turks and Arabs, has not even the semblance of truth. The rains of Æthiopia do not, in the increase of the Nile, consult the will of the monarch. If the river approaches at Napata within three days' journey of the Red Sea (see D'Anville's Maps), a canal that should divert its course would demand, and most probably surpass, the power of the Cæsars.

[152] The Abyssinians, who still preserve the features and olive complexion of the Arabs, afford a proof that two thousand years are not sufficient to change the colour of the human race. The Nubians, an African race, are pure negroes, as black as those of Senegal or Congo, with flat noses, thick lips, and woolly hair (Buffon. Hist. Naturelle, tom. v. p. 117, 143, 144, 166, 219, edit. in 12mo, Paris, 1769). The ancients beheld, without much attention, the extraordinary phenomenon which has exercised the philosophers and theologians of modern times.

sionaries, a Melchite and a Jacobite, embarked at the same time; but the empress, from a motive of love or fear, was more effectually obeyed; and the Catholic priest was detained by the president of Thebais, while the king of Nubia and his court were hastily baptised in the faith of Dioscorus. The tardy envoy of Justinian was received and dismissed with honour; but when he accused the heresy and treason of the Egyptians, the negro convert was instructed to reply that he would never abandon his brethren, the true believers, to the persecuting ministers of the synod of Chalcedon.[153] During several ages the bishops of Nubia were named and consecrated by the Jacobite patriarch of Alexandria: as late as the twelfth century Christianity prevailed; and some rites, some ruins, are still visible in the savage towns of Sennaar and Dongola.[154] But the Nubians at length executed their threats of returning to the worship of idols; the climate required the indulgence of polygamy, and they have finally preferred the triumph of the Koran to the abasement of the Cross. A metaphysical religion may appear too refined for the capacity of the negro race: yet a black or a parrot might be taught to repeat the *words* of the Chalcedonian or Monophysite creed.

Christianity was more deeply rooted in the Abyssinian empire; and, although the correspondence has been sometimes interrupted above seventy or a hundred years, the mother-church of Alexandria retains her colony in a state of perpetual pupilage. Seven bishops once composed the Æthiopic synod: had their number amounted to ten, they might have elected an independent primate; and one of their kings was ambitious of promoting his brother to the ecclesiastical throne. But the event was foreseen, the increase was denied; the episcopal office has been gradually confined to the *abuna*,[155] the head and author of the Abyssinian priesthood; the patriarch supplies each vacancy with an Egyptian monk; and the character of a stranger appears more venerable in the eyes of the people, less dangerous in those of the monarch. In the sixth century, when the schism of Egypt was confirmed, the rival chiefs, with their patrons Justinian and Theodora, strove to outstrip each other in the conquest of a remote and independent province. The industry of the empress was again victorious, and the pious Theodora has established in that sequestered church the faith and discipline of the Jacobites.[156]

[153] Asseman. Biblioth. Orient. tom. i. p. 329.

[154] The Christianity of the Nubians, A.D. 1153, is attested by the sheriff al Edrisi, falsely described under the name of the Nubian geographer (p. 18), who represents them as a nation of Jacobites. The rays of historical light that twinkle in the history of Renaudot (p. 178, 220-224, 281-286, 405, 434, 451, 464), are all previous to this era. See the modern state in the Lettres Edifiantes (Recueil, iv.) and Busching (tom. ix. p. 152-159, par Berenger).

[155] The abuna is improperly dignified by the Latins with the title of patriarch. The Abyssinians acknowledge only the four patriarchs, and their chief is no more than a metropolitan or national primate (Ludolph. Hist. Æthiopic. et Comment. l. iii. c. 7). The seven bishops of Renaudot (p. 511), who existed A.D. 1131, are unknown to the historian.

[156] I know not why Assemannus (Biblioth. Orient. tom. ii. p. 384) should call in question these probable missions of Theodora into Nubia and Æthiopia.

Encompassed on all sides by the enemies of their religion, the Æthiopians slept near a thousand years, forgetful of the world, by whom they were forgotten. They were awakened by the Portuguese, who, turning the southern promontory of Africa, appeared in India and the Red Sea, as if they had descended through the air from a distant planet. In the first moments of their interview, the subjects of Rome and Alexandria observed the resemblance rather than the difference of their faith; and each nation expected the most important benefits from an alliance with their Christian brethren. In their lonely situation the Æthiopians had almost relapsed into the savage life. Their vessels, which had traded to Ceylon, scarcely presumed to navigate the rivers of Africa; the ruins of Axume were deserted, the nation was scattered in villages, and the emperor, a pompous name, was content, both in peace and war, with the immovable residence of a camp. Conscious of their own indigence, the Abyssinians had formed the rational project of importing the arts and ingenuity of Europe;[157] and their ambassadors at Rome and Lisbon were instructed to solicit a colony of smiths, carpenters, tilers, masons, printers, surgeons, and physicians, for the use of their country. But the public danger soon called for the instant and effectual aid of arms and soldiers, to defend an unwarlike people from the barbarians who ravaged the inland country, and the Turks and Arabs who advanced from the sea-coast in more formidable array. Æthiopia was saved by four hundred and fifty Portuguese, who displayed in the field the native valour of Europeans, and the artificial powers of the musket and cannon. In a moment of terror the emperor had promised to reconcile himself and his subjects to the Catholic faith; a Latin patriarch represented the supremacy of the pope;[158] the empire, enlarged in a tenfold proportion, was supposed to contain more gold than the mines of America; and the wildest hopes of avarice and zeal were built on the willing submission of the Christians of Africa.

But the vows which pain had extorted were forsworn on the return of health. The Abyssinians still adhered with unshaken constancy to the Monophysite faith; their languid belief was inflamed by the exercise of dispute; they branded the Latins with the names of Arians and Nestorians, and imputed the adoration of *four* gods to those who separated the two natures of Christ. Fremona, a place of worship, or rather of

The slight notices of Abyssinia till the year 1500 are supplied by Renaudot (p. 336-341, 381, 382, 405, 443, etc., 452, 456, 463, 475, 480, 511, 525, 559-564) from the Coptic writers. The mind of Ludolphus was a perfect blank.

[157] Ludolph. Hist. Æthiop. l. iv. c. 5. The most necessary arts are now exercised by the Jews, and the foreign trade is in the hands of the Armenians. What Gregory principally admired and envied was the industry of Europe—artes et opificia.

[158] John Bermudez, whose relation, printed at Lisbon, 1569, was translated into English by Purchas (Pilgrims, l. vii. c. 7, p. 1149, etc.), and from thence into French by La Croze (Christianisme d'Ethiopie, p. 92-265). The piece is curious; but the author may be suspected of deceiving Abyssinia, Rome, and Portugal. His title to the rank of patriarch is dark and doubtful (Ludolph. Comment. No. 101, p. 473).

exile, was assigned to the Jesuit missionaries. Their skill in the liberal and mechanic arts, their theological learning, and the decency of their manners, inspired a barren esteem; but they were not endowed with the gift of miracles,[159] and they vainly solicited a reinforcement of European troops. The patience and dexterity of forty years at length obtained a more favourable audience, and two emperors of Abyssinia were persuaded that Rome could insure the temporal and everlasting happiness of her votaries. The first of these royal converts lost his crown and his life; and the rebel army was sanctified by the *abuna*, who hurled an anathema at the apostate and absolved his subjects from their oath of fidelity. The fate of Zadenghel was revenged by the courage and fortune of Susneus, who ascended the throne under the name of Segued, and more vigorously prosecuted the pious enterprise of his kinsman. After the amusement of some unequal combats between the Jesuits and his illiterate priests, the emperor declared himself a proselyte to the synod of Chalcedon, presuming that his clergy and people would embrace without delay the religion of their prince. The liberty of choice was succeeded by a law which imposed, under pain of death, the belief of the two natures of Christ: the Abyssinians were enjoined to work and to play on the Sabbath; and Segued, in the face of Europe and Africa, renounced his connection with the Alexandrian church. A Jesuit, Alphonso Mendez, the Catholic patriarch of Æthiopia, accepted, in the name of Urban VIII., the homage and abjuration of his penitent. " I confess," said the emperor on his knees, " I confess that the pope is the vicar of Christ, the successor of St. Peter, and the sovereign of the world. To him I swear true obedience, and at his feet I offer my person and kingdom." A similar oath was repeated by his son, his brother, the clergy, the nobles, and even the ladies of the court: the Latin patriarch was invested with honours and wealth; and his missionaries erected their churches or citadels in the most convenient stations of the empire. The Jesuits themselves deplore the fatal indiscretion of their chief, who forgot the mildness of the gospel and the policy of his order, to introduce with hasty violence the liturgy of Rome and the inquisition of Portugal. He condemned the ancient practice of circumcision, which health rather than superstition had first invented in the climate of Æthiopia.[160] A new

---

[159] Religio Romana . . . nec precibus patrum nec miraculis ab ipsis editis suffulciebatur, is the uncontradicted assurance of the devout emperor Susneus to his patriarch Mendez (Ludolph. Comment. No. 126, p. 529) ; and such assurances should be preciously kept, as an antidote against any marvellous legends.

[160] I am aware how tender is the question of circumcision. Yet I will affirm, 1. That the Æthiopians have a physical reason for the circumcision of males, and even of females (Recherches Philosophiques sur les Américains, tom. ii.). 2. That it was practised in Æthiopia long before the introduction of Judaism or Christianity (Herodot. l. ii. c. 104; Marsham, Canon Chron. p. 72, 73). " Infantes circumcidunt ob consuetudinem non ob Judaismum," says Gregory the Abyssinian priest (apud Fabric. Lux Christiana, p. 720). Yet, in the heat of dispute, the Portuguese were sometimes branded with the name of *uncircumcised* (La Croze, p. 80; Ludolph. Hist. and Comment. l. iii. c. 1).

baptism, a new ordination, was inflicted on the natives; and they trembled with horror when the most holy of the dead were torn from their graves, when the most illustrious of the living were excommunicated by a foreign priest. In the defence of their religion and liberty the Abyssinians rose in arms, with desperate but unsuccessful zeal. Five rebellions were extinguished in the blood of the insurgents: two abunas were slain in battle; whole legions were slaughtered in the field, or suffocated in their caverns; and neither merit, nor rank, nor sex, could save from an ignominious death the enemies of Rome. But the victorious monarch was finally subdued by the constancy of the nation, of his mother, of his son, and of his most faithful friends. Segued listened to the voice of pity, of reason, perhaps of fear: and his edict of liberty of conscience instantly revealed the tyranny and weakness of the Jesuits. On the death of his father, Basilides expelled the Latin patriarch, and restored to the wishes of the nation the faith and discipline of Egypt. The Monophysite churches resounded with a song of triumph, "that the sheep of Æthiopia were now delivered from the hyænas of the West;" and the gates of that solitary realm were for ever shut against the arts, the science, and the fanaticism of Europe.[161]

CHAPTER XLVIII (641-1185 A.D.)

Plan of the last two [quarto] Volumes—Succession and Characters of the Greek Emperors of Constantinople, from the Time of Heraclius to the Latin Conquest

I HAVE now deduced from Trajan to Constantine, from Constantine to Heraclius, the regular series of the Roman emperors; and faithfully exposed the prosperous and adverse fortunes of their reigns. Five centuries of the decline and fall of the empire have already elapsed; but a period of more than eight hundred years still separates me from the term of my labours, the taking of Constantinople by the Turks. Should I persevere in the same course, should I observe the same measure, a prolix and slender thread would be spun through many a volume, nor would the patient reader find an adequate reward of instruction or amusement. At every step, as we sink deeper in the decline and fall of the Eastern empire,

---

[161] The three Protestant historians, Ludolphus (Hist. Æthiopica, Francofurt, 1681; Commentarius, 1691; Relatio Nova, etc., 1693, in folio), Geddes (Church History of Æthiopia, London, 1696, in 8vo), and La Croze (Hist. du Christianisme d'Ethiopie et d'Arménie, La Haye, 1739, in 12mo), have drawn their principal materials from the Jesuits, especially from the General History of Tellez, published in Portuguese at Coimbra, 1660. We might be surprised at their frankness; but their most flagitious vice, the spirit of persecution, was in their eyes the most meritorious virtue. Ludolphus possessed some, though a slight, advantage from the Æthiopic language, and the personal conversation of Gregory, a free-spirited Abyssinian priest, whom he invited from Rome to the court of Saxe-Gotha. See the Theologia Æthiopica of Gregory, in Fabricius, Lux Evangelii, p. 716-734.

the annals of each succeeding reign would impose a more ungrateful and melancholy task. These annals must continue to repeat a tedious and uniform tale of weakness and misery; the natural connection of causes and events would be broken by frequent and hasty transitions, and a minute accummulation of circumstances must destroy the light and effect of those general pictures which compose the use and ornament of a remote history. From the time of Heraclius the Byzantine theatre is contracted and darkened: the line of empire, which had been defined by the laws of Justinian and the arms of Belisarius, recedes on all sides from our view; the Roman name, the proper subject of our inquiries, is reduced to a narrow corner of Europe, to the lonely suburbs of Constantinople; and the fate of the Greek empire has been compared to that of the Rhine, which loses itself in the sands before its waters can mingle with the ocean. The scale of dominion is diminished to our view by the distance of time and place; nor is the loss of external splendour compensated by the nobler gifts of virtue and genius. In the last moments of her decay Constantinople was doubtless more opulent and populous than Athens at her most flourishing era, when a scanty sum of six thousand talents, or twelve hundred thousand pounds sterling, was possessed by twenty-one thousand male citizens of an adult age. But each of these citizens was a freeman who dared to assert the liberty of his thoughts, words, and actions; whose person and property were guarded by equal law; and who exercised his independent vote in the government of the republic. Their numbers seem to be multiplied by the strong and various discriminations of character; under the shield of freedom, on the wings of emulation and vanity, each Athenian aspired to the level of the national dignity; from this commanding eminence some chosen spirits soared beyond the reach of a vulgar eye; and the chances of superior merit in a great and populous kingdom, as they are proved by experience, would excuse the computation of imaginary millions. The territories of Athens, Sparta, and their allies, do not exceed a moderate province of France or England; but after the trophies of Salamis and Platæa, they expand in our fancy to the gigantic size of Asia, which had been trampled under the feet of the victorious Greeks. But the subjects of the Byzantine empire, who assume and dishonour the names both of Greeks and Romans, present a dead uniformity of abject vices, which are neither softened by the weakness of humanity nor animated by the vigour of memorable crimes. The freemen of antiquity might repeat with generous enthusiasm the sentence of Homer, " that on the first day of his servitude the captive is deprived of one half of his manly virtue." But the poet had only seen the effects of civil or domestic slavery, nor could he foretell that the second moiety of manhood must be annihilated by the spiritual despotism, which shackles not only the actions but even the thoughts of the prostrate votary. By this double yoke the Greeks were oppressed under the successors of Heraclius; the tyrant, a law of eternal justice, was degraded by the vices of his subjects; and on the throne, in the camp, in the schools, we search, perhaps with fruitless diligence, the names and characters that may deserve to be rescued from oblivion. Nor are the defects of the subject compensated by the skill and variety of the painters. Of a space of eight hundred years, the four first centuries are overspread with a cloud interrupted by some faint and broken rays of historic light: in the lives of the emperors, from Maurice to Alexius, Basil the Macedonian has alone been the theme of a separate work; and the absence, or loss, or imperfection of contemporary evidence, must be poorly supplied by the doubtful authority of more recent compilers. The four last centuries are exempt from the reproach of penury: and with the Comnenian family the historic muse of Constantinople again revives, but her apparel is gaudy, her motions are without elegance or grace. A succession of priests, or courtiers, treads in each other's footsteps in the same path of servitude and superstition: their views are narrow, their judgment is feeble or corrupt: and we close the volume of copious barrenness, still ignorant of the causes of events, the characters of the actors, and the manners of the times, which they celebrate or deplore. The observation which has been applied to a man may be extended to a whole people, that the energy of the sword is communicated to the pen; and it will be found by experience that the tone of history will rise or fall with the spirit of the age.

From these considerations I should have abandoned without regret the Greek slaves and their servile historians, had I not reflected that the fate of the Byzantine monarchy is *passively* connected with the most splendid and important revolutions which have changed the state of the world. The space of the lost provinces was immediately replenished with new colonies and rising kingdoms: the active virtues of peace and war deserted from the vanquished to the victorious nations; and it is in their origin and conquests, in their religion and government, that we must explore the causes and effects of the decline and fall of the Eastern empire. Nor will this scope of narrative, the riches and variety of these materials, be incompatible with the unity of design and composition. As, in his daily prayers, the Musulman of Fez or Delhi still turns his face towards the temple of Mecca, the historian's eye shall be always fixed on the city of Constantinople. The excursive line may embrace the wilds of Arabia and Tartary, but the circle will be ultimately reduced to the decreasing limit of the Roman monarchy.

On this principle I shall now establish the plan of the last two volumes of the present work. The first chapter will contain, in a regular series, the emperors who reigned at Constantinople during a period of six hundred years, from the days of Heraclius to the Latin conquest: a rapid abstract, which may be supported by a *general* appeal to the order and text of the original historians. In this introduction I shall confine myself to the revolutions of the throne, the succession of families, the personal characters of the Greek princes, the mode of their life and death, the maxims and influence of their domestic government, and the tendency of their reign to accelerate or suspend the downfall of the Eastern empire. Such a chronological review will serve to illustrate the various argument of the subsequent chapters; and each circumstance of the eventful story of the barbarians will adapt itself in a proper place to the Byzantine annals. The internal state of the empire, and the dangerous heresy of the Paulicians, which shook the East and enlightened the West, will be the subject of two separate chapters; but these inquiries must be postponed till our farther progress shall have opened the view of the world in the ninth and tenth centuries of the Christian era. After this foundation of Byzantine history, the following nations will pass before our eyes, and each will occupy the space to which it may be entitled by greatness or merit, or the degree of connection with the Roman world and the present age. I. The FRANKS; a general appellation which includes all the barbarians of France, Italy, and Germany, who were united by the sword and sceptre of Charlemagne. The persecution of images and their votaries separated Rome and Italy from the Byzantine throne, and prepared the restoration of the Roman empire in the West. II. The ARABS or SARACENS. Three ample chapters will be devoted to this curious and interesting object. In the first, after a picture of the country and its inhabitants, I shall investigate the character of Mohammed; the character, religion, and success of the prophet. In the second I shall lead the Arabs to the conquest of Syria, Egypt, and Africa, the provinces of the Roman empire; nor can I check their victorious career till they have overthrown the monarchies of Persia and Spain. In the third I shall inquire how Constantinople and Europe were saved by the luxury and arts, the division and decay, of the empire of the caliphs. A single chapter will include, III. The BULGARIANS, IV. HUNGARIANS, and V. RUSSIANS, who assaulted by sea or by land the provinces and the capital; but the last of these, so important in their present greatness, will excite some curiosity in their origin and infancy. VI. The NORMANS; or rather the private adventurers of that warlike people, who founded a powerful kingdom in Apulia and Sicily, shook the throne of Constantinople, displayed the trophies of chivalry, and almost realised the wonders of romance. VII. The LATINS; the subjects of the pope, the nations of the West, who enlisted under the banner of the cross for the recovery or relief of the holy sepulchre. The Greek emperors were terrified and preserved by the myriads of pilgrims who marched to Jerusalem with Godfrey of Bouillon and the peers of Christendom. The second and third crusades trod in the footsteps of the first: Asia and Europe were mingled in a sacred war of two hundred years; and the Christian powers were bravely resisted and finally expelled by Saladin and the Mamalukes of Egypt. In these memorable crusades a fleet and army of French and Venetians were diverted from Syria to the Thracian Bosphorus: they assaulted the capital, they subverted the Greek monarchy: and a dynasty of Latin princes was seated near threescore years on the throne of Constantine. VIII. The GREEKS themselves, during this period of captivity and exile, must be considered as a foreign nation; the enemies, and again the sovereigns of Constantinople. Misfortune had rekindled a spark of national virtue; and the Imperial series may be continued with some dignity from their restoration to the Turkish conquest. IX. The MOGULS and TARTARS. By the arms of Zingis and his descendants the globe was shaken from China to Poland and Greece: the sultans were overthrown: the caliphs fell, and the Cæsars trembled on their throne. The victories of Timour suspended above fifty years the final ruin of the Byzantine empire. X. I have already noticed the first appearance of the TURKS; and the names of the fathers, of *Seljuk* and *Othman*, discriminate the two successive dynasties of the nation which emerged in the eleventh century from the Scythian wilderness. The former established a potent and splendid kingdom from the banks of the Oxus to Antioch and Nice; and the first crusade was provoked by the violation of Jerusalem and the danger of Constantinople. From a humble origin the *Ottomans* arose the scourge and terror of Christendom. Constantinople was besieged and taken by Mohammed II., and his triumph annihilates the remnant, the image, the title, of the Roman empire in the East. The schism of the Greeks will be connected with their last calamities and the restoration of learning in the Western world. I shall return from the captivity of the new to the ruins of ancient ROME; and the venerable name, the interesting theme, will shed a ray of glory on the conclusion of my labours.

THE emperor Heraclius had punished a tyrant and ascended his throne; and the memory of his reign is perpetuated by the transient conquest and irreparable loss of the Eastern provinces. After the death of Eudocia, his first wife, he disobeyed the patriarch and violated the laws by his second marriage with his niece Martina; and the superstition of the Greeks beheld the judgment of Heaven in the diseases of the father and the deformity of his offspring. But the opinion of an illegitimate birth is sufficient to distract the choice and loosen the obedience of the people: the ambition of Martina was quickened by maternal love, and perhaps by the envy of a stepmother; and the aged husband was too feeble to withstand the arts of conjugal allurements. Constantine, his eldest son, enjoyed in a mature age the title of Augustus; but the weakness of his constitution required a colleague and a guardian, and he yielded with secret reluctance to the partition of the empire. The senate was summoned to the palace to ratify or attest the association of Heracleonas, the son of Martina: the imposition of the diadem was consecrated by the prayer and blessing of the patriarch; the senators and patricians adored the majesty of the great emperor and the partners of his reign; and as soon as the doors were thrown open they were hailed by the tumultuary but important voice of the soldiers. After an interval of five months the pompous ceremonies which formed the essence of the

Byzantine state were celebrated in the cathedral and the hippodrome: the concord of the royal brothers was affectedly displayed by the younger leaning on the arm of the elder; and the name of Martina was mingled in the reluctant or venal acclamations of the people. Heraclius survived this association about two years: his last testimony declared his two sons the equal heirs of the Eastern empire, and commanded them to honour his widow Martina as their mother and their sovereign.

When Martina first appeared on the throne with the name and attributes of royalty, she was checked by a firm, though respectful, opposition; and the dying embers of freedom were kindled by the breath of superstitious prejudice. " We reverence," exclaimed the voice of a citizen, " we reverence the mother of our princes; but to those princes alone our obedience is due; and Constantine, the elder emperor, is of an age to sustain, in his own hands, the weight of the sceptre. Your sex is excluded by nature from the toils of government. How could you combat, how could you answer, the barbarians who, with hostile or friendly intentions, may approach the royal city? May Heaven avert from the Roman republic this national disgrace, which would provoke the patience of the slaves of Persia! " Martina descended from the throne with indignation, and sought a refuge in the female apartment of the palace. The reign of Constantine the Third lasted only one hundred and three days: he expired in the thirtieth year of his age, and, although his life had been a long malady, a belief was entertained that poison had been the means, and his cruel stepmother the author, of his untimely fate. Martina reaped indeed the harvest of his death, and assumed the government in the name of the surviving emperor; but the incestuous widow of Heraclius was universally abhorred; the jealousy of the people was awakened, and the two orphans whom Constantine had left became the objects of the public care. It was in vain that the son of Martina, who was no more than fifteen years of age, was taught to declare himself the guardian of his nephews, one of whom he had presented at the baptismal font: it was in vain that he swore on the wood of the true cross to defend them against all their enemies. On his deathbed the late emperor had despatched a trusty servant to arm the troops and provinces of the East in the defence of his helpless children: the eloquence and liberality of Valentin had been successful, and from his camp of Chalcedon he boldly demanded the punishment of the assassins, and the restoration of the lawful heir. The licence of the soldiers, who devoured the grapes and drank the wine of their Asiatic vineyards, provoked the citizens of Constantinople against the domestic authors of their calamities, and the dome of St. Sophia re-echoed, not with prayers and hymns, but with the clamours and imprecations of an enraged multitude. At their imperious command Heracleonas appeared in the pulpit with the eldest of the royal orphans; Constans alone was saluted as emperor of the Romans, and a crown of gold, which had been taken from the tomb of Heraclius, was placed on his head, with the solemn benediction of the patriarch. But, in the tumult of joy and indignation, the church was pillaged, the sanctuary was polluted by a promiscuous crowd of Jews and barbarians; and the Monothelite Pyrrhus, a creature of the empress, after dropping a protestation on the altar, escaped by a prudent flight from the zeal of the Catholics. A more serious and bloody task was reserved for the senate, who derived a temporary strength from the consent of the soldiers and people. The spirit of Roman freedom revived the ancient and awful examples of the judgment of tyrants, and the Imperial culprits were deposed and condemned as the authors of the death of Constantine. But the severity of the conscript fathers was stained by the indiscriminate punishment of the innocent and the guilty: Martina and Heracleonas were sentenced to the amputation, the former of her tongue, the latter of his nose; and after this cruel execution they consumed the remainder of their days in exile and oblivion. The Greeks who were capable of reflection might find some consolation for their servitude by observing the abuse of power when it was lodged for a moment in the hands of an aristocracy.

We shall imagine ourselves transported five hundred years backwards to the age of the Antonines if we listen to the oration which Constans II. pronounced in the twelfth year of his age before the Byzantine senate. After returning his thanks for the just punishment of the assassins who had intercepted the fairest hopes of his father's reign, " By the divine Providence," said the young emperor, " and by your righteous decree, Martina and her incestuous progeny have been cast headlong from the throne. Your majesty and wisdom have prevented the Roman state from degenerating into lawless tyranny. I therefore exhort and beseech you to stand forth as the counsellors and judges of the common safety." The senators were gratified by the respectful address and liberal donative of their sovereign; but these servile Greeks were unworthy and regardless of freedom; and in his mind the lesson of an hour was quickly erased by the prejudices of the age and the habits of despotism. He retained only a jealous fear lest the senate or people should one day invade the right of primogeniture, and seat his brother Theodosius on an equal throne. By the imposition of holy orders, the grandson of Heraclius was disqualified for the purple; but this ceremony, which seemed to profane the sacraments of the church, was insufficient to appease the suspicions of the tyrant, and the death of the deacon Theodosius could alone expiate the crime of his royal birth. His murder was avenged by the imprecations of the people, and the assassin, in the fulness of power, was driven from his capital into voluntary and perpetual exile. Constans embarked for Greece; and, as if he meant to retort the abhorrence which he deserved, he is said, from the imperial galley, to have spit against the walls of his native city. After passing the winter at Athens, he sailed to Tarentum in Italy, visited Rome, and concluded a long pilgrimage of disgrace and sacrilegious rapine by fixing his residence at Syracuse. But if Constans could fly from his people, he could not fly from himself. The remorse of his conscience created a phantom who pursued him by land and sea, by day and by night; and the visionary Theodosius, presenting to his lips a cup of blood, said, or seemed to say, " Drink, brother, drink "—a sure emblem of the aggravation of his guilt, since he had received from the hands of the deacon the mystic cup of the blood of Christ. Odious to himself and to mankind, Constans perished by domestic, perhaps by episcopal, treason in the capital of Sicily. A servant who waited in the bath, after pouring warm water on his head, struck him violently with the vase. He fell, stunned by the blow and suffocated by the water; and his attendants, who wondered at the tedious delay, beheld with indifference the corpse of their lifeless emperor. The troops of Sicily invested with the purple an obscure youth, whose inimitable beauty eluded, and it might easily elude, the declining art of the painters and sculptors of the age.

Constans had left in the Byzantine palace three sons, the eldest of whom had been clothed in his infancy with the purple. When the father summoned them to attend his person in Sicily, these precious hostages were detained by the Greeks, and a firm refusal informed him that they were the children of the state. The news of his murder was conveyed with almost supernatural speed from Syracuse to Constantinople; and Constantine, the eldest of his sons, inherited his throne without being the heir of the public hatred. His subjects contributed with zeal and alacrity to chastise the guilt and presumption of a province which had usurped the rights of the senate and people; the young emperor sailed from the Hellespont with a powerful fleet, and the legions of Rome and Carthage were assembled under his standard in the harbour of Syracuse. The defeat of the Sicilian tyrant was easy, his punishment just, and his beauteous head was exposed in the hippodrome; but I cannot applaud the clemency of a prince who, among a crowd of victims, condemned the son of a patrician for deploring with some bitterness the execution of a virtuous father. The youth was castrated: he survived the operation, and the memory of this indecent cruelty is preserved by the elevation of Germanus to the rank of a patriarch and saint. After pouring this bloody libation on his father's tomb, Constantine returned to his capital; and the growth of his young beard during the Sicilian voyage was announced, by the familiar surname of Pogonatus, to the Grecian world. But his reign, like that of his predecessor, was stained with fraternal discord. On his two brothers, Heraclius and Tiberius, he had bestowed the title of Augustus—an empty title, for they continued to languish, without trust or power, in the solitude of the palace. At their secret instigation the troops of the Anatolian *theme* or province approached the city on the Asiatic side, demanded for the royal brothers the partition or exercise of sovereignty, and supported their seditious claim by a theological argument. They were Christians, they cried, and orthodox Catholics, the sincere votaries of the holy and undivided Trinity. Since there are three equal persons in heaven, it is reasonable

there should be three equal persons upon earth. The emperor invited
these learned divines to a friendly conference, in which they might
propose their arguments to the senate: they obeyed the summons, but
the prospect of their bodies hanging on the gibbet in the suburb of
Galata reconciled their companions to the unity of the reign of Constantine. He pardoned his brothers, and their names were still pronounced in the public acclamations; but on the repetition or suspicion of
a similar offence, the obnoxious princes were deprived of their titles
and noses, in the presence of the Catholic bishops who were assembled
at Constantinople in the sixth general synod. In the close of his life
Pogonatus was anxious only to establish the right of primogeniture: the
heir of his two sons, Justinian and Heraclius, was offered on the shrine
of St. Peter, as a symbol of their spiritual adoption by the pope; but the
elder was alone exalted to the rank of Augustus, and the assurance of
the empire.

After the decease of his father the inheritance of the Roman world
devolved to Justinian II.; and the name of a triumphant lawgiver was
dishonoured by the vices of a boy, who imitated his namesake only in
the expensive luxury of building. His passions were strong; his understanding was feeble; and he was intoxicated with a foolish pride that his
birth had given him the command of millions, of whom the smallest
community would not have chosen him for their local magistrate. His
favourite ministers were two beings the least susceptible of human
sympathy, a eunuch and a monk: to the one he abandoned the palace,
to the other the finances; the former corrected the emperor's mother
with a scourge, the latter suspended the insolvent tributaries, with their
heads downwards, over a slow and smoky fire. Since the days of Commodus and Caracalla the cruelty of the Roman princes had most commonly been the effect of their fear; but Justinian, who possessed some
vigour of character, enjoyed the sufferings, and braved the revenge, of
his subjects about ten years, till the measure was full of his crimes and
of their patience. In a dark dungeon Leontius, a general of reputation,
had groaned above three years, with some of the noblest and most deserving of the patricians: he was suddenly drawn forth to assume the
government of Greece; and this promotion of an injured man was a mark
of the contempt rather than of the confidence of his prince. As he was
followed to the port by the kind offices of his friends, Leontius observed,
with a sigh, that he was a victim adorned for sacrifice, and that inevitable
death would pursue his footsteps. They ventured to reply that glory
and empire might be the recompence of a generous resolution, that every
order of men abhorred the reign of a monster, and that the hands of two
hundred thousand patriots expected only the voice of a leader. The
night was chosen for their deliverance; and in the first effort of the conspirators the præfect was slain and the prisons were forced open: the
emissaries of Leontius proclaimed in every street, " Christians, to St.
Sophia! " and the seasonable text of the patriarch, " This is the day of

the Lord! " was the prelude of an inflammatory sermon. From the church the people adjourned to the hippodrome: Justinian, in whose cause not a sword had been drawn, was dragged before these tumultuary judges, and their clamours demanded the instant death of the tyrant. But Leontius, who was already clothed with the purple, cast an eye of pity on the prostrate son of his own benefactor and of so many emperors. The life of Justinian was spared; the amputation of his nose, perhaps of his tongue, was imperfectly performed: the happy flexibility of the Greek language could impose the name of Rhinotmetus; and the mutilated tyrant was banished to Chersonæ in Crim-Tartary, a lonely settlement, where corn, wine, and oil were imported as foreign luxuries.

On the edge of the Scythian wilderness Justinian still cherished the pride of his birth, and the hope of his restoration. After three years' exile, he received the pleasing intelligence that his injury was avenged by a second revolution, and that Leontius in his turn had been dethroned and mutilated by the rebel Apsimar, who assumed the more respectable name of Tiberius. But the claim of lineal succession was still formidable to a plebeian usurper; and his jealousy was stimulated by the complaints and charges of the Chersonites, who beheld the vices of the tyrant in the spirit of the exile. With a band of followers, attached to his person by common hope or common despair, Justinian fled from the inhospitable shore to the horde of the Chozars, who pitched their tents between the Tanais and Borysthenes. The khan entertained with piety and respect the royal suppliant: Phanagoria, once an opulent city, on the Asiatic side of the lake Mæotis, was assigned for his residence; and every Roman prejudice was stifled in his marriage with the sister of the barbarian, who seems, however, from the name of Theodora, to have received the sacrament of baptism. But the faithless Chozar was soon tempted by the gold of Constantinople: and had not the design been revealed by the conjugal love of Theodora, her husband must have been assassinated or betrayed into the power of his enemies. After strangling, with his own hands, the two emissaries of the khan, Justinian sent back his wife to her brother, and embarked on the Euxine in search of new and more faithful allies. His vessel was assaulted by a violent tempest; and one of his pious companions advised him to deserve the mercy of God by a vow of general forgiveness if he should be restored to the throne. " Of forgiveness? " replied the intrepid tyrant: " may I perish this instant— may the Almighty whelm me in the waves, if I consent to spare a single head of my enemies! " He survived this impious menace, sailed into the mouth of the Danube, trusted his person in the royal village of the Bulgarians, and purchased the aid of Terbelis, a pagan conqueror, by the promise of his daughter, and a fair partition of the treasures of the empire. The Bulgarian kingdom extended to the confines of Thrace; and the two princes besieged Constantinople at the head of fifteen thousand horse. Apsimar was dismayed by the sudden and hostile apparition of his rival, whose head had been promised by the Chozar, and of whose evasion he was yet ignorant. After an absence of ten years the crimes of Justinian were faintly remembered, and the birth and misfortunes of their hereditary sovereign excited the pity of the multitude, ever discontented with the ruling powers; and by the active diligence of his adherents he was introduced into the city and palace of Constantine.

In rewarding his allies, and recalling his wife, Justinian displayed some sense of honour and gratitude; and Terbelis retired, after sweeping away a heap of gold coin which he measured with his Scythian whip. But never was vow more religiously performed than the sacred oath of revenge which he had sworn amidst the storms of the Euxine. The two usurpers, for I must reserve the name of tyrant for the conqueror, were dragged into the hippodrome, the one from his prison, the other from his palace. Before their execution Leontius and Apsimar were cast prostrate in chains beneath the throne of the emperor; and Justinian, planting a foot on each of their necks, contemplated above an hour the chariot-race, while the inconstant people shouted, in the words of the Psalmist, "Thou shalt trample on the asp and basilisk, and on the lion and dragon shalt thou set thy foot!" The universal defection which he had once experienced might provoke him to repeat the wish of Caligula, that the Roman people had but one head. Yet I shall presume to observe that such a wish is unworthy of an ingenious tyrant, since his revenge and cruelty would have been extinguished by a single blow, instead of the slow variety of tortures which Justinian inflicted on the victims of his anger. His pleasures were inexhaustible: neither private virtue nor public service could expiate the guilt of active, or even passive, obedience to an established government; and, during the six years of his new reign, he considered the axe, the cord, and the rack as the only instruments of royalty. But his most implacable hatred was pointed against the Chersonites, who had insulted his exile and violated the laws of hospitality. Their remote situation afforded some means of defence, or at least of escape; and a grievous tax was imposed on Constantinople to supply the preparations of a fleet and army. "All are guilty, and all must perish," was the mandate of Justinian; and the bloody execution was intrusted to his favourite Stephen, who was recommended by the epithet of the Savage. Yet even the savage Stephen imperfectly accomplished the intentions of his sovereign. The slowness of his attack allowed the greater part of the inhabitants to withdraw into the country; and the minister of vengeance contented himself with reducing the youth of both sexes to a state of servitude, with roasting alive seven of the principal citizens, with drowning twenty in the sea, and with reserving forty-two in chains to receive their doom from the mouth of the emperor. In their return the fleet was driven on the rocky shores of Anatolia; and Justinian applauded the obedience of the Euxine, which had involved so many thousands of his subjects and enemies in a common shipwreck: but the tyrant was still insatiate of blood; and a second expedition was commanded to extirpate the remains of the proscribed colony. In the short interval the Chersonites had returned to their city, and were pre-pared to die in arms; the khan of the Chozars had renounced the cause of his odious brother; the exiles of every province were assembled in Tauris; and Bardanes, under the name of Philippicus, was invested with the purple. The Imperial troops, unwilling and unable to perpetrate the revenge of Justinian, escaped his displeasure by abjuring his allegiance; the fleet, under their new sovereign, steered back a more auspicious course to the harbours of Sinope and Constantinople; and every tongue was prompt to pronounce, every hand to execute, the death of the tyrant. Destitute of friends, he was deserted by his barbarian guards; and the stroke of the assassin was praised as an act of patriotism and Roman virtue. His son Tiberius had taken refuge in a church; his aged grandmother guarded the door; and the innocent youth, suspending round his neck the most formidable relics, embraced with one hand the altar, with the other the wood of the true cross. But the popular fury that dares to trample on superstition, is deaf to the cries of humanity; and the race of Heraclius was extinguished after a reign of one hundred years.

Between the fall of the Heraclian and the rise of the Isaurian dynasty, a short interval of six years is divided into three reigns. Bardanes, or Philippicus, was hailed at Constantinople as a hero who had delivered his country from a tyrant; and he might taste some moments of happiness in the first transports of sincere and universal joy. Justinian had left behind him an ample treasure, the fruit of cruelty and rapine: but this useful fund was soon and idly dissipated by his successor. On the festival of his birthday Philippicus entertained the multitude with the games of the hippodrome; from thence he paraded through the streets with a thousand banners and a thousand trumpets; refreshed himself in the baths of Zeuxippus, and, returning to the palace, entertained his nobles with a sumptuous banquet. At the meridian hour he withdrew to his chamber, intoxicated with flattery and wine, and forgetful that his example had made every subject ambitious, and that every ambitious subject was his secret enemy. Some bold conspirators introduced themselves in the disorder of the feast; and the slumbering monarch was surprised, bound, blinded, and deposed, before he was sensible of his danger. Yet the traitors were deprived of their reward; and the free voice of the senate and people promoted Artemius from the office of secretary to that of emperor: he assumed the title of Anastasius the Second, and displayed in a short and troubled reign the virtues both of peace and war. But after the extinction of the Imperial line the rule of obedience was violated, and every change diffused the seeds of new revolutions. In a mutiny of the fleet an obscure and reluctant officer of the revenue was forcibly invested with the purple; after some months of a naval war, Anastasius resigned the sceptre; and the conqueror, Theodosius the Third, submitted in his turn to the superior ascendant of Leo, the general and emperor of the Oriental troops. His two predecessors were permitted to embrace the ecclesiastical profession: the restless impatience of Anastasius tempted him to risk and to lose his life in a treasonable enterprise; but the last days of Theodosius were honourable and secure. The single sublime word, " HEALTH," which he inscribed on his tomb, expresses the confidence of philosophy or religion; and the fame of his miracles was long preserved among the people of Ephesus. This convenient shelter of the church might sometimes impose a lesson of clemency; but it may be questioned whether it is for the public interest to diminsh the perils of unsuccessful ambition.

I have dwelt on the fall of a tyrant; I shall briefly represent the founder of a new dynasty,[1] who is known to posterity by the invectives of his enemies, and whose public and private life is involved in the ecclesiastical story of the Iconoclasts.[2] Yet in spite of the clamours of superstition, a favourable prejudice for the character of Leo the Isaurian [3]

[1] [With the reign of Leo III. Mr. Finlay's *History of the Byzantine Empire* commences—a very valuable work.—O. S.]

[2] Genealogy of the Isaurian dynasty:—

LEO III. Imp. *ob.* A.D. 741.

| Irene, d. of the Khan of the Chazars. | = | CONSTANTINUS V. COPRONYMUS, Imp. *ob.* 775. | = | Eudocia. |

| LEO IV. (Chazarus), Imp. *ob.* 780, *m.* Irene, an Athenian. | Nice- phorus. | Christo- phorus. | Nicetas. | Eudoxus. | Anthimus. |

Maria = CONSTANTINUS VI. = Theodata.
Imp. deposed 797, but his mother Irene reigned till 802.

Euphrosyne, *m.* Michael II.   Leo.

—S.

[3] [Though Leo is generally called an Isaurian, he was born at Germanicia, a city of Armenia Minor, in the mountains near the borders of Cappadocia and Syria. The family of Leo was a foreign one, and Finlay in his *Byzantine Empire* observes that he was probably called an Isaurian because the Isaurians appear to have been the subjects of the empire who had retained the greatest share of their original nationality.

A strange circumstance must be noted here, that the dates of forty-seven years in the eighth century from 726-7 to 773-4 are a year wrong. The Anni Mundi and the indictions, as Bury points out (*Later Roman Empire*, vol. ii. 425-7), do not correspond. The professor very cogently concluded from an investigation of the whole circumstances of the case, that Leo III. had packed two indictions into one year of twelve months, for the purpose of raising a double capitation tax, and that nearly fifty years later Constantine V. spread one indiction over two years (A.D. 772-4), so restoring the correspondence between Anni Mundi and Indictions, according to the previous method of computation. This reasoning was confirmed to Prof. Bury by one fact, the eclipse of the sun noticed by Theophanes under A.M. 6252, on Friday,

may be reasonably drawn from the obscurity of his birth and the duration of his reign.—I. In an age of manly spirit the prospect of an Imperial reward would have kindled every energy of the mind, and produced
a crowd of competitors as deserving as they were desirous to reign. Even
in the corruption and debility of the modern Greeks the elevation of a
plebeian from the last to the first rank of society supposes some qualifications above the level of the multitude. He would probably be ignorant and disdainful of speculative science; and, in the pursuit of fortune,
he might absolve himself from the obligations of benevolence and justice;
but to his character we may ascribe the useful virtues of prudence and
fortitude, the knowledge of mankind, and the important art of gaining
their confidence and directing their passions. It is agreed that Leo was
a native of Isauria, and that Conon was his primitive name. The
writers, whose awkward satire is praise, describe him as an itinerant
pedlar, who drove an ass with some paltry merchandise to the country
fairs; and foolishly relate that he met on the road some Jewish fortune-
tellers, who promised him the Roman empire, on condition that he should
abolish the worship of idols. A more probable account relates the
migration of his father from Asia Minor to Thrace, where he exercised
the lucrative trade of a grazier; and he must have acquired considerable
wealth, since the first introduction of his son was procured by a supply
of five hundred sheep to the Imperial camp. His first service was in the
guards of Justinian, where he soon attracted the notice, and by degrees
the jealousy, of the tyrant. His valour and dexterity were conspicuous
in the Colchian war: from Anastasius he received the command of the
Anatolian legions, and by the suffrage of the soldiers he was raised to the
empire with the general applause of the Roman world.—II. In this
dangerous elevation Leo the Third supported himself against the envy
of his equals, the discontent of a powerful faction, and the assaults of his
foreign and domestic enemies. The Catholics, who accuse his religious
innovations, are obliged to confess that they were undertaken with
temper and conducted with firmness. Their silence respects the wisdom
of his administration and the purity of his manners. After a reign of
twenty-four years he peaceably expired in the palace of Constantinople;
and the purple which he had acquired was transmitted by the right of
inheritance to the third generation.[4]

In a long reign of thirty-four years the son and successor of Leo,

August 15, clearly the annular eclipse of A.D. 760 on that day of the month
and week. The received chronology would imply that the eclipse took place
in A.D. 761, August 15, but astronomy assures us that there was no eclipse
on that day, nor was the day Friday.—O. S.]

[4] [During the latter part of the reign of Leo X., the hostilities of the Saracens, who invested a Pergamenian, named Tiberius, with the purple, and
proclaimed him as the son of Justinian, and an earthquake which destroyed
the walls of Constantinople, compelled Leo greatly to increase the burden
of taxation on his subjects. A twelfth was exacted in addition to every aureus
(νόμισμα) as a wall-tax. Cf. Theophanes; Schlosser, *Geschichte der Bilder-
sturmenden Kaiser,* p. 107.—O. S.]

Constantine the Fifth, surnamed Copronymus, attacked with less temperate zeal the images or idols of the church.[5] Their votaries have exhausted the bitterness of religious gall in their portrait of this spotted panther, this antichrist, this flying dragon of the serpent's seed, who surpassed the vices of Elagabalus and Nero. His reign was a long butchery of whatever was most noble, or holy, or innocent, in his empire. In person, the emperor assisted at the execution of his victims, surveyed their agonies, listened to their groans, and indulged, without satiating, his appetite for blood: a plate of noses was accepted as a grateful offering, and his domestics were often scourged or mutilated by the royal hand. His surname was derived from his pollution of his baptismal font. The infant might be excused; but the manly pleasures of Copronymus degraded him below the level of a brute; his lust confounded the eternal distinction of sex and species, and he seemed to extract some unnatural delight from the objects most offensive to human sense. In his religion the Iconoclast was a Heretic, a Jew, a Mohammedan, a Pagan, and an Atheist; and his belief of an invisible power could be discovered only in his magic rites, human victims, and nocturnal sacrifices to Venus and the demons of antiquity. His life was stained with the most opposite vices, and the ulcers which covered his body anticipated before his death the sentiment of hell-tortures. Of these accusations, which I have so patiently copied, a part is refuted by its own absurdity; and in the private anecdotes of the life of princes, the lie is more easy as the detection is more difficult. Without adopting the pernicious maxim, that, where much is alleged, something must be true, I can however discern that Constantine the Fifth was dissolute and cruel. Calumny is more prone to exaggerate than to invent; and her licentious tongue is checked in some measure by the experience of the age and country to which she appeals. Of the bishops and monks, the generals and magistrates, who are said to have suffered under his reign, the numbers are recorded, the names were conspicuous, the execution was public, the mutilation visible and permanent.[6]

---

[5] [Gibbon has omitted to mention that on the death of Leo III. Constantine's succession was contested by his brother-in-law, Artavasdus, Count of the Opsikian Theme who had married Leo's daughter Anna. Artavasdus defeated Constantine, was proclaimed emperor, and associated with him in the empire his eldest son Nicephorus. For nearly two years Constantinople was lost to Constantine (741-3), but in the last-named year Constantinople was taken by the troops of Constantine, and both Artavasdus and his son were put to death. There are coins extant bearing the impression both of Artavasdus and Nicephorus.—O. S.]

[6] [Constantine V. is accused of burning the library of Constantinople, founded by Julian, but one really cannot credit ninety per cent. of the lies which the monks fabricated against the man who strove to stamp out image-worship among them, and punished the clergy for their superstition. He had many faults, but he was manly and courageous, and he showed himself determined not to be led blindly by priestly advisers. He recovered Germanicia, Melitene, and Theodosiopolis from the Saracens, crushed an expedition sent by the caliph to besiege Cyprus in 746, exhausted the Bulgarian kingdom by a

The Catholics hated the person and government of Copronymus; but even their hatred is a proof of their oppression. They dissembled the provocations which might excuse or justify his rigour, but even these provocations must gradually inflame his resentment and harden his temper in the use or the abuse of his despotism. Yet the character of the fifth Constantine was not devoid of merit, nor did his government always deserve the curses or the contempt of the Greeks. From the confession of his enemies I am informed of the restoration of an ancient aqueduct, of the redemption of two thousand five hundred captives, of the uncommon plenty of the times, and of the new colonies with which he repeopled Constantinople and the Thracian cities. They reluctantly praise his activity and courage; he was on horseback in the field at the head of his legions; and, although the fortune of his arms was various, he triumphed by sea and land, on the Euphrates and the Danube, in civil and barbarian war. Heretical praise must be cast into the scale to counterbalance the weight of orthodox invective. The Iconoclasts revered the virtues of the prince: forty years after his death they still prayed before the tomb of the saint. A miraculous vision was propagated by fanaticism or fraud: and the Christian hero appeared on a milk-white steed, brandishing his lance against the pagans of Bulgaria: "An absurd fable," says the Catholic historian, "since Copronymus is chained with the demons in the abyss of hell."

Leo the Fourth, the son of the fifth and the father of the sixth Constantine, was of a feeble constitution both of mind and body, and the principal care of his reign was the settlement of the succession. The association of the young Constantine was urged by the officious zeal of his subjects; and the emperor, conscious of his decay, complied, after a prudent hesitation, with their unanimous wishes. The royal infant, at the age of five years, was crowned with his mother Irene; and the national consent was ratified by every circumstance of pomp and solemnity that could dazzle the eyes or bind the conscience of the Greeks. An oath of fidelity was administered in the palace, the church, and the hippodrome, to the several orders of the state, who adjured the holy names of the son and mother of God. "Be witness, O Christ! that we will watch over the safety of Constantine the son of Leo, expose our lives in his service, and bear true allegiance to his person and posterity." They pledged their faith on the wood of the true cross, and the act of their engagement was deposited on the altar of St. Sophia. The first to swear, and the first to violate their oath, were the five sons of Copronymus by a second marriage; and the story of these princes is singular and tragic. The right of primogeniture excluded them from the throne; the injustice of their elder brother defrauded them of a legacy of about two millions sterling; some vain titles were not deemed a sufficient compensation for wealth and power; and they repeatedly

series of campaigns, and showed himself the consistent enemy of all that savoured of superstition.—O. S.]

conspired against their nephew, before and after the death of his father. Their first attempt was pardoned; for the second offence they were condemned to the ecclesiastical state; and for the third treason, Nicephorus, the eldest and most guilty, was deprived of his eyes, and his four brothers, Christopher, Nicetas, Anthimus, and Eudoxus, were punished, as a milder sentence, by the amputation of their tongues. After five years' confinement they escaped to the church of St. Sophia, and displayed a pathetic spectacle to the people. " Countrymen and Christians," cried Nicephorus for himself and his mute brethren, " behold the sons of your emperor, if you can still recognise our features in this miserable state. A life, an imperfect life, is all that the malice of our enemies has spared. It is now threatened, and we now throw ourselves on your compassion." The rising murmur might have produced a revolution had it not been checked by the presence of a minister, who soothed the unhappy princes with flattery and hope, and gently drew them from the sanctuary to the palace. They were speedily embarked for Greece, and Athens was allotted for the place of their exile. In this calm retreat, and in their helpless condition, Nicephorus and his brothers were tormented by the thirst of power, and tempted by a Sclavonian chief, who offered to break their prison and to lead them in arms, and in the purple, to the gates of Constantinople. But the Athenian people, ever zealous in the cause of Irene, prevented her justice or cruelty; and the five sons of Copronymus were plunged in eternal darkness and oblivion.

For himself, that emperor had chosen a barbarian wife, the daughter of the khan of the Chozars; but in the marriage of his heir he preferred an Athenian virgin, an orphan seventeen years old, whose sole fortune must have consisted in her personal accomplishments. The nuptials of Leo and Irene were celebrated with royal pomp; she soon acquired the love and confidence of a feeble husband, and in his testament he declared the empress guardian of the Roman world, and of their son Constantine the Sixth, who was no more than ten years of age. During his childhood, Irene most ably and assiduously discharged, in her public administration, the duties of a faithful mother; and her zeal in the restoration of images has deserved the name and honours of a saint, which she still occupies in the Greek calendar. But the emperor attained the maturity of youth; the maternal yoke became more grievous; and he listened to the favourites of his own age, who shared his pleasures, and were ambitious of sharing his power. Their reasons convinced him of his right, their praises of his ability, to reign; and he consented to reward the services of Irene by a perpetual banishment to the isle of Sicily. But her vigilance and penetration easily disconcerted their rash projects: a similar, or more severe, punishment was retaliated on themselves and their advisers; and Irene inflicted on the ungrateful prince the chastisement of a boy. After this contest the mother and the son were at the head of two domestic factions; and instead of mild influence and voluntary obedience, she held in chains a captive and an enemy. The empress was overthrown by the abuse of victory; the oath of fidelity, which she exacted to herself alone, was pronounced with reluctant murmurs; and the bold refusal of the Armenian guards encouraged a free and general declaration that Constantine the Sixth was the lawful emperor of the Romans. In this character he ascended his hereditary throne, and dismissed Irene to a life of solitude and repose. But her haughty spirit condescended to the arts of dissimulation: she flattered the bishops and eunuchs, revived the filial tenderness of the prince, regained his confidence, and betrayed his credulity. The character of Constantine was not destitute of sense or spirit; but his education had been studiously neglected; and his ambitious mother exposed to the public censure the vices which she had nourished and the actions which she had secretly advised: his divorce and second marriage offended the prejudices of the clergy, and by his imprudent rigour he forfeited the attachment of the Armenian guards. A powerful conspiracy was formed for the restoration of Irene; and the secret, though widely diffused, was faithfully kept above eight months, till the emperor, suspicious of his danger, escaped from Constantinople with the design of appealing to the provinces and armies. By this hasty flight the empress was left on the brink of the precipice; yet before she implored the mercy of her son, Irene addressed a private epistle to the friends whom she had placed about his person, with a menace, that unless *they* accomplished, *she* would reveal, their treason. Their fear rendered them intrepid; they seized the emperor on the Asiatic shore, and he was transported to the porphyry apartment of the palace, where he had first seen the light. In the mind of Irene ambition had stifled every sentiment of humanity and nature; and it was decreed in her bloody council that Constantine should be rendered incapable of the throne: her emissaries assaulted the sleeping prince, and stabbed their daggers with such violence and precipitation into his eyes as if they meant to execute a mortal sentence. An ambiguous passage of Theophanes persuaded the annalist of the church that death was the immediate consequence of this barbarous execution. The Catholics have been deceived or subdued by the authority of Baronius; and Protestant zeal has re-echoed the words of a cardinal, desirous, as it should seem, to favour the patroness of images. Yet the blind son of Irene survived many years, oppressed by the court and forgotten by the world: the Isaurian dynasty was silently extinguished; and the memory of Constantine was recalled only by the nuptials of his daughter Euphrosyne with the emperor Michael the Second.

The most bigoted orthodoxy has justly execrated the unnatural mother, who may not easily be paralleled in the history of crimes. To her bloody deed superstition has attributed a subsequent darkness of seventeen days, during which many vessels in mid-day were driven from their course, as if the sun, a globe of fire so vast and so remote, could sympathise with the atoms of a revolving planet. On earth, the crime of Irene was left five years unpunished; her reign was crowned with external splendour; and if she could silence the voice of conscience, she neither heard nor regarded the reproaches of mankind. The Roman world bowed to the government of a female; and as she moved through the streets of Constantinople the reins of four milk white steeds were held by as many patricians, who marched on foot before the golden chariot of their queen. But these patricians were for the most part eunuchs; and their black ingratitude justified, on this occasion, the popular hatred and contempt. Raised, enriched, intrusted with the first dignities of the empire, they basely conspired against their benefactress; the great treasurer Nicephorus was secretly invested with the purple; her successor was introduced into the palace, and crowned at St. Sophia by the venal patriarch. In their first interview she recapitulated with dignity the revolutions of her life, gently accused the perfidy of Nicephorus, insinuated that he owed his life to her unsuspicious clemency, and, for the throne and treasures which she resigned, solicited a decent and honourable retreat. His avarice refused this modest compensation; and, in her exile of the isle of Lesbos, the empress earned a scanty subsistence by the labours of her distaff.

Many tyrants have reigned undoubtedly more criminal than Nicephorus, but none perhaps have more deeply incurred the universal abhorrence of their people. His character was stained with the three odious vices of hypocrisy, ingratitude, and avarice: his want of virtue was not redeemed by any superior talents, nor his want of talents by any pleasing qualifications. Unskilful and unfortunate in war, Nicephorus was vanquished by the Saracens and slain by the Bulgarians; and the advantage of his death overbalanced, in the public opinion, the destruction of a Roman army. His son and heir Stauracius escaped from the field with a mortal wound; yet six months of an expiring life were sufficient to refute his indecent, though popular declaration, that he would in all things avoid the example of his father. On the near prospect of his decease, Michael, the great master of the palace, and the husband of his sister Procopia, was named by every person of the palace and city, except by his envious brother. Tenacious of a sceptre now falling from his hand, he conspired against the life of his successor, and cherished the idea of changing to a democracy the Roman empire. But these rash projects served only to inflame the zeal of the people and to remove the scruples of the candidate: Michael the First accepted the purple, and before he sunk into the grave the son of Nicephorus implored the clemency of his new sovereign. Had Michael in an age of peace ascended an hereditary throne, he might have reigned and died the father of his people: but his mild virtues were adapted to the shade of private life, nor was he capable of controlling the ambition of his equals, or of resisting the arms of the victorious

Bulgarians. While his want of ability and success exposed him to the contempt of the soldiers, the masculine spirit of his wife Procopia awakened their indignation. Even the Greeks of the ninth century were provoked by the insolence of a female who, in the front of the standards, presumed to direct their discipline and animate their valour; and their licentious clamours advised the new Semiramis to reverence the majesty of a Roman camp. After an unsuccessful campaign the emperor left, in their winter quarters of Thrace, a disaffected army under the command of his enemies; and their artful eloquence persuaded the soldiers to break the dominion of the eunuchs, to degrade the husband of Procopia, and to assert the right of a military election. They marched towards the capital: yet the clergy, the senate, and the people of Constantinople adhered to the cause of Michael; and the troops and treasures of Asia might have protracted the mischiefs of civil war. But his humanity (by the ambitious it will be termed his weakness) protested that not a drop of Christian blood should be shed in his quarrel, and his messengers presented the conquerors with the keys of the city and the palace. They were disarmed by his innocence and submission; his life and his eyes were spared; and the Imperial monk enjoyed the comforts of solitude and religion above thirty-two years after he had been stripped of the purple and separated from his wife.

A rebel, in the time of Nicephorus, the famous and unfortunate Bardanes, had once the curiosity to consult an Asiastic prophet, who, after prognosticating his fall, announced the fortunes of his three principal officers, Leo the Armenian, Michael the Phrygian, and Thomas the Cappadocian, the successive reigns of the two former, the fruitless and fatal enterprise of the third. This prediction was verified, or rather was produced, by the event. Ten years afterwards, when the Thracian camp rejected the husband of Procopia, the crown was presented to the same Leo, the first in military rank and the secret author of the mutiny. As he affected to hesitate, " With this sword," said his companion Michael, " I will open the gates of Constantinople to your Imperial sway, or instantly plunge it into your bosom, if you obstinately resist the just desires of your fellow-soldiers." The compliance of the Armenian was rewarded with the empire, and he reigned seven years and a half under the name of Leo the Fifth. Educated in a camp, and ignorant both of laws and letters, he introduced into his civil government the rigour and even cruelty of military discipline; but if his severity was sometimes dangerous to the innocent, it was always formidable to the guilty. His religious inconstancy was taxed by the epithet of Chameleon, but the Catholics have acknowledged, by the voice of a saint and confessors, that the life of the Iconoclast was useful to the republic. The zeal of his companion Michael was repaid with riches, honours, and military command; and his subordinate talents were beneficially employed in the public service. Yet the Phrygian was dissatisfied at receiving as a favour a scanty portion of the

Imperial prize which he had bestowed on his equal; and his discontent, which sometimes evaporated in hasty discourse, at length assumed a more threatening and hostile aspect against a prince whom he represented as a cruel tyrant. That tyrant, however, repeatedly detected, warned, and dismissed the old companion of his arms, till fear and resentment prevailed over gratitude; and Michael, after a scrutiny into his actions and designs, was convicted of treason, and sentenced to be burnt alive in the furnace of the private baths. The devout humanity of the empress Theophano was fatal to her husband and family. A solemn day, the twenty-fifth of December, had been fixed for the execution: she urged that the anniversary of the Saviour's birth would be profaned by this inhuman spectacle, and Leo consented with reluctance to a decent respite. But on the vigil of the feast his sleepless anxiety prompted him to visit at the dead of night the chamber in which his enemy was confined: he beheld him released from his chain, and stretched on his gaoler's bed in a profound slumber: Leo was alarmed at these signs of security and intelligence; but though he retired with silent steps, his entrance and departure were noticed by a slave who lay concealed in a corner of the prison. Under the pretence of requesting the spiritual aid of a confessor, Michael informed the conspirators that their lives depended on his discretion, and that a few hours were left to assure their own safety, by the deliverance of their friend and country. On the great festivals a chosen band of priests and chanters was admitted into the palace by a private gate to sing matins in the chapel; and Leo, who regulated with the same strictness the discipline of the choir and of the camp, was seldom absent from these early devotions. In the ecclesiastical habit, but with swords under their robes, the conspirators mingled with the procession, lurked in the angles of the chapel, and expected, as a signal of murder, the intonation of the first psalm by the emperor himself. The imperfect light and the uniformity of dress, might have favoured his escape, while their assault was pointed against a harmless priest; but they soon discovered their mistake, and encompassed on all sides the royal victim. Without a weapon and without a friend, he grasped a weighty cross, and stood at bay against the hunters of his life; but as he asked for mercy, " This is the hour, not of mercy, but of vengeance," was the inexorable reply. The stroke of a well-aimed sword separated from his body the right arm and the cross, and Leo the Armenian was slain at the foot of the altar.

A memorable reverse of fortune was displayed in Michael the Second, who from a defect in his speech was surnamed the Stammerer. He was snatched from the fiery furnace to the sovereignty of an empire; and as in the tumult a smith could not readily be found, the fetters remained on his legs several hours after he was seated on the throne of the Cæsars. The royal blood which had been the price of his elevation was unprofitably spent; in the purple he retained the ignoble vices of his origin; and Michael lost his provinces with as supine indifference as if they had been the inheritance of his fathers. His title was disputed by Thomas, the last of the military triumvirate, who transported into Europe fourscore thousand barbarians from the banks of the Tigris and the shores of the Caspian.[7] He formed the siege of Constantinople; but the capital was defended with spiritual and carnal weapons; a Bulgarian king assaulted the camp of the Orientals, and Thomas had the misfortune or the weakness to fall alive into the power of the conqueror. The hands and feet of the rebel were amputated; he was placed on an ass, and, amidst the insults of the people, was led through the streets, which he sprinkled with his blood. The depravation of manners, as savage as they were corrupt, is marked by the presence of the emperor himself. Deaf to the lamentations of a fellow-soldier, he incessantly pressed the discovery of more accomplices, till his curiosity was checked by the question of an honest or guilty minister: " Would you give credit to an enemy against the most faithful of your friends? " After the death of his first wife, the emperor, at the request of the senate, drew from her monastery Euphrosyne, the daughter of Constantine the Sixth. Her august birth might justify a stipulation in the marriage-contract that her children should equally share the empire with their elder brother. But the nuptials of Michael and Euphrosyne were barren; and she was content with the title of mother of Theophilus, his son and successor.

The character of Theophilus is a rare example in which religious zeal has allowed and perhaps magnified the virtues of a heretic and a persecutor. His valour was often felt by the enemies, and his justice by the subjects, of the monarchy; but the valour of Theophilus was rash and fruitless, and his justice arbitrary and cruel. He displayed the banner of the cross against the Saracens; but his five expeditions were concluded by a signal overthrow: Amorium, the native city of his ancestors, was levelled with the ground, and from his military toils he derived only the surname of the Unfortunate. The wisdom of a sovereign is comprised in the institution of laws and the choice of magistrates, and, while he seems without action, his civil government revolves round his centre with the silence and order of the planetary system. But the justice of Theophilus was fashioned on the model of the Oriental despots, who, in personal and irregular acts of authority, consult the reason or passion of the moment, without measuring the sentence by the law, or the penalty by the offence.[8] A poor woman

[7] [Finlay in his *Byzantine Empire,* speaking of the foreign origin of Thomas the Cappadocian, or Thomas the Slavonian—for he has both titles: " His origin, by separating him in an unusual degree from the ruling classes in the empire—for he was like Michael the Second, of a very low rank in society— caused him to be regarded as a friend of the people, and all the subject races in the empire espoused his cause."—O. S.]

[8] [Finlay remarks that Gibbon has exaggerated the cruelty of the punishments inflicted by Theophilus, and Schlosser states that he has found no authority to justify the charge of excessive tyranny. But Bury thinks that

threw herself at the emperor's feet to complain of a powerful neighbour, the brother of the empress, who had raised his palace-wall to such an inconvenient height, that her humble dwelling was excluded from light and air! On the proof of the fact, instead of granting, like an ordinary judge, sufficient or ample damages to the plaintiff, the sovereign adjudged to her use and benefit the palace and the ground. Nor was Theophilus content with this extravagant satisfaction: his zeal converted a civil trespass into a criminal act; and the unfortunate patrician was stripped and scourged in the public place of Constantinople. For some venial offences, some defect of equity or vigilance, the principal ministers, a præfect, a quæstor, a captain of the guards, were banished or mutilated, or scalded with boiling pitch, or burnt alive in the hippodrome; and as these dreadful examples might be the effects of error or caprice, they must have alienated from his service the best and wisest of the citizens. But the pride of the monarch was flattered in the exercise of power, or, as he thought, of virtue; and the people, safe in their obscurity, applauded the danger and debasement of their superiors. This extraordinary rigour was justified in some measure by its salutary consequences; since, after a scrutiny of seventeen days, not a complaint or abuse could be found in the court or city: and it might be alleged that the Greeks could be ruled only with a rod of iron, and that the public interest is the motive and law of the supreme judge. Yet in the crime, or the suspicion, of treason, that judge is of all others the most credulous and partial. Theophilus might inflict a tardy vengeance on the assassins of Leo and the saviours of his father; but he enjoyed the fruits of their crime; and his jealous tyranny sacrificed a brother and a prince to the future safety of his life. A Persian of the race of the Sassanides died in poverty and exile at Constantinople, leaving an only son, the issue of a plebeian marriage. At the age of twelve years the royal birth of Theophobus was revealed; and his merit was not unworthy of his birth. He was educated in the Byzantine palace, a Christian and a soldier; advanced with rapid steps in the career of fortune and glory; received the hand of the emperor's sister; and was promoted to the command of thirty thousand Persians, who, like his father, had fled from the Mohammedan conquerors. These troops, doubly infected with mercenary and fanatic vices, were desirous of revolting against their benefactor, and erecting the standard of their native king: but the loyal Theophobus rejected their offers, disconcerted their schemes, and escaped from their hands to the camp or palace of his royal brother. A generous confidence might have secured a faithful and able guardian for his wife and his infant son, to whom Theophilus, in the flower of his age, was compelled to leave the inheritance of the empire. But his jealousy was exasperated by envy and disease: he feared the dangerous virtues which might either support or

Gelzer's opinion is much nearer the mark, who regards him as an insignificant, much-overrated ruler.—O. S.]

oppress their infancy and weakness; and the dying emperor demanded the head of the Persian prince. With savage delight he recognised the familiar features of his brother: " Thou art no longer Theophobus," he said; and, sinking on his couch, he added, with a faltering voice, " Soon, too soon, I shall be no more Theophilus! "

The Russians, who have borrowed from the Greeks the greatest part of their civil and ecclesiastical policy, preserved, till the last century, a singular institution in the marriage of the Czar. They collected, not the virgins of every rank and of every province, a vain and romantic idea, but the daughters of the principal nobles, who awaited in the palace the choice of their sovereign. It is affirmed that a similar method was adopted in the nuptials of Theophilus. With a golden apple in his hand, he slowly walked between two lines of contending beauties: his eye was detained by the charms of Icasia, and, in the awkwardness of a first declaration, the prince could only observe, that, in this world, women had been the cause of much evil; " And surely, sir," she pertly replied, " they have likewise been the occasion of much good." This affectation of unseasonable wit displeased the Imperial lover: he turned aside in disgust; Icasia concealed her mortification in a convent; and the modest silence of Theodora was rewarded with the golden apple. She deserved the love, but did not escape the severity, of her lord. From the palace garden he beheld a vessel deeply laden, and steering into the port: on the discovery that the precious cargo of Syrian luxury was the property of his wife, he condemned the ship to the flames, with a sharp reproach, that her avarice had degraded the character of an empress into that of a merchant. Yet his last choice intrusted her with the guardianship of the empire and her son Michael, who was left an orphan in the fifth year of his age. The restoration of images, and the final extirpation of the Iconoclasts, has endeared her name to the devotion of the Greeks; but in the fervour of religious zeal Theodora entertained a grateful regard for the memory and salvation of her husband. After thirteen years of a prudent and frugal administration, she perceived the decline of her influence; but the second Irene imitated only the virtues of her predecessor. Instead of conspiring against the life or government of her son, she retired without a struggle, though not without a murmur, to the solitude of private life, deploring the ingratitude, the vices, and the inevitable ruin of the worthless youth.

Among the successors of Nero and Elagabalus we have not hitherto found the imitation of their vices, the character of a Roman prince who considered pleasure as the object of life, and virtue as the enemy of pleasure. Whatever might have been the maternal care of Theodora in the education of Michael the Third, her unfortunate son was a king before he was a man. If the ambitious mother laboured to check the progress of reason, she could not cool the ebullition of passion; and her selfish policy was justly repaid by the contempt and ingratitude of the headstrong youth. At the age of eighteen he rejected her authority, without feeling his own incapacity to govern the empire and himself. With Theodora all gravity and wisdom retired from the court; their place was supplied by the alternate dominion of vice and folly; and it was impossible, without forfeiting the public esteem, to acquire or preserve the favour of the emperor. The millions of gold and silver which had been accumulated for the service of the state were lavished on the vilest of men, who flattered his passions and shared his pleasures; and, in a reign of thirteen years, the richest of sovereigns was compelled to strip the palace and the churches of their precious furniture. Like Nero, he delighted in the amusements of the theatre, and sighed to be surpassed in the accomplishments in which he should have blushed to excel. Yet the studies of Nero in music and poetry betrayed some symptoms of a liberal taste; the more ignoble arts of the son of Theophilus were confined to the chariot-race of the hippodrome. The four factions which had agitated the peace, still amused the idleness, of the capital: for himself, the emperor assumed the blue livery: the three rival colours were distributed to his favourites, and in the vile though eager contention he forgot the dignity of his person and the safety of his dominions. He silenced the messenger of an invasion who presumed to divert his attention in the most critical moment of the race; and by his command the importunate beacons were extinguished that too frequently spread the alarm from Tarsus to Constantinople. The most skilful charioteers obtained the first place in his confidence and esteem; their merit was profusely rewarded; the emperor feasted in their houses, and presented their children at the baptismal font; and while he applauded his own popularity, he affected to blame the cold and stately reserve of his predecessors. The unnatural lusts which had degraded even the manhood of Nero were banished from the world; yet the strength of Michael was consumed by the indulgence of love and intemperance. In his midnight revels, when his passions were inflamed by wine, he was provoked to issue the most sanguinary commands; and if any feelings of humanity were left, he was reduced, with the return of sense, to approve the salutary disobedience of his servants. But the most extraordinary feature in the character of Michael is the profane mockery of the religion of his country. The superstition of the Greeks might indeed excite the smile of a philosopher; but his smile would have been rational and temperate, and he must have condemned the ignorant folly of a youth who insulted the objects of public veneration. A buffoon of the court was invested in the robes of the patriarch: his twelve metropolitans, among whom the emperor was ranked, assumed their ecclesiastical garments: they used or abused the sacred vessels of the altar; and in their bacchanalian feasts the holy communion was administered in a nauseous compound of vinegar and mustard. Nor were these impious spectacles concealed from the eyes of the city. On the day of a solemn festival, the emperor, with his bishops or buffoons, rode on asses through the streets, encountered the true patriarch at the head of his clergy, and, by their licentious shouts and obscene gestures, disordered the gravity of the Christian procession. The devotion of Michael appeared only in some offence to reason or piety: he received his theatrical crowns from the statue of the Virgin; and an Imperial tomb was violated for the sake of burning the bones of Constantine the Iconoclast. By this extravagant conduct the son of Theophilus became as contemptible as he was odious: every citizen was impatient for the deliverance of his country; and even the favourites of the moment were apprehensive that a caprice might snatch away what a caprice had bestowed. In the thirtieth year of his age, and in the hour of intoxication and sleep, Michael the Third was murdered in his chamber by the founder of a new dynasty, whom the emperor had raised to an equality of rank and power.

The genealogy of Basil the Macedonian (if it be not the spurious offspring of pride and flattery) exhibits a genuine picture of the revolution of the most illustrious families. The Arsacides, the rivals of Rome, possessed the sceptre of the East near four hundred years: a younger branch of these Parthian kings continued to reign in Armenia,[9] and their royal descendants survived the partition and servitude of that ancient monarchy. Two of these, Artabanus and Chlienes, escaped or retired to the court of Leo the First: his bounty seated them in a safe and hospitable exile in the province of Macedonia; Adrianople was their final settlement. During several generations they maintained the dignity of their birth; and their Roman patriotism rejected the tempting offers of the Persian and Arabian powers, who recalled them to their native country. But their splendour was insensibly clouded by time and poverty; and the father of Basil was reduced to a small farm, which he cultivated with his own hands: yet he scorned to disgrace the blood of the Arsacides by a plebeian alliance: his wife, a widow of Adrianople, was pleased to count among her ancestors the great Constantine; and their royal infant was connected by some dark affinity of lineage or country with the Macedonian Alexander. No sooner was he born than the cradle of Basil, his family, and his city, were swept away by an inundation of the Bulgarians: he was educated a slave in a foreign land; and in this severe discipline he acquired the hardiness of body and flexibility of mind

---

[9] [The family of Basil I. was not Armenian, and the attempt to connect it with the royal line of Armenia must be entirely rejected (says Dr. W. Smith), adding, "there can be little doubt that Basil was a Slav." On the other hand, Prof. Bury says, "The Armenian descent of Basil is set beyond doubt by a notice in the *Vita Euthymii*, combined with the circumstance that a brother of Basil was called Symbatios. The settlement of Armenian families in Thrace by Constantine V. is attested by Theophanes. Hamza of Ispahan states that Basil was a Slav, but there is no evidence to bear this out."—O. S.]

which promoted his future elevation. In the age of youth or manhood he shared the deliverance of the Roman captives, who generously broke their fetters, marched through Bulgaria to the shores of the Euxine, defeated two armies of barbarians, embarked in the ships which had been stationed for their reception, and returned to Constantinople, from whence they were distributed to their respective homes. But the freedom of Basil was naked and destitute: his farm was ruined by the calamities of war: after his father's death his manual labour or service could no longer support a family of orphans; and he resolved to seek a more conspicuous theatre, in which every virtue and every vice may lead to the paths of greatness. The first night of his arrival at Constantinople, without friends or money, the weary pilgrim slept on the steps of the church of St. Diomede: he was fed by the casual hospitality of a monk; and was introduced to the service of a cousin and namesake of the emperor Theophilus, who, though himself of a diminutive person, was always followed by a train of tall and handsome domestics. Basil attended his patron to the government of Peloponnesus; eclipsed, by his personal merit, the birth and dignity of Theophilus, and formed a useful connection with a wealthy and charitable matron of Patras. Her spiritual or carnal love embraced the young adventurer, whom she adopted as her son. Danielis presented him with thirty slaves; and the produce of her bounty was expended in the support of his brothers, and the purchase of some large estates in Macedonia. His gratitude or ambition still attached him to the service of Theophilus; and a lucky accident recommended him to the notice of the court. A famous wrestler in the train of the Bulgarian ambassadors had defied, at the royal banquet, the boldest and most robust of the Greeks. The strength of Basil was praised; he accepted the challenge; and the barbarian champion was overthrown at the first onset. A beautiful but vicious horse was condemned to be hamstrung: it was subdued by the dexterity and courage of the servant of Theophilus; and his conqueror was promoted to an honourable rank in the Imperial stables. But it was impossible to obtain the confidence of Michael without complying with his vices; and his new favourite, the great chamberlain of the palace, was raised and supported by a disgraceful marriage with a royal concubine, and the dishonour of his sister, who succeeded to her place.[10] The public administration had been abandoned to the Cæsar Bardas, the brother and enemy of Theodora; but the arts of female influence persuaded Michael to hate and to fear his uncle: he was drawn from Constantinople, under the pretence of a Cretan expedition, and stabbed in the tent of audience by the sword of the chamberlain,

[10] [Finlay in his *Byzantine Empire* (vol. i. p. 300) controverts this statement, and shows that Thecla, sister of the emperor Michael, became Basil's concubine, not that Basil's sister became Michael's concubine. The royal concubine's name who married the chamberlain was Eudocia Ingerina, mother of Leo VI. —O. S.]

and in the presence of the emperor. About a month after this execution, Basil was invested with the title of Augustus and the government of the empire. He supported this unequal association till his influence was fortified by popular esteem. His life was endangered by the caprice of the emperor; and his dignity was profaned by a second colleague, who had rowed in the galleys. Yet the murder of his benefactor must be condemned as an act of ingratitude and treason; and the churches which he dedicated to the name of St. Michael were a poor and puerile expiation of his guilt.

The different ages of Basil the First may be compared with those of Augustus. The situation of the Greek did not allow him in his earliest youth to lead an army against his country, or to proscribe the noblest of her sons; but his aspiring genius stooped to the arts of a slave; he dissembled his ambition and even his virtues, and grasped, with the bloody hand of an assassin, the empire which he ruled with the wisdom and tenderness of a parent. A private citizen may feel his interest repugnant to his duty; but it must be from a deficiency of sense or courage that an absolute monarch can separate his happiness from his glory, or his glory from the public welfare. The life or panegyric of Basil has indeed been composed and published under the long reign of his descendants; but even their stability on the throne may be justly ascribed to the superior merit of their ancestor. In his character, his grandson Constantine has attempted to delineate a perfect image of royalty: but that feeble prince, unless he had copied a real model, could not easily have soared so high above the level of his own conduct or conceptions. But the most solid praise of Basil is drawn from the comparison of a ruined and a flourishing monarchy, that which he wrested from the dissolute Michael, and that which he bequeathed to the Macedonian dynasty. The evils which had been sanctified by time and example were corrected by his master-hand; and he revived, if not the national spirit, at least the order and majesty of the Roman empire. His application was indefatigable, his temper cool, his understanding vigorous and decisive; and in his practice he observed that rare and salutary moderation, which pursues each virtue, at an equal distance between the opposite vices. His military service had been confined to the palace; nor was the emperor endowed with the spirit or the talents of a warrior. Yet under his reign the Roman arms were again formidable to the barbarians. As soon as he had formed a new army by discipline and exercise, he appeared in person on the banks of the Euphrates, curbed the pride of the Saracens, and suppressed the dangerous though just revolt of the Manichæans. His indignation against a rebel who had long eluded his pursuit provoked him to wish and to pray that, by the grace of God, he might drive three arrows into the head of Chrysochir. That odious head, which had been obtained by treason rather than by valour, was suspended from ɩ tree, and thrice exposed to the dexterity of the Imperial archer: a base revenge against the dead, more worthy of the times than of the character of Basil. But his principal merit was in the civil administration of the finances and of the laws. To replenish an exhausted treasury it was proposed to resume the lavish and ill-placed gifts of his predecessor: his prudence abated one moiety of the restitution; and a sum of twelve hundred thousand pounds was instantly procured to answer the most pressing demands, and to allow some space for the mature operations of economy. Among the various schemes for the improvement of the revenue, a new mode was suggested of capitation, or tribute, which would have too much depended on the arbitrary discretion of the assessors. A sufficient list of honest and able agents was instantly produced by the minister; but on the more careful scrutiny of Basil himself, only two could be found who might be safely intrusted with such dangerous powers; and they justified his esteem by declining his confidence. But the serious and successful diligence of the emperor established by degrees an equitable balance of property and payment, of receipt and expenditure; a peculiar fund was appropriated to each service; and a public method secured the interest of the prince and the property of the people. After reforming the luxury, he assigned two patrimonial estates to supply the decent plenty, of the Imperial table; the contributions of the subject were reserved for his defence; and the residue was employed in the embellishment of the capital and provinces. A taste for building, however costly, may deserve some praise and much excuse: from thence industry is fed, art is encouraged, and some object is attained of public emolument or pleasure: the use of a road, an aqueduct, or a hospital, is obvious and solid; and the hundred churches that arose by the command of Basil were consecrated to the devotion of the age. In the character of a judge he was assiduous and impartial, desirous to save, but not afraid to strike: the oppressors of the people were severely chastised; but his personal foes, whom it might be unsafe to pardon, were condemned, after the loss of their eyes, to a life of solitude and repentance. The change of language and manners demanded a revision of the obsolete jurisprudence of Justinian: the voluminous body of his Institutes, Pandects, Code, and Novels was digested under forty titles, in the Greek idiom; and the *Basilics,* which were improved and completed by his son and grandson, must be referred to the original genius of the founder of their race. This glorious reign was terminated by an accident in the chase. A furious stag entangled his horns in the belt of Basil, and raised him from his horse: he was rescued by an attendant, who cut the belt and slew the animal; but the fall, or the fever, exhausted the strength of the aged monarch, and he expired in the palace amidst the tears of his family and people. If he struck off the head of the faithful servant for presuming to draw his sword against his sovereign, the pride of despotism, which had lain dormant in his life, revived in the last moments of despair, when he no longer wanted or valued the opinion of mankind.[11]

Of the four sons of the emperor, Constantine died before his father, whose grief and credulity were amused by a flattering impostor and a vain apparition. Stephen, the youngest, was content with the honours of a patriarch and a saint; both Leo and Alexander were alike invested with the purple, but the powers of government were solely exercised by the elder brother. The name of Leo the Sixth has been dignified with the title of *philosopher;* [12] and the union of the prince and the sage, of

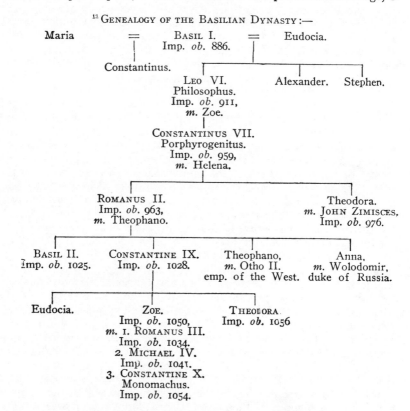

[12] Genealogy of the Basilian Dynasty:—

Maria == Basil I. Imp. *ob.* 886. == Eudocia.

Constantinus.

Leo VI. Philosophus. Imp. *ob.* 911, *m.* Zoe.

Alexander. Stephen.

Constantinus VII. Porphyrogenitus. Imp. *ob.* 959, *m.* Helena.

Romanus II. Imp. *ob.* 963, *m.* Theophano.

Theodora. *m.* John Zimisces, Imp. *ob.* 976.

Basil II. Imp. *ob.* 1025.

Constantine IX. Imp. *ob.* 1028.

Theophano, *m.* Otho II. emp. of the West.

Anna, *m.* Wolodomir, duke of Russia.

Eudocia.

Zoe. Imp. *ob.* 1050, *m.* 1. Romanus III. Imp. *ob.* 1034. 2. Michael IV. Imp. *ob.* 1041. 3. Constantine X. Monomachus. Imp. *ob.* 1054.

Theodora Imp. *ob.* 1056

[12] [Leo VI., "the Philosopher" (A.D. 886-912), typifies the idle spirit of conservatism as correctly as Constantine VI. does the aggressive energy of progress. He was a man of learning, a lover of luxurious ease, a conceited pedant, and an arbitrary but mild despot. Naturally of a confined intellect, he owes his title of "the Philosopher," or "the Learned," rather to the ignorance of the people, who attributed to him an acquaintance with the secrets of astrological science, than either to his own attainments or to any remarkable patronage he bestowed on learned men. Leo's works consist of some poetical oracles and hymns, and a treatise on military tactics. Leo

the active and speculative virtues, would indeed constitute the perfection of human nature. But the claims of Leo are far short of this ideal excellence. Did he reduce his passions and appetites under the dominion of reason? His life was spent in the pomp of the palace, in the society of his wives and concubines; and even the clemency which he showed, and the peace which he strove to preserve, must be imputed to the softness and indolence of his character. Did he subdue his prejudices, and those of his subjects? His mind was tinged with the most puerile superstition; the influence of the clergy and the errors of the people were consecrated by his laws; and the oracles of Leo, which reveal, in prophetic style, the fates of the empire, are founded on the arts of astrology and divination. If we still inquire the reason of his sage appellation, it can only be replied, that the son of Basil was less ignorant than the greater part of his contemporaries in church and state; that his education had been directed by the learned Photius; and that several books of profane and ecclesiastical science were composed by the pen, or in the name, of the Imperial *philosopher*. But the reputation of his philosophy and religion was overthrown by a domestic vice, the repetition of his nuptials. The primitive ideas of the merit and holiness of celibacy were preached by the monks and entertained by the Greeks. Marriage was allowed as a necessary means for the propagation of mankind; after the death of either party the survivor might satisfy by a *second* union the weakness or the strength of the flesh; but a *third* marriage was censured as a state of legal fornication; and a *fourth* was a sin or scandal as yet unknown to the Christians of the East. In the beginning of his reign Leo himself had abolished the state of concubines, and condemned, without annulling, third marriages: but his patriotism and love soon compelled him to violate his own laws, and to incur the penance which in a similar case he had imposed on his subjects. In his three first alliances his nuptial bed was unfruitful; the emperor required a female companion, and the empire a legitimate heir. The beautiful Zoe was introduced into the palace as a concubine; and after a trial of her fecundity, and the birth of Constantine, her lover declared his intention of legitimating the mother and the child by the celebration of his fourth nuptials. But the patriarch Nicholas refused his blessing; the Imperial baptism of the young prince was obtained by a promise of separation; and the contumacious husband of Zoe was excluded from the communion of the faithful. Neither the fear of exile, nor the desertion of his brethren, nor the authority of the Latin church, nor the danger of failure or doubt in the succession to the empire, could bend the spirit of the inflexible monk. After the death of Leo he was recalled from exile

married four times: (1) Theophano, who died 892; (2) Zoe, who died 896; (3) Eudocia Baiane, who died 900; (4) Zoe Carbonupsina. Nicolaus the Mystic, patriarch of Constantinople, refused to celebrate the fourth marriage, and was banished in February 907, being succeeded by Euthymius, who complied with the emperor's wishes.—O. S.]

to the civil and ecclesiastical administration; and the edict of union which was promulgated in the name of Constantine condemned the future scandal of fourth marriages, and left a tacit imputation on his own birth.

In the Greek language *purple* and *porphyry* are the same word: and as the colours of nature are invariable, we may learn that a dark deep red was the Tyrian dye which stained the purple of the ancients. An apartment of the Byzantine palace was lined with porphyry: it was reserved for the use of the pregnant empresses; and the royal birth of their children was expressed by the appellation of *porphyrogenite,* or born in the purple. Several of the Roman princes had been blessed with an heir; but this peculiar surname was first applied to Constantine the Seventh. His life and titular reign were of equal duration: but of fifty-four years six had elapsed before his father's death; and the son of Leo was ever the voluntary or reluctant subject of those who oppressed his weakness or abused his confidence. His uncle Alexander, who had long been invested with the title of Augustus, was the first colleague and governor of the young prince: but in a rapid career of vice and folly the brother of Leo already emulated the reputation of Michael; and when he was extinguished by a timely death, he entertained a project of castrating his nephew and leaving the empire to a worthless favourite. The succeeding years of the minority of Constantine were occupied by his mother Zoe, and a succession or council of seven regents, who pursued their interest, gratified their passions, abandoned the republic, supplanted each other, and finally vanished in the presence of a soldier. From an obscure origin Romanus Lecapenus had raised himself to the command of the naval armies; and in the anarchy of the times had deserved, or at least had obtained, the national esteem. With a victorious and affectionate fleet he sailed from the mouth of the Danube into the harbour of Constantinople, and was hailed as the deliverer of the people and the guardian of the prince. His supreme office was at first defined by the new appellation of father of the emperor; but Romanus soon disdained the subordinate powers of a minister, and assumed, with the titles of Cæsar and Augustus, the full independence of royalty, which he held near five-and-twenty years. His three sons, Christopher, Stephen, and Constantine, were successively adorned with the same honours, and the lawful emperor was degraded from the first to the fifth rank in this college of princes. Yet, in the preservation of his life and crown, he might still applaud his own fortune and the clemency of the usurper. The examples of ancient and modern history would have excused the ambition of Romanus: the powers and the laws of the empire were in his hand; the spurious birth of Constantine would have justified his exclusion; and the grave or the monastery was open to receive the son of the concubine. But Lecapenus does not appear to have possessed either the virtues or the vices of a tyrant. The spirit and activity of his private life dissolved

away in the sunshine of the throne; and in his licentious pleasures he
forgot the safety both of the republic and of his family. Of a mild and
religious character, he respected the sanctity of oaths, the innocence of
the youth, the memory of his parents, and the attachment of the people.
The studious temper and retirement of Constantine disarmed the
jealousy of power: his books and music, his pen and his pencil, were a
constant source of amusement; and if he could improve a scanty allowance by the sale of his pictures, if their price was not enhanced by the
name of the artist, he was endowed with a personal talent which few
princes could employ in the hour of adversity.

The fall of Romanus was occasioned by his own vices and those of his
children. After the decease of Christopher, his eldest son, the two surviving brothers quarreled with each other, and conspired against their
father. At the hour of noon, when all strangers were regularly excluded
from the palace, they entered his apartment with an armed force, and
conveyed him, in the habit of a monk, to a small island in the Propontis,
which was peopled by a religious community. The rumour of this
domestic revolution excited a tumult in the city; but Porphyrogenitus
alone, the true and lawful emperor, was the object of the public care;
and the sons of Lecapenus were taught, by tardy experience, that they
had achieved a guilty and perilous enterprise for the benefit of their
rival. Their sister Helena, the wife of Constantine, revealed, or supposed,
their treacherous design of assassinating her husband at the royal banquet. His loyal adherents were alarmed, and the two usurpers were
prevented, seized, degraded from the purple, and embarked for the same
island and monastery where their father had been so lately confined.
Old Romanus met them on the beach with a sarcastic smile, and, after
a just reproach of their folly and ingratitude, presented his Imperial
colleagues with an equal share of his water and vegetable diet. In the
fortieth year of his reign Constantine the Seventh obtained the possession of the Eastern world, which he ruled, or seemed to rule, near fifteen
years. But he was devoid of that energy of character which could
emerge into a life of action and glory; and the studies which had amused
and dignified his leisure were incompatible with the serious duties of a
sovereign. The emperor neglected the practice, to instruct his son Romanus in the theory, of government: while he indulged the habits of
intemperance and sloth, he dropped the reins of the administration into
the hands of Helena his wife; and, in the shifting scene of her favour
and caprice, each minister was regretted in the promotion of a more
worthless successor. Yet the birth and misfortunes of Constantine had
endeared him to the Greeks; they excused his failings; they respected
his learning, his innocence and charity, his love of justice; and the
ceremony of his funeral was mourned with the unfeigned tears of his
subjects. The body, according to ancient custom, lay in state in the
vestibule of the palace; and the civil and military officers, the patricians,
the senate, and the clergy approached in due order to adore and kiss

the inanimate corpse of their sovereign. Before the procession moved towards the Imperial sepulchre, a herald proclaimed this awful admonition: " Arise, O king of the world, and obey the summons of the King of kings! "

The death of Constantine was imputed to poison; and his son Romanus, who derived that name from his maternal grandfather, ascended the throne of Constantinople. A prince who, at the age of twenty, could be suspected of anticipating his inheritance, must have been already lost in the public esteem; yet Romanus was rather weak than wicked; and the largest share of the guilt was transferred to his wife, Theophano, a woman of base origin, masculine spirit, and flagitious manners. The sense of personal glory and public happiness, the true pleasures of royalty, were unknown to the son of Constantine; and, while the two brothers, Nicephorus and Leo, triumphed over the Saracens, the hours which the emperor owed to his people were consumed in strenuous idleness. In the morning he visited the circus; at noon he feasted the senators; the greater part of the afternoon he spent in the *sphœristerium*, or tennis-court, the only theatre of his victories; from thence he passed over to the Asiatic side of the Bosphorus, hunted and killed four wild boars of the largest size, and returned to the palace, proudly content with the labours of the day. In strength and beauty he was conspicuous above his equals: tall and straight as a young cypress, his complexion was fair and florid, his eyes sparkling, his shoulders broad, his nose long and aquiline. Yet even these perfections were insufficient to fix the love of Theophano; and, after a reign of four years, she mingled for her husband the same deadly draught which she had composed for his father.

By his marriage with this impious woman Romanus the younger left two sons, Basil the Second and Constantine the Ninth, and two daughters, Theophano and Anne. The eldest sister was given to Otho the Second, emperor of the West; the younger became the wife of Wolodomir, great duke and apostle of Russia; and, by the marriage of her granddaughter with Henry the First, king of France, the blood of the Macedonians, and perhaps of the Arsacides, still flows in the veins of the Bourbon line. After the death of her husband the empress aspired to reign in the name of her sons, the elder of whom was five, and the younger only two years of age; but she soon felt the instability of a throne which was supported by a female who could not be esteemed, and two infants who could not be feared. Theophano looked around for a protector, and threw herself into the arms of the bravest soldier; her heart was capacious; but the deformity of the new favourite rendered it more than probable that interest was the motive and excuse of her love. Nicephorus Phocas united, in the popular opinion, the double merit of a hero and a saint. In the former character his qualifications were genuine and splendid: the descendant of a race illustrious by their military exploits, he had displayed in every station and in every province the courage of a soldier and the conduct of a chief; and Nicephorus was crowned with recent laurels from the important conquest of the isle of Crete. His religion was of a more ambiguous cast; and his hair-cloth, his fasts, his pious idiom, and his wish to retire from the business of the world, were a convenient mask for his dark and dangerous ambition. Yet he imposed on a holy patriarch, by whose influence, and by a decree of the senate, he was intrusted, during the minority of the young princes, with the absolute and independent command of the Oriental armies. As soon as he had secured the leaders and the troops he boldly marched to Constantinople, trampled on his enemies, avowed his correspondence with the empress, and, without degrading her sons, assumed, with the title of Augustus, the pre-eminence of rank and the plenitude of power. But his marriage with Theophano was refused by the same patriarch who had placed the crown on his head: by his second nuptials he incurred a year of canonical penance; a bar of spiritual affinity was opposed to their celebration; and some evasion and perjury were required to silence the scruples of the clergy and people. The popularity of the emperor was lost in the purple: in a reign of six years he provoked the hatred of strangers and subjects, and the hypocrisy and avarice of the first Nicephorus were revived in his successor. Hypocrisy I shall never justify or palliate; but I will dare to observe that the odious vice of avarice is of all others most hastily arraigned, and most unmercifully condemned. In a private citizen our judgment seldom expects an accurate scrutiny into his fortune and expense; and in a steward of the public treasure frugality is always a virtue, and the increase of taxes too often an indispensable duty. In the use of his patrimony the generous temper of Nicephorus had been proved; and the revenue was strictly applied to the service of the state: each spring the emperor marched in person against the Saracens; and every Roman might compute the employment of his taxes in triumphs, conquests, and the security of the Eastern barrier.

Among the warriors who promoted his elevation and served under his standard, a noble and valiant Armenian had deserved and obtained the most eminent rewards. The stature of John Zimisces was below the ordinary standard; but this diminutive body was endowed with strength, beauty, and the soul of a hero. By the jealousy of the emperor's brother he was degraded from the office of general of the East to that of director of the posts, and his murmurs were chastised with disgrace and exile. But Zimisces was ranked among the numerous lovers of the empress: on her intercession he was permitted to reside at Chalcedon, in the neighbourhood of the capital: her bounty was repaid in his clandestine and amorous visits to the palace; and Theophano consented with alacrity to the death of an ugly and penurious husband. Some bold and trusty conspirators were concealed in her most private chambers: in the darkness of a winter night, Zimisces, with his principal companions, embarked in a small boat, traversed the Bosphorus, landed at the palace stairs, and silently ascended a ladder of ropes, which was cast down by the female attendants. Neither his own suspicions, nor the warnings of his friends, nor the tardy aid of his brother Leo, nor the fortress which he had erected in the palace, could protect Nicephorus from a domestic foe, at whose voice every door was opened to the assassins. As he slept on a bear-skin on the ground, he was roused by their noisy intrusion, and thirty daggers glittered before his eyes. It is doubtful whether Zimisces imbrued his hands in the blood of his sovereign; but he enjoyed the inhuman spectacle of revenge. The murder was protracted by insult and cruelty; and as soon as the head of Nicephorus was shown from the window, the tumult was hushed, and the Armenian was emperor of the East. On the day of his coronation he was stopped on the threshold of St. Sophia by the intrepid patriarch, who charged his conscience with the deed of treason and blood, and required, as a sign of repentance, that he should separate himself from his more criminal associate. This sally of apostolic zeal was not offensive to the prince, since he could neither love nor trust a woman who had repeatedly violated the most sacred obligations; and Theophano, instead of sharing his Imperial fortune, was dismissed with ignominy from his bed and palace. In their last interview she displayed a frantic and impotent rage, accused the ingratitude of her lover, assaulted, with words and blows, her son Basil, as he stood silent and submissive in the presence of a superior colleague, and avowed her own prostitution in proclaiming the illegitimacy of his birth. The public indignation was appeased by her exile and the punishment of the meaner accomplices: the death of an unpopular prince was forgiven; and the guilt of Zimisces was forgotten in the splendour of his virtues. Perhaps his profusion was less useful to the state than the avarice of Nicephorus; but his gentle and generous behaviour delighted all who approached his person; and it was only in the paths of victory that he trod in the footsteps of his predecessor. The greatest part of his reign was employed in the camp and the field: his personal valour and activity were signalised on the Danube and the Tigris, the ancient boundaries of the Roman world; and by his double triumph over the Russians and the Saracens he deserved the titles of saviour of the empire and conqueror of the East. In his last return from Syria he observed that the most fruitful lands of his new provinces were possessed by the eunuchs. "And is it for them," he exclaimed, with honest indignation, "that we have fought and conquered? Is it for them that we shed our blood and exhaust the treasures of our people?" The complaint was re-echoed to the palace, and the death of Zimisces is strongly marked with the suspicion of poison.

Under this usurpation, or regency, of twelve years, the two lawful emperors, Basil and Constantine, had silently grown to the age of manhood. Their tender years had been incapable of dominion: the respectful modesty of their attendance and salutation was due to the age and merit of their guardians: the childless ambition of those guardians had no temptation to violate their right of succession: their patrimony was ably and faithfully administered; and the premature death of Zimisces was a loss rather than a benefit to the sons of Romanus. Their want of experience detained them twelve years longer the obscure and voluntary pupils of a minister who extended his reign by persuading them to indulge the pleasures of youth, and to disdain the labours of government. In this silken web the weakness of Constantine was for ever entangled; but his elder brother felt the impulse of genius and the desire of action; he frowned, and the minister was no more. Basil was the acknowledged sovereign of Constantinople and the provinces of Europe; but Asia was oppressed by two veteran generals, Phocas and Sclerus, who, alternately friends and enemies, subjects and rebels, maintained their independence, and laboured to emulate the example of successful usurpation. Against these domestic enemies the son of Romanus first drew his sword, and they trembled in the presence of a lawful and high-spirited prince. The first, in the front of battle, was thrown from his horse by the stroke of poison or an arrow; the second, who had been twice loaded with chains, and twice invested with the purple, was desirous of ending in peace the small remainder of his days. As the aged suppliant approached the throne, with dim eyes and faltering steps, leaning on his two attendants, the emperor exclaimed, in the insolence of youth and power, " And is this the man who has so long been the object of our terror? " After he had confirmed his own authority and the peace of the empire, the trophies of Nicephorus and Zimisces would not suffer their royal pupil to sleep in the palace. His long and frequent expeditions against the Saracens were rather glorious than useful to the empire; but the final destruction of the kingdom of Bulgaria appears, since the time of Belisarius, the most important triumph of the Roman arms. Yet, instead of applauding their victorious prince, his subjects detested the rapacious and rigid avarice of Basil; and, in the imperfect narrative of his exploits, we can only discern the courage, patience, and ferociousness of a soldier. A vicious education, which could not subdue his spirit, had clouded his mind; he was ignorant of every science; and the remembrance of his learned and feeble grandsire might encourage his real or affected contempt of laws and lawyers, of artists and arts. Of such a character, in such an age, superstition took a firm and lasting possession: after the first licence of his youth, Basil the Second devoted his life, in the palace and the camp, to the penance of a hermit, wore the monastic habit under his robes and armour, observed a vow of continence, and imposed on his appetites a perpetual abstinence from wine and flesh. In the sixty-eighth year of his age his martial spirit urged him to embark in person for a holy war against the Saracens of Sicily; he was prevented by death, and Basil, surnamed the Slayer of the Bulgarians, was dismissed from the world with the blessings of the clergy and the curses of the people. After his decease, his brother Constantine enjoyed about three years the power or rather the pleasures of royalty; and his only care was the settlement of the succession. He had enjoyed sixty-six years the title of Augustus; and the reign of the two brothers is the longest and most obscure of the Byzantine history.

A lineal succession of five emperors, in a period of one hundred and sixty years, had attached the loyalty of the Greeks to the Macedonian dynasty, which had been thrice respected by the usurpers of their power. After the death of Constantine the Ninth, the last male of the royal race, a new and broken scene presents itself, and the accumulated years of twelve emperors do not equal the space of his single reign. His elder brother had preferred his private chastity to the public interest, and Constantine himself had only three daughters—Eudocia, who took the veil, and Zoe and Theodora, who were preserved till a mature age in a state of ignorance and virginity. When their marriage was discussed in the council of their dying father, the cold or pious Theodora refused to give an heir to the empire, but her sister Zoe presented herself a willing victim at the altar. Romanus Argyrus, a patrician of a graceful person and fair reputation, was chosen for her husband, and, on his declining that honour, was informed that blindness or death was the second alternative. The motive of his reluctance was conjugal affection, but his faithful wife sacrificed her own happiness to his safety and greatness, and her entrance into a monastery removed the only bar to the Imperial nuptials. After the decease of Constantine the sceptre devolved to Romanus the Third; but his labours at home and abroad were equally feeble and fruitless; and the mature age, the forty-eight years of Zoe, were less favourable to the hopes of pregnancy than to the indulgence of pleasure. Her favourite chamberlain was a handsome Paphlagonian of the name of Michael, whose first trade had been that of a money-changer; and Romanus, either from gratitude or equity, connived at their criminal intercourse, or accepted a slight assurance of their innocence. But Zoe soon justified the Roman maxim, that every adulteress is capable of poisoning her husband; and the death of Romanus was instantly followed by the scandalous marriage and elevation of Michael the Fourth. The expectations of Zoe were, however, disappointed: instead of a vigorous and grateful lover, she had placed in her bed a miserable wretch, whose health and reason were impaired by epileptic fits, and whose conscience was tormented by despair and remorse. The most skilful physicians of the mind and body were summoned to his aid; and his hopes were amused by frequent pilgrimages to the baths, and to the tombs of the most popular saints; the monks applauded his penance, and, except restitution (but to whom should he have restored?), Michael sought every method of expiating his guilt. While he groaned and prayed in sackcloth and ashes, his brother, the eunuch John, smiled at his remorse, and enjoyed the harvest of a crime of which himself was the secret and most guilty author. His administration was only the art of satiating his avarice, and Zoe became a captive in the palace of her fathers and in the hands of her slaves. When he perceived the irretrievable decline of his brother's health, he introduced his nephew, another Michael, who derived his surname of Calaphates from his father's occupation in the careening of vessels: at the command of the eunuch, Zoe adopted for her son the son of a mechanic; and this fictitious heir was invested with the title and purple of the Cæsars in the presence of the senate and clergy. So feeble was the character of Zoe, that she was oppressed by the liberty and power which she recovered by the death of the Paphlagonian; and at the end of four days she placed the crown on the head of Michael the Fifth, who had protested with tears and oaths that he should ever reign the first and most obedient of her subjects. The only act of his short reign was his base ingratitude to his benefactors, the eunuch and the empress. The disgrace of the former was pleasing to the public; but the murmurs, and at length the clamours, of Constantinople deplored the exile of Zoe, the daughter of so many emperors; her vices were forgotten, and Michael was taught that there is a period in which the patience of the tamest slaves rises into fury and revenge. The citizens of every degree assembled in a formidable tumult which lasted three days; they besieged the palace, forced the gates, recalled their *mothers,* Zoe from her prison, Theodora from her monastery, and condemned the son of Calaphates to the loss of his eyes or of his life. For the first time the Greeks beheld with surprise the two royal sisters seated on the same throne, presiding in the senate, and giving audience to the ambassadors of the nations. But this singular union subsisted no more than two months; the two sovereigns, their tempers, interests, and adherents, were secretly hostile to each other; and as Theodora was still averse to marriage, the indefatigable Zoe, at the age of sixty, consented, for the public good, to sustain the embraces of a third husband, and the censures of the Greek church. His name and number were Constantine the Tenth, and the epithet of *Monomachus,* the single combatant, must have been expressive of his valour and victory in some public or private quarrel. But his health was broken by the tortures of the gout, and his dissolute reign was spent in the alternative of sickness and pleasure. A fair and noble widow had accompanied Constantine in his exile to the isle of Lesbos, and Sclerena gloried in the appellation of his mistress. After his marriage and elevation she was invested with the title and pomp of *Augusta,* and occupied a contiguous apartment in the palace. The lawful consort (such was the delicacy or corruption of Zoe) consented to this strange and scandalous partition; and the emperor appeared in public between his wife and his concubine. He survived them both; but the last measures of Constantine to change the order of succession were prevented by the more vigilant friends of Theodora; and afer his decease, she resumed, with the general consent, the possession of her inheritance. In her name, and by the influence of four eunuchs, the Eastern world was peacably governed about nineteen months; and as they wished to prolong their dominion, they persuaded the aged princess to nominate for her successor Michael the Sixth. The surname of *Stratioticus* declares his military profession; but the crazy and decrepit veteran could only see with the eyes, and execute with the hands, of his ministers. Whilst he ascended the throne, Theodora sunk into the grave—the last of the Macedonian or Basilian dynasty. I have hastily reviewed and gladly dismiss this shameful and destructive period of twenty-eight years, in which the Greeks, degraded below the common level of servitude, were transferred like a herd of cattle by the choice or caprice of two impotent females.

From this night of slavery, a ray of freedom, or at least of spirit, begins to emerge: the Greeks either preserved or revived the use of surnames, which perpetuate the fame of hereditary virtue: and we now discern the rise, succession, and alliances of the last dynasties of Constantinople and Trebizond. The *Comneni*, who upheld for a while the fate of the sinking empire, assumed the honour of a Roman origin: but the family had been long since transported from Italy to Asia. Their patrimonial estate was situate in the district of Castamona, in the neighbourhood of the Euxine; and one of their chiefs, who had already entered the paths of ambition, revisited with affection, perhaps with regret, the modest though honourable dwelling of his fathers. The first of their line was the illustrious Manuel, who, in the reign of the second Basil, contributed by war and treaty to appease the troubles of the East: he left in a tender age two sons, Isaac and John, whom, with the consciousness of desert, he bequeathed to the gratitude and favour of his sovereign.[13] The noble youths were carefully trained in the learning of the monastery, the arts of the palace, and the exercises of the camp: and, from the domestic service of the guards, they were rapidly promoted to the command of provinces and armies. Their fraternal union doubled the force and reputation of the Comneni, and their ancient nobility was illustrated by the marriage of the two brothers, with a captive princess of Bulgaria, and the daughter of a patrician who had obtained the name of *Charon* from the number of enemies whom he had sent to the infernal shades. The soldiers had served with reluctant loyalty a series of effeminate masters; the elevation of Michael the Sixth was a personal insult to the more deserving generals; and their discontent was inflamed by the parsimony of the emperor and the insolence of the eunuchs. They secretly assembled in the sanctuary of St. Sophia, and the votes of the military synod would have been unanimous in favour of the old and valiant Catacalon, if the patriotism or modesty of the veteran had not suggested the importance of birth as well as merit in the choice of a sovereign. Isaac Comnenus was approved by general consent, and the associates separated without delay to meet in the plains of Phrygia at the head of their respective squadrons and detachments. The cause of Michael was defended in a single battle by the mercenaries of the imperial guard, who were aliens to the public interest, and animated only by a principle

[13] See table on opposite page.

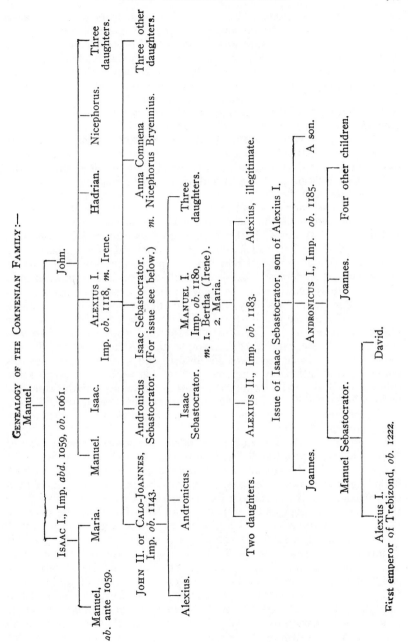

GENEALOGY OF THE COMNENIAN FAMILY :—
Manuel.

of honour and gratitude. After their defeat the fears of the emperor solicited a treaty, which was almost accepted by the moderation of the Comnenian. But the former was betrayed by his ambassadors, and the latter was prevented by his friends. The solitary Michael submitted to the voice of the people; the patriarch annulled their oath of allegiance; and as he shaved the head of the royal monk, congratulated his beneficial exchange of temporal royalty for the kingdom of heaven; an exchange, however, which the priest, on his own account, would probably have declined. By the hands of the same patriarch, Isaac Comnenus was solemnly crowned; the sword which he inscribed on his coins might be an offensive symbol if it implied his title by conquest; but this sword would have been drawn against the foreign and domestic enemies of the state. The decline of his health and vigour suspended the operation of active virtue; and the prospect of approaching death determined him to interpose some moments between life and eternity. But instead of leaving the empire as the marriage portion of his daughter, his reason and inclination concurred in the preference of his brother John, a soldier, a patriot, and the father of five sons, the future pillars of an hereditary succession. His first modest reluctance might be the natural dictates of discretion and tenderness, but his obstinate and successful perseverance, however it may dazzle with the show of virtue, must be censured as a criminal desertion of his duty, and a rare offence against his family and country. The purple which he had refused was accepted by Constantine Ducas, a friend of the Comnenian house, and whose noble birth was adorned with the experience and reputation of civil policy. In the monastic habit Isaac recovered his health, and survived two years his voluntary abdication. At the command of his abbot, he observed the rule of St. Basil, and executed the most servile offices of the convent: but his latent vanity was gratified by the frequent and respectful visits of the reigning monarch, who revered in his person the character of a benefactor and a saint.

If Constantine the Eleventh were indeed the subject most worthy of empire, we must pity the debasement of the age and nation in which he was chosen. In the labour of puerile declamations he sought, without obtaining, the crown of eloquence, more precious in his opinion than that of Rome; and in the subordinate functions of a judge he forgot the duties of a sovereign and a warrior. Far from imitating the patriotic indifference of the authors of his greatness, Ducas was anxious only to secure, at the expense of the republic, the power and prosperity of his children. His three sons, Michael the Seventh, Andronicus the First, and Constantine the Twelfth, were invested in a tender age with the equal title of Augustus; and the successsion was speedily opened by their father's death. His widow, Eudocia, was intrusted with the administration; but experience had taught the jealousy of the dying monarch to protect his sons from the danger of her second nuptials; and her solemn engagement, attested by the principal senators, was deposited in the hands of the patriarch. Before the end of seven months, the wants of Eudocia or those of the state called aloud for the male virtues of a soldier; and her heart had already chosen Romanus Diogenes, whom she raised from the scaffold to the throne. The discovery of a treasonable attempt had exposed him to the severity of the laws: his beauty and valour absolved him in the eyes of the empress; and Romanus, from a mild exile, was recalled on the second day to the command of the Oriental armies. Her royal choice was yet unknown to the public; and the promise which would have betrayed her falsehood and levity was stolen by a dexterous emissary from the ambition of the patriarch. Xiphilin at first alleged the sanctity of oaths and the sacred nature of a trust; but a whisper that his brother was the future emperor relaxed his scruples, and forced him to confess that the public safety was the supreme law. He resigned the important paper; and when his hopes were confounded by the nomination of Romanus, he could no longer regain his security, retract his declarations, nor oppose the second nuptials of the empress. Yet a murmur was heard in the palace; and the barbarian guards had raised their battleaxes in the cause of the house of Ducas, till the young princes were soothed by the tears of their mother and the solemn assurances of the fidelity of their guardian, who filled the imperial station with dignity and honour. Hereafter I shall relate his valiant but unsuccessful efforts to resist the progress of the Turks. His defeat and captivity inflicted a deadly wound on the Byzantine monarchy of the East; and after he was released from the chains of the sultan, he vainly sought his wife and his subjects. His wife had been thrust into a monastery, and the subjects of Romanus had embraced the rigid maxim of the civil law, that a prisoner in the hands of the enemy is deprived, as by the stroke of death, of all the public and private rights of a citizen. In the general consternation the Cæsar John asserted the indefeasible right of his three nephews: Constantinople listened to his voice: and the Turkish captive was proclaimed in the capital, and received on the frontier, as an enemy of the republic. Romanus was not more fortunate in domestic than in foreign war: the loss of two battles compelled him to yield, on the assurance of fair and honourable treatment; but his enemies were devoid of faith or humanity; and, after the cruel extinction of his sight, his wounds were left to bleed and corrupt, till in a few days he was relieved from a state of misery. Under the triple reign of the house of Ducas, the two younger brothers were reduced to the vain honours of the purple; but the eldest, the pusillanimous Michael, was incapable of sustaining the Roman sceptre; and his surname of *Parapinaces* denotes the reproach which he shared with an avaricious favourite, who enhanced the price and diminished the measure of wheat. In the school of Psellus, and after the example of his mother, the son of Eudocia made some proficiency in philosophy and rhetoric; but his character was degraded rather than ennobled by the virtues of a monk and the learning of a sophist. Strong in the contempt

of their sovereign and their own esteem, two generals, at the head of the
European and Asiatic legions, assumed the purple at Adrianople and
Nice. Their revolt was in the same month; they bore the same name of
Nicephorus; but the two candidates were distinguished by the surnames
of Bryennius and Botaniates: the former in the maturity of wisdom and
courage, the latter conspicuous only by the memory of his past exploits.
While Botaniates advanced with cautious and dilatory steps, his active
competitor stood in arms before the gates of Constantinople. The name
of Bryennius was illustrious; his cause was popular; but his licentious
troops could not be restrained from burning and pillaging a suburb;
and the people, who would have hailed the rebel, rejected and repulsed
the incendiary of his country. This change of the public opinion was
favourable to Botaniates, who at length, with an army of Turks, approached the shores of Chalcedon. A formal invitation, in the name of
the patriarch, the synod, and the senate, was circulated through the
streets of Constantinople; and the general assembly, in the dome of
St. Sophia, debated, with order and calmness, on the choice of their
sovereign. The guards of Michael would have dispersed this unarmed
multitude; but the feeble emperor, applauding his own moderation and
clemency, resigned the ensigns of royalty, and was rewarded with the
monastic habit, and the title of Archbishop of Ephesus. He left a son,
a Constantine, born and educated in the purple; and a daughter of the
house of Ducas illustrated the blood and confirmed the succession of the
Comnenian dynasty.

John Comnenus, the brother of the emperor Isaac, survived in peace
and dignity his generous refusal of the sceptre. By his wife Anne, a
woman of masculine spirit and policy, he left eight children: the three
daughters multiplied the Comnenian alliances with the noblest of the
Greeks: of the five sons, Manuel was stopped by a premature death;
Isaac and Alexius restored the Imperial greatness of their house, which
was enjoyed without toil or danger by the two younger brethren, Adrian
and Nicephorus. Alexius, the third and most illustrious of the brothers,
was endowed by nature with the choicest gifts both of mind and body:
they were cultivated by a liberal education, and exercised in the school
of obedience and adversity. The youth was dismissed from the perils
of the Turkish war by the paternal care of the emperor Romanus: but
the mother of the Comneni, with her aspiring race, was accused of
treason, and banished, by the sons of Ducas, to an island in the Propontis. The two brothers soon emerged into favour and action, fought
by each other's side against the rebels and barbarians, and adhered to
the emperor Michael, till he was deserted by the world and by himself.
In his first interview with Botaniates, " Prince," said Alexius, with a
noble frankness, " my duty rendered me your enemy; the decrees of God
and of the people have made me your subject. Judge of my future loyalty by my past opposition." The successor of Michael entertained him
with esteem and confidence: his valour was employed against three

rebels, who disturbed the peace of the empire, or at least of the emperors. Ursel, Bryennius, and Basilacius were formidable by their numerous forces and military fame: they were successively vanquished in the field, and led in chains to the foot of the throne; and whatever treatment they might receive from a timid and cruel court, they applauded the clemency as well as the courage of their conqueror. But the loyalty of the Comneni was soon tainted by fear and suspicion; nor is it easy to settle between a subject and a despot the debt of gratitude which the former is tempted to claim by a revolt, and the latter to discharge by an executioner. The refusal of Alexius to march against a fourth rebel, the husband of his sister, destroyed the merit or memory of his past services: the favourites of Botaniates provoked the ambition which they apprehended and accused; and the retreat of the two brothers might be justified by the defence of their life or liberty. The women of the family were deposited in a sanctuary, respected by tyrants: the men, mounted on horseback, sallied from the city, and erected the standard of civil war. The soldiers who had been gradually assembled in the capital and the neighbourhood were devoted to the cause of a victorious and injured leader: the ties of common interest and domestic alliance secured the attachment of the house of Ducas; and the generous dispute of the Comneni was terminated by the decisive resolution of Isaac, who was the first to invest his younger brother with the name and ensigns of royalty. They returned to Constantinople, to threaten rather than besiege that impregnable fortress; but the fidelity of the guards was corrupted; a gate was surprised, and the fleet was occupied by the active courage of George Palæologus, who fought against his father, without foreseeing that he laboured for his posterity. Alexius ascended the throne; and his aged competitor disappeared in a monastery. An army of various nations was gratified with the pillage of the city; but the public disorders were expiated by the tears and fasts of the Comneni, who submitted to every penance compatible with the possession of the empire.

The life of the emperor Alexius has been delineated by a favourite daughter, who was inspired by a tender regard for his person and a laudable zeal to perpetuate his virtues. Conscious of the just suspicion of her readers, the princess Anna Comnena repeatedly protests that, besides her personal knowledge, she had searched the discourse and writings of the most respectable veterans: that, after an interval of thirty years, forgotten by and forgetful of the world, her mournful solitude was inaccessible to hope and fear; and that truth, the naked perfect truth, was more dear and sacred than the memory of her parent. Yet, instead of the simplicity of style and narrative which wins our belief, an elaborate affectation of rhetoric and science betrays in every page the vanity of a female author. The genuine character of Alexius is lost in a vague constellation of virtues; and the perpetual strain of panegyric and apology awakens our jealousy, to question the veracity of the historian and the

merit of the hero.   We cannot, however, refuse her judicious and important remark, that the disorders of the times were the misfortune
and the glory of Alexius; and that every calamity which can afflict a
declining empire was accumulated on his reign by the justice of Heaven
and the vices of his predecessors.   In the East, the victorious Turks had
spread, from Persia to the Hellespont, the reign of the Koran and the
Crescent: the West was invaded by the adventurous valour of the Normans; and, in the moments of peace, the Danube poured forth new
swarms, who had gained, in the science of war, what they had lost in
the ferociousness of manners.   The sea was not less hostile than the
land; and while the frontiers were assaulted by an open enemy, the
palace was distracted with secret treason and conspiracy.   On a sudden the banner of the Cross was displayed by the Latins; Europe
was precipitated on Asia; and Constantinople had almost been swept
away by this impetuous deluge.   In the tempest, Alexius steered the
Imperial vessel with dexterity and courage.   At the head of his armies
he was bold in action, skilful in stratagem, patient of fatigue, ready to
improve his advantages, and rising from his defeats with inexhaustible
vigour.   The discipline of the camp was revived, and a new generation
of men and soldiers was created by the example and the precepts of their
leader.   In his intercourse with the Latins, Alexius was patient and
artful: his discerning eye pervaded the new system of an unknown world;
and I shall hereafter describe the superior policy with which he balanced
the interests and passions of the champions of the first crusade.   In a
long reign of thirty-seven years he subdued and pardoned the envy of
his equals: the laws of public and private order were restored: the arts
of wealth and science were cultivated: the limits of the empire were
enlarged in Europe and Asia; and the Comnenian sceptre was transmitted to his children of the third and fourth generation.   Yet the
difficulties of the times betrayed some defects in his character; and have
exposed his memory to some just or ungenerous reproach.   The reader
may possibly smile at the lavish praise which his daughter so often
bestows on a flying hero: the weakness or prudence of his situation
might be mistaken for a want of personal courage; and his political arts
are branded by the Latins with the names of deceit and dissimulation.
The increase of the male and female branches of his family adorned the
throne, and secured the succession; but their princely luxury and pride
offended the patricians, exhausted the revenue, and insulted the misery
of the people. Anna is a faithful witness that his happiness was destroyed, and his health was broken, by the cares of a public life: the
patience of Constantinople was fatigued by the length and severity of his
reign; and before Alexius expired, he had lost the love and reverence of
his subjects.   The clergy could not forgive his application of the sacred
riches to the defence of the state; but they applauded his theological
learning and ardent zeal for the orthodox faith, which he defended with
his tongue, his pen, and his sword.   His character was degraded by the
superstition of the Greeks; and the same inconsistent principle of human

nature enjoined the emperor to found a hospital for the poor and infirm, and to direct the execution of a heretic, who was burnt alive in the square of St. Sophia. Even the sincerity of his moral and religious virtues was suspected by the persons who had passed their lives in his familiar confidence. In his last hours, when he was pressed by his wife Irene to alter the succession, he raised his head, and breathed a pious ejaculation on the vanity of this world. The indignant reply of the empress may be inscribed as an epitaph on his tomb, " You die, as you have lived—A HYPOCRITE! "

It was the wish of Irene to supplant the eldest of her surviving sons, in favour of her daughter the princess Anna, whose philosophy would not have refused the weight of a diadem. But the order of male succession was asserted by the friends of their country; the lawful heir drew the royal signet from the finger of his insensible or conscious father, and the empire obeyed the master of the palace. Anna Comnena was stimulated by ambition and revenge to conspire against the life of her brother, and, when the design was prevented by the fears or scruples of her husband, she passionately exclaimed that nature had mistaken the two sexes, and had endowed Bryennius with the soul of a woman. The two sons of Alexius, John and Isaac, maintained the fraternal concord, the hereditary virtue of their race, and the younger brother was content with the title of *Sebastocrator,* which approached the dignity without sharing the power of the emperor. In the same person the claims of primogeniture and merit were fortunately united; his swarthy complexion, harsh features, and diminutive stature had suggested the ironical surname of Calo-Johannes, or John the Handsome, which his grateful subjects more seriously applied to the beauties of his mind. After the discovery of her treason, the life and fortune of Anna were justly forfeited to the laws. Her life was spared by the clemency of the emperor; but he visited the pomp and treasures of her palace, and bestowed the rich confiscation on the most deserving of his friends. That respectable friend, Axuch, a slave of Turkish extraction, presumed to decline the gift, and to intercede for the criminal: his generous master applauded and imitated the virtue of his favourite, and the reproach or complaint of an injured brother was the only chastisement of the guilty princess. After this example of clemency, the remainder of his reign was never disturbed by conspiracy or rebellion: feared by his nobles, beloved by his people, John was never reduced to the painful necessity of punishing, of even of pardoning, his personal enemies. During his government of twenty-five years, the penalty of death was abolished in the Roman empire, a law of mercy most delightful to the humane theorist, but of which the practice, in a large and vicious community, is seldom consistent with the public safety. Severe to himself, indulgent to others, chaste, frugal, abstemious, the philosophic Marcus would not have disdained the artless virtues of his successor, derived from his heart, and not borrowed from the schools. He despised and moderated the stately magnificence of the Byzantine court, so oppressive to the people, so contemptible to the eye of reason. Under such a prince innocence had nothing to fear, and merit had everything to hope; and, without assuming the tyrannic office of a censor, he introduced a gradual though visible reformation in the public and private manners of Constantinople. The only defect of this accomplished character was the frailty of noble minds —the love of arms and military glory. Yet the frequent expeditions of John the Handsome may be justified, at least in their principle, by the necessity of repelling the Turks from the Hellespont and the Bosphorus. The sultan of Iconium was confined to his capital, the barbarians were driven to the mountains, and the maritime provinces of Asia enjoyed the transient blessings of their deliverance. From Constantinople to Antioch and Aleppo, he repeatedly marched at the head of a victorious army; and in the sieges and battles of this holy war, his Latin allies were astonished by the superior spirit and prowess of a Greek. As he began to indulge the ambitious hope of restoring the ancient limits of the empire, as he revolved in his mind the Euphrates and Tigris, the dominion of Syria, and the conquest of Jerusalem, the thread of his life and of the public felicity was broken by a singular accident. He hunted the wild boar in the valley of Anazarbus, and had fixed his javelin in the body of the furious animal; but in the struggle a poisoned arrow dropped from his quiver, and a slight wound in his hand, which produced a mortification, was fatal to the best and greatest of the Comnenian princes.

A premature death had swept away the two eldest sons of John the Handsome; of the two survivors, Isaac and Manuel, his judgment or affection preferred the younger; and the choice of their dying prince was ratified by the soldiers, who had applauded the valour of his favourite in the Turkish war. The faithful Axuch hastened to the capital, secured the person of Isaac in honourable confinement, and purchased, with a gift of two hundred pounds of silver, the leading ecclesiastics of St. Sophia, who possessed a decisive voice in the consecration of an emperor. With his veteran and affectionate troops, Manuel soon visited Constantinople; his brother acquiesced in the title of Sebastocrator; his subjects admired the lofty stature and martial graces of their new sovereign, and listened with credulity to the flattering promise that he blended the wisdom of age with the activity and vigour of youth. By the experience of his government they were taught that he emulated the spirit and shared the talents of his father, whose social virtues were buried in the grave. A reign of thirty-seven years is filled by a perpetual though various warfare against the Turks, the Christians, and the hordes of the wilderness beyond the Danube. The arms of Manuel were exercised on Mount Taurus, in the plains of Hungary, on the coast of Italy and Egypt, and on the seas of Sicily and Greece: the influence of his negotiations extended from Jerusalem to Rome and Russia; and the Byzantine monarchy for a while became an object of respect or terror to the powers of Asia and Europe. Educated in the silk and purple of the East, Manuel possessed the iron temper of a soldier, which cannot easily be paralleled, except in the lives of Richard the First of England, and of Charles the Twelfth of Sweden. Such was his strength and exercise in arms, that Raymond, surnamed the Hercules of Antioch, was incapable of wielding the lance and buckler of the Greek emperor. In a famous tournament he entered the lists on a fiery courser, and overturned in his first career two of the stoutest of the Italian knights. The first in the charge, the last in the retreat, his friends and his enemies alike trembled, the former for *his* safety, and the latter for their own. After posting an ambuscade in a wood, he rode forwards in search of some perilous adventure, accompanied only by his brother and the faithful Axuch, who refused to desert their sovereign. Eighteen horsemen, after a short combat, fled before them: but the numbers of the enemy increased; the march of the reinforcement was tardy and fearful, and Manuel, without receiving a wound, cut his way through a squadron of five hundred Turks. In a battle against the Hungarians, impatient of the slowness of his troops, he snatched a standard from the head of the column, and was the first, almost alone, who passed a bridge that separated him from the enemy. In the same country, after transporting his army beyond the Save, he sent back the boats, with an order, under pain of death, to their commander, that he should leave him to conquer or die on that hostile land. In the siege of Corfu, towing after him a captive galley, the emperor stood aloft on the poop, opposing against the volleys of darts and stones a large buckler and a flowing sail; nor could he have escaped inevitable death, had not the Sicilian admiral enjoined his archers to respect the person of a hero. In one day he is said to have slain above forty of the barbarians with his own hand; he returned to the camp, dragging along four Turkish prisoners, whom he had tied to the rings of his saddle: he was ever the foremost to provoke or to accept a single combat; and the *gigantic* champions who encountered his arm were transpierced by the lance, or cut asunder by the sword, of the invincible Manuel. The story of his exploits, which appear as a model or a copy of the romances of chivalry, may induce a reasonable suspicion of the veracity of the Greeks: I will not, to vindicate their credit, endanger my own; yet I may observe that, in the long series of their annals, Manuel is the only prince who has been the subject of similar exaggeration. With the valour of a soldier he did not unite the skill or prudence of a general: his victories were not productive of any permanent or useful conquest; and his Turkish laurels were blasted in his last unfortunate campaign, in which he lost his army in the mountains of Pisidia, and owed his deliverance to the generosity of the sultan. But the most singular feature in the character of Manuel is the contrast and vicissitude of labour and sloth, of hardiness and effeminacy. In war he seemed ignorant of peace, in peace he appeared incapable of war. In the field he slept in the sun or in the snow, tired in the longest marches the strength of his men and horses, and shared with a smile the abstinence or diet of the camp. No sooner did he return to Constantinople, than he resigned himself to the arts and pleasures of a life of luxury: the expense of his dress, his table, and his palace surpassed the measure of his predecessors, and whole summer days were idly wasted in the delicious isles of the Propontis, in the incestuous love of his niece Theodora. The double cost of a warlike and dissolute prince exhausted the revenue and multiplied the taxes; and Manuel, in the distress of his last Turkish camp, endured a bitter reproach from the mouth of a desperate soldier. As he quenched his thirst, he complained that the water of a fountain was mingled with Christian blood. " It is not the first time," exclaimed a voice from the crowd, " that you have drank, O emperor, the blood of your Christian subjects." Manuel Comnenus was twice married, to the virtuous Bertha or Irene of Germany, and to the beauteous Maria, a French or Latin princess of Antioch. The only daughter of his first wife was destined for Bela, an Hungarian prince, who was educated at Constantinople under the name of Alexius; and the consummation of their nuptials might have transferred the Roman sceptre to a race of free and warlike barbarians. But as soon as Maria of Antioch had given a son and heir to the empire, the presumptive rights of Bela were abolished, and he was deprived of his promised bride; but the Hungarian prince resumed his name and the kingdom of his fathers, and displayed such virtues as might excite the regret and envy of the Greeks. The son of Maria was named Alexius; and at the age of ten years he ascended the Byzantine throne, after his father's decease had closed the glories of the Comnenian line.

The fraternal concord of the two sons of the great Alexius had been sometimes clouded by an opposition of interest and passion. By ambition, Isaac the Sebastocrator was excited to flight and rebellion, from whence he was reclaimed by the firmness and clemency of John the Handsome. The errors of Isaac, the father of the emperors of Trebizond, were short and venial; but John, the elder of his sons, renounced for ever his religion. Provoked by a real or imaginary insult of his uncle, he escaped from the Roman to the Turkish camp: his apostacy was rewarded with the sultan's daughter, the title of Chelebi, or noble, and the inheritance of a princely estate; and, in the fifteenth century, Mohammed the Second boasted of his Imperial descent from the Comnenian family. Andronicus, younger brother of John, son of Isaac, and grandson of Alexius Comnenus, is one of the most conspicuous characters of the age; and his genuine adventures might form the subject of a very singular romance. To justify the choice of three ladies of royal birth, it is incumbent on me to observe that their fortunate lover was cast in the best proportions of strength and beauty; and that the want of the softer graces was supplied by a manly countenance, a lofty stature, athletic muscles, and the air and deportment of a soldier. The preservation, in his old age, of health and vigour, was the reward of temperance and exercise. A piece of bread and a draught of water was often his sole and evening repast; and if he tasted of a wild boar or a stag, which he had roasted with his own hands, it was the well-earned fruit of a laborious chase. Dexterous in arms, he was ignorant of fear: his persuasive eloquence could bend to every situation and character of life: his style, though not his practice, was fashioned by the example of St. Paul; and, in every deed of mischief, he had a heart to resolve, a head to contrive, and a hand to execute. In his youth, after the death of the emperor John, he followed the retreat of the Roman army; but, in the march through Asia Minor, design or accident tempted him to wander in the mountains: the hunter was encompassed by the Turkish huntsmen, and he remained some time a reluctant or willing captive in the power of the sultan. His virtues and vices recommended him to the favour of his cousin: he shared the perils and the pleasures of Manuel; and while the emperor lived in public incest with his niece Theodora, the affections of her sister Eudocia were seduced and enjoyed by Andronicus. Above the decencies of her sex and rank, she gloried in the name of his concubine; and both the palace and the camp could witness that she slept, or watched, in the arms of her lover. She accompanied him to his military command of Cilicia, the first scene of his valour and imprudence. He pressed, with active ardour, the siege of Mopsuestia: the day was employed in the boldest attacks; but the night was wasted in song and dance; and a band of Greek comedians formed the choicest part of his retinue. Andronicus was surprised by the sally of a vigilant foe; but, while his troops fled in disorder, his invincible lance transpierced the thickest ranks of the Armenians. On his return to the Imperial camp in Macedonia, he was received by Manuel with public smiles and a private reproof; but the duchies of Naissus, Braniseba, and Castoria were the reward or consolation of the unsuccessful general. Eudocia still attended his motions: at midnight their tent was suddenly attacked by her angry brothers, impatient to expiate her infamy in his blood: his daring spirit refused her advice, and the disguise of a female habit; and, boldly starting from his couch, he drew his sword, and cut his way through the numerous assassins. It was here that he first betrayed his ingratitude and treachery: he engaged in a treasonable correspondence with the king of Hungary and the German emperor; approached the royal tent at a suspicious hour with a drawn sword, and, under the mask of a Latin soldier, avowed an intention of revenge against a mortal foe; and imprudently praised the fleetness of his horse as an instrument of flight and safety. The monarch dissembled his suspicions; but, after the close of the campaign, Andronicus was arrested and strictly confined in a tower of the palace of Constantinople.

In this prison he was left above twelve years; a most painful restraint, from which the thirst of action and pleasure perpetually urged him to escape. Alone and pensive, he perceived some broken bricks in a corner of the chamber, and gradually widened the passage till he had explored a dark and forgotten recess. Into this hole he conveyed himself and the remains of his provisions, replacing the bricks in their former position, and erasing with care the footsteps of his retreat. At the hour of the customary visit, his guards were amazed by the silence and solitude of the prison, and reported, with shame and fear, his incomprehensible flight. The gates of the palace and city were instantly shut: the strictest orders were despatched into the provinces for the recovery of the fugitive; and his wife, on the suspicion of a pious act, was basely imprisoned in the same tower. At the dead of night she beheld a sceptre: she recognised her husband; they shared their provisions, and a son was the fruit of these stolen interviews, which alleviated the tediousness of their confinement. In the custody of a woman the vigilance of the keepers was insensibly relaxed, and the captive had accomplished his real escape, when he was discovered, brought back to Constantinople, and loaded with a double chain. At length he found the moment and the means of his deliverance. A boy, his domestic servant, intoxicated the guards, and obtained in wax the impression of the keys. By the diligence of his friends a similar key, with a bundle of ropes, was introduced into the prison in the bottom of a hogshead. Andronicus employed, with industry and courage, the instruments of his safety, unlocked the doors, descended from the tower, concealed himself all day among the bushes, and scaled in the night the garden-wall of the palace. A boat was stationed for his reception; he visited his own house, embraced his children, cast away his chain, mounted a fleet horse, and directed his rapid course towards the banks of the Danube. At Anchialus, in Thrace, an intrepid friend supplied him with horses and money: he passed the river, traversed with speed the desert of Moldavia and the Carpathian hills, and had almost reached the town of Halicz, in the Polish Russia, when he was intercepted by a party of Walachians, who resolved to convey their important captive to Constantinople. His presence of mind again extricated him from this danger. Under the pretence of sickness he dismounted in the night, and was allowed to step aside from the troop: he planted in the ground his long staff, clothed it with his cap and upper garment, and, stealing into the wood, left a phantom to amuse for some time the eyes of the Walachians. From Halicz he was honourably conducted to Kiow, the residence of the great duke: the subtle Greek soon obtained the esteem and confidence of Ieroslaus; his character could assume the manners of every climate, and the barbarians applauded his strength and courage in the chase of the elks and bears of the forest. In this northern region he deserved the forgiveness of Manuel, who solicited the Russian prince to join his arms in the invasion of Hungary. The influence of Andronicus achieved this important service: his private treaty was signed with a promise of fidelity on one side and of oblivion on the other, and he marched, at the head of the Russian cavalry, from the Borysthenes to the Danube. In his resentment Manuel had ever sympathised with the martial and dissolute character of his cousin, and his free pardon was sealed in the assault of Zemlin, in which he was second, and second only, to the valour of the emperor.

No sooner was the exile restored to freedom and his country than his ambition revived, at first to his own, and at length to the public misfortune. A daughter of Manuel was a feeble bar to the succession of the more deserving males of the Comnenian blood: her future marriage with the prince of Hungary was repugnant to the hopes or prejudices of the princes and nobles. But when an oath of allegiance was required to the presumptive heir, Andronicus alone asserted the honour of the Roman name, declined the unlawful engagement, and boldly protested against the adoption of a stranger. His patriotism was offensive to the emperor; but he spoke the sentiments of the people, and was removed from the royal presence by an honourable banishment, a second command of the Cilician frontier, with the absolute disposal of the revenues of Cyprus. In this station the Armenians again exercised his courage and exposed his negligence; and the same rebel, who baffled all his operations, was unhorsed, and almost slain by the vigour of his lance. But Andronicus soon discovered a more easy and pleasing conquest, the beautiful Philippa, sister of the empress Maria, and daughter of Raymond of Poitou, the Latin prince of Antioch. For her sake he deserted his station, and wasted the summer in balls and tournaments: to his love she sacrificed her innocence, her reputation, and the offer of an advantageous marriage. But the resentment of Manuel for this domestic affront interrupted his pleasures: Andronicus left the indiscreet princess to weep and to repent; and, with a band of desperate adventurers, undertook the pilgrimage of Jerusalem. His birth, his martial renown, and professions of zeal announced him as the champion of the Cross: he soon captivated both the clergy and the king, and the Greek prince was invested with the lordship of Berytus, on the coast of Phœnicia. In his neighbourhood resided a young and handsome queen, of his own nation and family, great-granddaughter of the emperor Alexis, and widow of Baldwin the Third, king of Jerusalem. She visited and loved her kinsman. Theodora was the third victim of his amorous seduction, and her shame was more public and scandalous than that of her predecessors. The emperor still thirsted for revenge, and his subjects and allies of the Syrian frontier were repeatedly pressed to seize the person and put out the eyes of the fugitive. In Palestine he was no longer safe; but the tender Theodora revealed his danger and accompanied his flight. The queen of Jerusalem was exposed to the East, his obsequious concubine, and two illegitimate children were the living monuments of her weakness. Damascus was his first revenge, and, in the characters of the great Noureddin and his servant Saladin, the superstitious Greek might learn to revere the virtues of the Musulmans. As the friend of Noureddin he visited, most probably, Bagdad and the courts of Persia, and, after a long circuit round the Caspian Sea and the mountains of Georgia, he finally settled among the Turks of Asia Minor, the hereditary enemies of his country. The sultan of Colonia afforded an hospitable retreat to Andronicus, his mistress, and his band of outlaws: the debt of gratitude was paid by frequent inroads in the Roman province of Trebizond, and he seldom returned without an ample harvest of spoil and of Christian captives. In the story of his adventures he was fond of comparing himself to David, who escaped, by a long exile, the snares of the wicked. But the royal prophet (he presumed to add) was content to lurk on the borders of Judæa, to slay an Amalekite, and to threaten, in his miserable state, the life of the avaricious Nabal. The excursions of the Comnenian prince had a wider range, and he had spread over the Eastern world the glory of his name and religion. By a sentence of the Greek church, the licentious rover had been separated from the faithful; but even this excommunication may prove that he never abjured the profession of Christianity.

His vigilance had eluded or repelled the open and secret persecution of the emperor; but he was at length ensnared by the captivity of his female companion. The governor of Trebizond succeeded in his attempt to surprise the person of Theodora: the queen of Jerusalem and her two children were sent to Constantinople, and their loss embittered the tedious solitude of banishment. The fugitive implored and obtained a final pardon, with leave to throw himself at the feet of his sovereign, who was satisfied with the submission of this haughty spirit. Prostrate on the ground, he deplored with tears and groans the guilt of his past rebellion; nor would he presume to arise, unless some faithful subject would drag him to the foot of the throne by an iron chain with which he had secretly encircled his neck. This extraordinary penance excited the wonder and pity of the assembly: his sins were forgiven by the church and state; but the just suspicion of Manuel fixed his residence at a distance from the court, at Oenoe, a town of Pontus, surrounded with rich vineyards, and situate on the coast of the Euxine. The death of Manuel and the disorders of the minority soon opened the fairest field to his ambition. The emperor was a boy of twelve or fourteen years of age, without vigour, or wisdom, or experience: his mother, the empress Mary, abandoned her person and government to a favourite of the Comnenian name; and his sister, another Mary, whose husband, an Italian, was decorated with the title of Cæsar, excited a conspiracy, and at length an insurrection, against her odious stepmother. The provinces were forgotten, the capital was in flames, and a century of peace and order was overthrown in the vice and weakness of a few months. A civil war was kindled in Constantinople; the two factions fought a bloody battle in the square of the palace, and the rebels sustained a regular siege in the cathedral of St. Sophia. The patriarch laboured with honest zeal to heal the wounds of the republic, the most respectable patriots called aloud for a guardian and avenger, and every tongue repeated the praise of the talents and even the virtues of Andronicus. In his retirement he affected to revolve the solemn duties of his oath: " If the safety or honour of the Imperial family be threatened, I will reveal and oppose the mischief to the utmost of my power." His correspondence with the patriarch and patricians was seasoned with apt quotations from the Psalms of David and the Epistles of St. Paul; and he patiently waited till he was called to her deliverance by the voice of his country. In his march from Oenoe to Constantinople, his slender train insensibly swelled to a crowd and an army; his professions of religion and loyalty were mistaken for the language of his heart; and the simplicity of a foreign dress, which showed to advantage his majestic stature, displayed a lively image of his poverty and exile. All opposition sunk before him; he reached the straits of the Thracian Bosphorus; the Byzantine navy sailed from the harbour to receive and transport the saviour of the empire: the torrent was loud and irresistible, and the insects who had basked in the sunshine of royal favour disappeared at the blast of the storm. It was the first care of Andronicus to occupy the palace, to salute the emperor, to confine his mother, to punish her minister, and to restore the public order and tranquillity. He then visited the sepulchre of Manuel: the spectators were ordered to stand aloof, but, as he bowed in the attitude of prayer, they heard, or thought they heard, a murmur of triumph and revenge: " I no longer fear thee, my old enemy, who hast driven me a vagabond to every climate of the earth. Thou art safely deposited under a seven-fold dome, from whence thou canst never arise till the signal of the last trumpet. It is now my turn, and speedily will I trample on thy ashes and thy posterity." From his subsequent tyranny we may impute such feelings to the man and the moment; but it is not extremely probable that he gave an articulate sound to his secret thoughts. In the first months of his administration his designs were veiled by a fair semblance of hypocrisy, which could delude only the eyes of the multitude: the coronation of Alexius was performed with due solemnity, and his perfidious guardian, holding in his hands the body and blood of Christ, most fervently declared that he lived, and was ready to die, for the service of his beloved pupil. But his numerous adherents were instructed to maintain that the sinking empire must perish in the hands of a child; that the Romans could only be saved by a veteran prince, bold in arms, skilful in policy, and taught to reign by the long experience of fortune and mankind; and that it was the duty of every citizen to force the reluctant modesty of Andronicus to undertake the burden of the public care. The young emperor was himself constrained to join his voice to the general acclamation, and to solicit the association of a colleague, who instantly degraded him from the supreme rank, secluded his person, and verified the rash declaration of the patriarch, that Alexius might be considered as dead so soon as he was committed to the custody of his guardian. But his death was preceded by the imprisonment and execution of his mother. After blackening her reputation, and inflaming against her the passions of the multitude, the tyrant accused and tried the empress for a treasonable correspondence with the king of Hungary. His own son, a youth of honour and humanity, avowed his abhorrence of this flagitious act, and three of the judges had the merit of preferring their conscience to their safety; but the obsequious tribunal, without requiring any proof or hearing any defence, condemned the widow of Manuel, and her unfortunate son subscribed the sentence of her death. Maria was strangled, her corpse was buried in the sea, and her memory was wounded by the insult most offensive to female vanity, a false and ugly representation of her beauteous form. The fate of her son was not long deferred: he was strangled with a bowstring, and the tyrant, insensible to pity or remorse, after surveying the body of the innocent youth, struck it rudely with his foot. " Thy father," he cried, " was a *knave*, thy mother a *whore*, and thyself a *fool!* "

The Roman sceptre, the reward of his crimes, was held by Andronicus about three years and a half as the guardian or sovereign of the empire. His government exhibited a singular contrast of vice and virtue. When he listened to his passions, he was the scourge; when he consulted his reason, the father of his people. In the exercise of private justice he was equitable and rigorous; a shameful and pernicious venality was abolished, and the offices were filled with the most deserving candidates by a prince who had sense to choose and severity to punish. He prohibited the inhuman practice of pillaging the goods and persons of shipwrecked mariners; the provinces, so long the objects of oppression or neglect, revived in prosperity and plenty; and millions applauded the distant blessings of his reign, while he was cursed by the witnesses of his daily cruelties. The ancient proverb, that bloodthirsty is the man who returns from banishment to power, had been applied, with too much truth, to Marius and Tiberius, and was now verified for the third time in the life of Andronicus. His memory was stored with a black list of the enemies and rivals who had traduced his merit, opposed his greatness, or insulted his misfortunes; and the only comfort of his exile was the sacred hope and promise of revenge. The necessary extinction of the young emperor and his mother imposed the fatal obligation of extirpating the friends who hated, and might punish, the assassin; and the repetition of murder rendered him less willing and less able to forgive. A horrid narrative of the victims whom he sacrificed by poison or the sword, by the sea or the flames, would be less expressive of his cruelty than the appellation of the Halcyon-days, which was applied to a rare and bloodless week of repose: the tyrant strove to transfer on the laws and the judges some portion of his guilt, but the mask was fallen, and his subjects could no longer mistake the true author of their calamities. The noblest of the Greeks, more especially those who, by descent or alliance, might dispute the Comnenian inheritance, escaped from the monster's den: Nice or Prusa, Sicily or Cyprus, were their places of refuge; and as their flight was already criminal, they aggravated their offence by an open revolt and the Imperial title. Yet Andronicus re-

sisted the daggers and swords of his most formidable enemies: Nice
and Prusa were reduced and chastised; the Sicilians were content with
the sack of Thessalonica; and the distance of Cyprus was not more
propitious to the rebel than to the tyrant. His throne was subverted
by a rival without a merit, and a people without arms. Isaac Angelus,
a descendant in the female line from the great Alexius, was marked
as a victim by the prudence or superstition of the emperor. In a moment of despair Angelus defended his life and liberty, slew the executioner, and fled to the church of St. Sophia. The sanctuary was
insensibly filled with a curious and mournful crowd, who, in his fate,
prognosticated their own. But their lamentations were soon turned
to curses, and their curses to threats: they dared to ask, " Why do we
fear? why do we obey? We are many, and he is one; our patience is
the only bond of our slavery." With the dawn of day the city burst
into a general sedition, the prisons were thrown open, the coldest and
most servile were roused to the defence of their country, and Isaac,
the second of the name, was raised from the sanctuary to the throne.
Unconscious of his danger, the tyrant was absent—withdrawn from
the toils of state, in the delicious islands of the Propontis. He had
contracted an indecent marriage with Alice, or Agnes, daughter of
Lewis the Seventh, of France, and relict of the unfortunate Alexius;
and his society, more suitable to his temper than to his age, was composed of a young wife and a favourite concubine. On the first alarm
he rushed to Constantinople, impatient for the blood of the guilty; but
he was astonished by the silence of the palace, the tumult of the city,
and the general desertion of mankind. Andronicus proclaimed a free
pardon to his subjects; they neither desired nor would grant forgiveness: he offered to resign the crown to his son Manuel; but the virtues
of the son could not expiate his father's crimes. The sea was still
open for his retreat; but the news of the revolution had flown along
the coast; when fear had ceased, obedience was no more; the Imperial
galley was pursued and taken by an armed brigantine, and the tyrant
was dragged to the presence of Isaac Angelus, loaded with fetters, and
a long chain round his neck. His eloquence and the tears of his female
companions pleaded in vain for his life; but, instead of the decencies
of a legal execution, the new monarch abandoned the criminal to the
numerous sufferers whom he had deprived of a father, a husband, or
a friend. His teeth and hair, an eye and a hand, were torn from him,
as a poor compensation for their loss; and a short respite was allowed,
that he might feel the bitterness of death. Astride on a camel, without
any danger of a rescue, he was carried through the city, and the basest
of the populace rejoiced to trample on the fallen majesty of their
prince. After a thousand blows and outrages, Andronicus was hung
by the feet between two pillars that supported the statues of a wolf
and a sow; and every hand that could reach the public enemy inflicted
on his body some mark of ingenious or brutal cruelty, till two friendly
or furious Italians, plunging their swords into his body, released him

from all human punishment. In this long and painful agony, " Lord have mercy upon me! " and " Why will you bruise a broken reed? " were the only words that escaped from his mouth. Our hatred for the tyrant is lost in pity for the man; nor can we blame his pusillanimous resignation, since a Greek Christian was no longer master of his life.

I have been tempted to expatiate on the extraordinary character and adventures of Andronicus; but I shall here terminate the series of the Greek emperors since the time of Heraclius. The branches that sprang from the Comnenian trunk had insensibly withered, and the male line was continued only in the posterity of Andronicus himself, who, in the public confusion, usurped the sovereignty of Trebizond, so obscure in history, and so famous in romance. A private citizen of Philadelphia, Constantine Angelus, had emerged to wealth and honours by his marriage with the daughter of the emperor Alexius. His son Andronicus is conspicuous only by his cowardice. His grandson Isaac punished and succeeded the tyrant; but he was dethroned by his own vices and the ambition of his brother; and their discord introduced the Latins to the conquest of Constantinople, the first great period in the fall of the Eastern empire.

If we compute the number and duration of the reigns, it will be found that a period of six hundred years is filled by sixty emperors, including in the Augustan list some female sovereigns, and deducting some usurpers who were never acknowledged in the capital, and some princes who did not live to possess their inheritance. The average proportion will allow ten years for each emperor—far below the chronological rule of Sir Isaac Newton, who, from the experience of more recent and regular monarchies, has defined about eighteen or twenty years as the term of an ordinary reign. The Byzantine empire was most tranquil and prosperous when it could acquiesce in hereditary succession: five dynasties, the Heraclian, Isaurian, Amorian, Basilian, and Comnenian families, enjoyed and transmitted the royal patrimony during their respective series of five, four, three, six, and four generations; several princes number the years of their reign with those of their infancy; and Constantine the Seventh and his two grandsons occupy the space of an entire century. But in the intervals of the Byzantine dynasties the succession is rapid and broken, and the name of a successful candidate is speedily erased by a more fortunate competitor. Many were the paths that led to the summit of royalty: the fabric of rebellion was overthrown by the stroke of conspiracy, or undermined by the silent arts of intrigue: the favourites of the soldiers or people, of the senate or clergy, of the women and eunuchs, were alternately clothed with the purple: the means of their elevation were base, and their end was often contemptible or tragic. A being of the nature of man, endowed with the same faculties, but with a longer measure of existence, would cast down a smile of pity and contempt on the crimes and follies of human ambition, so eager, in a narrow span, to grasp at a precarious and short-lived enjoyment. It is thus that the experience of history exalts and enlarges the horizon of our intellectual view. In a composition of some days, in a perusal of some hours, six hundred years have rolled away, and the duration of a life or reign is contracted to a fleeting moment: the grave is ever beside the throne; the success of a criminal is almost instantly followed by the loss of his prize; and our immortal reason survives and disdains the sixty phantoms of kings who have passed before our eyes, and faintly dwell on our remembrance. The observation, that in every age and climate ambition has prevailed with the same commanding energy, may abate the surprise of a philosopher; but while he condemns the vanity, he may search the motive of this universal desire to obtain and hold the sceptre of dominion. To the greater part of the Byzantine series we cannot reasonably ascribe the love of fame and of mankind. The virtue alone of John Comnenus was beneficent and pure: the most illustrious of the princes who precede or follow that respectable name have trod with some dexterity and vigour the crooked and bloody paths of a selfish policy: in scrutinising the imperfect characters of Leo the Isaurian, Basil the First, and Alexius Comnenus, of Theophilus, the second Basil, and Manuel Comnenus, our esteem and censure are almost equally balanced; and the remainder of the Imperial crowd could only desire and expect to be forgotten by posterity. Was personal happiness the aim and object of their ambition? I shall not descant on the vulgar topics of the misery of kings; but I may surely observe that their condition, of all others, is the most pregnant with fear, and the least susceptible of hope. For these opposite passions a larger scope was allowed in the revolutions of antiquity than in the smooth and solid temper of the modern world, which cannot easily repeat either the triumph of Alexander or the fall of Darius. But the peculiar infelicity of the Byzantine princes exposed them to domestic perils, without affording any lively promise of foreign conquest. From the pinnacle of greatness Andronicus was precipitated by a death more cruel and shameful than that of the vilest malefactor; but the most glorious of his predecessors had much more to dread from their subjects than to hope from their enemies. The army was licentious without spirit, the nation turbulent without freedom: the barbarians of the East and West pressed on the monarchy, and the loss of the provinces was terminated by the final servitude of the capital.

The entire series of Roman emperors, from the first of the Cæsars to the last of the Constantines, extends above fifteen hundred years: and the term of dominion, unbroken by foreign conquest, surpasses the measure of the ancient monarchies—the Assyrians or Medes, the successors of Cyrus, or those of Alexander.